THE NEW
CAMBRIDGE MODERN HISTORY

VOLUME XII
(second edition)

THE SHIFTING BALANCE
OF WORLD FORCES
1898-1945

When the need for a new edition of this volume arose Dr David Thomson, the original editor, was unable, owing to other commitments, to undertake the task of producing a revised edition, and it was entrusted to a new editor.

THE NEW CAMBRIDGE MODERN HISTORY

VOLUME XII

THE SHIFTING BALANCE OF WORLD FORCES
1898-1945

A second edition of Volume XII
The Era of Violence

EDITED BY

C. L. MOWAT

CAMBRIDGE
AT THE UNIVERSITY PRESS
1968

Published by the Syndics of the Cambridge University Press
Bentley House, 200 Euston Road, London, N.W. 1
American Branch: 32 East 57th Street, New York, N.Y. 10022

© Cambridge University Press 1968

Library of Congress Catalogue Card Number: 57–14935

Standard Book Number: 521 04551 7

Printed in Great Britain
at the University Printing House, Cambridge
(Brooke Crutchley, University Printer)

CONTENTS

CHAPTER I

INTRODUCTORY SURVEY:
ON THE LIMITS OF MODERN HISTORY

By C. L. MOWAT, *Professor of History, University College of North Wales, Bangor*

CHAPTER II

THE TRANSFORMATION OF SOCIAL LIFE

By DAVID THOMSON, *Master of Sidney Sussex College and Lecturer in History in the University of Cambridge*

CONTENTS

CHAPTER III

THE WORLD ECONOMY: INTERDEPENDENCE AND PLANNING

By ASA BRIGGS, *Vice-Chancellor and Professor of History, University of Sussex*

CONTENTS

CHAPTER IV

SCIENCE AND TECHNOLOGY

By DOUGLAS McKIE, *Professor Emeritus of the History and Philosophy
of Science in the University of London*

CHAPTER V

DIPLOMATIC HISTORY 1900–1912

By J. P. T. BURY, *Fellow of Corpus Christi College and
Lecturer in History in the University of Cambridge*

CONTENTS

CHAPTER VI

THE APPROACH OF THE WAR OF 1914

By J. M. K. VYVYAN, *Fellow of Trinity College, Cambridge*

CONTENTS

CHAPTER VII

THE FIRST WORLD WAR

By BRIAN BOND, *Lecturer in War Studies, King's College,*
University of London

CONTENTS

CHAPTER VIII

THE PEACE SETTLEMENT OF VERSAILLES
1918–1933

By ROHAN BUTLER, *Fellow of All Souls College, Oxford*

CONTENTS

CHAPTER IX

THE LEAGUE OF NATIONS

By *the late* J. L. BRIERLY, *Professor of International Law in the University of Oxford*; revised and rewritten by P. A. REYNOLDS, *Professor of Politics, University of Lancaster*

CHAPTER X

THE MIDDLE EAST 1900–1945

By E. KEDOURIE, *Professor of Politics in the London School of Economics, University of London*

xi

CONTENTS

CHAPTER XI

INDIA AND SOUTH-EAST ASIA

1. India, by PERCIVAL SPEAR, *Fellow of Selwyn College and Lecturer
in History in the University of Cambridge*

2. South-East Asia, by D. G. E. HALL, *formerly Professor of the History
of South-East Asia, School of Oriental and African Studies, University of London*

I. INDIA

CONTENTS

CHAPTER XII

CHINA, JAPAN AND THE PACIFIC 1900–1931

By J. W. DAVIDSON, *Professor of Pacific History in the Australian National University*, and COLIN FORSTER, *Reader in Economic History in the Australian National University*

CONTENTS

CONTENTS

CHAPTER XIII

THE BRITISH COMMONWEALTH OF NATIONS

By J. C. BEAGLEHOLE, *Emeritus Professor of British Commonwealth History, The Victoria University of Wellington, New Zealand*

CHAPTER XIV

THE RUSSIAN REVOLUTION

By *the late* ISAAC DEUTSCHER

CONTENTS

CHAPTER XV

THE SOVIET UNION 1917–1939

By GEORGE KENNAN, *Professor in the Institute for Advanced Study, Princeton*

CONTENTS

CHAPTER XVI

GERMANY, ITALY AND EASTERN EUROPE
By Elizabeth Wiskemann

CONTENTS

CONTENTS

CHAPTER XVII

GREAT BRITAIN, FRANCE, THE LOW COUNTRIES AND SCANDINAVIA

By MAURICE CROUZET, *Inspecteur général de l'Instruction publique,*
Paris. Translated by K. LLOYD-JONES, *Lecturer in French,*
University College of North Wales, Bangor

CONTENTS

CHAPTER XVIII

THE UNITED STATES OF AMERICA

By Sir DENIS BROGAN, *Emeritus Professor of Political Science
in the University of Cambridge*

CONTENTS

CHAPTER XIX

LATIN AMERICA

By J. H. PARRY, *Professor of Oceanic History, Harvard University*

CONTENTS

CHAPTER XX

LITERATURE 1895–1939

By A. E. DYSON, *Senior Lecturer in English Studies, University of East Anglia*

CHAPTER XXI

PHILOSOPHY AND RELIGIOUS THOUGHT

1. Philosophy, by RENFORD BAMBROUGH, *Fellow and Dean of St John's College and Lecturer in Moral Science in the University of Cambridge*

2. Religious Thought, by the Very Reverend W. R. MATTHEWS, K.C.V.O., *formerly Dean of St Paul's*

1. PHILOSOPHY

2. RELIGIOUS THOUGHT

CONTENTS

CHAPTER XXII

PAINTING, SCULPTURE AND ARCHITECTURE

By M. E. COOKE, *Senior Lecturer in History and the History of Art,*
University College of North Wales, Bangor

PAINTING

SCULPTURE

ARCHITECTURE

CHAPTER XXIII

DIPLOMATIC HISTORY 1930–1939

By D. C. WATT, *Reader in International History in the*
London School of Economics, University of London

CONTENTS

CONTENTS

CHAPTER XXIV

THE SECOND WORLD WAR

By Sir BASIL LIDDELL HART

CHAPTER XXV

DIPLOMATIC HISTORY OF THE SECOND WORLD WAR

By Sir LLEWELYN WOODWARD, *formerly Professor of Modern*
History in the University of Oxford and Professor in the
Institute for Advanced Study, Princeton

CONTENTS

ACKNOWLEDGEMENTS

Thanks are due to the following for permission to reproduce copyright material in chapter xx: the Trustees of the Hardy Estate, Macmillan and Co. Ltd, the Macmillan Company of Canada Ltd and Crowell-Collier and Macmillan Inc. for 'The Shadow on the Stone' from *The Collected Poems of Thomas Hardy*; Mr Harold Owen, Chatto and Windus Ltd, and New Directions Inc., New York, for 'Futility' from *The Collected Poems of Wilfred Owen*; A. P. Watt and Son and Macmillan, New York, for lines from 'The Song of the Happy Shepherd,' 'Easter 1916' and 'Lapis Lazuli' from *The Collected Poems of W. B. Yeats*; Faber and Faber and Random House Inc., for lines from 'Spain 1937' by W- H. Auden, and Faber and Faber and Harcourt Brace and World for lines from 'The Waste Land' by T. S. Eliot.

CHAPTER I

INTRODUCTORY SURVEY: ON THE LIMITS OF MODERN HISTORY

W HEN Lord Acton was planning *The Cambridge Modern History* in 1896 he wrote of the venture:

It is a unique opportunity of recording, in the way most useful to the greatest number, the fullness of the knowledge which the nineteenth century is about to bequeath...

Ultimate history we cannot have in this generation; but we can dispose of conventional history, and show the point we have reached on the road from one to the other, now that all information is within reach, and every problem has become capable of solution.

Acton projected the *History* as a work of universal history, 'distinct from the combined history of all countries'.

It moves in a succession to which the nations are subordinate. Their story will be told, not for their own sake, but in reference and subordination to a higher series, according to the time and degree in which they contribute to the common fortunes of mankind.[1]

Few historians today have Acton's confidence that universal history or ultimate history can yet be written. Indeed, Sir George Clark, in his 'General Introduction' to the *New Cambridge Modern History*, disclaimed for historians of his generation the belief that it would be possible to write 'definitive history'. 'This new issue of the *Cambridge Modern History* has been planned neither as a stepping-stone to definitive history, nor as an abstract or a scale-reduction of all our knowledge of the period, but as a coherent body of judgments true to the facts.'[2] Its scope remained that of the original series: 'the history of that "civilisation" which, from the fifteenth century, spread from its original European homes, assimilating extraneous elements as it expanded, until it was more or less firmly planted in all parts of the world'.[3]

The last volume in the *New Cambridge Modern History* must necessarily begin by taking stock not only of the period with which it is concerned but with its place in the series or, rather, its place in 'modern history'. This was less essential for the editors of the last volume of the *Cambridge Modern History*. Published in 1910, and covering the period from 1870 to 1910, it was sufficient to call it 'The Latest Age' and to assume that it marked no end of an epoch, no real terminus. Its authors were spared the

---

[1] *The Cambridge Modern History: Its Origin, Authorship and Production* (Cambridge, 1907), pp. 10–14, quoted in E. H. Carr, *What is History?* (Cambridge, 1961), pp. 1, 145.
[2] *The New Cambridge Modern History*, vol. I (1957), p. xxxiv; cf. p. xxiv. [3] *Ibid.* p. xxxv.

I

knowledge that the first world war of modern history and of the twentieth century was only four years away, and that the continuity of the 'modern history' with which the twelve volumes had been concerned could not in future be taken for granted. None the less, their volume was far from being centred on Europe; its chapters included surveys of Egypt and the Sudan, the Far East, the British Empire in India, Japan, Latin America, the European Colonies, and a chapter on The Scientific Age.

The present volume virtually begins where its predecessor of 1910 ended, though several of its chapters go back to the beginning of the century. It ends in 1945, at a far greater distance from the time of its writing than was true of the earlier volume, which was for its latter stages practically contemporary history. In this volume some of the chapters refer perforce to events which have occurred after 1945. In all of them, whatever the nominal limits, the knowledge of the history of the world since 1945 has inevitably had its influence. How we view the period 1900–45 as a whole or in its parts is bound to be affected by our interpretation of the history of the last twenty years.

What, then, should be the theme of this volume, from the vantage-ground of 1966? The original edition was published in 1960, and reflected in its planning and its theme the spirit of the 1950s if not of the immediate post-war years after 1945. It was natural to entitle it 'The Era of Violence'. And no one would deny that violence characterised a great deal of the history it recorded—more so, perhaps, than in any earlier period of history, at least if the degree of violence and brutality, and the numbers of its victims, are reckoned in the balance.

As he surveys the twenty years or more since 1945, however, the historian may feel that violence has not been the main characteristic of this century. He notices the developments in the use of nuclear power for peaceful purposes as well as for its destructive force. He notes the achievement of parity in the ability to attack between the United States of America and Russia in 1957, and equally the first nuclear explosion in China in 1965. The danger of the proliferation of nuclear weapons has become clearer; but the very fact of this shows the universality of scientific and technical knowledge and discovery, and the need to recognise the condition that we are all members one of another. The exploration of space which has been proceeding seems to be competitive rather than co-operative, though clearly each team learns much, even if at one remove, from the work of the rival. Thus the launching of the first man-made satellite by the Russians in 1957 was followed by several manned flights of satellites of American and Russian manufacture in 1961.

Parallel with these developments were others transforming our view of the twentieth-century world. One was the sudden recognition that the world was in the midst of a 'population explosion' which was likely to produce a population of 5,000 millions by 1986 and 50,000 millions (or one person per square foot of the entire earth's surface) by 2110. Since 1850 the world population of 1,000 millions had doubled by 1930, increased to 2,326 millions by 1947 and to 3,000 millions in 1962, and was expected to reach 4,000 millions in 1977, a bare fifteen years later. The problems of food supply, and the contrast between the poverty of the majority and the well-fed affluence of a minority of the earth's peoples, were becoming more pressing. At the same time new fertilisers and pesticides and battery and factory methods of rearing animals for food promised an increase in food supplies while also threatening the balance of nature on which such supplies might depend. Yet again, discoveries in biology and genetics and contraceptives opened the way to limiting the increase of population, to moulding the physical characteristics of future generations, and to creating human beings by artificial means.

No less revolutionary were the other changes portended by new advances in science and technology. The development of computers and the process of automation promised to eliminate much routine work from industry and commerce. Not too little leisure but too much seemed likely to be the lot of ordinary men and women. Similarly, commercial aviation on the main routes across the oceans and between the continents only came into its own after 1945; diplomacy, business, tourism were much changed by the new speed of travel, measured in hours instead of days or weeks, and the apparent shrinkage of distances.

In these years (1945–65) world politics and the relations between countries and continents responded, though slowly, to the changes being made by science and technology. Power politics became polarised round two super-powers, the United States and Russia, who for long engaged in the rivalry of the 'Cold War'. The growth in power and influence and scientific mastery of the Chinese Republic since the middle 'fifties began to intrude upon this over-simple 'balance of power'. The recovery of western Europe, particularly of France and Germany and the other members of the Common Market (1957), raised up another, though lesser, force in world affairs. Other challengers of the old order were the newly independent countries of Asia and Africa and the Middle East which had risen from colonial status: first India, Pakistan, Burma and Ceylon in 1947; Ghana (1957), followed by the other British colonies in Africa; the overseas territories and colonies of France, Italy, Belgium and the Netherlands. From the first the new nations insisted on being treated on a level of complete equality with the old—a claim which Egypt vindicated by the nationalisation of the Suez Canal and by its resistance to the attempted Anglo-French invasion in 1956. The new nations came to constitute a majority in the United Nations. The rivalry between the white and coloured peoples, whether within a nation (as in the 'civil rights' campaigns in the United States in the 1960s) or between the nations, assumed a new dimension.

It is these circumstances which have forced historians to examine the whole nature of change in this century and to ask whether a new stage or a new epoch has been reached which demands a new kind of history and a new name. The editor of the first edition of this volume finds a 'more coherent and precise concept of world history' both possible and desirable in this century because for the first time 'the six continents of the world really matter to one another'. Interdependence and interaction provide 'the central theme of world history during the last fifty years'.[1] Another historian talks of 'the shifting balance of power between continents, nations and classes, through which we are living'.

The middle years of the twentieth century find the world in a process of change probably more profound and more sweeping than any which has overtaken it since the mediaeval world broke up in ruins and the foundations of the modern world were laid in the fifteenth and sixteenth centuries...This transition to what I have called the contemporary world...is not yet complete: it is part of the revolutionary change through which the twentieth-century world is passing...It is only today that it has become possible for the first time even to imagine a whole world consisting of peoples who have in the fullest sense entered into history...[2]

Similar reflections have led another historian to the conviction that 'modern history' has ended, and that recent or contemporary history cannot be thought of simply as the latest phase of modern history (the period of European history beginning with the Renaissance and the Reformation). 'Contemporary history is different, in quality and content, from what we know as "modern" history.'

One of the distinctive facts about contemporary history is that it is world history and that the forces shaping it cannot be understood unless we are prepared to adopt world-wide perspectives; and this means not merely supplementing our conventional view of the recent past by adding a few chapters on extra-European affairs, but re-examining and revising the whole structure of assumptions and preconceptions on which that view is based.

The first half of the twentieth century has all the marks of a 'period of revolutionary change and crisis' comparable to the 'social and intellectual upheaval at the turn of the eleventh and twelfth centuries' and to the period of the Renaissance and Reformation, one of the 'moments when humanity swings out of its old paths on to a new plane, when it leaves the marked-out route and turns off in a new direction'.[3]

With the problem of terminology here raised—what to call the new age of history—we need not be concerned. But the larger argument poses the question to what age of history the first half of the twentieth century

---

[1] David Thomson, *World History from 1914 to 1950* (Home University Library: Oxford, 1954), pp. 4–6.
[2] E. H. Carr, *What is History?*, pp. 112, 128, 135, 144.
[3] Geoffrey Barraclough, *An Introduction to Contemporary History* (London, 1964), pp. 2, 4.

belongs. Is it, as Barraclough contends, the 'watershed' between 'modern' and 'contemporary' history, a watershed extending from 1890, when Bismarck retired, to 1961, when President John F. Kennedy began his term of office? Does it mark the end of a chapter, or the beginning of a new chapter, or a time of transition partaking of two eras, old and new? To raise such questions is not to answer them. To define twentieth-century history as contemporary history, world history in a new sense, is not to write it; old habits of mind, old boundaries, persist, not least among historians. This volume can only hope to provide some of the materials for a judgement of the character of its period.

Of those forces making for a new kind of world and a new world history four at least were manifest in the opening years, before 1914. The 'dwarfing of Europe' and the power of nationalism outside Europe was foreshadowed at the beginning of the century by Japan's victory over Russia, an Asian nation defeating a European, 'a first glimpse of the future global age'.[1] This gave warning that the fate of Asia, and particularly of China, was not to be decided by the European powers. The creation of the Republic of China in 1912 was another portent, its significance masked for a generation by the civil wars and internal weakness which ensued (ch. xii). In Europe, the events of chief importance in the long run were not the rivalry of the Great Powers in the Balkans nor the diplomatic crises of 1905 and 1911 nor the competition in armaments, especially between Britain and Germany over naval strength; rather they were social, technological, scientific. It was not that society was transformed, but the assumptions which governed it were changing. There was greater class-consciousness, a sharper edge to industrial unrest, a stronger demand for more equality. The birth of the Labour party, the attack on the House of Lords, the legislation for social welfare (1908–11) were signs of a new temper and the efforts of government to placate it in Britain; and it was in 1911 also that the Bismarckian edifice of social security in Germany was completed. The technological and industrial changes were more gradual, and those affecting everyday living—refrigeration, canning, electricity, the telephone, the motor car—all had their beginnings in the late nineteenth century; as did the trusts and monopolistic corporations. The twentieth century opened, however, with two triumphs of invention fraught with global consequences: Marconi's transmission of wireless signals across the Atlantic in 1901, and Blériot's flight across the English Channel in 1909 (more significant, perhaps, than the Wright brothers' pioneer flight in an aeroplane in 1903).

It was, however, the scientists who even then 'had the future in their bones' (ch. iv). Becquerel's discovery of radioactivity in 1896, J. J. Thomson's discovery of the electron in 1897, Rutherford's demonstration in 1911 that the 'rays' emitted in radioactive disintegration were really

[1] *Ibid.* p. 101.

atoms, and equally the theorems of Planck and Einstein, pointed not merely to the transformation of physics but to the later exploitation of nuclear power. Here was a 'long revolution', continuing largely out of public sight between the wars, to its demonic revelation in 1945. Equally gradual was the advance of genetics, building on Mendel's forgotten work. The discovery of drugs to resist or cure disease was more dramatic: Ronald Ross and Walter Reed showed at the beginning of the century how malaria and yellow fever could be controlled—'western' scientists helping to transform the lives of millions in other continents. Ehrlich's discovery of salvarsan in 1909 was only one of a series, marked by the development of the sulfa drugs in 1935–8 and penicillin in 1940. All of this contributed to and rested on the growth of the scientific profession (itself an aspect of the rise of the professions which the nineteenth century had witnessed). The danger, coming from the steady and now commonplace manifestations of scientific progress, is that the giant weight and permeative force of science as an agent of change is too easily discounted, particularly over a period such as this, which was the seed-time for later harvests. Even the voice of the historian of science seems deceptively low-pitched:

The first half of the twentieth century proved to be a period of advance in science surpassing that of all preceding times in extent, in rapidity and in application; and in these fifty years the harvest of four centuries of modern science was reaped so thoroughly that it changed the whole aspect and outlook of our civilisation as well as our daily lives and our habits of thought.[1]

Into this world, barely disturbed by the first tremors of the changes to come, erupted the first of the two world wars of the half-century. Perhaps the first world war does not deserve its name; it was a European civil war with some fighting in side-shows outside Europe and it brought the United States into Europe as a belligerent. The older term, the Great War, puts it in its European context: the losses it inflicted, in blood and treasure, were far greater than those of any previous war. It was not, however, the human and material losses in Europe that made it significant in shaping the new world history. Rather, it was the succession of shocks and blows which it inflicted. Part of these were psychological. The war followed a century of general peace and of European hegemony, of growing international trade and of massive emigration from Europe. A world system of investment, credit and trade had seemed part of the permanent order of things, in which Great Britain was 'the conductor of the orchestra' (ch. III). Now the European states had weakened themselves and the old structure had disintegrated. The Austrian, German, Ottoman and Czarist empires were no more; in the quarter-century of King George V's reign (1910–36) five emperors and eight kings lost their thrones. The Russian Revolution might well prove the beginning of a

[1] See below, ch. IV, p. 88.

world revolution: the demonstration of communism in action, and the force of its example and propaganda, struck fear into the ruling classes and spread hope in much of the working class.

In all this the dwarfing of Europe had begun; its position of world leadership was undermined. The spirit of nationalism had been given new potency, particularly in India and in the Islamic world. Old patterns of trade and industry had been broken: new competitors appeared against the old suppliers, as Britain, in particular, found when her coal exports were displaced in Europe and her markets for cotton goods in India and Africa were invaded by the Japanese. The war had mobilised industry; but the expansion only left the contestants with surplus capacity. The war led to increased production of foodstuffs; at the end there was an apparent glut, and the slump in world prices held back the countries of primary production for a decade and delayed the recovery of world trade. True the interdependence which for centuries had made a world economy in trade a reality was not lost amid the movement towards higher tariffs and autarky; and planning, a feature of totalitarian, communist and democratic states alike, offered some hope of a better world order and a fairer use of the world's resources in some distant future (ch. III).

The more obvious legacy of the war was the 'great depression' of the early 'thirties and the rise of dictatorships in Germany, Italy, Spain, Portugal and several other countries (ch. XVI). Depression sapped the cohesion and the instinct for preservation in countries which remained democratic; in France and Belgium, and to a less extent in Britain, democratic government itself was under attack (ch. XVII). In Germany it gave an entry to Hitler and the Nazis to seize power and erect their totalitarian and militarist Reich and begin an internal reign of terror. Hitler's ambitions, the more frightening because they seemed nebulous and unlimited, were at least one of the causes of the second world war.

For a long time, however, the effect of the first world war in weakening European dominance and opening the way to a new era of world history was masked by the illusion of a return to the old order. International trade and credit revived, though clogged by the new war debts and reparations: the pound was restored to the gold standard at its pre-war parity with the dollar in 1925—a premature and unconvincing gesture. The League of Nations (ch. IX) seemed not merely a substitute for the old 'concert of Europe' but an improvement on it, world-wide but Europe-led. Soviet Russia, beset by the problems of economic planning and revolutionary social reconstruction (chs. III, XV), showed few signs of emerging as a new world power. The United States, equally responsive to war-born emotions of nationalism, retreated from open commitment to the European balance of power. On the other hand, the European overseas empires, swollen by the absorption of Germany's former colonies, were vaster and more impressive than ever; the British Empire had reached its greatest extent, and the sun never set on its Government Houses round the world.

Beneath the surface the European order was being eroded between the wars. Imperialism was in retreat. Perhaps J. A. Hobson's *Imperialism* (1904) was the first blow to its twentieth-century self-assurance: or had the Boer War already cast the first stone? The part played by the Dominions in the war gave them new status as independent states, and the new name for the British Empire, British Commonwealth of Nations, was not merely symbolic. In India the Congress party drew up a declaration of independence and Gandhi launched his civil disobedience campaign in 1919 (ch. XI, § 1), though it took a quarter of a century and a second world war to bring independence, and partition, to India. In the Middle East there were new states made from parts of the old Turkish Empire: true, British and French influence over them seemed secure, though Palestine's early history foretold the strength of Arab nationalism (ch. X). In Africa, the Caribbean and South-East Asia the colonies of the European powers felt little of the wind of change, though there were cautious efforts to bring educated natives into a share in government (chs. XI, § 2, XIII). The French colonies continued to be administered as permanent dependencies of metropolitan France, and 'assimilation' remained the goal. A policy very similar to Lugard's 'dual mandate' in the British colonies was expounded by M. Sarraut's *Mise en valeur des colonies françaises* (1923), emphasising the association of the native *élite* in the government, and economic development in the interests of the indigenous people. In the Belgian Congo (the Congo Free State ruled by Belgium after 1908) paternalistic administration and development of mineral wealth went hand in hand.[1]

How far the erosion of European power outside its own continent had gone was most clearly shown by the actions of Japan. It was in 1915, during the war, that Japan had presented its Twenty-One Demands on China, a claim to dominate China and much of Asia. Circumstances compelled a standstill; but Japan's invasion of Manchuria in 1931 was simply the resumption of the former claim (ch. XII). Behind it lay the rapid growth of population in the East, while Europe's rate of increase slowed down. Japan's population doubled in the sixty years before 1930; India's grew by 83 million between 1920 and 1940; in Java and the Kiangsu province of China the population density was over 800 per square mile (in Europe it averaged 184). This was not a matter of a growing rural population: in 1900 there were only 3 cities in Asia with over a million people; by 1960 there were 26 in the world's total of 69. 'It is no exaggeration to state that the demographic revolution of the half-century between 1890 and 1940 was the basic change marking the transition from one era

[1] Lord Hailey, *An African Survey* (rev. ed. Oxford, 1957), pp. 206 f.; R. Oliver and J. D. Fage, *A Short History of Africa* (London, 1962), pp. 210–11.

8

of history to another.'[1] 'The collapse of the European empires in Asia in 1941 was essentially a demographic failure.'[2]

The second world war made manifest what had been latent for the previous twenty years. It was indeed a world war, fought in Europe and Asia, the Atlantic and the Pacific, in the air as well as on land and sea. If the Western powers (the United States and Britain) with Russia defeated the Japanese bid for empire in Asia, in Europe it was a war of mutual extermination, though not pressed, like Laocoon's struggle with the serpents, to the extreme end. In it and after it the contours of the contemporary world were clear to see: the dwarfing of Europe, the end of colonial empires, the resurgence of the peoples of Asia and Africa, the predominance of two super-powers, the United States and Russia, the consolidation of revolutionary China, and the move into new realms of scientific discovery, space exploration, technical sophistication, and nuclear weaponry. The violence of the age had brought nemesis to Europe.

Among its victims the most tragic were the most innocent, the Jews. The age-old curse of anti-Semitism reached the ultimate in horror and evil under the Nazis. Jews were killed by the tens of thousands in the German concentration camps, 1,750,000 in Auschwitz alone. Of 6½ million Jews in Nazi-dominated countries in 1939 only 1½ million survived the war. In six years of war one-third of all Jews in the world perished; of Jews in Europe one-half, of those in central Europe three-quarters. A new word, genocide, was added to the vocabulary. As their historian has written, 'never in history had any section of mankind suffered so inhumanly'.[3]

It is always possible to take a hopeful or a pessimistic view about the future of mankind. Despair might have predominated in many countries at the end of the war. It did not. Twenty years later, though public war and private violence still rage, the historian is less likely to see violence as the mark of the age. Rather, he sees 'one world' as something more than a rhetorical term: a world which might rend itself in racial war or destroy itself in the collision of two super-powers, but which is increasingly bound together by common problems, common aspirations, and the world-wide effects of ever larger advances in science—discovering the 'secrets of the universe' and applying the knowledge to new ways of life.

Does this make the first half of the twentieth century a time of transition from old to new, from modern history to contemporary history? Has the time of transition ended? Is this the last chapter of modern history or the first chapter of world history? Perhaps the next *Cambridge History* will furnish the answer and Acton's 'ultimate history' at last be written.

[1] G. Barraclough, *Introduction to Contemporary History*, p. 87; see also pp. 71–4, 83.
[2] *Ibid.* p. 78.
[3] *Chambers's Encyclopaedia* (1955), s.v. Jewish history.

CHAPTER II

THE TRANSFORMATION OF SOCIAL LIFE

THE forty years before the second world war brought far-reaching changes in the ways of life and the standards of living of European peoples. These changes were wrought by historical forces and events which had diverse effects in different countries. When the twentieth century began Europe already fell into three fairly well-defined regions. Europe east of the Elbe remained essentially a peasant Europe, where industrialisation had spread slowly for some fifty years and where national consciousness had developed speedily, often on a linguistic, family or racial basis. Economically and socially eastern Europe lagged well behind most countries west of the Elbe. These, however, fell into two categories. The nations of the north and west—Scandinavia, the Low Countries, Britain, France, Germany, Switzerland—had pressed furthest with industrialisation and with other economic developments which usually accompanied it. They experienced urbanisation, capital accumulation and credit organisation, foreign trade, and higher general standards of living. Areas of the south and south-west—Spain, Portugal, southern Italy and southern Ireland—belonged geographically (and in certain respects historically) to the west, but in economic and social underdevelopment they more closely resembled the countries of the east. Spain and Portugal had won and lost large imperial possessions in the New World: the residue of past glories remained a drag on their modern development.

There were, inevitably, important exceptions to this tripartite division. Some of Austria was almost as industrialised as Germany, whilst parts of south-west France were as underdeveloped as southern Italy. But the three regions preserved broad characteristic differences which greatly affected the impact of twentieth-century changes on their social life. In the general balance of forces in the continent Germany was the pivot on which in their relations with one another the three regions turned.

Social changes were many and complex, as well as geographically diversified, but they may conveniently be considered as falling into two categories. There were changes in the size, structure and fabric of society, which included the growth and movements of population, the spread of towns and communications, the rise of new occupational groups and social classes. And there were changes in the functioning and pursuits of society, which included production and distribution of the greater wealth made available by technological change, the consumption and use of this greater wealth, and increasing acceptance of new purposes for society and the state, such as greater 'social justice' or 'social security'. Again, this distinction between structural and functional changes in society is far from rigid. Perhaps the profoundest change of all took place in the character and social role of the family, and this was at once both structural and functional. Throughout, interactions and correlations in time and place may be more significant than any one aspect of change considered separately. The transformation of society came about in the process of a continual interplay between three disparate factors: the fundamental conditions for economic growth, the social structure and aspirations of each community, and the political map of Europe in which state boundaries only partly coincided with either viable economic units or with communities socially and nationally homogeneous. Though infinitely complex the interplay is reducible to some kind of pattern, which in turn reveals something of the nature and development of European civilisation in the twentieth century.

During the first half of the twentieth century the world's population grew by more than 1,000 millions, which was a larger absolute increase than had occurred during the whole of the previous century. By 1940, however, divergencies between Europe and the other continents had not yet widened sufficiently to change the world's demographic balance decisively. The estimated totals were 1,608 millions in 1900, and 2,160 millions by 1940. Of these totals the share of Europe, apart from Russia, fell from 20 to 18 per cent. But until the 1920s the rate of growth of European population exceeded that of Asians and Africans: then it began to be exceeded by that of Asians and Africans. The decline in Europe's world supremacy in the twentieth century had this demographic basis. Internal rates of growth varied greatly, the largest proportionate increases occurring in the eastern and southern parts of Europe. By 1939 the rate of increase had become small in all countries of western and northern Europe, except the Netherlands. Although the population of Europe (including Russia) increased from some 423 millions in 1900 to 573 millions in 1940, nearly 100 millions of this increase took place within Russia.[1] Migration from Europe to other continents reflected these facts: the flow from eastern and southern Europe exceeding that from western and northern from 1896 onwards, the whole movement reaching a peak in 1913 and then declining sharply during and after the first world war.

Significant movements of people from one European country to another occurred frequently during the period, and for a wide variety of reasons. Central and eastern Europe were most affected. The long war, the post-war redrawing of frontiers, social revolution and political persecution all contributed to the upheaval. The Bolshevik Revolution, before the civil war ended, produced something between one and two

---

[1] *Cambridge Economic History of Europe*, vol. VI, part I (1965), pp. 59–63.

million refugees or exiles. Germany after 1919 absorbed some three-quarters of a million people whose homes lay mainly within the new Poland, whilst Hungary, much smaller and less industrialised, absorbed 400,000 from its border regions. There was a massive exchange, conducted under considerable coercion, between Greece and Turkey. The Nazi terror in Germany and the civil war in Spain sent many thousands more into exile. Restrictions on immigration imposed by the United States (1921 and 1924) and by the British Dominions meant that Europe between the wars had largely to deal unaided with its own population problems. The main country of reception now was France, underpopulated because of heavy war losses and a low birth-rate. Between 1920 and 1928 France accepted more than a million and a half foreign workers, mainly from Italy, Belgium, Poland and Switzerland. The number of resident foreigners per 10,000 inhabitants rose from 267 in 1901 to 691 in 1931. Elsewhere the prevalence of unemployment led to resistance to the admission of migrant workers from abroad. Apart from France, the internal European migrations were predominantly movements of compulsion or fear. The exodus resulting from selective persecution, such as flight from Bolshevik and Nazi terror, conferred great cultural benefits on the societies—usually the tolerant democracies—receiving them.

A further redistribution of population continued to occur within each country: the migration from countryside to town, matching the trend toward industrialisation and therefore now increasingly affecting the eastern European countries. The process continued sufficiently into the twentieth century to turn most Europeans into townsmen, and then it tapered off. 'Urbanisation', however, is a relative term, and towns which one society regards as relatively small and 'rural' another may regard as specifically 'urban'. Indisputably 'urban' units, of more than 100,000 inhabitants, were formed very early in Britain. Already by 1831 some 16 per cent of its population lived in such towns: it was 1936 before the same proportion of Frenchmen did so, and by then 40 per cent of British people did so. In 1939 there were 81 towns of this size in the Soviet Union, 57 in the United Kingdom, and 56 in Germany, but still only 17 in France. Throughout Europe as a whole, but at varying rates and to different extents, the number of large towns tended to increase. Between the 1880s and the later 1940s the populations of London, Glasgow, Amsterdam, Vienna and Naples doubled or nearly doubled; those of Birmingham and Lisbon nearly trebled; those of Madrid, Hamburg and Milan grew four-fold; those of Barcelona, Rome and Prague grew more than fivefold.

If the proportions of the population living in towns of more than 10,000 inhabitants be taken as a general index of undoubted 'urbanisation', Britain and the Netherlands were the most highly urbanised countries of Europe. By 1946 the percentages in each country living in towns of more than 10,000 were for Britain and the Netherlands 70; for Italy 53; for

Germany 47; for Belgium 45; and for France only 33.[1] Although most Europeans were now town dwellers, most were still small-town dwellers. But the uprooting of people from village life and rural occupations, their concentration into urban areas, and their subjection to the disciplines of factory work and office hours, were features of social change everywhere. More precisely, it meant in a period of expanding population that the numbers engaged in agriculture frequently remained static or shrank, while the increased numbers were almost wholly absorbed into expanding or new industries, or into the growing 'tertiary sector' of transportation, service or professional occupations demanded by a modern economy.[2]

Urban communities of large size usually developed around them 'suburban' areas, expanding outer layers from which many workers travelled daily to work in the city by trams, buses or railways. They were almost entirely industrial and business centres, large ports and capital cities. People living in such communities enjoy all the amenities but incur all the hazards of modern urban civilisation. They are subject to many different mass-pressures, and are among the first to feel the impact of an industrial slump and unemployment. They are most at the mercy of processes of inflation and of administrative control. At the same time, they are also more susceptible to forces of mass-suggestion and social unrest, more liable in times of disorder to slide into crime and riot. Large agglomerations of people exert a gravitational pull, attracting to themselves more and more incomers from home or abroad. In modern warfare they are especially vulnerable to attack from the air, as Rotterdam, Warsaw, Hamburg, Leningrad, London and other European cities were to give proof during the second world war.

On the other hand townspeople, although more exposed to the fluctuations of the modern economic system and to aerial attack, are also more open to new ideas and more liable to support movements which can provide greater security against the hardships of such fluctuations. They are better able to make effective organised protests against bad conditions. It is these urban masses in twentieth-century Europe which have given the main momentum to movements of social reform, as well as to the building of labour organisations, trade unions, and socialist parties. They have also been the main seed-beds of movements of unrest and violence. There have been few peasant revolts in Europe this century.

It is probable that before the first world war the disparities between town life and country life were sharper than after the second world war, despite the growth meanwhile of still larger urban and suburban areas. Until the appearance of cheap and fast road transport and the popularisa-

[1] C. P. Kindleberger, *Economic Growth in France and Britain, 1851–1950* (1964), pp. 249–50.
[2] Cf. Jean Fourastié, *Le grand espoir du xxe. siècle* (1947; rev. ed. 1963), for a famous discussion of the three sectors of activity and how they were affected by the intensity of technological progress this century.

tion of radio, the countryman was often virtually cut off from the amenities of the town in his daily life. Even the railways did not provide the great ease of movement which came with the internal combustion engine; and the cinema, unlike radio (and later television), was an amusement mainly of the towns. The tendency since the 1920s has been for agriculture to become more mechanised and for the villager to share more easily in the material facilities of the towns: for him to become more assimilated, thereby, to the outlooks and patterns of behaviour previously peculiar to townsmen. At the same time many things have conspired to take the townsman more into the countryside: the growth of annual holidays with pay and of cheap rail and road transport; a nostalgic 'return to nature'; the cult of the bicycle in France, of the *Wandervögel* in Germany, of youth hostels in Britain, of the Boy Scout movement everywhere; the upheavals and evacuations of war; the institution, even, of compulsory national service in peace-time, which almost every continental country had established by 1914 and which Britain accepted after 1939. Whether the final effect was to impoverish or to enrich rural life, it certainly helped to soften the differences between rural and urban populations and to create still greater homogeneity in national life. Where, as in France or Spain, or in much of eastern Europe, massive urbanisation was comparatively rare and the distinctive interests and methods of agriculture were more tenacious, disparities between rural and urban people remained both clear and significant. It is doubtful whether the impressive increase in international travel during these years greatly affected the matter. Travel across frontiers, whether for business or pleasure, is mainly between large towns, between ports and airports, or directed towards 'tourist centres'.

In the new conditions in industry in the twentieth century advantages did not lie entirely with the newer industrial countries as against the old, although eventually the balance of advantages and disadvantages probably did (chs. III, XIX). The United States were quick to improve and extend their highways for the benefit of the automobile, and their industrialists (notably Henry Ford) perfected the chain-belt techniques of mass production and the principle of paying workers enough to enable them to buy the motor-cars they made. Except when a country already had, as had Belgium and France after the post-war reconstruction of the 1920s, a system of good roads adequate for first-generation motor-cars, Europeans were slow to equip themselves to make use of the new inventions. Italy and Spain lagged behind the north-west, but even in Germany it was the 1930s before Hitler's preparations for war included the famous national network of *Autobahnen*. The first completed strip, from Frankfurt to Darmstadt, was opened in May 1935. In 1929 the Liberal party in Britain fought the general election with the programme *We Can Conquer Unemployment*. It urged a large programme of public works, including the building of a national system of trunk roads and ring roads round cities.

But annual capital expenditure in Britain on roads and bridges rose to only £19 million in 1931 and 1932, and by 1936 had fallen back to £8 million. On the other hand Europeans showed more enterprise than Americans in developing aviation as a commercial means of transport, and within Europe Italy and Germany outdistanced France by 1937. In 1920 the Dutch instituted a regular air service between Amsterdam and London, and throughout the 1920s European capitals came to be linked by regular commercial air services. In the course of the next decade the European colonies, too, became linked with the continental capitals by airlines. Strangely enough United States aviation meanwhile was mainly limited to military uses and to carrying mail. Internal commercial and passenger services developed later than in Europe, and it was the eve of the second world war before Europe and the United States were connected by a regular air service. The transatlantic telephone had existed since 1927.

As with development of transport and communications, so, in their exploitation of the new resources of energy and technology (ch. IV), European peoples varied considerably in enterprise and success. France was relatively slow to adopt the new industrial techniques, except in the outstanding instance of the automobile industry. The two large firms of Renault and Citroën, and to a lesser extent Peugeot, adopted mass production methods with the benefit of state credit and large state orders. Germany was quick to develop those industries in which, before 1914, it had enjoyed a special lead: notably the chemical, electrical, engineering and new textile industries. Sweden, which at the beginning of the century had just tipped in balance from a predominantly agricultural to a predominantly industrial economy, efficiently developed such appropriate new industries as pulp and paper-making, electrical products and engineering. At the other extreme, countries of southern and eastern Europe tended to remain producers of primary or extractive products. Spain adhered to farming and mining. Italy even by 1939 exported mainly fruit and market-garden produce, or textiles and other goods manufactured from imported raw materials.

The chief changes in the social structure and the balance of social interests implied by such tendencies contributed, in varying degrees, to blur the old division between the 'toiling masses', engaged in heavy labour involving little skill or limited skill, and the owners, managers or professional people who escaped such drudgery. Though the old dichotomy had never been as clear or as universal as social theorising implied, it certainly became increasingly unreal in this period. As occupational groups diversified in character and changed in balance, so the structure of each national society also changed, often in highly complex ways. The shrinkage of the *Lumpenproletariat* in favour of the skilled or clerical worker, the technician and the professional man or woman, may come to be seen as the greatest single social change of these years, at least in western Europe. Affecting as it did the daily lives of men and families and their attitudes to one another, necessitating a vast extension of popular education and technical training, transferring much effective power from both workers and capitalists to the managers and manipulators of modern society, this broad change was to become yet more evident with the applications of electronics and computers after the second world war.

At the beginning of the century Britain retained her position, won during the nineteenth century, as the world's most highly industrialised country. In 1910 the Board of Trade announced that, whereas 48 per cent of the population of England and Wales were engaged in manufacturing and mining, only 40 per cent of Germans, 33 per cent of Frenchmen and 30 per cent of Americans were so employed. In 1936 less than 30 per cent of Italians (gainfully employed persons over the age of ten years) were employed in industry; whilst nearly 48 per cent were engaged in agriculture, as compared with (in 1931) 35 per cent in France and only 6 per cent in Britain. The proportion of a nation's labour force engaged in agriculture declined everywhere in Europe during these decades. Even in a heavily agricultural country such as Denmark it fell slowly to 40 per cent by 1911, then more rapidly to 28 per cent by 1939. In the Soviet Union the decrease was dramatic, because of collectivisation and the extension of large-scale mechanised farming. Between 1926 and 1939 the number of Russians employed in agriculture fell absolutely by 10–20 per cent, and, in terms of a proportion of the total population, it dropped from more than 75 per cent to about 56 per cent.[1]

For a complex of reasons the 'thirties in Europe brought a sharpening of class conflicts and a widening of the gulf between capitalist and working-class interests. In France (ch. XVII) the outcry against the 'economic oligarchies' entrenched in 'financial feudalism' was a sharply defined version of a complaint raised in many other countries.

It was shown how 'two hundred families', through common stockholding, interlocking relationships, and similar devices, kept the posts of command of French economy firmly in hand, and publicity was given to the fact that fewer than 150 persons, most of them connected by marriage and family ties, held more than 1,900 seats in the administration of the most important corporations in the fields of coal, power, steel, oil, chemicals, railroads, banking, and insurance.[2]

From Germany's industrialists and financiers such as Alfred Hugenberg, Hjalmar Schacht and Fritz Thyssen, Hitler's National Socialist party received vital backing in its rise to power, but whether more from fear of communism or more from hopes of profitable rearmament remains in some doubt (ch. XVI). Thyssen later admitted, 'I have personally given altogether one million marks to the National Socialist party.'[3] Others,

[1] *Cambridge Economic History of Europe*, vol. VI, part 1 (1965), p. 24.
[2] H. W. Ehrmann, *French Labor from Popular Front to Liberation* (1947), p. 13.
[3] Fritz Thyssen, *I Paid Hitler* (1941), p. 133. He considered (p. 134) that 'all in all, the amounts given by heavy industry to the Nazis may be estimated at two million marks a year'.

such as von Krupp, opposed Hitler before he came to power but profitably supported the party once it had gained power.

In Spain social conflicts, which elsewhere either produced 'popular front' alignments of the left and centre to prevent fascist *coups*, or led to actual *coups*, resulted in both together and in prolonged civil war. Beginning in June 1936 as an army revolt against the Popular Front republican government (which communists had helped to power but in which, as in its French counterpart, they held no office), the Spanish civil war combined old and new internal schisms with international power rivalries in a most explosive mixture. The ferocious fighting which ensued had far-reaching social and psychological implications for the Europe of the 1930s. Against a background of economic slump which especially affected agricultural exports and metallurgical mining industries, and of political instability and anarchistic violence, its three years of bloodshed left Spain an impoverished and exhausted country, the battlefield of social and ideological enmities.

Here were ranged the masters of economic power in the country, led by the Army, and supported by the Church, that embodiment of Spain's past glory. All these believed that they were about to be overwhelmed. Opposed to them were 'the professors'—many of the enlightened middle class—and almost the entire labour force of the country, maddened by years of insult, misery, and neglect, intoxicated by the knowledge of the better conditions enjoyed by their class comrades in France and Britain and by the actual mastery which they supposed that the working class had gained in Russia.[1]

The forces most liable to disrupt societies which lacked the larger cohesiveness of strong national feeling were illustrated even more clearly in the experience of the Republic of Austria between the wars. The Treaty of Saint Germain forced together two radically different societies, the large, cosmopolitan industrial city of Vienna and the conservative, Catholic, agrarian provinces of the new republic. Geographical and administrative segregation of the social classes within one state resulted in the Social Democrats ruling the city with a rival Christian Social majority in the *Nationalrat*. In 1932, after a period of uneasy co-existence, of recurrent inflation culminating in economic slump, of interference from fascist Italy and frequent militant demonstrations, the country succumbed to the clericalist and authoritarian rule of Chancellor Dollfuss, who in 1933 suspended parliamentary government.

The structure of society in Europe, though changing in many different ways during these years under the pressures described, remained ultimately nationalist in character. It was not only that the peace settlement of 1919 redrew the map on more nationalistic principles: it was also that states which could not rely upon the cement of national community in face of the disruptive forces of economic distress, political ideology and social conflict tended to fall subject to dictatorship. This was as true of

[1] Hugh Thomas, *The Spanish Civil War* (1961; rev. ed. 1965), p. 159.

Russia in 1917 and the Austro-Hungarian Empire in 1918 as it was of Germany in 1933, or Spain in 1939.

The ultimate gains of the whole transformation of society by 1939 went most substantially to nationalism. States resorted to protectionist measures or to schemes of public works on a national scale in face of the economic slump. The democracies which most lacked national cohesion—Italy, Austria, Spain, Czechoslovakia—suffered disruption or the imposition of authoritarian rule. Within the single-party states of the 1930s it was in each instance the more nationalistic wing of the party which triumphed over the more reformist wing: Stalinists routed Trotskyists, Hitler and Himmler purged the 'second revolutionaries' in 1934, Mussolini and the imperialists had their way in Abyssinia and Spain and crushed internal fascist dissent. In Britain, Belgium and France national coalitions contrived to preserve national cohesion by moderate reforms and by withstanding the extremists of left and right. The main international organisations—the League of Nations, the Third (Communist) International, even the Roman Catholic church—were unable to hold their own against the powerful appeals of nationalist separatism. Already, in the colonial world, movements of national independence and unification were raising their heads—in India, the Far East, Africa (chs. XI, XII, XIII). This overriding fact coloured all social changes, whether of structure and fabric, or of working and purpose.

The commonest use to which the new wealth of society was put was, of course, improvement in the standard of living of some or all sections of the population. Both the extent and the incidence of better standards of living are, however, difficult to assess, not least because no entirely satisfactory test of 'standard of living' has been devised. Real wages are little guide in a rural society where a large part of personal or family income is in kind; or in a highly developed welfare state where a large part of real income takes the form of free or subsidised social services; or in a period (as this was in many countries) when married women are increasingly taking employment. Vital matters such as the general standard of housing and the kinds of food customarily eaten must enter into any comparison of standards of living in different countries, or even in one country at different times. So, too, the frequency of unemployment or of underemployment, and the degree of security against sickness and old age, are important components of any realistic criterion of well-being. Above all, since a standard of living is of no use without life itself, such data as the infant death-rate and expectation of life are useful indications of the medical services available, conditions of housing and nutrition, and the amount of human suffering endured.[1]

[1] Infant death-rate is the number of infants, per thousand born alive, who die during the first year of life. The expectation of life is the average age to which a person is likely to live if the death-rate of the year when he or she was born remains unchanged.

18

Measured by the tests of vital statistics, the United Kingdom made great and steady progress. In 1900–2, infants under one year old died at the rate of 142 per thousand; in 1920–2 at the average annual rate of 82; in 1930–2 at the rate of 67; in 1938–9 at the rate of 54.[1] By the same test France made equally rapid progress but at a lower standard. Her infant death rate averaged 161 per thousand in 1896–1900; 97 in 1920–4; 80 in 1930–4; and 71 in 1935–9. Although it was as high as 112 again in the critical year 1945, it more than halved (to 52) in 1950. In both countries the most striking improvement came after 1945. In the United Kingdom it fell from 49 in 1945 to only 31 in 1950. In 1950 Sweden, with only 21 per thousand, could claim the lowest infant mortality rate in the world. In most European countries it at least halved during the first half of the century, and dropped especially markedly between 1930 and 1950.

Similar improvements in the general expectation of life occurred during the period. Within the hundred years, 1850–1950, western civilisation added a full generation to the average length of life. In a number of the more advanced countries, during the fifty years before 1900, the expectation of life increased by about 2 years each decade; during the fifty years after 1900 increase was accelerated to about 3½–4 years each decade. As a result, and as some index of this new tenacity of life, the population of Europe excluding Russia grew from roughly 310 to 396 millions between 1900 and 1950. In this way Europe continued into the twentieth century, though with diminished momentum, its remarkable propensity to grow in population, despite declines in some national birth-rates and despite the heavy losses and dislocations of two world wars.

It was industrialisation, world trade, and improvement in methods of agriculture and transport that made it possible to maintain this increased population on a generally improving standard of living. Because the speed and the extent of industrialisation and the use of more scientific methods of production varied from one country to another, there remained wide disparities in their average standards of life: differences almost as great as those between European and non-European countries. In Spain the expectation of life at the age of one year in 1940 (52·4 for males, 58·8 for females) was still lower than that in France had been in 1900: and the infant mortality rate of Rumania in 1940 (188 per thousand) was about the same level as that of France a century before, and higher than that of India in 1940. In 1948 the Department of Economic Affairs of the United Nations surveyed differences in European standards of living and attempted to assess them comparatively in terms of the national income per head of the population in 1938, computed in terms of United States dollars. The range was as wide as from Great Britain (378) and the Netherlands (367) to France (236), Italy (127) and Greece (80). Regionally the range was highest in north-western Europe (362) and second highest in

[1] *Annual Abstract of Statistics*, no. 94, p. 35.

western Europe (262), with a sharp drop in central and north-eastern countries (132) and south and south-eastern including Italy (89). Before the second world war changes in the standard of living of Europeans had thus followed the familar regionalised pattern.[1]

Beyond such indications few valid generalisations can be made, save that broadly (though unevenly) there was notable improvement in physical health and length of life, and a general advance in the material well-being of the masses. This improvement included a general shortening of the working day and the working week, and even a contraction of the working life brought about by the tendency to raise the school-leaving age and to introduce a conventional age for retirement and superannuation. But material betterment was uneven for many diverse reasons. Whereas the large-scale migrations of the early decades improved both the standards of living of the migrants and the conditions of trade available to those who remained in Europe, the scale of migration overseas shrank considerably in the decades after 1914. In the Soviet Union under the first Five-Year Plan, and in the 'people's democracies' of eastern Europe after 1945, deliberate emphasis on capital investment for expanding heavy industry, at the expense of agriculture and immediate consumer goods, kept down the standard of living. Everywhere heavy expenditure on armed forces and armaments competed with consumer demands in the great dilemma of 'guns or butter'.

If wealth was more abundant, property was more insecure. The half-century was studded with wars, revolutions, and economic crises, each of which in turn wrought havoc with the previous distribution of wealth and social structure. The first world war brought the collapse of the old dynastic empires of Austria-Hungary, Turkey and Russia. This collapse involved the overthrow of much of the aristocracy and landed nobility. Throughout eastern Europe the old order went down in the violence of war and revolution. Within Russia, after the Bolshevik Revolution, land, factories, property of all kinds were confiscated. Power and control of wealth fell to new ruling cadres of party and state. In Germany landowners joined with the army and the new industrialists to retain political and economic power in their own hands; or, as in Hungary, they stemmed the tide of revolution by violent reaction. The great currency crash in Germany in 1923 ruined the bulk of the middle and *rentier* classes, and effected social upheaval at a level at which it had been evaded in 1919. During the world economic crisis of 1929–32 bankruptcies and mass unemployment brought ruin to many who had previously known prosperity. After 1933 the National Socialist régime confiscated the property of Jews and all who fell victim to the charge of political opposition. After 1939 the process was extended to all German-occupied territories. It

[1] *Economic Survey of Europe in 1948*, Department of Economic Affairs, United Nations (1949), p. 235.

was reversed by the post-war governments, who attacked collaborators and those who had profited from national misfortunes. In eastern Europe the new communist régimes after 1945 repeated much of the story of Russia after 1917. Meanwhile both world wars, and the political and racial persecutions of the inter-war and post-war years, resulted in a vast uprooting of millions of displaced persons and refugees who were left homeless and often destitute.

Which social classes gained or lost most by these upheavals it is difficult to determine. It is probable that the peasantry, still the substructure of much of Europe's economy, on balance gained from the changes. In eastern Europe they gained more land. The economic depression of the 1920s provoked government assistance for agriculture, greater mechanisation and more intensive cultivation. The 1930s were a period of steadily rising food production, and by 1939 agriculture was in a healthy state in most countries on the continent. The upheavals of war, German occupation, and liberation were accompanied by a steep decline in production and often by hunger and starvation. But except in the battle-areas these upheavals tended to hit urban rather than rural populations, and the strenuous efforts made, with American help, to restore European prosperity after the war brought a quick return to pre-war levels of production. The world shortage of food after the war meant high prices, official subsidies and encouragement, and frequently (as in France) a positive raising of the standards of living of the peasant above pre-war levels.

Landowners, though suffering less from inflation than the middle classes and less from currency collapse than the *rentier* class, suffered more from drastic confiscations. Industrialists, traders and shippers suffered from the world economic depression and from war-time confiscations, controls, and destruction. During the profound social revolution which occurred in Germany between 1923 and 1933, members of the middle classes whose incomes derived from salaries, pensions, small shops and businesses, the rental of real estate or interest on bonds or mortgages were usually reduced to great poverty. Meanwhile others gained: debtors, employers on a large scale, speculative investors, and farmers who, because they paid a fixed rent or owned their land, could benefit from rising prices. Industrial and agricultural workers, and many black-coated workers, suffered most acutely from mass unemployment during the world economic crisis. In most countries there appeared a persistent and growing army of unemployed. In Germany it approached 5 millions in 1930 and exceeded 6 millions by the beginning of 1932. In Great Britain it numbered 2 millions at certain times during 1921 and 1922, and reached nearly 3 millions in the years 1931–3. No European country suffered from mass unemployment more than Germany. France, being less dependent on foreign trade for her national prosperity, suffered less and later than either Germany or Britain.

21

4-2

Human anxieties, deprivations and destitution were the other side of the coin to the new abundance which modern technology made available to Europe. Amid plenty, poverty seemed more intolerable. This helps to explain the intensity and universality of the demand that the state should provide greater social security and undertake a more systematic redistribution of wealth. Repeatedly the normal hierarchy of wealth was violently upset. The divorce of economics from politics, which had underlain mid-nineteenth-century doctrines of *laissez faire* and free trade, could not survive such experiences. From the years before 1914 derived a more insistent demand for 'social justice', and with it a repertoire of devices by which greater social justice might be attained. The adoption and extension of these measures was, accordingly, a further main aspect of social change in this period.

The demand for social justice involved several interlocked procedures. It meant, first, completing that democratic revolution of the previous century which had moved towards universal suffrage and the extension of civic liberties and rights to all citizens. It meant, secondly, achieving greater social equality: an attack on extremes of wealth and poverty, a concern for greater equality of opportunity in education and for careers open to talents. It meant, thirdly, greater social security: protecting the individual and the family against the hazards and vicissitudes of an industrial society and an unstable world economy; providing safeguards against the poverty that could come from sickness or disability of the wage-earner, from periodic or chronic unemployment, from old age. It meant, finally, a new code of behaviour between different communities: extending self-government and civic rights to colonial peoples; co-operating with other nations in a rich variety of international bodies for promoting higher standards of living everywhere. So intense and so persistent was the general demand for greater social justice that by 1950 every European government was committed to such measures. The old division between economic and political activity was totally abandoned, and every state was engaged in implementing programmes of social security, economic regulation, and full employment. That intimate reciprocal relationship between state and society, government and nation, which was the outcome of both nationalism and democracy in the nineteenth century, was elaborated and carried very much further in the first half of the twentieth.

By 1900 most states of western Europe had either established universal suffrage or were approaching it. All Frenchmen of 21 and over had had the vote since 1870; all men in Germany since 1871, in Switzerland since 1874, in Belgium since 1893, in the Netherlands since 1896, in Norway since 1898. Although the minimum age varied the principle was generally accepted. Universal male suffrage was introduced in Sweden and Austria in 1907, Turkey in 1908, Italy in 1912. In Finland and Norway even women gained the vote in 1907. After 1918 the fashion for democratic government prevailed, and all the new states of Europe adopted democratic constitutions with universal suffrage. In 1918 women over 30 gained the vote in the United Kingdom; in 1919 women over 20 gained it in the German Republic. Turkey enfranchised women in 1934. By 1950 equal female suffrage became general throughout Europe. It was attained in Russia in 1918, in Britain in 1928, France in 1945, Italy in 1946, Belgium in 1948; and Switzerland remained the only outstanding exception. The general acceptance of equal political rights for both sexes had far-reaching but somewhat incalculable effects on representative government. It usually more than doubled the size of the electorate within a single generation. It compelled political parties to compete for the female vote in a way which may partly explain enthusiasm for systems of pensions for the widowed and aged, national health services and family allowances. The new electoral pressure of women reinforced other tendencies promoting the Welfare State.

The social revolution of twentieth-century Europe, which in most countries resulted in a new status for women, went much deeper in its causes than the agitation for female suffrage and much wider in its consequences than the extension of electorates. It was closely linked with the democratic ideal of equality, which emphasised the basic claim of every human being to equal civil and political rights. It was also part of a more comprehensive change of outlook in social life. This came with the decline in the infant mortality rate which freed women from the burden of frequent pregnancies; with more scientific facilities for birth-control and the fashion for smaller families; with opportunities for the employment of women (including married women) in offices, factories, restaurants and retail stores; with the extension of popular education to girls as well as boys; with a general demand for greater leisure and comfort. In Britain the average number of children per family was over five in the 1870s, three or four around 1900, but about two in the 1920s and 1930s. With the growing demand for female labour in factories and offices, domestic servants became more scarce, but the demand for them also declined. As housewives, women found their drudgery diminished by a host of labour-saving devices and by more abundant supplies of cheap soap, cheap furnishing materials, and more modern homes. Women in Britain and in some European countries supplied a large additional labour force in both world wars. Less economic subservience to their fathers or husbands made them more independent in spirit, more assertive of legal and social rights which legislatures, increasingly anxious to satisfy the demands of the new female electorates, readily granted. In the whole process cause and effect were usually indistinguishable. Again the change varied greatly in extent from one country to another, and it was discontinuous. The proportion of women in paid employment in France was less in 1926 than it had been in 1906. Female emancipation was often resisted by the influence of the

Roman church. The dictatorships of the inter-war years, especially the German, discouraged it and tried to raise the birth-rate and force women back into the kitchen and the nursery. In deference to this policy, the National Socialist régime in Germany failed to mobilise women for the war effort as thoroughly as did Great Britain.[1]

The eventual outcome in most countries, however, was a far-reaching transformation in the status and condition of women and of the most important single unit of social life, the family. What Professor Titmuss could claim for Britain of the 1950s was coming to be true, in varying degrees, of women in most European countries:

...it would seem that the typical working-class mother of the 1890s, married in her teens or early twenties and experiencing ten pregnancies, spent about fifteen years in a state of pregnancy and in nursing a child for the first year of its life. She was tied, for this period of time, to the wheel of childbearing. Today, for the typical mother, the time so spent would be about four years. A reduction of such magnitude in only two generations in the time devoted to childbearing represents nothing less than a revolutionary enlargement of freedom for women brought about by the power to control their own fertility.[2]

Moreover a woman aged 45 in 1931 could expect, on average, to live to the age of 73: in the 1890s she could have expected to live only to the age of 67. It may therefore be claimed that 'what these changes mean is that by the time the typical mother of today has virtually completed the cycle of motherhood she still has practically half her total life expectancy to live...For the generality of women in most societies of which we have any reliable records this is a new situation.'[3]

Sociologists are agreed that the family in these years underwent two important changes, though they disagree considerably about the significance of the changes. One was that the 'nuclear family' of parents-and-children became somewhat more important than the 'extended family' or 'kinship'. This happened chiefly because of the movements of population already noted, which for many destroyed the old bonds of neighbourhood and physical proximity, and because of the greater mobility and opportunities of labour in a modern industrial system. The other was that the nuclear family itself underwent important modifications because of the mother taking jobs and enjoying more personal freedom, its smaller size, and the growth of leisure. In general, it may be said that the family at all social levels became a more co-operative and less authoritarian community, more independent of the wider 'kinship' of grandparents, uncles and aunts, more likely to own specific property (the family house, the family

[1] The number of women employed in the German civilian labour force actually declined by about a quarter of a million during the first two years of war, and fell from 14,636,000 on 31 May 1939 to 14,437,000 three years later (see *Hitler's Europe*, ed. Arnold Toynbee and Veronica M. Toynbee, Royal Institute of International Affairs (1954), pp. 8, 226 and 234).
[2] R. M. Titmuss, *Essays on 'The Welfare State'* (1958), p. 91.   [3] *Ibid.* p. 93.

24

car) and to act as a separate group (the family holiday). This independence was in some ways buttressed by social services, giving in times of need support that was once given by the kinship, and through family allowances increasing the family's resources in some proportion to its responsibilities.

One feature of the history of the family in twentieth-century society calls for special emphasis. The major changes in its role and character have come about unintentionally as consequential effects of economic and social trends or world events, rather than as the results of deliberate policies or political enactments. The transformation brought about by industrialisation, population movements, improved standards of living and leisure has already been mentioned. In Germany and Britain in the 'twenties traditional parental authority was probably weakened more by mass unemployment, producing conditions in which the father might cease to be the family wage-earner, than by any legislative enactments. The two world wars caused more fundamental upheavals in family life than any events other than the world economic slump. British statistics of divorce, for example, show a steady low incidence of divorce from the beginning of the century until around 1918, when it sharply increased; then the incidence declined, though not to pre-war level, and remained steady until just before 1939; it increased again sharply until 1947, after which it again declined. Although other factors, including changes in the law such as the Matrimonial Causes Act of 1937, must be taken into account, it appears that wars are probably the greatest single cause of increased incidence of divorce.[1]

On the other hand, strenuously pursued governmental policies intended to change the habits or functioning of family life have conspicuously failed. Mussolini's efforts to boost the Italian family and the birth-rate proved to be powerless against the general European trend of the later 'twenties and early 'thirties towards lower birth-rates: and on this point fascist propaganda and inducements were backed up by clerical exhortations. Although Italy's population increased, from about 32 millions at the beginning of the century to roughly 37 millions in 1922 and nearly 43 millions in 1936, the increase was due neither to more marriages nor to a higher birth-rate. The rate of births actually fell from 32·7 per thousand in 1901–5 to 29·5 per thousand in 1922–5 and then to 23·7 in 1938. In 1938 Italy's net reproduction rate (1·131) was lower than that of the Netherlands, Spain, Portugal or even Bulgaria. The experience of the Soviet Union gave yet more dramatic evidence that even totalitarian régimes are relatively powerless against deep-rooted human habits and attitudes. After the revolution Bolshevik policy (though contrary to Lenin's own inclinations) was completely hostile to family life. Divorce was made easy, however often it was sought, birth-control and abortion

---

[1] See Griselda Rowntree and Norman H. Carrier, 'The Resort to Divorce in England and Wales, 1858–1957', in *Population Studies*, XL, no. 3 (March 1958).

were encouraged, all former external compulsions designed to preserve the family were abolished. For a few years, at least in the cities, family life seemed to have been shattered. But in the country at large the mass of the Russian people continued to fall in love, get married, raise children and build homes for their families. From 1936 onwards the Soviet government reversed its policy, lauded the family, reimposed external compulsions, and condemned 'free love and disorder in sexual life' as signs of bourgeois decadence.[1] An official policy which may more plausibly be claimed to have succeeded is the French system of family benefits and allowances, instituted in the form of a requirement of contributions from all employers in 1932, and elaborated in 1939 into a *Code de la Famille*. As implemented during and after the war the main purpose was to strengthen the family and boost the birth-rate. French birth-rates did, in fact, rise sharply after the war, and the contrast with pre-war trends was so sharp that many attributed the change to the generous system of family allowances and privileges since then granted to parents of large families. But even this is doubtful, and proof either way is virtually impossible.[2] By the time the rise in birth-rate became evident the system was not only incorporated into the still wider system of *Sécurité sociale* of 1945, but French society and social attitudes were undergoing the drastic upheavals of post-war reconstruction. Similar situations existed in other liberated countries.

Likewise, as regards housing, surprisingly few major states have a good record of successful policies. In many places slum-clearance and the building of workers' flats or of new housing estates were accomplished, but on a national scale such measures were seldom adequate to the basic problems. Urban and suburban development too often took place unplanned and without regard to the community's long-term interests. The second world war gave impetus to more radical rethinking of these problems by shattering many urban areas and imposing the need for systematic rebuilding.

Two ways in which governmental measures impinged much more decisively and significantly on social change were in the provision of free public education, and in the adoption of comprehensive systems of what, following the United States example of 1935, came to be called 'social security'. Such activities were common to democracies and dictatorships, and to both capitalist and communist régimes, and everywhere they became normal major activities of the modern state.

Already, by 1914, all Europe was being sent to school. Free compulsory education, at least at the primary level, was accepted as the normal or

---

[1] See Sir John Maynard, *The Russian Peasant and other Studies* (1942; 1962 ed.), pp. 521–5; Maurice Hindus, *Mother Russia* (1943). A law of July 1944 consolidated the new official attitude to the family, motherhood and parental authority.

[2] Cf. Laurence Wylie in *France: Change and Tradition* (1963), p. 191.

desirable arrangement in most countries. In France instruction had been free in all state primary schools since 1881, and compulsory for all children between the ages of 6 and 13 since 1882. In England a law of 1870 empowered local school boards to require attendance at primary schools; in 1881 compulsion became general, and ten years later elementary education became free. Comparable measures were passed during the same decades or earlier in most countries of north-western Europe, so that after 1900 their peoples were becoming increasingly literate. During the twentieth century literacy was similarly promoted in the Soviet Union after 1917, in Turkey under Mustafa Kemal, and throughout southern and eastern Europe, though often without complete success. In Portugal in 1950 more than 40 per cent of the population over the age of seven could not read or write; in Bulgaria in 1946 nearly a quarter of the whole population was illiterate.

The increase of literacy everywhere was accompanied by a great development of secondary and technical education and by expansion of university education. The number of pupils at French *lycées* and *collèges* doubled in the forty years before 1937: those going on to higher education much more than doubled. In Britain the Board of Education came into being in 1900, and the Act of 1902 prepared the way for a rapid growth of secondary education under central stimulus. This in turn generated a demand for the expansion of higher education. The Education Acts of 1918 and 1944 went far towards providing a complete system of national education, though British universities expanded more slowly than most. The number of students at British universities less than doubled in the forty years before 1939. The University of Wales was formed in 1903 and six new English universities were founded, at Birmingham (1900), Liverpool (1903), Leeds (1904), Sheffield (1905), Bristol (1909) and Reading (1926). In several other countries these years saw establishment of new universities. The Portuguese universities of Lisbon and Oporto were founded in 1911. In 1924 new Italian universities were founded at Bari, Florence, Milan and Trieste, and in 1944 at Salerno. The Danish university of Aarhus was founded in 1928, the Norwegian university of Bergen in 1946, but by that date many countries including Britain were beginning a new phase of rapid expansion of higher education and learning. The Soviet Union between 1917 and 1941 increased the number of its colleges and universities from 90 to 782.

In many countries, notably France, Germany, Italy and Belgium, this rapid expansion of state-provided or state-aided public education involved conflict between the state and the church, which had previously been the chief provider of education. This conflict was particularly acute where the Roman Catholic church predominated, and in France it precipitated the separation of church from state in 1905. In such countries the education provided in state schools and in teachers' training colleges was usually

27

positivist and secular, imbued with a strong spirit of anti-clericalism. A similar conflict revived under the dictatorships, which strove to indoctrinate the whole youth of the nation with their own secular ideologies. It recurred from time to time in the democracies, as in Britain after the Act of 1902, and in Alsace and Lorraine after their return to France in 1919.

These triumphs of liberal democracy in Europe were accompanied by a fundamental challenge to it. Even in the first decade of the century it became apparent that the developments already described might in aggregate move in either of two possible directions. They might tend, as liberal democrats expected and believed, towards the creation of a well-informed and thoughtful public opinion, seeking to use the power of the vote critically and reasonably, and in conformity with democratic ideals as these had been inherited from the rationalist democratic movement of the late eighteenth century. Or they might move in the direction of mass emotion, the subjection of public opinion to the power of propaganda, and the manipulation of the irrational impulses inherent in crowds and mobs. Popular education, movements for adult education,[1] the more responsible sections of the press and the provision of free libraries encouraged the tendency towards thoughtfulness and responsibility. Commercial advertising eager to capture the rising purchasing-power of the working classes, the sensational press made cheap by the support of advertisers, the more aggressive movements of nationalism, encouraged the contrary forces of irrationalism and mass excitement. Before 1914 it was clear that the second tendency was at least as probable and inherent an outcome of the new democracy as the first. Social theorists like Gustave Le Bon in France and Graham Wallas in England explored these questions with apprehension.[2] Popular hysteria and violence of feeling, such as were induced in Britain by the Boer War, in France by the Dreyfus Case, in Germany by the agitation for colonial and naval expansion, and in the United States by the Spanish–American War, revealed something of the capacities for violence endemic in the urban, nationalist and more literate societies of 1900.

What was new after 1900 was not human susceptibility to the arts of persuasion and propaganda. Great leaders in all ages had shown how opinion could be moulded. The popular associations of the nineteenth century had discovered all the arts of mass-agitation. Nor was it novel

[1] In Britain the universities of Cambridge, Oxford and London began extra-mural activities in the 1870s: the Workers' Educational Association was founded in 1903, its Swedish counterpart in 1908, and the French *universités populaires* between 1899 and 1903. The famous Danish People's High Schools dated from as early as 1844.

[2] Gustave Le Bon's *Psychologie des foules* appeared in 1895, Graham Wallas's *Human Nature in Politics* in 1908. Psychologists like William McDougall and sociologists like Gabriel Tarde developed, in the years before 1914, the more scientific study of social behaviour which then continued to make headway throughout the period.

28

for nationalist pride and aggression to capture popular enthusiasm. The novelties were the exposure of semi-literate urban populations to more intense and sustained pressure from propagandists of business and press, and the enhanced importance of the reactions of these populations because of universal suffrage, state activity and international tensions. The immense physical and emotional strains imposed by the four years of the first world war were quickly followed by the further expansion of media of mass persuasion in the form of the cinema, the radio, and large public meetings made possible by electrical amplification. Between the two wars it seemed that democracy had merely made the world safe for dictatorship. The monolithic parties of Soviet Russia, Fascist Italy, National-Socialist Germany, and their counterparts in some other states, seized and kept power by skilful manipulation of all the latest means for exploiting the irrational, pathological impulses of men and women in modern society. These forces, more harmlessly expressed by fashion, the hero-worship of sports favourites and film-stars, and the phenomena of song-crazes and best-selling novels, came to be harnessed to politics and (as in the propaganda which accompanied the Five-Year Plans in the Soviet Union) to economics. By 1950 television opened up still further possibilities of the same kind: and even in the most stable parliamentary democracies electioneering by film, radio and television became no less important than electioneering by poster, press and public meeting.[1]

States that were becoming increasingly democratic in structure and spirit also became providers of social services. Here, too, a certain pattern had been inherited from the later nineteenth century. By 1914 every European country outside Russia and the Balkans had relatively well-developed codes of factory and labour legislation. In the 1880s Bismarck had introduced legislation which equipped Germany with a comprehensive national system of social insurance against sickness, accident, and incapacity in old age, and in 1911 it was codified and extended to various classes of non-industrial workers, such as agricultural labourers and domestic servants. By 1913 some 14½ million people were thus insured, and codes of factory legislation and of child labour were added. Germany's neighbours, impressed by these measures, were quick to imitate them in whole or in part. In 1911 the United Kingdom introduced its first National Insurance Act, setting up a contributory scheme insuring a large part of the working population against sickness, providing for free medical attention, and insuring some categories of workers against unemployment. Belgium and Denmark, like Britain, imitated Germany's scheme of insurance against accident, sickness, and old age. Austria introduced accident and sickness insurance in the 1880s, Italy and Switzerland in the

---

[1] See R. B. McCallum and A. Readman, *The British General Election of 1945* (1947), ch. VII; H. G. Nicholas, *The British General Election of 1950* (1951), ch. VI.

1890s. In these years, too, Britain, France, Norway, Spain and the Netherlands passed legislation which obliged employers to compensate their workers for accidents which occurred during work. France introduced compulsory social insurance only in 1928. This expansion of state responsibility for the safety and well-being of its citizens, combined with the urbanisation of much of European society, brought about a general overhaul of local government and administration. By 1914 democratised and active municipal governments had endowed Europe with a great new equipment of public utility services of sanitation, water, gas, electricity and transport, and of hospitals, markets, laundries, slaughter-houses, labour exchanges, museums, recreation grounds, parks, libraries, schools, and all the other amenities of modern urban life.

The increased activities of government, both national and local, called for new fiscal policies. Until after 1871 direct income tax had been a device almost peculiar to Great Britain. With electorates of consumers indirect taxes became unpopular, and progressive direct taxation, scientifically assessed and collected in proportion to income or wealth, came into favour. In his budget of 1909 Mr Lloyd George included the whole gamut of fiscal devices which had been evolving in Britain for some years: heavy duties on tobacco and liquor, heavier death-duties on personal estates, which had first been introduced by Sir William Harcourt in 1894, graded and heavier income tax, an additional 'super-tax' on incomes above a fairly high level, a duty of 20 per cent on the unearned increment of land-values, and a charge on the capital value of undeveloped land and minerals. During the 1890s, *pari passu* with the great expansion of governmental expenditures on armaments as well as on social services, Germany and her component states, as well as Italy, Austria, Norway, and Spain, all introduced or steepened systems of income tax. French governments repeatedly shied away from it, though they resorted to progressive death duties in 1901, and it was 1917 before a not very satisfactory system of income tax was introduced. The great fiscal burdens of war accustomed people to heavier taxation. In 1920 the French ambassador, M. Paul Cambon, could remark to Mr Churchill: 'In the twenty years I have been here I have witnessed an English Revolution more profound and searching than the French Revolution itself. The governing class have been almost entirely deprived of political power and to a very large extent of their property and estates; and this has been accomplished almost imperceptibly and without the loss of a single life.'[1] If M. Cambon was exaggerating in 1920, he was perceptively prophetic, for his description became substantially true after the second world war. Already in 1937 it was calculated that 5 or 6 per cent of the national income was being redistributed from rich to poor.

A landmark in the history of social security in Europe was the *Report on*

---

[1] Winston S. Churchill, *My Early Years* (1930; new ed. 1947), p. 90.

Social Insurance and Allied Services published by Lord Beveridge in 1942. It won wide international acceptance as a social creed for the post-war world, even when the methods he proposed were unacceptable. It found fullest embodiment in the British National Insurance Act of 1946, the National Health Service Act of the same year, and the National Assistance Act of 1948, all passed by the Labour government. These measures unified the previous systems of insurance against sickness, disability, unemployment and old age into a national scheme of social security organised by the state, though leaving room for further voluntary provision; extended universally the provision of free medical and dental services; and ended the old poor law. A system of family allowances, also advocated in the Beveridge Report, was instituted in 1946; and on a much more lavish scale in France in 1945–6, as part of its General Scheme of Social Security. Comparable provisions had existed in Spain since 1939, and were instituted in Belgium in 1944 and Norway in 1946. Social security, the notion of public protection for the individual and the family against sickness, poverty, unemployment, squalor and ignorance, 'from the cradle to the grave', was the social ideal generated by the bitter experiences of the inter-war years.

These aims involved not only the provision of minimal social services such as public education, health services and old-age pensions, but the adoption by governments of a policy of 'full employment'. This policy was designed to forestall and prevent, by measures of currency and trade regulation and public investment programmes, a return of unemployment on a massive scale. Without full employment it was unlikely that social services could be maintained. It was now widely accepted in Europe that extremes of wealth and poverty should be avoided; that whilst national standards of living depended largely on world trade, the average standard of living in any country should be maintained at as high a level as possible by deliberate state action and regulation. The whole climate of opinion was completely changed from that of 1900, which outside Germany had distrusted state action. In most countries of eastern Europe more drastic policies of collectivisation were followed by the Communist governments which held power after the second world war.

Within the general pattern of promoting social welfare and security by state action and provision of social services, differences of circumstances and of emphasis left distinctive marks on each country's arrangements. Thus the French system was dominated by demographic policy, and used its family allowances and health provision to encourage large families. So did the Spanish system instituted after the civil war. The British system, being dominated much more by the problem of unemployment, gave priority to ensuring security for the worker against being out of work, ill or disabled, to the extent that even old age pensions came to be administered as, in part, an extension of unemployment relief and assistance. The Soviet system was so little concerned about demographic problems that in 1936 state aid was given to mothers only on the birth of the seventh child. In 1944, as part of the policy of reinforcing family life, it was made available on the birth of the third child. The Soviet Union, however, was much concerned from 1931 onwards with greater productivity, and aimed to give stronger incentives and higher rewards for skilled workers and for intensive work. Accordingly social benefits were made highly individual, and depended on such factors as length of service in one place and on levels of skill and of production. The United States Social Security Act of 1935 likewise envisaged widely differentiated benefits according to previous levels of income of the recipient, rather than a system of flat benefits or minimum subsistence needs, as in Britain. It was concerned to guarantee economic security rather than 'social security'. General world trends, as usually happened, assumed strong nationalistic colouring.

In most countries the general increase in national income, and the larger share of it enjoyed as personal incomes by the middle and the working classes, were reflected in mounting expenditure on amenities and luxuries. Coupled with greater leisure, greater affluence produced important changes in social habits and in economic structure. The whole structure of industry and business, especially of the distributive trades, was affected by the expansion of popular demand for consumer goods. Standardisation of products, qualities and packaging become more common. Multiple stores multiplied, though so did small shops. The American firm of Woolworth extended its mass-selling techniques to Britain in 1910 and to Germany in 1927. The French and other western nations then evolved comparable chain-stores, *Prisunic* and *Monoprix* appearing during the 'thirties. The departmental store originated in France and in the United States, whence it came to England by the turn of the century and spread after Gordon Selfridge opened his store in London in 1906. Meanwhile, too, the system of paying for goods on credit, by means of an initial payment and regular instalments, oddly called in England 'hire purchase', brought the more costly domestic goods such as furniture, vacuum cleaners, refrigerators and radio within the grasp of working-class homes.

Expenditure on luxuries inevitably increased in most western countries, and among the wealthy in eastern countries: on alcohol and tobacco, confectionery and entertainment, gambling and sports. The silent film became the most popular of all entertainments in the 'twenties, making Charles Chaplin a world figure. It gave way from 1929 onwards to the 'talking film', and even countries with a low standard of living came to be lavishly equipped with cinemas, whilst in large towns they became more palatial 'super-cinemas'. By 1937 British cinema-goers were spending

£40 million a year. Italy had some 9,000 cinemas with seating accommodation for 3½ million people; Spain nearly 4,000 with seats for 2 millions. Dancing became more broadly popular, especially among young people, and from Europe Britain imported the *palais de danse*, rivalling in its garishness of style (though not in extreme popularity) the equally 'palatial' new cinemas. The growth of commercialised sport of all kinds, together with new facilities for betting and gambling, produced such novelties as racing greyhounds after a mechanical hare (begun at Manchester in 1926), the totalisator for horse-race betting (introduced into England in 1928) and, leading favourite of mass gambling in the 'thirties, the football pools. By 1937 as much was spent on the pools in Britain as on cinema-going: after the war, much more was so spent, as new forms of mass entertainment dethroned the cinema from its inter-war supremacy.

The insatiable appetite of the masses for spectacular entertainment, exceeding even that for sensational news, led to two of the most significant phenomena of twentieth-century society: the popular press and the cult of sport. Their parallel and often interconnected growth emphasises several intrinsic features of social change: the immense importance of 'publicity' in modern society, the inherent tendency to commercialise all activities which have a mass interest, the pervasive force of politics in society, and the nationalistic, even chauvinistic, potentialities of all mass appeals.

In several ways it was France which led the way in the establishment of a popular daily press in Europe on the scale achieved in the twentieth century. In 1905 *Le Petit Parisien* sold 1,200,000 copies, and taken together it and *Le Petit Journal, Le Journal, Le Matin* and *L'Echo de Paris* reached some 5 million readers. The most popular daily press in Britain (as distinct from the Sunday press, which had always set the pace in mass circulations) did not achieve so large a public until the 1930s, and then did so by high-pressure salesmanship stunts, such as free insurance and free gifts for 'registered readers'. The German press was more avowedly political and more fragmented: in 1914 the Social Democrats alone had 110 daily newspapers whose total circulation was nearly 1½ million. The Italian press was normally of less importance, either socially or politically, though the northern cities had a few influential daily papers. The modern press with a mass circulation depends on a combination of several different factors: a modern technology of cheap and quick rotary printing; a speedy and efficient news-collecting service; almost universal literacy; organisation for speedy distribution over virtually the whole country; and —a crucial factor—a very substantial revenue from commercial advertising. The latter alone made it possible to sell papers cheaply enough for any working man to afford to buy his own copy. The modern newspaper is at once the product and the main vehicle of mass publicity.

Existing mainly on this basis, however, most of Europe's popular press, as well as much of its less commercialised and less popular press, was strongly political in attitude or even in ownership. In France there was a powerful tradition, from the first, that most papers were avowedly favourable to a political party or, at least, to the left, centre or right arcs of the political hemicycle: and leading politicians, a Clemenceau, Jaurès or Blum, came to be identified with the editing and writing of particular papers and journals. In Britain, too, popular papers were identified with a particular hue of politics or, as with the Northcliffe and Beaverbrook press, with the political views of the press baron who owned them. In Germany, Italy, Spain and most other countries similar affiliations grew up, even when mass circulations were clearly achieved by appealing to interests remote from politics, such as sporting news and comment and magazine features designed for women or children. The mass press, thriving most on sensational news and crises of acute national concern, usually tended also to be chauvinistic, presenting events abroad in a tone of excitement or alarm, handling issues of foreign policy from a patriotic man-in-the-street's point of view. During the competition in armaments before 1914, the more sensational press in each country kept alive the mood of alarm and fear which supported the arms race.

The evolution of sport showed precisely similar characteristics. It, too, changed from a selective social activity to a mass spectacle and a highly commercialised entertainment. Attendance of large crowds at sporting events was made possible by the erection of large modern stadia with electrical amplification and flood-lighting. The first modern Olympic Games were held in Athens in 1896, the Davis Cup was donated in 1900, the World Cup was first conceived in Paris in 1904, the *Tour de France* dated from 1903, the French *Grand Prix* from 1902, the Tourist Trophy Race from 1905. It was around the turn of the century that national and international tournaments of this kind came into fashion, and the vogue spread to practically all other sporting activities. With the internal combustion engine speed became a new challenge on land and sea and in the air. When so much money was involved sport became highly commercialised, for 'promotion' on so large a scale required investment of large sums.

It also, therefore, became highly professionalised. Efforts of the International Olympic Committee and of many separate national associations to preserve 'amateur status' led to considerable snobbery, hypocrisy, absurdity, recurrent controversy, and eventual failure. In the 1920s Mr John Kelly could not win the Diamond Sculls because he was a bricklayer, and so was disqualified as a 'manual worker': yet he won Olympic titles and became a millionaire, and his daughter, later made famous as a film-star, married Prince Rainier of Monaco. Records were so continually broken that nobody could sensibly compete without becoming so dedicated a trainee as to be in effect a 'pro'. Sport, and the attendant habit of betting, became so prevalent that none of the mass media could ignore it. News-reel films, radio programmes, as well as the press, necessarily devoted considerable attention to it. Special sporting papers, and professional sports correspondents and commentators, came into existence; sports champions rivalled film-stars as popular idols. Women claimed a place of eminence in certain sports, as in other social activities. As entertainment for the crowd sport might be a leisure-time occupation; for the most publicised participants it early ceased to be a pastime.

The last quarter of the nineteenth century, which saw the expansion of European civilisation throughout the world, saw also the propagation of European games throughout the world, especially by the British. Cricket did not catch on in the United States or Denmark, but football, lawn tennis and golf proved to be transplantable, most of all football. It has been suggested that mass attraction to sport reflects peculiar psychological needs of an industrial urban society.

It is chiefly through sport (at any rate in peace time) that male industrial workers can submerge themselves, if only as roaring spectators, in the communal will that 'their' team, the group with which they are identified, should win...It is possible to see the teams as organic communities, to let the imagination follow and endlessly discuss the fortunes alike of the group and of its component heroes, who provide a vicarious contact with the wild, the unforeseen, the forces of Nature...It is significant that the word 'style' is used of these activities, as of all the arts; a pointer towards the fact that sport should in truth be recognised as the folk art of industrial communities in particular and of urban society in general.[1]

Certainly sport in its mass forms serves well the ends of nationalism. The originator of the Olympic Games, the Baron de Coubertin, planned that only individual performers should win: it soon became the custom to speak of America, England or Russia 'winning' certain events. This was largely due to the sporting press, which depicted it in such terms to the public of each country. The alleged 'internationalism' of sport has therefore usually involved contests between national teams, however 'friendly', rather than between individuals divorced from any national context. It is no coincidence that the modern dictators invariably utilised sport as a vehicle of propaganda, to aggrandise themselves and their states at the expense of others: nor that sports stadia, with the susceptible mass audience prepared by community singing, parades, bands and the other trappings of sporting spectacles, became the favourite setting for party rallies, whether of the National Socialists in Germany or of the Communist party in Russia. That the sporting prowess of a few individuals out of many millions should be regarded as evidence of national virility and strength would be itself merely idiotic, were it not that the most powerful modern governments have assumed responsibility for choosing, training and financing national teams to win international contests. Governments and public opinion have been persuaded that pride, prestige and influence

[1] Renée Haynes in A. Natan (ed.), *Sport and Society: A Symposium* (1958), pp. 60-1.

are at stake in such contests. This could hardly have come to pass had not major national events become a folk ritual: as evidenced in the English Cup Final ritual at Wembley with the crowd reverently singing *Abide with me*, and the tendency for all such occasions to become as stylised as is bull-fighting in Spain. Here, perhaps, is the final comment on the transformation of social life in the twentieth century. Equally manifest in societies of east and west, of fascism and communism, democracy and dictatorship, capitalism and socialism, here is a trend which transcends all regional, national and ideological differences, because it combines irresistibly the strongest commercial, political, social and cultural tendencies of the age.

CHAPTER III

THE WORLD ECONOMY:
INTERDEPENDENCE AND PLANNING

THERE were so many changes in economic structure and relationships during the first half of the twentieth century, so many vicissitudes of fortune both for national communities and for social groups within them, that long before the outbreak of the second world war in 1939 it was clear that there could be no return to the theory and practice of international economic interdependence as both were understood in the world before the outbreak of the first world war in 1914. Although subsequent changes since 1939—and more particularly since 1950—have in some respects been even more drastic, there was such a sharp contrast in experience between the world before 1914 and the world after 1914 that contemporaries found it difficult to adapt themselves to new circumstances or to meet the challenge of new problems.

Before 1914, important economic changes, like the growth of the industrial power of the United States or the development of new technologies based on steel and electricity, took place within a system of specialisation which did not change as a whole: mutability in particulars seemed to be consistent with general stability. After 1918, serious maladjustments in the internal economies of the European countries, along with boom and slump of unprecedented dimensions in the United States, involved such dislocations and shocks to the international economy that there was a tendency to idealise the state of affairs before the debacle. At the same time critics were emerging who pointed to serious limitations and shortcomings. There were certainly substantial divergences of experience between different countries and between different years in the period before the outbreak of the first world war;[1] and while it is true that there then 'existed a much more closely-knit world community than today...only a very small part of the world belonged to it, as it excluded the larger part of mankind'.[2]

Such new interpretation takes into the reckoning the development of new economies, the emergence of new states and the expression of new aspirations; it also rests on an evaluation not only of the mechanisms of economic interdependence but of the forces making for 'planning' within and across economies. 'Interdependence' and 'planning', indeed, are

[1] S. Kuznets, *Capital in the American Economy* (Princeton, 1961); W. A. Lewis and P. J. O'Leary, 'Secular Swings in Production and Trade, 1870–1913' (*The Manchester School of Economic and Social Studies*, vol. XXIII, 1955).
[2] G. Myrdal, *Beyond the Welfare State* (London, 1958), p. 103.

37

twentieth-century themes which sometimes look to be completely separate and at other moments of time seem to converge. In the gloomy aftermath of the first world war, one of the outstanding economists of the 1920s and 1930s, J. M. Keynes, whose views on the possibilities of conscious economic control were radically to reshape economic policies after 1939, dwelt in retrospect both on the 'interdependence' and the 'automatism' of the pre-1914 system. In a well-known passage he wrote eloquently in 1920 of the 'extraordinary episode in the economic progress of man' that came to an end in 1914. Before 1914

the inhabitant of London could order by telephone, sipping his morning tea in bed, the various products of the whole earth, in such quantity as he might see fit, and reasonably expect their early delivery upon his doorstep; he could at the same moment and by the same means venture his wealth in the natural resources and new enterprises of any quarter of the world, and share, without execution or even trouble, in their prospective fruits and advantages... He could secure forthwith, if he wished it, cheap and comfortable means of transit to any country or climate, without pass-port or other formality, could despatch his servant to the neighbouring office of a bank for such supply of the precious metals as might seem convenient, and could then proceed abroad to foreign quarters without knowledge of their religion, language or customs, bearing coined wealth upon his person, and would consider himself greatly aggrieved and much surprised at the least interference. But, most important of all, he regarded this state of affairs as normal, certain and permanent, except in the direction of further improvements, and any deviation from it as aberrant, scandalous, and avoidable.[1]

Keynes appreciated without admiring. There was no nostalgia in his approach, for he also went out of his way to stress 'the intensely unusual, unreliable, temporary nature of the economic organisation' by which western Europe lived. Others, like the influential British Cunliffe Committee of 1918, which recommended that the overriding aim of British economic policy in the post-1918 world should be to return to the gold standard at the pre-war parity, overlooked many of the factors which Keynes took into account in his analysis. So too did most informed 'orthodox' opinion. Implicit in Keynes's analysis were many fundamental questions about the pre-1914 'system'. Which inhabitants of London behaved or could behave in this way? Why did some areas of the world outside Europe remain undeveloped? What was the price of 'dependency', particularly for primary producing countries? If all deviations from the system were thought to be 'avoidable', what of the fluctuations within it, some of which were socially as well as economically disturbing, not least in the 'advanced' countries? Was it sufficient to 'blame' the war, an exogenous factor, for all the strains and tensions that arose after it? Did not the change in the strategic position of Britain, around which late nineteenth-century international trade was organised, begin well before

[1] J. M. Keynes, *The Economic Consequences of the Peace* (London, 1920), p. 10.

1914, as did the growth of the United States economy, so that war, at most, accelerated processes which were already traceable? Some of these questions were already being asked before 1939, a few of them by critics of the 'system' even before 1914; others have been asked—in different tones of voice—since the second world war produced not only new dislocations but new approaches to the best way of dealing with them.

What is beyond dispute is that the international economy before 1914 was a product of nineteenth-century experience: it was unique as well as mortal.[1] It rested on the continuing growth of population in Europe; the free migration overseas in increasing quantities of both men and capital; the spread of machine industry mainly in western Europe but also, after 1870, in the United States and Japan; the development of an intricate network of communications, banking and insurance services; and the expansion, through specialisation, of multilateral trade. The combination of these forces, each with its own history, accounted for the special economic characteristics of the period from the late nineteenth century to 1914. It was in the late eighteenth century that the United Kingdom had initiated some of these changes, thereby securing a lead which later turned into a handicap, and it was in the last quarter of the nineteenth century that other countries, following different paths, 'caught up' or went ahead.[2] Germany, in particular, after its unification in 1871, began to challenge the United Kingdom as the principal industrial power in Europe. Russia, the population of which rose from 77 million in 1870 to 111 million in 1914, had its first industrial revolution during the 1890s—with improved communications, particularly railways, playing a crucial role. The European railway network as a whole increased from 140,000 miles in 1890 to 213,000 in 1914.

Although the birth rate in western European countries (except Holland) was falling during the last quarter of the nineteenth century and the largest proportionate population increases in the continent were taking place in the less developed south and east, the more industrialised west European countries took increasing advantage of the fact that they had been able to concentrate capital and labour on relatively small amounts of land with a high population density. Between 1900 and 1913 their industrial production increased by about a half.[3] Their specialised industrial populations, living at a relatively high standard of life, called for increasing supplies of food and raw materials which could only be obtained by fostering the primary industries of overseas countries and by

---

[1] See W. Ashworth, *A Short History of the International Economy* (London, 1962 ed.), p. 217.
[2] See A. Gerschenkron, *Economic Backwardness in Historical Perspective* (Cambridge, Mass., 1962).
[3] Organisation for Economic Co-operation and Development, *Industrial Statistics, 1900–1962* (Paris, 1964).

creating new transport services to move their products. During the last twenty years of the nineteenth century huge new regions of primary production were opened up—on a much greater scale than ever before—some of them dealing in new products, like rubber (Malaya and the Dutch East Indies), others in minerals and chemicals (Chile, Canada and the Congo), in cereals (Canada and the Middle West), fruit (South Africa), sugar (Cuba and Java) and meat (Australia, New Zealand and Argentina). Offices in London or Hamburg or Rotterdam controlled developments in Singapore or Shanghai or Santiago.

This was the geographical relationship; and in economic terms also the industrialised countries, which drew on cheap overseas labour but supplied the necessary capital and enterprise, found themselves able, in the last twenty years of the century, to sell the products of their industry and to buy primary products from overseas at very favourable terms of trade. Between 1900 and 1914 the terms of trade moved in the opposite direction, as the quantum of world trade in manufactured goods doubled while that of primary products increased by only two-thirds. Yet so great was European investment overseas in this period (about £350 million each year) that the trend was on the way to being reversed again as war broke out. This, then, was a world economy in which Europe was at the centre of economic power; and within Europe three countries—the United Kingdom, Germany and France—accounted in 1913 for more than seven-tenths of Europe's manufacturing capacity. In an age of coal and steel technology, these three powers produced 93 per cent of Europe's coal, 78 per cent of Europe's steel and 80 per cent of Europe's machinery.[1]

The United States had a far higher annual growth rate from 1870 to 1913 (4·3 per cent) than the United Kingdom (2·2 per cent), Germany (2·9 per cent from 1871) or France (1·6 per cent), and had moved ahead of Europe both in the mechanisation of agriculture and in the output of coal (producing 42 per cent of the world's supply), steel (41 per cent), and manufactures. Yet, because of its huge and expanding home market, it played a far smaller part than Europe in international trade. Sixty per cent of world exports of manufactured articles originated from the three leading European countries in 1913, and in the United Kingdom, in particular, the structure and organisation of industry—like the organisation of the money and capital markets—were geared to world trade. The British textiles industry, with its overseas sources of supply and its large overseas markets, was bigger than that of France and Germany combined, and Japanese competition had not as yet undermined its confidence. London—

---

[1] For these and other figures, see and compare League of Nations, *Industrialization and Foreign Trade* (Geneva, 1945); I. Svennilson, *Growth and Stagnation in the European Economy* (Geneva, 1954); C. Clark, *The Conditions of Economic Progress* (3rd ed. London, 1957); R. Nurkse, *Patterns of Trade and Development* (Uppsala, 1959); A. Maddison, *Economic Growth in the West* (New York, 1964); and A. Maizels, *Industrial Growth and World Trade* (Cambridge, 1963).

to a far greater extent than Paris or Berlin—was a world financial centre more than it was a national investment centre. Moreover, the services which it provided were dependent on a far more extensive trade than that which concerned the United Kingdom alone, either as an importer or an exporter, or the 'formal' Empire based on London. The financial institutions of 'the City' had world-wide connections, and supplied long-term capital through the new issues market and short-term capital through the bill market. Sterling acted as a common trade currency, and the cheapness and security of London's financial services encouraged regular and expanding international dealings.

Although it was becoming clear to far-sighted observers that the world's economic future would be determined in large measure by what happened in the United States, Europe still seemed to be firmly placed at the centre of international society. Even the great growth of American population was still being fed by large-scale immigration from Europe: eight and three-quarter million immigrants, indeed, entered the United States from Europe in the decade from 1900 to 1910, a majority of them from the south and east of Europe. These 'uprooted outsiders' were laying the foundations of a new society: they were also providing the manpower for a new economy, with a high rate of growth of output per head of population, higher wages and shorter working hours than in Europe, and more emphasis on new industries and on consumer goods. Yet neither the transformation of American life under fierce business pressure nor the industrial development of Japan under political direction—the number of Japanese machine looms increased from 19,000 to 123,000 in the decade before 1914—overshadowed Europe's role.

Again, it was possible to see in partial perspectives at the time what can now be seen clearly in retrospect—that over a long period the share of the United Kingdom in expanding world trade was declining (19 per cent in the years 1880–5; 14 per cent in the years 1911–13); that its position in certain export markets—South America, for example—was weakening in face of United States competition; that its industrial activity depended too much on 'traditional' nineteenth-century staples; that in steel as well as in 'new industries' its rivals were already ahead, with Germany, which gained greatly after 1871 from the acquisition of the ores of Lorraine, producing double Britain's output; that the decline in its agriculture (during a period of European agricultural development) entailed a huge and irreducible import bill for food; that, in short, its balance of payments position was vulnerable and its viability and resilience were in doubt. While there were enormous capital exports during the decade before 1914, payments for imports were always greater than current earnings from the sale of both goods and services. The long-term prosperity of the United Kingdom obviously depended heavily on the possibility of maintaining a large and growing income from interest payments overseas and on the rapid exploitation of new territories. Even had there been no war between 1914 and 1918 to diminish the United Kingdom's foreign assets, it is likely that the collapse of the pre-1914 boom would have had serious effects on the structure of the world economy.

Yet it is dangerous to exaggerate. In relation to the world economy before 1914, it was the United Kingdom which acted, in another phrase of Keynes, as 'the conductor of the orchestra'.[1] Some of its 'weaknesses', indeed, assisted the smooth running of the system. As the world's largest creditor country, the United Kingdom did not exploit its position to accumulate such large stocks of gold that it could drain the resources of other countries within the gold standard system. The payments transfers it managed—with the minimum of fuss—always allowed debts incurred by other countries in one area to be cancelled by credits earned in other areas. In this way, economic benefits were widely diffused and frictions reduced. The key equations of multilateralism were that the United Kingdom itself had a credit balance in its dealings with the primary producing countries, and that they settled their balance of indebtedness by an export surplus to the continental industrial countries and to the United States. The continental countries in their turn financed import surpluses with the primary producing countries and with the United States by export surpluses to the United Kingdom.

It was less the existence of the monetary mechanism of the gold standard or the 'rules' by which it operated than those conditions in which it was applied which maintained, although then never perfectly, world stability before 1914. Bank of England gold reserves rose from the mid-1890s, and there was a margin of comfort. Small countries were able to rest content, therefore, with keeping their rates of exchange around par in relation to London and not concerning themselves too much with the details of the functioning of an international financial system.[2] As far as capital was concerned, while political considerations influenced the volume and direction of both French and German capital movements, no political obstacles were ever placed in the way of free export of capital from London: in the seven years before 1914, for example, £600 million of British capital was provided for the construction of railways in countries, whatever their political system, which supplied Britain with foodstuffs and raw materials. Throughout the early years of the twentieth century, indeed, the United Kingdom annually invested a sum almost equivalent to the total current receipts in interest and dividends which it earned from accumulated overseas holdings of capital.[3]

[1] J. M. Keynes, *Treatise on Money* (London, 1930), vol. II, p. 307.
[2] R. S. Sayers, *Bank of England Operation, 1890–1914* (Oxford, 1930); P. B. Whale, 'The Working of the Pre-War Gold Standard', reprinted in T. S. Ashton and R. S. Sayers (eds.), *Papers in English Monetary History* (Oxford, 1953).
[3] For details see A. K. Cairncross, *Home and Foreign Investment, 1870–1913* (Cambridge, 1953).

Free movements of capital, stable exchange rates, and the 'legal order' provided by the gold standard (some, not only Englishmen, came to think of it as a moral order) facilitated international commodity trade. In that trade also, the special features of the United Kingdom position, including its 'weak' features, facilitated multilateralism. The United Kingdom's dependence on imports—in 1913, 63 per cent of its imports came from outside Europe—gave a fillip both to development and to trade; and within Europe itself not only did a number of European countries, like Denmark, look naturally towards London, but Germany, the United Kingdom's main industrial rival, was also a major source of supply of manufactured materials, like chemicals and dyestuffs (as well as a good customer for British products). Throughout the period before 1914 the United Kingdom remained 'dedicated' to free trade, resisting all counterarguments alike, whether they were based on reciprocity, on the importance of protecting threatened or new industries, on the need to increase domestic employment, or on the appeal for imperial preference. It also resisted pressure of vested interests, by falling back, usually fervently, on what in the course of less than a century had become fundamental liberal orthodoxy. In consequence, the free and open British market served by experienced wholesalers, brokers and bankers, and untouched by politicians, drew upon a large proportion of the world's total exports of staples and during business crises usually succeeded in absorbing all temporary surpluses.

The conception of a 'legal' or 'moral' order behind this intricate pattern of interdependence was challenged most articulately before 1914 at moments of business recession, as in the years 1907–8, when there were sharp downswings in the volume of economic activity and unemployment rose.[1] The United Kingdom suffered more from these downswings than Germany or France, and the United States, despite its more rapid rate of growth than Europe, also had more violent recessions. It is possible, however, to trace more persistent sources of discontent and disturbance. The tacit assumptions on which the system of interdependence was based concerned both the relationship of countries to each other and of governments to their peoples. The separation of economics and politics, reflected in the limited extent to which politicians interfered with international economic specialisation, depended largely upon the social framework and social pressures inside their countries. Businessmen were a highly organised group, even when pre-industrial values, inimical to 'acquisition' or to 'enterprise', persisted in national cultures. Politicians constituted an *élite*, even when they drew support from mass parties. Orthodox liberal economic theory, although it was not universally accepted, rested on the

[1] See W. L. Thorp, *Business Annals* (New York, 1926). Out of seventeen countries examined by Thorp, fifteen experienced a recession in 1907/8.

independence of the market. The 'dependence' of Africa and Asia on Europe was usually taken for granted.

Yet in the midst of this 'interdependent' world, there were forces pulling in a different direction. Most governments before 1914 found it increasingly necessary to interfere in economic relations both internally and externally. There were some spheres of economic organisation, like foreign investment, central banking and railways, which had important and obvious political and strategic implications encouraging governments to follow deliberate policies; there were also some governments which for reasons of tradition or exigency actively set out to intervene in economic processes. In consequence, while there was no attempt before 1914 to plan economies as a whole, there were many attempts to plan *within* economies or to regulate certain of their sectors. While there was no direct formulation of national policies to secure and maintain full employment, there was a growing interest in budget policy as a means of social adjustment. While quantitative import restrictions had not been developed, tariffs were freely employed. While the United Kingdom stood firmly by the principles of free trade, by 1900 45 per cent of its exports went to protectionist countries, and some of these, like Germany, conceived of tariffs as instruments of general national policy.

Thus, the historical origins of twentieth-century interventionism may be discerned in the interdependent pre-1914 world, and a conjunction of forces, most of them deriving from nineteenth-century sources, was responsible for the pattern of events. The first moves *within* economies began with the uneasiness of some of the privileged and the attack of some of the underprivileged on the inequalities of income distribution, the impersonalism of market forces, the cycle of family poverty and the conditions of industrial work. The extension of the suffrage was followed, or in some cases anticipated, by popular demand for a shortened working day and for increased social security. France, for instance, limited the working day to ten hours in 1900 and the working week to six days in 1906; Austria, following long after the United Kingdom, introduced factory inspectors in 1883 and a new industrial code in 1907. The victories of liberal democracy, however limited they were, always encouraged mass pressures. Some of their effects can be noted in the substitution of government spending policies for those based on retrenchment finance.[1] In 1908 Lloyd George could say that no one need be afraid of any taxes being taken off in his time, and a year later Winston Churchill, then a 'new Liberal', could declare that if he had to sum up the immediate future of democratic politics in a single word he would choose 'insurance'.

[1] See, for example, A. T. Peacock and J. Wiseman, *The Growth of Public Expenditure in the United Kingdom* (London, 1961); U. K. Hicks, *British Public Finances, Their Structure and Development, 1880–1952* (London, 1954).

The early stages in the gradual transformation of Lassalle's 'night watchman state' into the twentieth-century 'welfare state' can be traced in many parts of Europe before 1914. The motives, as usual, were mixed. Traditionalist paternalism, suspicious of the consequences of the growth of autonomous markets, might blend with progressive theories based on the need to secure more equal citizenship. Social insurance might offer right-wing groups the prospect of achieving political insurance. British insurance was by no means the first of such ventures on the part of governments. The German system of social insurance, inaugurated by Bismarck in 1881 and crowned in 1911 by the promulgation of a Workmen's Insurance Code of nearly 2,000 articles, the *Reichsversicherungsordnung*, began in part as an attempt to 'save' the German working classes from 'the siren song of socialism'. By 1914 there were more or less elaborate and comprehensive social insurance systems in the United Kingdom, France, Belgium, Holland, Italy, Denmark, Austria, Norway, Sweden and Switzerland. Social insurance was the spearhead of spending policy, even when it was financed out of contributions rather than directly from taxes, and when it was accompanied by the growth of 'trade boards' and the introduction of 'labour exchanges' it implied increasing state concern with the functioning of the labour market.

Yet if some moves towards greater interventionism within economies came from the demands of the underprivileged, others came from business circles themselves. The demand for protection was universal in the years from 1890 to 1914, although whether or not or to what extent it was conceded depended on local circumstances. A Swiss referendum in 1891 produced a vote in favour of higher duties; Swedish farmers secured a return to protection in their country in 1894; and in 1897 the German emperor suggested to Tsar Nicholas II, with no success, a general European Customs Union to protect Europe against United States competition. Everywhere economic rivalries—inside countries as well as between them—encouraged the imposition of tariffs. In some 'new countries'—Australia, for example—the relationship between industrialisation, investment and protection (labour politicians supported all three) was being underlined on party platforms. Tariffs, indeed, were conceived of in some countries not only as concessions to vested interests but as symbols of autonomy and as necessary instruments in the creation of national systems of political economy, free from the taint of *Manchesterthum*.

Along with tariffs, in some countries at least, went cartels and business concentration. While the United States produced trusts, like the United States Steel Corporation (1901), huge business organisations pioneered by 'titans', who have subsequently been heralded as the true pace-makers of planning, Germany produced market-sharing cartels, among them the Rhenish–Westphalian Coal Syndicate, created in 1893 and controlling half the coal production of the country, and the *Stahlwerkverband*, controlling almost the whole of steel production, in 1904. In France, where small business remained strong, the *Comité des Forges* was virtually controlled by six major firms. In all these cases big business was becoming a 'system of organised power'.[1] In the United States, by 1904, trusts controlled two-fifths of the manufacturing capital of the country, while in Germany there was a continuous line of development from private cartellisation and government assistance given to cartels before 1914 down to the 'economic planning' by the state (within a business framework) in the 1930s. Before 1914 many German economists already conceived of the state as the central regulator of the economic life of the community— a fact duly noted by the American institutional economist, Thorstein Veblen—and of business as the model of efficient organisation. During the first world war, in Germany and in the United States, as elsewhere, including the United Kingdom, state control had to be exercised through the mediation of businessmen and business organisations, and Walter Rathenau, who did much to build up the war-time economic apparatus of Germany, is reported to have said that he learned all that he knew of planned economy from his father, Emil, the managing director of the *Allgemeine Elektrizitäts-Gesellschaft*, founded in 1883. Walter Rathenau was himself the director of at least sixty-eight business concerns.

It is necessary to trace one branch of the pedigree of 'planning' back to such beginnings. While socialism remained a gospel, the so-called socialisation of large-scale enterprise was already a fact. Economists have noted the convergence of 'capitalism' and 'socialism' with a 'twilight zone' of intermediate and transitional forms,[2] and as early as 1911 one of them argued forcefully that the future of democracy depended upon its success in dealing with the problems of public ownership and regulation.[3] Certainly the growth of scale and the increasingly monopolistic structure of industry led to increasing scepticism about the relevance of classical theories of the market in twentieth-century conditions. It was clear that such scepticism, along with dissatisfaction with private ownership coupled with central control, would generate new schemes for control in the name of the community.

A third pedigree of 'planning'—through the discontents of dependent or 'colonial' societies—cannot be clearly traced back before 1914,[4] although just as the socially and economically privileged within 'advanced'

[1] R. A. Brady, *Business as a System of Power* (New York, 1943).
[2] A. H. Hansen, *Economic Stabilization in an Unbalanced World* (New York, 1932), p. 329. See also J. A. Schumpeter, *Capitalism, Socialism and Democracy* (4th ed. London, 1950); J. M. Keynes, *The End of Laissez Faire* (1924), reprinted in *Essays in Persuasion* (London, 1931); A. Berle and G. Means, *The Modern Corporation and Private Property* (New York, 1932).
[3] F. W. Taussig, *Principles of Economics* (London, 1911 ed.), vol. II, p. 411.
[4] Yet in 1906, after a bumper coffee crop, the state of São Paulo in Brazil decided to buy back part of the crop, hold it off the market and dispose of it at a more favourable season, an early example of 'valorisation'.

46

communities might sometimes anticipate criticisms which were later taken up by mass movements, so inside 'advanced' countries the critique of certain facets of 'imperialism', including its inequalities, was well developed by 1914. Critics in the United Kingdom, with the greatest and richest of the pre-1914 overseas empires, were most vociferous and influential, notably J. A. Hobson, whose *Imperialism*, later to be used by Lenin, was published in 1904. Yet, although there was much discussion of the statistics of 'exploitation' during the decade before 1914, and dramatic 'facts' relating to problem areas of development, like the Belgian Congo, received much public attention, when war broke out in 1914 it was not in any sense a war about 'colonialism' but rather 'a civil war within the partial world community of the rich nations'.[1]

During the *belle époque* of interdependence, the extent and timing of the benefits gained by different overseas countries varied greatly. Indian commerce greatly increased, for example, but Indian industry did not: entrepôts were more likely to develop than factories. South Africa, with its great mineral wealth and its relatively large white population, was opened up faster than East Africa. Different countries had different natural resources to offer—some in greater demand than others on the world's markets—and different social traditions, institutions and populations to encourage or inhibit adaptability and growth. The 'impact' of the West could be disruptive, constructive or more usually, perhaps, both, with the roads, railways, ports and harbours built during this period, symbols of enterprise and often triumphs of contractors' skill, remaining as valuable economic assets on which subsequent independent economic development might be based. The employment of Dutch capital in what is now Indonesia or of American capital in the Philippines provided economic foundations of this kind.

The one non-white country which made great independent economic progress before 1914—Japan—reconciled old traditions and new techniques, making use of elements of enterprise within the indigenous historic structure (see below, ch. XII). Yet its path of growth had much in common with that followed earlier by western European countries. Substantial increases in the relative size of the labour force in manufacturing were not accompanied at first by any big increase in productivity. This was secured as machine production, deliberately copied from Europe, became a matter of routine. Like the United Kingdom, Japan developed its industrial system on the basis of exports of manufactured goods—this was the 'leading sector' of its economy[2]—and it was favoured in its exploitation of new markets by the fact that the United Kingdom continued to pursue a policy of free trade. Textiles were the main export,

[1] Myrdal, *Beyond the Welfare State*, p. 109.
[2] See C. P. Kindleberger, *Economic Development* (New York, 1958) for models of development through foreign trade.

accounting for 32 per cent of Japan's total exports in 1900 and in the more variegated and advanced economy of 1913 for 30 per cent. Between these same two years, imports of textiles into Japan fell from 20 per cent of total imports to 5 per cent. The first world war did nothing in Japan to reverse or to decelerate long-term economic trends: indeed, since it was essentially a European war, it provided Japanese businessmen, like Japanese politicians, with new opportunities.

In Europe, however, there was a violent break in the continuity of economic development in 1914. The structure which had been built up during the previous century and had seemed to reach its culmination in the *belle époque* was destroyed for ever. That there was little recognition in 1914 of the kind of bill that would have to be paid added to the horror of paying it. At first, 'business as usual' was the slogan in 1914, and both Germany and the United Kingdom thought primarily of capturing each other's markets. It was only when 'knock-out blows' proved an illusion and the war settled down into a prolonged contest involving military attrition that the extent of the break with the psychology and economics of pre-1914 years began to be apparent. Another strain in the pedigree of twentieth-century 'planning'—planning for victory or for survival—can be traced back to the years of naval blockade and of trench warfare, much of it in the industrialised regions of Belgium and northern France. Once economics became the controlling factor in war, economies had to be controlled. The longer the war lasted, the more politicians found it difficult to reconcile the objective of winning the war with that of maintaining inviolate the autonomy of private business. Market mechanisms could not operate unchecked. Yet the transition to controlled systems was slow and hesitant, not usually the work of deliberate design, but shaped by the pressures of tightening scarcity and the insatiable needs of war production. Before 1914 there had been no detailed discussion, even in Germany, of the special 'political economy of war'. By the time that the war ended, however, administrators like Van Möllendorff were talking about *Planwirtschaft* while businessmen were continuing to sigh for a return to 'normalcy'. During the last years of the war an impetus was given to the demand for socialist planning, particularly when the more autocratic of the pre-1914 empires began to collapse.

The same essential problems faced all the belligerents in 1914, although recognition of their existence had to be forced on politicians by emergencies and crises. Large-scale modern wars involve organising the full employment of all available national resources, allocating them to various producers not only in the right order of priority but also in the right proportions at the right times, and in so arranging manpower, fiscal and financial policies that real resources are transferred rapidly to the war effort. All these implications of large-scale organised violence were less clear in 1914 than they were in 1918, and less clear in 1918 than they were in 1945. The first world war was full of surprises. The generals could not end it quickly, the factories could not produce sufficient munitions, civilians could not be neglected in the distribution of supplies, and criteria for dealing with the financial problem bore no resemblance to pre-war financial criteria. In trying to wrestle with these problems, governments faced all kinds of resistances, even resistances within their own ranks from those committed to doctrines of free trade or individualism. Although businessmen had to be associated with the framework of control in most countries, the *Politisierung* of economic life was not received with universal enthusiasm. A widely felt sentiment was expressed by Karl Helfferich, the director of the Anatolian Railway and the Deutsche Bank, when on being appointed to a new German economic department he wrote that the office would understand its task better if it returned as soon as possible to pre-war economic conditions.

It was Rathenau and not Helfferich who was most responsible for planning the economy of war-time Germany, the first of the belligerents to accept the challenge of full economic mobilisation. In August 1914 he was given extensive powers. As a result of his warnings about the danger of a breakdown in supplies, the war materials department (*Kriegs-Rohstoff Abteilung*) was set up in August 1914 to deal with conservation, production of substitutes (*Ersatz*) and planned distribution. By the end of the year, a whole range of technical offices for basic materials, such as metals, timber and wool, was in being. *Kriegswirtschaftsgesellschaften*, war-work agencies, acted as co-ordinating links between government and business. In November 1916 all the various branches of centralised authority were co-ordinated in a Supreme War Office (*Oberster Kriegsamt*), under the direct orders of General Groener, and in December a National Service Law made all men between the ages of 17 and 60 liable to be directed into the forces or the factories. The economic system now operated as a whole under close central direction.

More important even than this new economic structure were the attitudes it engendered. Rathenau himself claimed that the economic task was no longer one for individuals but for the whole community. He envisaged the war not so much as a battle between armies as a struggle between economic rivals. The final issue in the war, indeed, was not the victory or defeat of the German army, but the victory or defeat of the German economy. If the result—through organisation—should be victory, the task would be to go forward in peace as in war from private to collective economy, *Gemeinwirtschaft*.

In the United Kingdom there were less articulate or clear-cut formulations of new doctrines, although there was ample resort to new expedients. Although many steps were taken to control the economy before the political crises of December 1916, it was from that date onwards that key ministries like those of food and shipping began to function and the small War Cabinet provided a compact agency for central co-ordination. The War Cabinet reported that war, and especially the war events of 1917, had brought about a transformation of the social and administrative structure of the state, 'much of which is bound to be permanent'.[1] The process was cumulative. In the case of munitions, the War Office turned down a proposal in October 1914 that the government should take over the big armament firms and run them as a branch of the public service, and it was not until May 1915 that the Ministry of Munitions was created. In the same month Albert Thomas was given a similar assignment in France. The ministry faced difficult problems concerning priorities, allocations, prices and employment, which it met by extending control both vertically to cover raw materials supplies and horizontally to cover civilian needs as well as military requirements. In the organisation of manpower machinery devised in peace-time for different purposes—the labour exchange, for example—was used to regulate manpower needs. In the organisation of food supplies and shipping, steps were slow and less dramatic, but final ramifications were wide. Market mechanisms could never have accomplished what was urgent and necessary. The Ministry of Food, 'suppressing private enterprise completely, accomplished what private enterprise in this country could never have accomplished'.[2] The Ministry of Shipping focused attention on the necessity for a national import policy, which would provide for the needs of the economy as a whole. From the questions raised and the answers tentatively given to them a scheme of planning emerged. 'Hundreds of improvisations originating in shortages of sand-bags or shells or food, and the more fundamental scarcities of shipping and manpower had fallen together into a pattern. Very few people saw them as a pattern: fewer still saw the logic that informed it.'[3]

That there was a pattern is best revealed by examining the experience of the one belligerent which failed to build up a satisfactory machinery of war-time planning—Russia. Within a few months of the outbreak of war there was an acute shortage of guns and ammunition and insufficient industrial potential (despite a great pre-war leap) to provide for current military requirements. By the winter of 1916 economic disorganisation had reached an advanced stage. In that year, despite increased war demand, iron and steel production was down by 16 per cent and coal production by 10 per cent on the 1914 figures. There was no manpower policy, and the direction of 37 per cent of the Russian population to the army seriously crippled what was already an inadequate industrial effort. The food situation was disastrous. Although in 1916 the government adopted

---

[1] Cmd. 9005 (1918).
[2] W. H. Beveridge, *British Food Control* (1928), p. 338.
[3] W. K. Hancock and M. M. Gowing, *British War Economy* (1949), p. 29.

measures for controlling the grain trade and in March 1917 the new régime proclaimed the grain trade a state monopoly, there were acute food shortages, especially in the towns, and there was consequent severe political discontent. By 1917 it was clear that no further measures taken from the centre could be effective without a revolutionary impetus to drive them forward. Allied planning efforts had depended above all else on consent: planning in the revolutionary Russian situation would have to depend on force. The solutions the Bolshevik revolutionaries worked out for meeting problems of prolonged emergency and civil war were to have an important influence on the history of planning during the post-war years.

There was one other type of war-time planning which was important at the time and is interesting in retrospect. To replace the multilateral market systems of pre-war years, the Allies built up an extensive apparatus of international economic co-operation. During the early stages of the war an International Food Commission was set up in London in an attempt to secure an orderly distribution of supplies instead of a competitive scramble. Later developments included the evolution of two main groups of commodity organisations, one under a Food Council and the other under a Munitions Council. In addition, the Allied Maritime Transport Council aimed at applying the same principles of shipping pooling and allocation which had already been developed by the United Kingdom. This Council became the hub of the Allied machine of economic warfare. Yet such international planning involved no usurpation of the distinctive responsibilities of separate national governments. 'The international machine was not an external organisation based on delegated authority. It was the national organisations linked together for international work, and themselves forming the instruments of that work.'[1] When the machinery was destroyed in the holocaust of controls at the end of the war, all that remained were the separate national economic policies of the various individual states, and they were inevitably influenced by demands from business interests anxious to abandon war-time planning and in the words of the *Journal Officiel* in France, in December 1918, 'to re-establish freedom of business transactions with the utmost possible rapidity'.

The result of such pressure after 1918 was a general movement against planning. In the case of both the United Kingdom and Germany, the governments during the war had captured the commanding heights of the economy, although they had made little sustained attempt to limit profits while they regulated production. When the war ended, the collective purpose which had inspired the creation of the framework of control disappeared. A brief post-war boom, lasting until 1920, and the sharp contraction which followed it generated a conventional set of responses.

[1] J. A. Salter, *Allied Shipping Control* (London, 1921), p. 179.

The boom 'stirred starved appetites to new and clamorous life';[1] the slump destroyed the last vestiges of solidarity, forced conflicts between labour and capital to the surface, and pushed all the relics of war-time schemes into the melting pot. Some controls merely lapsed and nothing was done to renew them; others were deliberately jettisoned. 'During the war', wrote the imperialist liberal Lord Milner, 'a great deal of thought and really useful labour had been devoted, not only by the Ministry of Reconstruction, to making plans for the resumption of peaceful activities on better lines than those to which we had been accustomed in the past. In the disorganised scramble which began the moment the war was over, all these plans went by the board.'[2] In the international field the United States, with greatly enhanced economic power, exerted all its influence behind the drive to abolish inter-Allied control of raw materials. 'This government', wrote Herbert Hoover, 'will not agree to any programme that even looks like inter-Allied control of our resources after peace.'[3] The result was that not only did bodies like the Coal Control Department in Britain and the *consortiums* in France disappear, but bodies like the Allied Maritime Transport Council were dismantled. The disappearance of the international agencies made the task of world reconstruction more difficult. War conditions did not end with the end of hostilities, and collective disorganisation still called for collective effort. The fact that it was not forthcoming accentuated many of the problems of the next six or seven years.

If the machinery of planning was put out of action abruptly and decisively, it did not disappear without leaving a trace. In many governments—and in all oppositions—there were people and groups in favour of continued control of the economy. Möllendorff's plans in Germany for continued planning were abortive, but the constitution of the Weimar Republic laid down a system of workers' councils and economic councils with a National Economic Council (*Reichswirtschaftsrat*) at the top of the pyramid. Although the Council functioned only on a provisional basis after it came into being in 1920, the idea which lay behind it remained influential in Germany.[4] Gustav Stresemann, the outstanding figure in the middle years of the Weimar Republic, was the former chief bureaucrat of a large industrial organisation. In France, where some attempt was made to convert war machinery to peace-time purposes, so called 'mixed enterprises', partnerships of private and public capital, were created in the 1920s in industries like oil and petrol (the *Compagnie Française des Pétroles*), and a new bank, the *Crédit National*, set up to handle compensa-

[1] R. H. Tawney, 'The Abolition of Economic Controls' (*Economic History Review*, vol. xiii, 1943).
[2] Viscount Milner, *Questions of the Hour* (London, 1925), p. 24.
[3] Quoted in A. Zimmern, *The League of Nations and the Rule of Law* (London, 1938), p. 157.
[4] See G. Stolper, *German Economy, 1870–1940* (London, 1940).

tion payments and reconstruction allowances, was given official power to intervene in management.[1] A National Economic Council was created in 1924 to provide a forum for consultation between industrialists, workers and consumers, and plans were prepared to develop 'national equipment' (*outillage national*) in 1926 and 1929.[2]

There was one other legacy of war-time experience. When it became apparent that the world after 1918 was very different from that before 1914, the metaphors of war began to be revived and were employed in the planning 'campaigns' of the 1920s and 1930s. In the Soviet Union, massive by-product of Russian war dislocation, there continued to be agrarian and industrial 'fronts', 'battles' of production, 'brigade leaders' in the collective farms and 'shock' workers in the factories. In fascist Italy a 'Battle of the Grain' was proclaimed in 1925 'to free the Italian people from the slavery of foreign bread'. In National Socialist Germany a similar battle of agricultural production was announced in 1934 while the Labour Front was substituting for the trade unions 'a soldier-like kernel' of labour organisation and extolling the merits of compulsory labour service. All these schemes attempted to re-create the community of purpose and solidarity of interests which had made war-time planning possible: some were directly associated, indeed, with preparation for new warfare, for during the inter-war years memories of past war and thoughts about future war frequently overlapped.

The effects of the first world war on the development of planning went much farther, therefore, than the occasional continuity of institutions or the rebirth of metaphors. The post-war world, despite the apparent revival of multilateral trade between 1925 and 1929, was inherently unstable, and economic relationships within it had changed drastically. Historians may still argue about the extent to which the war itself was responsible for all the subsequent shocks and confusions of the inter-war years, particularly the Great Depression of 1929–32, the economic watershed of the period. Yet the wastes of war inside Europe, the dislocation of resources, the shifts of economic and geographical power outside Europe, the psychological and political transformation inside and outside, the disturbing financial consequences, both domestic and international, of the war and of the peace settlement were all obvious between 1918 and 1925. And even between 1925 and 1939, when it seemed that some aspects of the pre-war system had been 'restored', there were strains which led on directly to 1929 and 1931. While the effects of the war cannot be easily separated from the effects of other contemporary changes—of population, for example, or of technology—some, at least, of its direct consequences can

---

[1] A. Chazel and H. Poyet, *L'économie mixte* (Paris, 1963).
[2] For the significance of this see the official British report by R. Cahill, *Economic Conditions in France* (London, 1934).

be measured quantitatively. Moreover, it can be shown more generally, using the analogy of a pendulum, that the dislocation created by the war meant such a shock to the economic system that great swings followed, the greatest of them that of the Great Depression, and continued throughout the entire inter-war period.[1]

The wastes of war and the dislocation of resources had begun with manpower. It has been calculated that Europe (excluding Russia) lost from 20 to 22 million people as a direct or indirect result of the war, 7 per cent of its total population, and Russia about 28 millions, 18 per cent.[2] Between 1880 and 1913 the annual increase in Europe's population had been 2·3 millions; between 1913 and 1920 total population actually fell by 2 millions. During the same seven years, European manufacturing output fell by 23 per cent, while across the Atlantic that of the United States rose by 22 per cent.[3] European national incomes suffered too, and the income per head in the three large industrial countries—the United Kingdom, Germany and France—remained less in the mid-1920s than it had been in 1913. Industrial unemployment was a permanent feature of the economy, even when business revived. Agricultural production in Germany and France was lower in the years 1924–8 than it had been in 1913, while the output of food and raw materials in Oceania and Asia rose by 20 per cent between 1913 and 1925, in the United States and Canada by 25 per cent and in Latin America and Africa by even more. During the mid-1920s United States and Canadian grain production was 16–17 per cent more than the annual average of 1900–13. At the same time, new raw materials, like oil, challenged old European raw materials, like coal—crude oil output rose from 327 million barrels in 1910 to 688 million barrels in 1920 and 1,411 million barrels in 1930—and it was not until the late 1920s that coal output per man-shift in the United Kingdom reached the pre-war figure.[4] All in all, it has been estimated in straight economic terms that there was an eight-year setback to European industrial development as a result of the war. In the period from 1881 to 1913 European manufacturing output had risen on an average by 3½ per cent each year. If this rate of increase had been maintained during the war, the 1928 level of output would have been reached by 1921.[5]

Dislocation of resources was revealed at many points in the European economic system—for example, in transport in the breakdown of the European railway system and in the war-time over-expansion of the shipping industry, which led to serious post-war depression—and in

---

[1] Svennilson, *Growth and Stagnation in the European Economy*, p. 19. For the pendulum analogy, see R. Frisch, 'Propagation Problems and Impulse Problems in Dynamic Economics', in *Economic Essays in Honour of Gustav Cassel* (London, 1933).
[2] F. W. Notestein and others, *The Future Population of Europe and the Soviet Union* (Geneva, 1944), ch. III.
[3] Svennilson, *op. cit.* p. 18.   [4] *Ibid.* pp. 44–5.
[5] W. A. Lewis, 'World Population, Prices and Trade, 1870–1960' (*The Manchester School*, vol. XX, 1952).

excess capacity in iron and steel. The United Kingdom, in particular, suffered from dislocation of its economic pattern, just as Russia, and, in western Europe, France and Belgium, suffered most from direct damage; and by 1918 the proportion of United Kingdom industrial production which was exported overseas was little more than a half of what it had been in 1913. Throughout the 1920s stagnation in British staple industries caused serious concern to businessmen and governments alike, and there were few compensating gains in new industries. In one of the key nineteenth-century industries, textiles, closely geared to international trade, Japan even succeeded in penetrating the British home market. There were other kinds of dislocation or shift within the European economic pattern, notably in central and eastern Europe, where powerful large economic units were broken up and the number of nation states multiplied. Whereas before 1914 the population of Germany and Austro-Hungary taken together had substantially exceeded that of the United States, after 1919, of the twenty-nine European states, only five had more than forty million inhabitants and ten had less than five million. While market forces made for continued economic interdependence, political forces were re-emphasising the importance of sovereignty and of national frontiers. On ten German finished goods in 1913, the Austro-Hungarian tariff had amounted to 16–25 per cent. In Hungary in 1927 it was up to 34–54 per cent, and in 1931 to 42–61 per cent. Further east, partly for reasons of revenue raising, Rumania and Bulgaria built high tariff walls very quickly after 1919.

Even more disturbing in the 1920s than dislocation of resources, tariffs or the re-drawing of boundaries were internal inflation and a changed international balance of debtor–creditor relationships. Internal inflation—with prices rising from double to twenty times the pre-war level—was a general phenomenon, arising out of huge war-time budget deficits, which reached epidemic proportions first in central and eastern Europe and then in Germany. The German collapse was particularly serious. There were 250 German marks to the pound sterling in 1920—as against 20 in 1914—and in the last months of 1921 there were 1,000. In 1922 the figure soared to 35,000, and in the early autumn of 1923 the mark became worthless. Savings were wiped out, social relationships were seriously disturbed—the experience of inflation was as disturbing for large sections of the middle class as unemployment was for the workers—and Germany's capacity to pay reparations, a 'War guilt' payment on which the Allies insisted as part of the peace settlement, had to be re-viewed afresh. German financial collapse had been brought about not by the demand for reparations payments but by deliberate lack of fiscal responsibility. As a result of the collapse, however, the precarious relationships between reparations payments and war debts and between the Allies and the United States had to be re-assessed.

At the end of the war, all the European Allies were in debt to the United States, and all the Allies, except the United States, were in debt to the United Kingdom. Attempts by the United Kingdom in 1919 to have the war debts cancelled and three years later internationally to reduce the burden of debt proved unacceptable to both the United States and France; and the related problem of debts and of reparations (the United States refused to recognise the relationship) remained a major issue at international financial conferences until the 1930s.

Official debts and transactions arising out of them were only a part, if too big a part, of the story. Beneath the surface there were even more fundamental changes in international debtor–creditor relationships as a result of the war. United Kingdom foreign investments had fallen by 15 per cent in value between 1914 and 1918, and although by 1929, after a difficult struggle to restore the pre-war position, they had risen again above the 1914 level, it seemed to many contemporaries that the frontiers of investment had contracted and that a dangerous part of the long-term lending had been financed out of vulnerable short-term funds attracted to London from overseas. The City of London, still more interested in international finance than in British industry, was far less strongly placed internationally than it had been before 1914. In the meantime, the United States had become both the world's biggest creditor and its biggest capital exporter, with American foreign investments rising from about $2,000 million in 1913 to $15,000 million in 1930, 30 per cent of them being located in Europe. This may well have been too high a proportion: far less foreign investment moved into transport or into productive enterprises in 'undeveloped' areas than had been the case before 1914.

Equally serious, as far as Europe itself was concerned, dependence on the United States had become a prop of the system. Just as it would have been impossible to rehabilitate Europe without American assistance immediately after the end of the war—when the American Relief Association supplied food to the value of £291 million, only 29 per cent of which was paid for in cash—so it would have been impossible for European countries to pay either reparations or war debts, after 1923, without American loans. German reparations payments under the Dawes Plan of April 1923 (which brought the German financial crisis to an end) were met out of American loans, with the net import of capital into Germany during the period of the plan standing at between twice and three times the amount of the reparations payments Germany was called upon to pay. At the same time, limited German reparations payments to the ex-Allies were used by them to pay their annual war debts to the United States. 'Reparations and Inter-Allied debts', wrote Keynes in 1926, 'are being mainly settled in paper and not in goods. The United States lends money to Germany, Germany transfers its equivalent to the Allies, the Allies pass it back to the United States Government. Nothing real passes—no one is a penny the worse.'[1]

The continued existence of the circular flow depended on American capital, and, although American lending was to prove more jerky and less reliable than the pre-war British lending which had held the system together, the American economy seemed strong and resilient in the mid-1920s. While the United Kingdom was passing through its far from easy period of underemployment and industrial maladjustment, the United States was galloping through a roaring boom which carried much further the economic advances of the first world war, particularly in new industries with a future, like automobiles, rubber and electricity. Between 1925 and 1929 Europe also shared in much of the prosperity, as the volume of international trade rose by nearly 20 per cent (because of falling prices, only 5·5 per cent in value), with world production of foodstuffs and raw materials increasing by 11 per cent and manufactures by 26 per cent. Effective international economic aid to Austria and to Hungary, somewhat more sensible attitudes both to war debts and to reparations, and a widespread 'return to gold' were other signs of what optimists felt was genuine economic recovery. Sweden was the first of the European countries to return to gold in 1924, but most important in relation to the international economy was the United Kingdom's return a year later. (The move was strongly criticised by Keynes, who objected to a 'return' and looked for an alternative means of securing interdependence built on management of 'the actual system which had grown up half haphazard since the war'.)[2] Belgium followed in 1927 and Italy in 1928. Austria, Czechoslovakia, Estonia, Finland, Italy, Rumania and Yugoslavia adopted a gold exchange standard. Instead of holding gold as the backing of their currencies, they held claims on gold standard countries in the form of currency, bank deposits and securities. In such circumstances, the gold standard never quite operated in the classic form orthodox financiers expected of it or claimed that it had operated before 1914, nor were 'ordinary people brought up regularly against gold' in the form of coins as they had done before 1914. The system began to look suspect. Any serious strain in 'full' gold standard countries was likely to disturb gold exchange standard countries. Most countries had too small a stock of gold in relation to their liabilities. The United Kingdom was no longer in a position to 'manage the international system' on small gold reserves, while France, which stabilised the franc in 1926, at a level which undoubtedly upset competitive conditions in international trade, accumulated more gold than it needed.

Some of these problems could easily be overlooked between 1925 and

---

[1] In the *Nation and Athenaeum*, 11 September 1926.

[2] See J. M. Keynes, *The Economic Consequences of Mr Churchill* (London, 1925). For a contrasting view, see R. S. Sayers, 'The Return to Gold', in L. S. Pressnell (ed.), *Studies in the Industrial Revolution* (London, 1960).

1929, for if the existence of unemployment could not be ignored when sets of regular statistics appeared (a by-product in some countries of national insurance), it was often assumed to be a necessary feature of the system. Hidden from most people's view were the problems of the relationship between 'advanced' and 'developing' countries. Throughout the 1920s, world prices of food and raw materials remained low in relation to the prices of manufactured goods, yet there was a continuous increase of production which led to the accumulation of heavy unsold stocks. The world stock of wheat, for example, rose during the four 'good years' from 1925 to 1929 from around nine million tons to more than twenty million tons. Other international commodities, like sugar or coffee, which were produced in tropical countries as staple crops with low-income labour, offered an extremely precarious livelihood to the large number of individuals producing them. Dissatisfaction with the operations of the free commodity market was expressed most forcibly in the 1920s—and later in the 1930s—by monopolistic associations of producers, who tried to hold up the price of Canadian wheat or Brazilian coffee not by reducing output but by withdrawing or destroying stocks; yet they often received the support of their governments, which feared contraction of income from foreign trade, when they attempted, usually in vain, to resist falls in personal incomes. A characteristic example was the Stevenson scheme for the regulation of rubber prices put into effect in 1922 two years after the British Rubber Growers' Association in Malaya had decided to restrict output to cope with falling prices and one year after the British government had ordered an official enquiry. The scheme was dropped in 1928, to be succeeded six years later by an inter-governmental scheme, involving the Dutch Empire also.

Expressions of the dissatisfaction of plantation workers with the operations of the free market were less frequently heard in either colonial or independent societies than the complaints of business interests. They were less frequently heard, indeed, than the complaints of consumers in 'advanced' countries that whenever crops were destroyed there was, by a social paradox, 'poverty in the midst of plenty'. In fact, however, plantation workers were doomed to poverty so long as the patterns of land use and of farming and the whole economic structures of their countries remained unchanged. 'While statisticians juggled with figures for sugar quotas', it was noted in retrospect—and the note applied to many other primary producing industries besides sugar—'and while governments juggled with beet subsidies, the real cost of the maladjustment in the sugar market was measured by the sufferings of the Colonial workers attached to the industry.'[1] Social and economic problems were inextricably interconnected both in the primary producing countries and the 'advanced' countries. While primary producers, the more active they

[1] P. Lamartine Yates, *Commodity Control* (London, 1943), p. 53.

58

were, received lower incomes in return for their efforts and could not afford to buy manufactured goods, low-income consumers in 'advanced' countries, some of them unemployed, could not convert their wants into effective demand. The fact that many of the manufactured goods being produced were designed not for developing countries, but for the mass markets of the developed countries, like the fact that much of the investment of the period did nothing to change basic economic or social conditions in the developing countries represented in retrospect, at least, a failure both of opportunity and of responsibility.

The main reasons why the nature of this set of problems was not fully appreciated at the time were as much political as economic, although the fact that most of the highly industrialised countries were able by obtaining cheaper imports of food and raw materials to maintain, at least relatively, a strong international economic position and that, despite unemployment, the real income of their wage-earners increased, made it easier to ignore general economic vistas and responsibilities. There was, indeed, much less talk about this set of international economic issues than about the circle of reparations and war debts.

Between 1929 and 1933 the collapse of the United States economy and subsequently of many of the European economies provided more than adequate preoccupations in themselves. The optimism of the years 1925–9 was abruptly shattered by the Wall Street crash of October 1929, reaching a series of feverish climaxes on 24 October, 'Black Thursday'; on 29 October, 'the most devastating day in the history of the New York Stock Market' and possibly 'the most devastating day in the history of all markets',[1] when *The Times* industrial index fell by 43 points; and on three November days, the 11th, 12th and 13th, when the index fell by another 50 points. What began so dramatically was followed by the lingering 'Great Depression'. The recall of American funds from Europe meant not only a withdrawal of credit but that European banks had to meet their obligations in gold. There were consequent failures both of nerve and of institutional technique. The collapse became general, affecting men, money and materials. Everywhere in Europe and in other economically dependent parts of the world, like Australia and New Zealand, prices, output and trade declined rapidly and steeply; unemployment rose to alarming levels never before reached; international financial obligations were repudiated; and in most countries policy became concerned primarily with insulating the national economy from the effects of world-wide slump. Within a few months of the collapse it was difficult to realise that so very recently optimists had been convinced that 'the world as a whole' was 'advancing at an unprecedented pace to levels of prosperity never

[1] J. K. Galbraith, *The Great Crash* (London, 1955), p. 105.

59

before thought possible'[1] and in some cases predicting that the prosperity would go on for ever.

The 1929 American crash was followed not only by persisting hard times in the United States but less than two years later by financial collapse in Europe. Large and disturbing movements of short-term capital, 'hot money', had pressed dangerously on national reserves of gold and foreign exchange, and in some cases capital had moved speculatively from countries which needed it to countries which could not use it. The *Kreditanstalt* in Austria was saved in March 1931 only by advances from the Bank of International Settlements and foreign banks, including the Bank of England. Later in the year the crisis moved to Germany, where there had been both financial and political difficulties since 1928 despite a generous reorganisation and reduction of reparation payments under the Young Plan of 1929 which replaced the Dawes Plan. In June and July the German *Reichsbank* was in an extremely precarious condition, even after President Hoover of the United States proposed a one year moratorium on reparation and war debt payments on 21 June. International action to save Germany from financial collapse moved the crisis towards the United Kingdom, where gold was leaving the country at the rate of £2½ million a day and reserves were becoming ominously low. The fall of the Labour government in August 1931 and its replacement by a 'National' government temporarily halted the withdrawals, but by late September £200 million of gold had been lost in two months. On 21 September Britain suspended the gold standard, the prelude to a general movement off gold. By April 1932 twenty-three countries had followed Britain, and in seventeen others the gold standard was virtually inoperative. The monetary systems which had been so carefully and proudly rebuilt during the 1920s had been swept away.

Yet preoccupation with the fortunes of gold was not the most serious part of the story. The fall in prices was catastrophic. In the United States, in the sick economy of the 1930s, the Bureau of Labour's wholesale price index fell from 100 in 1929 to 63 in March 1933, and in the United Kingdom, which had not been a healthy economy even in the 1920s, the Board of Trade's index fell in the same period from 100 to 72. The prices of primary products, on which the income of the poorer countries of the world depended, fell even more sharply. The gold price of rubber in January 1933 was only 13 per cent of what it had been in January 1929, of wool 22 per cent, of silk 28 per cent, of copper 29 per cent, of cotton 34 per cent, of rice and coffee 41 per cent, of wheat 42 per cent and of sugar 50 per cent. While there was a reduction in the output of minerals, the volume of agricultural products did not fall, but the drastic drop in incomes led to a serious privation and to a sharp contraction in international trade. Between 1929 and the third quarter of 1932 the value

[1] A. Salter, *Recovery* (London, 1932), pp. 22–3.

of international trade shrank by more than 65 per cent, while the international trade of non-European countries fell to less than 30 per cent. In all the main industrial countries there was a sharp fall of production, a rise in unemployment, and a decline in exports. Taking 1929 as 100, United States production in 1932 was 54, that of Germany 53 and that of France 69. In Britain the figure was 84, but British exports in 1932 were only 63 per cent of those of 1929. American exports stood at 53 per cent, and French and German at 59 per cent.[1]

In such circumstances, there was recourse to many expedients and improvisations, some of them based on the simple maxim of *sauve qui peut*, others on the equally simple maxim of 'beggar my neighbour'. The United Kingdom abandoned free trade as well as gold in 1932: by the Import Duties Act a general 10 per cent tariff was introduced, with protective duties on some manufactured goods of up to 33⅓ per cent, and a year later an attempt was made at Ottawa to form an empire 'bloc', the main effect of which was to raise British tariffs on goods imported from outside the Empire. For many countries traditional economic instruments, like tariffs, seemed quite inadequate, and import quotas, control of marketing of home-produced products, price determination and regulation of capital investment and distribution were adopted. Such deliberate intervention to influence the operation of the market, however improvised in its origins, became a permanent feature of national economic policy.

The choice of instruments adopted, like their effectiveness, depended as much on political as on economic considerations. In Germany, where the number of unemployed rose to nearly six millions in 1932, the political tide moved in favour of the National Socialists, who in an atmosphere of tension and violence promised, certainly not on the basis of a carefully thought out economic programme, to abolish unemployment and guarantee national self-sufficiency. In countries like Belgium and Holland, where business interests were strong, government apparatus was designed to protect industrial capital and profits: attempts were made in 1932 (only to be blocked by Britain) to form a low-tariff zone in what is now Benelux. In the 'green international' countries of eastern and southern Europe, particularly hard hit, like primary producing countries outside Europe, by the fall in food prices, there was special political urgency in the old argument that agriculture constituted a special case in economics, and landlord and peasant interests had to be most carefully watched. Yet just as Britain blocked the agreement between Belgium, Holland and Luxembourg, so Germany and Italy (in 1931–2) blocked schemes for a Danubian customs union, this time on straight political grounds. Among the European countries only in Sweden, when the Social Democrats came into power in 1932 (in alliance with the Farmers), was there sufficient

[1] See League of Nations, *The Course and Phases of the Great Depression* (Geneva, 1931).

boldness to rely on unbalanced budgets and loan-financed public works to achieve 'a definitely expansionist mentality'.[1] In all the European industrial countries, however, the full social effects of the depression were 'cushioned' to some extent by the fact that they could maintain their imports of primary products at a relatively high level because of the disproportionately steep fall in import prices. The United Kingdom as the biggest importer benefited most. The average real income of the person at work was nearly as great in 1932 as in 1929, and even if the increasing number of unemployed are included, the average was only 10 per cent less.[2]

The United States, where industrial construction slumped from $949 million in 1929 to $74 million in 1932, made no effective contribution to international recovery during these difficult years. In addition to clinging to war debts, even after the unratified Lausanne Conference of July 1932 put a *de facto* end to reparations claims, the Americans followed a protectionist policy in international trade.[3] After the beginning of the depression the Hawley–Smoot Act of 1930 raised the already high protective duties imposed by the Fordney–McCumber tariff of 1922. It provoked a series of retaliatory measures in many parts of the world. 'The debts of the outside world to us', wrote the President of the Chase National Bank in 1930, 'are ropes about their necks, by means of which we pull them towards us. Our trade restrictions are pitchforks pressed against their bodies, by means of which we hold them off.'[4] Such contradictions reflected the large extent to which American economic policy was the product of powerful sectional business pressures.

At the same time, the fact that American farmers and workers were especially hard hit by the great depression made it inevitable that American politicians had to put America first, and there were many American economic 'nationalists' uninfluenced by business pressures who by 1933 found 'extolling the old *laissez-faire* liberal internationalism...harder and harder to bear'.[5] The reality of the position was brutally demonstrated in April 1933 when after the new President, F. D. Roosevelt, had sent a stirring message to the world stressing the need for international economic co-operation the American government abandoned the gold standard and devalued the dollar by 41 per cent at the very moment that a World Monetary and Economic Conference—the first and last genuinely inter-

[1] B. Ohlin, 'Economic Recovery and Labour Market Problems in Sweden', in the *International Labour Review* (1935), vol. XXI, pp. 498–501, 670–99.

[2] C. Clark, *National Income and Outlay* (London, 1937), p. 208.

[3] There was a *de facto* end to war payments to the United States after 1933, only Finland making any payments after December of that year.

[4] *Chase Economic Bulletin*, 14 March 1930.

[5] R. Tugwell, *Notes from a New Deal Diary*, 31 May 1933, quoted in W. E. Leuchtenburg, *Franklin D. Roosevelt and the New Deal* (New York, 1963), p. 200. 'The cat is out of the bag', wrote Tugwell later. 'There is no invisible hand, there never was' (*The Battle for Democracy*, New York, 1935, p. 213).

1ational conference to deal with economic problems since 1929—was
:onvening in London under the auspices of the League of Nations. Devaluation was conceived of as a means of raising the American internal
price level and strengthening farm incomes and Roosevelt rejoiced that
he 'old fetishes of so-called international bankers' were 'being replaced
by efforts to plan national currencies'.[1] Yet in so far as it in effect raised
United States tariffs by 60 per cent and gave a 40 per cent bounty to
American exports at a time when America already enjoyed a favourable
balance of trade and was importing gold, it had the effect of further increasing international disequilibrium. After this 'bombshell', it was not
surprising that the World Economic Conference failed to reach agreement
either on questions relating directly to currency or on proposals to
increase the volume of international trade. Its main achievement, indeed,
was further to extend or to reinforce international commodity controls of
a restrictive kind in relation to such products as wheat, rubber, sugar, tea,
tin and copper.[2]

Yet however unhelpful American policy was in relation to international
recovery, two points of qualification must be made concerning its general
role. First, it is by no means certain that a different American policy
would have made the World Economic Conference a success. The
pressures for independent national action were powerful everywhere, and
there was a universal contradiction between the facts of national economic
policy and the pious hope expressed by bankers and orthodox economists
that 'the gold standard remains the best available monetary system'.[3]
Secondly, President Roosevelt's apparent distaste for *laissez faire*, deflation and the adjustment of monetary policies to the vagaries of international capital movements was echoed in many circles in Europe.
Keynes, for instance, called his actions 'magnificently right'. His
vigorous actions in going forward to seek to meet the 'crisis' situation in
his country were seen as a triumph of purpose. There were over 13
million unemployed when he was returned to power, and the 'New Deal'
which he offered his people to meet this and other economic and social
challenges brought to an end a period of what has been called 'suspended
animation'.[4] While there was nothing revolutionary either in the philosophy or the purposes of the New Deal and there were many contradictory
tendencies expressed in it, it received widespread interest in all other parts
of the world, as did related American 'plans', like the Tennessee Valley
Authority scheme, introduced in 1933 as an imaginative attempt to
extend planning in the name of a return to the spirit and vision of the
American pioneer.

[1] Quoted in Leuchtenburg, *op. cit.* p. 202.
[2] See H. V. Hodson, *Slump and Recovery 1929–1937* (London, 1938), ch. VI.
[3] *Report of the Gold Delegation* (Geneva, 1932), p. 23.
[4] H. W. Arndt, *The Economic Lessons of the Nineteen-Thirties* (London, 1944), p. 42.

The first object of the New Deal was to pull the United States out of the slump, the second to widen the concept of social justice, and the third to balance the economic system. None of these objectives—and some of Roosevelt's friends as well as his opponents saw them as incompatible—involved any long-term overall plan, but they all implied increasing governmental intervention. Undoubtedly the American 'experiment', which had reached stalemate by 1938, after bitter arguments between different groups of presidential advisers and in face of increasing business resistance, stimulated great interest in the problems of planning both in America and in Europe. Alvin Hansen, the economist, might ask whether 'government intervention, made inevitable by the distress incidental to vast unemployment, has created a hybrid society, half-free and half-regimented, which cannot operate at full employment',[1] but in Europe the view was widely held that Roosevelt's 'strivings towards reconstruction and revival are as surely the outstanding example of reformed Capitalism as the Russian Five-Year Plans are of Socialist planning in the world today'.[2]

While the United States achieved this reputation, Sweden became known as 'the economic miracle' of the 1930s,[3] and New Zealand after an overwhelming Labour victory in 1938 consciously turned itself, despite international complications, into a 'welfare state'.[4] It was possible, indeed, for one well-known British economist to write (without enthusiasm) in 1934, 'we may not all be socialists now, but we are certainly (nearly) all planners'.[5] In retrospect, even given the American, Swedish and New Zealand experience, the remark seems exaggerated. There was still far less planning of economies than political interference within economies, and there was no general understanding of the economics of unemployment, despite the publication in 1936 of Keynes's *General Theory of Employment, Interest and Money*, which is one of the great twentieth-century landmarks in the history of economic thought. When 'planning' was discussed in the United Kingdom, which it often was, it did not entail more than strictly limited 'management', usually to meet the particular problems of specific industries by destroying excessive capacity and stocks or by 'rationalising' prices. 'Planning is forced upon us', wrote a young Conservative politician, H. Macmillan, in 1938, who on other occasions talked grandiloquently of 'an organic conception of society' as a counterweight to 'individualism and *laissez-faire*',[6] 'not for idealistic

---

[1] A. H. Hansen, *Full Recovery or Stagnation* (New York, 1938), p. 8.
[2] G. D. H. Cole, *Practical Economics* (London, 1937), p. 145.
[3] H. Dalton in B. Thomas *Monetary Policy and Crises* (London, 1936), p. x. See also M. Childs, *Sweden, the Middle Way* (London, 1937).
[4] J. B. Condliffe, 'The Labour Experiment in New Zealand', in *The Economic Record*, August 1957, pp. 153-4; W. B. Sutch, *The Quest for Security in New Zealand* (London, 1942).
[5] L. Robbins, *The Great Depression* (1934), p. 145.
[6] H. Macmillan, *The Spirit of Conservatism* (London, 1929), p. 103.

reasons but because the old mechanism which served us when markets were expanding naturally and spontaneously is no longer adequate when the tendency is in the opposite direction.'[1] The founding of the British Iron and Steel Federation in 1934, for example, was an example of a union of protectionism and 'a considerable measure of reorganisation'[2] which fell far short of general or even of limited economic planning. The Agricultural Marketing Act of 1933, which provided for the organisation of marketing schemes for commodities like milk, potatoes and hops, was in the same spirit.[3]

What was true of the United Kingdom was true of other countries. Italian fascist economists could write of *corporativismo* as a new order in which the distribution of labour and capital as well as the system of production could be planned in advance, but it was not until 1936 and 1937 that Mussolini emphasised the economic significance of increasing state intervention in industry; and as late as 1938 there was little co-ordination of the national economy through the action of the corporations. In France economic policy relied on quantitative import restrictions, as it did in a smaller country like Rumania, where the number of quotas rose from 120 in November 1932 to 500 in July 1933 (50 per cent of Rumania's imports). In both Italy and France (as in the United States) industrial production in 1937 remained less than it had been in 1929 when the Great Depression began.

Only in Sweden, where Ernst Wigforss was an outstanding finance minister and where economists were brought directly into the service of government, was there a sophisticated official approach to the dangers of deflation, yet even there external forces influenced the pattern of recovery, and deficit budgeting, thought of as contra-cyclical, did not wipe out unemployment. Paradoxically Wigforss had drawn many of his ideas from liberals and socialists in the United Kingdom,[4] where an unmistakable economic 'recovery' between 1933 and 1937 owed little or nothing to the strength of these ideas in official quarters, and depended rather on an 'untheoretical' combination of devaluation (embarked upon with such a display of reluctance in 1931), 'rationalisation', protection and cheap money. In a sense, the British recovery was a compensation for the stagnation of the 1920s: belated new investment, particularly in building, remedied serious under-investment during the 1920s. There was a kind of 'muddling through' to recovery which had little to do with 'planning'. In

---

[1] H. Macmillan, *The Middle Way* (London, 1938), pp. 7–8.
[2] Cmd. 4066, 4181 (1932); G. C. Allen, *British Industries and their Organisation* (3rd ed. London, 1951), pp. 109–12.
[3] For a more positive evaluation of 'the reassertion of state power' by the National government in England, particularly in the 'critical period' from 1931 to 1935, see S. H. Beer, *Modern British Politics* (London, 1964), ch. x.
[4] K.-G. Landgren, *Den 'nya ekonomien' i Sverige: J. M. Keynes, E. Wigforss, B. Ohlin och utvecklinger, 1929–39* (Stockholm, 1960).

the United States, Roosevelt was a pragmatist, not a doctrinaire, although his advisers included doctrinaires of different pedigrees with different programmes to advocate. At the international policy-making level, only the reports of the International Labour Organisation provided any kind of consistent if limited theoretical support for 'expansionism', through, for example, concerted international public works policies.

At the beginning of the Depression, as in the years of recovery during the late 1930s, the one comprehensive planning scheme in operation was that of the Soviet Union, where output rose rapidly during the 1930s. Yet as a result of the revolution of 1917 and the foundation of new economic policies in the 1920s, the Soviet Union had virtually disappeared from the international economic stage, and during the Depression remained insulated from the world economy. There was far less knowledge of its planning procedures than of the slogans used by its leaders, not least because the planning procedures were never very clearly elucidated even in the Soviet Union.

The Soviet planning system set out in a phrase of Trotsky's to bring aim and plan into the very basis of society, although at the beginning of the revolution the mechanisms of planning were still to be thought out as well as worked out (see ch. xv). 'There was nothing written about such matters in the Bolshevik textbooks, or even in those of the Mensheviks', wrote Lenin six months after the October Revolution. The machinery of planning in the Soviet Union, as in the case of war-time economic organisation, was the product of national emergency. It was at first tentative and hesitant, but it improved as a result of actual experience of economic administration, first in emergency conditions and then in the period of economic transformation under the First and Second Five-Year Plans. There was continual adaption and reorganisation within the Supreme Council of National Economy (VSNKh or *Vesenkha*), a body which came into existence as early as December 1917 and lasted until January 1932. Such fundamental problems as that of relating central 'steering' of the economy to local managerial effort in the 'trusts', the main units of nationalised production, were tackled by trial and error. There was no pre-existing conception of design. 'Socialist construction cannot proceed otherwise than gropingly', an official report put it in 1929, 'and, whenever practice is in advance of theory, faultless creativeness is impossible.'[1]

In the long run, the most important agency for drafting and co-ordinating Soviet plans was *Gosplan*, first set up in February 1921 as an advisory body attached to the Council of Labour and Defence. Yet *Gosplan*'s earliest tasks were 'perspective' plans of a somewhat abstract character, involving such general objectives as the extensive electrification of industry or the nationalisation of the corn trade. 'There is too much

[1] *Control Figures of the National Economy* (Moscow, 1928–9), p. 2.

talk of electrification, and too little about *current* economic plans', Lenin wrote to its chairman in 1921.[1] It was not until 1925 that *Gosplan* began to issue economic 'control figures' for the whole of the Soviet economy, and not until 1931, after bitter controversies, that the series of figures taken from separate industries became a system of figures related to an overall plan for the ensuing year. The creation of a Central Department of Economic Accounting (TSUNKhU) in the same year facilitated the necessary calculation of the 'material needs' (including the volume of investment) demanded by government policy. After the elimination of VSNKh in 1932, *Gosplan*'s co-ordinating powers greatly increased, and reforms of 1935 and 1938 emphasised its 'leadership' role. Although economic administration was left to other agencies—People's Commissariats or ministries, which increased in number from three in 1932 (heavy industry, light industry, and timber) to twenty in 1939—*Gosplan* established its position as the central headquarters of Soviet planning.

The basic problem of the Soviet economy throughout the 1920s and 1930s was that of transforming a relatively backward country into an extensively industrialised modern state without having to depend on private capitalists at home or on foreign investors overseas. The history of the transformation may be divided into three main phases—first, a period of war communism from the revolution of 1917 to March 1921, during which the state set out to capture the commanding heights of the existing economic system; secondly, a period of recovery and restoration accomplished within the framework of the so-called New Economic Policy (1922–7), which aimed at increasing the flow of goods to the markets, if need be by encouraging a strictly limited amount of individual enterprise; and thirdly, after strategic and controversial decisions, a period of intensive industrialisation and agricultural collectivisation, beginning with the announcement of the First Five-Year Plan in 1928.

The First Five-Year Plan began as a 'perspective plan', but it was discussed and reshaped frequently before efforts were made to implement it. Its keynote was a high rate of investment, particularly in heavy industry and in agriculture. During the first two years of the plan the objectives were secured without great difficulty, but in 1929 and 1930 many problems arose as a result both of inflationary pressure and the deliberate attempt by the government to force the pace of socialisation. In the case of agriculture, enforced collectivisation was pushed by vigorous coercion. In 1927, all the various forms of state and co-operative farming covered a mere 2 per cent of the peasants: by the beginning of March 1930 the figure had risen to 55 per cent and by 1936 to 90 per cent.[2] Coercion seemed the only means of solving the government's serious agricultural problems, which had proved intractable in the 1920s, and of making labour move from

---

[1] Lenin, *Collected Works*, vol. xxvi, p. 296.
[2] See N. Jasny, *The Socialized Agriculture of the USSR* (Stanford, 1949).

villages to towns; it was only at the cost, therefore, of great immediate hardship to large numbers of individuals and to the peasant class as a whole that agriculture was integrated (and even then imperfectly) into the general planning system.

The years 1929–31 marked the final capture by the state of the whole of the economic system, and the agricultural changes were paralleled by trade-union reforms, the dismissal of old leaders, a tightening up of factory discipline and the conversion of the unions into quasi-governmental agencies for raising productivity in the interests of the plan. There were also important fiscal and credit reforms, including the introduction of turnover tax in 1931, the creation of specialised investment banks in 1932, and the conferring on *Gosbank* of monopoly powers to grant short-term credits. These too had the same objective: to make the plan work. 'There is no fortress the Bolsheviks cannot take' was one of the key slogans of this drive.

The First Five-Year Plan, carried out in 'the hard years', set the model, but its successor, the Second Five-Year Plan, extending from 1933 to 1937, stressed practical advance and consolidation rather than gigantic leaps forward (see below, ch. xv). The economic atmosphere in which it was carried through seemed favourable. By 1935 it was considered safe to abandon rationing. In that year too a Collective Farm Statute, in force with little change until 1957, brought to an end the period of rural turmoil associated with 'revolution from above'. Subsequent increase in agricultural output was accompanied by rising industrial productivity, facilitated by the relative abundance of labour. New factories were well established, and began to add substantially to national output. In 1937 four-fifths of industrial output came from plants that were newly built or that had been reconstructed since 1928, while two metallurgical plants alone, Magnitogorsk and Stalinsk, had a productive capacity equal to that of the entire pre-1914 iron and steel industry.

The size of the Soviet economic system enabled it to pay smaller attention to foreign trade than would have been possible for a country more dependent on supplies of imports. On the basis of a great diversity of agricultural and non-agricultural materials, the Soviet Union was able to set up and operate plants which turned out most of the manufacturing products necessary for the development of the economy. From 1918 onwards international trade was monopolised by the State Commissariat for Foreign Trade. This monopoly enabled the government to maintain the rouble at an artificial value in terms of foreign currencies and to insist on an extremely tight import programme. In the critical years from 1929 to 1932 almost 90 per cent of imports consisted of goods for use in industry. Trade corporations specialising in the import or export of particular commodities worked closely within the framework of the plans, with *Gosplan* making known to them figures of essential import requirements and exportable surpluses. The Second Five-Year Plan explicitly limited exports to 'surplus products of the national economy' and imports to what could be paid for from such surpluses. In 1938, indeed, the total value of foreign trade amounted to only 24 per cent of the 1913 level (although it had been as high as 73 per cent in 1930, the peak year). Soviet planning was thus as independent as possible of world economic movements. It could even run directly counter to such movements, as it did in the Depression years when it dumped exports abroad at prices well below costs. It could also use trade as a political instrument, with long-term foreign contracts and agreements acting as useful political counters.

While during the late 1930s preparations for war distorted or even disrupted general economic advance in the Soviet Union, there was a sense in which, even apart from development within the war sector, the entire planned economy of the Soviet Union was throughout the whole of the inter-war years 'a sui generis war economy'.[1] All-out concentration of effort on major objectives determined by political authority—'campaign planning'—was associated with appeals to the patriotism and socialist consciousness of managers and workers alike. It was not merely foreign trade which 'politicised' markets and defied price-cost criteria. 'The price mechanism was hardly used for resource allocation at all, except to distribute to the citizens in an orderly way whatever happened to be available for them.'[2] In general, rational economic calculation was relegated to a minor place in 'the thought processes of the leadership', emphasis being placed throughout on plan as basic 'law', the will of the lawgiver, the conscious direction of the economy. 'Planning is no mere piling up of tables and figures unrelated to the course of fulfilment of the plan', Molotov proclaimed in 1939.[3] Fulfilment was a practical task, political and administrative, and it is significant that no general textbook of economics appeared in the Soviet Union between 1928 and 1954.[4]

Whatever the disadvantages of such a situation—disadvantages which have been widely commented upon by Soviet economists in the late 1950s and 1960s—Soviet planning, with all its miscalculations, its wastes and its coercion, undoubtedly appealed at the time and since both to groups in 'advanced countries' suffering from chronic unemployment and to 'backward countries' anxious for economic growth. The 'war' nature of the economy and the sense of 'strategy' which underlay Soviet development had a positive appeal in themselves. So too did the boldness of the vision. Before 1939 the Turkish Five-Year Plan and the Mexican Six-Year Plan

[1] O. Lange, *The Political Economy of Socialism* (Warsaw, 1957), p. 16.
[2] A. Nove, *The Soviet Economy* (London, 1961), p. 147.
[3] *The Third Five-Year Plan of the National Economy of the USSR* (Moscow, 1939), pp. 20-1.
[4] Nove, *op. cit.* p. 267. A textbook was being planned in 1941, when there were signs that the need for a 'new socialist economy' was felt by the authority. Even the word 'Statistics' dropped out of the title of the central accounting agency between 1931 and 1941.

were influenced by Soviet models: so, too, were some of the economic policies of the Soviet Union's non-Communist neighbour, Poland. It is since 1945, however, that the influence has become obvious and direct in Communist countries (all of them, except China, smaller and less favoured by nature than the Soviet Union) and that some at least among the many non-communist writers on 'development' have acknowledged that the Soviet 'path' to economic development has general relevance. As in war, 'the process (of growth) required the breaking of a succession of critical bottlenecks'. Marginal calculus was less important than sector planning, and people or groups standing in the way of sector planning had to have their power to curb or to resist destroyed. 'Total war, like planning development of poor and stagnant economies, involves marked and discontinuous structural changes, and resource allocation without reference to the market.'[1] Yet this is only one part of an analysis. The argument about Soviet planning continues, with the experience of other post-1945 plans—notably those of Communist Poland and Yugoslavia—influencing the debate in the Soviet Union itself.

German planning under National Socialism, unlike Soviet planning, accepted private enterprise and the economic institutions of capitalism. Within this framework the government assumed a firm control over manpower and production, distribution and banking, consumption and investment, and foreign exchange and trade. The aim of the government through what was called *Wirtschaftslenkung*, guided private enterprise, was to direct the economic machine for political purposes, ultimately, if occasion demanded, for the needs of war. Yet there was no full 'war economy' in Germany until after 1942. Armament expenditures, which rose regularly as a proportion of national expenditure from 1935 onwards, fitted Germany to embark upon *Blitzkrieg* but not to sustain prolonged war against powers like the United States, which had developed war production much more comprehensively. It has been estimated that half total investment between 1933 and 1938 was outside military facilities or basic industries.[2] There was, indeed, a certain vagueness about the criteria of German economic policy, as there was about the theories on which it should be based. 'Economic policy in the national socialist state', wrote one commentator, 'is determined by considerations of expediency, and, without prejudice, applies such means as are necessary in every given case for the welfare of the people.'[3] The term 'welfare' was elastic, including guns *and* butter,[4] even if the effect of government policy was to control inflation by limiting the freedom both of the wage-earner and of the entrepreneur. A

[1] B. Higgins, *Economic Development* (New York, 1959).
[2] B. H. Klein, *Germany's Economic Preparations for War* (Cambridge, Mass., 1959), pp. 14–15.
[3] L. Barth, *Wesen und Aufgaben* (Berlin, 1936), p. 26.
[4] A. S. Milward, *The German Economy at War* (London, 1965), p. 6.

wage-stop was coupled with strict limitations on the distributed dividends received by shareholders—a national incomes policy; exchange control and import restrictions regulated the balance of payments; and it was emphasised through every form of organisation and propaganda that there was a public or national dimension to all economic organisation. 'Private enterprises have become public trusts', wrote the *Deutsche Volkswirt* in 1937, 'the State is for all practical purposes a partner in every German enterprise.'

When the National Socialists took over in 1933 they found already in existence the two necessary components of their later policy—first, a highly organised industrial structure which had already been affected by the propaganda of 'rationalisation' in the 1920s, and, secondly, exchange control, first introduced in July 1931 to stop the flight of capital and which had become a point of departure for more extensive economic regulation. They made few economic innovations and had no agreed economic theory to support them—one section of the party, indeed, opposed all economic calculation as a form of excuse for a failure of will—but they were determined to make the economic system fit their aims. The existence of large-scale unemployment gave them an immediate objective in the shape of the promise of work for all: the dream of national self-sufficiency or at least of a sharp reduction in Germany's heavy dependence on overseas countries for raw materials, like iron, oil and rubber (only coal was in adequate supply from within) linked possible technological policy with trade.

Without the existing highly developed co-ordination of German business they could scarcely have evolved their own institutional structure. The Central Committee of Entrepreneurial Associations had been set up in 1920. The National Union of German Industry (*Reichsverband der Deutschen Industrie*), its most important member, had been formed in 1919 from a union of two older organisations, one going back to 1876 and the other to 1895. The influence and scope of the *Reichsverband* was wide-ranging, and its organisation, under the leadership of the most powerful industrialists in Germany, was complex, based on dual units, regional and functional. In 1932 the 29 industrial and 50 territorial organisations which belonged corporatively to it accounted for about 80 per cent of German industrial enterprise.[1] It was able to exercise considerable influence on the making of national policy. The National Socialist government, in establishing the National Economic Chamber (*Reichswirtschaftskammer*) and the Co-operative Council of Chambers of Industry and Commerce, at first conceived its task merely as the limited one of 'co-ordinating with the present national government the existing organisation of the vast field of German business administration'.[2] National Socialist

---

[1] K. Guth, *Die Reichsgruppe Industrie* (Berlin, 1941), p. 19.
[2] Dr Kurt Schmitt in 1934. See R. A. Brady, *The Spirit and Structure of German Fascism* (London, 1937), p. 266.

legislation, especially the 'Law on the Organic Structure of German Industry' of February 1934, made membership of the Chamber and of subordinate groups compulsory on all entrepreneurs, established the 'leadership principle', and laid down that the guiding rule of the system was 'never to act against the wishes of the government of the Reich'.[1] From 1934 onwards big business was clearly far more powerful than small business, and strengthening cartellisation and making it more comprehensive facilitated further concentration and control.

The government itself had a number of agencies at its own disposal. The Ministry of Economics, inaugurated in 1919, was a survival from the Weimar Republic, and Kurt Schmitt, minister in July 1933, made every effort to reconcile business to the new order.[2] So long as Hjalmar Schacht acted as minister—from August 1934 until November 1937—the ministry extended control over German banking and trade, and was drawn into difficult debates about the financing of rearmament. Schacht himself experimented freely with bilateral trade policies and sought to increase business opportunities and profits, but feared inflation and was an ultra-conservative opponent of deficit financing. After 1938, however, the Ministry of Economics, under Walter Funk, lost most of its influence. In the meantime, as emphasis passed from recovery to rearmament, the office of the Four-Year Plan had been set up in 1936 under the personal control of General Goering with immense powers on paper—above all, to increase the flow of synthetic materials (capacity for synthetic oil production was increased more than twofold between 1936 and 1939, while still remaining 45 per cent below the target figure) and to strengthen the hold of the National Socialist party over the economy. The first objective was clearly expressed by Hitler in an anti-Schachtian directive to Goering in 1936: 'the question of costs of raw materials is absolutely irrelevant, for it is preferable for us to produce more expensive tyres which are then available, than to buy theoretically cheap tyres for which the Ministry of Economics cannot allot the foreign exchange'. Hitler associated this statement with an attack on the 'capital system', linking Goering's duties with the second objective in the remark that if the industrialists refused to co-operate, 'the National Socialist State itself will know how to perform this task'.[3] The symbol of the second objective was the Hermann Goering steelworks on the Brunswick plain, the visible memorial of the National Socialist system, yet despite the existence of this and other ventures German steel production in 1939 exceeded that of 1929 only because of the acquisition of plant in Austria and Czechoslovakia.

The last of the government agencies, the army itself, had also built up

---

[1] Barth, *Wesen und Aufgaben*, p. 13.
[2] See A. Schweitzer, *Big Business in the Third Reich* (London, 1964), pp. 124 ff., 249 ff. Schweitzer brings out the conflicts between 'small' and 'big' business, pp. 524 ff.
[3] Quoted in Klein, *Germany's Economic Preparations for War*, p. 36.

its own economic departments from the top level downwards: General Georg Thomas, the officer concerned with this apparatus, was deeply concerned about the failure to co-ordinate and to extend national economic planning before 1939, while lacking the statistical or theoretical knowledge fully to support his case that Hitler would be taking an unjustifiable risk if he were to plan a war before the economy was ready.[1] Thomas's complaint that he was informed neither of total material requirements nor of strategic plans has been used by recent historians to prove the case that until 1942 Germany's economy in military terms was prepared only for small-scale quick wars which would not unduly disturb civilian standards or ways of life. It was, indeed, 'a cardinal policy of Hitler that war strategy was not a concern of economic planners', and since they were given only the inflated demands for men and materials of the various claimants 'it was impossible to put together a very intelligent picture of requirements'.[2] At the same time, the German armament firms were elevated to the position of *Wehrwirtschaftsführer* in 1935 and 1936, and their managers could act in a semi-military capacity.[3]

More important in retrospect than the elaborate structure of planning, which was far from producing an efficient, well-organised, industrial effort, was the experiment in reducing unemployment. Between 1933 and 1939 the Germans achieved what most of the private enterprise economies were eventually to proclaim during the second world war as the main goal of economic planning—full employment. Here again they inherited the strategy. In December 1932 a Commissioner for the Creation of Employment had been appointed, and two days before the beginning of the National Socialist régime an 'urgency programme' had been put into operation involving heavy public expenditure on roads, houses, public utilities and inland water transport. In May 1933 Hitler announced a plan for the abolition of unemployment. Sizeable public expenditures—not involving, as in the United States 'New Deal', any serious reliance on deficit budgeting or for that matter on new forms of taxation—associated with a revival of private investment led to substantial gains in total output and employment between 1933 and 1936. Unemployment fell to 1·6 million in 1936, approximately the pre-depression figure, and to less than 0·5 million two years later.[4]

The pursuit of full employment was coupled with extensive measures of labour and price control. Labour control, which began with the destruction of free trade unions, prevented wage-earners from pressing for wage increases in a sellers' market; price control was considered necessary not so much to 'regulate' the economy as to safeguard workers' loyalty and morale. The law concerning the Regulation of National Labour,

[1] Milward, *The German Economy at War*, pp. 24–5.   [2] Klein, *op. cit.* p. 38.
[3] Schweitzer, *op. cit.* p. 533.
[4] See C. W. Guillebaud, *The Economic Recovery of Germany, 1933–8* (Cambridge, 1939).

promulgated in January 1934, and the order of October 1934 substituted for the existing trade-union organisation a Labour Front and for collective bargaining and the right to strike 'enterprise communities' (*Betriebsgemeinschaften*) and 'enterprise rules'. Trustees of Labour (*Treuhänder der Arbeit*) were given wide powers to regulate the labour market as a whole. Only because of the existence of controls of this kind was the government's wage-stop effective: they were retained after recovery had been achieved, and they were associated also with moves toward a longer working day and towards labour direction. As far as prices were concerned, a Reich Commissioner for the Supervision of Prices had been appointed as early as December 1931, but in 1936 a new office, that of Reich Commissioner of Price Formation, was set up.[1] A Price-Stop Decree of November 1936 pegged prices to those of an arbitrarily chosen date, 17 October 1936, and prohibited all further increases in response to rising demand. There was talk in some circles, indeed, of the laws of supply and demand having been superseded. In fact, the Commissioner had wide powers to raise prices, and could claim that when he did so the higher production costs which were responsible for the rise derived from higher import costs or from the high costs of substitute materials.

All German internal policy depended, in fact, on vigorous control of foreign trade. Exchange control and refusal to devalue the mark had been pre-1933 policies, and Schacht's 'New Plan' of September 1934 followed naturally, albeit with greater energy and resourcefulness, from the work of his predecessors. Licences had to be obtained for any transactions involving an outflow of foreign exchange. All incoming payments from abroad had to be handed over to the Reichsbank, and as a check exporters were compelled to declare to the authorities the nature and value of the goods transferred out of the country. Imports were kept to a minimum, and interest and dividend payments to foreigners were first reduced and then restricted to payments out of export surpluses. Within the framework of regulation, trade discrimination, with varying rates of exchange for different types of transaction, was developed to its extreme practical limits. Wherever possible, imports were only drawn from countries willing to hold balances in marks and not in fully convertable currency. Special mark rates were adjusted in terms of the structure of each separate market. A regional bloc, mainly in southern and eastern Europe, was built up on the basis of bilateral agreements providing bulk turnover and long-term contracts.

There was no spectacular recovery of German exports as a result of these intricate measures: indeed, in relation to total industrial production exports declined from 22·5 per cent in 1933 to 13·1 per cent in 1938. By that

[1] Price controls had been ineffective between 1933 and 1936. The official cost-of-living index rose 7 per cent between 1933 and 1936 and wholesale prices by about 13·7 per cent (Schweitzer, *op. cit.* pp. 324–5).

74

year, however, only about one-fifth of Germany's foreign trade required and produced foreign exchange. The lines of trade were regulated in the interests of state policy, and in the business recession of 1938 it was not only the Communist Soviet Union but capitalist and National Socialist Germany which was insulated from the rest of the world.

Germany spent more on rearmament as a proportion of gross national product than any other of the other European powers between 1936 and 1939—the proportion rising from 3·2 per cent in 1933 to 5·5 per cent in 1935 and 18·1 per cent in 1938—yet in most other European countries, including the United Kingdom, increased rearmament expenditure—in the United Kingdom it followed the building 'boom'—was an important factor in the economic recovery of the late 1930s.[1] While such expenditure contributed to the demand for industrial raw materials and to the development of new forms of technology, it did little to mobilise to the full either national or international economic resources, including manpower. As industrial output increased, unemployment remained high, and there was talk in some circles of inevitable tailing off of growth or 'satiation', as Keynes called it, in 'mature' economies. Moreover, while after a long interval there was some improvement in Europe's relative position in world markets *vis-à-vis* that of the United States, a reversal of the trend of the 1920s, there was only a very limited revival of world trade.[2] Even as late as 1937 the volume of world trade was barely equal to that of 1929, and all official attempts to reduce tariffs and quotas and to stimulate greater freedom of trade, like those of Cordell Hull from 1934[3] and of Van Zeeland in 1938,[4] met with little response. The contrast between advancing industrial output and stagnating commerce remained striking. In the United Kingdom, for instance, the increase of 24 per cent in the volume of industrial production between 1929 and 1937 was accompanied by a fall in the volume of exports of no less than 16 per cent.

Both the constituents of world trade and the pattern of international payments altered during the 1930s. In 1937 the quantum of trade in foodstuffs was about 7 per cent below the 1929 level and in manufactured goods 14 per cent below, while in raw materials it was 12 per cent above. Such divergent movements were associated with inverse movements in relative prices. Industrial countries continued to enjoy extremely favour-

[1] See M. M. Postan, *British War Production* (London, 1952), ch. 2.
[2] Svennilson, *Growth and Stagnation in the European Economy*, ch. ix.
[3] Between 1934 and 1939 the United States concluded trade agreements with twenty countries, half of them in Latin America. In 1938, after protracted discussions, an agreement was reached with the United Kingdom.
[4] In April 1937 the British and French governments requested Van Zeeland, then Prime Minister of Belgium, to enquire into 'the possibilities of obtaining a general reduction of quotas and other obstacles to international trade': his report was published in January 1938.

able terms of trade as against the suppliers of primary products, thereby continuing to gain from the inability of 'underdeveloped' countries to raise their incomes or to diversify their economies. There were immense disparities in the national incomes per head of different countries and in their standards of living and their ability to use manufactured products.[1] Although there were still very few signs that such a situation provoked articulate and effective response, it was beginning to be realised that, if the demand for 'planning' arose in the poorer societies, it would probably take the form of 'a rational inference from an urge for development' and from 'the knowledge of the adverse circumstances' in which they found themselves.[2] Some of the reports both of the International Labour Organisation and of the League of Nations in the late 1930s directed attention to the links between economic and social policy. On the initiative of Australia, for example, the League in 1935 initiated an enquiry into 'nutrition in relation to health, agriculture, and economic policy'; and two years later a further enquiry into the broader problems of raising general standards of living was undertaken jointly by the League's Economic Committee and the International Labour Organisation. In 1938 the League appointed a committee to examine 'practical measures for preventing or mitigating trade depressions'.

There was an element of irony in this concern for welfare just at the time when warfare was preoccupying the minds of Europe's politicians. The international economic context in which the enquiries were launched was in some ways equally unpropitious. The market continued to set the terms of most international economic relationships—the price of cocoa, for example, fell calamitously by 40 per cent in the recession years 1937–8 —yet it was an imperfect market, tampered with by governments but not controlled.

State intervention was being gradually extended into the field of price formation and income distribution. As a result, some of the market incentives to transformation were weakened: the idea of national planning was, on the other hand, not so far advanced that governments were prepared to steer the development of the economy in a particular direction; or that state directives took over the functions earlier exercised by private initiative. Imperfections of the old liberal market economy were partly replaced by imperfections in state intervention.[3]

Bearing in mind both the precariousness as vantage-points of the years 1937 and 1938, and the dangers of relying too heavily on a comparison of index numbers over long periods of time, the pattern of industry and trade as it appeared on the eve of the second world war can be pieced together

[1] C. Clark, The Conditions of Economic Progress (London, 1940), ch. 2; A. Patel, 'The Economic Distance between Nations: Its Origin, Measurement and Outlook' (Economic Journal, vol. LXXIV, 1964).
[2] Myrdal, Beyond the Welfare State, p. 89.
[3] Svennilson, Growth and Stagnation in the European Economy, p. 36.

to illustrate which historical relationships within the international economy had changed and which had remained more or less the same since the beginning of the century:

World trends in population, production and trade, 1896–1938[1]

	Popu-lation	Production		Trade volume		1913 = 100 Trade unit values	
		Manu-factures	Primary Produce	Manu-factures	Primary Produce	Manu-factures	Primary Produce
1896–1900	90	54	76 (1900)	54	62	82	77
1911–13	99	95	93	94	97	98	98
1926–30	111	141	123	113	123	145	128
1931–3	117	110	120	81	116	100	68
1934–5	120	133	125	84	114	117	85
1936–8	124	158	135	100	125	120	93

From a more recent vantage-point, with the benefit of hindsight acquired since 1945, we can recognise not only that the late 1930s were 'transitional' years in relation to national and international economic policies, but that the break during this period in the historical relationship between indices of world manufacturing output and world trade in manufactures was 'a discontinuity due to special factors (trade and currency restrictions) operating to depress the level of trade'.[2] We can similarly recognise that some of the trade and currency restrictions, like the restrictions on output, were in themselves transitional examples of 'interventionism'.

In this transitional period, there was no world-wide monetary standard, and the attempt on the part of a few countries to cling to the gold standard proved as transient as had been the attempt on the part of the United Kingdom to 'restore' the international gold standard system in the 1920s. The prolonged effort by France to maintain the standard—and there were sufficiently strong French gold reserves to make this possible—entailed rigorous deflation and placed French business men in an unfavourable position *vis-à-vis* their foreign competitors. Moreover, there was inevitable pressure on wages to keep prices down, along with large-scale repatriation of foreign workers and a return of many French workers to the land, where they contributed to concealed unemployment. In 1936 a new Popular Front government in France decided that it was impossible to increase economic activity, at a low ebb in France, without devaluing the franc and maintaining parity through an exchange equalisation fund. Léon Blum's abandonment of the gold standard in September 1936 was a landmark in French economic policy, associated as it was with an attempt

[1] This table is based on Maizels, *Industrial Growth and World Trade*, p. 80.
[2] For a detailed analysis of the trends set out in the table see *ibid*. ch. 4. See also F. Hilgerdt, *The Network of World Trade* (Geneva, 1942), and R. de Oliveira Campos, G. Haberler, J. Meade and J. Tinbergen, *Trends in International Trade* (Geneva, 1958).

at a kind of French 'new deal' in social affairs.[1] In fact, there was no permanent improvement in France's position. Despite an immediate upsurge in economic activity, economic policies (no more strongly grounded in theory than those of Roosevelt or of the United Kingdom) clashed with social policies, and, after an alarming 'flight of capital' and months of further currency depreciation, France alone of the advanced industrial countries did not succeed in regaining its 1919 peak level of industrial production until after the second world war.

The other European countries which had stuck to the gold standard after 1932—including Italy and the Netherlands—put restrictions on the use of gold after 1936, and thereafter gold movements played little part in the maintenance of international exchange rates. The gold standard system had finally collapsed without any other 'system' taking its place, although after the French devaluation the United States, the United Kingdom and France pledged themselves in a Tripartite Monetary Agreement of September 1936 to take practical steps to ensure exchange stability, to seek 'the restoration of order in international economic relations', and 'to pursue a policy which will tend to promote prosperity in the world and to improve the standard of living'.

If the practical steps taken to maintain exchange stability were in part successful between 1936 and 1939, there were continued difficulties in relation to international payments and, because of the drying up of international investment, a failure adequately to achieve the most general of the objectives. The pattern of international payments in the late 1930s, like the pattern of international trade, bore many of the marks of the past, while showing some significant signs of change. Europe's trade continued to be characterised by a large import surplus into the United Kingdom and an export surplus from Germany, while world trade continued to depend on a European import surplus from the United States and a United States import surplus from the rest of the world. Yet the United States maintained a large annual export surplus throughout the 1930s (except in 1936), continued to drain gold from the rest of the world, and, despite Cordell Hull's plans for freer trade, contributed to the trend towards bilateralism which had been made a deliberate goal of German policy. At the same time, it had lost so heavily on its earlier capital investments overseas that it ceased to act as an international lender. In these circumstances, the United Kingdom no longer played its traditional role. Empire countries were no longer able to earn as much as they had done in the 1920s by selling their materials in Europe and the United States, while many manufactured goods were shut out by protection from the British market. The result was that bilateral exchanges between the Empire and the United Kingdom gained in importance. Never able to achieve an appreciable surplus on its current international transactions, the United

[1] R. Marjolin, 'Reflections on the Blum Experiment' (*Economica*, vol. v, May 1938).

Kingdom also ceased to invest overseas. On balance between 1930 and 1939 it actually imported capital.

There was clearly no place in the autarkical world of the 1930s for foreign lending of the old type, organised largely by private business on the basis of market incentives, yet foreign capital in the form of old-style lending or of new types of assistance was necessary if the 'underdeveloped countries' were to benefit from technical progress (a fact of life in the advanced' countries) and to achieve even limited economic and social advance. Relatively few long-term or short-term funds moved from industrial to non-industrial countries in the years immediately preceding the second world war. On the one hand, the risks of private foreign investment were considered too great and the instability of exchange rates created unfavourable conditions for expansion; on the other hand, there were no experiments in 'aid' or in 'redistribution'. At its best, the international economic specialisation of the late nineteenth century had served as something more than a device for using to the greatest effect the labour of a given number of human beings or the resources of a given group of countries: it had served as an engine of growth.[1] When it ceased to serve this purpose, the demand for something different to take its place was bound to grow. Those of the world's inhabitants who made up Western society were certainly better off on the eve of the second world war than they had been in the first decade of the century: economic instability had not meant economic or social stagnation. Yet for millions of people outside Europe difficulties and adversities were not confined to periods of depression: poverty was endemic, and social aspirations were severely limited.

The place of Europe within the international economic system on the eve of a war which was radically to transform both its economics and its politics can be set out in statistical terms. It had gained slightly over the United States as its newest industries—like automobiles and electricity— made up lost ground and also because discrimination against United States goods had been introduced as a deliberate element in certain national policies. Yet in other industries, notably textiles, Japanese competition had proved increasingly powerful during the 1930s,[2] and alongside all the new areas of European industrial development (many of them based on 'light industry' or the service industries and located near the large metropolitan conglomerations), there were 'depressed' areas, like South Wales, the north-east of England, the industrial zone around Lyons and parts of the Ruhr. Alongside new industries, like cement or rayon, there were old problem industries, like coal or cotton. There had been a move throughout the 1930s and throughout many parts of Europe towards larger economic

[1] D. H. Robertson, 'The Future of International Trade' (*Economic Journal*, vol. XLVIII, 1938).
[2] G. E. Hubbard, *Eastern Industrialisation and its Effect on the West* (2nd ed. London, 1938).

units in both old and new industries—evidence of further economic concentration—but size was no necessary guarantee of efficiency or of concern for what has subsequently been called 'research and development'; and in some countries, notably France among the most important, small units continued to predominate. The three most important economies of the years before 1913 accounted for less in Europe's trade in 1938 than they had done in 1913, yet, in spite of all the other changes, there had been little change in the proportion—40 per cent—of Europe's total exports being despatched outside Europe. The other 60 per cent had gone to other countries in Europe, constituting about half of Europe's total imports, the other half being imports from overseas:

Europe's exports and imports[1]

	1913		1928		1938	
	Percentage of total	Percentage of each national total going to Europe	Percentage of total	Percentage of each national total going to Europe	Percentage of total	Percentage of each national total going to Europe
			Exports			
United Kingdom	26·1	30·1	23·6	31·6	22·2	32·1
Germany	24·7	66·3	19·3	69·9	21·1	65·1
France	13·6	66·6	13·7	62·5	8·6	54·2
'Big Three' totals	64·4	51·7	56·6	52·2	51·9	49·2
Italy, Belgium, Luxembourg, Netherlands, Switzerland, Sweden	21·9	70·6	21·8	68·6	25·5	66·3
The rest	13·7	79·5	21·6	85·6	22·6	83·7
			Imports			
United Kingdom	26·9	37·5	27·6	38·9	31·0	31·0
Germany	21·2	40·7	17·8	47·1	50·3	50·3
France	13·3	46·5	11·2	42·7	9·9	33·7
'Big Three' totals	61·4	40·6	56·6	42·2	57·5	37·0
Italy, Belgium, Luxembourg, Netherlands, Switzerland, Sweden	24·7	59·3	21·7	61·0	22·5	62·6
The rest	13·9	70·3	21·7	75·9	20·0	75·3

[1] Table derived from Svennilson, *Growth and Stagnation in the European Economy*, pp. 173, 175.

If the precarious vantage-points of 1937 and 1938 are abandoned, problems of planning and interdependence on the eve of the world's greatest and most comprehensive war look different according to the choice of alternative later vantage-points. During the war years themselves and in the immediate aftermath of war, two incompatible conclusions were drawn by different writers and politicians from the 'failure' of the system before 1939—the first that restoration of unimpeded market forces was urgently necessary, the second that, 'in such conditions of disequilibrium as we shall have to expect at the end of this war, it will be impossible to rely on market forces to restore equilibrium'.[1] The first view was common in Europe and the United States,[2] the second predominant in the United Kingdom and in many countries outside Europe.

In the United Kingdom, in particular, special emphasis was placed on the need both to maintain full employment through Keynesian techniques of controlling the level of aggregate demand and to advance the complex of comprehensive or more comprehensive social policies to which the label 'welfare state' was soon attached. The name of William Beveridge was linked with both policies, since, in addition to popularising some of Keynes's ideas in his *Full Employment in a Free Society* (1944), he was the architect of 'Beveridgism', a far-reaching war-time plan for extended social security. In post-1945 Germany, by contrast, there was a reaction against 'the extremes of nationalism, autarky and government control'[3] and little interest in the economics of full employment. In the former German-occupied territories of Europe, the most difficult immediate task was that of identifying and relating on one side the practical short-term problems of reconstruction and on the other the long-term problems of development and growth. Yet once this task had been accomplished, there were differences of opinion about the range and scope of economic policy. While it was recognised that popular aspirations had changed as much as economic facts during the course of a prolonged period of what had been called 'total war', and that what had been acceptable before 1939 would not necessarily be tolerable after 1945, there were strong counter-currents favouring less rather than more planning. If the view was widely held in some circles that the frontiers of war-time planning should not roll back but should serve as a strategic base for new advances, in others there was strong dislike of all forms of *dirigisme*. In eastern Europe, Communism provided yet another set of ideas and techniques, while, outside Europe, new aspirations were beginning to influence policies, and the example of the Soviet Union was attracting wider attention in the 'undeveloped world' than it had done before 1939. Given this range of attitudes, opinions

---

[1] Arndt, *The Economic Lessons of the Nineteen-Thirties*, p. 300.

[2] W. Roepke, *La crise de notre temps* (Neuchâtel, 1945); *Internationale Ordnung* (Zürich, 1945); *Die Lehre von der Wirtschaft* (Zürich, 1946).

[3] The preface to the English edition of L. Erhardt, *Germany's Comeback in the World Market* (London, 1954).

and policies, it was obvious that the concept of international inter-dependence—a concept which had lost its universal meaning as the war-time world was divided into two highly organised *blocs* in a state of mutual blockade—would require new thinking in post-war conditions. 'An inter-national economic system which was based on the assumption of free private enterprise in *all* countries and the free operation of market forces the world over, which laid down rules that virtually lose all their meaning if applied to planned economies, and which explicitly borrowed methods of economic control that are essential instruments of planned economies, would clearly stand little chance of universal acceptance.'[1]

From a later vantage-point, somewhat different lessons have been drawn. It seemed for a time that the strains of adjustment after war and the divisions between nations threatened not merely the reconstruction of Europe but also material progress in general. By the end of the 1950s, however, high rates of economic growth in Europe during the 1950s, along with far-reaching moves towards greater integration, threw the record of the inter-war years into sharp relief. The increase in productivity achieved during the 1950s—an average of 3·5 per cent for twelve European countries—was twice the average for the whole period from 1913 to 1960. Only the United States had previously achieved a comparable increase, and the rate of increase had slowed down in the United States during the 1950s after a huge leap ahead during the second world war and the uneasy post-war period of international predominance, when Europe heavily depended on United States economic assistance. Throughout western Europe the rate of increase in output for every man employed was above that of any earlier period for which records were available. 'By the time that the decade ended, it had become clear that Western Europe was reaping the benefit of a significant change of trend, and that the change was not simply the reflection of a full employment policy which had put more people to work.'[2] It was not difficult in retrospect to claim that during the 1930s Europe had been suffering from 'the arterio-sclerosis of an old established, heavily capitalised economic system inflexible in relation to violent economic change. Low productivity in agriculture and many manufacturing industries, and widespread unemployment kept national output and income low, and blocked the road towards rapid general expansion.'[3]

In a changed and changing context, economists paid less attention to the economics of employment and more attention to the growth process, in some countries going beyond the limits of the Keynesian revolution of the 1930s by taking it for granted, in others treating it as irrelevant.

[1] Arndt, *op. cit.* p. 301.
[2] A. Shonfield, *Modern Capitalism* (London, 1965), pp. 4–5. Shonfield's figures are based on Maddison, *Economic Growth in the West.* See also United Nations, *Some Factors in Economic Growth in Europe during the 1950s* (Geneva, 1964).
[3] Svennilson, *Growth and Stagnation in the European Economy*, p. 52.

American economists had pointed the way in this field: now European economists took over.[1] Recognising that there were serious difficulties in making long-term statistical comparisons, economists none the less began to review historical experience, setting out their conclusions in tabulated form:

Recent and long-term annual national growth rates[2]

	Long-term rate			
	Starting year	Rate	1950–9	1954–9
United Kingdom	1857	1·2	1·7	1·6
United States	1871	2·0	2·2	2·2
Germany	1853	1·5	4·5	3·6
France	1855	1·5	3·6	3·3
Sweden	1863	2·1	2·8	3·0
Japan	1880	2·9	6·1	7·6

The margin of error increases the further back the figures go. At the same time, the figures expose a number of widely held misconceptions about the history covered in this chapter. There is little evidence to support the view that a stable population has been an obstacle to growth. Moreover, despite ambitious attempts at generalisation there is 'no convincing evidence' of any constancy or pattern in the international pattern of growth rates: the cataclysms of the past fifty years—two world wars and depression—have seemingly distorted and modified national growth rates and not simply interrupted trends. Nor can countries be separated out into those which 'normally' have grown fast and those which have not. With the significant exception of Japan,[3] nearly all countries have had fairly long periods of both rapid growth and of slow growth.

It is certainly too soon to find a satisfactory vantage-point from which to view what happened before the second world war. What happened in western Europe—and behind the averages there were substantial differences in rates of growth and in competitive power—must be related to what happened in eastern Europe and after 1917 in the Soviet Union: two international economic systems are now involved, neither of which is static. What happened in Europe as a whole must be related to what

[1] S. Kuznets, *Six Lectures on Economic Growth* (Chicago, 1959); O. Aukrust, 'Factors of Economic Development: a Memoir of Recent Research' (*Weltwirtschaftliches Archiv*, Band 93, 1964); P. D. Henderson (ed.), *Economic Growth in Britain* (London, 1966); R. Nurkse, *Problems of Capital Formation in Underdeveloped Areas* (New York, 1953). The pioneer *locus classicus* now became J. A. Schumpeter's *The Theory of Economic Development* (Cambridge, Mass., 1949): the German edition of this work had been published as early as 1911.
[2] D. C. Paige, F. T. Blackaby and S. Freund, 'Economic Growth, the Last Hundred Years', *National Institute Economic Review* (London, 1961).
[3] For an explanation of the Japanese position, see K. Kojima, 'Capital Accumulation and the Course of Industrialisation with Special Reference to Japan' (*Economic Journal*, vol. LXX, 1960); K. Ohkwa, *The Growth Rate of the Japanese Economy since 1938* (Tokyo, 1957); W. Lockwood, *The Economic Development of Japan* (2nd ed. Princeton, 1965).

happened outside Europe: after 1945 the growth in the number of independent states, with their economic and political pressures, transformed the modes and content of debate. What happened internally to economies must be related to patterns of international trade. During the 1950s the volume of trade in manufactures among industrial countries increased faster than it had done in this century, faster than production.[1] At the same time imports of manufactures by non-industrial countries rose rapidly and by semi-industrial countries (including many which had partially industrialised their economies during the second world war) less fast. Exports from primary producing countries (with the exception of oil) rose only slowly relatively to other sections in technology, a factor which needs detailed and specific analysis. Through the period since 1914 scientific industry in advanced countries has become less dependent on the agricultural and mineral products of the nineteenth and early twentieth centuries, although over short periods, at least, it has demanded and secured new products from 'under-developed' areas. Another factor influencing movements of imports and exports has been increasing demand for their own products, both food and materials, in the primary producing countries themselves.

In the light of recent enquiries, the position during the 1920s and 1930s may appear to be as unique and transient as was the position during the nineteenth century. It has already been shown clearly, however, that in changing circumstances expansion of trade between 'developed' and 'developing' countries depends on the easing of balance-of-payments difficulties either through increases in exports from non-industrial or semi-industrial countries or through loans and development grants. Much new thinking in this connection has historical perspectives, since it represents an extension in international terms of past thinking within individual countries—both about income redistribution and planning—to offset 'trends in inequalities'.[2] In the meantime, the net capital outflow from the industrial countries to the non-industrial and semi-industrial countries in 1958–60 represented only about 1 per cent of their gross national product:[3] this is a very small proportion as compared with United Kingdom exports of capital in the period from 1900 to 1913.[4] (See table on p. 85.)

Given the growing suspicion in the developing countries after 1945 both of privately supplied foreign capital and of governmental aid 'with strings attached', mutually acceptable concepts of economic 'interdependence' in changing historical circumstances clearly needed to be redefined.

[1] Maizels, *Industrial Growth and World Trade*, p. 384.
[2] D. Seers, 'International Aid: the Next Steps', a paper read to the Dar-es-Salaam Conference, 1964.
[3] Maizels, *op. cit.* p. 412. See also R. Prebisch, 'Towards A New Policy for Development', in Cmd. 2417 (1964), *United Nations Conference on Trade and Development: Final Acts with Related Documents*.
[4] A. K. Cairncross, *Home and Foreign Investment, 1870–1913* (Cambridge, 1953), p. 180.

Estimates of United Kingdom capital exports and the distribution of overseas investment[1]

	Net national income	Net export of capital	Estimates of distribution of investments (when known)				
			U.S.A. and Canada	South America	India and Ceylon	South Africa	Austra-lasia
1900	1,750	23·6	—	200 (Argentine only)	—	—	389
1902	1,740	9·8	205 (Canada only)	—	—	—	—
1911	2,076	171·3	1,061	587	351	351	380
1913	2,265	198·2	1,270	722	379	—	—

As for 'planning', there have been so many changes since 1945 both in theories and in techniques, objectives and policies, that it is possible to argue that planning is 'an activity of very recent origin, belonging to the 1960s rather than to the 1950s'.[2] In 'boom' conditions after 1950, long-term planning, employing a variety of instruments, more or less sophisticated, for the first time in years of peace began to be thought of in capitalist societies as the planning of whole economies and not simply planning within economies. In years of depression governments had resorted to 'regulation of single markets'—with business groups often 'willingly giving up more freedom of action than was actually necessary' and labour pressing for intervention on 'welfare' grounds.[3] In the changed conditions of the 1950s and early 1960s 'overall' planning in some countries, at least, began to take account not only of specific or short-range problems, including balance-of-payments problems, but of general tendencies towards distortions of market prices, of divergences between private and social costs, and of the need for long-term forecasting. The idea of shaping the development of an economy through 'modernisation' or through the assessment and formulation of future 'national needs' began to win new adherents. In countries like Germany and the United States, where there was continued suspicion of enhanced governmental powers, there was a development of planning techniques within large business firms, sometimes through the mediatorship of banks: here also there were 'lengthened perspectives', particularly in science-based industries, involving a sense of

[1] The estimates of national income—those of C. H. Feinstein—are conveniently set out in B. R. Mitchell and P. Deane, *Abstract of British Historical Statistics* (Cambridge, 1962), pp. 367–8. The figures relating to the export of capital and the distribution of investments are conveniently set out in Cairncross, *op. cit.* pp. 180, 185.

[2] Shonfield, *Modern Capitalism*, p. 220.

[3] A. J. Tinbergen, *Shaping the World Economy* (New York, 1962), p. 68.

planning strategy.[1] It has become possible, indeed, to trace a process whereby 'managerial practices and attitudes in the public and private sectors of most Western economies tend to become more similar'.[2] At the same time, the debate about economic planning in Communist societies has been opened up to cover such questions as the development of a 'less irrational' price structure, freedom of contract between enterprises, and more direct links between producers and consumers.[3] And, just as a process can be traced in capitalist countries which has led towards overlapping between private and public policies and practices, so there have been some planning processes (particularly those involving large-scale investment decisions) common to both capitalist and Communist countries. Again, the smaller undeveloped countries, where planning is a convenient and attractive slogan, face the greatest difficulties in practice in introducing planning in order to control their situation.[4] The minimum size required to secure both economies of scale in industry and the prospect of effective planning has risen as technology has changed and as planning techniques have become more highly sophisticated.[5] What effect this consideration will have on new forms of economic integration in the future remains as uncertain as what form economic 'interdependence' will eventually take.

[1] J. B. Quinn and A. M. Cavanaugh, 'Fundamental Research Can be Planned', *Harvard Business Review* (1964).

[2] E. S. Mason (ed.), *The Corporation in Modern Society* (Cambridge, Mass., 1959), p. 17.

[3] A. Nove, 'Soviet Planning: Reforms in Prospect', reprinted in *Was Stalin Really Necessary?* (London, 1964).

[4] For some of the difficulties, see G. Myrdal, *Economic Theory and Under-developed Regions* (London, 1957).

[5] E. A. G. Robinson (ed.), *Economic Consequences of the Size of Nations* (London, 1960).

CHAPTER IV

SCIENCE AND TECHNOLOGY

As the nineteenth century drew to its end, the mechanism and pattern of Nature seemed to have been revealed to the scientist in broad outline; and his researches appeared to some degree, especially in the physical sciences, to have assumed the form of investigations into a structure that was more or less known and established by the work of those who had gone before him. Scientific thought had already undergone three great changes that are properly described as revolutions, since they were no mere changes of emphasis but fundamental changes in outlook. They had all been effected in modern times and in western Europe. The seventeenth century had seen the revolution in mechanics and the foundation of modern physics, begun by Galileo and completed by Newton and marked particularly by the publication of Newton's *Principia* in 1687; in the eighteenth century there came the revolution in chemistry, brought about by Lavoisier's classic experiments and associated, so far as such events may be dated, with the publication of his *Traité élémentaire de chimie* in 1789, a date which still conveniently marks the foundation of modern chemistry; the revolution in biology was more recent, introduced by the publication of Darwin's *Origin of Species* in 1859. Biology had not kept pace with the physical sciences, but it too now seemed at last to have set out on its modern road; and the scientific mind appeared to be concerned at this period with what may be described in general terms as an increasingly refined anatomy of nature. The world around us, it was considered, was made up both in its living and in its non-living forms of a number of chemical elements. About seventy-five were already known, and it was recognised that there were probably others not yet discovered. The elements consisted of eternal and indestructible atoms: the atoms of any one element were alike and had the same weight, different from that of the atoms of every other element. The protean nature of energy was understood and its transformation from one form into another of its numerous manifestations, into mechanical or thermal or chemical or electrical energy, had been quantitatively determined in exact and refined experiments. The framework of the world was apparently known.

In the last few years of the century, however, the situation suddenly changed. In 1896 Becquerel discovered radioactivity and in 1899 Mme Curie concluded that radioactive atoms were unstable and that in the radioactive processes observed they were undergoing disintegration with release of energy; and meanwhile in 1897 Sir J. J. Thomson showed that the so-called cathode rays, discovered by Plücker in 1859, consisted of submicroscopic particles carrying negative charges of electricity: since they were produced in identical form from many different kinds of atoms, these particles, which he called 'corpuscles', and which were later renamed 'electrons', were a common constituent of atoms. Atoms, therefore, were not simple but composite; and some of them were unstable and disintegrating at measurable rates. These two discoveries, made at the very close of the century, ushered in the fourth revolution in science in modern times and opened to us the new world of atomic physics.

Science had, of course, been applied to some extent in industry even in the seventeenth century and still more in the nineteenth, but such application was not general and the links between science and technology were not close. Many of those engaged in politics realised the importance of scientific knowledge and its application in the modern world. Before the nineteenth century closed A. J. (later Lord) Balfour remarked of scientists: 'They are the people who are changing the world and they don't know it. Politicians are but the fly on the wheel—the men of science are the motive power.' But it was the first world war that effectively demonstrated to the modern nation-states and their governments the necessity of applied science for their economic and military survival.

So the nineteenth century ended with a fundamental and revolutionary change in the physical sciences and with some recognition that it was science that was moulding the world of the future.

The first half of the twentieth century proved to be a period of advance in science surpassing that of all preceding times in extent, in rapidity and in application; and in these fifty years the harvest of four centuries of modern science was reaped so thoroughly that it changed the whole aspect and outlook of our civilisation as well as our daily lives and our habits of thought. When men began some four hundred years ago to abandon the older ways of thinking and speculating about Nature and her workings, and to give up the practice of constructing systems of the world prematurely on shreds of evidence, they turned instead to the limited objective. They turned also to the 'explanation' that was to be accepted as 'true'—and this merely in the provisional and scientific sense—only if it agreed with indisputable and verifiable experimental fact. They had embarked upon a new adventure, much as other men went on voyages of discovery; and none could have foreseen that the knowledge that would ultimately be gained would presently outstrip their organised political capacity to control its application and to limit its use to beneficent ends, or that the customary freedom enjoyed by scientists for centuries in the publication of their discoveries would finally have to be taken from them in certain fields in the interests of military security and national survival. In the period now being discussed the invention of the internal combustion engine solved the problem of heavier-than-air flight and so gave us the aeroplane with its terrible powers of destruction in war; the advance of atomic physics has given us the atomic bomb, by which humanity holds in its own hands the very means of its extermination, perhaps of the destruction of 'the great globe itself' with 'all which it inherit', or perhaps of the mutation of living forms into new and monstrous evolutionary species. Man has for the first time become the master of his fate.

From its very beginnings, of course, modern science has been of consequence outside the study and the laboratory, beyond its immediate frontiers and often far beyond them. In the physical sciences, the heliocentric theory of Copernicus, set forth in his *De revolutionibus orbium caelestium* in 1543, displaced the habitation of man from the centre of the universe, about which the sun was believed to revolve for his benefit, to a minor planet in the solar system and gave him a less dignified and less important place in the material scheme of things; and, more recently, in the biological sciences, Darwin's theory of evolution as propounded in the *Origin of Species* in 1859 demonstrated man's remote and humble animal origin and removed him from his proud and privileged spiritual position of being 'a little lower than the angels'. From Copernicus to Darwin, however, these and similar advances, with such consequences on human thought and life as they might have, affected the minds of only a very small minority of men and the daily lives of probably none of them. The first half of the twentieth century brought great change in this respect; through the spread of education and the multiplication of a great variety of means for the popularisation and dissemination of scientific and technical knowledge, men and women of all classes everywhere, at least among the democracies, became aware that their survival and alike their destruction depended on the progress of science, or on how their rulers or the rulers of other peoples decided to apply that progress. These matters became clearer, however, and grimmer in their dread reality at the end of the second world war. We turn for the moment to earlier years and other fields in the half-century.

In the last fifty years there has been an unparalleled increase in our knowledge, not only of the complexity of the atom but also of the vastness of the universe, not only of the infinitesimally minute but also of the incomprehensibly great. When the century opened, the distances of only about twenty stars were known with any reasonable accuracy. As a result of the construction of new telescopes and of developments in photography the distances of several thousands have been determined accurately in the last half-century, and much has been learned thence about the size and structure of the cosmic system. The completion of the great 100-inch reflector telescope at Mount Wilson in California provided an instrument with greatly increased light-gathering power; and it soon became clear that there are galaxies other than our own, the so-called 'island universes', to the number of about a hundred million, all about the same order of size and all receding apparently from our universe, the Galactic System. The nearest is some 500 million light-years distant from us, that is, at the distance that would be traversed in 500 million years by light, which travels at a speed of 186,000 miles per second. The astronomer has, indeed, had to devise and adopt a new yardstick for his measurements, namely, the 'light-year', the distance travelled by light in one year, in order that he may be enabled to handle these huge and incomprehensible figures conveniently. The expansion of our world in these fifty years is enormous; its vast dimensions cannot be visualised by the human mind, and man, though the astronomers may show him to be 'a citizen of no mean city', finds his imagination incapable of realising its gigantic and colossal grandeur. Our own 'universe' has a diameter now calculated at about 100,000 light-years.

Cosmic space, therefore, so far as the great modern telescopes have probed, has been shown to contain an enormous number of 'island universes', all more or less of the same size and more or less evenly distributed. Some of them appear to be still in process of condensation and formation from glowing gaseous matter, or were so when the light by which our telescopes detect their existence and their state left them hundreds of millions of years ago on its long journey to our planet. Interstellar space, for long thought to be void, appears to be far from empty, since it contains much highly tenuous matter, this interstellar matter being comparable in amount with the stellar matter of the cosmos.

Much knowledge was gained during this half-century about the stars and about their chemical constitution and their evolution. The existence of 'giants' and of 'white dwarfs', which consist of very dense matter, as much as 10 tons to the cubic inch, and of variables of different kinds has been detected. It has also been shown that, in general, the main-sequence stars consist in all probability mainly of the element hydrogen, from which there are other reasons for supposing all the other chemical elements to have been formed. The process of probing space continues with ever more powerful telescopes, but the present century has already revealed much of the structure of the vast universe, or system of 'universes', with some knowledge of its evolution and its composition.

So far as this century has gone, these advances have brought an even greater sense of the vastness of the world and have reduced mankind, at least on the physical plane, to a creature of still more microscopic minuteness, yet taking such courage as he may in this awful immensity in which he finds himself from the circumstance that it is his mind that has penetrated to some extent its remote depths.

The hundred million universes, it has been shown, are composed ultimately, like man himself, of atoms, of those submicroscopic particles which the present half-century, after some beginnings at the close of the nineteenth century, has revealed as minute and complex worlds in themselves. Almost until 1900 the atom, in spite of the rise of a chemical atomic theory under John Dalton in the first decade of the nineteenth century, was, so far as science was concerned, merely a hard solid unstructured sort of infinitesimal billiard-ball, or, as Lucretius had described it two thousand years earlier, *solido atque aeterno corpore*. In 1897-9 Sir J. J. Thomson detected the first component to be known in the structure of the atom. This has since become familiar as the *electron*. Electrons were identical in all atoms from which they were obtained; and they proved to be particles carrying a negative charge of electricity, and possessing a mass very much smaller than that of a hydrogen atom, a mass presently shown to be about 1/1,850th of that of a hydrogen atom. The identification of a constituent common to all atoms recalled the dreams of the alchemists about the transmutation of the elements, and such changes were indeed effected later.

Shortly afterwards another particle was discovered in the structure of the atom, a particle charged with positive electricity equal in amount to the negative charge on the electron, and with a mass the same as that of the hydrogen atom. It was called a *proton*. It appeared that the atoms of the different chemical elements were formed of differently ordered assemblages of electrons and protons, the number of electrons in the atom of a particular element being the same as the number of protons, since the atom as a whole was electrically uncharged.

Then in 1911 Lord Rutherford introduced, to quote Sir Arthur Eddington, 'the greatest change in our idea of matter since the time of Democritus'. In his researches on radioactivity Rutherford had shown that the alpha rays, as they were called, which were emitted, like beta rays and gamma rays, in radioactive disintegration were in fact not rays, but positively charged helium atoms. Their mass was four times as great as that of a proton and they carried a charge double that of the proton. Also they moved at high speeds and had a high kinetic energy. They were known to pass through matter easily because of their great velocity and high energy, but Rutherford found that in so doing they occasionally suffered very large deflections. He concluded therefore that the inside of the atom was mostly empty, which would account for the observed fact that alpha particles in general passed through matter without deflection, but that the occasional deflections had been caused when the alpha particles had, in traversing the atoms, approached near a small central and positively charged nucleus or core. Thus the ancient solid atom, accepted from Democritus to Dalton and even for a century after Dalton had propounded his theory, was now revealed as a structure largely empty and consisting of a minute but massive central nucleus, with a positive electrical charge, surrounded at a distance by a peripheral shell of negatively charged electrons—a kind of solar system in miniature. Matter seemed, therefore, to be mostly empty space.

It appeared at the same time that protons and electrons, in some instances, might form two slightly different structures with slightly different atomic weights and therefore that the atoms of a given chemical element might exist in two forms with slightly different atomic weights. Up to this time the atomic weight of an element had been one of its supposedly invariable characteristics; but for such chemically identical atoms, with slightly different atomic weights but otherwise chemically indistinguishable, as now appeared to be possible, Soddy coined the name 'isotopes' in 1913 when he discovered the two isotopes of lead produced by the radioactive decay of uranium and of thorium respectively. In the same year J. J. Thomson in a study of positive rays discovered the isotopes of neon; and by means of the ingenious mass-spectrograph F. W. Aston showed in 1919 and in later years that most of the chemical elements were mixtures of isotopes.

The discovery that all atoms possessed two constituents, and that atoms differed chemically because of the different numbers of protons and electrons of which they were composed, brought science back to the long-rejected idea that matter was transmutable, a theory over which the alchemists had spent their lives and their fortunes, or some part of the fortunes of their patrons. Studies on radioactivity had already shown that certain elements were gradually undergoing change and disintegration, that uranium slowly passed into lead through a very long period of time and that thorium also underwent the same change. In other words, certain elements were being 'transmuted', but neither by the methods of the ancient alchemists nor according to their dreams; for, whereas they had hoped to convert base lead into noble gold or silver, Nature was slowly turning precious uranium into base lead. The first modern 'transmutation' was achieved by Rutherford in 1919, when he succeeded in obtaining hydrogen by bombarding certain light elements with alpha particles, and thus in producing a simpler atom from a more complex one. In 1922, however, Blackett concluded from similar experiments that oxygen was produced in the bombardment of nitrogen atoms with alpha particles, in this case a more complex atom being obtained from a less complex one by a 'transmutation' in which there was a building up rather than a breaking down. The rapid development of this work, by means of the cyclotron and later the atomic pile, has brought about many other transmutations: it has even led to the production of new elements, the so-called 'trans-uranic elements', those that fall beyond the heaviest element, uranium, in the chemist's Periodic Table. These new elements, such as neptunium, plutonium, americium, curium, berkelium and californium, were first produced in the laboratory; some of them have since been detected in minute proportions in pitchblende. The significant advance, however, is that the atomic physicist has, in this half-century, not merely transmuted elements but also produced artificial or synthetic ones.

Further striking advances in this field have led to the production of a number of radioactive, that is, unstable, isotopes of known elements, a result that has found many valuable applications. One that may be specially mentioned in passing is the use of radioactive carbon, or radio-carbon as this isotope of carbon is often called, in physiology and in medicine, whereby this substance may be traced in its passage through the organism by means of the external photographic detection of its radioactivity.

The use of radio-carbon has led also to the remarkable discovery that animal tissue shares with plant tissue what was long regarded as a unique function of the latter, namely, the utilisation of carbon dioxide, previously regarded as a waste product, in the building up of more complex substances; and it has also been shown that the oxygen evolved in photosynthesis by green plants under the action of light does not come, as was formerly supposed, from the decomposition of the carbon dioxide absorbed by the plant, but from the decomposition of water.

Since atoms, therefore, appeared to be assemblages of electrons and protons, every atom being electrically neutral because it was composed of an equal number of both kinds of particles, and since the proton had a mass about 1,800 times as great as that of the electron and, in fact, a mass that was practically equal to that of the hydrogen atom, it seemed that the proton, or perhaps the hydrogen atom, might be akin to the *protyle* or primary matter of the Greeks, from which all matter and therefore all atoms were made. A form of this ancient idea had been revived in the second decade of the nineteenth century by William Prout, a London medical practitioner, who had based his views on the somewhat inadequate evidence at his command that the atomic weights of the elements were whole numbers on the scale in which the weight of the atom of hydrogen was taken as unity—whereas, in fact, many of them were not integral. Prout thought that he had discovered in hydrogen the stuff of which all atoms and therefore all matter was composed, but for the moment the facts were against the acceptance of his hypothesis, although much time and exact experiment were given to further determinations of such important numbers as the atomic weights of the chemical elements. But in 1911 Barkla, in his studies on the scattering of X-rays, showed that the number of electrons in a particular atom corresponded to its place in the chemist's Periodic Table, in which the elements fall into well-defined series and groups when arranged in the ascending order of their atomic weights. In 1913–14 Moseley showed that the number of units of positive electricity (protons) on the nucleus of the atom of a chemical element gave its 'atomic number', which was, with certain exceptions—all long-standing anomalies—nothing more or less than its numerical position in the Periodic Table. In the modern form of the Periodic Table, subsequent to Moseley's work, the elements are arranged not in order of their atomic weights, but in that of their atomic numbers, since the latter are more fundamental, different isotopes of the same element having the same atomic number, and there are no anomalies.

Already, in 1901, Strutt had been attracted to Prout's hypothesis; and he had examined the eight most accurately determined atomic weights and shown mathematically that the probability of the total deviation of these atomic weights from a whole number being as great as found by experiment was about 1 in 1,000. He then examined in the same way a further eighteen other atomic weights which could not be so reliably determined, and concluded: 'A calculation of the probabilities involved fully confirms the verdict of common-sense, that the atomic weights tend to approximate to whole numbers far more closely than can reasonably be accounted for by any accidental coincidence. The chance of any such coincidence being the explanation is not more than 1 in 1,000, so that, to use Laplace's modes of expression, we have stronger reasons for believing in the truth of some modification of Prout's Law, than in that of many historical events which are universally accepted as unquestionable.'[1] The discovery of the electron and the proton as common constituents of all atoms, with the consequent revelation of atomic structure, and the remarkable discovery by Moseley of 'atomic numbers', seemed in the 1920s to have proved the truth of that 'modification of Prout's Law' foreshadowed in Strutt's conclusion, that the hydrogen atom in the form of its nucleus, the proton, was the primary stuff, so far as mass was concerned, of which all matter was made. And later came the conclusion that the main-sequence stars consist, in all probability, mainly of hydrogen, which therefore began to reveal itself as the *protyle* of the Greeks, the basis of all matter, terrestrial and celestial, although, of course, the Greeks excluded celestial matter as being of a different and permanent and unchanging nature. But, so far as the atom was concerned, simplicity soon disappeared with the discovery of fundamental component particles other than the proton and the electron, namely: the neutron (Chadwick, 1932), an uncharged particle with a mass equal to that of the proton; the positron (Anderson, 1933), with a mass equal to that of the electron, but a positive, instead of a negative, charge; a variety of mesons, particles with a short life and positively or negatively charged with electricity or even neutral; and, possibly, the neutrino, a neutral particle of very small mass. The structure of the atom, at first apparently simple, has since proved to be complex; and, although the atom now seems to be almost a cosmos in itself, its complex constitution and its fine structure have in these fifty years become subjects of experimental investigation.

Increasing knowledge of the atom and of its structure has largely broken down the barriers between the sciences of physics and chemistry. The terms 'atomic physics' and 'chemical physics' have come into use for special fields that overlap two sciences that are really but one, while at the

[1] *Philosophical Magazine*, 1901, vol. I, series vi, pp. 313–14.

ame time mathematics has entered into the science of chemistry to play almost as great a part as it plays in that of physics. Other developments associated with the study of living matter have brought into being the sciences of biochemistry and, more recently, biophysics. In biochemistry, in its brief half-century as an offshoot of chemistry, probably the most important advance was Gowland Hopkins's discovery of what were at first called the 'accessory food factors' and later known as the vitamins, those substances without which a diet, although it may supply ample energy to the organism, is inadequate for the maintenance of health. The vitamins, in small amount, are necessary ingredients of our daily bread; their absence causes what have been called the 'deficiency diseases', such as rickets, scurvy and so on. It is now known, for example, that Scott's South Polar Expedition (1910–12) was equipped with a diet satisfactory with regard to the energy that it would provide, but deficient in vitamin content, and that the expedition's tragic end was due to this cause. The results of the discovery of the vitamins and of wide development of knowledge in this field have brought inestimable benefit to the health of nations. Today some of these substances are in fact produced on the manufacturing scale. Another important group, essential to life and health, the hormones, produced in certain glands in the body and carried by the bloodstream to their points of action, was also discovered in this period by Bayliss and Starling (1902). Adrenaline was isolated by Takamine in 1901 from the suprarenal glands and thyroxine from the thyroid gland by Kendall in 1915. Insulin, isolated by Banting and Best from the pancreas in 1922, proved of great value in the treatment of diabetes mellitus; cortisone, from the adrenal cortex, isolated by Kendall in 1936, is being applied in the treatment of rheumatoid arthritis; and there are others, and some have been synthetised and some prepared on the manufacturing scale.

While the germ theory of infection had satisfactorily established itself, it now became clear that there are other and more minute agents of disease, namely, the ultra-filterable viruses, which can reproduce themselves only in living tissue. Some of these viruses, from plants, were isolated by Stanley in 1935 as crystals; they were found to be mostly complex protein substances or nucleo-proteins. The question of whether they are living matter is not yet capable of clear decision.

In organic chemistry, progress continued at an ever increasing pace. The characteristic work of the 'classical' organic chemist advanced farther in the isolation of substances that occur in or are associated with living matter, in the determination of their structure and their subsequent synthesis in the laboratory, and often in their production on the manufacturing scale if they proved of industrial or medical importance. Other organic chemists successfully applied the electronic theory of valency and molecular structure to chemical changes in order to explain the mechanism of the reactions between organic substances, which had previously found little or no explanation in the electro-chemical terms that had long be‹ used and applied in inorganic chemistry. Thus, the nineteenth centu closed with the science of chemistry, the science of which it is justly sa that it affects our daily lives more than any other science does, divid‹ into two distinct fields, organic chemistry on the one hand, and physic and inorganic chemistry on the other. The first half of the twentie century, by this wide application to organic chemistry of the methods ai theories of physical chemistry, has seen a unification of these two gre fields of chemistry, which is but part of that wider unification of the scienc of physics and chemistry that characterises the period.

A number of investigators in this half-century succeeded in the prepar tion of new drugs with the property of being deadly to bacteria and oth organisms of disease infecting the higher animals, while being general harmless to the host. The problem was approached deliberately and it w clear that it would be difficult. The component that would deal with t bacteria or other organisms must be combined with some other molecul group to form a new molecular grouping that would be innocuous to t host but yet retain the bactericidal properties of the first component. O of the first of these new drugs to be prepared was salvarsan, obtained Paul Ehrlich in 1909. It was fatal to the spirochaete of syphilis, but harr less to the subject; it revolutionised the treatment of this disease. S varsan was an organic compound of arsenic; the long and patient resear‹ involved in the prosecution of a problem of this kind is indicated by t fact that Ehrlich prepared over six hundred compounds by elabora syntheses before obtaining a product possessing the requisite propertic Other similar drugs for the treatment of such tropical diseases as sleepii sickness followed: but it was not until 1935 that Domagk showed th streptococcal infections could be treated in a similar way by means prontosil, a red organic dye-substance. After it had been realised th the effective part of the prontosil molecule was the sulphonamide grou the new drug, known as 'M and B 693', or sulphapyridine, was sy thetised by Ewins and Phillips and applied in 1938 in the treatment pneumonia and other 'killing diseases'. It has so greatly reduced t mortality from pneumonia that Osler's term for this formerly dread‹ disease, 'Captain of the Men of Death', a phrase which he derived fro John Bunyan, is no longer applicable. The sulphonamide drugs ha also proved an effective remedy in puerperal fever. The discovery of t antibacterial properties of penicillin by Fleming in 1929, and its successf development as an antibiotic by Chain and Florey in 1940, placed anoth powerful weapon in the hands of the physician. It was presently produc‹ on the commercial scale. Other antibiotics followed, including strept mycin, chloramphenicol and aureomycin, which have been used wi success in the treatment, respectively, of some forms of tuberculosis, typhus, and of virus diseases.

In the realm of crystallography, the chemical architecture of the molecule has been laid bare by physical methods in the pioneer work of Sir William Bragg and his son, Sir Lawrence Bragg, who devised the method of using a crystal as a diffraction grating for X-rays. From the spectra thus given, the arrangement of the atoms in the crystal molecule could be deduced. In this fascinating revelation of the patterns in which Nature builds, physics and chemistry have again combined; and the work of the Braggs and their pupils and other crystallographers has shown once again that these two sciences have become so closely linked as to be essentially one.

The discovery of the hormones, secretions of the ductless glands, as well as advances in our knowledge of the detailed chemical mechanism of the process of respiration, have been important developments in physiology in these fifty years. In neuro-physiology progress has been equally striking, especially Sherrington's researches on the integrative action of the nervous system, Dale's on the humoral transmission of nervous impulses and Adrian's on peripheral nerves. In physiology, and in the related science of histology, the instruments of the physical scientist have been partly responsible for the increased rate of progress; of these we may mention only X-ray diffraction methods and the improvements in microscopic technique, especially the ultra-microscope in the earlier part of this period and more recently the electron microscope.

Geology is another science in which the techniques of physics and chemistry have been widely brought into use in this present century, on the purely scientific side in elucidating the problems of geochemistry, and on the practical side in locating sources of valuable raw materials beneath the earth's crust. Today the geologist is called upon for scientific advice on many problems of our modern civilisation, apart from the location of new sources of raw materials for industry: water-supplies, building materials, the nature of soil and its suitability for various purposes, the sites for roads and houses. The study of the atmosphere by sending up carriers of recording instruments ranging from kites to the more recent powered rocket has shown that it consists of three very different layers: the troposphere, or lowest layer, a region of much movement and not of uniform temperature extending from the surface of the earth to a vertical height of about six miles; the stratosphere, above the troposphere and at a uniform temperature; and, above this, the ionosphere, beginning about thirty miles above the earth's surface and extending a further one hundred and twenty miles, increasingly ionised towards the upper layers and affecting the transmission of wireless waves, which it reflects. The circulation of the atmosphere and the formation of clouds have been increasingly studied, together with the many changes in this complex system. It appears that the causes of rain and snow and the formation of ice are not as simple as they were once supposed to be.

The search for sources of power, for coal and oil, has needed the services of the geologist, once the haphazard exploitation of former days had exhausted obvious supplies. The use of physical methods, such as the reflection of percussion or electromagnetic waves (wireless waves), or measurement of the minute changes in electric or gravitational fields, has been introduced to locate oil, water and a variety of minerals beneath the earth's surface. An interesting development in geological thought, in geophysics, was propounded in Wegener's theory of continental drift in 1915, to explain the distribution of the great land masses, the continents, on the earth's surface. Evidence was adduced to show that the various continents had in remote times gradually separated and drifted apart from one original land mass. The theory long remained a subject of lively debate but its acceptance was far from general.

However, it was the study of radioactivity that in the early years of this century provided the geologist with a reliable means of dating the formation of many of the strata that he studies. By laboratory measurements the physicist had established the rate of disintegration of radioactive substances, for example, into helium and radium-lead (an isotope of ordinary lead). It remained only to measure the proportion of lead and helium in radioactive minerals to establish the age of the rocks in which these minerals occurred. By this means, the geologist was shown to be correct in the estimates that he had made on purely geological data for the great age of many of the rocks, namely, hundreds of millions of years; indeed, the 'geological time' that he had demanded was in some cases now granted to him in overflowing measure without the scepticism that had on occasion formerly accompanied it. The passing of the half-century has also seen the geologist concerned in the location of sources of uranium and other elements of high atomic weight. The production of the atomic bomb at the close of the second world war, and the hopes of applying and developing the use of atomic energy, have led to an almost world-wide search for the necessary basic materials.

Meteorology is another science that calls to its aid the instruments of physics and chemistry; with these, more reliable daily weather forecasts have been made available, and mariners can be forewarned of bad conditions and farmers advised of good. State meteorological stations have been established by all civilised nations, and are a necessity for air travel, while the increased rapidity of communication brought about by means of wireless telegraphy has made more immediately available the data necessary for accurate forecasting of weather conditions.

But it is in physics itself that the most profound changes in scientific thought have occurred. While the nineteenth century closed with a firm belief in Newtonian mechanics, the researches of Max Planck on the radiation of heat disproved the older belief that energy was equally distributed among the different wave-lengths in which it was radiated by a black body; and energy appeared to be not continuous, as had been supposed, but discontinuous, discrete, almost corpuscular, so that it might be regarded as released in units or *quanta*. Where ν is the frequency of the emitted radiation and h a universal constant, which Planck called the 'quantum of action', the amount of quantity of energy emitted by a radiating body might be represented as the product of h and ν, or $h\nu$. Planck's quantum theory and his constant h have revolutionised the physicist's ideas on energy. Moreover, the development of the Special and the General Theory of Relativity by Einstein has shown that the energy (E) of a body is proportional to its mass (m) according to the relation $E = mc^2$, where c is the velocity of light *in vacuo*. Mass and energy have therefore lost their once so obvious difference and are now seen to be one and the same thing, or perhaps both imperfect expressions of one and the same incompletely understood idea, so that the laws of conservation of mass and of energy—the establishment of the latter being one of the great triumphs of the physics of the second half of the nineteenth century—really express the same idea from two different points of view. Indeed, the energy received from the sun may be largely due to the loss of mass that occurs when helium is formed from hydrogen, the change occurring in the sun, which is considered to produce the energy that it radiates.

With the rise of the Special Theory of Relativity, absolute space and time, together with the old mechanical ether, have been abandoned; and, under the Special Theory of Relativity, gravitation and electromagnetism (and light also, which was shown to be an electromagnetic phenomenon by Clerk Maxwell in 1873) have been unified in a new form of 'field physics'. The Newtonian world has been replaced by the four-dimensional space–time continuum; and thus the whole physical picture of the world has been changed, but rather by an extension than by an abandonment of Newtonian principles. The emission of light, too, since it is essentially a radiation, is discrete and it is emitted in units named photons. Since, however, earlier in this century light was considered to have the properties both of a wave and a particle, there was considerable development in the study of wave mechanics with the consequence that wave phenomena were recognised as statistical probabilities, as had also appeared in the study of heat radiation. Indeed, the statistical view, the view that a phenomenon occurs because it is the most probable among a number of possibilities, became widely applied in physics during the period with which we are here concerned.

The biological sciences have exhibited during this half-century a proliferation similar to that of the physical sciences; and genetics, which is concerned with heredity and variation, has developed so extensively that it is to be regarded as a science in itself, especially since, unlike physiology and biochemistry, it does not depend on the techniques of the physical sciences. When the century opened, it was realised that Mendel, whose work had begun at least as early as 1857 and had subsequently escaped the recognition that it properly deserved, had already discovered and established the principles of heredity experimentally. The situation was interesting. Darwin in his *Origin of Species* in 1859 had expanded the idea that he had put forward in collaboration with Alfred Russel Wallace in 1858 about a mechanism of organic evolution, namely, natural selection: it was in fact embodied in the full title of his book, *The Origin of Species by means of Natural Selection or the Preservation of Favoured Races in the Struggle for Life.* But Darwin's theory had been expressed in terms of small continuous variations and, before the nineteenth century closed, biologists had turned preferably to discontinuous variations or, as they were named, mutations. The theory of natural selection, oversimplified as 'the survival of the fittest in the struggle for existence', was presently supplemented by the explanation that 'particulate' inheritance, or Mendelian inheritance, is conveyed and controlled by the mechanism of *genes*— inherited factors or units existing in any individual in pairs, one derived from each parent. The *genes* are carried in the *chromosomes* of the cells and follow the Mendelian laws of inheritance. Probably the most important development in biology in this half-century has been the subsequent integration of Mendel's principles of heredity with the theory of natural selection.

In Mendelian genetics the hereditary units have been shown to maintain their identity, whereas Darwin had supposed that these factors blended. The advances of the recent half-century have now made it clear that evolution is governed by selection acting on Mendelian or 'particulate' inheritance, and in this way Darwinism has been more widely accepted in a new form. As for such theories of evolution as that of Lamarck, who based his ideas on the inheritability of acquired characters, such as might be produced by use or disuse, and who supposed that it was these changes induced in organisms that controlled the process of evolution, these views have in the second quarter of this century found wider acceptance in the Soviet Union for political reasons and not for their scientific validity.

In the last quarter of the nineteenth century an increasing number of finds of the fossil remains of Neanderthal man helped to establish the fact of human evolution. Then *Pithecanthropus* was found in Java in 1891 and afterwards *Sinanthropus* near Peking; in 1900 it was generally considered that Neanderthal man arose at some point between *Pithecanthropus*, the most ancient fossil form recovered, and *homo sapiens*, or modern man. In 1912 the famous Piltdown remains were found, since shown to have been the greatest scientific hoax ever perpetrated. The Steinheim skull, found in 1933, and the Swanscombe (Kent) skull found in 1935, together with numerous other finds, led to the rejection of Neanderthal man from the line of descent of *homo sapiens*, and to his relegation as an extinct offshoot. Many other varieties of human remains have come to light in this half-century, notable among these being *Australopithecus* from South Africa, found in 1925 and combining in remarkable ways the characteristics of man and ape. The descent of *homo sapiens* has, however, remained a problem.

The applications of science to medicine have been many and various in the period that we are here surveying. At the beginning of the century Ronald Ross had demonstrated that malaria was carried by mosquitoes that had bitten malaria patients and Reed in 1900 showed that the deadly yellow fever was similarly transmitted. These discoveries led to the control of the breeding places of the mosquito as a means of preventing these diseases and opened up large territories to cultivation and settlement: a spectacular result of the work on yellow fever was that it arrested the disease that had prevented the construction of the Panama Canal. In the treatment as opposed to the prevention of malaria, many new anti-malarial synthetic drugs have replaced quinine. Artificial immunisation was greatly developed also in this period: typhoid fever, hitherto the scourge of armies, had a negligible incidence in the first world war, and since then diphtheria has been similarly reduced. From 1940 onwards blood transfusion became a normal hospital procedure through improvement in the system of determining the blood group of the patient. One scientific discovery after another has been pressed into the service of medicine, notably X-ray photography.

The most significant change in our half-century from the point of view of technology is probably that we have separated ourselves from the horse and taken to the internal combustion engine in the motor-car and the aeroplane. The motor-car dates from the last decade of the nineteenth century, but it came into general use only after the first world war. The first aeroplane flight powered by petrol was that made by the Wright brothers in 1903; they flew 284 yards. In 1909 Colonel Blériot flew across the Straits of Dover. The first world war provoked development and design in aircraft; and in 1919 Alcock and Brown flew the Atlantic from west to east, while in the same year a passenger service between London and Paris was started. Successful helicopters and jet-engined aircraft date from the second world war, the demands of which, like those of the first world war, led to intensive development of this still novel and promising weapon.

In 1947 an aeroplane first flew faster than sound travels in air; and in the same year a flight of about 20,000 miles was made around the world. Long flights became common and large passenger aeroplanes were built. In another development of flight during the second world war flying bombs and rocket bombs were devised. Researches on rockets led to further speculations on the possibilities of flight to the moon, and of inter-planetary and even of space travel; and the sending out of artificial earth-satellites carrying recording instruments fitted with radio-transmitters was planned.

The internal combustion engine has replaced the horse where he was most familiar, namely, on the farm; and in this half-century, more particularly in the later part of it, the plough and all other agricultural implements have been powered by tractors. Much toil and drudgery have thus been avoided for both men and animals. In the home similar saving of labour has been achieved by the aid of electricity, especially in the working of the suction cleaner or so-called vacuum cleaner, and the washing machine, and also by the use of gas and of electricity for heating in place of coal.

Electricity has replaced gas as an illuminant in this period both in the home and in the factory, where also it has become the usual source of power. Its production on the large scale in hydro-electric plants—the so-called 'white coal' from 'falling water'—is now widespread where there is a sufficient supply and 'head' of water, that is, in hilly or mountainous rainy districts. Such schemes have carried electricity to the remote countryside as well as to the great cities; and in the later part of this half-century many countryfolk have in their homes passed from wood or coal or oil as fuel, and oil as an illuminant, to the use of electric power, without passing through the intermediate use of gas as did their fellows in the towns. In the same period electricity has brought broadcasting and television to town and country. The advance was rapid. In 1897 Marconi sent a message by wireless telegraphy a distance of eighteen miles, and in 1901 signals were successfully passed across the Atlantic. In the 1920s radio-broadcasting became general and it was followed by television after the second world war.

Wireless telephony was but another of those scientific inventions that men have misused. It might have been applied to break down the misunderstandings across frontiers. It all seemed so remarkable at first, and 'nation shall speak to nation' seemed about to be realised. When the nations did speak to each other by this medium, however, it was frequently the propaganda leading up to the second world war that they spoke, and the 'air' was often filled with raucous argument or, as some of them ensured by a warped sense of technology, noisy with the hideous blare with which they 'jammed' their rivals to prevent them from being heard by their own nationals. Statesmen and political leaders used this new method of communication to speak to audiences of nations; by its means messages could be passed to and from ships at sea and many lives were thus saved; and it had much to do with the urbanising of the countryman. Radio and television have proved valuable aids to education in the schools. They have brought the music, literature and art of the ages into the home and within the reach of the individual, even to his bedside when he is ill or old. But the control and the use of these great inventions with their almost boundless possibilities for the improving of men's minds have been and still are challenged and fought over by those who are more concerned with mass entertainment than with the preservation and dissemination of man's cultural inheritance. Science and technology, at last closely linked in our time, have lavished their gifts on a civilisation too immature to appreciate and use them properly.

The rapidity of modern technological advance, following the equally swift strides of modern science, is nowhere so evident as in the tapping of the vast source of energy in the atom. When Rutherford, first of the modern alchemists, in 1919 succeeded in transmuting certain light elements into hydrogen by bombarding them with the swift alpha particles emitted in the disintegration of radium, and Blackett in 1922 effected a similar transmutation of nitrogen into oxygen, these changes took place on a minute scale, because only a very small proportion of the atoms subjected to the bombardments underwent transmutation. But in 1931 Cockcroft and Walton in Cambridge developed an improved method for effecting such changes by means of a high-voltage apparatus; and Lawrence, working in the University of California, devised the cyclotron, the justly so-called 'atom-smasher', for obtaining charged particles with a high energy without the difficulty of using correspondingly high voltages. This ingenious contrivance was most successful. In 1932 Chadwick discovered the neutron as a further component in the structure of the atom, electrically neutral and with a mass equal to that of the proton. Fermi in 1933–4 showed that neutrons were very effective in atomic transmutations and that many new radioactive elements could be produced by bombarding various atoms with neutrons; and it was found that radioactive isotopes could be produced for all the chemical elements. In January 1939 Hahn and Strassmann in Germany reported that by bombarding uranium with neutrons they had obtained an isotope of barium, an element far removed from uranium and with an atomic number of 46, whereas that of uranium was 92. These atomic numbers, as we have seen, represent the nuclear charges of the atoms. It therefore appeared that something entirely new had been observed. This bombardment had not produced the usual result of merely removing from or adding to the bombarded nucleus one of the familiar particles such as a proton or an electron or an alpha particle: on the contrary, it had split the nucleus into two parts—atomic fission had at last been achieved.

The significance of this discovery was at once realised by scientists throughout the world. The opening of the second world war brought with it, however, the usual precautions of military secrecy, although the full possibilities of what had happened were not at first appreciated by the governments involved in the conflict. Within three years complete secrecy had been imposed and a team of physicists, American, British and Canadian, was officially organised to exploit the discovery of atomic fission for use in war. This application was no longer a scientific but rather an engineering problem. The first atomic bomb was dropped on Hiroshima on 6 August 1945, and the second on Nagasaki three days later. The governments of the United States, Great Britain and Canada had kept secret the technical information necessary for the manufacture of these atomic bombs; they had kept it from their allies, including the Soviet Union, and there was much criticism and resentment shown by the latter when this policy became clear and when it was maintained even after the conclusion of the war. Those who had been allies now split into two camps, one struggling to overtake the other's technical advance; and there were some 'leakages' of secret information and deliberate breaches of trust for political reasons. In six and a half years the application of the discovery of atomic fission, expedited by the exigencies of total war, divided the world in a race for technological superiority in the perfection of an offensive weapon capable of measureless material destruction and of shearing off whole nations in swift extermination. The democracies, comprising the United States of America and the nations of the British Commonwealth and of western Europe, were well ahead in 1945; but within another five years the Soviet Union narrowed this lead, and made and tested the first of a series of atomic bombs. In this uneasy tension civilisation faced a menace that seemed irremediable.

On the other hand, the sudden discovery of the availability of atomic energy brought a new source of power within the reach of those nations whose scientists were equipped to deal with such a problem and whose resources included the necessary materials, particularly uranium. Here again advance has been rapid; and, shortly after the close of the period with which this chapter is concerned, power stations supplying atomic energy were in operation.

The discovery of atomic fission had another and a quite different consequence, but this time within the world of science itself. From the beginnings of modern science in the sixteenth and seventeenth centuries scientists had published their work without any interference or censorship or ban by their rulers or governments. Now matters stood differently, and for the first time. Knowledge in a particular field of science, a branch of atomic physics, became of such vital interest to governments for the survival and military security of their peoples that it was declared secret, and those who worked in this field, mostly, of course, in special establishments and laboratories set up for that work, were forbidden to publish or communicate their work to others. Science, which had long and rightly boasted that it knew no frontiers, had to adjust itself to changed circumstances.

Developments in technology have been so numerous and so varied that any attempt at an inclusive summary would soon degenerate into a mere catalogue of invention, and so we shall refer only to a few of the more important. Metallurgical progress, for instance, has been most marked, especially in the production of a great variety of alloy steels. The special use of silicon steel in the cores of electromagnets dates from 1903 and effected considerable economies in electric power. Stainless steel, an alloy with chromium, has saved much domestic labour and has been of great benefit to the surgeon. Alloys with manganese, tungsten, nickel, vanadium, cobalt and molybdenum have added to the variety of metallic products necessary to our complex modern engineering; and in their different proportions there are some thousands of such alloys of steel with these different metals. This half-century has seen also a considerable development and application of the alloys of the light metals, notably of aluminium alloys for the aircraft industry. Aluminium, apart from its valuable quality of lightness, is particularly useful because of its further property of resistance to atmospheric corrosion by means of the thin film of protective oxide that is immediately formed on the clean surface of the metal when it is exposed to the air.

The pneumatic tyre, with all that it has meant to motor transport, has been mainly developed in this period; and a wide range of synthetic rubber substitutes with different properties was produced from 1930 onwards.

The first commercially produced plastic, bakelite, was made in 1908 and its production marked the beginning of what became a considerable industry: these plastics, or synthetic resins, are now so widely applied for many purposes to replace stone and wood and metal that one has only to look around to see them almost everywhere. Perspex, the first plastic to replace glass, was discovered in 1930, and polythene, a flexible plastic, came into production in 1939. Other plastics have been found useful as wrapping materials and electrical insulators.

Nylon, which can be formed into a thread and which replaced artificial silk as a fabric, dates from 1935. The earliest of these artificial fabrics, rayon, dates from the beginning of the century; it was followed in turn by cellulose acetate and then nylon; and towards the end of our period terylene proved successful.

Atmospheric nitrogen has been fixed by various industrial processes in the form either of nitric acid or of ammonia. The success of these processes proved of great benefit to agriculture and to the explosives industry, and brought to an end their dependence on such natural sources as the mineral nitrates of Chile. The successful invention of one of these processes in Germany is said to have been a factor in the decision to make war in 1914, since it appeared to indicate that an adequate future supply of nitric acid for the manufacture of explosives was assured even if imports from Chile were cut off.

Many new and improved dyestuffs have been manufactured in this period and they have added colour and variety to fabrics. Photography has been greatly improved with plates and films of varying sensitivity for different purposes; and what was at first a difficult and complicated process has passed successfully into the hands of countless amateurs. Insecticides in great variety have been invented, the best known probably being DDT, but careless or too general use of such remedies is said to destroy the pollinating insects as well as those that prey on the crops to be protected. Selective weed-killers, that destroy the weeds and leave the crop undamaged, have also been devised.

While the volume of agricultural production has steadily increased in this half-century by the application of scientific knowledge, the human race has multiplied even faster, and frequent warnings have been sounded that in a world populated by over 2,000 millions of people, increasing annually by 20 millions, a mere 1 per cent, disastrous shortages of food may well lie round the corner. In the West food supplies have so far proved adequate for an increasing population; in the East, however, this is, in general, so far from being so that birth-control has been recommended as the only solution against a threat of famine. The bringing into cultivation of hitherto untilled land has proceeded steadily, especially in those marginal areas where rainfall and temperature are only just sufficient for agriculture; and remedies for loss of soil by erosion, as in the 'dustbowls' of America, have been scientifically and successfully applied. In the later years of this half-century, however, surplus stocks of food have been amassed in some countries, with the threat of dangerous or even ruinous falls in prices, while at the same time the populations of whole tracts of the world have been underfed.

In the preservation of food, an important discovery in the refrigeration of meat carried in ships was applied in 1934. Two methods had long been in use: either the meat was frozen about ten degrees below the freezing-point of water, in which state it could be conveyed satisfactorily for great distances, for example, from Australia and New Zealand to Europe; or it was chilled to just below the freezing-point of water, and then it could be carried only for shorter distances, such as from America to Europe. Frozen meat deteriorated rapidly on being thawed, while chilled meat retained its quality and flavour but not its colour. It was discovered, however, that, if 10 per cent of carbon dioxide was added to the air in which the chilled meat travelled, the length of time in which it might be stored in this way was doubled, while the addition of a proportion of oxygen prevented the change of colour. This useful discovery was applied to other cargoes than meat in suitably adjusted atmospheres at the temperatures found necessary for these different products.

The domestic refrigerator is another invention that has come into common use in this period; and the so-called 'deep-freeze' for fruit and vegetables has followed it in preference to drying methods, the frozen materials preserving much of their freshness although only for a short time after thawing.

Ships have passed from coal to oil and from the steam engine to the steam turbine, which was first applied to drive a ship in 1894. The change from coal to oil has reduced the number of stokers to one-tenth. Time signals broadcast by wireless telegraphy have greatly helped the navigator since it is no longer necessary to calculate Greenwich mean time in order to determine the longitude of his ship's position. Other radio aids to navigation, particularly radar, which was first applied in 1936 to locate aircraft in flight, were developed during the second world war and these have, in effect, linked the ship with the shore for the purposes of controlling the direction of its course, while radar itself has reduced the perils of fog, darkness and icebergs.

Among many developments in communications the two most striking were the thermionic valve, which effected a fundamental change in method in wireless telegraphy and which came into general use about 1920, and the multiplex working of cables, by which a number of messages, often several hundreds, could be sent at the same time, an improvement dating from about 1930.

Colour cinematography and sound films were introduced in the late 1920s.

The progressive assembly technique in manufacture on conveyor lines or belts, with which Henry Ford was especially associated in America, originated in 1913 and later became a characteristic of modern industrial practice.

The world shortage of animal fats led to greater use of vegetable oils and fats; and the shortage of soap, arising from the shortage of fats, led to the production of 'synthetic' detergents in a great variety.

And so we might continue, enumerating one technological advance after another. The important thing for us to observe, however, about this half-century is that these advances have been made through a far closer alliance between science and technology than that seen in any previous age; and it is in this sense that our modern civilisation is properly described as scientific or technological. While the chance invention has still occasionally played its part in this period, it has been a part that is seen to be ever decreasing, both in extent and in quality, when contrasted with the conscious and deliberate exploitation of new scientific knowledge and its application to practical ends. That new knowledge has been won and its application has been effected in this half-century by the labours of one who has but lately come upon the scene, namely, the professional scientist; and to him it is now necessary to refer in greater detail.

The men who founded modern science were amateurs, not professionals; they were often churchmen interested in what was called 'natural philosophy' or they were men of wealth and social position with a similar attraction to the study of nature, and their education had in general been in classics and in mathematics and in theology; and some others had studied medicine for a profession. The universities did not teach science in our sense of the term and still less its applications. In the eighteenth century there were, however, a few special colleges in France and Germany for training in military and civil engineering and in mining, but the Ecole Polytechnique, founded in Paris in 1794 during the Revolution, was the first college concerned with the application of science. Developments in the nineteenth century were gradual. Germany led the way in multiplying technical schools of increasing standard, although it was not until 1899 that these institutions were raised to university status. In Great Britain, home of the Industrial Revolution, there was a similar slow progress towards technical education, and the teaching of science itself developed only gradually during the nineteenth century. The slow rise and growth of the newer university colleges and universities, after the foundation of University College, London, in 1826 had introduced the teaching of the different sciences into higher education, indicate lack of national alertness to the possibilities of applied science among the countrymen of Watt and Faraday. Gradually scientific studies were organised, even in the older universities. Both in Europe and in the United States there was scientific as well as technical education and young men, in small numbers, went into industry after such training. The idea of scientific research with the object of applying its results was not yet common, and scientists, outside the scientific departments of the universities, were not numerous. Further, higher education was regarded as education in the arts, and education in science, even in a university, was something that did not rank as high in the intellectual and social scale.

The twentieth century opened, however, with scientific education in the universities well established in Germany, and with the resounding recognition of technical education at the usual high standards of the German universities. In France the situation was much the same, science and technology having been long allied. Generally there was a deeper realisation of the necessity of science to industry, as voiced by A. J. (afterwards Lord) Balfour, who was quoted at the beginning of this chapter. In the earlier part of this century, however, there was a much keener realisation of this necessity in Germany than in any other country; and it was only as a result of the application of science in certain war industries during the first world war, coupled with a better understanding of the part that scientific research had played in the technical advances of German industry, that steps were taken in other countries for the promotion of similar advances and for the establishment of official or semi-official encouragement and financial aid for such technical or industrial research. In Great Britain the Department of Scientific and Industrial Research was instituted under a committee of the Privy Council while the war was still in progress: later a number of research associations were formed for different industries, the government subscribing 'pound for pound' with the different industries to finance these research associations; various research boards were organised; and the National Physical Laboratory was taken over. In the United States, the British reaction to the pre-war neglect of scientific and industrial research was not only understood and admired, but also imitated: a National Research Council was set up and National Research Fellowships were instituted. In France, since the close connection between science and technology was no new thing, there was less need for these new departures. In the Soviet Union, after the reorganisation that followed the revolutionary period, great attention was given to the setting up and equipping of technical colleges in great numbers. The general object of these movements in all these countries was the stimulation of industry to new developments by means of fundamental research and its application; and emphasis was laid on the connection between science and industrial efficiency and progress. For a time, however, the increasing number of young scientists trained in this way was not very considerable, and it was not realised that a new profession was in process of being formed, that of the professional scientist or the industrial scientist or the technologist, as he has been variously called; and it was only at the end of our period, during and after the second world war, that the professional scientist in large numbers found his place in industry and in the scientific branches of the civil services of the various governments. The nations had learnt that scientific knowledge and research were vital for their survival, and this gave the professional scientist an established place in the state. The state itself was often the only possible source for the heavy expenditure that scientific research required. Much of this had to be carried out in university laboratories; the staffs of university scientific departments had to be greatly increased; many industries had to set up their own research laboratories, often of a considerable size and with large technical and scientific staffs; research in pure science or academic research went on at the same time at an increasing rate, since science itself must progress in fundamental knowledge, and the advance of science and technology proved mutually stimulating; and the undergraduate and post-graduate student in science was no longer merely studying a particular science or sciences, but preparing himself for the practice of a profession much as the medical student had always done. At the beginning of our period, the chances of his doing so were small indeed; but such had become the life of the young scientist as the mid-point of the century approached.

Another development closely followed these changes. At the beginning of our period a graduate in science with inclinations towards research might work for two years with his professor or with another either at home or abroad, and with or without (but much more probably without) one of the few scholarships or grants then available; and then, if opportunity offered, he might find a place in some university department where he would be able to carry on with such research as his duties might give him time for. But it would normally be individual research, done by himself in the spare time left after his teaching and other duties; and it would be done at his own cost. Sir William Ramsay, as is well known, financed his classic researches on the inert gases from the fees that he earned as a consultant. In the early 1920s, however, the beginner in scientific research received a grant from one or other of such bodies as have been mentioned above; and it was given for a specific research under his professor or supervisor, and that research might or might not constitute a part of the attack on a large problem on which others might be working in the same laboratory. Later, after these beginnings, the young scientist might be one of a team working together on a problem, and it became less and less likely that he would be engaged in individual research. The organisation of such teams was a marked feature of much scientific research in the later part of our period. In Great Britain, for example, much of this kind of academic research was financed by the Department of Scientific and Industrial Research, the Medical Research Council, the various research associations, and individual industrial companies. Often the problem was precisely stated and the research organised as needing a staff of so many and as likely to take so long, but more often these details were not calculable. The speed and the urgency of much scientific research changed greatly in the times we are discussing; and the services of a variety of scientists trained in different sciences were often needed in collaboration on one problem. Such were the organisation and practice of science at the mid-point of the twentieth century.

Of the organisation of these great numbers of scientists throughout the world into their specialist societies in every country, it is scarcely necessary to mention any detail except that these scientific societies provided in their journals, maintained by the subscriptions of their members, the media for the publication of the bulk of the world's scientific research. In conjunction they organised also a service that compiled for publication classified abstracts of the latest memoirs in the journals dealing with each particular science. By this means the researcher was enabled to keep in touch with the latest advances in his own field and in any other in which he might be interested. Societies multiplied with the increasing complexity of science in this half-century, and their publications greatly increased. *The World List of Scientific Periodicals* gives valuable information on this point. The first edition of this useful work covered the period from 1900 to 1921 and included all journals published up to 1900 or brought out between that year and 1921, except those that might have escaped its net: the total was about 25,000. The second edition brought these details up to 1933: the number had increased to 36,000. The third edition brought them up to 1950: the number exceeded 50,000. As for the scientific books published and translated from one language into another, it would be difficult to form any estimate of the increase in their publication.

It will be noticed that between 1921 and 1950 the number of scientific periodicals doubled. Scientific periodical literature originated in the middle of the seventeenth century with the publication of the proceedings of the first national scientific academies; the number of such journals steadily increased. The data from the *World List* indicate that the total had reached 25,000 by 1921; much of this increase, it is known, occurred in the nineteenth century. It will be noted, however, that the number of scientific journals rose from 1921 to 1933 by 11,000 in twelve years, and then by a further 14,000 from 1933 to 1950 in seventeen years, from which six years of war should be deducted. This is characteristic of the whole period; and, looking a little farther back, to a century ago, we may say that, when the advances of the last hundred years are studied closely, it is found that by far the greater part lie in this half-century, and, similarly, when the progress of this half-century is analysed, it is evident that the greater part of it fell within the second quarter. The pace has steadily increased through these hundred years.

The historian of science surveying these fifty years, if he can detach himself from contemporary disputation and argument about the ethics of the application of scientific discovery to the waging of war, about remedies against the narrowness of scientific education, about the perils of technocracy, and about the urgent need for more and more scientists, looks upon a period of unparalleled and ever accelerated progress in science and technology. By far the greater part of it fell within the second quarter of the century, and much of it was expedited by the needs of two world wars and of the so-called 'cold war' as well. He will reflect sorrowfully that science, which began as the study of nature for its own sake, became in this age vital to the survival of nations in arms, and that in its disinterested pursuit of truth it was forced for the same cause to halt at frontiers where hitherto it had recognised none.

CHAPTER V

DIPLOMATIC HISTORY 1900–1912

BY 1900 the two dynamic forces of nationalism and industrialism had radically altered the balance of power throughout the world. Accompanied by increasing state control, they had extended European sovereignty to nearly the whole of Africa, led to new rivalries in Asia, and contributed to the spectacular development in wealth and strength of two non-European states, the U.S.A. and Japan. A further result was that the great powers in Europe were becoming greater, the small powers relatively weaker. Although the principal 'great powers' were still European, their relations with the peoples of other continents were of growing importance and the issues that divided them often concerned regions far beyond the confines of Europe. As the means of communication had multiplied in number and celerity, so the area and sensitivity of political repercussion had strikingly increased. By 1900 international relations were world relations in a sense unknown in 1800 or at the dawn of any previous century.

During the 1890s these relations underwent notable modifications. Bismarck had kept the peace of Europe, excluding the Balkan peninsula, for the best part of twenty years and the pattern of European relations had appeared relatively stable. But his fall in 1890, the uncertain temper of the brilliant, impulsive and indiscreet young emperor, William II, who dismissed him, and the uncertain policy of the lesser men who succeeded him and who, partly out of consideration for England, failed to renew the Reinsurance Treaty with Russia, but did renew the Triple Alliance (6 May 1891), inaugurated a period of fundamental change. Alarmed by the renewal of the Triple Alliance and by Anglo-German friendliness, Russia, whose relations with Germany had been cool even while the Reinsurance Treaty was in force, began to look elsewhere. The natural ally, dictated by strategical and economic, though not by ideological, considerations, was Republican France, whose statesmen were eager for Russian friendship, and the Franco-Russian Alliance (an exchange of letters agreeing to joint action for the maintenance of peace dated 27 August 1891 and a secret military convention of 18 August 1892 ratified by the two governments in the winter of 1893–4) brought about just that conjunction which Bismarck had striven to prevent. Although these agreements were wholly defensive and contained no 'suggestion of mutual support for the realisation of any positive ambitions', they gave France a feeling of security unknown to her since 1871 and caused misgivings in England as well as in Germany, since it was with France and

Russia that British interests chiefly conflicted. The balance of power was likely once again to become a European issue. This was a new factor in international relations and one which remained fundamental until the outbreak of the first world war. As yet, however, not all the eventual partners had taken sides, and the permanence of the new grouping had still to be tested. Although there were now two alliance systems, the nineties were characterised by such a complex fluidity of policies that they have been called the period of the 'interpenetration of alliances'.[1]

Outside Europe there were also changes of fundamental importance. The extension of European dominion continued apace and brought fresh menaces of conflict, while a new phase of expansion began for the non-European states, the U.S.A. and Japan.

In the Far East the ancient empire of China was the chief bone of contention. There, first in the field, England had by 1890 established a commercial and diplomatic pre-eminence based upon sea power. In the north, Russia aimed at securing an ice-free port to serve as the terminus of the great Trans-Siberian Railway, which she had begun to build in 1891 with the aid of French capital, and which was to transform the strategic position in North-East Asia. In the south, France's acquisition of Indo-China had been indirectly at Chinese expense, as had the British annexation of Upper Burma in 1885, and both powers were now able to penetrate into south China. Foreign concessions and commercial establishments in Shanghai and other great Chinese cities were eloquent witness to the economic stakes at issue. Indisputably China was the 'sick man' of the Far East, but, as in the Near East with Turkey, the European powers disagreed upon his treatment. Thus, whereas Russia favoured the amputation of outlying areas and opposed the open door for commerce, Britain championed integrity and the policy of free trade which had brought her two-thirds of China's modest foreign trade.

It was, however, the intervention of Japan in 1894 which made the Far Eastern question a major factor in international relations. Japan, who had so recently emerged from feudal isolation and astounded the world by her ability to assimilate western ideas and techniques, was in dispute with China over the Ryukyu Islands and Korea and determined to prevent their falling under European, especially Russian, control. After a brief and successful war, by the Treaty of Shimonoseki (17 April 1895) she obliged China to cede the island of Formosa and on the mainland the Liaotung Peninsula with its valuable ice-free harbour, Port Arthur, to grant her most-favoured-nation status in China, and to recognise the independence of Korea. This outcome was extremely unwelcome both to Russia, whose rulers were beginning to envisage the seizure of Manchuria and the eventual reduction of China to the position of a client

---

[1] For example, by G. Salvemini and W. L. Langer. See the latter's *The Diplomacy of Imperialism, 1890–1902* (New York and London, 1935), vol. I, p. 297.

state, and to Germany, who, with Russia's reluctant acquiescence, was planning herself to seize a Chinese port; and these two powers together with France, who felt bound to support Russia, demanded that Japan should hand back the Liaotung Peninsula. Japan complied, accepting an indemnity instead, but harboured a deep resentment against Russia and Germany, against whom she would one day take her revenge. Thus Far Eastern affairs had led to a loose coalition in Asia of those European powers who were on opposite sides in Europe. In effect their co-operation, which continued intermittently for another ten years, was a local manifestation of the sort of continental alliance against England so often urged by anti-British statesmen in Europe. China's self-appointed champions did not go unrequited. Russia soon received her reward, notably in a concession for the construction of the Chinese Eastern Railway, which facilitated her penetration into Manchuria, while France obtained railway concessions in the Yunnan area. Two years later the spoliation of China went a stage farther when Germany seized a base in Kiao-Chow Bay on 14 November 1897, and when, in March 1898, Russia, having declined English overtures for a 'partition of preponderance',[1] occupied the coveted Port Arthur, which she converted into a naval base. In both instances the European powers gained economic advantages in the adjacent territories and preferred to extort leasehold concessions instead of proclaiming outright annexation. This was a convenient new device 'whereby Foreign Powers might acquire the substance of colonial authority without a complete transfer of title'.[2] Inevitably the other powers felt obliged to seek some semblance of compensation, and accordingly England occupied Wei-hai-wei and France Kwang Chow Wan. The open-door policy had largely broken down, in spite of British and, subsequently (1899), American gestures to maintain it, and the struggle for 'spheres of influence' in China became the dominant concern.

These events had significant consequences. Chinese nationalist resentment manifested itself in the Boxer risings of 1900 in which the foreign Legations in Peking were besieged and many 'foreign devils', including the German Minister, met their death. At the same time Japan's feeling against Russia was embittered by the seizure of Port Arthur and she began to contemplate the possibility of war to prevent further Russian expansion. Her suspicions and those of England, throughout opposed to Russia's Chinese policy, were intensified when the Boxer risings enabled Russian troops to enter Manchuria in force. Thus, although the principal European powers and Japan combined to send an international force against the Boxers and to exact an indemnity from the Chinese govern-

[1] Lord Salisbury to Sir N. O'Conor, 25 January 1898. G. P. Gooch and H. W. V. Temperley (eds.), *British Documents on the Origins of the War, 1898–1914*, vol. 1 (London, 1927), no. 9. The 'preponderance' envisaged by Salisbury was economic, not territorial.

[2] G. F. Hudson, *The Far East in World Politics: A Study in Recent History* (2nd ed., 1939), p. 100.

ment, the Chinese question at the beginning of the twentieth century threatened to multiply the occasions of friction between the white nations. In particular, it had added a vast new area to the wide field in which British and Russian interests already conflicted.

In the Near East, however, Russia's preoccupation with Chinese questions resulted in an interlude in her traditional Balkan rivalry with Austria, and this happier state of affairs was confirmed by an agreement of May 1897, whereby the two powers renounced any conquests for themselves should the *status quo* in the Balkans be disturbed, and by the Muerzsteg Programme of 1903 in which they combined in efforts to settle the affairs of Macedonia. But this temporary improvement in Austro-Russian relations did not mean that Turkish affairs had ceased to be vexatious or significant. That shaky power had been shaken again by fresh stirrings of her subject nationalities, by risings in Armenia (1894), Crete (May 1896), and Macedonia. In 1895 England had threatened a naval demonstration to induce her to desist from solving the Armenian question by massacring the Armenians, and only the menace of Russian counter-measures had prevented the threat from being implemented. In Crete revolt had excited Greece to launch a hopeless attack upon Turkey, with the result that the Great Powers had intervened in order to prevent the conflict from spreading to the Balkans and had obliged the Turks to grant the Cretans autonomy under a Greek High Commissioner.

That Turkey had weathered these storms was, as so often before, largely due to the conflicting interests of the Great Powers. Traditionally, England had been the principal champion of Turkish integrity. But British influence at Constantinople had declined since 1879, and, as Salisbury despaired of Turkish reform and his colleagues, since the conclusion of the Franco-Russian alliance, were reluctant to risk the fleet for the protection of the Straits, control of the Nile valley had superseded the maintenance of Turkey as the chief British objective at the eastern end of the Mediterranean. The role of Turkey's champion had been assumed instead by Germany. Already in 1881 a German military mission had undertaken the training of the Turkish army and in 1888 a German syndicate had obtained a concession to build a railway from Ismid to Ankara. In 1889 the German emperor had paid a first visit to Constantinople and in 1898 at Damascus he demonstratively proclaimed his friendship for the Muslim world. The 1888 concession marked the beginning of a rapid extension of German economic influence. Naturally the German government favoured these developments, which received powerful backing from the able ambassador sent to Constantinople in 1897, Baron Marschall von Bieberstein. Within a few years he had acquired a dominant situation in the Turkish capital, while the efficiency of German 'promoters, bankers, traders, engineers, manufacturers, ship-owners and railway builders'[1] soon

[1] E. M. Earle, *Turkey, the Great Powers and the Baghdad Railway* (London, 1923), p. 37.

undermined French and British interests and created something like a German economic empire in the Near East. Most significant of all were the grant obtained by the German-controlled Anatolian Railway Company in 1899 to build a commercial port at Haidar Pasha on the Asiatic side of the Bosporus and the concession in principle of an extension of their railway from Konieh to Baghdad and the Persian Gulf.

To Turkey herself these developments seemed eminently desirable: railways would bring prosperity to backward districts of the empire and enable the government to move troops more rapidly to defend the frontiers or deal with internal disturbances, while the economic and diplomatic support of distant and seemingly disinterested Germany appeared the best guarantee of Turkish integrity. But so far as international relations were concerned this economic penetration could not but have a political significance. What alarmed other nations was the new projection of German power diagonally overland in an axis from Berlin to Constantinople which threatened to divide Europe in two. Such an axis cut across Russia's possible line of expansion to the Mediterranean through the Balkans, while the revival of Turkish power under German influence promised to frustrate Russia's age-long aspiration to control the Straits. Furthermore, the prolongation of the axis through Asia Minor to the Persian Gulf could be seen as a menace to British interests in Egypt and Persia. Thus, although the Deutsche Bank sought to enlist the aid of British, French and Russian capital to finance the construction of the Baghdad Railway, it was impossible for governments to regard this as a purely business undertaking. Russia had shown her alarm at the concession of Haidar Pasha; by the Black Sea Agreement of 1900 she forced the Turks to admit that any railway concessions in northern Anatolia and Armenia should be granted only to Russian citizens or to syndicates approved by the tsar; and she eventually withdrew her consent to the participation of Russian capital in the development of the Baghdad Railway. The British government on the other hand had been in favour of giving the railway an international character, but public opinion in England, already highly distrustful of Germany, made such an outcry against the participation of a British financial syndicate that they withdrew their support. This was a notable instance of the way in which diplomacy had sometimes to retreat in face of the new forces of publicity. The French government, impelled to follow Russia, likewise refused official backing, so that the Germans began the construction of the first section of the railway in 1904 without the financial aid of foreign governments. The intrusion of Germany into spheres long earmarked by other powers for themselves had introduced a new disturbing factor into international relations. In particular it imposed a new strain on the relations of Germany with Russia, France and England.

The third great area in which the European powers pursued their partitioning projects was Africa. Here the scene was dominated by the traditional colonial rivalry of France and England, the determination of Germany to make her influence felt, and the failure of the Italian attempt to conquer a new dominion.

English and French interests collided at many points but, whereas frontier disputes in the west were settled by an Anglo-French Convention of 14 June 1898, differences farther east were less easily composed. The main tension came with the struggle for control of the Upper Nile. For England, virtual mistress of Egypt since 1882, this was of vital concern, since the prosperity of Egypt depended upon the Nile waters. An attempt in 1894–5 to agree with France upon a definition of spheres of influence came to nothing. The French had never ceased to resent the fact that, largely through French timidity, the British had gained sole control of Egypt. Furthermore, some French colonial expansionists hoped to secure a continuous block of territory from the Atlantic to the Red Sea or Indian Ocean. For such a plan, as well as for applying pressure to Britain in Egypt, the Upper Nile region was of great importance, and in 1896 an expedition was sent to plant the French flag at Fashoda. In the same year Kitchener had been dispatched by the British government to reconquer the Egyptian Sudan, which had been evacuated in 1884, and in 1898 he captured Khartoum. On 25 September 1898, when he found Marchand's French troops at Fashoda and summoned them to withdraw, there occurred one of the gravest crises in Anglo-French relations since 1815. The British government mobilised the English press in support of its stand, Fleet Street being taken quite unusually into the direct confidence of the Foreign Office, and refused to negotiate until Marchand's force had been ordered to retire. For the second time in the 'nineties (there had been acute tension over Siam in 1893) England and France were on the brink of war. But the new French Foreign Minister, Delcassé, and his colleagues wisely recognised that France was in no condition to undertake a colonial war against the greatest naval power, and on 3 November they ordered the evacuation of the disputed territory. An Anglo-French Convention of 21 March 1899 demarcated the British and French spheres of interest in the region of the watershed between the Nile and the Congo and the problem of control of the Upper Nile was solved in favour of Britain.

The Fashoda crisis convinced an important group of French colonialists that France could no longer effectively challenge English rule in Egypt. Instead they urged Delcassé to offer England French recognition of her position in Egypt if she in turn would recognise French ambitions in Morocco.[1] This was the bargain which a few years later was to be the basis of the Entente Cordiale, but, in the aftermath of the Fashoda crisis,

[1] I am indebted for this and other points to Dr C. M. Andrew's forthcoming study of Delcassé.

Delcassé was still unwilling to abandon what remained of French rights in Egypt. Egypt excepted, however, he genuinely desired a swift and amicable settlement of the other points at issue between France and England, and early in 1899 Paul Cambon, the new French ambassador in London, made several attempts to reach an understanding with Salisbury. His efforts were, however, unsuccessful and in August 1899 Delcassé told the British ambassador that events had seemed to show 'the impossibility of keeping relations with England on a friendly footing'.[1] Delcassé was soon to see in English involvement in South Africa a fresh opportunity to challenge English rule in Egypt.

In South Africa the main conflicting interests were those of England and Germany, who had established herself in South West Africa in 1884; and the main cause of trouble was the economic development of the Boer Republic of the Transvaal. The gold rush of the 'eighties had led to the unwelcome influx into the Boer states of a large new white population which soon equalled and possibly outnumbered the original Boer stock. To these Uitlanders or foreigners the restrictive policies of the Boer President of the Transvaal became so irksome that revolt was openly plotted with the connivance of certain people in the adjoining British territories. But the Jameson raid of 1895, which attempted to precipitate such a rising, was a fiasco. Its most dramatic outcome was the intervention of the German emperor, whose congratulatory telegram to President Kruger on 3 January 1896 roused passionate resentment in England. Furthermore, the belief it encouraged in Kruger that he might rely on foreign support strengthened him in the intransigent attitude which led finally to the outbreak of the Boer War in October 1899.

Although Germany was helpless to intervene directly in South Africa, Britain's difficulties there and Portugal's financial troubles gave her an opportunity to exact a price for refraining from further encouragement to the Boers. This took the form of the Convention of 30 August 1898 in which the two powers defined their spheres of interest and the areas which they would occupy in the event of Portugal abandoning her colonies. But the good effect upon Germany of this dubious arrangement was undone by the colonial guarantee reaffirmed by England to Portugal in the following year in return for a Portuguese undertaking to stop the passage of arms to the Transvaal. The Germans felt that they had been tricked and the memory of this English 'perfidy' was undoubtedly a stumbling-block in the way of future Anglo-German arrangements. 'With these people', exclaimed the powerful director of the German Foreign Office, Baron von Holstein, 'it is impossible to enter into any engagement.'[2] Despite their mistrust, however, Germany during the Boer War refrained from taking

---

[1] *British Documents on the Origins of the War, 1898–1914*, vol. I, p. 212.

[2] Quoted in H. Nicolson, *Sir Arthur Nicolson, Bart, First Lord Carnock: A Study in the Old Diplomacy* (London, 1930), p. 128.

advantage of British isolation which others also wished to exploit. Thus, for example, Delcassé had at first hoped that Germany would join the Dual Alliance in a diplomatic initiative aimed at obliging England to honour her pledges to evacuate Egypt once order had been restored there. In March 1900, however, Germany declared that before considering intervention she must be assured of France's recognition of existing European boundaries. This would have involved French acceptance of Alsace-Lorraine as a permanent part of Germany, a requirement which Delcassé regarded as intolerable. Henceforth, believing that this was Germany's condition for Franco-German co-operation, he consistently rejected any idea of a *rapprochement* with Germany. Thus, just as events in South Africa had sown seeds of distrust between Britain and Germany which would not easily be eradicated, so the Boer War was a turning-point in Franco-German relations.

Colonial questions in Africa had thus led to grave friction between certain European powers; but they had generally been subordinated to European interests, and they had not materially hindered the process of bringing ever-larger areas of the African continent under more effective European control. Another European power, Italy, however, was less successful in her attempts at expansion, and her defeat at Adowa in 1896 by the Ethiopians, whom she had hoped to reduce to vassalage, dealt a blow to white prestige, changed the direction of her imperialist ambitions and had important repercussions upon Italian policy in Europe.

Meanwhile the 'nineties were no less significant for the new advances made by the U.S.A. There, nationalism of an expansionist character was once again in the ascendant. Its belligerent tone, manifested by President Cleveland in the British–Venezuelan boundary dispute of 1895, gave a new extension to the Monroe Doctrine and obliged an England pre-occupied by South African affairs to have recourse to arbitration. Still more important was the American war with Spain (April–August 1898), which led not only to the establishment of a United States protectorate over Cuba and the annexation of the Hawaiian Islands and Puerto Rico, but also to American assumption of direct rule over Guam and the Philippines. The annexation of the Philippines, the abrupt climax of long years of penetration into the Pacific area, was a striking departure from the traditional policy of confining American political responsibilities to the western hemisphere. Although it did not of itself involve the U.S.A. in Far Eastern rivalries, it meant that in the long run, territorially and strategically as well as commercially, she was much more likely to become so involved. However reluctantly and hesitantly, the Americans were beginning to assume the cares and ambitions of a world power to which their wealth and population already committed them.

Although these extra-European developments did not seriously affect the systems of alliance within Europe, they showed up the weak links in those systems, and the tension and danger of war created by such incidents as the Kruger Telegram and Fashoda gave rise to a sense of insecurity which impelled the major powers to seek to reinforce their positions. This reinforcement, which led to the completion of the alliance system, is a main theme of the next decade.

The sense of insecurity was increased by the growth of defensive armaments. The military budget of the German empire had nearly trebled since 1878 and those of England and France more than or nearly doubled. One way of relieving tension would have been by an agreed reduction of armaments and this was actually proposed by the tsar in 1898. The Russian note of 24 August suggesting an international conference urged that if armaments continued to grow there would be 'a cataclysm too horrible for the human mind to contemplate'. But the tsar's gesture, coming as it did shortly after Russia's seizure of Port Arthur, was met with incredulity and suspicion. Germany above all had 'no intention of binding herself in the question of military armaments',[1] and the only positive results of the first Hague Peace Conference (May–July 1899) were the establishment of a permanent court of arbitration and the adoption of two conventions relating to the rules of war. In the long run the Hague tribunal was to prove an enduring and important piece of machinery for the adjustment of international relations; but immediately the discouraging effect of the conference was to make clear that the armaments race would continue. Soon this would be a danger at sea as well as on land.

While the Hague Conference was still sitting, France on the initiative of Delcassé, who was preoccupied by the danger of the disintegration of Austria-Hungary after the death of Francis Joseph, renewed and extended her ties with Russia. On 9 August 1899 an exchange of letters took place in which 'the maintenance of the balance of power' was substituted for 'the maintenance of peace' as the prime object of the Franco-Russian alliance. This redefinition (later widely interpreted as implying that France would be readier to support Russia's Balkan ambitions) was intended by Delcassé as a statement of Franco-Russian opposition to Germany's supposed ambition to take Trieste, if Austria-Hungary broke up, and establish herself in the Mediterranean. At the same time the military convention, hitherto to last as long only as the Triple Alliance, was prolonged indefinitely, thereby ensuring that the Dual Alliance would survive any dissolution of Austria-Hungary. In 1900 the military arrangements between the two powers were also adapted to cover the risk of war with England, and an agreement to this end was ratified in 1901. In the

---

[1] 'Dass wir nicht gesonnen sind, uns in der Frage der militärischen Rüstungen nach irgendeiner Richtung hin zu binden, brauche ich hier kaum zu erwähnen', Bülow's instructions to Münster, the chief German delegate to the conference (*Die Grosse Politik der Europäischen Kabinette 1871–1914*, vol. xv, Berlin, 1927, p. 190). Cf. G. P. Gooch, *Before the War: Studies in Diplomacy*, vol. I (London, 1936), p. 196.

dawn of the new century both powers could consider war with England a danger which they must take into account. This did not mean that Delcassé had abandoned the objective of an understanding with England, but indicates that he still doubted its possibility.

At the same time a *rapprochement* between France and Italy ended a period of tension dating from the French occupation of Tunis in 1881. France naturally welcomed any opportunity to make the third partner in the Triple Alliance sit more loosely to her obligations, while Italy, baulked of Ethiopia, cast all the more longing eyes across the Mediterranean on the undeveloped Ottoman dependency of Tripoli. For any attempt on Tripoli to succeed, the goodwill of France, who held the adjoining Tunisia, was essential. New men, in Italy the Prime Minister, Rudini, and the Foreign Ministers, Visconti Venosta and Prinetti, in France Delcassé and Camille Barrère, sent to the Rome Embassy in 1898, helped to bring about the change. In 1898 a commercial treaty ended the customs war begun in 1888 which had damaged Italy more than France. On 14 December 1900 a secret agreement followed, whereby France promised Italy a free hand in Tripoli in return for recognition of France's interests in Morocco. The final triumph of French policy came in 1902 when Italy, who had just renewed the Triple Alliance for the fourth time and in doing so extorted an Austrian recognition of her interests in Tripoli, gave France a secret assurance that if France were attacked or obliged to declare war as a result of 'direct provocation' she would remain neutral. Her Mediterranean ambitions and skilful French diplomacy had thus led Italy to give an undertaking which was certainly not in accordance with the spirit of her obligations under the Triple Alliance which she had just renewed. Although the text was kept secret until 1920, a statement by Delcassé in the French Chamber claimed that France now had nothing to fear from Italy. In fact, however, the undertaking was equivocal. Despite the undoubted improvement in Franco-Italian relations manifested in 1901 by the visit of an Italian naval squadron to Toulon and subsequently by an exchange of visits between the heads of the two states, Italy, the weakest of the great powers, sat on the fence. Thus, while Germany was naturally irritated by what in the Reichstag her Chancellor affected to regard as an innocent flirtation, it was not until later that the flirtation was, as a French historian remarked, 'to develop into a liaison'.[1]

It was natural for France to seek to extend the circle of her friends. For her, isolation had been the penalty of defeat. For England it was less splendid or complete than used to be supposed. Yet England's abandonment of her relative aloofness and freedom from commitments because of a new sense of the need for security was a pregnant development. This

[1] M. Baumont, *L'Essor industriel et l'impérialisme colonial (1878-1904)* (Paris, 1937), p. 323.

sense of insecurity was the product chiefly of the Boer War and of fear of Russia, who until the Russo-Japanese War of 1904–5 appeared to most British statesmen and a considerable section of British public opinion to be a great and growing menace to British imperial interests.

At first England's most natural ally had seemed to be Germany. But early negotiations had come to nothing and, after the conclusion of the Franco-Russian alliance, which appeared to weaken England's international position, the German rulers inclined to believe that England would soon come cap in hand and enable them to extract a high price for their friendship. Although at times they indulged in frankly hostile dreams of a continental alliance for the destruction of the British Empire, their general policy was to keep a free hand as between Russia and England but to show that the hand was mailed and held a sharp sword. Thereby the kaiser was encouraged by his Chancellor, Bülow, to believe that he could play the role of *arbiter mundi*. So Germany entered upon a disconcerting course in which, in order to break the Franco-Russian alliance and to bring England to heel, she aggressively demonstrated her growing strength.

The first conspicuous example of this policy, the Kruger Telegram, was the first incident which made England feel that it would be wise to settle some of her differences and win a friend in Europe; but it was to Russia, not to Germany, that she turned, and a proposal by Salisbury for the mutual recognition of spheres of interest in Turkey was suggested as part of a wider settlement. This was the first of several such overtures, but, until her defeat by Japan, Russia saw in agreement with England a hindrance not an aid to her expansionist policy and she therefore turned a deaf ear.

It was above all the Far Eastern question which convinced an important section of British opinion, headed by the Colonial Secretary, Joseph Chamberlain, that the time had come to abandon isolation. Failing the U.S.A., and Japan, who was not yet disposed for an alliance that might provoke an armed clash with Russia for which she was still unprepared, Chamberlain turned to Germany. In 1898, in Salisbury's absence, he suggested a defensive alliance based upon 'a mutual understanding as to policy in China and elsewhere'. But China was not a vital German interest and Germany had no wish to side against Russia or to pull England's chestnuts out of the Far Eastern fire for her. By keeping a free hand she hoped rather to profit from the conflict between England and Russia which seemed so probable. The negotiations petered out and Chamberlain's subsequent public affirmation of England's need for an alliance with some 'great military power' aroused no enthusiasm in Germany or England. Indeed, an important factor in Anglo-German relations before 1914 was the lukewarmness or antagonism of British popular feelings towards Germany and the positive and increasing hostility of the great mass of

German opinion towards Britain. This mutual antipathy, which dates mainly from the Boer War, was all the more widespread since the development of a cheap popular press in both countries in the 'nineties, for neither country properly understood the workings of the press in the other and neither government was fully able to restrain the hostile outpourings of its own newspapers. In such circumstances a genuine alliance would have been very difficult to accomplish.

In spite of his failure, Chamberlain was loth to relinquish his dream of partnership between the big army and the big navy, so alien to the main tradition of British foreign policy, and, when the kaiser visited England in November 1899, he reverted to the theme of an alliance, this time between England, Germany and the U.S.A. But when in a public speech at Leicester he referred to 'the natural alliance between ourselves and the great German empire' he met with strikingly little support in England, criticism in the U.S.A. and a storm of hostile comment in Germany. Moreover, in the Reichstag Bülow poured cold water on Chamberlain's overtures and spoke of the need for a strong German fleet. The second German Navy Bill, introduced in January 1900, with its principle that 'Germany must have a battle fleet so strong that even the adversary possessed of the greatest sea power will attack it only with grave risk to herself', continued the potentially challenging policy inaugurated by Admiral von Tirpitz, who had become Minister of Marine in 1897. England was rebuffed and when, by the Yangtze Agreement of 16 October 1900, 'the only formal agreement for diplomatic co-operation ever made between Great Britain and Germany',[1] the two powers undertook to maintain Chinese integrity and the open door for trade 'wherever both Powers can exert influence', they soon fell out because they differed sharply over its interpretation.

The last attempt to bring about an alliance occurred in 1901. Originating probably with a personal initiative of Eckardstein, First Secretary of the German Embassy in London, and favoured again by Chamberlain and his friends, it developed on the German side into a proposal that England should join the Triple Alliance. But Salisbury saw no advantage—'the liability of having to defend the German and Austrian frontiers against Russia is heavier than that of having to defend the British Isles against France'[2]—and, as the Germans would be content with nothing less and were no longer interested in local co-operation, such as an alliance in the Far East mooted by Lansdowne, the new Foreign Secretary, these negotiations too were fruitless. If the Germans genuinely wished for Britain's friendship their insistence on her adherence to the Triple Alliance showed a lack of psychological insight, for, as the Anglo-French

[1] A. J. P. Taylor, *The Struggle for Mastery in Europe, 1848–1918* (Oxford, 1954), p. 393.
[2] *British Documents on the Origins of the War, 1898–1914*, vol. III, no. 86. Salisbury uses the words 'British Isles', although 'British Empire' would have been more appropriate.

entente was to show, a close association with Britain could operate without any formal ties. Bülow and his colleagues still believed that they had only to wait for England to renew her suit and pay the price. In spite of a plain hint by Chamberlain in April 1898, they could not think it possible that she would turn elsewhere. Their miscalculation was grievous.

Fresh tension in the Far East was part of the background to these negotiations. On the one hand, an alleged Chinese agreement to recognise Russia's hold on Manchuria alarmed Japan and led her to sound England for support against Russia. On the other, Russia's encroachments in Manchuria and Persia had made England still more conscious of her isolation. But it was not until he had failed both to enlist German aid in restraining Russia and to come to terms directly with Russia that Lansdowne contemplated alliance with Japan alone. At the same time Japanese statesmen were divided between the merits of an English alliance (desired by the war party) and a settlement with Russia. Thus, while the Japanese Ambassador, Baron Hayashi, was negotiating in London, Prince Ito was empowered to visit St Petersburg to explore the chances of an agreement with Russia. In view of their past experience the Japanese were by no means sure that either aim could be achieved. But, after the failure of renewed overtures to Russia, Lansdowne was convinced of the need for Japan's support, and so the Japanese had already committed themselves in principle to the English alliance when Ito reported that a Russo-Japanese agreement was also within the bounds of possibility. They could not have both and were reluctant to alienate England, who had abstained from interfering with their victory at Shimonoseki and had been the first to renounce extra-territoriality in Japan, by withdrawing when negotiations were so advanced. Thus on 30 January 1902 there was signed the treaty which marked England's abandonment of isolation in the Far East and strikingly emphasised the status Japan had won for herself among the nations (see below, ch. XII).

By the terms of the treaty, which was to last for five years, Japan appeared to gain more than England. By the first article each power recognised the other's special interests in China, but England also recognised those of Japan in Korea, whereas the Japanese had refused to extend their obligations to cover India, Siam and the Straits Settlements. By the second, if either power was involved in hostilities with another in defence of those interests the other was to preserve strict neutrality. By the third, if one of the signatories was at war with two powers in defence of those interests the other must come to its aid. In other words, England would be neutral if there was war between Russia and Japan, but would be bound to help Japan if France joined Russia. The treaty made war between Russia and Japan more likely, though this was not Lansdowne's intention, but it also made French participation more remote; for if 'France would not fight for the valley of the Nile, it was highly improbable that she would draw the sword for Korea'.[1] For England the important thing 'was not what was in *the* Alliance, but the fact that there was *an* Alliance';[2] had Russia and Japan agreed upon a common policy, British interests in the Far East generally might have been gravely menaced.

By relieving the pressure on her in the Far East the Anglo-Japanese alliance enabled England to reinforce her fleets in home waters. This new course of policy, in which Lansdowne sought 'to strengthen Britain's global interests by concentrating her military resources',[3] had its counterpart in the western hemisphere. The Hay–Pauncefote treaty of 18 November 1901 enabled the U.S.A. to proceed with the construction and defence of a trans-Isthmian canal, but in effect marked England's surrender of her naval supremacy in the Caribbean. Yet it led to a notable improvement in Anglo-American relations.

Although the Anglo-Japanese alliance made war between Russia and Japan more likely, it did not render it inevitable or preclude further attempts by Japan to settle her differences by negotiation. The deciding factor which led to conflict was the seizure of control over Russia's Far Eastern policy by an irresponsible militarist group.

In a military autocracy like Russia, when the autocrat was a man of weak will, as was Nicholas II, policy might oscillate violently because of the struggle of different interests to influence the tsar. The able finance minister, Witte, and most of his colleagues favoured a policy of peaceful penetration in China, but Witte's fall in August 1903 and the appointment of Admiral Alexeiev as viceroy in the Far East responsible directly to the tsar marked the ascendancy of a sinister camarilla, headed by an adventurer named Bezobrazoff, who envisaged war to gain their ends. In consequence Russia failed to carry out her undertaking of April 1902 to evacuate Manchuria, and after several months of negotiation in 1903 Japanese requirements for a peaceful settlement remained unsatisfied. At last, convinced of Russian bad faith, the Japanese determined upon the event for which they had long prepared. If there was to be war it should come at the moment of their choosing, when their naval armaments had been completed and before the Trans-Siberian Railway was finished. On 8 February 1904, without declaration of war, they opened hostilities by an attack on the Russian fleet at Port Arthur. The Russians were taken by surprise, lost command of the sea, and quickly suffered a series of reverses. Port Arthur fell on 2 January 1905, after a seven months' siege; Mukden was captured in March 1905; and the Russian Baltic fleet, which had sailed half way round the world in an endeavour to regain mastery of the China Sea, was annihilated on 27 May at Tsushima.

[1] G. P. Gooch, *Before the War*, vol. I, p. 22.
[2] W. L. Langer, *The Diplomacy of Imperialism, 1890–1902*, vol. II (New York and London, 1935), p. 783.
[3] J. A. S. Grenville, *Lord Salisbury and Foreign Policy* (London, 1964), p. 389.

Contrary to the expectation of most European military experts, Japan had defeated the Russian giant unaided, and once again, as in the Crimean War, but still more dramatically, the tsardom was shown to be a colossus with feet of clay. Grave disturbances broke out in various parts of European Russia and, no longer in any condition to fight, the tsar's government gladly accepted the American President Roosevelt's offer of mediation. By the ensuing Treaty of Portsmouth of 5 September 1905, signed a month after the renewal of the Anglo-Japanese Alliance with widened scope for a further period of five years, they ceded Port Arthur and the southern half of the island of Sakhalin together with the southern half of the railway they had built in Manchuria. They also recognised Japanese supremacy over Korea, which Japan formally annexed in 1910. In spite of the disappointment of her public opinion, Japan could afford to waive her claim to any indemnity beyond the cost of maintenance of prisoners of war: she had attained her objectives and her moderation paved the way for an improvement in her relations with Russia and an eventual second agreement (1907) for the division of Manchuria into Russian and Japanese spheres of influence. It was the first time that an Asiatic power had proved more than a match for a great European state in a major war. As Paul Cambon foresaw, although the war was confined to the Far East and involved neither France nor England, it was to alter the course of history and 'weigh upon the whole century'.[1]

In the meantime a most important change had been effected in the relations of the allies of Russia and Japan, namely, France and England.

The keys which opened the door to understanding and which explain French policy lay in Morocco, which was virtually an enclave in France's North African dominions and had a long and ill-defined frontier with Algeria. During the reign of an energetic sultan, Muley Hassan, foreign influences had been kept at bay; but after his death in 1894 the Moroccan realm showed signs of disintegration. Afraid that some other great power would seek to profit by its weakness to establish its own influence there and jeopardise the security of Algeria, Delcassé decided that it was urgent for France to obtain recognition of her special interests. Accordingly, having in 1900 secured Italy's blessing, in 1902 he began negotiations with Spain, the other Mediterranean state which by reason of its geographical position was particularly concerned with Moroccan affairs. They failed, however, because Spain was reluctant to act without the consent of the power which held Gibraltar. Meanwhile, however, a rebellion which threatened Morocco with anarchy disposed Lansdowne for the first time to consider an agreement on Morocco with France. For both powers the desirability of a settlement was emphasised by the risk of war in the Far East between France's ally, Russia, and England's new

[1] 'Tu es donc sur le théâtre d'événements qui peuvent changer le cours de l'histoire et qui vont peser sur le siècle entier.' *Correspondance, 1870–1924*, vol. II (Paris, 1940), p. 111.

partner, Japan. When, early in 1903, the breakdown of Delcassé's talks with Spain was closely followed by news that Lansdowne might be ready to negotiate, Cambon reported that Delcassé at last recognised that English support in Morocco must have a price in Egypt or elsewhere.

In the negotiations which opened in August 1902 Delcassé was ably seconded by Paul Cambon, and his task was made easier by the Francophil disposition of Edward VII, who had ascended the throne in January 1901. Furthermore, an exchange of visits by King Edward and President Loubet in 1903 helped to create better feeling between the two countries. But it was not until 8 April 1904 that the comprehensive agreement which was the basis of the subsequent Anglo-French Entente was signed. In the interim there had been much hard bargaining, since the discussions had broadened out to cover the whole range of colonial interests. For England, France's eagerness to secure herself in Morocco afforded an obvious opportunity to obtain France's formal recognition of England's position in Egypt: but both the Moroccan and Egyptian questions had their complexities and the hoary question of the Newfoundland fisheries caused unexpected difficulties, for, in return for the abandonment of their rights on the Treaty Shore, the French demanded territorial as well as financial compensation, and their request first for Gambia and then for an extensive area on the right bank of the Niger prolonged the negotiations for several weeks.

The final agreement took the form of three conventions. By the first France gave up her Newfoundland fishery rights, acquired at the Treaty of Utrecht, in return for the Iles de Los opposite Konakry and a rectification of the frontier between Gambia and Senegambia. The second regulated the condominium exercised by the two powers in the New Hebrides and delimited spheres of influence in Siam. By the third and most important, Britain recognised France's special position in Morocco in return for French recognition of the British position in Egypt. In addition there were certain secret articles, not disclosed until 1911, which provided for the eventuality of an alteration of the status of Egypt or Morocco, and in particular one which secured the interests of Spain should the sultan of Morocco at any time cease to exercise authority. The corollary of this was a fresh Franco-Spanish negotiation resulting in the secret Franco-Spanish convention of 3 October 1904, which defined Spain's sphere of influence and provided for her immediate right of action within it should both parties agree that the *status quo* could no longer be preserved. Thus Delcassé had gained the consent of three powers, Italy, England and Spain, to France's obtaining the lion's share of Morocco when the time proved ripe. But he had omitted to consult Germany, with the consequence that the Anglo-French Agreement, the crowning triumph of his career, was also to prove his downfall, although not the downfall of his policy.

This Agreement of 1904 was a common-sense settlement of outstanding disputes terminating a long period of friction. It reflected the predominantly imperial preoccupations of the Conservative government in England. It envisaged no alliance; and, except in the case of Morocco, it made no provision for future diplomatic co-operation. The very fact that its aims were limited, whereas those of the earlier Anglo-German negotiations were wide and ill-defined, probably helped towards its success. It was a concrete proof of the improvement in Anglo-French relations to which the altered tone of the British and French press already bore witness. The reality of this improvement was soon to be put to the test and to survive triumphant. Out of the trial came genuine *entente*.

Meanwhile other events disposed the two governments to co-operate. The growth of the German fleet led the British authorities in March 1903 to decide upon the creation of a new naval base at Rosyth and to transfer the greater part of their naval forces to home waters. French friendship was therefore desirable because of France's naval power in the Mediterranean, notwithstanding the decline of her general strength at sea since 1902. Both governments, too, were caused anxiety by the Russo-Japanese War and concerned to prevent it from spreading. Thus in October 1904, when the Russian Baltic fleet on its way to the Far East inadvertently fired by night on some Hull fishing vessels causing several casualties, French diplomacy played an important part in inducing the Russians to make prompt reparation. Henceforward the French, acutely aware of the perils of Anglo-Russian friction, were tireless in urging Britain to settle her differences with Russia even as she had settled them with France.

It was Germany who put Anglo-French friendship to its first serious proof. Germany's first reactions to the Anglo-French Agreement had been conciliatory and there had been no special emphasis on German interests in Morocco, but in reality the German Foreign Office was profoundly vexed. In fact Germany's diplomatic position had seriously deteriorated: Italy was no longer a reliable ally, Austria-Hungary was a prey to increasing internal difficulties, and the Franco-Russian Alliance and Anglo-French Agreement now seemed to threaten her with encirclement. The kaiser and his advisers were soon to develop a nightmare of *Einkreisung*. Moreover, they were irritated at not having been consulted. 'Not for material reasons alone', wrote Holstein, 'but even more for the sake of prestige must Germany protest against the intended appropriation of Morocco by France...If we let ourselves be trampled upon in Morocco, we invite similar treatment elsewhere.'[1] The timing of the protest required careful thought, and for some months after the first conciliatory declarations Germany maintained a sphinx-like reserve. It was

---

[1] *Grosse Politik*, vol. xx, pp. 208–9. Cf. G. P. Gooch, *Before the War*, vol. I, p. 247.
'...Lassen wir uns aber jetzt in Marokko stillschweigend auf die Füsse treten, so ermutigen wir zur Wiederholung anderswo.'

not until March 1905 that the world was startled by the kaiser's reluctant visit to Tangier and his resounding references to Germany's determination to protect her 'great and growing interests in Morocco'. The speech was the prelude to a powerful diplomatic offensive against France and the Anglo-French Agreement, accompanied by a violent press campaign.

There is little doubt that the timing and vigour of this apparent *volte-face* in German policy were affected by the Russo-Japanese War. Now that Russia was incapacitated Germany saw a striking opportunity to break the incipient Entente and get rid of Delcassé as Bismarck had got rid of Boulanger. Her desire to bring about Delcassé's fall was increased by Bülow's overriding concern for Germany's interests in the Far East and his fear that Delcassé might be invited to mediate in the war between Russia and Japan. There is evidence, too, that the German Chief of General Staff favoured a preventive war against France, but, although Bülow was ready to use the threat of war and his conduct was a vivid example of the way in which war remained an instrument of national policy, it is not clear that he wished to go farther. Delcassé's offer to negotiate was rejected and Germany demanded an international conference to discuss the Moroccan situation. If the French stood firm there was risk of war; if they yielded, they would also be humiliated. Delcassé urged firmness on the ground that Germany was bluffing and that English support was assured. This was going too far; although England was stirred by the challenge to Anglo-French relations implied by Germany's conduct, all Lansdowne had suggested was 'full and confidential discussion between the two Gov[ernmen]ts...in anticipation of any complications to be apprehended during the somewhat anxious period through which we are at present passing'.[1] Delcassé and his advisers, however, appear to have interpreted this statement in the light of unofficial assurances of military support which they believed to have been given by British service chiefs. But his colleagues placed less reliance on England, knowing that the British navy, her main strength, could not 'run on wheels',[2] and were painfully aware of Germany's military superiority. They rejected Delcassé's risky policy and he resigned on 6 June. Rouvier's offer of a Franco-German agreement was turned down by Bülow, and France was obliged to accept the proposal for a conference. It might now be hoped that France would realise that English support was worthless. When in the next month the kaiser secured a treaty with Russia which seemed to take the sting out of the Franco-Russian Alliance his elation was unbounded, for it looked as though the whole grouping of the European powers was about to be transformed to Germany's advantage. But what he beheld was a mirage.

The kaiser had encouraged the tsar to go to war with Japan, and in 1904, when war broke out, Germany, seeing an opportunity to try and

[1] *British Documents*, vol. III, no. 95.
[2] An expression used by the French Président du Conseil, M. Rouvier.

'mend the wire to St Petersburg', sent a draft treaty of defensive alliance to the Russian capital. Nothing came of it because the tsar felt that he would be bound to consult France if it were proceeded with; but Germany continued her courtship and strained her neutrality by coaling Russian ships, and in the following year in a *tête-à-tête* at Björkö in Finland, the kaiser persuaded the tsar to sign a treaty whereby, if one of the signatories was attacked by a European power, the other would support it in Europe. But the handiwork of the sovereigns was not found to be good in the sight of their absent ministers. Bülow, who thought that the words 'in Europe' made the treaty a liability when England with her vulnerable Indian empire was the enemy in view, actually went so far as to telegraph his resignation (which, however, he was persuaded to withdraw); while Lamsdorff at once declared such an arrangement impossible without reference to Russia's ally France, whom the Germans wanted to bring in only after the *fait accompli*. When the Russians sounded France about the possibility of extending the Franco-Russian Alliance to include Germany, they obtained the expected answer that French opinion would not tolerate a closer relationship. The tsar's consequent letter proposing an additional provision that the treaty should not apply in case of war between France and Germany ended the matter. In an alliance so emasculated Germany could have no interest and so, although never formally abrogated, the Treaty of Björkö was virtually stillborn.

These negotiations affected the development of the Moroccan question. So long as there was a chance of forming the grand continental alliance with France and Russia the Germans had been conciliatory in their demeanour towards the French after Delcassé's resignation. But, once that project failed, the Moroccan question remained the chief card to play against the Anglo-French Entente. The return of a Liberal government in England encouraged Germany to resume an uncompromising tone, and she looked to the international conference she had demanded to give her satisfaction.

Once again, however, she was doomed to disappointment. At the conference which opened at Algeciras on 16 January 1906 she gained only Austrian support on the most contentious issue, namely, the organisation of police in the Moroccan ports. Italy failed to back her, while Russia, urgently in need of a large French loan, stood firmly by France and England. The majority accepted the French view that the police organisation should be entrusted to French and Spanish officers; and the eventual compromise, incorporated in the Algeciras Act of 7 April 1906, whereby, while the sultan was to confide the organisation to French and Spanish officers, a Swiss inspector-general was to be superimposed who would make periodic reports to the Diplomatic Body on the functioning of the new police régime, was but poor consolation. The only advantage Germany had derived was the recognition that Moroccan affairs were a matter of international interest. To this extent France's desired freedom of action was restricted and the recognition meant that Germany could legitimately bring up the Moroccan question again should occasion arise. Apart from this, however, Algeciras was a serious check: Germany's diplomacy had overreached itself and her relative isolation had been publicly exposed; she had failed to obtain any tangible advantage for herself; and, last but not least, she had failed to break the Entente. Indeed the new Foreign Secretary, Grey, attached more importance to the Entente than Lansdowne. Not only had the British government given France their diplomatic support, but they had hinted that, in the event of a German attack upon France, England could not remain neutral. Furthermore, although he had refused to give France a written undertaking of armed support, Grey, without the knowledge of the Cabinet, agreed in January 1906 that staff conversations, already tentatively begun, should take place as a precautionary measure. It was expressly stipulated that these talks should be in no way binding on either government, but the fact that they could occur was of the highest significance and committed the British authorities more than they knew. England had returned unmistakably to her traditional policy of maintaining the European balance of power.

Although the Treaty of Björkö was secret, an indication that something was stirring the waters was conveyed by the Russian soundings in Paris and made a settlement of Anglo-Russian differences all the more desirable. The failure of Germany's schemes for an anti-British continental alliance, Russia's defeat by Japan, her co-operation with the Entente powers at Algeciras, fear of German influence penetrating Persia, and the change of policy favoured by Isvolsky, who became Russian Foreign Minister on 10 May 1906, all facilitated matters, and negotiations were formally opened on 6 June. Their progress was rendered slow by the internal instability of Russia and by public criticism in England of the measures taken to cope with it, by Isvolsky's understandable desire not to offend Germany and suffer the fate of Delcassé, and by the objections of the Russian General Staff; but eventually a convention was signed on 31 August 1907. From the British point of view the agreement, which related to three points of friction, Persia, Afghanistan and Tibet, was satisfactory since the main objectives were secured. Russia's recognition of the principle of Persian independence and integrity and the delimitation of spheres of influence within that country, her acknowledgement that Afghanistan was of special interest to England, and agreement to maintain Tibet as a buffer state under Chinese suzerainty, all appeared to check any further expansion menacing to the safety of India, which was England's paramount concern. Although the Persian problem would still cause the British Foreign Office many headaches, the great Anglo-Russian conflict of interests was virtually liquidated by the agreements.

The Anglo-Russian convention was negative in character: it contained no special assurances of friendship or co-operation and it was not welcomed in either country as the Anglo-French Agreement had been welcomed in England and France. Although it swung Russia slightly nearer to the Entente it did not preclude her from maintaining good relations with Germany; indeed Isvolsky was most anxious to do so and went out of his way to be co-operative, for instance at the ineffective second Hague conference in 1907. Nor, although Grey saw Russia as a counterpoise to Germany, was it part of a deliberate English design to encircle Germany. As has been well said, the two groups stood side by side rather than face to face and it was 'not a question of getting Russia to join England against Germany: it was solely a question of preventing Russia from joining Germany against England'.[1] Unfortunately, however, Germany saw in it an anti-German move, and this impression was strengthened when the tsar and King Edward VII met at Reval in June 1908. Unfortunately, too, the convention had the effect of shifting the main direction of Russia's foreign policy to still more dangerous waters. Checked by Japan in the Far East, prevented from further expansion in the direction of India, she turned once more to the Balkans.

But it was Austrian initiative which led to the first major Balkan crisis of the twentieth century. The Magyarising policy of the Hungarian government and the resentment it caused among their Serb and Croat populations intensified the racial problems of the dual monarchy. The deterioration of Austria's relations with Serbia since the sanguinary overthrow of the Obrenovich dynasty in 1903 and the tendency of the new Serbian rulers to look to France for money and munitions and to Russia for political support and to allow Belgrade to become a centre of Pan-Serb aspirations confronted the rulers of Austria with a foreign problem which was likely to be all the more difficult once Russia resumed an active interest in Balkan politics. So long as the Pole, Goluchowski, remained in charge, Austrian policy was cautious. But his replacement in 1906 by Aehrenthal and the appointment of Conrad von Hötzendorff as Chief of Staff brought to the fore men of more masterful stamp anxious to restore their country's declining prestige. Aehrenthal, who had been Ambassador at St Petersburg, was, like Isvolsky, Bülow and others, an example of the typical continental Foreign Minister trained in the narrow school of diplomacy instead of in politics. As he was reputed to be on excellent terms with the Russians and anxious to reconstitute the Three Emperors' League, his appointment was regarded as an earnest of Austria's desire to maintain friendly relations with Russia. But when his initial attempts at economic conciliation with Serbia broke down, largely owing to opposition at home, he embarked upon a coercive policy which quickly led to

[1] H. Nicolson, op. cit. pp. 234–5.

complications. His announcement early in 1908 of Austria's intention to build a railway to Mitrovitza in Turkey through the Sanjak of Novibazar, which separated Serbia from Montenegro, was intended as a warning to Serbia. But, made regardless of Russia's friendly intimation that complications might ensue, it virtually ended the Austro-Russian co-operation in the Balkans begun in 1897, and inaugurated a period in which the growing personal enmity of Aehrenthal and Isvolsky had the gravest consequences for European relations.

At first Russia made a counter-proposal for a railway from the Danube to the Albanian coast, and the next months might have witnessed no more than a competition in railway projects had not the general situation been transformed by the Young Turk revolution at Constantinople in July. By the Berlin Treaty of 1878 Austria had been accorded the right to administer the Turkish provinces of Bosnia and Herzegovina indefinitely and to garrison the Sanjak of Novibazar. The Young Turk revolution confronted Austria with the probability that the predominantly Serb populations of Bosnia and Herzegovina would demand the right to send representatives to the Turkish Parliament, now proposed, and that Turkey, infused with a new nationalism, would reassert her claim to full sovereignty over two provinces which Austria had in fact governed for thirty years. The grant of such demands was inconceivable for the Austrian rulers and Aehrenthal's remedy, approved by his government in August, was the annexation of the two provinces at a suitable moment, accompanied as a conciliatory gesture to Turkey by the withdrawal of Austrian troops from the Sanjak. 'Annexation', as has been said, 'would both solve the confused relations with Turkey and create an insuperable barrier against the seditious dream of a great South Slav kingdom; Serbo-Croat unrest, with nothing to hope for from Serbia, would be silenced, and the monarchy would now be free to accomplish the mission of economic betterment which thirty years of occupation had left unfulfilled.'[1] For the success of the scheme Russian support was essential, and negotiations to this end culminated in a secret interview between Aehrenthal and Isvolsky at Buchlau on 16 September. As a result Aehrenthal believed that he had secured Russian approval for the projected annexation, in return for Austrian support of a Russian proposal to modify the Straits régime so as to give the warships of the Black Sea powers free access to the Mediterranean.

But the plan miscarried. When Isvolsky went on to Paris and London he encountered difficulties. France was non-committal and England would not agree to his Straits proposals: the Cabinet felt no obligation to support Russia because of the recent Anglo-Russian agreements and was unmoved by Isvolsky's talk of the consequences for Anglo-Russian relations if his demands were not met. Meanwhile Aehrenthal, eager to secure Austria's share of the bargain, had declared the annexation of

[1] A. J. P. Taylor, *The Habsburg Monarchy, 1815–1918* (London, 1941), p. 260.

Bosnia and Herzegovina on 6 October, the day after the prince of Bulgaria, acting in collusion with him, had proclaimed his country's complete independence of Turkey and assumed the title of king. Thus Isvolsky's policy had broken down while Aehrenthal's had triumphed. Isvolsky had aimed at a *coup* in the Straits, a misdirected aim since the Russian people were more easily roused on behalf of the Balkan Slavs than by the old Straits question, but he had to return without this *quid pro quo* of the Buchlau bargain. Much mortified, he sought escape by asserting that he had been duped by Aehrenthal, demanding a European conference to discuss the Bosnian question, and encouraging the Balkan Slav agitation which followed upon the annexation.

Aehrenthal's attempt to solve the Serb problem thus led to a grave crisis which lasted for six months. To most European powers his action came as a shock. Although it made no practical difference to the two provinces, it was, as Grey wrote, the 'arbitrary alteration of a European Treaty by one Power without the consent of the others' and as such 'struck at the roots of all good international order'.[1] In consequence, England condemned the annexation just as she had condemned Russia's denunciation of the Black Sea clauses of the Treaty of Paris in 1870. To Germany the Austrian *fait accompli* was equally unwelcome. Bülow was indignant at not having been consulted beforehand by his ally and the kaiser saw his cherished Turkish policy in jeopardy. Yet Germany could not afford to see Austria weakened, and therefore supported Austria in her refusal of any conference which did not meet merely to confirm the annexation. Since the failure of the Björkö policy and the signature of the Anglo-Russian agreement Germany was all the readier to bolster up Austria by winning a diplomatic victory against Russia.

In the Balkans Austria's action had provoked a ferment: 'Turkey formally protested, and a boycott of Austrian goods began; Montenegro begged for frontier modifications and abolition of the fetters of the Berlin Treaty; in Serbia there was talk of war.'[2] As the rift between Austria and Russia became apparent so the bellicosity of the Serbs, who hoped for Russian aid, increased and Austro-Russian relations drifted into a state of dangerous tension. The decisive factor was the firm support given to Austria by Germany. After Bülow had rejected an offer of mediation by the Western Powers, Austria felt strong enough to demand Serbia's withdrawal of her opposition to the annexation, and when the Serbs complied but refused to give a written promise of future good behaviour she prepared for coercion. All in fact depended on Russia and Germany, for Serbia could not risk war without Russian assistance and Germany was determined to prevent that assistance from being forthcoming. On 22 March 1909 the German Ambassador in St Petersburg was instructed

[1] Viscount Grey, *Twenty-Five Years, 1892–1916* (London, 1925), vol. I, p. 175.
[2] G. P. Gooch, *Before the War*, vol. I, p. 403.

to obtain a definite reply to the question whether Russia accepted the Austrian note and the abrogation of the article of the Treaty of Berlin relating to Bosnia–Herzegovina. 'We should regard an evasive, conditional or ambiguous reply as a refusal. We should then withdraw and let things take their course.'[1] Unready to face another major war so soon after her defeat by Japan, Russia could only submit, whereupon Serbia too climbed down and gave the required guarantee. Turkey had already on 26 February acknowledged the annexation in return for an indemnity of some £2,400,000. Aehrenthal's triumph was complete.

But it boded ill for the future. So far from cowing the Serbs it antagonised them further and made Austria's Slav problem still more difficult. It was a blow to what international morality remained and, above all, a bitter humiliation for Russia, who had been helpless while Serbia was browbeaten and had to accept Austria's annexation of Bosnia and Herzegovina without compensation either in the Straits or elsewhere. In consequence, Germany's dreams of a continental alliance and Austria's visions of a new Three Emperors' League were farther than ever from fulfilment: still more so after the German emperor had rubbed salt into Russia's wounds by declaring that he had supported Austria 'in shining armour'. The Bosnian crisis did what neither the Anglo-Russian convention nor the meeting of sovereigns at Reval had been able to achieve: it created the Triple Entente. Although Russia was disappointed by lack of support from France and England and some British diplomats, aware of this, vainly urged Grey to convert England's *ententes* into alliances, she could not afford to retire into isolation, and co-operation with the Western Powers was the only alternative. Germany's attempt to mend the wire by an offer in 1910 to abandon support of Austria in the Balkans in return for a Russian promise not to help England against Germany came to nothing. Austro-Russian rivalry in the Balkans was again a dominating and dangerous factor in European politics. Moreover, the change in the Balkan balance of power had alarmed Italy, causing her to move still farther away from Austria, against whom Italian irredentist feeling was always strong, and to conclude the secret Treaty of Racconigi (24 October 1909) with Russia, whereby she undertook to support the Balkan *status quo*, should it again be threatened by Austria, in return for Russian recognition of her interests in Tripoli. In reply Austria tried to safeguard her position by promising not to make any new annexation without prior agreement with Rome to give Italy compensation. But, apart from German support, she was now isolated and, in consequence, her influence in the Balkans declined. Bülow had grievously miscalculated. By his unconditional aid to Austria he had committed himself to the support of

---

[1] '...Jede ausweichende verklausulierte oder unklare Antwort würden wir als eine Ablehnung betrachten müssen. Wir würden uns dann zurückziehen und den Dingen ihren Lauf lassen...' (*Grosse Politik*, vol. XXVI, p. 694).

methods and aims of which he disapproved and about which he had not been fully consulted. Furthermore, and still more ominous for the future, there was now a danger that Austria would take fresh risks, firm in the conviction that Germany would be obliged to stand by her. The roles had been reversed and it had been Germany's turn to play the part of 'brilliant second' to Austria. As in the Moroccan affair Bülow had hoped to break the Anglo-French Entente, so now his policy was explicable partly by his avowed desire to break 'the encircling ring'; and, as in 1905–6, it had precisely the opposite effect. The 'ring', hitherto mainly a figment of German imagination, began to assume reality. It was unlikely to dissolve so long as the thunder-clouds hung over the Balkans and the North Sea. Even as Austria's Balkan policy seemed a threat to Russia, so Germany's naval programme seemed an unprovoked menace to England.

Although the early German Naval Bills and jingoistic propaganda of the German Navy League had attracted much attention, the German naval programme did not become a diplomatic issue and a leading factor in Anglo-German relations until 1906. By this time the Moroccan crisis with its risk of war had made the British government aware that friction with Germany would inevitably increase the pace and burden of highly unwelcome competition in naval armaments. The Liberals who assumed office in 1905 were eager to reduce expenditure, and accordingly in 1906, welcoming the Russian invitation to a second Hague conference, they proposed a limitation of armaments. Such a proposal was hardly likely to be acceptable in Germany. By now, as a result of constant propaganda, the majority of the German people had come to believe that a big navy was essential for the maintenance of Germany's interests and prestige as a great power or, as Bethmann-Hollweg put it in 1912, 'for the general purposes of her greatness'. The implementation of the naval programmes was regarded as a fundamental point of policy. It was one of the few aims to which the volatile German emperor remained unflinchingly constant and its modification would probably have required a radical change of men and outlook. Moreover, England's proposals were necessarily suspect, for she now appeared to demand recognition of her naval superiority for all time. The Hague conference of 1907 therefore merely increased distrust. With no hope of international agreement to limit armaments, the only course left was that of direct discussions. Meanwhile the 'dry war' of the armaments race continued, since for Britain naval superiority was a matter of life and death and the pretension of Germany, the strongest military state, to bid for equality at sea was a grave risk to the balance of power.

At first the Germans were unwilling to negotiate, but eventually Bülow, constantly warned by Metternich, the German Ambassador in London, of the strength of English feeling (intensified by the belief, justifiably shared by the British government in the winter of 1908–9, that Germany had been accelerating the building of her ships), considered the possibility of slowing down Germany's naval construction in return for a promise of British neutrality. But Tirpitz's reply to such a suggestion in the spring of 1909 was unpromising—his suggested ratio of 3:4 was hardly likely to be acceptable—and before any overture was made to England Bülow had resigned and was succeeded, in June 1909, by Bethmann-Hollweg. Bethmann-Hollweg, a not very forceful civilian and a newcomer to foreign affairs, was unlikely to make a radical change in policy. He did, however, accept Bülow's notion of securing a political bargain, and negotiations begun in 1909 continued intermittently but fruitlessly until 1912. Bethmann's offer was to retard the German naval programme, not to reduce it, in exchange for British neutrality in case of an attack upon Germany. Such an undertaking would have been difficult for England in view of her commitments to other powers, even if the naval concessions offered had been greater; but her repeated assurance that the treaties and *ententes* she had concluded were not directed against Germany, and her offers to make an agreement on outstanding questions such as the Baghdad Railway, were not considered enough. Grey's proposals for exchanges of naval information also came to nothing and in 1911 negotiations seemed near a deadlock when a fresh Moroccan crisis blew up to imperil European peace and increase Anglo-German mistrust.

The Algeciras Act had not restored order to the Shereefian empire. In 1907 the sultan had been driven from his capital and a state of anarchy ensued which encouraged French penetration. However, in 1909, when both powers were preoccupied by the Bosnian crisis, Germany had come to an agreement with France which disquieted British opinion and seemed to foreshadow a new period of Franco-German co-operation. While both governments undertook that their nationals should be associated in the enterprises for which they obtained concessions, Germany expressed her 'political disinterest' in Morocco. But the economic side of the agreement gave rise to misunderstandings, especially when France proposed to build railways and refused to admit German personnel to run them on the grounds that this trenched upon her political interests. By 1911 relations had deteriorated, while fresh disorders impelled the French to send troops to Fez. The French government had already made overtures to Berlin for a revised agreement when the Germans reopened the Moroccan question with a startling gesture reminiscent of the Tangier incident of 1905. On 1 July a gunboat, the *Panther*, was sent to the closed Moroccan port of Agadir to protect alleged German commercial interests and the world was informed that since, in the German view, the occupation of Fez nullified the Algeciras Act, the time had come for a fresh 'friendly exchange of views'.

There was much to be said for the German argument that a military expedition like the French one to Fez was only too likely to turn into a permanent occupation and that France and Germany must reconsider their Moroccan arrangements; but Germany's manner of proceeding was open to serious criticism although Zimmermann, her Under-Secretary of State for Foreign Affairs, had argued that it was the only way to induce France to offer satisfactory compensation. For some days after the *Panther*'s arrival at Agadir, Kiderlen, now Secretary of State, imitated the sphinx-like silence of Bülow in the first Moroccan crisis and tension was acute. There was much uncertainty as to Germany's ultimate intentions: for instance, as there were no commercial interests in the Agadir region it was believed by many that she intended to demand or seize an Atlantic port. The French Foreign Minister had at first asked the British government to make a counter-demonstration; they refused this but warned Germany that they could not recognise any new arrangement which was come to in Morocco without them. Meanwhile Caillaux, the new Germanophil French Prime Minister, accepted the German suggestion of an 'exchange of views'. The Germans then revealed their hand. In return for recognition of France's complete freedom of action in Morocco they demanded practically the whole French Congo. When the French Cabinet on 17 July rejected their terms it seems that Kiderlen was ready to envisage war or at least to use the threat of it in order to intimidate the French into compliance. In these circumstances the attitude of England (who had on 13 July prudently renewed her alliance with Japan for a further ten years) was of decisive importance. On 21 July Grey told the German Ambassador in London that Germany's demands were excessive and that her action at Agadir still required explanation, and Lloyd George, the Chancellor of the Exchequer, who was believed in Berlin to be the leader of the pro-German section in the Cabinet, declared in a resounding speech at the Mansion House that if Britain were 'to be treated where her interests were vitally affected as of no account... peace at that price would be a humiliation intolerable for a great country to endure'. There was no mention of Germany or the Moroccan question, but the warning was clear, and the indignation of the German government and people showed that they knew that their bluff had been called—courteous assurances about Germany's intentions were speedily sent to London. Peace was preserved, but German prestige had suffered and there followed several weeks of hard bargaining between France and Germany during which there were twice threats of rupture and renewed rumours of war. Finally, a financial panic in Germany in September accelerated a settlement and on 4 November 1911 a fresh Franco-German agreement was signed. While Germany undertook not to impede French activity in Morocco and recognised France's right eventually to establish a protectorate there, France ceded part of the interior of the French Congo pointing towards the Belgian Congo (on which the Germans hoped to obtain a pre-emption) together with a strip of territory giving this new German acquisition access to the sea.

Although Delcassé's policy had triumphed in the end and France was now potentially mistress of Morocco, and although Germany had extended her colonial dominion at small cost to herself, the Agadir crisis left neither side content. In Germany Kiderlen, who had countenanced if not encouraged the public clamour for territorial compensation in Morocco, was strongly criticised, and the Colonial Secretary resigned in protest at the weakness of his policy; while in France the settlement was also attacked by colonial interests, and the discovery that Caillaux had conducted part of the negotiations independently of his Foreign Minister led in January 1912 to the fall of his Cabinet. He had indeed hoped to make the Moroccan question the basis of a general settlement of differences with Germany on the lines of the Anglo-French Agreement of 1904; but the hope was vain, for the methods of German diplomacy and the strong feeling roused in both countries made its realisation impracticable. Instead of bettering relations with Germany, Agadir had demonstrated once again the solidity of France's *entente* with England. In view of the risk of war, staff conversations had been resumed. England had already been making plans for the dispatch of an expeditionary force to France in case of emergency and now discussion of the technical details was pressed on apace. Still more conspicuous was the deterioration of Germany's relations with England, who now knew that for her the dominant questions of international relations were whether she intended to maintain the Triple Entente and whether she 'ought to submit to any dictation by Germany whenever she considers it necessary to raise her voice'.[1]

One further consequence of Agadir remains to be noticed. By opening the way to the French protectorate of Morocco, which was actually established early in 1912, it impelled Italy to move upon Tripoli. Already alarmed by Young Turk nationalism and fearing German competition, Italy believed she must act 'now or never'. On 25 September 1911, without warning, she published a statement of grievances against Turkey, and four days later, having rejected Turkish offers to negotiate, she declared war. The Treaty of Paris of 1856 guaranteeing the independence and territorial integrity of the Ottoman Empire, the Treaty of Berlin of 1878 which had reaffirmed that guarantee, and the Hague conventions to which Italy was a party were flung to the winds. She was determined to leave no time for outside intervention and had not even consulted her allies beforehand. She found her justification in the fact that three great powers, France, Austria and Russia, had all signed agreements giving her a free hand. A further blow had been dealt at international morality, and Italy's conquest and annexation of Tripolitania and Cyrenaica was the signal for the Balkan states to make a concerted attack upon Turkey. The new complications caused by the Balkan wars are part of the immediate prelude to world war.

[1] Sir A. Nicolson to Sir Edward Goschen, 24 July 1911 and to Lord Hardinge, 14 September 1911. Quoted in H. Nicolson, *op. cit.* pp. 347, 350.

CHAPTER VI

THE APPROACH OF THE WAR OF 1914[1]

T HE 'first world war' is a misnomer. Its causes were no more world-wide than its battlefields. The national antagonisms which exploded in it were European, and the alignment of the belligerent powers inside and outside Europe did not correspond to the lines of real cleavage between either the imperial interests of European powers or extra-European national ambitions. As world-wide causes have been assigned to the war, so also have causes comparatively remote in time. In each case the enlargement in retrospect of its true limits above all reflects the magnitude of the experience for contemporaries. But it accords as well with the preoccupations of various doctrinaire schools of international and national politics and history which have helped form popular interpretations of the war. The dogma, for instance, that war at this stage of history must express 'imperialist contradictions'—one not confined to Marxists—required that the war should be treated as global, while the doctrine current in post-war Europe that it was the necessary result of German authoritarian militarism required that the origins of the war should be traced back to the foundation of the second German empire.[2]

Most schools of interpretation, however, accept a distinction between remote and immediate origins of the war of 1914 and to most a dividing line in 1912 makes sense, if not for all the same reasons. Then began the crucial developments in two of the three main causes of the crisis of July 1914, or at least of the final order of battle, the alliance system and Balkan nationalism—the third being Anglo-German naval rivalry. Then, too, as distinct from those European issues, the last cause of conflict overseas had just been extinguished by a Franco-German agreement over Morocco.

The Moroccan convention of November 1911 licensed a French protectorate in exchange for territorial cessions in central Africa, and its critical reception by both French and German nationalists is one measure of its merits. In France, Caillaux's government which made it was replaced by the so-called 'great ministry' of Poincaré which accepted the settlement while appearing less disposed to further appeasement. It was one of Poincaré's first preoccupations to overhaul the Russian alliance, which

---

[1] The editor and author are greatly indebted to Dr A. E. Campbell for abridging the text of this contribution.

[2] The widest range of non-Marxist 'sociological' interpretation is comprehended in George W. F. Hallgarten, *Imperialismus vor 1914: Soziologische Darstellung der deutschen Aussenpolitik* (Munich, 1951; revised ed. 1962).

the Moroccan crisis had shown to be as inadequate a moral support for France as the Bosnian crisis four years earlier had shown it to be for Russia. But the crucial fact was that the Russians met Poincaré more than half way, for it was apparent that the next international crisis would be a Balkan one in which Russia had more to gain than France. The Russians therefore took the diplomatic initiative. The Balkan League developed early in 1912 under Russian patronage but without the co-operation or indeed full awareness of the French; it remained to commit them nevertheless to its risks.

Meanwhile it was in Germany that the Moroccan agreement was producing the most far-reaching repercussions. In the settlement with France Germany had, said Admiral Tirpitz, 'suffered a diplomatic check, and we must salve it by a supplementary naval bill'.[1] As Naval Secretary he gained the support of the Kaiser Wilhelm for this bill, usually known as the *novelle* of 1912, against the opposition of the Chancellor, Bethmann-Hollweg. Though loyal to it in negotiation, Bethmann was unsympathetic to the political strategy behind the German battle-fleet—that it would serve as a deterrent to British intervention in a continental war. Under Tirpitz's original 'risk theory', the German fleet had only to make victory so costly to the British fleet that it would be vulnerable to third powers, but this had become inadequate as the other naval powers, except isolationist America, had become British associates rather than potential enemies. The German fleet had therefore to aim higher—it needed at least a hope of victory—and Tirpitz, with a reasonable confidence in the superiority of German design, was thinking in terms of parity by 1920.[2] The competition in oceanic cruisers was secondary, but it kept for the navy the support of influential colonial and commercial pressure-groups.

British numerical superiority in up-to-date battleships had been sacrificed by the completion of the revolutionary *Dreadnought* in 1908. It was being regained, particularly since the slogan of 'two keels for one' had been accepted by the public and the Admiralty. But this naval competition strained the Liberal government's principles as well as their budgets, and when a forecast of the *novelle* reached London it found them ready to negotiate once more. The visit to Berlin of the supposedly Germanophil Secretary of State for War, Haldane, followed in February 1912. But the Germans asked for concessions over German colonial expansion, and over the continuation of the German Baghdad railway to the British-dominated Persian Gulf; they even asked for a declaration of neutrality. And when the text of the *novelle* was examined in London it was found to involve large increases in personnel, as well as the raising of a fresh battle squadron from some old and some new ships, while all that had been offered was postponement of these last. That

---

[1] Tirpitz, *My Memoirs*, vol. I (English edition, London, 1919), p. 211.
[2] E. L. Woodward, *Great Britain and the German Navy* (Oxford, 1935), p. 316.

was not worth colonial concessions, still less what amounted to the abandonment of the *entente* with France.

The kaiser may have gained a genuine impression that agreement had been reached during his talks with Haldane, although the latter had neither full powers nor full information. He affected indignation at being let down, but negotiations were allowed to drag on in London. The offer of a British declaration of non-aggression proved unacceptable, and Bethmann instructed the German ambassador in London that an agreement 'pledging England's neutrality and nearly amounting to a defensive alliance with us' was the sole condition which would justify the amendment of the *novelle*.[1] This fully endorsed Tirpitz's doctrine of the deterrent function of the German battle-fleet. Moreover, the deterrent had to be recognised by the British; the official tendency in London to treat the German fleet as merely a prestige symbol was resented as insulting.

The British answer to the *novelle* appeared in the Admiralty estimates of 18 July. British additional construction would be nearly double the new German increases, and these rates of building to maintain a ratio of 8:5 in battleships were maintained until the outbreak of war. But Tirpitz, in an inconsistent decision, slowed down building under the *novelle*. The British estimates were adjusted proportionately, and so the impulse was supplied for Churchill's proposal, repeated in 1913, for a 'naval holiday' with no new building for one year on either side. That was the last plan for naval limitation and it was ill-received in Germany as being, for technical reasons, favourable to Britain.

The naval stalemate, however, did not exacerbate relations. The German government still did not recognise that instead of imposing neutrality the uncompromising character of the naval challenge was making neutrality more obviously impossible. The idea of a 'political agreement' with Britain was to persist in German diplomatic strategy until the end. It did so without encouragement from London, but the two remaining themes in the Haldane negotiations, a colonial bargain and a Mesopotamian railway settlement, were more profitably taken up and developed slowly during the next two years into agreements stillborn on the outbreak of war.

The Anglo-German negotiations were alarming to the French and to the committed friends of France.[2] The French therefore exploited the refusal of a neutrality declaration to the Germans with a request for declarations about the Entente. They were helped by the simultaneous development of naval strategy. A reinforcement of the British battle-fleet in home waters from the Mediterranean was carried through, and, although it was formally declared to be unco-ordinated with French naval movements,

---

[1] Bethmann to Metternich, 18 March 1912, *Die Grosse Politik der Europäischen Kabinette, 1871–1914* (Berlin, 1922–7), vol. XXXI, no. 11406.

[2] The British Ambassador in Paris, Bertie, even incited Poincaré against his own government (R. Poincaré, *Au Service de la France*, Paris, 1927–33, vol. I, p. 170).

French battleships were transferred in the reverse direction so that a naval obligation to defend the Channel coast of France began to build up. It was rather to check than to establish this developing strategic link, that Grey decided to give it formal but secret definition in an exchange of letters with the French Ambassador on 16 and 17 November 1912. These expressly stated that the redisposition of the fleets involved no engagement, any more than the military and staff talks—which went back to 1906. But Grey's letter continued by promising consultation in case of an apprehended attack or a general threat to peace from a third power, and then recourse to the joint staff plans if action were decided upon.

This fundamental text of the 'Entente cordiale' was not disclosed outside the British Cabinet until the outbreak of war, except to the Russians earlier in 1914 as a concession to the French wish to formalise the Triple Entente. It was then, too, that British naval staff talks were secretly arranged with the Russians for the same diplomatic reason, though their strategic significance was negligible. Indeed, the independent bond between Russia and Britain was tenuous—the security that it gave to Russia came solely through British obligations or intentions towards France. Direct Anglo-Russian relations were still troubled by Russian political intervention in Persia. The Russians, Sazonov believed, could presume on ultimate British complaisance in Asia for the sake of 'political aims in Europe of vital importance'.[1] But the reverse process was also effective, and friction continued until July 1914.

While the Entente owed its 'triple' character to the two-way relationship of France within it, the rigour of the Franco-Russian alliance attenuated the British obligation to France. As Grey was to insist at the last moment in 1914, Britain was not morally bound to follow France in action imposed on the latter by a treaty such as Britain had deliberately refrained from concluding even with France, much less Russia. All the more was this the case when the French commitment to Russia became extended by the entanglement of Russian policy and prestige with the so-called Balkan League. The basis of the league was the treaty of alliance between Serbia and Bulgaria, signed on 13 March 1912.[2] Its ostensible purpose was to resist Austro-Hungarian expansion, but a secret annexe provided for the partition of Macedonia, the remaining Slav-speaking territories under Turkish rule. The Russians were accessory to the negotiations from the start; they were not merely implicated by the important provision that the tsar should arbitrate between the parties. Their motives were not solely adventurous, nor those of revenge for the diplomatic defeat over Bosnia in 1908–9. Fear of Austria-Hungary re-occupying the Sanjak of

---

[1] B. von Siebert, *Diplomatische Aktenstücke zur Geschichte der Ententepolitik der Vorkriegsjahre* (Berlin, 1921), pp. 205–6.
[2] 29 February, o.s. The texts of all the Balkan League treaties are to be found in the appendices to J. E. Guéchoff, *La Genèse de la guerre mondiale* (Berne, 1919).

Novibazar to keep Montenegro and Serbia apart and to push a projected railway through it all the way to Salonika was a genuine and early motive. Later the temptation of opportunities for Russia in the partition of Turkey came to the fore, although how the leadership of Balkan national ambitions was to bring Russia to the coveted control of Constantinople and the Straits had not been thought out.

The facts of the alliance between the Balkan states were incompletely revealed to their French allies by the Russians, in spite of pressing French enquiries, until Poincaré's visit to Russia in August 1912. When Poincaré did see the text of the secret Serbo-Bulgarian treaty he told Sazonov that 'France would not give Russia military aid over Balkan issues if Germany did not provoke the *casus foederis* of her own initiative, that is if she did not attack Russia'. The reference was to the military convention of 1892, which provided that 'if Russia is attacked by Germany or by Austria supported by Germany, France will employ all the forces at her disposal to fight Germany'. This was the basis of the Dual Alliance ratified in treaty form in 1894. But it had become increasingly obvious since 1908 that the emergency causing Russia to call upon the alliance would be an Austrian attack on a Balkan Slav state, followed by Russian intervention against Austria and in turn German intervention against Russia. Poincaré was in fact implying support in the new circumstances, otherwise the necessary reservation would have been that Russia should not attack Austria first. Reaffirming the alliance obligation without this caution, as Poincaré did in 1912,[1] meant that the defensive character of the alliance had been changed, or alternatively that Austria's Slav neighbours were henceforth included in it. There is little doubt that Poincaré yielded to Russian importunities for fear of losing the whole alliance, which he considered precious to France in its defensive form. That he does not make the point in his memoirs follows from his refusal to admit that the alliance was in fact transformed in Russian interests.

When Poincaré was in St Petersburg a conflict in the Balkans was imminent. Greece had joined Serbia and Bulgaria in a treaty concluded on 29 May, to which Montenegro had committed herself orally, and the whole Balkan League meant to take advantage of the continuing war between Turkey and Italy which had been one of the incentives to its formation and was now stimulating insurrection in Albania and Macedonia.

The Balkan crises tested Austro-German solidarity over the same strategic issues, if not in such a dramatic situation as that of 1914, and the question arises why they did not produce the same fatal result. The common supposition that Germany simply refused support to Austria-Hungary in 1912–13 and accorded it in 1914 misrepresents the course of events. Both Austrian policy and the German response to it were

[1] *Un Livre noir* (Paris, 1922–34), vol. I, p. 323; R. Poincaré, *op. cit.* vol. II, pp. 200 ff., 340 ff.

uncertain. Far from seeking to chastise the Serbs, the Austrian Foreign Minister Berchtold at first took the lead in diplomacy to ward off the crisis. He proposed joint admonitions to the Turkish government in favour of provincial decentralisation and warnings to the Balkan governments to keep the peace. German anxiety at this unilateral action was more an affirmation of the exclusiveness and solidarity of the alliance than the reverse.[1] And ultimately Berchtold's plan, with the added warning that the powers would not license changes in the territorial *status quo*, was accepted, the two most interested powers, Austria and Russia, being charged with acting on behalf of all. This promising concert of Europe had depended above all on Sazonov's revulsion at the apparition of Balkan nationalism which he had so casually invoked. It was both temporary and futile. The powers' joint action coincided with Montenegro's declaration of war on Turkey on 8 October and this was followed by Serbian, Bulgarian and Greek intervention ten days later, all without the Russian licence which the Slav states' mutual engagements contemplated.

The first crucial question which the war brought up was that of the Sanjak of Novibazar, which Austria had occupied until 1909, which was weakly held by the Turks and which the Serbs had to invade in order to join up with the Montenegrins. This challenge to Austrian prestige and strategic control Berchtold declined in advance, counting on later re-establishment of the *status quo*[2] but against the general staff's advice. No guarantee from Germany against Russian intervention if the Serbs were to be ejected was asked for, and that in spite of some evidence that it would have been given if asked.[3]

The main reason for the attachment of all the great powers to the *status quo* in the first diplomatic phase of the Balkan crisis was uncertainty as to who would win in a shooting war. The first few days of hostilities removed all doubts. The Bulgars drove through Thrace towards the Straits, and were just forestalled in Salonika by the Greeks. Meanwhile the Serbs reached the Adriatic. The Bulgars were stopped by Turkish resistance outside Constantinople, but their advance was unwelcome to the Russians. The Serbian successes threatened only the Austrians. At this point, therefore, Russian official policy and Panslav sentiment began to coalesce in sponsorship of the Serbs, while in Vienna an old idea was revived of building up Bulgaria as the rival Balkan nation in disgrace with St Petersburg.

Recent historians have entertained perhaps too easily the possibility for Austria of a reconciliation with the Serbs.[4] There was indeed a

---

[1] Kiderlen to Bethmann-Hollweg, 2 September 1912. *Die Grosse Politik*, vol. xxxiii, no. 12,135.

[2] L. Albertini, *The Origins of the War of 1914* (Eng. ed. I. M. Massey, London, 1952–7), vol. I, p. 387.

[3] *Oesterreich-Ungarns Aussenpolitik, 1908–1914* (Vienna, 1930), vol. IV, no. 4,022.

[4] For example, E. Eyck, *Das persönliche Regiment Wilhelms II* (Zürich, 1948), p. 643; Albertini, *op. cit.* vol. I, pp. 394–5; A. J. P. Taylor, *The Struggle for Mastery in Europe*, p. 491.

'trialist' school of thought which favoured equalising the status of the Slavs inside the empire with that of the Germans and Magyars. Such a move the Serbian government were believed to be ready to welcome if only Austria would tolerate their acquisition of an Adriatic port.[1] But, although overtures were made in the autumn of 1912 and again a year later, their sincerity must be suspect considering the secret influence in Serbia of nationalist extremists who had no use for compromise.

In their determination to keep the Serbs away from the Adriatic, the Austrians used the principle of nationality in persuading the powers to create the state of Albania. This block of non-Slav people, formerly under Turkish rule, covered the whole coastline from Montenegro to Greece but the Russian government pressed the Serb case for a free port on the coast, in particular Durazzo, if not a corridor to it as well. Tension between the two great powers rose to the pitch of reinforcing covering troops on both sides of the Galician frontier, a mutual demonstration which was to last for months. There was no demand from Vienna nor refusal from Berlin of support for intervention against the Serbs who had overrun part of Albania: sufficient German encouragement to maintain the war of nerves was gratuitous. The kaiser's utterances were, as usual, both inconsistent and emphatic. But Bethmann declared in a Reichstag speech on 2 December that 'if Austria in the course of securing her vital interests ...is attacked by Russia' Germany would fight.[2]

The Russian sponsorship of Serbian claims, however, was largely bluff. As early as 9 November the Serbs had been warned not to count on Russian support.[3] But Panslav feeling was running high in Russia, with militant devotees among the grand dukes and the general staff, so the Serb cause could not be brusquely abandoned. As it was, the suspicion of Russian apathy disconcerted Poincaré, and he complained to Isvolsky that Austrian military preparations were not being adequately countered.[4] Behind this seems to have been a conviction that Europe was near war, and that if Russia was not ready to draw off German as well as Austrian forces France would have to bear the brunt. Implicit, surely, was the new interpretation of the *casus foederis* for France which Poincaré had given in St Petersburg and Isvolsky maintained that he had since confirmed.[5]

The victorious Balkan allies and the defeated Turks concluded an armistice on 3 December and a peace conference opened in London. At the same time a conference of ambassadors of the great powers was formed there to supervise a Balkan and Aegean settlement. It immediately agreed on the status of Albania and the exclusion of the Serbs from the Adriatic—a decision followed by the Austrian renunciation of Novibazar.

---

[1] *Oesterreich-Ungarns Aussenpolitik*, vol. v, no. 5,005.
[2] Eyck, *Das persönliche Regiment Wilhelms II*, p. 639.
[3] Siebert, *Diplomatische Aktenstücke zur Geschichte der Ententepolitik*, p. 577.
[4] *Un Livre noir*, vol. I, p. 369. [5] *Ibid.* p. 326.

This conference reflected the disposition of the great powers to agree, and the issues between them were not directly affected by the break-up of the Balkan peace conference or by the resumption of the conflict as the so-called 'Second Balkan War'. What mattered was the incompatibility of Serbian victory and expansion with the prestige and therefore security of the Habsburg empire, and so, after the creation of Albania, the question of its future frontiers now overrun by the Serbs and Montenegrins became crucial between the Austrian and Russian governments. Where Austria-Hungary must stand and risk a general war Berchtold had certainly not decided in advance but the German Chancellor complained on 10 February that he was being kept in the dark. Indeed, at this time both Bethmann and Moltke were working to moderate Austrian policy.[1] Bethmann observed prophetically that it was 'almost impossible for Russia to look on inactive in case of a military operation by Austria-Hungary against Serbia'. It was not until six weeks later that the ambassadors' conference registered an Austrian concession over the disputed frontier villages of Dibra and Djakova, but relaxation of tension meanwhile between Vienna and St Petersburg and the stand-down of troops in Galicia are attributable to the German attitude.

That the Germans were blowing hot and cold was, however, shown in the Scutari crisis which followed in April 1913. That town, still held by the Turks and allotted by the powers to the new Albania, was invested in turn by the Serbs, who retired on Russian instructions, and by the Montenegrins under their king Nicholas (Nikita), who did not. A warning from the Austrian government that if the London powers did not jointly secure Nikita's withdrawal they would take independent military action was not discouraged in Berlin, and the Germans warned the French explicitly that if Russia intervened Germany would fight. Meanwhile Sazonov's actions had been at least as pacific as were Bethmann's in the preceding crisis, and he had admonished the Montenegrins for their 'passionate and foolish attitude', in opposition to the 'supreme interests of European peace'.[2] But no one believed that Panslav sentiment would allow Russia to abandon the Montenegrins, and the apparent danger of war was only averted by King Nikita's sudden submission. He is said to have gambled on the Vienna bourse over the crisis so that he could take his profit on ending it.

The Scutari episode held lessons. By the vicious conventions of twentieth-century politics and publicity the evacuation of Scutari without Austrian military action was to be regarded as a humiliation for the empire. So domestic criticism of Berchtold as a weak Russophil disposed him to more desperate courses, even if this was not immediately apparent. After the settlement of the Scutari problem the Balkan belligerents were

[1] *Die Grosse Politik*, vol. XXXIV (i), nos. 12,818, 12,824.
[2] Albertini, *The Origins of the War of 1914*, vol. I, p. 446.

brought back to London to negotiate, and their delegates finally signed the Treaty of London on 30 May. This reduced European Turkey to a bare hinterland of Constantinople and the Straits, the exact demarcation of the Greek and Bulgarian shores of the Aegean coast being entrusted to the great powers as was the disposition of the Aegean islands, while the partition of Macedonia was left to Serbia and Bulgaria to negotiate.

It was when these two states fell out that Berchtold returned to the plan of building up Bulgaria so as to encircle Serbia. Such an idea was unpopular in Berlin, above all because Rumania, the nominal satellite of the Triple Alliance, was also a rival of Bulgaria. Yet, in spite of her Hohenzollern King Carol, Rumania could not in the long run be held to the alliance. The intelligentsia were Francophil and the nationalist public of all classes saw their enemy in Hungary with its minority of a million or more Rumanians in the province of Transylvania. This the Germans failed to appreciate. After the ill-judged Bulgarian surprise attack on the Serbs and Greeks they maintained their objections to Austrian intervention to save the aggressor. It was expected, even by the bellicose Austrian chief of staff, General Conrad von Hoetzendorff, that Austrian action would bring in Russia, and it is doubtful how far Berchtold's warlike plans represented serious intentions. But, when Greece, Turkey and finally Rumania joined Serbia, the Germans disavowed their ally's policy by publicly approving the Treaty of Bucharest of 11 August 1913 and trying to incite the press to work for Berchtold's removal.[1] Nor was this all. This treaty and the Treaty of London left over certain questions for decision by the powers, and when the aspirations of Bulgaria and Greece conflicted the kaiser placed Germany in the opposite camp to the Austrians.[2] The latter found themselves in the same side as the Russians, whose immediate concern was to stop the Greeks from creeping up the coast towards Constantinople.

It was not until the autumn of 1913 that Berchtold won his first clear-cut diplomatic victory over the Serbs with German support. The Serbs were slow in withdrawing troops from northern Albania and indiscreetly avowed their hope of obtaining a frontier rectification. Cumulative warnings from Vienna were inadequate and were disregarded before the ultimatum of 18 October, which gave the Serbs a week to retire. The Germans were only informed of the note at the last moment (and the Italians after its dispatch). But the kaiser was enthusiastic. He even deprecated a peaceful solution, pointing out to General Conrad, 'The other [powers] are not prepared.'[3] This was true, since the last Austrian warning before the ultimatum had caused both Sazonov and the French to tell

---

[1] *Die Grosse Politik*, vol. xxxvi(i), no. 13,781, where the kaiser declared this aim.
[2] Wilhelm's philhellenic sympathies and his personal dislike of the king of Bulgaria worked in the same direction.
[3] Conrad von Hoetzendorff, *Aus meiner Dienstzeit* (Vienna, 1922–5), vol. iii, p. 470.

the Serbs to back down. The Serbs did so at once, but most striking about the success of Berchtold's undertaking was the appeal of the virtual *fait accompli* to the German government, in particular to the kaiser. It was as if consultation was really unwelcome, as if the principle was being established that Austria was responsible, morally and strategically, for her own Balkan policy and Germany only for its consequences.

The truth was that, apart from such an opportunist support of Austria-Hungary in a preventive war against 'Slavdom and Gaul', which the kaiser regarded as inevitable, no official German political strategy and certainly no clear war aims existed.[1] The kaiser was too volatile and yet fundamentally too conservative a European. Characteristic was his dictum that 'the true interests of Europe can be defended by the two main powers in the [two] groups, standing shoulder to shoulder, namely Germany and England'.[2] In world politics the 'yellow peril' interested him more than competition with Britain and he scoffed at what he called the 'crazy vision of an African colonial empire'.[3] Nor was the *Drang nach Osten*, the 'urge to the East', supposedly revealed in the Baghdad railway, by any means a dominant official preoccupation. German policy during the Balkan wars had not been appreciably affected by the German association with the equipment and training of the Turkish army since the 1880s, nor by the exploitation of this for diplomatic prestige in Turkey by Marschall von Bieberstein. The railway project was held up by booming Germany's shortage of liquid capital; military patronage was distinct, often competitive and not wholehearted because no one knew until after the outbreak of war in 1914 which great power camp the Turks would join.[4]

Not only Germany's but the other great powers' commitments in the decrepit Turkish empire were tested at the end of 1913. A new and large German military mission was invited to Turkey to rehabilitate the army once again. The news that a German general, Liman von Sanders, was to command the Constantinople army corps, as well as lead the mission, came in November as a shock to the Russians—perhaps a calculated one. In St Petersburg it seemed time to consider again the ultimate issues of war and peace in the question of the Straits. By January Sazonov was prepared to face general European complications in order to induce the Turks to drop Liman, and he proposed the occupation by all three *entente*

---

[1] The question of war aims (and by implication 'war guilt') has recently been revived by F. Fischer, *Griff nach der Weltmacht* (Dusseldorf, 1961) and in subsequent controversy, especially the same author's article, 'Weltpolitik, Weltmachtstreben und deutsche Kriegsziele' in the *Historische Zeitschrift*, vol. 199 (October 1964). His basis is the formulation of aims in the first month of war, the rest is largely retropolation, the association of politicians and officials with pre-war strategic and commercial collision courses which war-time peace aims expressed. The mapping of these courses by Hallgarten (*op. cit.* p. 329) is, however, filled in by Fischer's study of the Potsdam archives. A recent (1967) presentation of the controversy is in E. Lynar, *Deutsche Kriegziele 1914–1918*.

[2] *Die Grosse Politik*, vol. xxxvi(i), no. 13,781.   [3] *Ibid.* vol. xxxi, no. 11,422.

[4] Fischer, *H. Z.*, vol. 199 (see note 1 above).

powers of selected points in Asia Minor.[1] But it was already obvious that he could not count on such co-operation. The French had been prepared to protest to the Turkish government against 'handing the keys of the Straits' to the Germans,[2] but the British could not even go so far as that when they realised that their own adviser to the Turkish navy, Admiral Limpus, held an equivalent naval command to Liman's military one. In any case they feared an accommodation at their expense between St Petersburg and Berlin as more likely than a war.[3] But the immediate interest of Germany in a partition was overestimated in London. The Germans had designs on Turkish territory but were not ready for annexation. They wished, more than the Russians, to postpone the moment of partition.[4]

In the event a conciliatory solution was found in Berlin by promoting Liman to a rank which put him above a corps commander in Turkey and thus left him as adviser only. This concession overtook a ministerial conference at St Petersburg in January which was devoted to the emergency. There the Minister for War, Sukhomlinov, claimed that Russia was 'perfectly ready for a duel with Germany' if necessary, although the general staff was counting, with Sazonov, on French and possibly even on British support. The conclusion of the conference against risking war without *both* 'entente' partners deferred to the opposition of the premier, Kokovtsov—but Kokovtsov was about to leave office because of his incompatibility with the court régime.

The Liman episode had two serious consequences affecting the balance of war and peace six months later. There was a reappraisal of Russian strategy and armaments, and there was the emergence of a new and ominous ill-feeling in Russo-German public relations. Second thoughts made the Russian general staff conclude that an offensive in the Straits would have been impracticable, and led to fresh appropriations for the Black Sea fleet, the retention of conscripts with the colours and vigorous publicity for rearmament.[5] This was taken as provocation by German official and public opinion and set off a newspaper war probably stimulated by both governments. Soon the Allies, Austria-Hungary, and to a lesser degree France, were drawn into a 'controversy which could hardly be more embittered', as the British Ambassador wrote from Vienna, 'if a war were on the point of breaking out'.[6]

[1] Memorandum of 6 January summarised in *Der grossen Katastrophe entgegen* (Berlin, 1929) by Baron M. Taube (who was Sazonov's assistant), p 291.
[2] *Documents diplomatiques français, 1871–1914*, 3ème série, vol. VIII, no. 544. The French documents do not support the contention of E. Brandenburg (*From Bismarck to the World War*, Oxford, 1927, p. 461) and other German apologists that France was encouraging Russian belligerency (*ibid.* vol. VIII, nos. 598, 689, 694).
[3] *British Documents on the Origins of the War, 1898–1914* (London, 1926–38), vol. X (i), no. 180.
[4] Jagow to the German Ambassador in Constantinople in July 1913 (Brandenburg, p. 459).
[5] M. N. Pokrovskii, *Drei Konferenzen zu Vrorgeschichte des Krieges* (Berlin, 1920), pp. 66–7.
[6] *British Documents on the Origins of the War, 1898–1914*, vol. X (ii), no. 526.

The newspaper campaign in Russia linked Russian preparedness with admonitions to France. Russian public and official opinion was particularly anxious for the maintenance in France of the new law for three years' military service. The law had been passed in the spring of 1913, virtually simultaneously with the last great army expansion in Germany. Neither measure seems to have been definitely provoked by the other, but in each case the opportune competition reduced domestic criticism. Three years' service in France was the only way of making up for Germany's 50 per cent advantage in population and its higher birth-rate. The parties of the left were against it, but the premier in 1914, Viviani, had promised Poincaré to leave the law intact. Such a party compromise reflected the deeper tension in French than in Russian relations with Germany, even if the French press was more discreet. Exhibitions of German militarism, especially in Alsace or Lorraine, were given ominous importance. In both France and Germany parties of the left deplored the tension and an inter-parliamentary conference met at Berne in 1913 as a demonstration against nationalist alignments. Events proved its superficiality as well as frustrating its second annual meeting.

Britain was not remote from these agitations. The alarms in Russia led to pressure on Britain to tighten its links in the Triple Entente. The British royal visit to Paris in April stimulated French advocacy of the Russian plea and Grey gave way to the extent of linking the communication to the Russian ambassador of the Anglo-French agreement of 1912 with a move towards Anglo-Russian naval staff talks. The Germans got wind of this and were barely placated by Grey's prevaricatory answer to a parliamentary question to the effect that no agreements existed which would hamper Britain's free choice whether to wage war or not. They knew the facts, or an optimistic Russian interpretation of them, from purloined Russian documents.[1] Meanwhile the direct Anglo-German negotiations on extra-European issues, to which Berlin had probably attached too general a political significance, approached their conclusion. By the end of July no obstacle remained to the signature of the agreement for the hypothetical partition of the colonies of Britain's Portuguese ally. On 27 July the kaiser authorised the signature of the Baghdad railway treaty which exchanged British control of the Persian Gulf shipping for German control of the line to the Basra railhead. Linked with this treaty, and at least equally significant, had been a series of semi-private, semi-governmental tripartite negotiations in which the Turks shared, over oil and shipping interests—which were producing the incongruous result of the two rival imperial navies relying on the same local source of fuel.

The diplomatic stabilisation in the Near East and Africa—with its Far

---

[1] *British Documents on the Origins of the War, 1898–1914*, vol. x(ii), no. 548. E. Zechlin, *Hist. Zeitschrift*, vol. 199 (1964), suggests that the effect of this incident in Anglo-German relations was far-reaching; see especially p. 352, footnote 2.

Eastern parallel in the partition between Russia and Japan of claims on China beyond the wall—had no bearing on European antagonisms unless to free the protagonists entirely from other preoccupations. Contemporaries were in little doubt about the two crucial European factors: first the ripeness of the Habsburg empire for dissolution—or its converse the expansive force of Yugoslavism—and second the preponderance of the German army for good or ill. Jagow, the German Secretary of State, compared the prospects of Austria and Turkey in terms of 'a race between the two empires, which goes to pieces first' and deplored the lack of imperial sense among German Austrians.[1] Tschirschky, in Vienna, foresaw the latter joining Germany as the result of an eventual partition, and asked 'whether it really pays us to bind ourselves so tightly to this phantom of a state'.[2] Yet the Germans had little patience for the symptoms or the fancy remedies of the dying empire. They regarded the coming threat of the union of Serbia and Montenegro as irresistible, they deprecated a connection with Bulgaria and they continued to urge the conciliation of Rumania until that country's final defection was manifested by a Russian imperial visit in June 1914.[3]

That German military dominance obstructed the natural course of Slav liberation was not the sole grudge against it even of Russia. It was intolerable in itself. Sazonov's words are revealing. 'To feel the stronger and yet to give way to an opponent whose superiority consists solely in his organisation and discipline' was 'humiliating' and led to 'demoralisation'.[4] It was not known how unsystematic and—to give it its due—negative German foreign policy was behind its weapons. Alarmists could point to the domestic and foreign best-seller, *Germany and the Next War*, by the military publicist General Bernhardi, which demanded a final subjugation of France and revived Treitschke's aspersions on the 'unseemliness' (*Unsittlichkeit*) of world peace. And in fact, though not to public knowledge, these views sometimes echoed in the kaiser's mind, with a possible influence in official quarters, as when he wrote in 1912 of the 'eunuch-like' tendency to 'emphasise world peace'.[5] The temper of Europe was described in famous words by Colonel House, the American president's personal envoy on a peace-making mission whose very existence was significant enough. 'The situation is extraordinary. It is militarism run stark mad. Unless someone acting for you can bring about a different understanding there is some day to be an awful cataclysm. There is too much hatred, too many jealousies.' There was also, in spite of the German army, too much incompatible confidence among the general staffs—that built-in error of generals promoted for their leadership, not in counsel

---

[1] *British Documents on the Origins of the War, 1898–1914.* vol x (ii), no. 532.
[2] *Die Grosse Politik*, vol. xxxix, no. 15,734.
[3] *Oesterreich-Ungarns Aussenpolitik*, vol. viii, 9,902.
[4] *Mezhdunarodnye Otnosheniya v Epokhu Imperializma*, series iii (1931), vol. i, no. 289.
[5] *Die Grosse Politik*, vol. xxxiii, no. 12,225.

but in battle (or manœuvres) where euphoria is an indispensable virtue. They were not interested in deterrents but in victories.

While the tsar was driving in an outpost of the Triple Alliance on his visit to the king of Rumania, the kaiser was conferring with the Archduke Francis Ferdinand on Austro-Hungarian and Balkan problems at the latter's residence in Bohemia. Barely a fortnight later these issues were given a tragic twist by the assassination on 28 June of the archduke and his morganatic wife by a Bosnian Serb of Austro-Hungarian nationality, Gavrilo Princip. The murder was planned from Belgrade by the Serbian secret society *Crna Ruka* (the Black Hand) because Francis Ferdinand stood for Habsburg federalism and this threatened the establishment of a greater Yugoslavia. The young assassins declared this motive at their trial as a private one,[1] and the Austro-Hungarian government did not realise the scope of the organisation behind them. Still less did they know that its leader was Dimitriević, *alias* Apis, and that he was simultaneously head of the Black Hand and of military intelligence at the Serbian war office. Although Apis and his agents were in the Russians' pay it is highly improbable that this particular operation was helped by them or known at any level.[2] The case against the Serbian government rested upon the general licence, indeed encouragement, given to irredentist nationalism and the alleged supply of arms to terrorists by Serbian officials in the *Narodna Odbrana* (National Defence), an open patriotic association which the Austrians confused with the secret Black Hand. Austrian police intelligence was in fact as poor as their police precautions and the failure of these must be held to weaken their case against the Serbs. What remains uncertain is how much the Pašić government in Serbia knew of the Black Hand's plans and, if complicit, whether they were acquiescent or intimidated. It is fairly certain that they warned Vienna but too cautiously to be heeded.

The problem of war and peace set by the Sarajevo murder did not differ essentially from the emergencies in previous years when the Austro-Hungarian government had forgone the temptation of a *casus belli* against the South Slavs because of the risk of Russian intervention and the uncertainty of German counter-support. General Conrad thought the opportunity less favourable than earlier ones, while resolving that it must not be missed.[3] The gamble appealed to the court's and the bureaucracy's mood of studied desperation. By 1 July official opinion in favour of war was general enough for Tisza to protest to the emperor, after a ministerial council at which he was the sole dissentient, against the 'fatal blunder',[4] as he saw it, of using Berchtold's inadequate *casus belli*. But this time

[1] A. Mousset, *Un Drame historique, l'attentat de Sarajevo* (Paris, 1930) (text of interrogations), p. 151.
[2] N. P. Poletika, *Vozniknovenie pervoi mirovoi voiny* (Moscow, 1964), pp. 236–40.
[3] Conrad, *Aus meiner Dienstzeit*, vol. IV, p. 72.
[4] *Oesterreich-Ungarns Aussenpolitik*, vol. VIII, no. 9,978.

there was to be no mistake about German co-operation. A special mission was sent off to Berlin to sound out the senior partner in the Triple Alliance.

The message to the German kaiser which Count Hoyos presented on 5 July consisted of a letter from Francis Joseph covering a general memorandum on Austrian Balkan policy. This re-stated the Austrian plan of winning over Bulgaria as an ally against Serbia and a check upon the defection of Rumania, and warned that it was against Germany that Russian intrusion in the Balkans was really aimed. Neither document explicitly proposed immediate action, still less did they contain a plan for this, but the letter declared that future policy must be based on the 'isolation and reduction of Serbia'[1] and counted on the kaiser's agreeing that the 'focus of criminal agitation in Belgrade must not survive unpunished'.

Hoyos and the Austro-Hungarian Ambassador Szögyény found the kaiser in a receptive frame of mind, indignant at an act of regicide whose victim was a personal friend, yet impatient to dispose of urgent business so that he could leave the next day for his annual cruise with the German fleet. He hastened to give his concurrence in Austrian intentions subject to the formality of consultation with the Imperial Chancellor. Szögyény was able to telegraph at once that German support was promised even if it should come to war with Russia and that if the Ballplatz saw the 'necessity of military action against Serbia' the kaiser would regret to see them miss 'the present favourable moment'.[2] Before joining his yacht on 6 July the kaiser conferred briefly with representatives of the army and navy staffs—Moltke and Tirpitz were away. He warned them of the possible contingency of war with Russia and consequently with France as well, but he did not think Russia was 'ready to fight' and he did not apparently discuss Great Britain's position at all.

Consultation between the kaiser and the Imperial Chancellor, who arrived in Potsdam after the Austrians, was equally perfunctory; historians have long ago dissolved the myth of a full dress 'crown council' approving a war plan.[3] The result, according to Szögyény, was a confirmation of his master's undertakings by the Chancellor, in whose opinion, likewise, the present moment was most favourable for 'immediate action' [Einschreiten] against Serbia as the most radical and best solution.[4] The difference between his report of the Chancellor's assurances and Bethmann-Hollweg's own account in telegraphing to Tschirschky does not lead very far. Bethmann-Hollweg's telegram recorded the kaiser's agreement with the general Balkan policy proposed by Vienna—in which, as regards Bulgaria and Rumania, the Germans proceeded to co-operate—and added that as regards the 'questions at issue with Serbia' the kaiser 'would take up no

---

[1] Oesterreich-Ungarns Aussenpolitik, vol. VIII, no. 9,984.   [2] Ibid. no. 10,058.
[3] S. B. Fay, The Coming of the World War (1936 ed.), vol. II, p. 181.
[4] Oesterreich-Ungarns Aussenpolitik, vol. VIII, no. 10,076.

position since they extended outside his competence'.[1] But he would 'stand loyally on the side of Austria-Hungary'.

The claim on behalf of Bethmann that this lack of explicitness implied reservations has to contend with the fact that no positive hint, even in favour of moderation, was given to Vienna until nearly three weeks later, when the scope of diplomacy to prevent the outbreak of war was being narrowed by military policy solely concerned with its most advantageous timing. Meanwhile Tschirschky's interpretation of his instructions, pressing upon Germany's ally both a free hand and an unconditional guarantee, was continuously encouraged. In this neither the Chancellor nor the kaiser was deliberately picking a quarrel among the great powers: rather they were approving a supposedly unequal contest between one great and one minor power which they calculated could be localised. As to the consequences of miscalculation they showed themselves recklessly indifferent. The alignment of their potential enemies received no serious political and strategic appreciation. The charge of 'imposing' war, attributed to Germany in the Versailles treaty, was therefore misconceived. It was levity rather than a grand design which produced the fatal commitment. Where deliberation entered was in treating the commitment to Austria as more rigid than it necessarily was, and in making a virtue of preventive war against Russia and France out of the arguable necessity of ensuring an Austrian political victory over Serbia.

Armed with the encouraging German response, Berchtold obtained from a ministerial council on 7 July a decision in favour of provoking the Serbs to war in preference to exacting their diplomatic humiliation.[2] He argued that the Germans would see any sort of bargain as a 'confession of weakness which could not fail to react on our position in the Triple Alliance and the future policy of Germany'. This view was strengthened by Szögyény's reports of Berlin's impatience and of the opinion prevailing there that Russia was preparing for a future aggressive war, but was not yet ready for a defensive one.

Meanwhile a plan of action was taking shape. Tschirschky could report to Berlin on 10 July that a 48-hour ultimatum was to be delivered in Belgrade and that it would be for Berchtold a 'very disagreeable' solution if it were accepted.[3] But the Germans refused to help formulate the demands. They rejected responsibility for the form of the diplomatic operation while accepting its consequences. What the Germans did want was to speed up Austrian preparations, while foreign apprehensions were lulled by such deceptions as keeping both countries' chiefs of staff on leave. The Austrian timing of the ultimatum for 23 July was explained to Berlin as necessitated by the state visit to St Petersburg of Poincaré and Viviani

[1] *Die deutschen Dokumente zum Kriegsausbruch* (Charlottenburg, 1919), vol. I, no. 15.
[2] *Oesterreich-Ungarns Aussenpolitik*, vol. VIII, no. 10,118.
[3] *Die deutschen Dokumente zum Kriegsausbruch*, vol. I, no. 29.

between the 16th and 22nd of the month. It was better to wait till the French had gone home. But to Conrad Berchtold explained the delay by the need of getting in the harvest before mobilising, and by the process of investigation into the murder, as well as by the diplomatic problem.[1] The preparation of the case against Serbia was not plain sailing; the investigator sent to Sarajevo by the Ministry of Foreign Affairs could report no proof of even indirect responsibility, still less official complicity.[2] Nevertheless the terms of an ultimatum were drafted by 19 July and approved by a ministerial council and by the emperor, so that the text could be sent off on the following day, for communication to the powers after delivery of the note in Belgrade in the evening of 23 July. Its tenor had, of course, been known in Berlin for several days, but the Germans' interest in foreknowledge of the actual text seems to have been only in order to prepare the press.[3] The Secretary of State, Jagow, claimed that he criticised its severity to the Austrian Ambassador, but twenty-four hours after its receipt he was telegraphing to the major German embassies that he had no knowledge of its contents.[4] It was the predetermined German policy to turn a blind eye to the terms of the ultimatum.

The degree of collusion up to this stage between the two central powers is registered by a report from Schoen, the Bavarian representative in Berlin, on an interview with the Under-Secretary of State, Zimmermann, which he sent to Munich on 18 July. Schoen predicted the terms of the Austrian ultimatum, recorded the complete full powers (*Blankovollmacht*) given to Austria, and explained how the Germans, when giving immediate diplomatic support to the Austrian case, 'will claim to be as much surprised by the Austrian action as the other powers'.[5] Germany wanted the conflict localised, and hoped that Russian opposition might be no more than bluff, and that France and Britain might urge prudence in St Petersburg, but Schoen's information showed that even British neutrality was not expected if the balance of power appeared to be jeopardised by a threat to the existence of France. A still more authoritative explanation of the motives of German policy was given in a private letter from Jagow to Lichnowsky, who had been criticising from London the submission of German policy to Austrian interests. Arguing that Austria, Germany's only available ally, needed to chasten Serbia if she was to achieve 'political rehabilitation' and if 'the stabilisation of Russian hegemony in the Balkans', which he described as 'inadmissible', was to be averted, Jagow

[1] Conrad, *Aus meiner Dienstzeit*, vol. IV, p. 72.
[2] *Oesterreich-Ungarns Aussenpolitik*, vol. VIII, no. 10,252.
[3] *Die deutschen Dokumente zum Kriegsausbruch*, vol. I, no. 83.
[4] Jagow, *Ursachen des Weltkriegs*, p. 110. Bethmann-Hollweg also recollected his and Jagow's misgivings (*Betrachtungen zum Weltkriege*, vol. I, p. 139). These vital facts were in effect misrepresented by no less a scholar than Gerhard Ritter (*Staatskurst und Kriegshandwerk*, vol. II, p. 312) (who even got his dates wrong).
[5] *Die deutschen Dokumente zum Kriegsausbruch*, vol. IV, Anhang IV.

expressed hopes of localising the conflict. But, although he did not want a 'preventive war', it was a better moment for a show-down with Russia than it would be a few years hence. 'Then she [Russia] will overwhelm us with the number of her soldiers, then she will have built her Baltic fleet and her strategic railways. Meanwhile our group will become weaker all the time.'[1]

This was the Austro-German commitment at the beginning of the fourth week of July. Was it to any degree induced or confirmed by faults of commission or omission on what became the other side? Apologists for the central powers, while shuffling direct responsibility between Berlin and Vienna, have found it extenuated by a provocative attitude on the part of Belgrade, by the challenging consolidation of their front by the French and Russians, and by a misleading posture of neutrality on the part of Great Britain. There is some historical significance in all these charges, whatever their polemical bearing. Contemporary reporting from Serbia was partisan, but left no doubt that public opinion was excited; indeed an exchange of abuse with Austria had started in the press directly after the Sarajevo crime. The government's behaviour was, on the whole, correct; their offence was failure to initiate a Serbian investigation into the backgound of the assassination concurrently with the Austrian one. Coercion by the Black Hand or fear of damaging disclosures, rather than deference to public opinion, may account for their tactless passivity. But Pašić and his colleagues were showing no ardour for a sacrificial war of national liberation, and their fear of its imminence culminated in circular representations to the powers, protesting Serbian innocence and willingness to give Austria reasonable satisfaction, although this step did not effectively anticipate the Austrian ultimatum.

There is no evidence of Serbia having received any significant reassurance or suasion from the Russians from the beginning of the crisis until after the Austrian terms were announced. What mattered, however, was not the independent Russian reaction to signs of Austrian preparations— for these as we know were to be discounted as bluff in Vienna and Berlin —but the development of Franco-Russian solidarity, and the arrival of Poincaré and Viviani in St Petersburg unquestionably coincided with an increase in tension.

The French government had shown no more initiative in the Austro-Serbian question during the first fortnight of July than the other Entente powers, and on 15 July its leaders embarked on their planned visit to Russia with an agenda for consultation in which Serbia had a low priority compared, for instance, with the improvement of Anglo-Russian relations.[2] They were due to arrive on 20 July, to leave again on the 23rd and to be back in Paris on 28 July. These dates were kept, and during all that crucial period policy at the Quai d'Orsay was paralysed. So much is apparent from the positive and negative evidence of the French documentarv

[1] *Ibid.* vol. I, no. 72.   [2] Albertini, *The Origins of the War of 1914*, vol. II, p. 188.

material, including Poincaré's own memoirs. But the paucity of information about the Russian visit—which the published Russian documents barely supplement—is hardly to be explained by a lack of activity.[1] There can be no doubt that some immediate assurances were exchanged between the allied leaders. On 21 July Sazonov for the first time told the German Ambassador that Russia would not tolerate threats let alone military action against Serbia, her policy being, so he said, '*pacifique mais pas passive*'.[2] This attitude was endorsed by Poincaré himself on the same day in lecturing the Austrian Ambassador on the fact that 'Serbia has friends and thereby a situation dangerous to peace may arise'.[3] Yet the only ostensibly factual record of Franco-Russian agreement on joint policy during the visit is provided by a telegram of 24 July from the British Ambassador. Buchanan reported 'a perfect community of views' between France and Russia on European problems, and 'a decision to take action at Vienna with a view to the prevention of a demand for explanations or any summons equivalent to an intervention in the internal affairs of Serbia'.[4] No Franco-Russian counter-ultimatum in Vienna ensued, but the context suggests the recognition by the French government of the defence of Serbia's independence as a *casus foederis* for France. Poincaré's personal critics and revisionist historians have seized on the Russian visit as the culmination of a conspiracy between the two military allies.

In contrast, the diplomacy of Great Britain has been blamed even at this stage for an obtuse impartiality.[5] It is true that the German Ambassador told Grey as early as 6 July of the probable Austrian action and even of the possibility of German support. Lichnowsky's warning was confirmed as regards Austria by the British Ambassador in Vienna, and even the 'egging on' of Austria by Germany was detected by Crowe, the most acute of Grey's Foreign Office advisers, on 22 July. Yet on the same day Grey could tell the French Ambassador: 'Probably Berlin was trying to moderate Vienna.'[6] Although Grey impressed on both the Austrian and German Ambassadors his mounting anxiety, he made no imputations. And as late as 23 July he was speaking of a war between the other 'four great Powers' with British neutrality consequently implied.[7]

[1] *Documents diplomatiques français, 1871–1914*, 3ème série, vol. x, p. vi. P. Renouvin, 'La Politique française en juillet 1914' (*Revue de l'histoire de la guerre*, janvier 1937 (pp. 1–21)).
[2] *Die deutschen Dokumente zum Kriegsausbruch*, vol. I, no. 120.
[3] *Oesterreich-Ungarns Aussenpolitik*, vol. VIII, no. 10,461.
[4] *British Documents on the Origins of the War, 1898–1914*, vol. XI, no. 101.
[5] See, for example, Albertini, *op. cit.* vol. II, pp. 214–16
[6] *British Documents*, vol. XI, no. 72.
[7] Lichnowsky had been warned of much stronger language to Mensdorff though it was to include an offer to support 'moderate' (*gemässigt*) demands in Belgrade. In reporting this he added that Germany was counted on not to support the exploitation of the Sarajevo murder for Austria's Balkan ambitions—a caution which drew the kaiser's comment: 'An enormity of British shamelessness' (*Die deutschen Dokumente zum Kriegsausbruch*, vol. I, no. 121).

The hint of British neutrality was no doubt an avoidable mistake, and Grey's tendency to treat the German government as an uncommitted power, only less impartial than Britain, was certainly due to intellectual error as much as to a judgement of tactical expediency which subsequent evidence of second thoughts in Berlin to some extent justified. But the tendency has been to exaggerate and to antedate Grey's opportunity of influencing events. Whatever the defects of Grey's analysis before Austria-Hungary's commitment was completed, it was unthinkable to counter the latter by virtually guaranteeing Russia through France against Germany. Such an improvisation on the consultative pact with France—which was all the 1912 exchange of letters amounted to—would have required his colleagues' deliberate sanction. But there could be no question of seeking this yet in a cabinet divided already over the Ulster crisis. On the other hand, a private warning to Germany, without encouraging France and Russia, would have been a doubtfully practicable bluff and alien to Grey's straightforward methods. And to encourage Britain's Entente partners on his own responsibility would have involved the risk of leading them to 'face the ordeal of war relying on our support' only to find that this was not in the event forthcoming.[1] That risk could not be taken. If Grey did not regard British intervention as a means of averting war it was because his thinking was limited automatically by the realities of British politics.[2]

The fact remains that German policy did not hang upon British non-intervention. The German Foreign Office, as Schoen's report shows, expected British intervention if it was required to save France, while of the two strategic doctrines in vogue in Germany one disbelieved in British neutrality and the other disregarded the question. For the first of these, Tirpitz's blue water school, the world rivalry of the two naval, commercial and imperial powers must be the primary motive in German policy. Far from accepting war with Russia, Tirpitz would have had Germany seek a *rapprochement* at Britain's expense, for '*coûte que coûte* we must set the Whale against the Bear'.[3] Such a diplomatic revolution was also favoured by German conservatives of a very different stamp and supported by a strong pro-German faction at the court of St Petersburg.[4] The other school of strategy, without predilections for Britain or Russia, was that

[1] Grey, *Twenty-Five Years* (1935 ed.), vol. II, p. 158.

[2] It is a debating point rather than a historical one, since it did not enter into Grey's calculations, that an earlier British commitment, if it had not averted war, might well have placed Grey among the principal accused in the war-guilt controversy. He might not have been blamed for using war as an instrument of national policy but he would doubtless have been blamed for encouraging the French and Russians to do so. Poletika (*op. cit.* p. 504) finds Grey 'striving to bring about war more quickly'. Side by side with a mastery of familiar material this latest Soviet treatment shows striking ignorance of personalities and of group and class interests in Europe at the time.

[3] Von Tirpitz, *My Memoirs* (English ed.), vol. I, p. 174.

[4] This was a far less fanciful switch of policy than a tendency for France to combine with Germany and Britain against Russia, which some historians have managed to discern: for example A. J. P. Taylor, *The Struggle for Mastery in Europe*, p. 514.

of the Grand General Staff, which believed that the supremacy of Europe would be settled in battle on the plains of Flanders and Poland. Their timetable for the successive defeats of France and Russia did not leave room for the unimaginable introduction of a full-sized British army, nor for the long-term influence of sea power. Between these two schools the kaiser had blundered for years, not fully aware of their contradictions; but the policy of 5 July was that of the general staff.

The Austro-Hungarian ultimatum to Serbia was delivered in Belgrade at 6.00 p.m. on 23 July and its acceptance was required within 48 hours. The demands were formidable, but they were not disproportionate to the allegations which introduced them—still less to the unknown truth of Serbian intrigue. They included public repudiation of irredentist ambitions and the dissolution of the *Narodna Odbrana* among other concessions humiliating to Panslavism.[1] Russian susceptibilities were not acknowledged but acceptance of the risk of war was confirmed in a telegram to St Petersburg supplying the Austrian Ambassador Szápáry with a brief in support of the ultimatum. 'If', it began, 'Russia judges the time ripe for a final reckoning with the Central Powers the following instructions will be superfluous.'[2] This imputation ignored, of course, the common assumption in both camps that Russia would not be ready until 1917.[3] But it owed nothing to the theory—since so popular—that war offered tsarist Russia the last chance of national unity. Whether the revolutionary movement in Russia and the big political strikes of the summer of 1914 influenced the tsar and his advisers is unknown. But on the evidence Panslavism—the only vital political force favourable to the dynasty— was not exploited.

When the Austrian terms reached Sazonov he is said to have exclaimed: 'This means a European war.'[4] But in his interviews with the Austrian and German Ambassadors there was no sign of fatalism, only indignation. To the German Ambassador Pourtalès he gave the warning that 'if Austria swallows Serbia we will make war on her'.[5] This produced a deceptive reassurance, that Austria intended no annexation, which concealed in fact a plan to feed Serbia to the other Balkan nations. The headless French government responded non-committally, but the Italians objected to 'such far-reaching aggressive action' without consultation.[6] It already looked as if Italy would join the highest bidder or the most likely winner after the first battles; in Italy, as in Rumania, public opinion was favourable not to her allies but to the Entente. Even Grey's impartiality

[1] *Oesterreich-Ungarns Aussenpolitik*, vol. VIII, no. 10,395; vol. XI, Appendix A.
[2] *Ibid.* no. 10,685.
[3] The date set for a 'general settlement' according to the Serbian minister Jovanović. Albertini, *op. cit.* (Italian edition), vol. I, facsimile letter facing p. 400.
[4] Schilling, *How the War Began in 1914* (*Diary of the Russian Ministry of Foreign Affairs*) (London, 1925), p. 29.
[5] *Die deutschen Dokumente zum Kriegsausbruch*, vol. I, nos. 160, 205.
[6] *Ibid.* no. 156.

did not flatter Austro-German hopes of 'localising the dispute'. The provocation given to Russia seemed to him too strong, and he appealed for German action in Vienna as a part of four-power mediation.[1] The Russian reaction was not merely verbal. The Council of Ministers approved a plan of partial mobilisation against Austria to be applied at the appropriate moment. They also approved advice to the Serbs to withdraw from Belgrade and throw themselves on the mercy of the great powers. This has been interpreted as incitement to reject the Austrian ultimatum, but the full argument depends on an arbitrary reconstruction of missing correspondence.[2] And as late as 27 July the reply sent by the tsar to a Serbian appeal was distinctly equivocal. Meanwhile Sazonov's indignation did not prevent him from asking the Austrians for an extension of the time limit. But the chief aim of Russian diplomacy at this point was a British demonstration of solidarity with Russia and France. When Buchanan reported Sazonov's appeal for this, Crowe gave his opinion that France and Russia had already decided to accept the Austrian challenge so that the only question was whether Germany had determined on war. He suggested a warning to Berlin if France or Russia began to mobilise. But he failed to shake Grey's conviction that the British public would not sanction war over a Serbian quarrel.[3]

Since the Serbian reply did not amount to unconditional acceptance of the Austrian terms the Austrian Ambassador left Belgrade and the predetermined Austrian partial mobilisation—against Serbia only, not Russia—thereupon ensued. Actually the Serbs' own mobilisation had just preceded not only this but the delivery of their reply to the ultimatum, which they thus took at its word. Yet the Serbian note was highly conciliatory. About half the demands had been accepted outright, others had been evasively but deferentially answered. Moreover, an offer to submit the points left at issue to the international court at the Hague was added. The kaiser rightly called this a 'brilliant achievement for a time limit of only 48 hours', but the Austrians, he thought, had scored 'a great moral success' and 'all grounds for war disappear'. This was the common opinion in Europe, as the Austrians realised, but the powers were so strategically divided that the prospects of conciliation were seen to be poor. Pessimism aided the forces which were to justify it.

One proposal for conciliation had emerged already in the British plan for a conference, accompanied by a standstill in operations. Grey was influenced by gratifying recollections of the London conference of 1913, but the situations were profoundly dissimilar. In the earlier Balkan crises no great power had been an immediate party to the quarrel, nor had the Austro-Hungarian government been either single-minded or fully

[1] *British Documents on the Origins of the War, 1898–1914*, vol. XI, nos. 99, 116.
[2] For example, in Albertini, *op. cit.* vol. II, pp. 353 ff.
[3] *British Documents on the Origins of the War, 1898–1914*, vol. XI, no. 101.

supported by Germany. The value of a conference in 1914 would have been to gain time for compromise. But the desire for compromise was not general and each nation's military planners were known to believe—incompatibly with one another—that time was on the side of their adversary.

Although the German government agreed to four-power mediation in principle, they rejected the conference proposal on the ground that for Austria it would amount to a 'court of arbitration'.[1] The French and Italians accepted, but Sazonov announced his preference for direct talks with the Austrians, to be met a day later by Berchtold's refusal to discuss Austrian relations with Serbia on the basis of the ultimatum and the reply.[2] Next the British were told in Vienna that it was too late for mediation; in fact, the declaration of war on 28 July was deliberately intended to frustrate mediation. Berchtold said as much when asking the Emperor Francis Joseph's sanction two days earlier; it seems that the urging towards a *fait accompli* came from the German general staff.[3] In fact Austrian military planners did not want active operations before 12 August, and their bombardment of Belgrade was staged to end political measures rather than to open their offensive.

This first declaration of war was not decisive. Russian–Austrian talks continued, although Sazonov declared that they were manifestly futile.[4] German representations in Vienna were actually stimulated, but by this time the unity of command over German policy was questionable. Most serious was the effect on Russian preparations for war and hence on German relations with Russia. So-called 'premobilisation', involving some preliminary measures, had begun on 25 July both in Russia and in Germany. This phase, by custom not regarded as hostile, played a relatively small part in the rapid German process so that the far slower Russians were greatly the gainers. News of the declaration of war on Serbia raised, however, the question of active Russian 'mobilisation' (involving a call-up and all other measures towards operational readiness), partial or total. The military arguments for the more radical course were considered strong, and it was held that the chance of avoiding war was so slight that to lose no time was the first consideration. Developments during 29 July favoured these arguments, accepting the fallacy that the Germans would ever let the Russians get a move ahead. Evidence that there was some prospect of Austrian concessions was outweighed by news of the bombardment of Belgrade and a separate German threat to mobilise (fully) if Russia did not cease her minor military preparations.[5]

[1] *British Documents on the Origins of the War, 1898–1914*, vol. XI, no. 185.
[2] *Ibid.* vol. 179, no. 198. *Mezhdunarodnye Otnosheniya v Epokhu Imperializma*, series iii, vol. 5 (1934), nos. 116, 188.
[3] *Oesterreich-Ungarns Aussenpolitik*, vol. VIII, nos. 10,855, 10,656; *Die deutschen Dokumente zum Kriegsausbruch*, vol. I, nos. 213, 257.
[4] *British Documents*, vol. XI, no. 258.
[5] *Mezhdunarodnye Otnosheniya v Epokhu Imperializma*, series iii, vol. 5, no. 224.

There had been the usual muddle in Berlin; the quasi-ultimatum which Sazonov received from Pourtalès did not correspond to what Bethmann and Jagow were saying elsewhere.[1] But Sazonov was now convinced that the attack on Belgrade showed that the Austrians had only been negotiating to gain time.[2] He was converted to general mobilisation and agreed to persuade the reluctant tsar to sanction it. Recent reassurance of French support may have aided the Russian government's decision, but their ally was in fact far from approving such impatience.[3]

Hardly had the instructions for general mobilisation been approved than they were cancelled at the tsar's order and the partial mobilisation, of which the powers had already been notified, substituted. This was the result of a direct message from the kaiser to the tsar. The telegraphic correspondence between the two imperial cousins belongs to the period of second thoughts in Germany. Unfortunately the kaiser was too frantic and inconsequent and the tsar too weak and fatalistic to control the situation for good or evil. Until after he returned from his cruise the kaiser's influence had been wholly bellicose. But from the time he saw the Serbian reply, which seems to have been deliberately kept from him, the affectation of martial trenchancy and political infallibility in his comments and instructions began to alternate with self-pity, even common sense. It occurred to him that Austrian 'honour' might be satisfied by the seizure of Belgrade. This harmonised with the support which Bethmann-Hollweg had already begun to give the British move for mediation— stimulated without doubt by the diminishing prospect of British neutrality unless Germany could earn it. On the 27th Grey's guarded words to the German Ambassador about the scope of a European war caused Lichnowsky to warn Bethmann explicitly that 'in case of war we would have England against us',[4] so that the British offer of pacification in St Petersburg in exchange for similar action in Vienna should be followed up.

Bethmann sent on Lichnowsky's telegram to Vienna with his blessing. His object was probably to lessen German responsibility in the eyes of the world, but domestic politics also required that Germany should appear 'forced into war', as he explicitly stated.[5] Some saving clauses in his instructions to Tschirschky, in particular that the Ambassador should 'carefully avoid giving the impression that we want to hold Austria back',[6] also suggest that he was less preoccupied with averting war than with improving the grounds for waging it. Whatever Bethmann's own position,

[1] For example in *British Documents*, vol. XI, no. 263, and *Die deutschen Dokumente zum Kriegsausbruch*, vol. II, no. 385.
[2] *Oesterreich-Ungarns Aussenpolitik*, vol. VIII, no. 11,003.
[3] Poincaré, *Au Service de la France*, vol. IV, p. 385. The timing and meaning of assurances from the dispersed French ministers before the warning on 30 July from Viviani in Paris not to provoke German mobilisation is highly controversial. It is discussed exhaustively in Albertini, vol. II, ch. XIII.
[4] *Die deutschen Dokumente zum Kriegsausbruch*, vol. I, no. 265.
[5] *Ibid.* vol. I, no. 277.   [6] *Ibid.* vol. II, no. 323.

the increasingly strong remonstrances which he ordered in Vienna were almost certainly rendered ineffective by the Secretary of State, Jagow, as well as by Moltke. The Austro-Hungarian Ambassador in Berlin, Szögyény, reported on 28 July that the apparent German support for British proposals for mediation was only formal and that the German government were really 'decisively against heeding them'.[1] Whether or not Szögyény overdid Jagow's gloss on the Chancellor's views, Berchtold took him at his word and proceeded to treat the official German representations with calculated indifference. It is not known how faithfully Tschirschky interpreted the Chancellor's instructions, let alone his mood, but Bethmann's arguments and reproaches got merely evasive answers. The Austrians had concluded that a prestige victory would be valueless and that operations must go on.

Meanwhile the situation in Berlin had changed. Bethmann's last and most indignant telegram to Vienna was cancelled[2] and the kaiser's support in recommending the 'halt in Belgrade' to the Emperor Francis Joseph was too feeble and came too late.[3] The Austrians had successfully temporised long enough to let the mounting anxieties of the German general staff at Russia's military counter-preparations gain the ascendancy in German policy. On 29 July that body had formally warned the Chancellor of the decreasing lead in mobilisation which Germany would retain if Russian and French preparations went on. Military intelligence about these preparations overwhelmed Bethmann, late on 30 July, reinforced as it was by an interruption of the kaiser's pacific mood. For Wilhelm was indignant and despondent at news from London discountenancing a Hanoverian prince's report to him that George V reckoned on British neutrality.[4] Meanwhile Moltke had already been working against Bethmann in messages to Conrad in Vienna. 'Mobilise at once against Russia', he urged, 'Germany will mobilise.'[5] This injunction caused Berchtold to remark: 'Who gives the orders, Moltke or Bethmann?' Only the lack of co-ordination, indeed the division of power in Berlin, made it possible for the dependent ally to rebuff formal representations in favour of compromise from the superior power. It says more for Bethmann's loyalty than his trustworthiness as a historical source that he did not use this defence in his memoirs.

The impatience of the German generals on 30 July and the pressure they exerted on Bethmann and Conrad is sufficiently explained by the Russian measures of partial mobilisation; there is no need to assume a premonition

---

[1] *Oesterreich-Ungarns Aussenpolitik*, vol. VIII, no. 10,793.
[2] *Die deutschen Dokumente zum Kriegsausbruch*, vol. II, nos. 441 and 450. It had included the words: 'If...Vienna rejects everything it will prove that it absolutely wants war...and Russia will remain guiltless.'
[3] *DD* 368, 374, 400, 452.   [4] *Ibid.* no. 437.
[5] *Oesterreich-Ungarns Aussenpolitik*, vol. VIII, no. 11,033; Conrad, *op. cit.* vol. IV, pp. 152–3. Conrad's quotation of his own correspondence does not of course possess complete authenticity.

of the general mobilisation on the following day. For the partial mobilisation was known to involve all but three of the empire's call-up districts and the military as well as political significance of the fact that those omitted were the ones facing the German front was underrated. Still a decisive German reaction was forestalled by the further Russian step of general mobilisation, formally putting Russia in the wrong.

The Russian decision on 30 July, made public the next morning, was taken on purely military grounds, the impracticability of partial mobilisation, and the belief that German general mobilisation was imminent. The generals had pressed for the reversal of the tsar's last order of the previous day, and the weak and sanctimonious autocrat was driven against his pacific and Germanophil inclinations by Sazonov's advocacy into his habitual refuge of fatalism. The French made a last-minute plea for caution, but it is still not clear what bearing, if any, it had on the Russian decision. The relevant telegram of 30 July, while confirming the alliance obligations of France, suggested that Russia 'should not immediately proceed to any measure which might offer Germany a pretext for a total or partial mobilisation of her forces'.[1] This must be accepted as sent in good faith, but there are grounds for supposing that the warning was passed on late, imperfectly or not at all by the French Ambassador Paléologue, whose conduct throughout the crisis is suspect.[2] No such cautionary advice came from London. Rightly or wrongly it remained Grey's conviction that he must not exert influence when he could not accept responsibility for its indirect consequences.

The Russian general mobilisation was the decisive calamity. This is true even given the excuse that it was merely forestalling German action of the same kind. It is not certain that the Russian partial mobilisation was in fact inducing a German counter-move yet, in spite of Moltke's telegrams to Conrad. Moreover, Russian mobilisation was necessarily ineffective, for any attempt to reduce the German lead in the ultimate phase could be swiftly neutralised by Germany. Historians should not tolerate the illusion of the contemporary strategists that rapid mobilisation was all-important. Never has the dogma of the offensive been more prevalent; never, because of the lead of firepower over tactical mobility, has that dogma been less applicable.

Still, no one questioned in 1914 that general mobilisation by a great power must be followed by hostilities. The position was too competitive for the professionals to entertain the politicians' pretence that the Russian army could stay inactive on a war footing. The German government's immediate declaration of a state of war emergency (*Kriegsgefahrzustand*) on 31 July, followed by their ultimatum demanding the cessation of

---

[1] *Documents diplomatiques français, 1871–1914*, 3ème série, vol. XI, no. 305.

[2] This is the result of criticism of his evidence as much as the notoriety of his warlike views. See Albertini, *The Origins of the War of 1914*, vol. II, pp. 618–19

Russian military preparations, constituted only technically the initiative in aggression. But simultaneously they proceeded to extend their strategic initiative to the extremes demanded by the so-called Schlieffen plan.

That was a different matter. The famous plan, on which training and mobilisation had been based through twenty years of its evolution, from Schlieffen to Moltke, envisaged a 'lightning' (*blitzschnell*) offensive to knock out France before turning on Russia—which would be meanwhile held by a German defensive campaign. Tactically, that involved an approach march through Belgium to envelop the French left flank.[1] In this war on two fronts the west had priority, so a collision with France had to be brought on. Simultaneously therefore with the 12-hour ultimatum to Russia an 18-hour ultimatum went off for delivery in Paris demanding an assurance of neutrality. A request for free passage through Belgium had already been sent off for delivery in Brussels as soon as operations against France were due to start. But operations were delayed, for the French did not accept the initiative in declaring war. Had they acceded to the demand for neutrality the German Ambassador was to require further—so set was his government on the inevitability of a two-front war—the temporary surrender of two frontier fortresses as a guarantee. But when they neither promised neutrality nor declared war it was considered in Berlin that a short postponement of the onslaught would be just worth while in the hope of some French initiative or provocation which might affect the British attitude. The Germans were not going to compromise the Schlieffen plan for the sake of Great Britain; they had no alternative war plan and the challenge to Britain as a guarantor of Belgian neutrality must ensue. But whereas general war on the continent was seen in virtually all quarters to be inevitable within a few days once Russia and Austria had begun to mobilise, immediate British intervention was not. It was not appreciated in France or Germany—perhaps not in Britain itself—that Belgian neutrality rather than the fate and conduct of France would be the crucial issue.

Since Grey's admonitions on 27 July which had produced second thoughts in Berlin, the development of British parliamentary and public opinion had not kept pace with the requirements of effective diplomacy. Nor had the views of the Cabinet. Though the Liberal press was conspicuously divided, the bulk of the Liberal party's supporters were unprepared for war. Pacifist, and isolationist, they inclined to believe that war was financially impossible in the modern world as well as immoral, and that Germany as a great commercial power must be predisposed to peace. Did not Germany, furthermore, possess a powerful and internationally minded socialist movement, and great trade unions opposed to militarism?

---

[1] The incursion of the German armies into Holland as well had been dropped from the original plan: it was to be restored in the most thorough, though differently phased, use of the whole plan in 1940. G. Ritter, *Der Schlieffenplan* (Munich, 1956), gives its full history.

Many conservatives and most socialists also held one or other of these illusions. Moreover, of the putative allies, Russia was the classic enemy at once of the British Empire in Asia and of international socialism and democracy, while sympathy for France was counteracted by suspicion of her interest in a war of revenge.

These political inhibitions produced a schism in the Cabinet in the last week of peace. In Churchill's opinion the Cabinet would have 'broken up' if Grey had pushed ahead of events and sought authority for threats to influence them.[1] Public opinion was to unite on the issue of Belgian neutrality when it was nakedly presented by the Germans, but the Cabinet would not have united upon it as a hypothetical *casus belli* a few days earlier. How full and how early a commitment to intervention Grey wanted to make is not known. Two things are however certain. First, until the Russian general mobilisation order it was not 'too late' according to the contemporary strategists' conventions, even, for the Germans to have insisted upon compromise in Vienna. This could have been achieved with no more loss of face to Austria—indeed on more favourable terms—than at an earlier stage. Secondly, there was sufficient evidence, well before the Russian general mobilisation and without an explicit warning, for the Germans to reach the conclusion that Britain would intervene. That evidence of British intentions had no effect on the diplomatic situation was due to the fact that there was no more unity of command in Berlin than in London.

Grey did not press the Cabinet on the Belgian question; his limited objective was a guarantee to protect the northern coasts of France against the German fleet in view of the linked redistribution of French and British naval units which had left the Channel ports undefended. Meanwhile, confronted with the importunity of the French and German Ambassadors, seeking respectively intervention and neutrality, his warnings to the Germans were becoming a little stronger than his promises to the French. But not much. On 29 July the Ambassador in Berlin, Goschen, reported Bethmann's unwise plea for British neutrality on condition that France was not deprived of European territory; the answer made it clear that Britain could not afford to see France crushed.[2] On 31 July the mobilisation of Russia and Germany, the German declaration of war emergency and the German ultimata to Russia and France led Grey to require assurances from Paris and Berlin that Belgian neutrality would be respected, but he refused to offer Lichnowsky an assurance of British neutrality in return.[3] On the other hand, he was still refusing any commitment to France on 1 August, pointing out that French commitments to Russia were unknown to Britain. Officially the French government were not claiming a British military commitment but privately their Ambassador, Cambon, was raising the question of British honour.

---

[1] *World Crisis* (London, 1929), vol. I, p. 204.
[2] *British Documents*, vol. XI, nos. 293, 303.   [3] *Ibid.* no. 448.

It was not until 2 August that the British Cabinet was prepared to concede a guarantee of the French northern coasts. By then a formal assurance of support for intervention had come from the Conservative party, Luxemburg had been invaded, France and Belgium had begun to mobilise and the Belgians had made it clear that they would resist if their turn came.[1] The movement of the German army into Luxemburg had been accompanied by perfunctory allegations of imminent French incursions; the invasion of Belgium was being similarly prepared by a grotesque charge of unneutral conduct, and attempts began to create or invent incidents on Germany's frontier with France.

This propaganda made little impression. In contrast, the facts of French conduct eased the way for British intervention. Not only were French forward defences evacuated to avoid provocation but mobilisation was delayed until the commander-in-chief was threatening his resignation.[2] And the German ultimatum was met with the suggestion that news of promising developments in Austro-Russian relations made it premature.[3] In fact, these marked no advance. Sazonov had produced a new formula, but it did not offer a standstill in mobilisation or the 'halt in Belgrade'.[4] Berchtold, for his part, was merely repeating earlier prevarications. Meanwhile, German support for mediation had collapsed. Bethmann had become the advocate—for military reasons—of an early declaration of war on France, in spite of the obloquy: the opposition came from Tirpitz, not yet ready for a naval challenge to Great Britain. Once committed to a strong policy Bethmann was not strong enough to face modifying it in response to new developments. It was the kaiser who took most interest in a supposed British offer on 1 August to guarantee the neutrality of France if the German armies did not attack her.[5] What was actually said is still obscure; there was almost certainly confusion of thought, if not irresolution, in London. In contrast the fatal rigidity of German military and political thinking is shown by Moltke's embarrassment[6] and the harsh terms of the Chancellor's proposed acceptance. He would require Britain to 'engage herself with her entire armed forces for the unconditional neutrality of France during a Russo-German conflict', the scope and duration of which was 'for Germany alone to decide'.[7]

In the event, the declaration of war upon France and the final ultimatum to Belgium followed according to plan on 3 August, providing Grey with the ripe case for intervention which he made in his famous speech on that

---

[1] The international guarantee of Luxemburg differed from that of Belgium in being 'joint' only and not 'several' as well, thus involving a lesser obligation upon an individual guarantor. [2] Albertini, *op. cit.* (Italian edition), vol. III, p. 97.
[3] *British Documents*, vol. XI, no. 428.
[4] *Die deutschen Dokumente zum Kriegsausbruch*, vol. II, no. 421.
[5] *Ibid.* vol. III, nos. 562, 575.
[6] After resisting on logistic grounds the kaiser's proposal to turn the German army about for a march on Russia, Moltke went back to his office and burst into tears.
[7] *Ibid.* no. 578.

day. This was, on analysis, an admission that he had lost control of British foreign policy. But his hearers did not analyse, they accepted the identity of national interest and moral duty set before them. Grey did not ask for a vote for war. That followed the formality of an unheeded summons to Germany to stop the invasion of Belgium. The period of grace was used to pass German warships under British guns to Constantinople, where they dazzled the Turks into a military alliance.

Like the chance of British neutrality—if it existed—the chance of support from their nominal allies, Italy and Rumania, was discarded equally deliberately by the central powers. The race for the operational offensive had prevented the sequence of declarations of war taking the logical form of Russia against Austria, followed by Germany against Russia, and France against Germany. Hence technical aggression by Germany released the satellite allies, whose public opinion would not, in any event, have allowed them to fight.[1] Berchtold, who had ignored the German plea that Italy should be bribed with 'compensations', thought her neutrality was good enough.[2] Instead of their defecting allies, those allies' recent victims, Turkey and Bulgaria, were to join the central powers, though not at once.

In his last interview with the British ambassador, Goschen, Bethmann uttered the famous reproach that Britain was—in contrast to the other powers—going to war for the sake of a 'scrap of paper'. It was an error in political analysis as well as in public relations. The issue of Belgian neutrality indeed dissolved isolationism and pacifism in Great Britain as only a moral factor could do. But in taking the guilt out of distrust and jealousy of Germany it put these forces in the service of what was fundamentally balance-of-power politics. Elsewhere, without this sanction, the final challenges of the crisis fired nationalism equally beyond expectations. In countries where great political parties of the left professed adherence to an international socialist cause, in France and Germany, parliamentary solidarity with the government was virtually unanimous. Grey's appeal in the House of Commons for intervention on the side of law and order stirred no more conscientious enthusiasm than did Bethmann's declaration in the Reichstag that 'necessity knows no law', his promise that 'the wrong we do we shall try to make good' and his plea that 'whoever is threatened as we are can only think how to hew his way through'. The peoples did not ask for positive war aims and there were none fit to give them besides the will of France to recover Alsace and Lorraine. Neither the Germans nor the British had a ready-made imperial plan in stock; even the Austrians had no acquisitive purpose in the partition of Serbia, while the Russian territorial ambitions were at least as

[1] *Documenti diplomatici italiani*, quinta serie, vol. I, no. 101.
[2] *Diplomatisce Aktenstücke zur Vorgeschichte des Krieges 1914* (Vienna, 1919), vol. III, no. 117.

repugnant to their allies as to their enemies.[1] Each belligerent government was prepared to claim that the war was at the worst preventive, and each hastened to compile and publish a collection of its recent diplomatic correspondence, with exculpatory omissions and paraphrases, in order to prove more than this. These publications, distinguished in macabre cooperation by a different colour for each of the first six combatants, on the whole satisfied the intelligentsia of each country—in spite of the rival publications, soon available in translation—that the war was not merely a preventive but a defensive one.

[1] See note 1 on page 149 above.

CHAPTER VII

THE FIRST WORLD WAR

I N 1909 Norman Angell published his polemic *The Great Illusion*, in which he argued that the increasingly international character of trade, commerce and finance had rendered wars between sovereign states not merely unprofitable, but positively harmful to victors and vanquished alike. A decade earlier had appeared a remarkable six-volume treatise entitled *The Future of War in its Technical, Economic and Political Relations* by Ivan S. Bloch, a Warsaw banker. Bloch began on the sound tactical principle that firepower was bestowing ever greater strength to the defensive; so that in future wars infantry must take refuge in trenches or suffer fearful carnage. He envisaged wars of the future as enormous sieges, with famine as the final arbiter. Bloch, like Angell, concluded that war had become impossible—except at the price of suicide—since even the winners would suffer the destruction of their resources and risk social disintegration.

These and other warning voices made little impact on either soldiers or statesmen in the decade before 1914. The consolidation of the rival alliances, a succession of international crises, and the increasing likelihood of an explosion in the Balkans, were but the surface symptoms of a profound malaise. Politically these years provide a terrible indictment of the self-defeating quest for national security through secret diplomacy and armed might. Psychologically, too, nations were being conditioned for war: by propaganda; by the spurious application of the Darwinian struggle to the human species; by bitter class divisions; and not least by self-delusion as to the nature of war. The romantic view of war obscured both predictions like Bloch's and actual experience as recent as the fighting in Manchuria in 1905.

The conflict which began in August 1914 was not known to contemporaries as 'The first world war'. Its origins were essentially European; in the power struggle between Austria and Russia in the Balkans, and Anglo-French fear of German domination of western Europe. Yet the war, once loosed, rapidly gathered a momentum of its own, overflowed geographical boundaries and the control of European statesmen, and became truly world-wide in its repercussions. One of these, ironically, was that Europe itself emerged with diminished importance on the world stage.

If statesmen, by their vertiginous diplomacy of bluff and counter-bluff, brought Europe to the brink of the abyss after the assassination of Archduke Francis Ferdinand at Sarajevo, it was the General Staffs who gave the final push. Once Austria had declared war on Serbia on 28 July the generals' pressure for full and immediate mobilisation defeated the belated efforts of Grey and others to avert war. Years of preparation had been necessary to articulate the ponderous military machines for action. Victory was thought to depend on mobilising before the enemy. The General Staffs' assumption—and their political power—is necessary to explain why general mobilisation by Russia was speedily followed by the Central Powers and then by France and Britain. From that point the huge armies, rather than their creators, began to dictate events.

In retrospect it is astonishing that none of the belligerents was prepared either materially or mentally for a long war. Politically they anticipated a short struggle based on the traditional system of alliances, and militarily a contest between professional armies with the civil populations as spectators at a safe distance. Only slowly was the nineteenth-century concept of 'the nation in arms' replaced by the twentieth-century version of 'the nation at war'.

Germany was well organised in most respects for a short decisive war. Her well-tried system of conscription for two or three years' full-time training, followed by longer periods of reserve and landwehr service, gave her in 1914 an army of some five million men, including reserve corps, suitable for immediate employment at the front. The General Staff, the 'brain' of the German army, had been carefully selected and trained, and was unrivalled for professional knowledge and skill. Tactically the Germans had gauged the potentialities of machine guns and heavy howitzers and were much better equipped with both than their enemies. On the strategic plane the Germans had led the way in developing the military use of railways almost to an exact science. Not the least among Germany's assets was the army's high prestige in the hearts of the people.

None of these advantages was evident in Germany's ally. The Austro-Hungarian army numbered too many defeats in its recent history, and its racial mixture was a serious weakness which conscription had accentuated. In equipment and leadership it was inferior to Germany; and, worst of all, mistrust and friction had grown between the allies since the early 1890s, when German strategists began to give priority to the western front without keeping the Austrians informed of their plans.

On the Entente side France had made strenuous efforts to overcome her inferiority in potential military manpower—approximately 5,940,000 to 9,750,000—by training nearly every able-bodied male. In 1913 a highly controversial Army Law increased the period of conscript service from two years (adopted in 1905) to three, revealing a fear that the German army, also enlarged by recent legislation, was becoming more than a match for the French. Thus on the outbreak of war France could call on nearly four million trained men to Germany's five million: but with the significant difference that France placed little fighting value on her reservists. In the 1900s French military doctrine was founded on patriotic fervour and the offensive spirit, qualities which were allowed to conceal grave deficiencies in equipment and weapons. Her one first-class weapon, the 75 mm field gun, was consequently too heavily relied on. Russia's assets were her immense resources of manpower and the reputation of her troops for courage and stubborn endurance. Her leadership was poor, her troops ill-educated and her manufacturing resources were far below those of the great industrial powers. The British Expeditionary Force provided the *élite* of the Entente's forces, being indeed the best trained, best equipped, and best organised contingent with which Britain had ever started a war. In numbers, however, its 120,000 men only fitted it for a marginal role in 1914, considering that the Germans brought about one and a half million men into line against France in August, while the French Field Army numbered over one million. The British General Staff moreover, except for the unheeded Cassandra Lord Kitchener, was convinced that the war would be short and its own military contribution strictly limited.

The Central Powers' political preparations did not match their military planning. The participation of Britain released Italy, ever a doubtful ally, from her obligations under the Triple Alliance. Rumania's territorial greed for both Bessarabia and Transylvania caused her also to remain temporarily neutral, thus depriving the Central Powers of a flank attack on southern Russia and in turn exposing their own flank in the Danube plain. The allegiances of Bulgaria and Turkey would clearly be influenced by the opening moves of the war, as well as by fresh memories of the Balkan Wars of 1912 and 1913 in which they had been losers. Britain's prompt declaration of war, following Germany's invasion of Belgium, surprised the Central Powers but did not unduly perturb them. They underrated the B.E.F. and discounted the value of the Royal Navy in a short war.

Germany's central position and the depreciating asset of her alliance with Austria-Hungary gave her compelling reasons for staking all on a short war. This in turn led to concentration in the west. The German General Staff had become increasingly convinced since the 1890s that a quick decision was unobtainable on the eastern front, and in any case Russian finances might collapse if France were beaten. The gradual evolution of the plan designed to overwhelm France within six weeks was largely the work of Count Schlieffen, Chief of the German General Staff from 1891 to 1906. Schlieffen's greatest technical problem was how to prise open the French frontier so as to enable armies containing about a million troops to deploy. Between Luxemburg and Switzerland the frontier was naturally strong, and had been heavily fortified by the French since 1871. Schlieffen's solution, as befitted a professional technician unconcerned with politics, was to violate the neutrality of the Low Countries, place the numerical weight on his right wing, and aim at the encirclement of Paris. The idea of a modern Cannae became his obsession. The German centre and left wing would be deliberately left weak so that if the French chose to attack them they would only put themselves further into the net. Only a token force would be left on the eastern frontier to help the Austrians contain the slowly mobilising Russians, who could be crushed at leisure after the fall of France.

Schlieffen's successor, Helmuth von Moltke, altered some of the details of the draft plan of 1905, notably by cancelling the infringement of Dutch territory and strengthening the left wing. For these changes in the 'master plan' he was to be criticised—excessively so—after 1914, but it has recently been shown that Schlieffen himself grew increasingly worried about his plan, realising that he had solved intricate problems of manpower and movement only on paper. In fact the plan left so many problems unsolved and depended on so many assumptions of enemy reactions that one authority has called it 'a snare and a delusion'.[1] At best it was a bold gamble which required a superb commander and a great deal of luck if it was to succeed.

Germany certainly was fortunate in the reactions of the French High Command. General Michel, who in 1911 had accurately divined the German plan and proposed to meet it by a concentration in the north between Lille and Rethel with a defensive deployment elsewhere, was replaced as Chief of Staff by the offensive-minded Joffre. In 1913 the latter adopted Plan XVII which embodied an all-out offensive to break through the supposed German centre and to paralyse his communications. This plan was doomed to fail from its misreading of the enemy's distribution. Out of nearly a million and a half men deployed in the west, half were allotted to the three armies forming the right wing, nearly 400,000 to the two armies in the centre who were to advance through the Ardennes, and only 350,000 to the remaining two armies in Lorraine. The French threw in about 450,000 troops east of Metz and 360,000 into the Ardennes, leaving de Lanrezac, who had also grasped the German plan, with only 250,000 men to defend the vulnerable Belgian frontier.

Both the French offensives met with disaster. On 20 August they were defeated east of Metz at Sarrebourg and Morhange, and four days later were repulsed from the Ardennes with heavy losses—the wooded defiles cancelling the advantage of their 75 mm guns. But although beaten the French armies were not annihilated; by retreating in good order on to their rail communications they were soon in a position to send reinforcements northward as the main German threat developed.

Meanwhile, after entering Belgium on 4 August, the northern German armies had captured the great fortress of Liége—essentially a triumph for

---

[1] B. H. Liddell Hart in the Foreword to G. Ritter, *The Schlieffen Plan: Critique of a Myth* (London, Wolff, 1958).

their heavy artillery—forced the Belgian army to retire on Antwerp, and threatened to engulf de Lanrezac's 5th Army. Here the B.E.F., by its rapid shipment and deployment, was able to play a decisive part despite its small numbers. On 21 August the British reached the Belgian frontier and encountered the enemy. By the delaying battles at Mons (23 August) and Le Cateau (26 August) the vastly outnumbered British prevented the encirclement of the French left wing, and greatly added to Moltke's confusion since he thought they were still disembarking. Mistakenly deducing that the B.E.F. must be based on the Channel ports, the German 1st and 2nd Army commanders von Kluck and von Bülow missed excellent opportunities to cut them off from the retreating French.

As the German armies marched deeper into north-eastern France, in scorching summer heat, it slowly became clear to Moltke that the Schlieffen plan was not working out. The British, French and Belgian armies, though worsted in the frontier battles, had not been crushed— indeed they were retreating towards good communications and defensive positions, whereas the Germans, especially Kluck's army near the Channel coast, were outpacing their supplies. Real difficulties certainly existed but they were magnified in the Chief of Staff's mind. Moltke was an intelligent man and not lacking in courage; what he did lack was good health and its usual concomitant, self-confidence. He had never had full confidence in his predecessor's plan, and in the opening weeks of the war he made a number of errors which finally ended the possibility of a quick knock-out victory in the west. In the first place he did not keep sufficiently close to the front, setting up his headquarters first in Coblenz and later in Luxemburg. Since neither he nor his operations staff visited the front during August he lacked sufficiently fresh information to give orders to his army commanders. This underlined his second mistake of allowing his subordinates too much latitude as his famous uncle had done—though not without hazard—in 1870. On the right wing the energetic Kluck quarrelled with his pessimistic neighbour Bülow, while in Lorraine Crown Prince Rupprecht of Bavaria was allowed to press on his advance instead of retiring to draw the French into a trap. Thus by the end of August the Germans were advancing all along the line, and the outlines of the Schlieffen plan were already blurred. On 25 August Moltke made a third mistake in detaching six corps from the 2nd and 3rd Armies and dispatching them to Prussia. These and other questionable decisions need not have proved fatal to a more resolute commander, but by the end of August Moltke was approaching a physical breakdown. When, therefore, on 30 August Kluck turned his army south-east to maintain contact with Bülow, Moltke did not intervene and allowed the plan for the encirclement of Paris to be abandoned.

This gave the retreating allies the opportunity to counter-attack and Joffre, prompted by Gallieni, the Military Governor of Paris, ordered the about-turn and general offensive on 6 September (the battle of the Marne). Kluck was drawn into a separate battle with Manoury's newly formed 6th army and a thirty mile gap opened between him and Bülow. In fear lest Sir John French, commander-in-chief of the B.E.F., should throw his cavalry into this gap, Bülow began to retreat on 9 September. Kluck reluctantly conformed and Moltke, now a broken man, permitted a general retreat. This was a severe blow to German strategy, though tactically they avoided a serious defeat by taking up a defensive position behind the natural bastion of the river Aisne. Since Prince Rupprecht had failed to break through in the fortified area of Nancy, the only hope of a quick victory after mid-September lay in outflanking the allies to the north. Neither side possessed the means of mobility to achieve this manœuvre, and as the result of a series of checks the lines were extended from the Aisne past Amiens and Arras towards the Channel coast. In the process the original B.E.F. was virtually annihilated in stemming repeated attacks around Ypres in late October and November. Meanwhile Antwerp had fallen on 9 October but the bulk of the Belgian army escaped along the coast and made contact with the allies behind the line of the river Yser.

The German retreat from the Marne and the replacement of Moltke by Falkenhayn in mid-September clearly witnessed the failure of the Schlieffen plan. The margin of failure, however, was narrow and despite the strategic check the Germans were now in a most advantageous position. Nearly a tenth of France was in their hands and the occupied area contained the key to French industrial output; in fact 80 per cent of French coal, almost the whole of her iron resources and the great north-eastern factories were lost for the rest of the war. Germany's economy was correspondingly strengthened and—equally important—she could afford to let the allies do most of the attacking. Until March 1918 the lines of the great siege never changed as much as ten miles.

The opening encounters in the east had meanwhile revealed a characteristic pattern of the Russians suffering severely at German hands but themselves getting the better of the conflict with Austria. The Russian commander-in-chief, the Grand Duke Nicholas, promptly upset German calculations by invading East Prussia even though his armies were not fully concentrated. The Russian first and second armies, commanded by Rennenkampf and Samsonov respectively, outnumbered the Germans by more than two to one and had an excellent opportunity to crush them by a pincer movement in the region of the Masurian lakes. The two armies, however, showed no inclination to co-operate, possibly because their commanders had been personal enemies since a quarrel during the war with Japan. The German commander, von Prittwitz, lost his nerve in the crisis and was replaced, when he ordered a withdrawal behind the Vistula, by General von Hindenburg, who emerged from retirement, with

Ludendorff as his Chief of Staff. Rennenkampf's immobility on the eastern frontier and the Russians' folly in transmitting unciphered wireless orders enabled Ludendorff to turn the tables. Leaving only a cavalry screen before Rennenkampf he threw the bulk of his forces south against Samsonov. Under converging pressure Samsonov's army was almost destroyed and the commander committed suicide. Then receiving reinforcements from France, Ludendorff turned on Rennenkampf and drove him out of East Prussia. In these battles—of Tannenberg and the Masurian Lakes—the Russians lost a quarter of a million men and a vast amount of war material.

The psychological impact of Tannenberg would have been even greater had not the scales tilted against the Central Powers in Galicia. Two Austrian armies had invaded Poland but were halted by a Russian thrust against weaker forces protecting their right flank. By the end of August the latter had been driven back through Lemberg so that the Austrian Chief of Staff Conrad von Hötzendorf was obliged to withdraw his armies from Poland to avoid being cut off. By the end of September the Austrians had retreated almost to Cracow. In Poland the fighting raged back and forth throughout the autumn and the year ended with the Russians, exhausted and critically short of munitions, back on the line of the Nida and Dunajec rivers. Russia's exhaustion was balanced by the poor performance of the Austrians whose two attempted invasions of Serbia had both been contemptuously repulsed.

The miscarriage of the military plans gradually brought sea power into prominence. Although on the outbreak of war the British Grand Fleet outnumbered the German High Seas Fleet by 20 dreadnoughts to 13, there had been so many developments in the last decade—in gunnery, submarines, mines, wireless and aircraft—that superiority in capital ships would not necessarily assure Britain of victory in a great sea battle. For their part the German Admiralty adopted a Fabian policy. They would avoid a major fleet action until their minelayers and submarines had whittled away the enemy's superiority and would then seek the opportunity for a surprise stroke. This policy suited the natural defensive strength of Germany's naval bases but it had obvious drawbacks: it entailed the loss of Germany's overseas trade and greatly restricted her interference with the sea-borne supplies of Britain and her allies. Moreover the British Admiralty's cautious policy of preserving 'the fleet in being' deprived the enemy of opportunities to reduce the odds. Admiral Jellicoe did not rule out the hope of a Nelsonian victory but regarded his primary duties as preventing invasion, maintaining the security of the ocean routes and ensuring communications with the B.E.F. in France.

Outside home waters Britain suffered several humiliations before confirming her supremacy. In the Mediterranean two of Germany's fastest ships, the battle cruiser *Goeben* and the light cruiser *Breslau*, evaded

Allied attempts at interception and reached Constantinople, thus playing an important part in inducing Turkey to enter the war on Germany's side at the end of October 1914. Britain's naval concentration in the North Sea permitted Germany's commerce raiders a few months of expensive freedom. The light cruiser *Emden*, for example, led a charmed life in the Pacific and Indian Oceans until destroyed by the Australian cruiser *Sydney* on 1 November at Cocos Island. More serious was the defeat on the same day of Admiral Cradock's cruiser squadron by Admiral von Spee's more powerful cruisers *Scharnhorst* and *Gneisenau* at Coronel. This spurred the Admiralty to action. Admiral Sturdee was dispatched with the battle cruisers *Inflexible* and *Invincible* and these accounted for von Spee at the Falkland Isles on 8 December. By the end of 1914 Germany's power on the surface of the outer seas had been completely destroyed.

Early in the new year the war at sea began to take on a more frightful form. Britain's command of the ocean routes caused Germany to concentrate her efforts at the land termini and to rely increasingly on the submarine, hitherto considered a weapon for use in coast defence only, and against which British defences were wholly inadequate. The determination to pursue this anti-commerce policy was clinched by the victory of the British battle cruisers in an action off the Dogger Bank on 24 January. Since the policy of wearing down the Grand Fleet was failing Pohl, who replaced Ingenohl as Commander of the High Seas Fleet, proposed to Falkenhayn an offensive submarine strategy which, if it were to succeed, must be unlimited. Meanwhile, in January 1915, the Admiralty had advised British merchant ships to fly a neutral flag or no ensign in the vicinity of the British Isles, in order to increase the difficulties of German submarines. Germany retaliated on 4 February by declaring the waters round the British Isles, including the Channel, to be a war zone within which all enemy vessels would be sunk, and neutrals would sail at their own risk. This helped to free the British government from its feeling of moral obligation to uphold the Declaration of London of 1909 which, although never ratified by her, had hitherto hampered Britain's power to put maritime pressure upon Germany because of its interpretation of the rules on contraband of war and blockade. Britain now claimed the right to intercept all ships carrying goods to Germany and if necessary bring them into British ports for search. Serious friction with neutrals, especially the U.S.A., resulted but Germany forfeited her advantage by torpedoing the *Lusitania* off northern Ireland on 7 May. This pointless act of brutality directly affected the U.S.A. since over a hundred American lives were lost, and it dealt the first serious blow at her determination to remain neutral.

Britain's command of the seas enabled her or her allies to sweep up all Germany's overseas colonies—without difficulty in most cases. A New Zealand expedition captured Samoa in August 1914 and in September the

Australians took New Guinea. Japan, who entered the war in August 1914 as an ally of Britain, sent an expedition against the German naval base of Tsing-Tao on the Shantung peninsula, and eventually captured it early in November. In Africa Togoland speedily capitulated to the British, but the Cameroons was not finally brought under Anglo-French control until early 1916. General Louis Botha, formerly Britain's enemy, conquered German South West Africa and, equally important, put down a rebellion by disaffected Boers which—except for the Irish Rising at Easter 1916—was the only wartime revolt against Imperial authority. The outstanding exception to the easy conquest of Germany's overseas empire was German East Africa, her largest and richest colony. There, assisted by the terrain, the brilliant General von Lettow-Vorbeck distracted some 200,000 Imperial troops until the end of 1917. He himself continued a guerrilla resistance until after the armistice in Europe. The significance of these 'side-shows' lay perhaps less in their effect on the war in Europe than in their political repercussions on such countries as India and Japan for whom the war would otherwise have been remote in every sense.

In the long run Germany's submarine campaign and Britain's retaliatory blockade were to bring home the experience of modern war to the civilians of all the European belligerents. Early in 1915, however, it was in the air that it first became apparent that the war would no longer be confined to the military front. In 1914 the Great Powers were ill-prepared to adapt air power to military purposes, and consequently the value of aeroplanes on the western front was virtually restricted to reconnaissance. But from January 1915 Zeppelin raids began on the English coast, reaching their peak in the summer of 1916, to be followed by aeroplane raids. Initally there may have been some attempt to discriminate between military and non-military objectives, but it soon became evident that in a war for existence civilian morale had been added to traditional targets.

By the end of 1914 statesmen were all more or less bewildered by the failure of the generals to bring the war to the quick decisive conclusion for which alone they had prepared militarily, politically and above all economically. In 1915 attempts began to find some way out of the stalemate which, especially on the western front, was replacing a war of movement by the gigantic siege foreseen by Bloch. The problem prompted two main reactions: a variety of military experiments and a gradual civil adaptation to the 'long haul'.

Falkenhayn was one of the most intelligent generals of the war but he was confronted with an insoluble strategic dilemma by the failure of the Schlieffen plan and the resolute commitment of Britain to the defence of France. He believed that the Anglo-French armies would have to be beaten to end the war and that a decisive victory over Russia was unobtainable in 1915. Yet he appreciated that a war of movement, with the

179

promise of great territorial gains, was only possible on the eastern front. He had also to contend with the opposition of Hindenburg and Ludendorff, who naturally believed that theirs was the decisive theatre, and whose prestige with the emperor was high after their début at Tannenberg. Against his better judgement, therefore, Falkenhayn decided to concentrate against Russia in 1915 while standing generally on the defensive in the west. Great victories in the east did indeed result but France gained time to recuperate and Britain to mobilise her second-line and Dominion forces.

Where desire to preserve the territorial gains of 1914 influenced German strategy, the French were inflamed by determination to liberate their homeland. Concentration against the main armies of the enemy was also orthodox military doctrine, yet without any tactical solution to the supremacy of the defensive barrier it could only lead to disaster. The French offensives in 1915 in Artois, on the Aisne and in Champagne demonstrated chiefly that against resolute and skilful defenders the attackers invariably suffered more casualties. Britain's much smaller numbers and length of front[1] deprived her of an independent strategic voice, and in any case Sir John French firmly supported Joffre. Furthermore, this unqualified commitment to the French on the western front, combined with the fact that most of Britain's senior generals were now serving in France, made it almost impossible for the government to obtain objective service opinion on the best way to employ Britain's unexploited asset of sea power in support of the army. The western front remained the decisive theatre, if only because so few soldiers were prepared to think otherwise.

Although the defensive system on the western front was far from fully developed in 1915, the basic elements of trenches and barbed-wire entanglements supported by machine guns were nevertheless impregnable to infantry and horsed cavalry, particularly as Britain and France were pitiably short of heavy artillery and high-explosive shells. The Entente offensives followed a depressingly similar pattern. 'After air reconnaissance of the German positions, artillery pounded their wire, machine gun nests and trenches. After the barrage had been lifted to the enemy's rear—creeping barrages just in front of the advancing infantry were not practised until 1916—the infantry went over the top in waves about one hundred yards apart, with the men in each wave about six to eight feet from each other.'[2] The attackers usually carried the first line of trenches and sometimes the second before being halted by the enemy's reserves. Counter-

---

[1] In November 1914 the French held about 430 miles, the British 21 and the Belgians 15; a year later the British share had been increased to about 50 (see C. R. M. F. Cruttwell, *A History of the Great War, 1914–1918*, Oxford, Clarendon Press, 1934, p. 109 n.; I am greatly indebted to this work, and to B. H. Liddell Hart, *A History of the World War, 1914–1918*, London, Faber, 1934).

[2] T. Ropp, *War in the Modern World* (new rev. ed., New York, Collier Books, 1962), p. 246.

attacks then frequently re-established the lines on the original positions. At no point during 1915 did British or French attacks gain more than three miles.

The one real tactical innovation of the year was the German use of poison gas against the French sector at Ypres on 22 April. The Germans had actually experimented with a form of tear gas in Poland the previous January but the intense cold rendered it ineffective. As frequently happened, initial disappointment caused the German Command to put little faith in the new weapon. The inventor, an extremely able chemist Fritz Haber, was deprived of facilities for manufacturing shells and was obliged to discharge his lethal clouds of chlorine gas from cylinders. Furthermore, no reserves had been concentrated to exploit the confusion, so that although a four-mile gap was created by the flight of agonised troops the Allies were allowed time to seal it. Germany thus incurred the odium for introducing a novel weapon without gaining a compensating advantage, for the improvement of respirators on both sides soon reduced the effectiveness of gas attacks.

Joffre's strategic plan—designed to end the war in 1915—was for a pincer movement against the great bulge left by the German retreat in 1914. Anglo-French forces would attack in Artois and the French alone in Champagne. These offensives continued intermittently through the spring and autumn with negligible gains. The two sectors were too far apart to exert a direct effect on each other, and Joffre pursued the incompatible aims of a breakthrough preceded by long bombardments, thus throwing away the trump card of surprise. In 1915 France suffered nearly one and a half million casualties. The British too lost equally heavily in proportion to their numbers. Sir John French's conduct of the battle of Loos (25–26 September), where the New Armies were 'blooded', was severely criticised, and eventually led to his replacement by Sir Douglas Haig in December. At the same time French's Chief of Staff, Lieut.-General William Robertson, went home to become Chief of the Imperial General Staff (C.I.G.S.). This move brought an improvement in that the strategic direction of the war was removed from Kitchener's overburdened shoulders, but it also added a powerful voice to the 'Westerners' in London.

The boldest solution to the trench barrier in France was the 'Eastern Strategy' advocated in Britain by such influential Cabinet ministers as Churchill, Lloyd George and Kitchener. While differing in detail they agreed essentially that modern developments had so changed conceptions of distance and powers of mobility that a blow struck in some other theatre of war would correspond to the traditional flank attack—which in France was impossible. Such an operation would accord perfectly with Britain's traditional amphibious strategy, and would also bring into play the military resources of the Empire.

Unfortunately the prospects of an 'indirect approach' were marred from the outset by disagreements as to destination and objectives. Kitchener, whose prime anxiety was the security of Egypt, was for crippling Turkey by a landing in the Gulf of Alexandretta; Lloyd George favoured a Balkans policy designed to support Serbia; while Churchill's gaze was riveted on the Dardanelles even before the deadlock occurred in France. An added complication was the ambivalence of that aged firebrand Lord Fisher, whose complete co-operation, as First Sea Lord, was essential. Fisher had long envisioned a landing on the Baltic coast, and though he appeared to support an expedition to the Dardanelles early in 1915 he was at best lukewarm and never had faith in a purely naval assault. Such divergencies of view are commonplace; the tragedy was that profound disagreements were papered over by inadequate planning. Thus the Dardanelles expedition eventually dispatched fulfilled Lloyd George's warning of 1914 that 'Expeditions which are decided upon and organised without sufficient care generally end disastrously'.[1]

The decision to attempt to force the Dardanelles by naval action alone was undoubtedly inspired and engineered by Churchill. Unfortunately the interrelated problems of silencing the Turkish batteries and clearing the mines from the Narrows were never fully appreciated in London. When the navy failed in its only attempt to force its way past the Turkish defences on 18 March—by the smallest of margins, it subsequently appeared, for the Turks had exhausted their ammunition—Fisher's growing pessimism and Kitchener's willingness to send troops resulted in a muddled decision to attempt combined operations. These necessitated a fatal hiatus of six weeks which the Turks used well to fortify the Gallipoli peninsula. However, owing to a misunderstanding between the military commander, Sir Ian Hamilton, and Admiral Robeck, the army—with French participation—was left to bear the brunt of the campaign. Despite forfeiting surprise the initial landings on 25 April succeeded brilliantly, and there were to be several more occasions—notably on 6 August when fresh landings were made in Suvla Bay—when victory seemed within the Allies' grasp. It eluded them every time through a mixture of ill luck, lukewarm support from Whitehall and from Egypt, remarkable Turkish resilience and almost incredible blunders in execution. Sir Maurice Hankey, then secretary of the Committee of Imperial Defence, touched on two fatal flaws when he noted that the number of troops *needed* for this extremely difficult operation had never been coolly assessed— Hamilton was simply given those that could be spared, invariably 'too little and too late'; and too much depended on the (false) assumption that the Turks would put up only weak resistance.

[1] R. R. James, *Gallipoli* (London, Batsford, 1965), p. 14. I have relied primarily upon this admirable book in the following paragraphs though not fully sharing the author's conclusions. See also J. North, *Gallipoli, the Fading Vision* (London, Faber, 1936), especially pp. 83–100, for the strategic implications of the campaign.

Rather surprisingly Gallipoli rapidly degenerated into another 'trench front' and western front tactics were faithfully repeated there with similar results. Towards the end of 1915 the bold decision was made to cut losses and withdraw from the peninsula. Ironically the withdrawal was the most brilliant achievement since the landings in April.

This was a strategic defeat with far-reaching consequences. Gallipoli destroyed Hamilton's reputation, undermined Kitchener's and eclipsed Churchill's. In the long run it discredited Asquith too, although he personally was a 'Westerner'. Most tragically it appeared to damn the 'Easterners'' argument that there was an easier way to end the war than that of slow attrition of men and resources. After 1915 it was difficult for even the most fervent 'Easterner' to suggest more than token diversions from France, say to Italy or Salonika. After Gallipoli there seemed to be no short route to victory.

On the ultimate wisdom of the Gallipoli venture opinion remains divided. Was it, as Sir Basil Liddell Hart believes, 'a sound and far-sighted conception marred by a chain of errors in execution almost unrivalled even in British history'; or merely a wasteful distraction of resources from the decisive theatre? The problem is accentuated by uncertainty as to the precise objectives of the expedition. Could Russia have been kept in the war the gain to the Allies would clearly have been enormous. Some historians doubt whether the Allies had the vital munitions with which to supply Russia even had Constantinople been captured. This was true of 1915 but of the vast amount expended in the next two years in the west even a small proportion would have been invaluable to Russia. As for the manpower situation, with nearly half a million men cooped up in the Salonika bridgehead it is patently untrue that every man was needed for the western front. In sum, while the Dardanelles probably did present a glittering strategic prize, the precise consequences of the fall of Constantinople must remain a matter for speculation.

The painful process of civil adaptation to demands of near-total war was rendered doubly difficult by the excessive deference paid to the professional expertise of the generals in 1914.[1] Governments saw their task as to furnish the resources demanded by the military leaders to achieve decisive victory, thus ignoring Clausewitz's dictum that warfare constitutes a continuation of policy by other means. Only slowly did it dawn on the statesmen that the military experts were equally baffled by a war that transcended their experience and their imagination.

Though the war itself inevitably raised problems of civil–military relations for all the belligerents, the outcome in each case was to a large extent predetermined by political tradition. In Britain, for example,

[1] M. E. Howard (ed.), *Soldiers and Governments* (London, Eyre and Spottiswoode, 1957), pp. 11–86.

constitutional practice assigned authority to the political head of the War Office; in fact Kitchener's tenure of the War Office (1914–16) confused the issue so that Lloyd George achieved only an uneasy compromise as Prime Minister (1916–18), eventually securing the removal of General Robertson and Admiral Jellicoe but being obliged to retain Haig, whom he mistrusted, to the end. German experience, at least since the retirement of Bismarck, went in the opposite direction, and the war only brought this trend to a climax. By 1916 Hindenburg and Ludendorff were regarded as the indispensable saviours of Germany. They controlled strategy; compelled the dismissal of uncongenial ministers; and prevented any hope of a negotiated peace by their extravagant territorial claims. This domination of the Supreme Command over the civil government did more than lead Germany to military defeat: it fatally disrupted the constitutional fabric of the Reich. The French experience was different again. The army had grown increasingly unpopular since the Dreyfus affair, and, after mounting criticism of the High Command's conduct of the war through 1914–16, the failure of Nivelle's offensive was the last straw. Following in the tradition of Danton and Gambetta the French gave direction of the war to the Radical Clemenceau, who left no doubt as to where authority lay.

The generals' failure to win a quick victory presented their governments with the task of mobilising national resources on an unprecedented scale. In meeting this challenge governments not merely maintained mass armies in the field: they also virtually obliterated the distinction between soldier and civilian and transformed European society almost beyond recognition. These momentous developments can only be hinted at by touching on French unpreparedness in 1914 and the gradual British adaptation to the demands of total war.

French conviction that the war would be short, and hence that every fully trained soldier should be mobilised immediately, was encouraged by the prevalent military doctrine of the Nation in Arms, though little trust was placed in reservists.[1] Even the rare individuals, such as Colonel Mordacq, who were sceptical of the military arguments, still tended to believe that financial needs would bring the war to an end in a year at most. Thus the opening months of the war brought a traumatic shock. The Minister of War was appalled to find the daily demand for shells approximately 100,000 when he could provide only 12,000. Heavy artillery had been badly neglected on the assumption that it would be of little value in a war of movement. Several munitions factories closed because skilled workers had been allowed to rush to the colours. Worst of all the government showed little understanding of the need to preserve economic resources and control industrial production. On the eve of war no less than 15 million tons of France's total annual output of 21 million tons of

[1] R. D. Challener, *The French Theory of the Nation in Arms, 1866–1939* (New York, Columbia U.P., 1955), pp. 83–136.

iron ore came from the Briey Basin near Metz. Yet in the first week of the war this vital area was lost almost without fighting because, it was later revealed, no one in the High Command or the government had grasped the relevance of iron ore to the French war effort. The guiding assumption, that in a short war supply would not be a critical factor, would of course have seemed less ridiculous had the Schlieffen plan succeeded.

Britain's reluctance to depart from the traditional methods of sustaining a war was certainly not attributable to a 'nation in arms' policy, since she relied upon a small professional army and a reserve of Territorials who were not obliged to serve overseas. In one sense Britain was able to pursue her traditional policy until 1916 because the Channel and a powerful navy once again allowed time for gradual expansion of her armed forces. But the more complex demands of modern war beyond numerical expansion were only slowly understood and accepted. Widespread belief in a short and limited war effort was only part of the explanation. There were also the characteristic attitudes of 'antipathy to state action and indifference to science and technology' which obliged Asquith's government—and the country generally—to continue a policy of 'business as usual' until the spring of 1915.[1] What eventually shattered this complacency was the critical shell shortage that could no longer be ignored after the battle of Neuve Chapelle on 10 March 1915. When Sir John French leaked information about this to the press the government's credit was badly shaken. The creation of the Ministry of Munitions under Lloyd George, which followed in May, was a striking early example of government intervention in industry and restriction of trade unions that set a precedent for a flood of subsequent controls.

By 1915, also, the indiscriminate volunteering encouraged by Kitchener was seen to have exacerbated problems of war production, since so many skilled workers had been lost. Many of the trade unions dourly opposed the filling of these vacancies by unskilled or female labour until they had wrung certain guarantees from the government. By stages these acute problems of the allocation of manpower forced the government—a coalition of Liberals, Conservatives and Labour from May 1915—to admit the need for some measure of conscription, something quite unacceptable in 1914. National registration in August 1915 gave the first hint of compulsion, to be followed in January 1916 by conscription applying only to single men and widowers without children. Universal conscription became law in May 1916. Apart from its military value conscription had at least two important social consequences: it broke down the last barriers of prejudice against the full employment of women (only domestic service suffered); and for the first time it brought experience of war to a cross-section of the whole population, affecting one in three adult males.

[1] A. Marwick, *The Deluge: British Society and the First World War* (London, Bodley Head, 1965), especially pp. 39–44, 52, 56–85, 90–4, 151–86, 226–39.

Yet it is astonishing how reluctantly the sacred principles of *laissez faire*, namely, free trade, free currency and free enterprise, were given up. Through 1915, for example, Asquith hesitated to interfere to check rising prices, while the attempt to allocate war expenditure to particular tasks was only abandoned in July 1915 when the daily cost of the war to Britain reached £3 million. Moreover, despite weakening opposition to widespread nationalisation the government moved slowly even in 1916 so that even when Asquith resigned so important a matter as food control was still under discussion.

The advent of Lloyd George to the premiership, and a great increase in the strain of the war on Britain in 1917—especially through the submarine campaign—brought a surge of government activity which by the end of the war had left few aspects of public, or indeed private, life untouched. The railways, and the coal and shipping industries, for example, came under direct state supervision, over 200 factories were nationalised and nine-tenths of the country's imports were bought directly by the state. Food rationing and the drastic restriction of drinking hours ensured that no one entirely escaped the war's indirect effects. It was hardly surprising if most people by 1918 calmly accepted the idea of state collectivism. The *laissez-faire* principles of 'Liberal England' were included among the notable domestic casualties of the war years.

On the eastern front the Russian armies took another fearful hammering in 1915. The Russians attacked first and between January and April succeeded in driving the Central Powers back from southern Poland to the foothills of the Carpathians. Then on 1 May von Mackensen began his dramatic breakthrough at Gorlice-Tarnow in Galicia. His onslaught, after a short bombardment, surprised the Russians; they recoiled from the Carpathians in disorder, and by 14 May the Austro-German advance had reached the river San eighty miles from the starting-point. Meanwhile Italy had been preparing for war, though if possible she intended to secure her territorial claims from Austria, notably the ports of Trieste and Pola, without fighting. Haggling between Rome and Vienna continued throughout the winter of 1914–15 before Austria was finally outbid by the Allies—who could afford to be more lavish in their proffers of enemy territory. The secret Treaty of London, signed on 26 April 1915, promised Italy not only the Brenner frontier (including some 300,000 Germans) but also Istria and the larger part of Dalmatia. However, even Italy's tardy declaration of war on Austria in mid-May failed to check the advance. Przemyśl was captured on 3 June and Lemberg on 22 June. This Russian retreat, involving the loss of three-quarters of a million men in prisoners alone, only ended in October on the line from Riga on the Baltic to Czernowitz on the Rumanian frontier.

Meanwhile, a pincer movement had ended Serbia's gallant resistance at the third attempt. On 6 October von Mackensen and von Seeckt, his Chief of Staff, led Austro-German armies across the Danube, and simultaneously two Bulgarian armies struck westward into southern Serbia across the rear of the main Serbian army. This effectively cut off the Serbs from their British and French allies who were belatedly advancing from Salonika. Rather than submit to encirclement and surrender the Serbian forces split up and the survivors retreated westward through the Albanian mountains, some of them to find refuge in Corfu. The conquest of Serbia not only removed the threat to Austria's flank but also gave Germany free communication and virtual control over the Balkans and through Asia Minor to the river Tigris. On the other side their failure to link up with the Serbs in time left the Anglo-French forces with a seemingly pointless bridgehead at Salonika.

One other 'side-show' was opened in 1915. Britain's involvement in Mesopotamia was prompted by political rather than military considerations and the ensuing campaign remained peripheral to the war in Europe. An Anglo-Indian expedition captured Basra in November 1914 to secure Britain's oil supply from the Persian Gulf. The temptation to exploit this military success against the Turks proved too strong for the commanders on the spot so that by mid-1915 the British had advanced 180 miles up the Tigris to Kut. From there the egotistic General Townshend conceived the ambition of pressing on to Baghdad: his plan was optimistically sanctioned by the War Cabinet eager for success somewhere to offset failure in France. Townshend soon discovered he had underestimated Turkish strength; he was checked at Ctesiphon on 22 November and by 8 December was invested at Kut. After several relief attempts had been beaten off Townshend eventually surrendered on 29 April 1916. The Turks treated their 10,000 prisoners so barbarously that less than a third survived.[1]

In 1916 the centre of gravity shifted back to the western front, thus signifying the failure of Falkenhayn's compromise strategy of 1915. On the Allied side the close of 1915 saw the first, overdue attempt to arrive at a concerted policy. Meeting at Joffre's headquarters on 5 December the military chiefs adopted the principle of a simultaneous general offensive in 1916 by Britain, France, Russia and Italy. A series of preliminary attacks was planned for the opening months of the new year to use up Germany's reserves, while also gaining time for Britain's new armies to train.

These simultaneous offensives were never executed because Falkenhayn disrupted the Allied plan by striking first. His strategic appreciation at the end of 1915 was founded on the belief that Britain was the mainstay of the

[1] Cruttwell, *History of the Great War*, pp. 346–8; A. J. Barker, *The Neglected War: Mesopotamia, 1914–1918* (London, Faber, 1967).

enemy alliance. Britain herself could only be crippled indirectly through submarine warfare since Falkenhayn believed that the front held by her armies in France was unsuited to offensive operations. His solution was therefore to compel Britain to make peace by eliminating her allies. Russia was already nearing exhaustion, and Italy could be contained by Austria with a stiffening of German troops. Only France remained but she too, Falkenhayn believed, was nearing the end of her military effort. To break the will of the French people it was not necessary to break the trench deadlock: a policy of attrition would suffice. France could be bled to death if only the right objective could be found. Falkenhayn's choice fell upon Verdun. This fortified area threatened German communications; it presented a salient which could be 'nibbled away'; and above all its proud history endowed it with an emotional significance to the French which far transcended its military value. Falkenhayn's tactical plan was starkly simple: a series of continuous limited advances would draw France's reserves into the mincing machine of the German artillery. The attacker would economise in manpower by protecting his infantry with short, intense bombardments which would enable them to rush and consolidate new positions before the enemy could bring up his reserves to counter-attack. Falkenhayn's calculations of French reactions were sound, as were also his new tactics, but he seriously underestimated both the French determination in defence and the effects of attrition on his own men.

The German offensive, which began on 21 February, was assisted by French preoccupation with their own coming attack. Also Verdun's legendary impregnability was now illusory since the forts had been denuded of guns and were in use largely as shelters. The trench defences were shallow and the troops thinly spread. Yet somehow the first advances were checked, so that by the time Pétain took command of the defences early in March the first crisis was over.

France's allies sacrificed their preparations for the summer offensive in order to relieve pressure on Verdun. Haig took over the Arras sector from the French 10th Army, thus establishing a continuous British front from the Yser to the Somme; the Italians made their fifth unrewarding attack across the river Isonzo; and the Russians threw in their untrained masses against the Germans at Lake Narocz, near Vilna. These gallant gestures failed to halt the steady German advance towards Verdun, and at first casualty returns seemed to justify Falkenhayn's frightful calculations. When Fort Vaux fell on 7 June it seemed that Verdun was doomed.

Again the Russians attempted to relieve the pressure, both from the French at Verdun, and from the Italians who were being counter-attacked in the Trentino. Brusilov, commanding on the south-western front, began on 4 June what was supposed to be a distracting advance, but which developed into a major offensive. The Austrian 4th Army near Luck and their

7th Army in the Bukovina put up such weak resistance that Brusilov continued his advance for three months. Unfortunately he lacked reserves to exploit his breakthrough and by the time they had arrived from the northern front the Germans had rushed reserves to seal the gaps. Brusilov's attempts to renew the offensive after it had halted succeeded largely in exhausting his own army, and although he had taken 450,000 prisoners his huge losses—nearly a million in action and thousands more through desertion—broke Russia's offensive power and also brought revolution appreciably nearer.

Despite its ultimate failure Brusilov's offensive had far-reaching effects. It checked the Austrian attack on Italy, compelled Falkenhayn to withdraw troops from the western front and so abandon plans for a preventive blow against the British on the Somme, and also discouraged him from renewing the grinding attrition at Verdun. Brusilov's success against the Austrians also influenced Rumania in her fateful miscalculation to enter the war on the side of the Entente in August. Indirectly Brusilov's success was partly responsible for Falkenhayn's supersession by Hindenburg and Ludendorff. Falkenhayn's ultimate hopes for the Verdun offensive had not been realised, yet he had succeeded in so weakening the French armies that they were incapable of playing the major role in the projected summer offensive. Verdun in fact marks the end of France's seniority in the partnership on the western front, despite the fact that Generals Nivelle and Mangin had recovered most of the ground lost at Verdun by the end of 1916.

Thus the great offensive planned in December 1915 was barely recognisable in the Anglo-French attack on the Somme. These battles witnessed the début of the Kitchener armies and of the tank; and also the tacit acceptance of an attrition policy by the Allies.

After a week's bombardment, which sacrificed any possibility of surprise, the offensive began in brilliant sunshine early on 1 July. The new 4th Army, commanded by General Rawlinson, attacked with 13 divisions on a fifteen-mile front north of the Somme, while the French—their contribution greatly reduced—attacked with 5 divisions on an eight-mile front mostly south of the river. The absence of surprise, perfect visibility, and the failure of the bombardment to destroy the enemy's wire and machine guns, rendered the attackers' chances slim. Moreover, the tactics of an orderly advance in rigid lines proved suicidal. The attacks failed everywhere except on the extreme right where the French met weaker opposition. The appalling casualties—57,400—were the highest ever suffered by the British Army in a single day. A renewal of the offensive on 14 July with more flexible tactics actually penetrated to the German second positions but further progress proved impossible. Haig had gradually to modify his initial hopes of a breakthrough to capture Bapaume and Cambrai. The need to attack specifically to assist the French at Verdun disappeared in mid-July, yet Haig continued his methodical attacks for insignificant territorial gains until the winter rains obliged him reluctantly to order a halt in November.

Meanwhile, on 15 September the British first employed a novel weapon which was eventually to play a major role in breaking the trench deadlock, namely, the armoured fighting vehicle mystifyingly named 'the tank'. Pre-war experiments with motor-driven caterpillar-tracked vehicles had aroused little enthusiasm among senior officers. Only the insight and boldness of Winston Churchill as First Lord of the Admiralty had enabled Colonel Ernest Swinton and other tank pioneers to have the vehicles ready for action in 1916. Their first performance fell short of expectations. Only 49 tanks were available and 17 of these broke down before reaching the start line. Of the remainder only 9 were able to keep up with the infantry and these did make a good impression, particularly in clearing the village of Flers. Considering the crews' hurried training and the lack of time to correct mechanical faults it was not surprising that so many tanks had broken down. The prospects of piercing through the deep German defences were so dim by mid-September that it must remain doubtful as to whether the commander-in-chief was justified in experimenting with the one weapon which—given favourable circumstances— might have had a decisive effect.

The Somme campaign raised strategic issues which had their roots in the 'Easterners versus Westerners' controversy of the previous year and which were also to influence the conflict between Lloyd George and the High Command in 1917. The failure of the Gallipoli venture probably ended the possibility of a decisive blow at the weak flank of the Central Alliance. At any rate the orthodox view shared by the majority of British and French statesmen and generals was that Germany could only be defeated by a concentration of effort on the western front. It followed that the Allies must adopt an offensive strategy: the Germans' territorial advantage demanded it; financial considerations were urgent; and above all the political solidarity of the Entente depended on a continual striving for victory. French losses in the reckless offensives of 1915 and the Verdun bloodbath also entailed that the British must perform the lion's share of the attacking. These considerations dispose of some of the wilder criticisms of the British and French High Commands for the persistent offensives between July 1916 and November 1917, but they by no means provide a blanket justification for their methods of execution.

On the strategic level the British and French followed too literally and narrowly the principle of concentration on the decisive front, not realising that Germany's central position and greater efficiency in moving troops by rail enabled her to concentrate even more speedily wherever the greatest danger threatened.[1] Her repeated dispatches of reinforcements to

---

[1] For a clear statement of the 'Western' view see Field-Marshal Sir W. Robertson, *Soldiers and Statesmen, 1914–1918* (London, Cassell, 1926), vol. I, pp. 238–89.

save the Austrians amply demonstrates this advantage. Lloyd George and Churchill grasped the point that even if the western front was crucial—in the sense that defeat there could not be compensated for elsewhere—Germany's resources must nevertheless be stretched as far as possible to give frontal assaults any chance of success. Hence the plan to aid Serbia in 1915, and Lloyd George's frustrated design to reinforce the Italian front early in 1917. Tactically, the Allied generals—with a few exceptions such as Smith-Dorrien and Plumer—were slow to evolve more sophisticated methods than 'clumsy bludgeoning', and were too prone to reinforce failure rather than call off offensives to reduce losses. This attitude of dogged persistence was evident also in unwillingness to surrender hard-won ground even when, as on the Somme in the winter of 1916, the offensive had petered out in a marshy valley overlooked by the enemy. Thus although Haig and his Corps and Divisional commanders laboured under great difficulties in 1916—with mostly inexperienced troops, a strongly defended sector to attack, and uncertain French support—it remains the case that generalship was undistinguished.

Sir Douglas Haig personally had several admirable qualities as commander-in-chief, particularly his unruffled patience in dealing with the French, and his grasp of the enormous administrative problem. His gravest defects stemmed from his physical remoteness from the front, probably an unavoidable handicap, which was magnified by Haig's unshakeable confidence in victory—founded essentially upon religious faith—and his failure to appoint independent-minded staff officers who would tell him the truth, however unpleasant. In the last resort it was Haig's belief that the Germans could be beaten in 1916 that caused him to continue the Somme offensive after the pressure had lifted from Verdun. As hopes of a breakthrough faded he put his faith in the wearing down of the enemy, taking the most optimistic estimates of their casualties.[1] Haig's published papers do not reveal the critical intelligence that might have led him to an objective assessment of British, French and German losses.

At sea Germany's unrestricted submarine campaign was temporarily suspended in April 1916 because of growing friction with the U.S.A. It was this enforced change of policy that indirectly brought about the only major sea encounter of the war, the battle of Jutland. Late on 30 May the British Fleet left its bases on one of its regular sweeps through the North Sea; while early the following morning the German Fleet also put to sea with the hope of cutting off a section of the enemy. Admiral Sir John Jellicoe, commander-in-chief of the Grand Fleet, remained extremely cautious. Appreciating that he alone could 'lose the war in an afternoon', he was determined to fight a major battle only under very favourable

---

[1] R. Blake (ed.), *The Private Papers of Douglas Haig, 1914–1919* (London, Eyre and Spottiswoode, 1952), p. 175. The problem of casualty statistics is discussed later.

conditions. Early in the afternoon of 31 May Vice-Admiral Sir David Beatty, commanding the battle cruiser fleet, sighted five enemy battle cruisers. Impetuously he engaged, and, after losing two battle cruisers, came upon the main German battle fleet. His task now was to lure the enemy towards Jellicoe, but fog and eventually darkness foiled him. Nevertheless Jellicoe had manœuvred between the German Fleet and its bases and a great victory seemed possible. The chance was bungled, for although he was sighted Vice-Admiral Scheer, commanding the German battle fleet, managed to slip through the destroyer screen and regained the safety of home waters. Both sides claimed a victory. The Germans had a better case in the numbers of ships and tonnage sunk, yet Scheer had failed in his aim of engaging only a part of the Grand Fleet, and indeed was fortunate to escape without greater damage. The Grand Fleet remained intact and the stranglehold of blockade was unrelaxed. Failure to gain a decisive victory on the surface soon caused Germany to revert to submarine warfare—and on a wider scale. The sinking of neutral shipping off the coast of North America in July pointed to the almost inevitable consequence of America's entry into the war. After Jutland the great fleets played only a secondary role. Scheer was virtually paralysed when deprived of his flotillas for the submarine campaign; while Jellicoe was hampered by the diversion of his destroyer escorts to combat the submarine. In four years of war the great fleets were in action for barely half an hour.

The year ended bleakly for the Entente with the submarine dominant. Monthly losses in shipping rose from approximately 109,000 tons in June 1916 to 368,000 tons in January 1917. Most sinkings took place in the Mediterranean where Germany ran less risk of antagonising the U.S.A. This rising toll encouraged Germany's war leaders to re-open unrestricted U-boat sinkings in February 1917 on the calculation—or gamble—that the Entente would be beaten on land and by starvation before American participation became effective.

1916 ended, like 1915, with the defeat of one of the Entente's allies. Rumania had awaited an opportune moment to enter the war in pursuit of her greedy territorial claims, and Brusilov's offensive caused her to take the plunge in August 1916. It proved an unwise gamble. With Wallachia sandwiched between Austria-Hungary and Bulgaria no country in Europe was worse placed for defence. Only the Russians could possibly give her direct support but they regarded her with contempt.[1] Her troops suffered from pitiful equipment and wretched leadership. Moreover, by attacking into Transylvania she exposed her flank to a bitter enemy, Bulgaria.

[1] The Russian Chief of Staff Alexeiev thus expressed his bitterness to the tsar: 'Such are my feelings, that if His Majesty ordered me to send fifteen wounded soldiers to Rumania, I would on no account send a sixteenth' (quoted by Cruttwell, *History of the Great War*, p 295).

The Central Powers' campaign, initiated by Falkenhayn and executed by Ludendorff, was strategically perhaps the most brilliant of the whole war. While the main Austro-German army, under Falkenhayn, gripped the Rumanians in Transylvania, a Bulgarian army led by von Mackensen invaded the Dobruja, thus paralysing the enemy advance by a threat to his rear. Falkenhayn broke through the mountain passes into Rumania in mid-November while Mackensen withdrew his army from the Dobruja and crossed the Danube at Sistova. Both armies converged on the capital, Bucharest, which surrendered on 6 December. However, the bulk of the Rumanian army escaped northward to a secure front behind the river Sereth. There, re-equipped and re-trained by the French, they held out until March 1918.

The gain of three-quarters of Rumania provided a tonic for the Central Powers after the stalemate at Verdun and the Austrian collapse before Brusilov. Conversely the Entente was again humiliated through moving too slowly to support a Balkan ally. Materially Rumania was a valuable victim, providing Germany with supplies of oil and wheat without which her resistance could hardly have been prolonged until the end of 1918.

The close of 1916 witnessed important changes among the civil and military war leaders. In Britain Lloyd George replaced Asquith as Prime Minister. In June the former had gone to the War Office when Kitchener was drowned on a voyage to Russia. His advocacy of a more vigorous conduct of the war by a small War Cabinet under his own chairmanship eventually led to Asquith's resignation in December. The new Premier was critical both of the policy of attrition and of the ability of the High Command, yet in practice he failed to make drastic changes, primarily for two reasons: he was never politically secure, being dependent on Conservative support in the House of Commons; and he feared the outcome of a direct clash with the generals, whose popular prestige was by now formidable. Instead he relied on devious methods which only worsened the situation. Against this uneasy compromise with the 'brass-hats' must be weighed Lloyd George's dynamic leadership through a streamlined War Cabinet; his ingenuity in securing vital appointments, such as the recall of Churchill to the Ministry of Munitions; and his flair for promoting solutions—such as the convoy system—against expert conservatism.

In December also Joffre was removed by being made a Marshal and promoted to a sinecure. He had inspired confidence in the battle of the Marne and in 1915, but was clearly unequal to the unique problems posed by the trench deadlock. His successor was the most junior of the Army Commanders, General Robert Nivelle, whose reputation had been made at Verdun. Nivelle possessed the rare asset among first world war generals of a fluent and persuasive tongue. He converted Briand and, more surprisingly, Lloyd George to his plan for a lightning offensive to end the war in the spring of 1917.

Among the Central Powers Ludendorff was now virtually in control of strategy, both Falkenhayn and Conrad having been removed from the supreme commands. On 21 November Emperor Francis Joseph died, to be succeeded by the last Habsburg ruler, Charles VIII. The latter would gladly have made peace if only his ally had allowed him to negotiate separately. At the same time Lord Lansdowne's peace proposals were receiving publicity in Britain. Nevertheless tentative peace feelers from the Central Powers were firmly rejected on 10 January 1917. Mutual war weariness could not surmount the military obstacle: namely, that Germany would not surrender territorial gains while there was a hope of victory, while the Entente could not contemplate peace without the restoration of French territory and Belgian independence as a minimum. Even President Woodrow Wilson was soon to realise the impossibility of 'a peace without victory'.

Shortly before his replacement Joffre assembled a Conference of the army commanders at Chantilly to determine strategy for 1917. He and Haig agreed that the attrition process of the past year had left the German army near to breaking point on the western front. Further limited offensives to exhaust the enemy's reserves in the opening months of the new year could pave the way for a decisive victory in the spring. Joffre knew that French manpower resources were nearly exhausted and announced that this would have to be her last major offensive. With 'Western Front' opinion thus dominant General Cadorna's proposal, supported by Lloyd George, that the British and French should send reinforcements to Italy for a decisive blow against Austria, was disregarded.

The prospects of Joffre's unimaginative strategy were immediately affected by Nivelle's promotion. The latter not only promised a sudden breakthrough in contrast to Joffre's reliance on cumulative attrition: he also drastically changed the details of the plan. Joffre had intended the British to launch a major attack early in February to the north and south of the old Somme battlefield, with the French supporting them southward as far as the Oise. These attacks would be followed by a smaller French offensive in Champagne and—unless enemy resistance unexpectedly collapsed—the British would then switch their attack to Flanders. By contrast Nivelle intended the Somme offensives to provide the distraction for the major blow by the French in Champagne. Thus the French were now to play the major role and to assist them Haig was asked to take over the French line south of the Somme as far as Roye.

These alterations and others caused protracted friction between the Allies. Haig was pleased to hear that the French would make a bigger effort, but he insisted on certain conditions before taking over the French line since this obviously handicapped his plans for a Flanders offensive. These inevitable disagreements called for a unified control, but unfortunately the devious methods adopted by both Briand and Lloyd George, who tried to achieve this at the Calais Conference on 26 February by subordinating Haig to Nivelle, only increased ill-feeling between the generals and between the allies. Haig agreed to serve under Nivelle's direction during the offensive provided he could appeal to his own government in an emergency. Nivelle was left in the unsound position of directing an Allied campaign while simultaneously commanding the French army.

Ludendorff dislocated Nivelle's plan by an even more effective manœuvre than Falkenhayn's attack on Verdun the previous year. Anticipating a renewal of the Somme offensive, Ludendorff had an artificial line of enormous strength ('The Hindenburg Line') built across the arc Lens, Noyon, Reims some ten miles behind the front. Nivelle refused to believe the growing evidence that the enemy was preparing to retreat, yet this he did, beginning at the end of February and systematically devastating what traces of civilisation remained in no man's land. Supporters of attrition take this retreat as proof of the German 'defeat' on the Somme; critics regard it as 'a master stroke both in conception and execution' designed to thwart the enemy by surrendering useless ground. At any event Nivelle's offensive was left in the air, while Haig had no option but to concentrate on the Arras sector where the front remained unchanged.

Nivelle added to his difficulties by failing to adjust his plans and by boasting openly of his intentions. Moreover, when the major French offensive began near Reims on 16 April he possessed the confidence neither of his government, his ally nor even his army commanders. The attacks, which lasted until 7 May, penetrated up to four miles on a sixteen-mile front, but this limited success contrasted too sharply with Nivelle's own promises. In any case the French armies were crumbling in his hands. The combination of demoralisation among front-line troops at being ordered once too often to capture unbroken defences, with long festering grievances over lack of leave and wretched living conditions, caused mutinies to spread through the armies until by early May nearly half the units were affected.

Thus the poilus finally ended the cult of the reckless offensive. Pétain, who replaced Nivelle on 15 May, at once announced that the French must remain strictly on the defensive pending the arrival of American divisions, and the provision of more tanks and heavy artillery. By shrewdly combining firmness and reforms Pétain quickly restored order. Not even Pétain, however, could revive the French army's offensive power in 1917. The British had no option but to distract attention from the French front, so that Haig's persistent attacks in April and May were justifiable on political grounds. The Flanders offensive began auspiciously on 7 June with a model limited advance by Plumer's Second Army (with 'Tim' Harington as Chief of Staff). Surprise was assisted by the explosion of

19 huge mines under the enemy defences, and the infantry then succeeded in straightening out the Ypres salient by capturing the Messines ridge.

An unfortunate delay then occurred until the battle of 'third Ypres' (also confusingly known as Passchendaele) began on 31 July. In view of the controversy that still surrounds this offensive it must be stressed that Haig was no longer attacking at the insistence of the French. Indeed as early as 11 May Pétain made it plain that he was opposed to any big attack, and on 19 May he added that Haig's projected advance towards Ostend was certain to fail. Foch, whose usual preference for attacking was never in doubt, referred to Haig's plan on 2 June as 'a duck's march', and considered the whole thing 'futile, fantastic, and dangerous'. Even Robertson advised Haig to tone down his predictions that the campaign would yield decisive results.[1] In extenuation of Haig it should be noted that his determination to capture the Flanders ports Ostend and Zeebrugge was possibly influenced by Admiral Jellicoe's mistaken belief that unless these U-boat bases were captured Britain would soon be forced to make peace. Nevertheless it was for Haig and not the Admiralty to decide whether in fact this mission could be carried out from the land.[2]

Although the offensive made some progress in August and September, Haig's judgement was at fault in thinking that a breakthrough was feasible given the nature of the climate and the terrain. Meteorological records over the past eighty years showed that heavy rain could be expected from mid-August. Moreover, the 'swamp map' produced by Tank Corps headquarters to denote the bogs created by the destruction of the drainage dykes by the bombardment—begun on 15 July—showed 'a wide moat of liquid mud' over much of the sector to be attacked on 31 July. The Tank Corps was eventually ordered to stop sending these pessimistic reports to G.H.Q., and as Haig's most recent biographer comments, 'There is no evidence that Haig ever saw one of those "Swamp Maps"; had he done so, he might have felt differently about some of the reports he was receiving.'[3]

If the urgent need to capture the Channel ports partly extenuates Haig for the attacks in August, his motives for continuing the offensive into November long after that objective had ceased to appear attainable need careful scrutiny. Again it has been wrongly stated that Haig was attacking under French pressure, or because he doubted their ability to withstand a possible German attack. There is no contemporary evidence

[1] The references to Pétain are from Maj.-Gen. Sir C. E. Callwell (ed.), *Field Marshal Sir Henry Wilson* (London, Cassell, 1927), vol. I, pp. 349, 354–5. Foch's sarcastic remarks are quoted by B. H. Liddell Hart in *Foch the Man of Orleans* (Penguin ed. 1937), vol. I, pp. 253–4. Robertson's cautionary advice was prompted by distrust of Lloyd George; see J. Terraine, *Haig: the Educated Soldier* (London, Hutchinson, 1963), p. 330.

[2] Terraine, *Haig*, p. 334. See also Captain S. W. Roskill, 'The U-Boat Campaign of 1917 and Third Ypres', in the *Royal United Services Institute Journal* (November 1959), pp. 440–2.

[3] Terraine, *op. cit.* p. 342.

to support this view; on the contrary on 8 October, after a visit from Pétain, Haig wrote to Robertson that the French were quite capable of holding their own in defence and that there was no need for him to take over more of the French front.[1]

Haig's persistence was due neither to callousness nor to the alleged tactical necessity of gaining the Passchendaele ridge. The fundamental reason was that the optimism that had deceived him in 1916 was still colouring his judgement. Haig accepted the information fed him by his Chief of Intelligence, General Charteris, which strongly suggested that 'German civil and military morale were so near breaking point that a ruthless continuation of pressure might result not only in winning the battle but also in winning the war'. As late as 28 September he predicted 'decisive results' from the attack at Broodseinde, and only after its failure on 4 October did he settle for the limited object of the Passchendaele–Clercken ridge.[2]

There is ample evidence that the Flanders offensive succeeded in wearing down the strength and morale of the German 4th Army; but it is probable that the British troops suffered equally severely. Indeed, since the Germans were for the most part defending, and had adopted the sensible tactics of defence in depth with scattered strong points rather than lines, it would not be surprising if the attacker's morale was more severely strained. The demoralising effect of Passchendaele, as well as the more publicised shortage of men, has to be taken into account to explain the breakdown of British defences in March 1918.

The arguments for and against the policy of attrition must to a large extent depend upon casualty statistics, yet these have been notoriously difficult to assess. Among the numerous difficulties three may be mentioned. German figures relate to periods of time and sectors of the front and these do not always coincide with particular battles. Secondly, the sources on both sides frequently do not distinguish between killed, wounded, missing and prisoners. Lastly, many of the German records were destroyed during the second world war, while certain of the Allied returns have either disappeared or are inaccessible; so that disparities in the published accounts cannot be checked. These drawbacks have caused some historians to eschew statistics altogether, while others have manipulated them to support preconceived views. In particular one of the British Official Historians, Brigadier-General Sir James Edmonds, provided support for 'the Westerners'' view that German losses on the Somme in 1916 considerably exceeded those of the Allies; but his methods of

---

[1] Blake, *The Private Papers of Douglas Haig*, p. 258. The French then held approximately 350 miles to the British 100, but much of the French line in the far south towards the Swiss frontier saw hardly any fighting throughout the war.

[2] M. E. Howard quoting from the Haig papers in a letter published in the *R.U.S.I. Journal* (February 1960), pp. 107–9. See also B. H. Liddell Hart, 'The Basic Truths of Passchendaele', *ibid.* (November 1959), pp. 433–9; and Blake, *The Private Papers of Douglas Haig*, pp. 255–60.

reckoning have been shown to be completely unreliable.[1] Recent examination of available British, French and German sources does however point to one clear conclusion: the balance of comparative losses on the western front was decidedly against the Allies from 1915 to 1917 inclusive:

	1915	1916	1917
German losses: killed and missing	170,312	295,572	281,524
wounded†	677,916	896,879	776,943
Total	848,228*	1,192,451	1,058,467
French losses: killed and missing	330,000	300,000	145,000
wounded†	970,000	576,000	424,000
Total	1,300,000‡	876,000§	569,000
British losses: killed and missing	73,160	151,086	185,555
wounded†	239,867	500,576	564,694
Total	313,027	651,662	750,249

* Total losses may be slightly larger.   ‡ February to November only.
† Includes those who died of wounds.   § February to December only.

Losses in particular campaigns point to the same conclusion. For example, on the Somme (1 July to early November 1916) the highest German figure is 500,000 (undivided) compared with the British total of 419,654 (also undivided) and the French 204,253. At Verdun between 21 February and the end of August 1916 the French lost 317,000 to the Germans' 300,212. At Third Ypres (31 July to mid-November 1917) the British losses, according to the Official History, were 245,000;[2] the French lost 8,525 (dead and wounded only); and the German Fourth Army, covering a much wider frontage than that of the British offensive, lost between 175,000 and 202,000. Total deaths (from all causes) on the western front in 1914–18 were approximately as follows: British, 700,000; French, 1·3 million; German, 1·2 million.

But even if the numerical balance was clearly against Britain and France two further questions must be raised: did the Germans still lose more men than they could afford; and when and why did their will-to-win begin to decline? Although the attrition process never came near to exhausting German manpower, the effect of heavy losses did begin to exert a depressing influence from 1916, especially as the High Command became obsessed with the policy of counter-attack. By the end of 1917 manpower was posing a serious problem after the peak of 5·38 million for the Field Armies (on all fronts) had been passed in June. Even so in March 1918

[1] See M. J. Williams, 'Thirty Per cent: A Study in Casualty Statistics' and 'The Treatment of German Losses on the Somme in the British Official History' in the *R.U.S.I. Journal* (February 1964), pp. 51–5, and *ibid.* (February 1966), pp. 69–74. Dr Williams has generously provided me with a digest of his statistical researches into the British, French and German sources and the figures quoted in this section are his. The conclusions drawn from them however are my own.

[2] In Sir Basil Liddell Hart's estimation, however, the British suffered at least 300,000 casualties.

Germany had 5·1 million men in the Field Armies (with 3·8 million of these in the west) and a further 2 million approximately in the Home Army. A striking decline is apparent as a result of Ludendorff's offensives, for between March and July the Germans lost about 973,000 men, and over a million more were listed as sick. By October there were only 2·5 million men in the west and the recruiting situation was desperate. Even so the main German problem in 1917 and early 1918 was not so much numerical weakness as growing war-weariness combined with—and greatly influenced by—the increasing shortage of food. This view is supported by the marked increase in disciplinary problems, especially in home-based units, even while the Field Army was still advancing.

Thus no precise answer is possible as to the effectiveness of attrition. During 1914–17 the Allies, more especially the French, nearly bled themselves to defeat. German losses in those years, though much smaller than Allied generals believed, were still more than they could afford. The numerical imbalance only became of decisive importance from mid-1918 when the Germans had exhausted themselves by prolonged attacks and their morale had been undermined, while on the Allied side the exhaustion of France was more than counterbalanced by the arrival of the Americans.

Fighting in the West in 1917 did not end in the mud of Flanders. As hopes of a breakthrough at Ypres waned, the Tank Corps was permitted to plan a raid over the rolling downland near Cambrai. On 20 November Byng's 3rd army, preceded by nearly 400 tanks, achieved a remarkable break-in, advancing as much as 7,000 yards in places and capturing 7,500 prisoners and 120 guns. Unfortunately reserves of tanks and troops were lacking to press home the advantage while the two cavalry divisions available were inexplicably inactive. On 30 November a German counter-attack regained most of the lost ground, and also boosted their morale. British disappointment was somewhat eased by the greatly improved performance of the tanks.

The seriousness of the French army mutinies had been amazingly well concealed from friends as well as foes. Russia's long-impending military collapse could not be concealed, especially after the Petrograd rising of March 1917 which led to the deposition of the tsar. Briefly the Provisional Government gave promise that 'a peoples' war' would be vigorously continued, but the revolution had come too late. Revolutionary propaganda now provided the exhausted and dispirited troops with positive political reasons for ending the war. Brusilov was given the Supreme Command to make a last desperate offensive effort in July 1917. It failed, and, by the time of the Bolshevist seizure of power in October, the army had practically ceased to function. By the end of the year the Bolshevists had signed an armistice and the Allies had no reason to hope they would renew the struggle.

The issue starkly posed by the end of 1917 was: could America give effective assistance on land before the German troops released from Russia could overwhelm the exhausted Allies in the west? At sea the impact of America's entry into the war was felt almost immediately. Her co-operation with Britain converted the naval blockade into a stranglehold which was not impeded by respect for neutrals. At the same time the sub-marine menace to Britain's supplies gradually began to be mastered. It had been a close-run thing. Submarine sinkings mounted steadily to a peak in April 1917 when nearly one million tons of Allied shipping was lost. A convoy system was only reluctantly tested by the sceptical British Admiralty, yet the first experiment with a merchant fleet from Gibraltar in May proved a success. By September the assistance of American destroyers enabled trans-Atlantic shipping to be escorted in both directions; and at the same time the anti-submarine offensive was reinforced by special submarine-chasers, aircraft and a new type of mine. Germany had nearly won the war against commerce with a mere 140 submarines on active service of which seldom as many as 50 were operating at any time.[1]

The heavy losses in merchant shipping in the Mediterranean was one of the reasons why Italy was nearly defeated at the end of 1917. After the Italians' eleventh offensive on the Isonzo in August, Ludendorff decided that Austria could not be relied on to hold for another year, and to save his ally Italy must be crushed. His blow fell on the Caporetto sector on 24 October after a brief bombardment. In the disorganised retreat that followed General Cadorna lost 250,000 as prisoners and thousands more through desertion. He was replaced by Diaz after establishing a defensive line on the river Piave, covering Venice. Britain and France now rushed in reinforcements which would have been more valuable earlier in the year. The Austrians, having outdistanced their transport, failed in repeated attempts to turn the Italians' defences.

The Italian crisis brought one incidental benefit to the Allies: it led to the creation of a Supreme War Council at Versailles in November 1917. Another crisis was necessary to secure real measures of Allied co-operation, for initially the national representatives lacked executive authority; while neither Haig nor Pétain was willing to spare divisions to a general reserve.

The Allies' campaign in the Middle East, using Egypt as the starting-point in 1916, made rapid progress in 1917. On 9 December Jerusalem surrendered to Allenby after a brilliant mobile operation; and in Meso-potamia the British were now secure in Baghdad (see above, p. 187). These successes could not immediately sway the delicate balance in Europe. Russia was soon (2 March 1918) to sign the enforced peace at Brest-Litovsk, and Ludendorff was certain to get substantial reinforcements before the Americans were ready to participate in strength.

At the beginning of 1918 the initiative in the west clearly lay with

[1] Ropp, *War in the Modern World*, p. 262.

Germany. From November 1917 troop trains began to shuttle the bulk of German forces from the Russian front to France, so that by early March 1918 they had 193 divisions against the Allies' 173, counting the large American divisions as the equivalent of two British or French. Yet Ludendorff knew that he was struggling against time as well as with hitherto impregnable defences. The submarine campaign was failing; the effects of the blockade on the home front were becoming serious—for example a general strike occurred in Berlin in January; and above all American troops were now pouring into France. Ludendorff, like Moltke in 1914, gambled on complete success, since a limited advance would only drive the enemy back on to his communications while increasing the attackers' supply problem. For their part, if the Allies could withstand the forthcoming offensive they could expect victory through sheer weight of manpower and resources by 1919.

Despite ample warnings, Allied defensive preparations were inadequate. No government was willing to denude other theatres to reinforce France. Italy opposed the withdrawal of Allied troops sent during the Caporetto crisis; the French government insisted on maintaining the Salonika bridgehead; and a majority of the British Cabinet was eager to complete the victory in Palestine. Lloyd George and the War Cabinet also deliberately kept Haig short of reinforcements; considering that lives had been needlessly squandered by commanders with an irrational faith in the value of repeated offensives, they feared that large-scale reinforcements would only lead to further slaughter. Both sides had some grounds for their mistrust and neither was wholly free from blame. It is easier to see in retrospect that the government should either have given the commander-in-chief its confidence or else have replaced him even at the risk of a political crisis. Although mutual mistrust between Prime Minister and commander-in-chief was to cause bitter recrimination after the disaster in March, the connection between that disaster and the retention of reserves in England was not so obvious as has often been assumed.

In the first place Ludendorff was able to build up a five to one supremacy on the 5th Army's front without the British High Command taking alarm. Indeed on 2 March Haig believed his front was so strong that he doubted whether the enemy could be tempted to attack.[1] Secondly, through misreading enemy intentions the defensive precautions were inadequate. Thirdly, Ludendorff shrewdly dealt his main blow at the juncture between the British and French fronts. Relations between the Allies were at a low ebb mainly as a result of disputes as to how much more of the front the British should take over, and the vexed question of forming a general reserve. Thus inter-Allied controversy and miscalculation as well as shortage of men prepared the way for a German breakthrough.

[1] Blake, *The Private Papers of Douglas Haig*, p. 291. A good description of German preparations is given by B. Pitt, *1918: The Last Act* (Corgi ed. 1965), pp. 50–78.

When the offensive began on 21 March the Germans had a superiority of 69 divisions to 33 on the sixty-mile front between Arras and La Fère. Ludendorff's aim was to split the Allied armies and roll up the British against the Channel coast—a feat which Hitler's Panzer forces were to accomplish in 1940. Tactically the Germans showed a great improvement on the stereotyped efforts of previous years. The essence of the new method was infiltration. Specially trained groups of storm troops armed with light machine guns, light trench mortars and flame-throwers were to cross the trench lines, by-pass strong points and machine gun posts and try to penetrate to the enemy artillery. Ludendorff also grasped the importance of surprise: he relied on only a brief preliminary bombardment; distracting threats elsewhere; and full use of concealment, both by the artificial means of gas and smoke, and the natural cloak of fog. Lastly, though in practice he neglected it, Ludendorff was determined to apply the principle of using his reserves to exploit success rather than to revive sectors where the attack was flagging.

For five days all seemed to favour the attackers. South of the Somme the German 2nd Army carried all before it until checked by the old Somme battlefield, but north of the river the British defended tenaciously in the Arras sector. Ludendorff delayed fatally in moving reserves to the more successful flank, thus allowing the Allies time to recover from the initial shock. In fact he only narrowly missed a complete breakthrough. The British 5th Army was shattered, and Pétain momentarily contemplated breaking with his disorganised ally and retreating on Paris. This crisis at last brought the Allies unity of command, for at a hurried conference at Doullens on 26 March Ferdinand Foch was made Supreme Commander to co-ordinate operations. The immediate value of this appointment, as Haig shrewdly realised, was a generous flow of French reserves to the British front.

On 28 March Ludendorff renewed the battering of Arras, but lacking the assets of either fog or surprise he failed to dislodge Byng's 3rd Army. Again a little too late he switched his remaining reserves to support the advance on Amiens. When this advance halted on 30 March it had penetrated nearly 40 miles, and nearly 1,000 guns and 80,000 prisoners had been captured.

Ludendorff next attacked in Flanders, breaking through a sector weakly held by Portuguese troops on 9 April. By the end of the month the British had yielded all the costly gains of 1917, though Ypres itself still held out. The British suffered heavy losses but they denied the enemy a breakthrough.

Slowly the balance of manpower began to tip against Germany, though this was not apparent until the summer. Since the offensive began the British had lost nearly 300,000 men and 10 divisions had been broken up. Reinforcements were rushed from England, and divisions recalled from

Italy, Salonika and Palestine. The Germans, with 208 divisions now in France, still had the strength for further offensives but time was running out. Already in the March crisis General Pershing had relaxed his rule against the premature commitment of American troops, stipulating only that they should fight as complete divisions. From the end of April 300,000 Americans were arriving every month; by mid-July seven divisions were in action and fourteen more were preparing.

After a lengthy pause for recuperation Ludendorff attacked next on 27 May on the Chemin des Dames between Soissons and Reims. Shattered British divisions had been sent to this supposedly quiet sector to rest, but the French commander, Duchesne, had undermined an almost impregnable position by massing his infantry in the forward trenches where they became 'cannon fodder' for the skilfully sited German artillery. On the first day the Germans made the longest advance in the west since the onset of trench warfare. The centre advanced thirteen miles, crossing the rivers Ailette, Aisne and Vesle. As happened so often, however, slower progress on the flanks resulted in the formation of a vulnerable salient.

Paradoxically the very extent of Ludendorff's tactical successes proved an embarrassment. He had created two huge bulges and one smaller one in the Allied front, leaving his armies a prey to counter-attack as their impetus declined. The tide of battle began to turn in mid-July. On the 15th Ludendorff attacked near Reims but made little progress. Three days later Pétain, using masses of light tanks, counter-attacked on the Marne, causing the Crown Prince to retreat to straighten his lines. The planned offensive in Flanders was postponed, then abandoned. Gradually the initiative passed to the Allies and Foch never again lost it.

After a most promising beginning Ludendorff had forfeited the second and last chance of German victory in the west by persistently attacking the strongest centre of resistance. Even more serious, ultimately, than the physical losses sustained by Germany during these offensives was the blow to morale when the ragged, undernourished attackers discovered the Allied rear areas to be, by comparison with Germany, 'a land flowing with milk and honey'—or more literally with wine and bread. Disillusionment and defeatism now began to spread. A falling-off in the Germans' fighting qualities became noticeable in the summer of 1918, particularly in the increasing number who quietly surrendered. There was now real justification for Haig's previously unfounded belief that the end of the war was in sight.

The Allied advance opened on 8 August with an inspiriting victory. General Rawlinson's 4th Army and the French 1st Army struck east of Amiens and, using over 400 tanks, overwhelmed the forward German divisions. The psychological effect was far-reaching for Ludendorff later described this as 'the black day of the German army in the history of the war...it put the decline of our fighting power beyond all doubt'. Soon afterwards he shocked the kaiser by advocating peace negotiations before the situation deteriorated still further.

Foch now had sufficient manpower, artillery, ammunition and tanks to prevent the enemy from consolidating. Blow now followed blow in rapid succession; attacks which were checked were no longer pressed unprofitably but were suspended and resumed only when the enemy had been distracted elsewhere. The Germans now experienced the demoralising effects of steady if gradual retreat. By mid-September the Americans, in their first battle as an independent army, had erased the St Mihiel salient though at high cost; while the British 3rd and 4th Armies had reached the formidable Hindenburg Line.

Haig's unquenchable optimism now proved most valuable, for, undeterred by the doubts of French generals and the British government, he remained convinced that the war could be ended that year. He attacked the Hindenburg Line on 2 September, and after a week of skilful manœuvring penetrated the defences on the strongest sector of the Canal du Nord. The news of the cracking of the Hindenburg Line so alarmed the already despondent Ludendorff that he suffered a breakdown and on recovering urged the new Chancellor, Prince Max of Baden, to sue for an armistice at once. This he did on 3 October. The defeatism of the military leaders quickly infected the home front, so that, although the generals partially recovered their confidence towards the end of October, it was by then too late to rally the nation. The inexorable advance of the Allied armies further undermined the will-power of the German government and people. By the time the armistice was signed on 11 November, the Germans had been ousted from western Belgium and only a fringe of French territory remained in their hands. Foch was about to launch an attack in Lorraine which would for the first time have carried the war on to German soil.

It is tempting but scarcely possible to assign a precise order of importance to the causes of Germany's defeat. One problem is to weigh military defeats against domestic defeatism; or what is almost the same thing, the attrition of Germany's armies against the attrition of her people through the blockade. Clearly it would be unrealistic to distinguish too sharply between the home and military fronts: news of wretched conditions at home sapped the soldiers' will to fight; while the defeatism of the revered military leaders broke the last restraint against social revolution inside Germany.

Another problem is to decide which, if any, of the war theatres produced the decisive victory. Chronologically 'the Easterners' appear to have a strong case. In September 1918 the Salonika front was at last opened up by General Franchet d'Esperey and paid dividends for the half-million troops deposited there. Bulgaria capitulated on 30 September, and Turkey's end was hastened by the exposure of Constantinople to attack from Macedonia. In Palestine Allenby's final offensive, assisted by the Arabs under T. E. Lawrence's unorthodox leadership, began on 19 September. Brilliant mobile operations led to the fall of Damascus and Aleppo, and Turkey capitulated on 30 October. When the Austrians were defeated in the Trentino and on the Venetian plain the ramshackle Empire, which had endured remarkably well, at last disintegrated. Austria sued for an armistice at the end of October and signed one on 4 November.

However, it is unlikely that it was chiefly the collapse of her allies that caused Germany to surrender. Her military leaders had concentrated their forces and their hopes on the western front, and it was Ludendorff's failure to clinch victory between March and July that had led to disillusionment. The loss of her allies probably served only to confirm a foregone conclusion. Indeed the realisation by Austria—and even more Bulgaria—in the summer of 1918 that Germany was no longer strong enough to send reserves to their support probably accounts in part for the slackening of their own resistance.

In retrospect it is easy to see that once the rival alliances went to war in 1914 the consequence was likely to be a terribly wasteful struggle of attrition. Recent military history, notably the American Civil War and the Russo-Japanese War, suggested that the brief, decisive battle was a thing of the past given opponents inspired by patriotic fervour and with governments prepared to draw heavily on national resources.

In these circumstances the natural tendency to blame the full horror for the holocaust on the generals was misplaced; in particular it was falsely assumed that individuals could exercise strict control over the juggernauts. Not surprisingly armies numbered in millions tended either to break their nominal commanders—as with Moltke—or to submerge them in the business of administration—as tended to happen with Haig. It is noteworthy that generals who remained in high command in 1918 did eventually reveal ability to conduct a war of manœuvre—though only Allenby had the advantage of terrain that permitted truly mobile operations.

Thus while criticism of particular campaigns and individuals' shortcomings is legitimate it must be founded on what was practicable at the time and not some ideal standard. Equally the generals' pre-war education —in the widest sense—must be taken into account, for in the long run societies get the leaders they deserve.[1] The soldiers who rose to the

---

[1] R. Wilkinson, *The Prefects* (London, Oxford University Press, 1964), especially pp. 77–9, 83–9. For the German military tradition see Karl Demeter, *The German Officer-Corps* (London, Weidenfeld and Nicolson, 1965).

highest commands during the war were the *élite* of their profession; many had distinguished themselves before 1914 and a few were to do so in civil life after 1918.

By the end of the war the domination of the defensive was at last being challenged by new means of mobility, notably the tank, the motor vehicle and the aeroplane. The war had produced potentially revolutionary machines without as yet the techniques for their full exploitation. To these half-spelt 'lessons' of the war reactions differed widely. The French General Staff learnt too well the folly of their impetuosity, and in the 1920s fell back on a static defensive policy, epitomised by the construction of the Maginot Line. Britain, after pioneering the tank and leading the way in military aviation, practically turned her back on these achievements in the 1920s, and returned to the pre-war tradition of amateurish contempt for mechanisation. Germany, as might be expected of the loser, showed most willingness to follow the military logic of the new ways of warfare suggested by tanks and aircraft. By the mid-1930s she was again preparing to conduct a war of movement.

Dispassionately viewed in the context of world politics the war, though uniquely wasteful in lives and material, was not strictly pointless, except possibly for Germany, whose rise to industrial dominance in central Europe was only delayed. Three historic Empires collapsed irreparably as a direct consequence of military disasters, and from them new states were created and old nations resurrected. France regained the provinces lost in 1871, and Belgian independence was restored. The calamitous results of the pre-war anarchy in international relations led to the brave experiment of safeguarding international peace and justice through the creation of the League of Nations.

From another viewpoint the European belligerents were all losers in that the war marked—if it did not actually cause—a shifting of international power away from central Europe to North America on one side and, less obviously, to Soviet Russia on the other. More directly the war spread the infection of European nationalism to a wider world. Japan had already tasted the triumph of nationalist victory in 1905, and her successful participation in the war further encouraged her nationalist pride and imperial ambitions. In India the sense of privileges fully earned by self-sacrifice in the Imperial cause, and also the exposure of thousands of her citizen-soldiers to Western conditions and ideas, combined to inspire a new and more vigorous post-war phase in the movement for national independence. Similar reactions were evident among the self-governing Dominions, whose contribution to the Allied victory had been invaluable. The Dominions' war services gained them independent representation both at the Peace Conference and in the League of Nations. Henceforth there could be no question of Britain unilaterally committing them to uncongenial policies—as Canada demonstrated in 1922 over the Chanak crisis with Turkey. The Great War was, in short, the matrix of the Commonwealth.

Among the most ominous developments of the war were the deliberate encouragement of nationalist hatred, the enlarged role of the press in misleading the masses, and the raising of government-sponsored propaganda to the status of a major instrument of war.[1]

It was probably only in the last year of the war that Allied propaganda exerted an important influence on enemy morale. Austria-Hungary with its starving civilians and ragged, emaciated armies provided an excellent target. Literature in all the languages of the Empire was showered from aeroplanes on the enemy trenches and far behind the lines, stressing the tyranny of Austrian rule and exploiting racial antagonism. The effect was evident in the increased flow of deserters; while a Congress of Suppressed Nationalities held at Rome in April 1918 was warmly supported by the Allied governments.

The British propaganda campaign was now brilliantly directed by Lord Northcliffe, ably assisted by Lord Beaverbrook as Minister of Information. The leaflets dropped on Germany provided news which German censorship withheld. Maps demonstrated the progress of the Allied armies; the daily arrival of vast numbers of Americans in France was stressed; all the evils of the war were blamed on Prussian militarists; and hopes of a just peace were held out for a democratic Germany. By the end of the war Britain alone was dropping 140,000 leaflets a day over German lines. The Germans had been the first to use enemy propaganda but now they had no answer to this 'poison raining down from the sky'.

There is ample evidence—in the sudden slump in military morale, in widespread strikes and demonstrations, and in political crises such as Kühlmann's 'defeatist' speech in the Reichstag on 24 June 1918—that Allied propaganda played a decisive part both in breaking the German armies and in fomenting a revolutionary situation inside Germany. When Germany's military failure could no longer be concealed the deluded masses suffered a traumatic shock.

A massive propaganda campaign to strengthen one's own morale and cripple the enemy's was inevitable in an unlimited war, and at least the mixture of truth, lies and half-truths was less destructive than material attrition. Nevertheless, it was obviously a two-edged weapon whose evil effects could not be cut off with the armistice. Thus, for example, popular war hysteria ruled out any possibility of a moderate, conciliatory peace settlement in 1919; while Goebbels and others perfected and perverted war-time propaganda methods to support even more loathsome racialist policies in the inter-war years.

The neologism 'home front' aptly suggests the extent of civilian

[1] F. P. Chambers, *The War Behind the War 1914–1918* (London, Faber, 1939), pp. 494–537.

involvement in the war. Even in Britain, with its *laissez-faire* and anti-militarist traditions, the needs of war left few aspects of life undisturbed; British Summer Time and restricted licensing hours were among the permanent legacies. The most significant general trends were in the direction of strengthening the machinery of central government, extension of government activity through new ministries, and the imposition of controls that would have been unthinkable before 1914. Had the war stopped in 1916 a return to something like pre-war conditions might have been possible, but the final two years saw a transformation of European society which could not be reversed.

CHAPTER VIII

THE PEACE SETTLEMENT OF VERSAILLES
1918–1933

At eleven o'clock on the morning of 11 November 1918 the cease-fire sounded along the western front. It was the end of the first world war, which had killed not less than 10 million persons, had brought down four great empires and had impoverished the continent of Europe. The defeat of Germany, so long invincible to more than half the world, had been registered at dawn that day in the Armistice of Compiègne. Its heavy terms were in the main those proposed by Marshal Foch, the Allied generalissimo, and lay between the views of the British Field-Marshal Haig, who overestimated the German capacity for continued resistance and advocated more lenient conditions, and those of the American General Pershing, who had argued in favour of refusing an armistice and maintaining the Allied advance. This matched the attitude of the former president Theodore Roosevelt and a popular American demand for unconditional surrender. As it was, one month after the armistice, Ebert, head of the first government of the new German republic, greeted returning German formations at the Brandenburger Tor with the words: 'No foe has overcome you...You have protected the homeland from enemy invasion.'[1]

No less important in the long run than the terms of the armistice were the preconditions governing its signature. When the German government had applied to President Wilson on 4 October 1918 for an armistice it had adroitly proposed that peace negotiations, and not only those for an armistice, should be based upon the 'fourteen points' of his address of 8 January 1918, as amplified in his subsequent pronouncements. During the preparatory Allied discussion of armistice terms in Paris and Versailles at the end of October, the European Prime Ministers, Lloyd George, Clemenceau and Orlando, along with Sonnino, Italian Foreign Minister, were chary of committing themselves contractually to the frequent imprecisions of the fourteen points. Lloyd George asked: 'Should we not make it clear to the German Government that we are not going in on the Fourteen Points of peace?'[2] But Wilson's harbinger and confidant, Colonel House, threatened that, if they were refused as a basis, the United States might abandon her associates and conclude a separate peace with the enemy. By 5 November the American government was able to transmit to the German government in the Lansing Note a declaration by the Allied

---

[1] Friedrich Ebert, *Schriften, Aufzeichnungen, Reden* (Dresden, 1926), vol. II, pp. 127–8.
[2] Charles Seymour, *The Intimate Papers of Colonel House* (London, 1926f.), vol. IV, p. 167.

powers of 'their willingness to make peace with the Government of Germany on the terms of peace laid down in the President's address to Congress of January, 1918, and the principles of settlement enunciated in his subsequent addresses',[1] subject to two qualifications: first, the Allies reserved complete discretion concerning the freedom of the seas (point II)—an important success for Lloyd George against standing American resentment of the British doctrine of blockade; secondly, by the stipulation that the invaded territories must be 'restored' (points VII, VIII and XI) the Allies 'understand that compensation will be made by Germany for all damage done to the civilian population of the Allies and their property by the aggression of Germany by land, by sea, and from the air'[2]—a category much narrower than the possible but unrealisable claim to the whole of the direct cost of the war to the Allies, then estimated at around £24,000 million. Such was the so-called Pre-armistice Agreement respecting the fourteen points entered into in connection with the armistice with Germany, but not with the earlier armistices with Bulgaria, Turkey and Austria-Hungary, to which territories the points were largely relevant.

The Allied powers did not communicate to the German government the authoritative American commentary on the fourteen points provided by House, who, at the meeting of the Allied Supreme War Council on 29 October, pointed out that Wilson 'had insisted on Germany's accepting all his speeches, and from these you could establish almost any point that anyone wished against Germany'.[3] Certainly the commentary rendered the points rather more adaptable. For instance, the phrase 'open covenants of peace, openly arrived at' (point I) 'was not meant to exclude confidential diplomatic negotiations involving delicate matters'[4]—Wilson had explained this to the Senate. As regards the readjustment of Italian frontiers 'along clearly recognisable lines of nationality' (point IX) it was now suggested that 'Italy should have her claim in the Trentino, but that the northern part, inhabited by Germans, should be completely autonomous'.[5]

The American commentary likewise dealt gingerly with the 'open-minded, and absolutely impartial adjustment of all colonial claims' (point V) and subsequently, in initiating the discussion upon them in the first days of the peace conference, Wilson said that 'he thought all were agreed to oppose the restoration of the German Colonies'.[6] This principle, welcome to the British Empire, was adopted at once by the Supreme Council (24 January 1919) and later discussion turned upon its applica-

[1] *British and Foreign State Papers* (H.M. Stationery Office, London), vol. CXI, p. 650.
[2] *Ibid.* p. 651.
[3] David Lloyd George, *The Truth about the Peace Treaties* (London, 1938), vol. I, p. 80.
[4] *Papers relating to the Foreign Relations of the United States, 1918: Supplement I* (State Department, Washington, 1933), vol. I, p. 405.   [5] *Ibid.* p. 410.
[6] *Papers relating to the Foreign Relations of the United States: the Paris Peace Conference 1919* (Washington, 1942 f.), vol. III, p. 718. Hereafter cited as *The Paris Peace Conference 1919*.

tion, notably the form and attribution of mandates, the new instruments of trusteeship under the League of Nations (see ch. IX), whereby Allied powers took over the outlying territories of the German and Turkish empires. In this latter connection Lloyd George had already, at a brief Allied conference in London at the beginning of December 1918, used the great preponderance of British forces in the Turkish theatre to obtain Clemenceau's verbal agreement, honourably kept, to modify to British advantage the secret Sykes–Picot Agreement of 1916 for the disposal of the Turkish Empire; Palestine, which was to have been under international control, would now pass under British, and oil-bearing Mosul was to be transferred from the French to the British sphere of influence. The British Prime Minister also secured Allied recognition of the right of the battle-tested British Dominions to send delegates to the peace conference. Lloyd George was compelled, indeed, to concede what Castlereagh in like circumstance a century earlier had withheld, namely, his agreement that the freedom of the seas might be discussed; but when the conference came Wilson tactfully submerged this vexed issue of neutral rights under cover of his quest for a League of Nations without neutrals, in what he termed a 'practical joke on myself'.[1] Thus at the outset Lloyd George, reinforced by a fresh mandate from the British electorate in the Coupon Election of December 1918, had skilfully secured a strong position for Britain and had set her on the way towards obtaining much, if not most, of what she mainly aimed at on and across the seas as regards the suppression of the German fleet and colonies, the doctrine of blockade, her economic and strategic position in the Middle East on the route to India, and her constitutional evolution of empire.

If the initial position of Britain was stronger than that of the hard-tried continental allies, France and Italy, stronger again was that of America away across the Atlantic. It was, indeed, the strongest in the world. The United States, unlike the European allies, emerged from the war not poorer but much richer, with the others heavily indebted to her not only in gratitude for precious aid but also in hard cash to the extent of about £2,000 million. At the same time many Americans tended to think of themselves, despite their participation in the war, as impartially aloof from the rapacious feuds of old Europe. This attitude found divergent expressions, on the one hand in the isolationism of Senator Borah of the Republican party, and on the other in the idealism of President Wilson, the leader of the Democrats. His aspiration towards a finer ordering of international society had sent a thrill of hope through the war-weary world. It seemed that here at last was the old ideal of the philosopher-prince new-made in a professorial president with the power as well as the purpose to lead mankind into a more generous future. America

[1] President Wilson, speech at San Diego, 19 September 1919: Addresses of President Wilson (66th Congress, 1st Session, Senate Document No. 120: Washington, 1919), p. 278.

appeared the richest nation both in substance and in spirit so that even the old Tiger, cynical Clemenceau, believed or said he believed that she 'had opened a new and more splendid ethical era'.[1]

International relations were now to take an exciting jump ahead into the League of Nations. This was largely, though not entirely, done under Wilson's influence and he was the focus of expectation when he landed in Europe on 13 December 1918, the only head of a state who was, unwisely as many thought, to be a delegate to the Peace Conference of Paris. Preliminary meetings of the conference began a month later and it was formally opened in plenary session on 18 January 1919. Twenty-five allied and associated nations from the five continents were represented at this inauguration of the first peace 'congress of the world' (Wilson).

The delay in starting the conference was scarcely excessive considering the unexpected suddenness with which the war had ended; but once begun the conference, and specifically the Council of Ten comprising two representatives each of the Principal Allied and Associated Powers (British Empire, France, Italy, Japan, United States), still delayed in getting to grips with the main issues. Not only were the negotiators reluctant to show their hands too early but, instead of being able to concentrate upon the chief problems, the delegates discovered that they constituted 'a cabinet of the nations' (Lloyd George) subject to the pressure of current events. From the beginning the massive phenomenon of the Russian revolution loomed up behind the conference, as was indicated within its first week by the abortive Prinkipo Proposal.[2] In Berlin the Socialist government had indeed just crushed the Spartakist extremists by turning against them the militaristic free-corps, the beginning of the disappointment of the keen ambition of Lenin's Russia to promote a Communist take-over in Germany. This critical failure was to be reinforced by the suppression of the Soviet republics which were shortly to arise in Bavaria and Hungary. That, though, still lay ahead. For the present a wave of strikes further diminished confidence and dislocated the enfeebled economy of Europe, especially in Italy and England. In France, with her northern coalfields wantonly devastated by the Germans, coal production in 1919 was reckoned to be about 40 per cent of that in 1913. Furthermore, throughout the world, an epidemic of virulent influenza killed about twice as many people as the war had done.

[1] Conversation of 9 November 1918 with House, as reported by the latter: *The Paris Peace Conference 1919*, vol. I, p. 344.

[2] Lloyd George, who had personally advocated a hearing for Soviet Russia at the peace conference, hopefully proposed that all the warring factions in Russia should be called upon to observe 'a truce of God' and to be represented at a special conference to try to resolve the conflict under Allied auspices. Lloyd George was supported by President Wilson who drafted the Allied invitation of 22 January 1919 to attend such a conference at the Princes Islands, Prinkipo, in the Sea of Marmora. This venue reflected Clemenceau's refusal to have Soviet representatives in Paris. With French encouragement the White Russian authorities refused to have dealings with the Soviets, who for their part sent an insufficient and insulting acceptance. Thus the experimental Prinkipo Proposal came to nothing, and the allies in Paris were left to debate the uneasy pros and cons of further intervention in Russia.

Sickly Europe was short not only of coal and other raw materials, but also of food. Much was done here by the American Relief Administration under the influential Hoover, who became head of the Food Section of the Supreme Economic Council, judiciously constituted on 8 February 1919 by the Council of Ten in order to co-ordinate such organs as the short-lived Supreme Council for Supply and Relief, the Allied Blockade Council and the Allied Maritime Transport Council, and to correspond in some measure to the Supreme War Council on the military side. The Council of Ten was itself preoccupied about that time with executive matters of military and economic detail in connection with the renewal of the armistice with Germany and the relaxation of the blockade, which it had specifically maintained. The thirty-six-day Armistice of Compiègne, finally renewed at Trier on 16 February 1919, had been provisionally renewed on 13 December 1918 and again on 16 January 1919 when it was stipulated that 'in order to secure the provisioning of Germany and of the rest of Europe'[1] the German merchant fleet should be placed under Allied control for the duration of the armistice without prejudice to its final disposal, and under promise of 'suitable compensation' for its use. This was one of the additional demands which the Allies saw fit to make. These 'aggravations of the armistice' (Wilson) understandably incurred some moral criticism, but the demand for the German merchant fleet was, in view of the general shortage of tonnage caused by the German submarine campaign, a reasonable provision to facilitate the relaxation of the blockade in execution of the declaration in the original armistice convention that the Allies 'contemplate the provisioning of Germany during the armistice as shall be found necessary'.[2] The grim hunger in Germany was less severe than in some other parts of central Europe, but on 17 January the Allies declared their willingness to permit Germany to import a first instalment of 270,000 tons of food if the merchantmen were handed over forthwith. The German government, however, now refused to do so before it had received an Allied guarantee of specified deliveries. Complex negotiations ensued concerning terms of delivery and methods of payment. The French authorities, intent as ever upon German reparation for German devastation, were reluctant to allow Germany to pay in gold but were overborne by the forceful intervention of Lloyd George at a meeting of the Council of Ten on 8 March which led to the solution of the question six days later in the Brussels Agreement for the provisioning of Germany. Thereafter the food blockade of Germany was relaxed until it was finally raised on 12 July 1919 in consequence of her ratification of the peace treaty.

On the same day as the Brussels Agreement, 14 March, Wilson returned

---

[1] *British and Foreign State Papers*, vol. CXII, p. 899.
[2] *Ibid.* vol. CXI, p. 619. English translation of official French text as in H. W. V. Temperley, *A History of the Peace Conference of Paris* (London, 1920 f.), vol. I, p. 468.

THE SHIFTING BALANCE OF WORLD FORCES

to Paris after a month's absence. For as soon as the draft covenant of the League of Nations had been completed and laid before the full conference on 14 February he had left for Washington to face his critics in the Senate, where there was a Republican majority, before Congress adjourned. Wilson's concentration on the League of Nations was not, however, the only, or even perhaps the chief, psychological factor which combined with executive distractions to delay the primary task of concluding peace with Germany. For many, including keen young experts on the British and American delegations, the main interest lay less in the stern reckoning with Germany than in the benevolent creation of new nationalities like the Czechoslovaks and Yugoslavs in fulfilment of war-time Allied propaganda which had made of their liberation an idealistic war-aim such as Anglo-Saxon peoples generously crave. The time of the Council of Ten was much taken up with wearisome hearings of Central European and Near Eastern delegates and as late as 17 March Wilson 'insisted that peace should be made simultaneously with Germany, Austria-Hungary, Bulgaria, and Turkey'.[1] This impractical attitude was supported by Italy for practical reasons of self-interest in the dissolution of the Austro-Hungarian empire. It was partially reflected in the constitution, early in February, of the territorial commissions of the conference. There were commissions for Czechoslovak affairs, for Polish affairs, for Rumanian and Yugoslav affairs, for Greek and Albanian affairs, for Belgian and Danish affairs, but none specifically for German or Austrian affairs. Nor was this deficiency very satisfactorily remedied by the creation at the end of the month of the co-ordinating Central Territorial Committee and of later committees for considering enemy representations.

The effective improvement in organisation came in the last week of March when the Council of Ten contracted into the more secret and informal Council of Four, much as a century earlier at the Congress of Vienna the Committee of Eight had been effectively superseded by the Committee of Five. And on 25 March Lloyd George presented in his Fontainebleau Memorandum the first conspective review of the salient problems of peacemaking. At last they were hammered out between the four of them: Clemenceau, very old, in suede gloves, Wilson who 'believed in mankind but...distrusted all men',[2] Lloyd George who 'argued like a sharpshooter',[3] and Orlando, the only one who did not speak English. Subordinate to the Council of Four there was constituted a council of foreign ministers or Council of Five; and indeed Wilson and Clemenceau, more even than Lloyd George, did treat their respective Foreign Ministers, Lansing and Pichon, strictly as subordinates.

The conference now reached its crux over the claims of France in that

[1] Note by Colonel House: Seymour, *The Intimate Papers of Colonel House*, vol. IV, p. 401.
[2] Lloyd George, *The Truth about the Peace Treaties*, vol. I, p. 234.
André Tardieu, *La Paix* (Paris, 1921), p 113.

214

Rhineland region disputed between Frenchmen and Germans since the middle kingdom of Lothair was cast up in the wreck of Charlemagne's empire more than a thousand years before. The main French claims, already advanced in their clearest form in 1917, were two: first, that 'Alsace and Lorraine must be restored to us not in the mutilated condition in which they were left by the treaty of 1815, but with the frontiers as they existed before 1790. We shall thus have the geographic and mineral basin of the Saar';[1] secondly, the French government 'desire to see the territory to the west of the Rhine separated from the German Empire and erected into something in the nature of a buffer state'[2] against their more prolific German neighbours who had invaded France twice in one lifetime, in Clemenceau's. Wilson and Lloyd George opposed these claims, being rightly afraid of repeating in reverse Germany's provocation in annexing Alsace-Lorraine. Concentrated negotiation brought a sensible settlement by mid-April. It was decided that the territory of the Saar valley should be slightly enlarged and placed under a special administration of the League of Nations for fifteen years, after which its sovereignty should be determined by plebiscite; the mines of the Saar basin were given to France in compensation for her ruined coalfields. Clemenceau reluctantly and to the dismay of President Poincaré and Marshal Foch abandoned the demand for a buffer territory in return for three guarantees of security: first, a military guarantee by Great Britain and the United States of immediate assistance to France in the event of German unprovoked aggression; secondly, the demilitarisation of the west bank of the Rhine and of a fifty-kilometre belt on the east bank; thirdly, Allied occupation of the west bank and bridgeheads in three zones, one of which might be evacuated each five years up to fifteen years, or sooner if Germany had before then completely fulfilled her obligations. Wilson and Lloyd George were especially doubtful about Allied occupation but finally on 15 April Wilson agreed. That same day Clemenceau, in the presence of his friend House, instructed his secretary that the French press must cease its jeering attacks upon the thin-skinned president. They promptly ended. It was commonly supposed that this was more than coincidence and that Wilson had stooped to a disillusioning bargain. Meanwhile Lloyd George was temporarily absent in London; he did not much like the Wilson–Clemenceau agreement on occupation that he found upon return, but consented to it on 22 April.

Already on 18 April the German government had received an invitation to send plenipotentiaries to Versailles and on 7 May the draft treaty of peace was there communicated to Count Brockdorff-Rantzau, German Foreign Minister. Initially the general idea had been that some sort of 'preliminary peace conference' of the Allied powers would serve as a

---

[1] French note of 12 January 1917: *Papers respecting Negotiations for an Anglo-French Pact*, Cmd. 2169 of 1924, p. 2.

[2] Balfour, British Foreign Secretary, to the British Ambassador in Paris in connection with the foregoing note, 2 July 1917, *ibid.* pp. 3–4.

prelude to a full congress, which might include enemy delegates. Here, however, there prevailed even more than the usual haziness over procedure. For instance, Balfour had spoken in February of 'the final military proposals', which had originated in connection with renewing the armistice, as facilitating 'an important instalment of the Preliminary Peace'.[1] When nearly a month later the first report from a territorial commission, the Polish, was under discussion Lloyd George asked 'whether the Council proposed to define the frontiers of Germany finally on *ex parte* evidence alone. The other side had not been heard. It was not only a question of fairness to Germany but of establishing a lasting peace in Europe.'[2] But the idea of hearing the Germans before the treaty was in draft receded into the background, and when the first meeting did come on 7 May it was inauspicious. Count Brockdorff-Rantzau spoke sitting, unlike Clemenceau who preceded him, and said: 'We know the force of the hatred which confronts us here, and we have heard the passionate demand that the victors should both make us pay as vanquished and punish us as guilty. We are required to admit that we alone are war-guilty; such an admission on my lips would be a lie.'[3]

In his preceding speech Clemenceau had given the German plenipotentiaries fifteen days, subsequently prolonged by a week, in which to present observations in writing upon the draft terms. There followed a spate of German memoranda, often skilfully, sometimes speciously, argued. The main arguments were that 'the exactions of this treaty are more than the German people can bear'[4] and that in many respects they were in contradiction with the stipulated fourteen points. This comeback jolted the British representatives, who for one thing had tended, with their Allied colleagues, to compile the treaty piecemeal without always appreciating the heavy sum of the provisions. ('Instead of drawing the picture with big lines, they are drawing it like an etching', commented House.)[5] Also, the fourteen points had sometimes been rather lost from sight since Wilson had failed to follow them up with a detailed plan and had transferred his enthusiasm to the League of Nations, thus relaxing the American diplomatic initiative which House had secured at the armistice. Now, however, it was apparent that on some questions the Germans could make out 'an awkward case', as Balfour remarked at the session in Paris on 1–2 June of the British Imperial Cabinet at which the German observations were considered. A sincere and honourable desire to deal justly with Germany and a fear of renewed hostilities, if Germany should refuse the terms, combined to render the cabinet unanimous in charging the British Prime Minister to exert strong pressure to secure large con-

[1] *The Paris Peace Conference 1919*, vol. IV, p. 86.
[2] Lloyd George, *The Truth about the Peace Treaties*, vol. II, p. 984.
[3] *The Paris Peace Conference 1919*, vol. III, p. 417.
[4] *Ibid.* vol. VI, p. 795.
[5] Seymour, *The Intimate Papers of Colonel House*, vol. IV, p. 418.

cessions to Germany. These were resisted not only by Clemenceau but also by Wilson, who complained that the British were now afraid of the 'things that they insisted upon at the time of the writing of the treaty; that makes me very sick... They are all unanimous, if you please, in their funk. Now that makes me very tired.'[1]

Nevertheless Lloyd George surpassed Wilson on occasions, and now obtained important modifications. Back in March he had already secured the revision of the Polish Commission's territorial proposals, which were unduly drastic towards Germany according to the Wilsonian principle of ethnic self-determination; now he returned to the charge. Besides obtaining further modifications of the Polish frontier in Germany's favour, he overcame Wilson's reluctance to apply the process of self-determination to Upper Silesia, and met one of Germany's chief and legitimate grievances by insisting upon a plebiscite there instead of outright cession to Poland. Lloyd George failed, however, to surmount Clemenceau's refusal to reduce the fifteen-year period of allied occupation in the Rhineland. Nor did he get very far in his enlightened plea for the early admission to the League of Nations of Germany, who had offered to surrender the permitted remnant of her navy if this were granted her forthwith. Popular passions here as elsewhere complicated the task of the democratic peacemakers who, unlike their predecessors at Vienna, worked under the direct pressure of powerful criticism in press and parliament. It was the same with the question of reparation, concerning which Lloyd George had been instructed by the cabinet to aim at a modification 'in the direction of fixing the liability of the Germans to the Allies at a definite amount'[2] in place of the stipulation that the Allied Reparation Commission, which was to supervise the execution of Germany's financial obligations, would inform Germany by 1 May 1921 of her total liability.

Other things being equal, there was evident advantage, as the American delegation urged, in inserting the total in the treaty, and in the subsequent event its execution was gravely prejudiced by adding a delay in fixing the figure to the inevitable delay in paying a great indemnity. But other things were not equal. Lloyd George was well aware that Germany's capacity to pay was limited and furthermore that she must mainly pay by exports which would be particularly liable to injure the trade of her industrial competitor, Britain, stripped by war of foreign markets which had underpinned her nineteenth-century supremacy. The British Prime Minister, however, was saddled with his electioneering assurance that Germany 'must pay to the uttermost farthing', and he did not want to let his Conservative supporters 'throw him' on this issue.[3] Politics took

---

[1] Wilson at a meeting of the American Commission to Negotiate Peace, 3 June 1919 (stenographic report): *The Paris Peace Conference 1919*, vol. XI, p. 222.
[2] Lloyd George, *The Truth about the Peace Treaties*, vol. I, p. 719.
[3] Lloyd George to Colonel House, 6 March 1919: Seth P. Tillman, *Anglo-American Relations at the Paris Peace Conference of 1919* (Princeton, 1961), p. 239.

precedence over economics so that Lloyd George argued in the Council of Four that 'if figures were given now they would frighten rather than reassure the Germans. Any figure that would not frighten them would be below the figure with which he and M. Clemenceau could face their peoples in the present state of public opinion':[1] time, he now hoped, would promote moderation.

The British share in reparation would, under the terms of the Lansing Note, have been exiguous except for shipping had it not been that British argument, largely, and in particular by the memorandum of 31 March 1919 by high-minded General Smuts of South Africa, had secured the inclusion of service pensions and allowances in the category of damage done to civilians. Under cover of dubious reasoning which tarnished the Allied reputation, Germany's liability was thus at least doubled from somewhere about £2,000–3,000 million, which was what the British Treasury and Board of Trade had estimated that she could and should pay, to the much more uncertain region upwards of £6,000 million. The German delegation had in its observations mentioned the impressive-looking figure of £5,000 million as a possible maximum, but subject to such far-reaching conditions as the retention of colonies and foreign assets and to such technical qualifications that the amount actually to be paid would have been reduced out of recognition. This was considered an insidious and unacceptable offer. The provision for the determination of Germany's liability by 1 May 1921 was maintained, though Lloyd George secured agreement on 10 June that Germany might submit to the Allies within four months of the signature of the treaty any proposals for payment she chose to make in the way of offering either a lump sum, or labour and materials or 'any practicable plan'.[2] Germany did not avail herself of this concession.

The vigorous and voluminous Allied reply of 16 June to the German observations, while mainly controverting them, bore witness to the British initiative not only as regards reparation and Upper Silesia but also in a number of minor concessions to Germany as to the Pomeranian frontier, purchase of Silesian coal, the rate of German disarmament and, for instance, the international control of Germany's main waterways, which was a feature of the treaty. This Allied note gave Germany five days, subsequently extended to seven, in which to signify her acceptance of the revised treaty, failing which the armistice would lapse and the Allies would 'take such steps as they think needful to enforce their terms'.[3] These steps were to be in the first instance an advance in 'two bounds' by thirty-nine Allied divisions from the Rhine to the Weser and up the valley of the Main with the object of severing southern from northern Germany. Foch was authorised 'to commence his advance immediately

---

[1] Meeting of 9 June 1919: *The Paris Peace Conference 1919*, vol. VI, p. 261.
[2] Allied reply of 16 June 1919 to the German observations: *British and Foreign State Papers*, vol. CXII, p. 285.   [3] *Ibid.* vol. CXII, p. 253.

on the expiration of the armistice'[1] at seven o'clock on the evening of
23 June 1919. Meanwhile there was passionate opposition in Germany
to the terms, and a cabinet crisis whereby Bauer became Chancellor in
place of Scheidemann, who declared that the hand that signed such a
treaty must wither. On 22 June the Supreme Council shook the new
German government by rejecting its offer to sign under specific reserve
as to those articles (227–31) concerning German war-guilt and the surrender of Germans accused of war crimes. On the morning of 23 June
the Supreme Council, incensed by the scuttling two days previously of
the German battle-fleet interned at Scapa Flow, refused a German request
for a further 48-hour extension of the time limit. The Supreme Council
was again in session at five o'clock that afternoon, having not yet received
a German reply. The meeting concluded during an observation by Balfour,
recorded as follows by the adept secretary, Sir Maurice Hankey: 'As
to squeezing the Germans...(At this point M. Dutasta, followed by
Colonel Henri and Captain Portier, entered the room, with a note from
the German Delegation expressing willingness on behalf of the German
Republic to sign, under compulsion, a dishonourable peace...Orders
were given for guns to be fired. No further discussion took place).'[2]

At twelve minutes past three on the afternoon of 28 June 1919 in the
Galerie des Glaces at Versailles the German plenipotentiaries signed the
great treaty of 440 articles and sealed the defeat of that Second German
Empire which had been inaugurated in the same room, in victory, not
fifty years before. And it was five years to a day since the assassination at
Sarajevo.

By the Treaty of Versailles Germany in the west ceded to Belgium the
small districts of Eupen and Malmédy subject to conditions concerning
popular consultation, and returned to France the Alsace-Lorraine of
1870, accepting also the provisions with regard to the Saar and the Rhineland. In the south Germany 'acknowledges and will respect strictly the
independence of Austria' (article 80); the old frontier with the Austro-
Hungarian Empire was retained with the minor exception of a wedge in
Upper Silesia ceded to the new Czechoslovakia. In the east Germany conceded to reconstituted Poland a roughly ethnic frontier giving her Posen
and West Prussia with a corridor to the Baltic on the eighteenth-century
model in fulfilment of the stipulation in the fourteen points that Poland
'should be assured a free and secure access to the sea' (point XIII). In
this connection the German port of Danzig was constituted an outlet for
Poland as a free city under the auspices of the League of Nations, but
with no provision for subsequent revision as in the case of the Saar.
On the other side of East Prussia, Germany lost Memel, which eventually

---

[1] Decision of the Council of Four, 20 June 1919: E. L. Woodward and Rohan Butler,
Documents on British Foreign Policy, 1919–1939 (H.M. Stationery Office, London, 1946 f.),
First Series, vol. I, p. 18.   [2] *Loc. cit.*

passed to Lithuania. Plebiscites were to determine the attribution of Upper Silesia and of the East Prussian districts of Allenstein and Marienwerder: the provisions regarding Silesia and Marienwerder, as for Danzig, were substituted largely at British instance for originally proposed cessions to Poland. The outcome of the plebiscites, held under Allied administration, justified the British stand. Allenstein and Marienwerder were assigned almost entire to Germany as a result of overwhelming votes in July 1920, and in the Silesian plebiscite in March 1921 Germany secured approximately 60 per cent of the votes against 40 for Poland. The consequent division of Upper Silesia provoked a Polish insurrection under Korfanty and acute Anglo-French dissension before an award by the League of Nations in October 1921 partitioned the territory so that the smaller, but economically much the richer, part went to Poland. This difficult award satisfied neither party, but then the whole determination of Germany's eastern frontier on ethnic lines was highly complex, and in the main a creditably fair compromise was achieved. This did not, however, prevent especial resentment in Germany against a frontier which afforded so much to the hated Poles. The Silesian difficulty did not arise comparably in Schleswig since for that borderland the treaty specifically provided for a plebiscite to be held in two zones, the northern of which went to Denmark and the southern to Germany. In all, Germany lost, including Alsace-Lorraine, about $13\frac{1}{2}$ per cent of her territory, a roughly similar proportion of her economic productivity, and a little over 10 per cent of her population, some seven millions. She also lost all her colonies—a notable severity—all her merchant vessels over 1,600 tons gross and half those between 1,600 and 1,000 tons.

The Treaty of Versailles further provided for the disarmament of Germany. Conscription there was abolished, chiefly at the instance of Lloyd George against Foch, who saw danger in the resultant professional army, consequently limited to a mere 100,000 men. This miniature force was deprived of heavy artillery and tanks. The German navy was reduced to minor proportions, without submarines, and an air force was forbidden. (Wilson, however, had insisted, against the majority recommendation of the Aeronautical Commission of the peace conference, upon Germany's being permitted a civil aviation.) The disarmament was to be supervised by inter-allied commissions of control. The former German emperor was arraigned 'for a supreme offence against international morality' (article 227), but the Netherlands persistently refused to surrender him from his neutral asylum. Article 228 bound the German government to hand over for trial before Allied military tribunals all persons accused of complicity in the atrocities wherewith Germans had smirched their conduct of the war. The German government from the first did its utmost to evade this obligation and ultimately twelve accused were tried by the German Supreme Court at Leipzig. There they were either acquitted or received such inadequate sentences that in January 1922 an Allied juridical commission of enquiry recommended that the remaining accused be handed over for trial by the Allies. They, however, let the matter drop.

The other article which aroused the fiercest German resentment was the so-called 'war-guilt clause' whereby 'the Allied and Associated Governments affirm and Germany accepts the responsibility of Germany and her allies for causing all the loss and damage to which the Allied and Associated Governments and their nationals have been subjected as a consequence of the war imposed upon them by the aggression of Germany and her allies' (article 231). The Allies not unnaturally did consider this to be an affirmation of the truth, but it was intended to establish the potential extent of German responsibility in its financial bearing before proceeding to limit that financial liability along the lines of the Lansing Note. The article had been drafted, largely by the young American expert, John Foster Dulles, with the intention of achieving a compromise between the American viewpoint, adhering to the Note, and that of France and Great Britain, resigning themselves to its limitations. It was German propaganda which expatiated upon moral war-guilt in connection with an article which provoked no equivalent outcry from Austria or Hungary. The reparation settlement with Germany which this article introduced was as indicated, and included the short-term provision that, pending the fixing of the total liability by 1 May 1921, Germany should pay the equivalent of £1,000 million from which, however, there were to be deducted the expenses of the Allied armies of occupation and, with Allied approval, such supplies of food and raw material as they might judge 'to be essential to Germany to meet her obligations for reparation' (article 235).

Such were the main, but far from the entire, terms of the Treaty of Versailles. They were a severe imposition upon the new democratic régime of Weimar which had been stimulated in its origin by Wilson's objection before the armistice to treating with representatives of 'arbitrary power'. But, as Wilson said, 'the real case was that justice had shown itself overwhelmingly against Germany'.[1] That was the central verdict which most Germans would not accept, that and the sheer fact of defeat. They developed a telling propaganda against the treaty, bringing out wherever possible its inconsistencies, real and alleged, with the fourteen points. Attention was averted from the greedy and vindictive war aims which German arms had endeavoured to secure. In the peacemaking of the Allies, though, the measure of their good intentions was that they had sincerely adopted so high a standard in the first instance, and that a reproachful propaganda based upon it should have made them, as it did, apologetic. Seldom indeed has so stringent a treaty been framed with

[1] Meeting of Council of Four, 3 June 1919: *The Paris Peace Conference 1919*, vol. VI, p. 159.

such idealistic intent, a dichotomy which suggested to its prescient French critic, Bainville, that it was 'too mild for its severity'.[1] The opening for charges of Allied hypocrisy over a dictated peace was widened by the mismanagement of concluding an armistice with the enemy negotiated upon ambiguous terms and then, after permitting him to state his case in writing, indeed, but not in oral negotiation, imposing upon him the allied rendering of those terms.

The full significance of the peace can only be appreciated, however, if the settlement of Versailles be extended to embrace the treaties of peace with Austria (St Germain-en-Laye, 10 September 1919), Bulgaria (Neuilly, 27 November 1919) and Hungary (Trianon, 4 June 1920). This last was delayed first by a Hungarian lapse into Communism under Bela Kun (21 March–1 August 1919) and then by the ensuing Rumanian occupation of Budapest, which provoked admonitions from the Council of Heads of Delegations. These 'lawful heirs of the Council of Four' (Balfour, the British representative) toiled on for the second half of the peace conference, from the signature of the Treaty of Versailles until its entry into force on 10 January 1920; they mainly completed what Balfour called 'the immense operation of liquidating the Austrian Empire'.[2]

The resultant map of Europe was startlingly different from the old one. The empire was parcelled out among half a dozen 'succession states'. The German remnant of Austria became a top-heavy and economically precarious state of under $6\frac{1}{2}$ million inhabitants of whom nearly a third were concentrated in Vienna. Austria lost the South Tyrol to Italy but retained Klagenfurt by plebiscite and was awarded the Burgenland, where, however, Hungary managed to wrest back Sopron. Hungary was to lose most of all by dismemberment in obedience to self-determination; Croatia and Slovenia went, along with Bosnia and Herzegovina, to join with Serbia and later Montenegro in the new Yugoslavia; in the north Hungary yielded Slovakia, including a Magyar minority, to the new Czechoslovak republic, and in the east Transylvania, including another and less avoidable Magyar minority, to Rumania. (Here, as elsewhere, special arrangements were concluded to protect the rights of national minorities under the supervision of the League of Nations—see ch. IX.) Rumania was further aggrandised by gains in the Banat, Bukovina and, uneasily from Russia, in Bessarabia. This expansion could be mainly justified by ethnic arguments but they were scarcely applicable to Rumanian retention of the Dobrudja at the expense of Bulgaria, who was also to lose to Greece her Thracian outlet to the Aegean. If Rumania did well from the settlement so did Poland, back on the map after more than a century of sup-

---

[1] 'Une paix trop douce pour ce qu'elle a de dur'—8 May 1919: Jacques Bainville, *L'Allemagne* (Paris, 1939), p. 250.

[2] Meeting of the Council of Heads of Delegations, 19 August 1919: Woodward and Butler, *Documents on British Foreign Policy*, First Series, vol. I, p. 432.

pression. Having gained from Germany in the west, she now, with pent-up chauvinism, pushed out her frontiers in the east beyond the Curzon Line to include Eastern Galicia and adjacent territories after she had defeated the Soviet drive on Warsaw in the summer of 1920: a further critical failure of the revolutionary designs of Russia to the west. In the following autumn General Zeligowski's raid snatched Vilna from the Lithuanians and presented the great Allied powers with another Polish accomplished fact; they eventually sanctioned both these Polish gains in March 1923. The Polish dispute with Czechoslovakia over Teschen had been settled for the time being by an Allied award of 28 July 1920 partitioning the little duchy and thereby adding a small Polish minority to the Czech, Slovak, German, Hungarian and Ruthenian national groups which combined to make Czechoslovakia an ominous miniature of the defunct Habsburg monarchy.

Such, most briefly, was the balkanisation of central Europe with which the peacemakers were later reproached, not with full justice. For the settlement did, despite shortcomings, unravel a horrid tangle of conflicting claims and considerations broadly according to fresh concepts of ethnic self-determination. This principle was not, indeed, the invariable panacea which people then tended to suppose: much depended for instance upon the size and choice of the units selected for self-determination. Yet its strength in general was suggested by the way that the network of new frontiers on the whole survived the fluctuations of time; and where they were later altered it was not always for the better. Furthermore, the main features of this new national determination were already present when the settlement came to be drafted, since 1918–19 marked the disruptive success throughout the Austro-Hungarian empire of that national-liberal uprising which had been damped down seventy years before. Thus the responsibility of the great Allies might be held to lie less in their peacemaking than in their war-time propaganda which had so successfully preached the empire's dissolution. Nor were the drafters of the settlement so unmindful of wider economic considerations as was sometimes supposed. On 26 August 1919, for instance, they discussed a proposal involving 'a customs union from Danzig to Sicily'. Balfour remarked, however, that 'the proposal of establishing an entirely new customs system over half Europe alarmed him'.[1] And American opposition thwarted initiatives by Britain and other European Allies towards reviewing the economic position of Europe as a whole in relation to America, especially as regards currency, and drawing upon the experience of the Supreme Economic Council to constitute subsequent organs of economic co-operation.

The settlement did, however, contain elements of inherent weakness, especially as regards the main flaw in the logical application of self-determination. For while this doctrine was applied to Germany's detriment

[1] Woodward and Butler, *Documents on British Foreign Policy*, First Series, vol. I, pp. 547–9.

in Poland and elsewhere she was not allowed the benefit of it in the Sudetenland and Austria, where on 12 November 1918 the German-Austrian Republic had been constituted specifically as 'a component part of the German Republic', and claiming to include the Sudetenland. Article 80 of the Treaty of Versailles, matched in that of Saint Germain, did not prevent the framers of the new Weimar Constitution from providing for consultative Austrian participation in the German parliament preceding Austria's 'junction with the German Reich' (article 61). On 22 September 1919 Germany was accordingly compelled by the Allies to sign a declaration nullifying any article in the constitution which conflicted with the treaty. It would have been exceedingly difficult for the Allies to sanction such fresh additions to German territory and power but, as it was, Germany was left with a sense of injustice that could appeal to the victors' own principle of self-determination: a moral weakness in the Allied position which found its lodgment within twenty years.

Lloyd George had written in his Fontainebleau Memorandum: 'I cannot conceive any greater cause of future war than that the German people, who have certainly proved themselves one of the most vigorous and powerful races in the world, should be surrounded by a number of small States, many of them consisting of people who have never previously set up a stable government for themselves, but each of them containing large masses of Germans clamouring for reunion with their native land.'[1] Yet that was just what Lloyd George and his colleagues found it impossible to avoid. Smuts had written earlier, in 1918: 'Europe is being liquidated, and the League of Nations must be the heir to this great estate.'[2] It was a heavy heritage for so new and experimental an authority.

The unfashionable balance of power had broken down. The Concert of Europe had contracted by the autumn of 1919 to an uneasy western alliance. Attempts were then being made in Paris to strengthen this alliance by promoting the co-ordination of Belgian and Dutch defence against any eventual renewal of German aggression. This preoccupation already underlay the deliberations of the Commission for the revision of the treaties of 1839, of that 'scrap of paper' torn up by the German invasion of Belgium in 1914. Within two months of the signature of peace a British military representative informed members of this commission that the danger for Belgium of a repetition seemed to him 'to be chiefly for the time when Germany should have been able to arm herself anew and perhaps conclude an alliance with Russia, which might give birth to a rival of the League of Nations. This danger could not, however, arise for twenty or thirty years... The fact that the French frontier had been retraced towards the north along the Rhine made it more and more necessary for Germany to attack in Limburg. Germany would, therefore, become...more liable

---

[1] *Papers respecting Negotiations for an Anglo-French Pact*, Cmd. 2169 of 1924, p. 77.
[2] Lloyd George, *The Truth about the Peace Treaties*, vol. I, p. 622.

to oblige Holland to make war.'[1] The stubborn Dutch, however, were understandably suspicious of Belgian aspirations in regard not only to freer navigation of the Scheldt but even to the territories of Limburg and Dutch Flanders—the Council of Four had turned down a Belgian scheme for acquiring such slices of Holland and compensating her with German territory in Prussian Gelderland or East Friesland. A comprehensive revision of the settlement of 1839 was also stultified, partly owing to British refusal to guarantee Belgium unless she resumed her profitless neutrality.

As to the east, the Allied powers, hastily demobilised, were left with barely strength enough to evict from the new Baltic states of Latvia and Lithuania the ruthless German freebooters under General von der Goltz who, even after the peace treaty was signed, aimed at clamping down a teutonic domination there and so resuming the German drive to the east. The Supreme Council at Paris doubted its power to coerce, if necessary, even Hungary or Bulgaria. Balfour opined on 26 July 1919 that 'the Powers, which, eight months ago, were the conquerors of the world, could not, at the present moment, impose their will on an army of 120,000 men'.[2] Of the European conquerors Britain was bent upon reducing her continental commitments, France was wearied and Italy was embittered by her treatment at the peace conference.

If Italy's allies were unenthusiastic about her military performance in the war, Italy understandably resented the way in which they had concluded the Sykes–Picot Agreement behind her back, and was further put out when at the peacemaking she found herself less popular with them than her Adriatic rival, Yugoslavia, largely comprising Croats and Slovenes from the Austro-Hungarian empire, her main enemy. But Italy alienated her friends by her 'blinkered greed' (Lloyd George) in pressing not only her extensive claims under the secret Treaty of London but also her vociferous demand for Fiume, which that treaty had assigned to Croatia. The question of Fiume was accorded a symbolic significance beyond its intrinsic importance both by Italy, whose poet D'Annunzio seized it in a filibustering raid on 12 September 1919, and on the other side by Wilson, who, in refusing to concede it to Italy, matched Sonnino in stubbornness and had provoked the Italian delegation to temporary withdrawal from the conference by issuing an unseemly manifesto on 23 April 1919. Lloyd George warned Wilson of 'a growing feeling that Europe was being bullied by the United States'.[3] After much commotion the question was eventually left for direct settlement between Italy and Jugoslavia and dragged on until 1924 when most of Fiume was secured by Italy, who had earlier acquired Zara and Lagosta while renouncing her wider claims to Dalmatia

---

[1] Lieut.-Colonel Twiss at a meeting of great powers on the commission, 22 August 1919; Woodward and Butler, *Documents on British Foreign Policy*, First Series, vol. v, pp. iii–iv and 277–8.

[2] *Ibid.* First Series, vol. i, p. 207.

[3] Meeting of Council of Four, 3 May 1919: *The Paris Peace Conference 1919*, vol. v, p. 430.

under the Treaty of London. This Italian concentration on the Adriatic diminished her activity, if not in appetite, in other regions such as Africa where her interest in the direction of Abyssinia was indicated by her claim to British and French Somaliland and to the French holdings in the Djibouti–Addis Ababa railway. This claim being resisted, Italy in May 1919 offered to swap it for a mandate over the former German colony of Togoland on the other side of Africa. This also was unpalatable to Britain and France, who divided Togoland and the Cameroons between them, eventually under mandates. Italy had to be content, or discontent, with Jubaland in East Africa, ceded by Britain in 1924, and minor concessions from France on the Libyan border.

The Italian Prime Minister wrote to the British on 25 May 1919:

I cannot look forward without grave apprehensions to the future of continental Europe; the German longing for revenge must be considered in conjunction with the Russian position. We can thus see even now that the settlement to be arrived at will lack the assent of more than half the population of the European continent. If we detach from the block on which the new European system will have to rely for support forty million Italians, and force them into the ranks of the malcontents, do you think that the new order will rest on a firm basis?[1]

The might of Russia had for the present fallen away to the east and now that of America was to be withdrawn in the west so that, despite the residual League of Nations, European policies throughout the 1920s tended, with exceptions, to be cast upon a reduced scale. Wilson, back in America, suffered a paralytic stroke at the end of September 1919 and lingered on a broken man. Events swiftly suggested his partisan error in provoking the Republican party in the congressional elections of 1918 and in rejecting advice to include one of its leading members in the American Commission to Negotiate Peace. Strong opposition to the Treaty of Versailles had developed among those to whom a policy of splendid isolation seemed as desirable for America in the twentieth century as it had for Britain in the nineteenth. On 19 March 1920 the treaty finally failed to secure the ratification by the Senate required by the constitution. Such was the repudiation of the policy of the President who had assured his staff during their voyage to the peace conference that 'the men whom we were about to deal with did not represent their own people'.[2] America, having constrained the European allies to make peace upon the basis of an American programme, now left them to it.

Along with this repudiation went the American treaty of military guarantee to France which in turn, under the terms of agreement, released Britain from her undertaking. Thus did France find herself deprived of one of the main guarantees of security accorded her in return for renunciation of her demands in the Rhineland. No promising Anglo-French attempt

[1] Lloyd George, *The Truth about the Peace Treaties*, vol. II p. 883.
[2] Bowman Memorandum of 10 December 1918: C. Seymour, *op. cit.* vol. IV, p. 291.

to remedy this situation was made until the end of 1921 and even then negotiations flagged and eventually petered out, England having tried among other things to link them with lesser questions and France contending that the original guarantee of 1919 was humiliating to her because unilateral, and inadequate since it did not cover German 'indirect aggression' in eastern Europe. As the French Ambassador said in December 1921 to Lord Curzon, the touchy successor to the urbane Balfour: 'It would not cover us against a Polish Sadowa, which for Germany would be the best preparation for a new Sedan.'[1] If Poland was 'the linch-pin of the Treaty of Versailles' (Churchill), yet Balfour had earlier prophesied that, were she reconstituted, 'France would be at the mercy of Germany in the next war, for this reason, that Russia could not come to her aid without violating the neutrality of Poland'.[2] That, however, still rested with the future, as did the implications of Curzon's refusal now to pledge immediate British military aid to France if Germany should violate the demilitarised zone of the Rhineland. He admitted that the eastern frontier of France was 'in a sense the outer frontier of Great Britain herself', but refused to go beyond or undertake commitments in eastern Europe. France, deprived of her former Russian alliance, was left to seek such security as she could find in her traditional alternative, alliance with Poland (1921), and in association with the Little Entente, formed against Hungary in 1920–1 by Czechoslovakia, Rumania and Yugoslavia. Italy's rivalry with France in central Europe and the Balkans was indicated by her tendency to support Hungary, Bulgaria and Albania against these powers. This rivalry was significantly reduced in scale from the pre-war antagonism between Austria-Hungary and Russia, but was also the forerunner of a graver division. Already in August 1922, two months before Mussolini inaugurated the fascist era in Italy, an Austrian statesman had put it to Lord D'Abernon, British Ambassador in Berlin, that 'the real fact was that two incompatible alliances were fighting for the mastery in Central Europe: A North and South Alliance between Germany, Austria, and Italy. An East and West Alliance between France, Czecho-Slovakia, and Poland.'[3]

Britain viewed this French activity with a coolness verging on disfavour and there was ill-judged talk of a French domination of Europe: in fact the power of France was fragile. This was early suggested in the Middle East, where the positions were rather reversed, Britain being the principal exponent of a forward policy. Britain at the peace conference, secure in her

[1] *Documents relatifs aux négociations concernant les garanties de sécurité contre une agression de l'Allemagne, 10 janvier 1919–7 décembre 1923*, French Yellow Book of 1924, p. 92.
[2] Balfour in a conversation between Colonel House, Lloyd George, Balfour and Sir Edward Grey, 14 February 1916: Louis L. Gerson, *Woodrow Wilson and the Rebirth of Poland, 1914–1920* (New Haven, 1953), pp. 27–8.
[3] Lord D'Abernon, *An Ambassador of Peace* (London, 1929–30), vol. II, p. 101.

basic gains and dominant in Persia, indulged in two somewhat gratuitous and emotional policies, both calculated to antagonise Muslim populations. The first was a modern edition of ancient Greek colonisation upon the Ionian shores: a Greek expedition to Smyrna, largely Hellenic in population, was promoted in May 1919 by Wilson, Lloyd George and Clemenceau in accord with Venizelos, the persuasive Greek premier; this was during Italian absence owing to Wilson's manifesto of 23 April, and in order to forestall a repetition at Smyrna of independent Italian landings at other points in the zone allotted her by the secret Agreement of Saint-Jean-de-Maurienne. This agreement of 1917 was a corollary, in respect of Italy's rights, to the Sykes–Picot Agreement, but its validity was held by her allies to have lapsed owing to the defection of Russia. An unlikely project for affording Italy compensation in the Caucasus was turned down by the government of the shrewd Nitti, who had succeeded Orlando in June 1919.

The second British policy was the constitution in biblical Palestine of a Jewish national home, after centuries of Jewish dispersion, in accordance with the Balfour Declaration of 2 November 1917. Britain's attempt in Palestine to reconcile her obligations to the Arabs and to the Jews is a long, sad and separate story. A related problem, too, was how to reconcile her obligations to the Arabs under the Hussein–McMahon correspondence of 1915–16 (see ch. x) with those to the French under the Sykes–Picot Agreement, which was difficult since they were, in spirit at least, inconsistent. The French authorities wrongly suspected that their position in Syria was being disloyally undermined by the British, who in fact urged their Arab adherent, the Emir Feisal, to come to terms with them. In March 1920, however, Feisal defiantly assumed the title of King of Syria and Palestine and was expelled after France had, despite fierce Arab opposition, been designated as the mandatory for Syria at the allied Conference of San Remo on 25 April 1920. Then also British interests in Palestine and Mesopotamia emerged as mandates and an Anglo-French oil agreement was concluded, to be subsequently modified, however, in favour of the United States, which stood out for a share of the economic spoils of the Turkish Empire, with which they had not been at war, by pressing the principle of the Open Door stipulated for mandatory régimes. Such was the delicate adjustment in the Near East of national ambitions with the new international idealism.

The renunciation by Turkey of her Arab territories and of her suzerainty over Egypt and Cyprus was notable as being among the lasting provisions of the impermanent Treaty of Sèvres whereby the Allies made peace with Turkey on 10 August 1920. The details of this treaty, which left the Turks in Constantinople and the Greeks in Smyrna, both contrary to Curzon's judgement, and of the accompanying agreement allocating French and Italian spheres of influence in Turkey, are perhaps of greater interest in relation to the Eastern Question of the nineteenth century than to the peace settlement of the twentieth. For the treaty, delayed while the Allies waited upon the improbable event of America's deciding to assume a mandate for Constantinople or Armenia, remained unratified and stultified by the nationalist uprising which had meantime gathered momentum under Mustafa Kemal, largely impelled by the Greek occupation of Smyrna. This occupation was generally recognised at the time but never by its philhellenic champion, Lloyd George, to be a lamentable blunder. The ascendant Kemal set up a nationalist government in Angora (Ankara) over against that of the moribund sultanate in Constantinople, and by the Franklin–Bouillon Agreement of October 1921 France concluded with the nationalists a new and separate peace agreement apart from Great Britain. France failed to comprehend, and therefore mistrusted, British motives in maintaining what Curzon himself called 'the precarious and as I think worthless alliance of the Greeks'.[1] France and Italy now favoured the Turkish nationalists who finally routed the Greeks and entered Smyrna early in September 1922. This victory in turn menaced the small Allied forces still stationed upon the Asiatic shores of the Straits, a region where France and Italy habitually suspected British designs. They both withdrew their contingents from Chanak on 21 September 1922, leaving the British to make a stand alone. This they did with such fortunate effect that Mustafa Kemal agreed to a conference at Mudanya on 3 October 1922, the prelude to peace negotiations at Lausanne (see below, p. 291).

Lloyd George's eastern policy brought disaster to his favourite Greeks and an end to his own government on 19 October 1922. Curzon, however, remained as Foreign Secretary in the Conservative government of Bonar Law and, despite French intrigue, retrieved Britain's position by a personal triumph at the Lausanne Conference. As regards the two main British interests, satisfactory solutions were reached over the Straits and, eventually, Mosul. Thus by the Treaty of Lausanne of 24 July 1923 Britain after all came off at least as well in the Turkish settlement as did France or Italy.

The series of Anglo-French squabbles in those post-war years seemed almost to justify Paul Cambon when he wrote at the close of his twenty-years' embassy for France in London: 'I do not believe in the possibility of a rupture but everywhere, on every point, there is disagreement and the misfortune is that neither in Paris nor in London are they intelligent enough to reduce the disagreements to the essential points and disregard the trifles. It is easier to settle the big questions than the baubles. But men like Curzon or Leygues only care about the baubles.'[2] Certainly personalities played a part as always. The French came to distrust Lloyd

---

[1] Letter to Austen Chamberlain, 27 September 1922: The Earl of Ronaldshay, *The Life of Lord Curzon* (London, 1928), vol. III, p. 305.

[2] Letter to his son, 14 October 1920: Paul Cambon, *Correspondance 1870–1924* (Paris, 1940 f.), vol. III, p. 386.

George as being too pro-German and pro-Russian, and the British were alienated by the ungenerous legalism of Poincaré, French Prime Minister from January 1922 till June 1924. But these rubs were indications of a deeper psychological divergence which made the really big question, the treatment of Germany, not at all easy to solve. Briefly, Briand, Prime Minister between Leygues and Poincaré, spoke for war-scarred France in declaring (21 November 1921) that she could not disarm physically till Germany disarmed morally; whereas British statesmen sought a more cordial security through German goodwill by favouring her rehabilitation. They were impelled by motives psychological, the British being poor haters, political, being afraid of Communist Russia, and economic, seeking to stimulate that world trade which was Britain's mainstay. Time alone could, and did, demonstrate which thesis was the more nearly correct.

This divergence was thrown into relief by episodes in the execution of the peace treaty, as in Upper Silesia, and especially by the negotiations concerning reparation at the series of Allied conferences which distinguished the period 1920–2. Germany did not help Britain to help her. Her representatives created a bad impression upon their first appearance at the Conference of Spa in July 1920 with inadequate proposals regarding reparation backed by a most offensive speech by Stinnes, the German coal magnate; and again on 1 March 1921 at the London Conference they proposed 'indefensible' terms (D'Abernon), rejected the demands of the incensed Allies, and consequently provoked an extension of the Allied occupation to Düsseldorf, Duisburg and Ruhrort on 8 March, a sanction of marginal legality under the treaty. On 27 April 1921 the Reparation Commission announced its decision fixing Germany's total liability for reparation at the severe figure of £6,600 million. Also it found that, as regards the initial £1,000 million (20,000 million gold marks) which Germany was bound to pay by 1 May 1921, she was in default by at least 12,000 million marks. On 5 May the Allied governments communicated to Germany a 'schedule of payments' prescribing methods for discharging her obligations which in practice mitigated them, but included a demand for the payment of £50 million (one milliard marks) by the end of the month; a covering ultimatum stated that, if a satisfactory reply were not made within six days, the Allies would on 12 May occupy the Ruhr. After a governmental crisis in Germany, Wirth's administration accepted the Allied terms on 11 May, and had by August paid the first milliard marks, Germany's first cash payment. In these critical events Allied unity had been maintained, but so precariously as to promise ill for further strains ahead.

It was increasingly borne in upon Allied statesmen that the question of German reparation was closely related to that of Allied debts. They had been sharply warned off this delicate ground by the American Treasury in March 1919, but that July House wrote to Wilson in a prescient letter on

Anglo-American relations: 'Do you not think also that our people should be warned not to expect complete payment of loans to the Entente? Should they not be asked to consider a large share of these loans as a part of our necessary war expenditures, and should not an adjustment be suggested by us and not by our debtors?'[1] Wilson did not think so. Nor did Congress, which in February 1922 appointed a World War Foreign Debt Commission to collect the Allied debts by 1947 and impose a rate of interest not less than 4¼ per cent. Here the case of Britain was a special one, as being both debtor and creditor. For after America had entered the war she took over the traditional British position as banker of the alliance and Britain acted as broker for her European allies, contracting heavy debts in the United States, largely on their behalf. The Balfour Note of 1 August 1922 to the Allied powers reminded them that, exclusive of interest, they together owed Great Britain about £1,300 million, in addition to the £650 million due to her from Russia and £1,450 million as German reparation; for her part Great Britain owed £850 million to the United States. The note explained that American insistence upon payment compelled Britain to abandon her previous policy of refraining from asking for any Allied payments to her; the British government would nevertheless still prefer to remit all Allied war debts due to it, and the British share of reparation, as part of an all-round cancellation of war-indebtedness in 'one great transaction'. This statesmanlike proposal got a bad reception. The linking of war debts with reparations was opposed, for different reasons, both by the French and by the Americans, whose materialistic mood was reflected in President Coolidge's remark, 'They hired the money, didn't they?' The British government accordingly sent Stanley Baldwin and Montagu Norman, governor of the Bank of England, to Washington, where the American negotiators imposed such stringent terms that the British premier, Bonar Law, nearly resigned rather than accept them. Overborne, however, by considerations of party loyalty, he acquiesced. The British funded debt was fixed at 4,600 million dollars repayable over sixty-two years and subject to an average rate of 3⅓ per cent interest.

France had been a main beneficiary from the American loans which Britain was required to repay but Poincaré resented her trying to pass on the pinch. It added to the resentment which France already felt at being denied any priority of reparation for her devastated regions: their reconstruction, plus war pensions, was costing the French government half of its total yearly expenditure. In this heavy situation Poincaré was determined to secure 'productive pledges' from Germany, where inflation was mounting during 1922 and the government applying for, and partially obtaining, a moratorium on reparations. Productive guarantees chiefly meant for Poincaré the long-contemplated occupation of the Ruhr. At the end of December 1922 the Reparation Commission, by a vote of the

[1] *The Paris Peace Conference 1919*, vol. XI, p. 623.

French, Italian and Belgian representatives against the vigorous protest of the British, Sir John Bradbury, declared Germany in default on an insignificant delivery of timber, and on 9 January 1923, under the same conditions, declared a default in coal deliveries. Two days later French and Belgian forces marched into the Ruhr.

Bradbury had in the preceding August, as D'Abernon noted, gone 'out of his way to tell the Germans that, in the event of France taking isolated action, England would not interfere, but would adopt an attitude of "surly neutrality". The phrase has stuck in the German mind.'[1] It was a forecast as accurate as it was impolitic. With no united front against them, the German government ordered passive resistance in the Ruhr. This measure created dislocation and severely hampered the French in their attempt to draw economic benefit from an occupation which they compromised politically by fostering the separatist movement, by then weak, in the Rhineland, and by imprisoning local industrialists, who preferred inflation to providing reparation. The French, however, reckoned that they extracted over 1,300 million francs from Germany that year while the German government's recklessly defiant subsidising of idle hands in the Ruhr sent inflation rocketing, with values gone crazy with noughts—4,200,000,000,000 marks to the dollar at the peak in November 1923. This, more than 1918, was the true social revolution in Germany. But events were already on the turn. That November also witnessed the failure in Munich of Hitler's national-socialist coup, the climax of a year of extremist disturbance in Germany. Already on 27 September the ruinous policy of passive resistance had been abandoned by the new German government under Stresemann, formerly an intense nationalist, now a secret romantic with an unusual sense of practical moderation. By the end of November the Schacht–Luther financial reforms had already begun a feat of rapid recovery almost as remarkable as the inflation itself, and on 30 November the French government agreed to participate in an expert enquiry, favoured by the other Allied governments and by the United States, into the central question of Germany's capacity to pay reparation.

The enquiry was presided over by the American General Dawes and on 9 April 1924 it presented its report, known as the Dawes Plan. French delay in evacuating the Ruhr levered Germany into accepting the plan, and its adoption by France was facilitated by Herriot's succeeding Poincaré on 1 June. The resultant agreement between Germany and the Allies was signed in London on 16 August. The Dawes Plan was based upon the interrelated prerequisites of a balanced budget and a stabilised currency in Germany, the bank of issue being free from governmental control but subjected to supervision to protect foreign interests. The system of supervision was agreeable to France, less so the accompanying demotion of the Reparation Commission. By a similar adjustment, while

[1] Lord D'Abernon, *An Ambassador of Peace*, vol. II, p. 91.

the theoretical total of reparation due remained unaltered, Germany was in practice to pay on a much more moderate scale rising in five years from £50 million to the standard rate of £125 million, with special provision for the transfers to be operated by the recipients as a safeguard against a collapse of the exchange. In order to tide Germany over, a foreign loan of 800 million gold marks was raised, mostly in America. Foreign, especially American, capital was pumped into Germany, so that during the period 1924–8 she achieved an insecure prosperity and punctually discharged her obligations under the Dawes Plan. This seemingly satisfactory solution thus represented a financial roundabout whereby America lent to Germany who paid reparation to the European Allies who repaid debts to America. Such was the tangled legacy of war in which the nations had got caught up.

The Dawes Plan, however, marked the end of the worst of the post-war hangover. In 1925 European primary production first surpassed the level of 1913. Politically, the prospect of overcoming the frustration of Anglo-French friction was improved in October 1924 when the francophil Austen Chamberlain became British Foreign Secretary in Baldwin's new Conservative government. That government rejected, indeed, the diffuse idealism of the Geneva Protocol which its Labour predecessor had helped to elaborate (cf. ch. IX), but there was a swift demonstration of the beneficial effects of Anglo-French collaboration, in the interests of which Chamberlain revived the idea of a defensive alliance. Stresemann, who directed Germany's foreign policy from 1923 to 1929, perceived that 'a security agreement without Germany would have been a security agreement against Germany'.[1] On 9 February 1925 the German government presented to the French government a memorandum suggesting a pact for a considerable period between the powers interested in the Rhine, especially England, France, Italy and Germany, whereby they would undertake not to make war upon one another. This was a revised revival of an abortive proposal made by the German Chancellor Cuno in December 1922, and it was now blended with that of an Anglo-French alliance to constitute the Locarno Treaty of Mutual Guarantee, concluded together with pendant arrangements on 16 October 1925. By this treaty Britain, France, Italy, Germany and Belgium severally and collectively guaranteed the western frontier of Germany and the provisions of Versailles concerning the demilitarised zone. This agreement morally strengthened the peace settlement of 1919, since Germany now freely underwrote its attribution of Alsace-Lorraine, Eupen-Malmédy and the disarmed Rhineland, but materially weakened it since, in accordance with Stresemann's design, it circumscribed its military enforcement. But then for the British government, at least, military underpinning of its liabilities under the Pact of Locarno was scarcely

[1] Note by Stresemann, 1 July 1925: Eric Sutton, *Gustav Stresemann, his Diaries, Letters, and Papers* (London, 1935–40), vol. II, p. 98.

a very active concern at a time when the Prime Minister, Baldwin, was emphasising that 'any new obligation undertaken by His Majesty's Government must be pacific'.[1] Western Europe emerged for a space into 'the pale sunlight of Locarno' (Churchill).

The Pact of Locarno was to enter into force when Germany entered the League of Nations, which she did on 10 September 1926. A week later Stresemann and Briand lunched privately at a little hostelry with first-rate cooking at Thoiry near Geneva, and there waxed expansive over Stresemann's favourite theme of Franco-German economic collaboration, even, according to him, projecting it into Russia. In the west at the end of that month Germany, France, Belgium and Luxemburg formed an International Steel Cartel, a seminal initiative in the European economics of partnership from which Great Britain notably held aloof. At Thoiry Stresemann had further probed towards fresh relaxations of the Treaty of Versailles in return for German bolstering of the French economy. This did not commend itself, though, either to Schacht, the power of the Reichsbank, or to American interests.

American initiative, however, encouraged Briand towards a notable achievement in another direction. In 1927 he communicated to Kellogg, the American Secretary of State, a draft treaty for the renunciation of war between their two countries. After waiting six months to reply, Kellogg suggested in December that the proposed treaty be made multilateral. The outcome was the Pact of Paris or Kellogg Pact of 27 August 1928, whereby fifteen powers renounced war as an instrument of national policy, subject to some limited reservations, Great Britain for instance entering one concerning 'certain regions' in which she was vitally interested— a pointer towards the Suez Canal. By 1933 sixty-five nations had subscribed to this well-intentioned if somewhat indefinite undertaking.

These events illustrated the anxious preoccupation of the powers with regard to security in the aftermath of the war to end war. At the centre of the problem of security lay that of disarmament. Reparation and disarmament were the two main long-term obligations of Germany under the Treaty of Versailles, and the supervision of their fulfilment, respectively through the Reparation Commission and the Control Commissions working under the Conference of Ambassadors in Paris, was in the forefront of the policy of the Allies. In disarming Germany they had to reckon above all with General von Seeckt, a brilliant Prussian staff-officer, cultivated and withdrawn. Chief of the German army directorate (*Chef der Heeresleitung*) since the second quarter of 1920, Seeckt had begun by instructing commanders to cease measures for reducing the German army to the stipulated strength of 100,000 men since the German government were opposed to it. Seeckt, however, failed to induce the Allies at the Conference of Spa to permit double that number and eventually the

[1] Speech by Baldwin at Brighton, 8 October 1925: *The Times*, 9 October 1925.

reduction was effected, at least on paper. For Seeckt emulated Scharnhorst's subterfuge after Jena when he had secretly reconstituted the Prussian army in defiance of Napoleonic disarmament. Volunteers were rapidly passed through the army despite the limitation of enlistments to regulars for a twelve-year period under article 174. The recruitment of the so-called Black Reichswehr embraced the development of paramilitary organisations such as the Einwohnerwehr and Arbeitskommandos in violation of article 177 of the treaty. This was matched by illegal militarisation of the police, who were, indeed, liable to be especially important for maintaining internal order if military disarmament had been scrupulously observed, rather than evaded. Any loophole in the treaty was in fact ingeniously exploited: for instance, while it limited the number of officers to 4,000, it omitted to do likewise for non-commissioned officers, who were accordingly increased out of all proportion to the needs of a small army in accordance with Seeckt's aim of building up a military *élite* (*Führerheer*). Similarly, at the top, the general staff, prohibited by article 160, was maintained under a rich variety of subterfuges and engaged in equally forbidden activities such as plans for general mobilisation (violation of article 178) and for promoting military aviation, prohibited by article 198. Stocks of arms due for surrender were often hidden and the tasks of the Allied control commissions deliberately rendered difficult and unpleasant. Graver still, the German army was trained in the use of forbidden weapons such as armoured cars and tanks, Seeckt being a far-sighted exponent of mobile warfare. Nor were manœuvres with dummy guns and cardboard tanks a smiling matter when directed by the author of the grim definition: 'Warlike is meant not in the sense of the imitation of war, but in that of a preparation for a war.'[1]

By all-round evasion and violation of the treaty Seeckt created not a small army but a great army in miniature, its danger lying in its potentialities. Here considerations both psychological and economic entered in. Seeckt was determined to combat 'moral disarmament', of which, already in March 1922, D'Abernon, a good friend of Germany, wrote in Berlin: 'I not only doubt the existence of this at the present moment, but its bare possibility at any date. No one that I have met here would think a successful war morally reprehensible.'[2] On the economic side Seeckt perceived that what mattered was less the accumulation of obsolescent armaments than the co-ordination of manufacturing potential for military requirements. Here he secured the backing of Chancellor Wirth, who secretly subsidised the Krupp armament enterprise. That formidable concern concluded a formal agreement on 25 January 1922 with the German ministry of defence 'jointly to circumvent...the

---

[1] General von Seeckt. Cited, General Friedrich von Rabenau, *Seeckt: aus seinem Leben 1918–1936* (Leipzig, 1940), p. 503.
[2] Lord D'Abernon, *An Ambassador of Peace*, vol. I, p. 279.

provisions of the Treaty of Versailles'.[1] This activity was extended abroad, beyond allied reach. By 1925 Krupp held a controlling interest in the Bofors arms-works in Sweden, and was projecting the latest thing in heavy guns and tanks. German submarines were secretly built and crews trained in Holland, Spain and Finland. Even before the Russo-German Treaty of Rapallo in 1922 there were afoot clandestine arrangements foreshadowing the development in the Soviet Union of German artillery, tanks at Kazan, poison gas at Saratov, and at Lipetsk airbase fighters and dive-bombers. Training extended to staff-courses with Soviet officers. Even during the inflation of 1923 Wirth's successor, Cuno, had tentatively agreed on 11 July to finance German military collaboration with Russia to the tune of sixty million gold marks in the following year. Seeckt for his part considered that resurgent Germany should especially work with Russia, to destroy Poland. So had Wirth. He told Brockdorff-Rantzau, setting out after Rapallo as German Ambassador to Moscow: 'Poland must be disposed of. My policy is set towards this goal...It is...with my agreement that many things, too, have happened relative to the eastern frontier which are known only to a few besides myself. On this point I am in complete agreement with the military, especially with General von Seeckt.'[2]

In these views Seeckt, probably the most considerable soldier of the 1920s, was not, however, at one with their most eminent statesman, Stresemann, whose name stamped the pacific period of fulfilment and Locarno. Yet the divergence was rather less than might appear. Stresemann was largely aware of Seeckt's illicit rearmament, notably in Russia, and lied to D'Abernon in order to shield it. Pacific Stresemann was, though, in that in the time of German weakness he aimed at achieving his policy without war; but it was deep policy, deep and wide. It embraced 'the protection of Germans abroad, those 10 to 12 millions of our kindred who now live under a foreign yoke in foreign lands'.[3] In this connection Stresemann held as regards the South Tyrol, for instance, that 'the German qualities of Walther von der Vogelweide bear witness that Bozen (Bolzano) is within the German cultural community'.[4] Stresemann aimed at regaining Eupen from Belgium, and for him 'the recovery of the German colonies is an object, and a very present object, of German policy'.[5] For him too, moreover, a principal objective was 'the readjustment of our eastern

[1] Cited, Gordon A. Craig, *The Politics of the Prussian Army 1640–1945* (Oxford, 1955), p. 406.
[2] Cited, Herbert Helbig, 'Die Moskauer Mission des Grafen Brockdorff-Rantzau', in *Forschungen zur Osteuropäischen Geschichte* (ed. H. Jablonowski and W. Philipp; Berlin, 1954 f.), vol. II, p. 306.
[3] Letter from Stresemann to the former German Crown Prince, 7 September 1925: Sutton, *Gustav Stresemann, his Diaries, Letters, and Papers*, vol. II, p. 503.
[4] Speech in the Reichstag, 9 February 1926: *ibid.* vol. II, p. 454.
[5] Speech of 29 August 1925: *ibid.* vol. II, p. 314.

frontiers; the recovery of Danzig, the Polish corridor, and a correction of the frontier in Upper Silesia'.[1] It was in Stresemann's time and in accordance with instructions that Brockdorff-Rantzau on 20 December 1924 put it to Chicherin, Soviet Commissar for Foreign Affairs, that the 'solution of the Polish question, for Germany as well as for Russia, lay in the pushing back of Poland to her ethnographic frontiers',[2] as defined by her enemies.

In negotiating the pact of Locarno Stresemann was able to exploit Britain's standing refusal to underwrite French commitments in eastern Europe; he resisted all French attempts to secure in favour of her allies there a German undertaking 'to abstain from any attack. This obligation we undertook in the West, but we refused it in the East. Membership of the League does not exclude the possibility of war.'[3] D'Abernon's earlier suggestion to Stresemann of a 'reciprocal iron curtain'[4] between Germany and France in the Rhineland began to assume an ominous significance, and Stresemann saw 'in Locarno the preservation of the Rhineland, and the possibility of the recovery of German territory in the East'.[5] The settlement, as so often in German foreign policy, wore a two-faced aspect, fair to west, grim to east. There France's weakened position despite significant new treaties with Poland and Czechoslovakia was emphasised not only by Stresemann's gibes at those two countries but also by the further Russo-German treaty of friendship signed at Berlin on 24 April 1926. It was in pursuance of this 'fierce friendship' (Lloyd George) that Stresemann at Locarno had secured a critical weakening for Germany of article 16 of the Covenant of the League of Nations.

Stresemann, who exploited diplomatically the nationalist opposition against him in the German parliament, crowned his success against France at Locarno by presenting it as a concession to the Allies in return for which they adopted favourable 'reactions' towards Germany, notably by evacuating the Cologne zone by 31 January 1926. This first instalment of the evacuation of the Rhineland had been refused by the Allies the year before owing to 'the numerous defaults of the German government'[6] as regards disarmament. Here the Allied Military Control Commission was unable to pronounce itself fully satisfied even by 31 January 1927, when it was obligingly withdrawn. It declared in its final report a month later:

The Commission was confronted, in the German government, by a knowing and diligent adversary in regard to whom the Commission by itself possessed no means

[1] Letter to the former Crown Prince: *ibid.* vol. II, p. 503.
[2] Cited, Kurt Rosenbaum, *Community of Fate* (Syracuse, N.Y., 1965), p. 124.
[3] Speech of 14 December 1925: Sutton, *Gustav Stresemann, his Diaries, Letters, and Papers*, vol. II, p. 217.
[4] Lord D'Abernon, *An Ambassador of Peace*, vol. III, p. 101.
[5] Letter to Dr von Keudell, 27 November 1925: Sutton, *Gustav Stresemann, his Diaries, Letters, and Papers*, vol. II, pp. 231-2.
[6] *Note presented to the German Government by the British, French, Italian, Japanese and Belgian Ambassadors at Berlin, 4 June 1925*, Cmd. 2429, 1925, p. 3.

THE SHIFTING BALANCE OF WORLD FORCES

of constraint...The very history of the [military] control merges into that of the incessant obstruction by Germany of the demands and decisions of the Commission...But the shadows of a picture are not enough to mask its colours, and it should be acknowledged that the results attained are, such as they are, of capital importance...In achieving them the Commission for its part has dug the foundations of the building...which, since Locarno, is slowly beginning to rise from the ground.[1]

Such flowery apologetics suited official optimism. The weakness of those foundations, though, had already been suggested in mid-January 1927 by the new British Ambassador in Berlin, Sir Ronald Lindsay, who expressed to Stresemann his 'fears that there was still a strong spirit of militarism and revenge in Germany'.[2] In 1928 the German Cabinet specifically endorsed illicit German rearmament. By the Hague Agreement of August 1929, Stresemann's last big achievement before his death that October, the Allies undertook to complete the evacuation of the whole of the Rhineland by 30 June 1930. This evacuation was related to the adoption of the short-lived Young Plan whereby Germany's obligations for reparation were further reduced below those which she had assumed under the Dawes Plan with an eye to promoting the French evacuation of the Ruhr. Such was the outstanding success of Stresemann's policy of 'driving France back from trench to trench, as I once expressed it, since no general attack is feasible'.[3]

Germany pressed her 'peace offensive' (Stresemann) wherever she saw an opening, as in the preamble to Part V of the Treaty of Versailles wherein the disarmament of Germany was imposed 'in order to render possible the initiation of a general limitation of the armaments of all nations'. This, and a gloss upon it in the Allied reply of 16 June 1919 to the Germans, did not lay a contractual obligation upon the Allies to disarm, as German propaganda tried to make out, but they did constitute a moral obligation. This moral obligation was cancelled by German measures of rearmament in violation of the treaty. Though immediately defensive, they cast an ominous shadow ahead at a time when the ten-year rule in Whitehall exempted British service chiefs throughout the 1920s from anticipating a major war within the following ten years. And in general the victorious powers displayed a well-intentioned desire to work towards general disarmament.

At first this desire was, however, mainly manifest in the field which least affected Germany, the naval. The central issue here was Anglo-American competition, for during the war the United States had been building their navy up towards British strength and had, during the peace conference,

---

[1] Commission Militaire Interaliée de Contrôle en Allemagne, *Rapport Final*, of 28 February 1927 (Paris, 1927), pp. 512–14.
[2] Note by Stresemann, 15 January 1927: Sutton, *Gustav Stresemann, his Diaries, Letters, and Papers*, vol. III, p. 105.
[3] Letter to Lieut.-General von Schoch, 27 July 1925: *ibid.* vol. II, p. 58.

largely left unsatisfied British representations against continuing construction. American preoccupation here with Japan was evident at the Washington Conference of naval powers in 1921–2 which achieved both a political settlement in the Far East, where the Anglo-Japanese alliance was terminated in deference to American and Dominion wishes (see ch. xii), and an important agreement limiting naval armaments, signed on 6 February 1922. This pointed to the end of the naval supremacy of the Pax Britannica, gracefully accepted by a poorer, less ardent Britain, imaginatively exploited by the rival thrust of America. The agreement fixed a ratio in total tonnages for American, British, Japanese, French and Italian capital ships, prescribed a ten-year naval holiday in their construction, and limited their size along with total tonnages for aircraft-carriers; but it failed to secure any limitation by ratio for submarines, light cruisers and auxiliaries, chiefly owing to French obstruction which further strained Anglo-French relations. Anglo-American dissension, however, frustrated another attempt to reach agreement with the Japanese in these last categories at a naval conference in Geneva in the summer of 1927. A further naval conference was opened in London in January 1930 and after intricate negotiation produced on 22 April a three-power agreement between Great Britain, the United States and Japan whereby Japan had the right to build up to 70 per cent of British or American total tonnage in cruisers, destroyers and submarines, with parity at a low level in the latter. Franco-Italian rivalry in the Mediterranean defeated all efforts to include those powers in this agreement, and indicated the limitations to the considerable success achieved in naval disarmament. Another indication was the contemporary construction by Germany of the first 'pocket battleship', ingeniously designed to conform to the letter of the 10,000-ton limit imposed by the peace treaty while defeating its object by its unorthodox and powerful armament.

Military and aeronautical disarmament was more difficult to achieve than naval, both intrinsically and in its special relation to the problem of Germany. The protracted negotiations within the framework of the League of Nations which began with the appointment of the preparatory commission on disarmament in 1925 issued in a disarmament conference which opened at Geneva on 2 February 1932 (see chs. ix and xxiii). The success of this conference was ominously prejudiced from the start by Japanese aggression in Manchuria and in the end by the aggressive ascendancy of National Socialism in Germany.

The strength of the Nazi party jumped up in the elections of September 1930 from 800,000 votes to 6½ millions, to a peak of 13¾ millions in July 1932 (ch. xvi). Behind this phenomenon loomed the American slump on Wall Street in October 1929, the month that Stresemann died, and the ensuing economic blizzard which swept across Europe in renewed proof of the dependence of the old world upon the riches of the new. Swept away was the Young Plan of the preceding summer. The withdrawal of American credits revealed the insecurity of the German economy. The Austrian finances, in which German banks were closely interested, were apt to be delicate at the best of times, and in March 1931 the German government of Brüning tried to combine a bolstering of both economies together with a bold stroke of foreign policy by the surprise announcement of agreement to establish an Austro-German customs union. The project had to be dropped in the face of Anglo-French opposition. On 11 May 1931 the largest Austrian bank, the *Creditanstalt*, failed and precipitated the 'crisis within the crisis'. This spread across Germany to England, where the Labour government fell and the pound was forced off the gold standard on 21 September. Already in July the main European powers had, after some haggling by France, who had built up much the largest gold reserve after America, accepted President Hoover's timely proposal for a one-year moratorium on all payments of reparation and war-debts. In June 1932 a conference met at Lausanne to consider the situation upon the expiry of the Hoover Moratorium. There von Papen's 'Cabinet of Barons', which had just succeeded that of Brüning, secured an important success for Germany whereby reparation was at last abolished, subject to German delivery of bonds to the amount of £150 million. A 'gentlemen's agreement' reached on 2 July by Germany's creditors made ratification of this settlement contingent upon a satisfactory settlement between them and their creditors, namely, the United States. But America refused to cancel or reduce Allied war-debts and squashed the expedient adopted by Britain in 1933 of making token payments only. Thereafter the British government joined the French and others in defaulting on its payments, refusing, in effect, that the financial burden of the first world war should be inequitably shifted from Germany, no longer paying reparation, to the European Allies. And indeed even when Germany was paying reparation she had paid in practice not from her own substance and sacrifice, but from her loans and investments from abroad which amounted up to 1931 to some 35–8 milliard marks as against the total of 21 milliards which she had paid to the Allies during the same period according to the books of the Reparation Commission. Such was the sterile yield of a peace settlement which, after first applying the sanction of military intervention to enforcing reparation rather than disarmament, had come to rely, in the financial field even more than in others, upon the accommodating application of stringent terms instead of the reverse.

In the face of the economic blizzard the European powers huddled away from the expansive internationalism of the 'twenties, last manifest in Briand's plan for European union, into national economies behind tariff barriers, especially after America introduced the very stiff Hawley–Smoot tariff in 1929–30. This frustrated the conference which met at Geneva in February 1930 to devise a tariff truce. The era of free trade was finishing;

and, in totalitarian nations, the era of free thought. They were now joined by Germany, who, in the time of economic stress, turned to a creed which transcended economics, transformed politics and came to smash the settlement of Versailles.

Thus was the peace settlement after the first world war largely undermined in three waves, successive but overlapping, political, economic and psychological. Almost from the beginning it was compromised politically not only by errors of judgement which the peacemakers made at times in framing a very complex whole, but even more by the power-vacuum left, to German advantage, by the collapse of the Austro-Hungarian and Russian empires upon the one hand and by the falling away of the United States upon the other: a void too great to fill by the hopeful innovation of the League of Nations. This political insecurity was sharply accentuated in the 'twenties by economic crises of quite unforeseen extent, first the German inflation, the greatest in history, and then the world-wide slump. These not only vitiated the whole structure of German reparation and Allied war-debts but also demonstrated that, with the economic balance now tilted towards America in what was possibly the greatest shift of geopolitical stress since its discovery four centuries before, the victorious powers had failed to achieve an economic ordering of international relations which would afford stability to liberal societies in the twentieth-century phase of industrial capitalism. The 'thirties in turn demonstrated that the maintenance of the peace settlement was gravely menaced by unexpected phenomena not only economic but also psychological, ideological. The aftermath of the war to make the world safe for democracy witnessed a retreat from its liberalism into Communism in Russia, into Fascism in Italy and, most promptly disruptive, into National Socialism in Germany. Wilson, who had sought to make the Treaty of Versailles the palladium of international democracy, had intended that it should subject the Germans to 'a generation of thoughtfulness'.[1] But with many of them their thoughts turned largely inwards, obscure and festering, less to repentance than to revenge. And, whereas the Allied victors mainly came to look to politicians of rather ordinary capacity, the German vanquished found a leader of deep and evil inspiration. His mouthpiece proclaimed in advance (April 1928):

We enter parliament in order to supply ourselves in the arsenal of democracy with its own weapons. We are becoming deputies in order to paralyse the Weimar sentiment with its own assistance. If democracy is so stupid as to give us free tickets and salaries for this purpose, that is its own affair...We come as enemies! As the wolf bursts into the flock, so we come.[2]

So they came. On 30 January 1933 Adolf Hitler became Chancellor of Germany, of the Third German Empire.

[1] Meeting of Council of Ten, 12 February 1919: *The Paris Peace Conference 1919*, vol. III, p. 1002. [2] Dr Joseph Goebbels, *Der Angriff* (Munich, 1935), pp. 71–3.

CHAPTER IX

THE LEAGUE OF NATIONS

THE Covenant of the League of Nations formed Part I of each of the treaties of peace concluded after the first world war, and, when the first of these, the Treaty of Versailles, entered into force on 10 January 1920, the League began to exist. The incorporation of the Covenant in the treaties was a point on which President Wilson had strongly insisted at the peace conference; he looked to the League as a means whereby injustices and imperfections in the treaties would at some future time be corrected, and he probably foresaw that if the making of the League were postponed until after the treaties came into force there would almost certainly be no League at all. For the League this course had both disadvantages and advantages. On the one hand it led to the League's sharing in the unpopularity which assailed the peace treaties, for it could be represented by hostile or ignorant critics as merely an instrument which the victors had devised in order to rivet on the vanquished the injustices of the settlement. On the other hand the treaties had many provisions to which effect could only be given by a continuing organisation such as the League was intended to be, and by using the League for this purpose they ensured that it would at once be called on to play a part in great affairs and not be relegated to the obscurity to which, as Wilson had reason to suspect, some of his colleagues would have liked to consign it.

The drafting committee at the peace conference worked on the basis of a draft conflated by the British and United States legal advisers, Cecil Hurst and David Hunter Miller, from suggestions prepared by Lord Robert Cecil, General Smuts, a British Foreign Office committee under Lord Phillimore, and Colonel House. French and Italian drafts were hardly considered, and the finished Covenant thus reflected British and United States rather than continental ideas. The League emerged from the drafting committee possessed of no powers which could be described as supra-national or even in a strict sense governmental, with little more than the bare outlines of a constitution and free therefore to develop as experience might direct. It was to be an association of sovereign states pledged to co-operate with each other for specified purposes, and its effectiveness depended on these pledges being honoured. The institutions of the League were more in the nature of machinery designed to make it as easy as possible for the members to agree and act together than organs through which corporate action was to be taken, and 'the League' itself was little more than a name serving to describe the members collectively. It was clear too that the League would be an association more political than juridical in character, more in the tradition of the Concert of Europe, which, as many of the founders of the League believed, had served Europe well in the nineteenth century, than in that of the Hague Conferences, the work of which had counted for practically nothing in the war just ended. British opinion in particular hoped to find in the League an organisation in which the great powers would meet regularly and whenever an emergency made it desirable for them to confer, but in which the membership and the functions would no longer be limited to Europe: they would be served by a permanent secretariat, and they would accept some measure of accountability to the rest of the world.

The original members of the League were the signatories of the treaties of peace and a few other states invited in the treaties to accede to the Covenant. There was to be an Assembly in which all the members were represented, a Council, and a Secretariat headed by Sir Eric Drummond (later Lord Perth) as first Secretary-General. Under the Hurst–Miller draft the Council should have consisted of representatives of the great powers only, but in deference to the strong opposition of the smaller powers it was decided that while the great powers should be permanent members the Assembly should elect four others from time to time, and the number of these non-permanent members was progressively raised to eleven. A few functions were specifically assigned respectively to the Assembly or the Council, but the Covenant did not define their relations, and either of them was authorised to deal with 'any matter within the sphere of action of the League or affecting the peace of the world'.[1] This lack of differentiation was typical of the absence of rigidity in the Covenant as a whole and it led to no inconvenient results. The Assembly, contrary probably to the expectations of the founders, became the dominant organ, partly because it was able to secure control of the budget; it provided something wholly new in the intercourse of states and only possible in an atmosphere of courtesy and restraint such as normally prevailed at Geneva, a forum in which the smaller powers were free to criticise the great and the great did not refuse to explain and justify their conduct before the world. The Council, being a smaller body, meeting more frequently and therefore better able to act promptly, came to serve as a sort of executive committee of the Assembly, working out the details and supervising the execution of policies which the Assembly had accepted in principle. In conformity with the ordinary rule of international conferences the decisions of either body had normally to be unanimous, but this rule was subject to certain exceptions of which the most important were that matters of procedure might be decided by a majority, and the vote of parties to a dispute would not count against an otherwise unanimous Council or

---

[1] League Covenant Articles III and IV. Quotations from the Covenant are from the version printed in F. P. Walters, *A History of the League of Nations* (Oxford University Press, 1952), vol. I, ch. v.

Assembly report on the dispute with recommendations for its settlement. This rule of unanimity, however, had less influence on the practical working of the League than is sometimes supposed, because 'action' by the League consisted not in the taking of decisions with binding effect upon members, but rather in the formulation of recommendations and judgements to which members by their signature of the Covenant had undertaken to pay heed. The unanimity rule thus gave to a member not the power to veto League action, but the means of ensuring that its own rights and obligations should not be varied without its consent.

The Secretariat was the most original element in the constitution of the League. The previous practice of international conferences had usually been to rely for secretarial assistance on officials temporarily assigned to the work by the participating states, and the disadvantages of this method are obvious: it gave little chance for the development of a sense of corporate responsibility, and it left no machinery in being to give effect to the decisions of the conference. Sir Eric Drummond decided at the outset that the Secretariat of the League should follow a different plan: it was not to consist of national delegates, but of international servants whose first loyalty should be to the League. That ideal could not always be completely realised. It was not practicable, nor perhaps even desirable, always to treat questions of nationality as irrelevant in such matters as the recruitment of the members or the allocation of posts within the Secretariat, and some governments, especially after the rise of totalitarianism, sought to undermine the independence of the members by pressure which it was virtually impossible to resist. None the less, it is for its success rather than for its partial failure that this first experiment in the construction of a truly international civil service is chiefly remarkable.

The Council was directed by Article XIV of the Covenant to formulate plans for the establishment of a Permanent Court of International Justice, and one of its first acts was to set up a committee of jurists to advise it on this matter. The committee prepared a draft which the Assembly accepted as the basis of the statute of the court, and the court came into existence in the latter part of 1921. Its jurisdiction comprised 'all cases which the parties refer to it and all matters specially provided for in treaties and conventions in force'. Submission of disputes to the court was therefore voluntary, but the statute contained a provision, the so-called 'Optional Clause', by accepting which the members might, if they chose, recognise the jurisdiction as compulsory in the classes of disputes enumerated in the clause. As confidence in the court grew, after a few years' experience, this clause was widely accepted, though acceptances were often accompanied by reservations which seriously reduced their value. The court was in effect the judicial organ of the League and there were constitutional links between them. The judges were elected by the Assembly and the Council; the expenses of the court were borne on the

League budget; and besides its jurisdiction in contentious cases it was empowered to give an advisory opinion on any dispute or question referred to it by the Assembly or the Council. These links, however, never impaired the complete judicial independence of the court.

The prime purpose of the League was to achieve international peace and security. The Covenant included a variety of ideas, not all of them mutually consistent, by which this purpose was to be served. By Article x the members undertook 'to respect and preserve as against external aggression the territorial integrity and existing political independence of all Members of the League'. This seeming system of mutual guarantee did not, however, bind any member to take any specific action in aid of any other, for in case of aggression the Council was to 'advise upon the means by which this obligation shall be fulfilled'. The article remained in fact little more than a pious statement of principle; but it was unfortunately regarded by President Wilson as the core of the Covenant and his refusal to accept any compromise on it played a large part in the United States Senate's refusal to ratify the Treaty and the Covenant. There were, however, dangers in the article, clearly seen by Cecil, in that it might impose a rigidity on the international system (which the French desired) that would make it unable peacefully to cope with inevitable future pressures for change. Cecil's fears were in very limited degree met by the insertion of Article xix by which the Assembly was empowered 'from time to time [to] advise the reconsideration...of treaties which have become inapplicable and the consideration of international conditions whose continuance might endanger the peace of the world'. This article also remained largely a dead letter, and it is certainly arguable that the inability of the members to discover and operate effective procedures of peaceful change was a more serious weakness of the League than their failure to adhere to their perhaps inconsistent obligation to preserve each other's territorial integrity.

The second idea for achieving peace found expression in Article xi. 'Any war or threat of war' was declared to be 'a matter of concern to the whole League', and the League, acting as a commission of conciliation, was to take 'any action that may be deemed wise and effectual to safeguard the peace of nations'. Contrary to original expectations this article proved to be the one under which most of the disputes that came before the League were dealt with: its increased use reflected British views about the way in which the League machinery might most wisely be employed.

Thirdly, the League was to exercise a quasi-arbitral function over disputes, and in the last resort was to be an instrument for enforcing the peace. By Articles xii–xvii, which set out these functions, the members bound themselves to submit any 'dispute likely to lead to a rupture' to one of three procedures: to settlement by the Permanent Court of International Justice, to arbitration, or to enquiry by the Council; and in no case were they to resort to war until three months after the judicial decision, the arbitrators' award, or the report of the Council as the case might be, provided in the last case that the Council, apart from the disputing parties, had been unanimous. If in disregard of any of these undertakings a state should resort to war, the so-called sanctions were to become applicable to it. All the other members were then to sever all trade and financial relations with it, to prohibit all intercourse between its nationals and their own, to prevent all intercourse between its nationals and those of any other state whether a member of the League or not, and the Council was to recommend what armed forces the members should severally contribute to protect the covenants of the League. These provisions reflected what was believed to be one of the lessons of the war, namely, the overwhelming power of economic pressure, and therefore, whilst the provisions for economic measures were detailed and peremptory, those for military measures were left so obscure that it was never certain whether or not they imposed any actual obligation on the members.

War was thus neither excluded nor made illegal. Members might resort to war without breaking their obligations and so without exposing themselves to sanctions if the Council failed to reach unanimity in its report on a dispute, or if it found that a dispute arose out of a matter solely within the domestic jurisdiction of one of the parties (in which case it might make no recommendations for a settlement), of if at the end of the 'cooling-off' period neither party accepted the decision of the Court or the arbitrators or the report of the Council. In their caution the framers of the Covenant were realistic, but the possibilities that a state might with impunity resort to war came to be seen as 'gaps' in the Covenant. Much effort in the 'twenties was devoted to efforts to close these 'gaps'.

Before the League had even begun to exist it was dealt a grievous blow by the refusal of the American Senate to consent to the ratification of the peace treaties. The refusal meant much more than that the United States would be absent from the counsels of the League, serious as that alone would have been. It meant for League members, and for Britain and France in particular, that the League in being would be a different League from that which they had had in view when they accepted the Covenant. When the Covenant was before the British parliament not a single member expressed doubt as to the wisdom of accepting the sanctions provisions, though evidently their burden would be heaviest for a naval power; but these provisions took on a different aspect when it was seen not only that the burden would not be shared with the United States, but that the situation might easily arise where Britain would have to choose between reneging on her obligation to impose sanctions on an aggressor and leading a naval blockade and so denying that freedom of the seas which the United States traditionally so vigorously asserted. For the Dominions also, but particularly for Canada, the United States' absence profoundly altered the appearance of the enforcement provision of the Covenant. Primarily for this reason these provisions of the Covenant came under fire at the first meeting of the Assembly in 1920, when the Canadian representative proposed the elimination of Article x. The proposal was rejected, but it was renewed in the two following years, and in 1923 it led to an interpretative resolution which declared that it was for each state to decide for itself how far it was bound to employ its military forces in executing its obligations under the article. In 1921 the attack was extended to Article xvi and certain 'rules of guidance' were adopted for its application which had the effect of weakening its obligations. These amendments to the Covenant, that sanctions should not be applied immediately and completely but gradually and partially, and that all discussions on the subject should be entrusted to the Council, never acquired legal force because France refused to ratify them; but, on the only occasion when sanctions were applied in 1935, France was foremost in insisting that they should guide the League's action (see below, p. 259). All this was evidence of a trend of opinion which had already come to regard the collective security provisions as a dangerous experiment, and which, if it should prevail, would lead inexorably to a return to the pre-League system of every state relying for its defence on its own armed forces. It was clear also that it endangered a cause to which the League had already set its hand, that of the reduction of national armaments 'to the lowest point consistent with national safety and the enforcement by common action of international obligations', for the prospects of disarmament were inextricably bound up with those of security (see ch. viii).

The Allies had justified the disarmament of Germany in the Treaty of Versailles as being necessary to make possible a general reduction of armaments, and the Covenant had expressly charged the Council to formulate plans for this purpose. It was therefore inevitable, though it may have been unfortunate, that this problem should be among the first to be taken up by the League. A permanent military commission had been established by the Covenant to advise the Council, but it soon became evident that a professional body was more easily impressed by the difficulties than by the urgency of reducing armaments, and the first Assembly decided to establish another body to include lay as well as service members which became known as the Temporary Mixed Commission. The difficulties were not at first generally realised. Disarmament was a popular cause, on economic grounds, and because many believed that armaments were an independent cause of war rather than a sign that wars were still possible. The success of the Naval Conference of Washington in 1921–2 was thought by some to confirm the view that armaments could be dealt with in the main as a technical question; but in fact the Washington agreement was possible only because political issues were concurrently settled, because only the United States among the five powers that signed the agreement was economically able to engage in competitive building, and because the scope of the agreement was limited to capital ships. The political context of the League discussions was very different, for the lapsing of the United States guarantee to France (and the resultant lapsing of the British guarantee) in consequence of the Senate's rejection of the Treaty of Versailles had strengthened the hands of those Frenchmen who believed that Germany's greater potential strength must be balanced by heavy reparations, by a disparity in armaments, by alliances with the small countries of eastern Europe, and by using the League as a means of keeping Germany under control.

The political aspect of the disarmament discussions was accordingly soon seen to be fundamental, and in 1923 the Temporary Mixed Commission attempted a political approach in the draft of a treaty of mutual assistance which ingeniously combined the system of regional alliances which already existed and would, it was practically certain, have to be accepted, with a general system of security. The Council was to have power to determine an aggressor, but the obligation to use armed force against aggression was limited to states on the continent on which it occurred, and there was to be a guarantee for those states only which agreed to disarm. The treaty was rejected by the British government for various reasons, but chiefly because of the difficulty of reconciling the regional basis of the obligations with the relations between members of the British Commonwealth and with the world-wide responsibilities of the British navy, and though the British was not the only rejection it was decisive for the fate of the draft. The Assembly of 1924 therefore tried a different approach. The rejected treaty would have set up a security system side by side with that of the Covenant but on a different basis; the Geneva Protocol of 1924 accepted the Covenant, but sought to strengthen it. Britain and France, which this year for the first time were represented by their Prime Ministers, Ramsay MacDonald and Edouard Herriot, presented a joint resolution which became the basis of the Assembly's work. It was thought that a new key to the problem might be found in compulsory arbitration, the acceptance of which would offer a quasi-automatic test of aggression; in short, arbitration would make possible security, and security would then lead to disarmament. Compulsory arbitration would close the 'gaps' in the Covenant, for all disputes were to be settled by one of the means proposed in the Covenant, in the last resort by arbitrators whose decision would be final. Sanctions would thus be applicable to every resort to war and not merely, as hitherto, to war in breach of the Covenant. The whole plan, however, was to take effect only after a conference had adopted a disarmament plan, and the complexity of that problem was yet so little realised that it was proposed that the conference should meet in the following year and that in the meantime the Council should produce a draft plan for its consideration. In fact, it proved impossible to convene this conference until 1932.

During the debates on the Protocol MacDonald's Labour government had been in power in Britain, but before the British attitude was declared it had been succeeded by the Conservative government of Stanley Baldwin, and this decided to reject the proposals. It is unlikely that the change of government affected the issue, for when the Protocol came to be examined at leisure defects became apparent which had been overlooked or underestimated in the enthusiastic atmosphere of the Assembly. The claim of its authors that it ensured the final settlement of all disputes without exception was not justified by its terms; many of the most dangerous disputes are those which arise out of matters which fall within the domestic jurisdiction of one of the parties or in which one of the parties claims some advantage to which it has no legal right, and under the Protocol these could only have been decided on the basis of the existing legal situation, leaving them to continue on the plane of interests even though disposed of on that of law. Indeed, to some members of the League this was one of the merits of the Protocol, for it seemed to place an obstacle in the way of any revision of the territorial settlement. The new British government's decision to reject the document was, however, confirmed by the opposition of the Dominions, and, even had a Labour government been willing to take greater risks with the Protocol than the Conservatives, it could not have ignored this opposition. The reasons given by some of the Dominions for their rejection of the Protocol were not well founded, but their united opposition was significant of their fixed resolve on no account to increase the sanctions obligations to which they had committed themselves in the Covenant. The British rejection decided the fate of the Protocol as it had that of the draft treaty of 1923, but it is improbable that it could in any case have satisfied for long the demands of those members of the League that felt themselves insecure. The guarantees that it offered them were for practical purposes only those of the Covenant, and France and the countries associated with her had never regarded these as sufficient. It was founded on a diagnosis of the causes of the weakness of the League which was fundamentally mistaken; that weakness was not due to any juridical defect in the Covenant, but to the doubt whether, if the challenge should come, the League powers would, or in the absence of the United States whether they even could, confront an aggressor with the overwhelmingly superior force on which an effective security system depends.

Austen Chamberlain announced the rejection of the Protocol at Geneva in a speech, of which A. J. Balfour was believed to be the author, which caused some consternation by seeming to imply that in the absence of the United States the enforcement provisions of the Covenant had become unworkable. But he ended by suggesting that the Covenant might be supplemented by special arrangements 'knitting together the nations most immediately concerned, and whose differences might lead to a renewal of strife, by means of treaties framed with the sole object of maintaining, as between themselves, an unbroken peace',[1] a cryptic formula which seemed to foreshadow a new approach to the security problem. The speech was made at a time when the prospects for a general pacification had been greatly improved by the removal, at least for the time being, of the question of German reparations from the field of controversy through the acceptance in the closing months of 1924 of the plan of the Dawes Committee, and the consequent imminent withdrawal of the last French and Belgian troops from the occupation of the Ruhr. The special arrangements which Chamberlain had in mind clearly followed from a proposal by Gustav Stresemann, the German Foreign Minister, for a multilateral regional guarantee, and they took shape at the close of 1925 in the Treaties of Locarno. The negotiations for these treaties necessarily took place outside the League, since Germany was not a member, but the whole outlook for the League was transformed by the reversal of the French policy of holding Germany down by *force majeure*, the League being one of the means, if a poor one, for this purpose. The main provisions of the treaties were that France and Germany, and Belgium and Germany, undertook not to resort to war against each other, that Britain and Italy would immediately come to the help of the party attacked if this undertaking should be broken and would guarantee the frontiers between Germany and France and between Germany and Belgium, that commissions of conciliation would be set up between Germany on the one hand and France, Belgium, Poland and Czechoslovakia on the other, and that France, but not Britain or Italy, would guarantee the frontiers between Germany and Poland and between Germany and Czechoslovakia.

Locarno had a profound effect on the European situation and Austen Chamberlain was justified in calling it 'the real dividing point between the years of war and the years of peace'.[2] But its importance did not lie in its terms. Action under the British and Italian guarantees was to be automatic only if violation of the treaties took the form of 'flagrant' aggression, otherwise assistance was to be given only if the League Council confirmed that a violation had occurred. France's security was thus but little increased, and the British refusal to extend their guarantee to the Polish and Czechoslovakian frontiers with Germany denied the strategic unity of the France–Eastern Europe–Germany complex on which the French had hitherto, and rightly, always insisted. The importance of Locarno was rather that it opened a prospect that the chief danger to the peace of Europe, the age-long hostility between France and Germany, might at last be assuaged. For the first time since the war Germany had made a negotiated treaty with her former enemies; she had accepted the loss of Alsace

[1] League of Nations *Official Journal*, 6th year, no. 4: xxxiii Cl., p. 450.
[2] Quoted in A. Wolfers, *Britain and France between Two Wars* (Harcourt, Brace and Co., 1940), p. 260.

and Lorraine as final; and it had been arranged that she should enter the League and be elected to a permanent seat on the Council at a special Assembly to be held in March 1926. Unfortunately a hitch occurred in this arrangement at the last moment. Three other powers, Spain, Poland and Brazil, came forward as candidates for permanent seats, and as Spain and Brazil were already non-permanent members of the Council their votes were necessary for the election of Germany. It was generally felt that for any other member to be elected to a permanent seat would be a breach of faith towards Germany, and the Assembly dispersed without having reached any decision. Before the regular meeting of the Assembly, however, a compromise was arranged. The number of elected members of the Council was to be raised to nine; there was to be a new class of semi-permanent members who were to be re-eligible at the end of their normal three-year term, and it was understood that Poland would be one of these. Spain and Brazil withdrew their opposition to the election of Germany, but gave notice of withdrawal from the League; Spain retracted her notice before the two years' interval required by the Covenant had elapsed, but Brazil left the League.

The introduction of Germany into the League system as a great power permanent member of the Council made the unilateral disarmament provisions of Versailles anomalous, and accordingly the Final Protocol of Locarno included an undertaking by the signatories 'to give their sincere co-operation to the work relating to disarmament already undertaken by the League of Nations and to seek the realisation thereof in a general agreement'.[1] In pursuance of this undertaking the Council in December 1925 set up a preparatory commission for the world conference which it was still hoped to hold in 1926. The commission was, however, soon in difficulties. It found that on many questions of fundamental principle there was no sort of agreement among the states. Its technical sub-committees wrestled vainly with matters which might seem technical on the surface but were really rooted in widely divergent national interests. Even on the question of what the term 'armaments' should include, opinions differed widely: if military potential were to be included, all elements of a state's power—economic, geographic, demographic and so on—would have to be considered, some of these could not be quantified, and all were subject to changing values under the influence of scientific and technological discovery; whilst to exclude war potential altogether from the calculation would weight the balance heavily in favour of certain states. Other questions on which opinion differed were whether only men actually serving should be counted in a state's military forces or whether trained reserves should be included; whether there should be a budgetary limitation on the size of armaments; whether naval armaments should be reckoned on a basis of total tonnage or by categories of ships; how far

[1] *League of Nations Treaty Series*, vol. LIV, p. 299.

some form of international supervision could be devised to watch over the observance of any agreement that might be reached. There loomed also behind all these particular differences the shadow of the known determination of certain states to demand a firmer guarantee of their security as the price of any reduction in their armaments. The failure of the three chief naval powers, the United States, Britain and Japan, at a conference in June 1927 to reach agreement as to the limitation of non-capital ships added a new source of discouragement. It began to be evident that the preparatory commission was not far from a deadlock, but in 1928 an event occurred outside the League which seemed to open up once again the possibility of advancing towards disarmament by the political instead of the technical line of approach.

Shortly before the meeting of the Assembly of that year the Pact of Paris for the Renunciation of War, the so-called Kellogg–Briand pact, had been signed in Paris, and League members were now in the rather anomalous position of being parties to two systems for maintaining peace which were in some respects inconsistent with one another. The pact forbade any resort to war 'as an instrument of national policy', but the Covenant, owing to the existence of the 'gaps', allowed this in certain cases; the pact declared that the settlement of disputes should never be sought except by pacific means, but the Covenant did not absolutely ensure that every dispute should be settled in this way or even that it should be settled at all. If war, therefore, was now to be excluded, what, it began to be asked, was to be done about disputes which could not be settled peacefully? These questions had very little real importance, but on formal grounds there was no doubt a case for implementing the pact either by incorporating it in the Covenant or by setting up outside the Covenant a system for the settlement of disputes which might perhaps be accepted by the signatories of the pact who were not also members of the League. The former of these courses would have involved the closing of the gaps and thereby extending the sanctions to all wars, and, although the British government, departing for once from its policy of refusing further commitments, supported a plan to this effect, it was not accepted. Instead, the Assembly produced a plan for implementing the pact without amending the Covenant by a General Act for the Pacific Settlement of International Disputes which provided for conciliation commissions to be set up by each of the parties with every other party, for legal disputes to be submitted to the Permanent Court and non-legal disputes to arbitration. The Act was widely accepted, though in many cases with extensive reservations, but it was completely ineffective. It was a thoroughly doctrinaire document, prepared in haste and full of ambiguities. The conciliation commissions which the Act proposed were never found useful, and it was a retrograde step to substitute them for the Council, which was what the framers hoped would be the effect of the Act. For the Council had advantages which these commissions could never possess; it had prestige, its members were men of international reputation who were accustomed to working together, and it had means of informing itself on the facts and the law of the cases brought before it which had proved their value and which these ephemeral commissions could never command.

The Kellogg–Briand pact thus after all did little to improve the political context within which the preparatory commission for the disarmament conference was working, and by the time it eventually succeeded in producing a draft statement of principles in 1930 the general situation had greatly worsened as a result of the onset of the world economic crisis in 1929 and the emergence of Hitler's Nazis as the second largest party in the Reichstag after the elections of 1930. Even the draft statement did little more than set out the opposed positions on the issues in dispute, with little indication of how they might be reconciled, and it was accepted by a majority which did not include Germany, Italy or the U.S.S.R. The situation soon deteriorated still further as Japan invaded Manchuria and defied the League, but it was now thought to be impossible to postpone the meeting of the long-delayed world conference fixed for February 1932 (see below, chapter xxiii). From the outset, however, the German claim to equality overshadowed all the debates at the conference, and in June 1932 Germany threatened to withdraw. In December the rift was temporarily patched by an ambiguous formula which recognised in principle both Germany's right to equality and France's right to security, but did not show how the two were to be reconciled. Before the conference met again Hitler had become Chancellor of the Reich, and a few weeks later Japan gave notice of her intention to resign from the League, though she continued to take part in the conference. Britain attempted to save the conference from the impending wreck by presenting a new plan, to which Ramsay MacDonald gave his name, and when the conference adjourned for the summer of 1933 the plan after some difficult negotiations had been accepted as a basis for future discussions. But on the day the conference met again it was informed that Germany had withdrawn and was giving notice of her resignation from the League. The conference was never formally dissolved, but this was its death warrant. For the League the rise of Hitler had another sequel a year later in a complete reversal of the attitude of the U.S.S.R. In September 1934 the U.S.S.R. was elected to the League, with a permanent seat on the Council, and from that date until the outbreak of the second world war there was no more eloquent advocate at Geneva of the principles of the Covenant than her representative, Maxim Litvinov.

For some years after the peace settlement the mentality of war persisted over much of Europe, and the League, with no force at its command and no accumulated reserve of prestige behind it, was often unable to make its writ run when a state attempted to snatch by force or by fraud some advantage for itself and to face the world with a *fait accompli*. Its difficulties were increased by the existence of rival authorities, first in the Supreme Council of the Allies and later in the Conference of Ambassadors which they had set up in Paris to deal with matters left outstanding by the treaties. There was no clear demarcation of function between these bodies and the League, and the latter sometimes found itself excluded from matters which properly belonged to it, or else called in to deal with problems on which its rivals had been unable to agree and at a stage when they had become nearly insoluble. The first dispute to be brought before it was one between Sweden and Finland in 1920, and in this, which related to sovereignty over the Aaland Islands, it succeeded in arranging a settlement which both parties accepted. But a few weeks later a more difficult case arose. A Polish free-lance commander, Zeligowski, had seized the disputed city of Vilna in breach of an armistice which had left it in Lithuanian possession; he was in fact acting, though this was denied at the time, with the approval of the Polish government. The League Council tried vainly to induce the Poles and the Lithuanians to agree to an internationally supervised plebiscite, but in the end, in 1923, the Ambassadors awarded the city to Poland. Another successful act of aggression was the seizure by Lithuania in January 1923 of Memel, which was held by the Allies pending a decision as to its fate: by the time the matter was referred to the League Council by the Ambassadors the seizure was virtually accepted, but the Council was able to effect an arrangement which secured a measure of autonomy to the mainly German inhabitants of the city.

In August 1923 the League machinery was called upon to deal for the first time with an aggression by a great power. General Tellini, the Italian member of a commission which had been surveying the Greco-Albanian frontier on behalf of the Ambassadors, had been murdered, and the Italians, without waiting for any enquiry into the circumstances, demanded an indemnity from Greece and seized the island of Corfu after a bombardment causing serious loss of life. The Greeks appealed to the League, though declaring their readiness to accept any decision that the Ambassadors might make and thereby providing Italy with some technical justification for arguing that, as the dispute was in course of settlement by another authority, the League should refrain from interfering. The Council, however, declined to accept this argument and proceeded to negotiate a settlement under which the Ambassadors should investigate the responsibility for the murder and the Permanent Court should determine what compensation Greece should pay, 50 million lire being deposited pending the decision. Both the Ambassadors and the two parties accepted this settlement, but the matter of the Corfu seizure had not been dealt with, and the Ambassadors suddenly decided that Greece should pay the 50 million lire forthwith. It was clear that this was the price Italy had exacted for the evacuation of Corfu, that the seizure was not going to be considered, and that the League had been sidetracked. The Council had not been able to hold the scales even between a strong and a weak power. On the other hand it was widely felt that had the League not been in existence the dispute might have led to general war, and, although Italy had got much the best of it, none the less a great power had had to defend itself at the bar of world opinion—and Mussolini did in fact handle his relations with members of the League much more cautiously for the next eleven years. The results of the incident therefore were not wholly discouraging, and there seemed still to be a hope that with a fair field the machinery of the League might prove effective, and this hope seemed to be confirmed by the manner in which the League dealt with the next dispute to come before it. In October 1925, in consequence of an incident on the frontier between Greece and Bulgaria, Greek troops crossed into Bulgarian territory and Bulgaria at once appealed to the League. Drummond acted with speed and summoned the Council to meet within three days. The Council's President, Aristide Briand, confirmed this action and telegraphed to the parties exhorting them to stop all military action. On receipt of this telegram the Greeks countermanded an offensive they were about to launch, and the Council meeting in Paris succeeded in obtaining a cease-fire and proceeded to form a commission of enquiry to decide the merits of the dispute. The commission reported that the Greeks were largely at fault and the Council then fixed a sum which Greece was to pay by way of reparation. The complete success of the League on this occasion raised a hope that it had created a precedent which might be followed in future cases with equally good results. But the circumstances had been exceptionally favourable. Greece was a small power, the great powers had for once been united, and there were no political complications. The Council had acted much as the Concert had sometimes acted in the nineteenth century: Greece had been overawed and had submitted. Circumstances such as these were not destined to recur in the later history of the League.

The years that followed the Dawes Plan and the Locarno treaties were years of high promise for the League and there were signs that it had established itself as a normal and necessary part of international relations. The Foreign Ministers of the three principal League powers, Chamberlain, Briand and Stresemann, found it worth their while to attend in person practically every meeting of the Assembly or the Council, and the mutual confidence that grew up amongst these three became an important stabilising influence on the European situation. Most of the other European foreign ministers followed their example and became regular attendants at Geneva. The United States, though she showed no signs of being willing to join the League, had begun to look more benevolently on its work and to take part in many of its non-political activities, and in 1927 the U.S.S.R. began to do the same. For some years no major crisis occurred to test the soundness of the League's structure; and, though none of the great controversial questions—reparations, security, disarmament—had been solved, in the friendlier atmosphere that had begun to prevail they were ceasing to seem insoluble.

With the coming of the great economic depression of 1929 and the following years, the League's short period of optimism came to an end. In 1931 for the first time since 1923 it was faced with action by a great power that soon came to be seen as a direct violation of the Covenant. In September of that year Japanese troops guarding the South Manchuria Railway attacked and rapidly disarmed the Chinese garrisons in Mukden and neighbouring towns and drove out the provincial Chinese government. They claimed to be acting in defence of their interests and nationals in the South Manchuria Railway zone which were being threatened by China. The reality of this threat seemed plausible, since the Kuomintang government was bent on ridding China of foreign privileges and concessions, among them those of other leading League members. Japan's record in the League had hitherto been excellent, and in the absence of accurate information her representative's protestations were at first accepted at their face value. By the end of December, when the Japanese army had completed its overrunning of Manchuria, and when the genuine asseverations of the Japanese government that they intended no such thing had been shown to be irrelevant to the action of the army, it was already too late for effective action.

China had immediately appealed to the League under Article XI (see chapter XXIII). The Council's first idea of sending a commission of enquiry was abandoned in face of Japanese opposition and a United States refusal to co-operate. The Council then endeavoured to persuade Japan to withdraw her troops within the railway zone, and was assured that this would be done. By mid-October, however, it was clear that, far from withdrawing, the troops were still advancing, so on 24 October the Council proposed to fix a date by which the withdrawal was to be completed. The League's position had, it seemed, been strengthened by the agreement of the United States to allow a representative to sit in on the Council, but the representative was instructed to speak only when matters arising from the Kellogg–Briand pact were under discussion, and in fact he opened his mouth only once after the initial courtesies attendant upon his appearance. The Japanese delegate voted against the 24 October resolution and thus, under recent views of Article XI, nullified its legal validity. The Article XI conciliation procedure was thus shown to be wholly ineffective against a great power determined to have its way. As a last resort in December the Council belatedly decided to send a commission of enquiry of the five major powers (Britain, France, Germany, Italy and the United States), Japan concurring once China's sole condition that Japanese troops should first be withdrawn into the railway zone had been overridden.

Before the commission started the situation had deteriorated. Early in 1932 an anti-Japanese boycott and riots broke out in Shanghai, and Japan retaliated by bombing and moving in troops which were not withdrawn for several months. Three days earlier the Chinese had appealed under Article xv, thereby confronting the League with the possibility of the members finding themselves obligated to impose sanctions on Japan under Article xvi. They asked also, as the Covenant entitled them to do, that the appeal should be transferred to the Assembly, where the small powers, who felt their safety to depend on effective collective security, were in a large majority. A special Assembly met accordingly in March, resolved that it would not recognise changes brought about by means contrary to the Covenant or to the Kellogg–Briand pact, established a special committee to take over from the Council the task of seeking a settlement of the dispute (the first time that a specific political problem had thus been transferred), but decided, as it could hardly fail to do, to await the report of the Lytton commisssion of enquiry (so named after its British chairman). These many delays facilitated the maturing of the Japanese plans, and when at last the commission arrived in Manchuria it learnt that Japan had established a puppet government for a newly constituted 'independent' state of Manchukuo. The commission's report was received in Geneva in September and was considered successively by the Council and the Assembly. It was an authoritative document, giving full and fair consideration to the anomalous situation in Manchuria, but generally condemnatory of the scale of the Japanese action, and insistent in particular that China should be sovereign in Manchuria. The report was accepted in its main lines by the Assembly in February 1933, and a month later Japan gave notice of resignation from the League. There were, however, no means of enforcing the terms of the settlement proposed in the report, and the question of sanctions at this date simply could not arise even had the Assembly found, as it did not, that Japan had resorted to war in disregard of her Covenant obligations. But this was what she had in fact done. Aggression had been committed with impunity. The confidence of the smaller powers in the League had been gravely shaken, and a rift had developed between them and the major powers. The weakness of the collective security system as the great power members of the League were prepared to operate it had been mercilessly exposed.

While the League was still dealing with the Manchurian affair its attention had also been turned to two outbreaks of hostilities in South America. One of these arose out of a long-standing frontier dispute between Bolivia and Paraguay in the Chaco area, and fighting began there in June 1932. In May of the following year Paraguay formally declared war. A commission sent out by the League had no success, but the League did succeed in arranging an embargo on the supply of arms, at first against both belligerents, and later, after Bolivia had belatedly appealed to the League and offered to accept the recommendations of the Assembly, against Paraguay only. The embargo, although the United States supported it, was never completely effective, and each side in turn became obdurate as the shifting fortunes of the war favoured its cause. Finally the war ended in June 1935, not through any efforts of the League, but through the exhaustion of both sides.

In the other South American dispute the intervention of the League was more successful. In June 1932 a party of Peruvians, at first repudiated but later supported by their own government, seized a strip of undoubted Colombian territory near the village of Leticia and, Colombia having appealed to the League, the Council adopted a report calling for the immediate withdrawal of the Peruvians. There was a refusal to comply at first, but a change of government occurred in Peru and the two parties agreed to invite the League to send a commission to administer the disputed area while the withdrawal took place.

But any hope that still remained that the security system might be restored was destroyed by the war of 1935–6 between Italy and Ethiopia. The relations between these two countries first came before the League as a result of a clash between their troops in December 1934, at Walwal, a place near the undelimited frontier between Ethiopia and Italian Somaliland, when, on Italy's demanding compensation, Ethiopia appealed to the League under Article XI of the Covenant. At a meeting of the Council the next month it was arranged that the matter should be referred to arbitrators in accordance with a treaty between the two countries and that meanwhile consideration by the Council should be postponed. Italy delayed the appointment of the arbitrators and the tribunal did not meet until July, and in September it gave an award which exonerated both sides from blame. But long before this the Walwal incident had lost all importance, for Italy's warlike preparations were on a scale which made concealment of their purpose no longer possible, and as early as March Ethiopia had asked to have the dispute considered under Article XV as being 'likely to lead to a rupture'. Unfortunately her appeal coincided with the repudiation by Germany of the disarmament provisions of the Treaty of Versailles and Britain and France were exceedingly reluctant to take any action which might estrange Italy. The Council therefore several times postponed the matter and it was still engaged in preparing a report which would have contained the recommendations which it considered 'just and proper' for a settlement when, on 3 October, the Italian troops invaded Ethiopia.

Thus when the war began the dispute had been before the League in one form or another for about ten months, and there had been ample time for the 'cooling-off' process, in which the founders of the League security system had placed much confidence, to take effect. Here, however, the system had to deal with an aggression for which, as the Italian commander-in-chief, Marshal De Bono, later revealed, plans had been laid two years before, and the leisurely pace of the League had resulted not in a cooling of tempers but in facilitating the completion of the aggressor's arrangements. Until September the repeated procrastinations of the Council under British and French leadership caused growing despair among the now numerous and vocal supporters of the League in many countries of the world, including Britain. Mussolini's expectation that no more would be done than in the Manchurian affair was strengthened. But with a general election due within a year the British government could not ignore public opinion, and when the Assembly met in September the Foreign Secretary, Sir Samuel Hoare, declared that Britain stood with the League 'for the collective maintenance of the Covenant in its entirety, and particularly for steady and collective resistance to all acts of unprovoked aggression'.[1] Pierre Laval for France hesitantly and unconvincingly supported Hoare. Mussolini's decision to call the bluff by invading Ethiopia could not then be ignored, and on 7 October each of the members of the Council, with the exception of Italy, declared their government's agreement with a Council Committee's report that Italy had 'resorted to war in disregard of its covenants under Article XII of the Covenant of the League of Nations'.[2] Similar agreement was expressed in the Assembly on 9, 10 and 11 October by all members except Austria, Hungary and Albania (all under Italian influence), and Italy. By expressing their individual agreement with a report quoting words from the opening sentence of Article XVI, the members of the League accepted also the obligation to apply sanctions, and they proceeded to set up a committee to co-ordinate their further action.

Mussolini was almost certainly surprised by the speed and vigour of the League's reaction. He need not have feared. Literally applied, Article XVI required the members of the League immediately to sever all trade and financial relations with Italy, to prohibit intercourse with Italian nationals, and to prevent all financial, commercial and personal intercourse between Italians and the nationals of any other state whether a member of the League or not. But the Co-ordination Committee decided instead of this policy of complete non-intercourse to act under the Resolutions of 1921 (see above, p. 247). Members were advised in the first instance to ban imports from and loans to Italy, and also the export of certain raw materials; but these had the appearance of having been chosen so as not too seriously to inconvenience the Italians, and they did not include an embargo on oil, which, in the opinion of some competent judges, might have had a decisive effect on their operations. It may have been thought that, if time were given, the limited sanctions already being applied would be effective even without an oil embargo, and it is also possible that public opinion would sooner or later have forced the governments to impose it in spite of the risks of reprisal that it might have involved. But in the

---

[1] League of Nations *Official Journal*, Spec. Sup. no. 138, XVI Ass. p. 46.
[2] League of Nations *Official Journal*, 16th year, no. 11: LXXXIX Cl., p. 1225.

259

endeavour not finally to throw Italy into the arms of Germany the French maintained a prolonged and successful delaying action and at the beginning of May 1936 Ethiopian resistance collapsed thanks to the indiscriminate use of poison gas by the Italians on troops and civilians wholly without protection against it. After that it was clear that nothing short of military sanctions, which none of the major League powers was prepared to use, would affect the issue. At a meeting of the Assembly on 4 July, it was decided to lift the sanctions, and in December 1937 Italy gave notice of resignation from the League.

This was the decisive defeat for the League security system, not merely because there was far less excuse than in the case of Manchuria, but because the coercive sanctions procedure had for the first time been invoked under the influence of the high-sounding but hollow protestations of intent of the leading League powers, Britain and France. It was no longer possible to believe in the sincerity of their professed determination or in their will to uphold the Covenant. Never again was it seriously suggested that the peace enforcement provisions should be put into operation, and except for the expulsion of the U.S.S.R. after her attack on Finland in December 1939 the League remained henceforth a passive witness of the aggressions of the totalitarian powers. Its reaction to Hitler's annexation of Austria in 1938 was to strike Austria off the list of League members, and neither Czechoslovakia in 1938, nor Poland in 1939, thought it worth while to bring its case to Geneva. During these years there was a general feeling that some revision of articles of the Covenant which it was clear that the members did not intend to observe ought to be undertaken, and a number of different suggestions were brought forward. But the fundamental question at issue was whether the League should still be armed with some sort of coercive powers, possibly on a regional instead of a universal basis, or whether it should henceforth be merely a machinery for facilitating consultation and co-operation. That issue was still undecided when the war of 1939 broke out and no change had been made in the Covenant.

Supplementing these political and diplomatic means by which it was hoped that peace might be achieved, the League developed a wide range of activities in the field of international social and economic co-operation which were in part inspired by the thought that the problem of war might be attacked indirectly as well as directly by eliminating some of the causes of friction that make wars more probable. The initiation of these activities owed much to a famous pamphlet by General Smuts, *The League of Nations: A Practical Suggestion*, in which he urged that the League should be 'part and parcel of the common international life of States...an ever visible, living, working organ of the polity of civilization [functioning] so strongly in the ordinary peaceful intercourse of States that it becomes irresistible in their disputes...'.[1] Among the most important of the bodies

[1] Quoted in Walters, *History of the League of Nations*, p. 59.

constituted for these purposes was the International Labour Organisation established with autonomous status by a special chapter of the peace treaties. Its purpose was to further the improvement of conditions of labour by international action. It comprised (*a*) a General Conference consisting of four representatives of each member, two being government delegates, and two, representing employers and work-people respectively, chosen by governments in agreement with industrial organisations in their respective countries. Its functions were the making of recommendations for national legislation and the preparation of draft conventions requiring to be ratified by states before taking effect; (*b*) an International Labour Office, which was the secretariat of the organisation and was controlled by a governing body consisting of twelve government, six employers' and six work-people's representatives. Expenses were paid out of League funds, and membership of the League carried membership of the organisation, though non-League members might also be elected. It was happily shielded by the nature of its work from the political storms which the main body of the League had to meet, and it was significant for the development of some degree of co-operation across national frontiers between employers in different countries and between employees likewise.

A number of technical organisations were also set up under the general authority of the League Assembly and Council. The first of these was one on communications and transit, and in its main lines the constitution of this became a model for the later ones. It consisted of a General Conference which met at intervals of about four years and was composed of delegates of the governments, not all of which were necessarily members of the League; an Advisory and Technical Committee, meeting more often, and composed of individual experts not representing their governments; and a section of the secretariat. The committee advised the League, and when so requested individual governments, on matters within its competence; it was available to be used as a conciliation commission for the settlement of disputes on traffic questions; and it conducted investigations and prepared draft agreements for consideration by the General Conference. It formed a number of specialist committees dealing with rail transport, inland navigation, ports, electric power, and other special aspects of communications. The General Conference promoted international agreements on communications questions and from time to time it convened special conferences on particular topics. The general object of the Organisation had been laid down in Article xxiii(*e*) of the Covenant as 'to secure and maintain freedom of communications and of transit', and though that ideal was far from being realised it had some successes. Some of the conventions which it promoted were accepted and put into operation, but progress was less than it might have been, in part because matters of communications have political implications, and partly because the United States, the Soviet Union and Germany were unwilling to join in many arrangements which required world-wide agreement to be effective.

In the economic field the League had some early successes in handling some immediately urgent problems of reconstruction, notably in its work in the rehabilitation of the finances of Austria. Various countries had made relief loans to Austria, but these had served only as palliatives, there was no possibility of further loans, and it had become clear that nothing but a plan of radical reconstruction could avert a complete collapse of the Austrian economy. It was essential, however, before any such plan could be launched that states having reparation claims against Austria should agree to their deferment so as to enable her to offer the security necessary for any loan on an adequate scale. A special committee of the League Council carried through the difficult negotiations which were necessary for this purpose, and it was then able to put into operation a comprehensive plan, under the supervision of a League commissioner, of retrenchment and budgetary reform. This brought about a rapid improvement in the Austrian situation and kept the economy on an even keel until, with most of the rest of the world, it was engulfed in the great economic breakdown of the middle inter-war years. A reconstruction scheme modelled on that for Austria was later applied to Hungary.

The League was less successful in its efforts to introduce long-term improvements in the conduct of international economic relations. A general tendency towards more nationalistic economic policies gained ascendancy in the early 1920s, and against this the League could make little headway. Moreover, the two most crucial matters of international economic policy in the early years of the League were reparations and inter-Allied debts, and from both of these it was excluded. The first important enterprise of a general character was the organisation of a conference of financial experts at Brussels to consider remedies for the monetary chaos left by the war, but though the experts were practically unanimous in their recommendations these would have required, as the report pointed out, fundamental changes in the policies of nearly every state which governments were not willing, and perhaps not even able, to make. One result of this conference was, however, a decision to turn the provisional committee which had prepared it into a standing economic and financial expert committee with a section of the Secretariat to serve it. This was later divided into two separate committees for finance and economics respectively. In 1927 a World Economic Conference was held at Geneva after long and very thorough preparation, and this again resulted in an admirable report and recommendations, but any chance there may have been of effect being given to the recommendations was wrecked by the onset of the great depression two years later. In an endeavour to handle the problems of the depression a second World Economic Conference met in London in 1933, but the opposed views of Britain and France about the measures that were necessary, and the reversal of policy by the United States in the middle of the Conference, prevented any agreement being reached. Perhaps the most valuable legacy left by the League in the economic field was the series of studies and the collection and diffusion of economic information by its Economic Intelligence Service. The League could diagnose the causes of economic ills and prescribe the appropriate remedies, but it could not force those remedies on the patients.

Probably the work of the Health Organisation was the most permanently valuable of all the social services of the League. It began with the work of an Epidemics Commission formed to combat an outbreak of typhus and cholera which war and revolution had loosed upon eastern Europe, and this commission was soon afterwards used to assist the Greek government in the health problems arising from the influx of refugees driven from their homes in Asia Minor by the Turkish victories there. A permanent Health Organisation consisting of an Advisory Council of government representatives, a smaller Health Committee of specialists, and a section of the Secretariat, was created in 1923, and thereafter its work developed rapidly. The Epidemics Commission was enlarged into a permanent epidemiological service on a scale never before attempted for the collection of information on certain diseases and its distribution to national and port health authorities all over the world. Another branch of the Organisation's work was the standardisation of drugs, serums, vaccines and vitamins, which is essential to efficient collaboration between scientific workers in different countries, and the standards recommended have now been largely incorporated into national pharmacopoeias. An important new subject was taken up in 1935 when the Assembly asked the Organisation to collaborate with the International Labour Organisation and the International Institute of Agriculture in preparing a report on nutrition. When this report was issued in 1937 it revealed in a startling fashion how vast was the number of human beings who were either underfed or wrongly fed, and it led to the setting up of national nutrition committees in many countries to work towards the attainment of the standards recommended, which incidentally were soon to be found useful in the framing of war rationing schemes. Lastly the Organisation was able, when requested, to advise and help particular countries desiring to improve their health services; China in particular received invaluable help of this kind in a comprehensive programme of reforms involving the reorganisation of her quarantine service, the training of doctors and nurses, and the direction of a campaign against cholera and smallpox.

There were many other more limited but important fields in which the League promoted international co-operation. One great humanitarian work of the early days was that of Dr Nansen, who became the League's commissioner for refugees in 1921 and devoted the last years of his life to organising the resettlement of the scores of thousands of people who had lost their homes and nationalities through the war or the peace settlement. On an appeal from the Greek government this work was extended to grapple with the appalling problem created by the influx of more than a million persons from Asia Minor after the Turkish victories in 1922. Among the social evils attacked by the League were the traffic in women and children, on which a conference was held and a convention reached in 1921, and the traffic in dangerous drugs. The drug traffic created problems on which purely national measures had been found to be almost wholly ineffective, because of the ease with which drugs may be smuggled, and the profitableness of the trade. Its details were obscure, and the League first set itself to collect the facts; it then secured agreement on a system of licences for the export from and the import into each country of certain specified drugs, and this licensing system was then supplemented by limiting the manufacture in the producing countries as closely as possible to medical and scientific needs. The administration of the scheme was supervised by a Permanent Central Opium Board and an Advisory Committee. The last of the technical agencies to be established was the Committee on Intellectual Co-operation, of which the main purposes were to develop international contacts and to build an international consciousness among teachers, artists, scientists, authors and members of other intellectual professions. Even more than the other organisations, the Committee on Intellectual Co-operation was hampered by scepticism on the part of governments and by shortage of money.

The extreme parsimony of the financial provision that members of the League were willing to make was indeed notable: the average annual cost of the whole League, including the International Labour Organisation and the Permanent Court, and including the capital expenditure on its buildings, was about £1,600,000, of which the share of the United Kingdom was about £150,000. In these circumstances it was remarkable that the League was able, as the United States Secretary of State Cordell Hull wrote, to develop mutual exchange and discussion of ideas and methods to a greater extent and in more fields of humanitarian and scientific endeavour than any earlier organisation in history.

In the last years of the League the breakdown of the security system and the hostility of the totalitarian powers made it necessary to change the methods of working of the technical organisations. It had become useless to plan the holding of large conferences or to hope for the conclusion of conventions on matters of interest to states in general. Instead a practice grew of holding meetings of limited groups of states or of individual experts for the study of particular problems; sugar and wheat were among the subjects treated in this way. Interest shifted from the action of governments to the interests of the individual, and besides the question of nutrition already mentioned questions taken up in this way included the causes of economic and financial troubles, depressions, the trade cycle, the gold standard, and questions of hygiene and housing. There developed also an opinion in favour of greater independence for the social and technical organs, and on the eve of the second world war a committee under the chairmanship of Viscount Bruce proposed that a new central committee should be established to take over the responsibilities of the Assembly and the Council for these bodies, including the approval of their plans of work and their budgetary demands. A plan on these lines was subsequently adopted in the Economic and Social Council which the Charter of the United Nations constituted as one of its 'principal organs'.

Outside its two great functions of promoting international co-operation and achieving international peace the League had many and very various duties placed upon it by the treaties of peace. It was given, for instance, power to revise some few of the articles of the treaties and to settle some differences of interpretation; it had a part to play in settling the terms of the agreements into which Germany was required to enter; its consent was necessary to any alienation of the independence of Austria. But apart from particular acts such as these which it was required or empowered to perform it was given certain tasks of a continuing administrative character. One of these, contained in the Covenant itself, was the supervision of the mandate system, whereby colonies and territories of which the defeated powers were being deprived 'which are inhabited by peoples not yet able to stand by themselves under the strenuous conditions of the modern world' were to be placed under the 'tutelage' of more advanced nations as 'Mandatories on behalf of the League' (below, p. 292). The Covenant created a Permanent Mandates Commission to advise the Council and to receive an annual report from each of the mandatory powers, and in course of time this Commission accumulated a great store of experience of colonial problems; its members, who were individuals appointed for their special qualifications for the work and not as representatives of governments, learnt to appreciate the difficulties of colonial administration, and the colonial administrators often found the suggestions and criticisms of the Commission useful and came to realise that they were inspired by a genuine wish to co-operate and not by any captious spirit. Neither the Council nor the Commission had any power to coerce a mandatory power, but on the whole the system worked well.

The League was less successful in another somewhat similar task, that of supervising the observance of the Minorities treaties made between the great powers and certain states, such as Poland, Czechoslovakia, Rumania and others, which owed either their independence or an enlargement of their territory to the victory of the Allies. These treaties required the states concerned to accord certain rights to racial, religious, or linguistic minorities within their territories, and placed the observance of these rights under the 'guarantee' of the League. But they gave the League no means of enforcing this guarantee other than by the pressure of persuasion or publicity, and its effectiveness therefore tended to vary with the rise and fall of the League's own prestige. The Council evolved a procedure for dealing with petitions from the minorities which was reasonably good in view of the difficulties of the task; it laid down rules as to the receivability of petitions to be applied by the Secretariat, and it instituted a system of standing committees to examine those found receivable and to decide which of them it was necessary to bring before the full Council. This procedure was more effective than has sometimes been supposed, for it is usually judged by its failures, and these were publicly known; but when, as often happened, a grievance was settled without being brought before the Council, the matter was treated as confidential and the League did not always receive the credit to which it was entitled. But a fully effective system of minority protection is possible only if both the state in which the minority finds itself and the minority have learnt to be tolerant of differences, and in most of the countries with which the League had to deal this condition was far from being realised. The treaties ran counter to the sentiments of nationalism prevailing in most of the states bound by them, and it is possible that they sometimes encouraged irredentist feelings which could be represented as endangering the stability of the territorial settlement. They were resented too because they were felt to mark an inferior national status, especially since none of the great powers had been subjected to similar obligations, and one of them, Italy, was notoriously pursuing an opposite policy in the territories acquired from Austria-Hungary. Confidence in the system naturally declined in the last years of the League, and in 1934 Poland announced that she would no longer recognise the jurisdiction of the Council in minority matters.

Another difficult task laid upon the League by the treaties related to the settlement in the Danzig area. Danzig was a mainly German city, but its situation close to the mouth of the Vistula made it the natural port for Poland, as before the nineteenth century it had long been, and the obvious place for a Polish access to the sea. The Allies therefore sought to reconcile this important Polish interest with the principle of self-determination which they had accepted as the basis of the settlement by detaching it from Germany and constituting it a free city 'under the protection of the League'; its constitution was to be drawn up in agreement with a High Commissioner appointed by the League, and it was then to be placed 'under the guarantee' of the League. The arrangement included provisions limiting the autonomy of Danzig in the interests of Poland; she was to have the free use of the Danzig docks, to control the Vistula and the railway system within the city, to conduct Danzig's foreign relations, and to include Danzig within her customs frontiers. A High Commissioner resident in Danzig was to represent the League.

In view of the extreme complexity of the conflicting interests no settlement had any chance of permanency unless it was accepted by both parties as definitive, or, failing that, if it were not backed by some powers of enforcement. Neither of these conditions was satisfied. The High Commissioner's function was to mediate in disputes and to act as a guardian of the constitution, but he had no powers of government in Danzig; the League heard appeals from his decisions, and when disputes were taken to Geneva it often happened that a settlement was found possible in the calmer atmosphere prevailing there. But neither the League nor its commissioner could enforce a decision if either of the parties was obdurate. Fundamentally, Danzig–Polish relations were never more than one aspect of the relations between Germany and Poland; when these were good the affairs of Danzig ran smoothly; when German policy towards Poland became aggressive they deteriorated. In the last years before 1939 Berlin effectively assumed the direction of affairs in Danzig; the Nazi party had step by step established a dictatorship over the city; and the treaty settlement had completely broken down.

As compensation for the destruction of the coal mines of northern France the Treaty of Versailles required Germany to renounce the government of the Saar basin in favour of the League of Nations as trustee and to cede its coal mines to France outright. The League was directed to set up a governing commission of five persons—one Frenchman, one Saarlander, and three from countries other than France and Germany; and after fifteen years a plebiscite was to be held to decide between the maintenance of the treaty régime, union with France, and reunion with Germany, and if the latter were chosen Germany was to repurchase the mines from France. The commission made a rather unpromising start; the first chairman was a Frenchman, and some of his colleagues were suspected of a too Francophil bias. But even a perfectly constituted commission might have been daunted by the difficulties of the task entrusted to it. It had to organise an administration out of nothing in a politically backward area; it had been imposed on a resentful population which was kept in a state of perpetual unsettlement by the uncertainties of the plebiscite; and it was exposed to a constant stream of hostile propaganda from Berlin attempting to undermine its authority. With a change in the chairmanship and the entry of Germany into the League in 1926 the atmosphere improved and the commission succeeded in organising an honest and highly efficient system of government under which the territory prospered economically and financially. As the date of the plebiscite approached the position again deteriorated, and after Hitler's accession to power in 1933 the Nazis organised a reign of terror which seemed likely to make a fair conduct of the plebiscite impossible. In the end, however, thanks to the protection afforded at the last moment by an international force, the plebiscite passed off without disorder in January 1935 and resulted in an overwhelming vote in favour of reunion with Germany. On the whole the commission had successfully discharged a very difficult task, and incidentally had demonstrated that an efficient international government is not in all circumstances impossible.

After the meeting at which the U.S.S.R. was expelled in December 1939 the Assembly did not meet again while the war lasted, but the economic and social work was carried on, though necessarily on a restricted scale, and every effort was made to preserve the structure of the League and of its institutions intact and to assure the continuance of essential work. The International Labour Organisation moved to Montreal, the health section and the Central Opium Board to Washington, and the economic, financial, and transit work to Princeton, New Jersey. But as the war drew towards an end it became clear that the League would be replaced by a new organisation, and after the adoption of the Charter of the United Nations at San Francisco the chief concern of those responsible for the destinies of the League was to see that its activities were terminated in a manner worthy of the part it had played in world affairs. Representatives of the League and of the United Nations worked out a plan which was later approved by the twenty-first and last Assembly. The buildings and the Library at Geneva were transferred to the United Nations at an agreed valuation to become its European headquarters; the secretary-general was directed to afford every facility for the assumption by the United Nations of such of the non-political activities of the League as the new body might decide to assume; the Permanent Court was formally dissolved and replaced by a new International Court of Justice with a statute in almost identical terms; and provision was made for the continued existence of the International Labour Organisation as an autonomous institution in close relation with the United Nations. The League was dissolved by a resolution of the Assembly on 18 April 1946.

CHAPTER X

THE MIDDLE EAST 1900–1945

MIDDLE EASTERN history in the first half of the twentieth century may be looked upon as the working out of a crisis in society and politics—a crisis which began towards the end of the eighteenth century and from which in the end no geographical area and no section of society could remain immune. This crisis resulted from the contact between the traditional Muslim society, which seemed devoid of vigour, inventiveness and enterprise, and Europe, which was clearly in the ascendant, militarily superior, and full of complacent self-confidence, energy and reforming zeal. The initial European impact was military. From the first decades of the nineteenth century, Middle Eastern governments were becoming increasingly aware that European arms and military techniques were superior to anything they could command, and they proceeded to remedy their inferiority by the seemingly simple expedient of acquiring European arms and copying European military organisation. In this way they hoped both to parry the threat from Europe and themselves to threaten those of their neighbours who were tardier or more inefficient in adopting the new techniques.

But this exposure to European methods and ideas had many unexpected and disconcerting effects. We may first consider the case of the Ottoman Empire. Selim III (1787–1807) and Mahmud II (1808–39) between them destroyed the traditional Ottoman Army and laid down the basis for a European-model conscript army. Such an army required in turn a European-model centralised bureaucracy to administer it and, to lead it, a new type of officer, trained in European techniques and exposed to European ideas. But bureaucratic centralisation could not remain confined to military affairs, and by the end of the nineteenth century, as a result of increasing centralisation (and of the improved communications, such as the telegraph and the railway, which made centralisation feasible), the Ottoman State controlled its territory as it had seldom done in the past and regulated the affairs of its subjects more minutely than ever before. The introduction of European military techniques and administrative methods may then be said to have given a new lease of life to absolutism in the Ottoman Empire, and to have given a *coup de grâce* to such intermediary orders and institutions (for example the Janissaries, the craft and trade guilds and the autonomous religious communities) as had provided an element of practical constitutionalism to limit, effectively if informally, the utter plenitude of power which the ruler of the traditional Ottoman polity in theory enjoyed.

This increase in centralisation and absolutism required a new type of military officer and civil official trained in European military and administrative techniques and exposed therefore to European notions concerning politics and society. Since modernisation—which was initiated and carried out by the sultan and his entourage—did not manifestly make the empire better able to defend itself against European ambitions, this new class of European-trained officials and officers became increasingly disaffected towards the very régime which called them into being. They argued that the ills of the empire could not be cured by the adoption of mere techniques; that these ills could be cured only by the adoption of constitutional parliamentary government, which they believed to be the real foundation of European superiority. The first group successfully to promote these views was that of the Young Ottomans. Led by a high official and minister, Midhat Pasha, and exploiting a favourable conjunction of internal political turmoil and external military threat, they persuaded the new sultan, Abdul Hamid II, to promulgate in December 1876 a constitution which provided for a parliament and made ministers responsible to it. The first Ottoman parliament, with an elected chamber of 120 deputies, first met in March 1877 only to be dissolved by the sultan less than a year later, in February 1878. The sultan having prevented it from being put to the test, the Young Ottoman contention that salvation lay in making ministers responsible to a popular assembly and in encouraging local and provincial self-government remained a mere argument, an unfulfilled promise the ghost of which haunted the intellectual and official classes in the three decades of Hamidian rule which followed.

The Hamidian period saw a continuation of the trends to modernisation and centralisation which were dominant all through the nineteenth century in the Ottoman Empire. 'It would not be an exaggeration', writes Professor Bernard Lewis, 'that it was in these early years of the reign of Abdülhamid that the whole movement of the Tanzimat, of legal, administrative, and educational reform reached its fruition and its climax. And so, too, did the tendencies, already discernible under the *Tanzimat* regime, towards a new, centralized, and unrestrained despotism.'[1] One may in fact go on to argue that it was the very success of Hamidian policies in promoting education—both civilian and military—and in developing railways and telegraphs which brought about the downfall of the régime. More and more young men—eventually to become officers and officials—were exposed to European-style education and ideas, and thus became disaffected towards the régime which set up the schools and colleges in which they were educated, while improved communications spread these ideas to remote corners of the empire where they had hardly penetrated before. As a result, scepticism about the legitimacy of the traditional Ottoman institutions, a toleration, an expectation of change—whether peaceful or

[1] Bernard Lewis, *The Emergence of Modern Turkey* (1961), pp. 174-5.

violent—became widespread among the educated classes. Again, the increase in centralisation and absolutism in the three decades of Hamidian rule itself made easier the success of a *coup d'état*, the authors of which had now only to neutralise or topple the supreme authority in the state, i.e. the sultan, for them in turn to gain control of the empire and its military and administrative organisation.

This is what in effect happened in the Young Turk Revolution of 1908. In July of that year a group of young conspiratorial officers in the Third Army Corps stationed in Macedonia (with its headquarters in Salonika) started a mutiny which rapidly spread in the Corps and in the Second Army Corps stationed in Edirne. When it looked as though the troops which the sultan dispatched from Izmir against the mutineers were in sympathy with them, the sultan capitulated and on 24 July restored the Constitution of 1876 as the Salonika officers had demanded. But it became rapidly clear that the empire was not to be governed on constitutional, parliamentary lines. Until April 1909 there was an uneasy and indecisive sparring for power between the officers organised into a Committee of Union and Progress and Abdul Hamid, whose position was of course profoundly shaken but who still had some power and much influence. Whether or not inspired and encouraged by him, soldiers of the First Army Corps stationed in Istanbul mutinied on the night of 12–13 April, crying that the religion was in danger. This provoked a so-called 'Army of Deliverance' to march from Salonika on Istanbul, which they reached on 23 April. They crushed the counter-mutiny and the Committee of Union and Progress deposed the sultan and reigned in his place. But it became speedily apparent that autocracy was not transformed into constitutional government; rather the sultan's power passed to the officers who had dared to depose him. True, there were elections and there was a parliament, but it was not the deputies who controlled the government; on the contrary it was the government who manipulated elections and controlled the parliament. Power lay elsewhere; it was held by the officers who had carried out the *coup d'état* of July 1908 and who had foiled the counter *coup* of April 1909. As was shortly to be seen, such power was not amenable to constitutional limitation; gained through a *coup d'état*, it could be destroyed— not limited—only through a similar *coup d'état*. In 1911 there was a split within the Committee and opposition to its rule began to grow. The Unionists therefore dissolved the Chamber of Deputies in January 1912, and held a general election in which all but six of the returned members supported the government. This election became known as 'the big-stick election'. In July a group of officers known as the 'Saviour Officers' organised a movement in the army which succeeded in bringing down the Unionist government. The sultan—Mehmed Reshad, Abdul Hamid's successor and now a mere figurehead—appointed a new government, ratifying the choice of the 'Saviour Officers'. The Unionist parliament was dissolved and new elections held. In January 1913 a group of Unionist officers, led by Colonel Enver Bey (1881–1922), one of the authors of the original *coup* in 1908, burst into the Sublime Porte, where the cabinet was meeting, and in the fracas which ensued one of them shot the Minister of War dead. The cabinet was forced to resign at the point of the gun, and, until the end of the first world war, Unionist domination in the empire went unchallenged and unquestioned. The yearning of the official and educated classes for a modern constitutional parliamentary government thus finally found fulfilment in the replacement of the sultan's stable traditional autocracy by unstable military rule in which rulers gained and maintained their position by a constant and ready appeal to the sword. We may say in retrospect that for the Ottoman Empire and its successors the events of 1908–14 have an archetypal significance. They establish a modern and now familiar pattern of army intervention in politics—intervention planned and carried out by young officers in the belief that the European ideologies which inspire them can provide remedies for their political and social ills. These events also exemplify the crisis in representation which has increasingly overtaken Middle Eastern politics. The traditional rulers shared the same universe of discourse with their subjects, and in the course of the centuries autocracy had come to be mediated or tempered or checked by intermediate bodies which had either—like the *millets*—been instituted by the authorities for ease and convenience of government, or, like the Janissaries, arrogated to themselves, owing to the decay of the ruling institution, a quasi-independent position in the state. The officers and officials who now began to carry out *coups d'état* were isolated by their European ideas from the still traditional society the fate of which they were resolved to shape and direct. Again, the new centralised absolutism, of which these officers were the product and outcome, largely destroyed or emasculated the traditional intermediate bodies which had effectively if informally 'represented' the main interests of society and had served as their link with the central authority. In the European-style elections individual voters elected the candidates agreeable to the authorities, and the resultant parliaments could neither control nor check the government which had brought them into being. Representative institutions in fact signified an actual decrease of representativeness in the Ottoman body politic.

The other Middle Eastern state which proclaimed a constitution before the first world war was Iran. The conditions here were utterly different from those obtaining in the Ottoman Empire. Iran had not been touched by European influences during the nineteenth century to anything like the same extent as the Ottoman Empire, and had certainly not been subjected to that sustained and radical westernisation which the Ottoman sultans from Mahmud II to Abdul Hamid had initiated and carried through. The Iranian army, in particular, remained weak and backward, quite useless in war against an external enemy and hardly more useful in maintaining internal security. The most successful attempt at modernising the army had been that of Nasir al-Din Shah (1848–96). In 1879 he engaged Russian officers to train and command a Persian Cossack Brigade which until the reforms of Riza Shah (1925–41) remained practically the only modern— and effective—military formation in Iran. As a large modernised army did not exist, so its fateful concomitant, a numerous and important class of European-trained army officers, was likewise absent. By the same token, Iran remained an old-fashioned Oriental despotism, largely innocent of the centralised and levelling absolutism which was the consequence of the Ottoman reforms.

But of course Iran could not remain immune from European influence, whether political, economic or intellectual. Russia and Great Britain confronted each other in Iran as elsewhere in central Asia and were always seeking to establish and increase their influence and destroy that of their rivals. The European economy, world-wide in its extension, sooner or later brought Iran within its network through the activities of financiers and concession-hunters. The telegraph, first introduced in 1858 and extended after 1862 into a large network by a British concern, the Indo-European Telegraph Company, may stand as a symbol and index of the steady and cumulative increase of European influence in Iran. Beyond all these was the intellectual ferment which contact with Europe created and which until the last decade of the nineteenth century affected a few, albeit an influential few, of the learned and official classes.

The disturbance which European activity and European influences created in Iran is indicated by the so-called tobacco protest of 1891–2. Iran had known internal disturbances during the reign of Nasir al-Din Shah, the most serious of which were those messianic uprisings which the Babis fomented in the first years of his reign; but the tobacco protest had certain new features lacking in traditional agitations—which were to recur in the events leading to the grant of a constitution in 1906. The increasing intercourse between Europe and Iran had opened to the court and the official classes new vistas in the acquisition and consumption of wealth, and the grant of concessions—usually monopolistic—to exploit one or other of Iran's resources seemed an easy and painless way to acquire a substantial income. In 1890 the shah granted to a British concessionaire a monopoly of the production, sale and export of Iranian tobacco. The concession aroused widespread opposition in the country and it is interesting to examine which groups in Iranian society initiated and organised this opposition. The monopoly was seen as a threat to their interests by the native merchants and moneylenders, and they were prompt in voicing their objections. They were supported by the *ulama*, whose Shi'ism did not enjoin the same utterly passive obedience to the earthly ruler which was current in areas of Sunni dominance. Twelver Shi'ism, established as the official religion of Iran since Safavid times, considered the twelfth descendant of the Caliph Ali who had vanished in infancy as the legitimate ruler of the Muslim community, the Hidden Imam who would one day return to establish a reign of righteousness. In the meantime the authority to interpret the Holy Law was vested in the *mujtahids*, the theologians who, by their knowledge of holy writ and of precedents, are qualified to express the intentions of the Hidden Imam. The temporal ruler, whose authority would disappear at the coming of the Hidden Iman, was therefore bound to respect the authority of these *mujtahids* and to defer to their pronouncements. Two other features of Shi'ism served to enhance the position of the *ulama* and to make their concerted opposition to the ruler formidable. In the first place, some of the most revered shrines of Shi'ism, Karbala, Najaf and Kazimayn, lay in Ottoman Mesopotamia outside the control of the shah, and in them were to be found some of the most eminent *mujtahids* of the Shi'a world whose pronouncements would receive the ready and respectful acquiescence of the devout masses. And it is this popular devotion which, in the second place, gave the Iranian *ulama* influence and power in Iranian society. In the tobacco protest, these *ulamas*, fortified by fatwas emanating from *mujtahids* in Iran and Mesopotamia, exerted their influence—which proved decisive—against the concession. Their power was shown to be such that when they declared a boycott of tobacco and prohibited all forms of smoking, their prohibition was universally obeyed. The *ulamas* no doubt acted out of dislike for infidels and foreigners whose ways and whose ideas they shrewdly suspected of subverting sooner or later the traditional religion. As the struggle against the shah showed signs of being successful, they no doubt also came to enjoy this demonstration of their power and influence. The third group which worked with the merchants and *ulama* in organising and sustaining the agitation was rather different, less numerous and seemingly less powerful, but in retrospect it proves to have been the most significant. This group believed that the ills of Iran originated in its traditional institutions and that the only efficacious remedy was a radical one. In other words, these were the westernisers who were themselves westernised whether at first- or at second-hand. The Iranian westernisers, necessarily drawn from the official and intellectual classes, were a small group who began to propagate their views in the last decade or so of Nasir al-Din's reign. But they had to proceed very circumspectly, for, in a country where religion still had such a strong hold, a damaging charge of heresy could easily be levelled against them. To parry such a threat it would seem that some of them at any rate deliberately adopted the tactic of presenting their European notions in a Muslim garb. One of the most prominent of these reformers, Malkam Khan, openly discussed these tactics in an article on 'Persian Civilisation', published by *The Contemporary Review* in 1891.

As then Islam...[he wrote] is an ocean in which are accumulated all the sciences of the past times of Asia...then for any new law or new principle you wish to promulgate, you can find in that ocean many precepts and maxims which support and confirm what you want to introduce. As to the principles which are found in Europe, which constitute the root of your civilisation, we must get hold of them somehow, no doubt; but instead of taking them from London or Paris, instead of saying this comes from such an ambassador, or that it is advised by such a government (which will never be accepted), it will be very easy to take the same principle, and to say that it comes from *Islam*, and that this can be soon proved. We have had some experience in this direction. We found that ideas which were by no means accepted when coming from your agents in Europe, were accepted at once with the greatest delight when it was proved that they were latent in Islam. I can assure you that the little progress which we see in Persia and Turkey, especially in Persia, is due to this fact, that some people have taken your European principles, and instead of saying that they came from Europe, from England, France or Germany, have said: 'We have nothing to do with Europeans; these are the true principles of our own religion (and, indeed, that is quite true) which have been *taken* by Europeans!' That has had a marvellous effect at once.

This again was exactly the tactic which his associate, the famous Jamal al-Din al-Afghani (1838–97), pursued in Iran and elsewhere. For these modernisers the protest against the tobacco concession could be widened into a protest against the régime as a whole and could be made the occasion for demanding a limitation of the shah's power.

These three groups, then, merchants, men of religion and modernisers, though their motives were certainly not identical, found it possible to act in concert. Their agitation, thanks to the telegraph, spread across the whole of Iran. Supported by the Russians, who were afraid that the tobacco monopoly would increase the power and influence of their British rivals, it succeeded in eliciting a popular response such that the shah had no alternative but to cancel the concession.

The cancellation was a great blow to the authority of the régime. By giving in so unconditionally to pressure and popular agitation it cast doubt on its legitimacy and implicitly admitted the charges of despotism, greed and corruption which the more extreme of its critics had made. The tobacco protest publicised grievances which were to be heard again in 1905–6, when a constitution was granted, and it made familiar the notion that the shah and the government could be checkmated and perhaps overthrown by a popular uprising. The murder of Nasir al-Din Shah in 1896 showed the influence of the ideas spread during the tobacco protest, and the murder itself gave them further currency. The shah was murdered at the instigation of Jamal al-Din al-Afghani by a follower of his, Mirza Muhammad Riza. The murderer was essentially a simple man and politically quite unsophisticated. What he had to say in justification of his deed is therefore quite striking. He had murdered in the first place to avenge Afghani, 'that holy man and true descendant of the Prophet', whom the shah had seized and forcibly deported from Iran in 1891; but what moved him even more was the spectacle of

> thousands of poor Persian subjects who have fled from their own dear country from the hands of oppression and tyranny, and have perforce adopted the most miserable means of earning a livelihood...After all [he went on] these flocks of your sheep need a pasture in which they may graze, so that their milk may increase, and that they may be able both to suckle their young and to support your milking; not that you should constantly milk them as long as they have milk to give, and, when they have none, should devour their flesh from their body. Your sheep are all gone and scattered: this is the result of tyranny which you see.

For these reasons he had murdered the shah, and in no uncertain words threatened that, if Nasir al-Din's successor did not mend his father's way, he would suffer the same fate: 'If...he likewise adopts this practice and conduct, then this crooked load will never reach the halting-place.' When asked how he could reconcile his anxiety for his country with a deed which could possibly precipitate disorder and confusion, he replied: 'Yes, that is true, but look at the histories of the Franks: so long as blood was not shed to accomplish lofty aims, the object in view was not attained.'

Under Muzaffar al-Din Shah (1896–1907) the same conditions which led to the discontent of merchants, *ulama* and modernisers continued and perhaps worsened. Iran was becoming more and more embroiled in foreign debt, to service and to repay which required more revenues. This strained the Iranian fiscal system and evoked loud protests against foreign exploitation, official corruption and maladministration. Secret societies, or *anjumans*, became active. They were dedicated to the spread, particularly among the intellectual and official classes, of reforming and modernising notions. In 1904, in particular, various groups decided to come together and concert measures for the overthrow of despotism. A secret meeting of some sixty persons held on 28 May 1904 agreed on a programme of action consisting of eighteen articles, the sixteenth of which speaks of 'the bringing about of revolution'. The modernisers, as has been said, were always very careful to avoid any imputation of heresy, and it is interesting in this connection to note that article 14 of this programme required that whatever was circulated by the committee should conform to the laws of Islam so that no member could be accused of heresy, and article 17 required members not to take part in other than Islamic religious assemblies. Shortly afterwards, in February 1905, another group, known as the Secret Society, was formed the object of which, as stated in its programme, was to awaken the people to their rights, to remove tyranny and to seek ways of reforming abuses. In 1905 discontent came to a head, and there was widespread and open agitation against the shah, his ministers, and against Russian influence which was great and increasing. The Russo-Japanese War of 1904, in which a Christian European power was signally defeated at the hands of an Oriental power, and the revolution in Russia which followed the war, no doubt contributed to the effervescence, but the specific grievance which set in train the events leading to the grant of a constitution was the introduction of a new customs tariff in 1903 which the merchants considered onerous and oppressive. In 1905 the tariffs were enforced with greater severity and there were protests in various cities. In particular, a group of Tehran merchants took sanctuary in the shrine of Shah Abd al-Azim near the capital, whence they demanded redress for their grievances. The shah was then abroad, and his heir, who was acting as regent, pacified them by promising redress upon the shah's return. In the ensuing months tension between government and people in the capital as well as in the provinces did not abate. Incidents indicative of this tension were the ill-treatment of a *mulla* by the governor of Qazvin, the administration of the bastinado on the orders of the governor to a prominent religious leader in Kirman, and the firing by a troop of soldiers on a crowd demonstrating against the governor of Mashhad. These incidents in turn further exacerbated the situation. In December the Prime Minister accused some merchants of having raised the price of sugar; he seized them and had them bastinadoed. This led a group of merchants to protest by taking sanctuary in a Tehran mosque, where they were joined by a number of prominent *ulama* and their popular following. From this mosque they were expelled by a crowd at the instigation of another *mulla*, who was on the side of the authorities. The protesters and their following thereupon left the city for the sanctuary of Shah Abd al-Azim, where at the end there were some two thousand of them. A month afterwards there was still no prospect of their being dislodged. There they were, financed, provisioned and encouraged by their friends and perhaps also by prominent men who wanted to intrigue against the Prime Minister. To put an end to a state of affairs injurious to his authority and prestige, the shah issued an autograph letter to his Prime Minister which promised equality before the law, a code and the setting up of a ministry of justice to supervise its execution. This was presumably in response to a demand which one of the secret societies had made public the previous day. The shah's promise satisfied the protesters and they returned to Tehran. But it soon appeared that the promises were not being implemented and the agitation revived. The secret societies and the *ulama* who sympathised with them denounced despotism and put continuously before the public the shah's unfulfilled promise. In June, the Prime Minister tried to expel from Tehran two influential preachers; riots ensued and once again a large number of *ulama*, merchants and others took sanctuary, this time in Qum; the merchants and artisans of Tehran went on strike and the bazaars were closed; on 19 July another group took sanctuary in the gardens of the British Legation and so many joined them that by the beginning of August it was estimated that some 12,000 were camping in the gardens. Just as he felt compelled to give in on the previous January, so now again the shah retreated, dismissed his unpopular Prime Minister, and on 5 August issued a rescript setting up a national consultative assembly. Elections were held in September, and on 7 October the shah opened the assembly. It speedily proceeded to draft and vote on a Fundamental Law which the shah signed on 30 December. A supplementary Fundamental Law was promulgated on 7 October 1907.

When the agitation first began it was directed against financial and fiscal oppressions, and what its leaders openly demanded was the promulgation of a code of laws and reform in the administration of justice. The setting-up of constitutional and representative government may therefore be seen as the result of the shah's dilatory tactics which in the end left him no room for manœuvre. A constitutional representative government was probably what the modernisers and westernisers really desired, and they skilfully exploited the shah's weakness and impolicy. The Fundamental Laws of 30 December 1906 and their Supplement of 7 October 1907 provide examples of two incompatible outlooks within the Opposition—the Muslim traditionalist and the European modernist—and show that it is the modernist outlook which clearly prevailed. The traditional strain is exemplified in article 1 of the Supplementary Laws, which establishes Islam according to the Ja'fari sect (i.e. Twelver Shi'ism) 'which faith the Shah of Persia must profess and promote'. Article 2 is yet more unambiguously traditionalist. It states:

At no time must any legal enactment of the Sacred National Consultative Assembly, established by the favour and assistance of His Holiness the Imam of the Age (may God hasten his glad Advent!), the favour of His Majesty the Shahinshah of Islam (may God immortalise his reign!), the care of the Proofs of Islam [i.e. the *mujtahids*] (may God multiply the like of them!), and the whole people of the Persian nation, be at variance with the sacred principles of Islam or the laws established by His Holiness the Best of Mankind [i.e. the Prophet Muhammad] (on whom and on whose household be the Blessings of God and His Peace!).

The article went on to require the establishment of a committee of five theologians to whom proposed legislation would be submitted and who had the power to

reject and repudiate, wholly or in part, any such proposal which is at variance with the Sacred Laws of Islam, so that it shall not obtain the title of legality. In such matters [the article went on] the decision of this Ecclesiastical Committee shall be followed and obeyed, and this article shall continue unchanged until the appearance of His Holiness the Proof of the Age [i.e. the Hidden Imam whose reappearance will inaugurate the reign of Justice] (may God hasten his glad Advent!).

In contrast with this article, which from the outset remained inoperative, the Constitution abounded in provisions unmistakably European in provenance which clearly showed the influence of the westernisers. The second paragraph of the preamble to the Fundamental Laws, for instance, spoke of the right the shah was conferring on 'each individual of the people of our realm' to participate in choosing by popular election the Members of the National Consultative Assembly. Article 2 of these Fundamental Laws asserted that the Assembly represented 'the whole of the people of Iran, who thus participate in the economic and political affairs of the country'; article 8 of the Supplementary Laws, again, affirms: 'The people of the Iranian Empire are to enjoy equal rights before the Law'; article 26: 'The powers of the realm are all derived from the people' and article 35: 'The sovereignty is a trust confided (as a Divine gift) by the people to the person of the Shah.' This notion of a state composed of 'individuals' each of whom is endowed with 'rights', who are the source of public authority and who bestow 'sovereignty' on the ruler, is of course utterly at variance with the traditional Islamic theory of government. Equally at variance with both practice and theory was the separation of legislative, judicial and executive power which the Constitution enjoined, and the responsibility of ministers to the Assembly which it also prescribed.

As the sequel showed, it was hardly to be expected that a Constitution of this character, promulgated in such circumstances, could possibly operate in a country like Iran in a manner even remotely resembling the intentions and hopes of its authors. Muzaffar al-Din opened the Assembly on 7 October 1906. He died the following January and his son Muhammad Ali Shah (1907–9) succeeded him. From the start it was clear that he and his ministers were utterly opposed to the Assembly and that Russia was taking his part in the dispute. The authority of the shah having been seriously shaken and that of the Assembly hardly established, the maintenance of law and order became very difficult. Disorder broke out in the provinces and the authority of government disappeared. In August the Prime Minister, pro-Russian and opposed to the Constitution, was murdered by a member of a secret society. In December the shah, by arresting the new Prime Minister and other ministers who were in favour of the Assembly, tried to reassert his own unfettered power. Popular clamour in Tehran and the provinces foiled him for the time being. In February 1908 a bomb was thrown at his motor car, but the shah escaped. In June the Cossack Brigade bombarded and cleared the Assembly. Prominent popular leaders were arrested and two of them strangled without trial. On 27 June the shah dissolved the Assembly and abolished the Constitution as being contrary to Islamic law. Thereupon the *anjumans* of Tabriz, the capital of Azerbaijan, rose in rebellion, ousted the shah's men and held the town for some nine months, keeping a besieging force at bay. Other movements against the shah were organised from Rasht and from Isfahan. From the latter city a force of Bakhtiari tribesmen marched on the capital and, effecting a junction with a force from Rasht, entered Tehran on 13 July 1909. On 16 July Muhammad Ali, having taken refuge in the Russian Legation, abdicated. He was formally deposed at a meeting of the

Assembly that same evening and his twelve-year-old son Ahmad Shah (1909–25) proclaimed his successor.

Towards the end of 1909 elections for the second legislative session were held and the assembly met on 5 December 1909. Its record was quite as chequered as that of the first session. The Bakhtiari chieftains who were now preponderant in the government did not exactly have constitutionalism at heart; the country was in turmoil and the Russians ready to exploit the opportunity in order to establish and extend their position in the country. Some eighteen months after the inauguration of the second legislative session, in June 1911, matters came to a head. The ex-shah attempted to regain his throne by landing in Iran and fomenting a rebellion in which he was joined by Lur and Turkoman tribes whom he had tempted to his side. The rebellion was put down and the ex-shah forced to flee. But these events caused more disorder and anarchy in the country. To safeguard their interests in the south, the British landed troops in Bushire. The Russians took the opportunity to reinforce the troops they had stationed in the north ever since the summer of 1909. In May 1911 an American, Morgan Shuster, had been appointed Treasurer-General of Iran. This displeased the Russians, who began applying pressure on the Iranian government. This culminated in a forty-eight hours' ultimatum delivered on 24 November which demanded Shuster's dismissal. The government, knowing itself powerless to resist the Russians, wished to comply, but the Assembly wanted to resist. The government which had issued from the Bakhtiari march on Tehran in 1909, the object of which had been to re-establish the Constitution, now broke the deadlock by forcibly disbanding the Assembly and suspending the Constitution. This was practically the end of constitutionalism in Iran until the end of the second world war. Ahmad Shah attained his majority in July 1914; the opportunity was taken to resume parliamentary government. But the third legislative session met in the shadow of the first world war, which affected Iran in various disagreeable ways. The Germans and their Ottoman allies naturally did what they could to arouse opposition to the Russians and the British. Their task was made easy among the official and intellectual classes by Russian and British unpopularity, which stemmed from the constant intervention of these powers in Iranian politics during the past decade. German activities naturally elicited a Russian reaction. In November 1915 Russian troops seemed to be advancing on Tehran; the Assembly therefore broke up and most of its members fled to Qum. The Assembly was not to meet again until 1921. By then, the war and its aftermath had wreaked havoc with the government of Iran and had thrown up various contenders for power whose instincts and methods were certainly not constitutional. One of these contenders, Riza Khan, an officer of the Cossack Brigade, made himself master of the country by a military *coup d'état* and had himself proclaimed shah in 1925. Riza Shah ruled from

1925 to 1941 as an unchallenged despot. During his reign the Assembly met regularly, but it was no more than a decorative appendage of the régime.

The record of the two other constitutional régimes in the Middle East during this period was hardly more brilliant. Constitutionalism in the Ottoman Empire and in Iran was the outcome of a native movement of opinion, of a local reaction to the European challenge. In these two states constitutionalism may have been helped or hindered by the policies of the European powers. In Egypt and in Iraq, however, constitutional government was introduced and advocated by a European power, Great Britain. Egypt had been under British occupation since 1882 and since 1883 had been endowed with a Legislative Council and a Legislative Assembly, the functions of which were almost purely consultative. In 1913 the Legislative Council was abolished and the powers of the Legislative Assembly somewhat increased, but owing to the war its sittings were suspended in 1915 and never resumed. The aftermath of war saw Egypt plunged in an agitation against the British occupant, who had proclaimed Egypt a Protectorate in 1914. The British government eventually gave away to this agitation, and by the Declaration of 28 February 1922 recognised Egyptian independence. In 1914 Egypt was formally an autonomous part of the Ottoman Empire and its ruler had the title of khedive, a title bestowed by the Ottoman sultan. To symbolise Egypt's changed status under the Protectorate, the title of Egypt's ruler was changed to sultan, and to symbolise the era inaugurated by the Declaration of 28 February 1922 the ruler's title was once again changed—to king (*malik*). Egypt was to become a constitutional kingdom endowed with representative institutions and a responsible government. In April 1922 a committee was appointed to draft a constitution, and in October it submitted a draft which affirmed that sovereignty belonged to the Egyptian people, and which provided for elections and a parliament to which ministers would be responsible. King Fuad, who had unexpectedly become sultan on the death of his brother in 1917 and whose autocratic proclivities were well known, objected strenuously to the draft Constitution. He succeeded in making numerous changes which increased his own powers, and it was only after much pressure by Allenby, the British High Commissioner, that he approved the Constitution in its emasculated form in April 1923. Whether this or any other constitution would have been promulgated without British pressure is mere speculation, but it remains true that the British thought it necessary and desirable to press Fuad to grant a constitution. We may therefore conclude that they believed it feasible for an independent Egypt to become a constitutional monarchy with a representative and responsible government. The political history of Egypt under the monarchical constitution in fact continuously and systematically belied these expectations. The reason was the very same which accounted for the ill-success of Ottoman and Iranian constitutionalism, namely that western-style elections and representative institutions were incapable of representativeness and therefore incapable of providing constitutional and responsible government. Elections in Egypt under the monarchy, far from determining the character of the government in Cairo, were themselves determined by whichever faction happened to dominate the Cairo political scene. In 1923 the elections were overwhelmingly won by the Wafd, a populist movement created and controlled by Sa'd Zaghlul, who, inspired and instigated by Fuad in 1918, had challenged the British Protectorate. In 1923 he had the benefit of the king's support because his rivals had Allenby's support; it was indeed on behalf of these rivals that Allenby had pressed an unwilling Fuad to approve the Constitution. Zaghlul formed a government and during his period in office tried, by means of demonstrations and similar expedients, to intimidate Fuad into conceding him the primacy in the state. But his government lasted barely a year. The British Governor-General of the Sudan was murdered in November 1924 by terrorists connected with the Wafd. Zaghlul resigned and Fuad dissolved the parliament. He appointed a non-Wafdist ministry which immediately proceeded to conduct new elections. They resulted in a draw as between Zaghlul's supporters and the government's men. This was the only election under the constitutional monarchy the results of which did not correspond perfectly with the desires of whichever party happened to be dominant at Cairo. The reason for this undoubtedly was that the new government did not have enough time to destroy or neutralise Wafdist organisation which Zaghlul had been able to consolidate during his period in power. The new parliament met once in March 1925 and was immediately dissolved. The government dispensed with a parliament for more than a year and the king's influence was supreme. The British High Commissioner who succeeded Allenby, Lord Lloyd, judged this to be undesirable. He used his influence and power, which were still great— since the Declaration of 28 February 1922, while conceding Egyptian independence, had reserved the defence of Egypt, the security of British imperial communications, the protection of foreigners and the Anglo-Egyptian Sudan for continuing British control—to persuade the Egyptian government to carry out elections. This was a defeat for Fuad and the elections of May 1926 duly registered the fact by returning a Wafdist majority. The logic of constitutional responsible government would have therefore required Zaghlul to form an administration, but he was un-acceptable to Lloyd and a non-Wafdist became Prime Minister. The following year, Zaghlul having died, his successor Nahas made use of his parliamentary majority to compel his own appointment as Prime Minister. Shortly afterwards he fell foul of the British and, notwithstanding his large majority, Fuad dismissed him, dissolved the parliament and appointed as Prime Minister Muhammad Mahmud, the leader of the Liberal Consti-tutionalist party. He suspended the Constitution and ruled for a year without a parliament. In 1929 a Labour government came to power in Great Britain and wished to conclude an Anglo-Egyptian treaty. Such a treaty could not, in its view, possibly be negotiated and concluded except with a government which had the right to speak on behalf of the Egyptian people, and only a government enjoying a parliamentary majority had this right. Great Britain's position in Egypt lent great weight to such a view. Muhammad Mahmud's position became untenable. The subsequent elections ratified Muhammad Mahmud's—and Fuad's—setback by returning a large Wafdist majority. The Wafd formed an administration which failed to conclude a treaty with the British. The king dismissed it, and appointed Ismail Sidqi, a non-Wafdist, as Prime Minister. He dissolved the parliament, promulgated a new constitution which gave greater powers to the executive and held new elections. The electors returned a very large anti-Wafdist majority. This parliament lasted from 1931 to 1936 when Egypt was in effect governed by Fuad through a series of king's men. In 1936 the British once again wished to conclude a treaty with Egypt; once again they made it clear that they would negotiate only with an Egyptian government which could claim to represent Egypt; and it was again clear that they believed the Wafd to speak for the Egyptian people, or at any rate for a large majority of it. It therefore became clear that the royal policy had sustained a setback, which the electors duly ratified by returning a very large Wafdist majority. Nahas formed a Wafdist administration which signed the Anglo-Egyptian Treaty of 1936. Fuad having died the same year, he was succeeded by his son Faruq. He was a minor and assumed his powers only on attaining his majority in July 1937. He was as antagonistic to the Wafd as his father had been, and in December dismissed Nahas and appointed in his place Muhammad Mahmud, who dissolved the parliament elected in 1936. The Wafd thus sustained a defeat which the electorate ratified by returning a large anti-Wafdist majority in 1938. This parliament lasted until 1942 when the British, fearing the king's pro-Axis sympathies, forced him by a *coup d'état* to appoint Nahas Prime Minister. He held new elections at which a large Wafdist majority was returned. The second world war being nearly over in 1945, Faruq was able to dismiss Nahas. His successor dissolved the 1942 parliament and a large anti-Wafdist majority was returned. The 1945 parliament was the only one to run its full course under the constitutional monarchy. The 1950 elections returned a Wafdist majority, an outcome which may have been the result of an understanding between the king and the Wafd. The military *coup d'état* of July 1952 put an end both to monarchy and to parliamentary government.

In Iraq, too, constitutionalism, introduced and established by the British, proved—albeit for different reasons—a fiasco. Iraq was formed out of three ex-Ottoman provinces—Mosul, Baghdad and Basra—which the British conquered and occupied during the first world war. Conditions in these three provinces differed widely. The overwhelming majority in the south was composed of a Shi'ite semi-settled agricultural population accustomed to defer to its tribal leaders and to the *mujtahids* of Najaf and Karbala; the north had a majority of Kurds; the west and north-west contained a large agglomeration of Sunni Arab nomads. These and other disparate elements the British government forced in 1921 into one central-ised state controlled from Baghdad over which they placed, as king, Faisal, the third son of the Sharif of Mecca. Power in this overwhelmingly Shi'ite and Kurdish state was exercised by politicians and bureaucrats drawn from the Sunni Arab minority whose model and inspiration was the centralised absolutism of the Ottoman Empire whose servants they had hitherto been. To this centralising absolutism these men added an ideology, that of Arab nationalism, which they also wished to impose on this hetero-geneous and apolitical population. To all these complexities and potential conflicts, the British added the further complication of constitutionalism and responsible parliamentary government. A Constitution setting up a Parliament to which ministers were responsible was promulgated in 1925. Iraq was then not an independent state but a mandated territory, and the British High Commissioner had a supervisory, restraining and moderating influence. But even during this period it was apparent that elections went as the administration wanted them to go. After the mandate was termi-nated in 1932 elections and parliaments were only counters in the political game as it was played by the handful of politicians in Baghdad. Iraqi politics had a very narrow base and hence were highly unstable. In the period of the constitutional monarchy from 1921 to 1958 there was a total of 58 cabinets. This narrowness and instability tempted politicians to gain and hold power by extra-constitutional means. In 1934–6 they made use of tribal dissidence in the imperfectly policed south in order to force changes of government in Baghdad. These tribal rebellions were put down by the Iraqi army. The military officers, seeing how indispensable they were to the politicians, themselves started to intervene in politics in com-bination with this or that faction of politicians. The period 1936–41 there-fore saw a succession of military *coups d'état*. The last one, in April 1941, brought into power a pro-Axis government. This led the British to inter-vene and, until 1945, Iraqi politics were under British supervision. After 1945, owing to the increase in centralisation the tribal uprisings of the 1930s were no longer possible and by continuous purges and strict control the army was prevented from interference in politics; but eventually such measures proved useless and a military *coup d'état* in July 1958 made a bloody end of the constitutional monarchy. Between 1945 and 1958 the same narrowly based political game went on being played in the capital between a handful of politicians who manipulated elections and manœuv-red and intrigued each other out of office.

The constitutionalist movement in the Ottoman Empire and in Iran is a tribute to the prestige of the West in eastern lands; in Egypt and Iraq, however, constitutionalism is rather the direct outcome of European political pressure which was made possible by conquest and military predominance. The two decades following the second world war saw a progressive and ultimately almost complete withdrawal of European control from the Middle East. This withdrawal forms a stark and ironic contrast with the decades immediately preceding when almost the whole of the Middle East was under the control or influence of one or other of the European powers.

Significant European encroachment on Middle Eastern territories during the nineteenth century may be said to begin with the French conquest of Algeria, but the balance of power in Europe and the Mediterranean operated generally to prevent annexations or occupation for many decades. It was not until the early 1880s that France, following a bargain struck at the Congress of Berlin, formally established a protectorate over Algeria's western neighbour, Tunisia.

Great Britain, too, having landed troops in Egypt in 1882 to deal with the disorders consequent on 'Urabi's revolt, found herself exercising an effective if informal protectorate over this autonomous Ottoman province. Two other Middle Eastern territories came to be conquered and occupied by European powers before the first world war. Italy had had ambitions over Tunisia which the French protectorate disappointed. She therefore considered herself entitled to 'compensation', the only available territory to provide which was Tripoli, an Ottoman province. Having obtained the consent or acquiescence of the other European powers, the Italian government presented an ultimatum to Istanbul on 28 September 1911, alleging the maltreatment of Italians living in Tripoli and declaring its intention to land troops to protect them. The Ottoman government was given twenty-four hours to consent; but in spite of its conciliatory attitude the Italian government, determined it would seem to prove Italian prowess, declared war the following day. The Tripoli war dragged on for a year before the Ottomans were compelled by the Treaty of Ouchy signed in October 1912 to cede the province to Italy.

That same year by the Treaty of Fez France established a protectorate over the greater part of Morocco. Ever since the conquest of Algeria, Franco-Moroccan relations were inevitably strained. The frontier was undelimited or imperfectly delimited and clashes were therefore to be expected; French power was clearly superior and Morocco was a large sprawling country with an extensive Berber-populated mountainous area over which the sultan's authority was sketchy and intermittent. As the predominant power in North Africa France expected sooner or later to take control of Morocco. What stood in her way was not Moroccan military might but the objection and opposition of other European powers. British policy, in particular, had been to insist on Moroccan independence, but this policy was abandoned in 1904 in exchange for French acquiescence in the British occupation of Egypt. In the Anglo-French Agreement signed in April of that year the British government declared that 'it appertains to France, more particularly as a Power whose dominions are coterminous for a great distance with those of Morocco, to preserve order in that country and to provide assistance for the purpose of all administrative, economic, financial and military reforms which it may require'. The Anglo-French Agreement was followed by a Franco-Spanish treaty in September of the same year which allotted Spain a part of northern Morocco opposite Gibraltar; Italy was conciliated by being conceded a free hand in Tripoli. Germany, however, continued to oppose French ambitions; but in 1911 the French ceded a large tract of the Congo in exchange for freedom of action in Morocco.

The protectorate established in 1912 was for France the prelude of a long and costly process of pacification which went on intermittently until the mid-1930s. Morocco's condition in 1912 was pretty much as Sir Arthur Nicolson described it in a letter written when he was British Minister at Tangiers at the turn of the century.

The more I have seen of the members of the Government [he wrote] the more hopeless seems any prospect of reform or progress. The main policy and occupation of the Government is to set the tribes by the ears, to support one side, then wring money out of the beaten one, and then later, extort money out of the victors for assistance rendered. They wish to ruin the tribes, leaving them but the barest necessaries, so that they may be harmless. Their idea is that if a tribe becomes quiet and orderly it becomes rich (relatively) and that they will purchase arms and munitions and shake off subjection to the Government. No wonder that with this system the country is going backward and commerce languishing, and that merchants find it impossible to collect debts. It is rapacity, treachery, intrigue and misgovernment. I have been in most Oriental countries, but I have never seen such complete darkness as reigns here. The ignorance of the men I have met is simply incredible. It will all jog on thus till some move is made from outside, but once the rickety edifice gets the slightest push it will all come down.

But, far from coming down, the edifice was saved and immeasurably strengthened by French military action and administrative reform. It was a slow and very difficult operation, for the country was not pacified before the mid-'thirties. By then, the central government of Morocco though still under French control was potentially more powerful than any native Moroccan government had been for centuries. The centralisation of authority and the crushing of dissidence on which the French spent their treasure and their blood in fact made it possible for a nationalist movement after the second world war to organise a countrywide network of opposition and dislodge the Protectorate in a remarkably short time. What is true of Morocco is also true of Tunisia and of those Ottoman provinces which Great Britain and France occupied at the destruction of the Ottoman Empire during the first world war.

The first world war and its aftermath saw European control extend—albeit for a few decades only—over almost the whole Middle East. The Ottoman involvement in this war on the side of the Central Powers proved to have momentous consequences for this area, consequences which even now have not yet been fully worked out. The war meant the final and explicit abandonment of the traditional British policy of defending the independence and integrity of the Ottoman Empire. This policy, it is true, had ceased to command, in the two decades or so before the outbreak of war, the wide assent it enjoyed until the Congress of Berlin and after. There is no doubt that by 1914 the Ottoman connection had come to mean very little to Great Britain. This becomes clear when we consider how lukewarm was the effort to draw the Ottomans to the Allied side, or at least ensure their neutrality. But, though the independence and integrity of the Ottoman Empire was not by 1914 a vital and pressing British interest, no circumstances had yet arisen to compel the formulation of an alternative policy. The outbreak of war, however, now forced an explicit reconsideration of attitudes and policies. The proclamation of Egypt and Kuwait as British Protectorates was a first consequence of Anglo-Ottoman hostilities. Others, more far-reaching, speedily followed. The Gallipoli expedition embarked upon early in 1915 in order to destroy Ottoman power by the occupation of Istanbul immediately elicited a Russian demand for its possession in case of victory. The British and the French conceded the Russian demand in February–March 1915. It had been a cardinal principle of British policy to deny Istanbul and the Straits to Russia, and this therefore was a veritable revolution bound to have far-reaching consequences; to involve, in fact, the partition of the Ottoman Empire between Great Britain, France, and such other of their Allies as could make good a case for obtaining a share of the Ottoman domains. The British and the French agreed to a scheme of partition in discussions which began in November 1915. The Russians joined this scheme after securing some modifications in their favour. This partition scheme was embodied in the Sykes–Picot Agreement—so called after the chief British and French negotiators—which was signed in May 1916. In April of the previous year, the secret Treaty of London had promised Italy, if she were to join the Allies, an 'equitable share' in the partition of Asia Minor. This promise was in due course made good in April 1917 when by the Agreement of St Jean de Maurienne the British and the French promised the Italians Smyrna, the *vilayet* of Aidin and a large sphere of influence to the north. By mid-1917, then, Great Britain, France, Russia and Italy had secretly arranged to divide the Ottoman Empire among themselves in the event of victory. Great Britain was to acquire Mesopotamia up to the north of Baghdad and an enclave on the Mediterranean in Haifa and its surroundings. These two British territories would be linked, so to speak, by a large area comprising southern Syria, the Syrian desert and Transjordan. France was to acquire Lebanon and Cilicia and exercise paramount influence in the Syrian hinterland and the *vilayet* of Mosul. Russia, aside from Constantinople and the Straits, was also to acquire a large area of eastern Anatolia. Palestine was to be internationally administered.

These secret arrangements were complicated enough, but they were still more hopelessly tangled by other schemes and understandings. At the beginning of the war, the sharif of Mecca was encouraged by the British to plot a rebellion against the Ottoman Empire. Various vague and grandiose inducements were held out to him: an independent kingdom of the Hijaz, a transfer of the Caliphate from the Ottoman to his own dynasty, and the formation of an Arab state. Negotiations between him and the British High Commissioner in Egypt, Sir Henry McMahon, went on intermittently throughout 1915 and ended inconclusively in March 1916. The sharif made large claims and demanded an extensive Arab state; what McMahon was prepared to concede was much less. His letter to the sharif of 24 October 1915, which contained the British offer, whilst couched in misleadingly generous terms, in effect promised little of substance. D. G. Hogarth's summing-up of it still remains the most scrupulously judicious yet written:

> While it explicitly ruled out of negotiations all the Turkish-speaking districts which Husain [the sharif] had claimed as Arab, and all Arab societies with whose chiefs we already had treaties—while further, it reserved to French discretion any assurance about the independence of the Syrian littoral, or the freedom from tutelage of the interior, i.e. the districts of the four towns, Damascus, Homs, Hama and Aleppo—while by reserving other Arab regions in which France might have peculiar interests, it left Mosul, and even, perhaps, Palestine, in doubt—while, finally, it stated expressly that no guarantee for the unconditional delivery of either Lower or Upper Iraq to the Arabs could be given by us;—in spite of all these reservations it recognised an Arab title to almost all the vast territories which Husain had claimed, including Mesopotamia, subject only to limiting but not annulling conditions.[1]

We may add, further, that this offer, couched in these misleading terms, was in no sense a treaty with a recognised authority, but merely formed part of an inconclusive correspondence with someone whose title to speak or negotiate on behalf of the 'Arabs' was not self-evident. But in so far as this letter offered anything unambiguously or without qualifications—and it is difficult to see how it did so—what it offered, namely some kind of Arab state in Syria and Mesopotamia, was provided for in the Sykes-Picot Agreement; for in this agreement France and Great Britain pledged themselves to 'recognize and uphold' an Arab state or confederation of states to be set up in those areas of Syria and Mesopotamia which they were not to annex, but in which they would respectively exercise paramount influence.

[1] H. W. V. Temperley (ed.), *History of the Peace Conference of Paris* (1924), vol. VI, p. 126.

The way in which McMahon phrased his offer to the sharif was to lead to much trouble and contention later on, but that the offer fitted in with the arrangements of the Powers cannot be doubted. Another undertaking, the Balfour Declaration issued in November 1917, did not so fit in. It was a unilateral British declaration issued to the Zionists recording that 'His Majesty's Government view with favour the establishment in Palestine of a national home for the Jewish people, and will use their best endeavours to facilitate the achievement of this object'. This again was an ambiguous document the interpretation of which later gave rise to many disputes. But it was not only ambiguous, it was also in potential contradiction, not so much with McMahon's offer to the sharif, as with the Sykes–Picot scheme. This scheme proposed an international status for Palestine, and the 'establishment in Palestine of a national home for the Jewish people', most probably under British patronage, did not fit in well with such a scheme. And it is a fact that the Sykes–Picot scheme was becoming highly unsatisfactory in British eyes. The brunt of the fighting against the Ottoman Empire was being borne by British troops. It was British troops who fought in the Gallipoli campaign of 1915; British troops fought the Ottomans in Mesopotamia where they occupied Basra in November 1914 and Baghdad in March 1917; British troops, again, confronted the Ottomans in Sinai and were to be launched by Allenby in an offensive to capture Jerusalem in December 1917 and Damascus in October 1918. Why then should the French acquire such a dominant position in the Levant? There is little doubt that this was a main consideration in the policy leading to the Balfour Declaration. The Sykes–Picot scheme was also undermined by the British encouragement of sharifian ambitions. A tribal force raised by Faisal, third son of the sharif, had captured Aqaba in July 1917. Faisal had then been taken up by Allenby, who made him the commander of a so-called 'Northern Arab Army' which, when it could and as it could, served as an auxiliary to the British forces and operated east of the Jordan. In October 1918, having finally routed the Ottomans, Allenby allowed the sharifian troops to enter Damascus first and thus enabled Faisal to claim its conquest. He was appointed as military governor of Syria under Allenby's authority and thus allowed to disregard and defy the French in a territory where, according to the Sykes–Picot scheme, their influence was to be paramount. With Russia out of the war since November 1917, these developments meant that the Sykes–Picot Agreement was in ruins and that Great Britain and France had to come to a new *modus vivendi* in the Middle East.

The process was long-drawn-out, and may be said to have lasted from the Armistice of Mudros between the Ottoman Empire and the Allied Powers signed on 30 October 1918 to the Treaty of Lausanne concluded on 24 July 1923 after lengthy negotiations between Turkey—as the heartland of the Ottoman Empire now came to be called—and Great Britain,

France, Italy, Japan, Greece, Bulgaria and Rumania. The armistice found British troops occupying Palestine, Syria, the Lebanon, Cilicia, and in Mesopotamia the *vilayets* of Basra and Baghdad; immediately following the armistice British troops also occupied the *vilayet* of Mosul. This state of affairs tempted Lloyd George to try and persuade the French to give up or modify their rights under the Sykes–Picot Agreement. Immediately after the armistice the French did give up in favour of the British their claim to Palestine and to Mosul, but for the rest they were not to be persuaded. Deadlock ensued and lasted for a year. Finally Lloyd George gave up and concluded an agreement with Clemenceau whereby British troops would withdraw from Syria and the Lebanon and Cilicia, French troops replacing them in the latter two territories, and Syria remaining under Faisal's control. The change-over took place in November 1919. Earlier that year, in April, the Italians landed troops in Adalia to enforce their rights under the Agreement of St Jean de Maurienne. This was followed in May by the landing, under the protection of Allied warships, of a Greek army in Smyrna. Smyrna and its district contained a large Greek element. Venizelos, the Greek Prime Minister, who, during the war, had shown himself to be pro-Entente, had presented in February 1919 to the Paris Peace Conference a formal claim to the territory. The Allies, anxious also to prevent an Italian occupation of Smyrna, were persuaded. The Greek occupation—an occupation of a Muslim Turkish-speaking territory by the troops of a formerly subject nation—aroused widespread resentment and revived the will to fight in the country. These sentiments were canalised and organised by Mustafa Kemal (1881–1938), who not only led a successful military resistance to the Greeks and the Allies, but also in the process transformed the Ottoman sultanate into a Turkish republic, of which, until his death, he was the unchallenged autocrat. In 1919, Mustafa Kemal was an Ottoman general who during the war had distinguished himself in Gallipoli and against the Russians in eastern Anatolia. He was now in Istanbul, a city under Allied occupation where the sultan's government showed no will to resist the catastrophes that were falling upon the country. In May he got himself appointed as Inspector-General of the 9th army based on Samsun on the Black Sea, and from there began systematically organising resistance to the Greeks. At the end of 1919 he established himself at Ankara, which gradually became the effective centre of government, superseding in due course the Istanbul administration. From April 1921, Mustafa Kemal's troops began to get the better of the Greeks. A decisive battle was fought at Sakarya on 24 August 1921, and the Greeks were finally routed and Smyrna reoccupied on 9 September 1922. The revival of Turkish power led the Italians to think better of their occupation of Adalia, and in June 1921 they agreed to remove their troops from Asia Minor. After the battle of Sakarya the French, too, decided to evacuate Cilicia, and ended their military involvement in Turkey by the

Ankara Agreement of 20 October 1921. The British government then remained the only power involved in Turkish affairs and hostile to Ankara. After the occupation of Smyrna, Mustafa Kemal decided to evict the Greeks from eastern Thrace, which they had also occupied. To do so he had to cross the Dardanelles, which, after the Armistice of Mudros, was under Allied occupation. The Allied contingents included British, French and Italian troops; the two latter powers decided that they would not stand in Ankara's way, but Lloyd George was at first quite adamant that the British troops should stop the Turks by force. It nearly came to war at Chanak, but Lloyd George, finding himself isolated among the powers and within the Empire, finally gave way and by the Armistice of Mudanya agreed to the restoration of Istanbul and the Straits to Turkish sovereignty (see above, p. 229). With the conclusion of the Treaty of Lausanne the following year, no trace remained of any of the schemes for the Turkish-speaking areas of the Ottoman Empire which the Allies had concerted among themselves during the war.

This great and signal victory over the Greeks and their protectors enabled Mustafa Kemal to do away with Ottoman rule and to establish the régime at Ankara as the sole legitimate government of Turkey. The Sultan Muhammad VI Wahid al-Din, who had come to the throne in July 1918, had been very hostile to Mustafa Kemal and had acquiesced in the measures the Allies had taken against his movement. In November 1922 the Grand National Assembly enacted that the sultanate was abolished, but that the caliphate—now considered, in a manner completely untraditional, as a purely spiritual office—remained vested in the Ottoman house. Muhammad VI Wahid al-Din, having taken refuge aboard a British battleship, was considered as deposed and his cousin Abd al-Majid proclaimed caliph. The abolition of the sultanate left the headship of the state vacant. In January 1921 the Grand National Assembly had passed a 'Law of Fundamental Organization' which began by laying down that 'sovereignty belongs without reservation or condition to the nation'. Now, in October 1923, a year after the abolition of the sultanate, and in application of the law of January 1921, the Grand National Assembly proclaimed Turkey a republic, the president of which was elected by the Grand National Assembly from among its members. A Republic set up by the representatives of the sovereign people could, however, hardly harbour a caliph however 'spiritual' his functions. On 3 March 1924 the Grand National Assembly resolved that the caliphate was abolished, that the caliph was deposed and that all members of the Ottoman house were banished from Turkish territory. This was the end of the most ancient and venerable political office in Islam. This end was brought about by Mustafa Kemal Atatürk, a direct heir of the Young Turks and of their nineteenth-century westernising forebears. Mustafa Kemal, given his opportunity by the war and its aftermath, impelled his fellow Turkish-speaking Muslims to cease looking on themselves as Ottomans, subjects of the greatest Muslim state in the world, and to consider themselves instead as the sovereign citizens of a republic and members of a Turkish 'nation'. It was not only in Turkey that a great gulf opened between what the victorious powers had proposed and what finally came to pass. In Syria, in Palestine, in Mesopotamia too, the events overtook the tidy schemes of the Allies. In the autumn of 1919 French troops replaced British in the Lebanon, and Faisal, left in control of Syria, had to find and adopt some line of policy towards his powerful neighbours. He had hitherto been protected by the British, who made use of him in order to talk the French out of their claims in the Levant. The attempt failed, and the British withdrew, making it clear to Faisal that he had to reach some accommodation with their rivals. But Faisal was a weak man unable to check his turbulent followers, who forced on him a provocative and foolhardy policy towards the French. The border between Syria and the Lebanon became tense and insecure, and in March 1920 Faisal was proclaimed king of the United Kingdom of Syria—i.e. Syria, the Lebanon and Palestine! The French, in no mood to condone sharifian defiance, issued an ultimatum in July which required Faisal to accept French protection and control. Faisal, caught between French threats and his clamorous followers, dithered; the ultimatum expired and the impatient French marched on Damascus. A brief encounter at Khan Maisalun near Damascus on 24 July led to the rout of the sharifian troops. The French occupied the city, put an end to the sharifian régime and expelled Faisal from Syria. According to the Sykes–Picot scheme the Lebanon was to be annexed by France while Syria was to be under exclusively French influence. In the event, both Syria and the Lebanon became French-administered mandated territories. 'Mandates' seem to have been invented by General Smuts towards the end of the war and were included in the Covenant of the League of Nations which was incorporated in the Treaty of Versailles, signed on 23 June 1919. Article xxii of the Covenant explained the notion of a 'mandate' and its mode of operation:

To those colonies and territories which as a consequence of the late war have ceased to be under the sovereignty of the states which formerly governed them and which are inhabited by peoples not yet able to stand by themselves under the strenuous conditions of the modern world, there should be applied the principle that the well-being and development of such peoples form a sacred trust of civilisation and that securities for the performance of this trust should be embodied in this Covenant.

The best method of giving practical effect to this principle is that the tutelage of such people should be entrusted to advanced nations who by reason of their resources, their experience or their geographical position, can best undertake this responsibility, and who are willing to accept it, and that this tutelage should be exercised by them as Mandatories on behalf of the League.

By their public pronouncements during and after the war the Allies had made it very difficult for themselves to carry out the kind of scheme mooted in the Sykes–Picot Agreement. So, instead of annexations and protectorates, France and Great Britain acquired 'mandates' in the Middle East. The Allied Supreme Council meeting at San Remo in April 1920 had assigned to France the mandate for Syria and the Lebanon. France in due course established local administrations in both territories for the satisfactory performance of which she was responsible to the League of Nations.

The San Remo meeting also assigned to Great Britain the mandates for Mesopotamia and Palestine. According to the Sykes–Picot Agreement, Mesopotamian territory up to the north of Baghdad was to be under British control; but at the end of the war France ceded Mosul to the British, so that, when the mandate for Mesopotamia was assigned to her, Great Britain in fact controlled the three Mesopotamian *vilayets*. The country was then being administered from Baghdad by a Civil Commissioner assisted by Political Officers spread throughout the provinces. The future of the country, its form of government, whether British occupation would or would not continue: all these issues were highly uncertain, mainly because the British government was unable to formulate a clear, unambiguous policy. Further, the old Ottoman order had collapsed and had been replaced by a European Christian government, the ways of which were unfamiliar; again, as has been said, the country, particularly in its southern portions, presented a difficult problem of government. All these were so many factors of disorder which, after San Remo, came to be exploited by two groups: by the Shi'ite divines of Karbala, Najaf and Kazimayn, whose influence among the tribes of the south was great, and by the Sharifians established across the border in Syria. Each of these two groups wanted power for itself, but they united in the summer of 1920 in fomenting a serious revolt against the British. By the autumn the revolt was put down, but the British government, responding to a clamour for economy, decided that the mandate for Mesopotamia need not entail direct British occupation and administration of the country. They resolved to make the country a kingdom lightly policed by the Royal Air Force. In 1921 they offered its throne to Faisal, whom the French had evicted from Syria. The new kingdom was known as Iraq, an Arabic term adopted from the classical period of Islam. This was an indication that, in the eyes of Faisal and his followers, the new kingdom was meant to revive the Arab glories of the early centuries of Islam. In the meantime, Iraq was a British mandate. Article XXII of the League Covenant had specified that 'Certain communities formerly belonging to the Turkish Empire have reached a stage of development where their existence as independent nations can be provisionally recognised subject to the rendering of administrative advice and assistance by a Mandatory until such time as they are able to stand alone'. In application of this, the mandatory instruments for Iraq, Syria and the Lebanon, as approved by the League of Nations, required the Mandatories to facilitate their 'progressive development' as independent states. Such a provision of course meant that the Mandatory was always under challenge to show that the mandated territory was not yet ready 'to stand alone'. Such a challenge constituted the staple of Anglo-Iraqi politics in the decade following Faisal's accession. The British were not unwilling to be persuaded that Iraq should attain full independence, and in 1931–2, by a liberal distribution of promises of future good behaviour and a judicious exertion of pressure, Great Britain succeeded in obtaining the entry of Iraq into the League of Nations as a fully independent state. British policy in Iraq could not but influence the political situation in the French-mandated territories of Syria and Lebanon. The French themselves had had in 1925 a Druze rebellion to cope with in southern Syria which, owing to the difficult terrain, they had much trouble in quelling. Druze turbulence and maladroitness on the part of the French had precipitated the rebellion; Arab nationalists in Damascus extended the disturbances to Damascus and its environs and claimed that this was not a mere tribal rebellion such as the Ottomans had often had to cope with, but a national, Syrian, Arab revolt against French imperialism. It is with the slogans of Arab nationalism, and with the claim that the Syrians were ready and able 'to stand alone', that the French mandate was continuously challenged. The Popular Front government which came to power in France in 1936 decided to emulate the British example and concede independence to Syria and the Lebanon. Treaties were negotiated and signed, but they were not ratified owing to objections by the French parliament. The outbreak of war in 1939 was to affect profoundly the French position in the Levant.

The Palestine mandate differed from the other Middle Eastern mandates in that the Mandatory was not required to facilitate the progressive development of the country into an independent state. Instead, it made the Mandatory 'responsible for putting into effect' the Balfour Declaration which was incorporated in the preamble to the mandate. Zionist colonisation in Palestine thus had now a legal foundation. This did not mean—far from it—that it could proceed unhindered. The original inhabitants of Palestine were, in their great majority, Arabic-speaking Muslims, and they had always objected to Zionist settlement in the country. They were not slow to voice these objections in protests and riots the most serious of which in the first decade of the mandate were the so-called Wailing Wall Riots of 1929. A case can be made for the view that these riots and agitations were an attempt by the leaders of the Palestine Arabs to intimidate the Mandatory into abandoning the Zionist commitment, and that they would have died down as, on the one hand, the British showed that they were not to be intimidated and as, on the other, Jewish immigration proved unable to maintain its momentum. Both assumptions were reasonably accurate before 1933, but the coming of Nazism in Germany falsified them almost immediately. Jewish immigrants from Germany and other European countries began coming in a continuous stream. Great Britain also began to be threatened and hard-pressed by the European dictatorships in Europe and the Mediterranean; she was therefore much less ready to show firmness in the face of Arab protests, particularly when these came to be supported by Arabs elsewhere. A rebellion broke out in 1936 which led to the appointment of a Royal Commission (headed by Lord Peel) to investigate the problem anew. The Commission reported in 1937 that the Mandate as it stood was unworkable and proposed to set up a small Jewish state in part of Palestine while the rest of the country would be united with the Principality of Transjordan which in 1921 had been hived off from Palestine and was also a mandated territory. The British government first accepted this recommendation, but a year or so later declared it impracticable. It proceeded to convene a Jewish–Arab conference in an attempt to reach a negotiated settlement. This, the so-called Round Table Conference, met in London in February–March 1939 but failed to come to agreement. The British government thereupon issued a White Paper in May which drastically limited Jewish immigration into Palestine and severely restricted the areas of the country in which Jews were allowed to buy land.

It is clear that Great Britain embarked on this policy because she considered the cost of supporting the Zionists against the Arabs too high. By 1939 the Arabs were being increasingly wooed and encouraged by the Axis powers, and, as they occupied lands of strategic importance, it was considered that they had to be conciliated; hence the abandonment of partition, to which the Arabs had objected, and hence, too, the White Paper. But the Round Table Conference marked a significant departure in British policy towards the Middle East. The Conference was not merely between the Mandatory, the Palestinian Arabs and the Zionists—the parties immediately concerned. To it the British government also invited Egypt, Iraq, Saudi Arabia, the Yemen and Transjordan. This was to admit and concede that these states, presumably by virtue of being 'Arab', had the right to share in negotiations and decisions concerning Palestine. The British government, therefore, was prepared to recognise an 'Arab' collectivity and deal with it as such. In other words, this was to accept the claim of the Arab nationalists that there was one Arab nation which sooner or later had to be unified in one state. We may presume that the British government weighed and accepted these implications, and that the Round Table Conference was—among other things—an attempt to wean the Arab nationalist movement away from the Axis powers and to attract them to the British connection. This policy was defined and accentuated further when, in a speech of May 1941, Anthony Eden, the Foreign Secretary, promised 'full support to any [Arab unity] scheme that commands general approval'. British support of Pan-Arabian and Arab nationalism was further demonstrated in the Lebanon and Syria during the war. A year after French capitulation to Germany, in June 1941, Great Britain mounted an expedition against the Vichy régime in the Levant and quickly occupied the territory. A Free French contingent accompanied the British troops and Free French authority replaced that of Vichy in the mandated territories. At the start of the invasion, the Free French issued, under British pressure, a declaration promising complete independence to the Syrians and the Lebanese, which was endorsed and, so to speak, guaranteed by the British. The Free French, anxious to establish themselves as the champions of French greatness, were subsequently reluctant to implement this declaration to the full. In November 1943 they clashed with the Lebanese government, which, obviously sure of British support, had unilaterally ended the mandatory relation with France. The British government, by pressures and threats, compelled the Free French to accept the *fait accompli*. Again, a year almost after the liberation of France, the French clashed with the Syrian government in May–June 1945, and again the British government unequivocally sided with the Syrians. Their troops entered Damascus and disarmed the French. Thus ended, for the time being, the long rivalry that had opposed British and French in the Middle East ever since the first world war. The British were now the dominant power in the Middle East. In 1941, they had undone the recent Italian conquest of Ethiopia and, by 1943, Cyrenaica and Tripoli, conquered in 1912, were Italian no more. The French were now eliminated. The Arab states had, with British encouragement, conducted negotiations to achieve a measure of unity which had gone on from July 1943, and which had issued in March 1945 in the formation of a League of Arab States. Of this League Britain could justly consider herself the patron. But this appearance of dominance was highly deceptive. Great Britain was to emerge from the second world war gravely weakened and in no position to maintain an imperial stance. And, in the Middle East itself, a pro-Arab policy was a snare and a delusion. The fact is that there was not a single Arab state to be friendly to and to patronise, but rather a number of rivals and near-enemies each of whom claimed to be the only true promoter of Pan-Arabism. To support one of these rivals was to alienate the other, and, as speedily appeared after the war, British policy was wrecked on this dilemma. Speaking in the French National Assembly in the aftermath of the Syrian events of May–June 1945, the Foreign Minister, Bidault, uttered a warning which turned out to be truly prophetic. Addressing the British government he said: '*Hodie mihi, cras tibi.*'

CHAPTER XI

INDIA AND SOUTH-EAST ASIA

I. INDIA

A⊤ first sight it might seem that the obvious approach to Indian history from 1905 to 1947 would be the study of the development and triumph of the nationalist movement with its corollary of partition. Yet a little thought must modify this view. Indian nationalism itself, though much influenced by Western ideals and examples, had taken root in Indian soil to produce much which was unique in itself. Further, the Indian nationalist dialogue with the West had an economic aspect also; indeed, in the long run this proved to be one of its most potent ingredients. One cannot isolate political nationalism from economic issues, or both from the structure of Indian society. And here we find a conflict of ideas, values and behaviour patterns which suggest a movement in progress far deeper and more complex than political programmes or even economic changes. In fact what the sanguine reformers of the reform era had looked for in vain was beginning to materialise. Indian society had gone beyond the acceptance of this or that from the West from motives of duress or convenience; it was beginning to wish to integrate the new with the old; it was beginning to question some of the basic presuppositions on which it was itself based. A survey of the period must therefore be concerned not only with political and economic issues only but also with 'cultural' ones; not only with the signposts of westernisation, but with the evidence of assimilation and modification.

At the beginning of the century it might well have seemed to an observer that the British Empire was at its zenith. The government had apparently never been so strong or so vigorous; in the person of its representative Lord Curzon it was undertaking its own overhaul. Confidence was general, the sense of imperial mission strong and eloquently proclaimed. The movement towards the West was gathering strength and the westernised class steadily growing. The National Congress which expressed the political aspirations of this class and had drifted into criticism appeared so weak that Curzon could hope 'to assist it to a painless demise'.

When Curzon retired five years later the situation had changed dramatically. Public opinion was inflamed, conspirators were plotting and the government itself was apprehensive and perplexed. While political circles in Britain were absorbed with the Curzon–Kitchener controversy over the disposal of a seat in the viceroy's Executive Council, they missed the significance of the Bengali protests, soon augmented from the rest of India, at Curzon's administrative partition of Bengal. It was the Olympian disregard of these protests, even more than the act itself, which inflamed the sensitive Bengali nature. For the first time the Congress found itself with general popular backing in one part of India. This change in a few months was a portent; it alarmed some of the more staid Congressmen themselves who preferred speeches to processions and resolutions to prosecutions. The protest did not end with the act of partition; it strengthened the extremist wing of Congress with recruits who no longer believed in British good faith and it created a small but active terrorist movement, whose highlights were the murder of Curzon Wyllie in 1909, and the wounding of Lord Hardinge on his state entry into Delhi in 1912. The feelings of the articulate public were at the same time excited by the Japanese victory over Russia in 1904–5; this proof that the West was not infallible after all was reinforced by the revolutions in Turkey and Persia which occurred soon afterwards.

This was the situation which faced Lord Minto in India and John Morley as the new Secretary of State in London at the beginning of 1906. A distinct rift had opened between government and people and it threatened to grow wider. The next eight years record a determined effort by the government to close this rift without conceding a major change of policy. Morley and Minto agreed that Indians of the new classes should be brought into closer consultation with the government and associated more generously with the administration. Neither thought in terms of the parliamentary democracy which was the political faith, coming down from Gladstone and Ripon, of the Congress moderates. Minto's durbar plan was soon set aside, but then it was found that the government of India was so far committed to Western political forms and the new classes to the concept of parliamentary democracy that what was intended to be a consultative autocracy analogous to the Prussian and Japanese systems became in fact a preliminary step towards responsible government. With the bludgeon of repression in one hand and the torch of political progress in the other the government carried through the Morley–Minto reforms in 1909. An enlarged Imperial Legislative Council still had an official majority but the elective element was increased, supplementary questions could be asked and resolutions moved. Indians were appointed for the first time to the Executive Council in Calcutta and the India Council in London. The Islington Commission (1912) began to consider the admission of more Indians into the public services. Apart from these 'consultative' steps a notable innovation was made in the reservation of seats for Muslims in the councils at the instance of the founders of the Muslim League in 1906.[1] The plea was that poverty would exclude most Muslims from any property franchise roll and thus from elective public bodies. The plea was true but the crack in democratic principle thus created was to widen into the gulf of partition.

The reforms were followed by the revocation of the Bengal partition

[1] Founded 30 December 1906; first session December 1907.

298

and the removal of the capital from Calcutta to Delhi, the one calculated to please Bengalis, the other to please Indians as a whole. These measures must on the whole be pronounced a success. The moderate leader Gokhale was taken into something like partnership, and was able to win the support of the middle class for his 'moderate' line of co-operation and persuasion. Terrorism failed to spread and gradually died down; the extremist wing of Congress, led by the Maratha, Tilak, was defeated at the Surat Congress in 1907 and did not recover before the first world war; when Tilak was imprisoned for six years in 1909 no one stirred in his support in western India. Tilak's attitude in contrast to Gokhale's was the assertion of rights instead of the plea for concessions, opposition to the government to the limit of legality and the use of Hindu sentiment in stimulating anti-government feeling. His words were brave but the new class was not yet ready for these tactics. The Morley–Minto reforms are usually under-estimated. But they should be viewed in the context of the confident imperialist autocracy which preceded them. Where obstacles are great even modest progress may be vital. The reforms reached the logical limit of 'consultation', and with the political tide setting towards democracy the next step must go beyond that limit.

During these nine years India was stirring in other directions. The Tatas founded their Iron and Steel Company in 1907 and produced their first steel in 1913. The poet Rabindranath Tagore carried Indian literature to the world when his *Gitanjali* won him a Nobel Prize in 1912. There was a perceptible stirring, and this process, apart from that of the atavistic Arya Samaj, was generally in a Western direction.

The first impact of the war in 1914 confirmed this diagnosis. An outburst of loyalty brought from the princes offers of troops and service and from the middle classes votes of money and aid in recruiting. The government were able to send troops to France in late 1914, to Egypt for the defence of the Suez canal, and later to East Africa and Iraq, where their bravery won admiration and the failure of supplies discredit for the military authorities. India was denuded of British troops. No advantage, however, was taken of this enthusiasm, and as the war lengthened into years it gradually turned into impatience and discontent. Most significant was the change in the general Indian outlook. While the government marked time politically and allowed its young civil officers to join the army, Indian opinion rapidly stirred and matured. There was pride in the achievement of the Indian troops; Indians, it was clear, could fight as well as Europeans. There was horror and disillusionment at the fratricidal strife in Europe and the ferocity which both sides exhibited. Europeans behaved no better than Indians in the eighteenth-century wars. Thus the notion of European moral superiority was exploded. Then came the Russian Revolution of 1917 and President Wilson's Fourteen Points in 1918, with their recognition of self-determination. If the greatest autocracy could crash overnight, why should the Indian autocracy endure? And, if European peoples could determine their future, why not India? Indians considered themselves adult members of the world society; the Gokhale attitude of requests for concessions gave place to the Tilak line of demands and assertion of rights.

The British attitude to India had also changed, but not to the same extent. This explains why political reforms which were radical on any previous showing encountered major political opposition in the years after the war. The Declaration of 1917 promised 'the increasing association of Indians in every branch of the administration, and the gradual development of self-governing institutions with a view to the progressive realisation of responsible government in India as an integral part of the empire'. The constitutional Rubicon was crossed and led to the Government of India Act of 1921 which embodied the 'Montford reforms'.[1] By this measure official majorities were swept away from the councils (which were much enlarged), and some six million people were put on the registers to vote for the various legislative bodies. There was devolution of powers from the centre which prepared the way for later federalism. Indians were not given responsibility in the central government, but in the provinces a 'dyarchy' was created: ministers responsible to the elected councils worked alongside nominated official councillors as part of the provincial executive authority. The practice of joint discussion between ministers and councillors was encouraged. The ministers were to be in charge of 'nation building' departments such as education, and some financial elbow-room was provided in a division of the heads of revenue between the centre and the provinces. Along with this went a new attitude on the part of the still autocratic government of India under the leadership of the new viceroy, Lord Reading. The Rowlatt and Press Acts were repealed,[2] the unpopular cotton excise imposed in Lancashire's interest was first suspended and then abolished, factory and social legislation was begun, and a beginning made with the Indianisation of the officer cadre of the Indian army. The Lee Commission on the services looked to an equal division of the Indian Civil Service between Indians and British. Fiscal autonomy was granted and a tariff board created to administer it. Externally India received international status as a member of the League of Nations and was given a seat and a voice in the (then) Imperial Conference. The distinguished liberal leader Srinivasa Sastri headed government delegations and championed the cause of Indians in the dominions.

All this argues a great change of outlook; the political and social face of India in the 'twenties was in fact radically different to that of Lord Curzon's

---

[1] So called from its sponsors, Edwin S. Montagu, the Secretary of State for India (1917–22), and Lord Chelmsford, the Viceroy (1916–21).

[2] For the Rowlatt Acts see p. 301. The Press Acts of 1908 and 1910 made incitement to violence in the press felonious and gave government power to suppress newspapers in certain conditions.

time. Yet the government could not avoid a major collision with nationalism which left a rift not wholly closed till independence. The main reason
for this apparent contradiction is to be found in the transformation of the
Indian outlook already mentioned which caused officials returned from
war service to find they were speaking a different language to that of the
Indians, which they had formerly thought that they understood. The particular form which this clash took was due to the idiosyncrasies of one man,
Mohandas Karamchand Gandhi. At the end of the war in late 1918 Indian
opinion was restive and disturbed. It was irritated by food shortages, over-
zealous recruiting in the north, and governmental unresponsiveness; it
was stirred by the transformation of the world going on around it and
especially by President Wilson's advocacy of the cause of subject peoples.
There was a feeling of restive impatience and great expectation in the air;
what before would have been welcomed as a boon was now liable to be
scorned as an insult. It was in this situation that, while the Montford
proposals were still under consideration, measures known as the Rowlatt
bills were proposed to strengthen the law against subversive activities. To
the tense minds and taut nerves of the time this seemed an outrage and a
mockery of the newly professed democratic principles of the Montford
Report. They were carried by the official majority against the votes of all
non-official Indians in the Imperial Legislative Council. Gandhi, then but
four years returned from South Africa, stepped forward to organise *hartals*
or stoppage of work on the grounds of conscience, in the big cities. He
had found a moral issue and he had found a way of appealing to a general
Hindu, as distinct from a particular caste, feeling. Riots occurred, and at
Amritsar on 13 April 1919 a crowd was broken up by troops without
warning; 379 killed and 1,200 wounded were officially acknowledged. This
and the severities of the aftermath created an emotional gulf between British and Indians. The Hunter Commission, reporting on the event early in
1920, divided on racial lines, and the House of Lords gave support to
the general in command, while others raised a large subscription for him.
Gandhi declared that there could be no co-operation with a satanic
government. Again he struck a responsive chord, focusing the venerated
Hindu concept of *dharma* or duty on a political issue. The moderates, led by
Srinivasa Sastri, and constitutionalists such as the veteran Tilak, were
swept aside and the Congress followed Gandhi's lead for a non-co-operation campaign. At this moment his hand was strengthened by the support
of the Muslims, irritated and alarmed by threats to dismember Turkey,
the seat of the caliphate. The campaign lasted some eighteen months,
shaking the government as it had never been shaken since the Mutiny.
Nevertheless, the new constitution came into being and this, together with
alarm felt at outbreaks of violence and the Muslim Moplah rebellion in
Malabar, cooled enthusiasm until Gandhi himself was arrested early in
1922. Soon after, the abolition of the caliphate by the Turks took the

ground from beneath the Muslims' feet. By the end of 1922 the movement was over.

But India was not the same. The government continued to work the new constitution and many middle-class people, the backbone of the old Congress, were content with this for the present. But Congress itself was now under different and more determined leaders, with social roots reaching far deeper than before. Congress was dominated by Gandhi, who was henceforth the major architect of Indian independence. Gandhi had made his name as the lawyer-champion of the Indian community in South Africa, leading up to the Smuts–Gandhi agreement of 1913. It was there that he developed his ideas, deriving partly from his home in Gujarat and partly from Tolstoy and others: they included a belief in non-violence as a moral creed, and a fierce disapproval of Western society as being materialistic, based on greed, and subversive of morals. In India he expanded these themes and added his own mystical concept of *satya* or truth as the basis of all life and conduct. Gradually for him non-violence, which began largely as a political tactic of the weak against the strong, became a universal principle. To this creed he added an uncanny sense of Indian psychology which enabled him to express his political campaigns in terms which appealed to the general Hindu mind. To show his sympathy with the Indian poor and disapproval of Western materialism he adopted the peasants' dress of *dhoti* and *chadar*; the people in return hailed him as a *mahatma* or great soul.[1] This aura of sanctity gave him mass Hindu support which his political expertise enabled him to exploit. Sophisticated congressmen acquiesced in spinning and sermons for the sake of his political skill and national reputation; the masses accepted his politics and the imprisonment which periodically followed because they saw in him an embodiment of Hinduism and the guardian of Mother India.

Gandhi's method was to gather round him a band of faithful disciples called *satyagrahis* who spread non-violence as a faith for the few and as a tactic for the many. He promoted hand spinning and weaving in opposition to machine-made goods; he started a campaign for the admission of the large untouchable class into Hindu society. For him they were *Harijans* or sons of God. Thus he attracted the idealism of the age to himself and used it for his political ends. When Congress failed to follow his line he retired, confident that it could not long do without him. Gandhi turned Congress from a class to a mass movement; he nationalised nationalism. He did this by linking political nationalism with Hindu feeling. In some way it became a semi-religious concept. His reward was independence; the penalty he paid was partition.

In the mid-'twenties Gandhi had to recover his lost leadership. In England powerful conservative forces were not yet convinced that the Congress movement had any real roots in the country. During Gandhi's imprison-

[1] First awarded by Rabindranath Tagore but generally accorded from this time.

ment Congress under C. R. Das and Motilal Nehru decided to contest the next elections as the Swaraj party. The object was to bring the reforms to a standstill by making popular ministries impossible. Their success was only partial and they began to suffer erosion from politicians tempted by the prospect of office and influence. While these political doldrums endured the younger wing of Congress was growing visibly impatient with sterile parliamentary opposition and even less rewarding spinning. It accepted the Mahatma's analysis of the government but called for action instead of non-co-operation. It found in Jawarharlal Nehru and Subas Chandra Bose two youthful and charismatic leaders. They made their first visible impact on the Congress at its Madras meeting in 1928 when they carried a resolution for full independence against the wishes of their elders.

At this moment of frustration the government provided an issue by appointing the Indian Commission in 1927 under Sir John Simon's chairmanship to report on the working of the constitution as prescribed by the 1921 Act. The creation of the Commission earlier than was legally binding was intended as a gesture of goodwill but the all-white membership of it was interpreted as an insult. Opposition to the Commission provided a rallying point for all the Congress groups. An all-party committee led by Motilal Nehru devised a constitution as an Indian counterblast. By 1930 opinion had hardened sufficiently for Congress to demand a Round Table conference within a year to draw up a dominion constitution, under threat of civil disobedience. The government of Lord Irwin countered with its declaration in October that dominion status was the goal of British constitutional development, and made the offer of a Round Table conference to consider the next step. But Congress was adamant, and on this narrow margin Gandhi launched his second anti-government movement in April 1930. In making this decision Gandhi has been accused of bad faith and bad judgement. The motive which seemed to have moved him was not anti-government animus, for at first he recommended acceptance, but the state of the Congress. Left-wing sentiments were growing among the younger men, sharpened by the economic depression and stimulated by the spectacle of extremist movements in Europe, prescribing drastic remedies for drastic situations. Gandhi feared a left-wing revolt or even a breakaway, which would lead to a head-on collision with government, severe repression for which Congress was not ready, and the postponement of independence for a generation. So he decided to lead a non-violent movement himself, only regretting that Lord Irwin had made it so difficult for him to do so convincingly.

The struggle lasted nearly a year. The government was strained but did not crack, largely owing to Lord Irwin's resolution and balance. At one time 60,000 *satyagrahis* were in prison, but the Round Table conference met as planned, though without representatives of Congress. By 1931 it was clear that Congress could not overthrow the government. The Gandhi–

Irwin truce brought Gandhi to the second session of the conference, but when he proved intransigent and restarted the movement it was crushed quickly and severely. As in 1922 the public had had enough; the Congress a second time had overplayed its hand.

But these two years of turmoil left their mark and provided an important landmark on the road to independence and nationhood. At first Congress seemed to have disappeared, but in 1934 it re-emerged as strong as before. In fact the struggle demonstrated the strength as well as the weakness of Congress. It could not take over the country but it could hold it up; it could neither be broken nor suppressed for long. It was shown to be not only *a* force, but the major force in the country to be reckoned with. The realisation of this fact by the Indian government was important but still more so was the parallel realisation in Britain. The bulk of the Conservative party (Labour was already converted), now entering on a long spell of unchallenged government, realised that no settlement in India was possible without Congress participation, that the national movement was a reality which was growing in strength, that India could not for long be held down against her will in current conditions and that independence must therefore be planned for. If we must have an independent India we will have a conservative independent India, was their view. These were the assumptions upon which Conservative policy towards India in the 'thirties was based.

In India itself the movement saw a widening of the rift between the Muslims and the nationalists. The Muslim masses held aloof, which in itself caused resentment; the leaders were affronted by the refusal of the Motilal Nehru Committee to include separate or communal electorates in their proposed constitution. The intellectual Muslim nationalist M. A. Jinnah broke finally with Congress on this issue. Extremism, which feeds on action, grew in strength within Congress and began to display some terrorist offshoots. But socially there was an enlargement of spirit. Mass demonstrations and mass arrests drew and threw persons of all classes together. Here was an issue above caste, and the struggle tended to break down at least some of the external caste barriers. Particularly noticeable was its effect upon the women's movement. Hitherto the preserve of the westernised few, the movement now drew large numbers of women, attending demonstrations, addressing meetings, picketing liquor shops and courting arrest. Gandhi blessed them and distinguished congresswomen like Mrs Sarojini Naidu encouraged them. The foundation of their part in public life today was laid at this time. Even the fifty millions of the depressed classes felt this wind of change, for the spirit of brotherhood generated by the movement and Gandhi's prestige made many look more kindly on his claims for them.

The next few years in Britain saw the implementation of the new Conservative outlook on India. Despite the determined opposition of the group led by Winston Churchill and Lord Lloyd which caused a perhaps fatal two years' delay, a new constitution was elaborated as the Government of India Act of 1935. The Act was a blueprint for the constitution of independent India, but a constitution on conservative lines. A federal system replaced the unitary system of the past; this was designed to make possible the incorporation of the princes in a single Indian state, and it was balanced by the establishment of a Federal Court of Justice. There was to be full responsible government in the provinces and dyarchy or divided responsibility at the centre. The provincial electorates were enlarged to thirty million voters, with legislatures and second chambers to match. Clearly the next step could hardly be less than full dominion status. It was hoped that the federal system with its semi-local autonomy for Muslim-majority areas together with an elaboration of the system of communal electorates and reserfed seats would calm the fears of the Muslims and other minorities.

The conservative bias of the constitution was to be found not so much in the reserved powers of the Governor-General or in the continued power of parliament over India or in the property qualification for the franchise. All these could be removed without affecting the main structure. The parliamentary link was little more than an umbilical cord between political mother and infant and arrangements were in fact made for the Indian parliament to amend its own constitution in certain respects. The essence of the conservative principle lay in the treatment of the princes and it appeared in the guise of a revolutionary measure, the integration of the princes with the new federation. In return for the surrender of certain powers to the Centre they would retain internal autonomy in their states and they would gain a large influence in all-India affairs. They would do this by the nomination of one-third of the members of the lower and two-fifths of those of the upper house of Parliament. Since the central ministry would ultimately be responsible to the new parliament the political scales would be heavily weighted in favour of conservative ministries. It was the logical result of a long-standing princely policy of the government. Congress rule might not be excluded but an extremist Congress régime would be. Ironically, it was another conservative twist which undid these plans. Adhesion to the federation was to be voluntary and was not to come into force until half the states by population had acceded. Princely second thoughts and hesitations were thus given a further opportunity, and so gently was the policy administered that by the outbreak of the second world war not a single state had acceded. Negotiations were then suspended; by the war's end the princes found that time and events had passed them by.

These years in India saw two political developments. The first was the revival of the Congress as soon as civil disobedience was called off in 1934. But it was not the same Congress. Though chastened by the experience of running beyond the margin of mass support for the second time in twelve years it was also strengthened in resolve and unity. This latter gift enabled it to sweep the elections of 1937 under the new constitution, while the caution produced by the former induced it to form provincial ministries in six provinces out of eleven. They functioned with smoothness and efficiency until they resigned after the outbreak of the second world war. Within the Congress, however, a struggle was proceeding between its left and its right wing. The younger generation and lower-income groups were increasingly attracted to activist policies, looking to Jawarharlal Nehru with his militant democratic socialism and Subas Bose with his revolutionary idealism and dictatorial leanings. It was Gandhi's achievement during these years to keep the Congress united, allowing it neither to founder on the revolutionary rock nor to retire into elderly quietism. His method was to smother the radicals with promotion and then to control them by personal magnetism and the veteran vote in the Working Committee. He found Jawarharlal Nehru more amenable to this process than Subas Bose, and indeed established a personal ascendancy over Nehru which lasted until the eve of independence. He postponed a clash as long as possible, but when in 1939 Bose wanted a second turn as Congress president after the two terms enjoyed by Nehru, he drove him from office. This was a parting of the ways, for Nehru to the first premiership of India, for Bose to the leadership of the National Army in Burma. An offshoot of this activist sentiment was the rise of the Communist party during the 'thirties. It alarmed the government but it was too foreign and too secular seriously to challenge the Congress.

The second political development in the 'thirties was the rise of the Muslim League under Mohammad Ali Jinnah and the emergence of the concept of Pakistan. The Muslim community in India, one-fourth of the whole population, was already in eclipse when it was made the scapegoat of the Mutiny by the British. From this depressed condition it was rescued by Sir Sayyid Ahmad Khan (1815–98), who sturdily preached self-help, induced Muslims to accept Western education to put them into competition with the Hindus for the public services and to accept British rule as preferable to Hindu. His aim was a modernised Muslim community forming an essential component of a British Indian state. As soon, therefore, as the new National Congress began to think in terms of ultimate self-government he took alarm. Majority rule, he said, could only mean Hindu rule. He stood aloof from the Congress and carried most Muslims with him. Henceforward each move towards self-government provoked a Muslim demand for safeguards. The Muslim League was formed in 1906 as soon as reforms looked possible in the post-Curzon period. It demanded safeguards which were embodied in the Act of 1909 and extended with each instalment of reform. After the first world war there was a brief honeymoon with Gandhi's Congress when the Muslim supporters of the caliphate joined in the non-co-operation movement. But after the abolition of the caliphate in 1924 the previous process of mounting suspicion was resumed. Fear grew as the prospect of eventual independence became clearer and was fanned by uncompromising statements from extreme Hindu groups which the Congress was unable to control. As the 1935 reforms came into view the policy of withdrawal came into discussion. It was first put forward by Sir Muhammad Iqbal in 1930 and given the name Pakistan by Choudhri Rahmat Ali in 1933.

It was in this situation that Jinnah turned what had hitherto been a middle-class movement of disputed leadership against a background of mass quiescence into a dynamic mass movement. For long Jinnah had hoped for the integration of political Islam into the national movement. He was disillusioned by the terms of the Motilal Nehru report or proposed constitution in 1928 and exasperated by the attempt of the Congress to break up the League altogether in the United Provinces after winning the provincial elections there in 1937. Then Jinnah, a westernised lawyer-politician from Bombay who could not speak Urdu, appealed to the masses. He was helped by the smouldering Muslim distrust of Hindus and by the communal pinpricks administered by the minor officials of Congress ministries which he knew well how to exploit. When these ministries resigned in late 1939 he organised a successful thanksgiving day and the next year he adopted an independent Pakistan as the aim of League policy. There were two nations in India, he said, and they must each follow their own destiny.

The decade of the 'thirties saw the steady advance of the new India towards adult nationhood. In the economic sphere colonialism was giving place to a planned economy whose slogan was fiscal autonomy and symbol the Tariff Board. Created in 1923, the Board successfully protected the young steel industry from the effects of the depression of the early 'thirties and saved the cotton industry from the threat of cheap Japanese textiles. New industries like cement were founded and old ones like sugar-refining extended to make India independent of foreign supplies. By the second world war India was a country with modern industries if not an industrialised country; she ranked sixth in the list of the world's steel producers.

In education there was rapid expansion with the introduction of the teaching university on the British civic model and experiments in a federal collegiate system. Technical education began to develop. Primary education increased more in concept that in fact with Gandhi's basic education scheme and the Sargent plan for universal elementary education by 1970.[1] Nevertheless it went forward, especially in the Punjab. Women's higher education developed rapidly though female literacy was only half that of the men. Intellectual life acquired a new vigour. Formerly Tagore had been something of a lone star but now there appeared such

[1] Sir J. Sargent was Educational Adviser to the Government of India, 1938–46.

distinguished figures as Sir S. Radhakrishnan and Dr S. C. Das Gupta in philosophy, Sir J. C. Bose and Sir C. V. Raman in science, and Sir J. Sarkar the historian. In literature a whole school of young writers, practising in both English and the Indian languages, of whom Mulk Raj Anand and R. K. Narayan may be mentioned, studied current social and cultural problems with the help of western literary techniques. Indian music experienced a revival and Indian painters, inspired by Ajanta models, produced a distinctive school whose leader Abanindranath Tagore won an international reputation.

All these developments except the last two mentioned were Western in character, and even modern Indian music has been influenced by the West. The signs were that the West was gaining over Indian tradition in the intellectual and artistic fields. There were distinguished exceptions of whom may be mentioned Sri Arabindo of Pondicherry, the expounder of neo-Vedantism in mellifluous English, and Sir Muhammad Iqbal, philosopher and poet in Persian and Urdu, whose ideas provided an intellectual dynamic for the Pakistan movement. For the rest, traditionalist movements like the Arya Samaj made little progress. Gandhi's advocacy of a village economy and rustic philosophy was visibly faltering. His cap became a badge and *khaddar* a party uniform. On the other hand his Harijan and temple entry campaigns were openly hostile to Hindu orthodoxy. It could not therefore be said that there was yet any marriage of Eastern and Western concepts or any prospect of early intellectual or racial integration. But there were no longer defensive apologetics on the one side facing critical superiority on the other. There was an interchange of ideas, a running dialogue on a basis of adult equality.

In the summer of 1939 a casual observer in India might have considered the position not unhopeful. Congress ministries had worked in eight provinces for over two years while governments backed by both Hindus and Muslims firmly held Bengal and the Punjab. The Muslim League was loud in its protests but it had made little progress in the vital Punjab, and there was little evidence to show how far its roots had spread into the soil of popular Islam. The princes still hesitated to enter the federation but agents moved to and fro between their courts and it seemed that the Viceroy was determined to achieve success. Then came the outbreak of the second world war. It found India far less prepared for it than for the first world war. On that occasion there was an identification by India of herself with Britain; the British cause was the Indian cause; there was an outburst of princely loyalty and middle-class enthusiasm. But since then the British government had become 'satanic' in the eyes of many; the Congress was now the keeper of India's conscience. The Indian public had become adult in their attitude; their view of the crisis was detached and aloof; they were not unsympathetic to the Allied cause but were highly critical of British policy: they remembered the constitutional maxim which they had learnt at college: 'no supply without redress of grievances'. The war made little impact until the fall of France shocked the public into concern and anxiety. The British stand and the battle of Britain were viewed with growing admiration but little inclination to give unconditional aid; thereafter the mood of detachment returned until the Japanese action brought the war to the Indian doorstep in early 1942.

Neither of the two great parties officially supported the war or would allow their members to sit on the War Council which met in Delhi. But this did not prevent individuals from acting on their own. The war had a profound effect on Indian life and development. There was first the war effort. Indian troops took part in the desert campaigns of North Africa, where their 4th and 7th divisions won international fame, in Abyssinia and the Middle East. Later they were involved in the disastrous Malayan campaign leading to the fall of Singapore. Ninety thousand became Japanese prisoners, from some of whom Subas Bose recruited his National Army. After the fall of Burma they were concerned with the defence of the Indian border, winning laurels with the heroic defence of Kohima in 1944, and crowning their achievement with the recapture of Rangoon in early 1945. The record was impressive, but it moved the public to nothing like the extent of their forebears in the first world war. This again was evidence of the new Indian maturity in public matters. They were no longer surprised and gratified by Indian military achievement; they expected it and took it for granted.

But behind the front the social and economic consequences of the war were indeed great. The army was expanded from its peace-time strength of 175,000 to more than two millions. The men were drawn from the villages and they were much more evenly spread over the country than in the first world war. Many received the technical training demanded by mechanised warfare. Both the social impact on village life and the technical stimulus were proportionately great. This expansion helped to lay the foundation for the social and technical developments of post-war India. After the armed forces came the expansion of supplies. At first the army authorities were apathetic on the ground that an unmechanised Indian army could play no part in a mechanised war. But after the fall of France the attitude changed. India became a supply centre for the Middle East. The Viceroy, Lord Linlithgow, at his best in administration, organised the Eastern Group Supply Council. India came to supply 75 per cent of the total demands of this theatre. With the entry of Japan and America the pattern of supply changed, but industrial development went on faster than before. Tata's great steel works were extended and supplemented at Burnpur and elsewhere. The cement industry was greatly expanded to service the new airfields of eastern India, a new aluminium industry exploited the ample supplies of bauxite, and the mica industry was enlarged. These developments were far greater than those during the first

22-2

world war, and again laid a foundation for the policy of large-scale industrialisation of the post-war Indian government. The last shreds of colonialism were blown away in the effort to stop the Japanese.

A further effect of the war was the reappearance of famine in Bengal in 1943. Since the drawing up of the Famine Code in 1883 there had been no famine of hunger because imported food had sustained and relief work had occupied the cropless villagers. But when the Japanese occupation of Burma in 1942 cut off its rice there was no alternative external food supply on which to draw. The overall deficiency was not reckoned to be more than five per cent and the problem was one of distribution. But the railways were already strained by the east–west flow of military supplies from Bombay to Assam. To this was added a new north–south traffic in foodstuffs. The local governments proved quite unable to meet the situation or distribute fairly the supplies which came from the Punjab. The Viceroy, with ill-timed scruples about federal rights, remained aloof. The famine mounted amidst wringing of hands and profit taking until the new viceroy, Lord Wavell, visited Calcutta, put the British army on to distribution, and introduced rationing into all the chief cities as a measure of fairness. The subsequent enquiry commission estimated direct and consequential deaths at between one and a half and two millions. This famine was something of a portent for it seemed to show that the British were losing, not so much their capacity for administration as their vigour in taking decisions in a crisis.

The politics of the war began with the resignation of the Congress provincial ministries in protest at India's involvement in war without her consent. This is considered by many to have been the first tactical mistake of Congress because it removed its very real control from the administrative machine and inclined the government towards the less intractable Muslim League. A political deadlock then ensued, with interludes of negotiation until the end of the war. For the Congress there could be no participation in the war without self-government, for the government no constitutional settlement until after the war. The slogan 'after the war' hung heavily round the government's neck as did that of non-co-operation upon the Congress. Between the two the opportunity of understanding through joint action was lost. The discontents of a prolonged war, intensified with Japan's entry in late 1941, played into the hands of Congress; on the other hand the number of troops poured into the country from that time made any serious subversive effort hopeless. Meanwhile the way was cleared for the Muslim League. In 1940 it adopted Pakistan as its political goal and continued its propaganda unchecked. It won nearly every Muslim by-election and by the end of the war had a block of 25 seats out of an elected membership of 104 in the Central Assembly.

The Viceroy responded to the Congress tactics by offering an enlargement of his Executive Council, which he effected in August 1940, and a constituent assembly after the war. Gandhi, on the other hand, resorted once more to civil disobedience but arranged the campaign with such solicitude that the government was not seriously embarrassed. About 14,000 persons were in prison in early 1941, led by Gandhi's chief disciple Vinoba Bhave. So matters rested until the Japanese entry into the war created a new situation. The war was now on India's doorstep and her co-operation in defence was vital. It was time for a major effort and it was made in the form of a new constitutional offer conveyed by Sir Stafford Cripps, then freshly returned with his Moscow laurels, in March and April 1942. The offer was radical but the circumstances made it plausible to attribute it as much to Britain's dire need of support in a crisis as to generosity or foresight. A constituent assembly was to be called immediately after the war to draw up a constitution for an Indian Union with dominion status. The new state, like other dominions, would have the right of secession. The Indian states could join but the scheme would proceed without them if necessary. Minority rights were recognised by allowing a province to contract out of the new arrangement. The future seemed provided for but there remained the present, and it was on this rock that the offer foundered. Congress leaders were at first favourable but under Gandhi's influence they insisted on the full powers of a dominion cabinet for the proposed executive council of national leaders. Gandhi was reported to take a pessimistic view of British prospects; should the Congress draw a cheque on a failing bank? A little waiting, some increase in British extremity, and the whole government might fall to them.

The high hope of the offer produced a corresponding reaction. Gandhi anticipated in August the expected crisis of Japanese action in October by threatening mass civil disobedience because of the failure of the British to 'Quit India'. 'After all', he said, 'this is open rebellion.' The government interned the whole Congress committee and firmly repressed an attempted rising by the left wing at the cost of 900 lives and a million pounds of damage. Henceforth it was unchallenged. Congress, in missing this opportunity of controlling the government before the Muslim League was strong enough to interfere, lost its last opportunity of preserving a united as well as achieving an independent India.

With the end of the war in Europe a new situation arose. Dominion status must now come in some form or other. But it was thought that the war in Asia would last another year and that during that time the government could negotiate with the Indian parties from strength. Lord Wavell called a conference in June to form an interim cabinet on Crippsian lines but this broke down on the League's claim to represent all Muslims. The surrender of Japan in August 1945 set the stage for the final scene. Overnight the weightage of political factors was transformed. The British could no longer dictate or block the dictation of others. Their military strength drained away with rapid repatriation, and their governing purpose was undermined by a radical change of sentiment in Britain and in the world. The new Labour government was pledged to Indian self-government and was only concerned with ways of achieving it. Henceforth the British in India could argue and conciliate but not direct. With Indian sentiment in its then condition partition was inevitable. In the winter of 1945-6 a general election showed that the Muslim League dominated Muslim India as much as the Congress did Hindu India. The confrontation of the two parties was now clear and the leader of the smaller was a master tactician. At the same time a short-lived naval mutiny showed how narrow was the margin of authority still left to the British. From March to June a Cabinet Mission consisting of Lord Pethick-Lawrence, Sir S. Cripps and A. V. (later Viscount) Alexander made a major attempt to find an agreed settlement.[1] This broke down, nominally on the allotment of communal seats but really because neither side was willing to give up its respective goals of union and partition. Recriminations led to Jinnah's 'direct action day' of 16 August. The bloody riots which then afflicted Calcutta started a chain reaction in north India leading to endemic civil war in the Punjab from early 1947. In this mounting confusion and creeping anarchy the leaders on all sides were helpless; every move by one side was sabotaged by the other.

The London government met this situation by announcing in February 1947 the dispatch of Lord Mountbatten to wind up British rule not later than August 1948. After a final attempt at conciliation he worked out a plan for partition to which the parties agreed in June. He pushed forward with such speed that the actual handover was achieved on 14 August 1947. To Pakistan was allotted the West Punjab, Sind, Baluchistan, the Frontier Province and the Muslim majority areas of East Bengal and Assam, to the new India the remainder. A boundary commission settled frontier details. The Indian princes were released from their allegiance to the crown and urged to join one or other of the two states.

In this way the British–Indian controversy dissolved and was soon found to have left little but goodwill behind it. But it left in clearer relief the Hindu–Muslim controversy, which was not so much resolved as transmuted. The murder of an estimated half a million people on both sides and the migration of over ten millions at the time of partition in 1947 was the price for this transmutation of unresolved tension. On the other hand separation enabled each state to establish a strong government which could carry through modernisation programmes. For these the Indians, and to a much lesser extent the Pakistanis, found the foundation already laid by the British activities of the preceding quarter of a century.

[1] The Mission was in India from 24 March to 29 June 1946.

2. SOUTH-EAST ASIA

At the beginning of the twentieth century control over the vast area of mainland and islands now known as South-East Asia was almost monopolised by the Netherlands, Britain, France and the United States of America. Of the four the Dutch had been established the longest and possessed by far the richest empire. With its centre at Batavia, founded by Jan Pieterszoon Coen in 1619, Netherlands India, the 'girdle of emerald flung round the equator', comprised the whole Malay archipelago except the Philippines, newly acquired from Spain by the United States (Treaty of Paris, December 1898), north-western Borneo, the Portuguese half of Timor, and eastern New Guinea, the northern part of which was in German possession, the southern a British colony. The Netherlands Indies stretched for nearly three thousand miles from the north-west point of Sumatra to the eastern limit of Dutch territory in New Guinea, its breadth from north to south was roughly thirteen hundred miles, and it had a total land area of nearly 735,000 square miles. In 1900 the reduction of the whole area to Dutch rule was still incomplete. Much of it had been acquired only in the second half of the nineteenth century. The Achinese of north-west Sumatra, who had been fighting for independence since 1873, were not to be finally brought under control until 1908.

The British empire in South-East Asia was mainly continental. Its largest territory was the former 'Kingdom of Ava' (Burma), which had been annexed piecemeal to British India between 1824 and 1886. To the south of it lay the Straits Settlements of Singapore, Penang and Malacca, a crown colony, and the four Federated Malay States of Perak, Selangor, Negri Sembilan and Pahang, nominally independent sultanates under British protection. In 1909 Siam was to transfer to Britain her suzerain rights over the Malay states of Perlis, Kedah, Kelantan and Trengganu. In 1912 Johore was to come under British protection. In Borneo Sarawak, ruled by a nephew of the original Raja James Brooke, British North Borneo, administered by the chartered company of that name, and the sultanate of Brunei, were also British protectorates.

On the Mekong River and along the shores of the South China Sea France had been busy, from 1859 onwards, carving out for herself an extensive Indo-Chinese empire. It comprised the colony of Cochin-China in the extreme south, together with the protectorates of Annam and Tongking, Cambodia and Laos. Over the last named her control was still incomplete in 1900. The United States was the last western power to acquire any considerable territorial dominions in South-East Asia. After the Spanish–American war of 1898 Spain had been forced to cede the entire Philippine archipelago. Not until 1901, however, was American control finally established after intensive guerrilla warfare against a vigorous

313

Filipino independence movement, which the Americans themselves had previously nourished and armed against Spain.

The kingdom of Siam was the sole remaining independent state in the whole area. For years it had maintained an uneasy, precarious existence between the expanding empires of Britain and France. King Thibaw's attempts to play off France, then conquering Tongking, against Britain had led to the extinction of the Burmese monarchy and the annexation of Upper Burma. Siam's hour of crisis arrived when France used her new position in Vietnam to snatch the Laos kingdom of Luang Prabang from Siamese suzerainty and push the Siamese out of all their territories east of the Mekong. British administrators in South-East Asia were convinced that the French regarded their empire in Indo-China as a base for further advances, into China on the one hand and the Menam valley on the other, and even into the Malay Peninsula. The 'Paknam incident' of July 1893 was undoubtedly staged in the hope that Siam would lose her head and present France with a plausible pretext for another forward move. Actually it brought Britain and France to the brink of war, for British policy was to maintain an independent Siam as a buffer state between the Indian empire and French Indo-China. Prince Devawongse's admirable handling of the situation and British diplomatic pressure on France preserved Siam's independence for the time being. Then in 1896, after Anglo-French relations had again been strained almost to breaking-point over a quarrel between their respective boundary commissioners on the Upper Mekong, the two powers agreed to a joint guarantee of the independence of the Menam valley. But not until the Entente Cordiale of 1904 was Siam safely out of the wood.

In 1900 a new age of colonial exploitation had begun which was linking the East more closely than ever before to the productive system of the West. With the arrival of the internal combustion engine the tin, rubber and oil of South-East Asia became vital to Western economy. Private capital, directed by a few powerful corporations, was insisting upon the more efficient exploitation of colonies. Efficiency, in fact, was becoming the new administrative watchword, with Lord Curzon in India as its major prophet. But to the new generation of colonial administrators that was arising it was efficiency not merely for the sake of the profits of 'big business', but equally for the welfare of subject peoples. Kipling's 'white man's burden' had its Dutch counterpart in the 'ethical policy' of Van Deventer, whose article 'Een Eereschuld' (A debt of honour) in De Gids (1899) marks the beginning of the great change in the Dutch attitude towards their colonial peoples. Prosperity, however, was the prerequisite of social progress. The potentially rich but undeveloped countries of South-East Asia were too poor to support the heavy cost of improved social services. Hence in making them a happy hunting ground for private capital, colonial governments provided themselves with means for undertaking large-scale public works and promoting higher standards of public health and welfare.

Thus the economies of the South-East Asian peoples became dependent upon external markets and, in the cases of French Indo-China and the Philippines especially, closely linked with the economies of their metropolitan countries. The self-sufficiency of the indigenous village broke down with the rapid expansion in the production of cash crops and the change-over to a money economy; while the import of cheap manufactured articles from Europe and America had a depressing effect upon many of the local handicrafts, which had provided the peasant cultivator with a valuable supplementary source of livelihood. At the same time an un-paralleled increase in population, the result of better administration and of Western public health measures, caused social disintegration in many areas. In Burma there was a big movement of population into the Irra-waddy Delta region, especially after 1870, to expand its rice production, with British encouragement, so that by the end of the century Burma had become the world's largest producer of rice for export. The phenomenal increase in Java's population outran all the Dutch efforts to increase food production, and caused such intense pressure upon the land that the size of individual holdings, already too small with an average of $2\frac{1}{2}$ acres per family at the beginning of the twentieth century, tended still further to diminish, with serious effects upon the peasant's standard of living. But, bad as this situation was, it was better than that prevailing in the con-gested areas of the Red River valley of Tongking, where the depression caused by fragmentation of holdings was rendered worse through the acquisition by speculators of the communal lands which for centuries had been the village community's safeguard against poverty. In the Philippines the same tendency had begun to show itself by the end of the Spanish period in central Luzon and Cebu, where population pressure was aggra-vated by tenancy problems which the Americans, with their free-enterprise ideas, made no attempt to solve.[1]

Thus twentieth-century colonial rule failed to maintain adequate stan-dards of living for the peasant classes forming the overwhelming majority of the population of South-East Asia. The world slump, the full effects of which began to be felt in 1930, knocked the bottom out of the world market in South-East Asia's staple products. It revealed for the first time in its true proportions the problem of agricultural indebtedness, and brought home to the educated *élites* among South-East Asians the alarm-ing extent of the dependence of their economies upon those of the West. Peasant distress found expression in serious uprisings in Burma and Viet-nam, and in armed clashes between peasant organisations and landlords' private armies in the Philippines. In Indonesia Dutch control was too firm

[1] C. A. Fisher, in *South-East Asia, a Social, Economic and Political Geography* (London, 1964), pp. 161–94, surveys the main economic effects of Western domination.

and alert, having already been unsuccessfully challenged by left-wing revolutionary movements which came to a head in late 1926 and early 1927. A new and more intense nationalism was everywhere generated in response to Western rule. In its development Western education played a predominant role. The welfare state needed an increasing supply of trained indigenes in its expanding administrative services, as also did industry and commerce. The consequent development of secondary and higher education, based on Western methods and using Western languages as media of instruction, created a new intelligentsia which had been introduced to Western thought and organisation, Western history and science. They felt the influence of the scientific revolution that was transforming the outlook and techniques of the West. They were offered a new consciousness of their own historic past through the rescue, by Western archaeologists and scholars, of their ancient monuments and artistic treasures from ruin and oblivion, and the scientific study of their historical records. The impact of all this brought them a new self-awareness, and stimulated a renaissance bearing many resemblances to the European renaissance at the end of the Middle Ages. They deeply resented their relegation to a place of inferiority by westerners. They considered their culture to be as good as that of the West save in technology. Moreover, Western education was imparted with a Western-centred outlook which ignored indigenous modes of life and thought. Hence, by reaction, there was a revival of traditionalism which expressed itself in the identification of Buddhism in the Buddhist countries, and of Islam in the Islamic ones, with patriotism, in the re-assertion of traditional mythology, and in demands for greater recognition of national languages and literatures.[1]

National hatred was also whipped up against the foreign Asians whom Western economic exploitation of South-East Asia had attracted as immigrants, especially the Chinese and Indians. Their interest in, and support for, the intense nationalism, which developed in their own respective countries simultaneously with the South-East Asian national movements, militated strongly against their assimilation with the peoples among whom they lived, and made them a butt for their xenophobia.

Finally there was the influence of external events. The anti-Western Boxer rebellion in China in 1899, the rise of Japan as the self-styled champion of Asian rights and her victory over Russia in 1905, the Chinese revolution and the consequent deposition of the Manchu dynasty in 1912, and Gandhi's leadership of the Indian *swaraj* movement, all conveyed to the South-East intelligentsias a feeling of Asia arising and challenging Western domination. It was from their ranks that the leaders of the nationalist movements sprang. For them the doctrine of self-determina-

[1] On this point see Donald E. Smith, *Religion and Politics in Burma* (Princeton, 1965), pp. 52–7, 75–6 and 118; W. F. Wertheim, *Indonesian Society in Transition* (2nd ed. The Hague, 1964), pp. 209–17.

tion, enunciated by President Wilson among his 'Fourteen Points' for the settlement of Europe in 1918, had universal validity. It provided them with a rallying-cry against their alien rulers.

The awakening process began earlier in the Philippines than in any other South-East Asian country. This was only to be expected, since the Filipinos had been longer under Western rule than any other people of the area, and had been exposed to the most intense cultural pressure by Spain.[1] The islands had been closely tied to Mexico, and had made little economic progress. But in the nineteenth century, with the growth of much freer trade with the outside world, a prosperous middle class of Filipinos emerged, whose sons went abroad to study, and developed strong reformist ideas. Men of this class, such as José Rizal and Marcelo H. del Pilar, became the leaders of a nationalist propaganda movement demanding reforms, though not separation from Spain. But Rizal's moderate Liga Filipino was suppressed, only to be followed by a nation-wide revolutionary secret society, Katipunan, seeking to overturn Spanish rule by force. In 1897 it set up its own revolutionary government under Emilio Aguinaldo, but this was suppressed. A new rising in the following year became involved in the United States' war with Spain, and, as we have seen above, was ultimately crushed by the Americans after the transfer of the Philippines by Spain.

The United States' interest in the Philippines was purely strategic; but when the Americans became aware of the intensity of Filipino nationalism, they gave their promise that they would fully respect Filipino customs, habits and traditions, and provide for the 'amplest liberty of self-government'. They kept their promise. Moreover, realising that democracy demanded a much wider dissemination of education than under the Spanish régime, they set in motion a vast educational campaign with English as the medium of instruction. Education was America's most important contribution to the Philippines; expenditure upon it accounted for a much higher percentage of the colonial budget than in any other country of South-East Asia. They retained much of the framework of the Spanish administration, but injected a liberal dose of representative government into it, both at the centre and throughout the local divisions of provinces, municipalities and townships. This involved the formation of political parties, most of which began by agitating for immediate independence. From the first meeting of the Philippine Assembly in 1907 until the Japanese occupation in the second world war, one party, the Nacionalista, maintained complete dominance, chiefly through the leadership of three outstanding personalities, the American-trained lawyers Sergio Osmena (b. 1878) and Manuel L. Quezon, and the brilliant Manuel Roxas, a product of the University of the Philippines.

[1] The latest study of the subject is John L. Phelan's The Hispanization of the Philippines (Madison, Wisconsin, 1959).

THE SHIFTING BALANCE OF WORLD FORCES

Within a very short time the United States had introduced into the Philippines a form of democracy resembling its own; one, however, with severe limitations, for the landed gentry and the intelligentsia, interested solely in preserving their own social and economic privileges, were the effectual recipients of the powers transferred. Their manipulation of the administration reduced the majority of the owner-cultivators to share-cropping tenants or wage-earners. The inclusion of the Philippines in the United States tariff area in 1909 further strengthened the hands of the landlord class, for it favoured the large-scale production of sugar, abacá, coconut-oil and copra for export, with private corporations and large-estate owners in control. The expansion of such cash crops was achieved partially at the expense of food production, and the 'sugar-baron' became politically more powerful than the 'rice-baron'.[1] Further, the Philippines became more dependent upon the United States than any other country of South-East Asia upon its own metropolitan power, with the inevitable consequence of industrial underdevelopment.

By the 'thirties opinion in the United States began to veer strongly in favour of Philippine independence, and in 1934 Congress provided for a ten-year period of preparation for self-government and permitted the summons of a Philippine Constituent Assembly to draft a written con-stitution. In return for these concessions the United States was to retain its military and naval bases, until full independence was achieved.

No sooner, however, were the Philippines well and truly set on the road to complete self-government than the international situation began to darken both in Europe and in the Pacific. The Japanese invasion of China caused such alarm that Philippine policy took a sharp turn in the direction of closer association with America, and General Douglas MacArthur, appointed military adviser to the Philippine Commonwealth, began to raise and train a native army with the assistance of American funds.

During the first two centuries of their rule in Indonesia the Dutch were so eager to maintain their commercial monopoly that they paid no heed whatever to its effects upon native institutions. The cultuurstelsel, in-augurated in the first half of the nineteenth century, became the most effective system ever devised for the exploitation of native production, and yielded a vast colonial surplus, the batig slot, to the home govern-ment. Liberalism's prescription for the remedy of the evils which this wrought in Java was to open the door as wide as possible for private enterprise, again with no guarantee for the interests of the Indonesians. Hence the 'ethical policy' of the early twentieth century came as a sort of eleventh-hour repentance. Decentralisation was to be the method and the village community (desa) the chief means for enhancing native welfare. Little by little an elaborate village administration was built up. But so

[1] E. H. Jacoby, *Agrarian Unrest in South-East Asia* (New York, 1949), pp. 184–5.

318

great was the degree of Dutch paternal control that it was impossible for anything of the nature of real village autonomy to develop.

The first signs of Indonesian nationalism showed themselves early in the century in the activities of the gifted Raden Adjeng Kartini, daughter of the regent of Japara, whose letters, published in 1911, stimulated the release of a native spiritual energy which was a new phenomenon in Netherlands India. Both she and Dr Waidin Soedira Oesada, a retired medical officer, who began a campaign for the advancement of Java in 1906, looked to the spread of Western education as the means of salvation. In 1908 he founded the first nationalist association, Boedi Oetimo, 'High Endeavour', with a membership mainly of intellectuals and officials. It was soon followed, in 1911, by an association of a very different character. Sarekat Islam, a popular movement which, beginning as a combination of Javanese *batik* traders against Chinese exploitation, became within a few years a revolutionary political party holding national congresses, organising strikes and demanding independence. The Communist Revolution in Russia in 1917 had immediate effects upon the situation in Java. An energetic Communist section ('Section B'), closely in touch with Moscow, attempted to gain control over Sarekat Islam. Failing in this object, it formed the Perserikatan Komunist India (P.K.I.) and broke away from the parent body, which, although Socialist in outlook, remained firmly attached to nationalist and religious ideals. In 1922, under the influence of native graduates from Europe discontented with the status of natives in the government services, Sarekat Islam established relations with the Indian National Congress and adopted a policy of non-co-operation.

The post-war depression with its crop of industrial disputes presented the extremists with just the kind of opportunity they required for bringing about the maximum dislocation of political and economic life. Moscow regarded Java as a strategic centre of the highest importance. Through agents in Singapore, contact was made between the P.K.I. and the Chinese Communists. From 1923 onwards a series of revolutionary strikes, culminating in November 1926 in a sudden revolt, chiefly in west Java but also in the neighbouring parts of Sumatra, led the Dutch to take severe repressive measures. The Communist leaders and hundreds of their followers were interned in New Guinea and the movement petered out. In the following year Dr Soekarno's Perserikatan Nasional Indonesia (National Indonesian Party), which had attempted to imitate the Gandhi technique, was also broken up and its leader imprisoned. Firm repression and a strict censorship of the press checked the Indonesian political movement.

Much of the trouble of these post-war years was the result of disappointment at Dutch unwillingness to effect any real transfer of power. Their high-sounding promises meant very little in practice. During the first world war, in response to insistent nationalist demands for a greater share in the government, a Volksraad was brought into existence in 1917, but it had a

European majority, half its members were nominated, and its powers were narrowly limited. This development was associated with a general scheme of decentralisation in the provinces, but the new system was slow in taking shape, and was completed only shortly before the Japanese invasion. It represented the utmost concessions the Dutch were prepared to make.

The rapid expansion of the motor industry after 1900 revolutionised South-East Asia's position in world affairs. In 1938 the Netherlands East Indies, Malaya, French Indo-China, Siam, Burma, British North Borneo and Sarawak produced practically the whole of the world's rubber and more than half of its tin, with the United States as the chief purchaser and Malaya as the principal producer of both commodities. The great expansion in Malaya's rubber and tin production was achieved by British and Chinese enterprise and capital. It involved so large an influx of Chinese and Indian immigrants that by 1941 Malays formed no more than 41 per cent of the population and were outnumbered by the Chinese. They remained for the most part tenant farmers growing rice, too proud to be interested in the economic progress which transformed their country, and too shiftless to use the more modern methods placed at their disposal by the British.

It has been said that there has never been a race less politically minded and less interested in economic development. Hence the main problem that emerged was, in the words of Professor L. A. Mills, 'how to reconcile the legitimate interests of foreign capital and the immigrant races with the equally valid claim of the Malays to a larger share in the government of their own country'. As most of the Chinese and Indians were only temporarily in the country, the Malays alone developed any sort of Malayan patriotism. Before the Japanese conquest in the second world war this was limited to a very small middle class, which had absorbed a certain amount of Western education. Resentment against Chinese and Indians played its part, as also did the religious revival which occurred throughout the Muslim world after the first world war.

Indirect rule in the Federated States was a façade behind which the Chief Secretary at Kuala Lumpur and his dependent civil service ruled as it were a single unit, and with immense efficiency. In the Unfederated States advisers had to promote co-ordination of policy by means of advice and persuasion. The Straits Settlements were under a Governor assisted by an Executive Council and a small Legislative Council, all the members of which were appointed up to 1924, when two British members, elected by the Chambers of Commerce of Singapore and Penang, were added. The non-official members included one Malay and three Chinese. There was always an official majority which was bound to support the Governor's policy. In practice, however, much deference was shown to the views of the non-officials. There was strikingly little demand for any change in this form of government. British and Chinese economic interests feared the results of any relaxation of control by devolution of power to the sultans, but British administrators were not happy about the situation, and in the 'thirties a very stiff controversy raged around it. Finally a decentralisation policy was adopted; the Chief Secretaryship was abolished in 1935 and some additional powers transferred to the State Councils of the sultans. In this way the responsibility for the co-ordination of policy passed to the High Commissioner and his 'mouthpiece', the Federal Secretary, while the prestige of the sultans was enhanced. Up to the Japanese invasion in 1941 the Colonial Office in London remained firmly wedded to the policy of decentralisation, and further steps in that direction only awaited judgement of the effects of the changes introduced in 1935.

Burma, annexed piecemeal by the British between 1826 and 1886, was reunited as a province of British India at the time of the third, and final, annexation on 1 January 1886. The 'march to Mandalay' had been almost bloodless, but with the fall of the monarchy serious resistance on a national scale broke out and imposed upon the British a long and heavy task of 'pacification'. Afterwards Burma remained quiescent for a long period. At the beginning of the twentieth century its administration was very much like that of any other Indian province, with a handful of British civil servants at the top directing the operations of a hierarchy of Asian subordinates, among whom Indians held many of the key posts and were thereby a source of dissatisfaction to Burmese opinion. The urge for modernisation and efficiency was beginning to make itself felt in a big expansion of governmental functions involving the creation of specialist departments, and transforming the older paternal system into a bureaucracy. Now, for the first time under British rule, the wind of change began to blow at village level, with the creation of a new system of local administration based upon the village, and the increasing interference in its daily life of officials of the central government. At the turn of the century a swing was in progress away from the monastic schools, once of fundamental importance in Burmese life, to lay education maintained or aided by government, and with an emphasis upon secondary and higher education in English. The consequent resentment of the Buddhist monks, and the failure of the British administration to maintain the royal patronage of the *Sangha* after Thibaw's deposition, were important factors in the decline of monastic discipline, which became serious in the 1920s, and in an upsurge of anti-British agitation by nationalist monks, especially in the villages.

National sentiment among laymen expressed itself in the Buddhist revivalism of the Young Men's Buddhist Association, founded in 1906, and an agitation some ten years later for the prohibition of shoe-wearing at pagodas and other sacred places. External observers, however, thought the Burmese politically apathetic, especially when the announcement by Edwin Montagu in 1917 of his plan for the development of responsible government in India evoked from the Burmese only a demand for separation from India. How mistaken they were was demonstrated dramatically by the sudden outburst of popular indignation in 1920 when Burma was not included in the Montagu–Chelmsford plan for establishing dyarchy in the Indian provinces. The discontent expressed itself most forcibly in a students' strike in the newly established University of Rangoon and in government and missionary schools throughout the country, and in the organisation of a system of 'national schools' under a Council of National Education. The British government hastened to extend dyarchy to Burma, and in 1923 she received a new Legislative Council of 103 members, 79 of whom were elected on a democratic franchise. To it was assigned control over the departments of Education, Public Health, Forests and Excise through ministers chosen from its elected members.

The national movement now grew rapidly. The extremists, taking Ireland as their model, advocated violent revolution. The General Council of Burmese Associations boycotted the first elections to the Legislative Council, and secret *Bu Athins* carried on intimidation and a no-tax campaign in the villages. The distress caused by the Great Depression in 1930 led to increasing violence. An anti-Indian movement resulted in sanguinary riots in 1930, and again in 1938. In December 1930 full-scale rebellion broke out in the rice-producing regions worst hit by the slump; it was led by an ex-monk proclaiming messianic prophecies once associated with the monarchy.

Nevertheless, within its limits dyarchy worked. The legislature had a solidly nationalist majority, with which it often embarrassed the government, but never jammed it; and there were moderates anxious to promote social welfare. Their insistent demands, however, were for immediate self-government and separation from India. But the struggles among rival factions for power made the period of dyarchy singularly barren in reform legislation. In 1937, when India achieved provincial autonomy, Burma achieved separation together with a bi-cameral parliament and cabinet government. So much additional power was transferred that, even allowing for the governor's 'reserve' powers, the new government had effectual control over practically the whole range of the internal affairs of Burma proper; the Shans, Kachins, Karens of the hills and Chins were excluded from the scheme. The nationalists were still unsatisfied, but, had it not been for the menace of war in Europe, and the growing danger from Japan in the Pacific, Burma might have gradually and unobtrusively achieved dominion status without any major change in the framework of her constitution. It is significant that the nationalist agitation was confined to the Burmans: the non-Burman minority peoples saw the British as their protectors against the threat of Burman dominance.

National pride gave the initial stimulus in the creation of French Indo-China. It began with the chauvinism of the Second Empire and continued as a reaction against the humiliation of the Franco-Prussian war. The French never felt quite the same sense of responsibility for the welfare of their subjects as the British and the Dutch. They were bent on exploiting the wealth of the region for the benefit of France. Next to that, but a long way behind, and largely through force of circumstances, came the desire to spread French culture. Any idea of training the natives for ultimate autonomy was utterly repellent. The royal houses of Annam, Cambodia and Laos were left with a semblance of authority, but all real power was in the hands of the French Governor-General, who was the head of a highly centralised administration.

There was a curious inconsistency about French policy; for, while few French officials spoke the languages or could appreciate the outlook of the people they governed, a comparatively small coterie of French oriental scholars in the Ecole français d'Extrême-Orient, established at Hanoi in 1899, carried out the most remarkable researches into the languages, customs, history and archaeology of Indo-China, to use the term in its widest possible application.

But against that undoubtedly great achievement must be set the ruin of the native land economy over large regions in order to promote French agricultural colonisation, and the creation of a rich landowner class exploiting the labour of an ignorant, apathetic peasantry. Under French rule Indo-China became, along with Siam and Burma, one of the largest rice-exporting areas of the world. It became the most profitable of all France's overseas possessions. But the wages of the great mass of the people remained pitifully low, and it is small wonder that Communism developed stronger roots in French Indo-China than anywhere else in South-East Asia.

The Vietnamese, with a Chinese civilisation, are the most advanced culturally of the peoples of the Indo-Chinese Union. Vietnamese nationalism began largely as the product of the French-vernacular schools established for the training of native subordinates. To counteract it the French injected stronger doses of French culture through the higher schools and the University of Hanoi. But the opposite effect took place, and it was commented that the bitterest opponents of the French were those who knew the language best. Thus, when in 1907 Paul Beau as a concession to nationalism founded the University of Hanoi, such an outburst of the disease it was intended to cure resulted that in the following year it was closed, and was not reopened until 1917. The French made the same mistake as the British in Burma of neglecting vernacular education. As early as 1910 an observer noted significantly that the 'curves of crime and European education rose concurrently'.

The Vietnamese nationalist movement became a serious embarrassment to the French after the first world war, when the educated official class was stirred alike by the Western doctrine of self-determination and the

Indian Swaraj movement. Communism also became a potent force, and by 1925 there was a revolutionary party, mainly composed of students who imbibed their Communism from the Cantonese. In 1930 and 1931 there were small nationalist and Communist risings in Tongking, which the French ruthlessly suppressed with hundreds of executions. For years the anti-French movement was driven underground and largely lost its effectiveness.

In 1938 Japan, having delivered China a series of staggering blows in her second great offensive, which had begun in July of the previous year, announced the 'New Order' in East Asia. As publicly proclaimed it had two facets, the one anti-Communist, the other anti-Western. Two years later, at the moment of German military triumph in western Europe, she announced the creation of a 'co-prosperity sphere', and invited the various countries of South-East Asia to participate in it. South-East Asia had by that time become, in the production of the food and raw materials required by modern technological civilisation, incomparably the richest region in the world for its size. Of all its parts Netherlands India was the one most coveted by Japan, but all her attempts to persuade the Dutch to participate in the co-prosperity plan failed, and Japan realised that only by war could she achieve her objective.

It is a fact of some significance that up to the time when she committed herself to her great southward offensive in 1941 Japan had failed to stimulate in South-East Asian countries anything of the nature of a nationalist rising against the Western powers. Nor were the Japanese campaigns materially assisted by the nationalist movements in the various countries which they overran: nowhere were they welcomed as liberators. There were collaborators such as Ir. Soekarno and Mohammad Hatta in Indonesia and Ba Maw and Aung San in Burma; but there were equally sincere nationalists, such as the Sumatrans Amir Sjariffoedin and Soetan Sjahrir, who would have nothing whatever to do with the Japanese. The great mass of the people saw the tide of conquest roll over them with a sort of bewildered helplessness.

The astounding rapidity and ease with which the Japanese overran South-East Asia caused the Western powers a loss of prestige that was in many ways decisive. But it was not long before Japanese arrogance and brutality, and still more their ruthless exploitation of native manpower and economic resources, made them feared and detested. Everywhere resistance groups sprang up, often led by European officers left behind by the retreating armies or parachuted into the various countries. During the counter-invasion of 1945 the Burma National Army, largely organised by the Japanese, went over to the Allies and played a useful part in harrying the retreating Japanese.

The capitulation of the Japanese in August 1945 came so suddenly that in two regions where the Allied armies were not operating, French Indo-

China and Dutch Indonesia, there was a hiatus before Allied occupation could be carried out, and nationalist movements seized control, largely with Japanese assistance. Ho Chi-minh and his followers gained control over the puppet Annamite government, the emperor Bao Dai abdicated and the Republic of Vietnam was proclaimed. In Indonesia there was an unavoidable delay of over a month after the Japanese surrender before South-East Asia Command could begin the occupation of Java. Moreover, the Netherlands had been so recently freed from German occupation that the home government was unprepared to deal with the situation created by the sudden Japanese collapse. The way was open therefore for Soekarno, supported by Sjahrir and Hatta, to proclaim the Indonesian Republic. Neither France nor the Netherlands would recognise the authority of the new revolutionary governments in their pre-war empires, and both made preparations to regain as much as possible of their lost power.

In Burma and Malaya the British were welcomed as liberators and within a very few weeks were able to restore civil government. In both countries, however, the experiences of the war years had created a new political atmosphere. In Burma the British plan was to carry out rehabilitation measures for a short period under direct rule before restoring the constitution of 1937. Then elections for a constituent assembly were to be held, and the Burmese were to draft their own constitution as a self-governing dominion of the British Commonwealth. But Aung San, the commander of the National Army, and his associates of the *Dobama Asiayone* ('We Burmans Association'), demanded immediate complete independence. They had organised the nation-wide Anti-Fascist Peoples Freedom League and made it the focus of nationalist aspirations. Their experience of Japanese rule and of the 'independence' granted by Japan to Burma on 1 August 1943 had sharpened their desire for real independence, and they wanted to prevent foreign business interests from regaining their old position in the national economy. They effectively opposed every ministry formed by the British governor after the restoration of civil government, as well as British attempts to restore order and promote economic recovery. Accordingly in October 1946 Governor Sir Hubert Rance accepted their demand for an AFPFL-dominated Council of Ministers with Aung San as its leader. In the following January Aung San reached agreement in London with Mr Attlee's Labour government whereby his ministry was given full control over internal affairs, and Britain pledged herself to accept the verdict of a general election to be held in April 1947 to determine the form of self-government.

The most urgent question was the fierce opposition of the non-Burman peoples—the Shans, Kachins, Karens and Chins—against any arrangement involving Burman supremacy. The Aung San–Attlee agreement contained a proviso safeguarding their rights, and immediately after returning to Burma Aung San started negotiations which ultimately secured their agreement to the terms on which they would join the proposed Union of Burma; and these were duly written into the constitution. The Karens, however, stood out and demanded a separate state under British protection. But the fact that the great majority of them lived in Burma proper, forming a minority in every district where they were settled, made their demand quite impracticable, and Britain had—sadly—to reject it. This was one of Burma's unsolved problems when in July 1947 Aung San and most of his cabinet were murdered by the hired assassins of a political rival. Sir Hubert Rance at once nominated Aung San's close friend U Nu to the premiership, and it was with him that the British government negotiated the treaty by which on 4 January 1948 the Union of Burma became a sovereign independent state. Burma elected to become a republic outside the British Commonwealth. Thus at the outset did she manifest the isolationism which later came to dominate her policy.

Malay national sentiment realised itself as a political force for the first time during the war, and its rallying cry, 'Malaya for the Malays', became directed, after the Japanese departure, against the Chinese. British policy was to bring to an end the particularism of the individual states, which had facilitated the Japanese victory, and accordingly in 1946 all nine Malay states together with Penang and Malacca were joined to form the Malayan Union. The free port of Singapore with its preponderatingly Chinese population was excluded. With it Chinese would have outnumbered Malays in the Union. Moreover, the new union depended upon customs duties for most of its revenue. The Union was seen as a first step towards Malayan independence; but the transfer of sovereignty from the sultans to Britain and the generous citizenship rules for non-Malays caused so strong a Malay reaction that Britain yielded to their clamour. In 1948 a Federation took the place of the Union, the sultans regained their former powers, and the citizenship rules for non-Malays were stiffened up.

The anti-Chinese attitude of the Malays was an important factor in the Chinese-led Communist insurrection which began in 1948, and, though never with the faintest hope of success, caused the British authorities acute embarrassment and immense effort over a matter of years. It did not, however, adversely affect Malaya's constitutional progress, which was faster than that of any other colonial territory up to that time. Exactly how rapid was the transfer of power may be gauged from the following facts: Malaya's first general election was held only in 1955, and its Legislative Council then received its first elected majority; full independence within the British Commonwealth came on 31 August 1957. This would have been impossible but for the growth of co-operation in the national interest between its two major racial parties, the United Malays National Organization (UMNO) and the Malayan Chinese Association (MCA).

Singapore's progress towards independence was less rapid. Her strategic importance and the strength of her Communist front were factors militating against a complete transfer of power. It was only when, under Lim Yew Hock's leadership, firm action was taken against left-wing violence and subversion that the British government felt itself able to concede almost complete self-government, in June 1959, subject to special security measures. The leftist People's Action Party won the first general election. Its leader Lee Kuan-yew proved more than a match for the Communists. A realist in his assessment of Singapore's economic and strategic position, he became an ardent promoter of the island's reunion with Malaya.

To complete the story of the disappearance of the colonial régimes from South-East Asia one must turn now from the territories under British rule to those of the United States, the Netherlands and France. The Philippines was the first country in all South-East Asia to achieve independence, when the United States granted it in July 1946 in accordance with the promise made when the Tydings–McDuffie Commonwealth Act was passed in 1934. In Indonesia there was a long and cruel struggle between the Dutch and the Indonesian Republic proclaimed in August 1945. World opinion turned heavily against the Dutch when they began the first of what they termed 'police actions'. The intervention of the United Nations Security Council at the instance of India and Australia, and its creation of a Good Offices Committee to supervise the situation and promote negotiations, was an important cause of the failure of the Dutch attempt at a solution by force. In December 1949 the Netherlands and Indonesia reached an agreement whereby the latter's independence was established.

It was Vietnam's tragedy that her struggle for independence against France came under Communist direction, for after the Communist triumph in China late in 1949 it became merged in America's crusade against world Communism. When it became obvious that they could not crush Ho Chi-minh and the Viet Minh and its 'Democratic Republic of Vietnam', the French sought to build up the ex-Emperor Bao Dai as the national leader; but everyone knew that he was their puppet, whereas Ho Chi-minh was successfully challenging France. The recognition of his régime by China and the Soviet bloc was countered by the recognition of Bao Dai's by the United States and the powers associated with her; and American aid began to flow into Vietnam, via Paris. But as America became more and more committed to the struggle, particularly after the termination of the Korean war, France's effort began to flag before the determination and skilful generalship of the Viet Minh. It had little support from the Vietnamese, and became increasingly unpopular at home. American aid, however, mounted and with it pressure for a military decision. Hence the 'Navarre Plan', which came to grief in the disaster at Dien Bien Phu in May 1954. The French were outgeneralled in the operations leading up to it, but even more important was the material aid given by China. Her concern was rather over the security of her frontiers than over the interests of Vietnamese Communism. But the danger of the outbreak of another world war was now acute, with America ready with massive support for the French. Happily the forces pressing for a negotiated settlement prevailed, and in July under the joint chairmanship of Britain and Russia armistice agreements were signed at Geneva. Vietnam was provisionally partitioned at the 17th parallel of latitude with the Democratic Republic in control of the north and the Saigon régime, nominally headed by Bao Dai, in control of the south. It was provided that elections under international supervision were to be held in July 1956 to decide on the form of reunification. France withdrew from Indo-China, and the independence of the kingdoms of Cambodia and Laos became something more than a political formula. The elections were never held.

CHAPTER XII

CHINA, JAPAN AND THE PACIFIC 1900–1931

AT the beginning of the twentieth century, the countries of the Far East and the Pacific were regarded by the West from the standpoint of imperialism. Economically, they were important to it as sources of raw materials, fields of investment, and markets for manufactured goods. Politically, their relations with Western powers were conducted on terms of inequality. Some countries—especially China—had been compelled to grant the powers concessions in relation to trade and investment and jurisdiction in respect of the latters' nationals residing within their boundaries. Others had become colonies or protectorates. Even Australia, which became a federal Commonwealth in 1901, and New Zealand were not exceptions to the general situation. As high-income countries with predominantly European populations, they occupied advantageous positions within the framework of imperialism; but, though they possessed responsible government, they were subject to British control of their external relations. Japan alone had reached a stage at which the Western powers were beginning to treat her as a full member of the community of nations.

The international standing of Japan had been attained over a remarkably short period. Till the 1850s the country had maintained, for over two hundred years, a policy of seclusion mitigated only by limited contacts with the Chinese and the Dutch. But, within less than fifty years of its enforced entry into treaty relations with the Western powers, it had carried through a programme of political modernisation unequalled elsewhere in Asia. This adaptation to the circumstances of the new age was facilitated by the characteristics of Japanese social and political structure. Like Britain, Japan was an island country in proximity to a highly civilised continent. As such, it had been able to draw upon the cultural heritage of China, and at the same time, to develop a sense of its own distinctive identity. In these circumstances, the survival of clan loyalties had not prevented the early emergence of a unified system of government, though it had provided opportunities for the exercise of regional initiative. The political structure centred upon the Shogun and, through him, nominally upon the emperor, was an oligarchic one. Responsibility was diffused among the members of privileged groups; and decisions were reached by discussion and negotiation. This type of structure had encouraged the development of bureaucratic procedures and of a relationship between government and governed defined in terms of law and custom, rather than in those of personal authority. It had also provided channels for the

329

examination of proposed reforms and for their implementation by evolutionary means.

For more than half a century before the opening of diplomatic relations with the Western powers, groups within the Japanese *élite* had been discussing the need for political changes. The time was ripe for reform; and the action of the powers precipitated it. The office of Shogun, whose holder had for centuries exercised the powers of the emperor, was brought into disrepute by the humiliation inflicted by the West. But the motives of its antagonists were mixed. They were moved both by ambitions of a traditional order—rivalry towards the Tokugawa clan, which controlled the office of Shogun—and by their attitudes towards the West. Though some resented the inability of the Shogun to resist Western demands and others recognised that Japan's future was dependent on its adoption of Western methods, their differing lines of thought converged at the level of political action. In 1867, following the accession of a new emperor and a new Shogun, a demand was successfully made for the return to the imperial office of its full powers. In practice, this made the emperor dependent on those who had engineered the restoration.

During the succeeding thirty years the structure of the Japanese state was drastically reorganised. Feudal rights were terminated; a national army was formed; a uniform and comprehensive legal system was introduced; primary education was made compulsory; and a land tax was imposed to provide the government with an adequate revenue. In determining the character of these reforms, the Japanese government drew selectively upon the experience of the West. Contemporary developments in Germany were considered to be of special relevance. In particular, they provided a model for the constitution given to the country, in the name of the emperor, in 1889. This created a parliament, but limited its functions in relation both to legislation and to control of finance and denied it power to appoint or dismiss the cabinet. Through these changes, and a complementary reorganisation of administrative structure and procedure, Japan gained an efficient system of government in which a preponderant authority rested with the executive. Since the programme of reform was carried out as a consequence of the nominal restoration of the imperial power, it could not be questioned on grounds of legitimacy. On the other hand, by the establishment of a parliament and in other ways, it sought to satisfy the aspirations of those who had responded to the stimulus of contact with the West. Japan's resounding victory over China in the war of 1894-5 provided the Western powers with conclusive evidence of the success of the reorganisation.

Japanese policy had been one of enlightened conservatism. It had therefore been pragmatic, leaving virtually untouched those elements in the older social and political structure that presented no challenge to the new objectives. At the village level, for example, where government impinged most closely on the day-to-day activities of the conservative masses, local administration was little changed. And in other fields, where change was a matter of gradual evolution, rather than statutory enactment, traditional forms of organisation survived.

In the economic sphere, a framework for modernisation had been created by the establishment of capitalistic institutions. But, at the turn of the century, the impact of new industries and technology from the West remained limited. The great majority of Japanese still worked in agriculture, the production of handicrafts and fishing. Even in such areas of modern industry as existed, the introduction of new technical methods was more striking than any increase in the scale of operation. Cotton spinning was the main exception, with the emergence of large-scale factories in the 1890s; and there were as well several large government factories for military supplies, especially the arsenals at Tokyo and Osaka. In silk, power-driven filatures now accounted for half the production, although this was carried out in small establishments. Small-scale factory production also existed in such industries as cement, glass, beer and paper. In heavy industry development was meagre. Production of pig-iron amounted to some 25,000 tons, and practically the entire steel demand, which was only about a quarter of a million tons, was met from abroad. Similarly engineering and shipbuilding were on a very small scale, while coal output, although rising rapidly, was still only five million tons in 1895. The extent of the transformation in the economy is difficult to measure; but it seems that within manufacturing, where modern developments had probably gone furthest, something like three times as many found employment in the home as in the factory, and of course most factories were small and a far cry from modern Western establishments.

The effects of modernisation on the structure of the economy were by then beginning to be felt in the changing commodity composition of Japanese foreign trade. Raw silk was still the major export, but silk and cotton textiles and coal were rapidly increasing in importance. The development of the cotton textile industry began to show its effect on imports through the decline in importance of cotton fibres and yarns and the growth of raw cotton to some 20 per cent of total imports. Sugar and iron and steel products were other prominent imports. The opening of Japan to the West and the influence of foreign trade after the 1850s were the main causes of change in the Japanese economy, yet the reciprocal effect, that of Japan's entry into the international economy on world trading patterns, remained slight. Although by the end of the 'nineties foreign trade had risen in value to about a quarter of national income, it was still only some 6 per cent of Britain's trade; and only in silk was Japan a world trader on an important scale. An important limiting factor on the growth of foreign trade had been the almost inflexible suspicion of the Japanese government towards the importation of foreign capital, so that imports were limited in value by earnings from exports and whatever specie Japan could supply.

By 1900 Japan had created a basis for the conduct of political and economic relations with the Western nations on terms of equality. Her position was, in some respects, still a relatively weak or precarious one; but, economically as well as politically, the essential breakthrough was being achieved. Like China, she had been compelled in her original treaties with the powers to grant them extra-territorial rights and to accept a limitation on the customs duties she could impose on their products. In 1899 extra-territoriality was finally abolished and tariff autonomy virtually attained. Two years earlier she had joined the rest of the trading community on the gold standard and had begun overseas borrowing on a large scale. More generally, the strength of Japan's international position was a product not only of her external policies—diplomatic and military—but also of the recognition by the powers of the success of her internal reorganisation.

The position of China in 1900 was, on the contrary, the cumulative product of a succession of failures and defeats. In terms of domestic political structure, China had been for many centuries the largest country in the world subjected to the effective control of a single centralised administration. In those of external relations, her predominance in eastern Asia had been so great that she had recognised other states not as equals but only as tributaries. This heritage had, in itself, greatly complicated the task of adaptation to the conditions created by the expansion of the West. The government of China was cumbrous, slow to accept the need for change in either its principles or its procedures. The port cities on the coast and on the great rivers which were frequented by foreign merchants were distant from the capital at Peking. The scope and character of the threat to the ancient political order was not readily understood by those who alone had the power to take major decisions. The need to adopt a system of external relations based on the western concept of sovereignty was neither accepted nor even recognised.

The effect of the inherent restraints upon adaptation was intensified by the particular condition of the Chinese political system in the nineteenth century. The country was passing through a period of dynastic decline. The civil service was deeply penetrated by corruption. The Manchu garrisons, which were responsible for the maintenance of security, had lost most of their military prowess. The southern provinces were disaffected. Because of these circumstances, and because the dynasty itself was of alien Manchu origin, conformity with established conventions attained an overriding importance. In establishing themselves as rulers, the Manchus had become patrons and inflexible defenders of traditional Chinese culture. During their decline, they came to look upon sympathy towards innovation with increasing suspicion. The government service was dominated by men of unquestionable orthodoxy.

In these circumstances, the process of Western expansion in China was characterised by determined aggression, on the one side, and fumbling resistance, on the other. Agents of the West—primarily merchants, naval commanders and diplomats—took the initiative in ways that were sanctioned by the conventions of their own cultures; and many Chinese took advantage of the opportunities that their activities opened up. At each stage, resistance (or reluctance in collaboration) by the government of China was made the occasion for the presentation of further demands, to which the government, after a display of force by the Western powers, was compelled to agree. The scope of Western encroachment was limited only by the anxiety of the powers not to precipitate a complete breakdown of political order in China or, towards the end of the century, by their suspicion of each other's ambitions.

The difficulties of foreign merchants at Canton led to war between Britain and China in 1839 and the subsequent British victory to the signature of a group of treaties under which the powers gained their first substantial privileges. Five ports were opened to foreign trade; a customs tariff and a code of trade regulations were agreed on; and extra-territorial rights were granted to foreign residents. In addition, Britain obtained the cession of Hong Kong. As a result of these concessions, the foreign communities in the treaty ports developed into autonomous settlements completely removed from the jurisdiction of the government of China and providing a location for the establishment of modern commercial and industrial ventures. When the Chinese refused to discuss the extension of Western privileges in the 1850s, war was again resorted to; and new treaties were forced upon them. The number of open ports was greatly increased; the Yangtze river was opened to trade; and customs duties, which had already begun to be administered by a foreign-controlled customs service, were limited to 5 per cent *ad valorem*. By 1860 China was almost completely at the mercy of its Western invaders.

Thirty-five years later the Sino-Japanese war precipitated a further stage in China's collapse. Already the relationship between China and some of its former tributary states had been severed; and the country's northern frontiers had been encroached upon by Russia. In 1895 the terms imposed by Japan included a renunciation of Chinese suzerainty over Korea and the cession of Formosa. Japan's success was followed by a spate of fresh demands from the Western powers. Britain, France, Germany and Russia engaged in a scramble for concessions. Leaseholds were obtained over strategically or economically important areas; monopoly rights for the building of railways and the exploitation of minerals were conceded; and broad 'spheres of interest' were recognised. Within these latter, a particular power gained a prior claim to future concessions and an assurance that monopoly rights or leased territories would not be obtained by its rivals. The powers—including Japan—were preparing for the partition of China.

The modernisation of the Chinese economy in response to the opening of the country to Western influence remained slight. Until 1895 industrial change was almost negligible, and there were only several hundred miles of railways. The vast majority of Chinese still obtained their living from traditional occupations centred on agriculture. The government, which was unconcerned with the development of a modern economy, had borrowed only some £13 million up to 1894; and direct foreign investment was confined mainly to fields connected with trade, such as shipping, insurance and banking, and, to a small extent, to the illegal establishment of manufacturing in the treaty ports. Trade was the main avenue of Western economic influence. In value it was not large and totalled only about £50 million in the middle 'nineties. Exports were dominated by products of the traditional sector, especially tea, raw silk and silk goods, which still made up over half the total value in the 1890s. In the same years, opium still accounted for between 15 and 20 per cent of imports, but cotton products (both goods and yarn), which made up some 35 per cent of the total, had become the largest item. Though exact figures are unobtainable, it seems that during the nineteenth century Britain had by far the largest share of Chinese foreign trade. By 1900 Japan was challenging this position. But the British Empire as a whole still supplied almost half of China's imports and took about a quarter of its exports.

Economically therefore, as well as politically, China remained a classical field for the satisfaction of imperialist aspirations. The fact that it had not been subjected to the final ignominy of colonial rule owed little, if anything, to memories of its former grandeur and nothing to its present strength. To some small extent, its survival had been assisted by the American 'open door' policy, directed towards the maintenance of equality of commercial opportunity for the nationals of all the powers. But, fundamentally, it had maintained its nominal independence because none of the powers was willing to press its demands to the point at which it might have found itself at war with its rivals.

In the island groups of the Pacific, scattered over a vast area of ocean to the south-eastward of China and Japan, the powers had not been obliged to observe a similar restraint. In terms either of existing agricultural production or of known deposits of minerals, the islands were of limited value, though they were of importance to influential groups of merchants and investors in several Western countries. Strategically, some islands with good harbours were highly regarded as possible naval bases or coaling stations, and the groups nearest to the British dependencies in Australia and New Zealand had long been looked on with anxiety by the colonists, lest they should come under the control of an unfriendly power. The actual extension of political control was a consequence, in part, of arguments relating to their economic and strategic value. But, in part also, it was a result of circumstances of a different kind. In many island groups the activities of Europeans and Americans, as traders, planters, and labour recruiters, had made the establishment of a colonial form of government a prerequisite to the restoration of law and order. International rivalry in relation to the islands was not of sufficient importance to make it a likely cause of war.

By 1890 a substantial proportion of the major islands and island groups had been acquired by one or other of the powers. Fiji and south-eastern New Guinea were British colonies; New Caledonia and a number of archipelagos centred on Tahiti were French; north-eastern New Guinea, the northern Solomons and the Marshall Islands were German; and western New Guinea was part of the Netherlands East Indies. During the 1890s the process of partition was carried almost to completion. The territories annexed by the United States and Germany at this period were later of some significance in world politics. The former acquired Hawaii, Guam and eastern Samoa and the latter the Caroline Islands, the Marianas (apart from Guam) and western Samoa. Together with the American acquisition of the Philippines and with the new German concessions in China, these developments greatly enhanced the stake of both powers in Pacific affairs.

The period between 1900 and the outbreak of the first world war saw the completion of changes that had begun during the nineteenth century: the final collapse of imperial China; the full acceptance of Japan as a major power; and, with the agreement of 1906 making the New Hebrides an Anglo-French condominium, the settlement of the only remaining issue of political control in Oceania.

In 1900 a series of developments in the politics of the Far East was precipitated by a fresh manifestation of Chinese disorder. In May of that year adherents of an anti-Western sect, the Boxers, began destroying telegraph lines and damaging railways in north China. In June they entered Peking, where they massacred Chinese Christians, molested foreigners and attacked the legations. The Boxers had always been regarded as patriots, rather than rebels, by a section of the Chinese court and administration. When British forces set out from the treaty port of Tientsin to protect the legations and foreign nationals from Boxer aggression, they were opposed by imperial troops. When they captured the forts commanding the seaward approach to Tientsin, China declared war on the powers. This was the blind triumph of reaction, the decision of men—and of a woman, the empress dowager—whose judgement had been impaired by the humiliations that the West had inflicted on the old order in China. The viceroys of south China and the governor of Shantung, Yüan Shik-k'ai, promptly decided to suppress the war edict and maintain neutrality. In August an allied force entered Peking almost unopposed, and the court fled from the capital (above, ch. v).

A year later a peace protocol was signed. China was compelled to punish those responsible for the insurrection, to apologise for the murders of the German Minister and the Chancellor of the Japanese legation, and to permit the foreign occupation of the route between Peking and the sea. Some administrative changes were required; and a heavy indemnity was imposed.

The Boxer rising had, however, more far-reaching repercussions. Though the powers had acted together in suppressing it, they had done so in an atmosphere of increasing mutual suspicion. Throughout the joint action, they had been as much concerned with the advancement of their future national interests as with the solution of their immediate common problem. Moves by Russia in support of its position in Manchuria had, in particular, aroused the fears of the other powers.

Russian interests in Manchuria were centred upon the Chinese Eastern Railway. In addition, Russians were engaged in banking, coal-mining and shipping, and in administrative and trading functions associated with the construction and operation of the railway.[1] During June 1900 Boxer bands became active in Manchuria, and in July the government of China ordered its military forces to unite with them. Russia retaliated by obtaining the co-operation of the provincial governors and by bringing in troops. The result was a Russian military occupation of Manchuria, which was maintained after peace had been restored with China.

Russia's retention of the position it had gained during the period of disorder was, in itself, a threat to the interests of other powers. But it was interpreted by them in a broader context: by Japan in relation to its own increasing stake in Korea; by Britain in relation to Russian ambitions further west (particularly in Persia); and by them all in relation to Russia's intention, which had been evident throughout the Boxer incident, to play a lone hand in its dealings with China. In none of the countries concerned—including Russia—was the structure of politics monolithic: different groups favoured different policies. And the situation was one in which a number of alternative lines of policy seemed possible. In Japan there was support for an agreement with Russia, whereby the former would gain a free hand in Korea in return for its acceptance of the primacy of the latter's interests in Manchuria. In Britain it seemed to many that an agreement with Germany would provide the most effective support for the country's Far Eastern interests. But, in the event, the action that was taken by these two powers was the formation of the Anglo-Japanese Alliance of 1902.

Circumstances favoured such a move. During recent years, relations between the British and Japanese governments had been notably friendly, and significant elements in the public of both countries had expressed support for a closer association. None the less, both governments were

[1] Andrew Malozemoff, *Russian Far Eastern Policy, 1881–1904* (Berkeley and Los Angeles, 1958), pp. 124–76.

compelled to move with caution. Each would expose itself to domestic attack if it replaced the advantages of non-alignment by a commitment to joint military action without receiving adequate compensation. In the early discussions, the Japanese sought a formal recognition of their country's paramount interests in Korea and the British an extension of the terms of the proposed alliance to include the defence of India. But Britain was unwilling to be automatically involved in a war over Korea and Japan to accept commitments beyond the Far East. On the issue of limitation to the Far East, Britain gave way. In relation to Korea, a solution was found in the careful wording of the treaty. The two powers declared that they recognised the independence of China and Korea and had no aggressive intentions in relation to either country. On the other hand, they recognised that both possessed 'special interests' in China and that Japan was 'interested in a peculiar degree politically as well as commercially and industrially' in Korea. It would 'be admissible for either of them. . . to safeguard those interests if threatened either by the aggressive action of any other Power, or by disturbances arising' in China or Korea. If either party should become involved in war with a third power in the course of safeguarding its interests, the other should come to its aid only in the event of its enemy being joined by another power. The treaty was signed on 30 January 1902.[1] It was supplemented by an exchange of diplomatic notes. In these notes each power agreed to the use of its ports in time of peace by the naval vessels of the other and undertook 'to maintain, so far as may be possible, available for concentration in the waters of the Extreme East a naval force superior to that of any third Power'.[2] These provisions were of particular importance to Britain because of her worldwide commitments. But, since the notes were kept secret, they were necessarily excluded from the ensuing public explanations of the alliance.

In Britain, the alliance was justified by the government mainly on the ground that it stabilised the situation in the Far East. In addition to ensuring co-operation between Britain and Japan, it removed the risk that the latter might make an agreement with Russia to the detriment of the other powers. But in some quarters it was argued that it increased the danger of Britain's involvement in war and that Japan received far greater benefits than Britain. The latter point was, indeed, not without substance. The alliance placed Japan in a position to deal firmly with Russia, since it was now unlikely that other powers could come to Russia's aid if war should break out. The British navy—as a deterrent to potential antagonists or, if the worst should happen, as the active partner of the Japanese fleet—

[1] On the Anglo-Japanese alliance, see Ian H. Nish, *The Anglo-Japanese Alliance: The Diplomacy of Two Island Empires, 1894–1907* (London, 1966). For the text of the treaty of 1902, and a note on the treaties of 1905 and 1911, see John V. A. MacMurray (ed.), *Treaties and Agreements with and concerning China, 1894–1919* (2 vols. New York, 1921), vol. I, pp. 324–6.
[2] Nish, *Anglo-Japanese Alliance*, pp. 217–18.

provided the basis for a new sense of security. More generally, the alliance marked Japan's acceptance as a first-class power. For these reasons, news of its establishment was received in Japan with great enthusiasm.

For a time it appeared as if British hopes of stability in the Far East would be realised. Russia agreed to withdraw her troops from Manchuria. But, after the first stage of that operation had been carried out, Russian policy seemed to change. The remaining troops were not moved; and increased attention was given to the development of concessions both in Manchuria and in Korea. In fact, the changed character of Russian action seems to have reflected the uncertain balance of influence within the central government, rather than a firm decision to strengthen the country's position in the Far East.[1] But this was not evident to outsiders. Moreover, in a region where government was notoriously weak, the dividing line between the pursuit of economic interest and of political and military domination was not easy to define. The Japanese saw the situation as one that demanded a firm assertion of their own interests.

In June 1903 Japan decided to seek an agreement with Russia regarding their respective positions in China and Korea. The character of the proposals that were submitted in August was affected not only by the existence of the Anglo-Japanese Alliance but also by recent changes in Japanese politics. Although all the survivors of the 'elder statesmen' who had engineered the Meiji restoration of 1868 still occupied positions of influence within the government, the member of the group who was predominant at this period, Yamagata Aritomo, was the most authoritarian and aggressive of their number. He had engineered a change by which eligibility for appointment as minister for war or for the navy was restricted to serving officers of high rank; and, by his hostility to political parties, he had precipitated a decline in the vigour of parliamentary opposition to the executive. As a result, the Japanese terms for a settlement were severe ones. Russian recognition of Japan's 'preponderant interests' in Korea was to be unqualified, while Japan's reciprocal recognition of Russian interests in Manchuria was to be limited in ways that would not preclude the development of the Japanese position there. Negotiations continued for some months; but by January 1904 both countries realised that an impasse had been reached and were preparing for war.

Early in February the Japanese broke off diplomatic relations with Russia, landed troops in Korea, and attacked Russian naval vessels at Port Arthur, in the leasehold territory of the Liaotung peninsula, in southern Manchuria. These actions were immediately followed by the issuing of declarations of war by both Russia and Japan. In the ensuing fighting Japanese forces occupied the principal Russian centres in Manchuria and virtually destroyed the Russian Baltic fleet, which had been sent to the Far East in an attempt to destroy Japanese naval predominance.

[1] Malozemoff, *Russian Far Eastern Policy, 1881–1904*, pp. 177–249.

After their resounding naval victory, the Japanese proposed to President Theodore Roosevelt that he should invite the two powers to meet to discuss terms of peace. The President agreed to take this initiative; and a peace conference was held at Portsmouth, New Hampshire, in August and September 1905. While it was in progress, Japan's position was further strengthened by the publication of a revised Anglo-Japanese treaty, which extended the scope of the alliance to include the defence of British interests in India and gave more explicit recognition to Japanese hegemony in Korea. By the Treaty of Portsmouth, Japan gained Russian recognition of her paramount position in Korea, the transfer to her of the Russian lease-hold and railway in southern Manchuria (subject to the approval of China, which was readily given), and the cession of the southern half of the island of Sakhalin.[1] The terms of the treaty, and the military victory that lay behind them, confirmed Japan's position as a major power. But, in the long run, these developments were of greater importance in another way. They established Japan as a power with extensive interests on the mainland of Asia. Moreover, as Japan had hoped for even greater Russian concessions, they left the country—and especially its increasingly influential military group—with a sense of grievance. The Russo-Japanese war provided the foundations upon which later Japanese imperialism was based.

During the following years Japan consolidated her position in both Korea and Manchuria. In relation to Korea, where the interests of the other powers were small, the problems to be resolved soon became quasi-domestic ones. In Japan itself there were differences of opinion as to how full control should be established, and in Korea there was opposition to Japanese domination; but, once the powers had accepted the implications of Japanese hegemony, there was little external objection to Japan's decisions. In November 1905 Korea became a protectorate: Japan obtained control of the country's external relations and, in the following year, appointed a Resident-General at Seoul. In 1907, after the abdication of the king, Japan assumed control of domestic affairs. In 1910 the country was annexed.[2]

The Japanese position in Manchuria was a more difficult one. A Governor-General was appointed to the leased territory; and a corporation, in which half the capital was held by the government, was formed to control the railway and engage in a wide variety of other functions, including mining. Japan had obtained further rights from China when seeking agreement to the transfer of the Russian concessions; and, gradually, co-operation

---

[1] Payson J. Treat, *Diplomatic Relations between the United States and Japan, 1895–1905* (Stanford University, 1938), pp. 242–8; Edward H. Zabriskie, *American–Russian Rivalry in the Far East: A Study in Diplomacy and Power Politics, 1895–1914* (Philadelphia, 1946), pp. 115–30. For the text of the treaty, see MacMurray, *Treaties and Agreements*, vol. I, pp. 522–8.
[2] Hilary Conroy, *The Japanese Seizure of Korea: 1868–1910* (Philadelphia, [1960]), pp. 325–441.

between Japan and Russia in the development of their respective spheres of influence became closer. Under these conditions, Japanese investment rapidly increased. But Manchuria, unlike Korea, was a region of considerable interest to investors in other countries. In particular, British and American groups concerned with the building of railways obtained concessions from China that the Japanese considered to be in contravention of their own special rights. The antagonism generated by these moves led to nothing more serious for Japan than the reassertion by America of its 'open door' policy. But even this represented a challenge, and a potential danger, to Japanese imperialism.

As in the opening years of the century, the weakness of China remained a major source of trouble. The government, unable to defend the country's rights directly, saw advantage in stimulating dissension among those who sought to increase their encroachments upon them. But, though action of this kind may have somewhat reduced the scale of foreign investment, it did not affect the internal forces that were slowly bringing about the final collapse of the imperial régime.

After the Boxer rising, the autonomy of the provincial governments became more firmly entrenched. Where there was effective leadership, the provinces reorganised their local armies, improved communications, promoted industrial development, and established modern schools. Provincial leaders regarded this work as important not only in itself but also as constituting the only practical defence against foreign domination. Attempts to restore central control therefore encountered provincial opposition.

The central government was impeded no less, however, by factors that affected its operation even more directly: lack of finance; an inefficient and demoralised civil service; and—till her death in 1908—the baneful influence of the empress dowager, reactionary, jealous and intriguing. Partly for these reasons, even the more carefully planned and directed of government activities failed to achieve the expected results. The formation of a modern army led to an attack on the position of its organiser and commander, Yüan Shih-k'ai, by the empress dowager. The establishment of a constituent assembly, in preparation for the introduction of representative government, provided a forum from which its members launched a comprehensive attack on government policies. The decision to develop a national railway system precipitated the downfall of the empire itself, because its implementation both entrenched upon provincial interests and was to be financed by a foreign loan.

In 1911 an uprising against the central government occurred in the province of Szechwan, in the Yangtze valley, provoked by the railway scheme. This provided an opening for men whose political objectives were far more radical than those of the provincial leaders. In the treaty ports and overseas, younger Chinese had gained an appreciation of the political ideology of the West and developed a programme for reorganising China as a modern state able, like Japan, to handle its relations with the Western powers on terms of equality. Under the leadership of Sun Yat-sen, they had formed an organisation, the *T'ung-meng-hui*, to promote the realisation of their plans. This organisation was in touch, through the secret societies, with the rural population and, through army officers who had trained overseas, with the provincial governments. In 1911 the *T'ung-meng-hui* was prepared for risings in the provinces of the Yangtze valley. An explosion in a house at Wuhan where members were making bombs resulted in a police search that found evidence incriminating local army officers. These men forced their commander to lead an uprising against the dynasty. The rebellion quickly spread to other parts of central and southern China; and, on Sun Yat-sen's return from an overseas trip in December, he was elected president of a republican government.

The imperial government reacted to these moves by inviting Yüan Shih-k'ai to return to its service and lead the northern armies against the rebels. Yüan quickly achieved military victory; but he used it not to restore the imperial power but to reach agreement with the revolutionary leaders. In return for his undertaking to procure the abdication of the Manchu dynasty, which he accomplished, he was made president of the republican government, in place of Sun Yat-sen.

The new régime possessed an obvious source of strength, as an alliance between China's most experienced military leader and the revolutionary movement. But its weaknesses were both numerous and prospectively destructive. Yüan had no alternative to confirming the appointments of all those who held office at a provincial or regional level at the time of his own assumption of power. More importantly, his aims and those of the revolutionaries were markedly divergent; and the latter were seriously divided among themselves. Yüan was an authoritarian, who saw himself as the founder of a new dynasty. Sun Yat-sen and his personal supporters favoured a form of revolutionary totalitarianism. But another section of the *T'ung-meng-hui*, led by Sung Chiao-jen, wished to see China adopt the British system of parliamentary government. In pursuit of this objective, Sung persuaded several other revolutionary groups to join with the *T'ung-meng-hui* in forming a political party, the Kuomintang. The new government was adhering to the intention of its predecessor that an election should be held and a parliament be constituted in 1913. When it met, the Kuomintang, which had secured the election of the largest group of members, sought to obtain a constitution in which executive power would be vested in a prime minister and cabinet responsible to parliament. This objective conflicted directly with Yüan Shih-k'ai's quest for personal supremacy. Before parliament met, he had arranged the assassination of Sung Chiao-jen. Now, he declared the Kuomintang illegal and dissolved parliament.

Superficially, Yüan Shih-k'ai was well on the way towards the satisfaction of his ambition. In addition to destroying overt political opposition, he had obtained financial assistance from the powers. He proceeded to have a constitution drafted which concentrated authority in the hands of the president, and he had himself elected to this office for life. But, at a deeper level, most of the basic sources of weakness remained. The revolutionary movement still continued to work for a modernised China. The provinces still opposed the authority of Peking. The powers and their nationals still retained the privileges that had cut so deeply into Chinese autonomy. China had gained a new régime, but it still lacked a viable system of government.

The first world war, and the subsequent peace settlement, profoundly changed the political situation in the Far East and had a significant, though much more limited, effect upon the islands to the south. These changes were a product of the war as a whole. Military operations in the Pacific region were both restricted in scope and confined in time to the opening and closing stages of the war. They affected the eventual bargaining power of certain of the victors on particular issues; but, in relation to the more far-reaching changes that the war brought about, they were of minor importance.

The outbreak of war in Europe in August 1914 at once directly involved the Far East and the Pacific. Four of the original belligerents, Britain, France, Russia and Germany, were powers with major interests in China; and they were soon joined by Japan, as the ally of Britain. In addition, most of the island territories of the Pacific were dependencies of Britain, France or Germany, and Australia, New Zealand and Canada were British Dominions.

The centre of German military power in the Pacific was at Tsingtao, in the leased territory of Kiaochow, in Shangtung. Here a strongly fortified naval base had been built and the East Asia Squadron was stationed. The German island territories had few fortifications, but they possessed powerful radio stations able to maintain contact with naval vessels at sea. At the beginning of the war, most of the larger ships of the squadron were cruising in the Pacific and thus ready to attempt the disruption of enemy shipping and communications. The initial tasks of the Allies were therefore those of protecting shipping and of occupying the German island territories, in order to silence their radio stations.

In the early months of the war, the German navy inflicted sporadic damage on Allied shipping in the Pacific; but it was hampered by the lack of an adequate base other than Tsingtao, which was soon under attack by the Japanese. By the end of 1914 all the vessels of the East Asia Squadron had either been destroyed or driven into neutral ports by lack of coal.

The German colonies were taken with little opposition. A New Zealand expeditionary force, supported by vessels of the Australian and French navies, reached German Samoa at the end of August. The governor declined to surrender the territory to the Allied force, but he refrained from ordering that it should be opposed. Rabaul, the capital of German New Guinea, was occupied by an Australian force in September, without serious resistance, and the other ports in the New Guinea area later in the year. The isolated island of Nauru, important for its phosphate deposits, was taken by an Australian cruiser on its way to New Guinea. The occupation of the Marianas and the Caroline and Marshall Islands, which were also administered from Rabaul, presented no greater military hazards; but it raised important questions of Allied strategy.

When the Japanese government had offered the country's services to Britain, the Foreign Secretary, Sir Edward Grey, had been reluctant to encourage full-scale participation by Japan in the war. On the other hand, Britain stood in need of naval assistance in the Pacific. The British Ambassador at Tokyo therefore presented a formal request 'that the Japanese fleet should, if possible, hunt out and destroy the armed German merchant cruisers who are now attacking our commerce'.[1] It was hoped that this formula would restrict Japanese participation to naval action in the China seas. But Japan's ultimatum to Germany ignored the suggested limitation. When Japan declared war, after Germany's failure to comply with the terms of the ultimatum, it thus became necessary for Britain and Japan to determine the fields of operation of their naval forces. The agreement that was reached provided that the Japanese should patrol the waters north of the equator and the Royal Australian Navy those south of it.

The Marianas, Carolines and Marshalls lay within the area for which Japan had assumed patrolling responsibilities; but it had always been understood that their occupation would be carried out by the Australians. No expeditionary force had been dispatched, however, at the time of the Anglo-Japanese agreement. The Japanese therefore occupied the island of Yap, in the Carolines, where one of the German radio stations was situated, and explained that they were willing to transfer control to the Australians in due course. When an Australian force was about to sail for the German islands, however, rioting occurred in Tokyo in protest against the proposed transfer. Japan thereupon requested British agreement to her remaining in the islands. The request was accepted; and, on 3 December, the British government informed Australia that 'we consider it most convenient for strategic reasons to allow them to remain in occupation for the present leaving [the] whole question of [the] future [of the islands] to be settled at the end of [the] war'.[2]

[1] Quoted in A. Whitney Griswold, *The Far Eastern Policy of the United States* (New York, 1938), p. 181.
[2] Quoted in S. S. Mackenzie, *The Australians at Rabaul: The Capture and Administration of the German Possessions in the Southern Pacific* (4th ed. Sydney, 1937), p. 160.

This manœuvre, despite its apparent—though perhaps calculated—artlessness, was consistent with other aspects of Japanese policy. On the outbreak of war the governments of the United States and China had tried to secure agreement to the maintenance of the *status quo* in the Far East. But, in her ultimatum to Germany, Japan had demanded the transfer to her of the German leasehold at Kiaochow. She had accepted a British request for the inclusion of the words 'with a view to eventual restoration of the same to China'; and the Prime Minister, Okuma Shigenobu, had assured the world 'that Japan has no ulterior motive, no desire to secure more territory, no thought of depriving China or other peoples of anything which they now possess'.[1] But, on the issue of immediate occupation, the Japanese had stood firm.

Kiaochow was, indeed, of great importance to Japan. From the naval base of Tsingtao, a railway had been built, with German capital, running inland to Tsinan, and mining rights and other privileges had been acquired in the country thus opened up. These developments had turned Shantung into a German sphere of interest. As soon as Japan entered the war, she sent a naval force to invest Tsingtao and landed troops, supported by a small British force, in northern Shantung. Tsingtao fell on 10 November; and Japan then set up a military administration to control both the leasehold and the railway.

The government of China had sought to resolve its own problems in relation to the Allied landing by proclaiming a war zone within which it disclaimed responsibility for the actions of the belligerents; but neither side had accepted the definition of the zone. When Japan established a military administration, China protested. On 7 January 1915 it cancelled the war zone and demanded withdrawal of the Japanese forces, return of the leased territory, and payment of damages for operations outside the leasehold area. The government of Japan retaliated by accusing the Chinese of acting with 'want of confidence in international good faith and regardless of friendly relations' and by seeking a settlement of what were described as 'outstanding questions between Japan and China'.[2] On 18 January it presented the President of China, Yüan Shih-k'ai, with its Twenty-one Demands.

The dispute over the occupation of Kiaochow provided the occasion for, rather than the cause of, the Japanese *démarche*. Japan had been embittered by the action of Russia, France and Germany in 1895, when they had compelled her to abandon some of her demands upon China, and by the influence of the Western powers ten years later in causing her to moderate her claims upon Russia. Now, it seemed that she could greatly strengthen her bargaining position at the eventual peace conference by

[1] H. W. V. Temperley (ed.), *A History of the Peace Conference of Paris* (6 vols. London, 1920–4), vol. VI, p. 373.
[2] T. E. La Fargue, *China and the World War* (Stanford University, 1937), p. 27.

reaching a bilateral agreement with China while the other powers were occupied with the war.

The demands were arranged in five groups.[1] Group One dealt with Shantung, where Japan hoped to build up her position along the lines she had followed earlier in southern Manchuria. The Chinese government was required to 'give full assent' to any agreement Japan might later make with Germany regarding the Kiaochow leasehold and other German rights. It was required not to alienate land 'to any other Power'; but, on the other hand, it was to agree to the building of an additional railway by the Japanese. And, finally, certain towns were to be thrown open to foreign residence and trade. The demands in Group Two were concerned with southern Manchuria and the adjacent region of eastern Inner Mongolia. China was to recognise 'the predominant position of Japan' in both regions and to grant a number of concessions. The most important of the latter were: an extension for 'a further period of 99 years' of the lease of Port Arthur and Dairen and control of the South Manchuria and Antung–Mukden Railways; the grant of complete freedom to Japanese subjects to reside, acquire land, and carry on business in all parts of the two regions; and the acceptance of an obligation to consult Japan about any proposal involving the use of foreign capital or foreign experts. In Groups Three and Four, respectively, Japan demanded that the Hanyehp'ing iron and steel company should become a joint Sino-Japanese enterprise and that China should not 'cede or lease to any other Power any harbour or bay on or any island along the coast of China'. The wider ambitions of the Japanese were revealed most clearly of all by the demands in Group Five. These included provisions requiring China to employ Japanese as political, military and financial advisers, to place the police ('in localities...where such arrangements are necessary') under joint Sino-Japanese control, and either to purchase arms from Japan or to establish an arsenal under joint Sino-Japanese management. The full acceptance of the Twenty-one Demands would have reduced China to the status of a Japanese dependency.

In presenting the demands, the Japanese minister at Peking had enjoined secrecy upon the government of China. The latter realised, however, that only by allowing their contents to leak out could opposition to them be stimulated. Negotiations between the two governments therefore took place against a background of critical comment—not only in China and among the Western powers, but even in Japan itself. Moreover, Britain, as Japan's ally, had formally urged moderation. As a result, Japan dropped some of the proposals and withheld those in Group Five 'for later negotiation'. But she held to her demands for an extension of her leasehold and railway rights in southern Manchuria and for the final elimination of Germany from Shantung. After virtual agreement had been reached on

[1] Quotations from the text of the demands are from the Japanese translation. This is printed in full *ibid.* appendix I, pp. 241–3.

these terms, the Chinese government continued to prolong the discussions. The treaties, which the government knew would greatly damage its standing in China, were not signed till Japan issued an ultimatum.

The government of Yüan Shih-k'ai had suffered from the war in other ways than by its diplomatic capitulation to the Japanese. The financial aid that it had earlier received from the Western powers was not continued, nor were the funds of private investors in Western countries any longer available for development projects in China. When Yüan began to take steps to establish a monarchy, with himself as emperor, the military governors of the provinces rose against him. In concert with the party groups of the former parliament, they were discussing means of forcing his retirement from the presidency when he died on 6 June 1916.

After the death of Yüan Shih-k'ai, China soon relapsed again into political disorder. The former parliament was recalled; and the constitution that it had drafted, providing for an executive responsible to it, was brought into force. Since parliament was dominated by the Kuomintang and its allies, this arrangement did not resolve the fundamental conflict between the revolutionary movement and the military. A temporary compromise was achieved: Li Hüan-hung, the former Vice-President and a supporter of parliament, became President; and Tuan Ch'i-jui, a northern military leader, became Prime Minister. But the old conflict soon re-emerged, in relation, first, to provincial government (where the constitution could not be applied) and, then, to foreign policy.

When Germany, on 31 January 1917, announced her intention to resort to unrestricted submarine warfare, the United States decided to break off diplomatic relations with her and to urge all other neutral countries to take similar action. The American approach to China caused the Allies to reconsider their own attitudes, which had previously been in favour of Chinese neutrality. Japan decided to encourage China to join the Allies as soon as possible. The Japanese government shared the general belief that America's severance of relations with Germany would be followed before long by a declaration of war. It was thus anxious to avoid a situation in which China entered the war as a protégé of the United States, since this would be likely to lead to strong American support for China when the subject-matter of the Twenty-one Demands was considered by the peace conference. For different reasons, Britain and France also reached the conclusion that an early declaration of war by China was desirable. The Allies therefore outlined to China the advantages, primarily in terms of loans and concessions, that she could expect to obtain by joining them.

These two approaches—by America and by the Allies—were assessed by Chinese political leaders largely in relation to the domestic situation. Tuan Ch'i-jui quickly gave his support to the severance of diplomatic relations, since he hoped it would enable him to obtain financial assistance and thus reduce his dependence on parliament. For similar reasons, he came, a little later, to favour a declaration of war. Parliament, aware of his thinking, initially had reservations about the desirability of even the first of these moves; but it was won over by the prospect of aid. And on 14 March, after a favourable vote in parliament, China broke off diplomatic relations with Germany. Parliament's doubts regarding entry into the war were, however, more serious and more lasting. The economic and military arguments for doing so seemed of dubious validity: the Allies might not provide the financial assistance of which their representatives had spoken; and—after the outbreak of revolution in Russia—their victory appeared uncertain. But parliament was concerned, above all, with the increased power that a declaration of war would give to the military. This concern was greatly intensified when a conference of military governors, convened by Tuan, gave support to his war policy and when a hired mob attempted the direct intimidation of members of parliament.

These last events brought about the collapse of the uneasy alliance between parliament and the military. After the fall, successively, of the Prime Minister, parliament and the President, and a brief interlude during which a military leader attempted to restore the Manchu dynasty, Tuan Ch'i-jui returned to office as the head of a military government. In August 1917 this government declared war on Germany. A month later an alternative 'provisional government' in Canton, which had been set up by the Kuomintang members of the former parliament, recognised the action that had been taken. China was thus committed as fully as its chaotic political situation allowed to participation in the war.

The results of China's belligerency were, on the whole, disappointing both to the Chinese and to the Allies. China gained several useful concessions from Britain, France and the United States (which had entered the war in April), but no major financial assistance. The Allies received little help from China in the conduct of the war. Japan, continuing to pursue the path of self-interest, emerged as the principal beneficiary. In return for loans to the Peking government, it obtained further concessions and substantial control over Chinese military affairs.

During the latter half of 1917, the Japanese government was also attempting to win the support of the United States for its claims in China. Like the other Allied powers, Japan sent a war mission to Washington. While its ostensible purpose was the co-ordination of immediate war-time activities, the main objective of its leader, Ishii Kikujiro, was American recognition of Japan's 'paramount interest' in China. The American Secretary of State, Robert Lansing, at first countered Ishii's suggestion by proposing a Japanese–American declaration affirming respect for the 'open door' policy and the territorial integrity of China. Eventually a compromise was reached and embodied in the Lansing–Ishii Agreement of 2 November. In this document the United States accepted the argument 'that territorial propinquity creates special relations between countries, and, consequently, the Government of the United States recognizes that Japan has special interests in China, particularly in the part to which her possessions are contiguous'. The Japanese government, on the other hand, reaffirmed that it would 'always adhere to the principle of the so-called "open door"' and denied that it had any intention 'to infringe in any way the independence or territorial integrity of China'.[1] The wording of the agreement was not without ambiguity; and it was differently interpreted by its two signatories. To Ishii, it marked American recognition of Japan's position in southern Manchuria and acquiescence in the advancement of a type of Japanese 'Monroe Doctrine' for the Far East. To Lansing, on the other hand, Japan's 'special interests' had been recognised only in a geographical, and not a political, sense. Ishii probably had the better of the argument; but, in any event, he had secured American acceptance of a document that was likely to be useful to Japan—and embarrassing to America—in later negotiations.

Within a few days of the signing of the Lansing–Ishii Agreement, another event occurred to complicate further the Far Eastern situation. The Bolsheviks seized power in Russia. For the Allies, this had two important consequences: Russian co-operation with them was at an end; and, if the new government should survive, a separate peace would probably be made with Germany. While they were considering the military implications of the situation, a crisis arose in northern Manchuria. In the railway zone the Russian imperial government had gradually assumed complete administrative control, so that centres like Harbin were ruled as though they were Russian colonies. At this time Bolshevik supporters attempted to bring the administrator of the zone under their control. On behalf of the Allies, Chinese troops were sent to the area and successfully restored his authority.

The Allied action made the railway zone a centre for Russian anti-Bolshevik plotting. In the spring of 1918 a Russian irregular force moved across the frontier into Siberia; but, after its defeat in June by the Red Army, it retreated again into Manchuria. This event gave rise to fears, real or simulated, of an imminent Russian invasion and led to the dispatch of a Japanese force to the area. Meanwhile, the Allies had been discussing the landing of troops at Vladivostok to co-operate with anti-Soviet groups. Some of the principal arguments used in relation to this project were either unsound or disingenuous. It was contended that it might relieve pressure on the western front—by releasing 50,000 Czech troops who were marching east to offer their services to the Allies—and that it might facilitate the formation of an anti-Bolshevik government in Siberia. In reality, the thinking of the Allies was affected not only by considerations of this sort

[1] The text of the agreement is printed in *Papers Relating to the Foreign Relations of the United States, 1917*, pp. 264–5.

but also by their suspicions of one another. The Japanese feared that the Americans intended to seek concessions in Siberia from the Soviet government; and this increased their determination to give military support to the anti-Bolshevik groups already operating in the region. The Americans feared that the Japanese were planning yet another expansionist move, which made them unwilling to permit the latter to act alone. On these various grounds, a decision was taken in favour of Allied intervention; and in August and September 1918 Japanese, American, British and French forces were landed at Vladivostok.[1]

When the Allied powers signed an armistice with Germany on 11 November 1918, the world war came to an end; but in Siberia, as on the other borders of Russia, Allied military activity continued. It was not abandoned till all prospect of successful Russian opposition to the Communist régime had finally disappeared and till Japan had lost any chance of making territorial gains.

The situation in the Pacific at the end of the war differed very substantially from that which had existed at its beginning. Japan had extended her influence in Manchuria, taken over the German leasehold and other concessions in Shantung, and occupied the German Pacific islands north of the equator. Australia and New Zealand had occupied the German islands in the South Pacific. And the principal Allied powers and their satellites had made agreements with one another during the course of the war, some open and some secret, as to the benefits they should receive when they met in conference as victors. Russia had temporarily lost her influence as a Pacific power, as a result of the revolution, and Germany had lost her colonies and concessions through military defeat. These were the changes that would largely determine Allied decisions during the peace settlement.

But there had also been changes of a rather different order, less relevant to the substance of immediate negotiations but of greater importance in relation to the future balance of power and influence in the Pacific region. Both France and Britain had been weakened by the war, so that the former had lost the capacity to play a major role in the politics of the Far East and the latter the resources needed to restore its former naval predominance. Japan and the United States, on the other hand, had emerged from the war in far stronger positions than they had had when it began. Both countries were in a period of rapid economic growth; and, in both, the war had produced a sharpened awareness of the implications for internal security and prosperity of securing a settlement of international issues satisfactory to themselves. Russia was now controlled by a régime which, although it rejected the techniques and objectives of imperialism, was determined to establish its influence in China for ideological reasons. In

[1] On this episode, see James William Morley, *The Japanese Thrust into Siberia, 1918* (New York, 1957).

China itself change was less explicit. The old war-lords, who had exchanged the service of the empire for the pursuit of personal power, were still politically dominant; but they were served by men of a younger generation, often educated abroad, who were capable of reorganising administration at home or representing their country in foreign affairs on modern lines. And the government at Canton, inefficient and lacking in military resources as it was, none the less represented a broad-based national movement for political modernisation. The emergence of China as a modern state, though it had not yet occurred, was at least foreseeable. These were the changes against which the decisions reached during the peace settlement would be tested.

At the Peace Conference, which opened in Paris in January 1919, three of the matters that were discussed were of predominant concern to the Pacific: the disposition of the German Pacific islands; the settlement of the problem of Shantung; and a proposal by Japan for the inclusion in the Covenant of the League of Nations of a clause guaranteeing racial equality. In relation to the first two of these, the freedom of action of the conference was limited by secret agreements made during the course of the war. Early in 1917, when German submarine attacks were placing a great strain on Allied shipping, Britain had asked Japan to send destroyers to the Mediterranean. The request had been accepted in return for an undertaking by Britain to support Japanese claims to the German islands north of the equator and to the German concessions in Shantung. Japan, on her part, had agreed to support British claims to the islands which had been occupied by the Australians and New Zealanders.[1] The agreement had been reluctantly acquiesced in by the governments of Australia and New Zealand; and, shortly afterwards, France and Italy had entered into similar undertakings.

The problems facing the conference in regard to the German Pacific islands did not therefore include the choice of an administering authority but related only to the terms under which its powers should be exercised. President Wilson of the United States attached great importance to the principle of international trusteeship for ex-enemy territories unready for self-government; and this principle underlay the mandates provisions that were being incorporated in the Covenant of the League of Nations. Japan, on the other hand, claimed unfettered control over the Micronesian islands. Australia and New Zealand, which were to exercise the rights of the British crown in the former German territories in Samoa and New Guinea respectively, and to be associated with Britain in Nauru, adopted a similar line (as did South Africa in relation to the former German territory of South West Africa). In particular, they demanded the right to impose restrictions on trade and immigration. To resolve this impasse,

[1] H. W. V. Temperley (ed.), *A History of the Peace Conference of Paris*, vol. VI, pp. 634–7.

a new class of mandate—known as Class C—was provided for in the Covenant. 'There are territories, such as South West Africa and certain of the South Pacific Islands', the Covenant declared, 'which, owing to the sparseness of their population, or their small size, or their geographical contiguity to the territory of the Mandatory, and other circumstances, can best be administered under the laws of the Mandatory as integral portions of its territory...' By the use of this formula, the claimants were given the power to impose the restrictions they desired—which were already part of their own law. They were limited only by a general ban on fortification of mandated territories and by an obligation to protect the interests of the indigenous inhabitants. The compromise satisfied neither Wilson nor the prospective mandatories, but it was accepted, reluctantly, by both.

On the question of Shantung, unlike that of the Pacific islands, the Japanese had built up so strong a case for their claims that they were able to avoid the need for compromise. Apart from the promises of support that they had been given by Britain, France and Italy in 1917, they had obtained the formal agreement of China. In 1915, after the presentation of the Twenty-one Demands, the government of China had undertaken to accept any agreement that might be reached between Japan and Germany. In September 1918 it had agreed that the former German railway should become a joint Sino-Japanese concern and that Japan should finance the building of two important branch lines. Moreover, the Japanese contended that the United States had recognised their country's special interest in Shantung in the Lansing–Ishii Agreement. On the basis of these agreements, Japan demanded that the Kiaochow leasehold and the other German concessions should be handed over to her. The leasehold would eventually be restored to China. Only the economic concessions would be retained, and these would be dealt with in accordance with the existing Sino-Japanese agreement.

Despite the earlier commitments by the Peking government, the Chinese delegation at the conference passionately opposed the Japanese demand. Though its nominal leader, the Chinese Foreign Minister, was a politician of the old school, its dominant members were men of a younger generation who had received a Western education in China and later graduated from overseas universities. These men, like others of the returned-student group, were determined to work for the removal of the restrictions placed by the powers upon the exercise of China's sovereignty. As a consequence of the weakness and disorganisation of the government in Peking, they seem to have possessed a quite unusual freedom to develop their own lines of action in Paris. In addition, however, the Peking government was engaged, during the critical months of the conference, in trying to reach agreement with the provisional government in Canton on the restoration of unity in China. The forceful arguments of Chinese spokesmen in Paris were probably seen as helpful to this endeavour, both by diverting attention from critical discussions at home and by emphasising the government's vigorous defence of the country's interests.

The Chinese case, which was presented by V. K. Wellington Koo, was a mixture of legal argument and appeal to sentiment. Wellington Koo claimed that the German lease had been obtained by force and that the 1915 treaty with Japan had been signed by China under duress. Moreover, China had abrogated all treaties with Germany when she entered the war, so that the latter possessed no rights which could be ceded to Japan. But he also emphasized the position of Shantung as an integral part of China, a region of great current importance but also 'the cradle of Chinese civilization, the birthplace of Confucius and Mencius, and a Holy Land for the Chinese'.[1] On these grounds, he demanded the direct return to China of all rights in Shantung possessed by Germany at the outbreak of war.

The Chinese case, and the skill with which it was presented, received much favourable publicity in the world's press and aroused great enthusiasm among the western-educated group in China. As a result, the delegation increased its demands when the subject came up for final settlement. It asked for the abrogation not only of the 1915 treaty regarding Shantung but for that of all the treaties and agreements of 1915 and 1918, including those relating to Manchuria and Inner Mongolia. It had failed fully to understand the distinction between a debating success and the manœuvres of power politics. Japan's demands were accepted *in toto*.

But before Japan attained this victory she had been defeated on the third major issue of importance to her. In the League of Nations Commission, which was drafting the Covenant, the Japanese representative had moved for the insertion of a clause guaranteeing racial equality: 'The equality of nations being a basic principle of the League of Nations, the High Contracting Powers agree to accord, as soon as possible, to all alien nationals of States members of the League equal and just treatment in every respect, making no distinction, either in law or in fact, on account of their race or nationality.'[2] The subject was of great significance to Japan—and to other non-western nations—on grounds of prestige. But it was also of practical importance in relation to migration. For the latter reason, the Japanese draft was intensely disliked by the representatives of countries, such as the British dominions, which imposed restrictions on the entry of non-Europeans. Successive amendments to it by the Japanese, reducing it to a simple affirmation of the principle of racial equality, failed to mollify, in particular, the Prime Minister of Australia, William Morris Hughes, who threatened to arouse popular opposition in the dominions and the western states of America. In these circumstances, both President Wilson and the British representative on the commission abstained from

---

[1] The words are those of the official record of proceedings (quoted in La Fargue, *China and the World War*, p. 198).

[2] David Hunter Miller, *The Drafting of the Covenant* (2 vols. New York, 1928), vol. I, p. 183.

voting when the amended Japanese motion was put. When eleven out of seventeen votes were cast in its favour, Wilson declared that unanimity was necessary for it to be passed.

The decisions of the Peace Conference thus tended to confirm existing attitudes in both Japan and China. The Japanese delegation had gained its objectives when it had been able to rely on firm undertakings entered into during the course of the war; but it had failed when it was primarily dependent upon the goodwill of the Western powers. The benefits that had been obtained by China were little more than inevitable corollaries of the terms of reference of the conference itself. The war-time abrogation of treaties between China and both Germany and Austria-Hungary had been declared permanent. And the Chinese delegation, through its presence at the conference, had been able to create an awareness of the need for a general revision of the country's treaty relations with the powers. But no positive action had been taken towards China's emergence as a member of the family of nations. More generally, the atmosphere of the conference and the tone of public discussion in western countries had re-emphasised the division between East and West. Even Japan, although she was of necessity accepted as a great power, remained, in Western eyes, a part of Asia. Despite the formation of the League of Nations, the heritage of five centuries of European expansion still precluded the creation of an undivided world community.

For these reasons, amongst others, the world situation remained a troubled one; and, during the years immediately following the war, Britain, the United States and Japan all embarked on massive programmes of naval construction. The expenditure that these programmes entailed both hampered the economic development of the three countries and created financial difficulties for their governments. The increase in naval armaments resulting from them merely exacerbated the sense of insecurity that had given them birth.

One of the main sources of international tension was the situation in the Far East. The American and Japanese governments continued to regard each other's policy towards China with intense suspicion. From the American point of view, the position was complicated by the existence of the Anglo-Japanese alliance. This had always tended, the Americans considered, to make Britain tolerant of Japanese claims and was still more likely to do so in future, since Britain had lost her former naval predominance in the Pacific. The alliance was due to expire in July 1921. Would it be renewed and, if so, on what terms? This was a question of importance not only to the two signatory powers but also to the United States, the British Dominions and China.

During the early months of 1921, the British and American governments made their positions clearer to one another on the two major issues —the limitation of armaments and the future of the Anglo-Japanese alliance. By June the British government knew that the United States favoured the calling of a disarmament conference and desired that the alliance should be either abandoned or substantially modified. The American government, on its part, knew that Britain accepted the principle of naval parity with the United States and was willing to revise, though not to abandon, the alliance. It thus remained for the two powers to find a way of resolving the differences that still existed between them (and with other interested parties) and of giving effect to their eventual conclusions.

At the Imperial Conference which assembled in London in the second half of June, the Canadian Prime Minister, Arthur Meighen, assumed the role of mediator between Washington and London. He suggested, and his fellow Prime Ministers agreed, that there should be a conference on Pacific and Far Eastern problems between Britain, the United States, Japan and China.[1] This proposal became known to the American government in advance of its formal communication. In order to retain the initiative, it immediately invited the governments of Britain, Japan, France and Italy to attend a conference at Washington on the limitation of armaments. When the British proposal was officially received, the Americans suggested that the scope and, so far as necessary, the membership of the conference should be widened, so as to include Pacific and Far Eastern questions. And to this procedure the British government agreed.

Of the powers originally invited by the Americans, only Japan had reservations about accepting. The Japanese government was not unwilling to enter into discussions on the limitation of armaments. But it was suspicious of American motives in proposing the inclusion of Pacific and Far Eastern questions. Was not this an attempt to force the abandonment of the Anglo-Japanese alliance? Did not America hope to undermine the Japanese position in China in her own interests? The Japanese accepted the invitation but added the comment that they preferred 'to look forward to the future' rather than to engage in the re-examination of old grievances.[2]

In addition to those on the original American list, four countries received, and accepted, invitations to attend the widened conference: China, Belgium, the Netherlands and Portugal. These four were to be excluded from the discussions on the limitation of armaments but to participate in those relating to the Far East and the Pacific.

The Washington Conference was opened by President Harding on 12 November. The American Secretary of State, Charles Evans Hughes, was elected chairman. Hughes plunged at once into the main business of the conference by presenting specific proposals for the immediate reduction and subsequent limitation of the tonnage of capital ships. These proposals

---

[1] On this incident, see J. Bartlet Brebner, 'Canada, the Anglo-Japanese Alliance and the Washington Conference', *Political Science Quarterly*, vol. L, no. 1, pp. 45–58.

[2] Senate Documents, 67th Congress, 2nd session, no. 126, p. 755.

involved extensive scrapping of existing ships and acceptance of a ten-year naval holiday. The tonnage of capital ships possessed by the United States, Britain and Japan would be reduced by 40 per cent and then be limited to a maximum of 500,000 tons for the United States and Britain and to 300,000 tons for Japan.

Both Britain and Japan accepted the proposals in principle, but attached reservations. The most important were those of Japan. On the question of tonnage, agreement was finally reached on a slightly revised formula which allowed maxima of 525,000 tons to the United States and Britain, 315,000 tons to Japan, and 175,000 tons to the two smaller naval powers, France and Italy. But, in agreeing to this formula, the Japanese had insisted on the satisfaction of a further demand. They required that a halt should be called to the construction of naval bases and fortifications in the Pacific. This condition was eventually defined so as to exclude the metropolitan territories of the signatories (including the British Dominions, which were represented in the British delegation) and certain other areas (notably Hawaii); but it was to apply, most significantly, to the Philippines, Guam and Hong Kong.[1] The effect thus was to insure the Japanese mainland against naval attack from any possible base within convenient operational distance.

Concurrently with the naval discussions, the conference was considering the Pacific and Far Eastern questions that were before it. Most intimately connected with the naval problem was that of the Anglo-Japanese alliance. In view of the strength of American objections to it, the leader of the British delegation, A. J. Balfour, at first proposed its replacement by a treaty between Britain, Japan and the United States. But this was unacceptable to Hughes, who suggested the inclusion of France, in order to remove the danger of America's being outvoted by the combination of Britain and Japan. On American insistence, the new Four-Power Treaty was much weaker than the old alliance. It merely pledged the four powers to respect each other's rights in their 'insular possessions and insular dominions in the region of the Pacific Ocean'. If a controversy should arise between any of them on 'any Pacific question', there would be a joint conference; and, if any of them should, in respect of similar questions, be 'threatened by the aggressive action of any other Power', they would consult together.[2] In the event, even these consultative provisions were never invoked. The Four-Power Treaty became, as the Americans

---

[1] For the text of the treaties and agreements signed at Washington, and for a record of the proceedings of the conference, see *Papers Relating to the Foreign Relations of the United States, 1922*, vol. I, pp. 1–384. For British papers relating to the conference and its background, see Rohan Butler and J. P. T. Bury (eds.), *Documents on British Foreign Policy, 1919–1939*, First Series, vol. xiv: Far Eastern Affairs, April 1920–February 1922 (London, 1966).

[2] *Ibid.* p. 35. On the drafting of this treaty, see J. Chal Vinson, 'The Drafting of the Four-Power Treaty of the Washington Conference', *Journal of Modern History*, vol. xxv, no. 1, pp. 40–7.

intended and the Japanese feared, little more than a diplomatic device to end the Anglo-Japanese alliance.

The most important of the other regional questions were those relating to the position of China. On matters of general principle, the nine powers at the conference signed a treaty closely in line with the requests of the Chinese spokesman. They bound themselves to respect 'the sovereignty, independence and integrity of China', to provide 'the fullest and most unembarrassed opportunity' to China to establish a stable government, to maintain the principle of equal opportunity for the commerce of all nations, and to refrain from taking advantage of conditions in China for the purpose of seeking special rights or privileges. However, the procedure for the enforcement of these undertakings was limited to a 'full and frank communication between the contracting Powers' whenever, in the opinion of any one of them, 'a situation arose which involved the application of the Treaty'. The conference was thus happy to express liberal sentiments, in vague general terms, but cautious in committing itself to specific action in support of them.

The latter aspect of their thinking emerged clearly in the discussion of the Chinese government's points of grievance, such as the foreign control of customs tariffs, the existence of foreign leaseholds, and extra-territoriality. In respect of customs matters, the powers signed a treaty permitting China to impose significantly higher, though still limited, rates of duty; and a commission was set up to reform the tariff administration. Another commission was formed to investigate the working of extraterritorial rights, with a view to their future abolition, if possible. And other minor concessions were granted in relation to postal and radio services.

Among the most important of China's grievances were those concerning the position of Japan. These included the problem of Shantung. The Chinese government was anxious that the conditions for the return of the Kiaochow leasehold should be discussed, since it wanted to have the support of the other powers during the negotiations. But the Japanese were unwilling to have their own bargaining position weakened in this way. As the subject was too important to be left, the parties eventually agreed to a compromise by which discussions took place outside the conference, but with Hughes and Balfour present as observers. By the terms of the settlement which was eventually reached, Japan agreed to restore full sovereignty to China, together with the ownership of former German public properties. China, for her part, agreed to purchase the railways with money borrowed from Japanese bankers and to recognise certain Japanese interests in the mines. Japan further undertook to withdraw her troops and China to open the territory to foreign trade.[1] When this agreement was

[1] *Papers Relating to the Foreign Relations of the United States, 1922*, vol. I, pp. 948–60.

announced, Britain offered to surrender her lease of Weihaiwei, in order to restore to China full control over the whole of Shantung.

The Chinese also asked that the conference should review the Twenty-one Demands and Japan's special interests that were based upon them. Since the substance of some of the demands had already been disposed of, and since those in Group Five were now withdrawn by Japan, the major matters remaining for discussion were those relating to Japanese interests in southern Manchuria and eastern Inner Mongolia. In regard to these, the Japanese made two nominal concessions. They agreed to throw open to an international consortium their option over railway loans; and they disavowed their intention to insist on the appointment of Japanese as advisers in the administration of southern Manchuria. They insisted, however, on retaining their full rights in the Kwantung leasehold and the Southern Manchuria Railway. Southern Manchuria and Inner Mongolia were of steadily increasing importance to the economies of Japan and Korea; and the retention of control over the communications systems of the area had become a major object of Japanese policy.

During the three months over which it extended—from November 1921 till February 1922—the Washington Conference thus surveyed a vast range of problems; it analysed them in great detail; and it took firm decisions in respect of them. It thus brought clarity and precision into a wide range of international relationships in which doubt and uncertainty had ruled before; and, by doing so, it increased the prospects of future peace. But this was the real core of its achievement.

At the time, the conference was differently evaluated. Hughes described the naval treaty as 'perhaps the greatest forward step in history to establish the reign of peace'.[1] And Takahashi Korekiyo, the Japanese Prime Minister, described the decisions of the conference as 'a blessing to all mankind'.[2] These enthusiastic judgements were echoed by the world press at the time, and by men of affairs throughout the 1920s. But, in reality, the preservation of the peace required more than the formalising of existing relationships; and the diplomatic history of the following decade was, in part, a record of the collapse of the 'Washington system'.

The emergence of Japan as a great power had been made possible by the expansion of her economy. Though the scale of Japanese success in international politics was substantially increased by the high quality of her civil and military services, and by the skill and ruthless determination of her leaders, it had its basis in the facts of economic growth.

Between 1900 and the beginning of the great depression at the end of the 'twenties, total output in Japan is estimated to have grown at an annual rate of 4·2 per cent.[3] Since population increased from forty-four million to

[1] M. J. Pusey, *Charles Evans Hughes* (2 vols. New York, 1952), vol. II, p. 490.
[2] *Ibid.* p. 508.
[3] K. Ohkawa, *The Growth Rate of the Japanese Economy since 1878* (Tokyo, 1957), p. 248.

sixty-four million, at a rate of 1·2 per cent per annum, output per head thus expanded by 3 per cent annually, a rate which was probably unequalled elsewhere. The rewards of economic growth were by no means shared equally, but it is clear that very substantial benefits were felt throughout the population as a whole. Growth was based in the main on a transformation of the industrial structure as Japan moved closer to a modern Western pattern. This pattern had been by no means achieved by 1930, but the modern sector was by then firmly established. Almost half of the gainfully employed still worked in agriculture, an industry in which there was little change from the system of small farms and where some half of the farmers were tenants. Rice was still the main food crop, occupying well over half the cultivated area. In the production of raw silk, the second most important agricultural product, there had been a great expansion, so that by 1929 about two-fifths of all farming families were engaged in cocoon production as a secondary occupation. Manufacturing industry had expanded substantially and in 1929 employed 17 per cent of the occupied population but produced 27 per cent of total output. The most spectacular development was in silk and cotton, in which there was now little evidence of traditional methods and organisation. As a whole, the textile industry by then accounted for some 25 per cent of the industrial workers, and as many as half of those in factories with five or more employees. Thus Japanese manufacturing was heavily biased towards light industry, while heavy industry lagged in the general industrialisation. In the metal industry, steel output had reached over two million tons, but this met only some 70 per cent of Japanese demand; similarly in engineering, although output and range of products had expanded, for machinery as a whole Japan was still a large importer.

Modern industry was established in Japan at the same time as traditional occupations, living conditions and attitudes continued. The result was the emergence of a 'dual economy', which became particularly evident in the 1920s, when modern industry emerged as a significant part of the whole economy. In all sorts of ways—but especially in technology, incomes, working and living conditions—a gap existed between the modern and the traditional sectors to an extent unparalleled in Western society. Such a social and economic division virtually precluded the emergence of a Western democratic political system. Moreover, the control and ownership of the modern sector increasingly came into the hands of the Zaibatsu, the great Japanese family combines. These had originated in the early Meiji period in close association with government enterprise and were at the heart of the Japanese process of industrialisation. Economically, they contrasted with Western combinations in their freedom from legal restraint and in the breadth of their business activities, which spanned all fields of economic activity; in the 1920s they even moved into small-scale commerce and manufacturing. Socially, the Zaibatsu in their organisation were based on hierarchical status and authoritarian control, and so brought into modern industry many of the traditions of feudal Japan. Politically, their association with government became even closer in the 1920s. Principally because of the strength of the Zaibatsu and the almost unlimited supply of labour in the traditional sector, labour organisations remained extremely weak. The number of trade unionists had reached 285,000 in 1926, but they were only a small proportion of the work force. In the overall political and economic structure of Japan, labour organisations had almost no influence.

The degree of economic influence exercised by the West in Japan had been kept at a very low level by the method of financing industrialisation adopted by the Japanese between 1900 and 1930. Only in the period 1897–1913 did Japan rely at all heavily on foreign capital. In that period she borrowed some two billion yen, and it is some measure of the importance of this capital that it amounted to about 20 per cent of gross capital formation. Again in the 'twenties a further one billion yen was borrowed, but the growth of the Japanese economy in the intervening period made it of less importance. But borrowing was carried out almost entirely by the Japanese government and its agencies from private foreign lenders, so that foreign influence or direction was minimised. Direct foreign investment in private business in Japan did exist, but it was small both in relation to government borrowing and to total Japanese investment in business. Similarly, the role of foreign entrepreneurship in this period was small.

Between 1900 and 1930 Japanese economic contacts with the outside world through foreign trade expanded enormously. The quantity of both imports and exports grew roughly fivefold, and increased in total from 25 to 40 per cent of national income. Japan had now fully entered into the international economy and was dependent on world markets for her prosperity. Her position was similar to that of Great Britain in her limited range of natural resources, specialised skills, and insular position with its easy access to maritime trade. However, although Japan was now as dependent on international trade as Britain, her share of world trade was considerably smaller: it was 2 per cent in 1913 and 3 per cent in 1929, compared with Britain's 17 and 13 per cent for the same years. Thus the impact of the growth of Japanese foreign trade on world trade remained limited. Imports became increasingly dominated by food, industrial raw materials especially for textiles and, to some extent, machinery. The countries that particularly benefited from this trade were the United States and those of the British Commonwealth. The principal Japanese export continued to be raw silk, which grew in volume some eight times between 1900 and 1929; some 80 per cent of total output was exported in the 1920s, and the United States dominated the market. The most spectacular growth was in the second most important commodity, cotton textiles: the volume of cotton piece goods increased some sixteenfold

359

between 1900 and 1929, and in volume terms the main markets in 1929 were in Asia, with India taking 32 per cent, China 30 per cent, and the Netherlands East Indies 11 per cent. These two commodities dominated Japanese exports, so that in 1929 raw silk made up 37 per cent and silk and cotton manufactures 28 per cent of total exports. It was through these cotton exports in the 1920s that Japan gave warning of her growing development as an exporter of manufactures. Cotton was not a dynamic section of world trade, and Western exporters found it difficult to adjust to a new competitor. Japan was blamed, for example, for the decline of Britain's share of world trade in cotton piece goods from 65 per cent in 1909–13 to 34 per cent in 1928–9. Given the emphasis in Japanese imports on food and industrial raw materials, there was little in the Japanese market for Western exporters to soften the effect of Japanese competition in their own overseas markets. To a large extent, after the world war, Europe lay outside Japanese trading relations. Japanese competition was also felt in another depressed industry—shipping. In 1893 Japanese ships carried only some 8 per cent of Japanese foreign trade; by 1913 the proportion was a half, and following the shipping boom during the war Japan emerged with the fourth largest merchant marine, competing throughout the world and carrying some two-thirds of Japanese foreign trade. In the 1920s shipping receipts went a long way to meeting Japan's deficit in trade.

The development of Japanese economic relations with the outside world was affected by her acquisition of an empire, with which preferential relationships were established, and to a smaller extent by her special position in Manchuria. For economic purposes, in this period, the empire consisted basically of Formosa and Korea. Colonial trade amounted to some 10 per cent of Japanese foreign trade just before the world war and to about 20 per cent at the end of the 'twenties. Its economic development had been directed towards Japanese needs, and it emerged as a supplier of food and raw materials (especially sugar in Formosa and rice in Korea) and as a market for Japanese manufactures. Japanese capital was given a privileged place in its development, as was Japanese shipping in its trade. The real drive for empire development and co-ordination with the Japanese economy did not come until the 1930s, with the occupation of Manchuria and north China. Whether, on balance, Japan had gained any economic benefits from its empire before 1930 is doubtful. However, it is worth emphasising Japan's particular dependence on foreign trade and its particular interest in a relative freedom of trade and multilateral settlements. In fact, such a system largely existed, to Japan's benefit, up to 1930, and the special relationship established by Japan with its colonies was part of the undermining of the system which precipitated its collapse in the 1930s.

One of the most striking features of Japanese economic development between 1900 and 1930 was the increased involvement of the country in the world economy, so that changes in world economic conditions quickly affected economic and social affairs in Japan. Two spectacular and contrasting examples may be cited. The world war greatly expanded Japan's economic opportunities. European suppliers were cut off from markets they had previously held, and Japanese-manufactured exports and shipping services boomed. In particular, the war enabled Japan to replace Britain in its Asian cotton textile markets. In Japan this world demand led to rising incomes, employment and industrial expansion: it was a period of marked prosperity. All was not, however, to Japan's advantage: inflation and misused overseas reserves led to social disorders and difficult financial and trading conditions at the beginning of the 1920s. The opposite effect to that of the war was felt in Japan when the American depression began at the end of 1929. We have seen the importance of raw silk in Japan's exports, the dependence of about half the peasantry on its production and the overwhelming dominance of American demand. The American depression led immediately to a fall in raw silk prices of some 50 per cent during 1930, thus striking at the Japanese economy as a whole and especially bringing poverty to the countryside. The impact of world depression was a major factor in discrediting the liberal policy and the political leaders of the 1920s and setting the stage for reaction at home and aggression abroad in the 1930s.

In China, political impotence was both a cause and a consequence of the lack of economic development similar to that of Japan. It is significant of China's economic backwardness and political disorganisation that the data for the study of the country's economy during the period 1900–30 are themselves deficient.

Population appears to have been around 400–450 millions, and the increase in the period, if any, must have been small. By the end of the period the structure of employment of the work force had changed little. Some 80 per cent still remained in agriculture, and the proportion in the traditional sector as a whole would have been considerably higher, at some 95 per cent. The modern sector, then, remained small, and had grown only to the extent of producing about one-eighth of the national income.[1] Nevertheless, in spite of the continuing dominance of the traditional sector in the economy, China developed as a field for foreign investment, which by 1902 was valued at £162 million. It doubled to £331 million in 1914 and redoubled to £666 million in 1931.[2] Not all of this can be regarded as actual increase in real assets; and it has been estimated that, after making allowance for price rises, the real increase between 1902 and

[1] T. Liu and K. Yeh, *The Economy of the Chinese Mainland: National Income and Economic Development, 1933–1959* (Santa Monica, Cal., 1963), p. 132.
[2] C. F. Remer, *Foreign Investments in China* (New York, 1933), p. 58. The figures do not include the Boxer indemnity, initially worth £67·5 million. It was not in existence in 1902, amounted to £63·5 million at the end of 1913, and was insignificant in 1931.

1914 was about 90 per cent and between 1914 and 1931 about 20 per cent.[1] The greater part of this was direct investment by foreigners in firms in China (around 70 per cent), and the balance was made up of the obligations of the Chinese government. The direct investment was used mainly in railways and in areas associated with foreign trade; manufacturing took only some 10–15 per cent; and almost none went into agriculture. A very large part of the government borrowing was used for unproductive purposes: some two-fifths (in real terms) went on military and indemnity purposes, one-fifth on general government administration, while the balance was spent mainly on railways. Britain was the most important source of foreign investment in China, with roughly a third of the total over the whole period. Russia stood second to Britain in 1902, with an almost equal share, but by 1931 this position had been attained by Japan, and the Russian component had declined to less than 10 per cent. The direct investment of the foreign countries was heavily localised. At the end of the 'twenties, for instance, some three-quarters of British direct investment was in Shanghai and two-thirds of Japan's was in Manchuria.

In volume, the foreign trade of China doubled between the end of the 1890s and 1914 and then increased by a further 50 per cent by the end of the 1920s.[2] In value, it was in 1914 roughly equal to that of Japan, at 2 per cent of world trade, and it still maintained this proportion at the end of the 1920s. China, then, was not one of the world's great trading nations. As measured by the ratio of foreign trade to national income, trade was not very important to the Chinese economy. Estimates suggest that it was only some 12 per cent at its peak at the end of the 'twenties; and, since trade was growing much faster than national income in the intervening period, it must have been much lower at the beginning of the century. Silk and silk goods continued to be the most important export till almost the end of the period, although declining from 30 per cent of total exports in 1900 to 18 per cent in 1928. The effects of economic change accompanying foreign investment is shown clearly in the rise of exports of beans and of beancake from Manchuria, from 2 to 21 per cent of total exports at the end of the 'twenties, by which time it had become China's leading export. The effect of industrialisation on imports is seen principally through the development of a local cotton industry: between 1900 and the end of the 'twenties imports of cotton goods declined from some 20 per cent of imports to 15 per cent, and cotton yarn from 15 to 2 per cent, while raw cotton imports rose from nil to 7 per cent. At the same time China built up a considerable export (4 per cent of total exports) in cotton goods and yarn. During the period a marked change took place in the relative importance of the various countries trading with China.

[1] C. Hou, *Foreign Investment and Economic Development in China, 1840–1937* (Cambridge, Mass., 1965), p. 14.
[2] Y. Cheng, *Foreign Trade and Industrial Development of China* (Washington, D.C., 1956), pp. 258–9.

The increasing international use of Hong Kong makes it difficult to allocate trade to specific countries, but what is clear is the relative decline in European, especially British, trade with China, and the growth in importance of Japanese and, to some extent, American trade. Between them these two countries accounted for about half China's trade.

The bare statistics of foreign investment and trade in China show some important aspects of the economic impact of the outside world on Chinese economic development. But they reveal little of the broader framework that determined the special character of foreign trade and investment in China. The relative importance of the various countries investing in China was influenced by their political power in the region, and the great change during this period was the decline in the position of Russia and Germany and the rise in that of Japan. Moreover, this investment remained largely within the concession areas. By 1931 almost a half of all foreign direct investment was in Shanghai and almost two-fifths, mainly Japanese and to some extent Russian, in Manchuria. Railways—one of the early important fields of direct foreign investment—were built more for political and military purposes than for profit. Even the small part of government borrowing which was used productively in the building of railways, and not for indemnity for lost wars or servicing past borrowing, normally involved putting the construction and control of the lines in foreign hands. Almost all foreign loans before 1914 were secured by giving foreigners control over specific properties, revenues and taxes of the Chinese government. Even if the political implications of foreign investment are ignored, the economic effects are difficult to assess. On the credit side foreign investment was a means of introducing modern technology into China; it accounted for a large part of such modernisation as took place; in particular locations it provided the stability, law and social overhead capital—transport, public utilities, banking—which benefited Chinese as well as foreign enterprises.[1] On the other hand, the servicing of the foreign debt was a very heavy burden on central government finances, and the very success of foreign investment in its limited areas led to their isolation from the rest of China and the sustained existence of a very marked dual economy.

While investment tended to be localised, the effects of foreign trade were more widespread, though limited to areas near transport facilities, especially along the coast. The products of Western industry were made available to the Chinese, while export markets were provided for a wide range of products from the traditional sector. Generally speaking, throughout this period the 'open door' policy was observed in China's trade, with one major exception: by various means Japan was able to obtain

---

[1] Foreign capital was dominant in the fields of railways, shipping, foreign trade, iron and coal-mining, but in factory manufacturing one estimate places the Chinese share of total output in 1933 at 65 per cent (see C. Hou, *Foreign Investment*, pp. 127–301).

favourable treatment for her own goods in Manchuria, so that about two-thirds of that area's trade in the 1920s was with the Japanese empire. The outstanding characteristics of China's economic history during this period were the limited degree of modernisation and the small amount of foreign investment and trade. By 1914, when her share of world trade was roughly 2 per cent, China had received about $3\frac{1}{2}$ per cent of all foreign investment. At these levels, foreign trade and investment could not have effected a significant transformation of the economy, even if much of the investment had not been directed towards political ends. In part, the smallness of the foreign involvement can be explained in terms of the general lack of profitable opportunities in low-income countries with a high population density. But, in part also, it was a consequence of the Chinese failure to adapt to the needs of economic modernisation and of the political disorder that was endemic in the country throughout the period.

The acceptance, albeit reluctantly, by the Western powers of the erosion of their privileges during the 1920s reflected, in part, the small scale of their economic interests. For Britain, in 1929, investments in China represented only 5 per cent of her foreign investments and trade with China only 3 per cent of her external trade. For Japan, on the other hand, the changed position of China presented a substantial problem. Japanese investment in Manchuria, and the trade which was largely based upon her privileged position in that part of China, made important contributions to her national income. Moreover, she continued to look to Manchuria—as she had done since the beginning of the century—as a source of raw materials essential to her increasingly industrialised economy. By 1930 the position of Manchuria was the critical point in China's international relations.

Most of the forces that reshaped Far Eastern politics in the 'twenties had become apparent during the war or its immediate aftermath. But in the years following the Washington Conference the powers paid scant regard to them. They tended to ignore the broader implications of Japan's increasing industrialisation, of the emergence of a new generation of leaders in China, and of the Soviet Union's determination to play a major role in the region. This neglect was, in part, a consequence of their inability to comprehend the character or scale of these developments; but it derived, more directly, from their preoccupation with considerations of a different order. At Washington they had created a framework for international co-operation in the Far East; and current circumstances confirmed them in their resolve to confine their policies within it. Japan's economic ties with the United States provided her government with a powerful reason for eschewing expansionist aims in China. And, more generally, the disordered state of China encouraged restraint. Economic objectives—whether in relation to the development of trade or the payment of debts—could not be effectively pursued; and it was easy to argue that the time was not ripe either for the termination of extra-territoriality or for the restoration of tariff autonomy.

None the less, the powers had agreed at Washington to discuss China's demand for the removal of restrictions upon her control of the tariff. For several years action was postponed not only because of the general reservations of the major powers but also because France had declined to ratify the customs treaty. In 1925, however, after French ratification had been obtained, the Washington powers accepted an invitation from China to attend a tariff conference at Peking in October of that year. Detailed and carefully considered proposals for the restoration of tariff autonomy were presented by the government of China. These were accepted by the representatives of the powers, in so far as they related to the ultimate solution of the problem. But disagreement arose regarding the arrangements that should operate during a transitional period. The conference was unwilling to place substantially increased revenue in the hands of the Chinese while the country remained politically unstable. Since the Peking government controlled only a relatively small part of China, it seemed certain that much of the additional revenue would fall into the hands of rival war-lords and thus exacerbate the prevailing disorder. While the conference was in session, conditions in China further deteriorated. Fighting between rival factions cut communication between Peking and the sea; hostile demonstrations against the government occurred in the city itself; and, finally, in April 1926 the régime of Tuan Ch'i-jui fell from power. This last event was followed, perforce, by a suspension of the conference.

During the first weeks of the conference, the American Minister to Peking, in writing to Washington, had pointed to the unreality of discussing the attainment of long-term objectives with a government that might not be able to retain office 'for more than a few weeks or even a few days'.[1] As discussion proceeded, members of the conference also became increasingly aware of the element of fiction that underlay the whole policy of international co-operation in the Far East. And, after the final collapse of the conference, the governments which had been represented at it were forced to recognise the deficiencies of the 'Washington system' and to begin to redefine their positions upon a more realistic basis.

In their thinking upon China, the powers had failed, in particular, to take adequate account of the actions of Russia. The Soviet Union had reached a settlement of Russo-Chinese differences in a treaty signed with the Peking government in 1924; and, in doing so, it had emphasised its 'anti-imperialist' stand by abandoning any claim to extra-territorial rights for its citizens. But, of far greater importance, it had established close

[1] Quoted in Akira Iriye, *After Imperialism. The Search for a New Order in the Far East, 1921–1931* (Cambridge, Mass., 1965), p. 72.

relations with the Nationalist movement centred on Canton. With the help of Russian advisers, the Kuomintang was reorganised. It adopted a totalitarian structure resembling that of the Communist party in Russia; it developed methods for the mass indoctrination of workers and peasants; and it acquired a body of doctrine in 'The Three People's Principles' presented to it by Sun Yat-sen, as its president, in 1924. In addition, it entered into an alliance with the Chinese Communist party, which had been formed in Shanghai in 1921. These political moves were complemented by the creation of a revolutionary army. To provide leadership for this force that would be both technically competent and politically sound, a military academy was established near Canton, under the direction of Chiang Kai-shek.

The Russians had thus changed the situation in China in two important ways. Through their relations both with Peking and with the Nationalist movement, they had stimulated antagonism towards the Western powers and Japan. Through their assistance to the Nationalists, they had decisively shifted the balance of political power in the country. Before the arrival of Russian advisers, the Kuomintang had been kept together largely by its members' common acceptance of the need for political modernisation and by their loyalty to the person of Sun Yat-sen; and its government at Canton had been dependent for military support upon alliances with provincial leaders. Under Russian guidance, it had been transformed into a powerful revolutionary organisation, able to use both force and persuasion effectively in its pursuit of power.

When the tariff conference came to its ignominious end, the Kuomintang army was on the point of marching northward. Since the death of Sun Yat-sen in the previous year, the leadership of the movement had been weakened by antagonism between supporters and opponents of the link with the Communists; and this division continued to complicate the Nationalists' thrust for power. But, in relation to popular attitudes towards the advancing army, the dispute within the leadership was a factor of secondary importance. 'The ultimate cause of all the difficulties and sufferings of the Chinese people', the Nationalists had declared, 'lies with the aggression of the imperialists and the cruelty and violence of their tools, the nation-selling warlords.'[1] As the army passed through country where Kuomintang agents had been active among both civilians and provincial soldiers, it was received as a force of liberation. By the end of 1927 a Nationalist government, led by Chiang Kai-shek, was established at Nanking and was preparing to send the army north again to topple the enfeebled government that still survived at Peking, under the leadership of the Manchurian war-lord Chang Tso-lin.

From the beginning of the 'northern expedition' the powers had been compelled to take account of the Nationalists' success. But they had also

[1] Quoted *ibid.* p. 93.

been confronted by other evidence that the Chinese were no longer willing to tolerate encroachments upon the country's sovereignty. The Peking government, as well as the Nationalists, began to collect additional customs duties that the tariff conference had refused to authorise. Foreign privileges were frequently ignored in the treaty ports. And the demand for a fundamental revision of all treaties was asserted as uncompromisingly by northern merchants and industrialists as by the Kuomintang.

These developments produced a gradual change in the attitudes of the powers. Since the principle of international co-operation had been undermined by their dilatory and unrealistic approach to the situation in China during the preceding years, they began to act independently in defence of their national interests.

For Britain, the problem was a particularly complex one. Her interests were long established and substantial in scale, and they were largely concentrated in areas that were affected at an early stage by the Nationalist advance. For these reasons, a major share of Chinese antagonism to foreign interests was directed upon them. But, for the same reasons, Britain was the first of the powers to recognise the importance of establishing friendly relations with the Nationalists and of preparing for the time when they should have occupied Peking. The British government made it clear that it would be ready to discuss treaty revision and other matters as soon as political stability was restored. In the meantime, it sought to maintain a balance between the making of minor concessions and the defence of its major interests. Foremost among the latter was the British interest in Shanghai. When the growth of civil disorder seemed to endanger trade and investment and the security of British nationals in Shanghai, the British military establishment there was heavily reinforced. By this action—so much more clear cut than the conciliatory gestures and statements of intent by which the British government had hoped to gain Chinese goodwill—anti-British feeling was strengthened among both the Nationalists and the supporters of the Peking government.

The principal beneficiary of the British protection of Shanghai was probably the United States. The American government, like the British, hoped for the emergence of a stable régime in China which would be able to exercise the full powers of sovereignty; but it had been somewhat less conciliatory than the British in its general handling of the immediate situation. None the less, by being relieved of the necessity for military intervention in defence of American interests, it was able to preserve the country's reputation as China's firmest friend.

To Japan, the changed situation in China was of critical importance; but, since her interests were preponderantly in the north, she had some time in which to develop—and to reveal—her new strategy. In January 1927, when the Nationalist advance into north China seemed imminent, the Japanese Foreign Minister, Shidehara Kijuro, made a statement of policy in very general terms. The Japanese government, like those of Britain and the United States, declared that the Chinese should be left to settle their internal differences and affirmed its willingness to consider sympathetically Chinese demands. But it also stressed the need for close economic co-operation between the two countries and for the protection of Japanese interests. This statement, by its very generality, left Japan with ample scope for manœuvre; and, within the next few months, several events occurred that led to an increasing emphasis upon its more positive precepts and implications. In April a new government took office in Tokyo, led by Tanaka Giichi, a man of military background, who was firmly committed to the maintenance of Japan's position in Manchuria. A little earlier Nationalist soldiers had attacked foreigners and damaged foreign property in Nanking. Responsibility for these attacks was attributed to the Communist—and thus Russian-inspired—section of the movement. Japan was therefore able, without inconsistency, to give positive support to the Nationalist right wing, led by Chiang Kai-shek.

The January statement had not specifically mentioned Japanese interests in Manchuria. Essentially, Japan was concerned with the protection of her right to dominate the Manchurian economy and to integrate it with her own and with the maintenance of the administrative and other services that were necessary to the fulfilment of her economic objectives. A considerable range of views was held in Japanese circles as to how these interests could best be protected; but it was everywhere taken for granted that the Manchurian problem should be handled separately from that of relations with China proper.

Though Japanese leaders thus considered that the Manchurian problem was, in itself, of a special character, they recognised that their solution of it would affect their relations not only with China but also with the Western powers. For this reason, their thinking was influenced by consideration both of existing relationships and of expectations regarding the future. Those who were anxious not to disturb Japan's close links with the United States found in this, for example, a strong ground for favouring a solution that would leave substantial authority in the hands of a Chinese or Manchurian administration. Those, on the other hand, who believed that war with the United States was eventually inevitable regarded complete control as essential to Japan's defence. Differences of this kind, coupled with the vested interests of the military and civil groups concerned in the exercise of Japan's rights in Manchuria, greatly complicated the development of a clear-cut policy.

When the Chinese Nationalist army continued its move northward in 1928, the question of Manchuria became an urgent one for the government of Japan. Faced with the likelihood that Nationalist troops would soon reach the Manchurian border, it issued a statement of its own position. The Nationalists should not enter Manchuria and would be opposed by Japanese forces if they did so. Chang Tso-lin should retire from Peking but be permitted to form a separate government in Manchuria. On many grounds, this was a blatantly disingenuous proposal that ill concealed Japanese determination to detach Manchuria from China and control it through a puppet administration. But, up to a point, it was acted upon. The Nationalists, as their advance brought them towards Peking, offered to allow Chang Tso-lin and his forces to withdraw peacefully into Manchuria. Since his régime faced imminent collapse, Chang accepted the offer; but, when he reached Manchuria, the railway carriage in which he was travelling was blown up by Japanese army officers.

The Nationalist occupation of Peking marked the attainment, in a formal sense, of the objective towards which the revolutionary movement had been working since the formation of the *Tung-meng-hui* in 1905. China possessed a government that could claim jurisdiction over the whole of the country and that was committed to handling its relations with foreign powers on terms of equality. In reality, however, the Nationalists were still confronted by formidable difficulties. The leaders of the new government were deeply divided on basic issues of domestic policy. The government's actual authority in the provinces was very limited, so that it could neither obtain the revenue from land taxes nor disarm the private armies of the former war-lords; and in relation to Manchuria its position remained a particularly difficult one. At the end of 1928, after the failure of Japanese efforts to prevent it, the reunion of China and Manchuria was brought about; but the Manchurian government retained a large measure of autonomy, and the presence of the Japanese in the region created a further impediment to Chinese control. The internal weakness of the government did not prevent it, however, from adopting a strong foreign policy.

Soon after the occupation of Peking, the Nationalist government declared its intention of terminating all unequal treaties. This action evoked a generally sympathetic response. In accordance with their earlier policy statements, the Western powers signed new treaties that restored tariff autonomy to China; and, in doing so, they accorded recognition to the new régime. In the case of the United States, support for the government went considerably further. American advisers were sent to China; and American business interests provided financial and technical assistance.

Japanese policy towards China was both more complex and less unequivocal. The assassination of Chang Tso-lin had been an attempt by a section of the army to push the Japanese government further than it was prepared to go. Its organisers had hoped that it would create disorder in Manchuria and thus lead to the establishment of Japanese military control. In the event, they merely reinforced existing Chinese suspicions of their country's intentions, since neither the Japanese nor the Chinese government was willing to precipitate a crisis.

The position of the Tanaka cabinet was a difficult one. It believed that

369

the protection of Japanese interests in Manchuria required both an improvement in the country's relations with the Western powers and a curbing of the intransigence, and growing insubordination, of the army. But the powers had been alienated by the high-handed actions of the army; and the latter's support for an aggressive policy was strengthened by the evident unwillingness of the powers to act jointly with Japan. In these circumstances, the cabinet decided that it was essential to establish a close working relationship with the Chinese Nationalists. When Manchuria was reunited with China, the Japanese government therefore accepted the development without protest. Meanwhile, it had begun discussions with the Chinese regarding the restoration of tariff autonomy and the settlement of other matters that were in dispute between them. When agreement in principle was reached on these issues, it was followed by Japan's formal recognition of the new régime in China.

Shortly after this development occurred, Tanaka resigned from office. For some time he had been faced with growing opposition, as a result of his inability to bring to trial the officers responsible for the assassination of Chang Tso-lin. The new Prime Minister, Hamaguchi Osachi, and his cabinet were even more firmly committed to a policy of moderation in Manchuria and to seeking the co-operation of the Western powers. Primarily, they were influenced by economic considerations. They believed that the long-term interests of Japan would best be served by exposing its economy more fully to the ordinary pressures of international trade. They therefore removed restrictions on the export of gold and, by doing so, increased the country's dependence, during the subsequent period of adjustment, on the support of other major trading nations. But the new policy, by placing less emphasis on the economic links between Japan and Manchuria, directly affected the government's attitude towards China. The most important consequence of this diminished concern with the maintenance of special privileges was the replacement of the general agreement that had previously been reached on tariff autonomy by a formal treaty.

For the government of China, the treaty with Japan marked the successful conclusion of its struggle for control of the tariff. But it had been no less concerned with the removal of restrictions upon its jurisdiction over foreigners.[1] In April 1929 it had addressed notes to Britain, the United States and France seeking an early termination of extra-territoriality. During the following months, the powers made it clear that, while they favoured the gradual reduction of extra-territorial rights, they were not prepared to agree to their complete abrogation almost immediately, as desired by the Chinese. Their reservations were strengthened by the brash actions of the Chinese government at this time against Russian consular

[1] On this subject, see Wesley R. Fishel, *The End of Extra-territoriality in China* (Berkeley and Los Angeles, 1952), pp. 127–87.

and railway officials in Manchuria, which precipitated a brief armed conflict with the Soviet Union. And in 1930 and 1931, when the renewal of civil war in China emphasised both the tenuousness of the government's authority and the continued insecurity of foreign residents, their doubts increased as to whether the time was ripe for any radical change. None the less, negotiations were continued; and by the summer of 1931 both Britain and the United States had reached a substantial measure of agreement with China. In September, however, Japanese troops seized the city of Mukden, in Manchuria. The tragic significance of this event was quickly recognised: it weakened the position of the government of China far more disastrously than the disturbances of the immediately preceding years. Discussions on the ending of extra-territoriality were therefore suspended till the return of more settled times.

The resort to violence in Manchuria was not the result of a change in the policy of the Japanese government. The cabinet had not abandoned the economic and foreign policies that it had espoused on its accession to office in 1929; but the acceptability of those policies, and hence the effectiveness of the government itself, had been undermined by events. Japan's return to the gold standard had been closely followed by the onset of the world depression. The effect on the Japanese economy of falling prices and contracting markets was thus exacerbated by its recently increased exposure to world pressures. Nor could Japan obtain assistance from the United States or Britain, since they too were facing economic crises. The decline in incomes and employment was widely attributed to the defects of the government and its policies.

The growth of popular opposition greatly strengthened the hand of the military. The view that Japan's survival depended on the strengthening of her armed forces and the consolidation of her position in China, rather than upon her co-operation with the Western powers, now possessed mass support. High-ranking officers, both in Tokyo and in Manchuria, therefore prepared to take revolutionary action. A plot to overthrow the government in May 1931 had failed. But the seizure of Mukden on the night of 18–19 September marked the beginning of a period of military dominance in Japan.

At the beginning of the twentieth century, the international politics of the Far East and the Pacific had been dominated by the Western powers. By the 1930s those powers were, at most, reluctant imperialists. In China, their surviving privileges were retained mainly because the Chinese had been unable to resolve their internal problems. In the islands of the South Pacific, the continuance of their administrative responsibilities merely reflected their acceptance of common assumptions regarding the capacity of 'backward' peoples to govern themselves. In Australia and New Zealand, the residual powers that were still possessed by Britain were retained at the request of the governments of those two countries, which had been un-willing to accept the removal of restrictions upon their sovereignty that the Statute of Westminster made available to them.[1]

But the role that had once been theirs was now being assumed by Japan. The seizure of Mukden was followed by the complete conquest of Manchuria and the creation of the puppet state of Manchukuo. Inter-vention by the League of Nations, with the intention of restoring the sovereignty of China under conditions that would provide protection for Japanese rights and interests, was angrily opposed by Japan and led to her resignation from the organisation.

These actions further reduced political stability in the Far East. Since domestic political circumstances made withdrawal impossible, Japan in-evitably extended the scope of her aggression (see below, ch. xxiii). To counter increasing Chinese hostility, the Japanese built up their position in Inner Mongolia and in the north-eastern provinces of China proper by a combination of military action and political intrigue. In 1937 an armed exchange between Chinese and Japanese troops near Peking precipitated a full-scale invasion of China. The Nationalist government, forced to flee westward, established a new capital at Chungking; and in 1940 Japan installed a puppet régime at Nanking.

Japanese imperialism had reached maturity, however, at a period in which major international conflicts could be resolved only on a world scale. The seizure of Mukden and its consequences had encouraged both Italy and Germany similarly to flout world opinion; and with both these powers Japan made pacts. Japanese policy towards China was thus a major cause of the second world war; and its ultimate success or failure became a matter which only the results of that war could determine.

[1] See ch. xiii.

CHAPTER XIII

THE BRITISH COMMONWEALTH
OF NATIONS

NEVER had the British Empire been more unpopular in the world than it was when the nineteenth century passed over into the twentieth; never indeed had the idea of empire been more questionable in the eyes even of a number of the subjects of that empire; but never did the majority of Britons feel more justified in taking pride in the dominance which it exerted over so large a part of the earth's surface—its 'dominion over palm and pine'. The extraordinary, the frightful happenings in South Africa, where for a few months the British army was so ubiquitously beaten by elusive bands of bearded farmers, gave delight to those Europeans who now saw perfidious Albion in decline and fall. But Albion, though puzzled and perturbed, did not think of decline and fall; it sighed over its generals, sent out others, accepted help from the colonies ('the lion's cubs', in the language of the time, 'rallying to the dam'); and with tedious inevitability wore the farmers down. On 31 May 1902 the Boer leaders accepted the Peace of Vereeniging and British sovereignty. The readers of Kipling were reassured; the Union Jack, fluttering above the veld, marked the triumph of civilisation and efficiency; the way stood open for the pacifying efforts of Lord Milner's 'kindergarten', the young men from Oxford whose minds were suffused with the light of a liberal empire; and colonial Prime Ministers, like New Zealand's Richard John Seddon, released the ample folds of their homespun eloquence, congratulating and advising, upon a Mother Country that was both gratified and embarrassed.

Yet at that peak of victory men might well have been touched by anxious questionings. The disappointed enemies of Albion, could they have seen farther, might yet have had their comfort. For all was not lost to the overwhelmed and obscurantist old man, Kruger, to his defeated yet hopeful juniors Botha and Smuts. The Boer mind was not conquered: the treaty had promised self-government. The conquerors, it seemed, had at last learned the lesson proclaimed by Burke, that a great empire and little minds go ill together. They intended to be magnanimous; and the magnanimous empire, it became plain in the next fifty years, would cease to be an empire at all in any sense intelligible to older centuries. Even to the mid-nineteenth century, which had made the remarkable discovery of 'responsible government for colonies', the development of that responsible government might perhaps have seemed too extravagantly logical. Dominion, it was to become plain, could not be exercised over dominions.

26-2

Certainly the phrase 'dominion status' had not, in 1902, been invented. They were few, after all, who gazed on the word 'empire' with queasy stomachs. Earnest federalists there were who showed worry about the future of the empire. But to most people, Britons or colonials, imperial stability, like European stability, was in the order of things. Amid reasserted stability they did not pause to consider the implications for empire of the other British ideal of freedom: freedom, the instrument of magnanimity. There were Victorians, no doubt, who would have accepted as natural the Statute of Westminster, 1931; but would they have understood the extraordinary cohesive power that has gone with this flight from *imperium*?

The Victorian theory of empire was not, of course, simple, and was not static. It had dropped close economic control as one of its ingredients and objects. From a free-trade, still *laissez-faire* Britain the imperial statesmen looked out tolerantly enough, though a little uneasily, on self-governing colonies which had become steadily protectionist—and some of which, like New Zealand and its Australian sister, by 1900 had ceased to regard *laissez faire* as at all a tolerable social rule. In the imperial economy these communities, with Canada and Newfoundland, were still preponderantly 'primary producers'—the role of the southern ones accentuated by the brilliant success obtained in the refrigeration of meat and butter. But that did not affect the variety of their political development, under the benevolent metropolitan eye. The unitary system of small New Zealand or smaller, sparsely settled Newfoundland had little in common—save responsible government—with the thirty-year-old federalism of Canada, or with that other federalism which came into operation in the brand-new Australian Commonwealth on the first day of 1901. Nor were the two federations at all identical in design, in distribution of powers or in the power to adjust and amend: Australia was determined that necessary change should be as exclusively as possible an Australian concern,[1] while the Judicial Committee had been, and was still to be, one of the great interpreters of Canadian constitutionalism, and amendments to the British North America Act of 1867 could be made only by parliament at Westminster. Different from federal and unitary governments alike, different also in its place in world economics, was the Cape Colony, with its South African neighbours; poor in agricultural resources, leaning heavily on gold and diamonds, its politics complicated by the status of a governor who had at once to work with responsible ministers and, as High Commissioner, to control relations with Boers whether independent or conquered, and with native peoples under British rule inside South African geographical limits; a governor who was at once constitutional

---

[1] Nevertheless the decisions of the Judicial Committee of the Privy Council on some Australian cases, involving federal powers, carried to it on appeal have been of marked significance—for example, the judgements on marketing of 1936, and on the nationalisation of banks of 1949.

head of a self-governing colony and an administrative and diplomatic official responsible to England. But, though this was so at the beginning of the century, within a decade war, magnanimity, and economic necessity had done their work; and the Union of South Africa Act of 1909 created still another constitutional variant of that self-government which, according to Campbell-Bannerman's paradox of statesmanship, was better than 'good' government. It was neither federalism, nor, in the New Zealand sense, quite unitary, for the South African provinces had real powers. It could, by men like Botha and Smuts, be worked as good government; and the Union, in its relations to the imperial power, took its place securely enough as another of those dominions beyond the seas which owed allegiance to the crown but were, certainly, no longer simply colonies of England. An index of that subtle but far-reaching change had been the formal enlargement of the status of New Zealand from 'colony' to 'dominion' in 1907; though what precisely might be implied in that status, beyond compliment, was for legal conference. The Dominion of Canada was a Dominion; so, now, was New Zealand; so was Newfoundland; Australia was a Commonwealth; South Africa was a Union. Was there any difference, within the ambit of the Empire?

Whatever the answer to that question might be, there was no doubt of the difference between them and other parts of the Empire: those parts that before long were to be called in general, in distinction from Commonwealth and Dominions, 'the colonial empire': the moribund West Indies, into the economy of which Joseph Chamberlain had recently injected the stimulus of an Imperial Department of Agriculture; the large areas of the upper and lower Niger, just ceded by a commercial company to the crown, and the other territories of West Africa, fatal with fevers, waiting on the schools of tropical medicine founded in England in 1899; the Rhodesias, still smelling somewhat to tender consciences of the blood of the Matabele; the great Bechuanaland and Nyasaland protectorates; the other protectorates of Uganda and British East Africa, where the Foreign Office presided over economic penetration; the virtual protectorate of Egypt and the Sudan, the 'joint possession' of Egypt and Great Britain; Ceylon; the native states of Malaysia, and Singapore and Hong Kong, those two nodal points of an immense commerce, polyglot empires in themselves; in the great ocean to the south, a spatter of islands Polynesian, Micronesian, Melanesian—more or less exploited, more or less missionised, less rather than more administered. Here was an odd assemblage of bits and pieces, almost entirely the product of Victorian expansion; and very clearly, so the Edwardians as well as Victorians thought, unfit for self-government. Without civilised or scientific tradition, unacquainted with the amiable conventions of parliamentary debate, only a few years earlier large numbers of their peoples had stumbled in the long sad fettered lines of the slave trade, had speared one another or had their brains knocked out in fantastic varieties of savage experience; or had merely fished and picked coconuts. It was indeed clear that for them good government was better than self-government; that for them young empire-builders should drive the road and bridge the ford, direct plantation-labour and impose the Law. But was it—altogether—clear? What, after all, was good government? What was the Law? The decades immediately in the future were to see some questioning, some diversity of answer, on these points; and the lapse of another fifty years made it begin to seem improbable that a sharp line could be forever drawn, in constitutional status, between the dominions and the colonies, the free communities and the dependent empire.

And there was India. For India the division of centuries was to be a division of epochs, economic as well as political. Autocracy virtually untouched was attended in Lord Curzon's viceroyalty with uproar and indignation. What change would there be? How far was the Indian tradition inimical to self-government?

The historian, gazing back, can see change and at least some of the determinants of change. Most of the imperial fabric had been raised in a remarkably short space of time, in a world that strongly affected the fashion of building, and could not cease to affect it in a new century. Economic and social development on a world scale, two world wars and a vast depression, political and social revolution, the ground-swell of Asian unrest, were among the determinants. So also was political wisdom, in despite of vested interests: magnanimity in spite of the arguments of fear. In a remarkably short space of time the Victorian—or Edwardian—empire was gone, utterly destroyed, the insubstantial pageant of its imperial vision faded. And yet something remained for a future historian to define; the extraordinary British paradox remained; a 'Commonwealth' —whatever that term really meant—remained.

The development of the twentieth-century empire, then, on a basis of 'determinants', is a psychological development. The change of mind displays itself, for example, in unease at the speaking of the very word 'empire'. Men did not wish to be dominated—that had long been true in the settled colonies; it was to become true in a very short time in India, and rather more slowly, irregularly indeed, in large parts of the 'dependent empire'. But also they no longer wished to dominate. The imperialism of the 'nineties, part crude, part liberal, a good deal romantic, began to give way to a new attitude, rather sceptical, increasingly critical. The literature of imperialism began to be a literature of research, critical certainly, in which nineteenth-century humanitarianism was linked increasingly to a new ethnological approach, and to a determination to take full account of economic factors. Its critical role stimulated controversy (where the African colonies were concerned) reminiscent of the great days of Aborigines Protection a hundred years before. There was this difference, that in the course of the century it had become rather difficult for the reformer to be self-righteous; human association of all kinds had become too much the object of exhaustive examination.

It remains true that, in the greater part of the period now being considered, constitutional interest centres on the development of the relations of that group of communities which came to be called the British Commonwealth of Nations—of the United Kingdom and the dominions, the imperial metropolis and the semi-British societies who were exploiting the possibilities of responsible self-government. 'Semi-British' it is necessary to write; for, however much some dominions might glory in their British blood and tradition, the French-Canadians of Quebec, the Afrikaners of the Union, the Irish of the Free State (or Eire) made the problem of relations a perpetually unfinished one. The position of 'racial' minorities within the whole had been by no means so happily accommodated as enthusiastic persons were wont to assume in the early days of the century; the general British community as a reconciler of national differences had still some way to go.

It is this fact which is one of the underlying causes of the growing feeling of nationality in more than one dominion. French-Canadians showed no sign of being assimilated; their birth-rate was high, they were virtually a colonising people, as they spilled over into the other provinces of Canada; and wherever they went they carried the demand for special provision for their needs. Quebec remained a corner-stone of federal politics; its views of the world at large were a determinant in Canadian foreign policy that ministers would have ignored with peril certainly, and probably with disaster. But at least the French-Canadian was in a federation that managed to get along fairly peaceably within itself as the decades passed; he was not a republican; he was not tempted to take advantage of crisis by armed rebellion. In South Africa, on the other hand, there was an element never reconciled to British hegemony or even to British association; the war of 1899 threw off a last flurry in the rebellion of 1914; and this Afrikaner irreconcilability was the despair of many people who considered themselves reasonable. The Dutch Reformed church was a focus of tradition as compelling as the Catholicism of Quebec; in Afrikaans there was a language susceptible of literary development, and, as in Quebec, an infant native literature began to be consciously cultivated. The material unification of the world was to be offset, it seemed, by increasing cultural fission. In South Africa there was the added factor that the Afrikaner, with his distaste for the British association, considered himself also a member of a master race, the rock and fortress of European civilisation in the midst of the inferior millions of the native tribes. Here was complete intransigence, implacability emotional as well as political. Compared to this, the influence of an Irish strain in the population of

377

eastern Australia might seem quite negligible; yet, counting up the causes of Australian nationalism it would be wrong to omit that strain, with its determination not to be taken in by any branch of English policy anywhere. On the whole, however, the national sentiment of Australia was Australian, owing something to the continental nature and democratic social development of the country, and marked by a literature that was sometimes almost belligerently self-conscious in its cultivation of local colour. Only in New Zealand was national status uncomplicated by the existence of a national minority; for the Maori people, though in this period working out a sort of cultural and economic renaissance of extreme importance to itself, was not in the least concerned with status in an empire or commonwealth. A real feeling of New Zealand nationality, a thing felt in the bones, born of time and isolation, came only in the 'thirties and 'forties—or perhaps the first individual expression of it came only then. There were New Zealanders before.

For more than one reason, beyond national tradition, these communities began to feel, and to press, a separate identity; and in the complex twentieth-century world there was ample scope for difference of opinion. To speak in general terms, for fifty years their life was becoming steadily more complex, was being lived steadily on a larger scale. Economically by no means self-sufficient, they were yet building a wider basis for wealth, and were producing more of it. The old simple theory of imperial preference was going with the old simple relation of primary producer to metropolitan manufacturer and financier; even where, as in the case of New Zealand, that relation essentially remained, the impact of the Great Depression, followed by world war, urged a determination to manufacture; and the material of manufacture, even if not local, might not necessarily come from Great Britain. To take an example, the steel used in New Zealand towards the end of this period was largely the product of Australia. Australia, still with wheat and wool as fundamental exports, created heavy as well as light industries which had reached major importance by 1939; and, while the prairie provinces of Canada stood deep in their ocean of wheat, its industrialised eastern provinces joined the great manufacturing countries of the world. Populations were increasing, though the centre of white population still remained the United Kingdom; but, more important, they were increasing as native-born Canadians or Australians, with family ties concentrated in the one country, and with less and less tendency to think in terms of a 'mother-country', as the nineteenth-century sentiment of 'Home' steadily faded. To all this, in a world of trouble and strategic calculations, were added the facts and the implications of geography: the fact that Canada, sharing the economic life and philosophy of the United States, was becoming an American power; the fact that Australia, almost unconsciously, was becoming a Pacific power; the fact that Great Britain could no longer control all the oceans of the world; the fact, explicit as the decade of the 'forties opened, that not merely were the days of expansion over, but the prospect of power was a dwindling one.

This dispersed nationalism in itself, even in its early days, would have been enough to render null the theory of imperial federation that had attracted so many well-meaning people in the last twenty years of Victoria's reign: when the fourth Colonial Conference met in London in 1902 the issue was dead, and no later agitation, however ingenious and plausible the reasoning, could breathe life into it. The proposal brought before the Imperial Conference of 1911 by Sir Joseph Ward, the Prime Minister of New Zealand, was notable for the unanimity and scorn with which it was pulverised by his fellow statesmen. Yet in retrospect this proposal has a significance which is lost if it is regarded merely as an attempt to revive the dead cause. For Ward was not thinking merely of constitution-building, nor even of defence—which had already concerned Imperial Conferences a good deal. In 1902 Canada, breaking away from the general meagre support of the British navy, proposed to build a fleet of its own, an example followed with more immediate effect by Australia in 1907. In that year, however, there was common agreement over the foundation of the Imperial General Staff. Ward wished to improve on this, and to create a sort of 'Imperial Parliament of defence', which should control not merely naval and military matters, but the whole scope of foreign policy. His lower chamber elected on a population basis would certainly have deprived any partner except the United Kingdom of real power; and, apart from other details, the sacrifice of autonomy was too great a price to pay. Nor, argued Mr Asquith, could the United Kingdom possibly share control of foreign policy: there sovereignty must be unimpaired. But the desire for a share was precisely what lay behind Ward's imprecise scheme. Not merely was he conscientiously anxious for participation in the burden of defence: he was anxious also that dominions which might be called on to shed blood as a result of British policy should have some say in its formation.

Nor was New Zealand alone in this feeling, or, indeed, generally the most prominent in expressing it. Ward's inadequate exercise in federalism was, paradoxically enough, only one offshoot in a general growth of autonomy, which was leading the dominions inevitably, though hardly as deliberate choosers, towards an individual international status. (Nothing ever more admirably illustrated Cromwell's dictum that no man goes farther than he who knows not where he is going.) Their right to separate withdrawal from or adherence to British trade treaties was followed in 1907 by recognition of their right to negotiate their own trade treaties, subject only to final signature by a Foreign Office-accredited plenipotentiary. Then came the Anglo-American arbitration treaty of 1908, which bound Canada only with Canadian concurrence, extending thus the principle far beyond matters of trade. Nevertheless, in the drafting of the Declaration of London of 1909 (covering contraband and neutral trade in time of war, a result of the 1907 Hague Conference) the dominions were not consulted; and some dominion statesmen brooded. Thus, though Canada in 1910 legislated for itself over a fishery dispute with America, the 1911 Imperial Conference witnessed more than Ward's discontent. Australia protested at the failure to consult the dominions, and suggested, without pressing, direct communication between them and the Foreign Office. Canada differed: consultation, Sir Wilfred Laurier seems to have felt, would argue commitment, and commitment was exactly what French-Canadians would refuse. Nevertheless, in spite of Asquith's *non possumus*, some steps were taken. It was decided that in future the dominions would be consulted over the instructions to delegates to conferences, and over the signature of agreements which might concern them; while upon other international agreements, if time and circumstances permitted, their views would also be invited. The assembled statesmen were then given by the Foreign Secretary an intimate and comprehensive view of the subject-matter of European diplomacy which sent them home, having created a Committee of Imperial Defence, thinking furiously—not so much about the elasticity of the British constitution as about trouble to come.

The development of consultation was to be marked by hesitations, contradictions and nervous withdrawals. No one, it seems, can have suspected the total implications of the word; or measured against the brute facts of international relations a theory which involved all the circumlocutory possibilities of the sequence Foreign Secretary or Cabinet to Colonial Office (Dominions branch) to Governor or Governor-General to dominion Prime Minister and Cabinet and back again. The brute facts proclaimed themselves in the summer of 1914, when the dominions found themselves at war, without motion of their own, as completely and unequivocally as if their autonomy had reached no farther than that of the Isle of Wight. Paradox, however, is always round the corner. The war, begun in what might be described as so constitutionally reactionary a way, itself turned out to be a singular constitutional forcing ground. For the empire that seemed to calculating outside observers to be on the point of dissolution proved to have extraordinary powers of coherence, a tough inner spirit capable of creating new institutions according to its needs. Those needs brought dominion prime ministers to London, where their membership of the Imperial War Cabinet made consultation immediate and effective. So great was the success of this experiment, and so lively the feelings of unity that the common effort aroused, that, when the war-time Imperial Conference of 1917 met, there was general determination that somehow this happy state must be continued in time of peace. The dominions must be fully recognised as 'autonomous nations of an Imperial Commonwealth'. At a later conference the theory of an empire in which unity and autonomy had been so markedly reconciled must be somehow reshaped in accordance with reality.

But what was the nature of reality? It appears that even then there were different interpretations—that Massey from New Zealand, for instance, had been impressed chiefly by the unity possible in the midst of autonomy, Sir Robert Borden from Canada by the autonomy possible in the midst of unity; and Massey as politician was no more conservative than Borden. It was Borden who insisted that the dominions, having devoted themselves so unrelentingly to the purposes of war, and been consulted so freely, be consulted as freely in the making of peace; that dominion leaders could not simply trail subordinate in a British delegation, but must have an independent status of their own. Could the importance conceded to the lesser European countries be denied to these dominions? Could Smuts, who spoke the language of a new and better world, and was listened to, be ignored; could the astute and obstinate Australian Hughes be ignored? So dominion Prime Ministers signed the Treaty of Versailles, as somehow British, but also independent, negotiators; so their countries became members in their own right of the League of Nations created by that anomalous instrument. There seemed, to other people, to be a sort of gross cynicism about these proceedings, perfidiousness in Albion as ever; for were they not merely a means of gaining Britain five votes in the world parliament instead of one? They were not, but, to Europeans whose theories of sovereignty were logical and tight, to Americans whose continental federal system issued in a single foreign policy, the disclaimers might well seem hollow though bland. It was difficult for others to understand a system which many in Britain and in the dominions themselves tended to regard as dangerous nonsense; which was anyhow highly dubious in law; which was, as we can now see, merely constitutional work in progress. Nevertheless, irretraceable steps had been taken. New Zealand might refuse to accept the mandate for western Samoa except through a channel provided by the United Kingdom; Sir John Salmond, that extremely able constitutional lawyer, might return to New Zealand from the Washington Conference in 1922 insisting that the empire had undergone no essential change; but Canada and South Africa, at least, were quite convinced that a new status existed, and that it should continue to exist, and that British statesmen should not be allowed to forget it. And, by a miracle of convenience, this status seemed to provide a solution, at last, for the problem of Ireland.

The constitutional conference that had been expected after the war was not held. There were too many conferences, too many problems; and for the British government the most desperate problem was Ireland. Ireland was not a part of the Commonwealth at all, except in so far as it was part of a United Kingdom that was part of the Commonwealth:

except in so far as it was itself a 'mother-country', losing its sons and daughters to build up dominions and colonies overseas. In an empire those exiles did their best to be a disruptive force. The history of Ireland as a colony was a thing for academic specialists; what mattered to the great body of the Irish was their history as a subject race. In the first decade of the twentieth century they seemed at last to be issuing from that black period, with the promise of Home Rule from a Liberal government dependent on Irish National support; and Home Rule seemed to be realised in the enactment of 1914. But in Ulster there were Unionists prepared to rebel rather than to accept that Act; there were army officers prepared to resign their commissions rather than put down rebellion; and the importation of arms into Ulster was followed by the landing of arms in Dublin Bay and the organisation of the Irish Volunteers. European war reduced all this to small proportions in general feeling, so that the Easter Rebellion in Dublin in 1916, led by a small number of men deliberately offering up their 'blood sacrifice' to revivify Ireland, shocked their contemporaries and the English alike. Guerilla warfare broke out in 1919 and was savage on both sides, and was not brought to an end by the Government of Ireland Act of 1920, which partitioned the country into the six counties of Northern Ireland and the twenty-six of the rebels, with separate parliaments to control local affairs and a sort of federal relationship to Westminster. Only after the opening of the northern parliament in June 1921 did Lloyd George abandon the hope of reducing Ireland to quietude by force, and the rebels consent to a truce, sending to London the delegation that, under the threat of 'immediate and terrible war', accepted the treaty of 6 December. This treaty was approved by the *Dail Eireann* (the 'assembly of Ireland') and the Irish Free State came into existence, to be riven by a civil war imposed by the non-compromisers. But the new government was determined, and the country settled down for ten years to some sort of economic reconstruction, without violent disturbances of its theoretical constitutional position.

The treaty, however, did not prove to have solved the problem. For the Irish wanted clear definition, and that they could not be given in anything short of a republic. The real problem was the nature of their association with the Commonwealth. To well-wishing Commonwealth statesmen like General Smuts the solution seemed to lie in 'Dominion status', wherein, they held, lay all the constitutional flexibility the individual Dominions could wish for. But the other dominions did not have Ireland's history, and historically dominion status implied a close and willing association with Britain, a positive natural desire for the British connection. This was precisely what the Irish did not have. They had been invited to London to 'ascertain how the association of Ireland with the community of nations known as the British Empire can best be reconciled with Irish nationalist aspirations'; but it was the association with England that concerned them, and they were too well aware of the connotations of the word 'Empire'—a word that exerted its own tyranny. Nor has it been easy for any state not a dominion ever to feel quite sure of the virtues of dominion status. What they proposed at the treaty negotiations was, then, their own prescription of 'external association'—that is, absolute sovereignty in internal affairs, and association with Britain in external matters of common concern: Ireland, in fact, a republic outside the Empire but associated with it. It was this proposition that outraged the English political doctrinaire, for whom the symbols of sovereignty—common loyalty to the crown, recognition of the king as head of the state acting through a governor-general appointed by him, an oath of allegiance from members of an Irish parliament—still had a final value. It was these symbols that the Irish doctrinaire could not stomach: they made him the subject of an alien power, a man under dominion rather than the citizen of a dominion. Meanwhile where lay the truth, in the proceedings of every day? The Irish Free State was given the same constitutional status as 'the Dominion of Canada, the Commonwealth of Australia, the Dominion of New Zealand and the Union of South Africa', with more special reference to Canada: 'the law, practice and constitutional usage governing the relationship of the Crown and of the Imperial Parliament to the Dominion of Canada shall govern their relationship to the Irish Free State'. But what, again, was that law, practice and constitutional usage? What, to repeat, was the nature of reality? Certainly, if one were to judge from history, 'dominion status' could not be deemed to be static. Was its secret, then, development? And, if development, how far and how fast could it be allowed to develop? Was there, in fact, any theoretical limit, or might 'law, practice and constitutional usage' be in the end a sort of floating figment, 'a cloud that's dragonish'?

While such questions stirred uneasily in a number of minds, Canada affirmed its national opinion by negotiating a treaty with the United States for the protection of the North Pacific halibut fishery, signed at Washington by a Canadian minister alone, without the intervention of a British ambassador. This led to discussion at the Imperial Conference of 1923 about the mode of negotiating treaties, whence came general agreement over principles of consultation or information, whether the United Kingdom or a dominion should be primarily concerned. This in its turn was followed, within a year, by entire forgetfulness on the British part to consult the dominions over the Treaty of Lausanne; and the month of June 1924 saw almost simultaneously the Canadian Prime Minister reasserting the broken principle, and the Irish Free State dispatching its own minister to Washington. This latter step, an important one, though it again gave pause to the uneasy, was followed shortly by Canada; followed too, as convenience dictated, by the other dominions, in America, Europe and the Far East; so that in twenty years each one of them had its miniature Diplomatic List, and its problem of training young persons for the diplomatic life. In the meantime the uneasy were still further disturbed; and in 1926 a number of arguments were carried to London for settlement at the Imperial Conference of that year—the post-war constitutional conference at last, much more complicated than had seemed likely in 1917.

Constitutional advance within the Commonwealth (a term it was now becoming the habit to use) had been traditionally led by Canada. Canada was still advancing, but had at this stage been joined by the Irish Free State and South Africa. Each, or a considerable party in each, was deeply concerned about its status. The Irish found it impossible to reconcile their interpretation of their new dominion autonomy with treaty limitations. In South Africa the hegemony exercised for so long by Botha and then Smuts had been overthrown by the Nationalists—for whom, it seems, it was very necessary to assert the right of South Africa to secede from the Empire if it so wished. Party feelings were displayed more noisily over the design of a new South African flag, and the manner of flying it, a controversy which issued naturally enough from the thoroughgoing nationalism of the Union. The Commonwealth, or the Empire, could stand any number of flags, but could it admit secession? Canada had more than one trouble. In politics it had experienced a first-class crisis, and in law a serious rebuff. The crisis concerned the governor-general's prerogative. Had that personage still, when advised by his prime minister to dissolve parliament, a right to discretionary refusal, or was he bound to obey? Lord Byng, by refusing a dissolution to one minister and granting it to another, outraged Mackenzie King, who had been denied—and who denounced such procedure as a blow at the very heart of dominion freedom, a return to colonialism, a jeopardising of all the fruits of constitutional progress. For, if Canadian autonomy was real, then the Governor-General's prerogative, his discretion to bind or loose, could be no more real that that of the king in Great Britain. (The true measure of constitutional advance is indicated by the subsequent controversy, which centred not on any difference of degree in prerogative, but on whether the king himself had discretion or not.) In the legal sphere, feelings, though less excited, were no less upset. The issue arose on a criminal case, *Nadan v. the King*, carried on appeal to the Judicial Committee of the Privy Council. A Canadian act of 1888 had purported to abolish appeal to the Privy Council in criminal cases. The Privy Council now declared this abolition void: first, because appeals were regulated by the Judicial Committee Acts of 1833 and 1844—British legislation—and abolition by a Canadian act infringed the Colonial Laws Validity Act 1865; while, secondly, if that famous measure were not enough, the Canadian Act assumed extra-territorial power, which the Privy Council would not concede. Canadian laws, or the laws of any other dominion, could have force only within the dominion which enacted them; they could not affect a court elsewhere domiciled. So—concluded Canadian lawyers—Canadian justice was to be determined ultimately not by Canadian laws in Canadian courts, but by a clutter of transatlantic anachronisms, applied by transatlantic judges whose régime many Canadians disliked. The load of discontents was enough to ensure that that Imperial Conference of 1926 would not escape some difficult constitutional thinking. It is notable that Australia, New Zealand and Newfoundland had registered no dismay. Sensitive statesmen—one may instance Smuts in South Africa and Amery in England—had already been grappling with the problems both of principle and of formulation.

The celebrated Conference set up an 'Inter-Imperial Relations Committee' with a celebrated dialectician as its chairman. But it took the Committee a fortnight's hard work, as well as all the subtlety of Lord Balfour, to arrive at the point where it 'readily defined' the 'position and mutual relation of the group of self-governing communities composed of Great Britain and the Dominions'—which had, 'as regards all vital matters, reached its full development'. Italicised by a printer's mistake but none the less of singular importance, the definition proceeded. Its members were '*autonomous Communities within the British Empire, equal in status, in no way subordinate one to another in any aspect of their domestic or internal affairs, though united by a common allegiance to the Crown, and freely associated as members of the British Commonwealth of Nations*'. But, the report went on, the principles of equality and similarity, appropriate to *status*, did not universally extend to function. Diplomacy and defence demanded flexible machinery. The committee had endeavoured not only to state political theory, but to apply it to the common needs; that is, two aspects of what we may now, following the custom of the 'twenties, call 'dominion status', the domestic and the external—or, perhaps, status looked at from within the Commonwealth and from outside it—were both to be considered.

On the domestic side administrative, legislative and judicial forms admittedly were out of date. It was easy enough to alter the royal title now that Ireland was no longer part of a United Kingdom. 'His Majesty's Government in Great Britain' certainly had now no wish to impose the Judicial Committee on any of His Majesty's governments elsewhere. As for the governor-general, the committee could but generalise. The governor-general, certainly no longer the agent of the imperial government, personally represented the king, holding the same constitutional position (with, one assumes, whatever duties attached) as that held by the king in Great Britain: and it was accordingly thought fit that henceforth communication between government and government should be direct, and not through the royal representative. What should be done about the legislative power of the dominions it was less easy to say, though some things were obvious, and expert legal examination was recommended. In the sphere of external relations there was further definition of treaty-making procedure, and of dominion representation at international conferences—the general intent of which was that any dominion might have its own plenipotentiaries commissioned by the king on the advice of its own government. 'It was frankly recognised' that in foreign policy, as in defence—matters of 'function'—responsibility mainly rested, and must for some time continue to rest, with 'His Majesty's Government in Great Britain'. Nevertheless, as practically all the dominions were involved in some foreign relations, it was felt that neither they nor Great Britain could be committed to active obligations except with the definite assent of their own governments. And, indeed, none of the dominions was committed to the guarantee of French or German frontiers which Britain had given under the Treaty of Locarno. The appointment of dominion ministers in foreign capitals was approved, with the proviso that in their absence existing diplomatic channels should be used. But what of day-to-day consultations between His Majesty's government in Great Britain and His Majesty's governments elsewhere? Failing the Governor-General, some other functionary would have to be instituted.

The Prime Ministers separated with varying degrees of cheerfulness. The famous italicised formula gave pleasure in Canada and South Africa, where it, and the deductions drawn from it, seemed to concede with reasonable adequacy the main points then claimed by those communities—though certainly nothing had been said about secession. In Ireland pleasure depended on willingness to compromise; and still the emphasis of equality and free association went hand-in-hand with a common allegiance to the crown—a crown that was, to quote later Irish Prime Ministers, 'anathema in Ireland', and a crown (in more personal terms) worn by 'an alien king'. Nor was Ireland altogether satisfied with any theoretical limit on equality of function. In the other dominions satisfaction was not marked. Newfoundland, small in population and resources, could hardly make an effect in constitutional controversy, but neither Australia nor New Zealand was prepared at that moment for further advance into the doubtful region of autonomy, and New Zealand was indeed alarmed. To this dominion, in its colonial days so critical of British policy, Canadian, Irish and South African behaviour seemed to invoke the disruption of the Empire. Distrusting the new term Commonwealth, it wished neither for plenipotentiaries nor for political theory; into the proceedings of the next five years its political leaders were drawn with reluctance, and to the great enactment which was the culminating point of those proceedings, and indeed of the whole legal development of responsible government, it was stubbornly opposed.

That enactment was the Statute of Westminster, 1931. It was the logical result of the further consideration of administrative, legislative and judicial forms which the 1926 Committee had seen to be necessary—consideration given by the experts of the Conference on the Operation of Dominion Legislation and Merchant Shipping Legislation which met at London in 1929. It did not touch the Privy Council, however, except by implication; what the experts were concerned with were the limits on the legislative competence of the dominion parliaments—limits which had been imposed by, and did not exist for, the imperial parliament; limits which must be abolished if equality of status was to be real. These limits were drawn partly in the statutes by which the dominions had gained their constitutions, or in other statutes which by particular wording affected them; partly (as Canada had found) in that other fundamental statute, the Colonial Laws Validity Act, 1865; and partly in the obscure doctrine of extra-territoriality. There had been further limits on colonial autonomy, reaching far back into the history of imperial expansion, but these had disappeared in the process of conventional change. Under statute, for example, the crown could (except in the case of the Irish Free State) disallow dominion legislation—though such power had not been exercised since 1873; and statute provided for 'reservation', discretionary or obligatory, by a governor—that is, the withholding of his assent to a bill until the sanction of Whitehall should be obtained. Discretionary reservation had lapsed; obligatory reservation in some cases remained. Under the Colonial Laws Validity Act no dominion legislature could thrust aside these limits, even as no dominion legislature could (for instance) abolish appeals to the Judicial Committee; so that not merely was an abstract equality undermined but there was practical inconvenience. As for extra-territoriality, legal learning conflicted both as to the existence of the limitation and as to its extent. Something would undoubtedly have to be done to bring certainty into such spheres of law as fisheries, shipping, air navigation, marriage; while dominion shipping was affected still by imperial legislation. The Conference saw no way of removing the mass of anomalies except through an act of parliament at Westminster, and punctuated its report with draft clauses.

The draft clauses, discussed again at the Imperial Conference of 1930, were referred to the individual legislatures, who added further clauses to conciliate Canadian provinces and Australian states, always touchy over suspected federal aggrandisement; and in December 1931 the Act was passed. Like many statutes of profound constitutional importance, it does not illustrate by the nobility of its language or the rhythms of its prose its quite remarkable place in the development of an empire: as an application of a political theory which might well have exploited the combined eloquence of a Burke, a Chatham and a Fox, it was indeed remarkably flat. Its importance is not that of the memorable phrase but of the memorable deed. It is the final fracturing of the sovereignty of a centralised empire, with the remains of which unhappy legal conception the constitutional lawyers—confronted with the spectacle of one king advised by a multiplicity of governments—had to do their best. The very title of the act was significant: 'An Act to give effect to certain resolutions passed by Imperial Conferences held in the years 1926 and 1930.' It annulled for the dominions the Colonial Laws Validity Act, and declared the power of any dominion parliament to make laws having extra-territorial operation; it did away with all reservation; it declared that no future act passed at Westminster should apply to any dominion, unless a clause therein expressly stated that enactment had been requested and consented to by that dominion. The Canadian, Australian and New Zealand constitution acts were, at the request of those countries, excepted from the operations of the Statute. Australia, New Zealand and Newfoundland were excepted, indeed, altogether from the operation of the Statute until they should choose to adopt it through their own legislatures; so that loosing and binding were both voluntary. But how odd and irregular is constitutional development! It was in the year of the Statute that Australia, which held back from the operation of the Statute, took advantage of new procedure in the appointment of a governor-general to become the first dominion to elevate a native son to that post: for though, it was agreed in 1930, the governor-general represented the king, he must be appointed by the king on the advice of responsible ministers, and those ministers must be the ministers of the dominion concerned. This convention was as damaging to the old theory of empire as any statute could be. But before long the first fruits of the Statute of Westminster appeared in the abolition by Canada and the Irish Free State of appeals to the Privy Council; while South Africa, with a milder approach, opened its campaign by doing away with disallowance.

The peculiarity of the Commonwealth relationship, indeed, may be measured on the one hand by the Irish move outwards, and on the other by the fate which in 1934 overtook Newfoundland. That unhappy child of circumstance, smitten by economic depression as well as irresponsible administration, then saw no alternative to putting itself into the hands of receivers. Its relinquishment of dominion status was designed to be a temporary measure; in fact, having after some years of government by commission become again solvent, it found its post-war constitutional destiny not in resumption of its place as a dominion but in incorporation as a province of Canada (in 1949). Meanwhile separateness was mitigated by other facts of Commonwealth life. Whatever the difficulties of regular consultation, information could be given, and the flow of information from the centre to the perimeter and back again steadily increased in volume. The governor-general, decorating a formal niche, was superseded as government representative in his dominion by a high commissioner for the United Kingdom (the first such official had in fact gone to Ottawa in 1928); and,

though there was less business done directly between dominion governments, it was found useful for some of them to be politically represented
in one another's capitals also. Thus each dominion was building up a sort
of diplomatic pattern for itself, a reflection of its own needs, without
doctrinaire extension, both inside and outside the Commonwealth. Inside
the Commonwealth, as a sort of test case both of fundamental theory and
of procedure, men studied the constitutional history of the Abdication of
King Edward VIII in 1936; for with divided sovereignty and a multiplicity
of advisers, on an issue which connoted emotion, it was important to steer
opinion and legislation all the same way. The machinery worked; and the
Commonwealth was spared the embarrassment of more than one monarch.

The British, though they may be a self-governing people, are also a
conferring people. Nothing could be more striking, sometimes, than the
determination of this fragmented and disparate empire, or the greater
part of it, to work out a common policy; just as sometimes nothing could
be more striking than the determination of the individuals to go their own
way; so that to the outside observer the whole presents the perpetual
possibility of surprise, or of annoyance. Annoyance came from the Ottawa
Conference of 1932. It is interesting to mark the diverse implications of
the latest great revolution in British fiscal policy, the abandonment of
free trade under the impact of the Great Depression, and of that previous
revolution, the abandonment of protection nearly ninety years earlier.
For while free trade came before the colonies were their own masters
yet left them virtually at liberty to adopt what fiscal policy they liked—
was part, even, of the foundation of their political freedom—the later
event seemed to those same colonies, their autonomy sealed and blessed,
almost the return of a prodigal mother to the home. Was not there, at last,
to be introduced that system of Imperial Preference which had gilded the
colonial fancy three decades before, to pursue which Chamberlain had
abandoned office, which now, in an unstable world, might shore up the
staggering Commonwealth? The Ottawa Conference did not redeem these
high hopes, and the eloquence which played round that not very exactly
defined concept, 'the spirit of Ottawa', died away from a stage that was
being set for a different and more agonising performance. For the Ottawa
agreements, though they marked a considerable degree of determination
to work out a joint economic policy, and though they did materially help
certain groups—for instance, the coffee-growers of Kenya—were essentially opposed to the greatest possible recovery of world trade. The best
that could be argued for them as a whole, perhaps, was that, as it seemed
beyond the competence, or goodwill, of men to organise a rational economic system for the world, it was at least preferable to organise rationally
a smaller unit than to concede general chaos. But there could be no large
economic salvation for Britain merely in the empire, and the economic life
of the dominions had become so elaborated with industry that British

manufacturers, who were to have been encouraged, not infrequently felt rebuffed instead. Nor did the Australian and New Zealand producer of butter and meat feel more confident that his problems had been solved. The return of prosperity came with a world return; and there were critics who held that that return was impeded by the manful though not single-minded efforts of the statesmen of 1932. At least the historian may contemplate with some interest the process, without being involved too deeply in economic hypothesis.

This Ottawa Conference, with its underlying conception of an empire closing its ranks against the outside world, could not help implying a general foreign policy. Nevertheless, as the decade advances, what claims attention is again separateness. Or, to be more precise, as the international situation became more and more violently complicated and European politics more and more charged with doom, we see the dominions more and more struggling to work out their own foreign policies, which would reconcile their national interests with some sort of responsibility to civilisation in general; and at the same time, or perhaps alternatively, to maintain as a permanent and desirable thing the power and unity of the British association. This individuality might be the expression of a traditional attitude, as with Canada's reluctance to become caught in foreign entanglements; or it might be due to the emergence, with change of government, of strong personalities with convictions on international morality, as in New Zealand; or to the Australian realisation that potential markets and potential danger lay in the north; and in any case it went with a determination to scrutinise the foreign policy of the United Kingdom with care before giving it support. Naturally, in the mid-'thirties, dominion representatives found the League of Nations at once a peg for policy and a platform for its enunciation. They were certainly not dragged in the English wake; they reached their own conclusions about the application of sanctions to Italy during her Ethiopian adventure. In a time when collective security was greatly talked about and little heeded, when in 1936 the reform of the League was being considered, with no general determination either to reform it or to stand by it, Australia declared for automatic sanctions, economic and financial, and for regional pacts of mutual assistance; New Zealand and South Africa believed in taking the Covenant literally; while Canada deprecated the idea of force, or the notion that the League's central purpose was to maintain the *status quo*, and suggested the perfecting of the machinery of mediation and conciliation. They were all struggling against forces that took little account of dominion sentiments on collective security, or morality; in the last dreadful crises they fell silent; and in due course the blood of their sons and daughters was spilt.

Almost six years of hostilities completed, for the dominions, the assertion of their international status; some of them made independent declarations of war, and in 1939 South Africa decided only after war and neutrality had hung for some days in the balance. Constitutionally even more decisive, perhaps, was the neutrality of Eire. Eire: it is a new name, and an Irish name. We may look once more at Ireland. While the six northern counties clung with grim devotion to their union with England, the division between England and the Free State had steadily widened. It was a division different in kind, because different in feeling, from the widening autonomy of the other Commonwealth partners; for it entailed successive unilateral denunciations of the treaty of 1921, and there was no effective objection that Britain could possibly make. In 1932 de Valera, a survivor of 1916, and the Fianna Fail had come to power, and remaining in power for sixteen years applied themselves to a programme that was national both politically and economically. In 1937 a new constitution, drafted by de Valera, was ratified by plebiscite: there was now 'a sovereign, independent democratic State' called Eire; the governor-general had become an elected President, the oath of allegiance had become an oath of loyalty to the state. There was not yet a republic. While the country stood aloof from the abdication crisis, it was still prepared to use the new king as a constitutional convenience, for the one purpose of accrediting its diplomatic representatives abroad. Somehow the government of the United Kingdom was able to persuade itself that all this did not mean a fundamental alteration in the Irish position—i.e. that Eire remained a dominion; and the other dominions were able to agree. But was not this the triumph, in fact, of the concept of 'external association' brought forward, and so signally rebuffed, in 1921? In 1938 Britain handed back to Eire the 'naval ports' over which it had retained control since the treaty; but, amid the darkening international scene, de Valera forecast Irish neutrality as long as partition lasted. At least the neutrality, though it had some bitter consequences for Britain, was a friendly one; and, though it was regarded as an unhappy stand by the remainder of the Commonwealth, it was respected. The scrupulous respect exercised, above all, by the United Kingdom made plain as nothing else could the reality of autonomy. The Irish problem was not even then 'solved': Eire could not by now reconcile its national freedom, its peculiar sovereignty, either with status as a dominion, or with the tenuous bond of external association. It was not a member of the Commonwealth, said its spokesman, in 1947, when the war was over. Then what was it? Within two more years the final, compulsive, explicit step was taken, unimpeded by any of those who thereby ceased to be its partners. Nothing could more clearly register the change in the idea of empire over fifty years than the difference in the British attitude to the South African Republic in 1899 and the Republic of Ireland in 1949.[1] To confuse in words the issue, to baffle a tight constitutional logic as it had been baffled over the very beginnings of responsible

---

[1] Or, if we look ahead, to the Republic of South Africa, also seceding, in 1961.

government and colonial autonomy in the mid-nineteenth century, India had just, in 1948, given itself a republican constitution, and as a declared republic remained a member of the Commonwealth.

The war forced both Australia and New Zealand into greater legal autonomy. Australia found it necessary to put the powers of the Commonwealth beyond dispute by adopting the Statute of Westminster in 1942; New Zealand, after being entangled in complications which were a crown lawyer's nightmare, finally took the step in 1947. Dominions, too, were thrown into what was almost a new sense of geography, and what was certainly a new outlook on strategy, by the war's very course. Canada, besides sending an army to England and Europe, found itself interlocked with the United States in an Arctic strategy; Australia and New Zealand, with Singapore gone and the British navy vanished from the Pacific, found themselves interlocked with the United States in an oceanic strategy. Only South Africa found its traditional strategic position unchanged, with its interest in the Suez Canal, and its midway position, by a different route, between England and the East. For the others, this American interlocking gave new modes of 'consultation', with Washington sometimes the centre rather than London; or remoteness from England stimulated a greater sense of regional burdens, so that it was natural for the two Pacific dominions to work out their own Australian–New Zealand Agreement of 1944, the so-called 'Canberra pact', which insisted not only on a future common defence, but on common responsibility for the welfare of the island groups. They, it is notable, and none of the great powers, brought into existence the South Pacific Commission, with its accent on a new and more knowledgeable trusteeship. Nor is it unworthy of remark that after the war the British representative on the Allied Council in Japan—a rather powerless body, to be sure—was no English general or diplomatist, but an Australian. This was an autonomy and a co-operation undreamed of even in 1939. And still, amid the wreck and the reclamation of financial systems, as western Europe fought for stability, the process of consultation went on, the feeding of Britain proceeded; while once again the dominions, so different from the colonies of the nineteenth century, nevertheless began to think in terms of population and of labour, of new experiments in migration, of new adventures in industrialisation.

The dominions? Some of them were beginning to balk, to be restive, at the use of that convenient word. Was there in even it, for tender minds, some subtle angularity? With Canada the term dated from 1867, with New Zealand from 1907.[1] Did it carry with it, in spite of all that had passed,

---

[1] Changes in susceptibility are nicely balanced by changes in the administrative organisation of Whitehall. In 1907 the Colonial Office produced a Dominions Department. In 1925 this became the Dominions Office with a separate Secretary of State for the Dominions. In 1947 a further change of name resulted in the Commonwealth Relations Office, and a Secretary for Commonwealth Relations: and in these, within a few months, were absorbed the India Office and the Secretary of State for India.

the shadow, almost imperceptible but lingering, of the equality of status that was not equality of function? Had the 'group of self-governing communities' of 1926 really 'reached its full development' in that year? In fifty years, indeed, the whole world-entangled British complex had changed, in the facts and the philosophy of its construction, in its general policies and its general economics, in its social structure and its social relations— had changed so much that nothing that could happen to it in the future could be more surprising or more paradoxical than its past. But then were not the paradoxes logical after all?

To the consideration of this development must be added consideration of the colonies of what was still reckoned in the 1940s and 1950s as the dependent empire—a history exceedingly complicated and as interesting as that of the sovereign dominions. For, if the older dominions may be looked at from an agreed basis of objectivity whence passion has departed, the controversy that attends the relations of dominating and dominated societies has not ceased to brood over those entities, recently colonies and dependencies, that have come later to responsible government and independence. There was, in the middle of the century, much difference between Ceylon, which had, in 1948, become independent within the Commonwealth, and the communities of East and West Africa; Ceylon's constitutional problem, thus solved, was very different from that of Malaya or of the West Indies. Yet, no less than among the partners of the old Commonwealth, the history is one of government on a changing basis of social and economic life that produced a nationalism as fervent as anything in the history of Canada or Australia. It was more fervent, indeed; for the nationalism of the older dominions was a British or a European nationalism, not Asian or African; it presented no alien tradition or difference of colour. The changing relations between colonies and imperial centre were now complicated by precisely these things, just as nationalism itself was complicated by differences of language or of tribe. Superimposed on such traditions and such differences, and eagerly grasped, were the political institutions and parliamentary practice of Britain. It was a superimposition which came quite late and very suddenly.

In all this the overmastering fact is the poverty of the colonial peoples, though it was not for poverty but for the potentiality of wealth that adventurers first toiled up their rivers and through their forests; and certainly wealth has been extracted from them. Or, as in the West Indies, they exchanged outright slavery for slavery to world economics, and, while demand for their products fell, saw their population increased beyond the likelihood of providing for it at home. Thus, whether a colony were old or recently acquired, and whatever its administration, the spectacle it presented was almost always one of quite inadequate subsistence agriculture on soil of diminishing fertility for the overwhelming majority of its people;

393

or it might, as in East Africa, be that of a nomadic pastoralism. Not quite always; for in some cases a single crop for export revolutionised material life and involved its diversification, as cocoa did on the Gold Coast of Africa; or cotton and co-operative marketing might change for better the life of large areas of Uganda. Alternatively, mining by European companies, for copper in Northern Rhodesia or gold in—one need not look only at Africa—the mandated territory of New Guinea, might, in draining off male population, both complicate and impoverish the pattern of village life, without increasing real material prosperity. Poverty meant lack of community services—health, education, agricultural research and organisation, communications. Even where things were best, the basic conditions most favourable, as in Nigeria or the Gold Coast of Africa, the problems were enormous; where they were worst, as in the East African Protectorate, the twentieth-century model of the 'colony of exploitation', English plantation owners prospered only at the expense of a native population dispossessed of fertile soil. The generalisations are not altered essentially by the significance of particular colonial exports in the world's economy or by scientific methods of agriculture—by the fact that the plantations of Malaya, for example, produced before the second world war half the world's rubber and half its tin. For the 60 million people in British colonial or mandated territories at the outset of that war (of whom 80 per cent were in Africa) the Statute of Westminster, 1931, was certainly void of meaning.

On this material basis were worked out two conceptions of great importance for British colonial policy, that of the 'dual mandate' and that of 'indirect rule'. The first, the twentieth-century variant of the idea of the 'white man's burden', is prior logically though not chronologically to the second. On the imperial power, it argues, is laid a double burden: to see that the government of subject native peoples, and the development of the natural resources of their territories, are directed to the best interests of those peoples; and to see that in this process those natural resources are not denied to the world. The double burden is a double trusteeship. The conception was criticised as hypocritical, or at best an attempt to reconcile incompatibles. Certainly it rested on the assumptions that in the last analysis the governing power knew better than the governed peoples what was for their good, and that there was a sort of moral duty laid on those peoples to produce raw materials for the use of economically more advanced societies. But, granted that no indigenous people in any part of the world could hold off in perpetuity the agents of an alien economic life, however inimical that life was to the first principles of their own, the new conception had something to it. It was certainly an advance on naked exploitation: there was no inherent reason why administrators should be merely the agents of hypocrisy.

The 'dual mandate' received its classic exposition from one whose practice was fundamental also to the development of indirect rule, Lord Lugard,[1] though Lugard was by no means a sole discoverer. Thirty years earlier Sir Arthur Hamilton Gordon had worked on the same principle in Fiji; contemporary with Lugard was Sir William McGregor in Papua; the Germans in New Guinea, the Dutch in the East Indies, acted similarly. Indeed any colonial power, faced with responsibilities large in area and population, and small administrative resources of its own, was almost driven to some such solution to its problem. But it was certainly the Nigeria of Lugard and his successors that attracted most attention as a shining example. As a young soldier Lugard had been instrumental in the acquisition and pacification of much of Nigeria, where his great talent for administration, first awakened in East Africa, fastened on the possibilities of ruling through native agencies and institutions—throwing responsibility, or continuing it, where it had traditionally been, and placing on the officers of the British colonial service the tasks of general supervision, of advice, and superior justice, together with policy-making for the territorial area as a whole. 'Territorial area': for Nigeria consisted of a small coastal 'colony' where direct rule was carried on, and a vast hinterland, a 'protectorate': as did the Gold Coast, colony and protectorate, on a smaller scale, and the colony and protectorate of Sierra Leone. (Nor was the dichotomy confined to West Africa: a little later there was in East Africa the colony and protectorate of Kenya; the British South Africa Company was responsible both for the colony of Southern Rhodesia and the protectorate of Northern Rhodesia and Nyasaland; and there might be protectorates without a colony, like Uganda.) 'Territorial area', again, rather than native nation, or exclusive congeries of tribes or identical peoples or language groups; for the scramble for Africa had not resulted in territorial divisions that paid much attention to such things. Thus the powerful Muslim emirates of Northern Nigeria presented a different problem from that of the southern forest states; but all administrative problems, given patience and firmness, seemed amenable to indirect rule. Tribal authorities or institutions deemed decadent could, it was held, be encouraged into life again, or replaced; there was no need to impose an artificial uniformity on every part of a territory. The only uniformity was in the final subjection. Whatever exercise of powers might be tolerated, encouraged or delegated, there was a power in reserve—a power of law-making and taxation, the power 'to control the exercise of such subsidiary legislative powers as may be delegated to Native Authorities, to dispose of such lands as are vested in the paramount Power...and of course to raise and control armed forces'.[2] The system was under certain circumstances, as with the

---

[1] *The Dual Mandate in British Tropical Africa*, first published in 1922. Lugard was not the only man to think systematically (cf. Sir Donald Cameron's *Principles of Native Administration and Their Application*, Lagos, 1935). Cameron had got indirect rule going in Tanganyika, where he was governor, 1925–31.

[2] Cameron, *op. cit.* p. 24.

northern emirates, capable of brilliant success. It seemed equally successful in Uganda, where again there were strong native rulers. It could be or seem to be successful in places where indigenous authority had been less centralised or less stable: wherever there was some tribal authority, in fact, chief or council, who could be made the embodiment of local administrative and judicial powers, and be susceptible to the advice and guidance of the British district officer. Where there was an emir in Northern Nigeria, or a *kabaka* or king in Uganda, the system conferred an added authority on these magnates, maintaining a watchful eye on their courts and treasuries; elsewhere—in much of the East African protectorate territory, for example—it was very much a system of local government.

The system elicited much praise from those who practised it, and from many students of comparative government; and not unnaturally so. It seemed, from the ruler's standpoint, cheap, simple and efficient; the premium it placed on tradition and 'natural loyalties', in conjunction with good order, seemed admirable to the anthropologist; it had an appeal both to the hard-headed and to the romantic. From the standpoint of the ruling power, again, and of favourable imperial critics, it seemed to produce its justification in the war of 1914–18; for nothing, so the argument ran, could exceed the loyalty of the Africans who fought and carried in the campaigns both east and west, the armed and unarmed forces raised and controlled by the paramount power in a struggle which might seem in its origins but remotely concerned with the interests of African tribes. There were critics less favourable, however; as the century wore on certain disadvantages became apparent, and close students of contemporary African life were to think that as a constitutional safety measure the admirable system had perhaps been overdone. Though peace and good order were maintained, though native life was not broken up and destroyed in the name of an efficiency, political or economic, that was solely alien, though able chiefs were not forced into despairing idleness, though the sanctification of stalemate was not everywhere and always inevitable—as not a few district officers proved in the face of government poverty; though at the worst it could be said that direct government in such old-established colonies as the West Indies was no more enterprising and skilful—yet in another two decades it was becoming apparent that indirect rule had nothing to offer to the future. For no more than elsewhere was life in Africa immune to change; and the principal disadvantage of the system was its tendency to acceptance of a *status quo*, however mediocre, as a positive virtue—to the support, that is, as permanent realities of the outward forms of tribal rule, not always understood as what they were; to impotence in the face of economic and social change, to the perpetuation of native vested interests, to the ignoring of the legitimate unrest of the young; to a general lack of imagination on the part of administrators. There was little provision for education, either elementary or advanced. Nevertheless there was some, with the emphasis on education for the sons of chiefs. Education, western education, technical education, advanced education, became desperately necessary as the century itself advanced, unless Africa was to remain, in comparison with the rest of the world, indefinitely in an infantile state of economic, social and political tutelage. There were enough educated Africans both to resent this prospect and to make their resentment felt, as inevitable social change permeated the colonies, and spread its far and fading ripples through the protectorates. The clerk, the teacher, the journalist, the rarer lawyer or physician, though perhaps poised uncertainly between two cultures, had for his professional purposes little in common with the ancient purposes of his tribe, and might respect other leaders than his traditional ones; for him the institutions of power were, increasingly, western institutions. He could see clearly enough how the ultimate political power was exercised. There was therefore a paradox inherent in the whole system of African government, frankly puzzling to the liberal student and well-wisher of Africa. It was assumed that a united Nigeria, for example, would one day aspire towards some form of parliamentary government; yet for a people so backward (in western terms), so divided in religion and culture, 'who never knew any unity but that imposed by Britain upon this arbitrary block of Africa, that day will be very distant'.[1] Self-government was taken for granted, but was it possible that the issue from the paradox might some day be otherwise resolved?

The political traditions of Great Britain involve the assumption that self-government implies representative parliamentary institutions, and this is held also by the majority of educated Africans. It is implicit in the philosophy of indirect rule, however, that the nature of the political forms which may ultimately be involved should not be prematurely defined, and it is possible that a development deliberately based on African institutions may lead to some new type of self governing organisation.[2]

Thus went informed speculation on the eve of the second world war.

In Nigeria or the Gold Coast, meanwhile, or in Uganda or Bechuanaland, the condition of the native peoples was a happy contrast to that of peoples subject to the rule or the pressures of a white minority in Kenya, however the Colonial Office strove there to impose its safeguards and its benevolence; or of those hapless millions whose fate was being determined by the increasingly segregationist policy and uncompromising devotion to white supremacy of the Union of South Africa—and not white supremacy

[1] Margery Perham, *Native Administration in Nigeria* (1937). The quotation is from p. 360 of the 1962 edition.
[2] Lord Hailey, *An African Survey* (1938), pp. 134–5. A more forthright statement of this attitude came a few years later from Ernest Barker, *Ideas and Ideals of the British Empire* (1942): 'African self-government as it grows must be African: it must be a thing which is *sui generis*: it cannot be a mere imitation and a watery copy of European methods.' Barker, unlike Hailey, had no African experience; but he was a thoughtful and sympathetic historical and political scholar.

only, but, within the ambit of a white culture pattern, Afrikaner supremacy. In South Africa, it was becoming apparent, more than one British ideal was in decline. In Kenya—the East African Protectorate of 1895, which became the Kenya Colony in 1920—there grew up a classic example of racial confusion and exploitation, not resolved in the end without the worst sort of rebellion and repression, or until a period when the change in the aspect of protectorates and colonies was almost total. The people of the protectorate were nomads and pastoral; they had merely a subsistence agriculture; they did not have the traditional political organisation that would make indirect rule possible. Rational and effective administration, as well as the opening up of the country to European settlement which seemed axiomatically desirable, depended on communications. To work on the railway between Mombasa on the coast and Lake Victoria, Indians were imported, and after its completion in 1903 remained. Thus were installed the problems of the 'plural society'. By orders-in-council of 1901–2 European settlers were offered land on favourable terms in the fertile 'western highlands' which were transferred from Uganda to Kenya; and surveys for European settlement took in a great deal of land belonging to the Kikuyu tribe, land vacant at the time not merely because the people were nomadic but because their numbers had been reduced by smallpox. They did not cease to regard the land as properly theirs, and as their numbers again increased (an increase aided by peaceful government and modern medicine) their sense of grievance grew. Nor did the Masai tribe feel itself more justly treated. British settlers flowed in on to the best land of the country, falling sentimentally in love with it as a home for the free spirit, making the reputation of Kenya coffee, complaining of the lack of labour and of the reserves where potential labour for European farms preferred to spend its time; repeating the centuries-old pattern of the colonist who believes himself (not entirely without reason) as the founder of his adopted country's economic progress, deploring the inactivity in his interests of official persons, and demanding as of right a hand in his own government. In 1919 and 1920 the settlers and then the Indian minority were given elected representation in a legislative council; in 1927 the Indian seats (nominated and elective) rose to five (the Indians refused their co-operation for seven more years) and the Europeans to eleven, and the Arab community had one elected member. The interests of the great African population were represented by one nominated European, generally a missionary. To the demand (again true to pattern) from the settlers for an elected European majority on the council the Colonial Office replied that it could not surrender authority to any elected majority of non-Africans. It was an uneasy and unsatisfactory state of imbalance, economic and constitutional, over which controversy raged both in the colony and in Britain: the problems of the plural society were multiple.

The first world war had afflicted Britain with additional burdens under the mandate system—problems, even though the doctrine of trusteeship seemed to the optimistic to have enough sanction in existing practice to minimise them in British hands. But it was one thing to deal, relatively successfully, with Iraq and Trans-Jordan, which were not colonies at all; it was quite another to handle Palestine—a country which was being colonised by Jews in the face of Arab distaste, to the accompaniment of bombs and vicious murder, and presented a problem quite insoluble in colonial terms—a problem finally to be abandoned in 1948. The old German colonies, on the other hand, split up among members of the Commonwealth, could certainly be treated on traditional lines. To Britain went German East Africa or Tanganyika (where for some years the standards of social services were lower than under the Germans) and part of the Cameroons and Togoland in West Africa; these, as 'B' mandates, were virtually indistinguishable from British colonies. To South Africa went German South West Africa—which the South Africans, with no pedantic regard to the terms of the mandate, before long wished to incorporate completely into the Union. To Australia went the German part of New Guinea, which was administered until 1945 quite independently of the adjoining Australian territory of Papua; in that year the administrations were unified. To New Zealand went Western Samoa, the charming and difficult people of which made clear the inadequacy, for successful government, merely of confident good intentions. Nevertheless, under a later dispensation, it was Western Samoa that was the subject of one of the first Trusteeship agreements with the United Nations in 1947, and arrived at independence (a non-Commonwealth independence) in 1962.

The period between the two world wars was notable for discussion and development in both constitutional and economic spheres, discussion and development stimulated by the depression of the 'thirties, with the subsequent enquiries into the causes of misery and riot. Constitutionally, we see some experimentation with executive and legislative councils. In Ceylon, which among colonies may almost seem a spearhead of twentieth-century constitutional change, where increasing popular representation had been accorded on the legislative council since 1910, the official majority was abolished in 1920; in 1931 adult suffrage and a measure of responsible government were both granted. The country had a relatively high literacy level and an able educated class, and, though it had also a latent language problem, was without the bitter communal feuds that were to bedevil so much of the Asian future. It embodied all the elements of a successful unitary state. In 1920 Uganda was given both an executive and a legislative council. In 1923 the colony of Nigeria had elected members added to its legislature. In the same year Southern Rhodesia passed from the British South Africa Company to the crown as a self-governing colony; there were then 34,000 whites (to whom the franchise was confined) and upwards of 813,000 native Africans in the colony, approximately half of the area of which was set aside for European ownership. In 1924 Northern Rhodesia, also ceasing to be under company control, became a protectorate. About the same time ambitious voices were raised in various regions, where geography or economic interest seemed to justify the cause, in favour of some common administration, of amalgamation or federation. One such scheme was for the closer union of Uganda, Kenya and Tanganyika, a movement supported mainly by European communities and opposed by natives and the Indian commercial minority; favoured by the imperial government for certain limited purposes, discouraged as a whole in the absence of sufficient guarantees of native interests. It might be highly desirable to foster and integrate transport; but what general economic policy could subsume that of Uganda, where the alienation of land to Europeans was prohibited, and of Tanganyika, where European settlement was discouraged, and of Kenya, which its settlers preferred to regard as a white man's colony? How could closer union be imposed on systems of government so disparate? The outcome was an annual Governors' Conference, which met first in 1926. Another, for the union of the two Rhodesias, with possibly Nyasaland added in, was considered by a royal commission in 1927 and rejected, as it was by a second in 1939. Amid geographical conditions quite different from those of central Africa, the West Indies, with their queer congeries of representative and crown colony governments, and their history of abortive federal plans, were the scene of a developing West Indian regional consciousness; but a commission in 1932 could make no more of a scheme for federation, even on a small scale, than could its predecessors.

In the economic sphere the great step forward of this period, one of major social as well as economic importance, came at its end—came indeed as a climax of much of its worried thought, at a moment when the empire had again been plunged into world war. This step (for earlier ones we may go back as far as Joseph Chamberlain) was an extension of the policy of giving financial help for pressing colonial projects embodied in the Colonial Development Fund of 1929 (from which the British Treasury made grants to non-self-governing colonies and mandated territories); but this was also designed to stimulate British trade. The Colonial Welfare and Development Act of 1940 provided for free grants to the colonies, up to £120 million spread out over ten years, for expenditure under approved development plans on research, education, health and agricultural services, training of civil servants, labour and co-operative organisation, the development of local industries and communications—for, in fact, a systematic overhauling and reshaping of colonial resources in men and things. Large economic schemes were to be managed through development corporations in each area, an Economic and Development Council being established in London to advise the Colonial Office. Though the total was certainly quite inadequate for colonial needs, it was regarded not as a discharge of liability, but rather as a mode of breaking the vicious circle of poverty which stultified all self-help, a stimulation of potentialities as much as a particular grant-in-aid (and, there is no doubt, as a stimulation of colonial loyalties in time of war). The motive behind this new and hopeful advance harmonised with a movement for international collaboration over specific problems of trusteeship, designed to give badly needed improvement to the old mandates system. Beyond Africa, it was this movement that in different ways produced the Anglo-American Caribbean Commission in 1942, with its organs the Caribbean Research Council (which included French and Netherlands representation) and the advisory West Indian Conference; and, in the Pacific, the South Pacific Commission that was initiated by Australia and New Zealand, joined by those powers which were concerned also in the Caribbean, and inaugurated in 1947. Here, it could be said, was some attempt to work out formulated intention where earlier had been only wishes and vague hopes.

War, though it builds up empires, also helps to dissolve empires. The first world war, with its common effort, had been at once a sort of climax in imperial relations and a stimulator of great constitutional changes, so that in 1939 it was possible to talk in common phrase of the Commonwealth and Empire, two radically different components of the one vast structure: a Commonwealth linked together in free association, an Empire marked by subjection. After 1945 there was no halt to the free constitutional development of the Commonwealth—a point already made—as the relative importance of Britain the world power declined, and new varieties of foreign policy, new regional alignments, emerged. It was possible for Australia and New Zealand in 1951 to enter into a treaty with the United States—ANZUS—for 'Pacific defence', in which Great Britain did not participate, though all three, with other countries, were in the organisation called SEATO, set up by the South-East Asia Collective Defence Treaty of 1954. But no more was there a halt to the constitutional development of the Empire. The war which began in 1939 was fought on terms which almost forbade the existence of an empire, if subjection was to be the mark of empire; the attitude of the British people towards the concept of empire was undergoing a profound change; it emerged from war in 1945 unable much longer to bear the material, any more than the psychological, burden of empire. It was, in fact, not alone among western powers, a metropolitan power in retreat. The retreat, however, was also an advance; and with some hope, if not with entire faith, men planned for a new, an inter-racial, commonwealth.[1]

The immediate event, one on the largest scale, was the independence of India. The second, contemporaneous, was the independence as a dominion of Ceylon, where since its last political advance to 'semi-responsible'

[1] For the changes in India and South-East Asia see above, ch. XI.

government in 1931 there had been too much reservation of power, too little real autonomy, so that a new and considerably improved constitution in 1946 was followed almost inevitably by an act of parliament (the Ceylon Independence Act, 1947) and an order in council which had the effect of extending to Ceylon the provisions of the Statute of Westminster, 1931— an extension which was not, certainly, in the minds of the makers of that statute. In the West Indies there was greater hope than in 1932, from a conference of seven colonies that met in Jamaica in 1947 and set up a standing committee to work out the details. A federal constitution was evolved by 1958, only to break down almost at once in practice, with Jamaica and Trinidad emerging as separate dominions in 1962. In Nigeria the main colony, where alone there had been a legislative council, and the two regions, north and south, were in 1947 all given 'houses of assembly', with unofficial majorities, crowned with a legislative council for the whole country, also with an unofficial majority.

New concepts were taking hold on the African scene, being introduced by the ruling power to meet demands which were growing irresistible. These were Western, not African, concepts, and they killed indirect rule stone dead. The essential ones were government by elected representatives, and government through ministers on the British model. This was party government, and it was in the years immediately after the war that national parties proclaimed their existence—that is, parties whose primary demand was national self-government. Party divisions in the European sense could wait. The national, or rather nationalist, parties did not fail to get mass support; and the fact that a number of their leaders, young, educated, political-minded in a new way for Africans, spent periods in prison on charges of sedition did not lessen that support. In face of such demand no promise of parliamentary government in the distant future could make the slightest sense. By the end of the 1940s British officials and politicians were convinced of this; the next decade was thick with constitutions and constitutional conferences; and within a decade and a half the majority of Africans, for good or ill, were their own political masters.[1]

[1] The order in which the African countries attained independence within the Commonwealth was: the Gold Coast, as Ghana, 1957 (republic 1960); Nigeria 1960; Sierra Leone 1961; Tanganyika 1961 (republic 1962, United Republic of Tanganyika and Zanzibar, a few months later called Tanzania, 1964); Uganda 1962 (republic 1962); Kenya 1963 (republic 1964); Nyasaland, as Malawi, 1964; Northern Rhodesia, as Zambia (republic), 1964.

CHAPTER XIV

THE RUSSIAN REVOLUTION

THE revolution of 1917 broke out in the middle of the first world war, in which Russia, although belonging to an eventually victorious coalition of powers, suffered the heaviest defeats. The revolution may therefore appear to have been merely the consequence of military collapse. Yet the war only accelerated a process which had for decades been sapping the old order and which had more than once been intensified by military defeat. Tsardom tried to overcome the consequences of its failure in the Crimean War by the emancipation of the serfs in 1861. Defeat in the Russo-Japanese War of 1904–5 was immediately followed by an *annus mirabilis* of revolution. After the military disasters of 1915–16 the movement started again from the points at which it had come to a standstill in 1905: the December rising of the workers of Moscow had been the last word of the revolution in 1905; its first word in 1917 was the armed rising in St Petersburg. The most significant institution created by the revolution of 1905 had been the 'council of workers' deputies' or the soviet of St Petersburg. After an interval of twelve years, in the first days of the new upheaval, the same institution sprang into life again to become the main focus of the drama that was now to unfold.

When the events of 1917 are compared with the great French revolution or the English puritan revolution, one is struck by the fact that conflicts and controversies which, in those earlier revolutions, it took years to resolve were all compressed and settled within the first week of the upheaval in Russia. The classical prelude to other revolutions, consisting in disputes between the monarch and some sort of a parliamentary body, was lacking in 1917. The defenders of the old absolutism of the Romanovs had almost no say; they disappeared from the stage, as it were, as soon as the curtain was raised. The constitutionalists, who had wished to preserve the monarchy but to subject it to a degree of parliamentary control, had almost no chance openly to state their programme; in the first days of the revolution the strength of the republican feeling compelled them to fold up their monarchical banners and to pursue their objectives as constitutionalists *tout court*. No counterpart of the French states general or the English parliament existed. The main content of the events of 1917 was the struggle between groups that until recently formed the extreme wing of a clandestine opposition, the Russian Gironde (the moderate Socialists) and the Russian Mountain (the Bolsheviks).

The 'constitutionalist' phase of the revolution had actually been played out before 1917. In his October Manifesto of 1905, the tsar had promised to convene a representative parliament. But whereas Charles I or Louis XVI, before they were dethroned, had made to their national parliamentary institutions concession after concession, Tsar Nicholas II quickly recovered from the 'panic' of 1905 and reasserted himself as the autocrat of All the Russias. The political history of the years 1906–16 was marked by the continuous degradation of Russia's quasi-parliaments, the dumas. These were mere consultative bodies, without right to control the government; they were suspended or disbanded by the tsar's arbitrary edicts; and their members were not infrequently imprisoned or deported. In March 1917 there was thus no real parliamentary institution to serve as a platform for the contending parties or to provide a framework for their controversies. The soviet was destined to become the spectacular and powerful centre of the whole movement.

The warning of 1905 was wasted on tsardom. Not only did the autocratic government continue—it did so in an atmosphere of growing corruption and decadence, in which the bizarre Rasputin scandal was possible. The economic and social structure of the country remained unchanged, in all essentials. About 30,000 landlords were still in possession of nearly 70 million *dessyatin* of land.[1] On the other hand, 10·5 million peasants owned only 75 million *dessyatin*. One-third of the peasantry was completely landless. The technical level of agriculture was barbarously low: according to the census of 1910, 10 million wooden ploughs and *sokhas* and 25 million wooden harrows were in use and only 4·2 million iron ploughs and less than half a million iron harrows. Mechanical traction was almost unknown. More than one-third of the farmsteads possessed no implements at all, and 30 per cent had no cattle. No wonder that in the last years before the war the average yield of grain per acre was only one-third of that harvested by the German farmer and one-half of that harvested by the French peasant.

This stupendous burden of poverty was made even heavier by the annual tributes which the peasantry paid to the landlords—their value was estimated at 400–500 million gold roubles per year. More than half of the estates mortgaged at the 'Gentry's bank' were rented to the peasants for sharecropping or other feudal forms of rent. The landlord's share was often 50 per cent of the crop. More than half a century after the emancipation of the serfs the survivals of serfdom were numerous and strong, and in some parts, as in the Caucasus, 'temporary serfdom' openly existed until 1912. The demand for lower rents and for the reduction and abolition of 'servitudes' grew more and more insistent, until it was superseded by the clamour for the total expropriation of the landlords and the distribution of their estates among the peasants.

Such conditions made a gigantic *jacquerie* inevitable, sooner or later. The disorganising effects of the war heightened the explosive mood of

[1] 1 *dessyatin* equals 2·7 acres.

the peasantry. The successive mobilisations of 1914–16 deprived farming of nearly half its fit manpower; cattle were slaughtered *en masse* for the needs of the army; and the output of agricultural implements fell to 25 per cent of normal, while their import from abroad, on which agriculture had heavily depended in peace-time, stopped altogether. With the decline in production the burden of the rents became unbearable, and the peasants' hunger for land irresistible. In the interval between 1905 and 1917 only one major agrarian reform had been attempted: the Stolypin reform of November 1906 had intended to facilitate the growth of a layer of wealthy farmers, upon whose conservatism the régime could rely. But the effects of the belated reform were relatively insignificant, and they were largely undone by the war.

Agricultural poverty was matched by industrial backwardness. On the eve of the war, Russian industry produced 30 kilograms of iron per head of population, compared with 203 in Germany, 228 in Great Britain and 326 in the United States. The output of coal per head of population was 0·2 tons in Russia, 2·8 in Germany, 6·3 in Great Britain and 5·3 in the United States. The consumption of cotton was 3·1 kilograms per person, compared with 19·0 in Great Britain and 14·0 in the United States. Russia possessed only the beginnings of electrical and machine-building industries, no machine-tool industry, no chemical plants, no motor-car factories. In war the production of armaments was forced up, but output in the basic industries declined. In 1914–17 no more than 3·3 million rifles were manufactured for the 15 million men who had been called up. Industrial backwardness was inevitably translated into military weakness, despite the delivery of arms and munitions by Russia's western allies. Yet, by a strange paradox, Russian industry was in one respect the most modern in the world: it was highly concentrated, and the coefficient of concentration was higher than even in American industry at that time. More than half the Russian industrial proletariat worked in big factories employing more than 500 persons. This was to have its political consequences, for this unparalleled concentration gave the industrial proletariat a very high degree of organisation and political striking-power, qualities to which it owed, at least in part, its dominant position in the revolution. But before the leading class of the revolution was to display its strength, the weakness of the old régime was further aggravated by its financial bankruptcy. Russia's total war expenditure amounted to 47,000 million roubles, of which less than one-tenth was covered by ordinary revenue—foreign and domestic war loans amounted to 42,000 million roubles. Monetary inflation was rampant: ten times as much money as in 1914 circulated in the summer of 1917. When the year of revolution opened, the cost of living had risen to 700 per cent of pre-war. Strikes and bread riots frequently broke out in Petrograd,[1] Moscow and other industrial centres throughout 1916.

During the war St Petersburg was renamed Petrograd.

'If posterity curses this revolution, they will curse us for having been unable to prevent it in time by a revolution from above'—thus Maklakov, one of the leaders of the Liberal bourgeoisie, summed up the attitude of the court, the government and also of the Liberal middle class on the eve of the upheaval. True enough, the Liberal and semi-Liberal opposition in the duma had a premonition of the gathering storm. In August 1915, after military defeats which cost Russia 3·5 million men and entailed the loss of Galicia and Poland, a progressive bloc was formed in the duma. It embraced the Constitutional Democrats (Cadets), led by P. N. Miliukov and Prince G. E. Lvov; the Octobrists (led by A. I. Guchkov), that is conservatives who had given up the demand for a constitutional government and had reconciled themselves to autocracy; and a group of extreme right nationalists, whose spokesman was V. V. Shulgin. The progressive bloc confronted the tsar, rather timidly, with the request for a government 'enjoying the confidence of the country'. This formula did not even imply that the new government should be responsible to the duma—the bloc did not ask the tsar to limit his autocracy, but merely to make it more palatable. The main preoccupation of the progressive bloc was with the conduct of the war. The leaders of the bloc were alarmed by defeatist influences at the court. It was widely believed that various coteries counselled the tsar to seek separate peace with Germany. The clique around Rasputin, made powerful by the tsarina's mystical admiration for the illiterate and licentious Siberian monk, was especially suspect of defeatism. The leaders of the progressive bloc were united in the determination to pursue the war and were encouraged by the envoys of the Western powers in the Russian capital. There were stirrings of opposition in the supreme command. General Brussilov, the commander-in-chief, viewed with cautious, non-committal sympathy the moves of the civilian politicians. A plan of a conspiracy against the tsar was later attributed to another officer, General Krymov. If any such plans were hatched, none of them materialised. The tsar was strangely obstinate in his refusal to make concessions. The courtiers did their best to stiffen his attitude and to prevent him from calling in a Russian Necker or Turgot and from thus opening the sluices for revolution. On 3/16 September 1915 the tsar decreed a 'temporary dispersal' of the duma. He changed the government, but he did so in a way calculated to insult the progressive bloc and the opposition at large. Every reshuffling brought into the administration more and more odious figures and thickened the fog of defeatist intrigue. In two years of war, Russia had four Prime Ministers, six Ministers of Home Affairs, three Foreign Ministers and three Defence Ministers. 'They came one after another...[wrote Miliukov, the Cadet historian of the revolution] and passed like shadows, giving place to people who, like themselves, were only...protégés of the Court clique.' Late in 1916 the duma reassembled, and the leaders of the progressive bloc openly expressed their alarm. In a philippic, in which for the first time he openly denounced the tsarina herself, Miliukov repeatedly flung at the government the question: 'Is this stupidity or treason?' Once again the tsar replied in his customary manner: the speeches of the critics were confiscated, the duma itself was dispersed. The sluices were tightly locked against the tide of revolution, with the result that the flood was mounting ever higher until it would sweep away all barriers at once, and with them the age-old throne of the Romanovs.

The futility of all attempts to induce the tsar to change his attitude was for the last time underlined by the assassination of Rasputin, the court's 'evil genius', on the night of 17/30 to 18/31 December 1916. The 'Holy Monk' was assassinated by Prince Yussupov, a relative of the tsar, in the presence of other courtiers. The event demonstrated to the whole country the divisions in the ruling class—the assassins in fact aimed at destroying the pro-German influence at the court. For a while the hopes for a change in the method of government rose, but they were quickly disappointed. The tsar and the tsarina, resentful at the assassination of their 'Holy Friend', clung even more obstinately to their customary ways. Their behaviour was an object lesson—one that was thoroughly assimilated by the people—that the removal of one clique of courtiers would not bring about the universally desired change, that the resented state of affairs was bound up with the tsar himself, or, more broadly, with the entire monarchical order. Meanwhile the country was sinking into ever-deeper chaos: defeats in the field, starvation, orgies of profiteering and endless mobilisations continued; and the temper of the people was growing more and more restive.

Grey staff nonentities [wrote Trotsky]. . . would stop up all cracks with new mobilisations, and comfort themselves and the allies with columns of figures when columns of fighters were wanted. About 15 million men were mobilised, and they brimmed the depots, barracks, points of transit, crowded, stamped, stepped on each other's feet, getting harsh and cursing. If these human masses were an imaginary magnitude for the front, inside the country they were a very real factor of destruction. About five-and-a-half million were counted as killed, wounded and captured. The number of deserters kept growing. Already in July 1915 the ministers chanted: 'Poor Russia, even her army, which in past ages filled the world with the thunder of its victories. . . turns out to consist only of cowards and deserters.'

Yet, when at last the revolution came, almost nobody recognised it or gauged its elemental power. Like its great French predecessor, it was at first mistaken for a riot, and not only by the tsar, the court and the Liberal opposition, but by the revolutionaries. All were overtaken by the avalanche of events. The tsar continued to issue menacing orders up to the moment of his abdication. The Octobrist and Cadet leaders pressed for a change of the tsar's ministers after the tsar himself had become unacceptable to the country. Then they urged the tsar to abdicate in favour of his son or his brother after the insurgent people had rejected the dynasty as a whole and the republic had become a fact. On the other hand, the clandestine groups of socialists—Mensheviks, Bolsheviks, Social-Revolutionaries—thought that they were witnessing one of the successive bread riots when the riots turned out to be strikes and demonstrations culminating in a general strike; they were still deeply worried that the strike would be broken by armed force when the garrison of the capital joined in the revolt; and they were still wondering about the outcome of the whole struggle when they suddenly awakened to the fact that power lay in their hands. And then they began to look round, in deep embarrassment, to whom to hand it over. The revolutionaries themselves seemed hypnotised by the power of the old order after that order had disintegrated and collapsed.

This was, briefly, the sequence of events. On 23 February/8 March there were widespread strikes in Petrograd. Housewives marched in street demonstrations—this was the International Women's Day. A few bakers' shops were attacked by crowds, but, on the whole, the day ran its course peacefully. On the next day the strikes continued. Demonstrators, breaking through police cordons, penetrated into the centre of the city to protest against hunger and demand bread. Before they were dispersed, shouts of 'down with autocracy!' came from their ranks.

On 25 February/10 March all factories and industrial establishments in the capital were at a standstill. In the suburbs workers disarmed policemen. Military detachments were called out to break up demonstrations. A few clashes occurred, but more often than not the soldiers avoided firing at the workers. The Cossacks, who had been so prominent in suppressing the revolution of 1905, even supported the demonstrators against the police. On the following day the tsar, from his military headquarters, issued an edict disbanding the duma. The leaders of the duma were still afraid of defying the tsar's authority and decided not to convene the duma but to call upon deputies to remain in the capital. A committee of the duma was formed to keep in touch with events. On the same day the tsar ordered the general commanding the Petrograd garrison to suppress the movement immediately. In several places the military fired at crowds. In the evening the entire garrison was in a state of ferment, with soldiers holding meetings in barracks to consider whether they should obey orders to fire at workers' demonstrations.

27 February/12 March was the decisive day. New sections of the garrison joined in the revolution. Soldiers shared their weapons and ammunition with the workers. The police disappeared from the streets. The movement assumed such impetus that in the afternoon the government was completely isolated—its writ ran only within the Winter Palace and the offices of the Admiralty. The ministers still hoped to crush the revolution with the help of troops which the tsar had ordered to be moved from the

front to Petrograd. Late in the afternoon leaders of strike committees, elected delegates of factories and representatives of the socialist parties met to form the Council of Workers' Deputies (the soviet). On the morning of the following day it became clear that no troops from the front would rescue the government—the transport of those troops had been stopped under way by railwaymen. The garrison in the capital was completely revolutionised. Regiments elected their delegates, who were soon admitted as members to the soviet, the latter changing its name into Council of Workers' and Soldiers' Deputies. The soviet, commanding the complete obedience of workers and soldiers, was now the only *de facto* power in existence. It resolved to form a workers' militia; it took care of the provisioning of the capital; and it ordered the resumption of civilian railway traffic. Crowds stormed the Schlüsselburg Fortress, Russia's Bastille, and freed political prisoners. The tsarist ministers were placed under arrest.

Confronted with the accomplished fact of revolution and with the dominant position of the soviet, the duma committee, hitherto reluctant to challenge the tsar's authority, at last made up its mind to form a government. On 1/14 March the composition of a provisional government, presided over by Prince Lvov and including the Octobrists and Cadets, but not the socialists, was agreed upon. (Only the name of the *Trudovik* Kerensky was placed on the list of ministers, as Minister of Justice, but Kerensky was to assume office as an individual not representing his own party.) On the day of its formation, the provisional government sent Guchkov and Shulgin to the tsar in order to persuade him to abdicate in favour of Tsarevich Alexei. The tsar put up no resistance, but he resolved to resign in favour of his brother, the Grand Duke Mikhail, not in favour of the tsarevich. On 2/15 March he signed the act of abdication. Meanwhile Miliukov, Foreign Minister in the provisional government, publicly announced the abdication before he had learned about its details. He told a meeting of army officers that the tsar would be succeeded by his son and that until the new tsar came of age Grand Duke Mikhail would act as regent. The assembled officers protested that they could not return to their detachments unless the announcement about the regency was withdrawn. At the soviet Kerensky had already spoken in favour of a republic and had met with enthusiastic applause. The provisional government was divided, and the monarchist and republican ministers put their case before the Grand Duke Mikhail. Miliukov urged the duke to accept the succession, while Rodzianko, President of the duma, and Kerensky counselled abdication. The Grand Duke resigned; but the provisional government was incapable of pronouncing itself in favour of either monarchy or republic and decided to leave the issue open until the convocation of a constituent assembly.

From the first hours of their existence, the provisional government and the soviet of Petrograd confronted each other as virtual rivals. The soviet had no legal title with which to support its authority; it represented the forces that actually made the revolution, the workers and the soldiers. The provisional government had behind it the upper and the middle classes. Its legal titles were dubious. True enough, the tsar put his signature to the act appointing Prince Lvov to be the Prime Minister, but historians still argue whether he did so before or after the abdication. In the confusion of the eventful days the leaders of the new government, in all probability, forgot the niceties of constitutional form; and the tsar seems to have sanctioned the formation of Prince Lvov's government at a time when, in strict law, his sanction had no validity. Whatever the truth, the revolution had anyhow discarded the tsar as the legal source of power. The provisional government represented the last duma, which we know had been disbanded by the tsar before he abdicated. The duma had been elected on the basis of an electoral law, the product of Stolypin's *coup d'état* of 3/16 July 1907, which made it utterly unrepresentative. This circumstance accounts for the duma's unpopularity in 1917 and for its subsequent quiet and complete eclipse. But the chief weakness of the provisional government was that it was incapable of exercising real power. The middle classes which it represented were panic-stricken and politically disorganised—they could not pit their strength against that of the armed workers united with a rebellious army. The provisional government could therefore exercise its functions only if the soviets in Petrograd and in the provinces were ready to take their cue from it. But its social and political objectives were so strongly at variance with the prevailing radical mood that it could pursue those objectives only by devious and equivocal ways. The most influential ministers—Lvov, Miliukov, Guchkov—hoped for the restoration of a constitutional monarchy; they looked forward to the ebb of the revolution and were prepared to speed up that ebb, if possible; they were anxious to re-impose industrial discipline upon the workers and to avert agrarian revolution. Finally, they were determined to continue the war in the hope that victory would give Russia that control over the Turkish Straits and the Balkans which the secret London Treaty (1915) had promised her. None of these objectives could be disclosed without provoking dangerous bursts of popular indignation.

The soviets, on the other hand, were not only based on the working class (and, in Petrograd, on the garrison as well). Thanks to the mode of their election they were in the closest touch with the fluctuating popular moods and in the best position to rally the masses for any action. The deputies to any soviet were elected at the factories by the total mass of workers, and at the barracks by entire regiments. But the deputies were not elected for a definite term. The electorate at any time could recall any deputy, if it did not approve of his attitude, and elect a new one in his place. This was the original feature of the soviets, a feature which in later years they were to shed in practice, although not in precept. As representative bodies, the soviets were more narrowly based than parliaments elected by universal suffrage. They were a class organisation *par excellence*, and the mode of their election precluded any representation of the upper and middle classes. On the other hand, the soviets of 1917 represented their electorates much more directly and sensitively than could any normal parliamentary institution. The deputies remained under the constant and vigilant control of the electorate, and they were in fact frequently revoked. Through an almost ceaseless succession of by-elections the composition of the soviets changed with the moods in factories, barracks and on the land. Moreover, as the votes were cast not in territorial constituencies but in productive or military units, the capacity of the soviets for revolutionary action was enormous. Like gigantic strike committees, they issued orders to men in factories, railway depots, municipal services and elsewhere. The deputies were *sui generis* legislators, executive agents and commissars: the division between legislative and executive functions was extinguished. Towards the end of the February/ March revolution the Petrograd soviet became the leading body of the insurrection. It was to play that part once again after an interval of eight months.

Yet, after the events of February/March, the soviet did not so much ride the wave of revolution as it was carried by it. Its leaders were torn between the sense of their own power and the fear of using that power. On 2/15 March the Petrograd soviet issued its famous Order No. 1. This admitted soldiers' deputies to the soviet, called upon the soldiers to elect their committees, to take political orders from the soviet, and to carry out no directives that might contradict those of the soviet. Above all, the order warned the soldiers to keep watch on arms depots and to resist any attempt that might be made by the officers to disarm the rank and file. This was the first apple of discord between the provisional government and the soviet after the soviet had acknowledged the government's authority. The provisional government charged the soviet with undermining military discipline. On its part, the soviet, afraid of a counter-revolutionary attempt by the officers' corps, held that it could secure its own existence only through the allegiance of the army's rank and file. It was in its own interest therefore that it warned the revolutionised troops against attempts at disarming them. Order No. 1 aroused anew the soldiers against the officers; it also aroused the officers against the soviet. It raised the issue of the mutual relationship between the provisional government and the Petrograd soviet or the soviets at large. From the beginning that relationship bore all the characteristics of a dual power. The whole period from February/March till October/November can be viewed as a series of desperate attempts to solve that problem. All the time the two bodies were overlapping, stepping on each others' feet, trying to patch up their differences and to disentangle their responsibilities. The dual power was by its nature transitional. In the end either the provisional government or the soviets had to assert themselves and to eliminate their rival. The Cadet party and the officers' corps aimed at the elimination of the soviets; the Bolsheviks aimed at the elimination of the provisional government. Only the parties of moderate socialism hoped to consolidate the dual régime, that is, to transform the transitional constellation into something permanent.

The trend of events from the abdication of the tsar to the seizure of power by the Bolsheviks can be divided broadly into four phases:

In the first phase, lasting from 2/15 March to 3/16 May, the conservative and Liberal leaders of the landlords and the bourgeoisie alone held the reins of government and tried to mould the *de facto* republic in their own image and likeness. At the beginning of this phase, the leaders of the soviet[1] accepted the authority of the provisional government. Towards its end the representatives of the Liberal landlords and bourgeoisie were no longer capable of ruling by themselves. The first provisional government had been used up in the process of revolution.

In the next phase, from 3/16 May to 2/15 July, the first coalition of Liberals and moderate socialists endeavoured to save the bourgeois democratic régime. In this coalition, still presided over by Prince Lvov, the Liberals (Cadets) were the senior partners; but they stayed in office through the support of their junior partners, who at this time commanded a strong majority in the soviets. The need for a coalition government revealed that the bourgeois-liberal régime was at the mercy of moderate socialism, while moderate socialism was at the mercy of the soviets. By lending their support to the Liberal bourgeoisie, the leaders of moderate socialism appeared to their followers to be discarding their own principles. Towards the end of this phase they came to share the unpopularity of their Cadet partners. They might have saved themselves by breaking up the partnership and alone assuming power, but they could not bring themselves to make this step.

The third phase (3/16 July–30 August/12 September) was opened by an abortive revolution; it ended with an abortive counter-revolution. In the middle of this period the moderate socialists tried to salvage the coalition by assuming, at least in name, its leadership and forming a new government under Kerensky. But the bulk of the proletariat in Petrograd, although not yet quite ready to place the Bolsheviks in power, was already determined to break up the coalition. It menacingly confronted the moderate leaders with the demand that they alone (or they and the Bolsheviks) should assume office and openly exercise power in the name of the soviets. This was the essence of the semi-insurrection of the July

[1] 'Soviet' (in singular) refers to the Petrograd soviet throughout this chapter.

days, which was defeated by the moderate socialist leaders with the help of the army. It was during this crisis that Prince Lvov's government ceased to exist. Not only the workers and soldiers, but many of its middle-class supporters, had turned against it. The bourgeoisie was now divided: one section, whose influence was declining, still sought to preserve the alliance with moderate socialism; another and more powerful section had come to place its hopes on a counter-revolution capable of eliminating the soviets. That section of the bourgeoisie supported General Kornilov's counter-revolutionary *coup*. The *coup* was defeated by Kerensky but only with the help of the Bolsheviks. The defeat of the two abortive movements weakened, for a very short time, the uncompromising elements in both camps; it created a fleeting social equilibrium in which the attempt could be undertaken to galvanise the Cadet–Socialist coalition.

By the beginning of the fourth phase (30 August/12 September–24 October/6 November) both wings of the coalition had withdrawn from the government: the Liberal bourgeoisie because it sympathised with Kornilov, and the moderate socialists because they blamed Kerensky for having allowed Kornilov's plans to be hatched under the protective wings of his government. Kerensky was now able to form only a rump cabinet, the Directory, which was so much suspended in a vacuum that it took on the appearance of Kerensky's personal government. But, having defeated Kornilov with the help of the Bolsheviks, Kerensky found that the Bolsheviks had in the meantime gained a majority in the soviet of Petrograd. The revolution deepened. As the Bolsheviks came to sway the soviets, the moderate socialists tried to assert themselves outside the soviets, once again finding some common ground with the Liberal bourgeoisie. Thus the third and the last coalition was formed, which was to survive for one month only, a month filled with feverish Bolshevik preparations for the overthrow of the February republic.

The parties that confronted one another had existed and argued over the objectives of the anticipated revolution long before its outbreak. They had agreed that the upheaval would be anti-feudal and bourgeois in its objectives, a repetition in many ways of the great French revolution. Roughly up to the first world war it had been an axiom for all of them that Russia was not 'ripe for socialist revolution'—only Trotsky had denied that axiom as early as 1906. But in spite of this agreement on the broad historical perspective the cleavages between the parties had been deep. Unlike France in 1789, Russia had entered the era of bourgeois revolution at a time when she already possessed a very active and politically minded, though numerically weak, industrial proletariat, which was strongly imbued with socialism. In 1905 already that proletariat was the chief driving force of the revolution, a circumstance which could not but frighten the Liberal bourgeoisie, no matter how much the socialist theorists dwelt on the 'bourgeois' character of the revolution. The Liberal bourgeoisie refused to lead the anti-tsarist movement and rallied to the defence of the throne. Its reconciliation with tsardom was half-hearted: the Cadets still hoped gradually to convert tsardom into a constitutional monarchy, while the Octobrists made peace with the dynasty, such as it was.

This attitude of the middle class gave rise to a significant controversy in the Russian Social Democratic Workers' party. Its moderate wing, the Mensheviks, believed that, since the revolution could only be anti-feudal or anti-absolutist, the leadership in it would naturally belong to the bourgeoisie and not to the working class. For all its equivocal attitude, it was said, the bourgeoisie would eventually be driven by events to assume a directing role in the establishment of a parliamentary democracy on the Western European model. The Bolsheviks, and especially Lenin, argued that, as the bourgeoisie had passed or was passing into the camp of counter-revolution, only the industrial working class could lead the nation, or at least its majority, the peasants, in the struggle against the absolutist order. But, the Bolsheviks added, even though the revolution would be led by a class with socialist aspirations, it could not aim at establishing socialism in Russia before a socialist revolution had triumphed in western Europe. The revolutionary government would share out the landlords' estates among the peasants, set up a democratic republic and separate church from state; it would, in addition, introduce the eight-hour day and progressive social legislation; but it would not establish public ownership over industry or abolish private property at large—it would only substitute bourgeois forms of property for feudal and semi-feudal ones. Only after a period of intensive bourgeois development, the duration of which could only be a matter for conjecture, would the time come for socialist transformation. What was of immediate importance was that the working class should not shrink from leadership in the 'bourgeois' revolution and not wait, as the Mensheviks counselled, until the bourgeoisie took the initiative. It was with this perspective still in their minds that the Bolsheviks in Petrograd participated in the movement of February/March 1917.

Another significant difference between Mensheviks and Bolsheviks, one over which they had first split in 1903, concerned their methods of organisation. The Bolsheviks possessed a closely knit organisation with a distinct doctrine of its own, with carefully worked-out tactics and strict internal discipline, which allowed their central committee to plan its moves in the sure knowledge that its orders and instructions would unfailingly be carried out by the rank and file. The party had its recognised leader in Vladimir Ulyanov Lenin, in whose personality were blended such diverse qualities as enormous scholarship, the passionate temperament of the revolutionary, tactical genius and great administrative abilities. Lenin swayed his party by means of his powers of persuasion and through his moral authority rather than by means of that mechanical discipline which later became the characteristic trait of Bolshevism. Menshevism, on the other hand, was more or less shapeless in organisation and vague in matters of doctrine. One of its wings bordered on bourgeois liberalism, another on Bolshevism; in between these wings there was a wide range of intermediate positions. The Mensheviks had many gifted politicians, great orators and brilliant writers, but no national leadership capable of conducting a clear-cut policy. The February/March revolution found the party split into fragments. Tseretelli and Chkheidze, two Georgians, were its most authoritative spokesmen in the heyday of the February republic. Tseretelli had been a hard-labour convict under tsardom, and his martyrdom gave him considerable influence in the councils of the soviet and then in the coalition. Chkheidze had been the chief socialist spokesman in the duma. Tseretelli led the right wing of the party, Chkheidze spoke for its centre. On the extreme right stood Plekhanov, the founder of Russian social democracy, to whom Lenin, in his youth, had looked up as to his teacher and guide. On the left, Martov, the originator of Menshevism, headed the group of Menshevik internationalists. The *Mezhrayontsy* (Inter-borough Organisation) were former Mensheviks and former Bolsheviks who, for one reason or another, had stood outside their original organisations. Headed by Trotsky, this group was to join the Bolsheviks in July 1917. In the no-man's-land between Menshevism and Bolshevism there was Maxim Gorky's *Novaya Zhizn* (New Life), where freelance socialists expounded their views.

The Socialist Revolutionaries formed, like the Mensheviks, a loose federation of groups and individuals lacking coherent leadership. The party's traditions went back to the *Narodnik* movement, with its pro-muzhik attitude, its advocacy of a peasant socialism and its terroristic methods of struggle against tsardom. On the right wing of the party there were men who, like Kerensky, would have been at home in, say, the French radical party and who tried in vain to hypnotise the revolution with fireworks of parliamentary oratory. By Kerensky's side stood Savinkov, the ruthless romantic terrorist now converted into a good patriot and into an advocate of 'law and order'. The centre of the party had its most gifted spokesman in Chernov, Minister of Agriculture in the second coalition government, who had only recently, together with Lenin, taken part in the anti-militarist conference of socialists at Zimmerwald (Switzerland). The left wing of the party, most authentically identified with the old revolutionary strand of the *Narodnik* movement, was represented by the veterans Spiridonova and Natanson who were to join hands with the Bolsheviks in October/November. While the following of the Bolsheviks and Mensheviks was predominantly urban, the Social Revolutionary leaders, though they belonged to the intelligentsia, were the mouthpieces of the peasantry. The right wing spoke with the conservative voice of the wealthy farmers: the left was inspired by the peculiar peasant anarchism that had deep roots in Bakunin's country. But, on the whole, the Social Revolutionaries were inclined to look for guidance to the Mensheviks, especially in the first months of the revolution.

The belief in the 'bourgeois' character of the revolution, general in February and March, accounted, up to a point, for the puzzling behaviour of the leaders of the Petrograd soviet and for their readiness to acknowledge the government of Prince Lvov. This act seemed in perfect harmony with the Menshevik conception, according to which the bourgeoisie should form the provisional government in a 'bourgeois' revolution. It was not the socialists' job to participate in such a government; they could only support it from outside against attempts at counter-revolution, and at the same time they had to defend from outside, too, the claims of the workers against the bourgeoisie. To these principles the moderate socialists remained faithful in the first phase of the revolution, before they joined the Cadets in the coalition government. The attitude of the Bolsheviks was confused at first. They had been accustomed to think of the bourgeoisie as a counter-revolutionary force, and now they saw its leaders at the head of the first *de facto* republican government. What was to be the leading role of the proletariat in this revolution? Nurtured in a spirit of uncompromising opposition to the upper classes, Lenin's followers could not reconcile themselves with Prince Lvov, Guchkov, Miliukov, the leaders of the landlords and the industrialists. But, on the other hand, the belief that the revolution should stimulate the development of modern capitalism in Russia rather than attempt to introduce socialism pointed to the need for some conciliation. In his Swiss exile Lenin himself had already solved the dilemma: he had become convinced that the 'bourgeois' revolution was only a prelude to the socialist one, that the Russian working class should, with the support of the peasantry, overthrow the bourgeoisie and establish its own dictatorship. This was an important departure from his own previous prognostications, one that his followers in Russia had not yet made. Without Lenin's guidance, they vacillated between unreserved opposition to the provisional government and conditional support for it. In the days of the February/March revolution they were led by a few young radical men, of whom only Molotov was later to attain international fame. On 12/25 March, two of their more important leaders, Stalin and Kamenev, returned from Siberian exile and found the views voiced by Molotov and his friends to be imprudently hostile to the provisional government. Kamenev in particular counselled the Bolsheviks to adopt a more conciliatory attitude. Lenin, in his letters from Switzerland, was already expounding the ideas that were to underlie the October/November revolution, but from afar he could not induce the party to accept them. Thus in Petrograd, during the honeymoon of the February republic, Bolsheviks, Mensheviks and Social Revolutionaries, although differing from one another in traditions and outlook, still agreed on the 'bourgeois-democratic' limits of the revolution. Hence the idyllic mood of unity in the ranks of 'revolutionary democracy', a mood in which Bolsheviks and Mensheviks seriously considered their merger into one party.

The basic questions concerning the tasks of the revolution were complicated by the attitude of the parties towards the war. The Cadets and Octobrists hoped that the revolution would not prevent their government from waging war and preserving the continuity of Russian foreign policy. Under the secret London Treaty of 1915, we know, Russia had been promised control over the Dardanelles and territorial acquisitions in the Balkans. Miliukov, as Foreign Minister of the first provisional government, tried to reaffirm these objectives as the war aims of revolutionary Russia. But, in order to attain them, the army had to fight; in order that the army should fight, discipline had to be re-established in its ranks and the authority of the officer's corps had to be restored. The Liberal Foreign Minister became a consistent advocate of 'strong government'. But the restoration of discipline was possible only if the soviets willingly co-operated in this endeavour. Yet, even under the leadership of the most moderate socialists, the soviets could at best make only half-hearted attempts at exorcising the spirit of the revolution from the armed forces. For one thing, nearly all socialist groups and parties had been vaguely committed to anti-militarism. Most of them had denounced the war as a reactionary and imperialist adventure, as long as it had been conducted 'for the Tsar and the Fatherland'. The overthrow of tsardom made a big difference. It was now possible to claim that the character of the war had been altered and that Russia's revolutionary democracy, allied to the parliamentary democracies of France and Britain, was engaged in a life-and-death struggle against the reactionary monarchies of the Hohenzollerns and Habsburgs. This was what nearly all socialists (including some Bolsheviks) claimed in February and March—to this extent they became patriots or 'social-patriots'. But, precisely because they had come to accept the war for the reason just given, they could not openly embrace the war aims of the old régime. 'A democratic peace, without annexations and indemnities' was the slogan of the day. This and promises of a quick end to the war were believed in with deep earnestness by millions of hungry and unarmed soldiers in the trenches. It was enough for Miliukov to intimate in a note to the Western allies (18 April/1 May) that his government would honour the diplomatic and military obligations of the tsarist government and pursue its war aims to provoke a storm of protest all over Russia. It was over this issue that the first coalition broke down, after Miliukov had resigned from the ministry of Foreign Affairs and Guchkov from the ministry of War. The suspicion of the soldiers in the trenches and of the workers in the cities was for the time being allayed by the appointment of Kerensky to be the Minister of War. Yet, in the honeymoon of revolution, the socialist parties were not yet very seriously divided even in their views on the war; they still spoke and acted in a spirit of sentimental pacifism, which did not prevent them from half-supporting the war effort. The real cleavage was still to come.

From its first to its last day, the revolution was centred on Petrograd, and to a lesser extent on Moscow and other industrial towns. To the cities belonged the political initiative. But the revolution was by no means a purely urban affair. To paraphrase Marx's saying, the proletarian solo was powerfully supported, all over the country, by the chorus of an insurgent peasantry. From month to month and then from week to week the clamour rose for a root-and-branch reform in the countryside. By the middle of the year impatient peasants began to attack their landlords, burn their mansions and share out their land, until the whole movement acquired the impetus of a genuine peasant war. The disintegration of the army may be regarded as just one facet of this agrarian revolution. The army consisted largely of peasants, who expected the new régime to satisfy their demand for land and who then ascribed the government's procrastination to the fact that the landlords were so strongly represented in it. In truth, the Cadets and the Octobrists wished to avoid radical changes in the structure of agriculture. The moderate socialists had for a long time advocated agrarian revolution; but now they hesitated: should this revolution be carried out in the middle of war? Was not the abolition of landlordism so fundamental a matter that only a constituent assembly could deal with it? It might have seemed that in these circumstances the convocation of the constituent assembly should have been the government's most urgent business. Yet, each successive government kept postponing the assembly on the ground that political passions would be let loose in the elections, to the detriment of the war effort. The truth was that the 'political passions' had been let loose anyhow, and that every postponement of the assembly added fuel to them. The bourgeois ministers insisted on delay, fearing that an assembly convened at the height of the revolution would be too radical; and the socialist ministers sacrificed the assembly to save the coalition. Through their behaviour in this matter both Cadets and socialists unwillingly contributed to the eventual ascendancy of the soviets, which, apart from municipal councils, were the only elected representative bodies in existence. A constituent assembly convened early enough might have overshadowed the soviets and reduced them, in the eyes of the people, to sectional bodies trying to usurp power. In the constitutional vacuum of 1917 the opposite happened; something like a soviet constitutionalism took hold of the minds of the masses; and *vis-à-vis* the soviets it was the successive provisional governments, backed by no popular representation, who appeared more and more in the role of usurpers. The Bolsheviks were most insistent in calling for an immediate constituent assembly. They had not yet clearly thought out in what relationship the assembly and the soviets would stand towards one another, and it had hardly entered their mind that they themselves, the Bolsheviks, would convene the constituent assembly in a few months' time only to disperse it straightway. But, paradoxically enough, in advocating the rights of the assembly between February/March and October/November, this extreme party of the revolution also appeared to be more devoted to constitutional form than were the other parties. As to the great underlying issue of land reform, the Bolsheviks held no clear views at first. In the past Lenin had on many occasions spoken in favour of the nationalisation of land, which was in line with the collectivist outlook of his party. The idea that the large estates be shared out among the peasants, which the Bolsheviks were to do after their seizure of power, had been part and parcel of the programme of the Social Revolutionaries, not of the Bolsheviks; and the author of that programme, Chernov, was the Minister of Agriculture in the second coalition. Only one group of Bolsheviks, to which Stalin had belonged, had, in the previous decade, advocated the 'distribution' of land.

Thus on all major issues—the character of the revolution, the war and the land—the differences between the rival socialist groups seemed at first vague or superficial. The sharp line of demarcation that was to separate Bolsheviks from all other parties was drawn by Lenin only after his return from Switzerland in April 1917. His journey through Germany and Sweden had been arranged by Swiss socialists, after the British government had refused revolutionary émigrés permission to return through Britain. The German government was aware of Lenin's anti-war activities, and it hoped that his propaganda would sap Russia's military strength; but it did not expect that in a few months it would have to parley with Lenin as head of the Russian government. Nor did it expect the boomerang effect of Lenin's propaganda upon the German forces, one of the important factors in the disintegration of Germany's military power in 1918. Lenin, as is clear from documentary evidence, himself conducted no negotiations with the German authorities and took no obligation upon himself except to promise through the Swiss inter-mediaries that he would use his influence in Russia to secure, by way of compensation, the exit of some Germans from Russia. His unusual journey evidenced his anxiety to find himself as soon as possible in the centre of the revolution and there to assume the leadership of his party. He arrived with a clear idea of the course that Bolshevism was to steer. In his famous April Theses, and in a number of speeches, he forecast that the revolution would soon pass from its 'bourgeois-democratic' to its socialist phase and find its consummation in a proletarian dictator-ship. This should take the form of government by the soviets, a 'new type of state' best suited for the building of socialism. But, if all power was to go to the soviets, the workers ought to confront Prince Lvov's government with irreconcilable hostility. That government was the dictatorship of the bourgeoisie veiled only by the complicity of the moderate socialists. The Bolsheviks ought to do away with the ambiguity of their own attitude and to explain their position frankly to workers, soldiers and peasants until they, the Bolsheviks, obtained a majority in the soviets and were thereby entitled to wrest power from the bourgeoisie. Ambiguity was likewise inadmissible in matters of war and peace— the party must lend no support to the war, which, despite the change of the régime, was still 'imperialist through and through'. It was the task of the proletariat 'to transform imperialist war into civil war'. The land of the big landlords must be shared out among the peasants, this being the chief task in the 'bourgeois' phase of the revolution. The transition to the socialist phase would be speeded up by the outbreak of revolution in western Europe, which Lenin believed to be imminent. Meanwhile 'workers' control', or rather control exercised jointly by workers and capitalists, over industry would be a step towards socialisation. The new state would give the people incomparably more freedom than they could obtain under bourgeois democracy.

Having begun the revolution it is necessary to strengthen and continue it [thus Lenin addressed a meeting of soldiers shortly after his return]. All power in the state, from top to bottom, from the remotest village to the last street in the city of Petrograd, must belong to the Soviets of Workers', Soldiers' and Peasants' Deputies...There must be no police, no bureaucrats who have no responsibility to the people, who stand above the people; no standing army, only the people universally armed, united in the Soviets—it is they who must run the state. Only this power, only the Soviets, can solve the great question of land. The land must not belong to the feudal owners...Unite, organise yourselves, trusting no one, depending only on your own intelligence and experience; and Russia will be able to move with firm, measured, unerring steps towards the liberation both of our country and of all humanity from the yoke of capitalism as well as from the horrors of war!

This vision of the proletarian dictatorship, a state without police, bureaucrats and standing army, had an overwhelming appeal. Retrospectively, it may seem to have been a piece of sheer demagogy designed to wreck the remainder of any existing governmental authority. But such an interpretation of Lenin's attitude is disproved by his study *State and Revolution*, in which he developed the same ideas in a theoretical and scholarly manner, a study which could not have been written with an eye to the rewards of popularity but which reflected Lenin's profound conviction. In view of the subsequent evolution of the soviet régime, it is all the more important to remember how widely Lenin's vision of the proletarian dictatorship differed in 1917 from its materialisation in later years. Still another pronouncement of great significance, which Lenin made soon after his return, concerned the future of the labour movement in the world as well as in Russia. He advanced the idea of the third, the Communist International, made necessary, in his view, by the abandonment of class struggle and of socialist internationalism by the leaders of the Second International.

This set of ideas was at first received with stupefaction by many or most of Lenin's own followers. But, using all his powers of persuasion and helped by currents of radicalism in his party, Lenin soon converted most Bolsheviks to his views. On 14/27 April the Petrograd conference of the party passed Lenin's April Theses and shortly afterwards a national conference of Bolsheviks also endorsed them. This was in many ways the most momentous event since the tsar's abdication: the honeymoon of the first revolution, with its pretence of 'unity in the ranks of revolutionary democracy', was over; and the programme of the next revolution was now accepted by the party that was to accomplish it. In the national conference of Bolsheviks which passed Lenin's motions only 133 delegates took part, representing 76,000 members. In February the membership had amounted to less than 30,000. But the strength of Bolshevism consisted in the quality, not the quantity, of its membership. The average Bolshevik was an influential leader and organiser in his factory or workshop, increasingly capable of swaying the vast mass of workers who adhered to no party and even those who at first followed the Mensheviks.

After the collapse of the first coalition, in May and June, there was increasing evidence of popular disillusionment with the February régime. Municipal elections in the capital exposed the weakness of the Cadets, the party that predominated in the government; half the vote went to the Mensheviks; and some of the radical working-class suburbs voted solidly for Lenin's party. As a minority, the Bolsheviks displayed great tactical shrewdness and elasticity. Lenin made his party use every opportunity of putting its views before the masses, but he did not call for immediate revolution. For the time being, as long as the moderate socialists swayed the soviets, he ruled out any attempt on the part of the Bolsheviks to seize power. He urged the soviet majority, Mensheviks and Social Revolutionaries, that they themselves, without the Cadets, should form the government and thus justify the confidence which the working class placed in them. He advanced this policy at the first All Russian Congress of Soviets opened in Petrograd on 3/16 June, and it carried much conviction with the workers and soldiers who had followed the moderate socialists. The latter had just joined the second coalition government constituted by ten bourgeois and six socialist ministers. The Bolshevik agitators now raised the slogan 'down with the ten capitalist ministers', a slogan which stirred the suspicion, shared by the Menshevik and Bolshevik rank and file, of the bourgeois ministers. The more the Menshevik leaders clung to the coalition, the wider grew the gulf between themselves and their own followers. While the congress of the soviets was in session, its Menshevik-dominated executive committee called a demonstration for 18 June/1 July, hoping that the working class would on this occasion come out in favour of the coalition. But to the surprise and dismay of the moderate leaders, about half-a-million workers and soldiers passed before them with banners and posters carrying the inscriptions: 'down with the war', 'down with the ten capitalist ministers', and 'all power to the soviets'. Lenin had evidently gained for his tactics the support of the proletariat in the capital.

In the next few weeks the revolution reached a strange turn. The Bolsheviks had already behind them the workers and much of the garrison in the capital, but in the provinces the moderate socialists still wielded the greater influence. Lenin and Trotsky hoped that this 'lag' between the capital and the provinces would soon disappear. In the meantime they were anxious to avoid any decisive test of strength; they wished to postpone such a test until they could be reasonably sure that they could win it and that a Bolshevik government established in the capital would not be crushed by forces drawn from the provinces. Yet the impatience of their own followers in Petrograd led to the abortive rising of the July days. On 3/16 July the first regiment of machine-gunners, joined by sailors of the Baltic fleet and masses of workers, staged an armed demonstration, besieged the seat of the Petrograd soviet and menacingly urged the moderate socialists to transfer power to the soviets, in which they themselves had the majority. The Bolshevik Central Committee tried to curb the movement and to prevent it from becoming a real insurrection. The government brought front troops to the capital and suppressed the demonstrations. In the middle of these disturbances the news reached Petrograd of the collapse of the Russian offensive on the south-western front—the operation had been in progress since 18 June/1 July. The defeat, which was to lead to the final disintegration of the army, gave rise to violent recrimination. The Bolsheviks made themselves the champions of the ill-armed, ill-fed and ill-clad soldiers and charged the government with inability to put an end to orgies of profiteering by which food and clothing were withheld from the troops; they accused Kerensky, the Minister of War, of having undertaken the offensive under pressure from the Western powers, and they used the position at the front as an argument for peace. The government in its turn attributed the defeat to the subversive influence of the Bolshevik agitators in the trenches. As the demonstrations of the July days were being suppressed, the Bolshevik leaders were accused of being in the service of the German General Staff. The accusation, launched in a popular paper and supported with faked documents, released a storm of indignation in which it was easy for the government to inflict telling blows on Lenin's party. Officers' Leagues and other right-wing associations attacked Bolshevik headquarters, demolished the editorial offices of *Pravda*, and went out on punitive expeditions to the Bolshevik suburbs. On 6/19 July the government ordered the arrest of Lenin, Zinoviev, Kamenev, Kollontai and other Bolshevik leaders. Lenin and Zinoviev went into hiding, from which they were to come out only on the day of the October/November revolution. Trotsky, Kamenev and others were arrested. On 12/25 July the government reintroduced the death penalty for offences against military discipline committed at the front. On 18/31 July General L. G. Kornilov was appointed commander-in-chief in place of General Brussilov.

These events resulted in a 'shift to the right', the strength of which, however, was exaggerated at the time. Lenin, assuming that the soviets had played out their revolutionary role, advised his followers, as they assembled for their semi-clandestine sixth congress, no longer to advocate the transfer of power to the soviets. The leaders of the Officers' Leagues and other right-wing organisations considered the moment to be propitious for the final suppression of the soviets and all they stood for. In fact the strength of the soviets was still great, and the threat from the right provoked the moderate socialists to action. On 24 July/6 August the executive committee of the soviets confronted Prince Lvov with an ultimatum, in which it demanded the immediate and formal proclamation of the republic, the disbandment of the duma, and the prohibition of the sale of land until the passing of a land reform by the constituent assembly. Prince Lvov refused to accept these demands, and his government ceased to exist. The second coalition was formed under Kerensky as Premier and Minister of War. It inherited from its predecessor its internal divisions and its indecision. It satisfied neither of the parties who joined it. But now it was the turn of the right wing to strike.

For 12/25 August, Kerensky convened a 'State Conference' to Moscow, in which all parties and social and economic organisations were represented. The state conference was intended to enhance the prestige of the government; and it was convened at Moscow, where the Bolshevik influence seemed weaker than in Petrograd. The opening of the assembly, however, was marked by a general strike in Moscow, a meaningful reminder of the growing strength of Bolshevism in Russia's second capital. The conference itself revealed the widening gulf between left and right; that is, between the moderate socialists on the one hand, and the Cadets and military leagues on the other. The Conference also witnessed the incipient antagonism between Kerensky and Kornilov, the newly appointed commander-in-chief. Its debates were repeatedly interrupted by stormy ovations and counter-ovations staged now by the left and now by the right, now for Kerensky against Kornilov and then for Kornilov against Kerensky. The right wing hailed the commander-in-chief as the saviour of Russia, the man destined to reimpose discipline upon a disintegrating nation. The left acclaimed the premier as the defender of the revolution from both the extreme left and the extreme right. Outside the conference hall, the Prime Minister and the commander-in-chief reviewed rival military parades. In this antagonism, which was in part personal, major political differences were involved. Both Kerensky and Kornilov agreed on the need for a strong government vested with plenary powers. But Kornilov regarded the officers' corps as the chief prop of such a government and himself as the candidate for the dictator's post. Kerensky wished to free his government from the pressure of the soviets, but willy-nilly he had to rely on the soviets' support—he was himself still a member of the soviet executive committee. He had issued the order reintroducing the death penalty at the front. Kornilov wished capital punishment to be reintroduced all over the country, for offences against 'law and order'. Kerensky hoped to curb the aspirations of the soviets by using the army as a counterweight to them, while Kornilov's aim was the total dispersal of the soviets.

On 21 August/3 September Russia suffered another major defeat: Riga was captured by the Germans. The circumstances of that defeat were obscure. From the left came the charge that the supreme command deliberately ceded 'Red Riga' to the enemy. As to Kornilov, he used the fall of Riga as an excuse for his revolt against the government. On 25 August/7 September he ordered strong Cossack detachments to march on Petrograd and he openly withdrew his allegiance from the government. Kerensky denounced the commander-in-chief as a rebel and resolved to suppress the mutiny with the help of the Bolsheviks. He armed the Red Guards, appealed to the Baltic sailors and encouraged Bolshevik agitators to go out and meet Kornilov's troops. The Bolshevik propaganda among the latter was so effective that Kornilov's soldiers refused to obey his orders and to fight against Red Petrograd. On 30 August/12 September Kornilov was deposed from his post and arrested, and Kerensky became commander-in-chief in his place.

The abortive revolution of the July days had resulted in a temporary and superficial shift to the right; Kornilov's abortive counter-revolution was now followed by a momentous shift to the left. Its first, indirect manifestation was the collapse of the second coalition. No sooner had Kornilov moved against the government than the Cadets withdrew from it, either because they were in sympathy with the mutiny or because they refused to share responsibility for Kerensky's action. Simultaneously, however, the Menshevik and Social Revolutionary ministers, too, resigned. Their parties were inclined to blame Kerensky himself for a degree of complicity or negligence in the early stages of Kornilov's conspiracy. For nearly a month no regular government could be constituted. On 1/14 September Kerensky formed a Directory, composed of five ministers among whom he was the only personality of recognised political standing. His personal rule, or rather his personal incapacity to rule, which his Bolshevik critics exaggeratedly labelled as Bonapartism, was to bridge the gulf between the opposed political camps.

The shift to the left was more directly felt when on 31 August/13 September the Bolsheviks for the first time obtained a clear-cut majority in the Petrograd soviet. Trotsky, released from prison on bail, was elected President of the soviet, a post he had held in the soviet of 1905. Five days later the Bolsheviks were in a majority in the soviet of Moscow, and soon afterwards in most provincial soviets.

From this swing of opinion, Lenin concluded that the time had come for his party to seize power. From his hiding-place in Finland, early in September, he urged the Central Committee of his party to prepare for armed insurrection. This was the natural conclusion of Bolshevik policy as it had developed since April. The February/March régime, according to Lenin, had been made possible by the abdication of the soviets in favour of the provisional government, and this abdication had been effective because the moderate socialists had swayed the soviets. With the Bolsheviks in the ascendant, the soviets must regain full power. Since the government was not likely to bow to the will of the soviets, it must be overthrown by armed insurrection. The government too, and its Menshevik and Socialist Revolutionary supporters, felt that this was the logic of the situation, but they refused to believe that the Bolsheviks would act on it. Altogether apart from this, they were helpless in face of the overwhelming forces arrayed against the 'bourgeois democratic' republic. It was very difficult, if not impossible, for the moderate socialists openly to defy the authority of the soviets, an authority which they themselves had upheld on many occasions, merely because the soviets were now under Bolshevik influence. At this late hour Kerensky still refused to convene the constituent assembly. Instead, he convened a substitute for it, the so-called Democratic Conference, which was in session in Petrograd from 14/27 September to 22 September/5 October. Its main outcome was the formation of the so-called 'pre-parliament', an advisory body whose authority, since it lacked any mandate from the electorate and had no power to control the government, was very feeble. It was further weakened when the Bolsheviks, after some hesitation, decided to boycott the pre-parliament. The main task of the democratic conference had been to find ways and means for the reconstitution of a normal government in place of the rump Directory. But, even after the Bolsheviks had seceded, a majority of the conference voted against the renewal of the Cadet–socialist coalition. When Kerensky, three days after the end of the conference which he himself had exalted as the only representative assembly, defied its resolutions and replaced his Directory by the third and last coalition government, that government commanded even less authority than its predecessors. In theory it might have reasserted itself by appealing once again to the elements that had stood behind Kornilov. Lenin was firmly resolved not to give the third coalition enough time for that.

On 10/23 October the Bolshevik Central Committee met to discuss Lenin's scheme of insurrection. Lenin arrived from his hiding-place to urge that 'much time has been lost...The question is very urgent and the decisive moment is near...The majority is now with us...The situation has become entirely ripe for the transfer of power.' Two members of the Central Committee, Zinoviev and Kamenev, Lenin's close disciples and friends, were opposed to insurrection. A day after this session of the Central Committee they thus formulated their warning: 'Before history, before the international proletariat, before the Russian revolution and the Russian working class, we have no right to stake the whole future on the card of an armed uprising.' They urged the Central Committee to wait for the constituent assembly, which the government promised to convene and which would be swayed by a radical majority; they conceived the new state as a combination of a soviet republic with a parliamentary democracy and held that Lenin's policy would lead to débâcle. Lenin, they alleged, overrated the strength of the Bolsheviks and underrated that of the provisional government; he also believed that the Russian revolution would be saved by a socialist upheaval in Europe, whereas they denied the proximity of proletarian revolution in the West. Against these arguments Lenin repeated that it was no use waiting for the constituent assembly, for the government had so many times postponed its convocation and it would do so again; meanwhile the Officers' Leagues would have enough time to prepare a counter-revolution and establish their dictatorship. Lenin confidently predicted that, if the insurrection was speeded up, its opponents could muster only insignificant strength against it and that 'all proletarian Europe' would rise. His attitude was shared by ten members of the Central Committee: Trotsky, Stalin, Dzerzhinsky and others. Only Zinoviev and Kamenev cast their votes against his motion. The dramatic debate went on almost till the day of the rising; but to the end Zinoviev and Kamenev were outvoted; the majority of the party accepted Lenin's guidance.

While Lenin was the moving spirit of the insurrection and, from his hiding-place, prepared his followers for it, Trotsky was its actual leader and organiser on the spot. Lenin had urged his party to stage the rising in its own name, without paying attention to constitutional niceties, and to start it as an openly offensive operation against the government. Trotsky, however, was careful to place the insurrection in a wider political context, to conduct it under the auspices of the soviets and not only of the Bolshevik party, and to give it to the appearance of a defensive action designed to protect the revolution from a counter-revolutionary *coup*. His artful tactics greatly facilitated the Bolshevik victory: many of those who would have hesitated to support a rising staged, as it were, as the private affair of one party only, favoured the enterprise when it was backed by the authority of the Petrograd soviet or of the soviets at large;

and many who might have shrunk from an openly offensive action supported that action when it was justified on defensive grounds. In fact the rising had its defensive elements: the Bolshevik leaders, at any rate, were convinced that if they themselves delayed action they would be forestalled by another, and this time successful, counter-revolutionary *coup, à la Kornilov.*

But in what way could the 'transfer of power' to the soviets be accomplished? In June the first All Russian Congress of the soviets had taken place and had elected a central executive committee which was to convene the next congress in September. That central executive committee (*TsIK*) was still dominated by the Mensheviks and Social Revolutionaries even after the soviets on the spot had come under Bolshevik influence. The leaders of *TsIK* repeatedly postponed the second congress of the soviets, at which, it was clear, the Bolshevik party was certain to have a solid majority. In the end they yielded to pressure from the Petrograd soviet and convened the congress for the latter part of October, or for the beginning of November, according to the new calendar. The Bolsheviks linked the date of the insurrection to the forthcoming congress. After a last and final postponement, the congress was to be opened on 25 October/7 November. The insurrection was prepared to take place one day earlier so that the congress should be able at once to sanction its expected outcome, the formation of a Bolshevik government. The insurrection itself was carried out, on behalf of the Petrograd soviet, by the Revolutionary Military Committee which had been elected by that soviet. It was one of history's ironies that the setting-up of this revolutionary military committee had not been proposed by Bolshevik members of the soviet. In the first half of October Petrograd was astir with rumours, for which there appeared to be some basis in governmental statements, that with the advance of the Germans the city would be evacuated and the government would move to Moscow. The rumours were later officially denied but in the meantime, amid the panic and indignation to which they gave rise, the Mensheviks proposed that the Petrograd soviet should assume responsibility for the defence of the capital. To this the Bolsheviks readily agreed. The Revolutionary Military Committee was to keep in touch with the city's garrison, to acquaint itself with its disposition and to assess its strength. Ostensibly these activities served to prepare the defence against the Germans, but at the same time they formed the preliminaries to insurrection. Somewhat later Kerensky ordered a redistribution of military forces which again was ostensibly designed merely to strengthen the front, but which was meant to enhance the position of the government in the capital by sending the most revolutionary regiments to the front. The Revolutionary Military Committee vetoed this reshuffling of armed forces. Under Trotsky's guidance it sent its commissars to all the detachments stationed in and around

Petrograd in order to control the movement of troops. This was a challenge to the government and to the regular command, one which Kerensky could not leave unanswered. On 23 October/5 November he ordered the suppression of Bolshevik newspapers and issued writs for the arrest of the Bolshevik leaders who had been released on bail. The next day he indicted the Revolutionary Military Committee before the pre-parliament and ordered an enquiry into its activities.

While Kerensky was addressing the pre-parliament and indulging in belated threats against the Bolsheviks, the revolution had actually begun. His threats merely provided the Bolsheviks with a defensive pretext for the insurrection. The Revolutionary Military Committee had started it with its famous Order No. 1: 'The Petrograd Soviet is in imminent danger. Last night the counter-revolutionary conspirators tried to call the cadets and the shock-battalions into Petrograd. You are hereby ordered to prepare your regiment for action. Await further orders. All procrastination and hesitation will be regarded as treason to the revolution.' The plan of the military operations had been laid down with great precision by Trotsky, Podvoisky, Antonov-Ovseenko and Lashevich, members of the Revolutionary Military Committee. During the night from 24 to 25 October (6–7 November), Red Guards and regular regiments occupied with lightning speed the Tauride Palace, the seat of the pre-parliament, the post offices and the railway stations, the National Bank, the telephone exchanges, the power stations and other strategic points. While the movement which overthrew tsardom in February/March lasted about a week, the overthrow of Kerensky's last government took a few hours. On the morning of 25 October/7 November Kerensky had already escaped from the capital, hoping to rally front troops for the fight. At noon his government was besieged in the Winter Palace just as the tsarist government had been in the final phase of the February/March revolution. Within one night, almost without bloodshed, the Bolsheviks had become masters of the capital. The astonished population awakened in the morning to read posters announcing:

The Provisional Government has been overthrown. Governmental authority has passed into the hands of the...Revolutionary Military Committee which leads the proletariat and the garrison of Petrograd. The cause for which the people has struggled: the immediate offer of a democratic peace, the abolition of the landlords' property of the land, workers' control over production and the formation of a Soviet Government—this cause is now secure. Long live the revolution of soldiers, workers and peasants!

In the evening the second congress of the soviets was opened. The majority of its delegates (390 out of 649) were Bolsheviks. For the first time since July Lenin appeared in public to address the congress and to table two momentous motions on peace and on the land. His Decree on Peace called 'upon all belligerent nations and their governments to

428

start immediate negotiations for a just, democratic peace...without annexations...without the seizure of foreign lands and without indemnities'. The Decree on Land stated simply that 'landlord property is abolished forthwith without compensation'. While the congress applauded news of the arrest of the members of the provisional government, the first Council of People's Commissars was formed on 26 October/8 November with Lenin as its head, Trotsky as commissar for foreign affairs, Stalin as commissar for nationalities, Rykov (home affairs), Miliutin (agriculture), Shlyapnikov (labour), Lunacharsky (education), and Antonov-Ovseenko, Krylenko and Dybenko as the joint chiefs of the commissariat for military and naval affairs. The programme of this new government was still hazy in many respects. But its leaders were determined to establish a proletarian dictatorship and to gain for it the support of the vast mass of the peasantry which formed the bulk of Russia's population. They hoped to obtain that support by sharing out among the peasants 150 million *dessyatin* of land that belonged to the large estates. Their next immediate objective was to conclude peace. At the moment of the revolution they firmly believed that other European countries would so quickly follow Russia's example that the peace would be concluded between revolutionary proletarian governments of the main belligerent countries. The leaders of the new régime were less clear in their minds how far they should go in socialising industry—they nationalised the banks and transport but left most industries under the dual control of industrialists and workers. Finally, they set out to build up the soviets into 'a new type of state' superseding bourgeois democracy and representing workers and peasants on the basis of 'proletarian democracy'.

Frederick Engels once wrote that 'people who boast that they have made a revolution always find on the next day that they had no idea what they were doing, that the revolution made does not in the least resemble the one they intended to make'. Engels drew this generalisation mainly from the experience of the great French revolution, but its truth was up to a point confirmed by the fortunes of the Russian revolution and reflected in the deeds, beliefs and illusions of its actors. In April 1917 Prince Lvov boasted in a mood of elation: 'We can consider ourselves happy people. Our generation has been lucky to live in the happiest period of Russian history.' Only a few weeks later this 'happiest period' was in the eyes of the same man the blackest disgrace in Russian history. Kerensky in his heyday asked a meeting of soldiers: 'Is the Russian free state a state of mutinous slaves?...I regret that I did not die two months ago: I would have died dreaming the great dream that once for all a new life had begun for Russia, that we could live without the whip and the bludgeon, respect one another and administer our state not as did previous despots.' The disillusionment of men like Lvov and

Kerensky was growing as the revolution was using them up and throwing them overboard. They did not in any real sense *make* the revolution; they had no clear conception of its development; and in them the clash between illusion and reality was absolute.

The case of the Bolsheviks was different. They were the only party which in 1917 knew what they wanted and were capable of acting. They had a masterly understanding of all factors of the upheaval and they represented a profound historic urge of the Russian people. And yet they too were to find out that the revolution they made was different from the one they had intended to make. They too had yet to learn, in a long series of cruel lessons, that the assumptions on which they had acted had not been free from major and even tragic illusions.

On the eve of the October insurrection, in his controversy with Zinoviev and Kamenev, Lenin had stated his two main assumptions. He was confident that the revolution would justify itself *nationally*, that it would by supported by an overwhelming majority of the Russian people. He also believed that the revolution would justify itself *internationally*, that it was the prelude to imminent international revolution. His first assumption, that Bolshevism would be able to assert itself on the national, Russian scale, was soon vindicated to an extent of which he himself had not dreamt. For two-and-a-half years the Bolsheviks were to wage a savage civil war against White armies and foreign troops of intervention. If from this grim trial Bolshevism eventually emerged with flying colours this must have been due—in the last resort—to the deep popular appeal it had at the time. In one of its aspects the civil war was in fact a tense competition in which Bolshevism and the forces of the *ancien régime* tried to gain the support of the peasantry. This competition was won by Bolshevism. The 150 million *dessyatin* of land which the *muzhiks* obtained under the first decree issued by the Soviet government formed a wide and solid foundation for the new régime. In defending the Bolsheviks against the White generals and foreign interventions the Russian peasantry defended itself against the return of the landlords trailing behind the White armies. It may be argued that Lenin and Trotsky 'bribed' the peasantry; and in a sense this is true. But this does not alter the fact that the old system of land tenure was for the bulk of the Russian people an unbearable anachronism; that the peasantry's hunger for land had to be satisfied; that none of the old parties was willing or capable of satisfying it without delay; and that the agrarian revolution of 1917 gave the soviet system a stable foundation. So great indeed was the initial strength which the Bolsheviks acquired from it that it enabled them not only to outlast the civil war but to risk, about a decade later, a dangerous conflict with vast sections of the peasantry over the collectivisation of land and to outlast that conflict too. Into its own national soil Bolshevism had struck firm, indestructible roots.

The second assumption on which Lenin and Trotsky urged their followers to launch the revolution—the imminence of proletarian revolution in the West—was the half-illusory element in the beliefs and hopes of Bolshevism. It was only half and not altogether illusory, because the potentiality of revolution did exist in several European countries. But the potential did not become actual. When in November 1918 revolutions did break out in Germany and Austro-Hungary, they confined themselves to the substitution of bourgeois parliamentary republics for the old monarchies; they did not find their expected consummation in proletarian dictatorships. Moreover, these revolutions occurred later than the Bolsheviks had expected; and in the meantime the soviets had been compelled, by their isolation and war-weariness, to sign the 'shameful' Peace of Brest-Litovsk. In 1918–20 the sympathy of the European working classes for Soviet Russia was strong enough to hamper and eventually to bring to a standstill foreign intervention. To this extent Lenin was not wrong when he placed his hopes on 'proletarian Europe'. But his hopes had reached farther—he had looked forward to the revolutionary triumph of 'proletarian Europe'. He had always been acutely conscious of the 'backward, Asiatic' character of the Russian civilisation and he could not easily see how socialism could be achieved in Russia alone. In 1905–6, and for some years after, he had expected only a 'bourgeois-democratic' revolution in Russia, precisely for this reason. In 1917 he persuaded his party that the revolution could pass from the 'bourgeois-democratic' to the socialist phase, but he was also convinced that it could do so because it would not stop at Russia's frontiers. Once the revolution won in the highly industrialised and civilised countries of the West, so he repeatedly argued, the construction of socialism would assume an international character and advanced Europe would help Russia with machines, technical advice, administrative experience and education. In the meantime Russia had the political initiative of revolution; and in order to speed up the process the Bolshevik party set up the Communist International in 1919. However, towards the end of the civil war, or at any rate by 1921, it became clear that the bourgeois parliamentary régimes of western Europe had withstood the onslaughts of Communism, for the time being at least. Soviet Russia stood alone—a prodigy of devastation and poverty. A readjustment of the Bolshevik perspective was unavoidable, and not one but a series of readjustments followed. The first was the partial readmission of capitalism under the New Economic Policy (NEP) of 1921. The next was the enunciation by Stalin in 1924 of the doctrine of socialism in one country, the essence of which was the affirmation of the self-sufficiency of the Russian revolution. The vision of a joint advance of many nations towards socialism had faded for the time being, or become more remote. What replaced it or over-shadowed it was the vision of Russia's lonely progress towards the remote socialist objective through all the harsh trials of a state-controlled industrial revolution and of a forcible collectivisation of agriculture (ch. xv).

In another and equally important respect, too, the outcome of the revolution was to differ greatly from the expectations of its makers. 'We never anticipated that we would have to resort to so much terror in the civil war and that our hands would become so bloodstained': thus in October 1920 Zinoviev publicly confessed to a congress of German Independent Socialists at Halle. In the grim ruthlessness of the civil war the whole character of the revolutionary state was transformed. In 1917 Lenin advocated the Soviet system as a higher type of democracy, as a new state 'without police, bureaucrats and a standing army'. True enough, the possessing classes were disfranchised, and the new state was a proletarian dictatorship. But the disfranchisement of the bourgeoisie was at first considered to be a more or less provisional measure, dictated by an emergency; and, at any rate, the proletarian dictatorship was to give to the workers and peasants, that is, to the overwhelming majority of the nation, more political as well as economic freedom than they could obtain under a bourgeois democracy. By the end of the civil war the workers, and the peasants too, had been deprived of their political freedoms, and the foundations had been laid for the single party system. In the light of later events it has often been assumed that Lenin's party had from the outset deliberately worked to achieve this result, but this view is not borne out by the facts. It was only in the civil war, when the Bolsheviks were often unable to tell foe from friend, that they actually suppressed the parties of the opposition and established their own political monopoly, gradually and gropingly, under the pressure of events. In later years the sense of Russia's isolation in a hostile world coupled with the inertia of government by coercion prompted the final abolition of 'proletarian democracy' and the transformation of the Soviet régime into a terroristic police state. History's irony took a bitter revenge upon the men who had set out to build a state 'without police, bureaucrats and a standing army'. Yet, despite some Bolshevik illusions, which time and events dispelled either gradually or in the most violent manner, it cannot be doubted that the Bolshevik revolution, like the great French revolution before it, opened a new epoch not only in Russian history. The day of 25 October/ 7 November 1917 stands like a huge and indestructible landmark in the annals of mankind; and, although by no means all the implications of the upheaval then initiated have come to light by the middle of the century, the October Revolution can already be seen to have initiated Russia's extraordinary ascendancy as a world power, and also to have found a gigantic sequel in the Chinese revolution.

CHAPTER XV

THE SOVIET UNION 1917–1939

O N completion of their seizure of power in Russia's two capital cities, in November 1917, Lenin and his associates found themselves faced with two outstanding problems, both dangerously urgent. One was the need for consolidating and extending to the remainder of the country the power they now so tenuously held in the great urban centres. The other was the need for a clarification of the relationship of the new revolutionary Russia to the world war, then at the apex of its intensity. Russia was, after all, a belligerent; hostilities were still in progress; the situation could brook no delay.

The political grouping on which Lenin based his power—the Bolshevik faction of the Russian Social Democratic Labour Party—could scarcely have numbered at that time much more than 70,000 members in a country of some 160 million. This tiny following was concentrated largely in the great cities and a few outlying industrial communities. Although they had by this time gained control of the Petrograd and Moscow soviets, the Bolsheviki could not claim a majority even within the socialist component of the Russian political spectrum as a whole; and this component embraced only about half of the country's voting population. In the ranks of organised labour, in particular, their support was small, though increasing. In extensive outlying regions, such as the Caucasus and Siberia, they had only the merest smattering of followers. Their seizure of power in the great urban centres had been rendered possible by the far-reaching demoralisation of the army, the helplessness of the provisional government, their own ruthless employment of irregular armed units, the utilisation of the soviets of workers' and peasants' deputies as a screen for their action, and, finally, by their demagogic appeal to the peasantry to seize all large landed property—a move which, for the moment, neutralised whatever serious resistance might otherwise have been encountered in that vitally important quarter. But the victory was as yet a tenuous one. In many segments of the populace, far-reaching expectations had been aroused that had now in some way or other to be met or disarmed. Dangerous gaps remained to be filled in the structure of the Bolshevik authority.

In particular, the Bolshevik leaders faced a danger and embarrassment in their commitment to the convening of a constitutional convention to determine the future political system of the country. The demand for the early election of such a body (generally referred to in English usage as the 'Constituent Assembly') had long figured prominently in Lenin's political programme, and his followers had not hesitated to make an issue of the alleged dilatoriness of the provisional government in arranging the necessary elections. Preparations for such elections, however, were well in hand when the November overthrow occurred. There could be no question, now, of halting the process. Yet the elections were bound to produce an anti-Bolshevik majority.

The hostility that naturally prevailed against the Bolsheviki in the conservative, non-socialist sectors of the Russian public was not Lenin's greatest concern. These elements had already met with decisive political defeat in the fall of tsardom and the now irreparable disaffection of both peasantry and intelligentsia from their cause; and with the destruction of the old police system and the dissolution of the army they had lost their only effective weapons of self-defence. Lenin was also not seriously worried about his Menshevik rivals in the Social-Democratic movement. They had little popular support, except in one limited region: the Transcaucasus. The most serious danger lay with the S/R's—the Socialist Revolutionaries —and their extensive support among the peasantry. Elections to a Constituent Assembly would be bound to demonstrate the extensive popular support which the S/R's enjoyed, and to accentuate demands among these and other moderate-socialist elements for the establishment of a coalition government in which they might have a part.

With these dangers Lenin managed to cope, but only by the barest of margins. The demands for a coalition government were met by splitting the S/R party and taking its extremist and politically naïve Left Wing into an unstable political coalition. This association lasted only a few weeks (to the conclusion of the Brest-Litovsk Peace in March 1918), but long enough to obscure the issue and to provide a semblance of multi-party support, above all peasant support, during this crucial period.

As for the Constituent Assembly: the elections were held as planned, at the end of November 1917. The Bolsheviki turned out to have, even together with their Left S/R allies, something less than 30 per cent of the voting strength in the new body. The Assembly, convening in mid-January 1918, showed itself recalcitrant from the start to Bolshevik demands, and was then promptly suppressed and dispersed, by force of arms, on Lenin's orders. This action, its ominous implications notwithstanding, passed off for the moment without serious challenge in the general bewilderment and confusion of the Revolution; but the bitterness it aroused among the opponents of the Bolsheviki was understandably deep and lasting.

Even more serious, particularly in the strains it imposed on unity within the Bolshevik faction itself, was the problem presented by the need for defining the relationship of the new Russia to the war. Here, again, the Bolsheviki were forced to pay the price for previous demagoguery. They had long denounced the war as an imperialistic one, the issues of which were of interest only to the capitalist exploiters. They had not called for a separate Russian peace; they had denied, in fact, that this was what they wanted. They had called instead for the conversion of the 'imperialist' war into a civil one: for radical-socialist uprisings, that is, in all the warring countries, to be followed by the conclusion of a general socialist peace, on the basis of 'no annexations and no indemnities'. But they had in effect promised 'peace' to the Russian people. The situation with which they found themselves confronted, now that they were in power, failed to conform to this projected pattern. The working classes in the other warring countries did not rise up against their exploiters, in response to the Russian revolution. The western governments, still not overthrown, failed to respond in any way to the appeal for a general peace which the Bolsheviki issued within hours after their seizure of power. The powerful armies of Imperial Germany continued to confront the remnants of the Russian army, along the eastern front. They could not be expected to remain long quiescent. The Russian army, to the disintegration of which the Bolsheviki had so prominently contributed, was no longer an effective fighting force. The few units that retained some degree of discipline and fighting capacity were generally anti-Bolshevik in their political complexion. They could be employed in combat only at the risk that their bayonets might any day be turned against the new régime itself.

In these circumstances, there was only one realistic course to follow: namely, to sue for a separate peace on the best terms the Germans were willing to give. This course encountered such bitter opposition among Lenin's more hot-headed followers that the unity of the Party was rocked to the foundations before the process of capitulation could be completed. But, in the end, Lenin, who saw clearly where the necessities lay, carried the day. An armistice was concluded in early December. And on 3 March, after prolonged and angry negotiations, broken off for a time on Bolshevik initiative, a peace treaty was finally signed at the German headquarters for the eastern front, in Brest-Litovsk.

This treaty has come down in historical literature as a classical example of the draconic, punitive peace. Its terms were indeed severe. It represented a bitterly unhappy ending to Russia's long and costly participation in the first world war. But it must be remembered that the Germans were dealing here not with the legitimate Russian government which had opposed them earlier in the war, but, as they saw it, with a band of usurpers—political fanatics who had seized power in a single portion of the former empire and whose right to speak for the Russian people as a whole was as yet by no means demonstrated.

The greatest hardship of the Brest-Litovsk Treaty, from the Bolshevik standpoint, lay in the implied relinquishment on the part of the new régime of its claim to the Baltic States, Poland, and—above all—the Ukraine. The Germans, determined to have unimpeded access to the resources of the Ukraine for the benefit of their war effort, refused to treat with the Bolsheviki at all concerning the disposition of this region in particular, and insisted on concluding a separate peace with a small group of Ukrainian separatists—the so-called Rada—who were trying, in the aftermath of the breakdown of the old empire, to establish themselves as the government of an independent Ukraine. In addition to this, the Germans denied the right of the Soviet government to speak for Finland or the Baltic States. All this was of course a bitter blow to the Russian Communists, but it was a blow to their hopes rather than to their possessions. None of the regions in question was one in which they had yet succeeded in establishing their power (though they did succeed in seizing the Ukrainian centre of Kiev on the very day the peace between the Germans and the Rada was signed). Their claim to speak for the people of these regions rested, at the moment, primarily on their own ambitions, which the Germans, understandably, viewed with an emphatic lack of sympathy.

The Brest-Litovsk Treaty was entered into by both sides for wholly opportunistic reasons that implied no acceptance of the permanency or legitimacy of the other party. Coming as it did only some eight months before the collapse of the German war effort, its validity was of brief duration. Its execution was marked by many conflicts and disagreements between the two parties. But it yielded for the Bolsheviki what they at the moment most wanted: immunity from further military punishment by the Germans, and a period of respite in which to consolidate their power and to extend it to those parts of the former empire not overrun by the Germans.

The conclusion of the Brest-Litovsk Peace brought to an end the unstable governmental coalition with the Left S/R's. Their popular strength being largely in the Ukraine, they were particularly affected by the German occupation of that region. They viewed the Brest-Litovsk Treaty as a humiliating capitulation and refused to share responsibility for it. They were also estranged by the draconic means to which the Bolsheviki had been resorting for the extraction of grain from the peasants.

Prior to the seizure of power, Lenin had not hesitated to encourage the peasants to seize whatever land was not already in their possession. With a view to neutralising peasant resistance to the establishment of Bolshevik rule, he had even adopted *in toto* the agrarian programme of the S/R's, which abolished private ownership in theory while permitting in actuality a distribution of larger holdings among the poorer peasants. But the sharp ideological hostility entertained by the Bolsheviki for the peasantry, as a class, never really abated; and when, in the winter and spring of 1918, deliveries of food to the cities fell off disastrously as a result of the extreme disorganisation of the economy, the régime did not hesitate to resort to harsh and confiscatory measures to get grain to the industrial workers and to such armed units as were prepared to accept Communist leadership.

It was these practices, together with the Brest-Litovsk Treaty, that

THE SOVIET UNION 1917-1939

alienated the Left S/R's. Now, in the spring of 1918, they not only left the government, but struck out on an independent line, embarrassing the Soviet leaders by mounting a series of *attentats* against leading German officials (both the German Ambassador in Moscow and the military commander in Kiev fell victim to these assaults) and even in some instances attempting to challenge Soviet authority by armed force.

It was not only among the Left S/R's that violent opposition to the Communists was by now crystallising. In several outlying parts of the country, to which Bolshevik power had not yet been extended, political bodies or entities hostile, or at least resistant, to Bolshevik rule were now establishing their authority. Some were inspired by other socialists, primarily S/R's. Others proceeded from conservative elements, partisans of the old régime. These latter had even bridled at accepting the authority of the provisional government. They now had no intention of submitting peacefully to that of the Bolsheviki. Many of them had been stunned, initially, by the swiftness and audacity of the Bolshevik seizure of power; but by the spring of 1918 they had time to take the measure both of the slenderness of Bolshevik popular support and of the menacing intolerance with which the Communist leaders were pursuing a total monopoly of power. They now gathered for the counter-attack.

To these general national reactions, coming from people whose political aspirations related to the traditional Russian territory as a whole, there were added numerous separatist tendencies released by the recent collapse of the multi-national tsarist empire. Such tendencies were stimulated by the emergence of similar tendencies in the Austro-Hungarian Empire, as well as by the commitment of the Allied governments (and the Bolshevik leaders themselves, for that matter) to the principle of self-determination. In Finland, there was already in progress, by the spring of 1918, a bitter civil war between Communists and anti-Communists. One of the issues was the future relationship of that country to what was now a Communist Russia—a question soon to be decided in favour of complete independence. In the Ukraine, a separatism defiant of Bolshevik authority was being upheld by German bayonets. Similar particularistic tendencies were smouldering in a number of other regions of the former empire. By late spring of 1918, in short, the delayed political reaction to the Bolshevik seizure of power, fortified by centrifugal tendencies throughout the territory of the former empire, was beginning to make itself strongly felt; and political opposition to the Bolsheviki awaited only some special stimulus to bring it into full military activity.

This stimulus came in the summer of 1918, in the form of the Allied military intervention. Russia's departure from the war, accompanied as it was by the transfer of hundreds of thousands of German troops from the eastern to the western front and the opening up of the Ukraine to German economic exploitation, had caused intense excitement and alarm in the

Allied capitals—particularly in London and Paris. To Allied military planners, the total collapse of all military resistance to Germany in the east, occurring just as the last great German offensive was developing in the west, appeared as nothing less than a disaster. Around the time of the conclusion of the Brest-Litovsk Treaty, the wildest schemes were entertained in London and Paris for restoring some sort of fighting front in Russia, with a view to diverting at least a portion of German strength from the west. Initially, some of these schemes envisaged military support for the Bolsheviki. It was hoped that the Bolshevik leaders, with their hands thus strengthened, could be induced to scrap the Brest-Litovsk Treaty and to resume military operations against the Germans. For a time, in March and April 1918, Trotsky, now People's Commissar for War, took care not to discourage such hopes entirely. He feared that the Germans might disregard the treaty and resume hostilities, and was concerned to hold open the possibility of Allied support in such a contingency. By May, however, it was clear that the Germans, however severely they might interpret the Brest-Litovsk Treaty in other respects, did not intend any serious incursions on to the territory under Soviet control. With this, the Bolshevik leaders lost interest in military collaboration with the Allies; and opinion in the Allied capitals swung, accordingly, to the idea of military intervention in Russia in disregard or defiance of Bolshevik wishes. If resistance to Germany could not be restored in collaboration with the Bolsheviki, perhaps—it was reasoned—it could be restored in collaboration with other Russian political factions.

Most of the opponents of the Bolsheviki, particularly the conservative ones, still professed loyalty to the Allies and a desire to see Russia resume participation in the war. It is clear in retrospect that these professions were made more in the hope of enlisting Allied aid in the struggle against the Communists than out of any enthusiasm for the Allied cause or any serious intention of resuming hostilities against the Germans. The Russian army, after all, had now effectively ceased to exist. Nothing could have moved the mutinous peasant-soldiers, now largely demobilised, to go back into the trenches. At no time do the Allies appear fully to have realised that arms placed at that moment in the hands of any Russian faction would inevitably be used primarily against other Russians, in civil struggle, rather than against the Germans. But desperation bred wishful thinking. Extravagant claims as to the response that could be expected if only Allied troops were to set foot on Russian soil were given ready credence in London and Paris. And out of these desperate hopes came the decisions that led to the dispatch to Russia of the various minor expeditions known collectively as the Allied intervention.

Strictly speaking, the intervention may be said to have begun not with the dispatch of new military units to Russia but with the action of one Allied force that was already there. This was the Czechoslovak Corps, composed of Czechs and Slovaks (largely prisoners of war) hostile to the Austro-Hungarian Empire. This Corps had been stationed alongside the Russians on the eastern front before the latter collapsed. It was, by late 1917, theoretically under French command and hence in the formal sense an Allied force. In contrast to most of the Russian units along the front, it had retained its discipline, even after the November overthrow. But its position on the front was rendered untenable by Russia's withdrawal from the war. Arrangements were made, around the time of Brest-Litovsk, for its evacuation, via Siberia, to the western front. In May 1918, however, in the course of this evacuation, a conflict broke out between certain of the Czech units and the Communist authorities in western Siberia. In a matter of days the Czechs succeeded, somewhat to their own surprise, in seizing large sections of the Trans-Siberian Railway. Anti-Communist factions in this region naturally saw their chance and at once joined in the action against the Communists.

The Czechs enjoyed much sympathy in Washington. It was the situation resulting from their conflict with the Communist authorities in Siberia that led President Wilson (who understood the situation very poorly) to yield at long last to the pressures the French and British had been exerting on him since the beginning of the year and to consent to the dispatch of an American expeditionary force to eastern Siberia. The Japanese immediately followed suit by sending a much larger contingent, and for wholly different purposes. At the same time a mixed Allied force, under British command but with Americans forming the largest contingent of rank and file, was dispatched to north Russia (Archangel), where friendly political elements, at odds with the Bolsheviki, were pleading for their arrival. Finally, British expeditions, tiny in numbers but full of dash and determination, crossed the southern border of the former empire at two points, in the Trans-caucasus and Transcaspia, with a view to preventing the Turks and the Germans from capitalising too extravagantly on the collapse of the Russian military effort in that region.

These Allied expeditions were all minor in scale. Their purposes were incredibly confused. Naturally, they served everywhere to release and to stimulate military opposition to the Communists. In this way they un-questionably had much to do with the unleashing of the Russian Civil War. As a result of this association with anti-Communist Russian elements, together with the alarm and distaste produced upon them by Communist policies and views generally, many Allied officials in Russia unquestion-ably came to entertain a strong dislike for the Bolsheviki, to give credence to the abundant rumours that they were in league with the Germans, to regard them as inimical to the Allied cause, and to view it as one of the purposes of the intervention to bring about their overthrow. Yet, with the exception of the Japanese incursion into eastern Siberia, and a French expedition to southern Russia (not sent until after the armistice), the considerations leading to the dispatch of these expeditions were initially ones relating primarily to the prosecution of the war against Germany. Certainly the expeditions in north Russia, in Siberia, and in the Caucasus and central Asia, would never have been sent had there not been a world war in progress and had it not been thought that their activity in Russia would be useful to an Allied victory. That they were so slow in being withdrawn after the Armistice was attributable partly to technical difficulties, partly to inter-Allied misunderstandings and rivalries, partly to the extent to which they had by that time involved themselves with anti-Communist forces in the Russian Civil War. Except in north Russia, none of them became very seriously involved in military operations against Soviet forces. In no case was their eventual withdrawal the result of military necessity. They were withdrawn mainly because the termination of the world war removed the original rationale for their presence in Russia, and because the attempt to hold them there when hostilities had ceased elsewhere led to formidable problems of morale, but also because the grievous disunity prevailing among the various Russian factions with whom they found themselves associated made further military or political collaboration fruitless and unpromising.

While the Russian Civil War was thus touched off by the Allied intervention, it would be wrong to say that the intervention greatly affected its course. In the main theatres of the Civil War—the Urals, the Central Volga district, the Ukraine, the northern Caucasus, and the Crimea—the Allied expeditions (with the exception of the Czechs, and then only briefly) were scarcely a military factor. The Allied governments did give important help to the anti-Communist factions in the form of military supplies and financial aid. In many ways, however, the intervention, never popular with the Russian people, seems to have benefited, rather than damaged, the Bolshevik cause.

The term 'Civil War' is the one generally used to describe the whole complex of military events by which, in the period from mid-1918 to March 1921, the Russian Communists succeeded in eliminating those of their internal opponents who opposed them by force of arms and in extending the limits of their power to the boundaries that came to prevail throughout the period between the two wars.[1] While no one has succeeded in finding a better description for this long process of struggle, the designation could easily convey a misimpression. What transpired in Russia over those years in the way of armed violence failed in many respects to conform to the normal pattern of military conflict in which two clearly defined sides oppose each other over a single battle-line. Unity of purpose and command did indeed generally prevail on the Bolshevik side, but this was far from being the case with their opponents. The Communists were con-

[1] An exception was the Far East, where Japanese forces were not withdrawn until a later date.

fronted not with a single enemy, but with several of them. So great was the disunity among these latter that they often preferred fighting each other to fighting the Bolsheviki. In certain instances, they even allied themselves temporarily with the Bolsheviki in order to improve their prospects for destroying one another.

Military operations were for the most part on a small scale. There was a great premium on mobility, and a high degree of dependence, in the case of all parties, on what could be extorted from the local population in the way of food, transport and supplies. Lines and centres of communication were the normal objectives, the control of adjacent territory being more or less assumed. In these circumstances, territory changed hands, at least nominally, with bewildering rapidity. Indiscipline, pillage, licence of every sort, savagery of reprisal, and a fearful disruption of civilian life were the order of the day. Military operations directed to a coherent political–military purpose tended to merge with, and to become confused with, endless variations of local partisan activity, free-booting and sheer banditry.

In the early phases of the war, particularly on the Volga, in the Urals, and along the central Asian border, moderate socialist opponents of the Bolsheviki, especially the S/R's, played a certain part; but they were soon displaced, as a rule, by conservative army officer elements, contemptuous of the military qualities of socialist intellectuals and even more bitter and uncompromising in their opposition to Communist power. It is no exaggeration to say that, in the mutual antagonism prevailing between these two main forces opposing the Bolsheviki in the Civil War, the moderate socialists on the one hand and the conservative ex-officers and monarchists on the other, elements that hated each other no less than they hated the Bolsheviki, there lay the root cause of the failure of both. For the socialists were unable to conduct military operations without availing themselves of the military and administrative skills of the former ruling classes; whereas the latter were unable to raise reliable forces of common soldiers without availing themselves of the political appeal to the peasant masses which the socialists, particularly the S/R's, possessed. Neither party, in other words, was able to conduct a successful struggle against the Bolsheviki on its own resources alone. Yet mutual antagonism prevented any effective collaboration between them. At the heart of these antagonisms lay divergent attitudes, not so much towards the Bolshevik seizure of power, which all now deplored, as towards the first Russian revolution— the February Revolution—itself, which the socialists accepted and approved, whereas the conservatives did not. Admittedly, the superior discipline, determination and drive with which the Bolsheviki fought the Civil War contributed importantly to their success and deserve full recognition; but without this basic and unbridgeable division between its principal opponents it is permissible to doubt that Russian Communism, given its slender basis of active popular support, could have triumphed in the struggle.

In 1918, military activity in the Civil War was concentrated largely on the area between the Volga and the Urals, where the Czechoslovak uprising had touched off hostilities, and in north Russia, where the Allied intervention had had a similar effect. An episode incidental to the fighting in the Urals was the massacre by Red Guards in Ekaterininburg (16 July 1918) of the former Imperial couple, their five children, and a portion of the retainers of the Imperial household. This action appears to have been taken by decision of the local Communist authorities, in view of the approach of White forces to the city and the danger that the Imperial couple might, if alive, escape Communist control. The decision, however, was obviously within the framework of standing instructions from the Communist leaders in Moscow and received their tacit *ex post facto* approval.

The year 1919 saw the triumph of the Communist forces both in north Russia and in the area between the Volga and eastern Siberia. In the north, the withdrawal of the Allied contingents in late summer and autumn of 1919 left the local Whites demoralised, divided, and an easy prey to Communist vengeance. In the Urals and Siberia, after conservative elements, grouped around Admiral Kolchak, pushed the moderate socialists aside and seized control of the anti-Communist movement in late 1918, the Czechoslovaks, whose sympathies lay with the S/R's, lost heart for the struggle. The conservatives then found themselves unable to muster sufficient popular support to prevail alone. After some initial successes in early 1919 (which seriously misled the Allied statesmen in Paris), Kolchak's forces were routed and pushed rapidly back across Siberia. He himself was captured and executed in February 1920. In the further course of that year, Communist power was extended to all of western and central Siberia: to the point, in fact, where it encountered the lines of Japanese interest and influence. (The American forces were withdrawn from Siberia in the spring of 1920.) To avoid conflict with the Japanese so long as their forces remained in eastern Siberia, the Soviet leaders established in April 1920 a buffer state known as the Far Eastern Republic. This curious entity, governed by an unstable alliance of Communist and moderate-socialist figures, and resembling in some ways the Soviet satellite states of a later day, was liquidated in November 1922, after the departure of the last Japanese troops from the Siberian mainland, and its territory was then included in the Soviet state. Japanese forces remained, after that date, only in the northern half of Sakhalin Island, from which they were not withdrawn until 1925.

Meanwhile, the centre of military activity in the Civil War had shifted to the southern regions of European Russia. In the summer of 1919, forces under the command of General Denikin, pushing up from the northern Caucasus, overran much of the territory between Moscow and the Black

Sea. By October they had advanced as far north as Oryol. At that point, however, the fortunes of war changed abruptly. By the end of the year, Denikin had been driven back into the northern Caucasus. Here, in early 1920, his force was finally shattered and eliminated as a serious military factor.

At the time of Denikin's maximum penetration into European Russia, the Soviet leaders were faced with a simultaneous threat on their north-western flank, in the form of an attack launched from Estonia by the White general Yudenich. The approach of Yudenich's forces to the very suburbs of Petrograd, in late October 1919, marked for the Soviet régime the darkest moment of the entire Civil War; and their repulse and retire-ment, coinciding in time with the defeat of Denikin in central Russia, constituted the war's turning-point. After the triumph of the Communists in these encounters there remained, as a serious threat to their power, only the forces of General Wrangel, in the Crimea.

It was at this point that the Russian Civil War found its curious sequel in the dramatic Soviet–Polish War of 1920. In the absence of Russian representation at the Versailles Peace Conference, it had been impossible for the Conference to establish any agreed eastern boundary for the new Poland whose creation it had sanctioned. A boundary suggested by the western Allies and generally known as the 'Curzon line' (not greatly dissimilar to the border that exists today) did not satisfy the extravagant territorial ambitions which the Poles at that time entertained and for the realisation of which the domestic turmoil then prevailing in Russia seemed to offer such favourable prospects. Until the turning-point of the Russian Civil War had been passed and it had become clear that the Whites were not to be successful, the Poles held their hand. They did not wish to abet the victory in Russia of people even more hostile (as were most of the Russian conservatives) to the idea of an independent Poland than were the Bolsheviki themselves. But with the defeat of Denikin this danger seemed no longer to exist. In the spring of 1920 the Poles launched an attack which carried their forces to the Dnieper and culminated, in early May, in the capture of Kiev. To this challenge the Red Army, relieved now of the greater part of the internal threat, responded with great vigour and skill. The counter-attack not only wiped out these initial Polish gains but brought the Soviet forces by early August to the gates of Warsaw. Here they were halted and repelled, in a defensive action which owed its success partly to the excellence of Pilsudsky's strategic direction and partly to the jealousies and lack of co-ordination that plagued the Soviet command. The Polish counter-attack, adroitly aimed at the Soviet lines of communi-cation, forced upon the Red Army a retreat no less precipitate than had been their advance. The war ended with an agreement (sealed in the Peace of Riga, in March 1921) on the boundary line which was to endure down to 1939: a line more favourable to the Poles, indeed, that that which the

Allies had originally suggested, but short of the more sanguine Polish ambitions of the moment.

The termination of the war with Poland permitted the Soviet leaders to concentrate their entire military effort on the defeat of Wrangel. This task was soon completed, though not without severe fighting. With the evacuation of the last of Wrangel's forces from the Crimea in mid-November 1920, the Russian Civil War may be said to have come generally to an end. A minor epilogue remained to be played out in the suppression by the Bolsheviki (early 1921) of the independent republic which the Mensheviki had established in Georgia and which had for a time enjoyed formal Allied recognition.

Severe as had been the demands which the Civil War had placed on the energies and resources of the Bolshevik leaders, it had not prevented a certain simultaneous progress both in the consolidation of the structure of Communist power internally and in the regularisation of relations with other countries.

Theoretically, in the orthodox Marxist view, the disappearance of exploiting classes should do away with the necessity for any state power at all. In the Russia of 1917, however, the non-proletarian classes, particularly the peasantry, could not be regarded either as totally destroyed or as likely to be thus destroyed in any near future. This meant that some sort of a state structure, not identifiable with the Party as such, would have to exist. The necessity for total and final destruction of the old 'bourgeois' state structure had long been a cardinal element in the Marxist concept of the successful proletarian revolution. There could therefore be no question of restoring the apparatus of the tsarist state; something would have to be put in its place. For this problem, the various 'soviets of workers' and peasants' deputies', local and metropolitan, seemed to offer the best solution. It was in their name, after all, that power had been seized in November 1917. It was by the *ex post facto* sanction of the Third All-Russian Congress of Soviets that Lenin had justified his action in suppressing the constituent assembly, thus barring all other approaches to the establishment of any new structure of power at all. He and his party were in this way already committed, by implication, to the thesis that the soviets should constitute the basis for the new state structure. This concept was given formal recognition when the Fifth All-Russian Congress of Soviets, meeting in July 1918, approved the constitution of the first geographically delimited Soviet state: the Russian Soviet Federated Socialist Republic (R.S.F.S.R.), embracing those regions of the former empire to which Bolshevik power then extended. In theory, under this constitution, all state power was derived from the local soviets. In actuality, this principle was effectively negated, not only in the centralisation of authority in the periodically elected congresses of soviets which the Constitution itself provided, but even more in the total permeation and domination of all governmental processes by the Communist Party. So extensive was this domination that the governmental apparatus soon lost all semblance of independent authority; and its various bodies and offices, instead of respecting the lines of responsibility implicit in their own hierarchical structure, became the lifeless executive organs of those Party bodies whose area of geographical competence was similar to their own.

Thus the Party itself, the official designation of which was changed in March 1918 from 'The Russian Social Democratic Labour Party (of Bolsheviki)' to 'The Russian Communist Party (of Bolsheviki)', remained at all times the real and sole repository of absolute power. The physical suppression of political opponents began on a minor scale in the very first weeks of the new régime; but an attempt on Lenin's life (in which he was severely wounded) in August 1918,[1] coinciding as it did with the beginnings of Allied intervention, threw the Communist leadership into transports of anxiety and embitterment and evoked, as a reaction, the violent régime of terror against political opponents, real or potential, that was to endure with varying degrees of intensity for decades to come, and to be converted by Stalin, in the 1930s, into the instrument of his personal tyranny even within the Party itself. So jealous and ruthless was the use made of this instrument that within three of four years even the most pliant remnants of other radical-socialist parties or groupings, including the Left S/R's, the Anarchists, and the Mensheviki, had been totally suppressed and driven from participation even in the work of the local soviets. From 1921 on, if not earlier, the last pretence of the sharing of power with other socialist elements had been abandoned, and the Party's monopolisation of power was unlimited.

Meanwhile, during the final phases of the Civil War, progress had begun in the regularisation of relations with other countries. The first foreign governments to move in this direction were those of the border states of Estonia, Latvia and Lithuania, which, together with Finland, established normal diplomatic relations with the R.S.F.S.R. in 1920. All were of course anxious to fortify in every way possible their newly won independence; and diplomatic relations with the new régime in Russia were important from this standpoint in so far as they implied Soviet acceptance of the independent status. In March 1921, the British, for whom the way had now been smoothed by the ending of the intervention, concluded a trade agreement with Moscow, thus establishing a *de facto* relationship destined to blossom only some years later, and then after many vicissitudes, into permanent, *de jure* representation. The Germans soon followed the British example, as did Austria, Italy and the Scandinavian countries.

But at that time the world-revolutionary aims which the Soviet leaders freely confessed, and which they endeavoured by all means at their disposal to realise, still stood in the way of any more far-reaching normalisa-

[1] The *attentat* was perpetrated by Dora (Fanny) Kaplan, a Socialist-Revolutionary.

tion of relations with the outside world. The (Third) Communist International, established in Moscow in 1919 and dedicated to the spreading of Communist revolution to other countries, was no less plainly an instrument of the Russian Communist Party than was the Soviet government itself. Throughout the initial years of Soviet power, other governments would either hesitate to entertain any sort of relations with a régime whose leaders so cynically sought and promoted their overthrow, or would do so only with feelings of much discomfort and distaste.

The end of foreign intervention and the Communist victory in the Civil War not only opened up the possibility of diplomatic relations with foreign states but obliged the Soviet government to come seriously to terms, for the first time, with the problem of the attitude to be taken toward national and linguistic minorities within the Soviet sphere of power. Only a minority of the population of the former empire had been Great Russians. Even the Great Russians and the Ukrainians together had accounted for only some 62 per cent of the population. The R.S.F.S.R., as it emerged from the Civil War, included not all of the non-Russian elements of the former empire, but it included a considerable number of them. And, in determining their relation to the central Soviet power, the Bolshevik leaders faced a difficult dilemma. The minorities had contributed the greater part of the membership of the Social Democratic movement prior to the revolution. Their grievances had entered prominently into socialist criticisms of the tsarist régime. Their feelings could not now easily be ignored. A certain show of federalism was needed, furthermore, to encourage the spread of Communism to adjacent regions still not under Soviet control. On the other hand, a high degree of centralisation was called for not only by the temperamental inclinations of Lenin and his leading associates but also by the very requirements of the task of 'building socialism' to which they were now dedicated.

In the formal sense, the manner in which this problem was handled went through many variations, both in point of time and in point of differences between individual nationalities and minority groups. Suffice it to say that in general the problem was solved by conceding to the non-Russian elements various degrees of autonomy, or at least of the trappings of autonomy, on the *state* level, while retaining a total centralisation of power through the instrumentality of the Communist Party. The minority peoples, in other words, were obliged to content themselves with the external form rather than the content of a separate identity—a solution which left them free, as a rule, to employ their own language for governmental and educational purposes but placed very definite restrictions on what they might say when they used it. In the initial years of Soviet power, the régime went to considerable effort to reinforce this façade of autonomy by extensive use of native personnel in both party and governmental bodies. In the later stages of the Stalin régime, however, even this practice

446

was weakened, and relatively little effort was made to conceal a degree of Russian control scarcely different, in most instances, from that which had marked the final decades of tsardom.

In the winter and spring of 1921, as the Civil War and foreign intervention came to an end, the Soviet leaders found themselves faced with bitter and urgent problems of internal policy. Large sections of the country were in a state of economic ruin of which it can be said only that its physical evidences would probably defy the imagination of most people in the West. Industrial production was a small fraction of what it had been before the revolution. Living standards had declined drastically, even for the industrial workers who were supposed, now, to constitute the most privileged part of the population. The policy of extracting grain from the peasantry by forced and confiscatory collections was yielding diminishing and inadequate returns. It was clear that the multitude of peasant soldiers, now returning to their villages after demobilisation from the Red Army, would not be prepared to submit docilely to further such exactions. Most of them had supported the Communist side in the Civil War with no great enthusiasm—often only out of fear that a victory for the opponents of Bolshevism would lead to a restoration of the old régime and a re-establishment of the property rights of former landlords. Plainly, concessions would now have to be made to their economic interests if domestic peace was to be assured and if agricultural production, particularly marketable production, was to be revived.

On the industrial side, too, a new approach was essential. Larger industrial enterprises had been for the most part nominally nationalised in the preceding period of 'war communism'. To one extent or another these enterprises had been utilised, by makeshift methods, for the satisfaction of military needs. But this had been done at the cost of rapid depreciation of equipment, depletion of stocks, and deterioration of labour discipline. No adequate system of organisation and management had yet been established to replace that of the former private owners. So great was dissatisfaction among industrial workers that many of them were returning to the villages. The cities themselves were becoming seriously depopulated. The Russian proletariat, in the name of whose interests the Communists were exercising power, at its best a small minority of the population, was now threatened with something approaching extinction as a class.

Not only did these conditions threaten the essential economic and ideological basis of the régime, but the discontents they engendered were beginning to find support in, and to strengthen, opposition to the Bolsheviki within the socialist camp. In Petrograd, such tendencies came to the surface at the end of February 1921 in the form of widespread labour unrest, not dissimilar in many respects to that which had set off the downfall of tsarism in the same city just four years earlier. Here once

447

more, as in 1917, disaffection in the local garrisons magnified the dangers of civil disobedience. And again it was the sailors of the great naval base at Kronstadt, the same who in November 1917 had played so conspicuous a part in the Communist seizure of power, who were most deeply disaffected. Their dissatisfaction burst forth, at the beginning of March 1921, in a fully fledged mutiny, which the government was able to suppress only by military action on a serious scale.

There is no evidence to support the thesis, to which official Soviet historiography still adheres, that the Kronstadt mutiny was the result of counter-revolutionary, White Guard, or foreign capitalist inspiration. Its origins were wholly local—indigenous to the workers' and sailors' milieu in which it occurred. The demands put forward by the mutineers could stand, in fact, as a fairly accurate reflection of the aims for which both worker and peasant soldiers had conceived themselves to be fighting in the recent Civil War. These aims did indeed include the allowance of greater freedom of speech and political activity *within* the socialist segment of the population; but they took no account of the interests of the remainder (the so-called 'bourgeois' segment) of the population, and contained no advocacy of civil rights that would extend in that direction. They were not the sort of demands that would have reflected bourgeois, or foreign-capitalist, inspiration.

The response of the régime, not to the Kronstadt Uprising alone but to the general situation out of which it arose, took the form of the so-called New Economic Policy—generally known in its abbreviated form as the NEP (see above, ch. III). This change of policy did not find its expression in any single and comprehensive programme, promulgated at any one time. It was made up of a number of measures of relaxation, the first of which were taken in the spring of 1921—some even before the mutiny at Kronstadt. The most important of them was the abandonment—called for by Lenin at the Tenth Congress of the Communist Party in March of that year—of the policy of forced, confiscatory grain collections, and the substitution of a single tax in kind on agricultural production, after payment of which the peasant should be at liberty to trade on the open market with whatever further surplus he might have. In the course of the immediately ensuing months and years this measure was supplemented by others, the aggregate effect of which was to restore a limited market economy in food and other consumer goods, to permit an extensive revival of the handicraft and cottage industries, and to make possible the private operation, for profit, either by collective bodies (co-operatives, etc.) or by individuals, of small industrial and commercial enterprises. Heavy industry, transportation, finance, and numerous other aspects of economic life, enough, in fact, to constitute what the Bolsheviki themselves called the 'commanding heights' of the economy, remained fully under governmental ownership and control.

448

This new course was regarded by the Soviet leaders as a forced and temporary retreat from their central ideological goal of a wholly socialised economy—a retreat made necessary partly by the failure of the Communist revolution to spread to the remainder of Europe in the post-hostilities period (as they had initially hoped and supposed it would) but mostly by the fact that in the conditions of economic ruin then prevailing it was impossible to bring about a restoration of economic life without having recourse, if only partially and temporarily, to the stimulus of private incentive. A country in which the peasantry constituted some 80 per cent of the population was, even by Marxist definition, scarcely ripe for immediate socialisation. The NEP was conceived as a temporary expedient, reluctantly embraced, and due to be abandoned at the earliest convenient opportunity. But it was clear, to Lenin at least, and to the dominant group in the party, that this opportunity would not come at any early date—that the interlude would be at best a long one.

Just as the régime moved in this way to enlist the power of private incentive in the interests of economic recovery, it also moved to prevent any political capitalisation on this new leniency by moderate socialist or other opposition groups. As Stalin himself later said: 'in the dangerous conditions of the NEP' the party could tolerate no intra-party groupings. Repression of the Mensheviki and the S/R's (and also of the Anarchists, who had played a considerable role in the Kronstadt Uprising) was intensified after 1921. In the summer of 1922 such of the S/R leaders as could be found and apprehended were subjected to long public trial and a number of them condemned to death.[1] Meanwhile, at the Tenth Congress of the Party, there was established a series of rather vague new strictures on opposition activity within the Party, strictures which were to be extensively exploited in later years by Stalin for purposes which could scarcely have been envisaged at the time they were established.

The NEP was slow to yield its favourable economic results. On the agricultural side, its effects were delayed by the misharvest of 1921. This resulted from severe drought in certain of the main grain-growing regions, aggravated by the accumulated dislocations of revolution and civil war. It not only produced a major local famine, which took human lives by the millions, but it also caused a shortfall in marketable grain of several million tons. With vigorous help from Herbert Hoover's American Relief Administration and other foreign sources, as well as by energetic effort on the part of the Soviet authorities themselves, the effects of this disaster were contained and eventually overcome. In 1922 and 1923 crops were again reasonably satisfactory—amounting to some 75 per cent of pre-war production over the same area. But the temporary setback was severe.

---

[1] The death sentences were subsequently commuted in accordance with a personal promise given by Bukharin to socialist leaders abroad; but in certain instances the persons in question were never heard of again.

In industry, revival was slower and not uniform. Small local industries (food and leather, particularly) and handicraft production of many kinds were the first to revive. The revival of heavy industry, which remained under state control and required greater capital investment as well as higher managerial skills for its recovery, took considerably longer.

In the long run, however, the NEP served its purpose successfully. By the end of 1922, recovery was making rapid progress. It continued to do so into the mid-1920s. The greatest difficulties encountered lay less in the rate of recovery (except to some extent in the case of heavy industry) than in certain of its social and economic effects. The initial relaxations led in 1923 to a sharp crisis—the so-called 'Scissors Crisis'—in the development of the terms of exchange between city and country. A dangerous disbalance developed at that time between prices for industrial and agricultural products, industrial prices standing at 170–180 per cent of 1913, agricultural prices at levels closer to 50 per cent. The result was a natural inclination on the part of the peasants to withhold their produce from the markets and to fall back on various forms of subsistence farming or local exchange. The immediate crisis was overcome by the establishment of a system of price controls, under which prices on industrial goods were eventually brought down to more reasonable levels. But the episode served to make clear to the régime that, if one were to rely on private incentive as a means of bringing agricultural produce on to the market, there would have to be conceded to the peasant a heavy claim on the output of the reviving industry—a claim of such dimensions that it could not fail to complicate the accumulation of capital for further industrial development.

An even more significant effect of the NEP was increasing differentiation in the village as between weaker and stronger peasants. All counter-efforts of the régime notwithstanding, the more affluent peasant proved better able than his poorer neighbour to take advantage of the concessions the NEP involved. To Russian Marxists, trained to view all conflicts of economic interest between large groups of people as political encounters between cohesive social classes, functioning as conscious, organised actors on the political scene and locked in relentless mutual struggle for monopolistic political power, this strengthening of the economic position of the *kulak* was bound to appear as a species of political victory on his part and, by the same token, as a serious failure and humiliation of the régime.

Opinions differ as to how far the prosperity of the wealthier peasants really extended at the high point of the NEP. Some historians have accepted Communist claims that it exceeded anything known in tsarist times. For various reasons, this seems improbable. But one need not go this far in order to recognise that the recovery of Russian agriculture in the years of the mid-'twenties was rapid and impressive; that this recovery proceeded on the basis of private interest, operating within a market economy; that it led to a considerable strengthening of private farming, bringing much of it almost, if not entirely, to that modest level of prosperity it had enjoyed in the best of tsarist times, but that it also produced greater differentiations of income and greater inequalities in ownership and labour relationships than had existed in the immediately preceding period.

At this same time, a certain amount of private profit was of course being derived from the operation of the small industrial and trading enterprises which the NEP permitted. The extent of this too should not be overrated; but its effects soon became painfully conspicuous in the revival of luxury establishments of one sort or another—night clubs, gambling places, etc.—catering to the beneficiaries of this free enterprise.

All of this—the relative affluence of the *kulak* and the conspicuous consumption now flaunted by the so-called 'NEP men'—naturally aroused keenest disgust and impatience among members of the Party. Its effect was to lend fuel to the fires of a radical party opposition: of people who longed for the heroic days of revolution and civil war, who had never been able to adjust to the more mundane problems of the post-Civil-War period, and who were eager to find issues over which they could express their feelings of frustration and discontent. While these differences over the NEP did not represent a serious challenge to the stability of the Party, they were sufficiently serious to pre-empt a considerable portion of inner-party debate and activity during the period in which this policy was pursued. And their significance was increased, in the spring of 1922, by the fatal illness of Lenin and the crisis of leadership within the Party which that illness produced.

It was in May 1922 that Lenin suffered the first of his four strokes. He recovered sufficiently over the summer to enable him to resume work for a time in the autumn. In December, however, his condition deteriorated once more. On the 13th of that month a second stroke quite immobilised him. Over the winter he remained bedridden, but clear in his mind. Permitted by the doctors to dictate for brief periods each day, he took this means of putting on paper his thoughts on a number of questions that particularly troubled him. In March 1923 a third stroke inflicted an extensive paralysis, depriving him of the power of speech and leaving him a total invalid. It was in this condition, unavoidably removed from every connection with public affairs, that he remained, for some ten months, until his death on 21 January 1924. Only in May of 1924, after the passage of a further four months, was his political testament made known to selected Party leaders and responsibly considered by them. Thus gradually, over a period of a full two years, did the crisis of succession occasioned by his illness and death impinge itself upon the Party.

For Stalin, the great master of the gradual transition, this protracted quality of the crisis was unquestionably an advantage. So was the curious duplication of authority, as between Party and government, which marked at all times the Soviet structure of power. Lenin's ascendancy had been rooted less in his governmental position as Chairman of the Soviet of People's Commissars of the R.S.F.S.R. (this passed painlessly, after his death, to the relatively minor figure of Rykov) than in his personal authority among the senior leaders. Stalin, having assumed, in April 1922, the position of General Secretary of the Party, was already in firm organisational control of its central apparatus at the time when Lenin's illness began. At no time after that was there ever any question of his ability to exert a decisive influence over the voting in most of the senior Party bodies: the Central Committee, the Secretariat, the Organisational Bureau and the Central Control Commission—at least on day-to-day organisational questions. (The Politbureau, with its special competence for decisions of high policy, represented a partial exception.) But Stalin was at that time still a relatively obscure political figure, largely eclipsed in the public eye by Trotsky, Zinoviev and Kamenev. He lacked precisely that unspoken authority on which Lenin's power had rested. The dominant organisational position he had so gradually and quietly established for himself was already resented and opposed by a portion of the more radical Party leadership, including many people who had played a prominent part in the initial seizure of power and the Civil War. It was clear that any attempt on his part, around the time of Lenin's illness and death, to thrust himself forward openly as the successor to Lenin would be widely resented and self-defeating. Before anything of this sort could be contemplated, the more prominent figures had to become in some way discredited and disqualified in public view.

The problem Stalin faced in attempting to establish his ascendancy was greatly complicated by the fact that Lenin, throughout the period of his illness, plainly leaned towards Trotsky as the person best suited to succeed him in the direction of state policy if not in the day-to-day administration of the Party. Stalin, well aware of this inclination, took shameless advantage of Lenin's physical helplessness to reduce the latter's current influence on political affairs. He treated Lenin's wife, Krupskaya, on at least one known occasion, and probably on others as well, with a rudeness and inconsiderateness he would surely never have permitted himself had Lenin been in good health; and he invoked party discipline to prevent her from appealing to Lenin for support. At the same time, he persisted in the pursuit of practices and policies, notably in questions pertaining to his native Georgia, which he knew to be contrary to Lenin's strongest feelings. All of this clearly brought to the ailing Lenin a measure of excitement and distress of mind that could scarcely have failed to aggravate the illness. Lenin's second and third strokes both occurred at moments of high emotional disturbance, occasioned precisely by developments in which Stalin was prominently involved.

In later years, there would be suggestions and allegations (Trotsky, just before his own death, lent himself to them, though he never made the charge directly) that Lenin had been poisoned on Stalin's instigation. The preponderance of available evidence, however, does not support this thesis; nor does it seem likely that Stalin would have been moved, in the circumstances, to take any such step.

In December–January 1922–3 Lenin dictated from his sickbed the document which has become known as his political testament. Here he levied serious criticisms against Stalin, mentioning particularly his rudeness and disloyalty in personal relations, and called in effect for his removal from the position of Secretary-General of the Party. He pointed to Trotsky as the most able of his associates and, by inference, as the man best qualified to succeed him in the direction of affairs of state. (It seems doubtful that Lenin envisaged any one person as succeeding entirely to his unique position within the Party.) In accordance with Lenin's wishes, the testament was kept secret by his widow until after his death. At the time of the XIII Party Congress, in May 1924, it was revealed to a select group of party leaders. On this occasion, Trotsky, Zinoviev and Kamenev, acting with a blindness they would some day rue, connived at the suppression of the document (it was not even shown to the delegates to the Congress, though it had been Lenin's clear intention that it should be) and supported Stalin in the retention of all his Party offices.

It is evident that the disposition reflected by Lenin's testament became known to—or sensed among—the Party leadership long before its precise contents were revealed. The effect was to produce a defensive association of Stalin, Zinoviev and Kamenev, designed to keep Trotsky in check and to prevent him from succeeding to Lenin's authority. Signs of the existence of this grouping, which came to be known as the 'Triumvirate', were visible as early as January 1923. The high period of its effectiveness as a political alliance coincided with the period in which Trotsky appeared as a leading candidate for the succession. It did not come fully to an end until late 1925. By this time, Trotsky had not only abandoned his key position as People's Commissar for War and suffered a decisive loss of authority in the Party but had effectively eliminated himself as a candidate for the succession by publicly denying the authenticity of Lenin's testament when reports of it appeared in the foreign press.

In the measure that Trotsky became eliminated as a rival for the succession, Stalin addressed himself to the destruction of the political positions of Kamenev and Zinoviev. This involved initially the shattering of the local organisational strength these leaders had gained as bosses, respectively, of the Moscow and Leningrad organisations of the Party. The operation began in the summer of 1924 with the systematic undermining of Kamenev's position in Moscow. It was completed by January 1926, when Zinoviev's removal from the Leningrad post was followed by a ruthless purge and reorganisation of the Party apparatus in that city, conducted by Molotov under Stalin's direction. In this way the first and decisive phase of the succession crisis was brought to an end, two years after Lenin's death, with the emergence of Stalin in a position of clear organisational ascendancy within the Party.

The foreign relations of the Soviet régime had continued, meanwhile, to develop on the two conflicting planes that were to constitute their main theatres of activity for many years to come: the plane of the Comintern (i.e. relations with foreign Communist parties) where the effort was pursued, at least *pro forma*, to promote the overthrow of the governments of other great powers; and the plane of overt diplomatic relations, where the effort was made to co-exist advantageously with these governments so long as they continued to defy the efforts at their overthrow.

In Germany, regarded in those years as both the most important and the most promising target of revolutionary activity, grievous reverses were suffered in the failure of two major efforts mounted by the German Communists to seize power: one in the spring of 1921, the other in the autumn of 1923. Both of these failures had important effects on Soviet policy. They dampened hopes for any early extension of the Communist revolution to the remainder of Europe. They caused new importance to be attached to the shaping of Soviet relations with the capitalist world on the normal diplomatic and economic levels.

The need for trade with the Western governments and for the tapping of Western sources of financial credit made it desirable, from the Soviet standpoint, that normal diplomatic relations be established as soon as possible with all the leading capitalist powers. The governments of these powers hesitated, however, to take this step so long as the Soviet government continued to deny responsibility for the debts of former Russian governments and to refuse to make compensation to former owners for losses suffered by the nationalisation of foreign industrial and other property in Russia at the time of the Revolution. This issue, combined with the resentment felt in Western circles over the activities of the Comintern, served to delay general diplomatic recognition of the new Soviet régime. The first partial breach of the deadlock occurred, in April 1922, during the Genoa Conference, when the German government, still smarting under the strictures of the Versailles Treaty and anxious to ensure that Russia should not appear among the claimants on German reparations, broke ranks and concluded with the Soviet government the Rapallo Treaty, by the terms of which both parties relinquished all claims against the other and regular diplomatic relations were re-established. This weakened the position of the other Western powers in demanding debt settlements as a prerequisite to recognition. In January of 1924 the German example was followed by the Italians and the British (for quite different reasons in each case), and then by a whole series of other governments. In none of these instances was there any insistence on a prior debt settlement. This general movement of recognition included China and Japan, and involved the final departure (1925) of Japanese troops from the last bit of Soviet territory on which they had remained after 1922—the northern part of the island of Sakhalin. (A notable exception here was of course the U.S.A., which did not recognise the Soviet régime until 1933.) Generally speaking, it is thus possible to say that the general acceptance of the Soviet Union as a member of the international community, and the extensive normalisation of its relations with other great powers, coincided roughly in time with Lenin's death and the resolution of the succession crisis.

Hand in hand with these developments, not unsuitably, went the consolidation of the structure of the Soviet state into a single entity—the Union of Soviet Socialist Republics—under a new constitution, formally confirmed by the Second All-Union Congress of Soviets on 31 January 1924. The mid-1920s thus found the new Soviet state not only rapidly recovering, economically, from the ravages of war, revolution and civil war, but also constitutionally consolidated, emerging without instability from its first great crisis of personal leadership, and generally accepted into the international community; and, with this, the crucial period of trial and readjustment following upon the Revolution and the Civil War may be said to have come generally to an end.

A further three years would have to elapse, however, before the main domestic trends of this period—Stalin's successful struggle against the radical opposition (of Trotsky and Kamenev–Zinoviev) within the Party and the recovery of economic life—would reach their final culmination. After the smashing of their organisational strength within the Party, Kamenev and Zinoviev moved belatedly—much too late, in fact—to make their peace with Trotsky and to join forces with him, and with other Leftist elements within the Party, in the struggle against Stalin. From the summer of 1926 to the end of 1927, the Party was racked with the intrigues and polemics that attended this conflict. The leaders of what now emerged —the so-called 'United Opposition'—were organisationally helpless, but their prestige was great throughout the world Communist movement, both within and without Russia. Their platform was one that called for a reversal of the NEP, an early end to concessions to the peasantry and to private enterprise, a programme of rapid, intensive industrialisation, and an aggressive programme of revolutionary activity elsewhere, through the agency of the Comintern. Stalin, superior to them all in tactical skill, easily outmanœuvred them, and eventually brought about their expulsion from the Party and physical banishment from Moscow. But this took time; it was not fully accomplished until the turn of the year 1927-8. (Trotsky was forcibly exiled from Moscow to Kazakhstan in January 1928 and a year later deported entirely from the Soviet Union.) From the end of 1927, opposition from the Left was no longer seriously a thorn in Stalin's side.

The recovery of the economy had proceeded, meanwhile, at a generally satisfactory pace. By 1927 the quantitative production figures had either reached or were approaching pre-war levels. There were of course variations. Heavy metallurgy lagged behind. Electrification, on the other hand, had advanced well beyond anything achieved before the Revolution. In so far as one can judge from a somewhat confused and inadequate statistical background, agriculture too had largely, if not entirely, completed its recovery from the vicissitudes of the revolutionary period. Grain crops were now running in the neighbourhood of 80–90 per cent of the pre-war level, although the proportion of grain that could be brought on to the market and made available for non-rural consumption and for export fell considerably below the pre-war figure. Quality, to be sure, had not kept pace with quantity in the general process of recovery; and an increase of population (some 5–6 per cent over 1913) reduced the *per capita* significance of the 1927 levels of production. But it could fairly be said that by 1927 the advance of the Soviet economy, under the stimulus of the NEP, had reached a point where the outstanding problems of policy were no longer those of the restoration of production but rather those of determining along what lines further investment and development were to proceed. This raised new and momentous problems of policy.

The platform of the United Opposition was one that called in effect for an immediate and intensive effort to socialise the non-agrarian sector of the economy and to complete the industrialisation of the country—an undertaking that could proceed, obviously, only at the expense of the NEP. It wholly excluded the possibility that the economic development of the country should continue to proceed along lines that conceded permanency of status to any form of free enterprise. There is no evidence that Stalin was at any time opposed on principle to these views. But he evidently disagreed with the Opposition on certain points of timing, and was reluctant to change his course entirely before the Opposition had been crushed to a point where it could no longer take credit for the change. Until the end of 1927, he clung to a cautious middle ground, leaving it to Bukharin and other leaders of the future 'Right Opposition' to carry forward the more radical and enthusiastic defense of the NEP, while he himself moved quietly, in his skilful fashion, to take the edge off the arguments of the Left by limited concessions to its various demands.

The attacks levied against Stalin by the Left Opposition in these final years of its political vitality were by no means restricted to domestic policy. The criticisms directed to his handling of external affairs were if anything even more vehement and telling. The *de jure* diplomatic relations now established with the leading Western European countries had brought small profit to the Soviet leadership. Although the demands of the Western powers for debt settlements were no longer seriously pressed, long-term credits were, in the absence of such debt settlements, also not forthcoming.

The Soviet leaders had placed particularly high hopes on their relations with the German government. These relations had been fortified, since 1921, by clandestine arrangements of mutual convenience in the field of military collaboration. It had been the Soviet hope that German bitterness over the Versailles settlement would serve to produce that irreparable division among the leading Western nations on which prospects for the advancement of the world Communist cause were so largely predicated. But such hopes were premature. The stabilisation that occurred in Germany's relations with the Western powers in the period following the French occupation of the Ruhr in 1923, a stabilisation marked by the acceptance of the Dawes Plan, the creation of a stable German currency, conclusion of the Locarno treaties, and finally the admission of Germany to the League of Nations, made it clear that the Germans had no intention of basing their international position exclusively on the relationship with Moscow—that this tie was valuable, in fact, in German eyes primarily as a bargaining factor in Germany's dealings with other Western countries.

Relations with Britain developed even more unsatisfactorily. The effect of the *de jure* recognition extended by the Labour government of Ramsay MacDonald in early 1924 was largely nullified when that government fell from power, in the autumn of that year, as a result of the so-called Zinoviev Letter incident. Efforts conducted by the ensuing Conservative government to negotiate a debt settlement were unsuccessful. Ambassadors, consequently, were not exchanged. The already unhappy relationship was subjected to added strain by the resentment felt in Britain over the Soviet attitude towards the British General Strike of 1926. A year later, in May 1927, the British government broke off relations entirely, giving as its reason the results of a raid conducted by the British authorities on the premises of the Soviet Trade Delegation in London. It was 1930 before this new breach could be even formally healed.

In the Far East, an even more bitter disillusionment was suffered when the young and weak Chinese Communist party, attempting pursuant to Moscow's orders to co-operate with the Kuomintang in attacking the positions of the Western powers, was brutally crushed by the very political faction with which it was endeavouring to co-operate. This chapter of Soviet foreign relations is much too confused, and too full of baffling subtleties, to permit of any clear historical verdict as to personal blame for the disaster. But the United Opposition criticised Stalin savagely for his part in it, and drove him for a time sorely on to the defensive.

When the final crushing of the Left Opposition in 1927 liberated Stalin from harassment from the Left, the effects of these various disappointments and frustrations in external relations became clearly evident in his behaviour. Over an ensuing period of some years, he observed a marked caution and restraint in foreign policy, giving his attention primarily to domestic affairs and not hesitating to subordinate foreign to domestic considerations. On the Comintern level, sensitive to charges that he had lacked enthusiasm for the cause of world revolution, he set himself against all forms of collaboration with non-Communist elements, both nationalistic anti-imperialistic movements in Asia and the moderate socialist parties in Western Europe. At the same time he took the apparatus of the Comintern under closest personal control (lest it become another weapon of the Opposition against him) and used it primarily to further the national interests of the Soviet Union rather than those of world revolution. On the normal diplomatic level, he made no deliberate attempt to destroy the newly established diplomatic relations with the Western powers, but his behaviour showed that he placed little value on them. Three times in the period 1928–33, he strained Russia's relations with the governments of Germany, France and England, respectively, by staging propaganda trials, designed to shift to those governments and their agents the blame for various negative and embarrassing phenomena in Soviet life. In each case, when it was clear that things had gone too far, he made grudging concessions. But it evidently caused him no great concern that these abuses brought German–Soviet relations almost to the breaking point in 1928, or that in 1933 they caused the British to establish and maintain for a time an economic embargo against trade with the Soviet Union. He plainly considered that, in the disposition of these governments towards itself, the Soviet régime had little to lose.

It was not, however, in the foreign but rather in the domestic field that Stalin, once freed of serious pressure from the Left Opposition, instituted the most sensational and momentous changes in policy (see above, ch. III). These changes included not only the rapid termination of the NEP, in the sense of the suppression of the market economy in agriculture, in commerce and in industry, but also the physical destruction of the *kulak* class, the suppression of private farming itself as the principal form of agricultural organisation, the driving of most of the remaining peasantry into collective farms, and the pursuit, on a scale and at a pace hitherto undreamed of, of the goal of a total industrial and military autarky. That Stalin would move some distance to meet the criticisms of the Left Opposition, once its leaders had been placed in a position where they could no longer take credit for such a change of course, could have surprised no one. The programme actually put in hand, however, while pointing precisely in the direction the Opposition leaders had demanded, far exceeded in scope and in pace anything they had even envisaged. Not only were contemporaries flabbergasted by the suddenness and extremism of this change, but historians have been hard pressed to find the explanation for it.

It is not difficult to perceive the attraction of the principle of collectivisation as a long-term solution to the agrarian problems faced by the Soviet régime in the mid-1920s. Under the conditions of the NEP, in the absence, that is, of the resort by the régime to forceful and confiscatory measures for the collection of grain, the independent peasantry could be induced to part with its surpluses only at a price which appeared unacceptably high in the eyes of the régime—unacceptably high not just in monetary terms but especially in terms of the industrial output necessary to mop up the resulting purchasing power. Particularly was this true of the wealthier peasants. Not only did this drain on industrial output complicate the accumulation of the capital needed to support an intensive programme of industrialisation, but it left the régime with no certain control over the supply of grain for the feeding of the cities and the army, for the accumulation of military reserves, and for export. The unreliability of the open market in this respect was dramatically demonstrated in the winter of 1927–8, when severe difficulties were encountered in grain collections, and when it was estimated that something over two million tons were being withheld by the peasants in the hope of a rise in the governmental purchase price. It was clear, in these circumstances, that to continue to look to the independent peasant, and particularly the stronger one, as the principal source of urban food supply would be not only to tolerate a continued growth in influence on the part of what was regarded as a non-socialist element among the population, and to suffer a humiliating dependence on that element for one of the most vital requirements of the national economy, but also to forgo the possibility of a rapid industrialisation, and hence to remain in a position of military inferiority *vis-à-vis* surrounding capitalist powers.

The logical answer appeared to be the reorganisation of the agricultural process around collective associations of one sort or another in which the use of machinery would be possible and in which the government, having a higher degree of economic and administrative control, could have an assured source of cheap grain for the urban food supply, for military purposes, and for export.

There seems to be little doubt that this was the direction in which Stalin's thoughts, no less than those of the United Opposition, had been moving throughout the period of the NEP; and by 1927 conditions seemed ripe for more rapid progress in this direction. Until the end of 1919, however, the official calculations as to the pace at which it would be possible to effect such changes appear to have been relatively modest ones, envisaging the collectivisation of only a small percentage of the peasantry in the course of the next five years. (The First Five-Year Plan, approved in April 1929, and originally conceived to apply to the period up to autumn 1933, called for the collectivisation of only 18·6 per cent of the farming population.) How it came about that these calculations were suddenly revised, at the end of 1929, in favour of an intensive drive for the immediate collectivisation of the greater part of the peasantry, is still not entirely clear.

The activisation of policy towards the peasantry began in 1928, with

459

a large-scale action designed to extract, either by sheer confiscation or at very low prices and by use of force where necessary, the reserves of grain then in the hands of the more well-to-do proprietors. The resistance of the village to these measures was violent—more violent, apparently, than had been expected—and not entirely confined to the wealthier peasants. Plainly, the régime had seriously underestimated the solidarity of the village community in defence of the gains of the NEP. In the face of this situation, the campaign soon took on, in many places, the character of a conflict with the village as a whole.

Such developments were bound to cause tension between Stalin and the right wing of the Party. So long as he needed their support against the United Opposition, Stalin had co-existed relatively easily with Bukharin, Tomski, Rykov and the other Rightist leaders. The attack on the peasantry brought this co-existence to an end and unleashed a conflict scarcely less dramatic than the one recently conducted with the opposition groups on the Left. In some respects, this conflict was for Stalin the most difficult he had faced, for the Rightist position enjoyed some sympathy even among the ranks of his hand-picked personal supporters.

Here again, Stalin reacted by proceeding, skilfully and gradually, to destroy the political and personal positions of his leading opponents. But once more this took time. It was not until the autumn of 1929 that Bukharin, Rykov and Tomski had been driven from the senior Party bodies and forced to make public recantation of the views they had held against him.

Once the Rightist leaders had been thus disposed of, Stalin moved without delay to achieve not only the final and total 'liquidation of the *kulaks* as a class' but the immediate wholesale collectivisation, voluntary or otherwise, of the greater part of the remaining peasantry. The drive for these objectives was carried forward, with reckless brutality, during the winter of 1930. It involved the destruction, social or physical or both, of the whole of the more vigorous and competent portion of the peasantry, to the number of several millions of people; most of them were deported, under conditions that often fell little short of capital punishment, to forced labour in remote parts of the country. Peasant resistance was violent. The disruption brought to village life was enormous. Of particular gravity was the depletion of the livestock holdings. This was a consequence partly of deliberate slaughter by peasants reluctant to give up their animals to a common herd, partly of the losses from disease and neglect that occurred when small and previously well-tended herds were hastily thrown together into large aggregations. In this way the country lost within a year or two some 60 per cent of its farm-animal population—a catastrophe not just from the standpoint of food supply but also from the standpoint of the draught power and fertiliser available to the new collectives.

So frightening were the consequences of the sudden drive for general collectivisation that by March 1930, only three months after its inauguration, Stalin found himself obliged to call for a slackening of the pace. No sooner had this respite eased peasant resistance, however, than the pressure was resumed. By the end of the First Five-Year Plan period, 1932–3, some 60–65 per cent of the peasantry had been driven into the collectives. For the remainder it was only a question of time. It is unnecessary to emphasise that this development amounted to a new social revolution, comparable in profundity to that which had occurred between 1917 and 1921, and involving for the great rural population adjustments even more basic and drastic in their implications.

Hand in hand with this agrarian revolution-from-above there went a large-scale and extremely intensive programme of industrial construction and development, pursued with methods scarcely less violent. The initial phase of this programme, occupying the years 1928–32, came to be known to the world public as the First Five-Year Plan. Actually, this Five-Year Plan represented merely a listing of the various economic goals it was hoped to achieve over the period in question. Current direction and co-ordination of the process of industrialisation was effected, in so far as it was effected at all, by the day-to-day decisions of the ruling party organs, for which the original five-year estimates had no binding quality. It is evident that the First Five-Year Plan, as indeed the second and third ones that followed it, served in actuality as the external façade for an unpublished programme of military industrialisation, designed primarily to place the Soviet economy at the earliest possible time in a position of independence of foreign sources of supply in weaponry and military hardware of every sort.

In so far as the stated goals of the First Five-Year Plan are concerned, it can be said only that some were achieved, one or two were over-achieved, some were not achieved at all. The figure of 87 per cent, claimed by Stalin as the level of accomplishment of the planned objectives, is statistically meaningless (since it purports to strike an average out of values not mutually comparable) and gives a serious misimpression. A sampling of various indices would suggest that the overall level of fulfilment of the original objectives was closer to 50 than to 87 per cent. What was accomplished was the hasty construction of a great deal of new industrial plant, and, roughly speaking, a doubling of industrial production in quantitative terms. Qualitative standards, on the other hand, declined seriously over the period envisaged in the plan, as did labour efficiency. A great deal of the new plant was hastily planned, poorly geared to its economic environment, and shoddy in construction. No adequate indices of depreciation are available, but this must have been so rapid as to reduce greatly the value of what had been built, and to call for the replacement of much of it at an unduly early date.

What was achieved in the way of industrialisation between 1928 and 1933 was indeed formidable in scale. It constituted an important first step along the desired path towards military–industrial self-sufficiency. Involving as it did the selection of the Urals and western Siberia as centres for new construction in the metallurgical industry (notably the great new steel plants at Kuznetsk and Magnitogorsk), it laid the foundation for the major shift of heavy industry to the strategically protected interior regions that was to continue through later years and to be greatly intensified by the experiences of the second world war. But the costs of this great programme, in terms of waste, depreciation, inflated production costs, and depression of living standards, were enormous. It is difficult to believe that this was really the best, or indeed the only, way in which the general objectives of the First Five-Year Plan could have been achieved.

By 1932, as a consequence of what had been done in both agricultural and industrial fields, conditions in Russia were again appalling: worse than at any time since 1922. A large part of the peasantry was now, to be sure, formally collectivised. Yet overall grain production was still below the 1913 level and had shown no significant improvement. On the other hand, the percentage of the crop extracted annually from the peasantry, and made available for urban and military use, had increased. The livestock losses were of such an order that several years would have been required, even in the best of circumstances, to replenish the herds. The disruption of the agricultural process by the 'dekulakisation' and collectivisation campaigns had led, furthermore, by 1932 to a new famine in the main grain-growing regions, a famine of such seriousness as to take the lives of an estimated three to four million people and to raise the usual problems of depletion of seed grain. Rationing had had to be reintroduced in the cities and industrial communities. Meanwhile, nothing effective had been done to relieve the painful shortage of urban housing, now aggravated by the importation of new labour by the millions into the industrial communities; and the entire transportation system was overburdened to the point of breakdown. Hardship and suffering from depressed living standards were virtually universal.

Such conditions could not fail to find reflection on the political scene. Conducive as they were to the suspicion on the part of many senior people in the Party that the country was headed for a complete breakdown along the lines of 1917, they caused a number of the former oppositionists to endeavour to re-establish contact with one another and to try to re-create some semblance of political organisation, in order to be prepared for all eventualities. These efforts escaped neither the vigilance of the secret police nor the vengeful, secretive resentment of Stalin. More serious still was the fact that misgivings were now being aroused even among the ranks of those who up to this time had been Stalin's faithful supporters in the senior ranks of the Party. Such disaffection among the ranks of senior Stalinists, a factor which had already complicated the crushing of the Right Opposition in 1928 and 1929, was intensified by the hardships and reverses of 1932. There was a feeling that the cruelties of collectivisation had been excessive; that things had been driven too far and too fast; that too much brutality had been used; that even the working class was being alienated. There was a strong demand throughout the Party hierarchy for the introduction of a new note of humanity into the Party line: for the manifestation of a new concern for the feelings and the dignity of the individual citizen. This feeling found its moral epicentre in the writer Maxim Gorki; but it was to Sergei Kirov, Politburo member and Party chief in Leningrad, that people looked to give it expression on the political level. Although Kirov had made his career as a loyal follower of Stalin, he was widely believed to share, by this time, the general concern over the extremism of Stalin's recent policies.

It was in the midst of these stresses and strains, and probably not unconnected with them, that there occurred, in November of the unhappy year 1932, the sudden death of Stalin's wife, Nadezhda Alliluyeva. This event marked an important turning-point in the development of Stalin's personality. One notes just at this time in the historical record a marked increase in that exaggerated suspiciousness and ruthless vindictiveness, particularly with relation to persons in his own political entourage, to which Stalin had always been inclined, and which was now, in its pathological form, to plague the life of the Party and the country down to his dying day. It appears to have been at approximately this time that he began to demand the application of the death penalty against leading members of the various past opposition movements.

At this same time, Russia's international position, after some years of relative quiescence, became complicated by two new factors of great importance, both of which were destined to have a determining effect on Soviet foreign policy down to the second world war. The first of these was the advent of the National Socialists to power in Germany. Not only did this put an end to the pattern of German–Soviet relations that had endured since conclusion of the Rapallo Treaty ten years earlier, including the clandestine military arrangements, but it added to the difficulty of Stalin's personal position by rendering him vulnerable to the well-founded charge that, by his stubborn refusal to permit the German Communists to form a united front with the Social-Democrats in the preceding period, he had actually eased Hitler's path to power.

The second new factor was the conquest of Manchuria by the Japanese. This constituted a serious threat to Russia's military and strategic interests in the Far East. Being in no position at that moment to risk a military conflict, least of all on the Far Eastern borders, yet aware that any excessive conciliatoriness would merely whet the Japanese territorial appetite, the Soviet government compromised. It abandoned (through sale of the Chinese Eastern Railway in 1935 to Manchurian puppets of the Japanese) its claim, inherited from the tsars, to a special political position in the

Manchurian region. At the same time, it adopted an attitude of uncompromising firmness and vigilance in defence of the state frontiers of Siberia, and also of Outer Mongolia, which had long been a virtual Soviet protectorate. From this moment on, down to the final defeat of Japan in the Pacific War, the threat posed by the presence of strong Japanese forces along the sensitive borders of Siberia and Mongolia would be a constant source of apprehension to the Soviet leaders and one never absent from their thoughts and calculations as they addressed themselves to the problems confronting them from the European side.

These new factors were, as it happened, ones that affected United States interests scarcely less adversely than those of the Soviet Union. This, together with the accession of Franklin Roosevelt to the Presidency in 1933, established the preconditions for a breaking of the long diplomatic deadlock between the American and Soviet governments. Diplomatic relations, after an interruption of sixteen years, were resumed at the end of 1933. As in the case of Britain ten years earlier, the Soviet leaders, having won recognition without making significant concessions in the field of debts and claims, saw no reason to make such concessions once recognition had been obtained. The result, again, was that their hopes for major long-term credits were disappointed. Soviet–American relations, after much initial excitement, soon lapsed into a generally low and unhappy key. But the event took some of the sting out of Hitler's recent advance to power, and no doubt eased the change of Soviet policy which then ensued.

Faced with the threat of a general sweep of fascism over Europe, a threat highlighted by the evidences of great political tension in France in 1934, Moscow now reversed its position and began to encourage Communist elements in western Europe to unite their efforts with those of moderate-socialist and liberal groups in opposing the advance of fascism. Under Litvinov's able direction as Foreign Minister, far-reaching changes were introduced, during the period from 1933 to 1936, into Soviet relations with other Western countries. The Soviet Union entered the League of Nations, which its leaders had heretofore denounced as an agency of imperialism. Military alliances, ultimately ineffective but perhaps not momentarily without some small political effect, were concluded with France and with Czechoslovakia. These moves had, as their object, the checking or deflecting of an eventual German move towards the east.

Meanwhile, however, strange things were happening on the Soviet internal scene. With the completion of the First-Five-Year-Plan period, at the end of 1932, the pace of industrialisation and collectivisation was somewhat relaxed; economic life responded to this relaxation; and there was a corresponding—but still very relative—improvement in living conditions. Stalin, at the same time, as if to meet the demands for greater moderation and humanity of policy at least with relation to the non-Party masses, permitted the preparation, and the promulgation in 1936, of a new state constitution, ostensibly more liberal in spirit than the one it replaced. Far from reflecting, however, any greater liberality in practice, this document seems to have served primarily as a screen for something of a wholly contrary character: namely, a new determination on Stalin's part to exploit to the full the sinister resources of the police establishment with a view to stamping out not only every trace of past or existing resistance but even every remote possibility of resistance to his absolute personal rule, and to do this even if it had to involve the use of terror against the Party itself. Evidences of this tendency, increasing steadily in frequency and insistence in the period after 1932, naturally brought consternation to other senior Party figures and caused them to search for means of mutual defence. In this way Stalin's terror, originally conceived as a weapon against those who might have opposed him on other grounds, served to heighten the very contumacy it was designed to chastise and now became a weapon against those as well who had the temerity to challenge the desirability of the terror itself.

There is evidence that at the XVIIth Party Congress, in January 1934, Stalin met with some sort of opposition or rebuff at the hands of his senior colleagues in the Party. Kirov, in any case, appears to have been greeted by the members of the Congress with a deference, if not enthusiasm, which could not have failed to have aroused Stalin's ready jealousy and suspicion. Kirov, furthermore, was elected by the Congress to a key position on the Party's Secretariat: an appointment which presaged his early abandonment of the Leningrad post and removal to the central apparatus in Moscow. Before any such change could be implemented, however, and at a time, actually, when it seems to have been quite imminent, Kirov was murdered (in Leningrad, 1 December 1934). All that has become known, at the time and subsequently, of the background of this assassination points to a complicity somewhere in the higher echelons of the Leningrad police headquarters; and there have been suggestions that Stalin himself was not uninvolved in the affair. However that may be, Stalin exploited the development as an excuse for the launching of that extraordinary process of decimation of the existing official establishment of the country, not just in the Party but in the army, in intellectual life, and elsewhere, which went by the name of the 'purges' of the 'thirties. In so far as it had any specific focus, this action seems to have been aimed primarily against the old guard of the Party, particularly those whose experiences and memories reached back into the pre-1917 period, and those who had taken positions in opposition to Stalin during the 'twenties (in large measure, the two categories coincided). Yet the range of victims was by no means limited to Party members.

The purges had two evident purposes—closely related but distinguishable. One was the physical destruction of all those leading Communists who had opposed Stalin in earlier years. These were arrested and sub-jected to the full rigour of such pressures, psychic and physical, as a ruthless police system is capable of bringing to bear on an isolated and helpless prisoner. Those who could not be broken to the point where they were prepared to collaborate at their own humiliation by making public confessions to false charges were simply executed secretly, without public announcement. Those who could be induced to make such confessions appeared as defendants in the three great purge trials of 1936–8, after which they were, for the most part, executed on the strength of what they had confessed. The ordeal was thus a part of their punishment rather than an effort to establish their guilt.

The three trials followed closely the breakdown of the previous opposi-tion groups, the first being devoted to Zinoviev and Kamenev and persons close to them, the second, similarly, to the Trotskyites, the third to the Right Opposition. They provided the pretext for the execution, among others, of Kamenev, Zinoviev, Pyatakov, Bukharin, Rykov, Yagoda and Krestinski; but these represented only a small portion of the prominent Communists who fell victim to the purges.

Beyond these obvious individual targets, the purges appear to have been directed against entire categories of less prominent, but for the most part influential, persons—evidently persons thought capable either of sym-pathising with the leading victims or of being likely to form, tempera-mentally, a favourable soil for future opposition activity. In most of these cases, there was no question of any previous specific offence. The victims were skilfully manœuvred into assuming the main burden of their own destruction. An atmosphere was deliberately created in which the irrespon-sible denunciation of superiors or colleagues came to appear as the only likely means of purchasing immunity to one's own arrest and punishment, and that of one's family. As the process got under way, the offices of the secret police became literally inundated with such denunciations, and the prisons with their victims. The procedures by which such people were arrested and sentenced can scarcely even be called a mockery of justice, for in many instances no attempt was made to observe even the most elemen-tary judicial formalities. Each new arrest widened the circle of suspicion and denunciation and multiplied the number of victims. Before the process was halted (in late 1938, presumably in view of the growing danger of war), hundreds of thousands of people, numbers running in fact into the millions, had been either executed or driven off to prisons and labour camps under conditions in which the chances of any long and successful survival were poor. Even where death did not ensue, the effects on personality and physique were such as to deprive life, in many cases, of much of its meaning. Although not all of the inhabitants of the labour camps at that time were victims of the purges of the 'thirties, the fact that by the end of the 'thirties the total population of the camps obviously ran into millions gives some idea of the extent of the terror. And the effect on the Party itself may be gauged from Krushchev's revelation, at the XXIInd Party Congress, that the majority of the delegates to the XVIIth Party Congress of 1934, ostensibly the supreme body of the Party and of the land, were slaughtered off before another Congress could be convened, in 1939.

It is amazing that this huge wave of terror had no greater effect than it did on the life of the country at large. It was, of course, directed largely against members of the establishment; and there were usually ambitious underlings waiting to take their places. Simple people, particularly those who, like the peasants, had already suffered and survived their own encounters and conflicts with the régime, were relatively little affected; and foreign observers had the impression that many of them witnessed with no more than an embittered apathy this astounding process of self-destruction among their betters. Economic life, in any case, was not markedly set back, although here too there must have been some negative effect, if only from the disruption and high turnover of senior management. The Second and Third Five-Year Plans, less strenuously ambitious than the First, were relatively successfully promulgated. By 1939, living standards, except on the farms, had again advanced at least to the 1926-7 levels, and industrial production had increased several times over. Much of the increased industrial output went for military purposes, with the result that the Red Army was by 1939 extensively modernised in point of equipment and training. Its morale and efficiency had suffered, however, from the depredations of the purges; depredations that had affected not just the galaxy of marshals whose execution in 1937 so shocked the Russian and world public, but also a formidable number (probably about half) of the members of the senior officers' corps in general.

The years of 1936-8, which constituted the high point of the purges, were also marked with new trends in Soviet foreign policy. It is not to be excluded, in fact, that the two phenomena were importantly connected. By the middle of 1936 it had become abundantly clear to Soviet policy-makers that the Western powers, having acquiesced in Hitler's destruction of the Versailles Treaty and the German reoccupation of the Rhineland, would not be likely to oppose by force of arms any future expansion of German power to the east. Neither the moral support of the League of Nations nor the provisions of the Franco-Russian Pact could be expected to suffice for overcoming this lethargy.

This lesson was further driven home by the reactions of the various powers to the Spanish Civil War. The Soviet government at first adhered to the agreement arrived at among the powers for non-intervention in this conflict. When it became clear, however, as it did in the first weeks of the war, that the Germans and Italians were not prepared to respect this agreement, the Soviet government declined to be further bound by it and proceeded (October 1936) to give important military aid to the Republican cause. Air and tank units were dispatched. The initial defence of Madrid, in particular, seems to have owed its success largely to Soviet leadership and assistance. But, when it became clear that this example was not to be followed by the Western powers, that their role was to be a passive one and that they would not take serious steps to prevent a Nationalist victory, Moscow began to lose interest and to curtail its commitment. Signs of this loss of interest can be detected in the historical record as early as the first months of 1937; and it is not by accident that they were followed shortly by similar signs of an emerging interest on Moscow's part in arriving at some sort of a deal with Hitler—a deal which at best would turn the edge of the latter's ambitions westward and involve him in a war with the Western powers, and at worst would delay any German attack on the Soviet Union proper. Evidences of this purpose were clearly visible some time before the Munich agreement. They reflected not only growing doubt as to whether the Western powers could be induced to react with military means in the event of further German expansion to the east, but also a lively awareness of the delicate situation prevailing on the Man-churian–Mongolian frontier and a determination not to become involved, if this could possibly be avoided, in a two-front war with the Japanese and the Germans, from which the Western powers could remain aloof.

It is true that at the Munich Conference, and even later, in the abortive negotiations of the summer of 1939 with the British and French, the Soviet government maintained at all times a stance of readiness to oppose any further Nazi expansionism by force of arms, provided only the Western powers would do likewise. But the significance of this stance was weakened by the fact that Russia had no common border with Nazi Germany, whereas the Western powers in effect did. The pressures exerted by Moscow on the Western powers for joint military action against Hitler were in-variably, and not unnaturally, accompanied by demands for the right of passage of Soviet forces across the territories of Rumania, Poland and the Baltic states. But this was a prospect which the governments of those countries regarded as scarcely less dangerous to their independence and security than the expansionism of the Nazis. That Russia would gladly have made a token contribution to a war against Hitler at the time of Munich, had the British and French been willing to take up the gauntlet, is clear. That she would, or indeed could, have done much more than this, even in the event of the Rumanians and Poles permitting the passage of Soviet troops, is doubtful, if only for geographical and other military reasons. Had the Rumanians and Poles *not* permitted such passage—and they resisted it to the end—the Russian obligation could have been honoured with a regretful shrug of the shoulders. Moscow, in these circum-stances, risked little by her outward enthusiasm for collective security against Hitler.

This was the true background of the German–Soviet Non-Aggression

Pact of August 1939. Even in the summer of 1939, the Soviet leaders could perhaps have been prevailed upon (even this is not certain) to reject the German overtures and to join the Western powers in a common front against Hitler, if it could have been demonstrated to them that this would lead the Western powers to put up serious military resistance to any further German aggression; but, even then, this was something they would have consented to do only at a political price—namely, the establishment of a position of military ascendancy over the eastern European countries— which was unacceptable to the governments of those countries themselves and which the Western Allies were unwilling, at that moment, to pay. The Nazis, on the other hand, being less inhibited in disposing of the territory of others, were not adverse to offering to Moscow momentary gains (the occupation and incorporation into the Soviet Union of eastern Poland and the Baltic countries) which could presumably be easily nullified by a German attack if and when the resistance of the Western powers had been crushed. In these circumstances, Stalin opted for the German card, and agreed, in the secret protocol of the Non-Aggression Pact, to what was in effect a partition of eastern Europe with the Nazis. He presumably achieved, by this means, a delay in the necessity of facing Hitler's armies on the field of battle. He gained some space, to be traded for time, when the day of the German attack arrived. He succeeded in forestalling, at a particularly dangerous juncture, any further Japanese aggression against the eastern frontiers of Soviet power. But he forfeited, by the same token, whatever value the Polish, Rumanian and Baltic armies might have had, under proper encouragement, as supplementary impediments to the German military and political advance. He also brought, by the abruptness of the move, the greatest bewilderment to his admirers and followers in other countries throughout the world. Whether the net result was positive or negative is a question that will long be debated.

By August 1939, at the outbreak of the second world war, twenty-two years of Soviet power had brought momentous changes to the Russian and other peoples of the traditional Russian territory.

The population of the territory comprising the pre-1939 U.S.S.R. had risen from approximately 140 to 170 million. (It would presumably have risen by some ten to twenty million more had it not been for the civil conflict, the political persecutions, the man-made famines and the other hardships by which this period had been studded.) The rural population had shown no growth at all; that of the urban and industrial centres had more than doubled.

In agriculture—the pursuit that still claimed the energies of the greater part of the population—conditions of ownership and management had been thoroughly revolutionised. The traditional structure of the Russian village had been fundamentally altered. All but a negligible fraction of the peasantry was now employed either on state farms or on collective farms subject in reality to governmental control. Despite a 28 per cent increase in the population to be fed, output in major crops barely exceeded the 1913 level. The régime, on the other hand, was taking a higher proportion (34 per cent as opposed to 15 per cent) of the grain harvests for urban use. Livestock population, and with it the amount of draft power and fertiliser available to the agricultural sector, had still not fully recovered from the disaster of hasty collectivisation. It was evident that the régime, in introducing and retaining the system of collectivisation, had settled for a lower gross output of Russian agriculture in return for the privilege of having a larger control of what there was of it, of taking a larger proportion of it for urban and military use, and of taking that portion at a price determined by itself and not by the operation of a free market. The party could also have, for what comfort this was, the satisfaction of having 'socialised', at whatever cost, the agricultural process, and of having thus brought the great mass of the peasantry, for the first time, into an acceptable theoretical relationship to Marxist goals.

In industry a different situation obtained. There can be no disputing the impressive magnitude of the progress made, during the decade preceding the outbreak of the war, in providing Russia with the basic sinews of industrial strength. Statistics are neither adequate nor reliable for purposes of comparison; but selected key indices, such as those for iron and steel, suggest something like an average industrial growth rate of some 12–15 per cent, during the period since 1927, and a fourfold rise in productivity. This growth was, to be sure, not well balanced. Housing had been neglected, as had transportation. It is doubtful that living standards were, on balance, higher in 1939 than in 1913. The goal of military self-sufficiency, as the coming war was to show, had not been fully attained, though it was now no longer remote. Judged as an effort of military industrialisation, what had been accomplished in the 1930s was remarkable, and all the more so for the fact that it was carried through almost exclusively on the financial resources of the country itself, without resort to the long-term borrowing in foreign markets on which Russian industrialisation had been so extensively dependent in the pre-revolutionary period. The cost, on the other hand, had been great—in human mortality and in human discomfort. It is not too much to say that the well-being of an entire generation had been sacrificed to make possible this achievement. No statistical computation alone will ever strike the balance.

In cultural and spiritual fields, too, the life of the people had been profoundly affected. Education had made great strides (though no greater, it should be noted, than those that would have been made had the trends of the final years of tsardom been projected to this time). The role of the church in formal education had been wholly destroyed (not that it had ever been of major importance even prior to the Revolution) and the régime had done all in its power to destroy religious belief as well. But in the cities perhaps half of the people, and in the countryside even more, were still having recourse to the sacraments to dignify the great occasions of personal life; and a smaller but not insignificant number still went to church.

Twenty-two years of intensive ideological indoctrination had not been without effect on people's minds. The desirability of socialism, in the sense of governmental ownership and control of industry, was widely accepted. The collective farm system, on the other hand, remained odious to a large majority of those obliged to take part in it. By and large—as a result, not least, of the discouragement and disillusionment produced by the purges—the Marxist–Leninist ideology was losing its magic and its mystery. In the reactions, particularly, of the youth, it was passing from the status of a new and startling inspiration to that of a stultified state religion, increasingly inadequate as an answer to the problems—particularly the personal problems—of daily life.

In neither the intellectual nor the artistic fields had there been, over these twenty-two years, any lack of talented and earnest effort; but creativity, in every branch of art and science, had suffered precisely in the measure that it became the object of the attentions and ministrations of Party ideologists. The exact sciences, relatively resistant to ideological interpretation, carried on without serious difficulty; the social sciences, on the other hand, were grievously restrained and in some instances almost destroyed. Russian literature retained during the 1920s much of that extraordinary vitality that had sustained it over the preceding century; but the spirit and discipline of the purges were dreadfully unkind to literary creativity, and forced much of what was left of it to go underground. The theatre too maintained at all times its formidable technical strength and its great popularity as a form of artistic expression; but in the 1930s dramaturgy suffered along with the rest of literature, and the theatre shared this loss. The ballet, enjoying an almost total immunity from ideological harassment, carried on exuberantly as *the* great representational art of the Russian people; yet, even here, repertoire became increasingly stereotyped as the purges gradually throttled artistic initiative, and performances tended to take on the character of traditional ceremonies rather than that of a living art. Everywhere one could see, by 1939, the unfortunate effects of the extreme isolation from the major intellectual and aesthetic currents of the international community—an isolation which had varied in intensity, over the years, with the severity of the dictatorship, but had always exceeded the normal as well as the desirable, and had been carried finally, during the purges, to an extremity that had no parallel in the experience of modern European civilisation.

All in all, the Russian people found themselves, as the second world war

471

broke out, still in the midst of a process of profound social and economic change. In many ways, the progress made had been impressive. In particular the country had achieved, by dint of almost superhuman effort, and for the first time in its history, something close to military–economic self-sufficiency. But the achievement had involved an increasing, and finally almost total, regimentation of life. The cost had been measured not just in the comforts but also in the liberties of the people, and above all in their sense of identity and intimacy with the purposes of the régime. The loss in spontaneity, in individual initiative, in self-confidence, and in self-reliance, had been proportionate to the rigours of dictatorship. Fresh from the employment of terror on a sickening scale, the régime had no difficulty, now, in compelling the automatic obedience of those subject to its authority; but it would require, as the near future was to show, the challenge of external attack by an arrogant and contemptuous enemy to rouse this great and talented people once again to a spirit of real unity, and to fuse its spontaneous energies and enthusiasms with those of the régime in another great national undertaking.

CHAPTER XVI

GERMANY, ITALY AND EASTERN EUROPE

IN the Europe of the first fourteen years of the twentieth century, the political society of the greatest vitality was that of the German Empire. United within the curious federal framework provided by Bismarck, the Germans displayed different levels of political development, sharp social contrasts and conflicts, and yet a dominant centripetal tendency. The kingdom of Prussia extended from Aachen to Memel, from Flensburg to Kattowitz, right across the map of the new Germany: two-thirds, indeed, of the Germans were technically Prussians, and Prussia embraced the coalfields both of the Rhineland and of Silesia. The Prussian Landtag was elected according to the Three-Class system which gave far more representation, as well as strong administrative influence over the elections (which were indirect), to the rich. In the south-west public opinion was more justly mirrored in the Chambers of Baden, Württemberg and Bavaria, as it was in those of the northern city-states of Hamburg, Bremen and Lübeck: Bavaria, after Prussia the biggest member of the Federal Empire, had special rights of her own, and headed the Catholic minority interest against the Lutheranism of Berlin and the north.[1] The life of the ordinary German depended primarily upon the authority of the state in which he lived rather than on the imperial authority: he paid direct taxes for instance to the state of Prussia or Bavaria and only indirect taxes to the empire.

The Reichstag or Imperial Lower Chamber was elected by universal suffrage for men of 25 and over. It could legislate only in conjunction with the Bundesrat (which represented the member-states) and the emperor. It could criticise, but not control, policy. For Germany in 1900 was ruled by a royal autocrat who nominated the chief Imperial Minister or Chancellor: the Chancellor was responsible only to the emperor, not to the Reichstag or Bundesrat, of which ministers were not members. The senior civil service was provided by the landowning classes or their protégés; it too was responsible to the emperor. Successive Chancellors took some trouble to win the support of the deputies in the Reichstag, but they did not need to do so as the Reichstag had no effective way of blocking imperial expenditure, for instance on the army. When Bülow resigned in the summer of 1909 the reason, whatever was said, was that he had fallen out with the emperor, who chose the Secretary of State for the Interior, Bethmann-Hollweg, to succeed him for personal reasons. The criticism

[1] About 36 per cent of the whole population of the Hohenzollern empire was Roman Catholic.

473

of William's interview in *The Daily Telegraph* in the previous year gave the Reichstag an opportunity to assert itself which was not used.

The best thing to be said of the Germany of William II was that it was a *Rechtsstaat*: it guaranteed the rule of law. The press, though used by the government, was legally free, and the bureaucracy and judiciary incorruptible. A good illustration of these statements is the case of Maximilian Harden in 1907. Harden was a Jewish journalist of the kind German society despised; in his paper, *Die Zukunft*, he had attacked friends of the emperor's as exerting bad influence at court because they were homosexuals. When these people, Prince Eulenburg and Count Kuno von Moltke, the City Commandant of Berlin, brought a case for libel against Harden, in the first instance he won.

On the other hand the *Rechtsstaat* was all along menaced by the tortuous characters of Bismarck and Bülow but above all by William II. The kaiser had no serious regard for the constitution which gave him such tremendous powers, and he seemed readier to be impressed by the verdict of the duel than the verdict of the judge. He made the Germans familiar with noisy threats of violence and Byzantine attitudes; he habitually spoke as if political opponents deserved only to be persecuted. In his own intimate circle the Reichstag was often derided as 'the talking-shop' and from time to time a *coup d'état* to abolish the Reichstag was contemplated.

Part of the emperor's power depended upon the privileged position of the army, whose General Staff never really accepted civilian control of military policy any more than of military funds which were permanently guaranteed. The officers, both senior and junior, were linked through family connections with the big landowners and the higher bureaucracy. The fact that every German had to do military service made him directly aware of the power of the officer caste: it also brought the officers into a certain contact with Socialists as individuals they commanded.

The rapid and accelerating industrialisation of Germany since 1870 had brought increases and shifts of population and had transformed the country from a mainly peasant to a markedly industrial society. The percentage of the population living in towns rose from 47 in 1890 to 54·3 in 1900 and 60 in 1910. The new industrial employers had made every effort to identify themselves with the old ruling class, whose power seemed thus to have been rather fortified than not. In the universities, which were state institutions whose technical value was appreciated, the big majority of the professors at the beginning of this century were hotly nationalistic and, as such, supporters of the existing social order; the students were dominated by the various student *Corps*. Apart from their primitive habits of drinking and duelling over supposed insults, many of these bodies had tremendous snob value; they too were intensely nationalistic, mostly anti-Semitic, and they regarded Socialism as equivalent to high treason. Thus clashes between the student *Corps* and members of the rising Socialist trade

474

unions were liable to occur in the many university towns. The bureaucracy was largely staffed by the *alte Herren* or former members of the students' *Corps*; if one wanted a good position later on, it was essential to have the scars of a students' duel on one's face. In romantic revolt against the rigid organisation and the stiff conventions of the ruling classes a certain number of young people joined youth movements and became *Wandervögel*. This was in the spirit of *art nouveau*—called *Jugendstil* in German—and proved surprisingly sterile: 'Back to Nature' seemed to lead nowhere.

It is well known that Bismarck had tried to buy off the new industrial working class with a limited amount of social insurance, while seeking to crush those of its leaders who demanded more than this. In practice his methods emphasised the gulf between the classes and drove protesters towards Marxist socialism: German society seemed to them clearly to illustrate the dogma of the class war. In 1900 factory workers were still treated rather like military conscripts and the most powerful employers, such as the coal-king Emil Kirdorf, still tried to penalise trade union activity in the Rhineland.

Krupp's great iron concern at Essen was organised on patriarchal lines while the Saar coal mines, closely linked with the iron ore of Lorraine, were dominated by old *König* Stumm,[1] as the Baron was called, who died in 1901. The Saar miners were obliged to get his consent when they wished to marry, as if they were serfs. In the Silesian coalfields many of the workers were despised Poles who were just beginning to resent German rule. The election of Korfanty to the Reichstag in 1903 as their spokesman for the mining town of Kattowitz expressed this new feeling. Conditions of work in eastern Germany were undoubtedly worse than in the west and this caused a steady flow of population westwards to the Rhineland and a fair amount of emigration overseas. The population of the German Empire was 56·3 million in 1900, rising to nearly 67 millions in 1914. Though not so rich by most standards as Great Britain, Germany was expanding faster economically. Not unnaturally the German ruling classes displayed an arrogant self-confidence which delighted in assertions of the superiority of the German race. It is interesting to see how impressed so sensible and honest a person as Frau von Spitzemberg was by Houston Stewart Chamberlain's *Foundations of the Nineteenth Century* published in 1899: the critical attitude of the *Juden und Literaten* of Berlin made her feel more uneasy.[2]

Slowly and unsteadily nevertheless the ruling classes lost popularity in the years between 1900 and 1914; thus their power was undermined. Already in 1890 at the time of the fall of Bismarck the Socialists had gained more votes that any other party, though owing to outdated constituency

[1] Strictly speaking Freiherr von Stumm-Halberg, member of *Reichstag* and of Prussian *Herrenhaus*; he had considerable influence with William II.
[2] *Das Tagebuch der Baronin Spitzemberg* (1960), p. 403.

boundaries they only won 35 seats in the Reichstag: the Catholic Centre party gained most deputies at that time. Thenceforward the Socialists and the Centre were the two mass parties which, if they voted together against the government, could record the numerical, if not the political, strength of the opposition. Between the elections of 1890 and 1912 the Centre on average had a block of 100 deputies, while the Socialists in 1912 won 110 seats out of a total of 391 in the Reichstag, thus passing to the first place. During this period there were generally also about 40 Progressive deputies and about 30 representing the Danes, Alsatians and Poles who were hostile to the German government. The Progressives were, however, suspicious of the Socialists, although since Ebert had been appointed its secretary in 1906, indeed earlier, the Socialist party had shown itself predominantly revisionist. Thus criticism of the government, both in the Reichstag and, more cautiously, in the press, was possible and frequent and it grew in influence. Yet the system was pernicious because criticism was divorced from responsibility, the more so since no one would readily criticise who wished to keep in the favour of the authorities.

As in Hungary[1] education in Germany was offered only in the language of the state. This alienated some three million Poles in West Prussia (or, to the Poles, Poznania and Pomorze), as well as the Poles of Silesia. The Poles were treated contemptuously by the Germans as an inferior race. Further, German settlers, according to decisions made in 1886 and 1908, were sent to divide them from the Poles of Russia. Next door in Austria the Poles were treated as a favoured minority. Thus the German–Polish question by 1914 was explosive.

AUSTRIA-HUNGARY 1900–1914

To the south and south-east of Germany there lay the dominions of the Habsburgs ruled in 1900 by an old man of 70. Since 1867 the administration of Austria had been sharply divided from that of Hungary. Within Austria the authorities had haltingly admitted the non-German, mainly Slav, populations to certain rights, first and foremost that of being educated and tried in court in their own languages. In 1907 the Minister-President of the day, Freiherr von Beck, put an end to a system for electing the House of Representatives of the central *Reichsrat* by electoral bodies called *curiae* which gave German voters great advantages. He enfranchised virtually all men of 24 and over, and he grouped the constituencies so as to make them homogeneous nationally, not racially mixed. For some time the Germans of Austria had failed to recognise that they were a diminishing minority, but the new system made evident that Austria was predominantly Slav. The most flourishing Slav group was that of the Czechs in Bohemia and Moravia, with its own university in Prague—

[1] See below, p. 477.

it demanded a second one in Brno (Brünn) in Moravia. The Moravian Compromise of 1905 had arranged for the roughly proportional representation of Germans and Czechs in the Moravian Diet. The inability of the Czechs and Germans to come to similar terms with one another in Bohemia was, however, already in 1900 ominous, since for many reasons Bohemia was of great importance to the Monarchy. In all Austria (without Hungary) there were at this time about 9 million Germans; in Bohemia and Moravia together some 6 million Czechs and 3 million Germans; in Bohemia alone the Germans were rather more than a third of the population.

Austria also embraced the Poles of Galicia (some 4¼ million), the Ruthenes, Ukrainians and Russians of Eastern Galicia and the Bukovina (over 3¼ million), the Slovenes of Styria and Istria, the Croats of Dalmatia: in addition there were less than a million Italians in the Trentino, Trieste, Istria and a few in Dalmatia. The Chamber elected in 1907 was something of a federal parliament of nationalities; there were even two Russian-nationalist deputies, one Zionist and one Jewish democrat. Only the big Christian-Social and Social Democrat parties strove to rise above the racial battle while remaining predominantly German. It is noteworthy that for a long time Austrian members of parliament had been paid,[1] something unheard of in Germany or for that matter in Hungary.

Apart from the social and legal rights conceded to the different racial groups in theory if not always in practice, Austria was governed rather as Germany was: the Emperor Francis Joseph nominated his chief ministers, who were responsible to him alone. The *Reichsrat* in Vienna[2] was free to criticise as the *Reichstag* was in Berlin; the press was more or less free, though somewhat restricted by the powerful influence of the Roman Catholic church, which was closely linked with the dynasty. The administration was less efficient than that of Germany, but the force of racial circumstances made it more tolerant. The general atmosphere, beyond the world of the Court and the rather cosmopolitan aristocracy, was shabbier and more servile.

On the other side of the river Leitha, where Francis Joseph was king of Hungary, an entirely different system prevailed. Whatever people spoke at home, were it German, Slovak or Rumanian, except in Croatia-Slavonia they were compelled to be educated and tried in court as Magyars. A certain number of elementary schools organised confessionally were allowed to the non-Magyars, but they were in 1900 diminishing or losing their independence. Just as people in Vienna were often heard to say that German intransigence towards the Czechs in Bohemia would wreck the

[1] Bismarck had been particularly hostile to the payment of members long after it had been introduced in Austria.
[2] In 1907 the *Reichsrat* was given the power to legislate, but in fact the Imperial government legislated independently by special article as long as it survived.

Habsburg Monarchy, so they would deplore the policy of the Magyars for the same reason; to be forced to speak German at least had a practical advantage whereas to be forced to speak Magyar had none. The Archduke Francis Ferdinand, the heir to the throne, was known to resent the attitude of the Hungarians: partly a Neapolitan Bourbon by descent and largely so in outlook, it was what he regarded as Magyar insubordination towards the dynasty that he condemned as well as the Magyar contribution towards the disintegration of the Monarchy.

Like the Germans in Austria, the Magyars were a minority in Hungary, but owing to their policy of Magyarisation this minority was slowly increasing although the birth-rate of the non-Magyars was mostly higher. Since the franchise was exercised by a small, very largely Magyar electorate, and since the voting was public and police intimidation was used to deter voters from supporting non-Magyar candidates, the Chamber in Budapest was overwhelmingly Hungarian.

The chief non-Magyar subjects of the Crown of St Stephen were a number of Germans and Jews chiefly in the few towns and particularly in Budapest, and Slovaks, Ruthenes, Rumanians, Serbs and Croats. The latter two groups, sharing their language but not their religion, were legally guaranteed a fairly wide autonomy within the ancient Kingdom of Croatia. After a brief *rapprochement* between 1904 and 1906 relations between Budapest and Zagreb became strained: the Croats returned to their tradition of looking to Vienna for support and now beyond Vienna to Prague. The Slovaks, Ruthenes and Rumanians were mostly poor and often illiterate peasants, often too poor to care about their racial identity. The policy of the Magyar ruling class could not, however, prevent a certain encouragement from the Czechs for a few Slovak leaders, whose language was almost the same as Czech. Nor could it prevent generous sums of money for educational purposes being sent from the Rumanians of the Kingdom of Regat to the Rumanians of Transylvania.

Not only was Austria-Hungary increasingly anomalous in a Europe of nation-states: its very dualism emphasised the rift between the Slavs, who were divided between Austria and Hungary, and the German or Magyar ruling class which owned the big estates and often controlled industry. Thus the Slavs could nurse a grievance as the social underdogs, so that class and racial antagonisms tended to merge. The tide of socialism was rising. Thus the various Slav leaders, if and when they wished, could identify the emancipation of the Slav nations with a future reign of social justice. The dual system of Austria-Hungary was made even more explosive by the contrast between the relatively liberal administration of Austria and the conspicuous failure, between 1900 and 1914, to introduce anything of the kind into Hungary. It was almost ironical that, after Beck's reform of the franchise, less than 100,000 Rumanian voters in Austria were represented by 5 deputies in the *Reichsrat*. In the Hungarian

Chamber nearly 3 million Rumanians in Transylvania and the Banat were represented by 16 deputies—of whom one was Julius Maniu. (It is true that there were 516 deputies in the Viennese Chamber and only 453 in that of Budapest.) In Vienna the Rumanian deputies, in theory at least, could address the Chamber in Rumanian; in Budapest this was forbidden.

Of course things were not so simple as the racialist propagandists made them seem. Within Austria the Polish and Czech Slavs were on bad terms partly for social reasons. Many southern Slavs of the Monarchy before 1908 were sceptical about their brotherhood with the Serbs of Serbia. Many peasants throughout Austria-Hungary, together with the shop-keeper class as well as the nobility, regarded the rule of Francis Joseph as an inevitable and acceptable tradition; they were encouraged by their priests to do so and to spurn suggestions to the contrary from the 'traitor' Socialists of the towns. In Hungary, naturally, the Socialist party was small and weak, whereas in Austria in 1911 81 Social Democrats were elected and they dominated Vienna. It is interesting that many of the leaders of the Austrian Socialists, including Viktor Adler himself, had strongly nationalistic political roots. This was never true of German Socialist leaders before 1933.

Economically Austria lagged behind Germany. Industry was highly developed in Vienna, and in Bohemia, Moravia and Austrian Silesia which reached into the region of the great Silesian coalfields: the iron mines in Styria were important. But the proportion of the Austrian population which still lived on the land between 1900 and 1914 was noticeably higher than in Germany. Many of the peasants, German or not, had their own little farms, but the Austrian aristocracy—families such as the Schwarzenbergs—owned huge estates, particularly in Bohemia and Moravia. Hungary was far more backward in every way. Budapest was the only large town and industrial centre. The Hungarian magnates—the biggest landowners were the Esterházys—and the squires owned the land, many of the peasants living miserably as landless labourers, like serfs but detached from the land. The Hungarians were frequently in revolt against their union with Austria. Sometimes they complained of the use of German words of command in the Imperial and Royal Army.[1] But their favourite quarrel was with the customs union which in fact dated back to 1850; they complained that it prevented the development of Hungarian industry. Thanks to Jewish capital and drive, however, industry did develop in the years before 1914 so that the percentage of urban population rose to about 25. From 1900 to 1914 the population of Austria and Hungary together rose from some 45 to some 50 millions; looking back, the Dual Monarchy has been lauded precisely for supplying a customs-free zone in the Danube valley for this considerable population.

No sooner had the first elections after Beck's reform in Austria been

[1] *Kaiserliche und Königliche*, popularly abbreviated to *k-und-k*.

held than the Young Turk revolution in July 1908 reverberated through eastern Europe. Bosnia with Herzegovina had been administered by Habsburg officials since 1878: now in October 1908 the Austro-Hungarian Foreign Office and General Staff decided to annex Bosnia outright. It was a poor enough area but the majority of its inhabitants were Serbs or Croats, and the annexation was regarded by the Slavs as a German-Magyar affront to Serbia and the southern Slavs. It was really after this that Prague became south Slav headquarters with much talk of some kind of south Slav state in the future: thus the Germans of Bohemia had a new grievance against the Czechs. The loyalty of Slav political leaders to the Habsburg dynasty was shaken: Russophil tendencies among the Czechs were strengthened. Even the diplomatists of Imperial Germany had spoken for years of Austria-Hungary's inevitable disintegration and some Austrian Germans wished to be annexed by Germany. The annexation of Bosnia, followed by Russia's apparent acquiescence, made the more aggressive Germans believe that Austria might expand instead of breaking up. This was the choice. The idea of expansion merged into the idea of a German-dominated *Mitteleuropa* which was advocated by so enlightened a man as the German pastor and publicist Friedrich Naumann, as the best economic background for social progress.

THE BALKAN PENINSULA

The nationalistic ideals of the nineteenth century were still unsatisfied at the beginning of the twentieth, not only in Austria-Hungary and in German and Russian Poland but also throughout the Balkan peninsula; indeed they could only be satisfied there at the expense both of the Dual Monarchy and the Turkish Empire. The latter, ruled by the notorious Abdul Hamid, although in retreat for many years, still dominated the Balkans as it did North Africa; in theory the Turks still ruled Bosnia and Bulgaria. The Greeks were desperately dissatisfied on account of turbulent Crete and because Macedonia was still under Turkey. Macedonia was the Gordian knot of the peninsula; it was inhabited by a confusion of races each claiming the mastery. In the south there were Greeks, in the west Serbs and Albanians, in the north some Rumanians, and there were Turks scattered here and there. The biggest single group of Macedonians was considered by Bulgarians to be Bulgarian, and, ever since the abortive Treaty of San Stefano in 1878, Bulgaria had considered Macedonia to belong to her by right. The most famous Macedonian nationalist body, the terroristic 'Internal Macedonian Revolutionary Organisation' (I.M.R.O.), had been founded in 1893 to fight the Turks. In 1903 at Mürzsteg Austria-Hungary and Russia agreed to a programme for the administrative reform of Macedonia, and the other great powers supported them with the Turks.

The Balkan peninsula owed to the Turkish régime its squalid backwardness and lack of communications. Apart from the oil in Rumania it contained important metals, but any economic advance in the early years of the century was due to Austrian or German investors and technicians; the Germans were active in the Rumanian oilfields—indeed this was part of the German *Drang nach Osten*. In so far as the Serbs, Bulgars and Greeks had survived the Turkish conquest they had emerged as free peasants; only Rumania had an aristocracy of big landowners, against whom in 1907 their peasants revolted but were suppressed.

Through their kinship with the Serbs, Croats and—more remotely—Slovenes of Austria-Hungary, the Serbs of Serbia had become the chief south Slav centre of attraction. In 1903, after the gruesome murder of the former king and queen, the Karageorgević dynasty was restored in Belgrade in order to show greater national independence.

In July 1908, however, it was not the Balkan Slavs but the Turks themselves who carried through a revolution. A group of officers calling themselves Young Turks was able to force the sultan to acknowledge his forgotten constitutional obligations. At the same time the Young Turks became infected with the nationalism of the Slavs in the place of their former indifference; the Turks were no longer prepared to watch the corrosion of their power by hostile nationalism, but began to think in terms of an aggressive Turkish nation. In the circumstances the czar of Bulgaria quickly declared his independence and Crete declared its union with Greece in October:[1] it has been seen that the Austro-Hungarian authorities at the same time decided openly to annex Bosnia and Herzegovina, while the powers abandoned Macedonia to the Turks. The Russian government, which, however much it disliked Balkan revolutionaries, could ill afford to lose prestige among the Pan-Slav intellectuals, was obliged to accept the Habsburg annexation of Bosnia. But the word went round among all Slav sympathisers that it was a matter of *reculer pour mieux sauter*. At all events the emotional clash between those who felt hotly pro-German or pro-Magyar or pro-Turk, and the others who felt hotly pro-Slav, was violent; its effects merged into the two Balkan Wars and the first world war shortly afterwards.

The anomalies, the Balkan states which did not fit neatly into the German–Slav conflict, were Rumania and Greece, both proud not to be Slav. Although Rumanian feeling against Magyar oppression of the Rumanians in Transylvania was intense, there was also strong feeling against the Slavs of Russia and against the Bulgars over disputed frontier questions. This made possible Rumania's ties with the Triple Alliance favoured by her Hohenzollern dynasty. Not only did the Greeks clash with both Serbs and Bulgars in Macedonia but the Serbs and Bulgars, so closely related in every way, constantly quarrelled between themselves.

[1] This was only recognised by treaty in 1913.

The Albanians added the piquancy of being distinct from all the rest in race and language; they were a smaller racial group than any of the others, numbering only about a million.

After the Italian defeat of the Turks in Libya in 1911, Serbia with Montenegro, Bulgaria and Greece attacked Turkey; it was in fact Montenegro, a detached Serbian outpost, which first declared war in October 1912. The Turks were all but driven out of Europe. A quarrel between the victors caused Serbs and Greeks, now supported by the Rumanians, to attack the Bulgars in 1913. In this second Balkan War the Turks were able to creep back to the line of the Maritza river, but that was all. Crete was permanently attached to Greece. Thus the Balkan countries had freed the peninsula but no one was satisfied. The Bulgars refused to accept Serbia's conquest of most of Macedonia; on the other hand Austria-Hungary had insisted upon the creation of an Albanian national state in 1913 in order to prevent Serbia from reaching the western Balkan coast. A German–Slav explosion had not been fended off: it had been brought nearer, for an extended Serbia more than ever resented a Habsburg Bosnia reinforced by a Habsburg-protected Albania.

ITALY 1900–1914

After disastrous defeat in Abyssinia in 1896 and a dangerous collision between the government and the governed, especially in Milan, in 1898, with the turn of the century Italy entered into a period of conciliation and prosperity. When in 1900 King Umberto was murdered by an anarchist in revenge for the civilian casualties of 1898, his successor, Victor Emmanuel III, seemed able to turn over a new leaf. In February 1901 the enlightened radical, Zanardelli, was appointed Prime Minister: his right hand was Giovanni Giolitti as Minister of the Interior. These two men were the first Italians in authority to show understanding for Italy's new social problems. The king of Italy had a less thorough control of government than the emperors of Germany and Austria, and men like Zanardelli and Giolitti played up the powers of parliament—they were deputies and depended upon a parliamentary majority.

In the preceding decade, in spite of the lack of coal and iron, the industrialisation of northern Italy on a modern scale had begun. Milan had become a great industrial centre as well as Italy's financial and commercial capital. In 1899 the FIAT car factory was founded at Turin, whose life was transformed by this. The port of Genoa had been developed by the Ansaldo concern. Population increased quickly in evil conditions. Industrial profit was monopolised by the rich, who were absurdly favoured by the fiscal system. Although the franchise had been slightly extended since the foundation of the kingdom, only the better-off classes elected the deputies to the Chamber. The new industrial working class—still in 1900

smaller even in the north than that of those who worked on the land[1]—
had no political or social rights. It was, however, championed by a group
of intellectuals who had founded a Marxist Socialist Party (*Partito
Socialista Italiano*) in 1892, before the social question had had time to
ripen.

Zanardelli and Giolitti were no Socialists but they felt the injustices of
the Italian social system and they deplored the rigid conservatism of the
possessing classes. Giolitti, who succeeded Zanardelli as Prime Minister
in 1903 and ruled Italy with few interruptions until she entered the war,
was above all a benevolent opportunist. He thought it expedient to
integrate the new working class into the constitutional state by improving
social conditions and extending the franchise. The dominant Socialist
leaders of the early years of the century in Italy, men like Filippo Turati,
Ivanoe Bonomi and Leonida Bissolati, favoured moderate social reforms
which should put the working class in a better position to make further
gains. Hence to a considerable extent they were willing to play Giolitti's
game. Pragmatically the Italian state thus became not only constitutional
but also liberal: in spite of an elected mayor and corporation in each city
it was, however, over-centralised through the rule of the prefects appointed
by the Minister of the Interior.

A major problem in Italy in 1900 was the relation between the state and
the Roman Catholic church, since the overwhelming majority of Italy's
citizens were Catholics. The Vatican had been treated not ungenerously
by the new Italy; the popes, however, refused to recognise the kingdom,
which indeed they damned. In theory confessing Catholics were forbidden
to participate in the life of the lay state, though it was obvious that those
who were qualified to vote mostly did so. In the early years of the century,
many Catholics indeed criticised the policy of the Vatican. Those who
reacted to social change thought that the church should compete with the
Socialists for working-class support, saving the workers from the evils of
Socialist atheism. A particular group called Modernist considered that
Catholic dogma should not be static but adapt itself to social development.
Soon after his election in 1903 Pope Pius X condemned the Modernists;
he had, however, decided radically to modify the papal veto on voting in
elections. Henceforward the bishops in each diocese were to decide whether
or not their flocks should vote, and the decisions were more and more in
favour of doing so.

In 1911 Giolitti brought about an electoral reform which increased the
electorate from 3 to 8 million. In the general election which followed in
1913 the Catholic vote was obviously of the greatest importance. Giolitti,
by nature an anti-clerical, therefore came to terms with the head of the
Catholic Electoral Union, Gentiloni: in accordance with a pact named
after the latter, many of Giolitti's followers courted the Catholic vote by

---

[1] Actually about 35 per cent of the whole population.

promising to oppose divorce and support Catholic schools. Although there was as yet no prospect of a reconciliation between Vatican and Quirinal, Giolitti hoped to 'integrate' the Catholics too into the constitutional state.

The Age of Giolitti, as this pre-war period was called in Italy, saw the development of violent opposition to Giolitti's common-sense compromises, the more so since in southern Italy his bargains led to scandalous corruption. The extreme poverty of the south, which moved backwards rather than forwards while the north was becoming prosperous, was emphasised by the appalling earthquake at Messina in 1908. The historian, Salvemini, began to lead a campaign against Giolitti as a corrupter: he also began to preach help for the south from which he came.[1] From the Socialist side, the extremists led by Lazzari and Mussolini defeated the moderate leadership at the party congress at Reggio Emilia in 1912: very shortly afterwards Mussolini became editor of *Avanti*, the chief Socialist newspaper, and used it to attack Giolitti's opportunism. At the other end of things there arose a new Nationalist party which expressed the widespread feeling of boredom with Giolitti, and which demanded an aggressive foreign policy: the war against Turkey, which brought both Libya and the Dodecanese Islands to Italy, was to be only a beginning. The new nationalism was linked, through the poet D'Annunzio and the futurist Marinetti, with the literary and artistic movements of the day. It was in 1909 that Marinetti launched his first Futurist Manifesto in a Parisian newspaper; his *avant-garde* was surprisingly influential in Italy for the time being, certainly so long as it remained chauvinistic and bellicose.

When war broke out in Europe in the summer of 1914 Italy, though aligned for years with the central powers, had long come to terms in secret with France: this had made the Libyan war possible. In 1914 Giolitti and the moderate Socialists, keeping strange company with the General Staff and the Vatican, were against participation; the last two centres of influence were really pro-German. The Nationalists, in equally strange company with pro-French Radicals like Salvemini, wished to come in on the Allies' side. In the autumn of 1914 Mussolini launched an interventionist Socialist newspaper. In May 1915, after the territorial bribes offered by the Allies in the secret Treaty of London,[2] Italy declared war against Austria-Hungary.

---

[1] His wife and children were all killed in the earthquake of Messina.

[2] This treaty was signed on 26 April 1915; the Entente powers promised Italy the Trentino, Trieste with Istria, Dalmatia excluding Fiume, Spalato (Split) and Ragusa (Dubrovnik) but including the Adriatic islands and virtual possession of Albania.

THE AFTERMATH OF THE FIRST WORLD WAR

The most vocal opinion in Austria-Hungary, and more particularly in Germany, believed in the early years of the war that German domination over the Danube valley, all Poland (with some regional autonomy perhaps), the Baltic provinces and probably the fertile Ukraine would complete the creation of a Great-German world power. The Russian revolutions in 1917 and the Treaty of Brest-Litovsk in March 1918 only confirmed these beliefs although the price paid for the war by the civilian populations in food shortages was already exorbitant and the disintegration of Austria-Hungary was proceeding. From 1916 onwards the kaiser had practically abdicated in favour of the military leaders, Hindenburg and Ludendorff, who represented the chauvinism of the old ruling class. The parties in the Reichstag, however, who were opposed to this, gathered hidden strength. Centre, Socialists and Progressives pressed for franchise reform in Prussia if public morale were to hold, and at the same time worked for peace without annexations; in July 1917 a deputy of the Centre party called Erzberger brought forward a Peace Resolution in these terms which was passed. The Russian military collapse encouraged the arrogance of the German ruling class, while the Russian revolutions added to the anxieties of the Austrian government since they profoundly disturbed all the Slav populations. They followed, moreover, quickly upon the death of the old emperor in November 1916, who had left the young and inexperienced Charles to struggle with his heritage, with no august side-whiskers to help him.

In Italy, the defeat at Caporetto in October 1917 shocked the people into more serious efforts and national morale recovered. With Austria-Hungary's disintegration Italy stepped into a victor's role: the old Irredentist goals of Trieste and the Trentino were achieved, the south Tyrol up to the Brenner Pass being added to the Trentino, and Istria, Zara and several Adriatic islands to Trieste, though not, at first, Fiume. Thus Italy acquired a German-speaking 'minority' of about a quarter of a million and a Slovene and Croat one of about half a million. The social problems with which she was now overwhelmed were not diminished by these alien populations.

Most Italian peasants, particularly those from the south, had never until the war guessed at the living standards of their own northern compatriots; like the Russian and Magyar peasants they came home with new ideas. The Socialist leaders were excited, too, above all by the Russian revolutions. Opposed to them were the Nationalists and D'Annunzio's followers, who were full of indignation that Italy was not to gain still more territory. At the first post-war elections in November 1919, however, unlike the 'Khaki' elections in France and Britain, the Socialists and the Catholic *Popolari* polled best. In spite of acute economic difficulties the country seemed to settle down under a new Giolitti government in 1920: this government expelled D'Annunzio from Fiume, which he had seized in September 1919. During 1921, nevertheless, the position of the Socialists became much weaker. Their left wing split off to form the new Italian Communist party, while the constant strikes in industry irritated non-Socialist opinion and blew wind into the sails of the Nationalists and others on the right. Mussolini, the left-wing interventionist of 1915, had founded in March 1919 something which he called the Fascist Movement. Gradually Mussolini saw that an alliance with the Nationalists would give him greater power, and he increasingly accepted support from predatory bands of ex-servicemen who were hotly anti-Marxist and glad to take money from some of the industrialists in return for intimidating or beating up Socialists. During 1922 the situation in Italy deteriorated rapidly and the king and his advisers were at such a loss that they invited Mussolini, whose black-shirted supporters were threatening Rome, to become Prime Minister in October. Mussolini formed a coalition government in which all the major parties, including the Socialists, were represented. It was not until January 1925 that he followed Lenin's example and established a one-party state with only Fascist ministers. There seems no reason to suppose that in October 1922 he had any idea that this would be the consequence: nevertheless October 1922 became a landmark, particularly for all the enemies of liberal government. In 1924 it was still possible for Matteotti to indict Mussolini's terrorist election techniques: indeed Matteotti came within an ace of success, for his murder in June nearly overthrew Mussolini. Having failed to do so, its consequences impelled Mussolini to set up his whole-hog Fascist régime.

Fascism in Italy put an end to all freedoms. It infused a chauvinistic and pseudo-warlike tone into education and the arts. It increased the over-centralisation of Italian administration. Its economic results were not remarkable; it emphasised the protective character of Italian economic policy but failed to make Italy self-supporting, for instance in wheat. It was not anti-Semitic until later, it came to terms with the Catholic church in the Lateran Agreements of 1929, it preserved the Monarchy and the Senate set up by the *Statuto* of 1848. It even allowed Benedetto Croce to continue to publish his review *La Critica* with little interference.

After the German offensive in the spring of 1918 had failed and American participation on the other side was making itself felt, late in the summer the German military leaders ordered the civilians to make peace. Men like Erzberger and the Socialists, Ebert and Scheidemann, were left with the job of placating the Allies and their own outraged public opinion. Ludendorff disappeared in disguise to Sweden while the emperor took refuge in Holland and the other German dynasties dispersed. Despised trade-unionists and Catholics were left in charge while the defeated armies returned to their starving homes, and revolutionary talk ebbed and

486

flowed. Marx had destined advanced industrial Germany to be the cradle of Communist revolution. After the German military had helped him back to Russia Lenin always thought in terms of a Communist Germany as imminent. Yet, although German society was profoundly shaken, although all the old beliefs seemed to have collapsed, no fundamental social change took place. There was no expropriation of the landowners or industrialists, only an attempt to realise, in so far as defeat allowed, the political dreams of 1848: the result was the Weimar constitution. Like most new constitutions of the day it provided for male and female universal suffrage from the age of 20—in Prussia too—and for proportional representation, thus making new demands upon an inexperienced electorate. The President was to be elected by the people, but governments were to be made and unmade by the Reichstag, which was elected by the same people. For the first time there was to be a Minister of the Interior for the Reich—that ambiguous word remained—although the Prussian Minister of the Interior who controlled the Prussian police was more powerful.

The Treaty of Versailles, or at any rate its economic aspect, was harsh. The German nationalists, the old ruling classes and their supporters among the shopkeepers and peasants, used the so-called *Versailler Diktat* to discredit the liberalism of the Weimar Republic; they succeeded in accusing the civilians, who had borne the brunt of the defeat when Hindenburg and Ludendorff shirked responsibility, of 'stabbing the German Army in the back'. This monstrous lie preserved the gulf that stretched between the arrogance of Germany's former rulers with their supporters and the timid integrity of those who wished for political and social justice in twentieth-century terms. A certain levelling up did take place in German society between 1922 and 1924 thanks to the collapse of the currency and the disappearance of the nation's money savings. The inflation was partly due to Germany's inevitable plight after the years of war and partly to the Allies' reparation demands, but it was fostered by some of the more powerful industrialists: their property, like landed property, was all the more valuable (see above, p. 232).

The fiercest anti-Slav (and anti-Semitic) racialism had long been voiced by the Germans of the mixed Austrian crownlands like Bohemia and Styria. During the war these Germans had hailed the alliance with Berlin as the prelude to the real union of all Germans in the German-speaking lands and also in territory further east where the Germans formed at most an important urban element. When the central powers collapsed and the Allies forbade the union of Austria with Germany (precisely on account of all the *Mitteleuropa* talk), it was the Germans of Bohemia, of south Tyrol, of Novi Sad, of Transylvania, who felt most outraged. Instead of being regarded as the advanced element in the Habsburg empire they found themselves degraded to being 'minorities' in Italy or Rumania or the new Slav states of the Czechs and Slovaks or the Serbs and Croats. The German 'barons' of Russia's former Baltic provinces, the German landowners of Germany's former Polish territories, felt themselves to be humiliated in the same way. Many of them took refuge in the Weimar Republic, but they swelled the ranks of its disloyal citizens. They disliked its tolerance, racial and otherwise; above all they disliked its capital city. For Berlin quickly became headquarters of the new modern arts. Since the beginning of the century Berlin had had its sophisticated side, particularly its clever, sceptical Jewish journalists. Now this element became more conspicuous and exerted more influence.

The Russian revolution had caused the Spartakists, as a left-wing group called themselves, to break away as Communists from the traditional Social Democratic party of Germany. In January 1919 the Communist leaders, Liebknecht and Rosa Luxemburg, were murdered by Rightists in an affray in Berlin. These two turned out to be irreplaceable; insurgent attempts made by the German Communists in 1921 and then (in Hamburg and Saxony) in October 1923 were suppressed, the latter with the help of the Reichswehr. After an early and short-lived Communist régime in Bavaria (spring 1919), followed by a Bavarian threat to separate from Berlin and then an abortive revolt engineered by a group of fanatical nationalists led by an Austrian Jew-hater called Hitler supported by Ludendorff in November 1923, the Allies came to terms with the rulers of Germany over reparations. In the summer of 1924, after a new German currency had been introduced, the Dawes Plan was launched and five years of European recovery were initiated, five years to be associated with the name of Gustav Stresemann. Stresemann had been appointed Chancellor by Ebert in August 1923; in November his government was defeated, thanks to a hostile Socialist vote, but he remained as Foreign Minister until his death in October 1929.

Industrial development was now resumed in Germany with great success, particularly in light industry, and much building was undertaken: the necessary capital was largely provided by short-term loans from America. In the spring of 1925 Field-Marshal von Hindenburg was elected President of the German Republic in succession to Ebert, who had died. Stresemann, with his back covered by the Rapallo Treaty of 1922 with Russia, was already approaching Paris in the hopes of a détente and was disconcerted by this demonstration in favour of the old ruling class which was suspect abroad. With Briand's collaboration he was nevertheless able to arrive at the signature of the Treaties of Locarno in October (see above, ch. viii). These led on to the election of Germany to a permanent seat on the Council of the League of Nations in September 1926: there was no more reason for the Germans to feel outcast. Although a remarkable level of prosperity was reached there was a disagreeable tension between advanced Berlin, the centre of Prussian administration which was controlled for most of this period by a Social Democrat Prime Minister, Otto Braun, and the provincial world whether of landowners, shopkeepers or peasants who feared Berlin as revolutionary.

The position of the Viennese was not unlike that of the Berliners in these years. Only Vienna was harder hit by post-war circumstances for it was a huge city at one end of the fragment of the Habsburg Monarchy— *the Alpenländer*—which had become the first Austrian Republic. Although Vienna remained the great banking centre for central Europe and the Balkans, Austria was hit by the tariff barriers which sprang up around her. For now it was not only the Magyars but also the Czechs and Poles who wished to protect their own industries. The Austrian Republic was a federal one and Socialist Vienna was one of its nine *Länder*. Industry was concentrated in Vienna and so was poverty; the Socialist mayor and corporation, as soon as they could, built great blocks of workers' flats and naturally obliged the other householders of Vienna to help pay for them. This contributed to the anti-Socialist indignation of the clerical Christian Social party which was strong among shopkeepers and peasants throughout the eight other *Länder*. In the Austrian towns and at the Austrian universities there was above all German national, even racial, indignation over the fact that the Allies had vetoed the union of German Austria with Germany, and over the degradation, as it was felt to be, of other Germans in central and eastern Europe to be mere minorities in the successor states.

There were now three million Germans, who had indeed offered resistance to it, in the new Czechoslovak Republic based upon Prague, a city whose role, it has been seen, had been growing in the years before 1914. Czechoslovakia was in large part the child of an elderly Slovak professor of philosophy at Prague University called Thomas Masaryk, a man of splendid integrity and enlightenment. Six million Czechs supported it warmly, two million Slovaks formerly ruled by the Hungarians were glad now to be free to use their own language, and half a million Ruthenes and others in neglected Ruthenia were not sorry to escape from Magyar rule. Bitter rivalry between the Czechs and Germans of Bohemia was an old story and competition between them had probably stimulated economic development to its relatively high level. The Czechoslovak government subscribed to the Minorities Treaty drawn up by the League of Nations, and the Bohemian and Moravian Germans had their own schools and university. But the Czechs were the top dogs now, and small Czech officials in particular were certain to remind the Germans of this constantly.

Czechoslovakia adopted an advanced democratic constitution and initiated legislation for the redistribution of the land: most of her Germans felt that this constitution was worse than Beck's franchise reform of 1907, and the land reform seemed to them to be aimed only against the huge German-owned estates. The prosperity of the second half of the 'twenties, however, soothed the various susceptibilities.

After the war the Yugoslav Triune Kingdom of the Serbs, Croats and Slovenes was set up under the Serb Karageorgević dynasty. After the Austrian and Magyar landlords had left, like Bulgaria it had no aristocracy; it was a poor undeveloped peasant country, including Bosnia, most of the old Hungarian Banat and Macedonia as won by Serbia in the Balkan wars. Bulgaria, after all, had been on the losing side again between 1914 and 1918. Yugoslavia was particularly jealous of Italy, the more so after Mussolini was able finally to annex Fiume in January 1924.

Thus the Slovaks and the south Slavs had been liberated from the Magyars. More difficult and more important, Transylvania with its Rumanian majority had been handed over to Rumania: Maniu became leader of the Rumanian National Peasant party and was instrumental in putting through land reform here as well. It has been seen that Hungary before 1914 was highly explosive. Now all the non-Magyars except half a million Germans had been lost; in addition $1\frac{1}{2}$ million Magyars had been lost to Rumania and nearly $\frac{3}{4}$ million to Czechoslovakia and Yugoslavia respectively. After a brief Communist episode in 1919, when a Soviet republic was set up under Bela Kun, the magnates and squires of Hungary recaptured power. They did little to improve their society however: a tremendous campaign in favour of undoing the peace treaties of 1919 and 1920 deflected public attention from their 3 million landless peasants, probably the worst off in all Europe.

In some ways the most interesting of the post-war states was the new Poland: it began perhaps with the most severe handicaps. It had been a major battlefield; it started from zero with no natural frontiers and no port; it contained no highly developed industry except in the part of Upper Silesia which it obtained as a result of the plebiscite of March 1921. After the Russian troops were driven from Warsaw in August 1920, Soviet Russia was induced in March 1921 to accept a frontier which gave all her 'western lands' to Poland: thus about six million White Russians and Ukrainians who belonged to the Greek Orthodox or the Uniate church became the subjects of the Catholic Poles. Far more was to be heard of Poland's frontiers with Germany, although they could be much more easily justified. A good many Germans lived in the towns in Pomorze—which the Germans chose to call 'the Corridor'—and in Poznania or Posen. But there were only about 700,000 Germans in a Poland of over 30 millions, relatively a much smaller minority than the Germans in Hungary or Yugoslavia, not to speak of Czechoslovakia. The problem of a port for Poland was solved by making the German city of Danzig into an independent Free City within the Polish customs area and represented abroad by Poland. The Germans would hear nothing in defence of these frontiers; not even the Social Democrats accepted them, and to middle-of-the-road opportunists, such as Stresemann became, they were something to be abolished at the earliest possible moment. Thus Poland was faced by bitter animosities and great poverty from the start.

The Baltic provinces, which the Germans had intended to conquer, emerged from the war as the three small independent states of Estonia, Latvia and Lithuania; they expropriated their German barons, who mostly added to the *Auslandsdeutsche* in the Weimar Republic. Poland hoped to take the Baltic States under her wing but this plan broke down chiefly because Poland in 1920 seized the mixed town of Vilna from the Lithuanians, who regarded it as their capital. After this the Lithuanians could not be prevented by the great powers from taking the formerly German port of Memel, to which, however, a statute guaranteed by these powers offered autonomy.

Meanwhile a Turkish resurgence under an officer called Kemal Pasha caused the defeat and discomfiture of the Greeks in Asia Minor. At the conference at Lausanne in 1923 the Greeks were obliged again to recognise the river Maritza as Turkey's western frontier and to agree to evacuate about a million Greeks from Anatolia: some half million Turks were evacuated from Greece. Thus Greece, naturally very poor, had little time to put her house in order before the Great Depression.

Signs of political trouble appeared in eastern Europe in three countries before the Great Depression. In 1926 Pilsudski, the Polish general who had done most to liberate the Poles during the war, carried through a military *coup d'état*, oddly enough in conjunction with the Polish Socialists; it was aimed chiefly against the Peasant party, which was an Austrian inheritance. Pilsudski declared that parliamentary government had broken down, and imprisoned and later exiled the Peasant leader, Witos, who had sat in the *Reichsrat* in Vienna. Thereafter Pilsudski exercised authority through the army, allowing the Sejm or parliament to continue with diminished powers. In Austria after some Rightists involved in a skirmish in January 1927 had been acquitted, Socialist crowds burnt down the Viennese Palace of Justice in July. This exacerbated feelings between the Right and the Left in Austria, drawing the Clericals and Pan-Germans together against the Socialists. In 1928 parliamentary government began to break down in Yugoslavia because the Catholic Croats resented the rule of the Serb King Alexander and what they regarded as the primitive influence of the Serb Orthodox hierarchy and the Serb army and bureaucrats: the Croats claimed autonomy. The Croat leader, Radić, was shot at and mortally wounded in the Skupština or parliament by a Serb who went unpunished. In January 1929 the king proclaimed his own dictatorship and in September 1931 introduced a farcical constitution with open instead of secret voting. Thus the Great Depression hit the peasants of Yugoslavia when many of them already felt great bitterness against their government.

Until the autumn of 1929, however, political and social life had on the whole been consolidated: the peasant countries could sell food to the industrial ones: their own over-population, which was intensified by their poor standards of production, was still bearable. With the death of Stresemann (October 1929), which contributed to the strange collapse of confidence in the United States, capital was withdrawn from Germany, employment shrank and Germany reduced her imports of food. The vicious circle had begun.

THE GREAT DEPRESSION:
HITLER BECOMES GERMAN CHANCELLOR

In Germany towards the end of 1929 employment melted away so rapidly that the prosperous period seemed to have been a mere illusion. In Austria the prosperity had been less convincing in any case, and soon the streets of Vienna seemed crowded with beggars. The Socialist Chancellor of Germany, Hermann Müller, resigned, and Hindenburg called upon the leader of the Centre party, Heinrich Brüning, to succeed him in the spring of 1930. Behind Brüning, and far more than he ever realised, intrigues were concentrating upon plans to make Hindenburg more of a pre-1914 emperor, and to reduce the powers of the Reichstag accordingly: these intrigues emanated from a 'political general' called Kurt von Schleicher, a friend of the President's son Oscar. When in July 1930 Brüning failed to get the agreement of the Reichstag to some deflationary measures of his, Hindenburg, encouraged by Schleicher, enforced them by emergency decree. Brüning thought it correct to dissolve the Reichstag, which had been elected in May 1928 in the prosperous period.

Elections were held on 14 September 1930: the results were like a bomb-shell for Germany and for Europe. The number of Communist deputies increased from 54 to 77 and the National Socialist Party (Nazis) shot up from 12 in the last Reichstag to 107: they were now the largest party after the Social Democrats. These Nazis were the followers of the Austrian agitator, Adolf Hitler, who had ignominiously failed to seize power in Munich in November 1923. Upon release from prison, where he had begun to write *Mein Kampf*, at Christmas 1924 he had set to work to reorganise his followers, placing great emphasis upon his Storm Troopers or S.A. Large numbers of young men who could not fit into Weimar Germany were at hand even in the days of high employment. They were provided with a curious military type of uniform with jackboots and were declared necessary to protect Nazi meetings from Communist interruption. Basically they were intended to intimidate. With the slump their recruits multiplied rapidly since many ordinary young men could now find no work; feeling indignant and solitary they were happy to be clothed and employed and provided with formulated grievances against the authorities and slogans suggesting social salvation. It was particularly in the provinces that the S.A. flourished, not in Berlin: the Prussian authorities seemed more aware of the danger from them and placed obstacles in their path. The elections of September 1930 gave the Nazis their first big opportunity, which they did not waste.

With the new Reichstag Brüning became far more dependent upon presidential support and was indeed reduced to ruling by emergency decree. He tried to gain prestige by success abroad: in June 1930 the Rhineland had been evacuated by Allied troops. But with the Great Depression reparations payments under the new Young Plan were more resented than ever and so were the troubles of 'poor little Austria'. In the spring of 1931 Germany and Austria put forward a plan for an Austro-German customs union. Far from alleviating the crisis, this precipitated an intensification of it. The French resented what seemed to them a revival of *Mitteleuropa* and the plan was dropped. French pressure in Vienna was thought to have contributed to the collapse of the *Creditanstalt* there in May 1931: this caused repercussions throughout central Europe. It led straight to the suspension of private discount payments by the German Reichsbank on 20 June and contributed to the collapse of the Darmstädter bank in Germany on 13 July. The Hoover moratorium on 20 June had provided some respite (see above, ch. VIII). The next thing was the collapse of sterling with world-wide repercussions. Hitler's propaganda exploited the whole situation to the uttermost. Brüning, who misunderstood Hindenburg's backing, decided to work for his re-election as President and enrolled his own Centre party and the Socialists in support. Hitler, hastily acquiring German citizenship for the first time, decided to run against him: thereby he gained new outlets for his vast publicity although Hindenburg was re-elected in April 1932.

What was this National Socialism with which Hitler was trying to impregnate Germany? It was a crude claim that the Germans belonged to a superior race in whose interest other races were to sacrifice whatever profited—in Hitler's view—the Germans. The others might be called upon to abandon their territory, their education, their identity, even to be annihilated. Among the Germans themselves those who accepted National Socialism were encouraged to destroy the others without regard for any moral scruple. Hitler's creed was, however, presented with such skill as to exploit the whole malaise of German society. It claimed to be able to undo post-Versailles humiliations; it claimed to be about to abolish the rigid class distinctions which had largely survived into the Republic; it claimed to be able to find work and a fitting reward for every good German. It exploited to the full the antipathy felt by provincials towards the Jews who had made Berlin into the slightly hectic yet brilliant centre of modern art which it had become. Hitler did not then say what fate he intended for the Jews, but he sometimes spoke of the physical extermination of one's enemies. People discounted such talk as unrealistic; indeed many Germans approved rather of Italian Fascism with its compromises than of Hitler's real aims. After the clearest evidence of their destructive intentions Brüning decided in April 1932 that Hitler's Storm Troopers must be suppressed throughout the Reich. On being re-elected Hindenburg was asked to agree to this. But he had met Hitler by now and preferred Hitler's men to the Socialist *Reichsbanner* organisation which existed to defend the Republic. The upshot was that he dismissed Brüning, appointing Franz von Papen in his place with a team of ministers which, like those before 1914, did not depend upon Reichstag support but only upon the confidence of the head of the state. In July Papen suppressed Otto Braun's régime in Prussia(which had lost much support in elections in April) and held fresh national elections. Unemployment was still chronic and the National Socialists more than doubled the votes they had gained in September 1930. In August Hitler demanded to be Chancellor with full powers but Hindenburg refused this: thereupon Hitler insolently expressed his 'solidarity' with some S.A. men condemned to death for a political murder at Potempa. In the autumn unemployment did not rise as quickly as in the last three autumns and in elections in November the Nazis lost two million votes. In January 1933, making use of quarrels between Papen and Schleicher, who had been Papen's Minister of Defence, then his successor, Hitler agreed to be Chancellor with Papen as Vice-Chancellor and only two Nazi colleagues—Hitler could not wait for the economic recovery to become more obvious.

Hitler had taken office on condition that a fresh general election should be held on 5 March 1933 under the administrative control of the Nazis— he had brought into power with him Göring as Minister of the Interior in Prussia with a seat in the Reich cabinet and Frick as Reich Minister of the Interior. Hitler and Göring boasted that this would be the last election for a thousand years because the Nazis would know what to do with their majority. Between 30 January and 5 March a tremendous campaign of intimidation was organised. Already well-known opponents of Hitler began to vanish into prisons, where they were beaten up. The Reichstag Fire on 27 February gave the Nazis a wonderful opportunity within less than a week of the election; claiming that the fire was the signal for a Communist *coup d'état*, they declared a state of emergency, increased the arrests and muzzled the press. Interestingly enough Hitler did not win an absolute majority; the Centre and the Socialists were not shaken and he needed the support of the Nationalists, who supplied the majority of ministers in his cabinet, to give him 52·5 per cent of the votes for the Reichstag.

He was not deterred by such a trifle. The Communist deputies, mostly arrested by now, were not allowed to take their seats, and all the other deputies but the Socialists—a brave speech of protest came from their leader, Otto Wels—were dragooned into voting for full powers to Hitler, sanctioned by the Enabling Act on 23 March. By this time the first of the Nazi concentration camps had been established at Dachau near Munich. The Nazis said these were what Kitchener had invented in South Africa. They were nothing of the kind. They were carefully thought out places of detention where anti-Nazis were systematically tormented physically and psychologically for as long as the Nazis thought fit.

When Hitler became Chancellor of Germany, the Austrian Chancellor since the previous May had been the young Christian-Social politician, Engelbert Dollfuss. Hitler's coming to power excited all the different shades of pro-German feeling in Austria, since the Anschluss was the first point on his programme. It was easy for the Nazis to say that of course Austria was too small to survive alone and hence union with Germany was the only thing. In the circumstances Dollfuss dismissed the Austrian parliament as unworkable in March 1933.

The collapse of agricultural prices had not been so sudden for peasant Europe as the disappearance of jobs in industry in the German towns and in Vienna. But in the early 'thirties all social relationships were embittered by it. Except among the Serbs, Bulgars and Greeks it became easy to stir up peasant feeling against Jewish 'moneylenders'. Agitators who whispered that Communism protected society from depression found a ready ear among the Russophil Czechs, Serbs and Bulgars. The danger from Communism, real or imagined, inclined rulers to admire Mussolini and his methods increasingly. His autarkic or protectionist policy was lauded and imitated so that tariff barriers impeded the road to economic recovery. In Hungary and Rumania particularly, middle-class misfits, but also peasants, organised themselves into Arrow-Cross or Iron Guards advocating Fascist principles in coloured shirts. This introduced fear and blackmail into the general atmosphere: in Budapest, particularly, conditions resembled those in Berlin before Hitler came to power.

Mussolini had befriended Hungary since the Italo-Magyar treaty of April 1927; this meant that he sided with the Magyar revisionists against the Little Entente (Czechoslovakia, Yugoslavia and Rumania) and the peace treaties. The friendship between Rome and Budapest had a strongly anti-Bolshevik tang since the Magyars made much of their brief Communist spell under Kun: they knew, they said, what Communism really meant but they preferred to forget the White Terror which had followed it in Hungary.

In 1932 a half-German Hungarian officer called Gömbös became Minister-President of Hungary, thus superseding a period of the predominance of the magnates under Count Bethlen. Gömbös admired Fascist Italy but still more Nazi Germany. He did not realise that Hitler would later side rather with Rumania than Hungary: he did not realise the galvanising effect

Hitler's success would have upon the German minorities in Hungary, Poland, Yugoslavia, Rumania and Czechoslovakia: these were groups of people with little political consciousness beyond their fiery Germanness. In German Austria the tension seemed to become unbearable. With the German Socialists imprisoned or dispersed the Austrian Socialists felt caught in a trap. Since Austria was a Catholic country they were more anti-clerical than their German colleagues while the Austrian bishops denounced them as Communists. There was pressure from Italy against the Austrian Socialists because they had revealed gun-running between Italy and Hungary. At last in February 1934 there were four days of civil war between the Dollfuss government and the Austrian Socialists. There were tragic and far-reaching consequences. The Austrian Socialist party was suppressed after nearly fifty years, and its leader, Otto Bauer, with the help of the Czechoslovak Minister in Vienna, Fierlinger, went into exile in Prague. Italian influence seemed to prevail in Vienna, and in March 1934 Austria and Hungary made economic agreements with Italy in the Rome Protocols. But the unseen victor was Hitler; without the Socialists Austria could certainly not resist him and the rank-and-file Viennese Socialists were so embittered against the 'priests' and the new officials imposed on the capital that they were often willing to believe Nazi talk about being the workers' champions: this fitted into the traditions of the Austrian Socialists. The thousand mark visa charge imposed by Hitler in 1933 on Germans wishing to travel to Austria was calculated to cause grave economic suffering in the Austrian holiday resorts; this could be blamed back on to the Austrian government.

'GLEICHSCHALTUNG' IN GERMANY AND AUSTRIA

It was extraordinary to observe that Nazi Germany constantly lost sympathy yet won admiration: opinion in Europe evidently shirked the discreditable evidence which was painful, and jumped at the impressive slogans. After the Enabling Act all political parties other than that of Hitler were abolished, and the rights of Bavaria and the other *Länder* destroyed in favour of rigid centralisation under the Nazi party. The trade unions were suppressed in the spring of 1933 in favour of the Nazi Labour Front, and employers and workers transformed into leaders and following. The press was strangled. Every newspaper that survived became some sort of organ of the National Socialist party except for the *Frankfurter Zeitung*: this great liberal paper was allowed a little unreal liberty and survived until 1941. It suited the Nazis to parade this curious mascot— before the end, indeed, it became Hitler's property, a birthday present from his publisher, Max Amann, in April 1939. The effect of seeing and hearing party slogans at meetings, in the press, on the wireless, everywhere, warped the attitude of convinced anti-Nazis in spite of themselves.

Anti-Semitic action was at first sporadic. It began to be systematised in a boycott of Jewish shops ordered by the Nazi party for 1 April 1933. There was not much violence on that day. If foreign papers reported anti-Semitic incidents, the Nazis pointed out how peaceful things were on 1 April and blamed the Jews for stirring up world opinion against Germany. Gradually it was made impossible for a Jew to practise any profession: until 1938 it was left at that.

Early in 1934 Hitler ran into some unexpected difficulties. His two major aims were to destroy the Jews and to acquire territory in eastern Europe in order to plant German colonists there. The second of these aims was certain to bring war: therefore Hitler wished to build up a new, big, efficient army. His old friend Ernst Röhm, the chief of the Storm Troopers, wished the army to be absorbed by the S.A. men under his control. The Generals resented this idea, the more so since some of them knew that the S.A. were really a lot of terrorising thugs. Hitler was against Röhm's programme because it would make for a less efficient army. Hoping to cash in on the tension, some conservative protégés of Papen persuaded the Vice-Chancellor to make a public speech of protest against many of the characteristics of National Socialism at the University of Marburg on 17 June; it was evident that the speech was popular.

Hitler extricated himself from this situation with criminal brilliance. The most important piece of *Gleichschaltung* which had been going on behind the scenes was that of the police: by April 1934 the whole police machine had come into the control of Hitler's faithful creature Heinrich Himmler, who was also the *Reichsführer* of what was originally a special bodyguard in the S.A. The members of this bodyguard wore black uniforms (with brown shirts) and were called *Schutzstaffeln* or S.S. The evidence suggests that Himmler and his S.S. induced the army leaders to expect a S.A. revolt and the S.A. leaders to expect that the army intended to crush them. On 30 June and 1 July Hitler, using the S.S., arrested and had executed a number of S.A. leaders including Röhm himself. At the same time he had murdered the authors of Papen's speech and a number of others on the right, including Schleicher, who had criticised Nazi savagery. The whole thing was justified by Hitler in that he announced that his will was law. Thus the old legal system which had half survived since the days of William II was *gleichgeschaltet* together with the S.A.: this was the last of the *Rechtsstaat* until after 1945. After 1934 the Storm Troopers lost all importance, and German life was dominated by the S.S., who controlled the concentration camps. The summer which had seen Hitler's first meeting with Mussolini and the murders of 30 June and 1 July, a few weeks later witnessed the murder of Dollfuss by Austrian Nazis in Vienna[1] and culminated in the death of Hindenburg in August and Hitler's succession to

---

[1] The timing of this seems not to have pleased Hitler (or so he made it appear): the action in itself was certainly not unwelcome to him.

him. Hitler never used the title of President, but as head of state he was able to oblige every soldier in the army to swear an oath of personal allegiance to him.

From 1934 to 1938 life in Germany did not seem to change very much. Employment increased; it did so in other countries but received extra stimulus from German rearmament; conscription was officially reintroduced in March 1935 with its own social consequences. Unless one were a Nazi official foreign travel was restricted by the shortage of foreign currency which kept raw materials short. Schacht's financial brilliance at the Reichsbank and the Ministry of Economics made the best of the circumstances (see above, ch. III). Strikingly little was done about housing; Hitler after all was interested in colonising eastern Europe, not in enlarging the cities of German home territory.

Goebbels, the Minister of Propaganda, kept up an atmosphere of tension especially with regard to Germans said to be persecuted abroad: in the Saar until the plebiscite in January 1935, in Danzig, Memel, Czechoslovakia. After January 1934, when the Ten Year Pact with Poland was made, the Germans in Poland were forgotten until 1939. Goebbels was the master of Germany's artistic life now; the only important artist to come to terms with him was Richard Strauss, who became head of the Reich Chamber of Music. The schools and universities were caught up in the Nazi Youth organisations which put emphasis on para-military training. The old duelling Corps of the universities, which had survived through the Weimar Republic, were suppressed: Hitler disliked all aristocratic traditions. The Catholic church had at first extended something like a welcome to National Socialism, for the first positive recognition the Nazi state had received from abroad had been the Concordat in July 1933, and Hitler's hostility to Communism was welcomed by the Vatican. However, Catholic and Nazi doctrines were fundamentally irreconcilable, and Pope Pius XI became increasingly aware of this as his message to the German clergy, *Mit brennender Sorge*, made clear in March 1937. The German Protestants were divided in their reactions to National Socialism, but from the beginning those who followed Dibelius and Niemöller[1] protested; they enjoyed a certain support among Reichswehr officers (the future President Heuss and his wife were close friends of Dibelius). It should be added that Berlin with Hamburg was always less Nazi than the rest of Germany; National Socialism was less oppressive there and anti-Nazi jokes always circulated.

In September 1937 Berlin was obliged to parade for Mussolini. In November Hitler brought his plans up to date. This meant a final break with the old pre-1914 ruling class that winter, when Ribbentrop succeeded Freiherr von Neurath at the German Foreign Office. Generals Blomberg and Fritsch were disgraced and Hitler himself became commander-in-

---

[1] In July 1937 Niemöller was arrested.

chief. Ulrich von Hassell was dropped from the German Embassy in Rome, and when at last the new Ambassador was nominated he turned out to be Hans Georg von Mackensen, a Junker who had defected to the Nazis. At this time Papen, who might almost be described in the same terms, was recalled from Vienna, where in any case an Envoy was about to become superfluous. All these changes synchronised with the resignation of Schacht as Minister of Economics and his succession by a tool of the Nazi party called Walther Funk. Thus the decks were cleared for action.

CZECHOSLOVAKIA 1929–1938

At first Czechoslovakia was not seriously affected by the Great Depression: her finances were sound: she was fairly self-sufficient. The population, at any rate in Bohemia and Moravia, was reasonably well educated, and the constitution worked satisfactorily. Here in the 'twenties there seemed to be the new twentieth-century society freed of an alien aristocracy. Life in Prague competed with that in Berlin and Vienna; the intellectuals had the same strong bias to the left and their own special relationship with the Russians—life was less brilliant than in Berlin but a little saner, less isolated from its hinterland. An interesting figure of the day was Kafka's Milena. Before 1914 she had been a revolutionary Czech schoolgirl thirsting for national independence. Then there was Kafka and his early death; after translating his novels she became a literary journalist and a focus of Czech intellectual life. In the later 'twenties not only the Prague Jews but some of the other Bohemian Germans began to settle down to acceptance of the Czechoslovak Republic: Beneš's activities at the League of Nations —the Czechoslovak Foreign Minister presided over the Assembly of the League of Nations on the day of Germany's admission in September 1926 —added to its standing.

Their own circumstances and temperament made it difficult for the Czechs, whether Masaryk and Beneš or the general public, to grasp what began to happen all round them in the 'thirties. Stalin had chosen the path of despotism already in 1928. From the time of those elections in Germany in September 1930 the extreme racialism of the Bohemian Germans began to revive; the fanatics had remained fanatics but now people listened to them again. Since they lived on the fringes of the Republic, without big cities, Prague was their centre too. As the German economic crisis lifted and Hitler quickly took power, thus seeming to be the cause of the improvement, in Czechoslovakia the depression set in. It gravely affected, as depressions often had under the Habsburgs, the light industries of the Bohemian frontier districts where the Germans— Sudeten Germans, they now called themselves—lived. This caused great suffering for which the Czech authorities could be blamed. The old quarrel blazed up and now Nazi Germany began to finance Sudeten

German agitators with such success that a new Sudeten German party led by a certain Konrad Henlein polled 1,249,530 votes at a general election in May 1935; thus it had become the biggest party in the country, just ahead of the Czech Agrarians.

At the end of that year Thomas Masaryk, now 85, resigned from the presidency and was succeeded by Beneš; the new situation in central Europe was a challenge to everything he stood for. After the civil war in Austria the Czechs scarcely welcomed the corporate state of Dollfuss nor yet his murder by Austrian Nazis in July 1934 nor the succession of the clerical Schuschnigg. In the autumn of 1934 the U.S.S.R. was brought into the League of Nations with a permanent seat in the Council and Beneš decided to link himself with his French ally in making a cautious treaty with the Russians. This coincided with Henlein's election campaign and brought furious noises from all the nationalistic Germans; Beneš was betraying Europe to Bolshevism, they said, and making Czechoslovakia into a Russian air-base. Blow rained upon blow. Hitler used the opportunity provided by Italy's invasion of Abyssinia and quarrel with the League of Nations to remilitarise the Rhineland, an action which probably emasculated Czechoslovakia's treaty with France. Mussolini began to realise that feeling in Austria was not only anti-Italian—which it always had been—but also essentially *grossdeutsch*, and in acquiescing in advance in the Austro-German Agreement of July 1936 he in fact abandoned the cause of Austrian independence.

In his good-for-nothing days in Vienna, before he went to Munich in 1913, Hitler had been proudly old-style Austrian Pan-German. For him not merely 1919 but 1866 had to be undone, and Austria and Bohemia united with Germany. By November 1937 the 'Hossbach Memorandum' shows that he had decided to put all this in order: 'our first objective must be to overthrow Czechoslovakia and Austria simultaneously'[1]—this appeared as a single operation to him.

In Prague the Czechs remembered they had lived through bad times before but they did not intend to be beaten nor to lose the independence that had dawned so happily. The intellectuals still tried to put their hope in Russia, but a person so upright as Milena Jesenská realised that the Russia of the purging trials was both bad and weak, and she abandoned Communism.[2] Beneš naturally tried to placate the Sudeten Germans and to strengthen his defences. Even the Sudeten German Socialists who were in danger from Hitler were hard to placate, and strengthening his defences brought additional friction with the mass of the Sudeten Germans because they lived in the frontier districts but he could not count upon their loyalty.

[1] *Documents on German Foreign Policy*, Series D, vol. I, no. 19.
[2] She was arrested by the Germans in 1939 and died in the concentration camp of Ravensbrück in 1944. See *Kafkas Freundin Milena* by M. Buber-Neumann (1965).

Schuschnigg, who had succeeded Dollfuss as Chancellor of Austria, was an ambiguous character. With the intense German feeling of the Tyrolese he combined ardent Catholicism: the two together seemed to paralyse him. Like the Weimar authorities in 1931–2 he was, however, galvanised into some kind of action by the discovery of Nazi terrorist plans for Austria. At the instigation of Papen, Hitler's envoy to Vienna from 1934 to 1938, he agreed to visit Hitler in February 1938, and was browbeaten by the German Chancellor into a tentative surrender. On returning to Vienna he decided to make his own appeal to the Austrians by holding a plebiscite. Hitler may have feared the result. At all events he decided to seize Austria without for the moment attacking Czechoslovakia. On the contrary, when on 12 March the German army moved into Austria, the Czechoslovak Minister in Berlin was assured that no threat whatever to his country was involved (see below, ch. xxiii).

Already in 1933 Hitler's success in Germany had intoxicated the German minorities throughout eastern Europe. The absorption of Austria into Nazi Germany in March 1938 was like a second injection and all the Sudeten Germans except the Socialists rushed to join Henlein's Sudeten German party: they took care to know nothing of the ugly side of the Anschluss. The Czechs were surrounded by now—the Poles filled the only gap apart from Hungary—and it cannot be supposed that their partial mobilisation in May, which so much angered Hitler, really affected his plans appreciably. In his eyes a Czechoslovak democracy had no right to exist—it both hampered and irritated him. By the autumn of 1938 he wanted all the old pre-1914 Austrian *Lebensraum* under his control: he wanted it anyway but he began sometimes to admit that he wanted it as a preliminary to a war against the West.

Owing to the Munich conference (ch. xxiii) Hitler destroyed the first Czechoslovak Republic in two stages; it seems clear that he would have preferred to crush it by one quick war. By March 1939 when he set up the Protectorate of Bohemia and Moravia, a Slovakia dependent upon Germany, and gave Ruthenia back to Hungary, he had acquired tremendous economic power. The Anschluss had put under German control all kinds of central European banking and industrial connections. But in Prague the Czechs had built up something of an economic centre for the Little Entente. Czech bankers had invested considerable sums in Yugoslavia, an undeveloped country rich in copper, lead and bauxite: they had hoped to push their way into Rumania, the only European country other than Russia then known to produce oil, though in fact they could not readily compete with the big oil companies which were American, British and Dutch.

Since coming into power Hitler and his economic advisers, first and foremost Schacht, had seemed to come to the rescue of the east European peasantry by buying up their food produce. Germany, in view of her currency troubles, paid for such purchases in kind with whatever she needed to export. Ingeniously the smaller, weaker countries were made by Schacht to become dependent on her, their currencies linked with Germany's. Not very willingly the Yugoslav government had joined in economic sanctions against Italy during the Abyssinian war; instead of selling to Italy the Yugoslavs found they could sell more to Germany. (When the British stopped sending coal the Italians found the Germans could supply it.) The Hungarians similarly found that in spite of the Rome Protocols they could sell more to the Germans. With the seizure of Prague all former Czech investments came into German control, including of course the great Škoda armament works. A German *Mitteleuropa* had been created overnight. It was reinforced by the German–Rumanian Commercial Treaty of 23 March 1939. Oil was becoming more and more important. This treaty, which was concluded for at least five years, laid down that joint German–Rumanian companies were to intensify the exploitation of Rumania's oil and other natural resources. The Germans, who had been present here, it has been seen, before the first world war but then expelled at the end of it, now acquired 'free zones' in key positions in Rumania; they were to provide the necessary equipment for exploiting the oilfields. This treaty, the Germans presumed, would provide the model for further agreements ensuring them economic control throughout south-eastern Europe.

THE ATTACK UPON POLAND EXPANDS INTO
A SECOND WORLD WAR

In May 1939 the treaty which Mussolini called the Steel Pact was signed in Berlin between Germany and Italy. It was a frankly aggressive treaty which intensified the intimidation of Europe by Hitler and Mussolini. It misled world opinion in a way which suited Hitler in that it concealed the weakness of Italy behind Germany's strength. Almost immediately after the conquest of Abyssinia Mussolini had sent large contingents of Italian 'volunteers' to fight for Franco. In its timing the Steel Pact seemed to crown the success of Franco and the Axis powers in Spain after nearly three years' fighting. The Germans had not engaged more than small groups of airmen, but Mussolini had exhausted both his armies and his economic resources. As soon as he had signed the pact he began to be afraid of its consequences. Hitler, however, felt more assured. By now Mussolini had followed his example and introduced anti-Semitic measures into Italy. Beyond the frontiers directly controlled by the Germans, the governments of Hungary, Poland and Rumania were glad to buy favour in Berlin by anti-Jewish gestures. The time of annihilation was not to come for two years yet. But the existence of the scapegoat through which one could curry favour was one of Hitler's weapons in the war of nerves which he manipulated in such masterly fashion. Everyone's life in eastern Europe was affected, what they heard or read or said or saw stimulated anti-Semitism and discouraged tolerance.

It should, however, be observed that Hitler knew that German opinion was unenthusiastic about war. After the cool reception of his armoured division in Berlin in September 1938, in November he instructed journalists to work for greater bellicosity. The fact that this same month saw an organised pogrom all over Germany, the so-called *Reichskristallnacht*, with loss of life and much destruction of Jewish property was not accidental:[1] from this time onwards the German and Austrian Jews were systematically ruined economically. After Prague Hitler intended to liquidate Poland should it not prove pliant, and about this German opinion, in eastern Germany at least, was keener although the accompaniment of a pact with Soviet Russia was not likely to be popular.

After Pilsudski's death in 1935 Poland had been ruled by his former legionaries, the Colonels, of whom Joseph Beck was the most prominent. Beck was anti-Western, full of phrases about the understanding of the Austrian Hitler for Poland, and delighted to whip up feeling against Czechs over Teschen at the time of the Munich Agreement. Poland did indeed gain this latter territory at the beginning of October 1938. The Peasant party, submerged since 1926, was still almost certainly by far the largest party in Poland, and its leaders, in spite of endless chicanery from the government, were very active from the time of Pilsudski's death; they were indeed able to win remarkable successes in municipal elections in December 1938. They and their friend, General Sikorski, who was also a Galician, worked hard to warn their people that Hitler's friendship spelt mortal danger: the behaviour of the German minority in Poland began to look too much like the recent behaviour of the Sudeten Germans. Thus Beck's appeasement of Nazi Germany became very unpopular and the Polish Generals prepared resistance. But their equipment and technical knowledge were hopelessly out of date, and the country was one of the poorest, by any standards, in Europe. When Britain and France in the spring of 1939 offered to guarantee its frontiers Hitler decided upon a punitive expedition to put an end to Poland; this should teach the Western powers a salutary lesson that they seemed to have forgotten since Munich. Stalin's decision in August to come to terms with Hitler rather than with the Western powers facilitated Hitler's design (see below, ch. XXIII).

The destruction of Poland combined with the 'phoney' war against France and Britain did not seem to change life in eastern Europe for the time being: Hungary (enlarged by a big piece of Transylvania in November 1938) as well as Italy seemed to flourish on their neutrality. The Polish

---

[1] The *Reichskristallnacht* was the night between 9 and 10 November. The excuse had been the murder by a Jew of a German diplomatist in Paris, but Goebbels would have found another pretext easily enough.

war did, however, bring the realisation of Hitler's true aims much nearer in two ways. It caused an increase of tension in the Protectorate and a students' demonstration in Prague which gave the Nazis their excuse for closing the Czech university; this led on to the ending of all higher education for the Czechs, a part of the destruction of the national life of the inferior Slav races. Directly, the conquest of Poland provided the positive gain of *Lebensraum*. Rather more than the territory lost by Germany to Poland in 1919–21 was re-annexed to Germany and the Poles expelled from it. On 7 October 1939 Hitler appointed Himmler to be *Reichskommissar für die Festigung deutschen Volkstums* in charge of bringing in German colonists: this was not a moment too soon, for Himmler had already been perplexed as to where to settle Germans who had opted to leave the Italian South Tyrol after the Steel Pact. The Poles who were expelled from the homes their fathers and grandfathers had lived in under William II (when they had been a minority on the scale of the Sudeten Germans in Czechoslovakia but with no such 'minority' rights) were sent further east to what was denominated the *General-Gouvernement*; the Nazi authorities intended to neglect this economically so that Polish life there should be doomed to decay. The atmosphere in Germany itself was not very gay during the winter of 1939–40; sympathies were on the side of the Finns against Hitler's new friend, Stalin, in the 'winter war'.

Then came the euphoria of the seizures and victories of the spring of 1940 and the incredible collapse of France: almost suddenly the Germans were in occupation of Norway, Denmark and the Low Countries and very soon of France; from 10 June Italy was an ally, and Spain seemed to be so. Eastern Europe was either conquered or in economic subjection, and the U.S.S.R. apparently friendly. And yet victory did not bring an end to the war: the British Empire would not acknowledge defeat and in the autumn Italy began an unsuccessful war against the Greeks. The Soviet Union, moreover, had advanced not only into eastern Poland but also into the Baltic States and north-east Rumania: would there be a collision in the Straits near the oilfields or over Finland's resources in Petsamo? The problem of manning the German factories began to appear. This was one reason why the French prisoners were not repatriated; it also led to large numbers of Italian workers, as well as Polish ones, being sent to Germany. The growing labour shortage saved the Slav races; it even saved some Jews.

By the end of 1940 the war was not won. Hitler had decided in July that he must conquer perfidious Russia in order, he said, to destroy perfidious Albion. As a preliminary he must subdue the whole Balkan peninsula, occupy Rumania and Bulgaria, conquer the Greeks in Mussolini's wake, and cajole the Yugoslavs. When, however, towards the end of March 1941 the Yugoslav government agreed in return for big concessions to concur in the Tripartite Pact of September 1940 between Germany,

Italy and Japan, the population of Serbia and Montenegro erupted in protest. In August 1939 an agreement had been made between the Serbs and the Croats, but it had proved a disappointment partly because the Croats could not resist the hope that Axis pressure might extend their autonomy; the Serbs, on the other hand, suspected the Axis of wishing only to weaken the south Slavs and exploit their minerals. The Serb attitude was partly conditioned by Pan-Slav traditions, by hostility in the University of Belgrade to the Karageorge dynasty and its tsarist allegiance, and by suspicion of the Pan-Germans and the German Minority in Yugoslavia. Prince Paul, who had become chief regent for the new child-king when Alexander Karageorgević had been murdered at Marseilles in October 1934, was expelled, and young King Peter inaugurated his personal reign by appointing a new ministry under the chief of the air force, General Simović. This was tantamount to repudiating concurrence in the Tripartite Pact and incurred Hitler's fury and an immediate German attack at the beginning of April. Belgrade was savagely bombed and Yugoslavia fell to pieces for the moment. King Peter and his government took to flight, Slovenia was divided between Germany and Italy and Macedonia given to Bulgaria. The veteran terrorist, Ante Pavelić, was installed in Zagreb as dictator of the Croats under Italian protection. This was not what the Croat peasants wanted at all and their leader, Maček, was soon placed under arrest at his home. Serbia itself was placed under German military rule. The German army swept on into Greece, where a mixed German–Italian occupation was set up. Thus the whole of Europe from Copenhagen to Athens was occupied by German or Italian troops, and in the grip of the German Secret Police and S.S., which had become almost identical. Only Sweden and Switzerland retained their independence, apart from Franco's Spain and Salazar's Portugal. Hungary, like Slovakia, Rumania, Croatia and Bulgaria, was a dependent state subject to anti-Semitic and liberty-robbing pressures exerted by Himmler.

When Hitler attacked the U.S.S.R. in June 1941 he revived the old idea of a crusade against Communism: the slogan came in usefully again, though it had lost some of its appeal. Britain apart, an attack upon and partition of Russia lay at the heart of his ideology: the inferior Slavs must make room—*Raum*—for the German master-race and the orders given for the shooting of Communist commissars were soon equalled by a whole code of savagery aimed at the annihilation of the Russians, and at the German colonisation of their land.[1] Life in central and eastern Europe and in Italy became grimmer. For the officers and soldiers of the German army, although they advanced with extraordinary speed in 1941, there was scorched earth and icy cold rather than the pleasures of occupying Paris. Soon there were Russian prisoners to add to the labour in the German

[1] Cf. D.G.F.P. Series D, vol. XIII, no. 114. See also *Anatomie des S.S. Staates* by Buchheim, Broszat, Jacobsen and Krausnick (1965).

factories and a little later on German housewives were happy to find that they could procure Russian peasant girls as domestic servants.

With the war against Russia the reign of terror in Germany and German-occupied Europe was intensified, particularly so in Bohemia, where the Munich agreement had left bitterness against the West and had revived old Russophil sympathies. The Czechs lived in terror of being expelled;[1] in practice their labour was needed in German factories. By now there were Czech and Polish governments in exile in London. The Magyars and Rumanians, to some extent impelled by their old anti-Russian feelings, agreed to become belligerents at the side of the Germans against the U.S.S.R.

The reign of terror now included the extermination of the Jews by gassing. For in the summer of 1941 Himmler's second-in-command, Reinhard Heydrich, began to give orders to his subordinates such as Eichmann to carry out this 'Final Solution'; it was no accident that this same Heydrich was sent to rule Prague in September 1941 in the place of the 'Protector', Freiherr von Neurath, who went on sick leave. This was a case of the old ruling class leaving by the back door. The more urgent military problems of transport became, the more extraordinary it seemed— as well as unspeakably cruel—that trucks could always be spared to transport Jews to be gassed at Auschwitz. Part of the Nazi technique was to wrap up such crimes in tremendous mystery. Anyone who hinted at the truth was denounced as an enemy; thus ordinary people were terrorised into looking the other way and 'not knowing'. Since civilised people found it difficult to believe that such crimes were perpetrated in the twentieth century it was relatively easy to conceal them.

One of the most important events in the political and social history of central Europe in 1942 was the attempt made upon Heydrich's life in Prague at the end of May; in consequence he died at the beginning of June. He was the brains of the German Secret Police and probably irreplaceable, although evil processes which he had set in train, such as the liquidation of the Jews, continued. The attack upon his life had been carried out by an exiled Czech and Slovak flown in from Britain and was not without its symbolic significance. It inevitably brought about a fearful intensification of the Nazi reign of terror in the Protectorate: the Czechs, who had always been too matter-of-fact to put their case effectively before the world in the past, succeeded in imprinting upon the public mind the crime of the destruction that summer of Lidice and Ležáky, two villages near Prague where the men were massacred, the women sent to concentration camps and the children disappeared. The Czechoslovak government in exile in London succeeded in making Lidice into a byword.

Of all the countries which the Germans had occupied, the mountainous

---

[1] That Hitler thought of this is shown in the Hossbach Memorandum, D.G.F.P. Series D, vol. I, no. 19.

areas of Yugoslavia—Serbia, Bosnia, Montenegro—were the most promising terrain for guerrilla warfare, and this flared up very quickly. Unfortunately two opposed leaders appeared, Draža Mihailović who stood for a narrow, backward-looking Serb allegiance, and the Communist leader Josip Broz called Tito who was half Croat and half Slovene. The régime of Pavelić in Zagreb, involving the merciless killing of large numbers of Serbs and Jews, caused the Croats to become less hostile to Tito than they otherwise might have been. In November 1942 he felt strong enough to summon what he chose to call a National Assembly to Bihać in Bosnia, in fact a handful of Communists and sympathisers with them. From this time on, however, Tito's partisans took every opportunity to fight the Germans, while the followers of Mihailović lapsed into passivity or made bargains with the Italian forces of occupation. This state of affairs in Yugoslavia became a running sore of which Hitler was well aware.

Having come to a standstill at the gates of Moscow at Christmas 1941, Hitler had renewed the offensive in 1942. Towards the end of that year, in November, the Allies took him by surprise by landing in North Africa: at the same time the Russian resistance in Stalingrad also surprised him. The battle of Stalingrad, which became so famous, reverberated through central Europe and Italy all that winter, the Italian, Hungarian and Rumanian contingents suffering severely. At last came the thunderbolt: the German General Paulus and his men surrendered to the Russians on 1 February 1943, although it was known that Hitler forbade surrender.

In many ways Italy was the most interesting area of Axis Europe in 1943. Public opinion had betrayed little enthusiasm for Mussolini's declaration of war in June 1940, and the Greek war in October was unpopular from the start as well as unsuccessful. Economic difficulties multiplied, and Allied air raids increased. The Communist party had kept together certain cells in the industrial north and as the climate became more anti-Fascist their activity increased. In March 1943 the workers of the Fiat factories went on strike for compensation to bombed-out workers; some of the directors were known to be in sympathy, and the Fascist authorities seemed at a loss. When the striking in Turin died down, however, there were strikes in several big factories in Milan. These were the first serious strikes in Axis Europe. It should perhaps be added that the time to strike in Germany itself had passed, for the proportion of foreign slave labour (for this was what it came to) was now so high that strike action was out of the question. When Mussolini met Hitler at Klessheim in April his Under-Secretary for Foreign Affairs, Bastianini, told Ribbentrop that with so much labour unrest Italy could not continue the war. Mussolini was in poor health by now. The battle of El Alamein had put an end to his hopes in Africa in October 1942 and in May 1943 Tunis was lost to the Allies (see below, ch. xxiv). Knowing that the Italians wanted to make peace the Germans increased their personnel of various kinds in Italy and this made the Italians more anti-German. Over the Jews nearly all Italians were opposed to Nazi policy and they succeeded in putting spokes in Himmler's wheels. These things were reported to Hitler; the latter had taken a violent dislike to the king when he—the Führer—visited Italy in May 1938 and he now blamed Victor Emmanuel. There was something in this. The king of Italy had disliked coming into the war on Hitler's side and was cautiously considering the dismissal of Mussolini and putting out feelers towards peace. He was, however, afraid of popular pressure and he waited until late in July. By this time the Allies had landed in Sicily, meeting no serious resistance except from German troops. On 24 July Mussolini was induced to call together the Fascist Grand Council. Grandi and Ciano,[1] now Minister to the Vatican, put forward and carried an obscure motion in favour of restoring the king's authority. Victor Emmanuel had decided to appoint Marshal Badoglio in place of Mussolini, whom he dismissed and had arrested. Thereupon Fascism seemed magically to disappear overnight. Hitler, however, sent a special S.S. man to kidnap Mussolini on 12 September and he obliged the Duce to start a new Fascist Republic based on Lake Garda. For over eighteen months this Republic depending on Hitler fought a losing battle against the Monarchy backed by the Allies. In the spring of 1945 the German commanders in Italy surrendered unconditionally; Mussolini took to flight and was caught and shot by Resistance fighters. It had been a tragic and destructive period in Italy. Ironically the most active forces who fought with the Allies against the new Republic were republicans who hated the House of Savoy; they fought for a new reformed Italy, above all they fought against Fascism and National Socialism. In the end the Italian partisans who did this— it is worth remembering that some of them had fought against Franco in the Spanish Civil War—distinguished themselves as much as any Resistance fighters anywhere. Hitler was loth to abandon control of the north Italian factories although the workers in them were in some ways his most efficacious enemies in Italy.

The fall of Mussolini on 25 July 1943 after 21 years in office shook the Axis world profoundly; listening to the broadcasts of the B.B.C., as more and more dared to do now, people were adequately informed about it. In Germany the battle of Stalingrad had had its effect. In 1943, moreover, Allied air-raids were becoming much more powerful though it seems to be agreed that it was the disruption of communications rather than panic which counted. Indeed reactions in Berlin were not essentially different from those in London although these raids were more destructive and consequently the evacuation of Berlin was announced on 1 August 1943. From this time onwards those who could be moved were sent into the German provinces. Before this people had been evacuated perhaps to Silesia or East Prussia or even to the re-won 'West Prussia'. But now that

[1] Mussolini's son-in-law and Foreign Minister, 1936–43.

the Russians, though still distant, were advancing it was better to go to the *Sudetengau* or to Austria or Bavaria.

In a brutal police-state like that of Nazi Germany it was extraordinarily difficult to organise any effectual opposition. Indeed it was probably true that only people in key positions in the army could do so. General Ludwig von Beck, who was genuinely opposed to the Hitler régime, had resigned as Chief of Staff in 1938. Officers working with Admiral Canaris in his Intelligence set-up, the *Abwehr*, had prepared plans, but in 1943 the Secret Police arrested several key people there and early in 1944 arranged the dismissal of Canaris, taking over his powers. At last on 1 July 1944, less than a month after the Allied invasion of Normandy, Count Claus Schenk von Stauffenberg was appointed Chief of Staff to General Fromm who commanded the Reserve army. Stauffenberg was one of those who had become convinced that Hitler was a criminal who must be destroyed. On 20 July he took advantage of his new appointment in order to place a bomb near Hitler at a military conference in East Prussia and to find a pretext to leave immediately by plane for Berlin. Before he left he witnessed the explosion so that he thought himself able to report on arrival in Berlin that Hitler was killed; he and his friends had worked out plans for taking over control of the army in Paris and elsewhere. Alas for Stauffenberg, there were four mortal casualties at Rastenburg, but Hitler escaped with minor injuries. More excited than ever by this mark 'of the favour of Providence, the Führer launched a half-mad campaign of revenge and frightfulness against the various groups of people who had unskilfully conspired against him: the last nine months of his life were indeed a nightmare for Germany and the territories still occupied by the Germans.

The Allies' invasion of France had proved successful and on 23 August 1944 Paris was liberated. For eastern Europe, however, that day was more memorable on account of events in Rumania. Already in March of that year the Russians had conquered Bessarabia—in the same month the Germans fully occupied Hungary and suppressed the last vestiges of opposition there. Since the resignation of King Carol in 1940 a soldier, Marshal Antonescu, had governed Rumania despotically, not through the Iron Guard which he despised but along slightly more respectable lines: his energy, his patriotism and his anti-Semitism had satisfied Hitler. Although pushed aside by the pro-Fascist trend of the day, Maniu, like Maček in Croatia, had preserved a wide influence, especially on account of the protests he was known to have made when the Axis powers forced Rumania to cede territory to Hungary. The young King Michael, a contemporary of King Peter of Yugoslavia now in London, urged on by his mother and Maniu, on 23 August dismissed and arrested Antonescu and prepared for a Popular Front government. Two days later he and his advisers changed sides in the war, declaring war upon Germany. The oil-

509

fields of Ploesti, still of decisive importance, were thus put at the Russians' disposal. This was the end of German power in the Balkan peninsula for the second time since 1900. Bulgaria too changed sides and in October 1944 the Germans were driven out of Athens and Belgrade: Tito, whose partisans had made an important contribution to the liberation of Yugoslavia, was vindicated. In Greece a fight between Communist and nationalistic partisans was to continue for some time; there were no Soviet troops here to help the Communists.

Meanwhile on 1 August 1944 the Poles staged a rising against the Germans in Poland in the shadow of the advancing Russians; later in August there was a serious rising, joined by some Czech volunteers, against the German-protected régime in Slovakia. These events not only caused great suffering: they revealed the rift between the Western Allies and Soviet Russia which provided Hitler with his best hope, the strongest incentive to him to hold out. For the Russians for six weeks refused to allow Western aeroplanes to come to the Poles' help (these planes needed to re-fuel in the east if they were to do so) because this was the Polish nation in revolt, not the fringe of individuals who had become Communists. Thus the Germans were able to crush the uprising in Warsaw and massacre much of its population. The Russian attitude towards the Slovak rebellion was more ambiguous. The Germans were still able to suppress both risings just in time for a fresh crisis in Hungary. Here in the middle of October the regent, Horthy, had decided to swallow his Magyar pride and prejudice and beg peace from the U.S.S.R.; his commander-in-chief went over to the Russians. The Germans then put Hungary in the hands of the Arrow-Cross leader, Szálasi; they held out in Budapest till the following March, even launching a last attack there in February 1945. By this time the Russian armies had swept over Poland into East Prussia and Silesia, but in addition to a small portion of Hungary the Germans still controlled Bohemia, proverbially the key to Europe. It was not until April 1945 that American troops confronted Russian troops there and in Saxony and Brandenburg. The fate of central Europe was then decided, at any rate for the next generation, by unnecessary American anxieties about Japan; in order to ensure superfluous Russian support against the Japanese, the Americans withdrew and allowed Soviet troops to occupy Berlin, Vienna and Prague. None of these places was lost to the West for the moment, but the Russians had been given the power to take them, like Budapest, under their control. After the encirclement of Berlin by the Russians Hitler committed suicide on 30 April.

Social conditions in Axis Europe after the battle of Stalingrad were highly political; increasingly people joined the Resistance movements or helped them or at any rate hindered the authorities through sabotage. Most people in the towns went very hungry except the Germans themselves, whose cupboards turned out to be well stocked (unlike 1917–18). With the autumn of 1944 the Germans began to feel in danger east of the Elbe; the Western Allies would soon invade western Germany but one was less afraid of them. Thus, for the last six months of the war and during a phenomenally cold winter with air raids, wrecked railways and retreating troops, people were trying to go west and Berlin ministries to decentralise themselves. These migrations merged into the growing stream of refugees directly fleeing from the Russians and their protégés, the Polish Communists, who had by now succeeded in building up to something. It ended in the Polish–German *de facto* frontier becoming the line of the Oder and the Western Neisse rivers. All the Germans in Europe came to live west of this frontier, in a relatively small area, after 1945: otherwise there is only a group of about 250,000 German-speaking inhabitants in Hungary.

In the period from 1900 to 1945 profound social change took place in Germany, Italy and eastern Europe: for better and for worse the aristocracy dominant at the beginning had been destroyed by the end. The myth that the conspiracy against Hitler in July 1944 was due to 'feudal reactionaries' was nonsense; people from all classes of society were involved although the initiative came perforce from a group of officers, some with noble names. After this the Russian armies streamed into eastern Germany, precisely that part of the country where many of the big landed properties had survived. The widow of Bismarck's younger son, Bill, told Countess Dönhoff, who was riding to the West, that she was too old to leave the family estate at Varzin[1]—she did not wish to survive. The Russians came and she was never heard of again. At Löwenbruch in Brandenburg a Russian officer with his men prepared to have Frau von dem Knesebeck shot. But the eighty Russian prisoners-of-war who had worked on her estate protested with cries of 'Mamushka, Mamushka' which saved her life:[2] she had had the courage—and it required a great deal for it was strictly against Nazi rules—to treat them humanly. This was the swan-song of the east European aristocracy, its power and its way of life.

[1] See Marion Dönhoff, *Namen die keiner mehr nennt* (1964), pp. 36–8.
[2] Walter Keitel, 'Abend über Schloss Löwenbruch' in *Neue Zürcher Zeitung*, 21 January 1965.

CHAPTER XVII

GREAT BRITAIN, FRANCE, THE LOW COUNTRIES AND SCANDINAVIA

A T the beginning of the twentieth century, all the major European states could be characterised by their respect for the principle of the sovereignty of the people, and a social order founded on the predominance of a property-owning class composed of the aristocracy and the bourgeoisie. This was especially true of northern and western Europe; with the exception of republican France, the pattern of government was that of a constitutional monarchy supported by an electoral system based on property qualifications which usually excluded any popular elements from the elected assemblies. Political struggles were restricted to the two sections—conservative and liberal—of the ruling class—but neither of them ever thought of modifying the traditional structure of society in any way. Even socialism, still in its infancy, was not as yet strong enough to have any real influence on the pattern of society.

In the course of the following fifty years, however, the structure of society was to be shaken to its very foundations, partly because of the increase in population (although the rate of increase was slower here than elsewhere), but chiefly because of the rise of industry. This was to cause an upheaval in the social and professional distribution of the whole population, and, by altering the balance of power between the different classes of society, was to bring about a complete transformation of that society's institutions and mental attitudes. Two world wars and an economic crisis of unprecedented magnitude were to follow and in their turn speed up the rhythm of these transformations.

We are concerned here with those countries of north-western Europe which, before 1940 at least, were able to avoid a social revolution or a dictatorial régime, namely, Great Britain, France, Belgium and Luxemburg, the Netherlands and the Scandinavian countries. In general, the evolution of all these countries followed much the same pattern, although it is not always possible to establish a complete concurrence of events; there were variations which can be explained by differences in the character and tradition of each nation, by the differing stages of economic development and by problems peculiar to each one of them. Nevertheless, it is true to say that, throughout these countries as a whole, changes in the political and administrative institutions worked towards a democratisation of the representative system, an extension of the functions of the state, an upsurge of socialism which succeeded in curtailing the omnipotence of the former ruling class, and a levelling of living standards—which did not, however, prevent an unequal distribution of wealth and, to some extent, of power.

THE POLITICAL SYSTEM AND THE ORGANISATION OF SOCIETY AT THE BEGINNING OF THE CENTURY

France had adopted the principle of universal suffrage in 1848, but in Great Britain, although the Act of 1884 had increased the number of voters from four to five millions, the franchise was not universal, and plural voting was possible for persons owning houses or premises in several constituencies. In Sweden three-quarters of the citizens were denied the right to vote, and in Holland a property qualification was still in force, although it was reduced from ten florins to one in 1896; Belgium introduced a system of plural voting in 1893, whereby supplementary voting rights were granted to heads of families, citizens owning property worth 2,000 francs or providing an income of 100 francs, and those who had reached a certain level of education. But the proportion of voters to the population as a whole remained generally low: in France, 26·6 per cent (1898), in Belgium, 22 per cent (1900), in Holland, 11·9 per cent (1900), in Norway, 18·6 per cent (1900) and, in Sweden, 7·4 per cent (1902).

The bicameral system was in operation everywhere, but this system was always tempered by the extensive powers of the upper Chamber, drawn from a much narrower sector of the population than the lower Chamber, and also by the influence—considerable but highly variable—that still remained in the hands of the head of state.

The parliamentary system was as yet securely established only in a small number of nations: in Norway since 1880, in Denmark since 1901, and in Great Britain—a model admired by liberals everywhere, where the queen always chose as her Prime Minister the leader of the majority party. The system was less successful in France, where the large number of parties engendered instability in the government, and also in Holland, where religious and political allegiances gave rise to a variety of coalitions.

But alongside the old aristocracy which, with the exception of Norway, remained extremely influential, especially in the upper Chamber and at Court—in Belgium and Holland, in Sweden particularly and even in Great Britain—it was the bourgeoisie that governed, sustained by the clergy and the peasant masses who made up the greater part of the population, except in Great Britain. Representation was still wholly in the hands of the ruling class: in Great Britain, there were only two Labour members elected to the House of Commons in 1900; in France, it was only with the left-wing election of 1902 that 57 members of the *petite bourgeoisie* and of the working class were elected, and they made up

513

less than 10 per cent of the deputies; in Sweden, a lawyer became a minister, for the first time, in 1905.

The working class itself, numerically small and with its structure imperfectly delineated, remained in isolation. The trade union movement had its earliest and most important period of development in Great Britain, whereas its organisation was hampered in France by the memory of the Commune. The number of union members in Great Britain had grown from 500,000 in 1885 to 1,250,000 in 1900, but in France the *Confédération Générale du Travail* (C.G.T.) had only 121,000 members in 1902, when it merged with the *Fédération des Bourses du Travail*. On the other hand, French socialism was very active, although the movement was still divided into *Guesdistes*, who rallied to the banner of Marxism, and reformists. In Great Britain it was not until February 1900 that 129 representatives of the trade unions, the Social Democratic Federation (S.D.F.) (the only specifically Marxist organisation), the Independent Labour Party, and the Fabian Society, formed the Labour Representation Committee, which was given the responsibility of creating an autonomous group, wholly distinct from the other parties, to be known henceforth simply as the Labour party.

GOVERNMENT BY THE LIBERAL BOURGEOISIE 1900–1914

During the first years of the century, political rather than social problems prevailed. Political democracy could only be brought about by the granting of universal suffrage, by fortifying the parliamentary régime and by the transfer of power wholly into the hands of the middle class. It was over principles such as these that the two sections of the ruling class did battle—the conservative elements and the liberal elements, however they called themselves (the Liberal party in Great Britain and Belgium, the Radical party in France). The Liberals were supported by the working-class parties (Labour and Socialist), which were as yet of insufficient size to do more than assist in the struggle. With the gradual fulfilling of the Liberal programme and the resolving of fundamental problems of a political character, the nature of the collaboration between the Liberals and the Socialists was to become more and more uneasy. The Socialists, having grown impatient of promises and rights devoid of any concrete value, soon demanded structural reforms which their erstwhile allies were to refuse.

In 1899 a particularly serious crisis, the Dreyfus affair, had shaken France. The Republic had seen the army, the church and all those who sought a return to the past rise against her, and attack her with far greater violence than ever they had in the days of *Boulangisme*. The republicans, from the progressives—now become the *Alliance Démocratique*—to the Socialists, joined forces to support the Government for the Defence of the

Republic formed by Waldeck-Rousseau, which included, standing symbolically shoulder to shoulder, a Socialist, A. Millerand, and General de Gallifet, one of the *sabreurs* from the days of the Commune. The successive governments of Waldeck-Rousseau and Combes took five and a half years to settle the Dreyfus affair completely, for they had to purge the army high command, arrest and try the leading nationalists and, above all, reduce the influence of the church, a body of great conservatism which, at every period of crisis, had mobilised its members into supporting the anti-republican right-wing parties, in order to combat 'l'Ecole sans Dieu' and the 'faux dogmes' of 1789. The purpose of the Act of 1901 was to suppress the more compromised sections of the church ('les moines ligueurs' and 'les moines d'affaires') and to keep the others under the surveillance of the state. The rigorous application of this Act by Combes, who succeeded in getting the two Chambers to reject most of the requests of authorisation that came before them, gave rise to a dispute with the Vatican and the breaking off of diplomatic relations, and to the separation of church and state in December 1905. These measures were undertaken in an atmosphere akin to civil war, fostered by nationalist demonstrations each time an 'inventory' of the possessions of the church was drawn up or religious communities who resisted the enforcement of the Act were expelled.

The union of moderates from the Left Centre, the Left and the Socialists was consolidated by the *Délégation des gauches*, made up of representatives of all groups, who joined forces to take decisions of common importance, and which benefited from the dazzling eloquence of Jean Jaurès. Some moderates were, however, fearful of the recent turn of events and, by 1906, with the advent of the Clemenceau government, the disintegration of the coalition was already under way, the Socialists having passed a vote of censure on the brutal suppression of strikes in northern France.

During this period the two principal left-wing groups organised themselves finally into Radicals and Socialists. The 'Radical and Radical Socialist party', formed in 1901, was to be the dominant political party in France until 1940, with members in every government providing them with a *Président du Conseil* or taking over at least one of the key ministries dealing with internal affairs—the ministries of Education, of the Interior or of Agriculture. Representing the middle class and the *petite bourgeoisie* of the provinces, it stood for 'ordre' and for greater economies; whilst hostile to the wealthy upper class, it was antagonistic to the claims of the urban working class; it was conservative, chauvinistic, and distrustful of socialism, which was now becoming stronger. At its 1904 Congress, held in Toulouse, it proclaimed itself the 'parti du juste milieu', and in favour of private property. The representatives of the various socialist tendencies— *Guesdistes*, *Blanquistes* and Reformists in favour of participation in the government—were brought together by a Congress of Unity held in 1905.

They proclaimed their support for the decisions of the Amsterdam International of 1904, which had condemned reformism and participation in government, and became the Socialist party (S.F.I.O., *Section Française de l'Internationale Ouvrière*). Economic difficulties and the intellectual prestige of Jaurès consolidated its success: from 35,000 in 1905 its membership grew to 72,000 in 1914, and the number of votes gained leapt from 830,000 (with 51 candidates elected) in the 1906 election, to 1,400,000 (with 103 elected) in the 1914 election.

The unifying of the trade unions took place in 1902, with the C.G.T., which, through its general secretary, Griffuelhes, accorded its full support to a programme of revolutionary trade-unionism hostile to capitalism and state control, and favourable to direct action, acts of sabotage and strikes as a prelude to a general strike. Its complete political independence was proclaimed at the Congress held in Amiens in 1906. However, only 830,000 workers out of almost 7,500,000 wage-earners were trade union members, and only 300,000 had joined the C.G.T. French trade-unionism was thus a very different movement from its British counterpart; a minority group without any openly avowed connection with the working-class party, it drew its inspiration from a Marxist programme of class struggle and violent revolution. This hardening of attitude was the result of an uneasiness born of their disappointment with the left-wing coalition government—the *Bloc des Gauches*—with its meagre record of social reform; in 1904, military service had been reduced to two years, but exemptions had been abolished, and the length of the working day had been set at ten hours—in mixed establishments only. The demands of the workers had come up against a barrier of social conservatism erected by the Radicals. The government of Clemenceau had replied to working-class unrest and strikes by forbidding a demonstration on 1 May 1906 in favour of the eight-hour day, and by brutal, even bloody, repression, using the police and, against the miners of Courrières, the military. This repression, directed against electricians, building workers, dockers (1907) and construction workers (1908), culminated in legal measures to prevent the forming of trade unions by state employees—primary school teachers who had joined the C.G.T. and postal workers who struck in 1909. Serious disturbances also occurred in the south of France, where vine-growers complained of a slump in the wine market, mayors and municipal councillors resigned, crowds rioted, the sub-prefecture at Narbonne was burnt down, and there was a mutiny in the ranks of the 17th Infantry Regiment, which was recruited locally.

The 1906 election was a triumph for the coalition because of the application of the principle of 'republican discipline', whereby left-wing voters, there being no candidate with an absolute majority, voted at the second ballot for the left-wing candidate who had won the greatest number of votes. The left-wing coalition secured a majority, with 325 seats, whereas the right-wing parties were reduced to 174 seats; the 90 moderates of the Centre Left, whose co-operation had hitherto been necessary to form a majority, went over to the Centre Right. But unrest in the working class and amongst the lesser state employees was a source of concern for the bourgeoisie, and repressive policies further separated them from the Radical party. Conflict between the Socialists and the Radicals increased over other questions—the policy of an alliance with tsarist Russia (at that time repressing revolution with cruelty), the policy of hostility towards Germany, as advocated by Delcassé, the colonial policy which caused Jaurès to denounce the Moroccan undertakings of the 'parti colonial', just as, some years later, he was to support the policy of Caillaux which was aimed at easing the international situation after the Agadir incident. Not only the Right, but also a large section of the Radicals, disagreed with the Socialists on all these questions: they were concerned by the anti-military, pacifist propaganda of the trade-unionists, and by excessively frequent strikes. Moreover, it was feared that the greatly increased military and naval estimates, the expenses incurred through the voting of workers' pensions in 1909, the development of primary education and the purchase of the Ouest railway system would make it necessary to have recourse to the income tax proposed by Caillaux. Aided by nationalist propaganda which international tension further stimulated, the regrouping of the parties was now under way. With the lining up of the Entente Cordiale against the Triple Alliance, with Wilhelm II's initiatives in Morocco, with the humiliating dismissal of Delcassé in 1906, and the Agadir incident in 1911, there was a reawakening of nationalism strongly influenced by Catholicism, at a time when the latter was being firmly drawn towards the principle of integration with the state. The Right was given to a clamorous cult of Joan of Arc, beatified by Pope Pius X, to extolling the colonial work done by Marshal Lyautey, known not to be fond of the Republic, to titillating the chauvinistic and jingoistic patriotism of the *petite bourgeoisie*. The rupture came in 1910 when Briand broke a railway strike by calling up the men into military service and obtained a vote of confidence from a majority of Radicals, members of the Centre and of the Right. This new anti-Socialist majority was fully revealed when men of the Centre Left were appointed to three of the four most important posts of the régime—Paul Deschanel becoming President of the Chamber of Deputies, Raymond Poincaré President of the Republic, and Louis Barthou *Président du Conseil*; it was this same majority that voted the law extending the period of military service to three years.

With its unity re-formed, the Left was victorious in the 1914 election: on a platform of rejection of the three-year law and of opposition to 'the folly of armament', 300 left-wing candidates were elected, including 130 S.F.I.O. Socialists, as against 120 right-wing candidates. There was nevertheless a majority in favour of maintaining the three-year law.

Although no previous assembly had ever comprised such a large number of left-wing deputies, the slide to the right was undeniable since the Radical bourgeoisie now turned its back on its former allies, who, in its opinion, were calling for reforms that were likely to endanger the country, property, security and order.

Political evolution in the Scandinavian countries also worked towards a democratisation of institutions and the progress of the social-democratic parties. It was the least rapid in Sweden, owing to the greater influence of the aristocracy and monarchy there. Nevertheless, from 1906 on, the Right was, step by step, eliminated, and the Liberal party, created in 1901, finally secured a majority in the Lower Chamber. In 1907, electoral reform reduced the property qualifications for the Upper Chamber and limited plural voting; the size of the electorate was doubled and, by 1914, the Social Democrats had become the chief party in the country. The king had not yet fully accepted a parliamentary régime, however; on 6 February 1914, during a demonstration by 30,000 nationalist peasants, he openly declared himself in opposition to the Liberal government of Staaff, and forced it to resign. In Denmark from 1906 the left-wing opposition gained strength; the government of the Radical leader, Zahle, was brought to power by the peasantry, hostile to the great landowners, and by the Social Democratic party.

Democratic reform went deeper in Norway. It had been impeded by the struggle for independence which culminated, in June 1905, in the dissolution of the union with Sweden and in the creation of a constitutional monarchy confirmed by referendum. Henceforth the Liberal party was divided into two sections, the more progressive of which, the Venstre, joined forces with the Social Democratic party and formed the government from 1908 to 1919, except for the period 1909–12. Progressive legislation concerning the use of natural resources and foreign investment was passed. It was also in Norway that the powers of the monarchy were most reduced; the right of sanction in constitutional matters was suppressed in 1913, the coronation and consecration ceremonies having been abolished in 1908.

In Holland, where power remained in the hands of the three denominational parties, it was not until 1913 that the Liberal coalition and the Social Democrats obtained a majority in the Upper Chamber (55 seats out of 100) and introduced universal suffrage. The struggle was even harder in Belgium, where the Liberals, exasperated by the domination of the church, allied with the Socialists; their coalition succeeded in 1908 in forcing their opponents to consent to compulsory military service (previously a system of selection by drawing lots had been in operation, with facilities for substitution) and, in 1914, to compulsory primary education. There was much working-class unrest from 1906 on, and strikes were brutally broken. As elsewhere, this unrest split the Liberal party, some of whose members took fright: it took the shock of war to clear the final obstacles to the adoption of the eight-hour day and votes for women.

In Great Britain the election of 1906 was the signal for decisive changes. The electoral success of the Conservatives over the divided Liberals and the infant Labour movement in 1900, and the noisy celebrations of imperialist victory in the South African War, did not prevent anxiety over the economic situation from growing. Competition from Germany and the United States, and the protectionist policy of all the major powers, created many difficulties for British industry. As early as 1903 Joseph Chamberlain had proposed the adoption of an imperial preference system, which was to be the basis of a future imperial federation. Conservative opinion was split; many industrialists, chiefly Lancashire exporters, were hostile to this leap into the unknown. The Liberals were supported by the Trades Union Congress (T.U.C.), itself favourable to Free Trade, and by the Nonconformists, who were dissatisfied with the 1902 Education Act; in 1905 Balfour resigned. Campbell-Bannerman, a Liberal moderate, formed a cabinet of Liberal imperialists and Gladstonian radicals, including the trade-unionist John Burns, and won an overwhelming victory in January 1906; the Liberal party, out of power for ten years, won 399 seats, the Unionists (of whom two-thirds were Tariff Reformers) 157, Irish Nationalists 83 and Labour candidates 29.

The new government abandoned the imperialist policy, and passed the Trade Disputes Act in 1906, quashing the Taff Vale decision of 1901 which had threatened trade union funds. Campbell-Bannerman died in 1908 and was replaced by Asquith, with Lloyd George as Chancellor of the Exchequer. Many reforms were carried out: the reform of the army by Haldane, of the navy by Lord Fisher, the Old Age Pensions Act, awarding a weekly pension of 5 shillings to those over 70, and the voting of an eight-hour day in the coal mines. Above all, there were tax reforms to finance these measures, but which seemed to many people designed to produce a redistribution of wealth. The 1909 budget was aimed chiefly at the rich; it reduced income tax for heads of families, but levied a special tax on petrol and motor vehicles, and a duty of 20 per cent on the unearned increase in the value of land whenever it changed hands. The House of Lords rejected it. Two general elections were needed to secure these reforms and, at the same time, to take a decisive step forward towards democratisation by reducing the power of the Lords.

The conflict between the Liberals and the Lords was similar to the one that had existed in France for a century and which had attained a degree of unheard of violence in the course of the Dreyfus affair. For the Liberal bourgeoisie, the Conservative Lords had all the disdain of ancient noble families; for the numerous little men in the Liberal and Labour ranks— Lloyd George himself was the son of a schoolmaster and had been brought up by his uncle, a shoemaker—and for the newly rich middle class, they had nothing but contempt. They had undertaken a policy of systematic opposition to the Liberal projects. Lloyd George's defence of the budget was vigorous, and succeeded in making the Lords look odious and ridiculous. In January 1910 275 Liberal candidates were elected as against 273 Unionists, with 40 Labour members and 82 Irish Nationalists. The problems raised by the budget were thus resolved, but battle continued in the constitutional field: it was imperative to specify—and to limit—the powers of the Lords. The breakdown of George V's attempts at conciliation led to a further election, with another defeat for the Conservatives and the passing of the Parliament Bill, after the threat of creating a number of Liberal peers. The duration of the Lords' veto was reduced to two years, but, by way of compensation, the maximum life of a parliament was reduced from seven to five years.

These victories were made possible because the Labour party and the Irish members always voted with the Liberals, who in their turn could remain in power only by retaining this support. The alliance had therefore more solid foundations than its French counterpart; although soon to be imperilled, it was not yet broken. Great Britain now passed through a period of intense social discontent. The working class complained that it did not share in the general prosperity, with wages standing still and purchasing power diminishing. To these economic factors was added a feeling of growing frustration amongst the workers, who condemned their representatives for their feebleness and for following too closely in the wake of the Liberals, as, for example, when the latter refused to quash the Osborne judgement upheld by the Lords in 1909 (which jeopardised the trade unions' political levy); or again, when it was realised that the National Insurance Act of 1911, inspired by Bismarck's legislation for the working class, was to be financed not by the Treasury but in part by the workers themselves. It was therefore not surprising that the influence of syndicalism which dominated the French C.G.T. should have affected the British movement, as did that of the I.W.W. (Industrial Workers of the World) which was also favourable to strikes, boycott, the use of violence and a general strike. The Marxist tendencies of the small Socialist Labour party penetrated the ranks of the Labour party, and numerous tracts and pamphlets were issued denouncing the timorous and illusory policies of the Labour leaders and calling for direct action. The *Daily Herald*, which first appeared in 1912 and which George Lansbury edited from 1913, spoke in favour of energetic action and condemned the Liberal alliance. There followed a number of strikes in 1911, 1912 and 1913 among miners, railway workers, cotton textile operatives, seamen, dockers and naval dockyard workers, and the military was called in on Merseyside and in South Wales with, at times, resulting bloodshed. On the eve of the war, the Triple Alliance of miners, railwaymen and transport workers foreshadowed a general strike.

In another domain, the Liberals' obstinate refusal of votes for women exasperated the small groups of suffragettes, who now turned more frequently to demonstrations and violence. Furthermore, the serious nature of the Irish problem and the threat of civil war in Ulster halted social legislation and weakened the Liberals and their majority.

The Conservatives, like their French counterparts, were in fact far from resigned to their defeat. Beaten over their home policy in 1910, they now laid stress on imperialism and nationalism: supporters of the empire and the monarchy, they opposed the introduction of Home Rule in Ireland which was to come into effect in 1914, and they encouraged Sir Edward Carson to form an army of Ulster volunteers determined to resist it by force. This threatening move resulted in the creation of the Irish Volunteers, and the threat of civil war loomed nearer, aggravated by a mutiny of officers of a section of the British troops stationed in Ireland in March 1914.

Although the Liberal government carried forward its programme of social legislation (labour exchanges, 1909, health insurance and a limited scheme of unemployment insurance, 1911), the gap could only widen between the Liberals and the Labour supporters. The efforts of Liberal reformers who sought in no way to alter the existing social order were incapable of providing effective solutions to the political and social problems now being raised. The party that had been triumphant in 1906 began to fall into decline.

THE FIRST WORLD WAR AND ITS IMMEDIATE CONSEQUENCES
1914–1921

The outbreak of war in 1914 forced all the belligerent governments to settle a number of unforeseen problems. As for the neutrals, their day-to-day activities were also upset by the cataclysm, which spared them to a partial degree only; they too had to improvise solutions to the problems that now confronted them.

In the countries at war, a '*union sacrée*' was spontaneously set up. In France, there was a party truce, in spite of the assassination of Jaurès by a disciple of the *Action Française*. Strikes ended everywhere. Agitation by the suffragettes and the Irish came to an end in Great Britain, and even the most confirmed pacifists, such as Ramsay MacDonald, voiced their support for the recruiting campaign of September 1914. In France a government of National Unity was set up by René Viviani, which included Jules Guesdes, a Marxist Socialist, and Albert de Mun, a Conservative deputy. In Great Britain, Asquith formed a coalition government in May 1915, comprising 12 Liberals and 8 Conservatives, with Arthur Henderson of the Labour party and Lord Kitchener, War Secretary since the outbreak of war.

The violation of Belgian neutrality gave rise to widespread indignation, as did the reports—grossly exaggerated—of German atrocities in Belgium: added to this was the feeling of fighting for a right that had been violated. A wave of self-righteous patriotism and nationalist demonstrations of the most elementary sort swamped all spirit of lucid analysis. Resistance came from men like Romain Rolland, a few rare Socialists and Labour supporters, socialist trade-unionists on the Clyde and in South Wales, and the federation of metal workers in France.

Unanimity was, however, soon to disappear; as the war dragged on, the old differences came to the fore again. Reports from the front quickly showed up the scarcity and misuse of arms and munitions, the waste of human lives and material, and the arbitrariness of military leaders endowed with extensive powers and beyond governmental control. The murderous and ineffective offensives launched by General Joffre, and his absurd 'gnawing' tactics throughout 1915, earned him the most severe criticism both from the combatants themselves and from their representatives in the two parliaments. The Ministers of War, Messimy in 1914, Galliéni in 1915 and Lyautey in 1917, all complained of the encroachment of the High Command and of its resistance to any sort of control. In Great Britain, the campaign in the Dardanelles caused Admiral Fisher and its instigator, Winston Churchill, to resign, and the introduction of conscription in January 1916 brought opposition from Labour representatives and a number of Liberals. Criticism of the shortage of munitions and of the weakness of the governments resulted in the creation of the posts of Minister of Munitions, and brought to power men determined to conduct the war with ferocious energy: Lloyd George in December 1916 and Georges Clemenceau in November 1917. Power was thus concentrated in the hands of a few men: the War Cabinet, with five members (which became the Imperial War Cabinet in May 1917, with the addition of General Smuts and other Dominion representatives), and the *Cabinet de Guerre*, created towards the end of 1917, and comprising the *Président du Conseil*, and the Ministers of War, of the Navy, of Munitions and of Finance.

Veritable war-dictatorships were set up everywhere, for decisions had to be taken outside the parliaments, which were called upon to ratify them after the event. The Defence of the Realm Acts (D.O.R.A.), passed in 1914, placed all powers in the hands of the government in matters concerning the armed forces and the civilian population, including the power to detain people without trial. In France the same powers were conferred on the government by declaring a state of emergency. The necessity for secrecy in matters concerning military operations led to the extension of censorship of the press and of mail; it was held to be detrimental to national defence and the morale of the combatants to criticise the government's decisions, the behaviour of civil servants, profiteers and those who shirked at home. The press, particularly that of the left wing and of the opposition, such as *L'Homme Libre*—Clemenceau's *L'Homme Enchaîné*—was constantly having articles blacked out. These abuses, which were especially flagrant in France, were much fewer in Great Britain, where there was greater respect for the traditional defence of the rights of the individual.

Concessions were, however, wrested from the governments. In France, the two Chambers met in secret committees to hear reports that could not be made public, and control over the army was effected by 'députés en mission de contrôle'. The fact that the Cabinet was almost completely reshuffled seven times between 1914 and 1918—only once (the fall of Painlevé and his replacement by Clemenceau) was this caused by an unfavourable vote in the Chambers—bore witness to the gravity of the situation. Similarly in Great Britain, a coalition government was formed by Lloyd George as a result of revolt against Asquith's alleged indolence, which the Conservative leaders Bonar Law and Carson fostered, and which *The Times* helped on.

State surveillance was extended to many unexpected fields: agricultural and industrial production, transport, employers' profits, employees' wages, the length of the working day and disputes between employers and workers. Public administration was considerably extended; in Great Britain the Civil Service was doubled between 1914 and 1923, and new ministries were created—Munitions, Food, Pensions, Labour and Blockade in 1917, Air and Reconstruction in 1918. France witnessed the creation of undersecretaries or secretaries of state for Munitions, Food, Health, Military Aviation, Military Justice and the study of inventions of military importance.

Once again, social problems took on their former urgency. In 1915 trade union leaders relinquished the right to strike in exchange for the setting up of a national consultative committee and the appointment in every factory of works representatives. Similarly, in France, Albert Thomas, the Minister of Munitions, created workers' representative committees in factories concerned with the war effort. A labour force had to be found for these factories, entailing 'dilution' in Great Britain— the use of non-skilled labour—which resulted in protests, although the trade unions finally gave way. The Munitions of War Act banned strikes and instituted compulsory arbitration and powers to move a worker from one factory to another; it also prevented workers from leaving their jobs without a leaving certificate (abolished in 1917) and this, coupled with the rising cost of living (33 per cent from August 1914 to July 1915), caused the first major strike of the war, in the Clydeside area (February 1915), followed by the South Wales miners in July. The institution of shop stewards followed and soon spread—men chosen from the works floor, whose influence counterbalanced that of the trade union leaders, who were often suspected of collaborating with the government.

Thus, from 1916 on, the working-class movement revived. There was new interest in the International, which was divided into those for and those against the resumption of relations between the Socialist parties of the countries at war (in December 1916 the majority of members at the national congress of the S.F.I.O. had been in favour of this). The movement was also divided over the questions of participation at the Zimmerwald congress of 1915 and the Kienthal congress of 1916, the 'aims of war' and the Russian revolution. The Bolshevist programme of 'peace without annexations and indemnities' met with much favour amongst a large number of Socialists and Labour supporters. After visiting Russia with the French delegates Cachin and Frossart, Arthur Henderson, a member of the Labour party, declared that Britain should support the proposed conference of international socialists in Stockholm; this was approved by 1,840,000 votes against 550,000 at the conference of the Labour party held on 10 August 1917. But the issue of passports for Stockholm was withheld, and this caused Henderson to leave the War Cabinet. At the same period, strikes broke out in France, where, in May and June 1917, 71 industries were affected by strikes in St Etienne and Paris. And, behind the front lines at Le Chemin des Dames, the army, decimated and discouraged by the failure of Nivelle's murderous offensive of 16 April, mutinied. At the front itself, and behind the lines, weariness at a war that dragged on with no hope of a victory was felt everywhere. Clemenceau assumed the mantle of a veritable dictator, instigating the prosecution of businessmen and Radical and Socialist politicians—such as Malvy, the Minister of the Interior, and Joseph Caillaux—who were accused of defeatism or of relations with the enemy. He thus silenced every criticism of the war and of the total mobilisation of the country's resources to counter the German offensives in the spring and summer of 1918.

When the end came, the elation produced by victory and peace, and the illusion that it had been 'the war to end wars', were not enough to wipe out the memory of often useless losses, the ruin and the suffering of those four years. Bitterness and anger mingled with joy and relief, and a deep desire for change—a reaction against the uncontrolled discipline imposed by civil and military authorities—was encouraged by the example of the Russian revolution, which exalted the hopes of all those who had suffered so grievously and who were sickened at the sight of so many profiteers. Councils of soldiers were reported in Egypt in 1919. In Britain there were demonstrations among the troops over delays in demobilisation; during a riot in Glasgow the red flag was hoisted and several people were injured; there were strikes in the Yorkshire mines, the London Underground, and finally a general railway strike in 1919. In Ireland, after the Easter Monday rising in 1916, rebellion had spread and was, by now, a full-scale war. The time of 'the troubles' had started. In France, too, strikes broke out, and the violent protests against the continuance of the war, now being waged against Russia, caused a mutiny amongst several units of the Black Sea fleet.

Governments in England, France, Belgium, were thus forced to make concessions in order to deflate these dangerous popular movements. In France, the eight-hour day was made law (1919). In England Lloyd George, armed with unparalleled prestige conferred upon him by victory, very cleverly called for an early election. The Liberal party was now split into Asquithian Liberals, who never forgave Lloyd George for his questionable loyalty in 1916, and those who remained faithful to him. Threatened with isolation between Conservatives and Labour, now determined to fight alone, Lloyd George accepted an alliance with the former. There followed the 'coupon election' in which all the friendly candidates received a letter of endorsement signed by Lloyd George and Bonar Law. The coalition won 478 seats (335 going to the Conservatives), as against 28 for the Asquithian Liberals and 59 for the Labour candidates, who now represented the official opposition. Menaced by splintering as far back as 1914, the Liberal party was now ruined; these elections ushered in a period of twenty years of almost continuous Conservative hegemony.

However, under the direction of the 'Welsh Wizard' the coalition remained in power until October 1922. The Housing and Town Planning Act was passed in 1919, giving housing subsidies to local authorities, the University Grants Committee was set up, and, in 1920, the Unemployment Insurance Act was passed to overcome the problem of unemployment. In 1921 the one hundred and twenty railway companies were merged into four, and in 1922 the British Broadcasting Company was formed, with a broadcasting monopoly. But the economy committee under Sir Eric Geddes recommended economies that undermined part of Fisher's Education Act of 1918. The nationalisation of the coal industry demanded by the miners was rejected, though endorsed by a majority of the Sankey Commission. In Ireland, a vicious war composed of ambushes, the arresting of hostages, torture, and summary executions, in which Irish terrorists matched the Black and Tans (the British special police, one of whose exploits was setting fire to Cork), came to an end with the recognition of the Irish Free State as an autonomous unit within the Empire, with the exception of the six counties of Ulster (ch. XIII). This measure, which dissatisfied the Conservatives, contributed to the break-up of the coalition.

The return to political life was more slowly effected in France, with the election in November 1919 of a 'Chambre bleue-horizon' comparable to the post-war House of Commons in Britain. A new electoral arrangement, a compromise between the majority system and that of proportional representation, instituted the system of list voting on a departmental basis, the premium going to the majority candidate and the remainder of votes being shared proportionally. This resulted in a coalition of the Centre and Centre Right, the *Bloc National Républicain*, with 437 seats out of 613, the opposition consisting only of 68 Socialists and 88 Radicals. It was the most right-wing Chamber in France since 1876. Although Clemenceau had already crushed strikes caused by the rapid and sharp rise in the cost of living amongst workers in Paris (on 1 May), miners in the north, weavers in Rouen, railway and Métro workers, the victorious Right could not forgive him for having voted the eight-hour day and legal status for collective agreements, or for his anti-clericalism. In January 1920, he was passed over, as candidate for the Presidency of the Republic, in favour of Paul Deschanel, the moderate president of the Chamber of Deputies.

Belgium, which had been invaded, saw its wholly Catholic government move to Saint Adresse near Le Havre and become, by the addition of a few Liberals and Socialists, a government of National Unity. The occupied territory was administered by the Germans, who aggravated the disharmony between the two linguistic groups—Flemish and Walloon—by favouring the former; a Flemish university was created in Ghent, and a *Raad van Vlanderen* set up, which entailed the separation, administratively, of the two parts of the country. After the armistice, Albert I formed a government around a tripartite union—6 Catholics, 3 Socialists and 3 Liberals—and promised universal suffrage, trade union liberties, linguistic equality and the alliance of capital and labour. The election of November 1919—with suffrage extended to all the adult male population —resulted in an anti-clerical majority for the first time: 30 Liberals and 70 Socialists against 73 Catholics. Consequently, local electoral rights were extended to women in 1921 and the Catholics received, by way of compensation, an agreement on equal subsidies for state and private schools; liberty of association was conceded, as were old age pensions, the suppression of obstacles to the right to strike, and the eight-hour day.

The other countries of north-west Europe remained neutral. Although they doubtless profited considerably from providing Germany with raw materials and foodstuffs, they suffered as a result of submarine warfare, inflation and rising prices. They were forced to operate a policy of governmental intervention in order to regulate food supplies and prices by a complex system of distribution. They too found it necessary to censor the press in order to prevent newspapers from expressing support too overtly for one side or the other. All these measures dissatisfied public opinion, and it was again felt necessary to yield to popular pressure; thus Denmark introduced the eight-hour day, revised the constitution and extended suffrage to women at the age of 25. In Sweden, the Hammarsköld Cabinet, notoriously pro-German, was forced to resign in 1917, and was replaced by a coalition of Liberals and Social Democrats led by Hjalmar Branting—the first European government, outside France, to include Socialists. In Norway the introduction of proportional representation in 1919 ended representational inequality, which had been considerable, and proved favourable to the Social Democrats. Holland also adopted universal suffrage (as did Luxemburg in 1919) and the eight-hour day.

On all sides, universal suffrage reduced the role of the Liberal bourgeoisie to that of a make-weight or an arbiter (in Holland, Sweden and Great Britain) and encouraged the development of the popular parties (in Holland and Belgium). Where the Liberals did retain some of their importance, it was because they had taken over the role of the Conservatives. Wherever the parliamentary régime was firmly established, the rights of veto and dissolution fell into disuse, except in those cases where the latter was used to find a way out of an inextricable situation or to hasten the advent of urgent reforms. The only example of such a conflict was the case of the highly pro-German grand duchess of Luxemburg, who was forced to abdicate in 1919 and was replaced by her sister; and, with the referendum of 18 September 1919, the solution applied conformed in every way to the democratic principle.

THE INTER-WAR YEARS 1921–1939

When the peace treaties came into effect, serious problems faced the countries that had been at war. Great Britain had not been invaded, but she had suffered heavy losses of human life and materials, and she too had her 'devastated areas': industry which needed to be reconverted and re-equipped, the fleet to be rebuilt, former markets to be won back, American and Japanese (and before long German) competition to be faced; the national debt was very heavy, and the balance of payments was threatened. Exports had to be redeveloped and the pound restored to its old supremacy, for this had formerly been the condition of her prosperity.

In France the terrible bloodshed of the war had cost 1,750,000 lives, and the birth-rate fell below that of 1913; the ruins remained to be built upon, but the country's debts were made worse by having to pay for war damage and for pensions to war victims of all categories. The international situation was sombre. France and, to a lesser extent, Britain assumed an attitude of resolute hostility towards Russia, whose revolutionary propaganda they feared. Germany was also the subject of their distrust, all the more so since she seemed to be trying by all possible means to evade the restrictions of the Versailles 'Diktat'. France, particularly sensitive on this question, insisted on strict compliance with the terms of the treaty, with a narrow-minded adherence to the letter of the law symbolised by Poincaré. She contracted a series of onerous alliances with some central and eastern European countries and, at the same time, re-equipped and maintained the army at great expense.

Economic and social problems thus became the chief preoccupation of the government. Because of their technical character and urgency, parliamentary machinery produced only a meagre yield; decisions were made too late, or at the wrong time, and this resulted in disquieting stagnation which individualist political philosophy, of the sort that had made nineteenth-century Liberals see the state as the natural enemy of public liberty, did nothing to remedy. State intervention was looked upon with disfavour. But the industrialisation of society brought with it restrictions which were incompatible with certain liberties hitherto considered as essential and inalienable. The resultant crisis amongst Liberals became increasingly aggravated.

This crisis was accompanied by a transformation of the classes of society and of the balance of power between them. The working class, or rather the wage-earning class, grew in size and in importance. Although they remained in the minority, workers' organisations now became mass movements: in France the C.G.T. grew from 600,000 in 1914 to 2,000,000 in 1920; in Great Britain the Trades Union Congress, re-organised and now allied with Labour in a National Joint Committee, grew from representing 4,000,000 members in 1915 to 6,500,000 in 1919, and to 8,300,000 in 1920. The S.F.I.O. obtained 1,700,000 votes at the 1919 election (300,000 more than in 1914) and, in Britain, the Labour party flourished, reunified by Arthur Henderson and Sidney Webb, with its former structure reinforced by the creation of local branches. This laid a solid basis for expansion, supporting the programme of moderate democratic socialism drawn up by Webb, *Labour and the New Social Order*, which urged the planning of production and distribution. But, although the wind appeared to be in its favour, the working class was in fact irresolute and divided. The wave of enthusiasm caused in 1917 by the Russian revolution stimulated the left wing of the Labour party into hostility towards the policy of intervention in Russia; workers refused to load munitions bound for Danzig in 1920, and committees of action were set up to implement the slogan 'Hands off Russia'. But this unity went no further, for the direct action that the Communists were calling for was repugnant to the majority; and so the Communist party of Great Britain was founded in July 1920. Although it continued to influence intellectuals and certain trade unions in a very real way, it was to gain only scant success. In France the failure of the strikes in 1919 and the lack of success at the election of 1920 were discouraging, and the hopes of a rapid national revolution were destroyed. Opposition to Bolshevists and Reformists led to a rift in the Socialist party at the Tours Congress in 1920; the majority declared its adherence to the Third International and in favour of re-taining Jaurès's admirable newspaper, *L'Humanité*, whereas the minority rallied to Léon Blum. In the trade union movement, the majority remained in the reformist C.G.T. under Léon Jouhaux, and the minority formed the *Confédération générale du Travail unitaire* (C.G.T.U.), connected with the Communist party. This division resulted in an all-round weakening—in 1925 the C.G.T. numbered 50,000 only, and the C.G.T.U. 400,000.

The workers in both countries were thus to receive only a small share of the profits from this period of prosperity and rising prices which far outstripped the nominal rise in wages. The situation was aggravated by unemployment in Britain, with 858,000 out of work in December 1920 and 1,664,000 in March 1921. By May 1921 the figure had reached 2,500,000; it dropped to 1,400,000 in 1922, but never fell to less than a million until 1939. In France working-class unrest became sporadic and intermittent, and finally died out in discouragement.

Faced with a working class that was isolated, split and frustrated, the bourgeoisie too underwent a transformation. The old hierarchy had been thrown into confusion; landlords and property owners, people with fixed incomes, state employees, private employees and workers were all affected by the rise in the cost of living. But inflation benefited producers, middlemen and debtors. Social inequality was as great as before the war, and the new industrial bourgeoisie, made rich by war and reconstruction, feared the growth of the working class and its claim to restrict the employers' authority on the factory floor—even when the working class's programme was as moderate as Labour's. The 'divine right of the employer' brought him close to the traditionally conservative powers—the church, the army, and the former aristocracy that his forefathers had fought in the nineteenth century. During the war a particularly active and powerful pressure group, the Federation of British Industries, had been formed in Britain; similarly in France the *Comité des Forges*, the *Comité Central des Houillères*, the *Union Générale des Industries Métallurgiques et Minières* and the *Comité Central des Assurances* were formed. They all, directly or indirectly, worked towards influencing the judiciary and the financiers, and bringing pressure to bear on the decisions of the government and of the assemblies, all the more so since the economic scope of the state had widened and state protection was now indispensable for so many problems. These groups influenced the press, the administrative cadres who were responsible for the implementation of government decisions, and the elections—the *Union des Intérêts Economiques* shared out subsidies from the employers amongst candidates, and in 1924 the Radical party received funds from the *Comité des Assurances*. They also worked through family connections, through the social relationships uniting members of the ruling class, which was now tending to merge with the former clerical, conservative upper-class society whose reactionary ideology it absorbed. A new Right was thus brought into being which was no longer either liberal or parliamentary, which supported the nationalism that only the *Action Française*, founded in 1908, had stood for before the war. Drunk with the victory of 1918, and with the fact that France was now the strongest military power on the continent, the new Right showed systematic hostility towards 'eternal Germany' and refused to make any concessions to her. With disdain for humanitarian principles (according to Maurras, nothing but 'moonshine' and alien to French Catholic tradition) and for the League of Nations, it called for an authoritarian régime, which it considered to be the only one capable of formulating a policy of strength and greatness, the implementation of which could be possible only if the nation were united by stern discipline that was respectful of the traditional social hierarchy. Thanks to the coherence of its theories, untiringly repeated by its editor-in-chief, Charles Maurras, and to the talents of the polemicist Léon Daudet, the *Action Française* was highly influential in Conservative and Catholic circles (or, at least, for the latter until it was condemned by Rome in 1926). Its hate-ridden propaganda against 'métèques' (dagoes), Jews, freemasons, Communists and Socialists, and against 'capitalisme anonyme', the brutality of its *Camelots du roi* at public meetings, and its systematic calumny finally created an atmosphere of contagious violence. Its pseudo-anticapitalism drew to its ranks members of the *petite bourgeoisie*, tradesmen whose number had increased and whose profit margins were dwindling, craftsmen and minor industrialists working with out-of-date and inefficient equipment, and feeling themselves threatened by large combines and competition from more advanced countries. Anxious for the future, these groups of men, unenlightened, simple-minded and chauvinistic, were very ready to fall back on violence as a solution. Mussolini's Fascist blackshirts, which the *Action Française* praised and set up as a model, were recruited from identical social groups. 1924 saw the appearance of the Patriotic Youth Movement, organised to fight against Communism, to offer armed opposition if need be; in 1925, a dissident member of the *Action Française*, G. Valois, created a blue-shirted Fascist splinter group, the *Faisceaux*. These groups, taking the behaviour of the Communist party as an excuse to revive the spectre of the threat of revolution, sought thus to justify their use of violence and to acquire the support—and the subscriptions—of the right-thinking section of the public.

This anti-liberal, anti-parliamentary ideology was fostered and spread by the press, which was mostly in the hands of 'moneyed power'; the five major dailies (the so-called newspapers), all the Paris evening papers and almost all the magazines voiced their more or less open support for nationalist and conservative policies.

Whilst the political struggle in France had to do with the régime itself and with the principles upon which it was founded, political conditions were different in Great Britain. The division into Conservative and Labour fairly represented different conceptions of the production and distribution of wealth, but neither of the two parties sought to question the fundamental principles of the régime. Furthermore, the basically conservative character of the British working class coupled to its great unwillingness to adopt Marxist theory and practice directed the party towards moderation and caused it to reject vigorously all attempts, collective or individual, at affiliation with the Communists. In France, on the contrary, the existence of a powerful revolutionary party made both the unification of the Left and the creation of a durable majority impossible, and served only to aggravate the fears of a bourgeoisie all too ready to turn to the extreme Right and to look forward to the coming of a 'Saviour'. But in Great Britain the upper class felt itself less in danger, and the aristocratic element continued to play an important part in the House of Commons, comprising perhaps 40 per cent of its members between the wars.

There were thus, in both France and Great Britain, two quite separate populations drawn up against each other; caught between them, Liberalism was doomed to disappear or to cease being itself. The drama of the Radical Socialist party in France was that of the Liberal party in Great Britain. Similarly, in Belgium, the Liberal party after 1920, having completed its programme, found itself tugged in separate directions by the doctrinaire patrician class of the bourgeoisie, senior Civil Servants and industrialists who viewed the clergy unfavourably, but who were also fearful of working-class unrest, and by groups of primary school teachers and members of the *petite bourgeoisie* who were very hostile to the 'priest party'. The latter were to join forces with the Socialist party, as did many left-wing Liberals who rallied to the Labour party, thereby strengthening the moderate elements in both parties, whilst the groups with right-wing tendencies moved further towards the Right.

The weakness of European currencies was at once the cause and the occasion of these transformations. Governments and public opinion, long since accustomed to monetary stability, were thrown into confusion by its disappearance. The machinery of exchange and of the balance of trade broke down, provoking a rise in nominal wages and in the cost of living; the result was worsening inflation, the fall of the franc compared to the pound, and the rise of the dollar over both, with a consequent run on the franc and a flight towards safe holdings. Because of this, the capitalist oligarchy was able to impose its will on the governments, using the fall in value of national moneys as a lever to oust those that proved intractable and to return orthodox governments to power.

In Great Britain, Bonar Law succeeded Lloyd George in October 1922, with 345 Conservatives in the majority, against two rival Liberal factions —60 with Asquith and 57 with Lloyd George—and 142 Labour members. This was the first time that the Labour party had won more seats than the combined Liberal groups. When the ailing Bonar Law made way for Stanley Baldwin in 1923, a new election on the issue of a protective tariff reversed the majority. There were now 258 Conservatives whereas the Liberals, unified in the defence of Free Trade, numbered 159 and the Labour members 191. A Labour government was thus formed under Ramsay MacDonald in January 1924—since Labour was the larger of the Free Trade groups—but being in the minority and dependent on the

Liberals it was not able to undertake any specifically Socialist legislation. It fell after nine months over a minor issue, and was replaced by the Conservatives in the general election of 1924. The election was a further debacle for the Liberals, who lost 116 seats and were now reduced to 42, and for the Labour party, who won only 152 seats, although the number of votes cast for them—one-third of all those recorded—had gone up. The Conservatives gained 161 seats and won in all 415. There could have been no greater proof of the irremediable decline of the Liberal party.

The Baldwin government remained in office for five years, and, jointly with Briand, carried out a pacificatory policy in Europe (the Locarno Pact). At the same time, the Chancellor of the Exchequer, Winston Churchill, now back in the Conservative fold, pursued a policy of deflation; the return to the Gold Standard in 1925 set the pound at its former value once more, but also caused a reduction in exports, raising their price on the world market. It was also a cause of the General Strike which broke out in 1926. The coal-mining industry had for a considerable time been the one most affected by the export crisis and unemployment. Frequent strikes bore witness to its state of chronic crisis. A national coal strike against a reduction of wages began on 30 April 1926. It was supported by the General Strike (3 May) in which workers in the transport, gas, electricity, printing, building and heavy industries came out in sympathy. It was a trial of strength, for the Conservative government, determined to break the strike, had long since made arrangements to keep public services working, protected by the police and the army. Public opinion proved to be hostile to the apparent attempt to bring pressure to bear on the elected government; the trade union leaders, many of whom had been dubious about the strike in the first place, capitulated on 12 May. Mine owners took advantage of their victory to worsen the living conditions of the miners, and in 1927 the government passed the Trade Disputes Act, which banned sympathetic strikes and altered the unions' political levy. Trade union membership fell, and the revolutionary tendencies within the T.U.C. lost ground. The government took a few steps to ease social tension, including legislation for widows' pensions and contributory old age pensions, and the reform of local government. In 1928 the principle of equal electoral rights for members of both sexes was enacted, making suffrage completely equal and universal.

In France, events followed a similar pattern. The Radical coalition under Herriot, like the Labour interlude under Ramsay MacDonald, interrupted a sequence of Conservative governments. In both countries there was opposition between similar groups of interests—those of the ruling class and those of the working class—and it was by a more or less similar process that a solution was sought. But the pattern of events was not identical. France had not experienced the open wound of permanent unemployment, nor such a serious crisis as that of 1926. On the other hand, in France the extreme Right was much more virulent, and the very active Communist party made for constant tension. Nevertheless, each time a left-wing government came to power, a financial crisis succeeded in toppling it. The technique was simple: since tax payments were unevenly spaced over the year, the governments were forced to ask for loans from private banks, from the Bank of France and the savings banks, which in turn demanded guarantees and concessions. Moreover, the floating debt held by the banks—ninety-one million Treasury bonds in 1924—was a powerful weapon, because of the constant threat that they might be presented for redemption.

The 1924 election replaced the *Bloc National* by the *Cartel des Gauches*, a coalition of Radicals and Socialists, the latter offering their support but not their participation to Herriot. They wished, by their union, to reintroduce the anti-clerical legislation that the *Bloc National* had pushed into the background; in this way, they provoked the Catholics into forming the National Catholic Federation, presided over by General de Castelnau and directed by elements of the extreme Right. Mass demonstrations were organised in which the faithful affirmed their determination to resist the application of new measures. Furthermore, the Locarno Pact and appeasement with Germany were strongly criticised by the nationalists, and eventually financial difficulties gave the Right the opportunity to overthrow the government. To face the burden of reconstruction costs and the national debt (swollen by pensions and interest on loans, which were further enlarged by an over-generous evaluation of war damages), the government introduced measures intended to make the situation more healthy, to put an end to the flight of capital and to tax evasion—the 'carnet de coupons' and the 'carte d'identité fiscale'.[1] The Socialists in their turn called for the enforced consolidation of Treasury bonds and a tax on capital. The confidence of holders of savings faded away; the value of the franc, quoted at 90 to the pound in December 1925, fell to 165 in May 1926 and to 240 in July. The threat of a Socialist deputy to 'prendre l'argent où il est' was made much of by the press. Herriot, who had succeeded in obtaining the indispensable loans from the Bank of France only by giving up his projected 'carnet de coupons', was forced to draw back before the 'Mur d'argent'. Even so, he was overthrown by the senate. From then on, bankers used the threat of a 'plebiscite' amongst the holders of short-term bonds as a form of blackmail. Within two years, 1924–6, six governments were to follow each other; and the Radical coalition finally splintered in July 1926. Raymond Poincaré then formed a government which gained the support of the bankers and

[1] The 'carnet de coupons' would have made it possible to keep a check on the encashment of stocks and shares by their holders, and the 'carte d'identité fiscale' would have served as a record for checking statements made in income tax returns.

stabilised the franc at a quarter of its 1914 value; the majority of Radicals, having broken with the Socialists, lent their support to a right-wing financial policy. The system of a double ballot was re-established for the election of 1928, which gave the victory to the Right, thanks to a volte-face by Radical electors who, giving up the principle of 'Republican discipline', voted at the second ballot for the Right or Centre Right candidate rather than the Socialist heading the list after the first ballot. It was thus the Right and the Centre Right that governed France between 1928 and 1932, firstly with Poincaré and Tardieu, then with Briand and Laval, two *grands bourgeois* and two former Socialists gone over to the Right.

From 1931 in France, but elsewhere from 1929, Europe was in the grip of a depression which, although widespread, was not equally severe throughout the continent. More particularly, its consequences were not everywhere equally serious from the political point of view, as may be seen from a consideration of one of the most characteristic features of European history at this period—the spread of fascism. The whole of eastern, central and southern Europe was to succumb to the infection, whereas the countries of north-western Europe were able to resist until 1940. For some of these states, however (Great Britain, the Scandinavian countries, Holland), the upsurge of fascism was merely episodic, like a bout of passing fever. But elsewhere, in France and Belgium, it was much more, and was to have consequences which continued to be felt long after 1940. These two groups of states may therefore conveniently be dealt with separately.

The world-wide economic depression which followed the Wall Street crash was particularly severe in Great Britain, where, for almost ten years, unemployment had involved never less than 10 per cent of the labour force. In November 1929 there were 1,326,000 out of work; the figure leapt to 2,500,000 in December 1930, and was just under 3 million officially (perhaps 3·75 million actually) in 1931 and 1932. The MacDonald government, formed after the Conservative defeat in May 1929, was a moderate one, backed by 288 Labour members against 260 Conservatives; it depended for its existence, however, on the goodwill of the 59 Liberal members. The depression came as a shock for all three parties, and those who failed to perceive its real causes were many. Amongst these was, without any doubt, the Chancellor of the Exchequer, Snowden, who adopted a policy of the strictest orthodoxy and rejected any measures that might have resulted in a budget deficit. Almost alone to have understood what were the necessary steps to take was the small team grouped round J. H. Thomas, the minister in charge of unemployment, which was made up of Thomas Johnston, Sir Oswald Mosley and George Lansbury, and which drew up a plan of action. It was obstructed by Snowden, who contented himself with palliative measures—the Housing Act of 1930, to speed up slum clearance, the Agricultural Marketing Act of 1931, to help the farming community, and the Education Bill, which took the school-leaving age up to 15 and which was thrown out by the Lords. In July 1931 Sir George May's economy committee forecast a deficit of £120 million and proposed increased taxes and economies, chiefly the payments to the unemployed. The publication of this report created panic and the pound fell so sharply that even loans to the Bank of England from Paris and New York were unable to restore it. MacDonald resigned on 24 August and George V invited him to form a coalition government 'to save the pound'. The political consequences were serious. The trade union and Labour leaders opposed the 'National Government', except for 12 Labour members of parliament, whereas the Liberals and Conservatives supported it. The new government accepted many of the recommendations of the May committee. But it failed to save the pound: after a continued run on gold, it was necessary to abandon the gold standard, and the pound fell from $4.86 to $3.40. The ensuing election awarded the government a massive majority, with 554 Liberal, Conservative and National Labour members out of 615 members of parliament; the Conservatives gained three million votes, chiefly at the expense of the Liberals, with the Labour party losing 1,375,000 and retaining only 52 seats. The new government was predominantly Conservative. Neville Chamberlain, who replaced Snowden as Chancellor of the Exchequer, introduced Tariff Reform and thus instituted in February 1932 those duties that his father had advocated in 1903. Preferential duties were levied on imports from within the British Empire.

Henceforth, policy consisted in short-term measures taken under the force of circumstances by men who were prudent but incapable of understanding the new situation that had resulted from the slump in international trade and the upheaval that the ambitions and the armaments of the dictatorships had caused in the balance of power. These years 'that the locust hath eaten' were tragic ones, 'a time of tragically lost opportunities, of last chances never seized'.[1] In 1936 the Special Areas Act gave assistance to the transfer of workers to those regions where new industries were developing. Marketing boards and subsidies helped agriculture; a loan helped the completion of the *Queen Mary*. The production index (1929 = 100) had fallen to 84 in 1931, but rose to 93 in 1933 and to 124 in 1937, owing chiefly to the success of the building industry. The standard of living of those workers who had work rose also, thanks more to the balance of trade than to the efforts of the government, since foodstuffs and raw materials from overseas now cost far less as a result of the collapse of world prices. Nevertheless the standard of living of the unemployed, who remained numerous in certain 'distressed areas'—Tyneside, the

---

[1] David Thomson, *England in the 20th Century* (1964), p. 127.

Tees, Scotland and South Wales—continued to be low, geared as it was to the dole, which barely permitted workers to live at subsistence level.

At a time when fascism, exploiting the wretchedness and the despair of the unemployed, was spreading through central, eastern and southern Europe, the countries of north-western Europe were also, to a greater or lesser degree, attracted by the movement. Not even Great Britain was to escape from its clutches entirely. The movement founded by Oswald Mosley showed up all too clearly the disarray created in men's minds by the obvious failure of the traditional parties, and may be regarded as typical. Sir Oswald Mosley had been a member of the small group of Labour ministers which, in 1930, had drawn up a plan to combat the depression. Although his plan received the favourable attention of the annual conference of the Labour party and won over a million votes—it was defeated by 205,000 votes only—Mosley felt rejected and created a new party, the British Union of Fascists (B.U.F.) which comprised various fascist groups. He obtained the support of the *Daily Mail* and certain subsidies from Italy, and was thus able to set up local units with a fairly solid organisation behind them. The movement collapsed after a meeting in the Olympia hall in London in June 1934 when Conservative opinion was revolted by the brutality of its supporters in scuffles with the police and members of the Left, and by its violent anti-Semitism. The Labour party, in opposition since 1931, received a further defeat at the 1935 election, when it won 154 seats. The Spanish Civil War, the Abyssinian affair and the aggressive policies of the dictatorships aroused the party to the danger of war, but it opposed rearmament from distrust of the government. The leaders, essentially moderate, also opposed the setting up of a popular front in Great Britain and, at the beginning of 1939, they expelled Cripps for advocating it.

The uneasiness produced by the policies of Chamberlain, Prime Minister since 1937, spread throughout all the parties. Rearmament started in 1936 and was accelerated after the Munich settlement in 1938. Unemployment fell gradually from 1933, though there were 1,800,000 out of work during the winter of 1938.

The depression affected the three Scandinavian countries with varying degrees of severity. They followed Great Britain's example in abandoning the gold standard in 1931, and unemployment grew, chiefly in Denmark, where there were 200,000 men out of work in the winter of 1932, although in Sweden the figure was less than that for 1922. Malaise in rural districts also came to the fore at this time, especially in Denmark, where agriculture, relying chiefly on exports, was hit hard by customs barriers. The depression also resulted in the creation of a dangerous social tension, apparent in the development of Communism within the trade unions on the one hand, and in the creation of small fascist parties on the other. Only the Social Democrats were everywhere in the majority; since 1929 they had dominated the Danish parliament, they came to power in Norway in 1935 and regained the majority in Sweden in 1936. Their financial and economic programme was without originality, and was not even orientated towards Socialism. Like the old Liberal parties that they had now replaced, they were in agreement with the bourgeois parties in believing that state intervention was indispensable; they differed from them only on the question of how to effect this intervention. They were allied to the Agrarians in Sweden and Norway and to the Radicals in Denmark, in order to widen their political scope. They concentrated on promoting full employment, public works and increased wages, and on improving the peasants' lot with guaranteed prices and premiums on exports. The three countries made a customs agreement, the Oslo Convention (1931). The economic crisis was cut short in 1934 in Sweden, but not until 1936 in Denmark, which experienced serious strikes. The threat of fascism was thus without substance. In Denmark there were never more than three Fascist members of parliament, and in Norway, where Quisling founded the *Nasjional Samling*, and gained a measure of support amongst industrialists and army officers, no Fascist candidate was ever elected to parliament. Only in Finland did the extreme Right make any progress; since the acquisition of independence in 1917 and the ensuing civil war that lasted until 1920, difficult conditions had favoured such a development. Finland had adopted a presidential type of constitution and carried through a programme of agrarian reform. But the presence of a large Communist party and the proximity of Soviet Russia made the Finnish Right aggressive and uneasy and enabled them to secure the outlawing of the Communist party in 1923. Lapua's movement, nationalist and anti-Communist, organised a march on Helsinki by 12,000 peasants in 1930 and caused the government to fall. It was dissolved because of its excessive violence, but only to be replaced by a 'National Patriotic Movement' with distinctly fascist leanings, which in its turn was dissolved in 1938.

Dutch political life was perfectly calm by comparison, in spite of the great number of parties—seventeen, of whom there were never less than ten represented in the government. Stability was guaranteed by proportional representation, and the number of seats held by each party never varied by more than 4 per cent from one election to the next. Here too the Liberal party was growing weaker: reduced to ten members in 1918, it had fallen to four by 1937. The depression caused the devaluation of the florin in 1936 and the controlling of foreign exchange; Holland also joined the Oslo group. A small National Socialist party was founded by Mussert, an engineer, which was opposed by a government made up of Liberals and members of the religious parties, to which one Socialist member was added, for the first time, in 1939.

The fact that the depression struck France later than other countries may be explained by her archaic structure; except for certain sectors where a limited number of large firms had adopted modern production methods, France was still a country of artisans and small producers—more than a third of the wage-earners were still employed in undertakings comprising under five people, and in the field of commerce, 87 per cent of the businesses had five employees or less. The bourgeoisie was afraid of anything that looked like a spirit of adventure, and found investment and the renewal of equipment repugnant. Academic and political eloquence stressed the virtues of small-scale saving (the 'woollen stocking' method), small-scale farming, the craftsman class (which was supposed to be the only one capable of producing 'quality') and the superior nature of a so-called balanced economy—balanced in reality by a large mass of peasants who lived in wretched conditions. Technical progress was at times denounced as 'the source of economic anarchy and moral disequilibrium'. Technological progress was alleged to be the cause of unemployment, with the result that, during the few months before the depression hit France, men waxed eloquent about the prudence and the wisdom of pursuing a policy of stability, without realising that it was nothing more than the weakness of the country's production potential that was fending off the depression. The relatively low unemployment figure—1,000,000 in 1934–5, with over 3,000,000 partially out of work—was due to the fact that a great many foreign workers who had come to seek work in France were now returning home. It is therefore not to be wondered at that the ruling class, as blind when faced with the experience of the New Deal as they were ignorant of the theories of J. M. Keynes, sought to counter depression by the worst of solutions—deflation, ruinous economies in order to re-establish a balanced budget, whatever the cost, and a tardy decision to devalue the franc, in December 1936 (Great Britain having devalued in 1931 and the U.S.A. in 1933), at the very moment when other countries were overcoming the effects of the depression with policies of rearmament and public works. The steps taken were demagogic and ineffectual; rents and salaries of state employees were reduced by 10 per cent in 1935; state control of agriculture was introduced to improve the marketing of wine and sugar: new planting of vines was forbidden, and surplus crops were processed to make them useless for consumption. A Malthusian control was exercised over certain professions; it was forbidden to set up new shoe shops, *Uniprix* stores, and mobile shops. On the whole, this legislation penalised all profitable undertakings in order to protect small property-owners and small marginal producers whose costs were too high.

Traditional Liberalism was, to an increasingly obvious degree, incapable of solving the problem of the depression and countering the risk of war. The 'thirties thus saw the development, in France, as in all the

538

other liberal countries, of crises whose roots went very deep—the crisis of liberalism and of the parliamentary system. Both Chambers, in fact, were to see their functions restricted by the increasingly frequent application of 'decree-laws' and 'full powers' after 1934. The régime was all the more incapable of adapting the old political framework to modern economic problems for being under attack from a factious Right and a revolutionary Left. Up till now, there had been only governmental crises; now there was a state crisis. Public opinion was discouraged and exasperated by the repeated failures of the parties which came successively to power. The solutions put forward were varied. The Communist party, weak in Belgium, where the Workers' party refused any sort of alliance with it, was firmly established in France; the 1,000,000 votes it had gained in 1928 had grown to 1,500,000 by 1936. Its aim was a Communist régime brought about by revolution followed by a proletariat dictatorship as a temporary step. The advent of Hitlerism caused a change in tactics in favour of an alliance with the parties of the Left in a Popular Front to hold fascism and war at bay.

The Socialist parties were deeply divided amongst themselves. In Belgium, as in France, Marxism was being questioned by a wealth of revisionist doctrines. The most notable exponent was Henri de Man, who, after having lived for many years in Germany, where he taught at the University of Frankfurt, continued his work within the Belgian Workers' party. In 1927 he published *Au delà du marxisme*, in which he rejected the materialist interpretation of history in favour of a psychological one, stressing spiritual values, the spirit of equality and the feeling of universal brotherhood. 'The Socialist movement is as much the executor of democracy, which the bourgeoisie has deserted, as the accomplisher of the Christian ideal, which the Church has betrayed.' With *Socialisme constructif*, published in 1930, de Man moved even further from Marxism. The collapse of German socialism after January 1933 caused him to seek an answer to the threat of fascism—the depression must be strangled at the earliest possible moment, since it was propitious to fascism, by the re-establishing of full employment, the nationalising of credit and the creation of a mixed economy, partly nationalised—coal, electricity and a section of the steel industry—and partly open to private enterprise, this latter under the influence of the state through credit, commercial and fiscal policies. These were the aims of his 'Plan de Travail', which he persuaded almost the whole of the Workers' party to adopt at its Christmas 1933 Congress, and whose neo-Fabianism met with a reserved welcome from Léon Blum and de Vandervelde. Henri de Man became a minister in 1935, in both the Van Zeeland and Janson governments; but he was never able to put his Work Plan into operation, and, with his faith in parliamentary democracy shattered, he resigned in 1938.

The idea of a Plan having spread throughout French Socialist circles,

Montagnon presented a programme which drew its inspiration from this idea to the S.F.I.O. Congress in 1933. 'Socialism,' he said, 'in the present disorder, must be made to appear a haven of order and a pole of authority.' Adrien Marquet was to use much the same language: 'Order must be created, authority affirmed, the nation admitted', at which Léon Blum declared that he was 'épouvanté' (horrified). Marcel Déat, in his *Perspectives Socialistes*, published in 1930, exposed his ideas for 'socialising the nation'—capitalism was to be driven back by the use of the anti-capitalism of the middle classes, the artisans, small traders, small farmers and employers, since the fundamental problem was not the question of property, but of power and profits. And so Neo-Socialism came into being.

Reform of the state and of the parties was also the subject of study and planning by the Right and the Centre. In *L'épreuve du pouvoir* (1931) and *L'heure de la décision* (1934) André Tardieu, who had played a considerable part in the Centre Right over the previous decade, suggested a complete overhauling of the parliamentary régime: restoration of the state by strengthening the executive power and restricting the powers of the two Chambers, which would lose the right to initiate expenditure. Stability would be assured by using the right to dissolve parliament. He also proposed votes for women, the referendum, and the banning of strike action by state employees. Emmanuel Mounier, a Catholic of far less conservative outlook, founded in 1932 a review called *Esprit*, which was to become very influential. An apostle of 'personalism', he was both anti-capitalist and an enemy of bourgeois democracy and of socialism. This period saw the birth in right-wing circles of a great many more or less ephemeral movements which put forward plans for 'renovation', for creating a 'new order' with the intention of going beyond the old Right–Left dichotomy and of reconciling neo-liberalism and neo-traditionalism. Conservatives and Catholics were attracted to the idea of 'the corporate state' which, they believed, would put an end to class struggles and be a guarantee of social tranquillity. Attempts were also made by groups of the extreme Right to win the peasants over to the 'corporate state' idea, by means of an anti-parliamentary programme; the peasantry was the only 'healthy' element in the country, while the parliamentarians, 'pourris', 'vendus', were sacrificing its interests to those of industry and Jewish finance. There were only two realities within a strong state—one's work and one's family. Except for minor details, this was the platform on which the *Comité de défense paysanne* of Dorgères, the *Parti Agraire* of Agricola and the *Union des Syndicats agricoles* of Le Roy Ladurie now fought.

None of these movements was very influential; but this was not the case with those movements that were genuinely fascist. The examples of Germany and Italy spread to France, adding strength to the desire for direct action and the use of violence. The bourgeoisie, feeling itself in danger, responded with those same reflexes generated by fear that had led to the massacre of the insurgents in June 1848 and of the *Communards* in 1871. The anti-parliamentary tendencies of Boulangisme and an anti-Dreyfus type of nationalism reappeared in the form of armed Leagues using Nazi and fascist methods. A large number of those who felt threatened were not fascists, but they admired Mussolini who was establishing the reign of 'order', and they used the threat of the Leagues—and occasionally let them off the leash—to achieve their aims. The danger was thus a serious one, and the period 1934–6 was even more critical in France than that of the Dreyfus affair, for the factious elements were now receiving help from outside.

These Leagues were supported by the major reactionary and nationalist associations: the National Catholic Federation, the National Union of Combatants, the League of Tax-payers, the chief daily newspapers and the weeklies *Gringoire* and *Candide*. They grouped all those who longed nostalgically for a strong state into the storm-troops of the *Camelots du Roi*, the *Jeunesses Patriotes*, the *Solidarité Française* and the *Croix de Feu* organised, on a military basis, by Lt.-Col. de la Roque with the help of E. Mercier, the electricity magnate. These groups grew rapidly in importance. Others were the French Popular party created by Jacques Doriot after 1936, and the *Comité secret d'action révolutionnaire* (C.S.A.R.), known familiarly as the 'Cagoule', which stocked arms and received subsidies from the Fascists in exchange for carrying out acts of vengeance —the murder of Carlo Roselli—or of provocation, like the attack on the offices of the *Patronat Français* and the *Front Paysan*. The demonstration organised against the 'République des Camarades' on 6 February 1934 took advantage of the Stavisky scandal to call for a government that would put an end to disorder. The demonstration turned into a riot, twenty-five people were killed and many more wounded. Under pressure of this the Daladier government, although it had a majority in the Chamber, resigned and made room for a government under a former president of the Republic, Gaston Doumergue, a Radical gone over to the Right, and who now called a truce. His Cabinet contained one of the Neo-Socialist leaders (Marquet), one of the leaders of the ex-servicemen, and A. Tardieu, Marshal Pétain and Pierre Laval. Doumergue and his successor, Laval, adopted a policy of all-out deflation which, whilst it failed to improve the financial situation, succeeded in antagonising the greater part of public opinion.

The bloodshed of 6 February led to a regrouping of the forces of the Left. Those who were attached to the Republican ideal drew closer, and on 12 February a more or less complete general strike and massive demonstrations by workers in Paris and many provincial centres were organised in answer to the attempted *coup de force* of the 6th. Under the slogan 'le fascisme ne passera pas' there was a rallying of forces. Socialists and Communists signed a pact of 'unity of action', a 'committee for anti-

541

fascist action and vigilance' was set up under scholars like Paul Rivet and Langevin, which gained much support in intellectual circles, and all the left-wing parties without exception, from the Radicals to the Communists, formed a coalition for the defence of the Republic, known as the *Rassemblement populaire* or, more commonly, the *Front populaire*. Its programme consisted chiefly in a list of steps to be taken to defend liberty and peace, to restore purchasing power, to create the *Office du Blé* (to regulate the price of grain), to nationalise the Bank of France and, as financial measures, to create a fund for war pensions, to institute a progressive tax on income and to suppress tax evasion. No structural reforms were, however, implied by these measures.

The two major trade union movements joined forces in May 1936 and became henceforth the C.G.T. Elections held in May and June of the same year resulted in a majority for the Popular Front, with 378 seats, as against 220 for the Right and the Centre Right, the so-called 'national parties'. Communists (72) and Socialists (149) obtained more than a third of the votes and accounted for 57 per cent of the new majority. For the first time, there were more Socialists than Radical Socialists (109); but when they claimed power, as had happened formerly with Ramsay MacDonald and the Liberals, the new Socialist-inclined government was forced to rely on the Radical balance.

The victory of the Popular Front and the presence of a Socialist, Léon Blum, at the head of the government created a wave of enthusiasm in the working class, and the hope of an early improvement in its lot. From 26 May strikes broke out spontaneously but in a shape previously unknown in France, that of the 'sit-down strike', intended not to pave the way for nationalisation, as in Italy in 1921, but to foil any attempts at breaking the strike. The employers opened negotiations with the trade unions on 5 June which led to the Matignon agreements on the 7th— higher wages, recognition of trade union rights, obligatory collective agreements and the reduction of the working week to 40 hours with no corresponding reduction in earnings. This victory set the seal on half a century of trade union efforts; up till now, the great majority of employers had simply refused to accept the fact that there were trade unions, or to meet union representatives, to negotiate with them or sign collective agreements. Fifty-two years after the act that allowed them to be constituted, the trade unions had finally achieved full recognition as the representatives of the workers, and with this leap forward French social legislation made up for its previous backwardness in comparison with that of other industrial countries. The movement ebbed somewhat later, but agitation continued, especially when the employers had recovered from their great fear and tried to take their revenge by eliminating the union representatives and refusing to renew the collective agreements. Apart from the Matignon agreements and the law on holidays with pay, and also the *Code de la Famille* which, in July 1939, codified all the measures that had been passed concerning the family—in particular the obligation on employers to contribute to a 'caisse de compensation' for families (1931) and the principle of equal pay for men and women (1938) —the social balance-sheet of the decade had been bare.

As it happened, the Popular Front government remained in power for only one year. A drift to the Right began again in June 1937, and Daladier's Radical government in 1938 destroyed the most important of its achievements. In the long run it must therefore be considered a failure, partly because it coincided with acts of war born of repeated aggressions by the dictators—the reoccupation of the Rhineland, the conquest of Abyssinia, and especially the Spanish Civil War, in which the 'farce of non-intervention' made many left-wing thinkers lose patience with the softness of the British and French governments. Its failure may also be ascribed to the fact that its programme had not taken account of economic and technical difficulties, such as those caused by the delay in the devaluation of the franc, and the use of out-of-date equipment which made it impossible for the vast majority of undertakings to conform to the principle of three eight-hour shifts without excessive costs.

But the main reason for its downfall was the fear and the desire for revenge felt throughout the ruling class, and the alarm caused by the spectacular increase in trade union numbers. By the end of 1936, the C.G.T. numbered over 4,000,000 and the Communist party had doubled its membership to 380,000 between May and October 1936. Nor was the ruling class reassured to see a government in power which openly sided with the workers against the employers, and a prime minister who remained suspect in their eyes, even though he differentiated between 'the acquisition of power by revolution' and 'the exercise of power within the framework of a capitalist society'. Added to all this, it must be remembered that the employers were severely shaken by the sit-down strikes and the occupying of factories, and by the Matignon agreements which implied new duties that many small enterprises of a marginal nature were unable to perform; moreover the fact that their right to be 'masters in their own house' had been contested, that they had been threatened, insulted and humiliated, had wounded their pride.

This desire for vengeance was apparent in the way the employers reorganised themselves; the new Secretary General, C. J. Gignoux, set the belligerent tone with the *Confédération générale du Patronat français* which had taken over from the *Confédération générale de la Production française* and was now to be joined by a large number of small employers. There was no increase in output, but rather a deliberate holding back of production and a general refusal to invest; prices rose and the slowness of the recovery cancelled out all the advantages that the workers had gained, and they fell back on strike action. The value of the franc depreciated. In

June 1937 the senate refused to invest Léon Blum with the full powers he was asking for, and within eight months three successive governments were faced with an increasing number of difficulties which included the Anschluss, a second devaluation of the franc—to 58 per cent of its value under Poincaré—the Munich crisis and the difficulties of trying to implement the 40-hour week. In November 1938 Daladier suspended the act prescribing a 40-hour week; the general strike which followed was a failure because the working class was weakened by internal struggles between those for and those against the Munich settlement, between Communists and anti-Communists, between pacifists and those in favour of resistance to fascism. The division between the two major tendencies was so deep and the disarray of public opinion such that there followed a strange reversal of the traditional positions. From 1935 onwards, both the Left and the Right began to adopt attitudes towards the international problems which were completely the opposite of those they had formerly affected (a similar phenomenon appeared, rather less clearly, in England). The Left, attached to the idea of the League of Nations, to collective security and to sanctions, placed in the forefront of its concerns the defence of democracy, which it coupled with that of the nation, since both were threatened by the fascist intervention in Spain, by the claims of Italy and by the capitulation at Munich. Except for a very small anti-Communist section, pacifism was now rejected. The Right, so ferociously anti-German, hostile to any revision of the peace treaties, to disarmament, to the League of Nations and to the policy of appeasement, now felt that the greatest danger was represented by Bolshevism; it turned to pacifism since a war, even a victorious war, could be nothing other than disastrous, because Hitler, the bulwark of order, would be defeated. Whilst it still remained hostile to Germany, the Right attempted to direct Hitler's appetite for *Lebensraum* towards the plains of south-east Europe. The destruction of Czechoslovakia in March 1939 no doubt opened the eyes of many to the true nature of Hitlerism, but the unity of France was made impossible by Daladier's anti-working-class and anti-Communist policies, which alienated the greater part of the Left. There existed a sizeable and highly influential section on the extreme Right which refused to 'go to war over Danzig'. The defence of society was more important than the defence of the nation.

Political life in Belgium was as disturbed throughout this decade as it was in France, although not always for the same reasons. There was considerable governmental instability; proportional representation blunted the election results and the division of public opinion between the three parties led to coalition governments. Between 1928 and 1940 there were thirty governmental crises, frequently two or more a year. The Socialist party, which had been the great victor of the 1920 election, had fulfilled its basic programme of universal suffrage, trade union liberty, and progressive taxation of incomes and inherited estates. But it drew back before any real structural reforms and practically abandoned the socialisation of the means of production and the 'serment fiscal' (designed to check fraud and tax evasion), and contented itself with farming guarantees, holidays with pay for workers and the equalisation of the basic living wage. The reconstituted Catholic party, strongly influenced by the *Action Française*, was divided by working-class conflicts and by the Flemish question. The Liberal party, more and more tied to business circles, and committed to the defence of the most traditional sort of economic Liberalism, was extremely anti-Socialist; it abandoned its anti-clericalism and, in its social policies, moved ever farther to the right of the Catholic party. Like the Radicals in France, the Catholic party, a Centre party, swung sometimes to the Left, sometimes to the Right, and had a part in all the two-party cabinets. It was only at times of really severe crisis that a tripartite coalition was formed. The Belgian franc thus found itself in great difficulties in 1926, with the same results as those noted in London and Paris. The cabinet was taken over by a businessman, Emile Francqui, a vice-president of the important *Société générale* of Belgium. He was given full powers and proceeded to limit spending and introduce a new unit of currency, the *belga*, worth 5 Belgian francs, which he stabilised on the American dollar, at 175 francs to the dollar. More notably, the Socialists were forced to accept the transfer of all railway holdings to the state, to the *Société Nationale des Chemins de Fer*, whose shares were used for the enforced consolidation of Treasury bonds.

When the Great Depression came, it brought with it an even more severe crisis; the collapse of the rubber and copper markets led to a serious budgetary deficit and the number of men out of work rose to 300,000. Once again, the same orthodox treatment was applied: economies, lowering of the wages of state employees, customs tariffs, new taxes. The run on gold enabled the government of Theunis, Francqui and Gutt to return to power—the so-called 'Bankers' government', which, in pursuing a deflationary policy, reduced buying power and, in March 1935, abandoned parity with gold. The results were similar to those which the same policies had produced in France. Reaction against 'bourgeois Conservatism, the Popular Front and Communism' took two forms: an upsurge of nationalism in the Flemish area, and of *Rexisme* in the Walloon area. The latter was a fascist movement founded by Léon Degrelle, a product of the Young Catholics in Louvain, who leant heavily for his ideas on the *Action Française*; he denounced Liberal individualism and proposed that society be reorganised on the basis of the family and the trade guilds. The 1936 election brought heavy defeat to the three traditional parties; the Liberals lost 41,000 votes and one seat, the Socialists 112,000 votes and three seats (retaining 70 deputies) but the Catholic party lost 229,000 votes and three seats, with only 63 deputies in the new parliament. On the other hand, the Communists won six seats, the Flemish Nationalists (called *frontistes*) eight, and the Rexists, running for the first time, twenty-one seats, with 271,000 votes. Their electoral success was fleeting, for a few months later Degrelle, whom the clergy were by now combating, was beaten in Brussels by Van Zeeland, who won ten times more votes than him. In 1939, the Rexists held only four seats, although their influence was to remain strong.

Van Zeeland's government, which enlisted Henri de Man and Spaak, both Socialists, secured special powers for twelve months; it used them to devalue the franc once more (150 Belgian francs to the pound), and then abandoned free exchange by subscribing to the Oslo agreements, and adopted a Four-Year Plan. De Man, now the most important figure on the political stage, began leaning towards *Rexisme* and speaking of a national party 'of order and authority'; he was followed by Spaak, the first Socialist to become Prime Minister (in 1938). A new economic slump brought further unemployment and, when capital began to leave the country, produced a new monetary crisis. Socialist unity was shattered by the opposition of Vandervelde and Brouckere to Henri de Man and by the linguistic question. When Pierlot formed his Catholic–Liberal government after the 1939 election and abandoned all reform projects and major public works, the Socialist party passed over to the opposition.

As in France, although they kept their old names, the parties underwent profound changes. The only party to maintain its unity was the Liberal party, although it must be added that its membership was now low. The Socialists were divided into those who favoured orthodox measures, those in favour of planning, the partisans of Spaak, and those willing to co-operate with the Communists. Within the ranks of the Catholic party, there was opposition between the old Right, Christian Democrats, Boerenbonders, Flemish autonomists, Rexists and 'frontistes'. The confusion was aggravated by the personal politics of Leopold III, who did not attempt to conceal his contempt for the politicians and whose behind-the-scenes political activity earned him the outspoken condemnation of Pierlot.

THE SECOND WORLD WAR 1939–1945

All the liberal democracies of north-western Europe, with the exception of Great Britain and neutral Sweden, underwent occupation by the enemy. Alone amongst them to have a government that collaborated with the Germans was France: all the other governments sought refuge in Great Britain and carried on the war as best they could. Everywhere the occupying powers met with stubborn resistance.

Almost the whole of the British people accepted resolutely, from the very outbreak of the war, the entire gamut of those measures which, having been tried out during the Great War, were now reintroduced. Very wide powers were accorded to the government, new ministries and departments were created, but the control exercised by parliament was never interfered with, and the liberty of individual citizens was consequently always upheld. The nation's economic life was very strictly controlled in order to avoid the waste of manpower and materials, as well as to equalise living conditions as much as possible. Universal rationing, high taxes on unessential goods, the control of wages and of working conditions—such measures made it possible to maintain national unity in an atmosphere of goodwill and fraternity to a degree unknown during the Great War.

Furthermore the Cabinet formed by Winston Churchill in the darkest days of 1940 included six Labour members of parliament of whom two were members of the War Cabinet; their presence did not lead to the passing of any specifically Socialist legislation, but it was a guarantee that strict control was kept on all the national undertakings including banks and private enterprise. There was no regular opposition, either in parliament or in the country as a whole. Both the government and the parliament were mindful of the need to prepare for post-war reconstruction; one result was the report of Sir William Beveridge, a comprehensive plan of social insurance against illness, unemployment and want which laid the foundations of the future Welfare State.

The Labour party, chastened by past failures—and particularly by Ramsay MacDonald's 'betrayal' in 1931—prepared a realistic programme of reforms, *Let Us Face the Future*, placing in the forefront full employment and limited nationalisation. The somewhat hasty general election of 5 July 1945 found the party ready to defend a concrete programme of housing and social security which secured the votes of all those who remembered twenty-five years of insecurity and chronic unemployment. In spite of the enormous personal prestige of Winston Churchill, the Labour party won 393 seats (61 per cent of the total number, with 48 per cent of the total votes), the Conservatives 213, the Liberals 12 and the Communists 3. For the first time, Labour, with a clear majority, was able to put its programme into effect.

In France, the national unity created in September 1939 existed in no more than name. The strong passions that had been at work before the war had been ill concealed, and when the hammer-blow of invasion and the debacle came, a great wave of anti-republicanism, eager for revenge, was let loose. The enemies of the Republic sought consolation in the suppression of the hated régime, which they held responsible for the defeat. The old anti-parliamentary feelings became allied to a nationalism as anti-British as it was anti-German by tradition, and thereby silenced those who wished to continue the struggle. Intimidated by the violence of the anti-Republican propaganda, and by their own unpopularity, the deputies and senators summoned to a National Assembly at Vichy agreed to a proposal, put forward by Laval, that full legislative and executive powers be accorded to Marshal Pétain, with a blank cheque for the promulgation of a constitution founded on the new trilogy of *Travail, Patrie, Famille* which, on 10 July, replaced *Liberté, Egalité, Fraternité*: 80 votes were cast against the proposition, with 57 abstentions.

There ensued 'a sudden and anachronistic resurgence of the past'. Those who were victorious were inspired by the same principles as the reactionary Right—the outcome of political catholicism—which now 'took its revenge for the Dreyfus affair' and thus attempted to destroy all that had been achieved since 1789. The leading men of the new régime were supporters of Maurras, the men who had created the leagues; royalists, clericals and nationalists; authoritarians won over by fascism and National Socialism, and by the theories of de Man and Déat; the Catholic hierarchy, which believed that 'defeat is a Divine punishment for our anti-religious laws', and which was happy with a régime that attempted to put it in control of education—'Pétain is France; and France is Pétain', said Cardinal Gerlier—and senior civil servants glad to be rid of the control of trade unions and elected representatives. They constituted a very mixed bag, with interests and tendencies that were far from converging, where adventurers and utopians rubbed shoulders with anti-Germans and supporters of the Nazi system. There were thus various rival sorts of Vichyism, which fought and succeeded each other under pressure from the occupying forces.

There was nevertheless a measure of agreement over a certain number of principles and aims: suppression of universal suffrage and all forms of election; all authority was held to emanate from the state personified by Marshal Pétain. The régime was anti-Marxist, but also unfavourable to capitalism and big industry: its ideal was the small family enterprise; it called for a return to the land, 'which does not tell lies', it exalted the peasant, whom it saw as endowed with all the virtues, it founded its beliefs on the family, the guardian of morality and religion; it was respectful of the social hierarchy, the traditional defenders of order, the Church, the army and the upper class. To quote A. Siegfried, 'France had never known such an illiberal and completely arbitrary régime.' 'Le délit d'opinion' was restored, enforcing political conformity with retroactive effect. Freemasonry and the political parties were dissolved; the very title of 'Republic' disappeared, and the oath to the head of state was reintroduced. It was a 'régime d'ordre moral': the *Ecoles Normales* were suppressed, religious instruction was brought back into primary education, legislation concerning religious communities was suspended and private schools were subsidised. The creation of an oppressive department of Political Justice in 1941 led to the detention of Blum, Daladier and Gamelin in a military fort. The professional groups were organised—agriculture by the *Corpora-*

tion paysanne which was made up of trade unions and agricultural associations, industry by Committees of Organisation. The Charter of Labour forbade strikes and lock-outs, and claimed to have suppressed class warfare. Anti-Semitic legislation, which drew its inspiration from the Nuremberg laws, but which also drew on traditional Catholic nationalism, was also promulgated.

Alongside this nationalist, Catholic and anti-British Vichy, which predominated until April 1942, there was the Vichy of Laval, of Darnand, Doriot, Marion, Henriot, Déat, Abel Bonnard, all of them 'collaborators'; this was also the Vichy of certain pro-German elements from the worlds of banking and industry, like Barnaud, of the *Banque Worms*, and Lehideux, the son-in-law of Renault. All of these were Fascists and eager to integrate France into Hitler's continental system. After having attempted to be rid of Laval, by having him arrested (the 'plot' of 13 December 1940), Marshal Pétain tried to govern with the aid of P. E. Flandin and then of Admiral Darlan; but in the end he was forced to recall Laval. Thereafter the most important posts were given to men devoted to the cause of Germany. Economic collaboration grew more and more important; an anti-Bolshevist legion was set up to fight in Russia. At the same time the régime took on increasingly the characteristics of a police state; in 1941, Pucheu formed, from elements of the *Légion des Anciens Combattants* created by Pétain as a sort of single party, the S.O.L. (the *Service d'Ordre Légionnaire*), which was intended for police work; when Darnand became 'Secretary-General for the Maintenance of Order', the S.O.L. became veritable storm-troops comparable to the S.S., to be used in the struggle against democracy and the 'Jewish lepers'. In January 1943 the Militia recruited toughs from its ranks who acted as informers and arrested, tortured and shot Jews and members of the Resistance and of the Maquis, working with the military courts and the German police and army.

After the Allied landings in North Africa, the German occupation of the southern part of France strengthened the position of the collaborators; the Germans had no further reason to respect the fiction of an independent state. From the winter of 1943 on, many extreme collaborators entered the government, men like Cathala, Abel Bonnard, Bichelonne, Henriot, Déat, who attempted to maintain those services which the Germans needed in order to continue to be able to exploit the country. But it was obvious that the German cause was lost, and the traditionally conservative circles which had originally supported the National Revolution now became temporisers, as did the artful and the prudent.

In the other occupied countries the situation was far clearer; there were never any problems of conscience for the patriotic, who, whilst they obeyed their own feelings, were also conforming to the orders of their legitimate government.

The forms taken by the Resistance movements varied from country to country and from period to period. In the early days of occupation, the bourgeoisie and a large section of the middle classes and the peasantry—as well as the relatively small group of people already favourable to the Nazi cause—had a feeling of relief that, for them, the war was over and that the danger of Bolshevism at least had been definitively removed. Then, little by little, as the humiliation of defeat came to be felt more deeply, and, above all, as the real nature of the Germans showed itself in their behaviour, the spirit of the people revived. Men and women of all classes were roused to opposition by food shortages due to the black market and requisitioning, by the brutal and perverted police system, by the persecution of Jews and the execution of hostages, and by the introduction of forced labour. As the victory at Stalingrad and the Allied landings in North Africa indicated first a possible, then a probable, and finally a certain, defeat for the Germans, the local populations passed from defeatism to passive resistance and then to active resistance. Generally speaking, however, although the genuine Resistance movements in each country had the benefit of the sympathy and, at times, of the assistance of the major part of the population, they were in actual fact composed of a minority of courageous patriots who were prepared to give up their livelihood, to undergo torture and deportation, to sacrifice their lives for their country.

Sweden was the only state to remain neutral; but her position, between Germany and the U.S.S.R., was made especially difficult at the time of the Finnish War and after the fall of Norway and Denmark. Completely isolated and depending economically wholly on the Reich, she was forced to make concessions of a military nature, such as allowing the transit of troops (disguised as soldiers on leave) and material, and the setting up of secret hiding-places for submarines in Swedish waters. As the military situation of the Allies improved, Sweden had greater freedom of action; in 1943 the transit of individual German soldiers only was allowed, help was given to Danish Jews, and members of the Danish and Norwegian Resistance were able to train in Swedish camps.

Norway was able to oppose the German invasion for no more than two months; on 10 June after the evacuation of Narvik, King Haakon VII and his government withdrew to London. Legitimate resistance went on under Pascal Berg, the president of the Supreme Court, and Bishop Berggrav, and put up as much opposition as it could to the installation by the Germans of a puppet government under Gauleiter Josef Terboven. It was not until February 1942 that Terboven named Widkun Quisling, the head of the Norwegian National Socialist party, as leader of a national government. The response of the Resistance was shown in the resignation of senior civil servants and the formation of an 'Inner Front' which organised strikes, acts of sabotage (as in the heavy-water factory in 1943) and demonstrations against forced labour, which had been introduced in 1941. *Milorg*, the Military Organisation, under General Ruge, was able to send agents and information to London and Stockholm, and clandestine publications were distributed in abundance. The Germans, for their part, requisitioned all men between 18 and 55, closed down the University of Oslo and arrested 65 of its teachers and 1,500 of its students, and deported and executed members of the Resistance. The final months of occupation were made particularly difficult by the fact that the Germans adopted a 'scorched earth' policy as they retreated from the Russian advance and the attacks of Norwegian partisans.

The situation was somewhat different in Denmark, where King Charles X had remained and ordered all resistance to stop. The policies adopted by the government of Stauning, a Socialist, and by the Minister of Foreign Affairs, Scavenius, who favoured close collaboration with the Germans, went even farther—complete control of the Danish economy by the Germans, a very unfavourable rate of exchange, the removal of elements hostile to the new régime, the strengthening of censorship, and collaboration between the police and the magistrates' courts and the Gestapo. An election held in March 1943, with the permission of the Germans, showed how much opposition there was to these measures; Clausen's Danish Nazis obtained 2 per cent only of the total votes, and 3 seats, whereas the government coalition won 143; the Conservative party, the one most opposed to collaboration, won 40 per cent of the total votes. Here, too, the Resistance organised acts of sabotage, sending young people and information to London and Sweden and distributing clandestine publications. The movement became universal with the beginning of persecution of the Jews; the king opposed this personally, threatening to wear the 'yellow star' himself; strikes and acts of sabotage followed, leading to the proclamation of martial law and the arrest of army and naval officers. A general strike on 30 June 1944 was followed by another in September, after which the entire Danish police force was deported.

In Holland, where the population was considered to be of pure Germanic extraction, soon to be integrated into the Greater Reich, a less harsh régime was in operation, at least at the beginning of the occupation. The German High Commissioner, Seyss-Inquart, progressively introduced Nazi institutions and anti-Jewish laws, and dissolved all political parties and both Chambers. The only party allowed was the *Nationaal Socialistische Beweging*, led by Mussert, with, at the outside, 110,000 members. The sparseness of forests and the density of the population made guerrilla warfare almost impossible, but the democratic spirit, the religious convictions and the feelings of fellowship that existed amongst the Dutch people gave to their resistance certain original characteristics; it was, in particular, the persecution of the Jews, something that struck deep into the Dutch conscience, that led to the establishment of a movement which organised sabotage and espionage, and gave help to Jews and people on the run and those evading compulsory service. German repression was also particularly effective: over a period of two years the German police was able to arrest a great number of parachutists and seize a large quantity of material.

Luxemburg was also considered to be an authentically Germanic country and, step by step, was attached to the Reich under the jurisdiction of the Gauleiter of Trier and Koblenz. National Socialist laws were brought into application, the country was incorporated into the Wehrmacht, the Reichsmark introduced, and the use of the local language, Letzenburgish, was forbidden. But tenacious resistance was offered in the shape of public inertia, desertion, clandestine publications, the refusal to deliver requisitioned material and the formation of a Maquis movement in a country which lent itself effectively to guerilla activities.

In Belgium the king's refusal to leave the country and his unconditional capitulation, followed by his decision to regard himself as a prisoner of war at Laeken Castle and to abstain from all political activity, made the task of the Germans easier. Public opinion on the whole approved of the king's decision. The Germans also found that they were helped considerably by the large, pro-Nazi Flemish Nationalist party, by the Flemish Rexist party, the V.N.V. (*Vlaamische-Nationaal Verbond*), and by the Walloon Rexists who had now formed the Association of the Friends of the Greater Reich, the A.G.R.A. Life under the administration of the military régime was on the whole less difficult than in other occupied countries. Fairly soon after the Germans began to show sympathy for the Flemish activists, however, attitudes akin to those displayed during the occupation in the Great War reappeared. The country underwent rationing, and resistance was encouraged by the Catholic clergy, who never attempted to hide their condemnation of the collaborators and who protested against the deportation of workers. Strikes broke out in Liége, Verviers, La Louvière, Charleroi and Mons; acts of sabotage and violence took place, the escape networks organised for Allied prisoners of war and airmen were very active, and a secret army was formed. Along with the Belgian Legion, the Front for Liberty and other groups, the largest movement was the Independence Front directed by the Communists. The country was fairly rapidly liberated and the king, having fallen into disfavour after his visit to the Führer at Berchtesgaden in 1940 and his marriage in 1941, was obliged to leave the country. The regency was put into the hands of his brother, Prince Charles.

Resistance in France was more difficult to organise, and took a highly original turn because of the presence on French soil of the government presided over by Marshal Pétain. Loyalty to the head of the army, to a man universally respected, and the confidence that he inspired in building up a régime that corresponded to their ideal national state, led men of the

Right to vest him with a considerable amount of credit and to think that his way was without doubt the only appropriate way, given the situation. Many Frenchmen were thus brought to resignation, if not to collaboration. It was not until after the Montoire interview and the announcement of an actual collaboration policy, with the ensuing recall of Laval, that many came to think that the way of General de Gaulle, which was the most honourable, might also be the one most in keeping with the nation's interests. The result was that the struggle against the Germans became identified with the struggle against the Vichy régime. The French eventually became more or less actively hostile to the Germans and their allies, with the exception of those who feared that the defeat of the Germans would also mean the end of the traditional social order.

Resistance was, in fact, chiefly the work of men of the Left, with the help of some from the Right who were disgusted by the behaviour of the Germans and their allies from Vichy. Speaking from London on 18 June 1940 General de Gaulle had called on the French to continue fighting alongside Great Britain and to resist the Germans; 'France has lost a battle, but she has not lost the war.' He thus created an external Resistance, just at the time when an internal Resistance was spontaneously coming into being on French soil. It was chiefly due to the B.B.C., which secured first a French and then a world-wide audience for this unknown general, that his influence with the internal Resistance grew stronger. The Resistants regrouped, distributed clandestine publications and sent back information on the Wehrmacht. Establishing contact with them from outside was at first difficult. Special envoys sent by the British S.O.E. (Special Operations Executive) and the B.C.R.A. (*Bureau Central de Renseignements et d'Action*), directed by Colonel Passy, and material, radio transmitters and receivers sent through the same channels enabled the Resistants to co-ordinate their activities, and made it possible for General de Gaulle's emissaries to group the various movements round himself. In northern France, from 1940 onwards, in fact, men determined to resist had sought each other out and had found the means of contacting their British allies. Amongst this small number of isolated groups, mostly ignorant of each other's existence, the most important were the O.C.M. (*Organisation Civile et Militaire*) made up of military and bourgeois elements, and *Libération Nord*, chiefly composed of Socialists and trade unionists. In southern France, *Combat*, directed by a former officer, F. Frénay, was almost exclusively made up of men of the Left, as was *Libération Sud* founded by E. Astier de la Vigerie, and *Franc-Tireur* in the Lyons area. The Communists, either singly or in little groups, had been circulating clandestine pamphlets since the autumn of 1940; after the entry of Russia into the war, the party created a National Front and organised the armed groups known as the *Francs Tireurs et Partisans*. General de Gaulle's envoy, the former Prefect Jean Moulin, succeeded in persuading the various movements in the south to join forces; the *Mouvements de la Résistance* came into being early in 1942. In the north, unification occurred later, in May 1943, when representatives of the two main trade-union movements, the C.G.T. and the *Confédération française des Travailleurs chrétiens* (C.F.T.C.), six representatives of the political parties including the Communists, and eight from the various resistance movements joined together to set up the *Conseil National de la Résistance* (C.N.R.), under the presidency of Moulin as de Gaulle's delegate and commissioner of the *Comité national* in London. When Moulin was arrested, Georges Bidault replaced him. Consequently the whole of the Resistance was behind General de Gaulle when he set up the Provisional Government of the French Republic in Algiers (which was composed of representatives of the political parties, including two Communists, and members of the resistance movements) and especially when he called a consultative Assembly.

On the occupation of southern France, the *Organisation de Résistance de l'Armée* was formed, out of anti-Pétain elements of the pre-armistice army, dissolved by the Germans. The dropping of arms by parachute was organised after 1943, and escape networks enabled Allied airmen shot down by the Germans to reach North Africa, as well as volunteers for the army now being reconstituted there. Scores of intelligence networks functioned very actively. Attacks on German officers and individual soldiers multiplied, as did acts of sabotage, for which the Communists were chiefly responsible; by their intense activity they retaliated against the deportations and the executions of hostages. But serious misunderstandings developed between these men, who ignored the counsels of prudence sent to them, and the French and their allies in London and Algiers, mostly soldiers by profession, who had no more than a limited confidence in these spontaneously created groups acting under the orders of leaders unknown outside France, or else known to be Communists. These leaders complained that arms were being withheld from them or else being delivered in insufficient quantities, and alleged that this lack of confidence was the cause of the failure of certain Maquis operations in the Ain, the Alps (the plateau of Glières and the Vercors), the Massif Central (Mont Mouchet), Corrèze, Ariège and the Gard.

During the Normandy landings, two French armies took part in the fighting—the regular army, incorporated into the American army, and the clandestine army, the F.F.I. (*Forces Françaises de l'Intérieur*) who, according to General Eisenhower, were worth fifteen divisions to the Allies.

The régime established in France after the Liberation was organised not by the true Resistants, those who fought the Germans in France itself, but by the men from London and Algiers. They promised to carry out the programme of the C.N.R., but Left-wing influence was weak amongst them. But the leaders of the Right, most of them collaborators and supporters of the Vichy régime, had lost favour; the government was thus made up of Communists and Socialists, with one new party, the M.R.P. (*Mouvement Républicain Populaire*), which drew its inspiration from Christian Democrat thinking. This party gathered votes from the Right and thereafter acted as a check on the other parties, in much the same way as the Radical party had done before 1940.

In Great Britain, the Labour victory—it was only the second time since 1880 that the British Left had won a real victory in a general election—allowed the party to carry out its programme, which did not go beyond the framework of the Welfare State. Everywhere, in Scandinavia where they were in power, and in France and Belgium where they played an essential part on the political stage, the Socialist parties became reformist, eager to do their best for a capitalist society, but not to implement Socialism as their fathers had understood it twenty years earlier. The discovery of the military might of the Soviet Union, and the extension of this power into the very heart of Europe, gave rise to feelings of fear. The close financial and economic dependence on the United States which the need for reconstruction forced, whether they wished it or not, on the states of western Europe, could only strengthen the position of those elements hostile to a Socialist ideology. After the great blood-letting, in spite of appearances, the social structure of western Europe remained more conservative than ever.

CHAPTER XVIII

THE UNITED STATES OF AMERICA

IN the last year of the nineteenth century the American people re-elected William McKinley as President. By doing so, they ratified the liberation of Cuba and the annexation of Puerto Rico and the Philippine Islands. Probably not knowing what they were doing, and certainly unwilling to accept the full implications of their new situation, the American people had moved out on to the world stage, little better prepared for their new role than the Japanese had been when Commodore Perry's 'black ships' broke the centuries-old, self-imposed blockade of the island empire.

William Jennings Bryan, who had fought for the economically unfortunate, above all for the angered and impoverished farmer, in 1896, had fought in 1900 against 'imperialism'. But the sharp edge of discontent had been blunted by the flow of gold from South Africa and the Yukon, by a natural turn in the trade cycle, and the vague issue of 'imperialism' was not an adequate fighting theme. Flushed with an easy victory over an impotent Spain, and moving into a new boom period, the American people was convinced that it was living in the best of all possible republics, that it had nothing and no one to fear.

The politicians who felt this mood had no need to worry about re-electing the President and some of them took the chance to get out of the way an obstreperous hero of the brief Spanish–American war, Theodore Roosevelt, who had won the governorship of New York on the strength of his achievements with a regiment of irregular cavalry in Cuba. Possibly against his will, he was nominated for the vice-presidency. In Washington his great and unused energies were turned, for the moment, to the study of law. On 6 September 1901 the President was shot by a probably mad 'anarchist', Leon Czolgosz, and died on 14 September. Theodore Roosevelt was President of the United States.

The new President was just under forty-three, the youngest man ever to enter the White House. He was exceptional in other ways. Born in 1858, the Civil War was a vague memory for him, not a great crisis lived through as it had been for every one of his predecessors since Lincoln. He was the first Republican President since Johnson who was not a Civil War veteran and, although he was a vehement party man, his mother's family were Georgia Democrats and a paternal uncle was, and remained, a Cleveland Democrat. Not of a rich family by the new standards, he yet belonged to a stable and prosperous element in New York society. Graduating from Harvard, he had had a varied experience as state legislator, as ranch owner, as Police Commissioner, as Civil Service

Commissioner, as Assistant-Secretary of the Navy. But although active in politics he was not a politician as McKinley understood the term. He was the most versatile President since Jefferson and, if much of his knowledge was superficial, his interests, curiosity and sympathies were genuinely wide. His talent for dramatising himself was his greatest gift. His mannerisms were the delight of cartoonists and satirists. They were also the delight of the voters. Almost at once he made the presidency the centre of the political system as it had not been since Lincoln's time. He knew how to manœuvre, how to conciliate congressional leaders; he did not quarrel for quarrelling's sake. And, until he was re-nominated and re-elected in 1904, he avoided a show-down with the conservative elements who had hoped to bury him in the vice-presidency.

The impress on the American mind made by Theodore Roosevelt was greater than the positive achievement of his administration. Indeed, that impress was the main achievement of the administration. He made the federal government dramatic, impressive, popular. He also made it more modern. The new President had ideas on nearly all topics. He had plans for reforming the coinage on Greek models; he revived L'Enfant's plan for the development of Washington. He gave jobs to poets and naturalists as well as to former 'Rough Riders'. He exposed (with the help of a celebrated novel, *The Jungle*, by Upton Sinclair) the filth of the Chicago meat-packing plants. Although far from radical in his economic views, Roosevelt had none of the automatic sympathy with and admiration for the businessman that all his predecessors since Johnson, including Cleveland, had shared. Thus he intervened in the great Pennsylvania coal strike, but on the side of the miners. The effectively dramatised presidential attitude was a novelty in the White House and a welcome novelty. For the discontent that had exploded and died away in the Bryan campaign had taken a new and more relevant form. The Sherman Anti-Trust Act of 1890 had been a dead letter since the Cleveland administration had failed to enforce it in a prosecution that, some said, it had not pressed very effectively. The trusts had certainly flourished. Standard Oil, the best known and most hated, was stronger than ever and not only did the creation, in 1901, of the United States Steel Corporation unite all the great steel producers in one vast combine, but that corporation was capitalised at $1,400,000,000, just about the total of the national debt. And, as it was notorious that the assets taken over were not worth this sum, it was concluded that the promoters, J. P. Morgan and Company, were discounting the future profits of monopoly. When, therefore, the same banking house arranged peace between the warring Harriman and Hill railroad interests by the creation of the Northern Securities Company in 1902, public alarm was great and it was a triumph for the administration when the Supreme Court ordered the dissolution of the company in 1904, an election year.

The Roosevelt administration was marked by the development of two policies that were, among other things, presidential hobbies. Roosevelt had spent impressionable years in the west and he was deeply convinced of the necessity for conservation of natural resources. The policy of withholding national lands from mere exploitation went back as far as Cleveland, but Roosevelt extended the policy, especially the policy of preserving the forests, built up the forest service and dramatised the issue with a success that deeply marked future federal policy.

From his youth, Roosevelt had been fascinated by military affairs and, although protesting his love of peace, was deeply impressed by the reality of war. He supported the efforts of his war secretary, Elihu Root, to reform the army, but nothing could make the United States a great military power. The navy was another matter. Roosevelt begged, pleaded, argued for a big navy and he got it; and he watched the development of that navy with the keenest personal attention. As a gesture for peace through strength, he sent it on a cruise round the world, with only enough funds voted to send it half way, thus imposing on a reluctant Congress the duty of voting the funds to bring it back.

But not all his acts were mere gestures. When he came to office he reopened negotiations with Britain for a new treaty dealing with the 'Isthmian Canal' question. The second Hay–Pauncefote Treaty permitted the United States to fortify the canal. It was now necessary to decide between the Panama and Nicaragua routes: Panama was chosen and the Hay–Herran Convention was negotiated in 1903. But the Colombian senate refused to ratify the Convention and the canal might have been held up, or built in Nicaragua, had not a revolution conveniently broken out in the province of Panama. American recognition was given within three days and a treaty negotiated between Hay and Bunau-Varilla gave the United States the right to construct a canal in the territory of the newborn nation. Later, Roosevelt was to boast that he 'took the Canal'. Although American complicity in the convenient revolution was never proved, the episode poisoned the relations of the United States with Latin America for many years. In other ways Roosevelt wielded what, in one of his telling phrases, he called 'the big stick'. He interpreted the Monroe Doctrine to mean that the United States, if it kept European powers from using normal coercive measures to secure redress from the fleeting governments of the turbulent republics of the Caribbean, was bound, in turn, to impose a minimum of decorum on these republics. Thus the Dominican Republic was put under American supervision, not by a treaty, but by an 'executive agreement', and Olney's dictum in the Venezuela dispute, that the 'fiat' of the United States was law, was made to look like the truth, in this area at least.

Nor were greater issues avoided. The great struggle over the balance of power in the Pacific that led to the Russo-Japanese War saw American official, like unofficial, opinion deeply pro-Japanese. But Roosevelt, acting the part less of the honest broker than of the candid friend, persuaded the Japanese, who were, economically at least, at the end of their tether, to be moderate in their peace terms, and the Treaty of Portsmouth was concluded under American auspices in 1905. The balance of power was threatened in the Atlantic too, and, although less openly than at Portsmouth, Roosevelt supported the Franco-British position at the Algeciras Conference of 1906. Not since the end of the Napoleonic wars had the United States been of such importance in world politics; but then it had been as a patient, now it was very much as an agent.

There was no doubt (at any rate after the death of Mark Hanna, McKinley's manager) that Roosevelt would be re-nominated. The Cleveland Democrats capitalised on Bryan's discomfiture in 1900 and hoped to capitalise conservative discontent with Roosevelt, by nominating a conservative and little-known New York judge, Alton B. Parker, but 'big business' was not frightened enough of the President to back Parker; it contributed handsomely (although Roosevelt did not know or preferred not to know this) to the President's campaign funds. Parker lost many of the supporters of Bryan and gained little from the disgruntled Republicans. The campaign was a great personal triumph and, in the moment of victory, Roosevelt announced that he would not be a candidate for re-election. He was the first President in American history to be elected in his own right after coming to the presidency by mere succession, and he might have accepted the interpretation of the third term taboo pressed on him— that it meant two *elective* terms. But he burnt his boats and, all through his second term, suffered from the congressional knowledge that he would be out of office in 1909. His friends hoped and his enemies feared that he might change his mind, but he was determined to keep his word and even persuaded himself that a little less than eight years in the White House was enough for him and the country.

The second term was not sterile. A beginning was made with effective federal control of railway rates. Relations with Japan, which had rapidly deteriorated with the disappointment of the Japanese people with the terms of the Treaty of Portsmouth and with their resentment of anti-Japanese legislation in California, were nursed back to convalescence, if not health, by the President and his Secretary of State, Elihu Root. Work on the Panama Canal was pushed vigorously ahead after a great deal of initial confusion and squabbling. The President, when he quarrelled, managed as a rule to get the public on his side. His popular prestige was as great as ever and he was able to choose his successor. He had considered Root, but Root's corporation connections were considered too great a handicap and Roosevelt's choice fell on his Secretary of War, the vast William Howard Taft. The Democrats nominated Bryan, who did much better than Parker, showing where the Democratic strength still lay, in the south and west. But the country, seeing in Taft the heir of Roosevelt, voted for the President in choosing his successor.

The new President had never held an elective office before he entered the White House. As a federal judge, as Solicitor-General, as Governor-General of the Philippines, as Secretary of War, Taft had held high but subordinate office. He was now on his own. And he must have been conscious that he was only President because Roosevelt had chosen him as his successor. He began badly by getting rid of the whole Roosevelt Cabinet. He went on by taking the risk (one never taken by Roosevelt) of raising the question of tariff revision. The senatorial leaders, who had smarted under Roosevelt, began to take the measure of his successor and what they saw reassured them. For Taft believed in the separation of powers; it was not his function, he thought, to dictate to Congress or even to lead it. As a result the tariff bill (the Payne–Aldrich bill) which was finally presented to him was a parody of a revision. Taft might have stopped it earlier, might have forced modifications, but he accepted it and defended it. That part of his trade policy which might have redounded to his credit, the Reciprocity treaty with Canada, was rejected by Canada. This was not Taft's fault; if it was anybody's in the United States it was the fault of brash Democratic orators like Champ Clark, now Speaker of the House of Representatives. For the Democrats had capitalised on Republican disunion and had carried the House for the first time since 1892. In the House the middle-western insurgents had already combined with the Democrats to depose the autocratic Speaker Cannon. Even if the President had been willing to lead Congress, it was too late. And Roosevelt had returned from Africa and Europe suspicious and soon to be angry.

The wave of discontent with the old order, with the 'stand-patters', was far from spent. All over the country the voters were looking for a leader and Taft was not that. He felt, rightly, that he had not betrayed the trust that Roosevelt had placed in him. He resented warmly the charge that he and his Secretary of the Interior, Ballinger, had carelessly or corruptly alienated valuable parts of the public domain. He knew that his administration had been more active and more successful in prosecuting the trusts than had Roosevelt's. But Taft was a man of judicial temper and of physical and, to some extent, of mental lethargy. The revolting western radicals would have none of him. For a moment, it seemed possible that they would rally round Senator Robert Marion La Follette of Wisconsin, but La Follette could not compete with Roosevelt as a dramatic figure. And Roosevelt, still young, feeling like 'a bull moose', as he was to say, was under great pressure from his friends and his temperament to break with Taft. Shooting lions in Africa, visiting kings and emperors, receiving the Nobel prize for peace, or even giving the Romanes lecture in Oxford, were not enough for a man of such physical and mental energy, still only a little older than Lincoln had been when he entered the White House. Submitting to both pressures, Roosevelt became a candidate for the Republican nomination.

It is certain that he was the first choice of the average Republican voter, and it is probable that he was the only candidate who could have held the deeply divided party together. But Taft was resolved to fight and with him was most of the high command of the party, including such close friends of Roosevelt as Henry Cabot Lodge and Elihu Root. And the high command were ready to lose with Taft rather than win with Roosevelt and see the control of the party pass into dangerously radical hands. A President in office can always secure his re-nomination and Taft did so; but Roosevelt and his supporters, protesting that he had been robbed of the nomination, hastily founded the Progressive party and it nominated its hero.

This made a Democratic victory certain and, from the politicians' point of view, the obvious candidate was the Speaker of the House of Representatives, Champ Clark of Missouri. But Bryan, although even he had come to see that a fourth nomination was almost, perhaps quite, impossible, saw in Clark the nominee and ally of his old conservative enemies, the people who had nominated Parker in 1904. He threw his strength, which was still very great, to the only serious rival of Clark, the governor of New Jersey, Woodrow Wilson, who overtook the Speaker's early lead and was nominated.

The Democratic candidate was as unusual a phenomenon in American politics, in his way, as Roosevelt was in his. He had been in active politics for only two years when nominated. He had been a distinguished professor of political science and a famous President of Princeton University. He had been a standard southern, conservative Democrat, opposed to Bryan and Bryanism. But he fought and fought unavailingly to make Princeton 'democratic'. He became, to many, a martyr; he also became impossible as President of Princeton. He accepted the offer of the Democratic bosses to run for governor of New Jersey and was triumphantly elected. Again he became a national figure by quarrelling with the bosses, by defeating them and by advancing increasingly radical views. And it was as a radical, or at any rate as an advanced liberal, campaigning for 'the New Freedom', that he was triumphantly elected.

The new President was a devoted admirer of British constitutional practice. He saw himself both as President and as Prime Minister. When he was still President of Princeton University he had written that 'if he [the President] led the nation, his party can hardly resist him. His office is anything he has the capacity and force to make it.' He practised this doctrine. He disregarded the precedent set by Jefferson, who was no orator, and, instead of sending a long, written—and ignored—message to Congress, he addressed it in person, and Wilson was an orator. He had prepared and now pushed through a coherent programme of legislation. A bill reducing the tariff was introduced and passed by effective and dramatic appeals to the public and effective public and private pressure on Congress. The long-debated question of a reformed banking system was dealt with by the creation of the Federal Reserve System that provided for a far more elastic currency and a much better organised federal banking system. It also, in form, gratified the hostility to bankers of the agrarian radicals, whose leader, Bryan, Wilson prudently made Secretary of State.

He gratified Bryan in other ways: by tolerating, and to some extent gratifying, his desire to reward the faithful 'deserving Democrats' with patronage and by withdrawing support from the American bankers, who had been encouraged by the previous administration to meddle in the already troubled affairs of China. 'Dollar diplomacy' was deemed to be dead. True, Wilson was unlucky. In Mexico a real revolution was continuing. No Mexican government could carry out the normal obligations of a sovereign state. Many Americans had very real grievances against Mexico and Wilson was forced, he thought, to intervene and occupy Tampico to secure reparation for an insult to the flag. But he did succeed in getting rid of the 'usurper', Huerta, and, by accepting the mediation of Argentina, Brazil and Chile, he conciliated Latin-American opinion. He proclaimed that the Monroe Doctrine was not a form of protectorate and, although he continued intervention in the Caribbean, he steadfastly refused full-scale intervention in Mexico, contenting himself, in 1916, with sending a punitive expedition after Pancho Villa, who had raided American territory. The grant of greater autonomy to the Philippines, like the granting of American citizenship to the inhabitants of Puerto Rico, was proof of the same liberal, anti-imperialistic attitude.

But the war of 1914, as Wilson feared, pushed him, the longer it lasted, into the field of foreign affairs for which he was not prepared. It caused the resignation of Bryan from the Cabinet. The question of the American attitude to the two sides more and more preoccupied the President and the public. Legislation was not stopped. Labour unions were exempted (it was thought) from the anti-trust legislation; a Federal Trade Commission was set up to control business in the spirit of 'the New Freedom'. One of the most effective critics of big business, Louis Brandeis, was put, after a bitter fight, on the Supreme Court. The demand of the railway workers for a federal limitation of hours was granted in the Adamson Act and, at the end of his first term, Wilson could look back at a record of successful domestic leadership that few Presidents have ever equalled.

The reunited Republicans nominated Charles Evans Hughes, who resigned from the Supreme Court to run. Hughes was a stiff and tactless candidate and alienated some Progressive supporters he might have won. But Wilson's record was his chief asset, not only his domestic record, but the belief, summed up in a famous convention speech, that 'he kept us out of war'. It was to be an ironical reason for victory. The Democrats elected their President but barely kept control of Congress. Wilson, once re-elected, attempted to mediate between the warring powers, but the future of German–American relations was being settled in Berlin, not in Washington. The German high command decided to ignore the risk of American intervention which, they decided, would come too late to be effective and, a month after his second inauguration, Wilson led the American people into war. Wilson the reformer became Wilson the war leader. True, the United States was not an ally, only an 'associated power', but Wilson was the chief spokesman to his own people, to the allied peoples, to the German people, to the Russian people. Necessarily, the 'New Freedom' was neglected and the administration devoted more and more exclusively to the war. No American war had ever been run so efficiently, with so few scandals, with such a rapid mobilisation of the power of what was now the world's greatest industrial nation. The American people had reason to be grateful, but their gratitude, unlike their patriotism, was limited. The famous speeches that were heard round the world, culminating in the 'fourteen points' speech of 8 January 1918, had more enthusiastic audiences in tormented Europe than in a comparatively immune America.

The internal impact of the war was, by the standards of the time, very great. Conscription for service overseas was an unprecedented innovation. So were the economic controls like the imposition of limits on farm prices, the assumption of a general direction of the railways. The campaigns for the 'victory loans' were propaganda efforts unknown even in the Civil War and they were accompanied by a repression of dissent also unknown in the Civil War and more severe than anything found in Britain, France or Germany. The two 'Espionage Acts' seemed, to many, a gross breach of American tradition. German-Americans were the subject of an imbecile campaign of hostility, and radical dissenters began to suffer from legal and extra-legal repression. The President, absorbed in the conduct of the war and inclined to see in criticism and scepticism a reflection on his own moral purpose, was not as wisely magnanimous as Lincoln. He was, however, less inclined than Lincoln had been to act on a vague 'war power'. He went to Congress for his authority, but equally refused to countenance anything like the Civil War 'Committee on the Conduct of the War'. The Republican opposition, for the most part, supported all the war effort zealously; indeed, its most vocal members deplored the mildness of the President's language in his addresses to the German people and professed fear of a 'soft peace'. Wilson's refusal to give high command in the overseas army to Roosevelt and to Leonard Wood embittered their numerous Republican friends, and the President neglected to encourage, by close association with the administration, the numerous Republicans who wanted something more than victory. In the autumn of 1918 victory was in sight. So were the congressional elections and Wilson was induced to issue an appeal for a Democratic Congress. It is commonly asserted that this was a mistake. That cannot be proved or disproved. At any rate, the Republicans carried both houses.

Quite early in the war many Americans had pondered the problem of a 'League to Enforce Peace', and the President was determined to make that the basis of the new peace treaty. The war had been represented to the American people simply as a crusade for perpetual peace. That it might be that, and other things as well, had not been stressed and candid discussion of war issues was difficult under the régime of the Espionage Acts. Yet the loss of control of Congress did not shake Wilson's confidence in his mandate or his mission. He decided, against the advice of some close friends, to go to Europe himself. He neglected to take with him any of the eminent Republicans, like Taft, who might have carried weight in the party that now controlled Congress. Wilson in Europe was a Messiah at the very time that he was being disowned at home. For the American people was demobilising, psychologically as well as materially. The artificial character of much of the support for the war effort was now made manifest; so was the folly of imposing conformity. Germans, Irish and then Italians turned against the administration.

The Republican leadership took full advantage of the change. The new chairman of the Senate Foreign Relations Committee, Henry Cabot Lodge, packed the committee and led the campaign to impose reservations on the Covenant of the League of Nations that the President would refuse. Wilson, finally returning from Europe with a treaty of peace indissolubly tied up, he thought, with the Covenant, began a speaking tour to reconvert the country. Without the aid of wireless, Wilson undertook a task beyond his power and collapsed in Denver. He refused to compromise and any chance of American adherence to the League was over.

It was evident that the tide was turning against the Democrats, that the referendum that Wilson had called for would be hostile to his great design. The stroke which the President had suffered kept him from exercising his functions either as President or as party leader, and a sharp economic recession in 1920, the election year, further blighted the faint Democratic hopes. They nominated a former governor of Ohio, James M. Cox, an able and responsible newspaper owner little known outside his state, and, as a running mate, gave him the handsome and energetic young Assistant-Secretary of the Navy, Franklin D. Roosevelt. In the far more important Republican Convention the leading candidates cancelled each other out and the small senatorial group and some astute party managers imposed on the tired delegates an empty, idle, Ohio senator, Warren Gamaliel Harding. The platform was highly ambiguous, and eminent Republicans who had supported entry into the League could persuade themselves that the way to do it was to vote the Republican ticket. The managers of the campaign knew better. As a last and sole gesture of independence the convention nominated the governor of Massachusetts, Calvin Coolidge, for the vice-presidency. The election was a walkover; the Republicans carried every state outside the 'solid South' and carried Tennessee in it. The exile of the party that thought that it alone was fit to govern was ended. So was intrusion into the affairs of other nations. Once in office, any serious attempt to carry out the vague promises of the platform was abandoned and instead a separate peace was made with Germany. The 'great crusade' was over and disowned.

The years between the inauguration of Harding and the stock market crash of 24 October 1929 became, in retrospect, one of the least admired periods in American history, only comparable with the years that followed the Civil War. Each was a 'gilded age'. And, because the second era coincided with a profound change in the folkways of the American people, affecting domestic life, education, religion, sport, because a whole host of new forces attacked the older American ways, it was an era far more disturbed than the era of Grant. It lay between two catastrophic wars, in an age of change at least as profound as the age of the French Revolution and Napoleon. It would have been strange if the leaders in politics, in business, in religion, in education, had all been adequate in the crisis. Many were not and none were fully adequate. But they suffered a double condemnation since many of them claimed a competence that it was soon tragically demonstrated that they did not possess, and the outer world, on which a majority of the American people had gladly turned its back in 1920, refused to be excluded, refused to limit its sins and follies to those which did not affect the United States.

The landslide character of the Harding victory in 1920 was an affirmation of a nostalgia for the safe, stable American past that men thought, rightly, was threatened. It was a triumph for those sections of the Republican party which resented the concessions to 'progressivism' that had been forced on the party since the death of President McKinley. Yet the federal government did not quite go back to the old ways. A higher degree of control of the railroads was entrusted to the Interstate Commerce Commission and new obligations were imposed on the railways. Other instruments of federal control might be emasculated, as was the Federal Trade Commission; the spirit of the Republican administrations might be far more friendly to business rights (often disguised as states' rights) than had been true of the Wilson administration; but federal power could not but grow, if only because the new industries spreading into previously rural regions, the greater financial integration produced by the working of the Federal Reserve banking system, produced a 'more perfect union' that only the doctrinaire could ignore. The mere necessity of servicing the national debt, which had increased nearly twenty-five-fold since

1914, extended federal power and gave to questions of tax policy a new intensity of interest. It was possible to pass a temporary and then a permanent tariff law (the Fordney–McCumber Act of 1922), but this return to the principles of high protection did not merely, by being enacted, make the United States again a debtor nation or provide the dollar-hungry countries of Europe with means of buying American exports, above all of buying the products of the extension and intensification of American agricultural production that the war had fostered. Nor was it possible to limit the effects of the immigration restrictions that cut down to a trickle what had been a flood, and discriminated (as they were intended to do) against the 'new immigration' from eastern and southern Europe. 'America', said President Coolidge, 'must be kept American.'

That was also the view of less eminent persons. In the south there was a revival of the Ku-Klux-Klan. It was not, for long, confined to the southern states, although it tended, in the north, to be strongest in states like Indiana with a strong southern element in the population. Nor was its sole enemy the Negro. Its members had to be 'white, Gentile, Protestants'. It enforced the standards of fundamentalist Protestant morality by whipping, branding, castration, murder.

The uneasiness that led to the creation of the new Ku-Klux-Klan found other manifestations. It inspired legislation against the teaching of Darwinian evolutionary theory in the schools of several states; it inspired violent controversies within Protestant churches in which 'fundamentalists' (the term dates from this time) fought 'modernists'.

Politically, the most important achievement of this defence of the old American standards was the adoption of the eighteenth amendment to the Constitution in 1919. It provided not for the extension of the powers of Congress over the liquor traffic, but for the prohibition of 'the manufacture, sale or transportation of intoxicating liquors within, the importation thereof into, or the exportation thereof from the United States and all territory subject to the jurisdiction thereof'. It also provided that 'the Congress and the several States shall have concurrent power to enforce this article by appropriate legislation'. All states but Connecticut and Rhode Island finally ratified the amendment. Many states began by passing legislation reinforcing the main federal law, the 'Volstead Act', but zeal evaporated as it was discovered that mere law had very serious limits. Within a few years the administration of prohibition legislation, then the whole question of the wisdom and efficacy of the amendment, were one of the two or three burning themes of politics and one of the most significant lines of division between the old America and the new: the America of the countryside and the small towns, mainly north European in origin and Protestant in religion; and the America of the great new urban centres, where most of the population was of fairly recent immigrant stock, Catholic or Jewish in religion, and, in ways of life, ignoring some of the most cherished traditions and prejudices of the countryside.

Behind the fears for the American way of life lay equally potent discontent with some aspects of that life. The artificial markets created by the war had led to a fantastic overestimate of the permanent demand for American foodstuffs and raw materials like cotton. The prices of land soared as these expectations were discounted. Arable settlement moved in the war years and immediately afterwards into areas unsuited for ploughing except in exceptionally favourable seasons. Money was borrowed to buy land, to pay for improvements, to build schools and roads. The slump of 1920 wiped out many hundreds of millions of investments, turned many owners into tenants, wrecked the hopes of becoming owners of many more and left all the western and some of the southern states with a permanent grievance. They alone were not sharing in the golden stream that was flowing so freely in other regions. An alliance between the representatives and senators of both parties, the 'farm bloc', weakened party discipline. Behind and below the formal Republican triumphs there was this pool of discontent. And no Republican administration committed to the *ethos* of business could give the farmers what they wanted: some real, tangible, cash equivalent of the benefits flowing to industry from high tariffs. The new Republican administration had good fortune in its first year or two. The business recession of 1920 passed away and what was, with some minor lapses, an unprecedented boom began. The great American mass production automobile industry, personified by Henry Ford, was the delight of Americans and the wonder and envy of the world. Poverty was boldly asserted to be disappearing; the immense wealth produced by business was lavishly if not equally distributed.

Even the outside world seemed, for a moment, to be returning to sanity and solvency. The American government carefully avoided all commitments in Europe or Asia, but the two 'settlements' of the German reparations question were made under American auspices: the Dawes plan in 1924, the Young plan in 1929. The American government denied any moral or legal connection between the reparations debts owed by Germany to Britain, France, Italy and the debts these countries owed America, but the funds with which Germany paid the victors were provided by the American private investor and, in turn, were in the main paid over to the American government as part of the war-debt settlements negotiated in these years; settlements that, admitting the desirability of such payments, were in the presumed economic state of Europe generous—a view more strongly held in America than in Europe. In the Far East the Washington Treaty of 1922 which settled, for the time being, the ratio of naval power seemed, to the optimistic, to deal adequately with the situation created by the absence of Russian power, the decline of British and French power, the chronic civil war in China and the temptations that this situation offered to an economically expanding but hard-pressed Japan. Even when the stability of this settlement was open to more and more doubt, the Kellogg Pact of 1928, in which all the great powers, except Russia, renounced 'recourse to war...as an instrument of national policy', seemed to a legalistically minded people to mean the end of the threat of a renewal of the follies of 1914–18. It also made the disputes over armament conventions more unintelligible, more easily explicable in terms of the crude interests of bankers and munition makers. The discomfited Democrats themselves abandoned the cause of the League of Nations. And it was significant that, despite support from every President right down to the outbreak of the second world war, all attempts to get the United States to join the World Court broke down in the Senate.

Good fortune also attended the Republicans in a grim form, for the death of President Harding in 1923 relieved them of a burden that might have been fatal to their chances in 1924. Harding, if not quite as unfit to be President as criticism after his death alleged, and slowly learning his trade, yet had no serious executive or legislative experience and, if not so much a dupe of his corrupt friends as they suggested, was yet too tolerant of small-town grafters like his Attorney-General, Harry Daugherty, and men of desperate fortunes like Secretary of the Interior Fall. Soon rumours and then more than rumours of corruption began to spread. And they were rumours of corruption on a great scale, of corruption abetted by the Attorney-General and the Secretary of the Interior as well as corruption affecting lesser federal officers. Harding died before the storm broke. The Senate investigated scandals connected with the alienation of federal oil lands, with the administration of the Department of Justice, with the Veterans Administration. The evidence was abundant and conclusive: there had been no such plundering of the public assets since Grant's time. The new President hesitated but gave way. Three cabinet officers resigned; one was later imprisoned; the new administration cleaned house and the evil was interréd with the bones of Harding.

The new President, Calvin Coolidge, was of a very different type from the lush orator and small-town editor who had been foisted on the American people. He was a dry, Yankee lawyer, with experience of administration as mayor of Northampton and governor of Massachusetts and with a record of party regularity that had not involved him in being the dupe or accomplice of politicians like Harry Daugherty or Albert Fall. He gave to the White House, in an age of dissolving standards, a reassuring air of Yankee thrift, caution and taciturnity. The Republicans soon noticed that their new President was an asset and all the resources of publicity were devoted to building him up.

Inside the Democratic party the feud between city and country, the old and the new, took dramatic and suicidal form. The two chief candidates for the nomination in 1924 were William Gibbs McAdoo, Wilson's

Secretary of the Treasury (and son-in-law), and Alfred Emmanuel Smith, who was serving his second term as the phenomenally popular governor of New York. One was the candidate of the rural, evangelical, 'dry' sections of the party, the candidate favoured by William Jennings Bryan; the other was of Catholic Irish origin, a son of Tammany Hall, a 'wet', most manifestly a child of the 'sidewalks of New York'. The partisans of the two wrecked the convention and the chances of the Democratic party. The nominee, chosen almost in despair, was an eminent corporation lawyer, John W. Davis, who campaigned on the issue of corruption. It was not only that the issue was not very effective in a boom year, but a great part of the radical discontent of the country was drawn off to support the 'Progressive' candidacy of Robert Marion La Follette, the famous radical senator. In these circumstances, the victory of the Republicans was inevitable.

Coolidge, as much as Walpole, wanted to let sleeping dogs lie. The business boom continued and the Secretary of Commerce, Herbert Hoover, both encouraged the rationalisation of internal business, the standardisation of technical and of commercial practice, and encouraged American business to look abroad for ever-expanding markets. There were dark patches. The textile towns of New England were harder and harder hit by southern competition. Many coalfields faced crippling competition from fields either newer or easier to run because the miners' unions were weak or absent. The hopes of an expansion of organised labour that had risen high in the war were seen to be baseless. The unions barely held their own. In some areas they did not do even that. The radical forces that had rallied round La Follette were disorganised and demoralised. Communist zealots were active in fomenting strikes, in starting rival unions, in all kinds of agitation and propaganda, but what was the use in a country like the America of Coolidge?

As the presidential campaign of 1928 approached, there was only one doubt in the minds of the observers: would President Coolidge run? In an ambiguous statement he conveyed that he would not and that made it certain that the two candidates would be Herbert Hoover, the successful personification of the businessman in politics, and 'Al' Smith, now serving his fourth term as governor of New York. They were duly nominated and the campaign was of more significance than it seemed. For the nomination of a Catholic brought into the open the forces that had hidden behind the Ku-Klux-Klan. In no campaign in modern times had word-of-mouth slander played a greater part. And, with one important exception, in no campaign in modern times had the two candidates been closer in their programmes. Each asked for a mandate to carry on the business of the United States as it was being carried on. The one exception was that Governor Smith was hostile to the zeal with which, formally at least, the federal government was enforcing prohibition, while to Secretary

Hoover it was 'a great social and economic experiment, noble in motive and far-reaching in purpose'.

Again, there was little doubt of the issue. Prosperity was too widely spread, the 'golden expectation' of an even more rapid increase in wealth and in general well-being too generally shared, for an opposition candidate, even if he had not been a Catholic, Tammany New Yorker, to defeat the party that had wrought so well. And formally the Democratic party did worse than ever before, even losing five states of the solid south. But some observers noted that Smith got more votes than any Democrat had ever got, that he carried Massachusetts and Rhode Island and that everywhere in the great cities he showed a strength that no Democratic candidate had known for a generation. But the business candidate was elected and prepared to lead a business civilisation to greater heights. In less than six months the bubble burst. It is possible that earlier 'panics' were as severe as that which began with the break in the New York Stock Exchange. Earlier panics, too, had had marked political results. But the 'Depression' of 1929 which lasted, in one form or another, though with diminishing severity, until 1940 was more revolutionary in its impact than the previous 'panics' had been. It produced changes in American political and economic life as important as those produced by the Civil War, and more important than American intervention in the first world war or possibly even in the second.

In the first place, it accelerated developments in American governmental functions and in state and federal relations that would no doubt have come anyway. Isolationism had taken more forms than the drawing of American skirts away from Europe. It had been based on a belief that, inside America as well as outside it, dangers threatened the American way, dangers of state intervention in favour of labour, dangers of rudimentary state socialism, dangers of the use of the taxing power to redistribute income in accordance with some idea of social justice. It was not accidental or insignificant that the unions started and controlled by the great corporations should have been dubbed by the sponsors 'the American plan'. The same forces that produced political support for prohibition, for immigration restriction, that produced laws against 'radicalism', were at work in saving the United States from the contagious example of Europe. But, seen over a longer perspective, the forces, social and political, that were at work in the presidencies of the first Roosevelt and of Taft and during the first term of Wilson were only stayed, not stopped. They were stayed because the Republicans and their business allies claimed, plausibly, to be the natural, beneficent and successful leaders of the American people. 'The business of the United States is business', said Coolidge in an unguarded moment, but, taken out of its context as it was, the phrase did represent what most Americans thought. It was discovered, between 1929 and 1933, that the business leaders did not understand or could not control the great economic machine that they had claimed to have made and to know how to operate with more and more skill.

The inevitable result of the depression was to weaken, then to destroy faith in, the business class as a ruling class. Even as far as it was merely a matter of liquidation of speculation, it was serious enough and faith-destroying enough. Millions had been encouraged to speculate—in German securities, in Latin-American securities, in many much-touted American securities—and these investments proved of no more permanent value than losing tickets at a race meeting. Nor had most of these securities been marketed by fly-by-night entrepreneurs (although there were enough of them), but by great banks and by great bankers. Even had there been no more speculation, the credit structure was top-heavy. The long farm depression had, for years before the crash, been putting a strain not only on local banks, which failed in thousands, but on insurance companies, on loan companies, on holders of farm mortgages. The railroads were not in good shape, and even when well managed (and not all were) were under the strain of competition from the automobile, car and truck alike. As pressure continued, as banks insisted on payment of loans, as brokerage houses insisted on payment of margins, as money was lost in 'safe' banks and 'safe' securities, cautious and secure citizens found themselves as badly off as the mere gamblers. And, as scandal after scandal was revealed; as it was learned how the tax laws made it easy and legal for the rich-and-well-advised to avoid payment of income tax; as it was learned how the markets had been rigged; as towering pyramids of cards like the Insull utilities 'empire', or the less scandalous but equally insolvent Van Sweringen railroad 'empire' collapsed, discontent and distrust swelled into fear and anger. The American people, or many millions of them, had been betrayed by their natural leaders, so they turned to other leaders.

It was possibly unjust that this loss of faith should have been most visible in the change of the popular attitude to the new President. Herbert Hoover's reputation for ability, probity, industry, special competence, was not fictitious. But he had not only to deal with a world crisis, he had to deal with a domestic crisis for which his party, if not himself, was in part to blame, by its tariff policy, by its blind faith in the wisdom and trustworthiness of big business, by its illusion that the outer world could be ignored. Thus the only Republican answer to the crisis in America's balance of payments was to raise the tariff yet higher in the Smoot–Hawley Act of 1930, a piece of monstrously ill-timed legislation. Many were willing to believe that the two congressional authors of the Act did not know what they were doing, but could not believe that the President, the former energetic Secretary of Commerce, who had so pushed external trade, did not know it. Whether positive American co-operation in liquidating the war debts, reparations and the whole tangled web of

inextricable financial deals made in the boom years would have saved
Europe from the final crash no one knows. But the President could not
do more than offer a temporary moratorium. Congress and public opinion
would not let him do more. And, even if it was true, in part, that America's
troubles came from Europe, the American people had been taught for
over a decade to disregard the powers for mischief of the outside world.
It was too late to blame Europe now. The administration was blamed
instead.

It was blamed for many things, for some of which it had no responsibility. It may be doubted whether any administration would have dared
rigorously to limit the supply of money for speculative financing, thus
bringing an end to a boom that most Americans expected to last and
whose cessation they would have blamed on the politicians, not on the
bankers and businessmen. Believing at first that the collapse of the
market was merely a market collapse, a healthy shaking out of speculators,
the Hoover administration placed too much faith in faith, in reassuring
messages, in prophecies of speedy recovery 'just around the corner'. And
there were, in 1930, short periods of recovery, short periods of minor
booms, and the congressional elections of that year were less disastrous
than had been feared. The Republicans just lost the House and just held
the Senate.

It was in the second half of President Hoover's term that the rot set in.
It set in because, as the depression stayed and deepened, the problem of
what to do about it became the main theme of politics and one that
brought out sectional, party and class differences. After a decade of
budget surpluses there was a series of deficits. How were they to be met, by
higher income taxes, by closing the gaps revealed in the existing tax laws
or, in part, by a sales tax? A revolt of Democrats and insurgent Republicans defeated the sales tax in the House of Representatives. The insolvency of many railways, the threatened insolvency of many banks and
the many disastrous bank failures, the drying up of local credit, left the
federal government no choice but the underwriting of the credit structure.
One instrument of that underwriting was the creation of the Reconstruction Finance Corporation. But, for the insurgent members of Congress,
the theory behind the new corporation was exactly what the country had
been wrecked on. It was the theory of wealth and well-being percolating
down from above. They wanted aid for the unemployed to be provided
by the federal government, aid provided for bankrupt municipalities and
for states whose tax resources were drying up. Poverty was no respecter
of state lines and some of the poorest states had the most poor. It was
not until 1932 that the barriers the Hoover administration had set up
against 'raids on the treasury' began to go down. It was noted, bitterly,
that they did not go down until the depression had finally reached the
possessing classes. For the great corporations which had cut wages and

dismissed workers also maintained dividends, dividends not earned and not necessarily spent when received. The owners of tax-free securities (which successive Secretaries of the Treasury had tried to have abolished) still drew their interest, while all public services were cut—libraries, schools, roads, even prisons suffered from a wave of drastic economy that was thought, by many 'responsible' people, to be the drastic cure for the economic disease.

But not all voters or politicians were 'responsible'. A few listened to the heretical theories of John Maynard Keynes; others revived the old inflationary panaceas; the veterans, or most of them, wanted to be paid a bonus, now. Thousands of the veterans descended on Washington; the 'bonus army' was like Coxey's army of 1894. The veterans were finally expelled from their camp by troops using gas bombs. It was the equivalent of Cleveland's use of troops to break the Pullman strike in 1894. But it got far less applause and was one of the many burdens the administration had to bear in an election year.

Despite all the activity of Communists, of Socialists, of radicals of all types, it was to the regular opposition that the voters were turning. The Democratic nominee would be elected; the only question was his identity. The obvious candidate was Franklin Delano Roosevelt. Roosevelt had been elected governor of New York in 1928 when his chief, Al Smith, failed to carry his own state. He was re-elected in 1930 with the greatest majority in the state's history. He was the most 'available' candidate and, despite bitter opposition, he was nominated and broke all tradition by flying at once to the Convention and accepting the nomination on the spot. This disregard of tradition gave a welcome impression of energy and gave proof that the infantile paralysis from which the candidate suffered had not destroyed his energy. The Democratic platform, above all its double promise of a reduction in federal expenditure and support for the repeal of prohibition, won millions of voters away from the Republicans; for, to add yet another millstone to their burden, the Republicans had hedged about the fate of what the public insisted, wrongly, that the President had called 'the noble experiment'. Roosevelt carried forty-two states, including all the large states save Pennsylvania. The Democrats swept both houses of Congress and nearly all state offices and state legislatures. There was a mandate to do something, but there was then an interval of four months between the election and the inauguration of the new President. President Hoover stubbornly stuck to his policies, above all to measures designed to keep the dollar on gold. The President-elect, equally firmly, refused to underwrite the policies of the repudiated administration and party. The world situation grew worse. Hitler took power in Germany; an assassin almost succeeded in killing Roosevelt in Florida. The long-promised revival of business was postponed again because, said the Republicans, uncertainty about the policies of the new administration destroyed confidence. But that had been destroyed at least a year before.

The crisis that the new administration had to deal with had only been equalled, if ever, by the crisis that faced Lincoln in March and April 1861. Three years of deepening economic distress had undercut the foundations of many once strong and respected institutions. Few governmental units, cities, counties, states, were solvent. Social institutions designed for a rural society, charitable institutions designed for minor economic catastrophes or personal disasters, had had to face an ever-increasing strain. Under that strain they were breaking and what threatened to become an unmanageable mass of misery was poised like an avalanche. Social habits which had made for stability and discipline had been worn down. The 'bonus marchers' in Washington had been, for the timorous, only the precursors of the storm. If the angered veterans, if the desperate unemployed once began to move *en masse*, what could the local authorities, often bankrupt, with their reduced police forces, with their sullen citizens all around them, do? What meaning in this context had the traditional slogans of Americanism, the traditional precepts of self-help, of thrift, of sturdy independence? Indeed, the wonder was not that these attitudes were wearing out, but that they had lasted so long. The winter's discontent faced the new administration, and its situation was made dramatic, and the need for a dramatic solution made evident, by the collapse of the banking system. Banks had failed in increasing numbers: little country banks, great city banks. But now the machinery of banking and credit was grinding to a stop. More and more bank holidays were proclaimed until, on the eve of the inauguration, banks were closed in forty-seven states. And one of the first acts of the new President was to close all banks in the United States by presidential proclamation. Congress hastily ratified this action; no banks could be reopened except by permission of the federal government. The federal reserve banks were reopened first, then the solvent private banks. The first shock of the crisis had been met.

It is impossible to understand the 'New Deal' without bearing in mind the character of the crisis with which the new administration was faced. In his inaugural address, Roosevelt had said that there was 'nothing to fear but fear itself'. But the old sources of faith, trust in the regular way of doing things, in the businessman as the natural custodian of the governmental machinery—all these supports to faith had gone. They had to be replaced by new faith, faith in new ways of doing things, faith in the energy and audacity of the new administration. That faith was given abundantly and uncritically; it was near-treason to be critical. Franklin D. Roosevelt began his administration with a greater share of the confidence of his countrymen, especially but not exclusively of his electors, than any President had ever had, except possibly Jackson, Grant and Hoover.

The first months of the New Deal came to be known in retrospect as 'the Hundred Days'. But it was not a hundred days ending in Waterloo, but a hundred days ending in a feeling of hope and energy that the American people had not known since 1930. Again, in immediate retrospect, the period seemed to be completely dominated by the leadership of the new President; it was dominated by him, but not completely. He had been nominated by a coalition of the west and south, the same coalition that had nominated Wilson in 1912 and re-elected him in 1916. And that coalition still hankered after the old remedies, above all inflation by the use of silver or the issue of paper currency. The banking policy of the new administration was thus, in part, forced on it by the knowledge of the strength of the inflationary forces, by the knowledge that 'sound banking practice' meant for many, perhaps most Americans in 1933, an ingenious system of robbery. So the sprawling banking system was left unrationalised, for, although many hundreds of banks never reopened, the local banking system remained unaltered. The one great change was the imposition of a system of federal guarantee of deposits (at that time up to $5,000), a measure that shocked the orthodox, but which was essential if restoration of faith in banking and the restoration of the credit structure were to be possible. In the same way, the embittered farmers had to be given something tangible. The 'revolving funds', the marketing schemes with which the Republicans had attempted to cure the earthquake that was threatening to bring the rural credit structure down and which threatened to produce something like a *jacquerie*, were swept aside. Farmers were to be paid *not* to produce the excessively abundant crops which were driving down the prices below the bankruptcy level and the A.A.A. (Agricultural Adjustment Administration) came into being. In the field of industry, a corresponding effort was made to put an end to the much denounced evils of 'cut-throat competition'. This effort took shape in the most controversial experiment of the first New Deal, N.R.A. (the National Recovery Administration). N.R.A. lumped together, in a hastily and badly drafted statute, a number of remedies not necessarily consistent with one another. Like some other legislation of this time, it was in part designed to head off more radical measures, such as the Black–Connery bill that proposed to spread employment by imposing a thirty-hour week. Originally N.R.A. was to provide public works (carrying farther a remedy tried by the Hoover Administration); its functions included the relief of agriculture. But, by the time the law was enacted, these two fields of action had been allotted to others. The device by which the N.R.A. became best known, the 'codes of fair competition', were, again, originally planned only for the great, well-organised industries. But every type of business insisted on sharing in the guarantees against 'unfair competition'. Labour, too, wanted its share in guaranteed wages, in limitation of hours, in recognition of the sickly trade unions. Even the consumer was to be represented and protected. N.R.A. was launched under General Hugh A. Johnson with all the publicity that had been used for the 'Victory Loans'. The emblem of the 'Blue Eagle' was sported by great businesses and little. And since one object of N.R.A. was the raising of prices, people bought against the anticipated rise and caused a reversal of the long, downward spiral.

It was not only that this precautionary buying came to an end in a few months, but that not all firms played up, notably the great and, until recently, sacred firm of Henry Ford. Many minor businesses which had gladly sported the 'Blue Eagle' now began to repent it. Evasion of its obligations became more and more common, the hastily drawn-up codes were harder and harder to enforce. Labour, too, found that employment did not noticeably increase, and where it did it was not obvious that the codes deserved the credit. And the protection given to the unions, in the Act and in the codes, turned out to be illusory. By the time that the Supreme Court unanimously condemned the original act in *Schechter Poultry Corporation v. The United States* (1935) N.R.A. was already moribund. Few regretted its death except the President, and his public regrets may not have represented his real thoughts.

In other ways, the new administration turned its back on the policy of its immediate predecessor. That the new administration would tamper with the currency had been a resented Republican charge. But it promptly did so; the United States went off gold and the President 'torpedoed' the London economic conference by his refusal to discuss stabilisation, a decision that put further severe pressure on the remaining gold-standard countries, notably France, and acted both as a tariff barrier to European imports and a bonus to American exports. The new currency policy, if it horrified the orthodox, gratified that much more numerous group, the creditors, who had seen their real obligations rise steadily since 1929 (see ch. III). The foreign economic policy of the new administration, indeed its whole foreign policy in this period, was what came to be called 'isolationist'. The new Secretary of State, Cordell Hull, was a fervent Wilsonian, a believer in low tariffs and in international co-operation but, as yet, he had not the ear of the President.

The American people had discovered how little paper barriers to aggression meant when Japan destroyed the last remnants of Chinese authority in Manchuria over the heated protests of President Hoover's Secretary of State, Henry L. Simson, not backed up, even verbally, with any warmth by the British Foreign Secretary, Sir John Simon. The temper of the people was revealed in the Johnson Act of 1934, which forbade all credits to countries which had defaulted in payments on their war-debts to the United States. A special Senate committee, headed by Senator Nye, seemed to the uncritical to prove that one of the main causes of war was the selfish interest of bankers and munitions makers, the 'merchants of death'. A series of 'Neutrality Acts' prohibited trade in arms or the extension of credit to belligerents. The administration resisted, as far as it could, attempts to limit executive discretion, but it had to accept legislation designed, as was later said, to 'keep the United States out of the war of 1914'.

A more positive policy was inherited from the Republicans in the Latin-American field. A series of Mexican revolutions had further complicated the problems that plagued and perplexed Wilson. Confiscation of American property was answered by vehement demands for redress, to be obtained by force if necessary. The worst of the tension with Mexico was ended by Coolidge's ambassador, Dwight Morrow, although a formal settlement of American claims was not completed until 1942. Intervention in the Caribbean republics was ended (except in Haiti) and $25,000,000 was paid to Colombia in 1921 for unspecified losses, which meant the damage done by American policy at the time of the Panama 'revolution'. The Roosevelt administration carried farther the 'good neighbour' policy. After a revolution in Cuba, it consented to an abrogation of the Platt amendment of 1901 authorising American intervention to preserve order in the newly liberated republic. Haiti was evacuated and Pan-American conferences were used by Secretary Hull to build up a policy of 'hemispheric solidarity'. In the Philippines, where the Wilson policy of self-government had been to a large extent reversed by the Harding administration, the Roosevelt administration moved towards complete independence (a movement made easier by American pressure-groups hostile to competition of Philippine products inside the American customs barriers). The Commonwealth of the Philippines was created and it achieved complete independence in 1946.

Next to the bankers in public disesteem were the great power companies, and it was easy to get through Congress a measure, vetoed by several Republican presidents in a simpler form, for using federal installations of the late war at Muscle Shoals on the Tennessee River to produce power. But the Tennessee Valley Authority had more to do than improve navigation and, as an ostensible side line, produce power. The whole valley was to be rehabilitated by a government corporation, secured from political interference, with a broad commission to promote the general welfare of an especially backward region where the normal motives of capitalist development did not work. Attacked in the courts and shaken by internal feuds, the T.V.A. survived and throve, becoming one of the showpieces of the administration.

There were other new federal organisations created, like the Securities and Exchange Commission invented to police the stock markets. The powers of the Interstate Commerce Commission and of the Reconstruction Finance Corporation were extended. The foundations were laid of systems of unemployment insurance, administered by the states but largely financed by the federal government. The practice of 'grants in aid' was not new, but it was now vastly extended; children, widows, the unemployed, the blind, benefited. Behind the often inefficient and often bankrupt local units stood the federal government. Promises of cutting down federal expenditure, which had led to actual cuts in salaries and payments to veterans in the first few months of the new administration, were forgotten by the administration and remembered by its enemies; such enemies, including eminent Democrats like Al Smith, as those who founded the 'Liberty League'. But the tide was running one way. At the mid-term elections of 1934 the administration scored an unprecedented triumph: it increased its majorities in both houses. Republican chances were dim for 1936. Nor were they made brighter by the action of the Supreme Court in killing not only the unregretted N.R.A., but the A.A.A. and other social legislation. The conservatism of the majority of the Supreme Court had long been a source of resentment in the breasts of those who wished to use state or federal power to reduce economic inequality and temper the harshness of competition. The court seemed determined to prevent either the states or the Union from legislating in fields long occupied by European governments.

The Republican nomination in 1936 was not much worth having. It went to one of the few Republican politicians who had survived the deluge, Alfred M. Landon, the governor of Kansas. Landon was an old Progressive of 1912 with a good local record, but he was a bad speaker and he had bad luck. A terrible drought in 1934 was followed by an equally severe drought in 1936; the farmers were in no mood to hear sermons on government extravagance or states' rights. An overwhelming majority of the press, of business leaders, of sound, conservative opinion was against the President but, when the results were in, he had carried every state but Maine and Vermont, with a percentage of the popular vote only exceeded by Harding's in 1920. And in Congress the Republicans were further reduced until they found it difficult to do their share of the manning of committees.

The American people more definitely than in 1932 had given a commission to Franklin D. Roosevelt to reform the Republic. How would he interpret it? On 4 February 1937 the Democratic leaders in Congress were told: the 'court bill' was shown to them. It purported to be a bill for the general reform of the federal court system and many of the reforms were overdue. But the gist of the bill was a provision allowing the President to appoint not more than six new justices of the Supreme Court for every justice of seventy and over who had served ten years and did not retire; or, as its enemies put it, it was a bill to 'pack the Supreme Court'. It was bitterly fought; the Republicans wisely left the fight to revolting Democrats and it was discovered that, even after the election of 1936, there were institutions that the American people still treasured, no matter how bitterly they criticised them.

The threat to the court came, too, at a moment when moderate public opinion was alarmed by the wave of 'sit-down strikes' that had marked the great drive to create effective trade unions in the mass industries. This had been undertaken by the Committee for Industrial Organisations set up by the American Federation of Labor, headed by the leader of the miners, John L. Lewis. There were threats and rumours of revolution and disorder everywhere. There had poured into Washington, with the new administration, not merely the usual crowd of hungry office-seekers, but many thousands of young, ardent men and women anxious to have a hand in the saving of American society. And there had come others whose desire was to have a hand in the total reconstruction of American society on Marxist lines. They did not advertise their presence, but it was suspected in Washington, in Detroit, in Pittsburgh. But the great strikes, however suspect the leadership, succeeded. United States Steel, that had resisted attempts at unionisation so successfully in 1919, made peace with the new steel union. One after the other the other steel companies, and the automobile companies, recognised the unions. Only the stubborn individualist, Henry Ford, held out. But long before he gave way the Supreme Court had transformed its own position, and that of the unions, by validating the 'Wagner Act', passed in 1935, which had put the power of the federal law and administration behind the unions. Its constitutionality was contested, but by a majority of one the Act was upheld; a victory for organised labour that outweighed the split in the labour movement, for the American Federation of Labor expelled its committee and the unions which supported it. The 'Committee for Industrial Organisation' became the 'Congress of Industrial Organisations', keeping the now magic letters C.I.O.

Equally important was the effect of this and comparable decisions on the court fight. If the court was no longer an obstacle to social legislation, much of the driving force behind the 'court plan' would disappear. With each favourable decision, it did; the bill was rejected and the administration, within six months of its prodigious triumph, was defeated. Or was it? For justices now began to retire under new pension provisions and, before the end of his years as President, Roosevelt had nominated every member save one, and that one, Harlan F. Stone, he had promoted to be Chief Justice. The court ceased to be an obstacle to federal legislation and most of the original legislation of the New Deal was re-enacted, barring the unfortunate 'codes of fair competition'. Child labour, minimum wages, hours of work were now subject to federal legislation. A silent revolution in federal–state relations was accomplished.

But, if the New Deal triumphed in the courts, it did not triumph in all fields. Disastrous unemployment had been one of the main causes of the overthrow of the Republicans and, although the new administration or the flux of time had reduced the number of the workless, millions still depended on charity or on state or federal aid. In the first years of the New

Deal, various temporary bodies were set up to create work. One of these, the Civilian Conservation Corps, took young unemployed men into camps run, on a non-military basis, by the army, fed them, paid them and rehabilitated them. The C.C.C. was soon the only New Deal experiment that had hardly any enemies. Relief for older unemployed took two forms. In what came to be called the Works Progress Administration, temporary jobs were provided, some of them intrinsically useful, some not. And the head of the 'W.P.A.', Harry Hopkins, was suspected of diverting his resources into fields that were politically likely to be fruitful as well as beneficial to the unemployed. The other great spending agency, the Public Works Administration, under the vigilant and irascible Secretary of the Interior, Harold L. Ickes, was run on very different lines. Its projects were all long-term and of intrinsic value, and never in American history had such vast sums been spent with so little whisper of political or financial scandal.

But the unemployed remained. A drop in government expenditure brought about a 'recession' and in the congressional elections of 1938, although Democratic majorities remained abnormally large, the moribund Republican party of 1936 showed itself full of life and fight. And in the new Congress the President had to cajole, persuade, beg, instead of ordering.

Now the thoughts of the President were more and more turned outward. The economic and political isolation of the first years was abandoned. The efforts of the Secretary of State, by the system of reciprocal trade agreements, to make a breach in the lofty tariff wall, were supported by his chief. As the League of Nations collapsed before Italian aggression in Abyssinia, as Hitler occupied the Rhineland, as the Spanish Civil War presaged a greater, the President began to test American public opinion. In a speech at Chicago in October 1937 he advocated an economic quarantine of the aggressors (below, p. 710). Public opinion refused to follow. Munich shocked that opinion but did not change it, and all the President's efforts to get the Neutrality Acts amended failed. But, as the second world war drew nearer, the political aspect of the United States changed and what had only been a device of politicians fearful of losing the next election if the master politician was not in the field became a more serious possibility. Men who had no liking for the innovation, and were not necessarily worried about the election, began to worry about the fate of the United States and began to talk, more and more openly, of an unprecedented solution to the internal and external problem, a third term for the President.

That talk grew louder as the war came. In November 1939 the President forced through an amendment of the Neutrality Acts permitting the belligerents to buy war supplies on a 'cash and carry basis' and that, in 1939, meant that Britain and France could buy the war supplies they could pay for and take away in their own ships. It was an alteration of the law to the disadvantage of Germany. The great German victories of the spring and summer of 1940 made the re-nomination of Roosevelt a certainty. Great sums were hastily voted for armaments; two eminent Republicans were brought into the Cabinet as Secretaries of War and the Navy; the President began to consider how best to aid Britain, now alone and soon to be beleaguered.

The chief Republican candidates for the nomination had, unfortunately for themselves, committed themselves to a policy of strict neutrality before Hitler upset the confident expectation of a certain if slow allied victory. Senator Vandenberg, Senator Taft and the young District Attorney of New York, Thomas E. Dewey, were, to the surprise of all the professionals, beaten by Wendell Willkie, perhaps the darkest horse in American history. A few years before he had been a Tammany Democrat. He had only come into public notice as a vigorous defender of the utility companies, which he headed against the T.V.A. The presidency was the first public office he had ever aimed at. Willkie made a gallant campaign and it is possible that if the war had ended before the election he would have won it. But the war went on; the British stand excited admiration and anxiety. The President, by a series of agreements, aided Britain with destroyers, weapons, supplies in return for bases in the western hemisphere. Roosevelt won, and in the new Congress produced the scheme of 'Lend-Lease' in the form of a bill happily and deliberately numbered '1776'. If this was neutrality, it was neutrality of a totally novel kind. When Russia was attacked Lend-Lease was extended to her; but still the Germans held their hand. It was the Japanese who precipitated the decision and saved the administration from a more and more difficult situation. Refused any concessions by the United States, convinced that American support to China was the main reason why China could still resist, the military party in Japan took the same decision as the military party took in Germany in 1917. On 7 December 1941 the main Pacific fleet at Pearl Harbor on Oahu was wrecked from the air. A few hours later the main air force at Manila was wrecked on the ground. The United States was at war with Japan and, in a few days, with Germany and Italy, which supported their ally.

The role of the United States in the second world war was very different from that in the first. Then she had been an active belligerent for only a few months. Now she was in action from the day she was attacked and underwent a series of disasters with few parallels in her history. The loss of Corregidor ended resistance in the Philippines and, until the battle of Midway (June 1942), it was by no means certain that the Japanese could not successfully attack the Hawaiian islands, if not the mainland.

The manner of American entry into the war produced a far more real unity and energy than had existed in 1917. The scale of the war imposed a far more rigorous control of the American economy, a far more severe call on manpower. By the end of the war over 12,000,000 men were in arms and the United States was by far the greatest naval and one of the two greatest military powers in the world. The war was fought, too, with a more serious sense of the possibility of defeat and with less ideological emphasis than the first war had been. Roosevelt was in any case not such a master of the great oration as Wilson had been and neither the 'Four Freedoms' (January 1941) nor the Atlantic Charter (August 1941) had the effect of Wilson's speeches. And after America was a belligerent she had as an ally Soviet Russia, whose ruler had no intention of letting Roosevelt take the propaganda lead that Wilson had assumed in 1917–18.

Roosevelt's greatest achievement was as a war leader. Unlike Wilson, he had pondered the problems of war and of defence. He had built up the navy, even before 1939, as much as Congress allowed him to. He had, with great boldness and skill, managed to get Congress to agree to conscription in time of formal peace in 1940, and he chose and supported his war leaders with good judgement and resolution. Yet the first year of their participation in the war was one of frustration for Americans, and this was reflected in the near defeat of the Democrats in the congressional and local elections of 1942. But the tide had already turned. Allied armies landed in North Africa just after the elections; Guadalcanal was at last won in the Pacific; soon the Russians were to capture a German army at Stalingrad.

Public opinion was now prepared for American participation in a peace settlement; everyone was anxious to avoid or to forget the mistakes of 1919. A 'bi-partisan' foreign policy was preached and, to some extent, practised. At a series of Allied conferences, the higher strategy of the war was planned and the character of the peace outlined. Again, as 1944 approached, there was no question of who would be the Democratic candidate. The only change since 1940 was the dropping of the Vice-President, Henry A. Wallace, in favour of Senator Harry S. Truman of Missouri. The Republicans nominated Thomas E. Dewey, now governor of New York. By the time the election came, victory, as in 1918, was in sight, but it was not so near. Roosevelt was again elected and, in February of 1945, went with the British Prime Minister to Yalta to meet the Russian ruler, Stalin. Hitler's Germany was on its last legs; Mussolini's Italy existed only as a ghost. The net of American naval and military might was drawn, closer and closer, round Japan and already it was probable that the Americans would soon have in their power the most destructive weapon in the history of mankind, the atom bomb. Suddenly, to the surprise even of his intimates, Roosevelt died at Warm Springs in Georgia on 12 April 1945, a month before the end of the Third Reich.

Few Presidents have been more loved and hated. After his first few months, his support came mainly from the economically distressed or discontented; to the wealthier classes he became an object of hatred surpassing that evoked by his hero, Andrew Jackson. Under his administrations, if not solely or even mainly because of him, the whole economic and political balance of power in the United States was altered and, probably, the balance of power in the world; for a less bold and ingenious leader might have been at a total loss in the desperate year 1940. By his greatly extended use of the press conference and of wireless, above all in the 'fireside chats', he continually and effectively appealed to the people over the heads of Congress. Few Presidents have so completely overshadowed their colleagues and, indeed, opponents. Roosevelt's successor was hardly known to the public, but it fell to him to deal with the other Allied chiefs in the ruins of Berlin, to receive at Potsdam the news that the atom bomb tests had succeeded, and to authorise the use of the bomb against Japan. Already (26 June) a new international organisation, the United Nations, had been launched at San Francisco. On 14 August the Japanese surrendered.

The United States was the most powerful and richest nation in a world which her armies, navies, air fleets literally engirdled and all parts of which were, in various fashions and degrees, involved in American economic life and were dependants of American wealth and bounty. But it was not a confident and assured nation that looked back on its unprecedented achievement and power. For the old world in which America could keep to herself was gone for ever, gone in the bombs dropped on Hiroshima and Nagasaki, and in much else which the war had wrought. There was exultation, as in 1865 and in 1918, that 'the dreadful trip was done' but, underlying the euphoria of victory, a knowledge that nothing could now minister to them 'that sweet sleep which they owed yesterday'.

CHAPTER XIX
LATIN AMERICA

THE independence achieved by the states of Latin America in the nineteenth century was political only. These twenty-odd new nations, varying greatly in size, in peoples and in resources, suspicious of their former rulers and of each other, had one characteristic in common: a heavy dependence upon events and movements outside their own borders. As specialised primary producers, they had to rely on foreign markets to dispose of their goods and on foreign investment to develop their resources. As heirs of revolution and often victims of political and financial instability, many of them experienced active foreign intervention. In the nineteenth century the intervening powers were usually European; except for the episode of the Texan war, and the period of impotence during the American civil war, the United States government upheld Latin-American independence. It not only disapproved of European interference and influence; on the whole it refrained from interference itself. In the twentieth century, however, there was to be a dramatic exchange of political roles. European influence declined; North American influence increased; and some of the major Latin-American states began to move haltingly towards a real independence. The process was punctuated and accelerated by two world wars and a world depression of unexampled severity.

In 1898 Spain, after a brief war with the United States, lost the last fragments of a great American empire—Cuba and Puerto Rico. No longer feared and hated as an 'imperialist' power, Spain was to become the object of sentimental respect and affection and the centre of Pan-Hispanic feeling. Great Britain, though a colonial power, still by far the largest investor in Latin America, the principal source of manufactured goods and the biggest single market for food and raw materials, showed less and less inclination to political interference, especially since the growing naval power of Germany made it necessary for British governments to court North American friendship. France, despite a long record of interventions in the nineteenth century, seemed even less likely than Spain or England to become involved politically in Latin-American affairs.

In the United States, on the other hand, a rising national feeling, a growing sense of power, created a desire for a more aggressive interpretation of the Monroe Doctrine. The Venezuelan boundary dispute in 1897 had been made the occasion for strident pronouncements by North American statesmen. In inter-American affairs the United States was taking a resolute lead. The first Pan-American conference had met at Washington in 1889; a second was convened in Mexico in 1901. Pan-Americanism might appear to offer more solid advantages than a sentimental Pan-Hispanism or than vague proposals for a purely Latin-American league.

Pan-Americanism, however, with its assumption of common sentiment and common interests throughout the hemisphere, rested to some extent on an illusion. Most Latin-American states had closer kinship with Latin Europe than with Protestant North America, and for many South Americans Europe was physically more accessible than the United States, or indeed than other Latin-American countries. Pan-Americanism was largely the product of North American policy; it was long suspected of being an instrument of North American political and economic power, and for the first three decades of the new century it made little headway.

Among Latin-American states in 1900, four stood out from the rest as leaders in power, wealth and political stability. In Brazil, by far the largest state in area and in population, a military revolution in 1889 had ousted the Braganza monarchy. The resulting constitution, in 1891, had inaugurated a federal republic in which the several states enjoyed wide autonomy, including power to levy export taxes and to raise military forces, and in which the federal authority was relatively weak. Political leadership was shared between São Paulo and Minas Geraes, the coffee-growing and mining states of central Brazil. Government rested not upon the popular vote, nor upon party organisation, but upon a convention of balance of power between these two states, each of which provided four presidents between 1894 and 1930. Subject to this convention, a president could usually contrive to nominate his successor by an understanding with the governors of the states and with the majority in Congress, which first helped to manage the presidential election and then acted as arbiter of its legality. The system succeeded, as a rule, in raising men of marked ability to the presidential chair.

The political conventions of Brazil directly reflected the current economic trends. The country's prosperity, once based on sugar and tobacco, now depended upon the export of vast quantities of coffee, supplemented by wild rubber and other forest products from the Amazon basin. The coffee industry demanded the construction of ports and railways and, for this, capital was needed. A £10,000,000 loan, negotiated with the Rothschilds during a presidential visit to Europe, tided the country over a financial crisis in 1899. Rio de Janeiro and Santos grew from squalid waterfront towns into fine modern harbours in the early years of the twentieth century. The coffee economy of Brazil was built up by a steady flow of British, French and German capital, and of Portuguese, Italian and German labour; while most of the coffee was sold in the United States.

What coffee was to Brazil, beef and wheat were to Argentina. Much of the beef was exported to Great Britain. The production of beef suitable for the British market required enclosed pasture, good transport arrangements and elaborate processes of preparation. Barbed wire, the railway and the *frigorifico* were the instruments of Argentine prosperity, and for the most part British investors provided the capital, British and North American manufacturers the machinery. Rural society was patriarchal, with immense areas of good land in the hands of relatively few owners. It was this business-like landowning oligarchy, with its characteristic pride in good stock, which imported English pedigree bulls and developed the high quality, as well as the vast quantity, of Argentine beef production.

The large-scale export of grain began considerably later than the export of beef, but by 1904 its value was even greater than that of beef. The development of arable farming created a great demand for labour; and, like Brazil, Argentina attracted large numbers of immigrants, mostly Spanish and Italian. Many of these immigrants were seasonal visitors—*golondrinas*—who returned to Europe after each harvest; but more than three million of them made permanent homes in Argentina between 1880 and 1913.

As in Brazil, government, while adhering to constitutional forms, depended largely upon deals between members and groups of the landowning oligarchy. Subject to these deals, the presidents nominated not only their successors, but provincial governors, members of Congress, and most of the important officials. In Argentina, however, unlike Brazil, there was no longer a balance of influence between semi-autonomous states. Wealth and political power were more and more concentrated in the humid pampa area surrounding Buenos Aires, and in the capital itself. A radical party existed, which clamoured for free elections and occasionally staged revolts, provoked by the consistent manipulation of political affairs. These incidents were all confined to the capital, none aroused much popular interest, and none caused serious alarm. Conditions in general were stable. A series of conservative governments provided adequate and orderly administration in a time of rising prosperity, and appeared in little danger of being unseated by elections, financial crises, or accusations of corruption and extravagance.

Chile, the third of the so-called 'A.B.C.' powers of South America, was by far the smallest in area and in population. Most of the people lived by farming in the beautiful and fertile valleys of central Chile. As in Argentina, a small number of families owned most of the productive land; but methods of farming and estate management were conservative, paternal, somewhat feckless, and Chile, though an agricultural country, imported food. Most of the public wealth came from the copper mines of the western Cordillera, and above all from the northern coastal desert provinces, which yielded the world's chief supply of natural nitrates. The nitrates were dug and exported to the wheat-growing areas of the world by companies employing Chilean labour, but financed mainly by British, and later North American, capital. There was thus a serious and growing division between political power and economic reality. Political power, as in most Latin-American states, was in the hands of the landowning aristocracy, who controlled a Congress elected by a narrowly restricted franchise. Moreover, as a result of the civil war of 1891, the power of the executive had been so severely curtailed that Congress could always either control or frustrate the policy of the president. Inevitably the ruling oligarchy split into many shifting factions. Most governments were coalitions, most cabinets short-lived and unstable. Meanwhile the steady activity of the nitrate trade encouraged the growth of a commercial and professional middle class and of a small industrial labour force. The export tax on nitrates enabled social services and popular education to develop more rapidly than in most other Latin-American countries. In the long run these would inevitably prove powerful solvents of aristocratic government; but so long as the nitrate market remained firm the business of the country could be carried on, if not with conspicuous efficiency, at least with moderation and due regard for law, by a cultivated and, on the whole, remarkably public-spirited aristocracy.

Mexico, like Chile, depended for most of its revenue upon the export of minerals. The chief mineral products included gold, silver, lead, zinc, copper, antimony and, in the present century, petroleum; the first successful oil well was drilled in 1901. In Mexico, as in Chile, mineral resources were developed, railways and harbour works built, with foreign capital, by foreign engineers and managers and native labour. The great majority of Mexicans, however, lived by agriculture, upon the relatively small area of cultivable land afforded by an arid and mountainous country. The ownership of land was concentrated, to an even greater extent than in Chile, in a small number of very large, self-contained estates. Mexico lacked the racial homogeneity of Chile; persons of mixed blood formed a majority of the population, but the big *hacendados* were often of European descent, while most agricultural labourers were either Indians or *mestizos* in whom Indian blood predominated. Many landlords were absentees. Labourers were bound to the estates by a deep feeling for the land on which their forebears had lived, but which they no longer owned; and by *peonage*, a species of serfdom based upon truck payments on credit, keeping the *peón* in a condition of debt-slavery which, in custom if not in law, was usually hereditary. The land hunger of these dispossessed *peones* was the most striking characteristic of Mexican society, and was to prove in the twentieth century a powerful explosive force.

Mexico had been governed since 1876 by an efficient and ruthless dictatorship. Porfirio Díaz throughout his reign observed most of the forms of a federal constitution; but effectively he ruled his wild and heterogeneous country through an intricate network of jobs and personal loyalties. Judges, state governors, deputies in Congress were all his men, and so were the *rurales*, the highly efficient but arbitrary irregular police. A *mestizo* himself, he was not without a genial intuitive sympathy with his Indian subjects; but he did not seek, and could not afford, to offend the great landowners, and the incorporation of *ejidos*—village common lands —in private *haciendas*, whether by purchase, fraud or force, reached its peak in his time. He was no demagogue, and preached no military nationalist aggrandisement. His regular army, or at least its rank and file, was largely fictitious. His foreign policy included friendship with the United States, scrupulous service of acknowledged debts and adherence to treaties, and enthusiastic participation in schemes of international co-operation. The second Pan-American Conference met in Mexico in 1901–2; and in 1906–7 Mexico collaborated with the United States in an ambitious and statesmanlike plan for peace-making in Central America. At home, Díaz sought above all to exploit the most remunerative resources of Mexico, and to build impressive public works, by offering the most tempting terms to foreign investors. Mines, harbours, railways, factories, oilfields developed under foreign control and much farm and pasture land in their neighbourhood passed into foreign ownership, British, North American and German. Don Porfirio made himself famous, and his country liked and respected, abroad. At home he allowed his people to become strangers in their own land.

The chief economic and political characteristics of these four great states were present in varying degrees in most of the twenty-odd republics. Latin America in the early twentieth century was a land of promise, a magnet for the enterprise, the capital and the skill of more industrialised peoples. It was becoming a major source of a number of vitally important commodities. The government of most of its larger states was orderly, effective, sympathetic to investors. Its prosperity, if measured in terms of production, of exports and of public revenue, was rising steadily. All the Latin-American states, however, suffered from dangerous, but for the time hidden, economic and political maladies. They all depended for their revenues upon the export of one or two commodities, either foodstuffs or raw materials for industry. They were therefore extremely vulnerable to changes of price in the world market. They had nearly all become deeply indebted, through constant public and private borrowing from foreign sources, often at high rates, sometimes for unproductive purposes; and the willingness of European investors to throw good money after bad made it difficult to call a halt to this financial rake's progress. Most Latin Americans lived by agriculture, usually employing primitive and wasteful methods; they derived no direct and obvious benefit from the inflow of foreign capital or from the proceeds of the specialised export trades. They did not, as a rule, own the land they worked; if tenants or share-croppers, the terms of their tenure were often harsh and insecure. They had, therefore, a ready grievance.

Of those Latin-American countries which practised constitutional government, the majority were governed by somewhat theoretical constitutional rules, mostly borrowed from the constitution of the United States, owing little to the realities of Latin-American history and circumstances, commanding little general respect. The extremely artificial nature of 'federalism' in many states was an obvious example. The letter of the constitution often gave no indication of where real power lay. Constitutional remedies were so ineffective against powerful groups or personal interests that only revolution could effect a real change of administration; and 'revolution' often meant no more than an extra-legal demonstration calling for a change. The chief concession to realism in most Latin-American constitutions was the emergency power of suspending constitutional 'guarantees', entrusted to the president precisely to enable him to forestall such 'revolutions'. In many states constitutional government was a brittle façade; in some of the smaller states it hardly existed.

As in public affairs, so in more individual realms of spirit and mind the Latin-American peoples showed the symptoms of dependence upon imported and imperfectly assimilated ideas. Catholic Christianity was the outward religion of most people; but in many of the republics great numbers of Indians and *mestizos* hung between half-understood Christianity and half-forgotten local pagan cults. Among such people, as for instance in Mexico, a revolt against Christianity, once begun, was likely to be extreme. Even among people of European descent, with a few notable exceptions, the vital elements in Latin-American Catholicism were—and are—the foreign religious orders and foreign currents of Catholic thought. There had long been difficulty in maintaining the numbers and standard of the priesthood. The church, moreover, as a great landowner and a conservative force in politics, was disliked and feared by reformers, who tended throughout Latin America to be anti-clerical and sometimes anti-religious; though it is fair to add that most of them greatly underestimated the church's hold upon men's loyalty, and the secularising theories which they advocated, from positivism down to Communism, were themselves mostly imported from Europe. Avowedly religious people had long felt a vague sense of frustrated nationalism; some of them were uneasy in their allegiance to a church whose roots in America seemed uncomfortably shallow; but no satisfying alternative appeared. The Vatican was undoubtedly justified in regarding Latin America as a field of missionary endeavour; but no effort directed from Europe could, by itself, give to Latin-American Christianity the indigenous character which it lacked.

Many of the capital cities of Latin America were centres of vigorous intellectual life. Intelligent appreciation and discussion of serious literature, and to a lesser degree of music and the visual arts, had long been characteristic of educated town dwellers. Poetry never lacked an audience in any part of Latin America; but outside the towns literate people were very few. For the most part, literary activity was confined to relatively small groups of people and followed European models. It is true that *Facundo* or *Martín Fierro* could have been written nowhere but in Argentina, *Os Sertoes* nowhere but in Brazil; but, apart from exceptional works of genius, there had been little attempt at a development of independent culture, which would have meant a fusion of Indian and Iberian patterns of thought and expression. On the contrary, the liberal Latin tradition led to France, and French cultural influence was dominant at the end of the nineteenth century. For those who disliked French liberalism and French anti-clericalism, the most tempting alternative lay in a return to the Hispanic tradition.

In short, Latin America in 1900 was intellectually, economically and politically dependent upon the outside world. Its cultural life, though varied and active, lacked native self-confidence and drew its inspiration from abroad. Its economic and political life, though occasionally turbulent within its own area, assumed peace and stability elsewhere. Neither the national economies nor the national political structures were designed to withstand general adversity.

There was, indeed, no obvious reason for expecting adversity. Between the turn of the century and the outbreak of the first world war, the prosperity of Europe continued to overflow into Latin America. Progress was especially rapid in Argentina. The introduction of lucerne as a fodder crop, the substitution, from 1907, of a chilling process for crude freezing, the meticulous grading and pricing of fine stock, together built up an export trade in good beef unparalleled in the world. Buenos Aires became the greatest city of the southern hemisphere, and the centre of a railway system almost equal in extent to that of the United Kingdom.

In this period of rapid economic progress, however, three striking and significant developments took place which proved portents for the future. They were a peaceful but radical constitutional change in Argentina, an extremely violent social and political revolution in Mexico, and a remarkable growth of North American power and assertiveness in Central America and the Caribbean islands.

The Radical Civic Union, the precursor of the Radical party of modern Argentina, had been formed in 1892, and for twenty years devoted itself to the apparently hopeless task of electoral reform. Yet reform, when it came, was the work not directly of the Radicals, but of a member of that aristocratic caste which the Radicals wished to unseat—Roque Sáenz Peña, President from 1910 to 1913, a distinguished lawyer and a statesman of exceptional probity and devotion. Sáenz Peña, apparently from motives of pure conviction, insisted in 1912 on the passage of the electoral law which bears his name, providing for universal male suffrage and secret, compulsory voting. This revolutionary enactment—for so it was in the circumstances—by enfranchising the industrial and largely immigrant population of Buenos Aires, changed the whole basis of Argentine politics. Assisted by a daily press distinguished for responsibility and moderation, it promised a progressive liberalisation of government. It was also to reveal in time the dangers attending a sudden injection of democracy into a body politic largely unprepared for such treatment. Its first result was the election of Hipólito Irigoyen to the presidency in 1916, and the inauguration of a period of Radical rule broken only by revolution in 1930.

The Mexican revolution of 1910–11 was far more drastic and far-reaching. Its immediate causes included a financial depression in 1907, crop failures in 1907 and 1908, brutality in the suppression of the consequent strikes, and a wave of anti-foreign feeling and of political agitation. The armed rising which, in a few months, hounded Porfirio Díaz from office and from the country was led by a liberal theorist, Francisco Madero, with the conventional battle-cry of 'no re-election'; but it quickly threw up a host of other leaders—agrarian rabble-rousers such as Zapata, bandits like Pancho Villa, military adventurers like Huerta, the murderer and successor of Madero. Mexico suffered ten years of almost continuous civil war, and, since all parties looked to the United States as a source of arms, President Wilson's government was soon drawn into the conflict, supplying weapons to the self-styled constitutionalists under Carranza and denying them to Huerta. The inevitable incident occurred— an affront to American marines at Tampico: and in 1914 the United States intervened and seized the port of Vera Cruz. The intervention helped to remove Huerta, but failed to place the 'constitutional' party in power; and naturally it provoked universal resentment. An offer of mediation, however, made jointly by the 'A.B.C.' powers, enabled Wilson to withdraw without undue loss of dignity. The fighting went on; and eventually Carranza secured the presidency not by North American help, but by publicly accepting a programme in which he certainly did not believe—the agrarian reform programme of Zapata and his Indians. Thus in the midst of destruction, and almost unnoticed abroad because of the greater war then raging, a remarkable blueprint of a nascent new order was produced in the constitution of 1917, which is still the constitution of Mexico. Its political provisions contained little that was new; they repeated and expanded the radical and bitterly anti-clerical constitution of 1857, which the astute manipulations of Díaz had rendered ineffective. The most striking innovations were in the economic clauses. In article 123 a comprehensive, and for the time extremely generous, industrial labour code was written into the constitution. Article 27, more revolutionary still, proclaimed a reversal of the whole trend of Mexican agrarian history. It declared all land, water and minerals to be national property, private ownership existing only by an implied and conditional public

591

grant, and certain types of mineral-bearing land, including oilfields, being inalienable. It restricted the regions in which foreigners might acquire land and the terms on which they could hold and use it. It limited narrowly the area which might be owned by a single person or corporation, and forbade ecclesiastical bodies to hold land. It promised the restoration of all village common fields alienated since 1854, and authorised grants of land—presumably to be confiscated from private estates—to villages which possessed no commons. Agrarian bitterness had by that time reached such a pitch, and fighting was so widespread, that this drastic programme of redistribution was probably the only way of securing any semblance of peace. As it was, the opportunist Carranza failed either to govern or to keep his agrarian promises. He was driven out by his lieutenant, Obregón, in 1919, and soon afterwards murdered. Peace of a kind was achieved with the election of Obregón to the presidency in 1921; but nearly twenty years more were needed to enforce the new order, and an unpredictable length of time to make it work.

Meanwhile revolutions of another kind were shaking the small republics of Central America. The Spanish–American War had started the United States on a career of intervention which might become a career of colonial aggression. Puerto Rico was annexed in 1899. Cuba, the largest and richest of the Caribbean islands, after a short period of North American occupation, became politically independent in 1902; but the United States retained a base at Guantánamo and, under the Platt amendment, a right to intervene in the event of serious disorder. North American attention was drawn to the political affairs of the Caribbean countries by the prospect of a ship canal through Central America, and by the desire of the United States government to control the canal approaches. Shortly after the end of the Spanish–American War, two obstacles to the building of the canal, one diplomatic, the other territorial, had been removed. The diplomatic obstacle was the Clayton–Bulwer treaty of 1850. The British government agreed, after some discussion, to replace that instrument by the Hay–Pauncefote treaty of 1902, which provided for a canal controlled and fortified by the United States. The territorial obstacle was the attitude of Colombia to the project of a canal through Colombian territory. An opportune revolt broke out in the Panamá province of Colombia in 1903. United States naval forces were employed to prevent the intervention of the Colombian authorities; and the new republic of Panama, hastily recognised, agreed to a treaty giving the United States virtual sovereignty in the Canal Zone. This stroke of policy, while clearing the way for the canal, caused bitter and lasting resentment in Colombia, and did not pass unnoticed in the rest of Latin America (see also ch. xviii).

While Theodore Roosevelt was 'taking the Isthmus', the problem of defending the Caribbean approaches was complicated by the decision of the Hague Court of Arbitration in the Venezuelan debt dispute. This decision, by upholding the legality of the British, German and Italian blockade of the Venezuelan coast, placed a premium on the use of force as a means of collecting debts. It suggested the possibility of further European armed interventions, sanctioned by international law, in areas where American control was vital to the defence of the United States. The only hope of forestalling this possibility seemed to lie in police action by the United States government, to prevent defaults on just debts and disorders affecting foreigners. Accordingly in 1904 Theodore Roosevelt announced his so-called corollary to the Monroe Doctrine: a warning that the United States might be compelled to intervene in the affairs of Latin-American states in order to remove grounds for intervention by others.

The United States government already controlled, in effect, the affairs of Panama. In 1905 it negotiated an agreement with the Dominican Republic whereby the customs of that country were to be collected by North American officers, in order to remove occasion for European action. In 1906, to prevent a dangerous internal crisis, Cuba was reoccupied in accordance with the Platt amendment and the relevant provisions of the Cuban constitution. This second occupation lasted only until 1909, when an elected administration was duly installed; but advice, often unwelcome, continued to be proffered to the Cuban government. In the turbulent region of Central America a conference, in which Mexico took part, was convened at Washington in 1906–7 to formulate proposals for peace-making. The chief task of this conference was to prevent the kind of quarrel which arose from revolutions in one state being hatched in the territory of another. Its main result was an ingenious agreement to withhold recognition from governments which seized power by revolution. Thus within a few years the Roosevelt policy produced benevolent supervision in Panama, sporadic meddling in Cuba, and in Central America a new policy of non-recognition generally regarded—and resented—as a form of indirect intervention. These measures were not enough to keep the peace to the satisfaction of the United States, and President Taft, Roosevelt's successor, soon found his Central American policy drifting from a warning diplomacy towards the use of force. In 1909 Zelaya, the dictator of Nicaragua, whose aggressive designs abroad and xenophobia at home had repeatedly threatened the peace, was expelled in a revolution backed by North American commercial concerns. In 1912 American marines were landed in Nicaragua to prevent Zelaya from starting a counter-revolution. Nicaragua remained under North American tutelage, with one brief interval, until 1933. Two more armed interventions followed, both provoked by acute internal disorder, in Haiti and in the Dominican Republic. Haiti was occupied from 1915 to 1934, Santo Domingo from 1916 to 1924.

A naïvely cynical interpretation of these moves has applied to them the phrase 'dollar diplomacy'. It is true that Taft's Secretary of State, the egregious Knox, believed that a transfer of the public debts of the Central American republics from European to North American holders would be in the interests of peace; but he had great difficulty in persuading New York bankers to make loans to such governments as Haiti, Nicaragua, and the Dominican Republic. Only in Cuba were North American investments considerable at that time. No doubt the missionary zeal of conscious efficiency impelled North Americans to 'tidy up' these small, disorderly republics; but the principal considerations were strategic. In order to forestall possible European threats to the canal approaches, successive Secretaries of State were prepared to risk the alienation of Latin America. Of course, the policy of the United States was resented; it was unpopular at home, where it ran counter to deep-rooted traditions; it was naturally disliked in Central America, and over Latin America as a whole it gave rise to deep and lasting suspicion. In Argentina especially, journalists with ambitions for Argentine leadership in South America made the most of evidence of Yankee imperialism. The circumstance chiefly responsible for the strategic anxieties of the United States was the rise of German naval power. When, in 1914, the first great war against Germany began, the United States had hardly a friend in the Americas.

Latin America in 1914 was already far more important in world affairs than it had been in 1900. Politically, the participation of Latin-American delegates at the Second Hague Conference in 1907, and the intellectual qualities which they displayed there, had opened the eyes of Europe. The greater states of Latin America had become known and generally respected. Above all, their economic importance had greatly increased. Europe could not easily do without the food and the raw materials of Latin America, and Latin-American friendship became a valuable prize of belligerent diplomacy. In particular Germany, which in peace had ranked third among nations trading with Latin America, embarked upon an assiduous courtship backed by elaborate and costly propaganda. The most powerful counter-arguments were also provided by Germany, however, in the form of sinkings of neutral ships.

The Americas had no common policy towards the belligerents. The governments of Mexico and Venezuela were pro-German throughout, and in Chile, whose army was German trained, there were many German sympathisers. These three states, with Argentina, Colombia, Paraguay and El Salvador, remained neutral throughout the war, maintaining diplomatic and—as far as possible—commercial relations with all the belligerents. Chile, the most formidable naval power in South America, was subjected to a test of patience in 1915, when British warships sank the cruiser *Dresden* in a Chilean harbour—a gross infringement of neutrality for which the British government apologised. Argentine neutrality, though strictly correct, was distinctly favourable to the Allies, and especially sympathetic towards Italy, as was natural. Argentina won a notable diplomatic victory in 1917, when the German government made full apology and reparation for the sinking of three Argentine ships. In the latter half of 1917 Irigoyen had some difficulty in maintaining relations with Germany in the teeth of mass meetings and resolutions of Congress demanding rupture. Both Argentina and Uruguay gave material assistance to the Allies in the form of credits for the purchase of food.

The entry of the United States into the war inevitably affected the Latin-American position. Nearly all the states of Central America and the Caribbean joined the United States in making formal declarations of war. Peru, Uruguay, Bolivia and Ecuador broke off relations with Germany, and handed over to the Allies all German ships in their harbours. Brazil, whose foreign policy for years past had been conspicuous for statesman-like moderation and respect for international law, independently declared war on Germany in October 1917. This decision was immediately provoked by the sinking of Brazilian ships; but throughout the war most Brazilians had sympathised with the Allies, especially with France, which they regarded as the pattern and guide of Latin civilisation. Brazilian warships operated with the ships of the Allies in the Atlantic, though no military forces were sent to Europe. One important internal result of the war was a sustained attempt to 'Brazilianise' the German colonies in southern Brazil.

Politically, the chief effect of the war upon the Latin-American countries was their closer participation in international affairs. All the Latin-American states sooner or later joined the League of Nations, and most of them were original members. Membership fluctuated somewhat, disputes over the distribution of council seats being the occasion of several resignations; but many Latin-American states remained steadily loyal. The League appealed strongly to Latin-American idealism, and afforded a platform on which relatively weak states could make their voices heard. It is true that the presence in the Assembly of a large number of small states, with a voting power out of proportion to their physical strength, contributed to the air of unreality often characteristic of the deliberations of that body. It is true also that some states regarded the League as a counterpoise to the power of the United States and a substitute for the Pan-American system which the United States favoured. Naturally the absence of the United States from Geneva made political action by the League in the Americas extremely difficult. Nevertheless, Latin-American membership of the League was important and valuable. The technical organs of the League achieved much success in Latin America, and on one occasion the League was responsible—this time with the co-operation of the United States—for settling a serious dispute, between Colombia and Peru in 1933–4, over the Leticia territory (see above, pp. 257–8).

Economically the war had administered a sharp but temporary shock to Latin America. The supply of European capital and the stream of immigrants suddenly ceased. Exports to Europe dropped temporarily, through the diversion of shipping to other tasks, and then quickly recovered, thanks to the urgent demands of the Allies for food and raw materials. On the other hand, imports of manufactured goods from Europe dropped heavily, as European industry concentrated upon warlike needs. One result of this excess of exports over imports was a tentative industrial development in the A.B.C. states, especially in the manufacture of textiles for the home market, and the canning and preserving of food. This effort to achieve greater diversity and self-sufficiency in supplying home markets has continued persistently, though not steadily at the same speed, ever since. Another important result was a great increase, both absolute and relative, in imports from the United States. North American trade with Latin America held and further increased its war-time gains after the war, despite strenuous efforts by French and British firms, in the 1920s, to recover lost ground. On the whole, capital followed trade. In 1913 British investments in Latin America amounted to some $4,893 million; North American investments totalled $1,242 million, and were nearly all in Mexico and Central America, only $173 million being held in South American countries. In 1929 British holdings were $5,889 million, North American holdings $5,587 million including $3,102 million in South America.[1] North American investments followed much the same lines as British, but were more widely spread, less heavily concentrated in railways and other public utilities. Direct investment predominated. Most of the capital went into concerns such as mines, producing raw materials for export to manufacturing countries, and into transport developments ancillary to such concerns, rather than into industrial undertakings producing finished goods. Throughout Latin America the shifts of trade and finance during the war years and after thus produced not economic independence, but a partial change of masters, an overall increase in foreign capital invested, and a continued rise in apparent prosperity.

One or two important exceptions to this general trend require to be noticed. The war caused serious dislocations in the economic life of at least two of the leading states. Chile, though remote from the conflict, suffered heavily from its indirect results. Sodium nitrate is not only a fertiliser, but an ingredient in the manufacture of nitro-glycerine. During the war the Allies bought vast quantities of Chilean nitrate; but the Germans, cut off from Chile by the blockade, turned to the manufacture of synthetic nitrate and succeeded in supplying most of their own needs. After the war the use of synthetic nitrate became general. It was more expensive than the natural product; but the governments of the great powers all disliked dependence upon a remote source for an important

[1] M. Winkler, *Investments of United States Capital in Latin America* (Boston, 1929), pp. 275-83; *The Republics of South America*, Royal Institute of International Affairs (Oxford, 1937), p. 182.

munition, and preferred to make farmers pay more for fertiliser, in order to produce the raw material of explosive within their own territories. The Chilean share of world nitrate production fell from about 70 per cent at the turn of the century to 35 per cent in 1924 and 11 per cent in 1931.[1] It continued to fall in the 'thirties. At the same time the world market for copper was extremely unreliable. The population of Chile was too small to provide a market for extensive industrial production, and the drop in value of its two principal mineral products presented a prospect of economic decline for which no adequate remedy has yet been found.

The war had a serious effect upon the Argentine and Uruguayan beef industry. During the war the demand for chilled beef had been supplemented by a greatly increased demand for tinned or frozen beef. The product of the tinning process is of equal insipidity whatever the quality of beef used, and the high demand encouraged the breeding and sale of inferior animals. At the same time, a series of disastrous failures of the lucerne crop in the early years of the war made the production of good beef more difficult and expensive. The cattle industry was still in this disorganised state when the European slump of 1922 produced a sudden break in the market and made all but the best beef unsaleable. By 1925 the rubbish had been cleared and the industry was once again paying its way; but even then it had to make another readjustment to meet a demand for smaller beef joints resulting from the decline in the size of families in most parts of Europe. The chilling companies began to demand smaller beasts. The big shorthorn bullocks which had hitherto commanded the highest prices fell from favour and had to be replaced by stockier breeds such as the Aberdeen Angus. This change was still in progress when Argentina, with the rest of Latin America, received the staggering blow of the 1930 depression.

Apart from these troubled industries, Latin America throughout most of the 1920s was peaceful and prosperous. In Brazil cotton appeared alongside coffee as an important export crop and cattle (though of poor quality) increased considerably in numbers in the southern states. There was steady development in mining and in industry; Brazil, though lacking convenient coal, possesses large quantities of iron ore. In the arid northern states, post-war governments spent large sums on dams for water storage. There was a steady overall growth of population, both by immigration and by natural increase; and in the south, a slow but steady advance in state-sponsored colonisation. The most remarkable increase in wealth during this period, however, took place in the republics of the northern Andes, especially in Venezuela, where immense oil-fields were discovered. Venezuela was a backward pastoral and agricultural country; it still is, away from the cities, the oil-fields, and the more recently

[1] C. A. Thomson, 'Chile Struggles for National Recovery', *Foreign Policy Reports*, IX (1934), p. 288.

exploited iron-ore deposits. The export of oil began in 1918; by 1930 Venezuela was producing more than 10 per cent of the total world supply, and thanks to petroleum royalties was the only Latin-American state unencumbered by public debt. Nearly all the oil produced was exported, and nearly all production was—and is—in the hands of foreign firms, British and North American. The national economy came to depend, therefore, principally upon the price of oil in the world outside.

Peru, Colombia and Ecuador also developed oil-fields in the 'twenties, and all granted concessions to foreign capital for this purpose as well as for the development of public services. None of these countries, however, reached anything approaching the Venezuelan level of production, or became so dangerously dependent on oil. Colombia in particular enjoyed a period of very considerable prosperity and progress. The foreign trade of the country more than doubled, and expanding exports included coffee, cacao and sugar as well as oil. Two commercial and industrial cities, Cali and Medellín, in valleys far from the capital, grew rapidly, Medellín especially becoming an important centre of mining and textile manufacture in this period. Peru was more centralised than Colombia, more dependent upon its capital, Lima, and the near-suburban port of Callao. Peruvian society, moreover, was dangerously split between the isolated highland population, Indian and agricultural, and the people of the coast, largely European in outlook, concerned with commerce, mining, and to some extent industry. Despite these disadvantages, considerable development and diversification took place in the 'twenties. Peru exported copper, cotton, sugar and various other agricultural products as well as oil; and, as in the neighbouring countries, its economic life was largely and increasingly controlled by foreign capital.

One characteristic common to nearly all Latin-American countries in this prosperous era of the 'twenties was concern over the wages, working conditions and general welfare of industrial labour. The attention of governments was directed to problems of labour by the general desire to speed up the slow process of industrialisation. International discussion of such problems through the International Labour Organisation of the League of Nations stimulated interest, and so, no doubt, did the Mexican constitution of 1917. An advanced labour code became a matter of national prestige, a badge of membership of the comity of civilised states. Moreover, in most parts of Latin America mines, oil wells and factories were foreign-owned. Pressure brought upon foreign employers to raise wages and improve conditions was popular, patriotic, and politically safe. There could be no doubt of the need, by European or North American standards, for very considerable improvement of labour conditions. Argentina, Brazil and Chile all set up separate ministries or departments of labour, and they and several other states enacted labour codes, including such principles of social legislation as the eight-hour day, the right to strike, the minimum wage, and protection of women and children. Uruguay—once a battle-ground of *gaucho* armies, become peaceful and prosperous through the export of beef—and Chile embarked on schemes of national insurance. The volume and quality of legislation were impressive, but much of it was based on European and North American ideals and did not necessarily correspond to local needs. In most countries it hardly touched agricultural life, especially where employers were native and the personal relation between *patrón* and *peón* was strong. Even in industrial centres much legislation failed in its purpose because of the lack of adequate inspection. The activity of legislative bodies in many parts of Latin America has often seemed in inverse proportion to the ability to put laws into effect.

The movement to improve labour conditions came chiefly from above—from governments—rather than from below. Trade union organisation was weak everywhere; socialist movements, where they existed, were in infancy, and sometimes proscribed. A distinctive feature of the whole movement, however, has been the connection between industrial labour and the student population. Latin-American universities for the most part offer professional and technical training rather than general education; students are numerous; their organisations have considerable solidarity, and are often very active politically. Their activity usually issues in a vague clamour for reform rather than in support of a definite party programme, but it can be extremely vociferous and sometimes violent. In some countries it became in the 'twenties, and has since remained, a considerable political nuisance.

The governments which inaugurated all these programmes of social betterment in the 'twenties varied greatly in political form. In some countries, notably Colombia, the pre-war pattern of a landowning oligarchy governing through a discreetly manipulated constitution survived with little change. In Brazil the pre-war routine went on, though it was troubled by several abortive military outbreaks. In a few countries, constitutional radicalism was temporarily in the ascendant. The Radical party in Argentina ('Whig' would perhaps be a more descriptive title) had come to power as a result of the Sáenz Peña electoral reform. In Chile an analogous change of government took place in 1920. Alessandri, the new President, came from the northern province of Tarapacá and was avowedly the representative of labour and middle-class interests. The economic plight of the country and congressional opposition to proposals for reform compelled Alessandri to abandon the old 1833 constitution and to introduce a new one, ratified by plebiscite, which greatly increased the powers of the President. The outcome was a series of *coups d'état*, and from 1927 a military quasi-dictatorship, which carried into effect most of the provisions of Alessandri's reform programme. A pronounced characteristic of the radical parties in general was the intensely personal nature of their organisation. Irigoyen, the Argentine radical leader, who served twice as President, was known as the last of the *caudillos*; his personal control over every detail of party organisation and national government, his heavy-handed intervention in provincial government, recalled the methods of the old *caudillos*; but at least his actions came within the letter of the constitution. Several republics in the 'twenties, on the other hand, were governed without any serious pretence of constitutional forms, and carried through considerable programmes of development and reform by means of undisguised dictatorship. Unscrupulous politicians were learning the uses of an industrial proletariat as a support for unconstitutional power. Leguía, ruler of Peru from 1919 to 1930, was a man of humble origin whose seizure of power was supported by middle-class and labour interests, and whose programme included legislation for the protection of labour, general education, and redistribution of land, as well as the usual elaborate public works. A considerable part of the programme, especially in public works and in education, was put into effect by means of public loans raised in the United States. The perfect pattern of the radical dictator, however, was Juan Vicente Gómez, the uneducated *mestizo* who for twenty-six years, under various official titles, dominated the affairs of Venezuela. Gómez's armoury included all the now-familiar weapons of censorship, of secret police, of torture, of imprisonment without trial for political offences, of the distribution of responsible offices among those of the dictator's relatives who showed capacity and loyalty. Gómez ran Venezuela with ruthlessness and shrewd business efficiency. Like Leguía, he specialised in education and costly public works; but he was preserved from financial difficulties by the revenues from the oil industry. He died in his bed in 1935, still in office, immensely wealthy and universally respected. His nominated successor took over without serious commotion and the Gómez system lasted until 1945, when a revolution placed the Democratic Action party—a constitutionalist, middle-class body—in power.

Constitutional government, then, was by no means universal in Latin America even in the peaceful and prosperous 'twenties. On the other hand, the habit of revolution seemed to have been broken in most countries. To have broken it in Venezuela was Gómez's proudest boast. In leading states such as Argentina, which had known no violent change of government for half a century, stability and order were taken for granted. Everywhere great advances had been made in replacing the rule of force, of interest or of caprice, by the rule of law. Yet the underlying weakness, the excessive dependence upon the outside world, the failure to develop indigenous creative power, remained. World forces over which the Latin Americans had little control were to launch them into a period of disorder and distress.

The great depression of world trade which set in towards the end of 1929 struck Latin America almost immediately and with disastrous results. The Latin-American countries were more vulnerable, perhaps, than ever before. They depended upon foreign sources for many essential goods and services; they relied upon the export of a few basic commodities to pay for their very varied purchases. They were in many cases under contractual obligations to supply their customers, and the burden of their contracts was greatly increased by the fall in prices. Most of them were saddled with a heavy load of public and private debt. Their public revenues, out of which interest had to be paid and administration maintained, were drawn largely from export and import duties, which shrank alarmingly as trade declined. Faced with economic crisis, all governments except Venezuela and Argentina defaulted on their interest payments abroad; and all, perforce, reduced expenditure at home. Spending on works of capital development, on public health, on education, was drastically reduced. Governments and private concerns reduced their staffs. There was widespread unemployment—a new phenomenon in Latin America—followed by labour unrest, rioting and political revolts.

During 1930 and 1931 eleven of the twenty Latin-American republics experienced revolution; or, more accurately, experienced irregular changes of government; for these outbreaks were alike not only in their success, but, in most instances, in their relatively bloodless character. In some countries criminal proceedings were started against outgoing rulers—Leguía died in prison—but there were few assassinations or massacres. In general the revolutions took the civilised but extra-legal course of demonstration—ultimatum—resignation. It would be an over-simplification to attribute the outbreaks entirely to the depression. Bad business helped to make bad government intolerable. In every case there already existed social and political grievances to which the depression gave an opening. The commonest complaints were dictatorship, real or alleged, in some states; radicalism and pampering of labour in others; over-liberal terms offered to foreign capitalists; administrative waste and corruption; and the perennial grudge of the 'Outs' against the 'Ins'.

In Argentina the administration of Irigoyen was disliked by conservatives for its radicalism and by almost everybody else for its personal character, which concentrated a totally unmanageable mass of administrative detail in the hands of an upright but self-willed and narrow septuagenarian. It was not a dictatorship, but a creeping paralysis of administration, against which resentment grew. Irigoyen had forfeited labour support by an uncompromising attitude towards strikes in 1930. In September of that year an immense but well-organised and orderly demonstration in Buenos Aires compelled Irigoyen to resign. The demonstration was staged by students and the military. Its immediate consequence was a year of military rule under General Uriburu. An election was eventually held late in 1931, and General Justo took office as the head of an elected National Democratic—that is, conservative—government. The times were unpropitious for a conservative policy in the ordinary sense, and government tended to drift away from constitutional practice towards oligarchic rule of the old type. Finally, during the second world war, the oligarchy was displaced by a régime which bore at least a superficial resemblance to European fascism.

The revolution in Argentina was followed six weeks later by a widespread insurrection in Brazil. The coffee industry of Brazil had for some time been controlled by a valorisation scheme under which the government restricted the amount of production, bought the crop, stored it, and released quantities appropriate to the demand, in order to maintain the price. The scheme broke down inevitably and disastrously early in 1930, and the only way of disposing of vast quantities of unsaleable coffee was to burn it. To the resulting discontent the reigning President, Washington Luis of São Paulo, added a political grievance by giving official support to a Paulista candidate in the presidential election of 1930. As was customary in Brazilian elections, the official candidate was returned, and the conduct of the election gave great offence in Minas Geraes, the state which would have provided the next President according to long-standing political convention. The situation, with its threat of permanent Paulista government, was seized and exploited by the candidate of a third state, Rio Grande do Sul, which had been growing in wealth and population and now claimed a greater share in central government. Dr Getulio Vargas embarked upon civil war supported by Minas Geraes as well as by his own state of Rio Grande, defeated the forces of São Paulo, drove out the President, and set up a form of modified dictatorship, bolstered by two extensive constitutional changes designed to strengthen the power of the President and to reduce that of Congress and the state governments. The second of these enactments, in 1937, inaugurated a 'corporative' organisation reminiscent of fascist Italy; but Vargas was no Mussolini. His rule, though centralised and authoritarian, was neither arbitrary nor—except in dealing with revolts by alleged Communists—repressive. He himself displayed an engaging geniality and studied moderation. The great emperor Pedro II used to call himself the best republican in Brazil; Dr Vargas might similarly have said that, had he not the misfortune to be a dictator, he would have been a very democratic fellow.

The revolution in Chile was exceptional in being a successful revolt against military dictatorship. Chile probably suffered more severely than any other country from the depression; its export trade, already depressed, was for a time almost killed. Yet the Chileans, remote, poor, proud, eminently civilised, selected the inauspicious year 1932 for a return to constitutional government. The President inaugurated in that year, after two disputed elections and considerable disorder, was again Alessandri, liberal, upright and able, by far the most respected of Chilean statesmen. He governed for six years of modest recovery and careful administration, moving steadily away from his old radicalism towards a conventionally conservative policy. In his last years he adopted measures of active repression against socialists and Communists, which drove them to compose their differences and join with the radicals in a joint election campaign. Alessandri was thus succeeded in 1938 by Aguirre Cerda at the head of a 'popular front' coalition—itself a new and disturbing portent in Latin-American politics.

In Mexico there was no revolution in the ordinary sense. Mexicans considered that their country had been undergoing a continuous revolution since 1910. In the 'twenties, however, the process had slowed down. The old revolutionaries had become the new conservatives, and except for their anti-clericalism had forgotten much of the revolutionary programme. Obregón's successor, Calles, who either as President or as a power behind the President dominated Mexican politics from 1924 to 1934, publicly announced his opinion in 1929 that the land reform programme had gone far enough. In the early 'thirties distribution almost ceased. It is true that the industrial labour laws grew somewhat beyond what industry could safely afford; but the labour movement, like the government, was susceptible to jobbery, and trade union leadership became a road to affluence and power. Meanwhile there had been several armed revolts in the 'twenties, and the gun-toting tradition of Mexican politics was still alive. The general political tone of this phase of the Revolution is best expressed in the nickname given to Calles. He was called the *Jefe Máximo*—the Big Boss. Yet even in these circumstances the emotions supporting the Revolution were too ardent to be chilled by the economic blizzard from abroad. The depression produced not counter-revolution, but impatience with the slow progress of the Revolution. With the election of General Cárdenas to the presidency in 1934 the scene changed abruptly. During his six years of office most landowners possessing any considerable extent of good arable land were dispossessed of all but a small area. The expropriation was no longer confined to owners who had acquired land by illegal means, who farmed inefficiently, or who had given political offence. The mere size of an estate, and its proximity to a village which wanted land, was enough to justify seizure, and it became much more difficult to stave off expropriation by the payment of bribes. Forty-seven million acres of land were distributed among more than a million peasant families between 1936 and 1940, compared with some 20 million acres granted to three-quarters of a million in the previous twenty years.[1] Cárdenas's policy, much influenced by some aspects of Communism (Trotsky found asylum in Mexico), favoured the grant of

[1] P. E. James, *Latin America* (London, Cassell, 1943), p. 602. Detailed tables are collected in N. L. Whetton, *Rural Mexico* (Chicago, 1948).

ejidos to villages in common, rather than of plots in permanent ownership to individuals, who often used their plots to produce crops for
immediate subsistence, and nothing more. The hasty redistribution,
necessarily based on inadequate surveys, caused widespread disorganisation and, temporarily at least, a serious drop in production. The development of communal peasant farming posed urgent problems of capital and
management. A land bank system was started to lend money to *ejidatarios*;
but the collection of interest in small sums from many scattered borrowers
required an elaborate and costly organisation, and the operations of the
bank were mostly confined to promising villages in favoured localities.
The management problem was even more difficult of solution. Few
peones had experience of management, and, since *ejido* managers were
elected, they were often chosen on grounds of personal popularity rather
than of business ability. Nevertheless, some villages, particularly in the
now celebrated Laguna cotton-growing district, achieved considerable
success under the new system. It was confidently hoped that the problems
of leadership would prove easier of solution, as the determined efforts of
government to provide general education began to bear fruit. Meanwhile,
the price of revolution had to be paid in high cost of living, shaky national
credit, and uncertainty.

The revolution was avowedly nationalist as well as agrarian. One of the
most spectacular acts of the Cárdenas administration was the expropriation of the foreign oil companies in 1938, on terms of compensation which
could only be called derisory. A move to achieve native control of so
important a resource was understandable; but again a price had to be paid,
in foreign, especially British, resentment, and in the temporary deterioration of the industry. Whether through inexperienced management, or
intractable labour, or lack of capital for exploratory work, productivity
declined for a decade after expropriation. During the second world war it
became impossible even to import the necessary machinery for replacement, much less for development. Significant recovery did not begin until
the early 1950s.

The nationalism of the revolution was more than economic. The
plunder of the *hacendados* weakened and disrupted the cultivated social
and intellectual life, urban in character, French in tone, which their wealth
had supported. In the realm of the arts, a new and remarkable cultural
development came to take its place, self-consciously indigenous, based
largely upon Indian artistic tradition. Native Mexican art of the time was
most vigorous in the fields of painting and sculpture, less vigorous in
literary work. It was closely and grimly preoccupied with immediate
social problems, and this preoccupation set limits to its scope and its
appeal; but it represented genuine and original creative effort, and seemed
a presage of the growth of intellectual independence which Latin America
as a whole urgently needed.

To carry through the drastic changes of the 'thirties more than ordinary powers were needed, and President Cárdenas, supported by the army, industrial labour and the peasantry, was virtually a dictator. There was only one political party, the party of the Mexican Revolution. The dictatorship, however, was one of creative enthusiasm rather than of repression. Except in its persecution of the church and its ruthless invasion of property, it was tolerant of divergences of opinion and permitted outspoken public criticism of its policy. Most significant of all, when Cárdenas's term came to an end he attempted neither to seek re-election nor to evade the constitution by interfering in the administration of his successor.

Most Latin-American states in the 1930s showed a marked tendency to adopt more authoritarian forms of government. These forms could not fairly be called 'totalitarian'; most educated Latin Americans possessed too strong a sense of personal dignity to tolerate extreme dictatorship and too keen a sense of ridicule to be deceived by the cruder forms of racial myth. Governments, moreover, lacked the detailed administrative machinery which the 'totalitarian' state requires. There was, nevertheless, a very evident growth of self-conscious nationalism. In internal affairs it took the form of agitation and sometimes of financial discrimination against foreign capital—against the English railways in Argentina, against the nitrate concerns in Chile, and of course the oil companies in Mexico. Many of these undertakings had become notoriously unremunerative, and clearly the great days of foreign—or at least European—investment in Latin America were past. In some countries, legislation intended for the protection of labour was used as a means of discrimination against foreign employers. Most governments enacted anti-alien employment laws, limiting the number of foreigners who might be employed in industry or commerce. At the same time, the open-door immigration policy which had existed over most of Latin America came to an end. Restrictive legislation began in Brazil and on the Pacific coast with quota regulations aimed against the immigration of Japanese, who presented a difficult problem of assimilation and were generally disliked; but most governments wished also to protect the industrial and agricultural labour market, in a time of unemployment, against an influx of European wage-earners. In Argentina and Brazil, the principal immigration countries, restrictive legislation reached a peak of severity in 1938. Both countries still contained immense areas of empty land, and exceptions were made in favour of farming settlers; but few immigrants in the 1930s were of this class. Pioneer settlement was—and still is—hampered by lack of capital. Today there is little prospect in any part of Latin America of a revival of indiscriminate mass immigration.

Throughout Latin America renewed and strenuous efforts were made, particularly in developing industries, to achieve a greater degree of economic independence. Governments attempted to control the production of staple products—Brazilian coffee, Argentine wheat, Chilean nitrate, Bolivian tin—in the hope of maintaining prices. In foreign trade, barter agreements between governments began to replace the competition of the open market. Prominent among these was the Roca–Runciman agreement between Argentina and Great Britain in 1933, followed by other similar pacts which, whatever their economic justification, caused considerable resentment in the United States. Nationalism also took overt political forms. There were several acrimonious disputes between states, and one serious war between Paraguay and Bolivia over possession of the Gran Chaco. Bolivia, landlocked and disorderly, dependent for revenue upon the product of its foreign-owned tin mines, was defeated and suffered yet another loss of territory. Bolivian irridentism would, no doubt, have been a menace to the peace, but for Bolivian weakness. The resources of the country were further strained later, in the early 1950s, by a revolution of Mexican type which distributed the land of the big estates, armed the tin miners and nationalised the mines.

Nationalism, however, was clearly no panacea for Latin-American difficulties, and most governments knew and admitted that autarky, even if desirable, was out of the question in any foreseeable future. In many countries—though not in all—the 1930s saw a striking growth of enthusiasm for the Pan-American idea, and an elaboration of Pan-American arrangements for meeting and discussion. To some extent this was due to the decline in the prestige of the League of Nations, to Latin-American disappointment with the League's achievements, and disinclination to become involved in European quarrels which seemed to be passing beyond the scope of international discussion. In great measure, however, the revival of Pan-Americanism was assisted by changes in the foreign policy of the United States.

The Union of American Republics is an entirely voluntary association of theoretically equal sovereign states. It has no centralised administration and no constitution; few of its organs rest on formal conventions. Since 1910 it has maintained a permanent Bureau at Washington, which is a centre of research and propaganda as well as a secretariat for the periodical Pan-American conferences. The chief function of the Union is to facilitate the open discussion of matters of common interest to the American republics. The United States has always been the Union's chief sponsor; the chief obstacle to the work of the Union has been Latin-American suspicion of the United States. Many North American statesmen, notably Woodrow Wilson, insistently proclaimed their country's respect for the sovereignty of all its neighbours. These pronouncements appeared to be contradicted by the interventions in Mexico in 1914 and 1916–17, followed by a decade of uniformly bad relations; by the presence of United States forces—however few in number and helpful in intention—in Haiti, Santo Domingo and Nicaragua; by the Platt amendment;

by the non-recognition policy; by the economic power exercised in Cuba by the sugar corporations, and throughout the Caribbean by the United Fruit Company, an organisation far wealthier and more potent than the little republics in which it operated.

After the first world war it was generally thought that the strategic excuse for North American intervention in the Caribbean had disappeared. Resentment against the political and economic policy of the United States flared up in public speeches at the Havana Conference in 1928. The hostility then displayed gave a considerable shock to public opinion in the United States, and the year of the Conference saw the beginnings of a determined effort to improve relations with Latin America. The policy of the 'good neighbour' is closely associated with the name of Franklin Roosevelt. He was not responsible for the Clark memorandum, published in 1930, which explicitly repudiated the 'Roosevelt corollary'; nor for the appointment of Dwight Morrow, who as ambassador in Mexico did much to create friendly feeling and to postpone the Mexican onslaught on foreign property. The new policy reached its fullest expression, however, after Roosevelt became President in 1933. In that year, at the seventh Pan-American Conference at Montevideo, the United States accepted a resolution denying the right of any state to interfere in the internal affairs of any other state. The Buenos Aires Conference in 1936, which was opened by President Roosevelt himself, reaffirmed this principle in more explicit terms, and drew up a pact providing for consultation in the event of any threat to the peace of the Americas. The administrative organisation and procedure for carrying out this consultative pact were created by the eighth Pan-American Conference at Lima in 1938.

During this period of frequent conferences the United States government withdrew the last of its forces from Nicaragua and Haiti, rescinded the Platt amendment in 1934, and in 1936 voluntarily gave up its treaty right of intervention in Panama. Evidence of a radical change of policy was afforded not only by the actions of the State Department, but by its abstentions from action. North American investors abroad were left to shift for themselves. There was no intervention in Cuba during the anarchy of Grau San Martín's administration, and, when the Mexican government confiscated the foreign oil wells, the British Foreign Office was left alone to make futile protests and to break off diplomatic relations. Meanwhile a new and more liberal trading policy, initiated by Mr Cordell Hull under the Reciprocal Trade Agreements Act of 1934, found an effective sphere of operation in Latin America. By the end of 1939 agreements had been made with eleven Latin-American states.

The success of the 'good neighbour' policy was not universal. The Buenos Aires Conference, for instance, resolutely refused to endorse the neutrality legislation of the United States. There were sharp differences of opinion between Argentina and the United States over the procedure to be adopted to bring the Chaco war to an end, and over Argentine proposals for non-aggression pacts in which European states might be invited to participate. Not only were Argentine governments jealous of North American political leadership: the Argentine economy was complementary to that of Europe and directly competitive with that of the United States. Argentina today easily holds a record among American states for the non-ratification of international agreements.

Nevertheless, the Pan-American movement grew in strength, and its value became evident in 1939. Within three weeks of the outbreak of war the American foreign ministers met to establish a 'zone of neutrality' in the Americas and to set up a financial and economic advisory committee designed to reduce the economic consequences of the war in Latin America. In 1940, the emphasis having shifted from neutrality to defence, they met again at Havana, and devised a scheme for taking over the administration of European colonies in the western hemisphere in case of German victory in Europe. The Havana Conference also passed a resolution declaring that any attack by a non-American state would be considered an act of aggression against all the Americas.

An act of aggression against the United States took place towards the end of 1941, and early in 1942 the American foreign ministers met again, at Rio de Janeiro. This meeting—after a severe struggle in which Argentina led the opposition—recommended all American republics to sever relations with the 'Axis' powers. The co-operation of Latin America was now vital to the Allied cause, since the Japanese had possessed themselves of the chief sources, in the East, of tin, rubber, quinine, and a whole range of tropical products. The Latin-American states rose to the occasion. Mexico and Brazil declared war in the summer of 1942. Both in due course sent forces abroad. All the republics except Chile and Argentina broke off relations with the 'Axis' before the end of the Conference. Chile made the break in January 1943. Argentina broke off relations in 1944 and declared war in January 1945, obviously with a view to securing a place at the United Nations Conference. By that time Argentina was almost isolated politically, and its relations with the United States were deeply embittered. Argentina was not represented at the fourth conference of foreign ministers in 1945, but it eventually acceded to the final Act of Chapúltepec. This Act repeated the principle of common American resistance to aggression, and made it clear that the principle was to include aggression by one American state against another. Further, it provided for the first time a working definition of aggression, and committed states, if necessary, to the use of economic and military 'sanctions'. The Act of Chapúltepec thus marked, on paper, the metamorphosis of the Monroe Doctrine from a unilateral declaration of policy to a reciprocal system of regional security, within the proposed framework of the United Nations.

The strength and permanence of this system depended to a great extent upon the policy of the United States. The successes of the 'good neighbour' policy were achieved through the readiness of the United States to exercise exceptional restraint, and to make important concessions of immediate interests. There was still, however, considerable latent hostility towards the United States in Latin America. It broke briefly into clamour in Peru and Ecuador during the war, over the North American attitude towards a dispute between those countries about territory on the Upper Amazon. After the war most Latin-American states recognised, realistically if grudgingly, their dependence upon the United States for the general defence of the Americas against outside attack. The United States government, on its side, took great care to avoid open interference in the internal affairs of other American states. These attitudes and policies were enough to avert open hostility, if not to secure friendly co-operation. Nonintervention, however, was uneasily felt to be contingent, from the North American point of view, on good behaviour. It could hardly be maintained if, for instance, there should be a widespread development in Latin America of pro-Russian Communism.

At the time such a possibility seemed comparatively remote. Communist groups existed in most of the republics; they were often, and sometimes rightly, blamed for fomenting conspiracy and disorder; but they were small and relatively unimportant. It is true that the thought of the Mexican revolution owed much to Marx, but *agrarismo* was a Mexican phenomenon and had little in common with contemporary Russian totalitarianism. Indeed, both the theories and the policies of the revolutionary party in power in Mexico had become much less drastic, much more conservative, in the 1940s than they had been a decade earlier. Devices were found for avoiding the laws against concentrated estates, and no obstacles were placed in the way of the development of industry by private capital. APRA, the interesting left-wing party which came into power in Peru at the election of 1945, followed a similar route, though more briefly and much less effectively. *Aprismo* purported to be Marxist in political and social philosophy, but it recognised the importance of religion in social life, and accepted the need for the support of the middle class in the reform of society. It was strongly opposed to the influence of foreign capital, supported the idea of Pan-Latin-Americanism, and stressed the importance of the Indian races in American affairs. Its programme identified the most pressing task of any Peruvian government—that of bringing a dispossessed and poverty-stricken Indian peasantry into the main stream of national economic life. The APRA government achieved little; it was overthrown late in 1948, by a military insurrection which had widespread support among the employing and landowning classes. The soldiers and their allies thought, or affected to think, that *Aprismo* was dangerously close to Communism; but in fact APRA had moved steadily to the right during its period of office, and continued to do so after its overthrow. Ineffectual it may have been; it was not seriously revolutionary. Its political character-istics—a combination between the middle and professional classes and labour, and a tendency to move to the right when under pressure—were common to many moderate radical movements in Latin America, and a number of successful post-war governments were based on coalitions of this kind. Communism, which would not as a rule accept such a coalition, remained politically weak, though discontents of the kind on which it could thrive were widespread almost everywhere.

One of the major states of Latin America was until 1955 governed by a radical dictatorship of a fairly extreme kind. Argentina resembles Austra-lia in that, although its wealth comes from its immense rural resources, three-quarters of its population live in towns. Immigrants have always tended to seek employment in or near the towns, and urbanisation was accelerated by industrial development before and during the war. One-fifth of the population live in the capital. During the war, through the greatly increased demands for industrial production, especially (as in 1914) for tinned beef, labour in Buenos Aires received very high wages and became very powerful. After the war, with the falling-off of temporary demands and the attempt to resume normal pre-war trading, the labour in the canning factories and other concerns became extremely unruly. General Perón came to power as a result of a military *coup* in 1943 and a tumultuous election in 1945. His strength rested upon labour and the army, and was due to his gift of talking to the workers of the capital in language which they understood—simple, emotional and violent. His theme was an extreme left-wing nationalism, a promise to lead the wor-kers against the capitalist and the foreigner. His success in 1945 was probably assisted by the attempts of the United States Ambassador in Buenos Aires, Mr Spruille Braden, to rally opposition against him. This helped to explain the attitude of the government towards the United States. Unwillingness to compromise hindered trade negotiations with other states, notably Great Britain. National feeling insisted on the pur-chase in 1947 of the very unremunerative English railways—*el pulpo inglés*, the English octopus, as they were called in the *Peronista* press. The failure of the meat companies to deliver the beef which was to pay for the railways was due, not so much to ill-will or bad faith, as to labour trouble and general disorganisation in the trade. The economic life of Argentina was, indeed, in some disorder in 1949, despite its great potenti-alities.

Dictatorships of the *Peronista* kind remained rare in Latin America, at least in the greater states. In Mexico the revolution had lost its fierce urgency and constitutional government seemed firmly established. In Brazil the Vargas administration ended in 1945, and President Dutra correctly described his own government as one devoted to 're-constitu-tionalising' the political system. Chile and Uruguay each already enjoyed a long tradition of political stability. Over a great part of the area, therefore, the argument, so often advanced, that the economic difficulties of Latin America arose from the instability of Latin-American governments, seemed to have lost any force it might once have had. In the strictly economic field, major changes appeared to be on the way. The second world war, with its temporarily expanded demand for raw materials, especially minerals, and its curtailment of the supply of manufactured goods, had given a powerful stimulus to industrial development of the import-substitution kind. The process continued, under high protection, in peace-time. Heavy industry also made a beginning in Brazil, in Mexico and in Peru. In Brazil the building of the great Volta Redonda steelworks was hailed as a declaration of economic independence. Yet to assert, as some Latin-Americans did, that South America in 1950 was on the threshold of a development analogous to that of North America in the second half of the last century, was premature, to say the least. The whole area faced appalling difficulties. Many of the new import-substitution industries proved uneconomic in peace-time. Their products could not be sold abroad, and national markets were too small to absorb them. Agriculture in many sectors was neglected, technically backward, and stagnant. It lacked stimulus; for the world demand for primary products in peace was sluggish, compared with that for manufactured goods. New countries in Africa and elsewhere were emerging, moreover, as competitive producers of the export crops upon which Latin America had long relied. The area as a whole had never really recovered from the depression of the late 1920s. In 1932 the exports of Latin America to the rest of the world were less than half what they had been in 1928; and, while world trade thereafter recovered, Latin-American exports, in real terms, virtually stood still. The Latin-American share of world trade, expressed as a percentage, declined steadily from 1935 to 1940; rose from 1940 to 1945 in response to demand for raw materials; and again declined from 1945 to 1950.[1] The economic history of Latin America from 1930 to 1950, therefore, apart from the war years, had been one long continuous slump. Yet population was increasing by leaps and bounds, more rapidly, indeed, than in any other comparable area in the world. Unemployment was general in many countries, and became more apparent as hundreds of thousands of people migrated from the poverty-stricken countryside to the shanty-town slums of the big cities. The extent and speed of industrialisation needed to meet such a situation could not even be attempted, without foreign capital investment and foreign credit on an immense scale. These were not forthcoming. The only Latin-American countries which were able to earn foreign exchange in any considerable amounts were Venezuela, from oil, Mexico, from 'tourism', and Panama,

[1] *The Economic Development of Latin America in the Post-War Period* (United Nations, Economic Commission for Latin America, New York, 1964).

from the Canal. Significantly, these were the only Latin-American countries which combined—and still combine—a relatively high *per capita* income (by Latin-American standards) with a low annual rate of price inflation. Other countries either stagnated economically, or else pushed ahead with imaginative industrial schemes and ambitious public works to the accompaniment—as in Brazil—of ruinous inflation and consequent widespread distress. Of all the poorer areas of the world, Latin America in 1950 was the most literate, the most sophisticated in its leadership, the most evidently 'ripe' for rapid economic growth; yet of its major states probably only Mexico in 1950 showed any clear sign of such growth beginning. Latin America represented beyond question a political and cultural force, and a social and economic problem, which the world at large could not afford to ignore.

CHAPTER XX

LITERATURE 1895-1939

IN 1895 *Jude the Obscure* was published, Hardy's last, and perhaps his greatest, novel. It was promptly reviled by a majority of reviewers on both sides of the Atlantic, and burnt by a bishop, 'probably in his despair', Hardy suggested later, 'at not being able to burn me'; by so much had progress eroded the fervours of faith. The only long-term effect on the author, as Hardy also revealed, was that of 'completely curing' him 'of further interest in novel writing'. Fortunately it did not also cure him of the habit of poetry; and, meanwhile, *Jude* seems an excellent place to start.

In certain obvious ways, it is very modern; its treatment of human sexuality is more frank, if not necessarily more realistic, than one finds in any previous important English novel. The claims for naturalism made by Flaubert, Zola, Ibsen and other European writers were at last influencing the British tradition, as they might have done much earlier had it not been for the excessive public prudery of Victorian taste. But, like nearly all major novels, *Jude* is not primarily naturalistic. Its total impact has more the force of myth. To Hardy, as to many other progressive Victorians, modern life had come to seem a tragic affair. Jude and Sue pursue the romantic quest for self-fulfilment, but the very nature of things conspires against them. Certain of the sufferings arise, it is true, from social causes that might be alleviated; though Jude himself is rejected in his search for education, no laws of nature decree this fate. The gates of Oxford are fast shut, but the 'red-brick' colleges were rising. Forster's Education Act (1870) had removed many obstacles, and a Jude fifty years later would have found fewer frustrations of this kind. Again, Jude's sexual problems might have been less insoluble in the future. He might have found himself less fatally torn between two women representing so exclusively the one the bodily, the other the spiritual and intellectual, side of life—the earthy, coarse, good-natured, shrewd, uneducable Arabella, and the refined, well-meaning, incurably neurotic and destructive Sue. But, when this is said, certain aspects of Hardy's tragic context still seem beyond a solution, including perhaps the sexual make-up of Jude and Sue. There is Jude's strong animal instinct which delivers him— healthily, some critics have felt—to Arabella's coarser world. There is Sue's strangely tormented nature, which seems destined to destroy those who love her and whom she loves. Above all, there is the degree of sensitivity in Jude and Sue, which can scarcely expect peace in a suffering world. Almost, Hardy seems to be suggesting, Jude and Sue are in an

613   41-2

evolutionary cul-de-sac; such heightened sensitivity as theirs weakens the will to survive. Arabella is the one who will survive, whatever life offers, with her resilience in the face of suffering, her robust acceptance of the world as it is. But the evolution of higher sensitivity and intelligence begins to seem a dubious blessing. The man who suffers for worms and for rabbits may be destined to perish, a freak in our Darwinian, post-Christian world.

This perception hovers on the background, also, of Henry James's late novels—a roll-call of masterpieces as distinguished as any one could find: *What Maisie Knew* (1897), *The Spoils of Poynton* (1897), *The Awkward Age* (1899), *The Sacred Fount* (1901), *The Wings of the Dove* (1902), *The Ambassadors* (1903), and *The Golden Bowl* (1905). Through all these works one finds two deep, but ironically incompatible, insights. Intelligent, sensitive man needs, and must seek, a rich destiny—a destiny conceived, moreover, through personal relationships raised to the beauty of art. Yet personal relationships, even and perhaps especially when most sensitively cultivated, are characterised by ambivalence, and vulnerable to betrayal and death. The later James novels are masterpieces of subtlety, so rich that some readers have been repelled. Is the subtlety, they wonder, simply endless manner—manner calculated to add grace and interest to actually threadbare and sordid events? Yet James's achieved effect is virtually the opposite. He shows that certain people who might easily be dismissed as threadbare or sordid by a casual spectator may be living out intense dramas of heightened awareness but almost paralysed will. *The Wings of the Dove* sounds threadbare only if it is reduced to a naked plot level, and seen as the tale of two villains scheming for the money of a dying friend. In fact the leading villain on this reading, Kate Croy, represents 'life' even more strikingly than Millie Theale, her 'victim'; for, whereas Millie, despite her great love of life, is left merely to die exquisitely, Kate, if given Millie's money (which she certainly schemes for), could marvellously and richly live. The quality of 'life' is indeed James's central preoccupation, and, alongside it, the complications and corruptions which a society based on money and privilege must inevitably bring. The simpler moral judgements are, of course, present, and there is an important sense in which they remain true. Kate Croy herself, and her rich, domineering aunt Mrs Lowder, use and exploit people, and this is a cardinal Jamesian sin. Millie represents the exquisite delicacy which respects individuality and seems fulfilled in self-sacrifice, and this comes near to the Jamesian ideal. Merton Densher, again, is the kind of good-looking, well-intentioned, weak-willed young man who can be led unwittingly into a sordid plot through passion, but then incapacitated for the plot by a supremely magnanimous act of his intended prey; and this is an image of modern man to which James often returns. Teasing ambiguities make of James's later novels one of the supreme literary experiences, but, if a single aspect of *The Wings of the Dove* may be isolated for this present thesis, it is an insight that might remind us of *Jude the Obscure*. Kate and Mrs Lowder will survive and live lavishly, in their confident coarseness, while Millie and Merton Densher will not. The novel ends with Kate hurt but Millie dead, and Merton paralysed: even if sensitivity and conscience have the highest *potential* for life (and James showed this also in *The Spoils of Poynton*), it is people with great exuberance but a diminished conscience who are most likely actually to live. The modern world, if one can risk yet a further simplification, rewards heightened consciousness with heightened pain.

James's later novels were attacked by E. M. Forster for their stylistic density, but many of their values seem to be carried over into his own. His first novel *Where Angels Fear to Tread* (1905) was followed by *The Longest Journey* (1907), *A Room with a View* (1908), *Howard's End* (1910), and then years later by the last and greatest, *A Passage to India* (1924). Forster's novels are not without their ironic ambivalences, but characteristically he mediates these through a symbolism more explicit, if somewhat less resonant, than James's. Forster is a liberal humanist who continues to cherish his own moral values, whilst exploring their limitations in situations of choice and action so ironically that one comes to doubt their survival value in the modern world. Even democracy is afforded only two cheers, in its battles with tyranny; the best of a bad job, yes, says Forster, but no shining ideal. And his liberal heroes and heroines, who set out to 'connect' with their fellow men in humane benevolence, to transcend in art and friendship the sordid man-made barriers of class, colour and creed—these too are endorsed for their ideals and benevolence, but doomed by their frequent defects in elementary good sense.

In *Howard's End*, the story concerns two German sisters, Margaret and Helen Schlegel, who embody an enthusiastic liberal humanism, and confront the world with high hopes of setting it to rights. When they meet the wealthy and materialistic Wilcoxes, both sisters, after Helen's initial infatuation, are contemptuous; yet the Wilcox world of class gradations and business efficiency, of 'telegrams and anger', of sumptuous vulgarity with panic and emptiness somewhere just under the surface, is not to be simply derided as anti-cultural or 'anti-life'. Both sisters are themselves rich, and in the course of the novel they begin to understand the implications of their wealth. Confronted with the unfortunate Leonard Bast, a young man struggling with poverty and a tawdry marriage, and cut off by these things from the 'culture' to which he so desperately aspires, they realise how greatly their own commitment to art and to personal relationships depends upon the leisure of a privileged class. Their personal freedom is secured by investments, and these are produced and sustained by the Wilcoxes of the world, not by the Schlegels. There is a suggestion, even, that the liberal and artistic Schlegels may be parasitic upon the very

615

people whose material wealth they instinctively deride. In the novel, the two sisters take very different paths, which symbolise their individual reactions to this discovery. Margaret marries Mr Wilcox, and attempts a *via media*; perhaps she can 'soften' his way of life (but soften it without undermining it, one wonders?) whilst going fully half-way towards recognising its central validity in the modern world. Her marriage works, however, only fitfully and at low pressure; though allowances are made on both sides, and there is genuine friendship, the relationship is ill fitted to survive a moral crisis of the kind which Helen eventually precipitates. For Helen, refusing all compromise, rejects the Wilcoxes completely, and concentrates upon trying to make Bast the actual cultural equal of herself. The practical obstacles to this are underlined throughout the novel, with Forster's unfailing comic inventiveness. Eventually, perhaps in pity and desperation, though we are not fully shown this, Helen gives to Bast the gift of herself. The only 'connection' which will finally satisfy the appetite of her idealism for social realisation is the physical connection of sex. Some critics have seen in this a triumph of symbolism over psychological probability, but a woman like Helen, fiercely idealistic and fiercely intolerant of cant, might understandably drive her own sincerity to this supreme test. In giving herself to Bast, however, and conceiving his child, Helen produces merely a social disaster, in which her sister's marriage is tested almost to breaking-point, and Bast himself, in a typically ludicrous accident, is destroyed. The novel ends with ambiguities which, though more clearly defined than James's, avoid schematic simplicity. Though the Schlegels themselves are involved in muddle, and their ideals are forced by events towards Margaret's compromise and Helen's catastrophe, the next generation might still benefit from what they have done. The child of Bast and Helen will be the inheritor of Howard's End—once the home of the gentle, withdrawn first Mrs Wilcox, who represented so much of what was gracious and intuitive in the older England.

So Forster looks ahead, to the erosion of class-consciousness through democratic progress, perhaps (if one can use hindsight) to the welfare state. And in his later novel, *A Passage to India*, he again shows the liberal attempt to 'connect' Indians and Anglo-Indians across social pressures and barriers failing in the first generation, but holding some hope for future time. Since Forster's prevailing mode is comic rather than tragic, one is entitled to feel a certain optimism behind the gloom—an optimism partly justified, it may be, by the welfare and Indian legislation of Clement Attlee's post-1945 Labour government. Yet one feels, too, as one often does when reading Hardy and James, Forster's conviction of certain losses which time will never heal. Like most liberal humanists of the early twentieth century, he was aware of accelerating social changes, which must destroy much that was fine and serene in the old order, whether they also remedy the older evils or not. He was no longer able to entertain the full Arnoldian hope, attempted in Margaret's marriage to Mr Wilcox, of a middle class raised from philistinism to culture; still less could he foresee Arnold's 'raw, unkindled masses of humanity' transformed by decent wages and education into sweetness and light. Already, in Forster's writings, one detects certain characteristics that were later to be associated with Bloomsbury—an urbane and aristocratic irony, more conscious of its own precarious hold upon history than confident of its power to change things; a suggestion that the older humanism no longer represents the main current of history, but has become a backwater, a home for the dwindling élite.

The Edwardian novel would be distinguished if it could boast only James and Forster. But there were two other major practitioners in the mode, as it passed from its Victorian triumphs to a splendid late flowering. Kipling was still producing some of his best work—*The Second Jungle Book* (1895), *Stalky & Co.* (1899), *Kim* (1901), *Just So Stories* (1902), *They* (1905), *Puck of Pook's Hill* (1906), *The Brushwood Boy* (1907), *Actions and Reactions* (1909). And, though Kipling's reputation suffered a decline in his lifetime which lasted until comparatively recently, he is now being appraised as a major figure again. For too long, he was taken simply as a crude propagandist for imperial expansion, and discredited in the public mind along with that. The sadistic elements in his work were pointed to, but regarded as disabling; he was not credited with the insight into cruelty and violence which even the crudest post-Freudian writers are allowed to possess. Yet, even at the height of the reaction, major critics like T. S. Eliot, George Orwell, Edmund Wilson, Lionel Trilling and C. S. Lewis were fascinated by Kipling; they recognised the imaginative power, the mythic intensity of his writing, even if they remained scornful of his ideas. It has remained for more recent critics, and notably Noel Annan, to point out that Kipling's intellect is far more formidable than his critics have supposed.[1] While Hardy, James, Forster all in their different ways explored the limitations of romantic humanism, Kipling rejected the tradition outright. It rested, in his view, on a fallacy. Men are not naturally kindly and humane when freed from convention; their condition without Law is the Hobbesian one, nasty, poor, solitary, brutish and short. The public school boy in the dormitory, the soldier in India, the ordinary man in the street have their decencies, but decencies in permanent conflict with instincts that need to be curbed. When Kipling speaks of the 'lesser breeds without the law' he is not sneering, but reporting the truth as he sees it. The Law is the condition for civilised living, the condition outside which no man can hope to live in freedom. But is also positively a source of discipline, especially when it is reinforced, as in a public school or an army, by an astringent and testing mode of life. And, above all, it has glamour. When translated into the convictions of a caste or a club, an

[1] A. Rutherford (ed.), *Kipling's Mind and Art* (1964).

'inside' community, a perceived and envied élite, it offers excitement and self-respect by which to live. Kipling also saw, it seems, that men must exercise their authority and extend their boundaries or start, imperceptibly at first, to sink. In an individual life, as in empire, there is no standing still.

Ironically, it was precisely Kipling's realism about the ordinary man which alienated critics who prided themselves on their own realism about sex. Certainly the blend of cruelty, vulgarity, courage and latent decency which Kipling admires was unacceptable to those who took as axiomatic the superiority of Millie Theale to Kate Croy. Kipling's true position, though well on the political right, was safely clear of fascism; Noel Annan has suggested as immediate intellectual influences the European sociologists Durkheim, Weber and Pareto 'who revolutionised the study of society at the beginning of this century'. Such pointers help to confirm our feeling that the imaginative power of Kipling's novels springs from something more coherent than brash patriotism and unrecognised sadism. The strange underestimate of them in the late 1940s and the 1950s may come to seem as illuminating, in retrospect, of the retreat from empire, as the wildly hysterical overestimate of D. H. Lawrence which accompanied it. And it may be that, if Kipling's popularity returns in the near future, this will be not only because the British Empire needs its imaginative historian now it is over, but also because the values of empire are not so very unlike the values of economic survival: either one expands, says Kipling, or one dies.

The other major British novelist of this period is Conrad, a lone wolf in the English novel tradition. A Pole writing in a foreign language and living in exile, he has yet become one of the classics of English art. His first novel, *Almayer's Folly*, was published in 1895, and the next thirty years saw, among other work, *An Outcast of the Islands* (1896), *Nigger of the Narcissus* (1897), *Lord Jim* (1900), *Typhoon* (1903), *Nostromo* (1904), *The Secret Agent* (1907), *Under Western Eyes* (1911), *Chance* (1913), *Victory* (1915), *The Shadow Line* (1917), *The Rescue* (1920), *Suspense* (1925). It is a distinguishing feature of Conrad that he seldom writes about the domestic and middle-class scenes and people which have been so popular in English fiction. The relationship between the sexes, and even normal family relationships, interested him little. His main preoccupation seems to be with the moments when individuals are tested by circumstances, and challenged in loneliness to survive. Again and again his heroes are faced with the test of their manhood, either in actual storms and tempests at sea, or in the storms and tempests of life. The challenge is to develop courage and endurance, above all self-sufficiency, in a universe devoid of purpose, yet offering certain achieved ideals of responsibility and courage in the traditions of men. The heroic virtues become both the means of victory, and their own best reward. Conrad views certain human institutions, it seems, much as a Catholic views the Church. An individual sea-captain has to test himself against a role of high and proven courage; like a priest, he pits his success or failure in life against an accepted succession, of which he is part. Conrad has little time for the quest for personal fulfilment outside such testing frameworks; he scorns the pursuit of emotional satisfaction in a void. At times, he has seemed to some of his critics chillingly clinical; it has been postulated even that cold dislike for his characters might be the impetus of his art. But what more is such a view than a patent evasion?—an evasion the sentimentality of which Conrad would have been the first to detect.

In *The Secret Agent*, for instance, he depicts various paths that can lead to political anarchy, for idealistic men and even for men of unusual virtue, as well as for the evil and mad. And in Mrs Verloc he depicts a path leading to murder, for a woman who seems to call aloud for the understanding that also forgives. But Conrad himself can understand without forgiving; how can one find an easy formula of forgiveness without abdicating responsibility for what is actually done? It is true that he forbids us the luxury of simple condemnation, by depicting the good anarchists, and Mrs Verloc, with the kind of imaginative perception which kindles our fear. But equally he forbids us the luxury of armchair tolerance, by focusing very clear attention upon their deeds. The understanding is that they are casualties in life, and must inevitably suffer; that they are casualties dangerous, moreover, to the all-important order of society as well as to themselves. One can agree that the quality of analysis in such a novel is disturbingly astringent; but to call it 'inhuman' is to refuse the full insights of the novelist's art. Fortunately, Conrad has a wonderful richness to offer, as well as his sternness; the richness of perceived possibilities of greatness and adventure in a tragic world.

Emerging from this necessarily brief commentary upon the Edwardian novel, it is possible to point to at least one major common theme. All four of the novelists touched on, as well as Hardy, illuminate our need to cultivate endurance in the modern world. More and more, as Hardy implied in *The Return of the Native*, men will come to see their predicament mirrored not in the childhood quickness and curiosity of the ancient world, nor in the joyful dreams and rituals of medieval adolescence, but in the sombre, twilit glooms of Egdon Heath. Maturity has brought truth, but truth disillusion; Comte's Age of Positivism discovers few spiritual consolations to balance the loss. The young Yeats was already singing this theme in his early verses:

> The woods of Arcady are dead
> And over is their antique joy;
> Of old the world on dreaming fed,
> Grey Truth is now her painted toy...

Perhaps many other late Victorians, and Edwardians, were oppressed with such reflections, when they perceived that inexorable Duty must live on in a world unnourished by hope. In a tragic world, one's ideals must be human; in the human world, the betrayal of ideals seems the true tragic end. No wonder so many leading characters in fiction are left with only their own integrity and tried powers of endurance, as destiny darkens around them, and the world grows old.

One sees, indeed, how far these writers are from illustrating that mood of sunlit euphoria, all blue skies, cricket flannels and honeysuckle, in which the Edwardian innocents were once thought to have played. The liberals were exploring their own weaknesses with heartrending irony, while illiberals were robustly pushing their civilisation towards its collapse. And most of the minor writers too—H. G. Wells notably, but by no means solely—saw storm clouds of change and violence gathering over the civilised world. The forces which were to dominate European literature in the war years, and in the later years *entre deux guerres*, were already shaping—the qualification or outright rejection of liberal humanism, in Eliot, Hulme and a host of others; the perception that sensitive European man might after all be a small élite, left high and dry by history, and not the natural inheritor of the earth; the fear, so ironically reversing several centuries of optimism, that man was losing control of his own inventions, and might be doomed to be destroyed, like Frankenstein, by the monster he had so presumptuously made; above all, the myth of the final collapse of civilisation, 'the waste land', to which Eliot gave a central literary masterpiece as well as a name. In all these trends, one sees the political disturbances of the period reflected in literature. There is ample evidence for the view that such prolonged crises as the deteriorating relationship between Britain and Germany, the battle between Lords and Commons, the Home Rule crisis, the struggle for female suffrage, the growing alienation in industry between management and unions, the mounting rumours of international subversion and conspiracy, as well as the disturbing implications of new scientific inventions and changes, were profoundly influencing the ways in which men thought and wrote.

The literary greatness of the late Victorian and the Edwardian periods was in the novel, and it has seemed right to start from there. The poets were still no match for their great European contemporaries, though the fruitful influence of Baudelaire, Mallarmé and Laforgue might already be traced. In the early years of the twentieth century, there were some new and talented English poets, but only one genius. That was Hardy, who transformed himself with unparalleled versatility from a great novelist of one century into a great poet of the next. Hardy had written poems before, including some very fine ones, but his really memorable poems were written soon after the death of his wife, Emma, in 1912. When Emma died, he was released from the oppressive failure of his marriage into the most poignant memories of first love. Poems such as *After a Journey*, and

the one quoted here, express the agony of bereavement as purely and
movingly as poetry has ever done:

The Shadow on the Stone

I went by the Druid stone
That broods in the garden white and lone,
And I stopped and looked at the shifting shadows
That at some moments fall thereon
From the tree hard by with a rhythmic swing,
And they shaped in my imagining
To the shade that a well-known head and shoulders
Threw there when she was gardening.

I thought her behind my back,
Yea, her I long had learned to lack,
And I said: 'I am sure you are standing behind me,
Though how do you get into this old track?'
And there was no sound but the fall of a leaf
As a sad response; and to keep down grief
I would not turn my head to discover
That there was nothing in my belief.

Yet I wanted to look and see
That nobody stood at the back of me;
But I thought once more: 'Nay, I'll not unvision
A shape which, somehow, there may be.'
So I went on softly from the glade,
And left her behind me throwing her shade,
As she were indeed an apparition—
My head unturned lest my dream should fade.

The only comparable achievement of British art in the period is Elgar's.
An impression of some deep similarities between the mood of Hardy's
poems for his dead wife, and the great Oratorio, Symphonies and 'Cello
Concerto of Elgar, is perhaps worth recording.

The Great War occurred at a time of literary ferment, and some important new poets emerged. While Rupert Brooke celebrated the old
romantic concept of patriotism and glory, a poetry of war as the twentieth
century was to know it was being born. Wilfred Owen's *Futility* stands as
a poetic equivalent of the Tomb of the Unknown Warrior, a memorial to
an anonymous young man squandered:

Move him into the sun—
Gently its touch awoke him once,
At home, whispering of fields unsown.
Always it woke him, even in France,
Until this morning and this snow.
If anything might rouse him now
The kind old sun will know.

Think how it wakes the seeds,—
Woke, once, the clays of a cold star.
Are limbs, so dear-achieved, are sides,
Full-nerved—still warm—too hard to stir?
Was it for this the clay grew tall?
—O what made fatuous sunbeams toil
To break earth's sleep at all?

'My subject is War,' wrote Owen, 'and the pity of War. The Poetry is in the pity.' In *Futility* and a handful of other minor masterpieces he explored new techniques of language and rhyme to embody his pity: assonances and consonances instead of full rhyme, to challenge the ear; stark images of death and violence from which no aesthetic consolations could be drawn. Now in the middle of the 1960s, Owen's poetry has been given wide currency, through the revival of popular interest in the first world war, and in particular through Benjamin Britten's *War Requiem*. University students are more likely to be familiar with Owen's poetry than with Auden's or Graves's. Clearly, Owen's voice has come to seem especially valid in the atomic age. He marks the moment, in 1916 or 1917, when nearly everything that poets had written about war from the beginnings of literature became irrelevant to the future of man.

In Europe, the most striking war poet was Guillaume Apollinaire (1880–1918), whose *Calligrammes* (1918) include some of his greatest work. He died of Spanish 'flu in November 1918, within a week of Wilfred Owen. The other most important British poet of the war period was Edward Thomas, a writer of great sweetness and charm, who could sometimes achieve, in deceptively simple and pastoral poems, wonderfully vivid images of the world that was passing away. In *Adlestrop*, he captures the very essence of what was once a familiar railway experience. And suddenly, in the uncovenanted delight of a heightened moment, we hear them—the very last enchantments of the older England, still there, among the industrial and military threats; but for how long?

Yes, I remember Adlestrop—
The name, because one afternoon
Of heat the express-train drew up there
Unwontedly. It was late June.

The steam hissed. Someone cleared his throat.
No one left and no one came
On the bare platform. What I saw
Was Adlestrop—only the name

And willows, willow-herb, and grass,
And meadowsweet, and haycocks dry,
No whit less still and lonely fair
Than the high cloudlets in the sky.

And for that minute a blackbird sang
Close by, and round him, mistier,
Farther and farther, all the birds
Of Oxfordshire and Gloucestershire.

But already poetry was off on other tracks. Some years before the war, there had been a minor revolt. The group of poets published in anthologies by Sir Edward Marsh between 1912 and 1922, and now usually referred to as 'Georgians', had rejected the more stuffy and didactic aspects of *fin de siècle* versifying, whilst retaining certain other affinities with the late Victorian tradition. They continued to value lyricism, music, 'poetic' themes and imagery, and to believe that the poet's chief task is to console and uplift the human spirit by his creation of beauty. Sir Edward Marsh gathered together many of the best poets of his time, including Walter de la Mare, Edward Thomas, W. H. Davies and D. H. Lawrence, and his taste was by no means as narrow as later adverse critics have thought. He proved that a considerable market for poetry of this kind existed among ordinary intelligent readers, since his anthologies sold as poetry was not to do again until very recent times.

Yet the Georgian taste, catholic and popular within limits as it was, proved an irritant to another group of young poets. In 1913 the Imagists announced themselves in a Manifesto, and proclaimed entirely new principles for verse. Among their tenets was the notion that poetry must reach out to explore and encompass the whole of reality. In a world of great cities, motor-cars, aeroplanes, the poet could no longer write about pastoral feelings among pleasing scenes. The underlying notion of the imagists was that the poet must seek truth even before beauty. If he makes beauty his end, he may become simply escapist. Only if he engages with the fullest experiences of modern man can he revitalise language and create poems relevant to life. The Imagists believed that the Victorian conventions of diction, rhyme and imagery were played out; a pioneering sensibility requires experiments in form. So the demand of the 1913 Manifesto was for freedom, of style and content; and for the recognition, through such freedom, that poetic experience centres in the actual images that poets create. As T. S. Eliot was later to put it in his essay on *Hamlet*, the poet seeks an 'objective correlative' for his experience: 'in other words, a set of objects, a situation, a chain of events which shall be the formula of that *particular* emotion; such that when the external facts, which must terminate in sensory experience, are given, the emotion is immediately evoked'.

This notion of 'the image' is wide enough to include whole poems, and even whole plays and whole novels. The stress is on verbal precision and on the 'concrete'; but on the kind of precision and concreteness which, by capturing an experience completely, leaves the experience open and resonant, as it would be in life. So the imagist poet is inclined to forsake such normal literary conventions of communication as grammar and syntax, logical connections, traditional expectations of language and *genre*, and to think of poetry as working, rather, through 'imaginative order'. His stress falls on originality and precision; the only test of a poem is the test of whether it works. The life of images is in their own interplay, in juxtapositions which set up reverberations in the reader's conscious, or even unconscious, mind. *The Waste Land*, said Michael Roberts, in the famous Introduction to his *Faber Book of Modern Verse*,

possesses 'imaginative order', by which I mean, that to some minds it is cogent even before its narrative and argumentative continuity is grasped. This 'imaginative order' is not something arbitrary, specific and inexplicable. If the images which are used to denote complex situations were replaced by abstractions much of the apparent incoherence of the poem would vanish. It would become a prose description of the condition of the world, a restatement of a myth and a defence of the tragic view of life. But being a poem it does more than this; a poem expresses not merely the idea of a social or scientific fact, but also the sensation of thinking or knowing, and it does not merely define the tragic view, it may communicate it.

One sees clearly enough in such a formulation the influence of Baudelaire, Laforgue and Rimbaud; the affinities between Imagists and Symbolists amount to a debt. The 'image' becomes valued, like the French 'symbol', for its resonances; for its power to release overtones, suggestions, archetypes, just under the surfaces of conscious feeling and thought.

Eliot has been mentioned of necessity, and his importance to this great phase of modern poetry is sufficiently clear. It is of interest that he and Pound were the only distinguished poets associated with the imagist movement, and that both, like James before them, were American and European in almost equal degrees. The importance of imagism as a specific movement depends almost wholly on the work of these two—especially on Pound's *Canzoni* (1911) and subsequent volumes, and Eliot's *Prufrock* (1917). But the underlying importance of imagism was as a manifestation of 'the modern'; its manifesto was no doubt helped by the perception that Yeats's major verse, though wholly independent, was increasingly imagistic, and by the posthumous publication in 1918 of the poetry of Hopkins. Hopkins became so entirely a modern by adoption, that students are amazed to discover the dates (1844–89) of his birth and death.

But, at the same time, the central relevance of imagism was confirmed by the work of two important novelists, James Joyce and Virginia Woolf, whose experiments in the novel led them to define principles of 'imaginative order' akin to those of Eliot and Pound. The distinction between prose and poetry wore thin, and creative writers started to think of both as the release, through verbal precision, of imaginative truth. As soon as the novel is mentioned, however, one becomes aware of influences from Europe in the very near background. Just as the British modern poets were blood relations of Mallarmé, Valéry and Rilke, so the modern novelists discovered their closeness to Thomas Mann (*Buddenbrooks* 1901, *Tristan* 1903, *Der Tod in Venedig* 1913) and to Gide (*L'Immoraliste* 1902, *La Porte Etroite* 1909). Out of this whole ferment the word 'modern' emerges, and it is time now to take a closer look at that.

What is 'modern', in the sense that these writers appropriated it; what, if anything, does it mean? The argument has raged so fiercely, and shapelessly, that one can be grateful for the perspective provided in two recent books. The first is an anthology of documents taken from 'modern' writers defining themselves, *The Modern Tradition*, edited by Richard Ellman and Charles Feidelson, Jnr (New York, 1965). The second is Stephen Spender's *The Struggle of the Modern* (1963), which as its name implies is not only a definition of the modern, but also a polemical defence. The 'modern', in Spender's view, is a way of life before it is a literary programme. The situation of modern man is unprecedented, and his experiences need unprecedented forms of expression. As a social being he inhabits an industrial world which differs utterly from anything known before the mid-eighteenth century, both in its mode of living, with all the assumptions implied in that, and in its growing fear of world destruction. Cut off from traditional resources, he is denied an identity. There are no certainties for him of class or status, no moral, political or religious opinions that are generally received and operative in the social life. Yet, as the writer's difficulties increase, so do his opportunities. Perhaps he alone can offer insight, and even salvation, ironically diminished though his social role appears to be. He may even become, in his own estimation, an Atlas-figure, bearing the whole burden of the world's consciousness, the world's suffering, alone. But, by the same token, his situation can be profoundly depressing; how can a sensitive man take on such burdens and retain his poise? Little wonder that the 'modern' often defines itself pessimistically, in terms of riches and serenities lost in the past. Many of the moderns, including Eliot and Lawrence, looked back to historically happier times. For Eliot, there was the period before Dryden and Milton, when thinking and feeling were properly 'associated', and there was no split, as there has been since, between the two. For Lawrence, there was the primitivist vision of pre-industrial England, when men lived nearer to nature, and were their natural, spontaneous selves.

In a sense, this myth of a forfeited heritage is a much older tradition; its earlier exponents include many illustrious eighteenth- and nineteenth-century names. Naturally no two exponents agree on all the evil forces operative, so that the fall from grace has been variously placed. And naturally (the historian will perceive) there is much disreputable history; the literary tradition requires more Golden Ages than the past can conveniently hold. The tradition, then, is too venerable to be claimed as distinctively 'modern', but the moderns have fairly widely adopted it, along with frequent refinements of their own. Of particular interest is the modern attitude to the early Romantics. Instead of receiving adulation as enlightened precursors, these have often figured in a villainous role. In the writings of Hulme and T. S. Eliot they become scapegoats, almost, along with the liberal humanists, for our post-industrial fall. For what if the main enemy to man's serenity is *within* his citadel: if the 'holiness of the heart's affections' turns into the seething turbulence discovered by Freud? Divorced from any formal contexts or disciplines, might 'nature' not lead straight to the waste land itself? The romantic values of intense emotional feeling, of optimistic humanism, of 'sincerity', were to receive indeed a notable battering, not least from Eliot himself.

Such doubts can also be found (though D. H. Lawrence is an important exception) in a great many moderns. The satires of Aldous Huxley and Evelyn Waugh point a similar moral; the world of Kafka embodies the nightmare of living with the insoluble enigma of oneself. But merely to mention all these writers alerts us to a very basic danger: 'modern' writers are so highly distinctive and idiosyncratic, that generalisations about them are bound, if pressed, to break down.

For convenience, we might alight on two major modern masterpieces, both published in that literary *annus mirabilis* 1922. Joyce's *Ulysses* is often called a prose epic, and Eliot's *The Waste Land* the verse epic, or mock-epic, of its age. Joyce's *Ulysses* is modern both in its vitality and originality of language, and in its highly experimental form. A day in the life of Bloom, a contemporary Dubliner, is explored in very great depth. There is not plot of a normal kind, merely an accumulation of incidents, many of which might seem trivial if they were explored with less imaginative power. The realism of detail is so minutely faithful, that it becomes unfamiliar; the Circe episode breaks new ground in depicting urban squalor, but in doing so colours Dublin with the nightmare intensity of myth. (In this, Dickens was perhaps a more important influence than Zola.) At the same time, Joyce uses the technique which Proust and Virginia Woolf were also, through their very different sensibilities, exploring—the 'stream of consciousness', which follows the thoughts and feelings of an individual so closely that we experience events through his conscious, and to some extent his half-conscious or even sub-conscious, mind. This technique is realistic in its remarkable pursuit of inner realities; but, because the realities *are* inner, it can diverge from social 'realism' very sharply indeed. It can exist in ironic counterpoint, sometimes comic, sometimes tragic, with the external situation; or it can underline the entire isolation of the individual inside his own consciousness, where heightened sensitivity may have to be paid for with delusion, breakdown, or death. In Virginia Woolf, there is the further twist that her characters have the kind of abnormal consciousness which is often associated with mysticism, but which seems for them, rather, to emphasise a paralysing isolation in the self.

The greatest of all the stream-of-consciousness writers was Proust, whose vast *A la Recherche du Temps Perdu* (1913–28) explores so completely the possibilities of marrying this technique with symbolism, that a distinctive approach to literature has been rendered unworkable again. But mention of Proust returns one to the particular virtues of *Ulysses*: though Joyce never matches Proust in sheer depth of psychological insight and evocation, *Ulysses* is arguably closer to the centre of normal human life. The main fact about Bloom, and his wife Molly, is their sanity; our insight into them has the effect of healing, as well as deepening, our social sense. If there is a weakness in *Ulysses*, it is in its Homeric superstructure; the notion of counterpointing a modern day against the myth of Ulysses, whilst undoubtedly suggestive, produces effects not easy to define. Some of the parallels are too contrived to be taken seriously, and, whether mock-heroic deflation is or is not intended, the allusiveness is as likely to distract as to help. But perhaps over-allusiveness is a flaw in much modern literature. In creating deliberate obstacles for the reader, it is almost wilfully non-communicative; even *The Waste Land* is marred, while Pound's *Cantos*, for all their marvellous moments, are wholly wrecked.

The Waste Land is the other masterpiece of the *annus mirabilis*, a free-verse poem with occasional excursions into metre and rhyme. There is much allusion to earlier literature, and as in *Ulysses* the effect is primarily ironic, though whether the past is deflating the present or the present the past is not always clear. Does Eliot's modern neurotic beauty ('The Chair she sat in, like a burnished throne, Glowed on the marble. . .') mark a decline from Cleopatra, or might she be the reality behind Cleopatra herself? Eliot forces the question upon us, but does not solve it; if the answer is 'both', then the poem is odder than is usually thought. The poem is essentially an account of modern London, but London related to other great cities, now and earlier, and also to Dante's Hell. The following lines are a useful microcosm of Eliot's numerous levels of meaning:

> Unreal City,
> Under the brown fog of a winter dawn,
> A crowd flowed over London Bridge, so many,
> I had not thought death had undone so many.
> Sighs, short and infrequent, were exhaled,
> And each man fixed his eyes before his feet.
> Flowed up the hill and down King William Street,
> To where St Mary Woolnoth kept the hours
> With a dead sound on the final stroke of nine.

This evocation of rush-hour London is very beautiful, even though the suggestion *is* of lost directions in a spiritual fog. The crowd flows over the bridge as the river flows under it; the quotation places the crowd with the drifting souls of Dante's *Inferno*, neither good enough for salvation, nor bad enough for the really sadistic torments of Hell. But what one is most captured by is the extraordinary resonance. No doubt St Mary Woolnoth does strike nine like this, as Eliot's notes assure us, but the effect is nearer to Charon (in Dante's same Canto) waiting to bear the souls of the lost into Hell.

The main framework of Eliot's poem is in two death-and-resurrection cycles, the ordinary round of months and seasons, and the persistent pagan and Christian myths of a dying god. The temporal cycle in the poem holds no hope of salvation; April is the cruellest month, waking from winter forgetfulness into the suffering of life. Our modern world is a scene of aridity, staleness, delirium, broken images; a world mirrored in loneliness and sterility, in episodes of sordid and despairing sex:

> At the violet hour, when the eyes and back
> Turn upward from the desk, when the human engine waits
> Like a taxi throbbing waiting,
> I Tiresias, though blind, throbbing between two lives,
> Old man with wrinkled female breasts, can see
> At the violet hour, the evening hour that strives
> Homeward, and brings the sailor home from sea,
> The typist home at teatime, clears her breakfast, lights
> Her stove, and lays out food in tins.
> Out of the window perilously spread
> Her drying combinations touched by the sun's last rays,
> On the divan are piled (at night her bed)
> Stockings, slippers, camisoles, and stays.
> I Tiresias, old man with wrinkled dugs
> Perceived the scene, and foretold the rest—
> I too awaited the expected guest.
> He, the young man carbuncular, arrives,
> A small house agent's clerk, with one bold stare,
> One of the low on whom assurance sits
> As a silk hat on a Bradford millionaire.
> The time is now propitious, as he guesses,
> The meal is ended, she is bored and tired,
> Endeavours to engage her in caresses
> Which still are unreproved, if undesired.
>
> Flushed and decided, he assaults at once;
> Exploring hands encounter no defence;
> His vanity requires no response,
> And makes a welcome of indifference.
> (And I Tiresias have foresuffered all
> Enacted on this same divan or bed;
> I who have sat by Thebes below the wall
> And walked among the lowest of the dead.)
> Bestows one final patronising kiss,
> And gropes his way, finding the stairs unlit...

She turns and looks a moment in the glass,
Hardly aware of her departed lover;
Her brain allows one half-formed thought to pass:
'Well now that's done: and I'm glad it's over.'
When lovely woman stoops to folly and
Paces about her room again, alone,
She smoothes her hair with automatic hand,
And puts a record on the gramophone.

No hope for man is envisaged through the social or political framework. The only hope is from a religious dimension; but the religious hope is itself involved with the waste land imagery, and poised between delirium and joy. The mysterious stranger in the Emmaus road episode may be the risen Christ, over death victorious; or he may be the final illusion of delirious men dying of thirst. Later Eliot became a Christian, and with hindsight one can read the poem as a movement towards faith. But faith is present in the poem only through enigma; the positive experience is of sickness in society, and boredom with life.

And this poses a very interesting problem; why was the poem received, by Michael Roberts and others, as a report on our modern society as it is? The more obvious interpretation is as an image of the poet's personal neuroses; the world can indeed appear like this, one realises, but seldom to anyone in normal health. Part of Eliot's success is in his vivid evocations; undeniably there are moments of depression for most of us as Eliot depicts them, and the accumulation of such moments in major poetry can make them seem more typical than they are. There *are* very broken-down and bitchy old women in public houses, but is the public-house dialogue in part II of the poem typical even of a cockney public bar? To anyone who enjoys London public houses there is no self-evident connection between the 'hurry up please', the noise and chatter of closing time, and the collapse of civilised values beyond recall. Perhaps it is a danger in the imagist method that so few readers notice the oddity of Eliot's associations; if spelled out in more conventional language, this would immediately be seen. And of course the whole poem might alert us to certain other forces behind Eliot's depression: the suggestion that a 'small house agent's clerk' can be nothing but 'carbuncular'; the equation of political changes in eastern Europe with the descent of the barbarian hordes.

These comments are not to throw doubts on the poem's greatness, but to question the kind of reputation it has acquired. *The Waste Land* seems a morbid and unusual poem rather than a mirror of English society; it is not a mirror, surely, but a distorting mirror, with the distortion somewhere in the poet himself. What must interest us is the number of intellectuals who clearly accepted it at its face value; why did Eliot's extreme pessimism awaken an echo in so many hearts? Fear of the future, and of international chaos, must be one answer; fear of human nature, as the Great

War had shown it to be, another. Perhaps the new psychology added to a prevailing sense of breakdown and confusion; perhaps it was less easy for sensitive men to adjust to accelerating changes in the 1920s than it has since (apparently) become. But also, there was a general desire among creative writers to find salvation, and *The Waste Land* mirrors a widely felt spiritual malaise. Some writers, like Eliot himself and later Auden, moved to Anglo-Catholicism; some, like Graham Greene and Evelyn Waugh, to Roman Catholicism; some, like Aldous Huxley, Yeats and Lawrence, to a variety of mysticisms; some, like the poets of the 'thirties, to Marxism, or to other robust political faiths.

The 1920s is a period so rich in western literature, that a survey of this kind can attempt little more than a listing of names. In America the theme of the waste land was undertaken by Scott Fitzgerald (the phrase is actually used in *The Great Gatsby*, 1925), but Fitzgerald infused into it his own splendidly human warmth. *The Great Gatsby* is a novel of the highest worth and perfection; if it is surpassed at all on its own ground, then this is only by Fitzgerald's most ambitious novel *Tender is the Night* (1934), which was received tepidly by its original critics, but already stands out as a major work of our time. In *Tender is the Night*, a young doctor, Dick Diver, is shown at the moment when he starts to go downhill. He marries a highly neurotic wife, Nicole, in ambiguous circumstances; Nicole's rich relations want, in effect, to buy her a permanent doctor, but Dick, who knows this, marries chiefly for love. In the course of the novel, he succeeds in curing Nicole, but more in his role of husband than as doctor. At the end, his wife is whole again, but he is broken. The tragedy is that Nicole, despite everything, has the hardness needed for survival; when the cure is completed, she is free to be independent again. The doctor's reward is to become redundant; but, when the doctor is also husband, and his energies have been exhausted, emotional collapse seems the inevitable end. Yet Dick's acceptance of Nicole was taken in full knowledge of its probable outcome, so that his downfall suggests the kind of moral already encountered in Hardy and James. Perhaps superior sensitivity in the modern world *is* no more than a crippling handicap: yet a handicap which few of us would be without.

In Europe, Gide's *Si le grain ne meurt* (1926) established new standards of autobiographical honesty, and André Breton's *Nadja* was a portent of surrealism in 1928. But the most remarkable writer of the 'twenties was Kafka, whose two great works (*The Trial*, published posthumously 1925, *The Castle*, published 1926) are central nightmares of our time. In each, a semi-anonymous character is caught up in a situation of increasing complexity, where his efforts to understand lead to deepening bewilderment, and his efforts to survive are frustrated by events. There seems to be some prophetic sense of the impending fascist terror; the literal enemies are politicians and bureaucrats behind the scenes. But the novels are political prophecy only incidentally; as allegory, they explore modern man's quest for religious truth. The obvious suggestion is of gods non-existent, or hostile, or at the very least inaccessible (though it could be claimed that a kind of dark Barthian Protestantism, which rejects human reason and morality and defines God as 'Wholly Other', underlies the events). And, of course, Kafka's novels can be seen as the product of a morbid sensibility; at least one eminent doctor has found them a case-book example of paranoid delusions, and little more. But, if so, a highly significant question again confronts us: why should modern man so readily find in paranoid delusions his image of truth? With Kafka one cannot suspect a shrinking from sexuality as one does in Eliot, or any simple distaste for the lower class. His vision is the deeper nightmare which Orwell's *1984* later embodied, when it had been hideously authentic-ated by the history of later times. What are we to say of an age when men who morbidly think themselves persecuted really are persecuted; when events that ought to be clinical fantasies turn into political truths?

The English writer of the 1910s and 1920s who has received most attention is D. H. Lawrence, and at first sight he may appear to offer a powerful counterblast to so much gloom. From his successful *Sons and Lovers* (1913) he progressed through numerous short stories and novels, including the two novels generally accepted by Lawrentians as his master-pieces, *The Rainbow* (1915) and *Women in Love* (1920), to his last, and most posthumously controversial novel, *Lady Chatterley's Lover* (1928). Undoubtedly these works were written with extraordinary vigour, and with fine imaginative insight into people and places. Yet their underlying *raison d'être* seems often prophetic; Lawrence was a messianic writer, who became increasingly bitter as he judged himself rejected by the world.

At the heart of his vision is a passionate romanticism. He believed in man's vast potentiality for vitality and happiness, and resented social attitudes that put the human spirit in chains. In his essay *Democracy* he discerns three modern enemies to individual fulfilment: worship of the average, the uniformity of dullness; worship of The One, the uniformity of self-immolation; and the cult of 'personality', the uniformity of a conformist social façade. Against these enemies he proclaims 'individual-ism', which is the individual's cultivation of inner riches, the organic flowering of his unique, spontaneous self. But it is important to remember that Lawrence did not believe in solitary flowering. Men need human relationships, especially family relationships, to fulfil themselves, and it is in studying these, with exceptional insight and delicacy, that Lawrence is often at his best. One of his basic convictions was that body and mind are not divided; 'Man is one,' he wrote, 'body and soul; and his parts are not at war with one another.' In place of the older notion that the mind is our 'higher' part, and our body the 'lower', Lawrence poses a fruitful equality of the two. Sexual love is humanly good, and humanly necessary, but there must be a total meeting of mind, spirit and body in the physical act. Like Blake, whom he clearly resembles, Lawrence believed that the giants of human passion control one another if freed from restriction; a man's tenderness and loyalty protect him from promiscuity far more effectively than a negative religious commandment, or a legal rule.

Lawrence's power in depicting his vision cannot be questioned, but his novels are not as unclouded as this would suggest. He could also be destructive and sadistic; these impulses are present from the beginning of his work to the end. His views on sex were apt to be strangely qualified. Sometimes he presents it as an initiation beyond human relationship into mystical experience; sometimes he concentrates, as in *Lady Chatterley's Lover*, on the physical act—Lady Chatterley's desertion of her husband, and the undercurrent of revenge and violence in Mellors's life with her, depart strikingly from his normal views. One detects in the later Lawrence a growing frustration. Confronted with tragic elements in the human predicament, including the loss of youth and vitality, he looks for human scapegoats. His tirades take on a note of hysteria, and his positive vision ceases to ring true. Towards the end of his life, he became fascinated with death and resurrection. His later poems are a preparation for some new life on the other side of the ultimate darkness, and his phoenix symbol assumes religious overtones of a mystical kind. Had he lived, he might have developed as a religious writer, and followed the mystical path of his admirer, and apparent polar opposite, Aldous Huxley. He will remain one of the most fascinating of modern writers, especially when he has been rescued from his friends.

The inter-war years, though serious, had their lighter moments; it was a great time for cranks and eccentrics, pioneers and prophets, exotic scandal and revolt. The popular press was creating the taste by which it was enjoyed (like Eliot); its sensations chart zestful as well as painful headline news. This is the ethos in which the two major ironists flourished —Aldous Huxley (*Crome Yellow* 1921, *Antic Hay* 1923, *Point Counter Point* 1928, *Brave New World* 1932, *Eyeless in Gaza* 1936, *After Many a Summer* 1939), and Evelyn Waugh (*Decline and Fall* 1928, *Vile Bodies* 1930, *Black Mischief* 1932, *Handful of Dust* 1934, *Scoop* 1938). Both writers engage with the world of upper-class exoticism, the Mayfair smart set, the bright young things, the press barons and the messianic pretenders, the fashionable corrupters and the ageing corrupt. Both find in the gaiety of this world an edge of desperation, a waste land sport over various kinds of abyss. In Huxley, the satire is always cutting, with a hard, sharp edge of fear. His heroes seem to parody Lawrence's hopes of sexual salvation, and it is not surprising that he moved off, through renunciation of the flesh, towards a mystical faith. Evelyn Waugh, though fully as amusing as Huxley, and sometimes almost more outrageous, is always a little in love with the world that his satire rejects. 'Youth is brief, and Love has wings; Time will tarnish, 'ere we know, The brightness of the bright young things...' Yet Waugh's ruthlessness reflects a final coldness towards, or contemptuous dismissal of, his people; he seldom seems as serious as Huxley, behind his façade.

In Huxley and Waugh the world of broken images turns into farce and absurdity; in other writers, as the 1930s wore on and the storm clouds darkened, it became a challenge to sterner things. In 1930 Auden published his first volume, and during the 1930s he and a group of young poets akin to him became famous. Some of the relevant names and volumes are: W. H. Auden, *Poems* (1930), *The Orators* (1932), *Dance of Death* (1933), *Look Stranger* (1936); Louis MacNeice, *Blind Fireworks* (1929), *Poems* (1935), *Earth Compels* (1938), *Autumn Journal* (1939); Stephen Spender, *Poems* (1933), *Vienna* (1934), *Still Centre* (1939); C. Day Lewis, *Beechen Vigil* (1925), *Country Comets* (1928), *Transitional Poem* (1929), *From Feathers to Iron* (1931), *Magnetic Mountain* (1933), *Time to Dance* (1935), *Overtures to Death* (1938). These 'poets of the '30s', as they have since been called, were all very youthful poets, 'poets exploding like bombs', as Auden has it in *Spain 1937*. Their verse matches great freshness and energy with strong social commitment; for the first time since the very early nineteenth century, a group of poets was actively campaigning for a political cause. Their position involves a basic critique of capitalist society. Spender writes about the unemployed as the drifting flotsam of society in a poem which explicitly refuses to embroider their predicament with art. The poetry, as for Owen, is in the pity; and the pity, now, is a revolutionary challenge to the world. As the 1930s unfolded, 'the enemy' was totally identified with fascism. The Spanish Civil War engaged these poets passionately, as it engaged, of course, many other writers, including those like Orwell who were less enthusiastically Left wing. Auden's *Spain 1937* is the best of several poems written on this war—a call to fight for the survival of civilisation while there is still time to fight; a reminder that man alone shapes the destiny of the modern world:

> The stars are dead; the animals will not look:
> We are left alone with our day, and the time is short and
> History to the defeated
> May say Alas but cannot help or pardon.

These poets of the 'thirties were exciting and influential rather than outstanding—yet their standards were exacting, and Auden, at least, is one of the metrical masters of modern verse. In this, he was equalled in the 1930s only by Dylan Thomas, whose early poems arrived on the literary scene like a portent with *Eighteen Poems* (1934), though his best work was not until the late 1940s and early 1950s, just before his death. The poetic freshness of Auden and MacNeice is often metrical and verbal—

exuberant intelligence, and pleasure in intelligence as a good in itself. But Dylan Thomas's power over language is more deeply original. He can make the most familiar ideas and phrases sound new minted; his control over complex syntactical structures and complex stanza forms became more and more remarkable with the years.

There were at least two other striking poetic voices on the English scene, Robert Graves and Edwin Muir—both fine, if more traditional, poets who achieved their greatest fame at a later time. And, in America, the modern movement was continued through a host of important poets— Conrad Aiken, Marianne Moore, Wallace Stevens, John Crowe Ransom, Allen Tate, Hart Crane, E. E. Cummings, Richard Eberhart, to name only a few.

Even so, one may feel in the late 1920s and the early 1930s that the novel was holding its own with poetry: though there may be no new novelists of the eminence of James, Conrad, Mann, Kafka and Scott Fitzgerald, there are a number very high in the second rank. In England, Graham Greene and George Orwell; in America Faulkner and Hemingway, with perhaps Steinbeck as a third. Of these, Graham Greene received wider recognition in Europe than most of his English contemporaries. In the 1930s, he offered a series of grim 'entertainments' which proved a prelude to many greater achievements, and notably, in 1938, *Brighton Rock*. The novelist's triumph in *Brighton Rock*, as in several later novels, is to present his own faith only in its most paradoxical form. The destiny of Pinkie, the delinquent young hero, is presented with almost Jansenist determinism, and the priest's attempts to console Pinkie's wife at the end of the novel seem designed to show the powerlessness, even the irrelevance, of faith. None the less, Greene convinces us that there are orders of reality outside the vision of Ida Arnold, the courageous, happily pagan barmaid who tracks Pinkie down. Without qualifying her attractiveness, which is continually manifest, he presents his tormented Catholics as inhabiting a more real, if more terrible, world. Against her secular code of 'right and wrong' is posed the religious view of Good and Evil. Pinkie is evil, but he is also Catholic; his drama is the mystery of iniquity.

As a novelist, Graham Greene has the rare gift of combining plots attuned to the conventions of the thriller with explorations of complex moral and religious concern. The quality of compassion in the novels is deepened by the sense of evil, but we are never allowed to forget that compassion itself may be infected; Greene can make his highest values at home in hell.

In temperament and values Orwell seems poles apart from Greene, but he produced visions of evil, especially just before his death in the late 1940s, which make certain joint literary influences unusually plain. Both writers were profoundly influenced by Dostoevsky and Kafka, in their creation of criminal outcasts suffering the traditional torments of the damned. Like many other central twentieth-century figures, Orwell can seem oddly contradictory—a rebel by instinct, yet an admirer of Kipling; a martyr in his life for working-class values, yet the writer who produced the *Animal Farm* sheep and the *1984* proles. Sir Richard Rees has discerned in Orwell four apparently conflicting strands, the rebel, the paternalist, the rationalist and the romantic. And he has reminded us that Orwell was a man in whom a passionate love of justice and a passionate bitterness were apt to meet.[1] The hero of *Keep the Aspidistra Flying* seems prophetic of the 'angry young man' of the 1950s—a man whose social anger, though born in idealism and outrage, turns by degrees to bitterness and negation, an 'evil mutinous mood' to use Orwell's term. Throughout the early Orwell, however, there is clear common sense as well as impassioned honesty; and, underlying everything, the clear-eyed acceptance of Everyman's plight in a tragic world. Perhaps no literary documents evoke the mood of the 1930s more memorably—*Down and Out in Paris and London* (1933), *Burmese Days* (1934), *A Clergyman's Daughter* (1935), *Keep the Aspidistra Flying* (1936), *The Road to Wigan Pier* (1937), *Homage to Catalonia* (1938), *Coming Up For Air* (1939).

Such brief comments would not be complete without the mention of certain European chronicles of the new dark age—Antoine de Saint Exupéry's *Vol de nuit* (1931), Louis-Ferdinand Céline's *Voyage au bout de la nuit* (1932), André Malraux's *La Condition humaine* (1933)—and, of course, of Christopher Isherwood's two *tours de force*, *Mr Norris Changes Trains* (1935) and *Goodbye to Berlin* (1939). J.-P. Sartre's *La Nausée* appeared in 1938, and 1939 saw the completion, after fourteen years, of Joyce's *Finnegans Wake*.

Drama has been absent from this discussion, since, though it is always relevant to the 'modern', it has developed to laws of its own. More insistently even than for poetry and the novel, a consideration of drama needs a European frame. In the background are the formidable figures of Ibsen and Strindberg, the former one of the great tragic dramatists from any period, the latter fascinating and influential, if somewhat less great. Ibsen's early plays up to and including *A Doll's House* were mainly preoccupied with social problems. His people found themselves trapped in a repressive society, which utterly opposed any joy or freedom in life. The women, in particular, were reduced to toys and dolls. *A Doll's House* (1879) shows a woman breaking out of these moulds in search of fulfilment. She needs courage, clearly, to affront society and to risk her security; courage especially to risk hurting those close to her, with the further resulting harm to herself. She needs the kind of courage, moreover, which can involve itself in insoluble moral ambiguities; if anyone says that Nora is simply a lying and heartless mother, who can ever completely

[1] Sir Richard Rees, *George Orwell: Fugitive from the Camp of Victory* (1961).

deny this, including herself? But, given courage, victory is not impossible. At the end of *A Doll's House* Nora's decision, though costly, is basically justified; she has proved that a sensitive and adult woman can bring herself to behave with the degree of freedom which would come with fewer difficulties to the depraved. We are left feeling that her courage might help eventually to change society, so that such freedom might become less exceptional, less ambiguous and tainted, with time.

With *Ghosts* (1881), however, Ibsen's sense of ambiguities deepens, and his great phase as a tragic dramatist really begins. His later plays develop Sophoclean patterns of irony; the deadly power of the Past allies itself with an unpropitious society, to destroy those seeking dangerous freedoms of aspiration and joy. The equivocal nature of idealism becomes ever more apparent; perhaps the idealists and liberators are more dangerous in the last analysis, more tainted and unrealistic, than such open enemies of joy as Pastor Manders and Kroll. Ibsen's later plays explore the complex contradictions and delusions of those whose aspiration or idealism lifts them above the crowd; his leading characters become destructive through the very conditions inherent in their choice. It is possible to feel that characters like Solness and Hilda in *The Master Builder* (1892) are too purely immersed in delusion to be fully tragic. But *John Gabriel Borkman* (1896) can be read as a universal tragedy of overreaching modern man.

Strindberg carried the tradition of the neurotic, or mad, hero much further than Ibsen. His main theme is of basic and inescapable human conflict, between man and woman, master and servant, the weak and the strong. In *Miss Julie* (1888), the twin battles of sex and class are played out against a background of impending revolution and social violence. The later plays become more symbolic, and at the same time more characterised by Strindberg's peculiar coldness; in the preface to *Miss Julie* he actually discusses tragic pity as a somewhat ignoble extension of personal fear. But his situations, of people destined to torment and destroy one another, some through neurotic weakness, some through sanity manifesting itself in forms almost wholly cruel, were fruitful to the whole modern tradition. The themes are taken up by two much more warmly human tragic dramatists, Eugene O'Neill inside our period, and Tennessee Williams just outside. They anticipated some of the chillier discoveries of the coming science (or art) of psychiatry; they provided dramatic formulae which influenced writers as diverse as Sartre and Pinter.

Meanwhile, the years 1895–1905 saw the major achievements of Chekhov, another dramatist whom one would name, with Ibsen, among the truly great. Chekhov's people are typical sensitive and frustrated products of a decaying society, tormented with their helplessness, and reduced to vague hopes for some future when people will be less doomed to futility than themselves: *The Seagull* (1896), *Uncle Vanya* (1899), *The Three*

Sisters (1901), *The Cherry Orchard* (1904). These plays are not called 'tragedies' by Chekhov, and they culminate in no tragic catharsis; there is too much futility for catharsis, the suffering is too near to the absurd. Yet the suffering is never wholly naked nor wholly ridiculous; a richly elegiac note pervades and transforms the plays. Even in *Uncle Vanya*, where the hero's attempt to rise to tragic action collapses in farce, our final impression is not of absurdity, but of poignant lyricism—in Helena's boredom, Astroff's fury, Vanya's self-knowledge, Sonia's movingly ambivalent final speech. Chekhov's importance to the historian of drama is chiefly as an influence, an explorer of the borderland between tragedy and farce. But his real importance is far more than as simply an influence: he is the greatest, as well as the first, dramatist of the absurd.

In English drama the period is dominated by Shaw, a superbly comic dramatist, but scarcely of the same stature as Ibsen and Chekhov. Shaw defended Ibsen vigorously against his detractors in *The Quintessence of Ibsenism* (1891), but, while he did justice to many of Ibsen's subtleties, his main concern was with the dramatist of social reform. Ibsen interested Shaw as a dramatist who used the theatre as a moral challenge to society, posing problems that might still, with courage and honesty, be solved. Shaw himself was a great believer in reason; he pioneered ceaselessly for good sense on a very wide variety of social topics, as a selection from his many titles amply shows: *Plays Pleasant and Unpleasant* (1898), *Three Plays for Puritans* (1900), *Man and Superman* (1903), *Major Barbara* (1905), *The Doctor's Dilemma* (1911), *Pygmalion* (1912), *Androcles and the Lion* (1916), *Heartbreak House* (1919), *Back to Methuselah* (1921), *St Joan* (1924), *The Apple Cart* (1930), *The Millionairess* (1936). An underestimate of Shaw today often rests on a simple lack of historical insight; much of what he fought for is now either taken for granted, or written off as simply cranky and not worth the time. And another cause for underestimating Shaw may be the modern underestimate of intellect; critics are unwilling to admit that intelligence can be a sparkling and legitimate pleasure in itself. Yet there is the possibility, too, that Shaw's drama was unduly polemical; there is some minimal truth in the jibe that the Prefaces are more important than the Plays. Shaw relied too exclusively on reason to support the dramatic experience; we miss the symbolic and imaginative resonances that seem always to be part of the greatest art. Like Wilde and Butler, both of whom he admired, he delighted in shocking his audiences —for the sake of the shock itself, because he was impish, but still more for the salutary moral purpose behind the shock. But his plays are rigidly ruled by reason, even in their shock tactics; the speeches are over-rhetorical, and the characters seem imprisoned in their ideas. Shaw's solutions to social problems often rest on patent oversimplifications and omissions. He falsifies—or overlooks—the complexities of human emotions: he ascribes evil too simply to abstract ideals, or economic trends.

With the lapse of time, Shaw's plays remain amusing and highly readable or viewable, but they refuse to look as significant as they should. The significance was more for their own time than for all time. By the highest tests, they remain in the second rank.

In the early twentieth century the theatre was dominated, even apart from Shaw, by Irish dramatists. During the Edwardian years there were the highly poetic plays of Yeats, and the equally poetic, though technically prose, plays of Synge. Synge's main dramas fall within a very short period: *In the Shadow of the Glen* (1905), *Riders to the Sea* (1905), *Well of the Saints* (1905), *Playboy of the Western World* (1907), *Deirdre of the Sorrows* (1910). They are characterised by a highly stylised rhetoric, consciously Irish, and attuned to the general tragic music of life. Whether Synge picks great mythical figures like Deirdre, or the peasants and tinkers of his own time, he brings out both the joy of life and the sadness of transience and death. One is teased (as in Pinter) by a sense that his speech rhythms are highly authentic, yet nearer to ritual than to daily life. The vitality and humanity of his characters co-exist with something very like their opposite; 'In *Deirdre*, for example, the characteristic falling cadences give a curiously retrospective quality to the emotion as if the lovers from the beginning were contemplating their own story, already past.'[1] More than usually (even) in tragedy, one is conscious of the beauty of the telling in the sadness of the tale. There is the distinctive recurring music of the cadences: 'It's getting old she is, and broken'—and, more liturgically, 'May the Almighty God have mercy of Sheamus and Patch, and Stephen and Shawn; and may he have mercy on my soul, Nora, and on the soul of everyone is left living in the world.' During the plays, Synge's delight in the wildness of nature and the lives of simple people mingles with the inevitability of transience. At the end, one is reminded of the tragic tradition of a few survivers left over a body or a grave, all passion spent.

Equally Irish, but otherwise almost wholly contrasted, was Sean O'Casey, whose most famous dramas arise directly out of the Irish 'troubles': *The Shadow of a Gunman* (1923), *Juno and the Paycock* (1925) and *The Plough and the Stars* (1926). O'Casey's plays have more realism than Synge's; their dialogue, whilst being equally distinctive, is less ritualistic, nearer to the rhythms of everyday speech. Technically uneducated, he learned his creative art from other dramatists, especially Shakespeare. His weakness, undoubtedly, was for the over-colourful and the melodramatic. In *The Plough and the Stars* Nora's development from normal sanity through extreme tension to madness is not wholly successful; one feels so little potential for greatness in the other characters that Nora does not symbolise the tragedy of Ireland as she should. But in *Juno and the Paycock* the main characters are drawn with greater subtlety, and Juno herself is built on a fully tragic scale.

[1] Ronald Gaskell, 'The Realism of J. M. Synge', *Critical Quarterly*, vol. v (1963), p. 247.

O'Casey's main inspiration was his turbulent relationship with Ireland; when the unpopularity attendant upon this drove him into self-imposed exile, he never recaptured his original fire. A class-conscious, obsessively anti-Catholic Irish patriot, he was better placed than most men to enjoy unpopularity; nor was he helped by his peculiarly mixed attitude to the troubles themselves. For others, there was a transforming magic in the days of martyrdom; Yeats, in his great poem *Easter 1916*, celebrates men removed from the 'casual comedy' of ordinary living into the grander, more permanent world of the heroic dead:

> I write it out in a verse—
> MacDonagh and MacBride
> And Connolly and Pearse
> Now and in time to be,
> Wherever green is worn,
> Are changed, changed utterly:
> A terrible beauty is born.

But for O'Casey, casual comedy co-exists with heroism; and beyond casual comedy, bitter satire, as the former Irish militant shows corruption, fear and absurdity behind the heroes themselves. No doubt the mid-'twenties was a tactless time for such exposures, when independent Ireland was at last emerging; O'Casey's kind of honesty is seldom popular at the best of times. Yet his plays still retain their tremendous freshness and vitality—the lives of the poor in the Dublin tenements, the human fecklessness and courage, humour and resilience, in a testing time. Though they are plays of hotblooded anger, they are the work of a craftsman. They seem nearer to direct imaginative experience than most of Shaw.

At the same period the American Eugene O'Neill was making an impact; never a great impact, since he has remained, even until the present, the most underrated dramatist of our time. The earlier plays were admittedly oversimplified, with crude situations, and characters defined too simply through tricks of speech. But, as he developed through his middle period, his tragic vision deepened; the use of myths released his sense of family tragedy, and his explorations of human failure become more and more moving. From early plays like *The Emperor Jones* (1921) and *Anna Christie* (1922) he moved on through *Desire Under the Elms* (1924) and *The Great God Brown* (1926) to *Strange Interlude* (1928) and *Mourning Becomes Electra* (1931). His two greatest plays belong to a later period—*The Iceman Cometh* (1946) and *Long Day's Journey Into Night*, discovered after his death. When the history of that period comes to be written, these will certainly take their place with works by Sartre, Camus, Brecht, Arthur Miller, Tennessee Williams and Genet, among major drama in a period once parochially thought of, in England, as waiting for Beckett.

A final word about the revival of poetic drama in the 1930s. Though there were one or two interesting left-wing plays (Auden and Isherwood, *The Dog Beneath the Skin* (1935) and *The Ascent of F. 6* (1936); Stephen Spender, *Trial of a Judge* (1938)), the only major plays to emerge were T. S. Eliot's *Murder in the Cathedral* (1935) and *The Family Reunion* (1939). *Murder in the Cathedral* was written to be performed in Canterbury Cathedral, and represents an early attempt to rescue drama from the commercial theatre and restore it to a more serious stage. Eliot returned to the Greek dramatists for his model, partly in order to enhance his religious theme, and partly, he said later, to escape the pervasive influence of Shakespeare upon English dramatic verse. The Chorus has a double function, as in several Greek plays. It represents the attitudes of normal, humble Christians to their Archbishop's crisis, and at the same time evokes a mounting atmosphere of fear and impending doom. The temptations of Becket are a reminder that Eliot also learned his craft from English Morality drama. They culminate in the unexpected fourth temptation, when the Archbishop's inner pride becomes incarnate, and he is invited to 'do the right deed for the wrong reason'. As the play progresses, the audience is continually drawn in: first through the Chorus, which moves freely about among it; then as congregation for Becket's Christmas sermon; and then as the actual object of temptation, when the Archbishop's murderers step out of the frame of the play. By this time, it is easy to see how Eliot relates his historical episode to the mood of the 1930s, though less easy, perhaps, to accept his own premises as they become apparent. None the less, the play does not simply descend to being a direct moral challenge. The poetic texture is marvellously rich, and its impact, in a church or cathedral, makes it the best specifically Christian play in the English tongue.

In *The Family Reunion* Eliot takes on an even more ambitious theme, of family doom and guilt in a claustrophobic setting. His method here challenges direct comparison with Ibsen; a comparison which serves to show, however, how decisively limited Eliot's dramatic gifts were. The ritualistic quality has the effect of slowing the action and depersonalising the characters; one has the odd sense of witnessing an elaborate puzzle, where the subtle ironies of moral behaviour and the traumatic events alike seem deprived of their proper power.

In 1939 Christopher Fry wrote *Boy with a Cart*, but neither his later plays, nor Eliot's, could infuse real life into poetic drama. *Murder in the Cathedral* remained an isolated success. Another twenty years was to pass before the authentic rebirth in England of drama with the imaginative intensity of poetry. Then it was to come through Beckett and Pinter, a development that neither Eliot nor Fry could have foreseen.

Perhaps we may conclude with a poem by the greatest British poet of the time. Yeats has so far been mentioned only on the periphery, but, though he evades most of the generalisation about 'modern' literature, he remains among the greatest moderns of them all. In 1937 he published *Lapis Lazuli*.

I have heard that hysterical women say
They are sick of the palette and fiddle-bow,
Of poets that are always gay,
For everybody knows or else should know
That if nothing drastic is done
Aeroplane and Zeppelin will come out,
Pitch like King Billy bomb-balls in
Until the town lie beaten flat.

All perform their tragic play,
There struts Hamlet, there is Lear,
That's Ophelia, that Cordelia;
Yet they, should the last scene be there,
The great stage curtain about to drop,
If worthy their prominent part in the play,
Do not break up their lines to weep.
They know that Hamlet and Lear are gay;
Gaiety transfiguring all that dread.
All men have aimed at, found and lost;
Black out; Heaven blazing into the head:
Tragedy wrought to its uttermost.
Though Hamlet rambles and Lear rages,
And all the drop-scenes drop at once
Upon a hundred thousand stages,
It cannot grow by an inch or an ounce.

On their own feet they came, or on shipboard,
Camel-back, horse-back, ass-back, mule-back,
Old civilisations put to the sword.
Then they and their wisdom went to the rack:
No handiwork of Callimachus,
Who handled marble as if it were bronze,
Made draperies that seemed to rise
When sea-wind swept the corner, stands;
His long lamp-chimney shaped like the stem
Of a slender palm, stood but a day;
All things fall and are built again,
And those that build them again are gay.

Two Chinamen, behind them a third,
Are carved in lapis lazuli,
Over them flies a long-legged bird,
A symbol of longevity;
The third, doubtless a serving man,

Carries a musical instrument.
Every discoloration of the stone,
Every accidental crack or dent,
Seems a water-course or an avalanche,
Or lofty slope where it still snows
Though doubtless plum or cherry-branch
Sweetens the little half-way house
Those Chinamen climb towards, and I
Delight to imagine them seated there;
There, on the mountain and the sky,
On all the tragic scene they stare.
One asks for mournful melodies;
Accomplished fingers begin to play.
Their eyes mid many wrinkles, their eyes,
Their ancient, glittering eyes, are gay.

This wonderful poem turns on a word, and explores the resilience of man and of art. Of what use is art, in a world of crisis? The word 'gay' is first an abuse, a badge of the irresponsible; but the abuse, says Yeats, is hysterical, even if we are, as the women fear, to be destroyed. In the artist's gaiety there is a hope beyond tragedy, a miracle somewhere in the hinterland between life and art:

Gaiety transfiguring all that dread...

But this gaiety is not escapism; it is a supreme conquest, in the light of which even the death of a civilisation may be faced:

All things fall and are built again,
And those that build them again are gay.

The miracle of these lines is their effrontery. The insupportable burden of the first!—the granite-like assurance of the second. But what is this transfiguring gaiety which the poem asserts? If not of Hamlet the character nor of Hamlet the actor, of Hamlet the idea perhaps—Hamlet removed into the Byzantine permanence of art? In a sense, no doubt this *is* what Yeats is saying: all art is 'gay' in its formal exuberance, for the artist creating, for the actor or audience re-creating, however grim the tragedy and desolating its relevance to life. But the gaiety, the resilience, 'belong' neither to the artist nor to the art; their saving existence is somewhere between the two. And so the poem's main image is of the lapis lazuli, depicting its gay old men. The gaiety is theirs, as we see them before us; yet the gaiety comes from human originals long since perished, for where but in human eyes can the light be seen? And then again, art can perish, like the men who create it; it is itself a thing that may fall and be built again. In the poem's splendid central section, Yeats achieves a highly distinctive triumph; he not only asserts his theme but enacts it, as the lost work of Callimachus returns to life in his lines. How Yeats evokes the grace and delicacy of the vanished artist!—calls back to it, across the dark backward and abysm of time. And how relevant, later, that the very cracks in the lapis lazuli should have become part of its intrinsic beauty; that art should have assimilated the normal erosions of time. The interaction between art and life reminds us of Keats—the Grecian Urn especially—but Yeats is saying finally different things. The Grecian Urn records an unhealed, a tormenting dichotomy, of intensity and permanence fated never to meet. One work of art (the Urn) gives birth to another work of art (Keats's poem), but the original lovers recede from us, and the artists themselves recede in the time-scale of their art. In Yeats's *Lapis Lazuli*, a work of art dies, but is recalled by another artist—the art depends on the artists as much as the artists upon the art. Just as the gaiety may have permanence neither in a living old man nor in a lapis lazuli figure, yet the two together attest the strength of gaiety in a tragic world, so the human spirit, Yeats demonstrates, has its resilience in creation; in creating and re-creating, *there* is the triumph of life. And this moves us back to the poem's last, and most unforgettable, image, of the transforming gaiety somewhere between the onlooker and the art. The poet, contemplating the art, becomes engaged with it; 'I delight to imagine', he says. His delight is touched off by the art, then in turn re-creates it. The old men desire music, and music is played for them. Somewhere between the poem and its audience the miracle happens, 'Accomplished fingers begin to play.' And meanwhile Yeats's own accomplished fingers reach for a pencil. On the brink of 1939 and of European destruction, the artist testifies:

> Their eyes mid many wrinkles, their eyes,
> Their ancient, glittering eyes, are gay.

CHAPTER XXI

PHILOSOPHY AND RELIGIOUS THOUGHT

I. PHILOSOPHY

PHILOSOPHY is a continuing conversation. Its texture and structure, its methods and results, are closely similar to those of an evening's talk in a crowded room. Somebody who comes along afterwards to give you an account of what was said, whether he speaks as a direct ear-witness and participant or as a more or less ill-informed reporter, will present a picture that is distorted in one or more of a number of characteristic ways. It will oversimplify or overcomplicate, dramatise too much or too little; a monologue about a dialogue can never do full justice to its changes of key, pitch and tempo. Unless the history of philosophy is itself written as a conversation, it will not be likely to represent accurately the conversation that is philosophy.

Although philosophers from Socrates and Plato to Hegel and Wittgenstein have spoken of philosophy as dialectical, most philosophers, and nearly all non-philosophical readers and observers of philosophy, have failed to take seriously enough its dialectical, conversational character. Both in the conduct of philosophy itself, and in writing the history of philosophy, they have been too attached to political or even military analogies: to pictures of philosophers as forming parties or regiments, following leaders, firing at each other across gulfs, canyons or unbridgeable torrents, or shouting at each other across the floor of a House firmly held by stable coalitions, with only rare and abrupt changes of power.

These images are especially attractive, and at least as dangerous as usual, in attempts to present a picture of what has happened in philosophy in the twentieth century. There is much talk of a 'revolution in philosophy'. It is obscurely supposed that until about 1900 there was a Conservative government of Absolute Idealists, who were then routed by a vigorous alliance of Empiricists, Realists and Pragmatists, and that they in turn formed a popular front with extremist Logical Positivists, who soon took over the party and the country and held them until the sweets of office softened them into the more moderate Linguistic Philosophers who now have such an irresistible majority that they can afford to be deaf to the growing whispers of counter-revolution.

The inaccuracy of this comfortably neat account becomes plain as soon as we look at the detail of the philosophical situation at the turn of the century, and in particular at what is widely quoted as the first shot in the revolutionary war: G. E. Moore's 'The Refutation of Idealism'.[1] But to

[1] *Mind*, 1903, reprinted in *Philosophical Studies* (1922).

look at this classic document, or at F. H. Bradley's *Appearance and Reality*, one of the leading texts of the Idealism against which it is directed, is also to understand what makes the false picture plausible:

The principle of organic unities, like that of combined analysis and synthesis, is mainly used to defend the practice of holding *both* of two contradictory propositions, wherever this may seem convenient. In this, as in other matters, Hegel's main service to philosophy has consisted in giving a name to and erecting into a principle, a type of fallacy to which experience had shown philosophers, along with the rest of mankind, to be addicted. No wonder that he has followers and admirers.

But three pages later, just when we may be thinking that here is a clarion-call to a quite specific revolt, Moore writes:

And at this point I need not conceal my opinion that no philosopher has ever yet succeeded in avoiding this self-contradictory error: that the most striking results both of Idealism and of Agnosticism are only obtained by identifying blue with the sensation of blue: that *esse* is held to be *percipi*, solely because *what is experienced* is held to be identical with the *experience of it*. That Berkeley and Mill committed this error will, perhaps, be granted: that modern Idealists make it will, I hope, appear more probable later.

'The Refutation of Idealism' is a contribution to a conversation in which Hegel and Bradley, but also Berkeley and Mill, had been engaged. Moore is challenging all of them and all other philosophers, on a point of common concern to all of them. He is in conflict with his predecessors but therefore also in contact with them. His demonstration that *esse* is not to be identified with *percipi*, though it was indeed one of the forerunners of much that is most characteristic of the British philosophy of the twentieth century, was also a discussion of issues that had preoccupied philosophers in Britain, Europe and America for several centuries at least.

To look at some of Moore's other work is to complicate the picture still further. *Principia Ethica* (1903) shows the same determination to be clear, detailed and concrete: its epigraph from Butler—'Everything is what it is and not another thing'—became a slogan for common-sense, analytical philosophy; but it also allies itself with Bradley and with H. A. Prichard in defending the autonomy of ethics against the naturalist utilitarianism of John Stuart Mill.

Bradley's *Appearance and Reality* (1893) was one of the great and dominant texts in philosophy at the turn of the century. Here was an Anglicised Hegelian Idealist, at once complaining that the intellect characteristically distorts reality and setting out to show by systematic reasoning what the nature of reality is and must be like. In such papers as 'The Conception of Reality' (1917)[1] Moore analyses the arguments (and the ambiguities) by which Bradley arrived at his surprising and dramatic conclusions that Time and Space are unreal, that external relations are logically impossible, that nothing short of a complete description of everything can be more than partially true.

---
[1] *Ibid.*

But Bradley was not the only English-speaking Idealist of that generation, and Moore was far from being the only or the only kind of critic of Idealism. In America Josiah Royce defended an epistemological version of Idealism which helped to provoke C. S. Peirce and William James into their pragmatist and empiricist doctrines. Like Moore, they emphasised the complexity and subtlety of thought and its objects, against the monistic tendencies of the Idealists. In Cambridge Moore and his near-contemporaries Bertrand Russell and A. N. Whitehead were taught and influenced by J. M. E. McTaggart, whose pluralist personal Idealism was expounded with an analytical circumspection that remained characteristic of Cambridge philosophy long after nearly everybody had ceased to believe that the universe is a series of eternal selves.

There are still further obstacles to the production of any neat diagram of early twentieth-century philosophy. Herbert Spencer was still alive, and Darwin's evolutionary biology continued to preoccupy a varied group of philosophers in England and America. In continental Europe there was Bergson's vitalist philosophy, which had links both with the voluntarist strand in pragmatism and with the insistence of the Idealists that the intellect distorts reality. The growth of the natural sciences also had a decisive effect on E. H. Haeckel, whose *Riddle of the Universe* (1899) was one of the most widely read books of its day.

Far more important for the immediate future of philosophy were the preoccupations of Husserl, Brentano, Meinong, and above all Frege. All these were concerned, though they differed in their idioms and in their conclusions, with a cluster of questions in ontology and epistemology which were to be among the central themes of philosophy in the subsequent decades. In retrospect Frege looms largest in this group. His researches in the foundations of arithmetic pioneered a road that led to Russell and Whitehead's *Principia Mathematica* (1910–13), one of the landmarks in the whole of philosophical history.

The consequences of this attempt to reduce mathematics to logic, and of Russell's major supporting works, spread far beyond that field into almost every area of philosophy. F. P. Ramsey, whose posthumous collection of papers *The Foundations of Mathematics* (1931) was one of the products of the same enterprise, described Russell's 'theory of descriptions' as 'a paradigm of philosophy'. Having solved the puzzle about fictional and imaginary entities by formal deductive analysis, and so annihilated Meinong's world of shadowy entities, Russell and his friends were ambitious to achieve greater conquests still by wielding Russell's slogan that one should wherever possible substitute logical constructions out of known entities for unknown and *inferred* entities. Russell's *The Analysis of Mind* (1921) and *The Analysis of Matter* (1927) were contributions to this programme. Mind was seen as reducible to behaviour, and material objects to 'sense-data'. *Analysis* was the watchword: logic was 'the essence of philosophy'. The achievements of physicists, logicians and mathematicians provided the stimulus to philosophers that had once been provided by theological, ethical and biological preoccupations.

Moore was much less programmatic than Russell, but he dealt with some of the same topics and used similar methods. His *Philosophical Studies*, collected in 1922, treat, among other things, of 'The Nature and Reality of the Objects of Perception', and 'External and Internal Relations' in an informal, but nevertheless rigorous, logical idiom. (The latter paper introduces the notion of *entailment* which was to continue to be discussed at Cambridge and elsewhere until the present day; but it did so in the context of an enquiry into and a refutation of the Idealist doctrine that all relations are internal.)

Here again we must pause to look at links that cross time, space and subject-matter. The reductive epistemology of Russell and his followers had been foreshadowed in outline by the classical British Empiricists and by J. S. Mill, and in greater detail by some scientifically oriented writers of the late nineteenth century, both at home and abroad. Ernst Mach's *Science of Mechanics* (1883) was translated into English in 1893, one year after the appearance of the influential and widely read *The Grammar of Science* by Karl Pearson. An English edition of Hertz's *Principles of Mechanics* (1894) was published in 1899. These works are of such a date and of such a character as to refute any suggestion that the 'Cambridge Analysts' were introducing something wholly unprecedented into philosophy.

The same works have a further importance for the philosophical history of this period, and one which again connects British and continental philosophy closely together. The stream of positivistic empiricism in England became a flood-tide only when the influence of the 'Vienna Circle' and of Wittgenstein's *Tractatus Logico-Philosophicus* was felt and was absorbed.

Ludwig Wittgenstein came to Manchester to do research in engineering in 1908. His growing interest in logic and the foundations of mathematics led him to Cambridge to work with Russell, who wrote an Introduction to the *Tractatus* when it was published with an English translation in 1922. Here was a manifesto which had all the confidence and all the trenchancy that could be hoped for by a band of radical philosophical reformers, or all the arrogance and all the dogmatism that could be feared and castigated by the many surviving exponents of older traditions:

the *truth* of the thoughts communicated here seems to me unassailable and definitive. I am, therefore, of the opinion that the problems have in essentials been finally solved.

Defenders and detractors alike were tempted to forget the next sentence:

And if I am not mistaken in this, then the value of this work secondly consists in the fact that it shows how little has been done when these problems have been solved.

Both sides attended more closely to the claim that most questions and propositions of traditional philosophy were *senseless*, and to the famous last section of the *Tractatus*:

6.53. The right method of philosophy would be this. To say nothing except what can be said, i.e. the propositions of natural science, i.e. something that has nothing to do with philosophy: and then always, when someone else wished to say something metaphysical, to demonstrate to him that he had given no meaning to certain signs in his propositions. This method would be unsatisfying to the other—he would not have the feeling that we were teaching him philosophy—but it would be the only strictly correct method.

6.54. My propositions are elucidatory in this way: he who understands me finally recognises them as senseless, when he has climbed out through them, on them, over them. (He must so to speak throw away the ladder, after he has climbed up on it.)
He must surmount these propositions; then he sees the world rightly.
Whereof one cannot speak, thereof one must be silent.

But the *Tractatus* is much more than a manifesto. It is already recognised as a classic work of philosophy. Like many another classic, it is obscure, compressed, lending itself to rival interpretations, needing some at least of the abundance of commentary and annotation that has already flowed over it.

Here it is possible to do no more than to mention some of its themes and doctrines. Wittgenstein's own summary in the Preface declares that

the book deals with the problems of philosophy and shows, as I believe, that the method of formulating these problems rests on the misunderstanding of the logic of our language. Its whole meaning could be summed up somewhat as follows: What can be said at all can be said clearly; and whereof one cannot speak, (see above) thereof one must be silent.

His acknowledgement to 'Frege's great works and the writings of my friend Mr Bertrand Russell' prepares the reader for the preoccupation with problems of mathematics, logic, meaning and necessity. Disciples and critics have found in it a 'picture theory of meaning', according to which language *mirrors* the world, and what a sentence has in common with a state of affairs is a *form* or structure which cannot, therefore, be explained or expressed *in* language, but which 'shows itself'; and the theory of 'Logical Atomism' which Russell had expounded, with acknowledgements to Wittgenstein, in *The Philosophy of Logical Atomism* (1918)—the theory that analysis requires the existence of 'ultimate simples'. Debate continues on whether Wittgenstein can be credited or debited with such explicit and formal *theories*: the book is aphoristic, literary, apophthegmatic, rather than systematic and formal in the manner of Russell and Frege. What is clearer is that it offers an account of the nature of logical necessity which was to be characteristic of later positivist thought. The propositions of mathematics and logic are represented as tautologies, which, because they are true in all possible states of affairs, '*say nothing*' about the world. A contradiction, which is true in *no* state of affairs, is also *senseless*. *Sense* belongs only to 'the propositions of natural science' which are 'what *can* be said'.

Wittgenstein's logicist colleagues and disciples were less happy about the mystical streak in the *Tractatus*, the references to God and death and 'what is higher'. They were content to note that Wittgenstein consigned these topics to that realm 'whereof one cannot speak' and they did not too closely enquire whether he would have dissented from Ramsey's remark that 'Theology and Absolute Ethics are two famous subjects which we have realised to have no real objects'. It was Ramsey again who wrote: 'What we can't say we can't say, and we can't whistle it either.'

Wittgenstein did not belong to the Vienna Circle, though he was acquainted with some of its members, but there was certainly some community of spirit between the *Tractatus* and the more straightforwardly and formally positivist writings of Schlick, Carnap, Neurath, Feigl, Hahn and the other members of what became a concerted movement of empiricist, anti-metaphysical philosophers. It is important not to exaggerate the unity of this school: there were internal debates and differences about the exact nature of the verification- or meaning-criterion by which metaphysics was to be banished into limbo, and about the nature of the 'basic propositions' or 'protocol-statements' on or out of which the world was to be 'logically constructed'. But they did constitute a conscious and formal school: they met for discussions, they held conferences, they published journals.

Similar ideas were introduced to English readers by Ogden and Richards in *The Meaning of Meaning*. The first edition of 1923 already alludes to Wittgenstein and Russell, and also (to remind us again of deeper roots) to C. S. Peirce. But the somewhat casual references to these writers give no sufficient impression of what the work must have owed to philosophical discussion in Cambridge and the debt that such discussions owed in turn to news from Vienna.

It was not until 1936, with the publication of A. J. Ayer's *Language, Truth and Logic*, that the general reader in English-speaking countries had access to a systematic and avowed presentation of the doctrines of the Vienna School. Ayer's preface begins by acknowledging that his views 'derive from the doctrines of Bertrand Russell and Wittgenstein which are themselves the logical outcome of the empiricism of Berkeley and David Hume'. He goes on to express a large debt to Moore, though he recognises that Moore and his followers 'are not prepared to adopt such a thoroughgoing phenomenalism as I do, and that they take a rather different view of the nature of philosophical analysis. The philosophers with whom I am in the closest agreement are those who compose the "Viennese circle", under the leadership of Moritz Schlick, and are commonly known as logical positivists.'

In spite of these generous acknowledgements, and of many more specific references in the text of the book, *Language, Truth and Logic* had much of the air of a radically new departure in philosophy, and it was received or rejected as such by many philosophers of all persuasions. It is a masterpiece of clarity and force of exposition, and though it is doubtful whether it contains an original idea of any importance, it did a great service to the progress of philosophy by presenting, in a form in which they could be clearly understood and therefore clearly discussed, ideas which were as important as they were unfamiliar to most philosophers of the day. It is a mark of the book's incisiveness and of the grace of its style, as well as of the immense readership that these qualities won for it, that only in very recent years has it been possible for professional philosophers to persuade their non-philosophical friends that there are any philosophers in England who are not logical positivists, or that logical positivism owes anything to any other text than this.

Ayer is certainly thoroughgoing. The first chapter is entitled 'The Elimination of Metaphysics' and its final sentence reads: 'The traditional disputes of philosophers are, for the most part, as unwarranted as they are unfruitful.' The book offers 'a definitive solution of the problems which have been the chief source of controversy between philosophers in the past'.

Metaphysics is eliminated by a revised version of the Vienna School's criterion of literal meaningfulness:

The criterion which we use to test the genuineness of apparent statements of fact is the criterion of verifiability. We say that a sentence is factually significant to any given person, if, and only if, he knows how to verify the proposition which it purports to express—that is, if he knows what observations would lead him, under certain conditions, to accept the proposition as being true, or reject it as being false. If, on the other hand, the putative proposition is of such a character that the assumption of its truth, or falsehood, is consistent with any assumption whatsoever concerning the nature of his future experience, then, as far as he is concerned, it is, if not a tautology, a mere pseudo-proposition. The sentence expressing it may be emotionally significant to him; but it is not literally significant. And with regard to questions the procedure is the same. We enquire in every case what observations would lead us to answer the question, one way or the other; and, if none can be discovered, we must conclude that the sentence under consideration does not, as far as we are concerned, express a genuine question, however strongly its grammatical appearance may suggest that it does.

Ayer acknowledges the kinship of his iconoclasm with Hume's onslaught on the metaphysics of the medieval schools:

Of Hume we may say not merely that he was not in practice a metaphysician, but that he explicitly rejected metaphysics. We find the strongest evidence of this in the passage with which he concludes his *Enquiry Concerning Human Understanding*. 'If', he says, 'we take in our hand any volume; of divinity, or school metaphysics, for instance; let us ask, Does it contain any abstract reasoning concerning quantity or number? No. Does it contain any experimental reasoning concerning matter of fact and existence? No. Commit it then to the flames. For it can contain nothing but sophistry and illusion.' What is this but a rhetorical version of our own thesis that a sentence which does not express either a formally true proposition or an empirical hypothesis is devoid of literal significance?

The chapter giving 'A Critique of Ethics and Theology' was perhaps the most blood-stirring or spine-chilling. Christians were offered the cold comfort of an assurance that their beliefs shared with those of atheists and agnostics the stigma of being 'not false, but senseless'. Moral judgements were described as 'partly expressions of feeling, partly commands'. 'Ethics without propositions' became the slogan of a school of moral philosophers. The most detailed and careful presentation of this account of morality was given by C. L. Stevenson in *Ethics and Language*. It became fashionable for bright young things to use the word 'emotive' or the crushing retort 'that's a value judgement' as a stopper of all serious conversation about morals, politics, religion, literature and art. (Many of them are still doing it, though their brightness is tarnished and their youth has faded.)

Ayer's phenomenalism was representative of his doctrines on all the main problems of philosophy. He offered *reductions*, analyses in the Russellian manner: minds, numbers, concepts, propositions, material things, past and future, all were logical constructions, not inferred entities. No other possibility was considered.

Even outside the ranks of the banner-waving positivists, much of the philosophical work of the 'thirties was of a similar temper. Gilbert Ryle in 'Systematically Misleading Expressions' (1932)[1] underlined some lessons of the current distinction between sentence forms and the 'logical forms' of the facts that the sentences expressed. Plato's universals were banished by diagnosing the linguistic confusions that had given them birth. Ryle had some misgivings about the way in which his work was pointing:

But as confession is good for the soul, I must admit that I do not very much relish the conclusions towards which these conclusions point. I would rather allot to philosophy a sublimer task than the detection of the sources in linguistic idioms of recurrent misconstructions and absurd theories. But that it is at least this I cannot feel any serious doubt.

In 1936, the same year as *Language, Truth and Logic*, there appeared an article that pointed in another direction: John Wisdom's 'Philosophical Perplexity'.[2] Wisdom's work had already passed through several phases. His book *Problems of Mind and Matter* (1934) belonged to an earlier Cambridge, the Cambridge of Ward and Stout and McTaggart, to whom he was linked by the teaching of Moore and Broad. In a series of papers on 'Logical Constructions' (*Mind*, 1931–3) he had joined in the fashionable search for logical equations as solutions of philosophical problems. Now, after a spell at St Andrews, he had returned to Cambridge to find

[1] *Proceedings of the Aristotelian Society*, 1931–2. [2] *Ibid.*, 1936–7.

Wittgenstein in full cry, and the quarry included 'the author of the *Tractatus*'. According to this second Wittgenstein, he and his colleagues had rightly identified 'misunderstandings of the logic of our language' (*Tractatus*, Preface) as the source of philosophical confusion, but they had misunderstood the nature of the disease and the mode of treatment appropriate to it. They had themselves been misled by language, misled into thinking that philosophical questions and statements were as similar to scientific and mathematical statements in their logical character as in their forms of expression. 'The craving for generality' could be mortified by attention to details and *differences*. Analysis must give way to *description* before philosophers could be freed from 'the idea that the meaning of a word is an object' and other beguiling illusions.

Wittgenstein's new ideas soon gained wide currency, partly by oral transmission, partly by the circulation of typescript notes of his lectures (the 'Blue and Brown Books', which were not published until 1958), but mainly by the work of Wisdom and other pupils. Wisdom exaggerated his great debt to Wittgenstein: from Wittgenstein he had learned that philosophers spoke paradoxically, putting familiar expressions to unfamiliar uses and hence misleading themselves and others. But he saw more clearly than Wittgenstein had seen that in these paradoxes there is penetration as well as confusion. Here Wisdom was developing the lessons of Wittgenstein's own remark in the *Tractatus* that 'what the solipsist *means* is of course correct'. Wisdom elaborated these points in numerous articles in the philosophical journals, and notably in a series on 'Other Minds' (*Mind*, 1940–3). After the unhistorical and often antihistorical bias of the positivists, here was somebody who emphasised the continuity of philosophy: the links between the new linguistic epistemology and the metaphysical ontology of the traditional philosophers. His philosophical practice already adumbrated his later account of 'The Metamorphosis of Metaphysics' (British Academy, 1961).

Language, Truth and Logic continued to receive critical attention both from traditionalist thinkers like A. C. Ewing, who kept Idealism alive in Cambridge while all about him were succumbing to what C. D. Broad called 'the syncopated pipings of Herr Wittgenstein's flute' and from others such as M. Lazerowitz and C. L. Stevenson, who were sympathetic to Ayer's radicalism but who wished to prune some of his excesses. Broad himself continued to write philosophy in the manner of the Cambridge analysts of a slightly earlier day; he allowed in spite of the new critics that there was scope for 'speculative philosophy' as well as for the 'critical philosophy' that he practised himself. Such books as *The Mind and its Place in Nature* (1925) and *An Examination of McTaggart's Philosophy* (1933–8) have virtues of sanity, acuteness and disinterestedness which can now be seen more clearly than they were seen by partisans of the new movements of the 'twenties and 'thirties.

Meanwhile in Oxford there flourished a school of common-sense, down-to-earth philosophers who were unknowingly preparing the way for the 'linguistic' philosophy that took Oxford by storm in the years just before and after the second world war. Cook Wilson, like W. E. Johnson and Moore at Cambridge, emphasised the importance of 'normal usage' before this became a modish slogan. Joachim, Prichard, Joseph, J. A. Smith and (among a younger generation) H. H. Price differed from each other in many ways, but they had in common a determination to be concrete, detailed and *sensible*, to avoid the large enthusiasms of some nineteenth-century metaphysicians and to deal with problems thoroughly and piece-meal. These virtues, and the corresponding limitations, were to be transmitted to the younger philosophers who would acclimatise 'Cambridge philosophy' to its Oxford environment.

R. G. Collingwood, also in Oxford, kept alive an interest in philosophy of history and in aesthetics, as well as in natural philosophy and the traditional problems of metaphysics, while his younger contemporaries concentrated on more narrowly logical and epistemological issues and did not even read the Continental authors on whom he drew—Croce, Gentile, Dilthey and Hegel. Collingwood's *Autobiography* (1939) gives a partial but valuably corrective picture of Oxford philosophy between the wars. Samuel Alexander's *Space, Time and Deity* (1920) and some of the works of Whitehead (e.g. *Process and Reality*, 1929) were grand metaphysical productions which seemed to more fashionable philosophers merely grandiose.

The neglect of these thinkers and their themes was accompanied by a disregard of the Continental authors to whom they were more nearly akin. The complaint of the general public that academic philosophers ignored all that was most important and most vital in the general intellectual life of the century had great plausibility. Marx was read by economists and by the politically active; Nietzsche by those whose primary interests were literary rather than philosophical; Kierkegaard by theologians and philosophical amateurs; Freud by everybody. But none of these thinkers, with the possible exception of Freud, was even on the fringe of the consciousness of many practising philosophers in those years.

During the inter-war years there was correspondingly a comparative neglect of historical studies in philosophy, and of nearly all fields of philosophical enquiry outside logic and epistemology: ethics, philosophy of religion, philosophy of history, aesthetics, political philosophy. It would be possible to draw up a long and distinguished list of exceptions, but they would nearly all be the work of men who were out of sympathy with the prevailing philosophical mood. A. E. Taylor, John Burnet, Henry Jackson, F. M. Cornford and Sir David Ross made outstanding contributions to the study of Greek philosophy, but Ross and Taylor were old-fashioned in their independent philosophical work and the others were not original philosophers at all. Work on the history of modern philosophy was also largely confined to those who drew their philosophical sustenance from the earlier periods that they wrote about, or who were inactive in substantive philosophy. G. R. G. Mure wrote on Hegel, A. C. Ewing on Idealism, N. Kemp Smith on Descartes; Collingwood's original works (*The Idea of Nature, Speculum Mentis, The New Leviathan*) were systematically historical in method and approach. But after Russell's *Philosophy of Leibniz* (1900) there was for several decades no full-scale work on a great philosopher of the past by a leading philosopher of the modern movement.

The philosophy of religion was similarly isolated. F. R. Tennant's *Philosophical Theology* (1928–30) had something of the concreteness and common sense of the Cambridge analysts of his day, but like Sir Charles Oman, H. H. Farmer and others he worked independently of the main movements of thought among his philosophical contemporaries.

In spite of Russell's active concern with political and social questions, much the same is true of political philosophy in this period, but an important exception to this and to many tempting generalisations about twentieth-century philosophy is provided by Sir Karl Popper. Though it was not translated into English until 1958, his *Logic of Scientific Discovery* (*Logik der Forschung*, 1935) gives him a distinguished place as a philosopher connected with the Vienna School but always independent and critical of its slogans. His thesis that falsifiability and not verifiability is the mark of scientific propositions became widely known and accepted outside the ranks of professional philosophers even before it was available in English.

Even better known is *The Open Society and its Enemies* (1945), which combined a detailed and highly critical consideration of Plato, Hegel and Marx with a philosophical defence of 'the open society' and of a piecemeal, empirical approach to social and political problems. This is almost the only important philosophical work of its day to have direct relevance to the larger historical and political events of the century, and like the same author's *The Poverty of Historicism* it has been widely read by historians and social scientists and by the intelligent public at large, to a degree that can be rivalled by few recent works of philosophy.

Like Laird in his *Recent Philosophy*, any chronicler of twentieth-century philosophy must apologise for mentioning so many names and for omitting so many names. Eddington and Jeans, Poincaré, Jeffreys and Keynes, Tarski and Gödel, Dewey and Schiller, Reichenbach, Hempel and Bridgman, Gilson and Maritain, Bosanquet, Green and Rashdall, C. I. Lewis and Waismann all deserve more than the mere mention which is all that can here be given to them. Most of them are important, and the others are important at least as having been thought by many to be important. The omissions are as varied as the inclusions. To add still more names would be to reinforce an emphasis on the variety of twentieth-century philosophy without finding reason to withdraw a complementary insistence on the cross-connections which give it the unity of a conversation. The same unity and the same variety can be seen in what has happened and is still happening in the post-war philosophy that falls outside the scope of this chapter and this volume.

Wittgenstein's Preface to the *Philosophical Investigations* is dated 1945, but the book was not published until 1953, two years after his death. It is a landmark by reference to which most of the most significant post-war philosophy can be located, whether by comparison or by contrast. Many recent writers are pupils and followers of Wittgenstein: John Wisdom, Rush Rhees, Morris Lazerowitz, Norman Malcolm, Elizabeth Anscombe, Peter Geach. Numerous others who were not his pupils and are not his disciples nevertheless show and acknowledge his deep influence: D. M. MacKinnon, D. F. Pears, Stuart Hampshire and P. F. Strawson are prominent examples. Two of the most influential figures on the post-war philosophical scene, Gilbert Ryle and J. L. Austin, have written important books and articles in which his name is seldom or never mentioned, but whose evident kinship with his work calls for no recondite explanation. A. J. Ayer and H. H. Price at Oxford, R. B. Braithwaite and Casimir Lewy at Cambridge, like many others in other places, have produced work that is more in the spirit of the earlier Cambridge philosophy of Russell, Moore and Broad than in that of the later Wittgenstein. There are two large classes of active philosophers who are firmly opposed to the work and influence of the later Wittgenstein: the traditionalist metaphysicians (Ewing, Blanshard, Mure) and logical empiricists and philosophical logicians (Quine, Goodman, Carnap) whose interests link them closely with the Vienna Circle, the *Tractatus* or *Principia Mathematica*.

This account began with a warning against parochialism in time. It must end with a warning against parochialism in space. It has become commonplace to deplore the gulf between Anglo-Saxon and Continental European philosophy in the mid-twentieth century. But the differences are exaggerated both by critics of contemporary British philosophy who hold up Sartre and Camus and Heidegger and Jaspers as models to imitate, and also by neo-positivist and linguistic philosophers who hold up the same Continental philosophers as warnings of the snares that threaten those who are not vigilant in the preservation of their emancipation from ancient metaphysics.

Since most philosophers at all times and in all places are bad philosophers, and since even the best philosophers are occasionally guilty of folly and absurdity, it is easy for both parties in this wrangle to compile *sottisiers* from the works of their opponents' heroes. But the idea that either side has a monopoly of serious concern with the central problems of philosophy is one that will not survive the examination that it is at last receiving. German-, French- and English-speaking philosophers have read the same philosophical classics and inherited from them substantially the same preoccupations. There are differences of idiom between one place and another, but they are no more important than the differences of idiom between one time and another, or between different philosophers who share the same time and place. Not all philosophers at all times and in all places are equally interested in all philosophical problems, and the differences of stress between Continental and Anglo-Saxon philosophers at the present time are simply one illustration of this truism.

Jean-Paul Sartre is one of a number of Continental philosophers in whom British philosophers are becoming increasingly interested. The nature of his work exemplifies the wider situation. His *Esquisse d'une théorie des émotions* (1939, translated 1962) deals with problems in the philosophy of mind which have been prominent in British and American philosophy, where they have been associated, as they are by Sartre himself, with the work of William James and Freud. It has been widely recognised that *L'Existentialisme est un humanisme* (1946, translated 1948) is relevant to contemporary discussion of the nature of moral reasons and judgements. *L'Être et le néant* combines these two fields of interest, together with an epistemological preoccupation very close to that of many British philosophers. One section is entitled *L'Existence d'autrui*—which would be a good title for a French edition of Wisdom's *Other Minds*. Meanwhile some of the work of Ayer and Ryle and Austin and Wittgenstein is being read in Italy, Germany and France. The conversation continues.

2. RELIGIOUS THOUGHT

The distinction between 'religious' and secular thought is probably unreal and certainly difficult. The first half of the twentieth century seems, in retrospect, to fall, in this respect, into two contrasting periods—before 1914 and after 1918—the first characterised by a close relation between philosophy and religion, the second by a tendency to fall apart, influential philosophers holding that metaphysical statements are meaningless and theologians that Revelation needs no support from human reason. At the opening of the century Herbert Spencer was still alive and his agnostic theology of the 'Unknowable', which he derived from the Anglican Dean Mansel, was under fire from the rising school of Idealists. Positivism, of the Comtist type, was widely held as a philosophy which harmonised with the scientific outlook, and the proposition that the only genuine knowledge is scientific knowledge was widely accepted. About this time the word 'Naturalism' came into use as a general term for a scientific metaphysic which, with more or less emphasis, rejected the idea of God. Since this controversy on Naturalism was about the nature of truth and the limits of knowledge, it concerned many thinkers who would not have claimed to be theologians. The institution of the 'Gifford Lectures', which were explicitly devoted to the consideration of belief in God in the light of reason without resort to authority or alleged revelation, secured that the great themes of God, Freedom and Immortality were continually being examined from many points of view. The second period saw the emergence of a new form of naturalism which maintained that statements which could not be verified or 'falsified' by sense experience were unmeaning. This extreme position proved untenable, but a prevailing view among English-speaking philosophers is that metaphysics, and consequently rational theology, are not possible. One result of this has been to concentrate religious thinking more on the idea of revelation and the nature of religious experience. A sign of the times is that, whereas in the early years of the century the Philosophy of Religion threatened to take the place of lectures on doctrine, in more recent days Systematic Theology and Dogmatic Theology have resumed their sway in the theological curriculum.

Before passing on to a brief account of theological developments, some reference must be made to influences which affected most of the religious thinking in the half century. Two writers of an earlier period, Kierkegaard and Nietzsche, stimulated many religious minds. The philosophy which has been labelled 'Existentialism' is alleged to stem from Kierkegaard, no doubt correctly, but the forms which it takes are so protean, ranging from Atheism to Catholicism, that it remains a puzzle. Perhaps its most obvious effect has been to reinforce the reaction against reason in religion and to encourage the emphasis on will, decision and 'commitment' in religious experience. A comparison between Kierkegaard and Blaise Pascal is illuminating; both were converted by a *saltum mortale* which took no account of 'the God of the philosophers', both were men of exceptional intellect and literary power. Another pervading influence is the new development of psychology. Sigmund Freud was of the opinion that he had proved religion to be an illusion, a 'universal neurosis', and it cannot be denied that he has caused much searching of heart and revision of concepts among those theologians who have given serious attention to his writings, but how much of his theory of the Unconscious will survive the criticism, which continues, we cannot tell; the same remark applies, with even greater force, to the work of his pupil and rival C. G. Jung. Without doubt, both have important contributions to make to our understanding of religion; the analytical philosophers could perhaps help us to estimate the significance of the symbols and myths which they employ. Some continuing influence on religious thought has come from the attempts to find some 'meaning' in history. Benedetto Croce and Giovanni Gentile were Idealists who attributed absolute value to history, in the sense that to them history was the manifestation of Spirit. This point of view obviously has a direct bearing on the Christian doctrine of

Providence. So too have the speculations of Oswald Spengler and Arnold Toynbee on the nature of history. Spengler's *Der Untergang des Abendlandes* was published at the end of the first world war and caused a sensation by its pessimism and atheism. Toynbee's elaborate *Study of History* has had a notable influence on religious thinking, largely because, while more learned and comprehensive than Spengler, he dwells on the enormous importance of religion for the understanding of history and outlines, as it were, a doctrine of Providence for scientific historians.

Very much of the best thinking of the time was directed towards the question of the nature of religion, the conception of God in the light of modern science and the bearing of new knowledge on the traditional doctrines of Christianity. Pringle Patterson's *Idea of God*, which restated the doctrine of theism from the Idealist point of view, had considerable influence and was a distinguished essay in interpretation. Clement C. J. Webb devoted a long life of reflection to the study of the history of natural theology and the philosophical aspects of the belief in divine personality. Dr Tennant, in his *Philosophical Theology* and other shorter writings, brought an acute and analytic intelligence to bear on the central dogmas of religion, approaching them with the presuppositions rather of the realistic Cambridge school than with those of idealism. Hastings Rashdall, in his *Theory of Good and Evil* and his *Doctrine of the Atonement*, gave to the world two substantial works in which deep theological and philosophical knowledge were blended. Though an idealist, he was opposed to absolute idealism and held the empirical idealism of Berkeley. To these names we may add that of W. G. de Burgh whose writings on the relation between morality and religion and on the place of reason in religion, *The Life of Reason*, came at the end of the period and have the interest of summing up a tendency of thought in which many thinkers had taken their part. Nor may we forget two philosophers who concentrated attention on the moral argument for a religious view of the world—Professor W. R. Sorley and Professor A. E. Taylor. The latter, who had begun his philosophical career as a disciple of Bradley, illustrates a movement of religious thought which had wider significance than the development of an individual mind. He abandoned the pantheistic conclusions of absolutism and ended with a view which was at least not far removed from that of Thomas Aquinas.

All the authors mentioned in the preceding paragraph were concerned to maintain the validity of religious experience and the essential truth of the central affirmations of Christianity, but it cannot be said that in all cases the theologians were grateful for the services of the would-be defender of their science. The modifications and limitations which some of the philosophers of religion would have introduced into the accepted doctrines appeared to many to be dangerous departures from revealed truth and to this feeling we must ascribe the fact that two of the best minds of the Anglican church in these years, Dr Rashdall and Dr Tennant, were not given the recognition and influence they deserved. The times in fact were not propitious for the calm discussion of religious ideas, for from the outset of the century the Christian religion was passing through a severe crisis in which, as it seemed, there were more urgent problems than those which the detached thinkers debated. The leaders of the churches were confronted with a wide falling away of the people from public worship and from any serious allegiance to 'organised religion'. Though this fact is not the only important factor which affected religious thought from 1900 to 1950 it is one to be constantly borne in mind.

Religion, being a social activity as well as a subjective experience, is necessarily more directly linked than philosophy with the vicissitudes of history, and the crisis of western civilisation which culminated in the two world wars is reflected very clearly in the somewhat abrupt changes in theological currents which have occurred. The nineteenth century bequeathed to the twentieth two unsolved theological problems. The first was how to reconcile the results of natural science with the world-view which seemed to be implied in the Christian faith, and the second was how to assimilate the results of the historical criticism of the Bible and the conclusions of the students of comparative religion.

When the century began, a powerful and earnest body of Protestant Christians in Great Britain, America, Germany and most of the European states had adopted a theology which is named, chiefly by its critics, Liberal Protestantism. The principal features of this type of Christian belief were a minimising of the supernatural and dogmatic aspects of Christianity and a 'return to the Gospels'. In them, it was thought, the dominant idea was that of the Kingdom of God. Liberal Protestantism, therefore, placed the Kingdom of God at the centre of its interpretation of the religion of Christ, but it concentrated attention on the coming of the Kingdom in this present world excluding, so far as might be, those elements in the Gospels which suggest the 'other-worldly' aspect of the Kingdom. The 'social gospel' became identified in the minds of some with the idea of progress, which, in the first decade of the century, was regarded as almost certain, if not inevitable. The greatest name associated with Liberal Protestantism is that of Harnack, whose *History of Dogma* is one of the major influences in the intellectual ferment of the time. In this work, distinguished by wide learning, Harnack sustained the thesis that the original Christian experience which created the New Testament had been so interpreted by Greek philosophy that it had been transformed from its primitive simplicity into a series of theological propositions and an elaborate sacramental and hierarchical system. The popular *Das Wesen des Christentums*, which reproduced lectures given by Harnack to students in Berlin, was an eloquent plea for a simplified Christian faith consisting in two fundamental affirmations—the fatherhood of God and the brother-hood of men. It would be unjust to Harnack and the very numerous 'liberal' theologians who were in sympathy with him to say that they ignored such weighty matters as sin, redemption and the Incarnation; they aimed rather at a revaluation of these doctrines in the light of what they supposed to be the simple message of Jesus. T. R. Glover's *The Jesus of History*, which was widely read in England and America, is an attractive example of the writing produced by this type of Christian scholarship. The study of the religions of the Hellenistic age, to which Glover also contributed, was an additional factor in the problem. The researches of Reitzenstein, Cumont and others led to a clearer understanding of the importance of the 'mystery cults' and the question was raised how far the transformation of the primitive Christian gospel was due to the influence of the mystery religions and whether the process had not already been begun by St Paul, who was alleged by some to have borrowed ideas and phrases from pagan rituals.

The writings of Harnack were in part the occasion of the modernist movement in the Roman Catholic church. Catholic scholars in France, Germany, England and Italy were conscious of the need for relating the teaching and practice of the church with modern scientific and historical knowledge, and some at least were dissatisfied with the intransigent attitude of ecclesiastical authority to all concessions to the thought of the new age. At the same time, they were firmly convinced that the church was the providential bearer and protector of the life of the spirit. The Abbé Loisy, meeting the challenge of Harnack and Liberal Protestantism, attempted to develop a new kind of Catholic apologetic in his two short but effective books, *L'Evangile et l'église* and *Autour d'un petit livre*. Accepting a criticism of the sources at least as drastic as Harnack's, he tried to show that the gospel and the church were inseparable and that the living tradition of worship in the church was the substance of the Christian religion. In England two eminent theologians were associated with the modernist movement, George Tyrrell and Baron F. von Hügel. The latter, though certainly a modernist in his critical views, was probably not a philosophical modernist; and he escaped the papal condemnation which overtook his friends. For the Roman church, or at least the Vatican, repudiated the new apologetic and the programme of accommodation to modern knowledge. Modernism was banned as a heresy in 1907 and there followed a drastic 'purge' of the seminaries and the parochial clergy. To all appearance the movement was defeated in the Roman church and perhaps it had in the end its greatest influence on the liberal wing of the Anglo-Catholic section of the Anglican church. Loisy and Tyrrell continued to write. The former became more agnostic than believing and his *Birth of Christianity* would be hard to reconcile with his *Gospel and the Church*.

The social gospel had a different complexion in the Anglican communion. Its exponents, the so-called Christian Socialists, Charles Gore and Henry Scott Holland, based their teaching on the Incarnation and on the Catholic doctrine of the Incarnation to the defence and explanation of which Gore's principal books were devoted. Bishop Gore represents one of the chief trends of Anglican thought in the first thirty years of the century and was one of the outstanding personal influences. The liberalism of his earlier period, when he contributed to *Lux Mundi*, was always of a strictly limited character and in later life he stood for an orthodoxy which was prepared to silence those clerics who went farther in criticism of traditional doctrines than the acceptance of the positions of *Lux Mundi*. Nevertheless, he was always half a liberal and it is interesting to note that his 'kenotic' theory of the Incarnation is now repudiated by Anglo-Catholic theologians who find this leader of the Catholic party of yesterday too liberal for today.

The first world war was a heavy blow to the optimism of Liberal Protestantism. The dream of the permeation of society by the principles of Christianity was clouded though not destroyed. The League of Nations was, in great measure, the creation of Christian idealism and it failed chiefly because the spiritual power which made it was not sufficient to sustain it. The hopes of the 1920s and the disillusionments of the 1930s had their repercussions in religious thought, but there were also other disturbing causes which arose within theology itself.

The 'historical Jesus' who leads mankind into the Kingdom is the central figure of idealistic Christianity. He is a universal figure, modern at any rate in the sense that He speaks in language which has significance for our time. This figure had been constructed by selecting from the Gospels those traits and words which are consonant with our ways of thinking and dismissing the rest. The Apocalyptic school of New Testament interpretation protested against this picture on the ground that it left out the most important element in the story. They pointed out that the first three Gospels are deeply imbued with the ideas and imagery of Jewish Apocalyptic. Albert Schweitzer caused the greatest perturbation with his book *The Quest of the Historical Jesus*, in which he insisted that Jesus was 'a Jew of the first century'. Other works, *The Mysticism of St Paul* in particular, followed the clue of Apocalyptic, and the striking and attractive personality of Schweitzer, together with his devoted labours as a medical missionary, made him one of the most important religious spirits of our time. The extreme Apocalyptic view of the Gospels has been criticised and eminent scholars still reject it altogether, but on the whole it may be said that the contentions of Schweitzer and those who agreed with him in his principal positions, such as Professor Burkitt, have left a permanent mark on New Testament interpretation and on the conception of the Kingdom of God in the teaching and experience of Jesus.

44-2

The question of the nature of the religious experience was raised, as we have seen, by the new psychology and much active theological discussion was directed to the refutation of the fundamental scepticism of the Freudians. A positive contribution to the problem was made by Rudolf Otto's *The Idea of the Holy*, in which he developed a theory of 'the numinous' as a distinctive feeling which exists at all levels from that of unreasoning, shuddering dread to that of awe and reverence. Otto linked his theory with the theology of Schleiermacher, the philosophy of Fichte and the religion of Luther and carried his line of thought farther in a penetrating study of *Mysticism, Eastern and Western*. For reasons not easy to discover he had a larger following in England and America than in Germany. He is one of the authors of the time whose writings will probably be of permanent value and his doctrine of the 'irrationality' of the divine has not yet been placed in its proper perspective.

In the ferment of conflicting theories perhaps the systematic theologian is at a disadvantage, because he finds no firm ground of accepted presuppositions under his feet, but noteworthy efforts were made to restate the orthodox doctrines for contemporary minds. Dr Gore, at the end of his career, returned to the defence and exposition of the Christian beliefs about God, Christ and the Church; Dr A. C. Headlam, beside books on the *Life and Teaching of Jesus* and *The Atonement*, produced the first volume of a system of theology which he did not live to finish. William Temple, archbishop of Canterbury, was through most of these years probably the most effective exponent of a liberal kind of orthodox theology. His wonderful powers of memory and of lucid statement enabled him to pour out books in spite of his absorption in the practical work of the church. Three of his books, *Mens Creatrix, Christus Veritas*, and *Nature, Man and God*, contain the essence of his thinking and display the movement of his mind from a 'broad Church' to a more traditional standpoint.

We have already observed in passing that an interest in mysticism appeared in more than one quarter and it may be suggested that one of the causes operating to quicken this interest was the uncertainty both of the social and of the intellectual background. Men sought for some basis for life and found no reassuring answer in the idea of progress or in the dogmas of the church. They looked within for the foundation and many found it there. The list of distinguished students of mysticism is long and we can notice only a few of them. Dr W. R. Inge, in his *Christian Mysticism* and in his lectures on *The Philosophy of Plotinus*, did much to widen the understanding of mysticism and to persuade those who were suspicious of it that it was worthy of serious attention. Evelyn Underhill, in her *Mysticism* and many other books, brought the words of great mystical writers home to the general reader and had an influence on wide circles through her spiritual conferences. Baron F. von Hügel was a religious thinker who brought a unique acquaintance with contemporary continental scholarship and philosophy to the service of a liberal Catholic theology, but his most memorable book, *The Mystical Element of Religion*, was a detailed study of St Catherine of Genoa on which was based an investigation of the nature and significance of the mystical experience. The London Society for the Study of Religion, which von Hügel founded, was a meeting-place for some of the finest spirits of the 1920s and 1930s. Two of its members, Claude Montefiore, the Jewish scholar and student of the Gospels, and Edwyn Bevan, the expert on Hellenistic culture and author of a valuable book on *Symbolism*, must be named.

In the year following the end of the first world war Karl Barth came into prominence and since that time his 'dialectical' theology of crisis has been a major feature in Protestant thought. Though it can hardly be said that Barth has any disciple or colleague who accepts all his positions and he has conducted lively controversies with some who were at one time members of his school, such as Gogarten and E. Brunner, his influence may be discerned in the majority of Protestant theologians since about 1925 either by way of agreement or of criticism. At the beginning of our period there were those who placed so much faith in the philosophy of religion that they expected it to take the position formerly occupied in the church by dogmatic theology; at the end we find a powerful movement which repudiates all connection with philosophy and presents a dogmatic based on the Bible as the only divine truth open to men. The conception of the Word of God is central for Barth and he draws a sharp distinction between it and all the wisdom and spiritual experience of humanity. The Word of God comes into the world as a direct and unrelated act of God. It is not to be criticised or validated by human reason, which, being corrupt through the Fall, is incapable of passing judgement on the Word. The root of Barth's hostility to every form of philosophical theology is his denial of the 'analogia entis', that is, of any 'image of God' in man from which he could rise by a process of analogical inference to any knowledge of God. The Barthian theology represents the extreme form of the reaction against Liberal Protestantism and 'rational' religion. It is, as the name 'Theology of Crisis' implies, a movement evoked by the menace of the historical situation, but it may have more permanent importance than that, for it is, on one side of its doctrine, a revival of elements in Christianity which have their origin in St Paul.

A brief reference is all that space permits to the contribution of Russian and Eastern Orthodox writers. The exile of many Christian scholars from their native land has enriched the religious thought of the West. The names of Franks and Bulgakov must be passed over with a bare mention though the former has given us an excellent exposition of a philosophical type of mysticism which is not afraid of the idea of the church. Nicolas Berdyaev, in a long series of books, presented a philosophy of religion and a theology which attracted attention partly by its difference in method and inspiration from all Western religious thought. Neither the Scholastic logic and metaphysics nor the Reformation are among the fundamental sources of his thought, which is moulded chiefly by the tradition of Orthodox theology, Marxism and German philosophy. He writes rather as a prophet than a philosopher though his works are full of references to philosophy of all ages and many nations; he does not argue but states his conclusions in an oracular manner. Towards the end of his life he was interested in the permanent value and truth of the Apocalyptic vision of history, a subject which he had approached through his two most significant studies, *The Meaning of History* and *The Destiny of Man*. Probably his really important contribution was his frank recognition of the necessity of 'mythological thinking' in religion and his attempt to elucidate the nature of myth in Christian belief. It is remarkable that many orthodox theologians hailed Berdyaev as an ally in spite of the obvious tendency of his mind towards positions which would be distasteful to the traditional dogmas both of Protestants and of Catholics. Many reasons may have contributed to this, the stimulating character of Berdyaev's thought, the obscurity of his writing and the obtuseness of the orthodox.

Anyone who studies the religious thought of the first half of the twentieth century with the purpose of finding clues to probable future development may well judge that the most hopeful sign of the times is the fact that the Ecumenical movement for Christian unity has emerged from two world wars more vigorous than ever. In the sphere of theological thinking, the Ecumenical spirit has shown itself by a change of method in discussion. In place of controversy 'dialogue' is the fashion, and theologians aim less at refuting errors of those who disagree with them and far more at understanding. Anticipation of the 2nd Vatican Council (1962–4) stimulated restatement of doctrinal positions in the Roman Catholic church, which proved to open new approaches to such notable points of difference as Justification; an example of eirenic analysis of this type is the treatise by Dr Hans Küng on the theology of Karl Barth (*Justification: the Doctrine of Karl Barth*). From the Protestant standpoint, memorable studies of Systematic Theology have come from Reinhold Niebuhr and Paul Tillich, both of whom exercised powerful influence in America and Great Britain. Co-operation in religious thinking is a recognised fact in the sphere of scholarship as in the case of the Dead Sea Scrolls (discovered in 1960); it is becoming more and more recognised in the central concern of theology—the doctrine of the Being of God and of man's salvation. We may say, at least, that so far as Christian thought is concerned the day of anathemas is done.

CHAPTER XXII

PAINTING, SCULPTURE AND ARCHITECTURE

Painting

THE first half of the twentieth century saw the creation of modern art, that is, a revolutionary art which broke with traditional ideas of representation; and since the public now looked at nature with eyes conditioned by photography, the gap between artist and public widened. Modern art grew out of impressionism and therefore began in Paris where impressionism had matured; but when impressionism was shown on a large scale at the Paris World Fair of 1900 it became international, and modern movements began to develop in Germany, Italy and Russia while the art of Paris itself became cosmopolitan. In France orthodox painting continued to be organised round the annual Salon from which the jury excluded all advanced work, so that the avant-garde had been forced to organise on its own, setting up first *ad hoc* impressionist exhibitions, then in 1884 the Salon des Indépendents and in 1903 the Salon d'Automne. So art was organised into conservatives and radicals like contemporary politics.

In 1900 two movements were dominant—divisionism and symbolism. The divisionists following Seurat tried to make impressionism scientific by painting in complementary colour dots which fused at a short distance. The symbolists followed Gauguin into rejecting science for poetry; they neither imitated nor analysed but sought a pictorial equivalent for nature in broad colour zones closed by decorative lines. During the next ten years three other artists came to be understood: Van Gogh, whose fierce colour and tempestuous brush stroke keyed painting to the expression of emotion; Cézanne, who, struggling to realise his sensations before a motive by modulating small colour planes, combined the freshness of impressionism with the solidity of a new classic structure; and the Douanier Rousseau, whose naïve realism invested objects with an aura of wonder.

The years before 1905 seem in retrospect an introduction. While the young Picasso drew circus folk in a style of emotive realism, Vuillard and Bonnard wrote a postscript to impressionism in colourful interiors and street scenes. The first modern art was created by the fauves between 1904 and 1908. A *succès de scandale* at the 1905 Salon d'Automne caused by the violence of their colours gave them their name of 'wild beasts'. Colour was indeed their preoccupation. They used it raw, neither darkened to model nor toned by atmosphere, with abrupt transitions and strident harmonies where those of the divisionists had been complementary, while in order to further decorative richness and uninhibited brushwork their pictures were flattened and their forms simplified.

There were two sides to fauvism, one exemplified by Vlaminck, the other by Matisse. Vlaminck adapted the swift strokes and burning colour which for Van Gogh had been the outcome of unbearable tension to express passion for its own sake; Matisse, starting with Gauguin, sought by juxtaposing colours a new pictorial architectonic rendered lyrical by arabesque. The impressionists had pioneered these ideas but used them descriptively, while for the fauves nature was a starting-point and the picture an end in itself. They recorded emotions, not facts; but by emotion they meant aesthetic sensation for they had no story-telling, social or moral aims. Though less radical in practice than in theory, keeping much description, impressionist subject-matter and sunny mood, their concern that colour as such should be the prime element in picture-making still underlies the moiety of contemporary art.

Cubism was the logical counterpart of fauvism, a revolution of form succeeding a revolution of colour, an intellectual against a sensuous, a puritan against a hedonist art. It is generally accorded three over-lapping phases: proto-cubism 1907–9, analytic cubism 1909–12 and synthetic cubism 1912–14.

Proto-cubism began with Picasso's 'Demoiselles d'Avignon' (1907), a large picture of five nudes whose angular forms seem 'hacked out with an axe'. Perspective and chiaroscuro are replaced by a play of surface planes which convey some sense of space and solidity without hollowing the canvas. The heads of the two right-hand figures made more radical deformations than any hitherto, probably under the influence of negro sculpture. The nose of one is folded flat on the face and so asserts what became a cubist principle—the right to portray objects simultaneously from different viewpoints.

During 1908 Braque, influenced by Cézanne, experimented with con-structing pictures from low-toned colour planes; thereafter the two artists developed cubism side by side. In 1909 Picasso concentrated on emphasising the surface planes of a nude model seen from shifting view-points, so that the figure appeared faceted like a crystal and stressed haptic rather than visual sensations. The object though simplified re-mained distinguishable, but in 1910 planes were allowed to penetrate the body, cut into each other and interweave with those of the back-ground, so that the image became fragmented until the object ceased to be identifiable and the artist had reached the brink of abstraction. But abstrac-tion seemed an impoverishment and at once Picasso withdrew, though only slightly. When in 1911–12 the climax of analytic cubism was reached in pictures such as Picasso's 'Clarinet Player' and Braque's 'Portu-guese', the object which was the artist's starting-point could still be glimpsed through the pattern of interpenetrating and translucent planes and overall texture of little bricks of paint. So cubism remained a realist movement not only because its point of departure (guitars and guitar players, bottles, newspapers, etc.) were taken from the artist's immediate environment, but because appreciation of it turns on the interaction between what is left of reality in the fragmented image and the structural pattern.

In 1911-12 Picasso and Braque introduced into their pictures pieces of wall-paper, newspaper, etc., thereby asserting the traditional medium to be no more sacred than the traditional image and that pictures might be made from anything, even rubbish. 'Papier Collé' (as this was called) carried further the cubist probe into pictorial reality and space. The scrap of newspaper was reality itself, not pictorial illusion, the scrap of wall-paper painted with imitation wood-graining was at once reality and illusion, while both were parts of the picture and so negated perspective, emphasised surface and took their places in a composition of toned and textured planes.

When the object's total disintegration was almost reached, analytical cubism could move only into the abstraction it had rejected and it was papier collé which opened a road through the impasse. Coloured papers began to be used, and this helped to bring colour back into a movement hitherto concentrated on design, but to bring it back as an element of design which by the advance and recession of planes furthered the articulation of the picture. A picture made from cut-outs tended moreover to fewer parts, larger and more defined, and so towards clarity. Above all the cut-outs suggested a new starting-point, for the artist ceased to break down an object into a near-abstract pattern, but arranged shapes until an image which stood for a guitar, a bottle, etc., had emerged. Gris was the purist of this synthetic process; Picasso and Braque remained empirical, always ready to ignore theory when they felt it a constraint. Yet Picasso's 'Three Musicians' (1921) is probably the masterpiece of synthetic cubism. Built of shapes which resemble cut-outs in their hard edges and abrupt super-impositions, it achieves everything—image, space and recession—by manipulating these coloured planes. And much earlier, at least by 1914, cubism had established what the fauves had only adumbrated—that the picture was a thing in itself subject to its own and not to nature's laws.

Analytical cubism began with the object it disrupted, but the group 'Section d'Or' (exhibited Paris 1912) began with pictorial elements. They subordinated appearances to a structure of mathematical proportions, and tried to make colour scientific, as Seurat had, by subjecting it to their numerical canons. They held colour to be the prime element and thus might have fused the cubist and fauve streams had any of them been great enough: as it was they inspired the 'Orphism' of Delaunay. His true subject was the natural and spontaneous life of colour, and by 1913 he had developed a motive of concentric coloured disks into a symbol of atmospheric luminosity which was at once dynamic and abstract. His associate Léger, starting with the cones and cylinders which Cézanne had sought in nature, made a similar transition to dynamic abstraction in terms of form.

Unlike the French movements, Italian 'Futurism' began with a literary and political manifesto, that of Marinetti, published in Paris in 1909: the past should be forgotten, its museums burnt, and a future of machinery, cities, noise, speed and war passionately embraced. A year later a group was formed in Milan with a programme to implement this philosophy in paint. Divisionism suggested the colours, cubism the techniques, for expressing not particular actions but dynamism itself. Balla painted the several stages of an action simultaneously, Boccioni drew lines of force to depict the 'Dynamism of a Street'; but their pictures remained anecdotal until they exchanged the attempt to represent a movement for its presentation by an abstract equivalent (e.g. Boccioni's 'Dynamism of a Cyclist' (1913)).

Expressionism is associated with Germany, where the influence of the Norwegian Munch (who had adapted Van Gogh's passion and Gauguin's line to the expression of bourgeois anxiety) had been profound. In 1905 the group 'die Brücke' was formed at Dresden (Kirchner, Schmidt-Rottluff, Heckel, etc.), creating an art like that of the fauves but acid in colour and anguished in mood. From 1912 its style became more unified and national, and, drawing inspiration from African sculpture and Gothic wood-cuts, sacrificed structure to intensity of feeling. On the outskirts of the group expressionism was applied by Nolde to religious art and by Kokoschka to the portrait. Yet the greatest expressionist was perhaps the Parisian Rouault, who from 1904 painted prostitutes and clowns, advocates and judges, savagely and pityingly sublimating all in his images of Christ.

A fresh phase of expressionism was launched by the 'Blaue Reiter' group in Munich in 1911. Unlike 'die Brücke' it was international both in composition and outlook, and was unified less by style than by its use of fauve–cubist formal discoveries for psychological ends. Franz Marc applied the techniques of Delaunay to convey the beings of animals in their habitat; while Kandinsky, leader and theoretician of the group, was influenced by memories of Slav folk art and the Byzantine church murals of his native Russia. His early landscapes had the broad colour zones of Gauguin, but their mesmeric and disturbing colours rendered them not so much decorative as mystical. This appeal to the inner eye increased at the expense of the ostensible subject-matter until in 1910 the latter disappeared. Thereafter Kandinsky used colour in abstract and informal shapes, whose conflicts in a space rather mental than pictorial expressed the turbulent disharmonies of the human soul. In these pictures the abstract expressionism of the 'fifties had its source.

Pre-1914 abstraction was not a movement but resulted logically from the formal preoccupations of fauves and cubists, and emerged simultaneously around 1910–12 in several countries to demonstrate that pictures could be made from form alone. Picasso had turned back in 1910, but Mondriaan pressed cubist analysis to its end, stylising a tree until only verticals and horizontals remained. Yet even at this early date abstraction was various. For Delaunay it symbolised light, for Léger an ordering of volumes, for Boccioni movement, and in Kandinsky's hands it not only acquired psychological overtones but was freed from geometrical as well as natural form. Thus Kandinsky reached one extreme; the Moscow Russians reached the other. Larionov made pictures from light and dark diagonals ('rayonnism') and Malevitch from squares and triangles ('suprematism') and in 1917 the latter painted the ultimate in logical purification—a white square on a white ground.

Expressionism excepted, the discovery of new formal modes had been the object of each several art movement, but around 1913 painters called metaphysical or fantastic found a new subject-matter in the content of dreams. Chagall, a Russo-Parisian, through peasant colour and cubist geometry created a dream world where memories of his Vitebsk ghetto jostled the Eiffel Tower, calves became visible in cows' bellies and heads and bodies lived contentedly apart. Chirico, an Italo-Parisian, painted classical arcades with sharp clarity and exaggerated perspective; headless statues or the shadow of an unseen presence inhabit a piazza ended by a clock, a factory chimney or a train behind a wall. So clarity conceals mystery as in pictures by Rousseau; but Chirico's magic is chilling and forebodes catastrophe. Here painting turned away from the rational to prepare the way for surrealism.

1905–14 was the period of invention when almost all the great discoveries were made so that the between-wars would be a period of fulfilment. Yet the academies were still dominant and neither the fashionable world nor the general public understood the new art, which, whenever it was put on exhibition, created a scandal widely thought to be its purpose. Matters were better than they had been for the impressionists, for now an avant-garde was recognised as normal. Impressionists and post-impressionists had been first condemned then accepted: this was the new pattern. The avant-garde, now extended from Paris to other major cities, was both conscious of its role and confident in its future. A few bold dealers (Kahnweiler), a few bold collectors (the American Steins and the Russian Schukin) were persuaded, and the leading artists could make a living. In France and Britain the museums fought a stiff rearguard action, but audacious directors appeared in Germany—a first breach in the official wall. The art of this period was related to society less by the social consciousness of 'die Brücke' or the self-conscious modernity of the futurists than by its experimental attitude. The artist in probing the nature and resources of painting became a research worker who paralleled rather than symbolised the contemporary achievements of science.

Its style perfected, cubism ceased to destroy and it was Marcel Duchamp who continued the attack. Between 1911 and 1914 he 'debunked' many accepted sanctities: love, by revealing woman as an arrangement of flues; inspiration, by techniques of chance; machine efficiency, by his 'Cocoa-Grinder'; art itself by 'ready-mades' (mass-produced objects mounted like sculpture). Amid the mass slaughter of 1916 his sophisticated scepticism became the nihilism of Dada which demanded a romantic anarchy for both art and society. Defeated Germany gave this philosophy a ready welcome, and both there and in Paris the Dadaists made nonsense verse and nonsense pictures to mock rationality, held provocative exhibitions and childish demonstrations to shock the world into recognising its own insanity. Yet Dada had lasting results. The collages of Ernst and Schwitters developed for satirical what cubism had invented for formal reasons, the 'ready-mades' argued that the whole world was potential art, while Arp pioneered a new bio-morphism by his insistence that the artist must parallel, not imitate, nature so that his wood reliefs grew in his hands like fruit on a tree. Finally, an understanding of Freud brought realisation that Dada nonsense was not nonsense but symbolised subconscious desires. At which point Dada evolved into surrealism.

The origins of surrealism were literary and its manifesto was published in 1924 by the poet Breton. The poets sought to explore the subconscious by automatic writing and the artists looked for equivalent techniques, sacrificing formal considerations to the discovery and presentation of a disturbing and irrational imagery by any helpful means, even illusionist realism. Thus Max Ernst used (*inter alia*) collage to find and juxtapose unrelated images and displace them from their natural setting—like a canoe and a vacuum-cleaner making love in a forest. The effects were to startle the spectator, to make him question the inevitable rightness of everyday reality, and to show him poetry in the absurd. Dali's horrific and photographic visions advertised the cult, but its true artist-poet was the Catalan Miró, who rejected illusionism for abstract shapes which he used less as elements in a formal pattern than as emblems of a mythological world. Miró transcended surrealism, and in his hieroglyphs developed a range of expression which ran from the gay to the horrible or the obscene, but his particular gift was to preserve the insights and spontaneous reactions of primitives and children in a precise, subtle and intellectual art. Miró owed something to Klee, whose art also was rooted in the subconscious, which he plumbed to the primordial depths where he believed all things to originate. Klee sought emblems of this primitive realm which should make visible the formative processes rather than the finished products of nature, and his method was to begin with formal elements—line, tone, colour—until an image suggested itself which he would consciously perfect. Though his pictures are tiny, personal, fanciful and apparently slight, his command of structure developed from the discoveries of fauves, cubists and Delaunay, and explained in his 'Pedagogue's Notebooks', was nowhere excelled. It is by this combination of formal organisation with psychic improvisation that he united the two mainstreams of modern art and became one of its most significant painters.

Against surrealist unreason and uncontrolled expressionism, there emerged in the early post-war years an ultra-rational trend which sought discipline in a stricter geometry. One source was the cubism of Gris, who started with an abstract order which he progressively modified by concrete identifications ('out of a cylinder I make a bottle') until a self-sufficient intellectual structure acquired a foothold in reality. Ozenfant's 'Purism' (Manifesto, Paris 1918) reversed this process, abstracting form from jugs as Poussin from the nude. Standard shapes resulted which might have unified this painting with industrial design had it had force enough. Instead it was Léger who revealed and idealised technological society. In his 'Grande Déjeuner' (1921) the figures are assembled from machined forms in industrial colours among industrial products, yet achieve a monumental and leisured serenity in their mechanised utopia. Mondriaan went further. Rejecting images and associations he reduced his forms to a grid and his colours to primes. His 'Neo-Plasticism', he insisted, constituted in the mutual relations of these simple elements a new and man-made reality of absolute form; it was an art of pure contemplation whose aim was to render visible a universal harmony independent of the natural order. Kandinsky, stimulated by the constructivists, turned from his informal abstractions which had exteriorised human emotion to free arrangements of geometric forms. At times these were as absolute as Mondriaan's, at others, in their interactions in cosmic and microcosmic space, they seemed emblems of universal conflict within a natural order fundamentally indifferent to man. All these trends were institutionalised by the German Bauhaus which Gropius founded in 1919, where artists were to design buildings with all their contents (murals, light sockets, machinery, furniture) so that art should rejoin craft under the aegis of architecture and the artist should be re-integrated in society. The Bauhaus created modern art-training, grounding it on the study of basic design in terms of particular materials; while its two greatest teachers—Kandinsky and Klee, studying the elements of point, line, plane and colour—strove to formulate the laws of form.

From 1918 until the end of our period Bonnard, Matisse and Braque continued to develop their personal styles uninfluenced by art movements, depressions, revolutions or wars; Bonnard on the basis of impressionism, Matisse of fauvism and Braque of cubism. No new principles were involved, but each artist thoroughly explored the possibilities of his style and their pictures are among the finest of the period. Picasso was cubist, neo-classic, surrealist and expressionist by turns, even all at once. From 1915 he began to alternate Ingres-like drawings with cubist works, and in the early 'twenties joined the return to order by painting monumental figures in an adaptation of Poussin. His cubism of the time makes no concessions to representation but the planes are simplified and clearer. Even before the war he had made a few paintings which in retrospect look surrealist, but from 1927 surrealism became a major element in his art. With the Spanish Civil War he became emotionally involved in the tragedy of the decade. All his invention and technique now served an art of ferocious distortion whose first monument was the huge 'Guernica' (1937) and which he continued in a long series of seated women and still lifes until 1945.

Before 1910 only Sickert's impressionist realism broke the sterility of British painting, so the public were scandalised when in 1910–12 Roger Fry staged two exhibitions of modern French art. Then Wyndham Lewis launched 'Vorticism', a futurist-inspired rebellion which fell a victim to the war and his deficiencies as a painter. Complacency was absolute in the 'twenties save for the eccentric Spencer, but in 1933 'Unit One' was formed with Read as spokesman, Axis as its magazine and Nicholson, Hepworth and Moore among its members. All lived in Hampstead; and when for a few years they were joined by notable refugees (Mondriaan, Gabo, Gropius, etc.) they generated the most exciting artistic atmosphere in Europe. Climax came in 1936 with international exhibitions of abstraction and surrealism, for a year later the 'Euston Road Group', moved by unemployment and the threat of fascism to reject an art which seemed to them irrelevant to life, led a return to impressionist realism. 'Unit One' dissolved but Nicholson continued geometrical abstraction, Sutherland discovered a modern romantic landscape, and these with the sculptors Moore and Hepworth preserved British art in its new audacity and scale.

In the United States it was the impressionist realism of the 'Ash Can School' which first attacked the academies. But artistic Americans looked to Europe, and some were so daring that a small gallery for modern French works—the New York '291'—could establish itself by 1909. In the vast Armory Exhibition of 1913, amidst uproar, mockery and some enthusiasm, American and French modernism was seen by more than 100,000 people in New York alone. Some of the great modern collections were now started, while Gallery '291' began to sponsor Americans trained in revolutionary Paris or Berlin, so that by 1917 modern art had a firm foothold.

In the between-war years an isolationist and chauvinistic reaction took place, both with the public and among artists who resented the collectors' preference for Europeans. A romantic and regionalist naturalism became the vogue, and after the depression 'art for art's sake' was consciously replaced by social and political commitment. The early New Deal helped artists with commissions, but two events turning on private patronage were more important: the foundation in 1929 of the Museum of Modern Art in New York, based on the Bliss collection, and the attracting of leading artist refugees to America. As in Hampstead an exciting artistic climate was born in a small and outlawed group led here by Jackson Pollock, which, exploring a form of abstract expressionism based on new techniques of psychic improvisation, produced the American 'Action Painting' so soon to burst upon the world.

Sculpture

After the death of Michelangelo sculpture declined, for art turned to effects of light and space which favoured painting. This phase reached a climax with impressionism, and with its exhaustion painting returned to object and picture plane and sculpture recovered. Its modern history is the story of that recovery, largely through movements launched by painters.

It began with Rodin, who in himself summed up romanticism, realism and impressionism, but who joined his use of these to a fresh understanding of Michelangelo, from whom he learned something purely sculptural—the expression of movement through tactile values. Like Degas, he never forgot inner muscular tension even while his surfaces expressed the play of light; but unlike Degas he preserved not only the Renaissance technique but its full heroic humanism, and this, while it added to his stature, made him the culmination of an old rather than the primitive of a new tradition.

Maillol led a reaction to neo-classicism, the only movement Rodin had not absorbed. His re-working of Greek sculpture was in terms of nature, so that his 'Chained Action' (1905) combines generalised and static volumes with the animality of Courbet, but his revival of humanism kept Maillol also within the nineteenth century.

German expressionism was in sculpture a classic heresy, so that Lehmbruck, its most talented exponent, preserved Maillol's clarity even through elongated and emotive forms.

Fauve sculpture is limited to Matisse, who transposed composition by colour into composition by plastic form. It becomes modern through a change of emphasis, for form and medium now precede representation. A comparison between 'Reclining Nude' (1907) and 'Jeanette V' (1911) illustrates this by a growing readiness to exaggerate single forms for the sake of tactile and architectonic order.

Bondage to the natural figure was broken by cubism, futurism and Brancusi. Picasso's 'Head of a Woman' (1909) is straight translation of his 1909 pictures into three dimensions; thereafter, though a little late,

Lipchitz and Laurens provide a sculptural analogue for each cubist phase. Though sculpture still takes its cue from painting it remains only slightly behind in the destruction of tradition and the creation of new images, and by 1922 had acquired independent validity; e.g. Lipchitz's 'Homme Assis' (Breton granite) has not only the planar structure of synthetic cubism but the ponderous monumentality of stone.

Futurist sculptures were among the movement's most vital creations. Nowhere did Boccioni express his conception of space–time more success-fully than in his 'Development of a Bottle in Space' (1912) while Duchamp Villon's 'The Horse' (1914) is a potent and abstract image of mechanical energy.

Brancusi's organic abstraction owed nothing to painting for he sought always for the sculptural essence, striving to express an idea through the fewest and simplest shapes. His 'Kiss' (1908) conveys action with minimum detail and minimum impairment of the block, his 'Mrs Meyer' (1910) reduces portrait to four curved forms, while his 'Bird in Space' (1919) captures almost in a single ovoid both form and flight.

Cubist iconoclasm had spread from traditional forms to traditional media and led Picasso through papiers collés to constructions in space. These were still pictorial—that is, to be viewed frontally—and it was the constructivists who developed the idea into three full dimen-sions. Meduniezsky's 'Construction 1919' is sculpture made from a ring, a triangle and two strips of bent metal, and so anticipates Kan-dinsky's geometrical abstractions. It was neither carved nor modelled but built, and indeed some constructivist assemblages suggest architect's models.

Dada produced sculpture almost more naturally than painting, such as Marcel Duchamp's 'Ready-Mades' and the satirical constructions of Ernst and Schwitters. If the surrealists were less witty they were more creative, and indeed surrealist sculpture betters much surrealist painting because it is unliterary. Thus Giacometti's 'Spoon Woman' (1926) conjures up a disturbing presence through subtle undulations rather than by any double image, and Lipchitz's 'Figure 1926–30'—two intersecting pincers topped by an abstract head with glaring eyes—is a true nightmare. And if Picasso's 'Figure 1928', half-human and half-horse, is related to his contemporary paintings it is because the latter are sculptural. The fundamental vocabulary of modern sculpture was complete by 1930, though development and exploitation continued of which only brief indi-cations are possible here.

Picasso in two periods of sculptural activity (1928–34 and 1940–5) used many materials and many styles. His work ranged from thin figurines and obscene surrealist monstrosities to objets trouvés and near-naturalism, his techniques from welded iron to twisted paper. If he produced no masterpieces his unrivalled inventiveness made his œuvre a rich quarry of ideas. Matisse by contrast produced few surprises, but his series 'The Back' culminated in two works of monumental grandeur.

Naum Gabo, a pioneer of Russian constructivism, added transparent plastics to wood and metal, which with its abstract geometry made his work of the 'twenties look like scientific instruments or photographs of astrophysical phenomena. Pevsner's related constructions suggest rather biological science: animalcula under the microscope, dissected membranes or birds' wings. The American Calder made constructions of sheet metal more overtly animal ('Whale', 'Black Beast', etc.) but is best known for his mobiles—Miró-like forms in coloured sheet which move freely in the wind. More prophetic was Juan Gonzales, whose sculpture in wrought iron and harsh angular shapes could easily belong to the 'fifties.

In the biomorphic wing the two leading figures were Jean Arp and Henry Moore. Less exquisitely refined than Brancusi, less suggestive of immense meanings compressed into a hieroglyph, Arp's 'Human Concretions' are shaped like stones or nesting birds and palpably breathe with inner life. Moore, far greater in range and in powers of development, has yet at the centre of his œuvre one dominant conception, the reclining figure at once woman and landscape which stands for the enduring, regenerative and procreative forces of the earth (e.g. 'Recumbent Figure, Green Hornton stone, 1938'). Moore in his work of the 'thirties not only founded the English school of sculpture but, more than any of her painters, brought England back into the mainstream of Western art.

Architecture

In the nineteenth century social and industrial revolution required a new architecture. New building types such as railway stations and department stores evolved, and in them new materials like iron and glass made possible unsupported spans and better lighting. But only in temporary or utilitarian structures such as the Crystal Palace, Paddington Train Shed or the Garabit Viaduct could these facts be admitted. Elsewhere, as at the Albert Hall, an engineer's structure was clothed in stone and a period style.

Inspired by Ruskin, William Morris attacked this dishonesty, arguing that the present age should imitate the methods and not the style of the Middle Ages; that it should base art on craft to give it roots in society. He devised a new ornament freshly stylised from plant forms to replace the machine-made and tasteless decoration in which everything was smothered. His own house (built in 1859 by Philip Webb) replaced pomp by domesticity, showed its bricks and structure, and was planned in terms of function rather than of symmetry and façades. Charles Voysey continued this reticence into the 1890s. His homes too had period flavour without period detail, but were lighter and more suburban. Contemporary were the Garden City (city in the country) experiments which made a first attack on the squalor of industrial housing. But the whole Art and Craft movement was flawed by Morris's rejection of the machine which was becoming the central fact of civilisation, so that after 1900 it lost relevance.

Machine-age architecture began in Chicago, where Louis Sullivan invented a form for the high office block. His 'Guaranty Building' (1895) is free of historical reminiscence, and expresses both its function (shops underneath, offices above) and its structural steel cage.

About the same time an attempt to escape historicism was made in Europe with the creation of 'Art Nouveau'. This was a decorative style of free-flowing curves owing much to Morris, but wilder, more exotic and anti-rational. Through its general application to objects, furniture, china, jewellery, book-plates, it unified an interior ensemble; but it could also be truly architectural. Thus Horta's 'Maison du Peuple' (Brussels, 1896–9) by using iron and glass effected a light spatial transparency; while the undulations which pervaded not only the structure of its auditorium but its façade and its plan took away all sense of the utilitarian. In Barcelona Gaudi was still more extreme, building a stone palace of swaying forms like sea-hollowed caves (Casa Mila, 1905–10), an architecture plastic and untrammelled as sculpture.

Most hopeful of these movements was that in Chicago, where Sullivan had cleared the way for the expression of the industrial city; but in 1893 the Chicago World Fair launched a fresh phase of neo-classicism which swept through America and Europe to remain largely dominant until 1945. The growth of the New York skyscraper belongs therefore to the history of engineering.

Sullivan's great pupil, Frank Lloyd Wright, made his chief contribution before 1914 in the field of the suburban villa, for his skyscraper projects remained unbuilt. This was a paradox, for social and technical change did not become marked in the domestic field until after 1920, with the motor-car, the servant shortage and the gradual mechanisation of services. Wright's 'Robie House' (Chicago, 1909) shows its modernity in sweeping horizontals, expressive of machine-cut efficiency, and purposive movement across the plane, while its spreading cantilevers (roofs over verandahs) begin to blend interior and exterior space. Asymmetrical and irregular massing disrupts the traditional box shapes which are cut by intersecting planes like those of contemporary cubism. The inside looks backward to the countryman's cottage; it is dark, a refuge, where little diamond panes make even glass a barrier; but the shifting room heights, and the planning which forces space into a continuum through wide openings from a central hearth, are as disruptive of the room box and as cubist as the outside. Inside and out, brick, stone and wood show where possible the natural surfaces. Wright's one monumental industrial work, the 'Larkin Office Block' (Buffalo, 1904), is also natural brick. A stark cube with blank double towers at the corners, it turns its back on the city and looks inwards into its own glazed hall whose secure space flows easily into galleries.

As Art Nouveau declined into commercial extravagance, a Scotsman, Mackintosh, like Wright sought a new monumentality. His 'Glasgow Art School' (1898-1909) adumbrates the two main lines on which modern architecture was to develop, the subjective or expressionist and the objective or rational. Its front windows are grids and rational; but its entrance, and the library with its tall forms rising from the hillside, are expressionist. The library interior is different again; its spatial interplay of post and beam, half decorative, half structural, anticipates de Stijl.

Clear separation between the main tendencies begins in Vienna, where Mackintosh was greatly admired; Olbrich's 'Hochzeitsturm' (Darmstadt, 1907) is expressionist, Wagner's 'Post Office Savings Bank' (Vienna, 1905) is rational. Where the 'Hochzeitsturm' is brilliantly inventive—five-fingered tower, roofs in cubic geometry, window bands that cut round corners—the interior of the post office is classically simple. Horta had used iron and glass as instruments of whimsy; with Wagner they express the smooth efficiency of the machine. Finally with Loos's 'Ornament and Crime' (1908) Vienna gave rationalism a fighting dogma. Loos's 'Steiner House' (Vienna, 1910) showed in practice how architecture might be returned to its basic elements, undecorated stereometric volumes.

But it was in Germany that modern architecture matured, in both its aspects. Hermann Muthesius, who had studied English Art and Craft, founded the 'Deutsche Werkbund' in 1907 with similar aims save for one difference—the artist-craftsman was to make, not the individual and therefore expensive object, but the prototype for machine reproduction. Art and craft were reoriented towards industry and a mass society.

In the same year Peter Behrens was appointed chief designer to the electrical combine A.E.G., to shape their products, their literature and their buildings. In his 'Turbine Factory' (Berlin, 1909) he strove to discover a form for such buildings and achieved a masterpiece, but one which was classical and expressionist, rational and irrational at once. To carry the massive and oversailing roof the stanchions appear like columns strengthened at the corners by giant stones, which results in a Greek temple converted to the expression of industrial power. Yet the factory is rational in that the stanchions reveal their steelness and are linked only by glass; it is irrational in that they are really arches flowing without break from base to crown, while the ponderous corners are thin concrete and carry nothing.

The masters of contemporary architecture—Gropius, Mies van der Rohe and le Corbusier—all worked in Behrens's studio, so that when a lavishly illustrated book on Frank Lloyd Wright was published in Germany the chief sources of the first modern (so-called 'international') style came momentarily together. Results were immediate, for the workshop of Gropius's 'Fagus Factory' (1911–13) is the first entirely modern building. It continues the work of Behrens, is still a temple, but its shape is the crystal cube typical of the international style a generation later. Romantic monumentality has gone; in its place is the translucent recti-linear elegance of a glass sheath which, hanging proud of its piers, is visibly unstrengthened at the corners. Where Behrens was personal and glorified the roar of dynamos, Gropius was objective to symbolise the quietly efficient and anonymous corporation.

At the Werkbund Exhibition (Cologne, 1914) Gropius took up Behrens's theme. His 'Machine Shed' is a temple without columns whose stretched and moulded skin expresses only its function—the enclosure of industrial space. In the office block of this model factory he invented another motive for the international style—the cylindrical glass tower which houses and reveals a spiral staircase. Yet Gropius's planning is not modern. Both factories were composed by elements, i.e. of separate buildings. In the Fagus Factory grouping was by function merely; in the Model Factory (where there was no function) it was axial and symmetrical, i.e. academic.

If Gropius led the rational–classic wing of German architecture, Poelzig, Berg and Taut constituted its so-called expressionist, which, if less pure, is more dramatic and formally inventive. Poelzig's 'Water Tower' (Posen, 1911) sums this up. Its enormous cylindrical volumes intend an aggressive impact, but they spring from its functions as tank and exhibition gallery. His 'Chemical Factory' (Luban, 1911) is freely planned after the English manner, while Taut for his 'Glass Pavilion' (Cologne, 1914) invented the lattice or geodesic dome.

French contribution to modern architecture lay in the development of reinforced concrete. Among the first large buildings in this material was the 'Tourcoing Spinning Mill' (1895) where François Hennebique re-placed walls by a light concrete grid with glass infilling. His aims were practical—to resist fire and increase light; and he was so successful that both material and method spread rapidly for utilitarian building.

But it was Auguste Perret who turned a practice into an aesthetic. In his '25 bis Rue Franklin' (Paris, 1903) he supported a high block of flats with six cantilevered stories on posts of unimaginable thinness. Though he used decorated tiles, frame and cantilever were visibly the basis of the façade; so that here Perret brought concrete within the classic principles of trabeation by adapting them to proportions based on weightlessness and the preponderance of voids. His methods were apparently true to his materials, but they were not so in fact, for ferro-concrete is naturally monolithic and performs best in arcuate forms. Hennebique showed this in his spiral staircases for the 'Petit Palais' (Paris, 1898) and his ideas were taken up by engineers. Thus Maillart constructed bridges from curved concrete slabs (Tavanasa Bridge, Grisons, 1905) while Freyssinnet's huge airship hangars with their parabolic arches (Orly, 1916–24) equal in achievement the great Victorian train sheds. But the only architect to work on these lines was Max Berg, a German individualist whose 'Centenary Hall' (Breslau, 1910–13) is a modern version of the Pantheon, where curving girders and openwork dome anticipate Nervi.

There remain two prophets—the Frenchman Garnier and the Italian Sant' Elia. Garnier's 'Cité Industrielle' (1901–4, published 1917) is a detailed blueprint which shows not only house blocks with white façades, terraces and roof-gardens, but studies their setting and the separation of city functions—work, residence, leisure and transport. The futurist Sant' Elia in his 'Projects 1914' gave romantic glimpses of a skyscraper city with multi-level circulation, which provided an emotional charge to inspire necessary rethinking of a whole way of life.

Actual town-planning was most advanced in Holland, where Berlage's 'South Amsterdam' (begun 1915) was based on the broad street and residential block; which if less adventurous than the plans of the visionaries was both more essentially civic and more suited to the facts of population than the garden city.

1919–23, the aftermath of war, was a period of uncertainty, protest and adventure which favoured expressionism; and, because the coming leaders, little employed on building, turned to imaginative projects, it was a heyday of ideas.

As a neutral, Holland was the first to build; but the expressionism of the Amsterdam School (Eigen Haard Estate, 1917–21) was whimsical, a late product of the secure world of art nouveau. True expressionism was German, declamatory yet also functional. Even Mendelsohn's 'Einstein Tower' (Potsdam, 1921), which surprisingly calls to mind a submarine, has an odd logic, for it is the 'periscope' of a basement observatory; and while its streamlining is irrational its moulded forms derive from the plastic nature of concrete, though for lack of the necessary skilled labour it was actually built in rendered brick. Hoger's 'Chilehaus' (Hamburg, 1922) was just as practical and as metaphorical, exploiting a corner site to suggest a high prow and tiered decks curling away in waves. But some works have been called 'expressionist' that are not rhetorical. Their architects denied that certain functions meant certain forms, restudied function and were thereby prompted to invent new form, e.g. Haring's 'Cowhouse' (Garkau, 1923).

The Dutch group 'de Stijl' (founded 1917) made a reappraisal of form itself, going back like Loos in 1910 to its elements. But where Loos had seen architecture as a simple aggregation of closed volumes (especially the box) de Stijl, taking one hint from Wright and another from cubism, either broke open the box to compose in planes, or caused the boxes themselves so to intersect and interrelate as to destroy their separateness in a new continuum. Such buildings could no longer be grasped from a single viewpoint; they must be appreciated in space–time by walking round and by walking through. Both methods are combined in Van Doesburg's 'Project for a Private House' (1923).

In the same period, Werkbund ideas for the union of art and craft and their realignment with architecture and industry culminated in the foundation of the Bauhaus under Gropius (Weimar, 1919). Although both expressionism and de Stijl were influential, it was a variety of functionalism (akin to Haring's) which came to predominate. Here the artist founded his inspiration on a reassessment of function in terms of materials and machine production, so that by 1930 a contemporary style of furniture, fitments and typography had been created.

Its approach to architecture can be illustrated by Mies's unbuilt projects. The 1919 skyscraper owes its queer fortress shape not to expressionism but to the aesthetics of the glass wall; it was composed for reflections instead of shadows. The brick villa of 1923 explores de Stijl, and the linking of inner and outer space by walls continued from within. The office block of a year earlier is structural–functional; its long concrete horizontals alternating with bands of glass were to have a vast commercial progeny after 1930.

It was Gropius, however, who led the return to order in Germany. Already in 1922 his project for the *Chicago Tribune* employed the structural prose of the original Chicago school; but his opportunity came when the Bauhaus moved to Dessau, for its new building (1925–6) was the first of these large projects to become reality. The workshop block developed the rectangular shape and glass curtain of the Fagus Works, but now the piers are hidden and the basement set back so that it floats on air. Each wing is an element—workshop, design school, hostel, administration—and each receives its own functional expression. But the elements are welded into sculptural unity via the legacy of de Stijl; spatial volumes, each having its own identity, flow freely into others in a composition where every change of viewpoint brings new revelations of form.

Holland produced a contemporary rationalism in the flats of J. P. Oud (The Hook, 1924–7), but still more significant was the work of le Corbusier, who in Paris was occupied with his 'Citrohan' projects: a conception of the house which converted Sant' Elia's visions into a precise and revolutionary plan. The house was to be a 'machine for living in' on the analogy of a car. It was to consist of a simple cube, manufactured from standard parts, supported on posts so that walls could be glazed and partitions moved, finished for easy maintenance and equipped instead of furnished—even the garden would be built-in. These cubes would be assembled into blocks, self-contained with their own local shops and garages, and standing in spacious grounds made possible because their concentration would release land. Accessible but well away, multi-level highways would carry their inhabitants to tall slabs in the city centre which would hold factory, office and store. His 'Pavilion de l'Esprit Nouveau' (Paris Exhibition, 1925) was the prototype for such a house.

The new ideas spread rapidly so that the exhibition at Weissenhof in 1927, with flats by Mies, Gropius, Oud, Corbusier and others, revealed that a new style had emerged. This, the 'International Style', was rectangular and white, it had black roofs carrying terrace gardens, flat façades with balconies, and windows that were punched holes or unbroken bands. It abhorred decoration, relying for its aesthetics on bare geometry and good proportions which, it claimed, arose naturally from new functions and materials. In fact they were a free choice to symbolise machine efficiency, for neither concrete nor modern living enforced square forms.

If the freedom of the expressionist period was now lost, the new stylistic restrictions were creative. Mies's 'Barcelona Pavilion' (1929) shows some of its spatial possibilities. Here, above its stylobate, rich marbles contrast with white, glass with reflecting pools and bright steel; while opaque, translucent and transparent walls lead a space defined only by floor and roof in a slow rhythm, newly classical in its serenity, which makes no distinction between within and without. By contrast, le Corbusier's 'Villa Savoie' (Poissy, 1928–30), its lower floor withdrawn, poises, a closed cube on thin stalks. Inside is another geometry, for ramps, terraces and partitions which might be curved or of glass create a spatial continuum subtle and complex as that of Mies.

In the competition for a League of Nations Palace (Geneva, 1927) Corbusier applied on a larger scale the lessons of the Bauhaus, expressing separate functions in separate wings yet joining all in a free sculptural unity which respected the site. His wedge-shaped auditorium, with its roof slung to give unhindered vision and parabolic to perfect the acoustics, created a new type. Though he lost the commission to the conservatives, officials and governments had been forced to study his plans and to realise that modern architecture answered real problems. The failure of the building actually erected—it ignored function and wrecked the site— made this the last major victory for traditionalism, and at last Corbusier received a few large commissions. The modernists, infuriated by defeat, formed C.I.A.M. (Congrès International d'Architecture Moderne), an organisation which did much to publicise, much to unify and something to narrow the international style.

The 'twenties created a style; the 'thirties diffused and diversified it. They began disastrously with the great slump and the rise of dictatorships which ended modern architecture in Russia and Germany during this time. But the refugees from Nazism spread their ideas, and, while the movement itself became aggressively doctrinal to combat hostility, this did not inhibit its leaders, who, coming together until the Weissenhof Exhibition, now increasingly diverged.

Corbusier's rejected plans for a Palace of the Soviets (1931) exemplified the fertility of his invention. There was to be a vast auditorium whose roof should hang from splaying girders resting at one end on posts and suspended at the other from a gigantic parabolic arch, and displayed as confidently as the buttressing of a gothic apse. His 'Swiss Pavilion' (Paris, 1932) was quite differently uncompromising. It was a square slab daringly cantilevered from massive legs, yet its staircase tower curved gracefully, while the attached communal rooms at ground level ended in a wall of irregular stone, a resounding denial of machine aesthetic. For a much larger slab (the Ministry of Education at Rio, 1936–45) he was only consultant, but here he conceived the prototype for innumerable post-war skyscrapers. In the brise-soleil, a concrete grid covering its southern flank, he invented not only a necessary corrective to the glass curtain for hot countries, but a new stylistic feature big with sculptural and decorative potential. The execution of this building by the Brazilians Costa and Niemeyer began the flourishing modern school of Latin America.

Little had occurred in England since 1900, but there were signs of reviving energies when Owen Williams erected a modern factory for Boots Ltd (Beeston, 1930–2). The arrival of refugees gave a fresh impetus. Gropius joined with Fry to design Impington College (Cambridgeshire, 1933), a freely planned school which was the beginning of British primacy in this sphere, while Lubetkin inspired two other modern buildings—'Highpoint Flats' (Highgate, 1933) and 'Finsbury Health Centre' (London, 1938).

Architecture in America was historicist or commercial; even Wright's 'Californian Houses' were inspired by Mayan temples, and were brilliant rather than modern. The 'Rockefeller Centre' (New York, 1931–40) marked an advance, for though expressionist it was planned as a group. But Europeans brought the real change. The Swiss Lescaze shaped the first skyscraper in the international style (the Saving Fund Society Building, Philadelphia, 1932), unique in America for twenty years, while the Viennese Neutra brought the same style to the domestic house (Lovell House, Los Angeles, 1927–9).

The exhibition of European achievement by the Museum of Modern Art in New York in 1932 made a great impact, not least on Wright whom it inspired to a second creative phase. His 'Usonian' houses were an adaptation of his earlier style to simplicity, standardisation and low-cost production; while his 'Falling Water' (Bear Run, 1936) magnificently combined bold international-style cantilevers in white concrete with a rough stone tower in exquisite harmony with its natural setting.

These achievements were consolidated by the arrival of Gropius and Mies. Gropius at Harvard was the greatest teacher of the new generation; while Mies, commissioned to design the campus of the Illinois Institute of Technology, was through his buildings the greatest influence on their style. His plan for the campus (1940) continues the flowing classicism of his Barcelona Pavilion; while the buildings themselves, square boxes of bricks, steel and glass, return to that surprising blend of industrialism with the Greek temple practised by Behrens, but with the expressionism left out. A style of tasteful compromise characterised Scandinavia of which the masterpiece was 'Stockholm Town Hall' (1909–23); but in 1930 Gunnar Asplund burst into full modernity with the light elegance of his 'Swedish Pavilion' (Stockholm Exhibition, 1930). 'Bella Vista Flats' (1933) marked the appearance of Arne Jacobsen in Denmark, but it was Finland who in Alvar Aalto produced a new master. In his 'Vipuri Library' (1927–35) he made the ceiling of the lecture theatre undulate to satisfy the requirements of acoustics, and thereby demonstrated even more forcibly than Corbusier how curving forms could be rational; while his 'Villa Mairea' by using curves and natural materials harmonised a modern villa with the countryside.

Mussolini's dictatorship, though hampering, was not fatal to modern architecture in Italy. Terragni's 'Casa del Popolo' (Como, 1932–6) is the perfect graft of the international grid on to the Renaissance palace. Engineers were even freer, and among them Nervi was a true architect. His 'Florence Stadium' (1930–2) has a cantilevered roof which is poised apparently on air; a feat even exceeded by the Spaniard Torroja, whose 'Madrid Grandstand' (1935) uses light curving slabs like corrugated iron to the same end. Maillart in his pavilion at the Zürich Exhibition in 1939 (which rises like a sheet of bent paper at architectural scale) demonstrated just as dramatically the constructional if not the aesthetic possibilities of shell concrete. These engineers, together with Freyssinnet, revealed how unnecessarily restrictive were the post and beam methods of the international style.

Architects are dependent upon expensive patronage which is given inadequately and late, so an epilogue is needed to reveal contemporary masters at their full stretch. Corbusier's 'Unité d'Habitation' (Marseilles, 1947–52), an assemblage of 'Citrohan' units, realises one of the self-contained blocks in his imagined cities. But its stumpy legs, fire escape, the variegated brise-soleil, above all the abstract roof garden, are powerfully sculpturesque, while the concrete is both exposed and roughened; all of these aggregate to a total rupture with the weightlessness and machine polish of his earlier style. In his chapel at Ronchamp (1950–5) he abandons even square forms, and his architectural sculpture becomes as free and irrational as that of Gaudi. At Chandigarh (Punjab, 1954–65) he planned a city, but the emphasis was no longer sociological but on individual great buildings and their mutual relations. Similarly Mies in his 'Crown Hall' of 1952 on the Illinois campus develops his industrial temple to its ultimate perfection as an enormous and undivided room; and in his 'Seagram Building' (New York, 1958) applied the precision of the Parthenon architects to the glass slab. Nervi has redeemed the promise of Berg, and Candela that of Torroja, so that the international begins to take its place among traditional styles, though its fundamentals of function, material and structure are as valid as ever.

CHAPTER XXIII

DIPLOMATIC HISTORY 1930-1939

BY the end of 1930 the precarious international order established at Versailles had begun to totter and crumble. In western Europe, the German Foreign Minister Stresemann's successors were being driven by unemployment and the rocketing growth of the Nazi party to abandon his policy of gradual revision of Versailles for a policy of adventurism from weakness. In south-east Europe and the Mediterranean, Franco-Italian amity was breaking on France's refusal to consider the Italian position on disarmament and in the Balkans. In eastern Europe, the Soviet drive for collectivisation had weakened the vital link with Germany without providing the Soviets with any alternative way out of their isolation. And in the Pacific, by the terms of the London Naval treaty of 1930, Britain and the United States had driven the extreme Japanese nationalists in the army and elsewhere to plot external adventure against China in Manchuria and internal revolution as the only alternatives to what they saw as national humiliation.

These largely political issues were linked and made more extreme by the steady spread of the economic crisis. Europe's recovery after the war and the disastrous German inflation of 1923 rested on a precarious but little-understood system of international trade which, being rigidly anchored to gold, had inadequate reserves of liquidity and was burdened with the extra task of handling the immense transfers of funds involved in the payment of reparations by Germany to the victors and of war-debts by the victor countries to the United States. A major part of the extra liquidity necessary to cover this had been provided by a high volume of short-term loans at high interest rates, mainly from the United States. Some of this capital had already begun to be repatriated for investment in the great stock market boom in the United States as early as the end of 1928. The great crash of September 1929 had caused the recall of much more. There remained a very large volume of 'hot money', which, as depression spread in the United States, itself began more and more to seek refuge in France, providing that country with reserves of confidence and financial strength which it did not hesitate to turn to political advantage during the economic crisis of 1931-2.

Germany and Austria were particularly hard hit by the financial crisis (ch. xvi). In Germany, opposition to the Young plan for the settlement of Germany's reparation obligations united industry and finance with extreme nationalism and rocketed the Nazi vote in the Reichstag elections of September 1930 to 107 seats, second only to the Social Democrats.

Failing to obtain a revision of the Young plan from Britain, France and the United States in negotiations in November–December 1930, the German government turned, in search of a diplomatic victory, to the idea of a customs union with Austria. Driven by their own economic weakness the Austrians agreed. A preliminary protocol was signed in Vienna in March 1931.

To world opinion this seemed a preliminary to that union of Germany and Austria which had been forbidden by the peace treaties. At a time when only immediate international aid could have prevented the collapse of Austria's largest bank, the Vienna *Creditanstalt*, the financial weakness of both signatories made the realisation of their plans both impossible and irrelevant to their position. As large-scale withdrawals of funds from Germany and Austria continued, Britain stepped into the breach with heavy loans to both countries. Anxiety as to the fate of the remaining American funds drove President Hoover of the United States in June 1931 to propose a year's moratorium on all war-debts and reparations payments. French desire to use Germany's weakness to force her to abandon the customs union, end her pressure for revising the Treaty of Versailles, and break her links with the Soviet Union, held up the implementation of the Hoover proposal for a vital three weeks.

During this period the run on Germany's banks spread from foreign to domestic credits. The German government sought help from both Paris and London; but France's demands were impossible for Germany to accept in the state of German domestic opinion. And, from the middle of July, the pound began to come under the same severe pressure as the Reichsmark, at a time when the Hoover moratorium prevented Britain recovering the large sums loaned to Germany, Austria and Hungary. On 24 August the Labour government in Britain split bitterly on the measures of domestic economy necessary to bolster the pound. The new National government abandoned the gold standard entirely in mid-September, announcing measures of economy which led to a mutiny in the British fleet. Deserted by Britain, the German government made a virtue of necessity and abandoned the Customs Union project on 3 September 1931, concluding that only a wide-ranging political understanding with France could secure a revision of reparations. For the moment France's policy had triumphed and the initiative lay entirely in her hands. But it was not to survive the spread of the financial crisis to France while Britain's financial position recovered. French strength was an illusion and the French use of it made her no friends for the period of weakness that followed.

The financial crisis in Britain coincided with the total breakdown of international order in the Far East. This order rested essentially on Japanese goodwill towards China and her Anglo-American sponsors. For, although the Nine Power Treaty of Washington had in 1922 bound its signatories to respect the political and territorial integrity of China, the Five Power Naval Disarmament Treaty, signed at the same conference, had, by fixing the battleship strength of America and Britain in a 5:5:3 ratio with Japan and prohibiting any fortified bases between Hawaii, Singapore and Japan, deprived the Anglo-Saxon powers of the naval power to intervene against Japanese aggression. The 'incident' in Mukden, the capital of Southern Manchuria, on the night of 19 September 1931, which led the Japanese forces in that province, ostensibly there to protect the South Manchuria Railway, to occupy all of Manchuria and proclaim it an independent state under the name of Manchukuo, was organised, in fact, by a small group of influentially placed Japanese officers. But they were reacting against a combination of Chinese nationalist pressure designed to drive the Japanese from Manchuria, Anglo-American diplomatic pressure which had imposed at London in March 1930 a second naval disarmament treaty on Japan which they regarded as nationally humiliating, and a growth in civilian power in Japan which they believed to be undoing the independent status of the armed forces under the Japanese constitution (ch. xII). Their action caused the Japanese Cabinet to resign, after it had failed to control them. And the diplomatic pressure which was organised in Washington and at the League of Nations against Japan would probably have failed on this inability of the Japanese Cabinet to control the Kwantung Army, even if lack of force and divided counsels had not rendered it even more ineffective.

This was amply demonstrated when, on 28 January 1932, the Japanese Navy answered a Chinese boycott of Japanese goods by an amphibious operation against Shanghai. The League of Nations had reacted to the Manchurian incident by dispatching an investigatory commission under Lord Lytton, a former viceroy of India. American impatience with Japanese action led Secretary Stimson of the United States on 7 January 1932 to announce the Stimson doctrine of non-recognition of changes of régime brought about by force. But, while the British government began to work for League acceptance of this doctrine, the Shanghai incident led to a misunderstanding between the two countries which was to inhibit their co-operation in the Far East for several years. His knowledge of American impotence and President Hoover's resistance to any involvement led Stimson, in a letter to Senator Borah, the Chairman of the Senate Foreign Relations Committee, to threaten abrogation of the Four and Five Power Treaties. A sense of defencelessness and a fear that public gestures would strengthen rather than defeat extremism in Japan led the British to prefer to work for an armistice in Shanghai and Japanese withdrawal. But they achieved this, on 3 April 1932, only at the cost of a total loss of American confidence in British guts and goodwill.

Neither American condemnation nor the carefully conciliatory proposals for a settlement advanced by the Lytton report in October 1932 could restrain the Japanese. Though British action at the League Assembly meeting in December 1932 prevented the smaller members from provoking a direct clash with Japan in which Britain's armed forces, crippled by ten years of financial stringency and the effects of the financial crisis of 1931, would have had to bear the brunt, the Japanese rejected all attempts at mediation by the League of Nations and on 24 January 1933 announced their withdrawal from the League.

The collapse of the projected German–Austrian Customs Union left France with the momentary leadership in central Europe. The French chose to use it not to achieve a reconciliation with Germany but to build up still further the barriers against any revision of the Treaty of Versailles. For the Danube basin the government of M. Tardieu launched, on 5 March 1932, a plan for a free trade area to unite Austria, Czechoslovakia, Hungary, Rumania and Jugoslavia, with a reconstruction loan from France, Britain, Germany and Italy to back it. Since France, with her offer of ten million pounds sterling, would have provided the bulk of the financial backing, the other three powers combined to thwart the scheme at a conference in London in April 1932. But its effect on Italy, already disturbed by France's persistent refusal to accept her claims for parity in naval armaments, was to destroy entirely the French alignment of Mussolini's foreign policy. In April Mussolini dismissed his Foreign Minister, Count Grandi, to the ambassadorship in London and took over the Foreign Ministry himself. Italian policy turned towards Germany on the disarmament issue; while in central Europe Mussolini exerted himself to capture control of Austria by subsidising the paramilitary nationalist Heimwehr organisation and supported Hungary against the Little Entente.

France was equally unsuccessful in dealing with the Soviet Union. At the height of the crisis over the Austro-German Customs Union, in August 1931, relations had improved so much as to allow the initialling of the draft of a Franco-Soviet non-aggression pact. But the French insistence on Soviet settlement with her western neighbours broke down on Rumanian obstinacy. And the Soviet authorities whose overriding aim at the moment was to preserve tranquillity on their western frontiers resented French pressure as offering them little to offset a deterioration of their relations with Germany. The prospect of a united Europe under French hegemony at the same time aroused their deep-rooted ideological fears that the capitalist world would seek a way out of the contradictions which, in their view, had created the world slump, in a crusade against the Soviet Union.

These fears were intensified by the French disarmament plan, advanced on 5 February 1932 at the opening of the World Disarmament Conference in Geneva. The Conference itself had been in gestation since the middle 1920s. But the annual sessions of its preparatory commission had produced only a draft convention on which none of its members were agreed. The new French plan demanded compulsory arbitration backed by an international police force as a preliminary to disarmament. As such it denied the German claim to equality of rights, now seen in Berlin as the only hope of the Brüning cabinet's survival against the rising tide of Nazism; faced the Soviets with the chimera of a capitalist crusade; and confronted British determination not to accept any further commitments. To the United States government it appeared to be a device to throw responsibility for the breakdown of the Conference on the known unwillingness of the United States to co-operate formally with League action against an aggressor.

While the Conference argued, the French position was steadily eroded as devaluation in Britain brought financial stability to London and drained 'hot money' away from Paris. The British delegation exerted themselves behind the scenes to bring Germany and France together; only to see this in turn torpedoed by President Hoover, driven by the exigencies of the forthcoming presidential election to make, in June 1932, an appeal for an all-round cut of one-third in treaty strengths. For the United States this only applied to ships which Congress were already unwilling to authorise. For Britain it meant reduction in forces already below the level deemed appropriate to defend her national security. For the Disarmament Conference as a whole it offered a welcome way out of the impasse which had developed between France and Germany.

This impasse, as it happened, had been played out less at Geneva than at the Conference which met in mid-June at Lausanne to attempt to solve the problem of German reparation payments after the expiry of the Hoover moratorium. Brüning's government had finally fallen at the end of May 1932. Brüning's successor, Franz von Papen, attempted to solve all Germany's difficulties at one stroke by the offer of a Customs Union, a consultative pact and military staff arrangements in return for French agreement to cancellation of reparations and equality of rights for Germany's armaments. But the scheme was too revolutionary to inspire overmuch French confidence in its offerer; and M. Herriot, the new French Premier, preferred the British offer of a consultative agreement with a secret proviso designed to preserve a common front against Germany.

Von Papen made a further approach, with equal lack of success, to the French in August 1932. Thereafter, rebuffed, he retreated into an ultra-nationalist stance, expressed in September 1932 by withdrawal from the Disarmament Conference until the German claims for equality of rights were acknowledged. At that moment such withdrawal was of symbolic significance only, as the general Conference had seized on the disruption introduced by President Hoover's intervention as an excuse to adjourn while confidential negotiations sought to restore some hope of an agreed outcome to its deliberations. The effects of von Papen's offer did not, however, end there. In eastern Europe, both Poland and the Soviet Union, feeling threatened by a Franco-German rapprochement, concluded a non-aggression pact on 25 July 1932. And Poland's example was to be followed by France herself, alarmed by von Papen's recoil into nationalism and by renewed British pressure to find a basis for Germany's return to the Disarmament Conference. On 29 November 1932 the Franco-Soviet non-aggression pact was signed in Paris. Its conclusion nerved the French to agree on 11 December 1932 to a Five Power declaration on German equality of rights 'in a system which would provide security for all nations' which made it possible for Germany to return to the Disarmament Conference. The concession came too late, however, to preserve Germany from Nazism. On 30 January 1933 Adolf Hitler, the Nazi Führer, was appointed Chancellor of Germany.

While the embodiment of *revanche* was climbing to power in Germany, the United States was turning away from Europe. The presidential election of November 1932 had returned to power a Democratic President and a Congress dominated by hostility to the notions of international financial co-operation, determined to solve America's economic and financial problems in isolation, and ambivalent in its attitudes towards European problems and the League of Nations. President Roosevelt refused to collaborate in any way with the outgoing Republican administration during the five months between his election and his inauguration at the end of March 1933. The crisis over European war-debt payments to the United States, which arose with the expiry of the Hoover moratorium on 15 December 1932, found the United States government unable to take any initiative. Britain paid her instalment with a warning that without some adjustments she anticipated a general breakdown. France defaulted; and American opinion turned more against Europe.

Worse, however, was to follow. Despite vaguely encouraging noises made by the new President to visiting statesmen (Prime Ministers MacDonald of Britain, Herriot of France, Reichsbank President Schacht of Germany), Roosevelt was to set himself against any measures of international financial stabilisation and to neglect his Secretary of State's plans for reducing the barriers to world trade. On 20 April 1933 he freed the dollar from the gold standard. And, when the World Economic Conference met in London in June 1933 to attempt to work out some measure of international financial co-operation to put an end to the panic movements of international capital which had fragmented the world's financial system into three great blocs, dollar, sterling and gold, and was shortly to drive Germany into total financial isolation in a permanent siege economy, Roosevelt chose publicly to denounce the only positive proposal to emerge from the conference in terms which made it clear that he placed domestic economic recovery above international recovery.

The collapse of the World Economic Conference was followed by increasing default on their war-debts by America's other creditors. The predominantly isolationist Congress retaliated in 1934 with the Johnson Act, which denied access to the American capital market to any foreign government in default on its war-debts. At the same time, American opinion turned more and more against Europe, reinterpreting history to make America's entry into the first world war the product of British propaganda and the machinations of American armaments and war-loans dealers, fearful of losing their investment through an Allied defeat. By 1935 the Senate had imposed on a reluctant President neutrality legislation, making it mandatory on him, in the event of an international conflict in which America was neutral, to ban the export of arms to any belligerent, whether aggressor or victim. Those powers in Europe pledged by the League Covenant to protect the international *status quo* against aggression, if necessary by military sanctions, were at one stroke debarred from access to the industries of America.

While the government and people of the United States were thus withdrawing from the reserve benches to the grandstands of the international arena, the new German Chancellor was planning a progressive unilateral dismantlement of the Peace Settlement as a preparation to launching Germany on a course of world conquest. In *Mein Kampf*, written nine years earlier in the aftermath of the French invasion of the Ruhr, he had advocated the exploitation of British and Italian fears of France. He was now to use these same countries as his tools against the Peace Settlement. Ordering the creation of an air force and the expansion of Germany's army and navy to make Germany a major military power by 1938, he began by focusing his foreign policy on a rapprochement with Poland and the union of his native Austria with his adopted Germany (ch. xvi).

But for their alarm over his Austrian policy, where he both underestimated the strength and determination of the Christian Social Chancellor, Engelbert Dolfuss, and proved unable to control the Austrian Nazis, the powers did not react very strongly at first to Hitler's advent to power. They were engaged principally in attempting to take the Disarmament Conference one stage further and restraining France's demands for security before disarmament. The Poles reacted very strongly in March 1933 to Nazi activities in Danzig, ostentatiously reinforcing their troops on the Westerplatte; but thereafter they allowed themselves to be mollified by German approaches. The belief, encouraged by Polonophil historians after 1945, that Marshal Pilsudski, Poland's dictator since 1926, had proposed to France a pre-emptive strike against Germany, would seem to be mistaken. Only the Soviets, already alarmed by Japanese pressure on their interests in Manchuria and along the Amur river, reacted positively against Hitler. In the summer of 1933, the Soviets ended the clandestine co-operation with the German Reichswehr. And Soviet diplomacy began to orient itself strongly towards France.

To the British, their intelligence on Hitler's measures clandestinely to rearm Germany was alarming; though British opinion had already accepted that some measure of German rearmament was inevitable. Hitler's speech of 17 May 1933 supporting the British disarmament plan, released to the Geneva Disarmament Conference in March 1933, was taken as proof that he could restrain his hotheads, while, to Mussolini, Hitler represented at first a welcome ally against the expansion of French influence in eastern Europe and the pro-French bloc of Little Entente countries in the League of Nations. In March 1933 Mussolini had proposed a Four Power Pact between Britain, France, Germany and Italy, with the aim of substituting a Great Power tetrarchy for the parliamentarianism of the League of Nations (which he found offensive), and of securing an agreed revision of the 1919 Peace Settlements in eastern Europe. The pact itself was concluded, in a very emasculated form, on 7 June 1933. This was followed by the Austrian crisis as Hitler stepped up radio propaganda, economic pressure on and sabotage within Austria, and Dolfuss appealed for British support against Germany and permission to increase the size of the Austrian army to 30,000 by the recruitment of a short-service militia. Britain and France issued a joint démarche in Berlin on 7 August 1933 and Mussolini assured Dolfuss of Italian military support in return for Dolfuss's strengthening his régime's anti-Socialist stance.

Common opposition to Hitler's designs in Austria was gradually to ease Franco-Italian tension. More important in the circumstances of the summer of 1933 was the effect of this German pressure on Austria, when taken with reports of German clandestine rearmament, on Anglo-French relations and the fate of the Disarmament Conference. The British Cabinet realised that their hopes of any success in this one remaining area where international co-operation still seemed to function had been much affected by Hitler's actions. For the first time France's fears for her security did not seem over-exaggerated. Sir John Simon, the British Foreign Secretary, therefore accepted a French proposal that an agreed international supervisory system should be set up and tested in practice for a period of four years before German equality of rights in the field of armaments was accepted. A British draft incorporating this revision of the MacDonald draft was therefore submitted to the Disarmament Conference in October 1933. On 14 October 1933 Hitler replied by withdrawing Germany not only from the conference but also from the League of Nations.

The combination of Japanese and German withdrawal from the League in the same year set fire to British anxieties as to the very weak state of her armed forces, especially in the light of reports of German rearmament in the air. In the winter of 1933–4 the Defence Requirements Sub-Committee of the British Committee of Imperial Defence laboured over the problems of British defence deficiencies. Their final report, given to the Cabinet in

February 1934, pinpointed the dangers to British security from Japan and Germany. The arms programme they recommended struck the British Treasury as beyond the capacity of Britain's economy, still weak from the strains of 1931, to support. With the consideration by the full Cabinet of the D.R.C. report began a debate, in which arguments of financial weakness in the face of the costs of adequate rearmament were used to urge a policy of avoidance of conflict by judicious concession, which was to persist until the winter of 1938.

The Defence Requirements Committee judged Japan the closer in time to aggression against British interests, but Germany the greater threat to them in the long run. Their report led to a serious examination of the possibilities of an understanding with Japan, seemingly more rather than less belligerent as a result of her success in Manchuria. Japanese aggressiveness was fired in the winter of 1933 by the increasing evidence of Chinese willingness to turn to Europe for aid and assistance in making herself a modern power. T. V. Soong, the Chinese Finance Minister, was active in Europe and in Washington. The number of League of Nations advisory and assistance missions to China seemed on the increase. For modernisation of her armed forces, China turned to Germany, inviting Field-Marshal von Seeckt, architect of the German army after 1919, to advise on the development of an élite army; a German military mission and Italian and American air missions were active in training the Chinese armed forces. The Japanese authorities felt again the threat to their position in the Far East that a China modernised in her military forces, economically healthy and politically united, would constitute. On 17 April 1934 Eiji Amau, spokesman of the Japanese Foreign Ministry, issued a statement claiming a special position for Japan in the maintenance of peace in the Far East and proclaiming Japanese opposition to all foreign military and economic aid to China, whether bilateral or multilateral.

The British government protested very forcefully against the Amau statement. Thereafter, however, it made strenuous efforts to persuade the United States authorities into a joint policy on naval disarmament, which would counter the more extreme nationalist elements in Japanese policy. Both the Washington and London Naval Treaties were due to expire at the end of 1936, and both Japan and France were threatening to denounce them. The prospect of a new naval arms race—twelve of Britain's fifteen capital ships were due for replacement after 1936—gave their efforts an added spur; the more so as the Cabinet apparently concluded in June 1934 that what little revenue could be spared for Britain's defence deficiencies should be spent on remedying Britain's virtually total defencelessness in the air, and that naval construction would have at the least to be postponed. They failed, however, to carry the United States with them, since the Americans were persuaded that Japan's financial strength was itself not adequate to the demands of a major naval role or the hazard of war. Japan duly denounced the naval treaties on 31 December 1934. Her encroachments into north China continued throughout the following year. The German withdrawal from the League had been rather differently viewed in London and in Paris. In their attempt to save something from the wreck the British government had turned to the idea of agreeing to legitimise German rearmament in return for some German contribution to international security. French reactions were delayed by a serious internal crisis arising from the Stavisky financial scandal and the right wing demonstrations which accompanied it (ch. xvii). The Doumergue Cabinet set up on 7 February 1934, with Louis Barthou as Foreign Secretary, leant very heavily towards the idea of containing Germany by agreements with Italy and the Soviet Union. Litvinov's preference for collective agreements led him and Barthou on 18 May 1934 to propose an Eastern Security agreement on the lines of the Treaty of Locarno to be backed by a Franco-Soviet pact of assistance. The French Cabinet had already made it clear that Britain's schemes were unacceptable when on 17 April they used the occasion of an increase in Germany's defence budget to turn down flat a German offer, elicited by British and Italian mediation, to limit her new army to three hundred thousand short-service men with only 'defensive' arms.

Germany was well armoured against the Eastern Locarno proposals by the successful culmination of Hitler's wooing of Poland in the German–Polish non-aggression pact of 26 January 1934. The Poles viewed with suspicion and hostility the French efforts to redress the European balance by calling in Soviet Russia. And, despite Barthou's efforts, undertaken under British pressure during Barthou's visit to London 9–11 July 1934, to make the proposals formally less obviously designed to control Germany and to diminish Poland's international status, both Germany, on 10 September, and Poland, on 27 September, 1934, had no difficulty in finding pretexts to reject them. The deterioration in Germany's international position in 1934 came not from the *rapprochement* between France and Russia but from her own internal crisis and from the breakdown of Hitler's Austrian policy.

Since the summer of 1933, German pressure on Austria had driven Dolfuss steadily into the arms of Mussolini, a development encouraged if anything by France and Britain, despite Dolfuss's own efforts to maintain a degree of independence. In January 1934 the Italians virtually ordered him to suppress the Austrian Social Democrats by force. The resultant military action, taken on 12–16 February, so alienated opinion in Britain and France as to make Dolfuss Italy's prisoner. On 17 February the British, French and Italian governments issued a joint declaration on the necessity of maintaining Austria's 'independence and integrity'. But the real situation was shown on 17 March, when representatives of Italy, Austria and Hungary signed the Rome Protocols, providing for joint consultation. Hungarian opposition prevented the Italians strengthening this into a Customs Union. But the result established Italy firmly in central Europe, where stability now rested on an uneasy balance between Italy's revisionist associates and France's allies in the Little Entente. A Franco-Italian break would deliver them all equally into German hands.

For the moment Hitler preferred to force the pace. Meeting with Mussolini in Venice on 15–16 June, he believed he had secured Italian support for his hopes of securing the entry of prominent Austrian Nazis into the Dolfuss Cabinet. The degree of his error was revealed in the aftermath of the putsch attempted, probably without his complete foreknowledge, by a group of Austrian S.S. on 25 July (ch. xvi). Their murder of Dolfuss not only shocked world opinion, already severely shaken by Hitler's purge of the leadership of the German S.A., together with selected former enemies and rivals, on 30 June 1934, but it provoked Mussolini to move four divisions to the Italian border with Austria—and laid the way open for direct Franco-Italian co-operation against Germany.

The main remaining obstacle to this co-operation was Yugoslav fear of Italy. Yugoslavia in fact answered the move of Italian troops to the Brenner by a similar military movement. Attempting to remove these Yugoslav anxieties, on 9 October 1934, Barthou fell victim, together with King Alexander of Yugoslavia, to assassination by Croat terrorists, formerly organised, trained and financed by Italian and Hungarian authorities.

Barthou's successor, the former Premier, Pierre Laval, continued his policy, while altering the emphasis. As between Italy and the Soviet Union he preferred Italian support. And he thought much more of conciliating than of coercing Germany. His preference thus lay more for a Europe of the Four Power Pact than a Soviet alliance. And he revived the Eastern Locarno scheme as a means of avoiding that alliance, rather than, as Barthou had designed it, as a screen for its conclusion. His amiability towards Germany led him to co-operate in a tranquil settlement of the Saar question, where, under League supervision, a plebiscite held on 13 January 1935 duly voted the territory reunited with Germany. His main effort went into the approach to Italy. On 7 January 1935, meeting Mussolini in Rome, he concluded with him a series of agreements which settled all the outstanding colonial issues between them, and recognised Italian pre-eminence in Abyssinia, while aligning the two countries in Europe in favour of a Danubian Pact against any threat to Austrian independence, and against any unilateral repudiation by Germany of the restrictions on her freedom to rearm imposed by the Treaty of Versailles. Military staff conventions, actually negotiated in June 1935, supplemented and reinforced these agreements.

Meanwhile the British Cabinet had emerged from its examination of Britain's defence deficiencies profoundly disturbed by the intelligence of Germany's clandestine rearmament, but very undecided what to do about it. Some pressed for condemnation of Germany and encouragement of Franco-Italian co-operation. But the Foreign Secretary, Sir John Simon, and his supporters still hoped to barter the legitimisation of German rearmament for a comprehensive European settlement which would satisfy British—and French—anxieties on security. Germany should rejoin the League, accept the Eastern Locarno and the declaration of February 1934 on Austria. Simon urged these ideas on Laval in Paris on 22 December 1934.

More detailed Anglo-French talks followed in London on 1–3 February 1935. The French ministers showed themselves determined not to accept the British scheme unless their own security *vis-à-vis* Germany was increased. They proposed an air convention to guarantee the signatories of Locarno against sudden air attack, which contemporary opinion believed could well prove so overwhelming in its strength as to make conventional invasion by land unnecessary. The final communiqué of 3 February 1935 outlined such a scheme to be part of a general settlement which would also include an agreed abrogation of Part v of the Treaty of Versailles. The proposal was put to the German government. But Hitler sensed in it Britain's reluctance to take any stronger action. And, when the British government sought on 4 March to justify a measure of rearmament by reference to Germany, and the French proposed to increase the period of conscript service from one to two years, Hitler seized the occasion to denounce Part v of Versailles unilaterally and to proclaim the reintroduction of conscription in Germany.

His action nearly resulted in the cancellation of the visit to Berlin planned by Sir John Simon and Anthony Eden. Despite French and Italian misgivings, however, they went ahead, holding prolonged conversations with Hitler over 25–26 March. Hitler, who had in the meantime also announced the formation of a German air force, overwhelmed the two ministers with protestations of his friendship for Britain. The only positive proposal he made, however, was of an Anglo-German agreement which would exclude naval competition between the two countries. This was of some interest to that section of British official opinion that was worried by British naval weakness and the threat from Japan. The main British reaction to the visit, however, was the increased need for Britain to mediate between France and Italy and Germany.

The need was the more urgent in that France had summoned Britain and Italy to a conference at Stresa on the German action and also appealed to the Council of the League of Nations. More importantly still Laval had been driven by his colleagues to the final stage of the Franco-Soviet negotiations. At Stresa on 11–14 April the French and Italian statesmen decided on staff agreements, concluded in May and June 1935, on military and air collaboration against German aggression in Austria or on the Rhine. All Sir John Simon could do for Britain was to prevent the final communiqué being too open in its condemnation of Germany. At the Council meeting in Geneva on 15–17 April the pattern was repeated. And on 2 May 1935 with the blessing of her allies in eastern Europe, including Rumania but not Poland, the Franco-Soviet Pact of Mutual Assistance, whose provisions would operate even without unanimous agreement in the Council of the League, was signed in Paris. A Soviet–Czech pact on similar lines, save that it only became operative *after* the invocation of the Franco-Soviet pact, was signed on 16 May in Prague.

The conclusion of the Franco-Soviet pact marked the pinnacle of French policy against Germany. But its basis was almost immediately to be destroyed by the conclusion of the Anglo-German Naval agreement of 18 June 1935, and the Italian attack on Abyssinia, which brought Italy into direct conflict with Britain and the League of Nations. Hitler's offer to discuss naval armaments with Britain fitted into the scheme Britain was evolving for a new naval treaty to replace those Japan had denounced. But, on the arrival of a German delegation in London on 5 June, led by Hitler's personal ambassador, Joachim von Ribbentrop, the Germans refused to take part in any naval talks unless the British accepted a bilateral agreement fixing German naval strength at 35 per cent of that of the British Commonwealth. The British Cabinet accepted this as something which would at least tie Hitler down in one sphere. But European opinion saw in the agreement British condonation of Germany's denunciation of Versailles. French and Italian reaction was particularly bitter.

The conclusion of the agreement coincided with a marked sharpening in Anglo-Italian relations over Abyssinia. Italian designs on Abyssinia dated back to before their defeat at Abyssinian hands at Adowa in 1896. In 1906 Britain, France and Italy had agreed to divide Abyssinia into spheres of influence, Italy obtaining the lion's share, in the event of a breakdown in Abyssinian government. During the period of Franco-Italian rivalry in Abyssinia in the 1920s, France and Germany sponsored Abyssinia's admission to the League of Nations, although Abyssinia was still an anarchic-feudal state, ridden with slavery, the writ of whose central government ran only fitfully through its territories. Britain had declared her lack of interest in the whole of Abyssinia save the headwaters of the Nile in Lake Tana, in the Anglo-Italian exchange of notes of December 1925. The Italo-Abyssinian Agreement of 2 August 1928 seemed to have given Italy the necessary springboard for establishing her economic predominance there.

By 1934, however, it was clear that the new Negus of Abyssinia, Haile Selassie, was determined to resist Italian encroachment. That same year Mussolini seems to have decided to use his central position as Austria's guarantor to secure Abyssinia and round off his East African dominions. A frontier incident at Wal-Wal, a group of wells in the undemarcated frontier areas between Italian Somaliland and Abyssinia, provided an excuse for action, the more so as Abyssinia rejected Italian protests and appealed to the League. At their meeting in Rome on 3–7 January Mussolini had secured Laval's agreement to the establishment of Italian predominance in Abyssinia; though it seems unlikely that Laval expected Mussolini to challenge the League of Nations by using force. But similar Italian efforts to secure British cognisance failed in the light of the aroused state of British opinion against Italy after Abyssinia's appeal to the League. British and French attempts to mediate between Italy and Abyssinia were similarly thwarted by exaggerated Abyssinian confidence in the ability of the League to restrain Italy.

By the middle of June 1935, the British Cabinet, reinforced in their conviction that no direct British interests were involved by the report of a commission headed by Sir John Maffey, were caught in the cross-pressures between the violently anti-Italian sentiments of British opinion, the reluctance of their diplomatic advisers to do anything which would antagonise Italy and drive her into Germany's arms, and the advice of the Chiefs of Staff that Britain's arms were hardly adequate for war with Italy and that the inevitable losses attendant on such a war might well so weaken the navy as to destroy its chances of deterring Japan from aggression in the Far East.

In June, with Eden's visit to Rome, and again in Paris in tripartite Anglo-Franco-Italian talks, the British attempted in vain to persuade the Italians to accept some kind of economic advantage in Abyssinia and to abandon their plans for military occupation. Their failure led them to accept that the Covenant of the League, especially Article xvi with its provisions for economic sanctions, would have to be invoked; but that, to be effective, and to avoid a purely bilateral conflict with Italy, Britain could go no further or faster than she could carry the French, whose military and naval co-operation in the Mediterranean was deemed essential. To rally the opinion of the smaller powers who would have little to risk and much to gain from successful League action against Italy was to prove much easier than to move the French. Sir Samuel Hoare's speech of 11 September to the Assembly of the League of Nations (he had succeeded Sir John Simon as Foreign Secretary in June) produced an illusion of world unity against aggression which Laval's reluctance to estrange France from her one ally against Germany was to deprive of any real power against Italy.

Sure of French obstructionism, Italy duly attacked Abyssinia on 3 October. The League replied by denouncing Italy as an aggressor and invoking economic sanctions against her (ch. ix). The detailed examination of the goods, export of which to Italy was to be embargoed, revealed a good deal of special pleading. Austria and Hungary refused to take part; and Soviet exports to Italy showed little variation from their normal level. The real sticking point, however, was the extension of the embargo to oil, coal and steel, a proposal on which Laval successfully postponed discussion until well into the New Year. British attempts to secure more determined French support met with French reluctance to do anything without a definite promise in return of British military aid should Germany remilitarise her Rhineland frontier with France. This gave added inducement to British attempts to evolve with Laval's aid a formula with which they could mediate between Italy and Abyssinia. The final details of such a formula were settled between Hoare and Laval in Paris on 7–8 December 1935. They envisaged the retention by Italy of most of the areas of Abyssinia then under her military occupation, and the establishment of a still wider zone in which, under League auspices, Italian economic predominance was to be linked with the economic development of Abyssinia. In return Abyssinia was to be given direct access to the sea by the cession to her of part of Italian Eritrea.

The plan, leaked to the Parisian press, raised such a storm of public denunciation both in Britain and France as to destroy its signatories. But Eden, who succeeded Sir Samuel Hoare as British Foreign Secretary, appeared to have no alternative policy other than that of waiting until the rainy season in Abyssinia ended active military hostilities and made a new mediation possible. Flandin, who succeeded Laval in France, remained as determined to resist the introduction of oil sanctions as his predecessor, while devoting even more effort to attempting to secure from Britain reinforced guarantees against German violation of Locarno. In this Flandin had no more success than had Laval. Indeed the new British Foreign Secretary, having concluded that the Rhineland was not an issue on which Britain should go to war, was once again being lured by the idea of using Hitler's alleged desire to free himself from Versailles legitimately as a means of securing a European settlement.

The idea was as ill timed as it was ill considered. During the long winter of 1935–6, Mussolini had been gradually making it plain to Hitler that he would no longer stand by France. In mid-February 1936 Hitler took preliminary soundings in Rome preparatory to the remilitarisation of the Rhineland. And on 7 March 1936 he sent small peace-time garrisons into the Rhineland towns, taking care, however, not to come too close to the frontier, accompanying his action with an offer to return to the League of Nations and to conclude non-aggression pacts with all Germany's neighbours.

The action could not have come at a worse moment for the French government. Of her east European allies only Czechoslovakia and Rumania supported her. The Yugoslavs prevaricated. The Poles offered to honour their alliance; but this only became operative if German troops crossed the French frontier, which was not the issue. The Belgian government, driven by the need to secure Flemish support for their own rearmament programme, had only the previous day given notice to terminate the

Franco-Belgian alliance. The failure of economic sanctions against Italy virtually ruled out any hope of League action against Germany. And the French army, entrenched behind the great fortifications of the Maginot Line, contemplated an inroad into the Rhineland only with the utmost reluctance.

The French government appealed to the signatories of Locarno and to the members of the Council of the League of Nations. But they appealed in vain. The refusal of the Belgian government, from a country much weaker than France whose security was equally affected by the German action, to associate themselves with the French demands greatly weakened their stance; while German diplomatic pressure was brought to bear on a number of the weaker members of the Council. The crucial role, however, was played by Britain, where opinion had been captured by Hitler's offer to return to the League and negotiate a general European settlement, and whose only available military support was tied up in the Mediterranean against Italy. Assurances were given to France and Belgium of British military assistance in the event of a German attack; and preliminary staff talks were in fact held in London on 15–17 April 1936. But the main British effort was devoted to trying to pin Hitler down to new talks on security in western Europe. The negotiations were to drag on until the end of 1937, Eden's patience being matched by the procrastination of the Germans. But in these fourteen months the whole shape of Europe had changed (cf. below, pp. 740–1).

The collapse of sanctions against Italy after the Italian entry into Addis Ababa on 6 May 1936 a month ahead of the rainy season on which Eden's hopes of a mediated settlement had been pinned, and the German success in remilitarising the Rhineland without Western molestation, were followed by a wholesale withdrawal by the smaller nations of the League from the previous systems of collective security. In the Council of the Little Entente, Rumanian leadership secured a renewed avowal of support for collective security at its Belgrade meeting on 6–7 May. But the Rumanian Foreign Minister, Nicolai Titulescu, was manœuvred out of office at the end of August and thereafter Rumania edged closer to Germany and Italy. Yugoslavia took pains to reduce the old tension in her relations with Italy and Hungary, and initiated negotiations with Bulgaria which were to lead to the conclusion of a pact of friendship in January of the following year. The Greek Premier, General Metaxas, used the meeting of the Balkan powers in Belgrade on 4–6 May to make it clear that Greece would accept no obligations outside the Balkan peninsula.

A major German trade offensive along the Danube was also not without influence on some of the Balkan states. That this offensive did not have the far-reaching effects attributed to it at the time is shown however by the case of Turkey. She took pains to secure her Mediterranean frontiers by maintaining good relations with Britain and doing what she could to improve them with Italy. Her main effort, however, was put into her more immediately Asian frontiers. In July 1936 she convened a conference at Montreux which, against bitter Soviet opposition, gave her complete freedom to refortify the Dardanelles. In September she protested bitterly at the French agreement with the nationalists of Syria, looking towards Syrian autonomy, and opened a crisis which was only ended in May 1937 after the intervention of the League Council, separating the Hatay, the partly Turkish-inhabited province of Alexandretta, from Syria and placing it under a special régime. And in July 1937 she mediated successfully between Iran and Iraq, and brought them together with Afghanistan into the so-called Oriental Entente, signed at the Shah's summer palace at Sa'dabad on 8 July 1937.

Sanctions against Italy were in fact lifted by the League on 15 July 1936. On 1 July the Foreign Ministers of the four Scandinavian countries, and of Holland, Spain and Switzerland, signed a joint declaration expressing their unreadiness to accept any future application of sanctions. The Scandinavian states were to go on to a much more far-reaching declaration at Copenhagen two years later (23 July 1938), together with Holland, Belgium and Luxemburg. Switzerland also made clear her return to the traditional tenets of neutrality.

The most far-reaching developments, however, were in Belgium and in the United States. The Belgians began by accepting staff talks with Britain. But, as it became clear that Germany had no intention of concluding a new collective treaty of guarantee with her western neighbours, the Belgian king issued on 14 October 1936 the text of a speech to the Cabinet proclaiming a new policy 'exclusively Belgian', aimed at 'placing us apart from the conflicts of our neighbours'. On 24 April 1937 the French and British governments agreed reluctantly to release her from the terms of Locarno, while reaffirming their own guarantees of Belgian integrity and on 13 October the German government followed suit.

The events of 1935–6 were watched with equal concern in the United States. The League embargo on trade with Italy was answered by an embargo on arms trade with Italy. But the administration had no power to impose a more far-reaching embargo and American trade in oil, trucks, iron and steel with Italy nearly doubled in the month of October. The Hoare–Laval proposals destroyed attempts to secure a 'moral embargo', and led the isolationist and pacifist elements to propose far more drastic neutrality legislation, leaving little or no discretion to the President. The debate raged over the years 1936–7. The final Neutrality Act of 1 May 1937 put an automatic embargo on arms sales, loans, travel on belligerent ships and arming of American ships trading with belligerents. Other exports to belligerents could be brought, at the President's discretion, under the requirement that all title to them should be transferred to the belligerent purchasing them before the goods left the United States, the so-called

'Cash-and-Carry' clause. Its effect was virtually to close the American arms industry to Britain and France, and to face the British government with the need, in any war against Germany, to finance the war on cash and not, as in 1914–18, on credit.

The most crucial effects of the events of October 1935–March 1936 were however felt by the states on Germany's south-eastern frontier, Austria and Czechoslovakia. The Italo-Abyssinian war destroyed Italy's ability and willingness to come to Austria's help. The Austrians turned briefly to Prague and Belgrade. But negotiations failed on the insistence of the Slav powers that the Austrian authorities should formally renounce any intention of restoring the Habsburgs—an infringement of Schuschnigg's monarchical plans which he was unwilling to accept. Thereafter the internal struggle for power in Austria and Mussolini's preference for an Austrian alignment with Germany rather than the western democracies drove Schuschnigg to make his peace with Germany. By the so-called 'Gentleman's Agreement' of 11 July 1936 Germany recognised Austria's independence and promised non-intervention into her internal affairs. In return Schuschnigg agreed to allow representatives of the Austrian national opposition (i.e. pro-German but not overtly Nazi) into his Cabinet, promised to conduct a foreign policy parallel to Germany's, and allowed the German press full freedom to circulate in Austria. Ostensibly a settlement, in fact the agreement amounted only to a temporary licence to survive granted by Germany to Austria. As for Czechoslovakia, she was now totally isolated in central Europe, her only protection the willingness of France to court a general European war to protect her.

The events of this crucial period had, in fact, totally shattered the international order established in the 1920s in Europe, and had revealed only too thoroughly the military and psychological inability of the principal European guarantors of that order to defend it against unilateral revision. They had revealed too that, despite the illusion of collectivity established by the Covenant of the League of Nations, the only real defence of that collectivity lay with the European great powers. The principal of those powers, Great Britain and the Soviet Union, were, however, under continuing pressure throughout the period, as a result of the earlier break of security in 1931–3 in the Far East. The year 1934, as earlier related, had seen an abortive attempt by Britain to sound out the possibilities of a new Pacific settlement—defeated by the continuing unwillingness of the United States either to accept a settlement favourable to Japan or to join Britain in setting up a barrier against further Japanese encroachments. It had also seen the elimination by Soviet Russia of any commitments in advance of her own Asiatic frontiers by the negotiation of the sale of her interests in the Chinese Eastern Railway to Japan. The final transfer of those interests was agreed in March 1935. The Russians coupled this, however, by greatly strengthening their position in Outer Mongolia and in Sinkiang. The Far

Eastern army was heavily reinforced and a policy adopted of answering any trangressions of the frontier by Japanese troops by immediate counter-attack. There was a succession of military clashes with Japanese forces throughout 1935 along the frontiers between Manchuria and Outer Mongolia. On 12 March 1936 the Soviets signed a Protocol of Mutual Assistance with the Mongolian authorities.

The main Japanese effort in 1935–6, however, was directed into China. It took two forms. From Tokyo Japanese diplomatic pressure was exerted both to attempt to exclude Western aid to China and to bring China herself into subordinate alliance with Japan. In northern China, the Kwantung army and its offshoots sought to expand Japanese influence into the five provinces of northern China. The principal Japanese weapon was presented to them quite gratuitously by the United States, where, under the pressure of senators from the mountain states, legislation was adopted in August 1934 to raise the dollar price of silver. The effect was to drain China steadily of the silver which was essential to back her currency. In October 1934 the Chinese government attempted to end the export of silver by imposing a massive export duty on it; but the only effect was an immense increase in smuggling, at once seized on and encouraged by the Japanese as a weapon of economic pressure both against the Chinese government and against Western, mainly British, economic and financial interests in China. Under the threat of an imminent collapse of their currency the Chinese appealed both to Britain and to the United States for financial assistance. The United States was unwilling either to intervene or to modify their silver legislation. The British hoped still to maintain the *status quo* in the Far East in view of the increasing threats in Europe. They were, however, again unable to carry the United States with them, and swung therefore gradually towards a more outspoken criticism of Japanese actions which they backed by dispatching Sir Frederick Leith-Ross, principal Economic Adviser to the Cabinet, to China to advise on currency reform.

In the meantime Japanese diplomatic pressure was expressed in a series of negotiations carried out throughout the year with Chiang Kai-Shek and the Chinese Premier, Wang Ching-Wei. Wang was inclined to favour agreement with Japan on any terms, but the publication in October 1935 by the Japanese Premier, Hirota, of his 'Three Principles' for a settlement, when taken with the activities of the Kwantung army in north China, caused a great surge of popular anti-Japanese feeling such as to render any settlement with Japan on these terms a political impossibility. The 'Three Principles' were: an anti-Communist alliance; the abandon-ment of attempts to play off one foreign nation against another; economic 'collaboration' in terms heavily weighted in Japan's favour. These terms, first advanced early in May 1935, were not, however, far-reaching enough for the Kwantung army, which in May 1935 began a series of operations in

Jehol, Hopei and Inner Mongolia designed to withdraw these provinces completely from control by Peking and turn them into Japanese satellites. The Ho–Umetsu agreement of 6 July 1935 established what they wanted in Jehol. In November 1935 the establishment of the Hopei–Chahar Political Council gave them what they wanted in these two provinces.

The Leith-Ross mission attained nothing so far as the Japanese were concerned. But it did help the Chinese to solve some of their economic problems by nationalising silver in November 1935. American agreement to the purchase of fifty million ounces of silver the same month was of further assistance in establishing a new basis for China's currency. Shortly thereafter the price of silver in the United States returned to its normal level. Encouraged by this the Chinese, with British advice, adjusted the existing terms to British bond holders on to a much easier basis and embarked on an ambitious programme of railway and industrial expansion in which British, French and German firms participated on a bilateral basis; and in April 1936 Chiang concluded an extensive arms agreement with Germany in which raw materials were bartered against extensive arms deliveries.

The Japanese reaction to all these developments was extreme. On the one hand the Japanese army opened negotiations secretly with von Ribbentrop as Hitler's representative for an agreement to combat the Soviets. On the other hand the internal struggle broke out in February 1936 into a mutiny by one faction of the army and an attempted *coup d'état* in Tokyo. Its defeat, paradoxically, greatly enhanced the political strength of the rival faction—so much so that the Japanese Foreign Ministry was overruled, and negotiations with Germany for the Anti-Comintern Pact were renewed. One aim was to secure a diminution of German aid to China. More important, however, was to secure Japan's northern frontiers with the Soviet Union so as to make possible a more vigorous drive into China and the South Seas. The 'Basic Principles of National Policy' adopted by the Japanese Cabinet on 11 August 1936, despite a certain genuflexion to the need to maintain friendly relations and to attain her aims by peaceful means, made it clear that the 'Imperial Way' to be followed by Japan was one of 'overseas expansion' and the establishment of the nation as the 'stabilising power' in East Asia.

The Anti-Comintern Pact was signed in Berlin on 25 November 1936. Its public terms spoke entirely of joint agreement to combat international Communism, and invited the participation of other states. A secret protocol signed on 24 October bound the signatories to support each other diplomatically, though not militarily, if either were involved in war with the Soviet Union. Its terms were immediately known, through intelligence channels, to the Soviet Union and to Britain. And the subsequent efforts of the Japanese Foreign Office to exploit it diplomatically by negotiating a *rapprochement* with Britain were watched with as much alarm in Moscow as they were greeted with suspicion in London. The various commissions, etc., set up by the pact never functioned, its importance being mainly symbolic and the use made of it by the two signatories mainly propagandistic. In Germany it was the work of von Ribbentrop, rather than the Foreign Ministry, who found much more importance in the negotiation of the agreements of 21 October 1936 with Italy, which marked the formation of the Axis.

The driving force in the negotiations which led to the signature of the German–Italian agreements in October 1936 and to Mussolini's speech of 2 November proclaiming the Axis was provided by Italy rather than by Germany. Italy had greeted the end of sanctions with a good deal of suspicion; and Mussolini and his entourage were inclined to use the *de jure* recognition of Italy's conquest in Abyssinia and of the king of Italy as the real yardstick by which they judged the goodwill of those states which had so lately been applying sanctions against them. Mussolini had, in fact, emerged from the conquest of Abyssinia convinced of British hostility towards him and of the need for closer relations with Germany. In time, these convictions might have subsided—there were after all plenty of potential causes of German–Italian friction, especially over Germany's new trade drive in the Balkans and in German relations with Yugoslavia. But the election of a government of the Centre and Left in France in June 1936 under the leadership of M. Blum the French Socialist (the so-called 'Popular Front' government), and still more the outbreak of civil war in Spain on 15 July 1936, provided him with a completely new set of reasons for cleaving to Germany.

In its origins the revolt of the Spanish generals on 15 July 1936 against the Centre–Left government elected in January 1936 sprang from purely Spanish causes. There is little or no evidence of prior knowledge of the generals' plans by either Germany or Italy (although Italian arms had been being given to Spanish right-wing groups under an agreement concluded in 1934). But, once their revolt had failed to overturn the Spanish government in the way military *pronunciamentos* had so often overturned Spanish governments in the past, the Spanish military leadership used every available channel to appeal to Italy and Germany for arms; and, within a fortnight of the outbreak of the civil war, Italian and German arms and aircraft were flooding into the Spanish military strongholds in Majorca and in Morocco.

In its turn the Spanish government appealed for military aid to France. The Blum government was deeply divided, and the British advice, given to Blum when he visited London at the end of July, at best was hostile to the Spanish government. British conservative opinion had been bitterly shocked by the anti-clerical excesses and the massacres of nationalists in government-held territory; and the British government dreaded the danger of yet another European war springing from Spanish causes, as had the war of 1870-1. Delbos, Blum's Foreign Minister, found a way out of the dilemma by proposing an agreement between the European powers not to intervene in Spain with arms supplies, financial support or volunteers. The proposal, accepted by all the powers by the end of August 1936, led in turn to the proposal of an international committee to supervise the agreement. But by the date of its first meeting on 9 September 1936 it was clear that the agreement was not being honoured. Portugal, Germany and Italy were pouring arms into Spain in support of the Spanish nationalists; and early in September the first cargoes of Soviet arms and advisers began to reach the Spanish government forces. At the same time, Comintern agents began to take hold of the small groups of non-Spanish volunteers fighting with the Spanish government forces, to build out of them the International Brigade. As the Spanish nationalist forces were beaten off in their first assault on Madrid, so Germany and Italy in turn sent military units, euphemistically described as 'volunteers', to supplement and spearhead the nationalist attack on the capital, and on the Basque republic in the north. For the next eighteen months, European diplomacy was dominated by the issues arising from the war in Spain.

German motives in this were quite clear. Initially, their main motives were economic: the lure of Spanish copper and other mineral resources. From that, Hitler developed the hope of a Franco-Italian war in the Mediterranean which would enable him to settle accounts with Austria and Czechoslovakia. German military involvement in Spain was thus strictly limited to armour and aircraft, German military strategists profiting by the opportunity to try out the *Blitzkrieg* tactics they had been evolving in staff studies since the late 1920s. Soviet motives are more obscure. The civil war in Spain was immensely useful to them as a means of building up support in France for an anti-fascist front, and they got a certain amount of propaganda value out of it in Britain. They attempted to transform the Non-Intervention Committee into an instrument of collective security. And, just as Hitler hoped to use the war to embroil France with Italy, so they very well may have hoped to use the war to embroil Britain and France with Germany, and divert Germany's military effort westwards.

The Russians were well informed as to the progress of German–Japanese negotiations. And it was in this period that the great purges of Stalin's opponents began, purges which in the following year were to strip the Soviet military leadership of all but a minute percentage of its senior members and affect in all between 30 and 40 per cent of the entire Soviet officer corps. The result was to destroy the image of Soviet military power in Europe's eyes and to remove any possible alternative source of leadership in the Soviet Union apart from that of Stalin himself. It is significant therefore that it was in this period, November 1936–February 1937, that Stalin chose to approach Hitler through the medium of David

Kandelaki, a fellow-Georgian, the head of the Soviet trade mission in Berlin, to propose a German–Soviet understanding. The approach was rejected with the comment that such negotiations would be possible in the future if Russia developed into an absolute despotism based on the military —an ominous foreshadowing of the Nazi–Soviet pact of August 1939.

For the British and French governments the main motive in the policy they followed in the Non-Intervention Committee was to attempt to manœuvre Germany and Italy into withdrawal from Spain, as a preliminary to yet another attempt to negotiate a European settlement. As the war progressed, and Italian support of General Franco, the nationalist leader, became more outrageously overt, so their own counsels became more divided, Anthony Eden and successive French governments being driven into a progressively more anti-Italian stance, while other elements, most notably Neville Chamberlain, who became Prime Minister in Britain at the end of May 1937, were driven to ignore Spain entirely in their efforts to obtain an opening for new negotiations.

The Italian régime, by contrast, never seems thoroughly to have thought out its reasons for intervening in Spain. Possibly Mussolini genuinely believed his own propaganda, seeing himself the champion against a would-be Soviet take-over in Spain. His efforts were so thwarted that Italian aid to the Spanish nationalists gradually escalated until, especially after the Italian defeat at Guadalajara in March 1937, withdrawal would have been synonymous with defeat. Yet for Italy the Spanish adventure was disastrous. Unpopular at home, it set Italy against Britain and France, and drove her willy-nilly into Germany's arms, while Germany steadily took over her economic and political position in the Danube basin. In the economic sphere it drained Italy of arms and money, and prevented any recovery from the effects of sanctions. Spain converted Mussolini from Hitler's equal into his satellite.

Italy's relations with Germany at least until the end of 1937 were made continuously uneasy by the fears of an Anglo-German *entente*. Not only did this govern the negotiations which led up to Count Ciano's visit to Berlin in October 1936—the protocols then signed largely represented Italian attempts to tie Germany down on issues such as relations with the League of Nations, and on the negotiations for a security pact in western Europe, where the Italians feared lest Germany's desire for good relations with Britain might lead Germany to accept proposals which would leave Italy isolated. Even thereafter, the Italians found that they were forced to moderate their own policy towards Britain in accordance with German moves.

Their position was rendered the more difficult by the waiting game Hitler was playing. In the summer of 1936 he launched a new rearmament programme, the Four-Year Plan, designed to make Germany more self-sufficient and to put her in a position to risk major war in Europe by 1940.

In his relations with Britain he seemed, from his defence of his British policy to Ciano in October 1936, still to have hoped to secure British agreement to German hegemony in Europe by beating the anti-Comintern drum. But the yardstick he selected during 1936–7 by which to test Britain's readiness to fall in with his plans was that of British willingness to discuss the return to Germany of her former colonies. And on this Britain was in no position to meet his demands, even had there been any real support for the idea in Britain, since German South West Africa was under South African control, and Australia had taken over the German position in New Guinea. During his colonial propaganda campaign he came to overestimate the fissiparous forces in the British Empire; and by the end of 1937 he had apparently concluded that Britain was to be counted permanently among his enemies. In the summer of 1937 the new orders issued to the German armed forces for the first time envisaged the possibility of war with Britain. The marked solidarity of Anglo-French relations under Eden and Delbos presumably strengthened him in this view. And there is a good deal of evidence to suggest that he regarded the crisis which led to the abdication of Edward VIII, subsequently duke of Windsor, in the winter of 1936–7, as the planned removal by the Conservative leadership of a Germanophil monarch.

It is one of the many paradoxes and misunderstandings that led to the outbreak of war between Germany and Britain in 1939 that Hitler's change in attitude towards Britain developed *pari passu* with the advent to power in Britain of a man more determined to re-establish good relations with Germany, if that were possible, than any of his predecessors. Neville Chamberlain, the new British Prime Minister, was not the naïve pacifist his enemies depicted. He always regarded Germany as a disturbing, disruptive force. But he believed that it was essential to try to come to a settlement in Europe if that were possible; and he was very impatient of the formal obstacles placed in the way of such a settlement by the existing treaty structure. From a strong supporter of collective action and sanctions in 1935, he had by 1937 become a convinced advocate of bilateral negotiation on the detailed removal of grievances between the major powers.

He was impelled in these views by four main sets of considerations. The Imperial Conference, which met in May 1937, revealed that the British dominions were generally opposed to British involvement in a European war. Treasury investigations, set on foot while he was still Chancellor of the Exchequer, showed that Britain could not afford to *attain* the level of armaments deemed necessary to enable her to contain Germany in Europe, Italy in the Mediterranean and Japan in the Far East, nor *maintain* the level of armaments deemed necessary to enable her to contain Germany and Japan, once that level were attained—at least not without permanently weakening the British economy. Chamberlain believed Japan to be genuinely unappeasable; and he had little real confidence in American willingness or ability to restrain Japan in China. Lastly, he was convinced, not altogether wrongly, that a second war would be disastrous for European civilisation, and that some kind of co-existence should be possible once Germany's and Italy's legitimate grievances had been satisfied.

His advent to power was marked by three developments: the dispatch of a new Ambassador to Berlin, Sir Nevile Henderson, with instructions to do his utmost to improve Anglo-German relations; the invitation to the German Foreign Minister, Baron von Neurath, to visit London; and the initiation of direct contacts with Italy to end Anglo-Italian tension. The first of these was disastrous; and a crisis in the Non-Intervention Committee enabled Baron von Neurath to evade the British invitation. Nevertheless the news of the invitation was enough to drive the Italians to take up, momentarily, the idea of Anglo-Italian talks. Their action began a series of contacts which was eventually to lead to the resignation of the British Foreign Secretary, Eden, and the establishment of Chamberlain's policy and personality as dominant over all other trends of thought within his Cabinet and party.

After the abandonment of sanctions against Italy in July 1936, Eden had devoted a good deal of effort to re-establishing good relations. Once the establishment of the Axis had removed Italian fears of isolation, Mussolini had welcomed these moves and had concluded on 2 January 1937 the so-called Anglo-Italian 'Gentleman's Agreement' on the *status quo* in the Mediterranean. His secret dispatch of large contingents of Italian 'volunteers' to Spain both before and after the signature of the Agreement was taken by Eden as evidence of Italian deceit. From February to June 1937 Anglo-Italian relations steadily deteriorated. Mussolini's exploitation of the Arab revolt in Palestine, with propaganda, money and arms deliveries, greatly exacerbated this process. In July Italian fears of a new Anglo-German *rapprochement* led to an exchange of letters between Chamberlain and Mussolini; and an agreement to begin talks on a settlement. But Italian submarine attacks on ships bound for Spanish ports, which escalated at the end of August to the sinking of a British merchant ship, the S.S. *Woodford*, and an attack on a British destroyer, H.M.S. *Havock*, caused their suspension.

Instead Eden called an international conference at Nyon. The French, who had originally proposed such a conference, supported him; and the conference set up a system of international naval patrols in the Mediterranean with orders to sink any unidentified submarine encountered, the lion's share of the patrolling being taken by British and French naval units. Italian submarine activity was hastily suspended. Mussolini retaliated, however, with a major military concentration in Libya, where his troops could move with equal ease against the British in Egypt or the French in Tunisia. And, while he was careful to reassure Britain and France of his willingness to resume talks, he was much more concerned to obtain reassurance in his turn from Hitler. His visit to Berlin at the end of September 1937 he had originally proposed as a central European conference, including representatives of Poland, Austria, Hungary and Yugoslavia. But Hitler was able to avoid the commitments which might have emerged from such a meeting by playing on Mussolini's vanity. The meeting of the two dictators took place, as a result, with little or no political conversation. Mussolini returned to Rome, more enthralled with Hitler's personality, but no stronger either in central Europe or in the Mediterranean.

At the end of October 1937, then, the European position was as follows: the Soviet Union was plunged in the nightmare of Stalin's purges—nominally allied to France and Czechoslovakia though there were no military agreements to give the alliance teeth, doing her best in Spain and at the League of Nations to embroil Britain and France with the Axis. In central Europe, Czechoslovakia confronted Germany in isolation. Her allies in the Little Entente had made their peace with the Axis powers—her enemies, Poland and Hungary, had abated none of their enmity. Italy and Germany were tied by an Axis, in which Germany was increasingly the stronger partner, Italy apparently on a collision course with Britain and France over Spain. The Scandinavian powers, Switzerland and Belgium had retreated into neutrality. Britain and France were holding closely together; but economic weakness was hampering their rearmament efforts and, in France, the enemies of the government were becoming increasingly pro-fascist. And in the Far East Japan was now engaged in full-scale hostilities against China.

From the Japanese point of view, their situation in China had deteriorated markedly since the summer of 1936 despite the conclusion of the Anti-Comintern Pact. The most alarming development had been the conclusion of a truce between the Chinese nationalist government and the Communists after the kidnapping of Chiang Kai-Shek by dissident Chinese troops in December 1936. The basis of the truce was to be the organisation of a common anti-Japanese front. While negotiations for such a front were in progress, the Soviet authorities, who seem to have had no hand in either the kidnapping or the negotiations between Chiang and the Communists, proposed, in April 1937, a Soviet-Chinese mutual assistance pact. Their main motive seems to have been anxiety over the Japanese approaches to Britain mentioned earlier which continued until June 1937. But a contributory factor may well have been their own military weakness in consequence of the continuing military purges; although the full weight of these was not felt in the Soviet Far Eastern forces until the winter of 1937-8, an incident between Japanese and Soviet forces on the Amur river in June 1937 had already led the Japanese military to write off the Soviet Far Eastern army as demoralised by the purges.

On 7 July 1937 fighting broke out between Japanese and Chinese forces near the Marco Polo bridge in northern China. Local negotiations failed and the incident, which, unlike that at Mukden in September 1931, does not seem to have been planned on either side, escalated until the two nations were locked in full-scale war. It was not to end until the Japanese surrender, under the American atomic bombing, in August 1945. Overconfidence and a great wave of anti-Japanese feeling in China was answered by an increase of army strength and extreme nationalism in Japan beyond the power of the more moderate political elements to control. Peking fell to Japanese forces at the end of July and on 13 August fighting spread to Shanghai. On 13 September the Chinese government appealed to the League of Nations.

The Chinese appeal raised again the question of League sanctions, and of the difficulty of organising pressure on Japan without prior agreement with the United States, a difficulty felt most acutely by Britain and France. But, whereas in 1931–2 this situation had led to Anglo-French differences and to Britain appearing to act as a brake on American initiative, British anxieties over Shanghai and the confidence engendered by the close Anglo-French co-operation in the Mediterranean now led Britain to be the initiator, while the United States, led by Secretary of State Hull and Roosevelt himself, supplied a very effective brake.

The first British approach to Washington was made shortly after the initial Sino-Japanese incident. The proposal for a joint offer of 'good services' was rejected, Hull professing to prefer parallel rather than joint action, and seeing in the fighting an occasion for continuing the moral education of the world against the use of force rather than for joint action to prevent it. The prospect of the League invoking Article XVI against Japan, however, led Britain to ignore this rebuff and invoke the Washington Nine Power Treaty of 1922. A conference of its signatories and other powers duly met in Brussels at the beginning of November.

Before the conference could meet, however, President Roosevelt had succeeded in confusing its members entirely by a speech, delivered at Chicago on 5 October 1937, calling for a 'quarantine' of aggressor states. His ideas seem to have developed from the plan for common American neutrality advanced by the American delegation at the Inter-American Conference at Buenos Aires the preceding December; and, from his subsequent reactions to Japanese acts against American interests in China, the proposal seems to have marked a stage in his gradual movement towards the idea of common economic action against states committing aggression. As an idea it was hardly adequately developed enough to warrant the intense international and national interest it aroused. Never was Roosevelt's habit of thinking out loud so disastrously demonstrated; since it led Eden to devote himself over the next three months to the chimera of joint Anglo-American action against Japan. His failure did

710

much to discredit his policy and to confirm Chamberlain in his search for bilateral agreements with Germany and Italy for the removal of their 'legitimate' grievances.

The American delegation arrived at Brussels without any plan of action save that of inviting Japan to attend the conference. The smaller powers at once made clear their determination to avoid any scheme for economic sanctions against Japan. And, when Japan's refusal to send a delegation to Brussels became clear, the American delegation's attempt to discuss co-operation with Britain and France, both of whom wanted united action against Japan, was angrily repudiated by the State Department and Roosevelt in their anxiety that the United States would be manœuvred into being either the spearhead of action or the scapegoat for inaction. The conference therefore adjourned on 24 November after issuing a communiqué in which only Hull could find any satisfaction.

In the meantime the military situation in China had deteriorated very markedly. In September and again early in November the Japanese government had offered Chiang Kai-Shek through German good offices terms which would have confirmed Chinese government in north China and withdrawn the Japanese forces from north China in return for an end of anti-Japanese activity in China, a common Sino-Japanese front against Communism and the re-establishment of *de facto* relations between China and Manchukuo. But, just as a desire to forestall any positive action by the League or the Brussels conference played its part in inspiring the comparative moderation of those terms, so the false hopes these aroused in the Chinese made them unacceptable. In the first week of December, Japanese troops entered Nanking and by the end of the year virtually the whole of China's coast line lay under Japanese control. The collapse of her hopes of Brussels now led China to indicate her willingness to accept Japan's terms at precisely the moment when their military victories had enabled the hotheads of the Japanese army to overcome the civilian Cabinet's predilection for negotiations. On 14 January 1938 the Japanese broke off all negotiations and all relations with the Chiang government and announced their intention of moving towards the setting-up of a new Chinese government with which it could collaborate.

Their action coincided with the temporary abandonment by the British government of any attempt to enlist American support against Japan. On 27 November and again on 13 December, after Japanese aircraft had sunk the U.S.S. *Panay*, an American gunboat on the Yangtse-Kiang, and attacked H.M.S. *Ladybird*, a British gunboat which was accompanying her, the British had proposed a joint Anglo-American naval demonstration, only to be rebuffed. The full news of the *Panay* incident which reached Washington only after the rebuff of the second British approach led some elements in Roosevelt's administration, notably Henry Morgenthau, the Secretary of the Treasury, to propose joint Anglo-American economic action; but the British in their turn refused to accept anything except political and military agreement. In January 1938 an American naval officer, Captain Ingersoll, visited London and concluded an 'informal agreement' on the course to be followed should Britain and America be involved in war with Japan. But the plan was so tentative and long term that the British authorities in fact dropped a third proposal for joint action to prevent Japan taking over the administration of the Chinese Maritime Customs, preferring to negotiate directly with Japan on a bilateral basis instead.

In Washington, the continuing debate on how best to oppose Japan led Roosevelt on 11 January 1938 to address a message to London proposing that he should call an international conference to reach agreement on the essential principles to be observed in the conduct of international relations, including reduction of armaments, equal access to raw materials and the laws of war. The proposal struck Neville Chamberlain, temporarily in control of the British Foreign Office in Eden's absence on holiday, as both unreal and likely to interfere with the progress of his negotiations for the appeasement of Germany and Italy. Eden's belated opposition secured a withdrawal of his original reply requesting Roosevelt to stay his hand. But Roosevelt by now had had second thoughts, prompted by Chamberlain's indication that *de jure* recognition of the Italian conquest of Abyssinia was under consideration, and did not return to the charge. Eden's position was the more weakened and Chamberlain's the more confirmed in his drive for a settlement with the dictators.

This drive had only been reinforced by events in the Far East, and by the outcome of the long examination of Britain's rearmament effort which was concluded early in 1938. The ever-increasing costs even of those measures which were already agreed on had led the British Cabinet at the end of 1937 to limit Britain's defence effort only to the defence of British territory at home and overseas and the protection of her trade routes, leaving co-operation in the defence of the territory of her allies as something probably beyond Britain's financial strength. This decision was reinforced by the categorical statement by the British Chiefs of Staff, reiterated early in February 1938, that Britain's forces could not face a major war in 1938 and were inadequate to meet her existing defence commitments. It was essential therefore to explore every means of reducing the number of Britain's potential enemies.

By the autumn of 1937 Chamberlain himself seemed to have become increasingly discontented with the slow tempo of the Foreign Office's approaches to Germany and Italy, as with the ease with which events in Spain or the Mediterranean had been allowed to disrupt the approaches planned to Germany in June 1937 and to Italy in July and October. Eden's emphasis on the need to move *pari passu* with the French he found equally burdensome. German propaganda for a return of her colonies had awakened yet again the idea of legitimising Germany's demands as part of a general settlement which had so weakened Britain's policy towards Germany after her withdrawal from the League of Nations and in the months preceding the reoccupation of the Rhineland. A German invitation to Lord Halifax, Chamberlain's closest associate in the Cabinet, issued in October 1937 was eagerly seized on. Halifax visited Berlin and Berchtesgaden in November 1937, holding a long conversation with Hitler in which he outlined Britain's willingness to support a change in the *status quo* in central Europe providing this was achieved without the use of force. The German failure to react to this move left Chamberlain only the more convinced of the need to pursue the matter more actively.

The British move was the more important in that, by the end of 1937, no French government had any alternative, short of an outright surrender to Germany, of following wherever Britain led. If Britain was on the whole isolationist where central European affairs were concerned, and beguiled by the prospect of a settlement, France was so bitterly divided that an independent anti-German policy was almost inconceivable. If Britain's rearmament effort was flagging, and the Treasury determined not to allow it to weaken her financial recovery, the French effort was pitiable, hamstrung by trade union agitation for better working conditions, and the French franc was in a state of almost continuous decline. Chautemps and Delbos, who came to London at the end of November 1937 for talks with Chamberlain and Eden, viewed Chamberlain's policy with scepticism shading into outright distrust. But they were unable to gainsay his proposals. And Delbos's subsequent tour of France's allies in eastern Europe only underlined the total isolation of Czechoslovakia from Poland as from her former associates in the Little Entente. This isolation was underlined in January 1938 by Molotov's bitter criticism of France in the final session of the Supreme Soviet, and by the Soviet closure of all but a handful of the foreign consulates in Russia, steps which underlined Russia's retreat into a new isolationism.

Hitler's uncanny gift for sensing the weaknesses of his opponents had already shown him the way ahead (ch. xvi). On 5 November 1937 he had used the occasion of a meeting of his senior service commanders, ostensibly called to settle the disputed question of priorities in German steel production, to outline his readiness, so soon as international conditions permitted, to strike at Austria and Czechoslovakia. A Franco-Italian war in the Mediterranean or the spread of civil war to France seemed the most likely alternatives. Otherwise he was prepared to wait until Germany's armament drive had sufficiently outdistanced those of Britain and France, whom he characterised as hate-crazed opponents of Germany. Halifax's offer to help him to meet his demands in central Europe as a kind of silver medal for good behaviour he did not find attractive. In December 1937 the standing orders for the German armed forces were revised so as to put the main planning emphasis on war with France and Czecho-slovakia, with the main German drive against the Czech defences. And early in February 1938 he reorganised the command structure of the armed forces so as to put the main command in his own hands. The Defence Minister and the Chief of Staff were forced out of office. Baron von Neurath, the Foreign Minister, was elevated to the chairmanship of a Reich Council that was never to meet, and his creature, von Ribbentrop, rescued from the failure of his embassy in London, was made head of a thoroughly purged Foreign Ministry. Yet as so often in these years Hitler's own actions precipitated events and brought upon him the crises he sought in a manner quite unlike that he had planned for.

The first crisis burst over Austria just as his purge was being completed. It arose originally from the resentment of the Austrian Nazi party at the manner in which, since the Austro-German agreement of 1936, it had been neglected by Germany in favour of the policy recommended by von Papen of working to infiltrate into the Austrian government representatives of the much more respectable crypto-Nazi 'National Opposition'. This resentment led to a plot for a new *coup d'état* against the Austrian government, the plans for which fell into the hands of the Austrian police when the party offices in Vienna were raided on 22 January 1938. This capture gave Schuschnigg the confidence to accept the invitation to meet Hitler which von Papen had so long been pressing on him. And it was his acceptance in turn which enabled von Papen to escape Hitler's purge and fix 12 February as the date for the meeting. Schuschnigg's hope was that he could also reach a settlement with the 'National Opposition' before that date; but, failing to realise that they were hand-in-glove with Berlin, he failed to realise that he was destroying any chance of his resisting Hitler's pressure in advance.

At his meeting at Berchtesgaden on 12 February he found himself confronted with demands much greater than he was prepared to concede, to be met within a week, and confronted too with a great parade of military force. Back in Vienna he seems to have decided that his only chance of resistance was a carefully prepared nation-wide plebiscite in favour of Austrian independence. No support was likely from Britain or France; and Italy, while prepared to use the crisis to force Britain to negotiate with her on a Mediterranean settlement, was not prepared to support Austria against Germany. Chamberlain forced Eden's resignation on the issue of opening negotiations with Italy after a meeting with Grandi, the Italian ambassador in London, on 19 February. But, when news of Schuschnigg's intention leaked out on 8 March, Mussolini advised him against it.

Schuschnigg's plan threatened the downfall of Hitler's whole Austrian policy. On 10 March therefore he ordered military preparations for the immediate invasion of Austria and demanded the cancellation of the plebiscite. This granted, on 11 March, he followed it by demanding Schuschnigg's resignation and his replacement by the leader of the 'National Opposition', the German stooge, Artur Seyss-Inquart. Actual invasion by German troops was as unwelcome to Seyss-Inquart as it was to the Austrian Nazis and the Austrian government. But the refusal of the Austrian President to appoint Seyss-Inquart and Hitler's discovery that Italy would not intervene cleared the way for direct invasion. On 12 March German troops crossed the frontier. The next day in his old home town of Linz Hitler proclaimed the union of Austria with Germany.

The successful annexation of Austria marks the opening of a new and much more reckless phase in Hitler's foreign policy, and one in which international events were to be wholly dominated by his actions (ch. XVI). Strategically it turned the flank of the Czech fortress system, leaving all Bohemia thrust like a peninsula into German-controlled territory. Almost unanimously, Europe's governments assumed that Hitler's next target would be the union of the three million Sudeten Germans into his Reich. That this was for him only a preliminary, or rather an excuse for the destruction and absorption of the Czech state, they were not yet ready to believe. The slogan of self-determination and revision of Versailles blinded them to Hitler's real aims as to his hatred of the Czechs and their state.

The origins of the Sudeten German problem went back to the rise of Czech nationalism in the nineteenth century and its national identification with the old crownlands of the Habsburg empire, Bohemia and Moravia. In 1918 the Sudeten Germans had proclaimed their union with Germany, only to find their movement suppressed by Czech military action and themselves incorporated into the new Czechoslovak state by the Treaty of Versailles. During the 1920s the main political parties among the Sudeten Germans had collaborated with the Czech state, entering into the Agrarian Coalition government in 1926. Only the extreme nationalists, among whom a small Nazi party was to be found, had opposed them. Economic grievances in the years of the world economic depression and the rise to power of Hitler in Germany led in 1933 to so great an accretion of Nazi strength that the party was dissolved by Czech police action. The German Foreign Ministry took the opportunity to encourage the emergence of a new political movement under a young youth leader, Konrad Henlein. With secret financial support from the ministry his party, the *Sudetendeutsche Partei* (SdP), won 44 out of the 66 German seats in the Czech elections of April 1935, making them the second largest party in the Czech parliament. Thereafter Henlein had concentrated on winning sympathy abroad, especially in Britain, for his party and claims against the Czech state; in which he had been remarkably successful. The flat contradiction between the forcible incorporation of three million Germans into Czechoslovakia and the slogan of national self-determination had always pricked the Anglo-Saxon conscience; and the slavishness with which Czechoslovakia had followed the French line at the League of Nations in the 1920s had not won her any goodwill in British government circles. Already in November 1937, Chamberlain had made it clear to Chautemps and Delbos that British opinion would not support involvement in a war with Germany over Czechoslovakia.

The Anschluss was therefore followed immediately by discussions both in London and in Paris on the Czechoslovak question. In Paris, a new government headed by Blum, but retaining Delbos as Foreign Secretary, took office on 13 March. On 15 March, at a meeting of the *Comité de la Défense Nationale*, they heard General Gamelin tell them that the French army was unready for war, and that the prospects of its being able to help Czech resistance against a German attack were viewed very pessimistically. Blum and Delbos refused to accept this; but renewed diplomatic soundings in eastern Europe revealed Czechoslovakia still to be totally isolated. On 8 April the Blum government fell. Edouard Daladier, a man of more rhetoric than understanding or determination, became Premier, Georges Bonnet, a devious and pacific-minded schemer, Foreign Minister.

In London the Chiefs of Staff were, if anything, more pessimistic. Britain, they advised, could not prevent Germany overrunning Czechoslovakia. To enter a war with Germany would be to embark on a long struggle in which Italy and Japan could be expected to intervene at their own chosen moment. They could not foresee a time when, even with the aid of France and her allies, Britain could withstand such a triple attack. In 1938 Britain was definitely not ready for war, and to embark on war would entail a grave risk of defeat. Their advice reinforced the Prime Minister in his belief that resisting German pressure on Czechoslovakia was no responsibility of Britain. And on such a weak military hand he was not inclined to bluff. In his speech to Parliament on 24 March 1938, which was to become the sacred text of British policy, he said that the Sudeten question was one internal to Czechoslovakia, and should be settled at that level. Britain had no obligations to Czechoslovakia other than those contained in the Covenant of the League. He warned Germany that, if war should break out, it was unlikely that it would be confined to central Europe. Privately, it was agreed that any obvious anti-German front must be avoided, and pressure brought upon Prague to meet the Sudeten demands, and upon Paris to influence Prague in the same sense.

In Moscow the main anxiety appears to have been to counter the appeasement policy of Britain and France and embroil them with Germany while avoiding anything likely to involve them in a direct clash with Germany. On 17 March Litvinov did his best, via the foreign press correspondents, to urge common resistance to Germany. But the Soviet Union's own obligations to Czechoslovakia only became operative if France first honoured hers. Soviet troops could only come to Prague's aid by crossing the territory of Poland or Rumania, both adamantly opposed to the entry of Soviet troops into their countries. Moscow left to Paris the task of persuading them to alter their stand. Litvinov further proposed a conference of Britain, France, Czechoslovakia, the United States and the Soviet Union. The rejection of his proposal by Britain, France and America only underlined the exclusion of the Soviet Union from European politics for the next twelve months.

The preoccupation shared by London, Paris and Moscow with the prospect of a German move against Czechoslovakia was justified by Hitler's own moves. On 28 March he told the SdP leaders that it was his intention to 'solve the Czech problem in the not too distant future', and instructed them to advance demands beyond those the Prague government could be expected to concede. Thus, when the Czech government, under Anglo-French prompting, opened negotiations with Henlein, they were confronted with eight demands, advanced in his speech of 23 April at the SdP Conference held in Karlsbad (Karlovy Vary), which would have made the Sudeten territories virtually autonomous within the Czech state. In the meantime, Hitler had ordered his armed forces to redraft the standing orders of December 1937 to comprehend the changed strategic situation after the annexation of Austria. And on 5-8 May he visited Italy and offered Mussolini a direct military alliance.

This offer Mussolini refused. Despite his acquiescence in the annexation of Austria, he had been alarmed by the arrival of German troops on the Brenner. Extremist Nazi propaganda in the South Tyrol and German activities in Jugoslavia had further irritated him. On 18 April he had finally succeeded in negotiating an agreement on the Mediterranean and Middle East with Britain by which Britain at last promised to recognise Italy's conquest of Abyssinia in return for a cessation of Italian pressure in Libya and the Middle East, and a withdrawal of Italian volunteers from Spain. As Hitler arrived in Rome, negotiations for a similar agreement with France were in progress. Hitler returned to Germany disillusioned and empty-handed. Five days later the Franco-Italian negotiations broke down and Mussolini attempted to return to the German offer, only to find that Hitler had had second thoughts. Their occasion was the so-called 'week-end' crisis of 20-22 May.

The crisis was occasioned by the association of reports of heavy German troop movements towards the Czech frontier with a break in Sudeten German contacts with the Czech government on the eve of the Czech local elections. On 20 May these reports led the Czech government, under pressure from its military advisers, to call a general mobilisation (the reports were ominously similar to those which had preluded the occupation of Austria), to call one class of reservists and various specialists, in all about 50,000 men, to the colours. British enquiries in Berlin the same day were met with indignant denials that any untoward troop movements were in fact in progress; and investigations by the British military attaché and his staff failed to disclose anything on the scale reported. The British and French governments however made warning démarches in Berlin on 21 May, the British following this with a special appeal by Halifax to Ribbentrop the following day. The German denials were widely hailed in the Western press as a major defeat for Hitler.

Hitler had, in fact, not yet decided on the timing of his next moves on Czechoslovakia. When the crisis opened he was considering the draft orders designed to put the Wehrmacht in a state of readiness to act against Czechoslovakia when he felt the political moment warranted it. The Anglo-French action and the comments of the Western press on these seem to have acted on his unstable personality like a red rag to a bull. On 24 May he ordered his naval staff to draw up plans for an immense increase in naval strength, as Britain and France were now to be considered as Germany's bitterest enemies. On 30 May he announced his intention of crushing Czechoslovakia at the first available opportunity. The Wehrmacht were to be prepared for action by 1 October. The opportunity was to be created by the political leadership working through the Sudeten leader, Henlein.

In London and Paris the effect of the 'week-end' crisis seems to have been to determine both governments not to allow any repetition. Pressure on the Czechs to reach an accommodation with the Sudetens was greatly increased. Neither government seems to have been aware of Henlein's German direction; which made any idea of a compromise being found completely impossible. Renewed negotiations between the Czechs and the Sudeten leadership, in fact, took place in the first week of June, and the Czechs went a very considerable way to meet the Sudeten demands. True to his instructions from Hitler, however, Henlein found grounds for rejecting them; and the Czech leadership on their side had a good deal of resistance to overcome within the governing coalition.

The failure of these negotiations led the British to turn to the idea of sending a mediator to attempt to evolve a compromise acceptable to both sides. The proposal was discussed in Paris on 20 July between Lord Halifax, who, as Foreign Secretary, accompanied King George VI on his state visit to Paris, and Bonnet. Initial Czech resistance to the idea was abandoned after Britain and France had threatened to abandon Czechoslovakia to her fate in the event of a German–Czech war. The chosen negotiator, the former Cabinet minister, Lord Runciman, arrived in Czechoslovakia on 3 August. With this action the British government, despite their professed lack of interest in central Europe, assumed an open responsibility for the solution of the Sudeten dispute and the protection of Czechoslovakia, which it was to prove impossible to evade.

During the month of August it became clear, despite Lord Runciman's mission, that a Sudeten settlement was in fact impossible. The Sudetens duly rejected a third set of proposals submitted to them on 2 September by the Czech authorities. In desperation the Czech President forced on his Cabinet the total acceptance of Henlein's Karlsbad programme. This was duly announced to the startled Sudeten negotiators on 6 September. But the approach of 1 October and the opening of the Nazi party rally in Nuremberg in the first week of September had already made all this out of date.

The critical event was Hitler's speech to the party rally on 12 September. But during August the German propaganda build-up had been such as to convince world opinion that a German declaration of war might be expected to coincide with the rally. Once again Hitler's political and psychological warfare got ahead of his military timetable. On 27 August the British Chancellor of the Exchequer, Sir John Simon, repeated the warning contained in Chamberlain's speech of 24 March. But Chamberlain was already turning his thoughts to a further move.

The increasing pressure was used as an occasion for a renewed Russian intervention. Since the Sudeten crisis opened Soviet diplomacy had been devoted to attempting to stiffen Czech resistance to Germany and to incite Britain and France to join in a 'grand alliance' against aggression. Questions as to how the Soviet Union could help Czechoslovakia were answered by animadversion to Polish and Rumanian unwillingness to allow transit or overflying rights to Soviet troops. The offer of a grand alliance was made twice, over the period 17–22 March, and again in talks between Litvinov, the Soviet Foreign Minister, and Bonnet on 12 May in Geneva. From that date until the end of August, the Soviet authorities made no new move except to repeat assurances that they would honour their obligations to Czechoslovakia.

The apparent imminence of a German attack on Czechoslovakia now drove Litvinov to one final attempt to secure a common front against Hitler. On 26 August the Soviet Ambassador in Paris urged Bonnet to show more firmness in the Czech question. On 2 September Litvinov answered French queries as to how the Soviet Union proposed to aid Czechoslovakia in the light of Poland and Rumania's attitude to the transit problem by proposing the employment of the machinery of the League of Nations and asking for immediate staff talks. On 10–12 September Litvinov followed this with talks in Geneva with Comnène, the Rumanian Foreign Minister, and Bonnet. Comnène remained opposed to all talk of Soviet troops passing through Rumania. Bonnet evaded Litvinov's pressure for staff talks, pleading British resistance, and ignored his renewed appeal to activate the League machinery. Both Bonnet and Chamberlain preferred to exclude the Soviet Union from their designs, suspecting a Soviet scheme to involve them in war with Germany. The Soviets on their side were still unprepared to act except within the framework of their alliance with Czechoslovakia, that is, in the case of prior

French support of Czechoslovakia, and with the backing of the League of Nations to justify the passage of their troops through Rumania.

Hitler's speech was delivered on 12 September. It was preceded on 7 September by an incident in the Sudetenland in which two Sudeten Germans were killed by a Czech gendarme, an incident which gave the Sudeten leadership the excuse needed to enable them to evade discussion of the latest Czech proposals. Hitler's speech was venomous and bellicose; and was followed immediately by an outbreak of disorders staged by extremists of the SdP which in places, especially in the Egerland, reached the scale of open rebellion. The Czechs retaliated by proclaiming emergency law and moving troops and police into the affected areas in force. The SdP leadership and the bulk of the SdP storm-troops took refuge in Germany, and the SdP itself was proscribed. For the moment there was even a movement among former SdP moderates to form a new party to resume negotiations with the Czech authorities.

Hitler's speech and the subsequent disorders in the Sudetenland caused panic in Paris and led Chamberlain to embark on his plan, pondered since the end of August, of a direct meeting with Hitler. At Berchtesgaden on 15 September Hitler demanded from Chamberlain the secession of the Sudetenland to Germany, and the detachment of Czechoslovakia's Hungarian and Polish minorities. On Chamberlain's pressure, he agreed, however, to discern ways and means of implementing 'self-determination' if Britain would accept the principle. Returning to London on 16 September, Chamberlain persuaded his Cabinet to accept the secession of the Sudetenland to Germany and the issue of a guarantee to the remainder of the Czechoslovak state. Cession seemed preferable to a plebiscite as demanded, *inter alios*, by Mussolini, which the Czechs themselves turned down completely. On 18 September, meeting under the prospect of immediate Czech mobilisation, Chamberlain persuaded the French ministers Daladier and Bonnet to accept the principle of cession of all districts with a German majority and an exchange of populations in other areas. Joint Anglo-French proposals in this sense were submitted to President Beneš the following day. In the early hours of 21 September the Czech Cabinet finally accepted these proposals after their initial rejection of them had been met with a flat statement by the British and French ministers in Prague that this would involve immediate German invasion and the repudiation of the French alliance. Before accepting the Anglo-French proposals Beneš enquired what the Soviet attitude would be in the event of France not honouring her obligations to Czechoslovakia. The Russian answers were too hesitant and too equivocal, being linked with a Czech appeal to the League of Nations, to overcome Beneš's reluctance to break with the West and give substance to German allegations that Czechoslovakia was merely a tool of Bolshevism.

On 22 September therefore Chamberlain met Hitler at Godesberg with the news of Czech acceptance of his Berchtesgaden proposals. He was flabbergasted to be met by a flat statement that this was no longer enough. In the first place there were the demands of Poland and Hungary. In the second place Czech troops and police must be withdrawn from the areas inside the German language frontier by 1 October at the latest. Chamberlain then broke off negotiations, and there followed an exchange of letters in which Hitler reiterated his demands. On the evening of 23 September at a second conversation Hitler handed over a map showing the areas immediately to be evacuated by Czech troops and further areas in which a plebiscite was to be held on the basis of residence before October 1918, that is, before the establishment of the Czechoslovak state. Chamberlain extracted a slight extension of the time limit for evacuation from Hitler and returned to London. Before the second meeting with Hitler, he had already agreed to withdraw British objections to Czech mobilisation (partial French mobilisation followed the same evening). He also agreed, however, to transmit these new German proposals to the Czechs; whose note rejecting them *in toto*, but agreeing to treat with the Poles, was received in London on 25 September.

Both French and British Cabinets agreed on rejecting the Godesberg proposals. On 25 September Bonnet and Daladier flew again to London to concoct the next step. The conference stretched into the following day. Under brutal and persistent questioning into the reality of France's ability to conduct war, Daladier accepted on 26 September a British proposal that a new appeal should be addressed to Hitler, which should include a warning that, if France went to war with Germany as a result of a German attack on Czechoslovakia, Britain would support her. The appeal reached Hitler before, but did not prevent, his delivery of a violent and bellicose speech at the Berlin *Sportpalast* demanding total evacuation of the Sudetenland by 1 October or war. The appeal was delivered by Sir Horace Wilson, Chamberlain's agent; he did not give Hitler the accompanying warning until the following morning.

It is from this date that Hitler seems to have lost some of his determination on war. Orders to mobilise were issued that day (27 September) but in secret. A contributory factor may have been the marked lack of enthusiasm shown by the population of Germany in general and Berlin in particular to the military demonstration he staged in Berlin that evening. A British declaration, based on a conversation in Geneva with Litvinov on 24 September, that the Soviet Union would also support France cannot but have added to his uneasiness.

That evening, however, the British evolved a further set of proposals providing for a tripartite German–Czech–British conference to arrange for Czech evacuation of the Sudetenland, drawing up of a new frontier, and the future revision of Czechoslovakia's treaty relationships. Simultaneously Chamberlain made a radio appeal for peace in which he spoke of a 'quarrel in a faraway country among people of which we know nothing', and spoke of continuing efforts for peace. On 28 September Chamberlain delivered a fresh appeal to Hitler, accompanying it with a simultaneous appeal to Mussolini. He offered to come to Germany for a new four power conference to settle all Germany's essential demands. Before the appeal was delivered to Hitler, Mussolini intervened also to suggest the postponement of German mobilisation in terms which suggested that Italy's previous readiness to support Hitler (staff conversations between the German and Italian armed forces were just about to begin) was about to disappear. He followed this with a second message suggesting a four power conference. This Hitler had no real choice but to accept.

The conference met in Munich in the afternoon of 29 September. Hitler saw Mussolini, who already knew the German proposals, first. At the conference Mussolini advanced the German proposals as though they were his own. No forceful objections being made to his draft by either Chamberlain or Daladier, the final draft of the agreement was signed shortly after midnight the same day. It provided for the cession of the entire Sudeten territory to Germany, its evacuation by Czech troops and officials to begin on 1 October and be completed by 10 October under the supervision of a five power Commission (the four signatories and Czechoslovakia). Certain disputed areas were to be the subject of plebiscites. Britain and France would guarantee the new boundaries against unprovoked aggression, Germany and Italy following suit when the Polish and Hungarian claims had been settled. Only when the agreement had been signed was it presented to the Czechs.

The Czech government found itself faced with the alternative of fighting Germany on her own or capitulating. Against Germany her forces were approximately equal, save in the air; moreover they lay behind long-prepared fortifications. But the prospects of Hungary and Poland joining in made things very different. They addressed one last appeal to the Soviets; but were forced to decide on the proposals before a Soviet reply could be received. To preserve Czechoslovakia from war they accepted the proposals, which stripped them of all their fortifications and left them defenceless.

On 30 September Chamberlain met Hitler briefly and secured his signature to a hastily prepared Anglo-German declaration, drafted by Chamberlain's staff on his instructions, binding Hitler to settle 'any other questions that may concern our two countries' by consultation. On this document he was to build short-lived hopes of a new settlement in Europe, the aim towards which he had been working since the summer of 1937. With this his own personal triumph was complete, as much with the German people as with those of France and Britain.

Yet the Munich settlement in fact represented a total defeat for that policy. It destroyed the remains of the Versailles balance. It left all eastern and south-eastern Europe open to German colonisation. It greatly weighted the military balance towards Germany not only by handing over the equipment of the Czech army and ending the threat to Germany's south-eastern frontiers, but also by putting under German control the whole Skoda industrial armaments complex. Finally it enlisted both Hungary and Poland firmly on Germany's side.

The Polish government had nursed the issue of Teschen to divide them from Czechoslovakia since 1919. From 1933 onwards they had attempted to play the role of a great power in central Europe, a role which led in 1937 to Colonel Beck enunciating the doctrine of the *intermarium*, a zone stretching from Scandinavia to Italy and the Balkans, to be led by Poland in agreement with Italy. To this Czechoslovakia was the principal obstacle, rendered more hateful by her Soviet connections. Indeed, continuing hostility to the Soviet Union was one of the main elements in Beck's policy of balance at this time, and there were some Polish–Japanese contacts, designed by Beck to reinforce the anti-Soviet elements in Japanese policy. In conversations with Admiral Horthy in February 1938 and Count Ciano in March and in visits to the principal Baltic and Scandinavian capitals in the summer of 1938, Beck had alternately discussed the need for a common Polono-Hungarian frontier and adumbrated the idea of the *intermarium* as a block to further German expansion. With the intensification of the Czech crisis in August 1938 Polish demands had been advanced 'in steps' as Beck put it on 8 September with Germany. On 20 September a formal claim was made on Teschen and Polish military preparations began, only to be brought to a complete halt on 27 September by a Soviet warning and ominous Soviet troop concentrations on the eastern frontier. On 25 September when Czech rejection of the Godesberg terms made war seem inevitable, the Czechs offered to cede Teschen to Poland to buy security for their northern flank. Munich, however, said nothing of Poland's claims.

Hungary by contrast now followed a more cautious path, driven by anxiety as to the possible attitude of Czechoslovakia's associates in the Little Entente, Jugoslavia and Rumania. In April her demands for staff talks with Germany were ignored, so that later pressure by Goering in June and July on Sztojay, the Hungarian minister in Berlin, and on Horthy himself on his visit to Berlin at the end of August, was no more successful. Nor could the Hungarians extract guarantees from Rome. Both Germany and Italy set too much store on the pro-Axis course followed by Stoyadinović, the Jugoslav Premier. Instead Hungary felt constrained to negotiate an agreement with the Little Entente powers, signed at Bled on 28 August. This did not prevent the Hungarians from advancing the claims of their own minority in Czechoslovakia on 22 September. But it prevented any of the powers meeting at Munich from taking them any more seriously than those of the Poles.

In the discussion of 30 September between Chamberlain and Hitler, reference was made by Hitler to the Spanish civil war and to the Sino-Japanese conflict. The Spanish civil war had, in fact, lost a good deal of its central position in international affairs as a result of the new German drive in central Europe and the collapse of the Spanish Republican front in the north in April 1938. For a time it seemed as if German and Italian forces would no longer be needed; but the reopening of the French frontier for arms deliveries to the Republicans thereafter and a great flood of Soviet aid led to the re-establishment of the military stalemate. The German and Italian governments decided reluctantly to continue to maintain their forces on Franco's side, and there was a recrudescence, largely ignored in the tensions of the Czech crisis, of air and submarine attacks on British ships trading with the remaining ports in Republican control. The sharpening of the Czech crisis in August and early September was viewed with great alarm by the nationalist authorities, who feared that they would be the first object of French attack in the event of a Franco-German conflict. Franco in fact declared his unconditional neutrality at the height of the September crisis, greatly to the disgust of the Axis leaders. In November 1938, however, he was again the beneficiary of large-scale German aid. Simultaneously, the Soviet authorities seem to have abandoned any hope of widening the Spanish conflict so as to involve the West with Franco's Axis supporters. The international brigades were withdrawn the same month, and the collapse of the Republican forces in Catalonia and in central Spain followed in March 1939. On 27 February 1939 Britain and France formally recognised the Franco régime.

In the Far East the principal developments in 1938 followed the same indecisive pattern as in the previous year. China leaned heavily on Soviet aid; this did not, however, prevent new Sino-Japanese talks on a settlement in the summer of 1938 which broke on Japanese intransigence. The Japanese army, obsessed by the need to discourage Soviet aid, opened contacts in January 1938 with Ribbentrop, through the Japanese military attaché in Berlin, General Oshima, on transforming the Anti-Comintern Pact into a military alliance. In July 1938 German aid to China was finally cut off and the German military advisers recalled. At the same time draft German proposals were sent to Tokyo by a special Japanese emissary. The Japanese authorities decided to take them up, but on two conditions: that the alliance should be principally directed against the Soviet Union, and that the treaty should be defensive. The collapse of the Sino-Japanese talks was followed by a marked hardening of the Japanese attitude as the Ugaki Cabinet was replaced in September by one headed by Prince Konoye; and Japanese military action was now devoted to gaining control of the whole Chinese coast line. Canton and Hankow fell to Japanese attack that month. In August bitter fighting on the

Soviet–Manchurian border at Chang Ku-feng between Soviet and Japanese forces showed that, despite the spread of the Stalinist purge to the Soviet Far Eastern forces (their commander, Marshal Blyukher, was executed in November 1938), they could still give a very good account of themselves.

The Munich agreement gave Hitler the command of eastern Europe; but it preserved the rump of the Czech state he had determined to smash. It opened the way for him to move either eastwards or westwards, either against the Ukraine and the Soviet Union, or against France and Britain. Although there seem to have been those in his entourage, notably Goering and Koch, the Gauleiter of East Prussia, who wanted to move eastwards, the course and outcome of the Czech crisis, whose resolution had given not Hitler but Chamberlain the plaudits both of the world and of the German crowds, seem to have settled Hitler in favour of making his next great move against France and Britain. First, however, he had some unfinished business: rump-Czechoslovakia had to fall, the German flag to wave over Prague. Then there was the Memel. And finally there were Danzig, the Corridor and Poland. That, for Hitler, these were only side-shows is shown by the drive he put into negotiations to transform the Anti-Comintern Pact into a triple alliance against the West, by the lengths he went to to negotiate a settlement with Poland, by the priority he gave to building up the German navy and by the orders he issued for staff talks with Italy.

His grand design was, however, more grandiose than well designed. In the first place he had to re-establish his control over Poland and Hungary, both eager to establish a common frontier across Slovakia and Ruthenia. The task, complicated by his failure to understand for a month or so the strength of Slovak separatism, and Goering's encouragement of the Ukrainian nationalists of Ruthenia, was only achieved with Italian aid, and the severest pressure on Budapest. By the Vienna award of 2 November 1938 Hungarian frontier claims against Slovakia were settled, and the Hungarians induced to demobilise. German economic courtship of Rumania was increased, and the Slovaks shown they could rely on German protection. Support for the Ruthenes was thereafter withdrawn. On 21 October and 17 December directives prepared the Reichswehr for the march into Prague. The new Czech government attempted to appease Berlin, but in vain. Early in February 1939 the Slovaks were incited to press for independence from Prague. Negotiations between Czechs and Slovaks broke down on 10 March. Summoned to Berlin and given the go-ahead on 13 March, the Slovak leader, Tiso, proclaimed Slovakia's independence the following day. The Ruthenes followed suit. That same evening, the Czech President, Hacha, also summoned to Berlin, was bullied into requesting a German protectorate. At 6 a.m. on 15 March German troops entered Bohemia and Moravia. The protectorate was proclaimed the following day. Hungarian troops engulfed the unfortunate Ruthenes. Czechoslovakia was no more.

This was the littlest part of the grand design, and the only part to go right. Its very success upset everything else; but the other parts of the design had already run into trouble. An indispensable part was settlement of Danzig and the Corridor (chs. IX, XVI). Hitler and Ribbentrop spent five months trying to persuade the Poles to accept their offer, compensation in the Ukraine for the reversion of Danzig to Germany, and the grant to Germany of sovereignty over a six-lane autobahn through the Corridor. Invited to join the Anti-Comintern Pact, the Poles rightly saw this as an invitation to accept satellite status, without realising that the balance of power had swung irretrievably against any chance of their maintaining a position of true independence. The Germans urged the generosity of their offer at Berchtesgaden on 24 October 1938 to Lipsky, the Polish Ambassador; in Berlin on 19 November; in Warsaw on 15 December; in Munich on 5 January, when Colonel Beck was Hitler's guest; in Warsaw, at the end of January, when Ribbentrop returned the visit. The Poles temporised, evaded, procrastinated. Instead, on 19 November 1938, they concluded a new agreement with the Soviet Union. And Colonel Beck dreamed of Polish colonies, to be obtained in the new colonial carve-up for which he thought Hitler was pressing the British. In the effort to demonstrate German goodwill Ribbentrop ran relations with the Soviet Union, with whom new trade talks were due, to a total standstill; all in vain.

Nor were the negotiations with Japan and Italy any more successful. The Japanese army and the Konoye Cabinet pressed for a general treaty which would isolate China and bring the Kuomintang to capitulate; but it is clear that for them its main weight had to be against Russia. The Italians were much less sympathetic. Given the first draft during the Munich conference, Ciano consigned it to the 'file and forget' category. Mussolini was not anxious to jeopardise ratification of the Easter agreements with Britain, and was alarmed by the prospect of being odd man out in the Berlin–Tokyo relationship. Ribbentrop, descending suddenly on Rome on 28 October 1938 to obtain signature of the alliance, was rudely rebuffed. The Anglo-Italian agreement was ratified on 16 November.

A fortnight later, on 30 November, the Italian Chamber of Deputies staged an organised demonstration, calling for the return to Italy of Corsica, Nice, Savoy, Tunis. The French government reacted toughly. By 2 January Mussolini, who had already been pressing for German–Italian staff talks, told the Germans he was ready and willing to sign the alliance. Four days later the Japanese Cabinet collapsed. In its successor, headed by Baron Hiranuma, the element of caution was more strongly entrenched. Successive drafts and counter-drafts were exchanged in vain. The majority in the Japanese Cabinet would not accept a treaty which they could not justify both at home and in London and Washington as being purely directed against the Soviet Union. British and American pressure (both countries were well informed on the course of the negotiations despite the secrecy with which they were cloaked) only reinforced their objections. Ribbentrop insisted on an alliance which would operate against Britain and distract and dissipate British strength away from Europe; again, in vain.

In the meantime, German plans for war against Britain were maturing. On 26 November the High Command of the Wehrmacht (OKW) issued Hitler's orders for staff talks with Italy. Their aim was war with Britain and France, to knock France out by a direct breach of the Maginot line and to drive British influence finally from the European mainland. In December the navy's plan for a fleet to defeat British sea power by a *guerre de course* on the surface, the Z-plan, was finally approved. Preparations to denounce the Anglo-German naval agreement were discussed, though in the meantime the proprieties were observed. At the end of the year Anglo-German naval conversations legitimised the growth of the German submarine fleet to parity with that of the British Commonwealth. And early in January Hitler signed an order giving the German navy priority in the allocation of steel and other vital raw materials over the German army and the Luftwaffe.

A major factor in whipping Hitler on against Britain was the British reaction to Munich. The settlement itself was acclaimed in London as opening a new era of Anglo-German relations. But it soon was apparent that this was not intended to be one in which British armaments would again be as weak as in September 1938. New measures of rearmament were announced and set in motion. And, while it was clear that the British government were prepared to concede German hegemony in central Europe, it was also clear that elsewhere, including the colonial issue, their attitude had much hardened. They thus raised no objection to France negotiating an agreement on the same lines as the Anglo-German declaration. And such an agreement was in fact signed by Bonnet and Ribbentrop in Paris on 6 December 1938. But when Chamberlain and Halifax visited Paris on 24 November they urged the French to escalate their arms programme. They placed some hopes on a series of economic negotiations with Germany. But the anti-Jewish pogroms staged in Germany on 10 November so incensed British opinion that, when Chamberlain and Halifax visited Rome in January 1939, one of their purposes seemed to be to appeal to Mussolini to get Hitler to see reason.

At the same time increasing reports were reaching British intelligence of German plans for new aggressions. In late December these all reported a new move eastwards. But in January an attack on the Netherlands or directly, by air-bombardment, on Britain was foreshadowed. On 24 January Halifax alerted Washington and Paris. Early in February, the

British began to press for staff talks with the French. The French replied by urging Britain to adopt conscription. In mid-February the Cabinet, overriding both the Chancellor of the Exchequer and the Prime Minister's rearguard action, decided to equip an expeditionary force to fight in France. It was at this moment that news arrived of the German march into Prague, over a week-end just after Sir Samuel Hoare had unwisely been seduced into speaking of the dawning of a golden age of peace.

With the German march into Prague, Hitler destroyed completely any chance he might have had of completing his grand design against Britain and France. The ruin of his schemes was, however, not his action in annexing an immense population of non-Germans into German rule, though it made any further exploitation of the doctrine of 'national self-determination' and the Western Versailles guilt-complex impossible, while providing his enemies with a useful counter-argument. It was the atmosphere of war-nerves which the suddenness of his action created in Europe which was to bring about the defeat of his plans.

The first reaction came on 17 March when the Rumanian minister in London, M. Tilea, appealed to Britain for aid against alleged German demands for a monopoly position in Rumanian trade, which, he said, had the character of an ultimatum. The British reaction was to move at once to the idea that a settlement with Germany was only possible if Hitler could be shown that further expansion would involve a European war. On 18 March therefore enquiries were addressed to all the Balkan states, to Poland and to the Soviet Union, to ask what their attitude would be in the event of a Rumanian appeal for aid to resist German aggression.

The move was immediately welcomed by Litvinov, the last embodiment in the Soviet Union as in Europe of the idea of collective resistance to Germany. Since the Soviet Union's exclusion from the Munich conference his influence in Moscow had been waning, as the Soviet Union retreated into isolation. In February he had made an abortive attempt to organise a Black Sea pact which would strengthen Rumania and Turkey against German pressure. The real trend of Soviet policy had been revealed on 10 March in Stalin's speech to the eighteenth congress of the Soviet Communist party, with its celebration of Soviet armed might and its denunciation of the democracies for their misguided hopes that the Soviet Union would 'pull their chestnuts out of the fire'. Since Munich the only Russian moves of any diplomatic importance had been to conclude the November 1938 agreement with Poland and to withdraw entirely both their own advisers and the international brigades from the Spanish republic, leaving it to its fate.

The British initiative must have come to Litvinov as his last chance. On 18 March he replied by proposing a conference of the British, French, Rumanian, Polish, Turkish and Soviet governments to meet immediately in Bucharest to discuss common action. The proposal struck the British as dilatory and verbose. In its stead they proposed a declaration by Britain, France, Poland and the Soviet Union that they would immediately consult on joint resistance to any threat to the political independence of any European state. Litvinov's proposal was dismissed as 'premature'. By 22 March it had become clear that any hope of Poland participating in a joint declaration or conference with the Soviet Union was illusory. With this Litvinov's hopes of collective action faded, and the Soviet authorities seem to have concluded that Britain still had no serious intentions of standing up to Hitler.

On 21 March Hitler made his last attempt to persuade Poland to join his camp. The next day his forces marched into the Memel. In reply the Poles mobilised three age groups, and on 23 March and 28 March rejected entirely the German proposals on Danzig, stating that any attempt at unilateral action over Danzig would lead Poland to declare war. In London alarmist reports of German military moves against Poland led Chamberlain to act on the proposal for a declaration unilaterally. On 31 March he announced to a startled House of Commons that if Poland felt herself threatened and compelled to resist that threat by force Britain would come to her aid, a declaration which made Warsaw formally the arbiter of Britain's entry into war. This guarantee represented so extraordinary a move that, although at once accepted by the Poles, it was not taken seriously either in Berlin or in Moscow. Intended as a deterrent to Hitler, it remained strictly incredible, since, without an Anglo-Soviet alliance or Soviet–Polish military co-operation, there was no way of supporting Poland against German attack. Only the Poles believed they could stand up to German might.

To the Soviets the British action represented yet a further attempt to use them only as a backstop for British policy. Presumably to test British sincerity, they proposed staff talks on 6 April, and on 18 April a ten-year alliance. At the same time, Soviet diplomatists began to hint in Berlin that the Soviet Union was interested in improving relations with Germany. The real Soviet worry, however, seems to have been at the progress of British policy in the Balkans. Here the British had been very much aided by local fears of Italy. The German action in Prague had stung Mussolini to renewed rage. He had long pressed for staff talks with Germany on common action against the democracies, and early in March Hitler had agreed to them taking place purely at a technical level. On 5 April these opened in Innsbruck. On 9 April Mussolini's forces invaded Albania; as a tit-for-tat for Prague, he gave Germany no more warning than he had had of the Prague operation.

The Italian action reacted in turn on Britain, whose main diplomatic effort was now put into the attempt to make Turkey the keystone of a Balkan bloc guaranteeing Rumania against aggression. British and French guarantees were given to Rumania on 13 April. Their drive had sufficient success for a while to alarm the Soviet authorities. On 22 April M. Potemkin, the Soviet deputy Foreign Minister, was dispatched on a tour of the Balkan capitals. But by the time he arrived in Ankara the Soviet authorities appear to have concluded that Britain was simply using them as a final backing for British policy; while in London the Foreign Office were beginning to feel anxious that the Soviet Union was giving very little in return for the indirect guarantee to her security contained in the British guarantees to Poland and Rumania. On 15 April Moscow was therefore invited to issue parallel guarantees to these countries. Litvinov preferred to take up a French suggestion; on 18 April he offered a ten-year alliance against German aggression only to find his proposal again rebuffed. On 4 May, therefore, he was dismissed and replaced as Foreign Minister by Molotov. For the next ten weeks Molotov was to exert himself to convince London and Paris that without Soviet aid their system of guarantees was pointless, and that such aid would only be forthcoming on terms which would ensure Poland and Rumania acting as a glacis for the Soviet Union. Eventually realising that this was impossible, the Soviet leadership was to turn to Nazi Germany.

For the Russian proposals were basically impossible for Britain and France to concede. It proved impossible to persuade Beck, when he came to London in early April, and thereafter, that Poland would have to accept Soviet aid, or to persuade M. Gafencu, the Rumanian leader, to moderate his outright opposition to a Soviet military presence in Rumania. The British were intent on something which would deter Hitler and lead him to the conference table, not on a military alliance which would destroy him. They did not therefore weigh Soviet military aid very high; their experts expressed grave doubts as to the Soviet capacity, after the great purges, to attempt anything more than a determined defence against a German aggression.

The main impact of Litvinov's fall was felt in Germany. The issue of the British guarantee to Poland and the progress of Britain's dam-building negotiations in eastern Europe both alarmed and infuriated Hitler. At the end of March he instructed his Chief of Staff to prepare orders for war with Poland, though these were at first only defined as a 'precautionary complement' to preparations for war in the west to be implemented when Poland could be isolated diplomatically. His army was also ordered to prepare for a sudden *coup de main* against Danzig alone, if the political situation made this possible. During April his anger mounted, especially as his diplomacy failed to prevent Anglo-Turkish co-operation. On 28 April he answered Britain's adoption of conscription by denouncing both the Anglo-German naval agreement concluded in 1935 and the German–Polish non-aggression pact of 1934. On 6 May Ribbentrop proposed to Ciano that they should conclude a bilateral alliance without waiting any more for Japan to overcome her hesitations. The German–

Italian alliance, the 'Pact of Steel', was, in fact, signed on 22 May. Hitler was, however, well aware that this alone would not be adequate to give France and Britain pause. If he could detach the Soviet Union from the West, this would be a very different matter.

The first approach to Russia was made on 20 May by the German Ambassador in Moscow. His reception by Molotov was, at first sight, so discouraging that Hitler's advisers nearly despaired. He persisted however, and fresh conversations were opened at the end of May. In the meantime, the first signs of pressure by the Danzig Senate on Poland began to appear. And on 23 May Hitler revealed to his generals his intention to attack Poland 'at the first available opportunity'. He made it clear that he intended to do his best to isolate Poland first. But if Britain and France intervened then he was prepared for a showdown with Britain. Japan might be used to restrain Russia; it was not impossible, however, that Russia might show herself uninterested in Poland. German diplomacy was now directed to detaching Rumania from Poland, to stepping up pressure on the Danzig issue, and to detaching the Soviet Union from the West.

It was not until the end of July that Hitler judged the time to be ripe. In the intervening two months there was one major crisis, during which it seems that consideration was given in Berlin to the alternative plan of a *coup de main* against Danzig. But the main German drive to disrupt Britain's efforts to construct a Balkan bloc around Rumania was only partially successful. Turkey accepted a British guarantee on 12 May and, after bullying France to transfer the Sanjak of Alexandretta entirely into Turkish sovereignty, a French guarantee also. On the Soviet front Hitler simply had to watch and maintain contact with Moscow while the British steadily gave way under Soviet pressure only to find that the agreement they sought was still out of their reach. A British draft of a pact linked to the League Covenant was rudely rejected on 27 May. Molotov then demanded its extension to cover the Baltic states of Finland, Estonia and Latvia. A new British draft was rejected on 22 June. On 1 July Molotov demanded a Soviet alliance with Poland and Rumania, adding too that the treaties should be operative in the case of 'indirect aggression', a concept which he defined so as to raise the suspicion in London that the pact was intended to cover Soviet action against any government they disliked and wished to overthrow. On 23 July Molotov suddenly demanded that staff talks should begin forthwith.

His motives in doing this are still unclear. But he may have been influenced by knowledge of the talks held in London in mid-July between Dr Wohltat, a senior official in Goering's Four-Year Plan organisation, and Sir Horace Wilson, the Permanent Under-Secretary in the British Treasury, and Robert Hudson, President of the Board of Trade. On the British side these seem to have represented a last attempt by those who believed in the evidence of a moderate element in Hitler's entourage to lure him away from the path of violence in Europe by the prospect of far-reaching concessions in the common exploitation of markets and raw materials in Africa and elsewhere. These conversations, never more than demi-official on the British side, also involved proposals for disarmament negotiations, non-intervention declarations, recognition of German economic primacy in south-east Europe, and, in some versions, a large-scale British loan. To Molotov they must have raised the spectre of renewed Soviet isolation and spurred him on to strengthen those circles in Britain who regarded this kind of talk as totally unrealistic.

The studied deterioration in relations between Danzig and Poland during June and July lent force to the arguments of this latter school. After the crisis of the last week in June, fresh disputes arose in mid-July over the difficulties placed by the Danzig authorities in the way of the Polish customs inspectors. The Poles instituted economic reprisals, and at the end of July the Danzig Senate, on Hitler's orders, dispatched a deliberately provocative note to the Polish government threatening reprisals against the Polish customs inspectors. At the same time Ribbentrop sounded the Soviets as to the possibility of a political agreement. On 3 August he received a positive reaction. Hitler appears to have decided now that conditions were right for the isolation and annihilation of Poland.

The Wilson–Hudson–Wohltat talks certainly played a part in convincing Hitler that the British guarantee for Poland was bluff; more important was the reluctance of the British Treasury to extend Poland a loan to purchase armaments and the delays both in the talks on an Anglo-Polish alliance and in the Anglo-Soviet negotiations. In addition, elements of the Japanese army in China, furious at the resistance in Tokyo to the conclusion of the alliance negotiations with Germany, had done their utmost to provoke a war with Britain by blockading the British concession at Tientsin. Only very skilful diplomacy on the part of the British Ambassador in Tokyo and strong American pressure had succeeded in averting a conflict. To Hitler the signs of a breakdown in the British front against Germany must have seemed ripe for exploitation.

On 4 August the Poles replied to the Danzig Senate that action against Polish officials in Danzig would be regarded as an act of violence against the Polish state. Hitler summoned the Nazi Gauleiter of Danzig to Berchtesgaden, and ordered him to step up the pressure so as to provoke a Polish attack on Danzig. A bellicose German note was given to the Poles on 9 August, to receive, the following day, an equally violent and uncompromising reply. German military preparations were ordered to be completed by 24 August.

At this point Hitler's own plans began to disintegrate. The negotiations with Russia went well. On 14 August Molotov proposed a non-aggression pact, while the Soviet army leaders fenced with the Anglo-French staff missions sent to Moscow on Molotov's invitation. In a series of messages Hitler beat down the Soviets' attempt to fence further and on 21 August Ribbentrop arrived in Moscow. Two days later the Nazi–Soviet non-aggression pact was signed, together with a secret protocol dividing Poland and eastern Europe into German and Soviet spheres of influence. The order was given for Danzig to provoke a breach with Poland. Hitler harangued his generals yet again on the isolation of Poland and the cowardice of Britain and France. And the order for the German attack on Poland was set for 4.30 a.m. on 26 August.

The events of 25 August were to prove Hitler wrong. At 4.30 p.m. Hitler heard that Britain, so far from being deterred by the conclusion of the Nazi–Soviet pact, had gone ahead and signed a formal alliance with Poland. At 6 p.m. he heard that Italy would not support him. At the time of the signature of the Pact of Steel, Italy had stipulated that there should be no major war in Europe for at least two years. Count Ciano, the Italian Foreign Minister, had only realised the true direction of German policy at the beginning of August. On 11 August he had descended on Berchtesgaden, only to be lectured by Hitler and Ribbentrop in a manner which he took to be arrogant, stupid and deceitful. On his return, he had succeeded in persuading a reluctant Mussolini that Italian entry into war was impossible. Much shaken, Hitler countermanded the orders for attack and the German troops returned to their barracks. The same day the Japanese government broke off her alliance negotiations with Germany, in horror at Germany's union with the country against whom the Anti-Comintern Pact had originally been concluded. Japanese troops were in fact engaged in a major military clash with Soviet troops at Nomonhan on the borders of Outer Mongolia. Several divisions were committed on each side and Japanese casualties in the fighting, which lasted until mid-September, were very heavy.

For a day or so it seemed that Hitler had been decisively defeated. But Hitler had always been half-prepared for war with Britain and France, and he had already gone too far to recoil. Had his dispute with Poland been genuine there might have been a chance for a mediatory proposal. Instead, he evolved one final scheme to isolate Poland diplomatically. The Poles were to be invited to negotiate in Berlin and the negotiations then broken off in such a way as to put the blame on the Poles; the planned attack on Poland would follow immediately. The scheme involved the preparation of what could be represented to the British as a genuine compromise. With Goering's assistance, and the use of a neutral intermediary, a Swedish businessman, Birger Dahlerus, these proposals were discussed with the British government. At the same time, 28 August, a new date, 1 September, was set for the attack on Poland.

The scheme foundered on three points. The Poles refused to send a plenipotentiary to Berlin at such short notice despite very considerable

British pressure, and the British did not feel that they could be forced to do so. The actual handing over of the draft German proposals was so mishandled by Ribbentrop that they barely reached the British in time for government consideration let alone to make any real impact on British opinion, which by now had largely accepted the inevitability of war. And the military timetable was too rigid to allow any time for manœuvre. The German attack on Poland duly followed at dawn on 1 September.

At this point the French Cabinet, clutching at straws to avoid a war no one wanted and to which large parts of French opinion were bitterly opposed, persuaded Mussolini to propose a new four-power conference. After thirty-six hours' delay a revolt of opinion both in parliament and Cabinet forced the British government to issue an ultimatum demanding the withdrawal of German troops from Polish territory within two hours. The French declaration of war followed six hours later. The second world war had begun.

CHAPTER XXIV

THE SECOND WORLD WAR

TWO new means of action, or instruments of warfare, that became prominent in the first world war were the principal causes of military discussion and controversy during the interval that followed —the aircraft and the tank. In those twenty years they met more doubt and criticism than recognition of their potentialities. Yet when the second world war came they largely dominated its course—especially in the opening stages.

Another new instrument, a naval one, was of earlier origin, but was allowed no adequate chance to prove its powers until the first world war. This was the submarine. Only after the *surface* duel between the battle-fleets had clearly become barren, by the middle of the war, was the submarine given such a chance—in the hands of the inferior naval power, Germany. But then, in 1917, it became dominant in struggle at sea, and by its potency in blockade brought the superior naval power, Britain, to the verge of defeat by starvation. Yet after that war it soon fell into neglect, and the possibility of a revival of its threat was discounted by the bulk of naval opinion, which clung to the illusion, and faith, that the battleship was again the mistress of the seas—so that when the next great war came in 1939 even Germany had only a handful of submarines. But these soon became an important factor, and, as their numbers increased, a vital one— even though their effect was never quite so great as in the previous war.

There was a similar discount, and disparagement, of the effect of aircraft on surface craft, both directly and indirectly, while such tests as the navies carried out were designed, and distorted, to show the continued supremacy and invulnerability of the battleship. It became evident that its existence was an article of faith rather than a matter of technology susceptible to scientific test.

Here it should be noted, and emphasised, that all three of the new instruments, although often described as weapons, were more truly weapon-carriers. They were means of conveying shells, bombs or torpedoes to operatively close quarters where they could have the maximum effect—in other words, giving *mobility-cum-flexibility* to weapons.

A recognition of this basic common quality is of importance because it brings out the major change in warfare that such new instruments produced—the development of mechanical power to the point of domination over manpower.

The significance of such a change was obscured because the diminution in the number of men employed in a fighting function was offset by the

735

increased proportion employed to assist and maintain them administratively. Moreover, this was apt to be increased beyond real need as a way of absorbing the surplus manpower that became available when war came and old-style forces were mobilised, regardless of need and of equipment available, under the influence of former concepts.

In such circumstances the issue of a prolonged war could still be decided by exhaustion of manpower.

Nevertheless, this condition should not obscure the deeper lesson that, in modern warfare, there has been a great depreciation in the value of manpower compared with mechanical power. A nation that is deficient in mechanical equipment is not likely to have a chance of prolonging the war if exposed to attack by a well-equipped nation. However many men the former can put in the field, their value will be discounted by their mechanical inferiority, and the war be quickly lost. In such a case, although the attacker may happen to enjoy a superiority in manpower as well as in mechanical power, the real cause of the decision will lie in his mechanical advantage. This was very clearly shown in the course of the Italian invasion of Abyssinia in 1935-6. Yet most of the European powers, particularly France, did not heed the portent.

After the first world war the victorious armies had remained content to perpetuate the technique of 1918. But a few of the younger soldiers of the British army—which had rather hesitatingly taken the lead in developing the tank—became the prophets of a new era of mechanised warfare in which high-speed tanks, or, as some argued, the combination of tanks and bombing aircraft, would open the gates of the future.

At the same time the Air Staff in Great Britain, under the leadership of Lord Trenchard, propounded the view that the bomber would be the decisive factor in any future war, and would suffice in itself to produce a decision—by destroying the industrial resources of the opposing power. That view came to be associated with the writings of an Italian general, Douhet, but had actually been a primary article in the Royal Air Force creed long before Douhet's theory had gained currency. Proceeding from the fact that aircraft could move in three dimensions, it was urged that, instead of striking at the opposing army, which blocked the way, the air force should hop over it and concentrate on destroying the cities and industrial resources that had in earlier times been covered by the army.

Having been established as a separate service, the R.A.F. had a natural tendency to develop its own distinctive theory as a way to justify its own existence. This separateness helped to protect it when the post-war pressure for economy became severe, and to aid its growth when such pressure eased—in contrast to the way that the Royal Tank Corps suffered as a junior part of the army. But it tended to make the R.A.F. unco-operative in contributing to the development of a combined theory, or even taking part in exercises with tanks.

THE SECOND WORLD WAR

The tank-cum-air theory received more attention in defeated Germany than it did among the victorious powers, while another quarter highly receptive to the new idea was the new Soviet Union which had emerged from the Russian Revolution. In either case, the idea of such a compound key, applied in the military sphere, was more favoured than that of a purely bombing key, applied in the national sphere as a whole.

When the next great war came, twenty-one years after the last, the tank-cum-air theory was put into practice by Nazi Germany. It achieved a speedy triumph over Poland in 1939, and a greater one over the western Allies in 1940. The German army's leaders have amply acknowledged that they adopted the theory from its exponents in Britain, and benefited much by close attention to the practical tests that had been carried out there—before they had any armoured forces of their own.

Why were its foster-parents so much quicker than the original parent-country to appreciate and cultivate its potential powers?

The first, and most obvious, explanation is that this new technique of mechanised warfare, combining tank force and air force to attain a multiple effect, was naturally suited to the purpose of aggression—since it offered an increased prospect of rapid success in the offensive.

To peace-desiring and peacefully minded countries it seemed a superfluous luxury: a needless addition to the premium they were paying for their national insurance policy. When budgets were already strained by the debts of the first world war, it seemed to their directors desirable to eschew any change of methods and means that might increase the burden. It was cheaper—on a short view—to preserve the forces in their old-established form.

A further explanation, based on the experience of history, is that armies learn only from defeat. That explains why an army which has been victorious in one war so often loses the next war. Victory induces complacency—satisfaction with things as they are. It takes disaster to jolt an army, or a nation, out of the rut of traditional ways.

After victory had crowned their efforts in 1918, the military chiefs of the Allied powers were unduly content with their instruments. They were even inclined to go back to the instruments of 1914. Since several of them were cavalrymen they exalted the virtues of an arm for which they had an affectionate attachment, regardless of the small part that horsed cavalry played in comparison with its scale.

The psychological effect of this 'vested interest in obsolete knowledge' was illustrated in a public declaration which Lord Haig made in 1925. In a little book called *Paris, or the Future of War*,[1] the present writer had just set forth a picture of future mechanised warfare, on land and in the air. Very different, however, was the view of the most influential British

[1] Published by Kegan Paul, in the *Today and Tomorrow* series.

soldier, the commander-in-chief of Britain's armies in France in the last war:

Some enthusiasts today talk about the probability of horses becoming extinct and prophesy that the aeroplane, the tank, and the motor-car will supersede the horse in future wars. I believe that the value of the horse and the opportunity for the horse in the future are likely to be as great as ever... I am all for using aeroplanes and tanks, but they are only accessories to the man and the horse, and I feel sure that as time goes on you will find just as much use for the horse—the well-bred horse—as you have ever done in the past.

Nevertheless, the advocates of the new idea prevailed so far that in 1927 the first complete mechanised force that the world had seen was experimentally formed, on Salisbury Plain. Its trials were so successful that the Chief of the Imperial General Staff spoke of creating 'armoured divisions'. But a conservative reaction soon set in, and in 1928 this first mechanised force was disbanded—a high officer announcing to the Press at the time: 'Cavalry are indispensable. Tanks are no longer a menace.'

In 1929 the War Office was persuaded to approve the issue of the first official manual of mechanised warfare, and it made sufficient impression to pave the way for a revival of a trial armoured force in 1931. A year later this was dropped, but revived again after a year's interval. A step forward, a step back—such was the fluctuating course of progress.

Despite constant opposition, the new technique was by degrees worked out in practice during these years. Among those who took a leading part in its development, special tribute is due, first, to the far-ranging theoretical vision of Colonel Fuller, and then to the practical contribution made by Colonels Lindsay, Broad, Pile and Hobart, and Major Martel. It was Hobart who, commanding Britain's first permanent armoured formation in 1934, brought the new technique close to perfection.

At that moment, when Britain's rearmament programme was about to be launched, after the unmistakable signs that Nazi Germany was rearming rapidly, Britain had both the minds and the means to maintain her original lead in mechanised warfare.

Unhappily, the heads of the War Office, in a pronouncement on policy, declared their obstinate conviction that 'We should go slowly with mechanisation'. Thus the Germans were given the chance to leap ahead. Meantime, the mechanised experts of the British army were hobbled, or shelved, apparently as a precaution against their inconvenient persistence.

This treatment was the more unfortunate for Britain's prospects because the knowledge gained in developing the new offensive technique had led to the discovery of an effective counter-technique—in a combination of mines to delay it, anti-tank guns to check it in co-operation with one's own concealed tanks firing from stationary positions, and the latter then thrusting back when the attackers were in disorder. But it had taken fully ten years to gain official acceptance for the offensive technique, and even then in a half-hearted way. So it was perhaps too much to expect that the antidote could have been approved and prepared in time, unless the war had been postponed until 1945.

A survey of the basic factors in the problem which faced Britain led one towards certain conclusions, mutually linked. First, that, in face of the growing strength of anti-tank defence, the best chance for applying the new offensive technique lay in starting with the advantage of surprise and a superiority in tanks and aircraft. Secondly, that the peace-seeking policy of France and Britain would inevitably deprive them of this opportunity. Thirdly, that, in these circumstances, their only hope lay in developing the powers of a 'defensive-offensive' strategy—and in providing the necessary modern means for it. One had to deal with the facts, instead of indulging in dream-offensives that could have no chance of realisation.[1]

With the French the soothing effects of victory were magnified by the pressure of economy, and also by their faith in conscription. Victory had left them with a mass of war material that soon became obsolete, but which they were unwilling to scrap—whereas by enforcing Germany's disarmament they cleared the ground for her to make a fresh start, unencumbered by the old tools, and the mental habits that these inculcated.

The enforced abolition of conscription in Germany, which lasted until 1935, also compelled her generals to concentrate on producing an army of high quality and mobility—whereas the French, by clinging to conscription, degenerated into a militia-type army that became less efficient as the period of service was reduced. Moreover, the leading French generals were so satisfied with their success in 1918, and so sure of their own superior military knowledge, that they were the most complacent of all —and thus the most reluctant to envisage any radical change of technique. The hindrance was increased by the way that, in the French army, tanks formed part of the infantry and cavalry, and had long been divided between these two arms, instead of forming a new and distinct arm.

During the years since the second world war there has been an outpouring of evidence both from documentary archives and from the memoirs of the political and military chiefs, especially the latter. Indeed, the military chiefs on the Allies' side have been so vociferous, and their contentions so sharply opposed, that it might truly be said that peace brought a fresh kind of war—the 'war of the generals'.

This chapter is focused on the main areas of controversy—which are naturally those theatres where the war was conducted on a partnership basis, without any one power having a clearly defined and accepted

[1] See B. H. Liddell Hart, *Europe in Arms* (2nd ed. 1938), especially chs. 7, 23, 24, 25; *The Defence of Britain* (1939), especially chs. 1–5, 20; *The Liddell Hart Memoirs* (1965), vol. I, especially ch. 12 and Entr'acte; vol. II, chs. 1 (pp. 24–8), 4 (pp. 161–2, 172), 5 (pp. 188–9, 200–4), 6 (pp. 241–6, 253–5), Epilogue (pp. 280–1).

predominance in the direction of operations. This condition requires a concentration on the western and Mediterranean theatres, with a relatively brief treatment of the Russian and Pacific theatres. In such a context, too, it can only touch lightly on the more purely sea and air operations—over which controversy has been less, and on a lower level.

There are two principal questions to determine. Were the operations conducted in a way fitted to achieve the military aim—and the ultimate political object? What were the errors that can be picked out as having a great effect on the course and issue of the war?

The answer to the main questions can be reached by examining the war phase by phase—the phases that formed its turning-points, adverse to the Allies from 1939 to the autumn of 1942, and then in their favour increasingly.

This catastrophic war, which ended by opening Russia's path into the heart of Europe, has been called by Churchill 'the unnecessary war'. In striving to avert it, and curb Hitler, a basic weakness in the policy of Britain and France was their lack of understanding of strategical factors. The British statesmen of that time were more ignorant than the French in this respect, and the major share of the responsibility falls on Baldwin, for his inertia in facing problems, and on Chamberlain for his unrealistic way of tackling them.

Through lack of strategic sense, the western Allies slid into war at the moment most unfavourable to them, and then precipitated an avoidable disaster of far-reaching consequences. Britain survived by what appeared to be a miracle—but really because Hitler made the same mistakes that aggressive dictators have repeatedly made throughout history.

When the tide eventually turned against Hitler—as a result of his turn away to attack Russia, and of America's entry into the war—the Allies forfeited the post-war prospects by pursuing the illusion of 'victory'—the destruction of the immediate antagonists without regard to the future.

In drawing up a balance-sheet, it is important to examine the pre-war phase—for that was where the causes of the opening disasters in the war can be traced.

In retrospect it has become clear that the first fatal step, for both sides, was the German re-entry into the Rhineland in 1936. For Hitler, this move carried a twofold strategic advantage—it provided cover for Germany's key industrial area in the Ruhr, and it provided him with a potential springboard into France.

Why was this move not checked? Primarily, because France and Britain were anxious to avoid any risk of armed conflict that might develop into war. The reluctance to act was increased because the German re-entry into the Rhineland appeared to be merely an effort to rectify an injustice, even though done in the wrong way. The British, particularly, being politically minded, tended to regard it more as a political than as a military step—failing to see its strategic implications.

But a further, and decisive, factor was French military unreadiness for prompt 'fire-extinguishing' action. In *The Remaking of Modern Armies* (1927), and subsequently, the present writer had emphasised that the pattern and doctrine of the French army was dangerously out of date and lacking in flexibility—so 'rigid' and 'ponderous' that 'under the test of a future war it might break down altogether'. He urged that the prime need for France was to create 'a mechanised striking force of highly trained long-service volunteers, to form a spearhead'—prior to the mobilisation of the conscript mass.

Charles de Gaulle took up this argument and proposal, making them the theme of his striking little book of 1934, *Vers l'armée de métier*. Paul Reynaud urged the same idea—the need for a mechanised spearhead of professional troops. But nothing was done to carry it out.

That military factor—the lack of such an immediately available spearhead—was primary in point of time. It became a check on any riposte to Hitler's Rhineland move before political hesitation on the part of the British government increased the restraint. What Reynaud and de Gaulle have said about this handicap is borne out by the detailed record of high-level discussions given in General Gamelin's *Servir*, vol. II, and by the accounts of the ministers who urged prompt and vigorous action, particularly the Prime Minister, Sarraut, and Paul-Boncour, and Flandin, then Foreign Minister.

When the French Cabinet met on the morning of 8 March 1936, the Minister of War, General Maurin, stated that any intervention in the Rhineland would require a large-scale mobilisation of reservists. Indeed, according to Flandin, Paul-Boncour, and Mandel, he insisted it would require 'general mobilisation'. That grave prospect damped down the urge for immediate action that had been marked the previous day. The other two service ministers were equally discouraging. It was only after this that the decision about action was put off, and left to wait on the British government's attitude—which proved negative, on political grounds.

In his 1938 moves Hitler again drew strategic advantage from political factors—the German and Austrian peoples' desire for union, the strong feeling in Germany about Czech treatment of the Sudeten Germans, and the widespread feeling in the Western countries that there was a measure of justice in Germany's case in both issues.

But Hitler's march into Austria in March laid bare the southern flank of Czechoslovakia—which to him was an obstacle in the development of his plans for eastward expansion. In September he secured—by the threat of war and the resultant Munich agreement—not merely the return of the Sudetenland but the strategic paralysis of Czechoslovakia.

In March 1939 Hitler occupied the remainder of Czechoslovakia, and thereby enveloped the flank of Poland—the last of a series of 'bloodless' manœuvres. This step of his was followed by a fatally rash move on the British government's part—the guarantee suddenly offered to Poland and Rumania, each of them strategically isolated, without first securing any assurance from Russia, the only power which could give them effective support.

By their timing, these guarantees were bound to act as a provocation—and, as we know now, until he was met by this challenging gesture Hitler had no immediate intention of attacking Poland. By their placing, in parts of Europe inaccessible to the forces of Britain and France, they provided an almost irresistible temptation. Thereby the Western powers undermined the essential basis of the only type of strategy which their deficiency in mobile striking forces made practicable for them. For, instead of being able to check aggression by presenting a strong front to any attack in the west, they gave Hitler an easy chance of breaking a weak front and thus gaining an initial triumph (cf. above, pp. 725 ff.).

The most extraordinary feature of this period was the statesmen's belief that the guarantee given to Poland, which was a strategic absurdity, could be a deterrent to Hitler—and the only one who voiced a warning of its folly was Lloyd George. Churchill, who could also see its weakness, and natural consequence, spoke in favour of it.

Hitler, being strategically minded, was quick to realise that only Russia's aid could make it effective. So, swallowing his hatred and fear of 'Bolshevism', he bent his efforts and energies towards conciliating Russia and securing her abstention. It was a turn-about even more startling than Chamberlain's—and as fatal in its consequences.

On 21 August Ribbentrop flew to Moscow, and the pact was signed on the 23rd. It was accompanied by a secret agreement under which Poland was to be partitioned between Germany and Russia.

This pact made war certain—in the intense state of feeling that had been created by Hitler's rapid series of aggressive moves. The British, having pledged themselves to support Poland, felt that they could not stand aside without losing their honour—and without opening Hitler's way to wider conquest. And Hitler would not draw back from his purpose in Poland, even when he came to see that it involved a general war.

Thus the train of European civilisation rushed into the long, dark tunnel from which it only emerged after six exhausting years had passed. Even then, the bright sunlight of victory proved illusory.

On Friday 1 September 1939 the German armies invaded Poland. On Sunday the 3rd, the British government declared war on Germany, in fulfilment of the guarantee it had earlier given to Poland. Six hours later the French government, more reluctantly, followed the British lead.

Within less than a month Poland had been overrun. Within nine months most of western Europe had been submerged by the spreading flood of war.

Poland was badly handicapped by her strategic situation—the country being placed like a 'tongue' between Germany's jaws, and Polish strategy made the situation worse by placing the bulk of the forces near the tip of the tongue. Moreover, these forces were out of date in equipment and ideas, still placing faith in a large mass of horsed cavalry—which proved helpless against the German tanks.

The Germans at that time had only six armoured and four mechanised divisions ready—but, thanks to General Guderian's enthusiasm, and Hitler's backing, they had gone further than any other army in adopting the new idea of high-speed mechanised warfare that had been conceived twenty years earlier by the British pioneers of this new kind and tempo of action. The Germans had also developed a much stronger air force than any of the other countries—whereas not only the Poles, but the French also, were badly lacking in air power, even to support and cover their armies.

Thus Poland saw the first triumphant demonstration of the new *Blitzkrieg* technique, by the Germans, while the Western allies of Poland were still in process of preparing for war on customary lines. On 17 September the Red Army advanced across Poland's eastern frontier, a blow in the back that sealed her fate, as she had scarcely any troops left to oppose this second invasion.

The German forces had crossed the Polish frontier shortly before 6 a.m. on 1 September; air attacks had begun an hour earlier. The Luftwaffe operated in a very dispersed way, instead of in large formations, but it thereby spread a creeping paralysis over the widest possible area. Another weighty factor was the German radio bombardment, disguised as Polish transmissions, which did much to increase the confusion and demoralisation of the Polish rear. All these factors were given a multiplied effect by the way that Polish overconfidence in the power of their men to defeat machines led, on the rebound, to a disintegrating disillusionment.

In the north, the invasion was carried out by Bock's Army Group, which comprised the Third Army (under Küchler) and the Fourth Army (under Kluge). The former thrust southward from its flanking position in East Prussia, while the latter pushed eastward across the Polish Corridor to join it in enveloping the Poles' right flank. The major role was given to Rundstedt's Army Group in the south, which was nearly twice as strong in infantry, and more in armour. It comprised the Eighth Army (under Blaskowitz), the Tenth (under Reichenau), and the Fourteenth (under List). The decisive stroke, however, was to be delivered by Reichenau, in the centre, and for that purpose he was given the bulk of the armoured forces.

By 3 September—when Britain and France entered the war—Kluge's advance had cut the Corridor and reached the Lower Vistula, while Küchler's pressure from East Prussia towards the Narev was developing. What was more important, Reichenau's armoured forces had penetrated to the Warta, and forced the crossings there. By the 4th Reichenau's spearheads had reached and crossed the Pilica, fifty miles beyond the frontier. Two days later his left wing was well in rear of Lodz, and his right wing had driven into Kielce. The Polish armies were splitting up into unco-ordinated fractions, some of which were retreating while others were delivering disjointed attacks on the nearest enemy column.

Meanwhile, near the Carpathians, List's mobile forces swept across the Dunajec, Biala, Wisloka, and Wislok in turn, to the San on either flank of the famous fortress of Przemysl. In the north Guderian's armoured corps, the spearhead of Küchler's army, had pushed across the Narev and was attacking the line of the Bug, in rear of Warsaw. Thus a wider pincer-movement was developing outside the inner pincers that were closing on the Polish forces in the bend of the Vistula west of Warsaw—where the largest remaining part of the Polish forces was trapped before it could withdraw over the Vistula. To the advantage which the Germans had gained by their strategic penetration was now added the advantage of tactical defence. To complete their victory they had merely to hold their ground—in face of the hurried assaults of an army which was fighting in reverse, cut off from its bases.

While the big encirclement west of the Vistula was being tightened the Germans were now penetrating deeply into the area east of the Vistula. Moreover, they had turned both the line of the Bug in the north and the line of the San in the south. From East Prussia, Guderian's armoured corps drove southward in a wide outflanking thrust to Brest-Litovsk. On List's front, Kleist's armoured corps reached the city of Lwow on the 12th. Although the invading columns were feeling the strain of their deep advance, and were running short of fuel, the Polish command-system was so badly dislocated that it could not profit either by the enemy's temporary slackening or by the stubbornness that many isolated bodies of Polish troops still showed.

Then on the 17th came the Russians' advance across the eastern frontier of Poland. The German and Russian forces met and greeted each other on a line running south from East Prussia past Bialystok, Brest-Litovsk, and Lwow to the Carpathians. Their partnership was sealed, but not cemented, by a mutual partition of Poland.

Could France and Britain have done more than they did to take the German pressure off Poland? On the face of the figures of armed strength, as now known, the answer would, at first sight, seem to be 'yes'.

The German army was far from being ready for war in 1939. The Poles and French together had the equivalent of 130 divisions against the German total of 98 divisions, of which 36 were in an untrained state. Out of the 43 divisions which the Germans left to defend their western frontier, only 11 were active divisions, fully trained and equipped, whereas the French General Staff planned to deploy 85 there. It is thus natural that the German generals, when interrogated after the war and in their memoirs since, have all declared that their western front would have been broken if the French army had made a serious effort to attack it.

But Hitler's strategy had placed France in a situation where she could only relieve pressure on Poland by developing a quick attack—a form of action for which her army was unfitted. Her old-fashioned mobilisation plan was slow in producing the required weight of forces, and her offensive plans were dependent on a mass of heavy artillery which would not be ready until the sixteenth day. By that time the Polish army's resistance was collapsing.

The responsibility for the French army's incapacity to deliver a prompt attack lies partly with its successive chiefs from Pétain to Gamelin, who were all wedded to slow-motion ways of warfare, and partly with the political leaders, who clung to the belief that a massive army raised by conscription was the cheapest and safest form of national defence assurance. Both the military and the political leaders ignored or discounted the arguments and warnings uttered by Reynaud and de Gaulle.

On the other side of the Channel, a few progressive military thinkers had urged that the best contribution that Britain could make to the defence of the West was by the early intervention of a strong air force and a small and highly efficient mechanised force of two or three armoured divisions— to offset French weakness in these means. That view momentarily gained favour in 1937. But, after Munich, the French political and military chiefs pressed their allies to adopt conscription in order to produce a large army on the old lines. Their views were shared by the British General Staff, which was also wedded to old-style ways, and by a growing proportion of the Cabinet.

Eventually, after Hitler's move into Prague, the British government abandoned its former military policy and introduced conscription. That decision diminished the effective contribution that Britain might have made, by absorbing industrial resources to equip the mass army now projected. When war came a force of four infantry divisions was sent to France while a build-up to 55 divisions was planned. By the spring of 1940, 13 British infantry divisions had arrived in France, but no armoured division—which would have been far more effective in the circumstances. The one tank brigade that was on the scene counter-attacked at Arras with such effect, on the mind of the German Command, as to cause a pause in the panzer drive towards Lille and Dunkirk.

The rapid overrunning of Poland was followed by a six months' lull— christened 'the Phoney War' by onlookers who were deceived by the surface appearance of calm. A truer name would have been 'The Winter of Illusion'. For the leaders, as well as the public, in the Western countries spent the time in framing fanciful plans for attacking Germany's flanks—and talked about them all too openly.

In reality, there was no prospect of France and Britain ever being able, alone, to develop the strength required to overcome Germany. Their best hope, now that Germany and Russia faced each other on a common border, was that friction would develop between these two mutually distrustful confederates, and draw Hitler's explosive force eastwards, instead of westwards. That happened a year later, and might well have happened earlier if the Western allies had not been impatient—as is the way of democracies.

Their loud and threatening talk of attacking Germany's flanks spurred Hitler to forestall them. His first stroke was to occupy Norway. The captured records of his conferences show that, until early in 1940, he still considered 'the maintenance of Norway's neutrality to be the best course' for Germany, but that in February he came to the conclusion that 'the English intend to land there, and I want to be there before them'. A small German invading force arrived there on 9 April, upsetting the British plans for gaining control of this neutral area—and captured the chief ports while the Norwegians' attention was absorbed by the British naval advance into Norwegian waters.

The prime responsibility for this fiasco rested on Churchill, who had re-entered the government on the outbreak of war as First Lord of the Admiralty, and from September on had pressed for drastic action to cut off Germany's supply of Swedish iron ore, by stopping its transportation through Norwegian neutral waters. He recognised that this would provoke the Germans to 'fire back', but argued that 'we have more to gain than to lose by a German attack upon Norway and Sweden'. His unrealistic views, and sweeping disregard for Scandinavian neutrality, were supported by Daladier and Reynaud in turn, and also by Gamelin. His mind and theirs were filled with dreams of attacking Germany's Baltic flank by opening up a new theatre of war in Scandinavia. The outcome soon showed how unrealistic they were. But the mismanagement of the Allies' action—the way that a small German force was allowed time to establish itself and then push back into the sea a larger Allied force—was due mainly to the fumbling of the British planners and executants, under the direction of Admiral Pound and Field-Marshal Ironside.

The British counter-moves were slow, hesitant, and bungled. When it came to the point of action the Admiralty, despite its pre-war disdain for air power, became extremely cautious and shrank from risking ships at the places where their intervention could have been decisive. The troop-moves were still feebler. Although forces were landed at several places with the aim of ejecting the German invader, they were all re-embarked in barely a fortnight, except from one foothold in Narvik—and that was abandoned a month later, after the main German offensive in the west. The dream-castles raised by Churchill had come tumbling down. They had been built on a basic misconception of the situation, and the change in modern warfare—particularly the effect of air power on sea power.

The German force that captured the capital and chief ports of Norway in the opening coup was astonishingly small. It comprised seven cruisers, fourteen destroyers, a number of auxiliary ships, and some 10,000 troops— the advance elements of three divisions that were used for the invasion. At no place was the initial landing made by more than two thousand men. One parachute battalion was also employed—to seize the airfields of Oslo and Stavanger. This was the first time that parachute troops had been used in war and they proved very valuable.

But the most decisive factor in the German success was the air force; the actual strength employed in this campaign was about 800 operational planes and 250 transport planes. It overawed the Norwegian people in the first phase, and later paralysed the Allies' counter-moves.

On the evening of 7 April British aircraft actually spotted 'strong German naval forces moving swiftly northward' across the mouth of the Skaggerak, towards the Norwegian coast. Churchill says: 'We found it hard at the Admiralty to believe that this force was going to Narvik'— in spite of a 'report from Copenhagen that Hitler meant to seize that port'. The British fleet at once sailed from Scapa, but it would seem that both the Admiralty and the admirals at sea were filled with the thought of catching the German battle-cruisers. In their efforts to bring these to battle they tended to lose sight of the possibility that the enemy had a landward intention, and lost a chance of intercepting the smaller troop-carrying warships.

It was unfortunate, and also ironical, that the British minelaying operation should have absorbed and distracted the Norwegians' attention during the crucial twenty-four hours before the Germans landed. As for the Norwegians' chances of rallying from the opening blow, this was diminished by their lack of fighting experience, peaceful spirit, and out-of-date military organisation.

The weakness of the resistance was all too clearly shown by the speed with which the invaders raced along the deep valleys to overrun the country. If the resistance had been tougher, the melting snow on the valley-sides—which hampered outflanking manœuvre—would have been a more serious impediment to the German prospects of success.

The most astonishing of the opening series of coups was that at Narvik, for this far northern port was some 1,200 miles distant from the German naval bases. Two Norwegian coast-defence ships gallantly met the attacking German destroyers but were quickly sunk. Next day a British destroyer flotilla steamed up the fiord and fought a mutually damaging action with the Germans, and then on the 13th these were finished off by the inroad of a stronger flotilla supported by the battleship *Warspite*. But by this time the German troops were established in and around Narvik.

Further south, Trondheim was captured with ease after the German ships had run the gauntlet of the batteries dominating the fiord—a hazard that had dismayed Allied experts who had considered the problem. By securing Trondheim, the Germans had possessed themselves of the strategic key to central Norway, though the question remained whether their handful of troops there could be reinforced from the south.

At Bergen, Stavanger, and Kristiansand the Germans suffered some damage from the Norwegian warships and batteries, but had little trouble once they were ashore. In the approach to Oslo, however, the main invading force suffered a jolt. For the large cruiser *Blücher*, carrying many of the military staff, was sunk by torpedoes from the Oscarsborg fortress, and the attempt to force the passage was then given up until this fortress surrendered in the afternoon, after heavy air attack. Thus the capture of Norway's capital devolved on the troops who had landed on the Fornebu airfield; in the afternoon this token force staged a parade march into the city, and its bluff succeeded. But the delay at least enabled the king and government to escape northwards with a view to rallying resistance.

The capture of Copenhagen was timed to coincide with the intended arrival at Oslo. The Danish capital was easy of access from the sea, and shortly before 5 a.m. three small transports steamed into the harbour, covered by aircraft overhead. The Germans met no resistance on landing, and a battalion marched off to take the barracks by surprise. At the same time Denmark's land frontier in Jutland was invaded, and after a brief exchange of fire resistance was abandoned.

The occupation of Denmark went far to ensure the Germans' control of a sheltered sea-corridor from their own ports to southern Norway, and also gave them advanced airfields from which they could support the troops there.

Once the Germans had established a lodgement in Norway the best way of loosening it would have been to cut them off from supply and reinforcement. That could only be done by barring the passage of the Skaggerak, between Denmark and Norway. But it soon became clear that the Admiralty—from fear of German air attack—was not willing to send anything except submarines into the Skaggerak.

There still appeared to be a chance of preserving central Norway if the two long mountain defiles leading north from Oslo were firmly held, and the small German force at Trondheim was quickly overcome. To this aim British efforts were now bent. A week after the German coup, British landings were made north and south of Trondheim, at Namsos and Andalsnes respectively, as a preliminary to the main and direct attack on Trondheim.

The advance south from Namsos was upset by the threat to its rear produced by the landing of several small German parties near the top of the Trondheim fiord, supported by the one German destroyer in the area. The advance from Andalsnes, instead of being able to swing north on Trondheim, soon turned into a defensive action against the German troops who were pushing from Oslo up the Gudbrand valley and brushing aside the Norwegians.

As the Allied troops were badly harried by air attack, and lacked air support themselves, the commanders on the spot recommended evacuation. The re-embarkation of the two forces was completed on 1 and 2 May —thus leaving the Germans in complete control of both southern and central Norway.

The Allies now concentrated on gaining Narvik—more for 'face-saving' purposes than from any continued hope of reaching the Swedish iron mines. The original British landing in this area had been made on 14 April, but even when their forces in this area had been built up to 20,000 troops— five times the occupying power's strength—their progress was still painfully slow. Not until 27 May were the Germans pushed out of Narvik town—and by that time still more dramatic events had arisen to the west of Europe that led to the Allies' early abandonment of Narvik, their last foothold in Norway.

For Hitler's next stroke had been against France and the Low Countries on 10 May. He had started to prepare it the previous autumn, when the Allies rejected the peace offer he made after defeating Poland—feeling that to knock out France offered the best chance of making Britain agree to peace. But bad weather and the doubts of his generals had caused repeated postponements from November onwards. Meanwhile the German plan was radically recast. That turned out very unfortunately for the Allies, and temporarily very lucky for Hitler, while changing the whole outlook of the war.

The old plan, with the main advance going through the canal-lined area of central Belgium, would in fact have led to a head-on collision with the best part of the Franco-British forces, and so would probably have ended in failure—shaking Hitler's prestige. But the new plan, suggested by Manstein, took the Allies completely by surprise and threw them off their balance, with disastrous results. For, while they were pushing forward into Belgium, to meet the Germans' opening assault there and in Holland, the mass of the German tanks (seven panzer divisions) drove through the hilly and wooded Ardennes—which the French General Staff, and the British too, had always regarded as 'impassable' to tanks.

Crossing the Meuse with little opposition, they broke through the weak hinge of the Allied front, and then swept on westwards to the Channel coast behind the backs of the Allied armies in Belgium, cutting their

749

communications. This decided the issue—before the bulk of the German infantry had even come into action. The British Army barely managed to escape by sea from Dunkirk. The Belgians and a large part of the French were forced to surrender. The consequences were irreparable. For when the Germans struck southwards, the week after Dunkirk, the remaining French armies proved incapable of withstanding them.

The Battle of France is one of history's most striking examples of the decisive effect of a new idea, carried out by a dynamic executant. Guderian has related how, before the war, his imagination was fired by the idea of deep strategic penetration by independent armoured forces—a long-range tank drive to cut the main arteries of the opposing army far back behind its front. A tank enthusiast, he grasped the potentialities of this idea, arising from the new current in military thought in Britain after the first world war.

The German invasion of the west opened with dramatic successes on the right flank, against key points in the defence of Holland and Belgium. These strokes, spearheaded by airborne troops, occupied the Allies in such a way as to distract attention for several days from the main thrust—which was being delivered in the centre, through the hilly and wooded country of the Ardennes, towards the heart of France.

The Hague, the capital of Holland, and the hub of its communications, at Rotterdam, were attacked in the early hours of 10 May, by airborne forces, simultaneously with the assault on its frontier defences a hundred miles to the east. The confusion and alarm created by this double blow, in front and rear, were increased by the widespread menace of the Luftwaffe. Exploiting the disorder, German armoured forces raced through a gap in the southern flank and joined up with the airborne forces at Rotterdam on the third day. They cut through to their objective under the nose of the Seventh French Army, which was just arriving to the aid of the Dutch.

On the fifth day the Dutch capitulated, although their main front was still unbroken. Their surrender was accelerated by the threat of close-quarter air attack on their crowded cities.

The invasion of Belgium also had a sensational opening. Here the ground attack was carried out by the powerful Sixth Army under Reichenau (which included Hoeppner's XVI Panzer Corps). It had to overcome a formidable barrier before it could effectively deploy. Only 500 airborne troops were left to help this attack. They were used to capture the two bridges over the Albert Canal and the Fort of Eben Emael, Belgium's most modern fort, which flanked this waterline-frontier.

By the second morning sufficient German troops had arrived over the canal to burst through the shallow Belgian line of defence behind. Then Hoeppner's two panzer divisions (the 3rd and 4th) drove over the un-demolished bridges and spread over the plains beyond. Their on-sweeping drive caused the Belgian forces to start a general retreat—just as the French and British were arriving to support them.

This breakthrough in Belgium was not the decisive stroke in the invasion of the west, but it had a vital effect on the issue. It not only drew the Allies' attention in the wrong direction but absorbed the most mobile part of the Allied forces in the battle that developed there, so that these mobile divisions could not be pulled out and switched south to meet the greater menace that on 13 May suddenly loomed up on the French frontier—at its weakest part, beyond the western end of the incomplete Maginot Line. For the mechanised spearheads of Rundstedt's Army Group had meantime been driving through Luxemburg and Belgian Luxemburg towards France. After traversing that seventy-mile stretch of the Ardennes, and brushing aside weak opposition, they crossed the French frontier and emerged on the banks of the Meuse—early on the fourth day of the offensive.

What proved fatal to the French was not, as is commonly imagined, their defensive attitude or ' Maginot Line complex', but the more offensive side of their plan. By pushing into Belgium with their left shoulder forward they played into the hands of their enemy, and wedged themselves in a trap—just as had happened with their near-fatal Plan XVII of 1914. It was the more perilous this time because the opponent was more mobile, manœuvring at motor-pace instead of at foot-pace. The penalty, too, was the greater because the left shoulder push—made by three French armies and the British—comprised the most modernly equipped and mobile part of the Allied forces as a whole.

The German advance through the Ardennes was a tricky operation, and an extraordinary feat of staffwork. Before dawn on 10 May the greatest concentration of tanks yet seen in war was massed opposite the frontier of Luxemburg. Made up of three panzer corps, these were arrayed in three blocks, or layers, with armoured divisions in the first two, and motorised infantry divisions in the third. The van was led by General Guderian, and the whole was commanded by General von Kleist. To the right of Kleist's group lay a separate panzer corps under Hoth, which was to dash through the northern part of the Ardennes, to the Meuse between Givet and Dinant.

These seven armoured divisions formed only a fraction of the armed mass that was drawn up along the German frontier ready to plunge into the Ardennes. Some fifty divisions were closely packed on a narrow but very deep front. The chances of success, however, essentially depended on the quickness with which the German panzer forces could push through the Ardennes and cross the Meuse.

The race was won, though with little margin. The result might have been different if the defending forces had been capable of profiting from the partial checks caused by demolition that were carried out according to previous plan. It was unfortunate for the security of France that these demolitions were backed by no adequate defenders.

Guderian's attack was concentrated on a 1½-mile stretch of the river just west of Sedan. The assault was launched at 4 p.m., led by the panzer infantry in rubber boats and on rafts. Ferries were soon in operation, bringing light vehicles across. The river salient was quickly overrun, and the attackers pressed on to capture the Bois de Marfée and the southern heights. By midnight the wedge was driven nearly five miles deep, while a bridge was completed at Glaire (between Sedan and St Menges) over which the tanks began to pour.

The bridge was heavily attacked by the Allied air forces, which enjoyed a temporary advantage as the weight of the Luftwaffe had been switched elsewhere. But the anti-aircraft artillery regiment of Guderian's corps kept a thick canopy of fire over the vital bridge, and Allied air attacks were beaten off with heavy loss.

By the night of the 16th the westward drive had gone more than fifty miles further, towards the Channel, and reached the Oise.

The issue had turned on the time factor at stage after stage. French counter-movements were repeatedly thrown out of gear because their timing was too slow to catch up with the changing situations, and that was due to the fact that the German van kept on moving faster than the German High Command had contemplated. The French chiefs had based their plans on the assumption that an assault on the Meuse would not come before the ninth day. That was the same time-scale the German chiefs had in mind originally, before Guderian intervened! When it was upset, worse was to follow.

The French commanders, trained in the slow-motion methods of 1918, were mentally unfitted to cope with panzer pace, and it produced a spreading paralysis among them.

Reynaud made a move to replace Gamelin—summoning Weygand, Foch's old assistant, from Syria. Weygand did not arrive until the 19th so that for three days the Supreme Command was in a state of suspense.

On the 20th Guderian reached the Channel, cutting the communications of the Allied armies in Belgium. Moreover, Weygand was even more out of date than Gamelin, and continued to plan on 1918 lines. So hope of recovery faded.

On the 16th the British Expeditionary Force had made a step back from its advanced line in front of Brussels. Before it reached its new position on the Scheldt, this had been undermined by Guderian cutting communications far to the south. On the 19th the Cabinet heard that Gort was 'examining a possible withdrawal towards Dunkirk if that were forced upon him'. The Cabinet, however, sent him orders to march south into France and force his way through the German net that had been flung across his rear—though they were told that he had only four days' supplies and ammunition sufficient for one battle.

Gort, though arguing that the Cabinet's instructions were impracticable, tried an attack southward from Arras with two of his twelve divisions and the only tank brigade that had been sent to France. When this counter-stroke was launched on the 21st it had boiled down to an advance by two tank battalions followed by two infantry battalions. The tanks made some progress but were not backed up, the infantry being shaken by dive-bombing. It is remarkable, however, what a disturbing effect this little tank counterstroke had on some of the German higher commanders. For a moment it led them to think of stopping the advance of their own tank spearheads. After the flash-in-the-pan at Arras the Allied armies in the north made no further effort to break out of the trap, while the belated relief offensive from the south that Wegyand planned was so feeble as to be almost farcical.

On the evening of the 25th Gort took the definite decision to retreat to the sea, at Dunkirk. Forty-eight hours earlier, the German panzer forces had already arrived, on the canal line only ten miles from the port!

Next day the Belgian army's line cracked in the centre under Bock's attack, and no reserves were left at hand to fill the gap. King Leopold had already sent repeated warnings to Churchill, through Admiral Keyes, that the situation was becoming hopeless. Most of Belgium had already been overrun and the army had its back close to the sea, penned in a narrow strip of land that was packed with civilian refugees. So in the late afternoon the king decided to sue for an armistice—and the 'cease fire' was sounded early the next morning.

The British retreat to the coast now became a race to re-embark before the German trap closed—notwithstanding French protests and bitter reproaches. It was fortunate that preparatory measures had begun in England a week before. Admiral Ramsay, commanding at Dover, had been placed in operational control on the previous day, the 19th. A number of ferry-craft, naval drifters and small coasters were at once collected for what was called 'Operation Dynamo'.

In the days that followed the situation became rapidly worse, and it was soon clear to the Admiralty that Dunkirk would be the only possible route of evacuation. 'Dynamo' was put into operation on the afternoon of the 26th—twenty-four hours before the Belgian appeal for an armistice, and also before the Cabinet had authorised the evacuation. At first it was not expected that more than a small fraction of the B.E.F. could be saved.

In the next three days the air attacks increased, and on 2 June daylight evacuation had to be suspended. The fighters of the R.A.F., from airfields in southern England, did their utmost to keep the Luftwaffe at bay, but, being outnumbered and unable to stay long over the area, because of the distance, they could not maintain anything like adequate air cover. The oft-repeated bombing attacks were a severe strain on the troops waiting on the beaches, though the soft sand blanketed the effects.

Far more material damage was done over the sea, where the losses included six destroyers, eight personnel ships, and over two hundred small craft, out of a total of 860 British and Allied vessels of all sizes employed in the evacuation.

It was very lucky that the German navy made very little attempt to interfere, either with U-boats or E-boats. Happily, too, the evacuation was favoured by extremely good weather. By 30 May 126,000 troops had been evacuated, while all the rest of the B.E.F. had arrived in the Dunkirk bridgehead—except for fragments that were cut off during the retreat.

By midnight on 2 June the British rearguard embarked and the evacuation of the B.E.F. was complete—224,000 men had been safely brought away, and only some 2,000 were lost in ships sunk en route to England. Some 95,000 Allied troops, mainly French, had also been evacuated. On the next night every effort was made to bring away the remaining Frenchmen, despite increasing difficulties, and 26,000 more were saved. Unfortunately a few thousand of the rearguard were left—and this left sore feelings in France.

By the morning of the 4th, when the operation was broken off, a total of 338,000 British and Allied troops had been landed in England. It was an amazing result compared with earlier expectations, and a grand performance on the part of the navy.

At the same time it is evident that the preservation of the B.E.F. would have been impossible without Hitler's action in halting the panzer forces outside Dunkirk twelve days before, on 24 May.

Hitler had been in a highly strung and jumpy state ever since the breakthrough into France. The extraordinary easiness of his advance, and the lack of resistance he had met, had made him uneasy. The effects can be followed in the diary that was kept by Halder, the Chief of the General Staff. On the 17th, the day after the French defence behind the Meuse had dramatically collapsed, Halder noted: 'Fuehrer is terribly nervous. Frightened by his own success, he is afraid to take any chance and so would rather pull the reins on us.'

Hitler's doubts revived as his panzer forces swung northward, especially after the momentary alarm caused by the British tank counter-attack from Arras, slight as this was. They were reinforced when he visited Rundstedt's headquarters on the morning of 24 May, a crucial moment. For Rundstedt, in his review of the situation, dwelt on the way that the tank strength had been reduced in the long and rapid drive, and pointed out the possibility of having to meet attacks from the north and south, particularly from the latter direction.

On Hitler's return to his own headquarters in the afternoon, he sent for the commander-in-chief, and gave him a definite halt order—Halder that evening mournfully summarised its effect in his diary: 'The left wing, consisting of armoured and motorised forces, which has no enemy in front of it, will thus be stopped in its tracks by direct orders of the Fuehrer. Finishing off the encircled enemy army is to be left to the Luftwaffe!'

If Hitler had felt that his halt order was due to Rundstedt's influence, he would almost certainly have mentioned it after the British escape among the excuses he gave for his decision, for he was very apt to blame others for any mistakes. It seems more likely that Hitler went to Rundstedt's headquarters in the hope of finding further justification for his own doubts and for the change of plan he wanted to impose.

At the same time there is evidence that even the Luftwaffe was not used as fully or as vigorously as it could have been—and some of the air chiefs say that Hitler put the brake on again here.

All this caused the higher circles to suspect a political motive behind Hitler's military reasons. Blumentritt, who was Rundstedt's operational planner, connected it with the surprising way that Hitler had talked when visiting their headquarters: 'He then astonished us by speaking with admiration of the British Empire, of the necessity for its existence, and of the civilisation that Britain had brought into the world. He compared the British Empire with the Catholic Church—saying they were both essential elements of stability in the world. He said that all he wanted from Britain was that she should acknowledge Germany's position on the Continent.'

Hitler's character was of such complexity that no simple explanation is likely to be true. It is more probable that his decision was woven of several threads. Three are visible—his desire to conserve tank strength for the next stroke, his long-standing fear of marshy Flanders, and Goering's claims for the air force. But some political thread may have been interwoven with these military ones in the mind of a man who had a bent for political strategy and so many twists in his thoughts.

The new French front along the Somme and the Aisne was longer than the original one, while the forces available to hold it were much diminished. The French had lost 30 of their own divisions in the first stage of the campaign, besides the help of their allies. (Only two British divisions remained in France, though two more that were not fully trained were now sent over.) In all, Weygand had collected 49 divisions to cover the new front, leaving 17 to hold the Maginot Line.

The Germans, by contrast, had brought their 10 armoured divisions up to strength again with relays of fresh tanks, while their 130 infantry divisions were almost untouched.

For the new offensive the forces were redistributed, two fresh armies being inserted to increase the weight along the Aisne sector, and Guderian was given command of a group of two armoured corps that was moved to lie up in readiness there. Kleist was left with two such corps, to strike from the bridgeheads over the Somme at Amiens and Peronne respectively, in a pincer-move aimed to converge on the lower reach of the Oise near Creil. The remaining armoured corps was to advance between Amiens and the sea.

The offensive was launched on 5 June, initially on the western stretch between Laon and the sea. Resistance was stiff for the first two days, but on the 7th the most westerly armoured corps broke through on the roads to Rouen, and the Germans met no serious resistance in crossing the Seine on the 9th.

Kleist's pincer-stroke did not, however, go according to plan. The right pincer eventually broke through on the 8th but the left pincer, from Peronne, was hung up by tough opposition north of Compiègne. The German Supreme Command then decided to pull back Kleist's group and switch it east to back up the breakthrough that had been made in Champagne.

The offensive there did not open until the 9th, but then the collapse came quickly. As soon as the infantry masses had forced the crossings, Guderian's tanks swept through the breach towards Chalons-sur-Marne, and then eastward. By the 11th Kleist was widening the sweep and crossed the Marne at Chateau-Thierry. The drive continued at racing pace to the Swiss frontier—cutting off all the French forces in the Maginot Line.

As early as the 7th Weygand advised the French government to ask for an armistice without delay, and next day he announced—'the Battle of the Somme is lost'. The government, though divided in opinion, hesitated to yield, but on the 9th decided to leave Paris. It wavered between a choice of Brittany and Bordeaux, and then went to Tours as a compromise.

On the 10th Italy declared war. Mussolini had been belatedly offered various colonial concessions, but spurned them in the hope of improving his position with Hitler. An Italian offensive, however, was easily held in check by the French.

The French Cabinet was now divided between capitulation and a continuance of the war from North Africa, but only decided to move itself to Bordeaux, while instructing Weygand to attempt a stand on the Loire.

The Germans entered Paris on the 14th and were driving deeper on the flanks. On the 16th they reached the Rhône valley.

Meanwhile Weygand had continued to press the need for an armistice, backed by all the principal commanders. In a last-hour effort to avert this decision, and ensure a stand in Africa, Churchill made a far-reaching proposal for a Franco-British Union. It made little impression, except to produce irritation. A vote was taken upon it, a majority of the French Cabinet rejected it, and it turned into a decision for capitulation. For Reynaud resigned, whereupon a new Cabinet was formed by Marshal Pétain and the request for the armistice was transmitted to Hitler on the night of the 16th.

On the 22nd the German terms were accepted, and the armistice became effective at 1.35 a.m. on 25 June, after an accompanying armistice with Italy had been arranged.

Britain was now the only remaining active opponent of Nazi Germany. But she was left in the most perilous situation, militarily naked while menacingly enveloped by a 2,000 mile stretch of enemy-occupied coastline. Even though the bulk of the British army had got away safely, it had lost most of its arms. If the Germans had landed in England any time during the month after the fall of France there would have been little chance of resisting them.

Naval interception would have been difficult, slow, and uncertain. The British fleet was kept far away in the north—to keep it out of the reach of the Luftwaffe. For the moment the Channel 'tank-ditch' was a more effective shield than sea power.

Britain's land forces could have done little to stop the enemy if his troops had actually got ashore. Although the army managed to escape from the debacle in France, it had left the bulk of its weapons and equipment behind. Barely five hundred guns of any sort and two hundred odd tanks remained in the country for use by the troops who had to defend Britain's shores. Months would pass before the factories could turn out sufficient weapons to make up the quantity lost at Dunkirk. There was only one near-fully-equipped division in the country. Even by mid-July there were only two.

The Home Guard could contribute large numbers of men, and plenty of spirit, but suffered from a lack of equipment and training until long after the threat of invasion had passed. Originally formed in mid-May, under the title of 'Local Defence Volunteers', a quarter of a million men between sixteen and sixty-five years of age enrolled within a week, and the total reached about 300,000 by the end of that month. But rifles were available for barely 100,000, and the rest had to depend on primitive improvised weapons such as bludgeons and pikes. By the end of July the force had risen to a total of nearly half a million, renamed the Home Guard on the 31st of that month, but it received few further rifles until late in the year. Indeed, even by the spring of 1942 when the numbers of the Home Guard were over one and a half million men, a quarter of them were still without a rifle or other personal weapon.

Happily the Germans' bid to gain command of the air, as a preliminary to invasion, was frustrated by the superb efforts of the fifty odd squadrons of Fighter Command—under the masterly direction of Air Marshal Sir Hugh Dowding and Air Vice-Marshal Park, who commanded No. II Group in south-east England. Even on the modified figures ascertained since the war, they brought down a total of 1,733 German fighters and bombers by the end of October, for a loss of 915 British fighters. (The

Germans' initial strength was over 1,300 bombers and an equal number of fighters, while the British defence had barely 600 fighters serviceable and available at the outset.)

In August and September 1940, the threat of invasion had been partially eclipsed by the fight overhead, for air supremacy, that was dramatically epitomised by the title of the 'Battle of Britain'. This in turn was succeeded by the prolonged night-time 'blitz' of London and other main industrial centres. The strain was severe, and the defence largely ineffective.

But there were other saving factors, of even more importance. The first was that Hitler and his service chiefs had made no preparations to invade England—nor even worked out any plans for such an obviously essential follow-up to their defeat of France. He let the vital month slip away in hopeful expectation that Britain would agree to make peace.

Even when disillusioned on that score, the German preparations were half-hearted. When the Luftwaffe failed to drive the R.A.F. out of the sky in the 'Battle of Britain', the army and navy chiefs were glad of the excuse thus provided for suspending the invasion. More remarkable was Hitler's own readiness to accept excuses for its suspension.

The records of his private talks show that it was partly due to a reluctance to destroy Britain and the British Empire, which he regarded as a stabilising element in the world, and still hoped to secure as a partner.

But beyond this reluctance there was a fresh impulse. Hitler's mind was again turning eastward. This was the key factor that proved decisive in preserving Britain.

If Hitler had concentrated on defeating Britain, her doom would have been almost certain. For, although he had missed his best chance of conquering her by invasion, he could have developed such a stranglehold, by combined air and submarine pressure, as to ensure her gradual starvation and ultimate collapse.

Hitler, however, felt that he could not venture to concentrate his resources on that sea-and-air effort while the Russian army stood poised on his eastern border, as a threat to Germany on land. So he argued that the only way to make Germany's rear secure was to attack and defeat Russia. His suspicion of Russia's intentions was all the more intense because hatred of Russian Communism had so long been his deepest emotion. He also persuaded himself that Britain would agree to peace once she could no longer hope for Russian intervention in the war.

As early as 21 July, at the first Conference on the hastily drafted plans for invading England, he declared his conclusion: 'Our attention must be turned to tackling the Russian problem.' Planning for it started immediately, though not until early in 1941 did he take the definite decision.

As an alternative course Hitler's naval adviser, Admiral Raeder, had repeatedly urged him to concentrate on crippling Britain indirectly by capturing the keys of the Mediterranean. But Hitler showed little interest in such projects and opportunities—he was obsessed with Russia.

That was the more fortunate for Britain, since her overseas positions had been put in grave peril already by Fascist Italy's entry into the war in June 1940—on Mussolini's impulse to exploit France's downfall and Britain's weakness—as well as by Japan's growing threat in the Far East.

Initially, the extension of the war to the Mediterranean turned out to Britain's advantage, as it offered her a chance for counterattack, in an area where sea power could exert its influence. Churchill was quick to seize it—in part too quick. Despite the misgivings of the service chiefs, he sent to Africa part of Britain's scanty reserve of equipped troops, even while the homeland lay under imminent threat of invasion. His bold decision was justified by the way that Wavell's mechanised forces, although small, soon smashed the out-of-date Italian army in North Africa, besides conquering Italian East Africa. They could have driven on to Tripoli, and thus cleared the enemy completely out of Africa—but were halted in order to provide the means of sending a British force to Greece.

When Hitler's attack on the West had reached a point—with the breach of the impoverished Somme–Aisne front—where the defeat of France became certain, Mussolini had brought Italy into the war, on 10 June 1940, in the hope of gaining some of the spoils of victory. It appeared to be an almost completely safe decision from his point of view, and almost certainly fatal to Britain's position in the Mediterranean and Africa.

There was nothing available for the moment to reinforce the small fraction of the British army that guarded Egypt and the Sudan against the imminent threat of invasion from the Italian armies in Libya and Italian East Africa. Numerically, these armies were overwhelmingly superior to the scanty British forces opposing them, under General Sir Archibald Wavell. There were barely 50,000 British troops facing a total of half a million Italian and Italian colonial troops.

On the southerly fronts, the Italian forces in Eritrea and Abyssinia mustered more than 200,000 men, and could have pushed westwards into the Sudan—which was defended by a mere 9,000 British and Sudanese troops—or southwards into Kenya, where the garrison was no larger. On the North African front a still larger force in Cyrenaica under Marshal Graziani faced the 36,000 British, New Zealand and Indian troops who guarded Egypt. The Western Desert, inside the Egyptian frontier, separated the two sides on this front. The foremost British position was at Mersa Matruh, 120 miles inside the frontier and some 200 miles west of the Nile Delta.

The situation was all the worse because Italy's entry into the war had made the sea route through the Mediterranean too precarious to use, and

759

reinforcements had to come to Egypt by the extremely roundabout Cape route—down the west coast of the African continent and up the east coast into the Red Sea.

But it was not until 13 September that the Italians, after massing more than six divisions, began a cautious move forward into the Western Desert. After advancing 50 miles, less than half way to the British position at Mersa Matruh, they sat down at Sidi Barrani, and there established themselves in a chain of fortified camps—which were too widely separated to support one another. Week after week then passed without any attempt to move on. Meanwhile reinforcements reached Wavell, including three armoured regiments—rushed out from England in three fast merchant ships, on Churchill's initiative.

Wavell now decided that, as the Italians did not come on, he would sally forth and strike at them. The stroke was planned, not as a sustained offensive, but rather as a large-scale raid. Wavell thought of it as a sharp punch to stun the invaders temporarily while he diverted part of his strength down to the Sudan, to push back the other Italian army there. Thus, unfortunately, no adequate preparations were made to follow up the overwhelming victory that was actually gained.

The British force under General O'Connor consisted of only 30,000 men, against an opposing force of 80,000—but it had 275 tanks against 130. The fifty heavily armoured 'Matildas' of the 7th Royal Tank Regiment, impervious to most of the enemy's anti-tank weapons, played a particularly decisive role in this and subsequent battles.

On the night of 7 December the force moved out from the Matruh position on its 70-mile approach through the desert. Next night it passed through a gap in the enemy's chain of camps, capturing three of these in turn on the following day, and the cluster around Sidi Barrani on the 10th—with a total bag of nearly 40,000 prisoners.

The remnants of the invading Italian army, after recrossing their own frontier, took refuge in the coast-fortress of Bardia. There they were speedily isolated by the encircling sweep of the 7th Armoured Division. Unfortunately, there was no backing-up infantry division at hand to take advantage of their demoralisation. For Wavell had planned to take away the 4th Indian Division as soon as Sidi Barrani was captured, and to bring it back to Egypt for dispatch to the Sudan. Thus on the third day of battle, when the routed Italians were running westwards in panic, half the victor's force had been marching eastwards—back to back! Three weeks elapsed before the 6th Australian Division arrived, from Palestine, to aid in continuing the British advance.

On 3 January 1941 the assault on Bardia was at last launched, with twenty-two Matildas of the 7th Royal Tank Regiment leading the way— as 'tin-openers'. The defence quickly collapsed and by the third day the whole garrison had surrendered—with 45,000 men. The coastal fortress of

Tobruk was attacked on 21 January and fell next day—yielding a bag of 30,000 prisoners.

But Churchill's imagination was now chasing a different hare. Following the scent of his old venture in the first world war, and stimulated by the way that the Greeks were standing up to the Italians, he pictured the possibility of creating a powerful combination of the Balkan countries against Germany. It was an attractive picture, but in the actual circumstances unrealistic, for the primitive Balkan armies had no power to withstand Germany's air and tank forces, while Britain could send them very little.

Early in January Churchill had pressed the Greeks to accept a contingent of British tank and artillery units, to be landed at Salonika. But General Metaxas, then head of the Greek government, declined the proposal, saying that the force offered would be likely to provoke a German invasion without being nearly strong enough to counter it.

This polite rebuff from the Greek government coincided with O'Connor's capture of Tobruk, so the British government now decided to allow him to push on another step and capture the port of Benghazi. On 3 February, however, air reports showed that the enemy was preparing to abandon Benghazi, and retreat to the Agheila bottleneck, where they could block the route from Cyrenaica into Tripolitania. O'Connor immediately planned a bold stroke to intercept the enemy's withdrawal, employing only the depleted 7th Armoured Division and dispatching it across the desert interior with the aim of reaching the coast-road well beyond Benghazi. It had about 150 miles to go, from its position at Mechili—the first long stretch being across extremely rough country. It moved off with only two days' rations and a bare sufficiency of petrol.

By the evening of the 5th, its two columns had established blocking positions across the enemy's routes of retreat. By the morning of the 7th the Italians had abandoned their efforts to break through, and 20,000 men had surrendered, while over 100 tanks had been lost or abandoned— of which nearly all were newly arrived cruiser tanks. The British cutting-off force here mustered only 3,000 men, with 38 cruiser tanks. When Bardia and its garrison fell, Anthony Eden had coined a new version of Churchill's famous phrase, saying 'never has so much been surrendered by so many to so few'. That was even more true of the crowning victory at Beda Fomm.

The radiance of victory, however, was soon dimmed. That was due to top-level decisions in London. The complete extinction of Graziani's army had left the British with a clear passage, through the Agheila bottleneck, to Tripoli. But just as O'Connor and his troops were hoping to race on there—and throw the enemy out of his last foothold in North Africa— they were definitely stopped by order of the British Cabinet. What had produced this somersault? Metaxas had died suddenly, on 29 January, and the new Greek Prime Minister was a man of less formidable character. Churchill saw an opportunity of reviving his cherished Balkan project, and was prompt to seize it. He again pressed his offer on the Greek government—and this time they were persuaded to accept it. On 7 March the first contingent of a British force of 50,000 troops landed in Greece.

Churchill had reverted to his old fault of seeing and attempting too many things at the same time. He dreamed of opening up a new theatre of war in the Balkans, and marshalling the countries there for a combined attack on Germany's flank. Overborne by his personality, the British Chiefs of Staff and Wavell assented to his unrealistic project. But the Germans promptly swept into, and over, Yugoslavia and Greece—and the British were driven to a second 'Dunkirk'. While still shaken, they were also ejected from Crete.

The British force (of approximately 3 divisions) under General Wilson had been moving into position on the central sector, between the main Greek armies (of 14 divisions) facing the Italians in Albania and the smaller Greek force (of 3 divisions) near Salonika. It was to cover the approaches to southern Greece, and take under command the three weak Greek divisions already assigned for that purpose. Before it could get into position the Germans had struck, on 6 April. Ten days previously the Yugoslav government, after being coerced into a pact with Hitler, had been overthrown by an officers' coup headed by General Simovitch. Hitler had promptly decided to invade Yugoslavia and Greece simultaneously, reshuffling the German forces and reinforcing them for the enlarged operation—from 18 divisions to 28, of which 7 were to be panzer divisions (out of his total of 17 in Europe). They were supported by about a thousand aircraft.

Within barely a week, by 5 April, one of the three corps of List's Twelfth Army, now in Bulgaria, had been moved across to the south-eastern frontier of Yugoslavia, opening fresh supply routes, while Kleist's panzer group was switched north-westward to that country's central frontier close to Belgrade, the capital. At the same time Weichs's Second Army was assembled in southern Austria ready, along with Hungarian forces, to invade the northern half of Yugoslavia.

The attack opened with a devastating air bombardment of Belgrade and other centres. Then the land thrusts disrupted the Yugoslav Army, which soon collapsed under their multiple pressure. Meantime List's two westerly corps quickly overran Greece's shallow coastal strip in Macedonia and Thrace, while his third corps drove into the south of Yugoslavia. Reaching Skoplje on the second evening, 7 April, it separated that country from Greece, made touch with the Italian Army in Albania, and was free to swing southward into Greece, along with the neighbouring German corps (of List's army).

Besides cutting off the retreat of the main Greek armies in Albania, the Germans thus turned the flank of Wilson's force before his British troops were even in position. On 10 April Wilson began a withdrawal, which developed into a quickening series of rearward moves as the Germans successively bypassed his inland flank. By the 21st, when his troops were still holding the Thermopylae line, 130 miles south of the original position, it was agreed with the Greek government that the British force should be evacuated. This evacuation, from the southernmost ports of Greece in the Peloponnese, began on the night of the 24th and most of the remaining troops were taken off by the 28th. The bulk was taken to Crete.

In Yugoslavia and Greece, Hitler's new armoured forces had proved as irresistible as in the plains of Poland and France, despite the mountain obstacles they met. They had swept through both countries like a whirlwind and knocked over the opposing armies like ninepins. Field-Marshal List's army alone captured 90,000 Jugoslavs, 270,000 Greeks and 13,000 British, at a cost to itself of barely 5,000 men killed and wounded, as later records showed. (At the time British newspapers estimated the German loss as over a quarter of a million, and even a British official statement put them as 'probably 75,000'.)

Crete became the Germans' next objective—although Hitler himself was a reluctant convert to the scheme. He had wanted to break off the Balkan campaign after reaching the south of Greece, but General Student, the commander of the airborne forces, gained Goering's support on 21 April; he then succeeded in convincing Hitler that it was practicable—and desirable. He was allowed to use for the purpose Germany's one parachute division, her one glider regiment, and a mountain division—to be transported by air.

At 8 a.m. on 20 May some 3,000 parachute troops were dropped on Crete. The island was held by 28,600 British, Australian and New Zealand troops, along with two Greek divisions amounting in numbers to almost as many. But there were merely half a dozen tanks, and air support was lacking.

The attack had been expected, as a follow-up to the Germans' conquest of the Balkans, and good information about the preparation had been provided by British agents in Greece. But the airborne threat was not regarded as seriously as it should have been—especially by the commander in Crete, General Freyberg.

By the first evening, the number of Germans on the island had been more than doubled, and was progressively reinforced—by parachute drop, by glider and from the second evening onwards by troop-carriers. These began landing on the captured Maleme airfield while it was still swept by the defenders' artillery and mortar-fire. The ultimate total of German troops brought by air was about 22,000. Many were killed and injured by crashes on landing, but those that survived were the toughest of fighters, whereas their numerically superior opponents were not so highly trained and were still suffering from the shock of being driven out of Greece.

On the seventh day, the 26th, the British commander in Crete reported: 'in my opinion the limit of endurance has been reached by the troops under my command...our position here is hopeless'. Coming from such a stout-hearted soldier as Freyberg, V.C., this verdict was not questioned. Evacuation began on the night of the 28th, and ended on the night of the 31st—the navy suffering heavy losses from the enemy's dominant air force in its persistent efforts to bring away as many troops as possible. A total of 16,500 were rescued, including about 2,000 Greeks, but the rest were left dead or prisoner in German hands. The navy had well over 2,000 dead. Three cruisers and six destroyers were sunk. Thirteen other ships were badly damaged, including two battleships and the only aircraft-carrier then in the Mediterranean fleet.

The Germans had some 4,000 men killed, and about twice as many wounded. Thus their permanent loss was less than a third of what the British had suffered, apart from the Greeks and local Cretan levies. But, as the loss fell mostly on the picked troops of Germany's one existing parachute division, it had an unforeseen effect on Hitler that turned out to Britain's benefit.

For Hitler did not follow up his third Mediterranean victory in any of the ways expected on the British side—a pounce on to Cyprus, Syria, Suez or Malta. A month later he launched the invasion of Russia, and from that time on neglected the opportunities that lay open for driving the British out of the Mediterranean and the Middle East. If his forfeit was mainly due to his absorption in the Russian venture, it was also due to his reaction after the victory in Crete. The cost depressed him more than the conquest exhilarated him. It was such a contrast to the cheapness of his previous successes and far larger captures.

Besides the losses in these disasters, the British paid a double forfeit in Africa. For the pause there allowed time for the arrival in Tripoli of a German panzer force under Rommel, sent by Hitler to the aid of the collapsing Italians. Although not strong, its swift surprise advance on 31 March sufficed to sweep the British out of Cyrenaica and back to the frontier of Egypt. Churchill then hustled Wavell to make a hasty fresh effort, and, when this grandiloquently named 'Operation Battleaxe' failed in June, he sacked Wavell—who was replaced by Auchinleck.

The image of Rommel now filled Churchill's eye to the exclusion of all else. To eject him, Churchill poured most of Britain's available forces into Africa. The renewed and enlarged British offensive, called 'Operation Crusader', had been launched on 18 November. This time Churchill's efforts had provided the British forces (now entitled the Eighth Army) with over 750 tanks—more than twice as many as Rommel had, and a third of his were poorly armed Italian tanks. But the German tanks were much better handled tactically than the British and a proportion of them had a heavier gun. Moreover Rommel skilfully manœuvred to bait the British into bull-like charges where they were trapped by his concealed anti-tank guns. In consequence, he was able to turn the tables on his opponents in the first few days of the battle, despite their 4 to 1 superiority in the air (and the fact that two-thirds of his meagre number of aircraft were Italian). The way that he hit back threw the attackers into such confusion that the commander of the Eighth Army, General Cunningham, thought of breaking off the battle. In the crisis Auchinleck flew up from Cairo to take a personal grip on the situation, and persisted in pressing the offensive. The Eighth Army was given a new commander, General Ritchie, and a large number of reinforcing tanks and troops were brought up. Eventually, after two more weeks of hard struggle, superior weight prevailed and Rommel's depleted forces were pushed out of Cyrenaica.

Now at last, in Christmas week, Rommel received the first small batch of reinforcements—two tank companies and a few batteries of artillery—that had reached him since the battle had begun, a month before. With this aid he repulsed a British attempt, launched on Boxing Day, to storm the position near Agedabia where he had halted his retreat. Then, on 21 January, he suddenly sprang like a tiger upon opponents who had assumed him to be badly lamed and too weak to move. His unexpected pounce and swift series of blows threw the Eighth Army into disorder, and drove it to abandon most of the ground it had gained. It managed to halt on the Gazala–Bir Hacheim line, just west of Tobruk.

For that abortive effort to knock out Rommel, Britain paid heavy penalty (which reacted on her Allies too)—the forfeit of her positions in the Far East. The chief of the Imperial General Staff, Sir John Dill, had emphasised in May that 'it has been an accepted principle in our strategy that in the last resort the security of Singapore comes before that of Egypt'. He had deprecated neglecting the defence of the Far East in favour of an early offensive in Africa. But Churchill rebuffed the warning, and confidently declared that 'in any case Japan would not be likely to besiege Singapore at the outset' even if she did enter the war.

Churchill's blind neglect of the Far East defences was the more extraordinary because it had long been an axiom of British policy that if Japan's oil supply were cut off by an embargo she would be bound to strike back. In July that drastic step was taken by Roosevelt and Churchill simultaneously, to enforce their demand for a Japanese withdrawal from Indo-China. Yet both Britain and the United States were caught napping when Japan at last struck on 7 December—and nothing adequate had been done to strengthen the defence of Singapore during the five months' interval.

That was a much worse error, and far more serious in its consequences, than any of which Dill's successor, Alanbrooke, complained. (Characteristically, Churchill had become impatient of Dill's doubts and removed him from office, a week before the Japanese landed on the Malay Peninsula in rear of Singapore, thus confirming Dill's warnings.)

The only compensation, which eventually outweighed all else, was that the simultaneous attack by the Japanese on America's Pacific bases brought the United States into the war. That in the end proved fatal not only to Japan but to Hitler.

The German invasion of Russia was launched on 22 June—a day ahead of Napoleon's date. The panzer forces quickly overran the Soviet armies that were immediately available and within less than a month had driven 450 miles into Russia—three-quarters of the way to Moscow. But the Germans never reached there.

On 3 February 1941 Hitler had approved the final text of the Barbarossa plan, after a conference of his military chiefs at Berchtesgaden. The enemy's strength in western Russia was estimated at 155 divisions, including sixty tank brigades. The Germans could muster only 121 divisions, of which seventeen were armoured, for the attack. Moreover the number of armoured divisions had been raised to that figure only by halving the scale of tanks in them—a dilution, contrary to the views of the tank experts, that Hitler decreed to increase the apparent number of such divisions. The comparative figures did little to allay doubts among the executive generals.

Hitler's original timetable was upset by the events in the Balkans (above, p. 762). He had a deep fear of British intervention in the Balkans, close to his Rumanian sources of oil supply, and that fear increased after Mussolini had attacked Greece in October without consulting his partner. Hitler was very annoyed, and found little consolation in the repulse that the Italians suffered. For the appearance in Greece of a small instalment of British aid made it likely that a larger one would follow—and it did. Hitler had gained a dominating position in the Balkans by inducing Bulgaria and Yugoslavia in turn to come under his wing, but this did not satisfy him, so he had decided to occupy Greece as further cover to his Balkan flank, before invading Russia. The overthrow of the government of Yugoslavia by a military revolt caused Hitler to make a bigger effort, and detach larger forces to subdue Yugoslavia simultaneously with Greece. Both were quickly overrun, and the British were driven to re-embark. But, when Hitler took the decision, he had felt compelled to put off the invasion of Russia from mid-May to mid-June. Because of the lateness of the spring and bad weather, however, he could not have started it until a week or so earlier.

Hitler and the Army Command had different ideas from the start of the planning—and never reconciled them.

Hitler wished to secure Leningrad as a primary objective, thus clearing his Baltic flank and linking up with the Finns, and tended to disparage the importance of Moscow. But, with a keen sense of economic factors, he also wanted to secure the agricultural wealth of the Ukraine and the industrial area on the Lower Dnieper. The two objectives were extremely wide apart, and thus entailed entirely separate lines of operation.

Brauchitsch and Halder wanted to concentrate on the Moscow line of advance—not for the sake of capturing the capital, but because they felt that this line offered the best chance of destroying the mass of Russia's forces which they 'expected to find on the way to Moscow'. In Hitler's view that course carried the risk of driving the Russians into a general retreat eastward, out of reach.

In the first phase, however, it was agreed that the centre of gravity should be in the sector of Bock's Army Group just north of the Pripet Marshes, and along the route from Minsk and Moscow. Here the major part of the armoured forces were employed—Bock being given two panzer groups (of nine panzer and seven motorised divisions) to act as spearheads, and fifty-one divisions in all.

Leeb's Army Group on the northern flank, near the Baltic—with one panzer group (three panzer and three motorised divisions), and thirty divisions in all—had bare equality to the Russian forces facing it. Rundstedt's Army Group, south of the Pripet Marshes, was given one panzer group (five panzer and three motorised divisions) and thirty divisions in all—a total much less than the forces opposing it.

The panzer pincers of Guderian and Hoth quickly made two deep incisions, and on the sixth day met at Minsk, 200 miles inside the frontier. Behind them the infantry pincers closed in at Slonim, but they were not quick enough to complete the encirclement before the bulk of the enveloped Russian armies forced their way out of the trap.

A second attempt, aimed to surround them near Minsk, was more successful, and nearly 300,000 were captured—although large fractions had managed to escape before the encirclement was sealed. The size of the bag gave rise to a wave of optimism, even among the generals who had been apprehensive about Hitler's decision to invade Russia. Halder wrote in his diary on 3 July: 'It is probably not an exaggeration when I contend that the campaign against Russia has been won in fourteen days.' On that day Guderian's leading troops had reached the Dnieper—320 miles deep into Russia and half-way to Moscow.

The German higher command then thought it best to wait until their own infantry masses came up, but that would have meant up to a fortnight's delay, so Guderian decided to tackle the Dnieper with his panzer forces alone. His attack was successful, and, after overcoming the Dnieper line on 10 July, he reached the city of Smolensk on the 16th and drove quickly on to the Desna river.

Guderian urged the importance of keeping the Russians on the run, and allowing them no time to rally. But Hitler reverted to his own original idea for the next stage of operations. The panzer forces were to be taken away from Bock, in the centre, and sent to the wings—Guderian's panzer group was to wheel southward to help in overcoming the Russian armies facing Rundstedt in the Ukraine, while Hoth's panzer group was to turn northward to aid Leeb's attack on Leningrad.

Once again Brauchitsch temporised, instead of at once pressing for a different plan. He argued that, before any further operations were started, the panzer forces must have a rest to overhaul their machines and get up replacements. Meanwhile the high-level discussion about the course to be followed went on, and it continued even after the panzer forces could have resumed their drive. None the less, another encirclement, at Kiev, was a great success, and raised rosy expectations. Guderian thrust downward across the Russians' rear while Kleist's panzer group thrust upward. The two pincers met 150 miles east of Kiev, closing a trap in which 600,000 Russians were caught. But it was late in September before the battle ended, as poor roads and rainy weather had slowed down the pace of the encircling manœuvre.

The renewed advance on Moscow began on 2 October. Its prospects looked bright when Bock's armies brought off a great encirclement round Vyazma, where a further 600,000 Russians were captured. That left the Germans momentarily with an almost clear path to Moscow. But the Vyazma battle had not been completed until the end of October, the German troops were tired, the country became a morass as the weather got worse, and fresh Russian forces appeared in the path as they plodded slowly forward.

Brauchitsch and Halder, as well as Bock, were naturally the more reluctant to call a halt because of their earlier struggle in getting Hitler to accept their arguments for capturing Moscow rather than pursuing objectives in the south.

So the push for Moscow was resumed on 15 November, when there was a momentary improvement in the weather. But, after two weeks' struggle in mud and snow, it was brought to a halt twenty miles short of Moscow. On 2 December a further effort was launched, and some detachments penetrated into the suburbs of Moscow, but the advance as a whole was held up in the forests covering the capital.

This was the signal for a Russian counter-offensive of large scale, prepared and directed by Zhukov. It tumbled back the exhausted Germans, lapped round their flanks, and produced a critical situation.

The forfeit of Moscow was not compensated by what the armies attained in the south. After the great round-up at Kiev, Rundstedt overran the Crimea and the Donetz basin, but was frustrated in his drive for the Caucasian oil-fields. He then wanted to fall back to a good defensive line on the Mius river, but Hitler forbade such a withdrawal. Rundstedt replied that he could not comply with such an order, and asked to be relieved of his command. That was in the first week of December— simultaneously with the repulse at Moscow.

The same week Brauchitsch asked to be relieved on grounds of sickness, the next week Bock did likewise, and a little later Leeb resigned when Hitler rejected his proposal for a withdrawal on the northern front near Leningrad. So all the four top commanders departed.

Hitler appointed no successor to Brauchitsch, but took the opportunity to make himself the direct commander-in-chief of the army.

The Red Army's winter counter-offensive continued for over three months after its December launching, though with diminishing progress. By March it had advanced more than 150 miles in some sectors. But the Germans maintained their hold on the main bastions of their winter front.

What were the key factors in the German failure?

(i) The autumn mud and winter snow were the obvious ones.

(ii) But more fundamental was the Germans' miscalculation of the reserves that Stalin could bring up from the depths of Russia. They reckoned on meeting 200 divisions, and by mid-August had beaten these. But by then a further 160 had appeared on the scene. By the time these in turn had been overcome, autumn had arrived, and, when the Germans pushed on towards Moscow in the mud, they again found fresh armies blocking the route.

(iii) Another basic factor was Russia's continued primitiveness despite all the technical progress achieved since the Soviet Revolution. It was not only a matter of the extraordinary endurance of her soldiers and people, but the primitiveness of her roads. If her road system had been developed comparably to that of the West, she would have been overrun almost as quickly as France.

(iv) Even as it was, however, the invasion might have succeeded if the panzer forces had driven right on for Moscow in the summer, without waiting for the infantry—as Guderian had urged, only to be overruled on this occasion by Hitler and the older heads of the army.

The winter in Russia proved a terrible strain and drain on the German forces—and they never fully recovered from it. Yet it is evident that Hitler still had quite a good chance of victory in 1942, as the Red Army was seriously short of equipment, while Stalin's grip on it had been shaken by the heavy initial defeats.

Hitler's new offensive in 1942 swept quickly to the edge of the Caucasus oil-fields—on which Russia's military machine depended. But Hitler split his forces between the double objectives of the Caucasus and Stalingrad. Narrowly checked here, he wore down his army in repeated bull-headed efforts to capture the 'City of Stalin', becoming obsessed with that symbol of defiance. Forbidding any withdrawal when winter came, he doomed the army attacking Stalingrad to encirclement and capture when Russia's newly raised armies arrived on the scene late in the year.

At the outset the *Blitzkrieg* tactics had scored once again—but for the last time. A quick breakthrough was achieved in the Kursk–Kharkov sector, and then Kleist's panzer army poured down the corridor between the Don and Donetz rivers. Surging through the gateway to the Caucasus, it reached the more westerly oil-fields round Maikop in six weeks.

This was Russia's weakest hour. Only an instalment of her newly raised armies was yet ready for action, and even that was seriously short of equipment. Fortunately for Russia, the attackers were also much weaker than in 1941. Hitler tried to fill the gaps with Rumanian, Italian, and Hungarian troops, using them to cover his long flank—and that substitution turned into a fatal liability at the end of the year.

When Kleist drove on from Maikop towards the main oil-fields of the Caucasus he was first halted by running short of petrol, and then hung up in the mountains, where he met stiffer resistance as well as a stiffer obstacle.

At the same time his own forces were progressively drained in order that Hitler might reinforce the divergent attack on Stalingrad. Here, the first onset was barely checked, but the resistance hardened with repeated hammering, while the directness of the German strokes simplified the Russians' problem in meeting the threat. Hitler could not bear to be defied by the 'city of Stalin', and wore down his forces in the prolonged effort to storm it. Meanwhile the new Russian armies were gathering on the flanks.

The counterstroke was launched on 19 November, and was well timed. It started in the interval between the first strong frosts, which harden the ground for rapid movement, and the heavy snows, which clog manœuvre. North-west of Stalingrad, Russian spearheads thrust down the banks of the Don to Kalach and the railway running back to the Donetz basin. South-east of Stalingrad the prongs of the left pincer thrust westward to the railway running south to Tikhoretsk and the Black Sea. After cutting this line they pressed on towards Kalach, and by the 23rd the encirclement was completed. It was welded more firmly in the days that followed, enclosing over 200,000 of the enemy. General von Paulus's army attacking Stalingrad was left isolated.

Meanwhile, another powerful Russian force had burst out of the Serafimovich bridgehead and spread over the country west of the Don bend. This outer-circle movement was of vital importance, for it dropped an iron curtain across the more direct routes by which relieving forces might have come to the aid of Paulus. Thus the German reply, in mid-December, was delivered from the south-west, beyond the Don. But this hastily improvised advance was checked a long way short of the beleaguered army, and then gradually forced back by Russian pressure on its own flank. With the frustration of this attempt any hope of relieving Paulus passed, for the German Command had no reserves for another attempt.

The disaster at Stalingrad left the Germans with a far longer front than they could hold with their depleted strength. Withdrawal was the only saving course, as the generals urged, but Hitler obstinately refused to sanction it. Hitler's forces were suffering, increasingly, the consequences of strategic overstretch—which had proved the ruin of Napoleon.

The Germans were already paying the penalty of overstretch in the Mediterranean. The Italians' breakdown in North Africa had led Hitler to send German reinforcements there, under Rommel. But, having his eyes fixed on Russia, Hitler sent only enough to bolster up the Italians, and never made a strong effort to seize the eastern, central and western gates of the Mediterranean—Suez, Malta and Gibraltar. So in effect he merely opened up a fresh drain on Germany's strength, which ultimately offset the success of Rommel's counter-thrusts in postponing for over two years the clearance of North Africa.

The Germans were now stretched out along both sides of the Mediterranean and the whole coast line of western Europe, while trying to hold a perilously wide front in the depths of Russia.

The same overstretch became a fatal factor for Germany's new ally. The Japanese stroke at Pearl Harbour, with naval aircraft, temporarily crippled the U.S. Pacific fleet, and the immediate sequel was that it enabled the Japanese to overrun the Allied positions in the south-west Pacific—Malaya, Burma, the Philippines and the Dutch East Indies. In this rapid expansion, however, they became stretched out far beyond their basic capacity for holding their gains. For Japan was a small island state, with limited industrial power.

Initially it had been the British who had paid forfeit for overstretch—while both they and the Americans had to pay forfeit for being taken by surprise.

In July 1941 President Roosevelt had sent his personal adviser, Harry Hopkins, on a mission to London to convey his misgivings about the wisdom of Churchill's policy and a warning of the risks involved elsewhere—'by trying to do too much' in the Middle East. The American military and naval experts endorsed the warning, and expressed the view that Singapore should be given priority over Egypt. None of these arguments altered Churchill's view. 'I would not tolerate abandoning the struggle for Egypt, and was resigned to pay whatever forfeits were exacted in Malaya.' But he did not really expect danger there. He says: 'I confess that in my mind the whole Japanese menace lay in a sinister twilight, compared with our other needs.' It is thus painfully clear that the responsibility for Malaya's inadequate defences rested principally with Churchill himself—and was due to his insistence on launching a premature offensive in North Africa.

The chain of errors did not end there. After the decision to cut off Japan's oil supplies, Churchill 'realised the formidable effects of the embargoes', and a month later proposed the dispatch of what he called a 'deterrent' naval force to the East. The Admiralty were planning to assemble there the *Nelson*, the *Rodney*, and four older battleships, together with a battle-cruiser and two to three aircraft-carriers. Churchill preferred to employ 'the smallest number of the best ships', and proposed to send one of the new *King George V*-type battleships, with a battle-cruiser and aircraft-carrier, saying: 'I cannot feel that Japan will face the combination now forming against her of the United States, Great Britain and Russia... Nothing would increase her hesitation more than the appearance of the force I mentioned, and above all a *K.G.V.* This might indeed be a decisive deterrent.'

Accordingly the *Prince of Wales* and the battle-cruiser *Repulse* sailed for Singapore—but without any aircraft-carrier. The one that had been earmarked ran ashore in Jamaica and had to be docked for repairs. There was another actually in the Indian Ocean, and within reach of Singapore, but no orders were given for her to move there. Thus the two big ships had to depend for air cover upon shore-based fighters and these were scanty.

The *Prince of Wales* and *Repulse* reached Singapore on 2 December. Five days later a 'war warning' signal had been issued to the U.S. Navy that 'an aggressive move by Japan is expected within the next few days'. On 6 December a large Japanese convoy of transports, escorted by cruisers and destroyers, was reported to be sailing from Indo-China in the direction of Malaya.

Meanwhile a Japanese naval force (with six carriers) was approaching Pearl Harbour, in the Hawaiian Islands, the main U.S. naval base in the Pacific. Early on 7 December the Americans were caught napping by an attack there. The stroke was made ahead of the declaration of war, following the precedent of Port Arthur, the Japanese opening stroke in the war against Russia.

Until early in 1941 the Japanese plan in case of war against the United States was to use their main fleet in the southern Pacific in conjunction with an attack on the Philippine Islands, to meet an American advance across the ocean to the relief of their garrison in the Philippines. That was the move that the Americans were expecting the Japanese to make, and their expectation had been reinforced by the recent Japanese move down to Indo-China. But Admiral Yamamoto had in the meantime conceived a new plan—of a surprise attack on Pearl Harbour. The striking force made a very roundabout approach via the Kurile Islands and came down from the north upon the Hawaiian Islands undetected, then launching its attack before sunrise, with 360 aircraft, from a position nearly three hundred miles from Pearl Harbour. Four of the eight American battleships were sunk and the others badly damaged. In a little over an hour the Japanese had gained control of the Pacific.

Japan's opening stroke in the south Pacific was equally effective. The

Japanese invasion convoy crossed the Gulf of Siam unmolested and on the night of the 7th began disembarking its troops at three points high up the Malay Peninsula. Next evening Admiral Phillips gallantly sailed north from Singapore with his two big ships to strike at the transports, although no shore-based air cover could be provided so far north. Soon after daylight on the 10th he was caught off Kuantan by a force of some 80 Japanese bombers and torpedo-bombers from their base at Saigon in Indo-China. They swooped down on the *Prince of Wales* and *Repulse* in nine successive waves, and both ships were sunk.

By these strokes the way was cleared for an uninterrupted seaborne invasion of Malaya and the Malay Archipelago. While the main Japanese striking force had been steaming north-east towards the Hawaiian Islands, other naval forces had been escorting troopship convoys into the south-west Pacific. Almost simultaneously with the air attack on Pearl Harbour, landings began in the Malay Peninsula as well as in the Philippines. The former were aimed at the great British naval base at Singapore, but there was no attempt to attack it from the sea—the kind of attack which the defence had been primarily designed to meet. The approach was very indirect.

While landings were made at two points on the east coast of the Malay Peninsula, to seize airfields and distract attention, the main forces were disembarked on the Siamese neck of the peninsula, some 500 miles north of Singapore. From these landing-places in the extreme north-east the Japanese forces poured down the *west* coast of the peninsula, successively outflanking the lines on which the British forces attempted to check them.

The Japanese profited not only by their unexpected choice of such a difficult route but by the opportunities for unexpected infiltration which the thick vegetation often provided. After almost continuous retreat for six weeks the British forces were forced to withdraw from the mainland into the island of Singapore at the end of January. On the night of 8 February the Japanese launched their attack across the mile-wide straits, got ashore at numerous points, and developed fresh infiltrations along a broad front. On 15 February the defending forces surrendered, and with them was lost the key to the south-west Pacific.

In the main Philippine island of Luzon, the initial landings north of Manila had been quickly followed by a landing in the rear of the capital. Under this dislocating leverage, and the converging threat, the American forces abandoned most of the island and fell back into the small Bataan Peninsula before the end of December. There, by contrast, they were only open to frontal assault on a narrowly contracted front, and succeeded in holding out until April before they were overwhelmed.

Long before that, and even before the fall of Singapore, the Japanese tide of conquest was spreading through the Malay Archipelago. On 24 January different Japanese forces landed in Borneo, Celebes and New

Guinea. Three weeks later they launched an attack on Java, the core of the Dutch East Indies, after the island had been isolated by flanking moves. Within a further three weeks, the whole of Java had fallen into their hands like a ripe plum. But the apparently imminent threat to Australia did not develop.

The main Japanese effort was now directed in the opposite direction, westwards, towards the conquest of Burma. The direct but wide-fronted advance from Thailand upon Rangoon was an indirect approach to their major object on the Asiatic mainland as a whole, the paralysis of China's power of resistance. For Rangoon was the port of entry for Anglo-American supplies of equipment to China, by way of the Burma Road. At the same time, this move was shrewdly designed to complete the conquest of the western gateway to the Pacific, and there establish a firm barrier across the main routes by which any overland Anglo-American offensive might subsequently be attempted. On 8 March Rangoon fell, and within a further two months the British forces were driven out of Burma, over the mountains, back into India.

The Japanese had thus secured a covering position so strong by nature that any attempt at reconquest would be badly handicapped and bound to be a very slow process. A long time passed before the Allies built up forces sufficient to attempt the recovery of Japan's conquests—beginning at the eastern end. Here they benefited from the preservation of Australia, which provided them with a large-scale base close to the chain of Japanese outposts.

Once America's strength developed, and Russia survived to develop hers, the defeat of the Axis powers—Germany, Italy and Japan—became certain, as their combined military potential was so much smaller. The only uncertainties were how long it would take, and how complete it would be. The most that the aggressors, turned defenders, could hope for was to obtain better terms of peace by spinning out time until the 'giants' became weary or quarrelled. But the chances of such prolonged resistance depended on shortening fronts. None of the Axis leaders could bear to 'lose face' by voluntary withdrawal, and so clung on to every position until it collapsed.

The turning-point against Japan came with the Battle of the Coral Sea in May 1942, and was clinched by the Battle of Midway the next month—the first naval battles in history where the ships never sighted each other nor fired a shot. For they were conducted by long-range air action, and Japan's loss of five aircraft-carriers in them crippled her sea–air power. But, although the tide had turned in the Pacific, a long time passed before the turn became very marked.

It was 7 August 1942 before a strong American naval task force landed a Marine division at the new Japanese-built base of Guadalcanal in the

Solomons, and six months passed before the island was completely re-conquered. That was only after a very tough struggle on land and a series of naval battles. Meantime the Japanese had landed in New Guinea, and, although foiled by the Australians in their effort to capture Port Moresby, on the south coast, they clung on to their westerly footholds until the summer of 1944—despite increasing pressure from an Allied force built up to ten divisions.

From the autumn of 1943 onward, however, the tide had begun to move faster as General MacArthur and Admiral Nimitz, on their respective lines of advance along the chain of islands, developed the method of bypassing some of the links in the chain, and leaving their garrisons isolated, while thrusting deeper and deeper into Japan's outlying rings of defence. Her overstretch was made fatal by this bypassing strategy.

Against Germany, the tide turned later but moved faster from the moment of the turn.

The failure of Hitler's 1942 offensive in Russia—his second gamble on victory—did not itself produce the disaster which followed in the winter. The fatal step was Hitler's obstinate refusal, when winter came, to let Paulus's army withdraw from its far-advanced position on the edge of the Volga at Stalingrad. How the Stalingrad army could have saved itself was shown by the way that the Caucasus army did save itself, under worse conditions—for it had pushed much deeper. Although constantly menaced in flank and rear, Kleist's army got back to safety through the bottleneck, while the Russians were held at bay. That long retreat in the depths of winter was one of the most remarkable feats of extrication from a trap in all history. Moreover, when the Russian advance approached the Dnieper in February, after capturing Kharkov, the German armies on the southern wing mounted and delivered a counter-stroke—under Manstein—which pierced the hinge of the advance and rolled back the Russian armies in confusion, recapturing Kharkov.

But this evidence of the defensive capacity which the German armies still possessed had a too exhilarating effect on Hitler. He would not listen to arguments for a withdrawal to the Dnieper line, and decided to take the offensive again in the summer—though the German strength was much depleted and Russia's increasing all the time. By contrast, the Russian army had improved a lot since 1942 both in quality and quantity. The flow of new equipment had greatly increased as well as the number of new divisions, and its numerical superiority was now about 4 to 1.

The German offensive was at last launched on 5 July on the Kursk sector, and into it Hitler threw seventeen armoured divisions—almost all he had. Both the pincers got entangled in the deep minefields which the Russians had laid—forewarned by the long preparation of the offensive—and failed to secure any large bag of prisoners, as the Russians had withdrawn their main forces out of reach. On 12 July, as they began to pull out, the Russians launched their own offensive, which thus had the recoil-spring effect of a counter-stroke.

In the second half of August the Russian offensive was more widely extended, and, though it did not make headway very fast, its alternating strokes kept the scanty German reserves scurrying from sector to sector. Skilful commanders like Vatutin, Konev, and Rokossovsky were quick to exploit thin stretches of the broad front. Before the end of September they had reached the Dnieper and established a wide range of bridgeheads beyond it. While attention was focused by Vatutin's threat to the famous city of Kiev, Konev burst out of his bridgehead at Kremenchug and went half-way to severing the great bulge formed by the Dnieper Bend. The Russians' fresh stroke here reached the mouth of the Dnieper early in November, closing the exits from the Crimea and isolating the enemy forces there.

Hitler's chief consolation was that his northern armies, after falling back from Smolensk in September to a line covering the Upper Dnieper, succeeded in repelling five successive Russian offensives between October and December. The assaults here were mainly delivered astride the Moscow–Minsk highway. As they came along an obvious line and on a narrow front, the well-knit defence proved superior despite a numerical inferiority of about 1 to 6. It showed how Hitler might have spun out the war if his strategy had been wiser—and less self-exhausting.

But Russia's survival and her subsequent advance owed much to the distraction caused by the amphibious flexibility inherent in sea power and the widespread threat it created. The effect, as revealed by analysis, was greater than has ever been realised. In 1940 the Germans committed 95 per cent of their strength to the offensive against the West. When they attacked Russia in 1941 they ventured to use barely 70 per cent of their strength there—because they felt it was necessary to guard the vast coast line of the countries they had conquered against the threat of British seaborne attack.

When that threat was increased by America's reinforcements and by a growing scale of assault shipping, the distraction became much larger. Nearly half the Germans' strength was drawn away from the Russian front *before* the western Allies even set foot in Normandy. Moreover, less than a quarter of the troops drawn away from Russia were facing the coming cross-channel attack. Such was the effect of sea power *as a threat*— a ubiquitous and incalculable threat of launching an invading force ashore anywhere along an 8,000 mile stretch of Europe's coast line.

The turn of the tide in the Mediterranean came earlier than in Russia. In the spring of 1942 Churchill had again urged early action, pointing out that the Russians were fighting desperately, and Malta, closer at hand, was being reduced to an extremity by Kesselring's sustained air attack. But Auchinleck, who had a shrewd sense of the technical and tactical defects of the British forces, wished to wait until Ritchie's strength was raised to a level sufficient to make sure of nullifying Rommel's superiority in quality. Finally Churchill, overruling his arguments, decided to send him definite orders to attack which he 'must obey or be relieved'.

Rommel, however, struck first. On the moonlight night of 26 May he passed round the flank of the British position with his three German divisions, followed by the one Italian armoured and one Italian motorised division, leaving the four Italian unmotorised divisions to 'make faces' at the Gazala line, and the divisions holding it. His flank stroke caught the British armour ill-positioned, and it came into action piecemeal, and was badly knocked about.

But despite Rommel's opening success he did not succeed in cutting through to the sea, and thus cutting off the divisions in the Gazala line, as he had hoped. His panzer divisions had a shock on encountering, for the first time, the Grant tanks with 75 mm guns that America had provided—200 of them had already reached the Eighth Army and Rommel had been unaware of that when launching his attack. He himself says: 'The advent of the new American tank had torn great holes in our ranks... far more than a third of the German tanks had been lost inside of one day.'

His renewed effort to reach the sea on the second day brought little progress and more loss. After another abortive day he ordered his striking force to take up a defensive position. That was a precarious position. For it lay beyond the fortified British Gazala line, and left him separated from the rest of his forces by the British garrison and their far-stretching belt of minefields.

During the days that followed, the British air force rained bombs on this position, which was aptly christened 'The Cauldron', while the Eighth Army attacked it on the ground. Yet by the night of 13 June the whole outlook had changed. On the 14th Ritchie abandoned the Gazala line, and started a rapid retreat to the frontier which left the troops in Tobruk isolated. By the 21st Rommel had captured that fortress and 33,000 men in it, together with an immense amount of stores. It was the worst British disaster of the war except for the fall of Singapore. Next day the remainder of the Eighth Army abandoned its position on the frontier near Sollum, and beat a hasty retreat eastward through the desert with Rommel on its heels.

What had caused such a dramatic turn-about? Rarely has there been such a tangled battle, and the threads have never been properly unravelled. The basic clue is to be found in Rommel's notes: 'Ritchie had thrown his armour into the battle piecemeal and at different times, and had thus given us the chance of engaging them on each occasion with just enough of our own tanks...'

777

Rommel's calculation worked out all too well. The British persisted in a series of piecemeal assaults on his position, at heavy cost. Such direct assaults proved the worst form of caution. While beating them off, he overwhelmed the isolated 'box' at Sidi Muftah held by 150th Infantry Brigade, which lay behind his back, and cleared a passage through the minefield for his supplies. He also tackled the still more isolated 'box' at Bir Hacheim on the southern flank that was held by the 1st Free French Brigade under General Koenig.

Meanwhile the British tank strength had melted from 700 to 170, and most of the reserve tanks had been used up. In one of his sudden ripostes Rommel had also captured four regiments of artillery—a very important bag. He now struck eastward, on 11 June, and cornered most of the remaining British armour between his two panzer divisions, forcing it to fight in a cramped area where he could batter it with converging fire. By nightfall on the 13th it had shrunk to barely 70 tanks. While he had lost many himself in the three weeks' battle, he now had an advantage of more than 2 to 1 in tanks fit for action—and, being in possession of the battlefield, he could recover and repair many of his damaged tanks, unlike the British.

Next day, as the British were falling back, Churchill sent an emphatic message saying: 'Presume there is no question in any case of giving up Tobruk.' He repeated this admonition in telegrams on the 15th and 16th. That long-distance advice from London conduced to the crowning blunder. For the hasty step of leaving part of the Eighth Army in Tobruk, while the rest withdrew to the frontier, gave Rommel the chance to overwhelm the isolated force in Tobruk before its defence was properly organised. The consequence of that disaster was the headlong retreat into Egypt of Ritchie's surviving force, with Rommel in hot chase. In maintaining this pursuit Rommel was greatly helped by the huge haul of stores he had made at Tobruk. General Bayerlein, the Chief of Staff of the Afrika Korps, stated that 80 per cent of Rommel's transport at this time were captured British vehicles!

Ritchie's intention was to make a stand at Mersa Matruh, and fight out the issue there with all the forces he had left, reinforced by the New Zealand Division which was just arriving from Syria. But on the evening of 25 June Auchinleck took over direct command from Ritchie. After reviewing the problem, he cancelled the order and decided to fight a more mobile battle in the Alamein area.

It was a hard decision, for not only did it mean many difficulties in getting away troops and stores, but it was bound to cause fresh alarm at home, particularly in Whitehall. In taking the decision, Auchinleck showed the cool head and strong nerve of a great soldier. It proved fortunate, for Rommel was racing forward so fast that his spearhead burst through the front south of Matruh on the 26th and reached the coast road behind.

But the withdrawal had been ordered just in time, and the bulk of the encircled troops were able to force their way through before the ring was firmly welded.

At Alamein, Auchinleck was not content with stopping Rommel, but sought to turn the tables decisively. How near he came to succeeding is shown by a letter that Rommel wrote on 18 July—'Yesterday was a particularly hard and critical day. We pulled through again. But it must not go on like that for long, otherwise the front will crack. Militarily, this is the most difficult period I have been through.' Fortunately for Rommel, the British troops were as exhausted as his own, and soon afterwards Auchinleck in turn had to suspend his attacks. But Rommel's closing reflection was: 'Although the British losses were higher than ours, yet the price which Auchinleck had had to pay was not excessive. What mattered to him was to hold up our advance and that, unfortunately, he had done.'

It is now clear that this first Battle of Alamein was really the turning-point, although Churchill's account and war memoirs have obscured the fact. Moreover, British reinforcements were now streaming into Egypt by sea.

Although Auchinleck had 'stemmed the adverse tide', as Churchill recognised and said, it was not so apparent that the tide had actually turned as can be seen in retrospect. Rommel still stood barely sixty miles from Alexandria and the Nile Delta—disturbingly close. Churchill was already thinking of making a change in the command, and his inclination turned into decision after finding that Auchinleck strongly resisted his pressure for an early renewal of the offensive, and insisted that it must be deferred until September in order to give the new reinforcements time to become acclimatised and have some training in desert conditions. So, after further discussion, Churchill telegraphed to the other members of the War Cabinet in London that he proposed to appoint Alexander as commander-in-chief, and to give the command of the Eighth Army to Gott—a surprising choice in the light of this gallant soldier's fumbling performance as a corps commander in the recent battles. But Gott was killed in an air crash next day, on his way to Cairo. Montgomery was then, fortunately, brought out from England to fill the vacancy.

But an ironical result of these changes was that the resumption of the British offensive was put off to a much later date than Auchinleck had proposed.

During August only two fresh formations arrived to reinforce Rommel— a German parachute brigade and an Italian parachute division. Both came 'dismounted', for employment as infantry. By the eve of the attack, which Rommel was planning to deliver at the end of August, he had about 200 gun-armed tanks in his two panzer divisions, and 240 in the two Italian divisions. But the British tank strength at the front had been brought up to a total of over 700 (of which some 160 were Grants).

Rommel had to depend on achieving surprise in time and speed. He hoped that, if he broke through the southern sector quickly, and got astride the Eighth Army's communications, it would be thrown off balance and its defence disjointed. But when the attack was launched, on the night of 30 August, it was found that the mined belt was much deeper than expected. At daylight, Rommel's spearheads were only eight miles beyond it.

As a result of Rommel having to wheel north earlier than he had intended, the attack fell directly on the 22nd Armoured Brigade, and on that alone—but not until late in the day. For continued air attacks, and the delayed arrival of fuel and ammunition convoys, had such a retarding effect on the advance that the Afrika Korps did not begin even the shortened northward wheel until the afternoon. Even when morning came on 1 September there was still such a shortage of fuel that Rommel was forced to give up the idea of carrying out any large operation that day. The diminished attacks of the German armour were successively checked, by a reinforced defence. The *Panzerarmee* now had only one day's fuel issue left in hand—a quantity sufficient only for about sixty miles movement for its units. So, after a second night of almost continuous bombing, Rommel decided to break off the offensive, and make a gradual withdrawal.

For the troops of the Eighth Army, the fact of seeing the enemy in retreat, even though only a few short steps back, far outweighed the disappointment of failing to cut him off. It was a clear sign that the tide had turned. Montgomery had already created a new spirit of confidence in the troops, and their confidence in him was confirmed. Tactically, too, this battle has a special interest. For it was not only won by the defending side, but decided by pure defence, without any counter-offensive—or even any serious attempt to develop a counter-offensive.

Seven weeks passed before the British launched their offensive. An impatient Prime Minister chafed at the delay, but Montgomery was determined to wait until his preparations were complete and could be reasonably sure of success, and Alexander supported him. So Churchill, whose own position was at this time very shaky after a series of British disasters since the start of the year, had to bow to their arguments for putting off the attack until late in October, when the second Battle of Alamein began.

By that time, the British superiority in strength—both in numbers and quality—was greater than ever before, the Eighth Army's fighting strength being 230,000, while Rommel had less than 80,000, of which only 27,000 were German. More striking still is the comparison in actual tank strength. When the battle opened the Eighth Army had a total of 1,440 gun-armed tanks, of which 1,230 were ready for action—while in a prolonged battle it could draw on some of the further thousand that were now in the base depots and workshops in Egypt. Rommel had only 260 German tanks (of which 20 were under repair, and 30 were light Panzer II's), and 280 Italian tanks (all of obsolete types)—so that, in terms of reality, the British started with a 6 to 1 superiority in numbers fit for action, backed by a much greater capacity to make good their losses. In fighting power, for tank *versus* tank action, the British advantage was even greater, since the Grant tanks were now reinforced by the still newer, and superior, Sherman tanks that were arriving from America in large numbers. Moreover, Rommel had lost his earlier advantage in anti-tank guns. In the air, the British also enjoyed a greater superiority than ever before. This amounted to more than 1,500 first-line aircraft, whereas the Germans and Italians together had only some 350 serviceable in Africa to support the *Panzerarmee*.

But even more important for the issue of the battle was the indirect and strategic action of the air force, together with the British navy's submarines, in strangling the *Panzerarmee*'s sea-arteries of supply. The heaviest loss of all was the sinking of oil tankers, and none reached Africa during the weeks immediately preceding the British offensive—so that the *Panzerarmee* was left with only three issues of fuel in hand when the battle opened, instead of the thirty issues which were considered the minimum reserve required. That severe shortage cramped countermanœuvre in every way.

The loss of food supplies was also an important factor in the spread of sickness among the troops. The most important 'sick casualty' of all was Rommel himself. He flew back from convalescence in Austria on 25 October—to take charge of a defence which had by then been deeply dented and had lost nearly half its effective tanks that day in fruitless counter-attacks.

The battle became a process of attrition—of hard slogging rather than of manœuvre—and for a time the effort appeared to hover on the brink of failure. But the disparity of strength between the two sides was so large that even a very disparate ratio of attrition was bound to work in favour of Montgomery's purpose—pressed with the unflinching determination that was characteristic of him in all he undertook. Within the chosen limits of his planning, he also showed consummate ability in varying the direction of his thrusts and developing a tactical leverage to work the opponent off balance.

The chance of cutting off Rommel, however, was lost because the pursuit was not sufficiently indirect or extensive in its circling sweep.

Once Rommel had slipped through the jaws of his armoured pursuers, he did not pause until he had reached his favourite backstop position near El Agheila at the far end of Cyrenaica—700 miles back from El Alamein. But this time the odds against him were too heavy to permit any riposte or even a long-sustained stand at El Agheila.

A pause of three weeks occurred before the Eighth Army could bring up its strength and mount an offensive against the El Agheila position.

Just as the offensive developed, Rommel began to slip off, and, although a flanking manœuvre succeeded in cutting off his rearguard, this managed to break through and get away before the 'strategic barrage' was properly cemented. Rommel halted again on the Buerat position, a further 200 miles back. He stayed there three weeks, but, when the Eighth Army closed up and launched its next offensive, in the middle of January, he fell back again. This time he made an almost continuous withdrawal for 350 miles, past Tripoli, to the Mareth line inside the frontier of Tunisia. His decision was the consequence not merely of his weakness of force and the sinking of the majority of his supply-ships, but of the new situation produced by the Anglo-American invasion of Morocco and Algeria in November under Eisenhower. That move had closely followed the El Alamein offensive, some 2,500 miles distant at the other end of North Africa.

The landings near Algiers reduced the distance from Bizerta to barely 400 miles. At that moment, a mere handful of motorised troops could have run through to Bizerta and Tunis without hindrance except from the mountain roads. Alternatively, either seaborne or airborne landings nearby would have met scarcely any opposition. But the naval authorities were chary of attempting even small-scale landings so far ahead of air cover, and the overland advance was too cautious. Meantime, the Germans' reaction was swift, though the landings had taken them by surprise. From the third day onwards they began to rush troops to Tunis in all available troop-carrying aircraft, as well as in small coasting vessels. Although the total was still small, it was just sufficient to check the leading troops of the Allied First Army when these reached the immediate approaches to Tunis two and a half weeks after the initial landings.

The result of this check was a five months' deadlock in the mountainous arc covering Bizerta and Tunis. Nevertheless, this failure worked out to the Allies' advantage in the long run. For it encouraged the enemy to continue pouring reinforcements across the sea to Tunisia, where the Allies could cut off their supplies through developing the stranglehold of superior sea power, and then cut off their retreat.

The 1943 campaign in Tunisia had opened, however, with a German counter-stroke that gave the Allies a bad shock. It came just when their two armies—the First from the west, and the Eighth from the east—seemed about to crunch the Axis forces between their jaws. The Axis command aimed to forestall that danger by dislocating both jaws, and for such an aim the conditions had become more favourable than was apparent on the surface of the situation. By now the reinforcements sent to Tunis had been built up into an army, under General von Arnim, while at the same time the remnant of Rommel's army was acquiring fresh strength, and equipment, as it came nearer to the supply ports in its westward retreat.

The American 2nd Corps (which included a French division) was the immediate target of the counter-stroke. Its front covered 90 miles, but was focused on the three routes through the mountains to the sea, with spearheads at the passes near Gafsa, Faid and Fondouk. At the end of January, the 21st Panzer Division made a sudden spring at the Faid Pass, overwhelmed the French garrison before American support arrived, and thus gained a sally-port. On 14 February the real blow came, starting with a fresh spring forward from the Faid Pass. Opening out as the American armour came forward to meet it, the 21st Panzer Division pinned the Americans in front, turned their left flank, and drove round their right flank to catch them in the rear. The Americans, however, had collected in strength on the line of approach to Thala, and held on so stubbornly to the Kasserine Pass that the Germans did not break through it until the evening of the 20th. Next day they drove into Thala, exhausted, and were pushed out by the British reserves that had now arrived there. So on the 22nd the Germans, realising that their chance had passed, broke off the attack and began a gradual withdrawal.

Until 26 February Montgomery had got only one division forward facing the Mareth line. For once he was worried, and his staff worked feverishly to redress the balance before the blow came. By 6 March, when Rommel struck, Montgomery had quadrupled his strength—besides 400 tanks he had now over 500 anti-tank guns in position. Thus in the interval Rommel's chance of striking with superior force had vanished. The attack was brought to a standstill by the afternoon and the Germans' loss of fifty tanks was a serious handicap in the next phase of the campaign. By then they had also lost Rommel, who had gone back to Europe, sick and frustrated.

The Eighth Army's attack on the Mareth line was launched on the night of 20 March. The main blow was a frontal one, intended to break through the defence near the sea and make a gap through which the armoured divisions could sweep. At the same time, the New Zealand corps made a wide outflanking march towards El Hamma in the enemy's rear, with the aim of pinning down the enemy's reserves that were placed there. The frontal attack failed to make an adequate breach. So, after three days' effort, Montgomery changed his plan, side-stepping inland and sending the 1st Armoured Division to follow up the New Zealanders' threat to the enemy's rear.

Then, in the early hours of 6 April, the Eighth Army attacked the Wadi Akarit under cover of pitch darkness. That tactical innovation resulted in a penetration, though the exploitation was checked by the Germans when daylight came. The rapidity of the retreat from the Wadi Akarit, and its success in evading the Allied attempts at interruption, gave the Germans a chance to evacuate their forces to Sicily, if they had chosen that course. The Supreme Command, however, was led to attempt a prolongation of the campaign in Africa, rather than draw in its horns and base its defence of Europe upon the southern shores of Europe. Even in Tunisia it tried to hold too extensive a front for its resources—a 100-mile perimeter—in the endeavour to preserve both Tunis and Bizerta. Stretched between those two 'horns of a dilemma', it provided the Allies with an ideal opportunity to exploit the advantage of having alternative objectives.

Before playing his hand, Alexander reshuffled his cards. On 20 April the offensive was opened by the Eighth Army with an attack on the enemy's left flank. But the coastal corridor became very narrow beyond Enfidaville, and the advance soon slowed down, coming to a halt on the 23rd.

Meantime Alexander again reshuffled his hand. Leaving only a screening force in the right centre near Goubellat, he moved the bulk of the 9th Corps over to the left centre, concentrated it behind the 5th Corps, and reinforced it with two picked divisions from the Eighth Army—the 7th Armoured and 4th Indian. Arnim had little chance of perceiving the deception, or of readjusting his dispositions after the blow fell, because of the Allies' command of the air. The highly concentrated assault of the 9th Corps, now under General Horrocks, was launched in the starlit but moonless early hours of 6 May. The stunned defenders of the gateway were soon overrun by the infantry of the 4th Indian and 4th British Divisions. The overstretched defence was not only thin but had little depth. Then the concentrated tanks of the 6th and 7th Armoured Divisions drove through the breach. But they lost time in dealing with various small pockets of German resistance. By nightfall they had only advanced a few miles beyond the breach and were still some fifteen miles from Tunis.

Next morning, however, it became clear that the opposing army as a whole was still paralysed by the combined air shock and strategic shock to such an extent that it could not develop any tactical counter-measures. By the afternoon the leading troops of the British armoured divisions had swept into Tunis. The 6th then turned south, while the 7th turned north, to spread dislocation. Almost simultaneously, the Americans and French poured into Bizerta. Enemy resistance dramatically collapsed on the northern half of the front. The enemy command had been caught off its balance, and then its machine was thrown out of gear by the combination of air pressure overhead and tank impact on its back. Dislocation of control was the primary cause of collapse, while the breakdown of communications accentuated the demoralising effect of lack of reserves and disruption of supplies. Another factor was the closeness of the enemy's bases to the broken front. That deepened the depressing sensation of fighting with their back to the sea—a sea now dominated by the Allies' sea power and air power.

The resulting 'bag' of the whole German–Italian army in Africa cleared the way for the Allies' re-entry into Europe—which might otherwise have been blocked. The success of their follow-up landing in Sicily in July produced the downfall of Mussolini and the quickly following surrender of Italy. That in turn cleared the Allies' path to the Italian mainland in early September. But the Germans were quicker in reacting to the emergency than the Allies were in exploiting the opportunity, and their advance up the mountainous peninsula became sticky and slow. The German generals, under Kesselring, ably made the most of the obstacles, while the Allied generals showed much less ability to overcome them—though Guillaume's handling of the French corps was a shining exception.

Significantly, the distracting effect caused by the Allies' amphibious flexibility diminished when the ubiquitous threat was translated into an actual landing. By June 1944 they were employing in Italy a strength in troops double that of Kesselring. That was not a good investment proportionately, and justified the American argument for breaking off the offensive there after the strategic airfields in the south were gained. Moreover, its continuance did not draw German reserves away from Normandy, nor prevent them reinforcing Normandy, as the British hoped—and have claimed.

The only claim that can be made for the strategic effect of the Italian campaign, as an aid to the success of the Normandy landing, is that without its pressure the German strength on the Channel front might have been increased even more. The scale of the assault and immediate follow-up forces there was limited by the number of landing craft available, so that the Allied forces employed in Italy could not have added to the weight of the Normandy landing during its crucial opening phase.

On 6 June 1944 the main Allied armies, which had been built up in England for a cross-Channel invasion, landed in Normandy. Here success was certain if they could firmly establish themselves ashore in a bridgehead big enough to build up their massed strength and swamp the Germans' barricading line. For, once they broke out, the whole width of France would be open for the manœuvre of their armies, which were fully mechanised, whereas the bulk of the German forces were still on a horse-transport basis.

The Germans' defence was thus doomed to eventual collapse unless they could throw the invaders back in the sea in the first few days. But in the event the move-up of their panzer reserves was fatally delayed by the paralysing interference of the Allied air forces, which had a 30 to 1 superiority over the Luftwaffe in this theatre.

Even if the invasion of Normandy had been repulsed on the beaches, the Allies' now tremendous air superiority, applied direct against Germany, would have made her collapse certain. For, even if the will to fight had survived the increasingly intense bombardment, organised resistance would have become impossible—through the paralysis of communications and the destruction of essential supplies.

Until 1944 the strategic air offensive had fallen far short of the claims made for it, as an alternative to land invasion, and its effects had been greatly overestimated. The indiscriminate bombing of cities had not seriously diminished munitions production, while failing to break the will of the opposing peoples and compel them to surrender, as expected. For collectively they were too firmly under the grip of their tyrannical leaders, and individuals could not surrender to bombers in the sky.

But in 1944–5 air power was better directed. Besides cramping and often paralysing the counter-moves of the German armies, it was applied with ever-increasing precision and crippling effect to the key centres of war production that were vital to the enemy's power of resistance. In the Far East, too, the master key of air power made the collapse of Japan certain, without any need for the atom bomb.

The main obstacle in the Allies' path, once the tide had turned, was a self-raised barrier—their leaders' unwise and short-sighted demand for 'unconditional surrender'. It was the greatest help to Hitler, in preserving his grip on the German people, and likewise to the war-party in Japan. If the Allied leaders had been wise enough to provide some assurance as to their peace terms, Hitler's grip on the German people could have been loosened long before 1945.

Three years earlier, envoys of the widespread anti-Nazi movement in Germany made known to the Allied leaders their plans for overthrowing Hitler, and the names of the many leading soldiers who were prepared to join such a revolt, provided that they were given some assurance about the Allied peace terms. But then, and later, no indication or assurance was given them, so that it naturally became difficult for them to gain support for a 'leap in the dark'.

Thus 'the unnecessary war' was unnecessarily prolonged, and millions more living needlessly sacrificed, while the ultimate peace merely produced a fresh menace and the looming cloud of another war. For the unnecessary prolongation of the war, in pursuit of the opponents' 'unconditional surrender', proved of profit only to Stalin—by opening the way for Communist domination of central Europe.

Under the shield of a vastly superior air power the Allies' footholds in Normandy were soon expanded into a large bridgehead, eighty miles wide. Although the German army managed to keep them penned in there for nearly two months it was never able to deliver any dangerous counter-stroke.

On 25 July the U.S. First Army launched a fresh offensive, 'Cobra', while the recently landed Patton's Third Army was ready to follow it up. The last German reserves had been thrown in to stop the British thrusts near Caen, on the west. On the 31st the American spearhead burst through the front at Avranches, on the other wing. Pouring through the gap, its tanks quickly flooded the open country beyond.

The bulk of the German forces in the west had been thrown into the Normandy battle, and kept there by Hitler's 'no withdrawal' orders until they collapsed—and a large part were trapped. The fragments were incapable of further resistance for the time being, and their retreat—largely on foot—was soon outstripped by the British and American mechanised columns.

On 31 August the spearheads of Patton's army crossed the Meuse at Verdun, a hundred miles to the south. Next day, patrols pushed on unopposed to the Moselle near Metz, thirty-five miles farther east. There they were barely thirty miles from the great industrial area of the Saar on the German frontier, and less than a hundred miles from the Rhine. But the main bodies could not immediately follow up this advance as they had run out of fuel.

On 3 September one armoured spearhead of the British Second Army swept into Brussels—after a seventy-five mile drive through Belgium from its morning starting-point in northern France. Next day another drove on to Antwerp and captured the vast docks undamaged before the surprised German base units had a chance to carry out any demolitions. There it was less than 100 miles from the Rhine, at the point of entry into the Ruhr, Germany's greatest industrial area. If the Ruhr was captured Hitler could not maintain the war. That same day the spearheads of the U.S. First Army captured Namur, on the Meuse. On this flank there was now a gap a hundred miles wide facing the British. No German forces were yet at hand to fill it. Rarely in any war has there been such an opportunity.

But, just as complete victory appeared within easy reach, the Allies' onrush petered out. By mid-September the Germans had thickened up their defence all along the front, and above all on the most northerly sector. That was the more unfortunate since Montgomery was now mounting another big thrust there, to the Rhine at Arnhem, on 17 September. In this he was planning to drop the recently formed Allied Airborne Army to clear the path. This thrust was checked by the enemy before it reached its goal, and a large part of the British airborne troops, dropped at Arnhem, were cut off and compelled to surrender.

The next month was spent by the U.S. First Army in grinding down the defences of Aachen, while Montgomery brought up the First Canadian Army to clear out the two 'pockets' of Germans which commanded the passage up the Scheldt estuary to Antwerp, and thus blocked the use of the port. Clearing these pockets proved a painfully slow process, which was not completed until early in November. Meanwhile the German build-up along the front covering the Rhine was progressing faster than that of the Allies, despite Germany's inferiority in material resources. In mid-November a general offensive was launched by all six Allied armies on the western front. It brought disappointingly small gains, at heavy cost. After that, the Germans were even able to stage a powerful counter-offensive before Christmas, in the Ardennes, with two panzer armies. It took the U.S. First Army by surprise, broke through the front and almost reached the Meuse, causing great alarm and confusion before being checked. Then Montgomery and Patton closed in and squeezed out the bulge it had made.

The price that the Allied armies paid for the missed opportunity in early September was heavy. Out of three-quarters of a million casualties which they suffered in liberating western Europe, half a million were after their September check. The cost to the world was much worse—millions of men and women died as a result of that extension of the war. Moreover, in September the Russian tide had not yet penetrated into central Europe.

On the eastern front, the dominant factor in the campaign of 1944 was that the German front remained as wide as ever, while the German forces were shrinking. As a natural result the Russian advance continued with little check except from its own supply problem—and, owing to the Russians' simpler requirements, that problem was less of a handicap than in any other great national army. The Russians' summer offensive was launched on 23 June, north of the Pripet Marshes, soon sweeping the Germans out of Belorussia and north-east Poland. On 14 July the next stroke came, south of the Marshes. By the end of the month the Russians also reached the Gulf of Riga, while in the centre they penetrated to the suburbs of Warsaw, and the Polish 'underground' leaders there were encouraged to give the signal for a rising.

It was a moment of general crisis for the Germans. In the west their front in Normandy was collapsing, while their rear was shaken by the repercussions of the plot to kill Hitler and the purge that followed. But an astonishing rally came in August, beginning at Warsaw. Three S.S. armoured divisions arrived at the crucial moment, and delivered a counter-stroke which threw back the Russian advance forces. This gave the Germans a breathing space in which to suppress the Polish rising. But the change was not confined to that sector—for by the end of the first week of August the Russians were held up almost everywhere. They had advanced up to 450 miles in five weeks—the longest and fastest advance they had yet achieved. They were now suffering the natural effect of over-stretching their communications, and had to bow to that strategic law. Six months were to pass on the Vistula before they were ready to mount a fresh drive.

The temporary deadlock was broken by a change of direction—a new Russian move in the south, on the Rumanian front. Rumania quickly capitulated, Bulgaria was then overrun, and the Russians pushed through the Transylvanian Alps into Hungary.

At the opening of 1945 the western half of Poland was still in Germany's grip, but the Russian High Command was now well prepared to exploit the fundamental weaknesses of the German situation. The mounting stream of American trucks had enabled them to motorise a much larger proportion of their infantry brigades, and thus, with the increasing production of their own tanks, to multiply the number of armoured and mobile corps for exploiting a breakthrough. At the same time, the new Stalin tanks strengthened their punch.

The Russian offensive opened on 12 January, when Konev's armies were launched against the German front in southern Poland. After they had pierced the enemy's defence, and produced a flanking menace to the central sector, Zhukov's armies bounded forward from their bridgeheads nearer Warsaw. That same day, the 14th, Rokossovsky's armies struck north into East Prussia. At the end of the first week the offensive had been carried 100 miles deep, and was also 400 miles wide by now—far too wide to be filled by such scanty reinforcements as were belatedly provided. By 31 January Zhukov's mechanised forces reached the Lower Oder, only 40 miles from Berlin. But the Germans' defence benefited from being driven back to the straight and shortened line formed by the Lower Oder and the Neisse. On this line their front was barely a quarter of its former width— less than 200 miles from the Baltic to the Bohemian mountain-frontier. That great reduction of the space to be covered went far to balance their loss of strength. By the third week of February the front in the east was stabilised, with the aid of German reinforcements brought from the west and from the interior.

Although the Russians were balked, it was the menace of their imminent approach to Berlin that led Hitler to decide that most of his fresh drafts must be sent to reinforce the Oder, whatever the risk to the defence of the Rhine. The way was thus eased for the passage of the Rhine by the American and British armies.

By 21 March Patton had swept the west bank clear of the enemy along a seventy-mile stretch between Coblenz and Mannheim, cutting off the German forces in that sector before they could withdraw to the Rhine. Next night, Patton's troops crossed the river almost unopposed. By this time Montgomery had completed his elaborate preparations for the grand assault on the Rhine near Wesel, a hundred and fifty miles downstream. Here he had concentrated 25 divisions. The thirty-mile stretch of river where he planned to attack was held by only 5 weak and exhausted German divisions. On the night of 23 March the attack was launched after a tremendous bombardment by over 3,000 guns, and by successive waves of bombers. The leading infantry, supported by amphibious tanks, crossed the river and established bridgeheads, meeting little resistance.

When the advance developed, much the most serious hindrance came from the heaps of rubble created by the excessive bombing efforts of the Allied air forces, which had thereby blocked the routes of advance far more effectively than the enemy could. For the dominant desire of the Germans now, both troops and people, was to see the British and American armies sweep eastwards as rapidly as possible to reach Berlin and occupy as much of the country as they could before the Russians overcame the Oder line. Few of them were inclined to assist Hitler's purpose of obstruction by self-destruction.

As the end drew near, Hitler's illusions continued to grow, and he counted on some miracle to bring salvation almost until the last hour. On 12 April the news reached Hitler that President Roosevelt had died suddenly. Goebbels telephoned him, and said: 'My Führer, I congratulate you. Fate has laid low your greatest enemy. God has not abandoned us.' This was the 'miracle', it seemed, for which Hitler had been waiting— a repetition of the death of the empress of Russia at the critical moment of the Seven Years War in the eighteenth century. So Hitler became convinced that the Alliance between the Eastern and Western powers would now break up through the clash of their rival interests. The hope was not fulfilled and Hitler was driven a fortnight later to kill himself—as Frederick the Great had been about to do, just when his 'miracle' had come to save his fortune and his life.

Early in March Zhukov had enlarged his bridgehead over the Oder, but did not succeed in breaking out. Russian progress on the far flanks continued, and Vienna was entered early in April. Meanwhile the German front in the west had collapsed, and the Allied armies there were driving eastward from the Rhine with little opposition. They reached the Elbe, 60 miles from Berlin, on 11 April. Here they were halted by top-level decision. On the 16th Zhukov resumed the offensive, in conjunction with Konev, who forced the crossings of the Neisse. This time the Russians burst out of their bridgeheads, and within a week were driving into the suburbs of Berlin—where Hitler had chosen to remain for the final battle. By the 25th the city had been completely isolated by the encircling armies of Zhukov and Konev, and on the 27th Konev's forces joined hands with the Americans on the Elbe. But in Berlin itself desperate street-by-street resistance was put up by the Germans, and was not completely overcome until the war itself ended, after Hitler's suicide, with Germany's unconditional surrender.

The war in Europe came to an end officially at midnight on 8 May 1945, but in reality that was merely the formal recognition of a finish which had taken place piecemeal during the previous week. On 2 May all fighting had ceased on the southern front in Italy, where the surrender document had actually been signed three days earlier still. This, the first of the three official acts of surrender, was the most significant, for it was signed while Hitler still lived, and in disregard of his authority. Moreover it was the conclusion to 'backstairs' surrender moves which had started on that front nearly two months before.

On 2 September the representatives of Japan signed the 'instrument of surrender' on board the United States' battleship *Missouri* in Tokyo Bay.

The second world war was thus ended six years and one day after it had been started by Hitler's attack on Poland—and four months after Germany's surrender. It was a formal ending, a ceremony to seal the victors' satisfaction. For the real ending had come on 14 August, when the emperor had announced Japan's surrender on the terms laid down by the Allies, and fighting had ceased—a week after the dropping of the first atomic bomb. But even that frightful stroke, wiping out the city of Hiroshima to demonstrate the overwhelming power of the new weapon, had done no more than slightly hasten the moment of surrender. This surrender was already sure, and there was no real need to use a weapon under whose dark shadow the world has lived ever since.

By the spring of 1945 Japan was palpably incapable of checking the Americans' two-pronged Pacific counter-offensive. In January MacArthur's forces had completed the conquest of Leyte Island, their first foothold in the Philippines, and made another jump forward—on to the main island of Luzon. By the end of February they had regained most of this great island along with the capital, Manila. More important than the recapture of territory was the wearing down of Japanese air strength in the struggle—their loss was estimated as more than 9,000 aircraft. It heavily drained the fighter strength available for the defence of Japan, and was the more important because Admiral Nimitz's forces, making another leap forward, had captured the Marianas in the summer of 1944—thus enabling airfields to be established from which heavy bombers could develop a bombardment of Japan, 1,500 miles beyond.

The Japanese hold on Burma had also been broken—by the converging pressure of the forces, predominantly British, under Admiral Mountbatten's command. Following the repulse of the Japanese invasion of India in 1944, Slim's Fourteenth Army advanced into central Burma, regaining the city of Mandalay in March 1945. Then it drove on south, opening the road to Rangoon.

Meanwhile the Americans had made another big leap forward, by-passing Formosa. On 1 April they landed on Okinawa, one of the Ryukyu islands, midway between Formosa and Japan. The shock of that news, coupled with the Russians' ominous notice of terminating their neutrality pact with Japan, precipitated the fall of Koiso's Cabinet on 5 April, and Suzuki then became Prime Minister. Okinawa was not finally cleared until mid-June, but its fate had been sealed in the first week, when Japan's last and latest modern battleship, the *Yamato*, had been sunk by American aircraft on 7 April after sallying forth from Japan in an attempt to intervene. This was a forlorn hope, for there were no aircraft carriers left to escort the *Yamato* after the loss of four in the October battle off the Philippines.

It was evident that, once the island was captured, the Americans would soon be able to intensify their air bombardment of Japan itself, as the airfields were within less than 400 miles of Japan—barely a quarter of the distance from the Marianas. Terrific damage had already been inflicted by the bombing attacks from the Marianas—the effect being much increased since the spring when the Americans largely changed over from high-altitude attacks in daylight with high explosive to lower-level night attacks with incendiary bombs. In a single night's attack, on 9 March, over 1,600 tons of incendiary bombs were dropped on the capital, Tokyo, and some 15 square miles of the city were burnt out, while 185,000 people were killed or injured. By the end of May three million of Tokyo's population had been rendered homeless, and by August over nine million altogether in the 66 cities selected for destruction.

The hopelessness of the situation was plain to any strategical mind, but Admiral Suzuki and his peace-seeking Cabinet were entangled in a knotty problem. Acceptance of the Allies' demand for 'unconditional surrender' would appear like a betrayal of the forces in the field, who might refuse to obey a 'cease fire' order if there was any demand for the removal of the emperor, who in their eyes was not only their sovereign but also divine. It was the emperor himself who moved to cut the knot. On 20 June he summoned to a conference the six members of the inner Cabinet, the Supreme War Direction Council, and there told them: 'You will consider the question of ending the war as soon as possible.' Eventually it was decided that Prince Konoye should be sent on a mission to Moscow to negotiate for peace—and the emperor privately gave him instructions to secure peace at any price.

The Americans became independently aware of Japan's desire to end the war, for their intelligence service intercepted and read—by the cipher-breaking means called 'Magic'—the messages from the Japanese Foreign Minister to the Japanese Ambassador in Moscow. But President Truman and most of his chief advisers were now as intent on using the atomic bomb to accelerate Japan's collapse as Stalin was on entering the war against Japan before it ended, in order to gain an advantageous position in the Far East.

There were some who felt doubts, and among them was Admiral Leahy, Chief of Staff to President Roosevelt and President Truman successively, who recoiled from the idea of employing such a weapon against the civilian population—'My own feeling was that, in being the first to use it, we had adopted an ethical standard common to the barbarians of the Dark Age'. But the scientists who were closest to the statesmen's ears had a better chance of gaining attention, and their eager arguments prevailed in the decision—aided by the enthusiasm which they had already excited in the statesmen about the atomic bomb, as a quick and easy way of finishing the war. So on 6 August the first atomic bomb was dropped on Hiroshima, destroying most of the city and killing some 80,000 people—a quarter of its inhabitants. Three days later the second bomb was dropped on Nagasaki.

The news of the dropping of the Hiroshima bomb reached President Truman as he was returning by sea from the Potsdam Conference. According to those present he exultantly exclaimed: 'This is the greatest thing in history.' The effect on the Japanese government, however, was much less than was imagined on the Western side at the time. Russia's declaration of war on 8 August, and immediate drive into Manchuria next day, seems to have been almost as effective in hastening the issue, and the emperor's influence still more so. Meantime the government announced by radio its willingness to surrender provided that the emperor's sovereignty was respected—a point about which the Allies' Potsdam Declaration of 26 July had been ominously silent. After some discussion President Truman agreed to this proviso, a notable modification of 'unconditional surrender'.

Why then was the bomb used? Stalin's demand at Potsdam to share in the occupation of Japan was very embarrassing, and the U.S. government was anxious to avoid such a contingency. A second reason was revealed by Admiral Leahy: The scientists and others wanted to make this test because of the vast sums that had been spent on the project—two billion dollars. One of the higher officers concerned in the atomic operation, the code name of which was the 'Manhattan District Project', put the point still more clearly: 'The bomb simply had to be a success—so much money had been expended on it...The relief to everyone concerned when the bomb was finished and dropped was enormous.'

Twenty years later, however, it is all too clear that the hasty dropping of the atomic bomb has not been a relief to the rest of mankind.

Much the worst of the Allies' military errors were before the United States was brought into the war, by Japan's colossal misjudgement—and especially those of the first nine months. But the 'unconditional surrender' policy not only tended to prolong the war and its exhausting effect but was fatal to the prospects of a good and stable peace. Although it has the appearance of a political error, it was really a basic error in grand strategy. The direct responsibility for it was due to Roosevelt and Churchill, but their adoption of such an unwise and short-sighted demand was supported by popular emotion, while their strategic advisers failed to raise any objections to the foolish formula until experience brought proof of its drawbacks. In the end it was tacitly abandoned when dealing with Japan.

No great military errors were made on the Allied side in the years from 1942 to 1945, following America's entry into the war. The wrangles of the generals, in their memoirs, are largely over secondary matters which made no great difference to the issue—and it is very doubtful whether the alternative courses that some of them favoured would have done much to shorten the war or diminish its cost.

It was the combination of superior industrial power and superior material resources with sea power that turned the tide and settled the issue. Generalship had no great effect in accelerating the tide. At the best, it was competent in developing a leverage, and careful in avoiding the extravagantly futile sacrifice of life that had exhausted the armies and the manhood of nations in the first world war. But it was never masterly—in the real sense of the term. The few generals on the Allied side who showed flashes of brilliance were also those most apt to commit blunders.

It is evident, too, that some of the generals have claimed, or let their protagonists claim for them, more than their due—and also have complained about their allies more than is justified.

Alanbrooke's claim, as voiced by Bryant,[1] is that he conceived the strategy that won the war, induced the Americans to follow it, and that its purpose was 'to make possible a simultaneous attack from across the Channel and from Russia' that Hitler would be unable to counter, by 'drawing and keeping his strategic reserves south of the Alpine ranges'. Bryant also asserts that Alanbrooke formulated this strategy, and 'forecast' its course, on becoming Chief of the Imperial General Staff in December 1941. But Alanbrooke's own diary provides no evidence that any such far-sighted, comprehensive and subtle design was in his mind. Instead, it shows that his main purpose then was simply to reopen the Mediterranean as a traffic route to the Far East.

Close examination of Alanbrooke's diary also shows that he was slow to grasp, and dubious about, further developments in the Mediterranean area. In June 1942 he was opposed to Roosevelt's and Churchill's projected landing in French North Africa, doubting both its practicability and its value, although he came round subsequently to accept the plan. When the landings succeeded, his diary streams with criticism that the advance to Bizerta and Tunis was not being pushed faster, and for this it blames Eisenhower. His criticism of the slow pace was justified, tactically. But it shows that he had not developed any such subtle luring strategy as is now claimed. For the slowness of the advance became the unintended means of drawing Hitler and Mussolini to pour large reinforcements into Tunisia—where Allied sea power isolated the Axis forces and compelled their surrender in May 1943.

That huge 'bag' left Sicily stripped of forces to defend it, and only this naked state made possible the successful invasion of Sicily and Italy on which Alanbrooke had set his mind. Moreover, during the previous winter he had been in conflict with the American Chiefs of Staff, headed by General Marshall, who wanted to close down operations in the Mediterranean in order to launch the cross-Channel attack against Normandy in 1943. Ironically, it was the slow progress of their advance into

[1] Sir Arthur Bryant, *Triumph in the West, 1943-46* (1959), p. 197.

Tunisia that nullified the Allies' hopes and led them to agree that the next move should be against Italy—as Alanbrooke desired—since it was now too late to mount the cross-Channel attack that year. It was the logic of events resulting from loss of time, more than logic of argument, that swung the Allied strategy towards the invasion of Italy. But, although Alanbrooke's wish was conceded, his hopes were soon disappointed again by the slow progress after the landing, and he vented his disappointment in renewed criticism of the American leaders.

The memoirs of American generals, on the other hand, express doubts about Alanbrooke's and Churchill's wholehearted acceptance of the adopted plan that the invasion of Italy in 1943 should be followed by the invasion of France in 1944. Their doubts, and their suspicions that the British were hoping to sidetrack the cross-Channel venture, will be re-kindled by a number of entries in Alanbrooke's diary. As late as October 1943 he records the receipt of a note from Churchill 'wishing to swing the strategy back to the Mediterranean at the expense of the Channel'—and remarks: 'I am in many ways entirely with him.' The following week he records that Churchill argued the case for the Mediterranean 'as opposed to' the cross-Channel attack, and himself terms the latter 'very problematical'. While recognising that the Americans would strongly object to putting it off again, or to any Balkan move, he remarks: 'I am tired of seeing our strategy warped by their shortsightedness.'

The British strategic plan, however, received a bad knock at the Teheran Conference at the end of November, through Stalin's reinforcement of the American arguments against it. That was ominous, and ironical. For the Americans, according to Harry Hopkins's diary, had expected the Russians to team up with the British at Teheran in favour of a Balkan rather than a Normandy operation in 1944—an expectation which showed their blindness to the long-range political aims of Stalin's strategy. He naturally wished to see the British effort kept well away from eastern Europe, and turned from Italy towards France.

So Churchill and Alanbrooke were pushed into a definite commitment which neither of them liked. Indeed, almost on the eve of the Normandy landing, Alanbrooke wrote in his diary that he was 'torn to shreds with doubts and misgivings...The cross-Channel operation is just eating into my heart'—and feared that it would prove 'the most ghastly disaster of the war'. Even after victory in Normandy was complete, he continued, at successive stages of the advance into Germany, to express pessimistic doubts about the prospect of early victory in that quarter.

But from the time of the Normandy landing Alanbrooke ceased, and Churchill too, to have any important influence on the course of the war—or on its sequel. Both strategically and politically, American influence became overwhelmingly predominant, and dictated the Allies' course. Indeed, when the British Prime Minister began to see the ominous consequences of the 'unconditional surrender' policy, which he had so lightly adopted in company with Roosevelt, he was powerless to modify it. He had in effect become, as he earlier proclaimed himself, merely the American President's 'lieutenant'.

In the tactical field, a British influence was sustained by Montgomery—first as executive commander of the Allied forces in Normandy, and then, after the break-out, as commander of the British in this theatre of war. The inter-allied conflict now became mainly a tug-of-war between Montgomery on the one hand, and Bradley—plus his insubordinate subordinate Patton—on the other hand, with Eisenhower as the rope.

In the first stage, until Eisenhower took over charge in the field, Montgomery was the chief target of criticism—and came under heavy fire from the American generals both at the time and in their memoirs later. It is easy to understand how his manner irritated them—both Eisenhower and Bradley were marvellously patient until exasperated beyond endurance. But much of the criticism is not borne out by analysis of the operations. On the whole, his plan of levering the enemy off balance was ably conducted, and the checks suffered in its development were more the fault of the executants, British and American.

In regard to the exploitation of the break-out, Eisenhower has been the chief target of criticism—particularly from the British, and above all from Montgomery. The failure to end the war in 1944 is attributed by them to Eisenhower's belief in a 'broad front' advance, in contrast to a concentrated thrust along one line, as Montgomery desired. But analysis reduces the significance of this difference, and of the whole argument that it was decisive in the frustration of the Allied pursuit from Normandy towards the Rhine. For the allotment of supplies given to Patton, so that he could continue his advance on the right wing, was merely 500 tons a day more than it had while halted—and the total, 2,500 tons, was only a small fraction of what was sent to the left wing, where Montgomery was advancing along with Hodges. Moreover, the extra allotment to Patton was much less than what was wasted on the left wing through various miscalculations, particularly a superfluous airborne attack near Tournai that Montgomery planned, which entailed a loss of over 800 tons of supplies a day for six crucial days before it was cancelled.

Most fatal of all to the prospect of reaching the Rhine, and preventing the disorganised enemy rallying, was the British pause from 4 to 7 September after reaching Brussels and Antwerp. That is hard to reconcile with Montgomery's declared aim, in his drive from the Seine, 'to keep the enemy on the run straight through to the Rhine, and "bounce" our way across the river before the enemy succeeded in reforming a front to oppose us'. *Persistent pace and pressure* is the key to success in any deep penetration or pursuit, and even a day's pause may forfeit it. The lengthy pause at Antwerp was due partly to a general tendency to relax and rest after the dash from the Seine, but also to the over-confident assumption that the Germans were incapable of rallying.

Underlying these mistakes in the pursuit was a deeper one. For the root of all the Allied troubles at this time of supreme opportunity was that none of the top planners had foreseen such a complete collapse of the enemy as occurred in August. They had not made the necessary preparations for exploiting it instantly by a rapid, long-range thrust. It is beside the point for them to blame each other for mistakes and delays in the follow-up. Basically they were all at fault before it started.

CHAPTER XXV

DIPLOMATIC HISTORY OF THE
SECOND WORLD WAR

THE fundamental differences between the democracies and the dictatorships, National Socialist, Fascist or Communist, in the second world war can be seen in their diplomacy as in their military strategy. The conciliation of neutrals, the maintenance of smooth relations between allies, a realisation that in the long run national claims must take account of the interests of other powers, all these features of a prudent diplomacy were far more evident on the side of the democracies. German policy since Bismarck, whether under William II or under the Weimar Republic, had never been remarkable for a sense of limits. Hitler exaggerated the faults of earlier régimes; the crude maxims set out in *Mein Kampf* really represented the sum of his political ideas just as the *Blitzkrieg*, a sudden and overwhelming deployment of superior force, was his favourite method. He carried out important diplomatic moves mainly by personal interviews in which he could use his tactics of bluster and cunning.[1] He paid little attention to his professional advisers—indeed he regarded the German Foreign Office as politically unreliable—and rarely tried to get the free, wholehearted assent even of his allies. At his meetings with Mussolini Hitler did nearly all the talking; his Foreign Minister Ribbentrop, who reflected his master's qualities as far as his limited ability allowed, was no less domineering at his interviews with Ciano, and the German military chiefs hardly troubled to hide their contempt for the Italians. There was no German–Italian liaison at a high level corresponding to the Anglo-American Combined Chiefs of Staff at Washington. Mussolini reached the conclusion very soon after he had brought Italy into the war that Hitler was less concerned to satisfy Italian territorial demands than to conciliate France (at least temporarily, though he never intended to keep his promises to the Vichy government). Mussolini undertook his attack on Greece without consulting the Germans; Hitler disapproved of it because he thought that it might lead to British action such as the bombing of the Rumanian oil-fields. In return Hitler did not tell Mussolini of his intention to attack Russia until a week before the German offensive opened. It is not to be wondered that Mussolini, who now had no escape from the consequences of abetting German aggression, was anxious that the Germans in Russia should not succeed too easily since a complete

---

[1] General Franco was one of the few lesser figures whose bland self-assurance Hitler could not shake. Franco kept Hitler waiting for an hour before their meeting at Hendaye in October 1940, and insisted on taking his usual siesta after lunch.

German victory would mean the reduction of Italy to vassalage. There were no detailed German–Italian plans of action in 1942 to meet a possible Allied landing in North Africa. In the final attempt to hold Tunisia, where the Italians hoped for political control, the Germans practically disregarded their presence.

Hitler's relations with Japan were more distant and necessarily more careful. He could not bully the Japanese or do much to influence their decisions; he was a little disturbed over the extent of their early victories and, according to Goebbels's diary, uneasy about a possible 'Yellow Peril'. To the Russians Hitler was as distrustful and deceitful as they were to him. The Russo-German economic agreement of February 1940 allowed Germany twenty-seven months for carrying out her deliveries to the U.S.S.R., while the latter had to fulfil their promises within eighteen months.[1] Hence, when, in December 1940, Hitler decided to attack Russia, he knew that Germany would not have to implement her part of the bargain.

Hitler could not even feel certain of the subservient French government installed at Vichy. He exaggerated the chances of spirited action by this group of defeated and defeatist figures who continued, under the nominal direction of a secretive old man, the personal intrigues which had disfigured the last years of the Third Republic. At the same time Hitler did not attempt a real conciliation of French sentiment; the virtual annexation of Alsace-Lorraine, the deportation of Frenchmen, the outrageous costs of the army of occupation, the refusal to return French prisoners of war, the execution of hostages, destroyed any chance of genuine collaboration except from a few politicians, industrialists or military men of poor judgement. After the entry of the United States into the war the French industrialists who had been willing to take a profitable part in a German-controlled Europe—which at least would not be Communist—began to have their doubts about an ultimate German victory.

The German inability to think politically in terms other than those of force and exploitation showed itself in the fate of the 'New Order' announced for Europe in September 1940. There was anyhow no likelihood of organising Europe as a single community under German leadership in a manner satisfactory to the nationalities concerned. The concept of the 'New Order' was based on muddled National Socialist thinking about 'living space' (*Lebensraum*), but, in spite of the vague terms in which it was expressed, the idea of a large, ordered community in a régime of planned production and exchange might have had an appeal to European peoples wrecked by war; Great Britain might thus have been left in isolated and hopeless resistance to a continent which preferred peace and material prosperity under German direction to the prospect of endless

[1] The reason for this difference was that Russia was supplying, mainly, raw materials, whereas Germany was sending finished goods which had to be manufactured.

fighting.[1] Unfortunately for the Nazi propagandists, Hitler was never much interested in the plan; although he boasted of a 'thousand year Reich', he continued to think almost exclusively in terms of conquests and annexations. The 'New Order' was dropped in theory before the Germans had to abandon it in practice. Strange as it seems in retrospect, the Germans had not provided for a long war, and, when in 1943 they found themselves fighting a war for survival, they intensified their plunder and exploitation of conquered countries and their suppression of public and private liberties. The treatment of the Jews throughout the war was not only a lasting stain on the German character—no alibi is possible for the Germans as a nation—but was also politically and militarily irrelevant to the chances of victory, and merely added to the detestation of German rule by all civilised men.

The diplomacy of the U.S.S.R. resembled that of the Axis powers in its lack of scruple; there was little to choose between the Russian attitude towards the Baltic States and the German attitude towards the smaller neutrals or between German and Russian behaviour towards the Poles. Russian, like German, diplomacy was under the close direction of a dictator and his immediate confidants. The combination of Stalin and Molotov remained unbroken throughout the war. German as well as Allied negotiators were baffled by Molotov's blank negatives and unwillingness to consider the claims of any state other than the U.S.S.R. Russian ambassadors had little freedom of negotiation; foreign ambassadors in Moscow, as Sir Stafford Cripps (British Ambassador, 1940–1) found to his dismay, rarely saw Stalin or even Molotov. The Soviet leaders were suspicious of their allies, and apt to take or pretend offence over trifles. They often exaggerated their suspicions for their own purposes, but there was a substratum of genuineness in them if only because the Russians could not believe that the Western powers were not as crafty and deceitful as themselves. During their period of collaboration with the Germans the Russians distrusted Hitler's offers but accepted under protest every German move against them, while they seized all territory within their reach which might be to their military advantage. Thus, on 30 August 1940, the Germans surprised them by guaranteeing what remained of Rumanian territory after the return of half of Transylvania to Hungary, and after the Russians themselves had taken Bessarabia and northern Bukovina. When German troops entered Bulgaria in March 1941 the Russians did no more

[1] The Vichy minister Baudouin described one of Churchill's speeches in August 1940 about fighting a long war until victory as 'ce fatalisme de destruction' (P. Baudouin, *Neuf mois au Gouvernement* (1948), p. 309). The British Foreign Office realised the danger of the German propaganda. They proposed that Keynes should broadcast a practical answer that Great Britain had more to offer to Europe in the form of an order based on sterling and linked with the free societies of the Commonwealth than Germany could provide in an order based on the mark and subject to German economic domination.

than protest, though they were now threatened with attack from the south against the Ukraine, the centres of industry around Stalingrad, and the oil-fields of the Caucasus. They could hardly have carried further their appeasement of Germany in the summer of 1941. Hitler did not give them the option of anything less than complete military surrender since he was determined to destroy once and for all Russian armed strength.

After the German attack, one form of Russian political action—propaganda in the German interest against Great Britain—ceased, though the Russians continued indirectly to harass British plans by demands for the opening of a second front long before an operation of this kind had a chance of success. Maisky, their Ambassador in London, openly encouraged the critics of the British government.[1] In these circumstances there could be no co-operation with Great Britain on such close terms as that between the British and Americans. Churchill attempted a personal correspondence with Stalin, but it was never very cordial on the Russian side; in June 1943 the correspondence seemed like coming to an abrupt end owing to the British inability or, as Stalin chose to put it, unwillingness to open a second front in western Europe.

Inevitably, therefore, as the war took a more favourable turn for the Allies, in large part owing to the Russian successes, Soviet policy towards them became more distant, secretive, and deceitful. The Russian view of the future was that they must continue to defend themselves against the consequences of a victory of the capitalist democracies as well as against a possible revival of German aggression. The Russians thought in old-fashioned military terms; they had tried between 1939 and 1941 to extend their own frontiers to form a glacis against Germany; they intended to reconstruct this glacis by controlling the governments of all the states on their western borders and as far as their armies could reach. Until they were in occupation of the territory they wished to control, they had to temporise and engage in 'double talk' with the British and Americans about the re-establishment of national independence and freely elected governments in the countries liberated from German rule.

American diplomacy was totally different from that of the U.S.S.R. and the Axis dictatorships. The President had greater personal power than a British Prime Minister, but Roosevelt's freedom of action, until after 1941, was more restricted by a highly organised public opinion. Roosevelt and most of his advisers were aware of the danger to the United States from a German, and still more from a German–Japanese, victory. The United States might well be excluded from the raw materials of the Middle and Far East and German influence might spread in Latin America. After the

[1] The Foreign Office thought it better to disregard the extent to which Maisky abused his position as an ambassador, but Eden felt it necessary to speak to him about the matter in September 1942.

destruction of political liberty in Europe Hitler would want to undermine democratic institutions everywhere in the western hemisphere. Most Americans, however, in spite of their dislike of dictatorship and sympathy for Great Britain and France, did not feel responsible for the survival of democracy in Europe, still less for the survival of the British Empire; their first care was that the United States should avoid what, in the mood created by revisionist historians (and German propaganda), seemed to have been a mistaken policy of intervention in the first world war. As late as July 1939 Congress had refused to repeal the clauses in the neutrality legislation which prevented belligerents from buying arms in the United States. Roosevelt was able to get this embargo removed early in November 1939, but United States ships were forbidden to carry munitions to belligerents or to enter areas designated by the President as combat zones. At a conference of American republics held at Panama in October 1939, a 'security zone' was established to exclude acts of war from the seas around the western hemisphere (except for Canada and the 'undisputed colonies and possessions of European countries'). This declaration of Panama was not valid in international law; the British navy disregarded it at the battle of the River Plate. The only method of enforcing it would have been by belligerent action which was just what the Americans were unwilling to take. The surest way of avoiding American involvement in the war would have been to persuade the belligerents to end it; Roosevelt sent Sumner Welles, Under-Secretary of State, to London, Paris, Rome, and Berlin in February–March 1940 to sound out the possibility of a negotiated peace. The British and French were afraid that Welles might suggest a settlement which would leave Hitler in power, and would therefore be only an uneasy truce. The German invasion of Norway and Denmark took place before any sequel could be given to Welles's discussions.

The collapse of France revealed to the American public their danger. The French and Dutch possessions in the western hemisphere might fall into German hands; the prospect of a defeat of Great Britain was far more alarming. The United States would then have to protect herself, and Latin America, on two oceans with a navy adequate only for one of them. A considerable section of American opinion at the time of the French defeat believed that Great Britain was now a bad risk and must be left to her fate while the people of the United States concentrated on their own defence. Fortunately the President thought otherwise.

The danger of the Axis powers getting control of territory in the New World was met by a resolution of Congress that the United States would not recognise the transfer of territory in the western hemisphere from one European power to another. A meeting of American republics at Havana in July 1940 supported the resolution (with Argentina at first disagreeing). Roosevelt had to fight a presidential election in November 1940. He was re-elected, but he failed to get the Republican party to accept a 'bi-partisan' foreign policy and had to declare that Americans would not be sent abroad to fight in a foreign war. On the other hand he maintained his plan to include British requirements in future American defence programmes. After his re-election he could be firmer about aid to Great Britain. He suggested 'Lend-Lease' in December 1940. Earlier, in September, on the announcement of the Tripartite pact between Germany, Italy, and Japan,[1] the President had decided, after consultation with Great Britain, that, if the United States were forced into war, she would act offensively in the Atlantic and defensively in the Pacific. This plan to deal first with Germany became the basis of Anglo-American strategy. Secret staff meetings began at Washington in January 1941; out of these meetings arose at the end of the year the Combined Anglo-American Chiefs of Staff Committee which became the organ for co-ordinating and directing the war effort of the two powers.

From this time Anglo-American co-operation was continuous. This co-operation was closer on the military than on the diplomatic side; it was less easy to work out a 'combined' diplomatic policy dealing with long-range interests than a military policy concerned with the immediate aim of defeating a common enemy; even so, the 'defeat of the enemy' itself did not have quite the same meaning for the British and the Americans. The normal diplomatic liaison, however, was supplemented by Churchill's personal correspondence with Roosevelt. Churchill began this exchange (with the Prime Minister's approval) when he was First Lord of the Admiralty; the original purpose of his messages was merely informative, but, after Churchill himself became Prime Minister, and especially after the United States entered the war, the correspondence became of the highest importance in the framing of policy. The personal liaison was also valuable because the relations between the President and the American Secretary of State were less close than those between the British Prime Minister and Foreign Secretary. Churchill was the more active correspondent; from May 1940 he sent about a thousand messages and received about eight hundred, mostly in the form of replies. There was a certain risk that Churchill, though he kept the Foreign Office informed of what he was writing, might emphasise too strongly his personal views. Furthermore, in the latter part of the war Roosevelt was a little uneasy, and perhaps a little jealous, of Churchill taking the lead in policy-making. Americans in all spheres of joint action tended to be on their guard against British skill in negotiation. Even in the early days of staff conversations the Americans were warned by their own authorities that the British would have drawn up their proposals 'with chief regard for the support of the British Commonwealth. Never absent from British minds are their post-

---

[1] The Tripartite Pact pledged the signatories to mutual aid if any one of them were attacked by a power not already taking part in the European war or the hostilities in China. The only power likely to make such an attack was the United States.

war interests, commercial and military.'[1] Churchill's powers of persuasion were regarded with caution. The American Admiral Leahy wrote of Harry Hopkins, another of the President's confidants, that 'nobody could fool him, not even Churchill'.[2]

In the first months of the war one of the urgent tasks of British diplomacy was to persuade neutral countries, and especially the United States, to accept measures necessary for enforcing the economic blockade of Germany. The term 'economic warfare' rather than the older term 'blockade' was used to cover the effort to dislocate the economic life of Germany by preventing her from maintaining her overseas trade or obtaining commodities essential for the prosecution of the war. The British government in this early period was over-confident about the effects of economic warfare just as the Germans relied too much upon the *Blitzkrieg*. The Germans did not realise until too late the need to mobilise all their economic resources; the British overlooked the fact that, until the expensive failure of the *Blitzkrieg* against Russia, the Germans were not using up their reserves of material and productive power, and were therefore not being brought to a standstill by the denial of imports from overseas.

British negotiations with the neutrals were carried out in detail by representatives of the Ministry of Economic Warfare attached to the Diplomatic Missions,[3] though the Ambassador would take personal control of any business likely to cause political tension. In view of past American sensitiveness to British interference disputes over the interpretation of maritime rights might well have had serious consequences. There was indeed a time early in 1940 when the War Cabinet thought it necessary to send (jointly with the French) a special mission to discuss with the Americans the machinery of the blockade as it affected the interests of the United States. The mission reached a satisfactory agreement, and special war trade agreements were also made with the Scandinavian and Low Countries, Switzerland and, Greece, and, on a smaller scale, with Spain, Yugoslavia, Hungary and Rumania. The collapse of France, the Axis occupation or control of the Atlantic and Mediterranean coasts of Europe, changed the central problem of economic warfare. The war trade agreements with countries now under Axis control disappeared; the British navy could not spare enough ships from the protection of Great Britain and British merchant shipping to patrol the whole of the Atlantic and Mediterranean seaboard. The surest way of cutting off enemy supplies was by agreements with the producing countries. The United States was

---

[1] M. Matloff and E. M. Snell, *Strategic Planning for Coalition Warfare* (U.S. Army in World War II) (1953), pp. 29–30.

[2] W. D. Leahy, *I Was There* (1950), p. 138.

[3] For the diplomacy of economic warfare, see W. N. Medlicott, *The Economic Blockade* (History of the Second World War, Civil Series, 1952, 1959).

the most important of these countries; hence American acceptance of the 'navicert system'[1] and of import quotas to Germany's neighbours was essential. American co-operation was not complete until after Pearl Harbour, but it was largely extended in the summer of 1941 not only by the pre-emption of commodities which might otherwise have reached Germany, and by the 'freezing' of German, Italian, and Japanese assets, but also by the removal of restrictions forbidding United States merchant vessels from carrying goods to Great Britain, and by the provision of American naval escorts for convoys in the western Atlantic. From September 1941, ships of the United States navy were authorised to attack Axis warships found in the western zone.

While Anglo-American co-operation was gradually approximating to a military alliance, the United States was exercising a certain pressure on the Vichy government and making the Japanese more hesitant than they might otherwise have been. Pétain and his colleagues still held to their two fundamental errors that a British defeat was inevitable, and that Germany would allow France to contract out of the war and even, as Laval hoped, to manœuvre herself into a favourable position in a German-controlled Europe. The Vichy ministers were resentful against Great Britain for having, as they alleged, pushed France into a war for which she was not prepared, and then for the failure to give her adequate help. They were angry at British support of General de Gaulle, since every success for his Movement lessened Vichy chances of getting concessions from the Germans. The Foreign Office received vague approaches from members or agents of the Vichy government during the late autumn of 1940, mainly through the French embassy at Madrid; these approaches were obviously attempts to stop British aid to de Gaulle and to prevent the extension of the British blockade to French trade with North Africa. The meetings between Pétain and Laval and Hitler at Montoire in October 1940 suggested Franco-German collaboration beyond the terms of the armistice. The only possible method of influencing Vichy in this matter was through the United States. At Churchill's request Roosevelt warned Vichy that a surrender of the French fleet would have a serious effect upon Franco-American relations. The British government, which hoped more of Weygand in North Africa[2] than of Pétain at Vichy, made suggestions for a *modus vivendi* in which the French would promise neither to attack colonies which joined de Gaulle, nor to allow their ports or territories to be used as bases for attacks on Great Britain; the British government, in return, would discuss concessions about French trans-Mediterranean trade. Nothing came of the proposals; the French economic demands were too high.

[1] A 'navicert' was a certificate obtained from British representatives in an exporting country that goods destined for European countries were not intended for Germany.

[2] General Weygand had been appointed Delegate-General of the French Vichy government in North Africa in September 1940.

After the failure of these approaches the Foreign Office lost hope of Vichy; Admiral Darlan[1] was as collaborationist and anti-British as Laval, without Laval's astuteness. The Americans, however, still thought that concessions might have an effect upon Weygand. For this reason they decided to send a limited quantity of supplies to North Africa. The British government thought this plan useless and even dangerous, but were willing to let it be given a trial. The German attack on Russia did not affect Vichy policy. In May 1941 Pétain had made a strongly collaborationist broadcast. After the opening of the Russian campaign he was sure that the Germans would be in Moscow and on the Don by the end of the year and would then return to defeat Great Britain.

The American entry into the war did not encourage Pétain to make overtures to the Allies. He merely regretted American belligerency; he told the United States Ambassador at Vichy that, if the Germans insisted upon an alteration in Franco-American relations, France would have to agree; otherwise she would remain neutral. None the less, although the Americans were as anxious as the British to keep Franco-German collaboration within the bounds of the armistice, they were now more hopeful again of French support in the event of an invasion of North Africa. They resumed in July 1942 the supplies to North Africa which they had cut off for a time after the return of Laval to power in April. There was at this period considerable difference of view between Churchill and the Foreign Office about policy towards Vichy. Churchill, though he did not expect the Vichy ministers to take any overt action to resist German demands, tended to think with the Americans that they would change their attitude when they could safely do so. The Foreign Office believed that Pétain would always be defeatist; that Laval and Darlan were not just trying to placate the Germans, but had committed themselves entirely to a German victory. Hence the Vichy government would never bring France or North Africa into the war until it was too late for a *volte-face* on their part to make a contribution to victory.

The counterpart to the more optimistic American view about Vichy, or, at all events, about North Africa, was their lack of sympathy with General de Gaulle. Since his recognition by the British government (28 June 1940) General de Gaulle had not won as much support as he had hoped either among prominent Frenchmen—few of whom had come to England to join him—or in the French colonial empire, though here the adherence of French Equatorial Africa to his movement was economically and strategically valuable. General de Gaulle was not easy to deal with; his concern for the honour and status of France too often overlooked the fact that French recovery depended upon an Anglo-American victory. He was causing difficulties for Great Britain in Syria and the Lebanon, where,

[1] Admiral Darlan became Vice-Premier and Minister of Foreign Affairs in February 1941.

when these former French mandated territories were recovered from Vichy control mainly by British arms, General de Gaulle had agreed to a proclamation granting independence. He continually postponed the implementation of this grant, and alleged that British pressure upon him to carry it out in detail was an attempt to get rid of French influence in the Levant. Early in 1942 General de Gaulle did great harm to his chance of improving relations with the American authorities. The British government had suggested that he should be allowed to take over the French islands of St Pierre and Miquelon off the coast of Newfoundland, and at this time under Vichy control.[1] The Americans refused the suggestion; they did not want to offend Vichy, and were pledged not to allow a transfer of sovereignty in the case of possessions of non-American powers in the western hemisphere.[2] General de Gaulle, however, sent Free French warships to seize the islands. The British government had great difficulty in persuading the President to accept a compromise under which the Vichy authorities (to the satisfaction of the inhabitants) withdrew from the islands and Canadians and Americans jointly supervised the wireless installations.

In spite of these and other troubles, the British view was that General de Gaulle should still be supported since no other Frenchman was likely to take his place as a leader of French resistance. Many of the difficulties with the general had arisen because the British government had promised him support without securing his consent to any obligations to themselves, and the French National Committee which he had set up consisted of his own nominees. Anglo-American policy should therefore be to use the recognition of the Committee by the United States as an occasion to re-define its status. In the new definition (July 1942) General de Gaulle's name did not appear; the Committee was described as one of Frenchmen collaborating with the United Nations.[3] The Allied landings in North Africa, however, brought further trouble. The Americans did not want General de Gaulle to be associated with the operation because they thought that he had only a small following in North Africa; he was not told of the landings until after they had taken place.[4] The fact that the Americans were supporting another French general—Giraud—whom they mistakenly expected to get more local backing put matters wrong politically from the start. General Eisenhower's willingness to use Admiral Darlan at least temporarily as the head of the French administration in North Africa was even more disastrous. British as well as Free French

---

[1] There was a powerful wireless station on St Pierre which could be used to guide German submarines.

[2] See above, p. 802.

[3] At General de Gaulle's request the name of his Movement was changed from 'La France libre'—Free France—to 'La France Combattante'—Fighting France.

[4] General de Gaulle would have been more hostile if he had known that Roosevelt had proposed to address Pétain as 'my dear old friend'.

opinion was shocked at what seemed an act of political cynicism, whatever military reasons might be alleged in its favour.

The assassination of Darlan (24 December 1942) saved the Anglo-American alliance from a severe strain, but the conflict between de Gaulle and Giraud remained. In the end, although the Americans took a long time to recognise the facts, General de Gaulle, who was abler and more adroit, as well as having far more claim to represent French resistance groups, became head of a new French Committee of National Liberation, but Roosevelt refused to recognise this Committee as competent to take over the civil administration of France between the liberation of the country and a general election. Churchill shared Roosevelt's distrust of de Gaulle. The Americans suggested that something like the Allied Military government which functioned in Italy should be set up in France until a plebiscite could be held on the future government of the country. The Foreign Office realised that the French people, after their liberation from the Germans, would fail to understand why they had to submit to Anglo-American control outside the zone of military operations; hence, though Roosevelt refused to admit the fact, there was no alternative to General de Gaulle and the French Committee. The President held to his view until after D-day. General de Gaulle would have been wiser to have accepted this somewhat absurd position in the certainty that within a very short time the French people would show their support for him. Instead he refused at first to allow any of the French liaison officers attached to the Allied Expedition to go to France until he had American signature to an agreement about their duties. Churchill, in spite of his anger with General de Gaulle, made another appeal to Roosevelt, who finally gave way, though until mid-October 1944 he would not recognise the French Committee as a Provisional Government.

From the outbreak of war British and American diplomacy in the Far East aimed at keeping Japan from fighting on the German side. After the French collapse the difficulties of Great Britain gave the Japanese an opportunity, which even the more cautious among them could hardly resist, to establish themselves in an impregnable position in China and east Asia generally. The Vichy government could not oppose a Japanese move into Indo-China; British chances of resistance depended upon American support. The United States government did not believe that Japan could be held back except by force, but in 1940 the American navy was in no position to risk a war in the Pacific. Hence the Americans recommended temporary British compliance with Japanese demands as far as might be necessary to avoid war. The British government agreed to close the Burma Road (over which supplies were sent to China), though they set a time limit of three months during which efforts were to be made by Japan to secure a satisfactory peace with China. Since the Japanese were unwilling even to discuss terms which the Western powers regarded as reasonable for China, the Burma Road was re-opened. Japanese policy was indeed clear, though from their point of view the timing was fatally wrong. Japan signed the Tripartite Pact a few days before the failure of the German air force to open the way for the invasion of Great Britain; the attack on Pearl Harbour coincided with the failure of the German *Blitzkrieg* against the U.S.S.R.

The final unsuccessful negotiations with Japan were undertaken by the United States; British policy was to keep close to the Americans. Thus in July 1941 when the Americans froze Japanese assets (after the Japanese occupation of southern Indo-China), Great Britain took a similar step, though there was always a risk that, if Japan retaliated only against the British and Dutch possessions, the United States might not intervene. For a time the diplomatic negotiations were complicated by the attempt of less extreme elements in the Japanese government to reach a direct understanding with the United States. The latter did not expect these discussions to succeed, but thought that they offered a chance at least of postponing a Japanese attack. The discussions reached a critical point in November. The Japanese negotiators warned the Americans on 18 November that, unless the United States gave up economic sanctions against them, war was inevitable. The Americans asked for the withdrawal of Japanese troops from Indo-China. This condition was not accepted. Hull, the American Secretary of State, then considered offering a *modus vivendi*— an arrangement for two or three months which would have allowed time for a comprehensive settlement—on the basis of the withdrawal of most of the Japanese forces from Indo-China in return for a considerable lightening of the economic embargo. The Foreign Office thought that the concession demanded from Japan was inadequate; they told Hull, however, that the British government had confidence in his handling of the negotiations, and left it to him to decide on the next step. After the Chinese had protested strongly against the *modus vivendi*, Hull, without consulting the British government, decided to abandon it. The Foreign Office instructed Lord Halifax to repeat the British view in favour of an *interim* agreement as such. Hull's answer was that it was too late to revert to the *modus vivendi*. On 7 December the Japanese delivered a surprise attack on Pearl Harbour.[1]

There was a wider divergence between British and American views over China. American opinion (endorsed by the President) was much more hopeful about the political future of China. The British view was that General Chiang Kai-Shek had little chance of remedying the incompetence

[1] Sir R. Craigie, British ambassador to Japan, thought that, if Hull had continued discussions about a *modus vivendi*, the Japanese might have postponed their decision to go to war. The Foreign Office did not take this view, and seem to have been right, though the possibility cannot be ruled out that, if Japan had put off her attack even for a week, the German failure before Moscow might have brought a change in Japanese policy.

and corruption of his government; that aid to China was not the best way to defeat Japan, and that after the war China would not be, as Roosevelt expected, a stabilising force in the Far East. The Americans were inclined to regard this assessment as due to British imperialism. General Chiang Kai-Shek did not improve matters by trying to interfere in the internal affairs of India. In 1943 Great Britain and the United States signed treaties with China for the surrender of extra-territorial rights. From this time the Americans took over practical responsibility for Chinese relations with the Allies. The British government watched anxiously the continued disruption of General Chiang Kai-Shek's authority, and the consolidation of Communist power, but Great Britain had no means of changing the situation for the better.

About the time of the Japanese attack on Pearl Harbour, Eden, the Foreign Secretary, went to Moscow to explain British proposals for Anglo-Russian political co-operation during and after the war. He found that the Russians wanted to be assured at once of British recognition of their annexation of the Baltic States and of territory up to the Curzon line in Poland.[1] Stalin and Molotov refused to accept Eden's protest that he had no authority to agree to territorial changes and that Great Britain was pledged to the United States not to make any such changes during the war. The War Cabinet did not reply immediately to the Russian demands. They came round, however, to the view that, although these demands conflicted with the Atlantic Charter,[2] they would have the greatest difficulty in refusing them. Apart from the risk that Stalin might make a separate peace with the Germans if the Western powers refused his claim to the frontiers of the U.S.S.R. before the German attack, there would be far less chance of getting Soviet co-operation after the war if Great Britain, at a time when she could do little to relieve the pressure on the Russian armies, refused to allow Russia in the future the frontiers which she regarded as essential to her defence. In any case the Russians, if they drove back the Germans, would reoccupy the territories in question and the Western powers would be unable to turn them out. Hence it seemed realistic generally to accept the Russian claims and, in so doing, to try to limit them, especially in regard to Poland. Nevertheless this surrender of principle was a significant and dangerous step which Great Britain had refused to take in the Anglo-Franco-Russian negotiations of 1939 and which was harder to justify after the announcement of the Atlantic Charter. The British government had now allowed the Soviet rulers to 'get away with' make-believe

---

[1] I.e. the line drawn up by the Allied Supreme Council in 1919, and recommended by Lord Curzon in 1920 during the fighting between the Russians and the Poles as the best practical approach to an ethnographical Russo-Polish frontier. The line had two variants at its southern end; one of them included Lwów in Poland and the other excluded it. Some confusion arose because Churchill and Eden seemed for a time unaware of this fact.

[2] See below, pp. 811–12.

and 'double-talk' to describe action incompatible with the independence of small states. Once this surrender had been made, similar claims would be less easily resisted.

The Russians did not wait long before trying to enlarge the scope of their diplomatic victory. Molotov came to London in May 1942 with proposals for an Anglo-Russian treaty in which not even local autonomy would be allowed to the Baltic States and Great Britain would not be consulted about the fixing of the Russo-Polish frontier. The British government refused these proposals and suggested merely a post-war Anglo-Russian alliance against the recurrence of German aggression without mention of frontiers. The Russians agreed to the treaty, but showed that they had not abated their claim to decide for themselves how much of Poland they intended to take. If there had been any doubt about their ruthlessness in this matter, they dispelled it in 1943 when, in spite of appeals from Churchill, they broke off relations with the Polish government in exile in London on the pretext that the Poles suspected them of responsibility for the massacre of Polish officers and men at Katyn.[1] The Russians had already introduced various administrative measures unfriendly to Poles who had taken refuge in Soviet territory or had been deported to it on Soviet orders. They were now likely in their victorious advance to re-enter Polish territory; their attitude was ominous for the future of the Polish nation.

The terms of the Anglo-Russian treaty of 26 May 1942 envisaged the organisation of 'like-minded states...for common action to preserve peace and resist aggression in the post-war period'. This phrase represented the stage reached in Allied plans for post-war security. In the early part of the war Great Britain could not give any precise definition of post-war plans; no one could foresee when the war would end, or what states would have become involved in it. The initiative in a positive statement came from the United States. In August 1941 Churchill and Roosevelt met on board ship in Placentia Bay, Newfoundland. At Roosevelt's suggestion they drew up, somewhat hastily,[2] a joint declaration of the broad principles upon which both countries were acting. This declaration, the so-called Atlantic Charter, laid down that the two countries sought 'no aggrandisement, territorial or other,' for themselves, and that they desired no territorial changes which did not 'accord with the freely expressed wishes of the peoples concerned'. They respected 'the right of all peoples to choose the form of government under which they will live' and wished

---

[1] The balance of opinion in Great Britain and the United States was, and is, that the Soviet government, and not the Germans (who were equally brutal elsewhere in their treatment of Poles), were responsible for this massacre at Katyn (near Smolensk).

[2] Evidence of haste in drafting may be seen in the omission (criticised in the United States) of any direct reference to freedom of religion. There is no official text of the Atlantic Charter, as a signed document, in the British archives.

self-government to be restored to peoples forcibly deprived of it. They held out to all states, 'victor or vanquished', equal freedom of access to trade and raw materials and would try to bring about international economic collaboration, social security, and conditions providing freedom from fear and want; they would deny armaments, 'pending the establishment of a wider and more permanent system of general security', to nations threatening aggression, and would further all measures which would 'lighten for peace-loving peoples the crushing burden of armaments'.

The British government realised that the issue of this declaration implied an American claim to take a leading part in the peace settlement, and that, in order to avoid unfortunate consequences like those following the use of Wilson's loosely worded Fourteen Points as the basis of an armistice and peace treaty, it was desirable to consider more precisely how the terms of the Charter could be given practical effect. The next step, however, came from another American initiative. On his visit to the United States in December 1941 Churchill was given a draft declaration binding the signatories to secure the defeat of the 'Axis forces of conquest' and reaffirming the 'purposes and principles' of the Atlantic Charter. This 'Declaration of the United Nations'[1] was again drawn up in unnecessary haste, to the dissatisfaction of the War Cabinet. The Russians, whose aims were on different lines, also criticised the document.

For a time, however, the anti-Axis powers were too much occupied with the military situation to give much thought to the post-war organisation of peace. The Foreign Office drew up a number of memoranda of which the general tenor was that Great Britain should try to get a World Security Organisation controlled by the four great powers.[2] The Foreign Office also suggested the establishment of an Inter-Allied Armistice and Reconstruction Commission to deal with the restoration of economic and political life in Europe after the war; this commission might develop into a Council of Europe on which all European States (including Great Britain and the U.S.S.R.) and the United States would be represented. Churchill was specially interested in the possibility of a Council of Europe leading to a United States of Europe.

Eden went to Washington in March 1943 for informal talks on post-war questions. He found general approval of the idea that the four powers should act as something like an executive committee of the United Nations, but the Americans had not yet worked out a detailed scheme. There was still a feeling that the planning of the World Organisation must remain in the background. The Foreign Office considered that the prerequisite of any plan was that the great powers must remain in agreement; British policy

---

[1] Roosevelt suggested the term 'United Nations': the simpler word 'alliance' would have raised constitutional difficulties in the United States.

[2] The United States, Great Britain, the U.S.S.R. and China. The British argued strongly that France could not be left out or put in a position below that of China. The State Department favoured the British view, but Roosevelt would neither exclude China nor include France.

should concentrate on maintaining this agreement before beginning, in Sir A. Cadogan's words,[1] to 'design all the outworks of the future Palace of Peace'. It was also necessary first to get acceptance of a common policy on the terms of an armistice and the occupation of enemy countries. There was as yet no decision on the treatment of Germany—whether the Reich should be broken up into a number of separate states, or whether large areas on its frontiers should be detached or whether some form of decentralisation would suffice. The only matter upon which a pronouncement had been made was a demand for unconditional surrender. Roosevelt had suggested this demand to Churchill at their meeting at Casablanca in January 1943. Here again an important political decision was taken almost casually (though Roosevelt had discussed it with his military advisers); the Americans wanted to avoid the ambiguity of the armistice terms of 1918. 'Unconditional surrender' was also a vague term; surrender of what, by whom, and on whose behalf?

It is a matter of opinion whether this demand was expedient. Churchill, who consulted the War Cabinet, would not have extended it to Italy, but Eden and Attlee (Deputy Prime Minister and Leader of the Labour party) thought that Italy should be included. Churchill's view was that the demand might discourage the Italians from making a separate peace. In fact they surrendered unconditionally after the fall of Mussolini and the loss of Sicily. They would not have surrendered earlier, and their 'unconditional surrender' was mitigated for them by a promise that in a peace treaty account would be taken of their subsequent co-operation with the Allies. The demand for unconditional surrender was also modified in the case of the Axis satellites in south-east Europe. Before the cross-Channel invasion of 1944 there was some Anglo-American discussion whether a definite set of terms should be substituted for unconditional surrender. Churchill explained in parliament in February 1944 that unconditional surrender did not mean that the Germans would be treated in a barbarous way but that there would be no pre-armistice bargaining. Churchill in fact thought that the terms which at that time the Allies were planning to enforce would alarm the Germans far more than a vague demand for unconditional surrender. German resistance was senselessly prolonged not because of the Allied insistence upon unconditional surrender, but because Hitler, who could expect no mercy for himself or his associates, was too crazed to admit defeat, and an internal revolution in Germany was impossible without the active support of the High Command as long as the internal machinery of the dictatorship was working.

A meeting of the three Foreign Ministers at Moscow in October 1943 carried a little nearer to decision both the question of the treatment of Germany and that of the post-war organisation of security. The Americans

[1] Permanent Under-Secretary of State for Foreign Affairs.

813

introduced a four-power Declaration on General Security which envisaged 'the necessity of establishing at the earliest practicable date a general international organisation, based on the sovereign equality of all peace-loving states, and open to membership by all such states, large and small, for the maintenance of international peace and security'. The declaration was made public on 30 October, and the three powers agreed to an informal exchange of views about the nature of the organisation. Eden persuaded his colleagues to accept a more limited and directly practical proposal for a European Advisory Commission to suggest ways of dealing with European problems after the fighting. The Moscow meeting was held to prepare for a conference of the three Heads of Government. This first meeting of Churchill, Roosevelt and Stalin was held at Teheran in November 1943. The purpose of the Conference was mainly military, but there were important, though inconclusive, discussions on the treatment of Germany; the question was referred to a special committee under the supervision of the European Advisory Commission. No agreement had been reached by September 1944—the British Government had not even settled on their own policy—when Roosevelt persuaded Churchill (before the arrival of Eden) at a conference in Quebec to accept an extraordinary plan put forward by Morgenthau, United States Secretary of the Treasury, and supported by Lord Cherwell (Churchill's adviser on scientific questions), for eliminating German 'war-making industries', and leaving the country with an economy primarily agricultural and pastoral. This plan, which the Foreign Office strongly opposed, would have put upon the Western allies the burden of maintaining a starving population. The President himself soon abandoned it.

At the Yalta Conference in February 1945 the Russians brought forward something like the Morgenthau plan by asking not only for the political dismemberment of the Reich, but for German payment of reparations in kind to an extent which would have reduced the heavy industry of the country by about 80 per cent. The British ministers at the conference would agree only to a further study of dismemberment; they did not reject the principle of a single payment of reparations in kind—on a large scale—followed by annual deliveries of goods over ten years, but they dismissed the Russian figures—an equivalent of 20,000 million dollars (of which the U.S.S.R. would receive one half)—as far beyond German capacity of payment. Stalin therefore had to accept the appointment of a tripartite Commission to recommend a definite figure.

Soon after the return of the British ministers from Yalta the Treasury submitted to the War Cabinet a paper on German reparation and dismemberment. This paper argued conclusively that the Russians were making an impossible attempt to combine the maximum of reparation with the maximum of dismemberment, and that their proposals would impoverish the whole of western Europe and endanger its political stability.

Furthermore, as in the case of the Morgenthau plan, the proposals for reparation would have the severest effect on the industrial area of western Germany which fell within the zone of occupation allotted by the Yalta Conference to Great Britain. The burden of dealing with the inevitable distress would fall on the British people, who would in fact be paying a very considerable part of the reparation received by Russia. Within a short time the Russians gave up the idea of dismemberment; the Commission on reparation failed to agree, and the problem was left to the tripartite conference at Potsdam (July 1945).

At this last of the three war-time meetings of the British, Americans and Russians, the latter repeated their demands; the British again rejected their figure. The Americans, who did not intend to exact reparation for themselves, though they would not forgo their claim, finally proposed, as part of a compromise on the main issues in dispute at the conference, that each of the three powers should take reparation in kind from their own zone of occupation, and that the Russians, who had already removed large quantities of machinery from their zone, should be given additional deliveries from the zones of the Western powers; the latter would also find the share allotted to the smaller Allies. The Russians, in return, promised to provide coal and foodstuffs from the German territory occupied by themselves and the Poles and from which western Germany had drawn supplies before the war.

There was some talk—again inconclusive—about the future World Organisation at the Teheran Conference. Early in 1944 the British and United States governments began to work out detailed schemes with a view to discussions with the Russians[1] before inviting representatives of other governments to a general meeting. A British committee drew up proposals in five memoranda which were shown to a meeting of Dominion Prime Ministers in London in May 1944, and were then submitted to the War Cabinet. The proposals were for a World Assembly on which all member states would be represented and a World Council consisting of representatives of the four powers and a number of other states. The World Council would take the initiative in action to maintain peace, and all the members of the organisation would be bound by its decisions. The memoranda did not attempt at this stage to lay down detailed rules of procedure. There were no proposals for an 'international police force' to keep the peace; the practical difficulties of the selection, maintenance, location and command of such a force seemed insuperable.

British, American and Russian delegations met to consider the various proposals at a conference at Dumbarton Oaks, near Washington, in

[1] The Americans continued to insist on the inclusion of China as the fourth great power and as a leading member of the Organisation; they were, however, now willing to give France a permanent seat on a World Council as soon as the Organisation had been set up. Discussions with the Chinese took place at Dumbarton Oaks (Washington) after the meetings between the British, American and Russian delegates.

August and September 1944. The British and Americans were in general agreement. The main difference with the Russians was over the question whether a permanent member of the World Council should vote in a dispute to which it was a party. The three powers agreed that in decisions involving action against aggression a unanimous vote of the permanent members should be required. If, however, a permanent member were allowed to vote in a dispute to which it was a party, it could block action against itself, since its adverse vote would destroy the unanimity of the permanent members; in other words, a vote in such circumstances would be a veto. The British view was that the smaller powers, especially the Latin American states, and members of the British Commonwealth not having a seat on the Council, would object to a veto by which, for example, Great Britain could prevent any action against herself whereas Canada might not be able to do so. The Americans at first thought that the Senate might insist upon the right of veto; later they changed their minds. The Russians would not give up the veto; the question therefore had to be left to a meeting of the three heads of governments.

Before this meeting took place (at Yalta) Field-Marshal Smuts had suggested to Churchill that it might be desirable to accept the Soviet view. The Russians were arguing that the Western powers suspected their willingness to co-operate with them; they regarded the veto as a test case whether the U.S.S.R. was really being treated as an equal. In any case the possession of a veto might enable the Western powers to prevent Russia from action of which they disapproved. A section of American opinion continued to support the veto as a safeguard against a combination hostile to American interests. The British delegation had suggested a compromise in which a veto would be allowed against positive action by the Council but not against the investigation of a dispute or the presentation of proposals for its settlement. Early in December Roosevelt also suggested a settlement on these lines. At the Yalta Conference the Russians accepted the compromise, but raised demands which they had previously made for the separate representation of each of the sixteen constituent Republics of the Soviet Union. They now limited their demand to membership for two or three of them. The British and Americans agreed that the constituent republics had no independent foreign policy and that their inclusion would merely add to the voting power of the U.S.S.R. On the other hand, the British government wanted to secure separate representation for the great self-governing Dominions of the Commonwealth, whose claims were very much stronger. In the end the Ukrainian and White Russian Republics were given separate membership.

The general conference for the establishment of the United Nations opened at San Francisco on 25 April 1945. The meeting was nearly postponed owing to the Russian refusal to fulfil the agreement reached at Yalta about the constitution of an independent provisional Polish government. The Russians also asked that Poland should be represented at the conference by the puppet government under their control at Warsaw. The Western powers rejected this demand. Apart from the addition of a chapter on trusteeship and the compromise on the veto the Charter of the United Nations accepted at San Francisco differed little from the Dumbarton Oaks draft. The British delegation suggested the title 'United Nations' for the Organisation;[1] they would have chosen one of the smaller European states for the headquarters of the secretariat.[2]

The negotiations at Dumbarton Oaks and San Francisco did not encourage optimism about the unanimity of the great powers upon which the successful working of the United Nations depended. The record of the Potsdam Conference (16 July–2 August 1945) was even more ominous for the future. The Russians had excluded the Western powers from a share in the affairs of Bulgaria, Hungary, and Rumania. The Foreign Office thought it useless to dispute Russian predominance in the areas of south-east Europe under the control of their armies, but they believed that the Western powers should make a stand over Poland. On entering Polish territory the Russians had set up a government predominantly Communist in character and had ruled out the return of the exiled Polish government in London. They had previously embarrassed the latter by insisting on immediate public consent to the surrender of Polish territory east of the Curzon line (and of the variant excluding Lwów from Poland). They were killing or deporting members of the Polish Underground Movement. In the early autumn of 1944 they had done nothing to assist the revolt which the army of the Underground Movement had begun against the Germans in Warsaw on the approach of the Russian forces.

The British and Americans had tried at Yalta to safeguard Polish independence by getting the Russians to agree to the constitution of a Polish provisional government including, as well as members of the puppet government, non-Communist Polish leaders from Poland and abroad. As soon as the Yalta Conference was over, the Russians invented pretexts for delaying the formation of this new government. They clearly intended neither to include Poles who were not subservient to their control nor to allow the holding of free elections in Poland. Churchill wanted Great Britain and the United States to take a firm line with Stalin over the failure to honour the Yalta agreement; he pointed out to the Americans that the issue went far beyond the fate of Poland. The Polish problem was a test between the Russians and the Western powers of the meaning to be attached to democracy, sovereignty, independence, representation, or free

[1] The Foreign Office would have preferred 'Union of Nations', but the Americans rejected the term as implying too close an association of states.
[2] The British delegation thought that, if the Russians objected to Geneva or any other place in western Europe, Copenhagen, Prague or Vienna would have been suitable.

elections. Churchill wrote shortly before Roosevelt's death that, if the three powers could not agree on the Polish question, the World Organisation would have little chance of success. Churchill also appealed more than once to Stalin; he told him that 'there is not much comfort in looking into a future where you and the countries you dominate, plus the Communist parties in many other States, are all drawn up on one side, and those who rally to the English-speaking nations... are on the other. It is quite obvious that their quarrel would tear the world to pieces.'

Churchill wanted an immediate three-power meeting to secure the implementation of the Yalta agreements; meanwhile he would have had the British and Americans stand at full strength on the lines of their advance into Germany, and would have refused to withdraw from the areas allotted to Russian occupation until the Russians had given way over Poland. Roosevelt's over-confidence at Yalta in his ability to secure Russian co-operation was maintained by President Truman. Truman was perhaps a little more suspicious of British policy;[1] he was anxious to avoid 'ganging up' (in Roosevelt's words) with the British against the Russians. The Americans therefore would not press for the immediate meeting which Churchill thought necessary. Before the three powers met at Potsdam the Poles, who could not now hope for anything better, had agreed with the Russians on the composition of a provisional government. The Russians controlled more than half the seats in the new government. They left no doubt about the character of the 'free' elections which they had promised to hold. While the Potsdam Conference was in session the British chargé d'affaires at Warsaw reported that already things were 'moving in the wrong direction' and that the assembly brought together by the new government was 'not a people's democratic assembly, but a voting machine carefully parked on them'. In the final stage of the conference Bevin, the Labour Foreign Secretary, did his best to secure a promise of free elections in return for British consent to the Russian demand for the extension of the Polish–German frontier to the western Neisse. The British view had been that the new frontier should not go beyond the Oder; Churchill wrote later that he would have refused any further extension, but it is doubtful whether Great Britain could have prevented Stalin from getting what he wanted, especially since the Americans were willing to accept the western Neisse frontier as part of the general bargain to break the deadlock at the conference. The last phase of Allied diplomacy thus brought nearer to fulfilment Churchill's sombre words about Allied disunity rather than Truman's more confident hope of postwar co-operation between the three powers whose armed forces had defeated Germany, Italy, and Japan.

[1] Truman has written in his *Memoirs* (vol I [1955], p. 164) that at the end of April 1945 he was 'trying to get Churchill in a frame of mind to forget the old power politics'.

INDEX

(The reader should refer to the analytical list of contents for the treatment of major themes.)

835

Pound, Ezra, American poet, 624
Pourtalès, Count Friedrich von, German diplomatist, 160, 163
Price, H. H., British philosopher, 653, 655
Prichard, H. A., British philosopher, 645, 653
Princep, Gavrilo, assassin of the Archduke Ferdinand, 153
Prinetti, J., Italian foreign minister, 121
Prinkipo proposal (1919), 212
Privy Council, Judicial Committee of, 374 n., 384, 387
Proust, Marcel, French writer, 627
Prout, William, British physician, 93–4
Puerto Rico, 119, 556, 562, 584; annexed by the United States, 592

Quezon, Manuel L., Filipino leader, 317
Quine, M. V., British philosopher, 655
Quisling, Vidkun, Norwegian traitor, 537, 550

Radhakrishnan, Sir Savepalli, Indian philosopher, 308
Radić, Stiepan, Croat leader, 491
Raeder, Erich, German admiral, 758
Rainier, Prince of Monaco, 34
Rameau, Sir C. V., Indian scientist, 308
Ramsay, Sir Bertram, British admiral, 753
Ramsay, Sir William, British scientist, 110
Ramsey, F. P., British mathematician, 646, 649
Rance, Sir Hubert, Governor of Burma, 325–6
Ransom, John C., American critic, 634
Rapallo Treaty (1922), 236, 454, 463, 488
Rashdall, Hastings, British theologian, 654, 658–9
Rasputin, Grigori, Russian monk, 404, 406; assassinated, 407
Rathenau, Walter, German industrialist, 46, 49
Rawlinson, Sir Henry (baron), British general, 189, 203
Read, Herbert, British writer, 672
Reading, Marquess of (Rufus Isaacs), viceroy of India, 300
Reed, Walter, American physician, 6, 101
Reichenau, Walter von, German field-marshal, 743–4, 750
Reichenbach, Georg von, German philosopher, 654
Reitzenstein, R., German theologian, 660
Reparations Commission (1921), 230; Dawes plan (1924), 232; Young plan (1928), 240; Lausanne Conference (1932), 688
Reynaud, Paul, French prime minister, 549, 741, 745–6, 753, 756

Rhineland, 475; French demands (1919), 215, 226–7; occupation, 230, 233; evacuation, 237–8, 493; German reoccupation, 467, 543, 740; remilitarisation, 500, 698–9
Rhodesia, 375, 395; Northern, 400, 402; Southern, 399
Ribbentrop, Joachim von, German foreign minister, 498, 506, 696, 703–4, 714, 718, 724, 726–34, 798
Richards, I. A., British literary critic, 649
Riga, 423; Peace of (1921), 443
Rilke, Rainier Maria, Austrian poet, 625
Ritchie, Sir Neil, British general, 765, 777–8
Riza Khan Shah of Persia, 273, 280–1
Rizal José, Filipino nationalist leader, 317
Robeck, Sir John de, British admiral, 182
Robertson, Sir William, British field-marshal, 181, 184, 196–7
Roca–Runciman trade agreement (1933), 606
Rocque, Colonel de la, leader of French Croix de Feu, 541
Rodin, Auguste, French sculptor, 673
Rodzianko, Mikhail, president, Russian Duma, 409
Rohe, Mies van der, American architect, 677, 680, 682
Röhm, Ernst, chief of Nazi Storm Troops, 497
Rokossovsky, Konstantin, Soviet general, 776, 789
Rolland, Romain, French writer, 522
Rommel, Erwin, German field-marshal, 764–5, 771, 777–83
Roosevelt, Franklin Delano, United States president (1933–45), Democrat
  first term, 573; second term, 578; third term, 581; fourth term, 582
  World Economic Conference (1933), 62–3, 689
  'good neighbour' policy, 607; quarantine speech, 710; proposed conference (1938), 712
  second world war, 771, 796, 801–3, 805, 810–13; relations with Churchill, 771, 803–4; with de Gaulle, 807–8; Atlantic Charter, 811–12; 'unconditional surrender', 786, 813; Teheran (1943), 814–15; Yalta (1945), 815; d. 583, 790
Roosevelt, Theodore, United States president (1901–9), Republican
  first world war, 209, 563
  Russo-Japanese war, 126, 339, 559; central and south America, 592–3
  career, 556–7; 'the big stick', 558
Root, Elihu, United States secretary of state, 559, 561
Roselli, Carlo, Italian politician, 541
Ross, Sir David, British scholar, 653